Yearbook on

International

Communist Affairs

1977

Yearbook on International Communist Affairs

1977

EDITOR: Richard F. Staar

Associate Area Editors:

Eastern Europe and the Soviet Union	Milorad M. Drachkovitch
Western Europe	Dennis L. Bark
Asia and the Pacific	Ramon H. Myers
The Americas	William E. Ratliff
Middle East and Africa	Lewis H. Gann
International Communist Front Organizations	Witold S. Sworakowski

HOOVER INSTITUTION PRESS
STANFORD UNIVERSITY, STANFORD, CALIFORNIA

Hoover Institution Publication 170

CONTENTS

The Americas

Middle East and Africa

INTRODUCTION

The purpose of the 1977 *Yearbook on International Communist Affairs*, the eleventh consecutive volume in this series, is to provide basic data and preliminary evaluations concerning organizational and personnel changes, attitudes toward domestic and foreign policies, and activities of Communist parties and international front organizations throughout the world. Much of the information comes from primary source materials in the native languages. Profiles on each party include founding date, legal or proscribed status, membership, electoral and parliamentary (if any) strength, leadership, auxiliary organizations, domestic activities, ideological orientation, views on international issues, attitude toward the Sino-Soviet dispute, and principal news media. Identity as a Marxist-Leninist party remains the criterion for inclusion and, hence, pro-Soviet, pro-Chinese, Castroite, Trotskyist, as well as other rival Communist movements are treated whenever applicable.

Excluded from the Yearbook are Marxist liberation movements and Marxist ruling parties that specifically disclaim being Communist. The Frente de Libertação de Moçambique (FRELIMO), for example, governs the People's Republic of Mozambique. It has announced a Marxist program and is organized on the basis of "democratic centralism," but is not, properly speaking, a Communist party. The Movimento Popular de Libertação de Angola (MPLA) rules most of the People's Republic of Angola; it derives support from Soviet advisers and Cuban armed forces in a continuing struggle against opposition. The Partido Africano de Indêpendencia de Guiné e Cabo Verde (PAIGC) is the ruling party of Guinea-Bissau. MPLA and PAIGC both share FRELIMO's general orientation; they also have been excluded.

The ruling movement in the Congo People's Republic, the Parti Congolais du Travail, claims to be Marxist-Leninist; its leaders state that they are Communists committed to "scientific socialism." But the party is not regarded as an orthodox Marxist-Leninist movement by its peers. The president of the Congo People's Republic has stated that, while Marx's writings remain valid, they must be adapted to local conditions. The ruling Somali Revolutionary Socialist Party, while likewise committed to establishment of "scientific socialism," is in a similar category. The same applies to the National Front in the People's Democratic Republic of Yemen and the Party of the People's Revolution in the People's Republic of Benin (previously known as Dahomey).

Leftist organizations of an oppositional type, such as the Mouvement National pour l'Indépendance de Malagasy (Monima), the Eritrean Liberation Front, as well as the so-called national liberation movements in Bahrain, the Cabinda enclave, former Spanish Sahara (Polisario), Rhodesia (ZANU and ZAPU), and South-West Africa (SWAPO) are not discussed. Omitted also because of insufficient data are groups such as the Communist parties of the Faroe Islands, Lesotho, the Malagasy Republic, Malta, Nigeria (the Socialist Workers' and Farmers' Party), Saudi Arabia, and Senegal, even though their Marxist-Leninist orthodoxy may not be in dispute. The following is a brief summary of *Yearbook* highlights in 1976.

USSR and Eastern Europe. The Communist Party of the Soviet Union (CPSU) held its 25th Congress between 24 February and 5 March. It confirmed the undisputed leadership of Leonid I. Brezhnev. The congress failed to bring forth any surprising or innovative elements, and confirmed the trend toward stabilization and security for middle- and upper-level party cadres. It did not address the increasing stagnation at the top level, nor the succession to Brezhnev, who became 70 in December. The previous month, two new faces appeared on the political scene: Aleksei Shibayev (61) became trade union chief, a post left unfilled 18 months; and Yakov Ryabov (48) was named a Central Committee secretary, replacing Defense minister Dimitri Ustinov.

Despite a prevalent domestic political calm, the Soviet republic of Georgia continued to remain a trouble spot for the regime, and party organizational problems also persisted in the Ukraine. A hard line toward dissenters continued, with punishment such as psychiatric confinement remaining a common occurrence. Nonconformists were purged from the USSR writers' union. However, an unprecedented U.S.-mediated exchange of political prisoners involved leading Soviet dissident Vladimir Bukovsky and secretary-general Louis Corvalán from the Communist Party of Chile in mid-December.

A new five-year plan was launched in January and it was appraised in the West as being more realistic, especially in view of the fact that the major goals of the previous plan had not been fulfilled. A good harvest of 224 million tons improved the agricultural situation, after the catastrophic one in 1975 (only 140 million tons), although the USSR continued purchases of American grain, making the trade balance for the first nine months of 1976 about 12 to 1 in favor of the United States.

Foreign policy in general during 1976 followed the broad outline of Brezhnev's report to the 25th CPSU Congress, at which he said: "In today's conditions, our party's activity in the international arena is unusually broad and diversified; there is now probably no spot on earth in which the state of affairs does not have to be taken into consideration, in one way or another, in the formation of our foreign policy." This succinct description of Soviet global interests reflected achievements and setbacks, as well as diplomacy and party policy around the world.

Moscow's prestige and influence particularly increased throughout Africa, following the MPLA victory in Angola. The new Cuban-supported government received additional Soviet military assistance in May, while a treaty of friendship and cooperation was signed with its representatives at Moscow in October. At the same time, a separate agreement on cooperation was concluded between the CPSU and MPLA. The USSR established diplomatic relations with the Philippines, stepped up its activities in Laos (officially recognized as a Communist-ruled state), and sent a large delegation headed by Mikhail Suslov to the 4th Congress of the Vietnamese Workers' Party at Hanoi in December. Soon after Mao Tse-tung's death, Soviet leaders hinted at normalization of relations with mainland China. This did not materialize and the new Chinese leader, Hua Kuo-feng, accused the Kremlin of hoping for violent turmoil in China when Mao died.

The Middle East is where the USSR suffered its most visible setbacks. President Anwar Sadat abrogated the 1971 Soviet-Egyptian treaty of friendship and cooperation in April. Syrian military intervention in Lebanon was followed by a deterioration of relations between Damascus and Moscow. Iran's military buildup, through acquisition of advanced American weapons systems, also displeased Soviet leaders. Improvement in ties with both Jordan and Libya could not compensate for the foregoing.

Soviet-U.S. relations fluctuated throughout the year. A treaty limiting underground nuclear explosions for peaceful purposes was signed at the end of May, and economic contacts between the two states continued at a high level with trade turnover almost reaching $2.5 billion. However, little if any progress could be registered in talks on arms reduction in Europe or on SALT II. One of the difficulties in following up the November 1974 preliminary agreement at Vladivostok involved the issue of whether to include Cruise missiles (U.S.) and Backfire bombers (USSR) within the ceiling of 2,400 strategic delivery vehicles allowed to each side. On two occasions, addressing a Central Committee plenum in October and at a Kremlin dinner for American business and government executives the following month, Brezhnev insisted on the necessity of achieving a new long-term agreement on limitation of offensive strategic weapons.

Two specific issues — the meaning of "détente" and implementation of agreements reached at the

July-August 1975 Helsinki Conference on Security and Cooperation in Europe—in particular complicated Soviet-U.S. relations. Adverse public reaction to many facets of USSR foreign policy induced President Ford to drop the word "détente" from public statements. Conversely, in his 29 June speech to the East Berlin conference of European Communist parties, Brezhnev accused the West of noncompliance with the Helsinki principles. What especially alarmed U.S. analysts were estimates concerning the Soviet drive to achieve military superiority, a conclusion based on a year-end intelligence estimate of USSR strategic objectives and submitted to President Carter in January 1977.

The major inter-party event of the year was the conference of top leaders from 29 European Communist movements, held at East Berlin the end of June. The fact that preparations for the meeting took almost 20 months, with 16 sessions required to agree on formulas acceptable to all participants, indicated that Moscow had lost its former dominant position. Moreover, speeches by French, Italian, and Spanish representatives insisted on autonomy and the right of each Communist party to decide its own domestic as well as international political line. Brezhnev, who headed the Soviet delegation, took a conciliatory stand. While apparently accepting the foregoing arguments, he continued to emphasize the importance of "proletarian internationalism"—a concept traditionally understood to mean CPSU domination. The final conference document omitted any mention of that concept but extolled the "great ideas of Marx, Engels, and Lenin," as well as international Communist solidarity.

The summit meeting in East Berlin was heralded by the Soviet press, as the "outstanding event of our time." Western commentators were of two minds in appraising its significance. According to some, the gathering represented a "triumph for national communism," a harbinger of disintegration in the previously monolithic Communist world, certifying the birth of Western "Euro-communism" as distinct from Comunist theory and practice in Eastern Europe. Other commentators saw in CPSU flexibility a design to restore Communist solidarity, helping West European parties in their domestic political maneuverings while enlisting their full support for the basic tenets of USSR foreign policy.

Soviet readiness to compromise at the East Berlin conference contrasted with an apparent decision not to tolerate any relaxation of USSR control over Eastern Europe. At a Council for Mutual Economic Assistance meeting which took place also in East Berlin only two weeks later, Soviet representatives pushed ahead with plans for closer integration of bloc economies with that of the USSR. Likewise, a political consultative session of the Warsaw Treaty Organization, held at the end of November in Bucharest, established a committee of WTO foreign ministers and a new unified secretariat for the purpose of "continually improving the mechanism of political collaboration." Brezhnev's state visits to Yugoslavia and Romania also during November, despite words about respect for the independence of these countries, testified to Soviet anxiety that future political developments in those two states might be detrimental to Kremlin interests.

Developments in some of the East European countries revealed the existence of domestic ferment which must be of major concern to USSR leaders. This unrest has several causes, the most immediate being popular dissatisfaction with the economic situation and expectations resulting from the humanitarian principles enunciated in the Helsinki declaration. Announcement on 24 June by the Polish government that prices for basic foods would be raised substantially (meat and grains by 40 percent, sugar by 100 percent) precipitated workers' strikes, public protests, and even riots. The proposed increases were withdrawn within 24 hours, and the regime promised to rebuild contacts with citizens as well as promote a new type of "socialist democracy." The powerful Roman Catholic church hierarchy later in the year protested reprisals against workers who had been jailed or fined for participating in the demonstratons. Moscow indicated a readiness to defuse a potentially explosive situation, and reportedly provided Warsaw with the equivalent of almost $1.5 billion in long-term loans.

In the German Democratic Republic, whose Communist movement held its congress in May, the hard line was strongly reemphasized, despite mounting ferment among GDR intellectuals. A new party program stressed dictatorship of the proletariat. Opposition to any reconciliation with the Federal Republic of Germany was reiterated, along with the intention to further tighten economic integration with the Soviet bloc. The regime relentlessly promoted youth indoctrination, insisted on military preparedness, and applied repressive measures against nonconformists. On the other hand, an upsurge in demand for the right to visit or emigrate (more than 100,000 applications) to West Germany, self-immolation of a clergyman, and a protest by prominent intellectuals against repressive policies testified to the existence of underlying discontent. Manifestations of dissent were also perceptible in Czechoslovakia, although the government remained unswerving in its subservience to the Soviet Union and maintained the situation under control. In early January 1977, it arrested some of the 300 prominent citizens who had signed "Charter-77," a manifesto petitioning for implementation of constitutional rights.

As in the recent past, Hungary enjoyed a more relaxed atmosphere than most of its neighbors. The twentieth anniversary of the 1956 revolution passed unnoticed in public, as if the population had become resigned to trade its relative economic well-being for the loss of national independence and democratic freedoms. The main economic preoccupation in Romania centered on establishment of targets for the 1976-1980 five-year plan, especially in view of agricultural shortages. Tightening totalitarian control, the ruling party adopted in November its ideological action program, an indigenous version of "permanent revolution." Distinctive features include political indoctrination of children starting at age four, along with accelerated patriotic education embracing the entire population. Patterns of Romanian foreign policy remained basically unchanged, although signs of improvement in ties with the USSR and the other Warsaw Pact countries could be noticed. Special emphasis was placed on cultivating relations with non-aligned countries. As in the past, Bulgaria maintained total loyalty to the Soviet Union. At the 11th Congress of its Communist party, held a month after the one in Moscow, Todor Zhivkov extolled "fuller and more organic rapprochement between Bulgaria and the USSR."

Developments in Yugoslavia remained dynamic as well as contradictory. The distinctive institution of workers' self-management became codified in a new law on associated labor. The economic situation, still unstable, improved with a drop in the inflation rate and a decline in the adverse foreign trade balance. Persecution of political opponents, both pro-Soviet and pro-Western, continued. Most publicity dealt with trials of "Cominformists." Tito met with Brezhnev twice, at East Berlin in June and Belgrade in November. Although the communiqués formally acknowledged Yugoslav views, uncertainties about Soviet intentions in a potential post-Tito crisis could not be dispelled.

In its Adriatic corner, Albania continued in self-imposed isolation. A new constitution was promulgated on 28 December. Further purges in the higher echelons of the party and the armed forces were announced at the Seventh Party Congress the previous month. Despite an earlier rapprochement with Yugoslavia, tension between the two countries increased toward the end of the year with Enver Hoxha denouncing Tito by name. Albania also refused to attend the Balkan conference at Athens earlier in the year. Even its relations with China appeared to be less cordial. The Soviet Union remained the "revisionist" enemy, and the Albanian party did not participate in the East Berlin Communist summit conference.

Western Europe. During the year, two principal themes continued to dominate both domestic as well as foreign attitudes and activities of these Communist movements: "unity of the Left," and détente between Communist-ruled states and capitalist countries. Both themes were highlighted at the conference of 29 parties, held in East Berlin at the end of June. Their successful application could be seen in Italian election results earlier that month. Not only are the Italian and French parties the largest non-ruling ones in the world, but 15 among Western Europe's 22 Communist movements have representation in parliaments.

The conference at East Berlin opened in the hope that it would strengthen unity among participating Communist parties. Representatives from Denmark, Greece, and Ireland, writing in the September issue of *World Marxist Review*, concluded that the final document represented a ". . . common communist platform for promoting détente, durable peace and social progress, for rooting out reaction and fascism, but [was] also . . . an earnest call for joint action by all individuals and organizations who want a Europe of peace and prosperity." The conference document supposedly received unanimous endorsement. However, it was neither signed nor approved formally but merely issued. It stressed willingness of participants to cooperate "with all democratic forces, especially with socialist and social-democratic parties, in the struggle for peace, democracy and social progress." Cooperation among Communist parties would be voluntary and based on "principles of equality and sovereign independence of each party, non-interference in internal affairs, and respect for their free choice of different roads in the struggle for social change of a progressive nature and for socialism."

Unlike similar conferences in the past, the role of the CPSU was not emphasized. The French party leader, Georges Marchais, made no reference at all to it. Santiago Carrillo, general secretary of the Spanish Communist Party, stated that ". . . diversity must be accepted once and for all. There will be no schism, if nobody puts his own position forward as dogma. . . . For years, Moscow was our Rome. . . . We regarded the great [Soviet] October Revolution as if it were our Christmas. . . . Today we have grown up. More and more we lose the character of being a church." Italian leader Enrico Berlinguer added: ". . . free debate of ideas . . . is one way to increase the force of attraction of Socialism, particularly among the younger generations." He made it clear that ". . . the models of socialist society followed in the countries of Eastern Europe do not correspond to the peculiar conditions and orientations of the broad working-class and popular masses in the countries of the West."

Other activities of Communist parties in Western Europe suggest that the movement toward "unity of the Left" has gained momentum which is likely to continue at least for the next few years. It should receive a major test in the 1978 French parliamentary elections. Many of West Europe's other Communist parties have been focusing also on establishment of electoral coalitions with socialist parties. This has been true especially in Italy and Finland, but also to a lesser extent in Britain, Norway, Portugal, Cyprus, Sweden, and Greece.

At the same time, it should be emphasized that "unity of the Left" has not always been successful, as the case of Portugal shows. Another example was the West German national elections in October, when the Communist party won only 0.3 percent of the votes and no parliamentary seats (it is one of only seven West European Communist parties not represented in the national legislature). The previous month, a Swedish coalition of moderate parties ousted social democrats after more than four decades in power. The Communist party of Sweden lost two of its 19 seats in parliament, after receiving only 4.7 percent of the vote, compared with 5.3 percent in 1973. Serious disagreements arose within several of the West European movements concerning the degree of cooperation with socialists, most notably in Norway, where a major party split occurred, but also in Greece, Sweden, Finland, Switzerland, and Britain.,

The most significant events occurred in Italy. After national elections in June, the Italian movement (PCI) clearly emerged as the strongest non-ruling Communist party, with considerable power and influence at both local and national levels. It had won 34.4 percent of the vote, an increase of seven points over the previous election in 1972, and acquired 228 of the 640 seats in parliament. Although the PCI did not participate in the coalition headed by the Christian Democrats, party leader Berlinguer declared that the Italian cabinet would remain in office only as long as PCI deemed it useful. In addition, Italian Communists participate directly in the administrations of six among the 20 regions, and indirectly in four others. They control 2,715 of the 7,900 municipalities and 39 of the 93 province capitals, including Rome. Furthermore, the PCI claims to have registered 170,000 new members during the first nine months of the year, and just over half of the party's 1.8 million members have joined since 1968. Not only do these statistics indicate PCI strength, but they also illustrate Berlinguer's maxim: "In order to change society, one must have access to it."

What appears to be emerging is a new era of the "united front," in which social, political, and economic values are undergoing continuous challenge. Communists in many West European states hope to gain power through alliances with social democrats, left-wing Catholics, and others. As a result, they seek to convince the voters that they would act in their own nations' interests rather than as Soviet agents.

In the course of the year, an effort to change the Communist "image" was especially evident in rejection of "proletarian internationalism" (i.e., adherence to CPSU positions and policies) by most of West Europe's Communist parties, whose leaders spoke clearly against this concept during the East Berlin conference. The Spanish movement sought legal status, and leader Carrillo was quoted as stressing that democratic and pluralistic systems must be respected. His arrest in Madrid on 10 December led to demonstrations in six Spanish cities. Before the end of the year, he had been released on bail.

The 22d Congress of the French Communist Party (PCF) in February renounced "dictatorship of the proletariat." It adopted the new slogan "Socialism under the Tricolor." Party chief Marchais called for a strategy of broad political and social alliances and "democratic" attainment of power. The PCF sought to expand its left-wing alliance with the socialists and its own role in that alliance. Marchais's report to the congress, remembering what had occurred in Chile and Portugal, stressed that (1) once conditions are ripe, it is necessary to proceed fast enough to create an irreversible situation, and (2) adventurist slogans and actions which could sabotage the movement should be avoided.

On the basis of political developments Western Europe's Communists are still far from achieving their goals. Failure of the Portuguese party to consolidate its power (its coalition won less than 18 percent of the vote in the December local elections) and near success of the Italian movement in gaining power directly suggest that the future may be uncertain. But Communist activities over the past year also serve as clear evidence that the parties have made considerable progress. It also seems clear that most of the movements in Western Europe are concerned to a large degree with establishing their credibility as members of electoral coalitions. Moreover, the idea of working within existing parliamentary structures to achieve "social progress" and political power is common to almost all of them.

Rather than appeal to the older generation which remembers the violence that communism brought to both Eastern and Western Europe during the years immediately following World War II, the movements today focus their attention on youth, women, and non-worker groups. They emphasize principles of compromise and political pluralism, respect for private property and the church, and commitment to the parliamentary system. Yet they have always stressed and will continue to proclaim the necessity to transform bourgeois society.

Asia and the Pacific. The major event in the Asian Communist world was the death on 9 September at age 82 of Mao Tse-tung. Remarkable developments occurred soon after his death. Mao's widow, Chiang Ching, and her three radical associates in the Politburo (Wang Hung-wen, Chang Chun-chiao, and Yao Wen-yuan) were arrested on either 6 or 7 October along with a number of their supporters. Hua Kuo-feng and his supporters then assumed control over the erstwhile strongholds of the radicals, including the urban militia, the Shanghai party organizatin, and indeed the capital itself. Throughout the rest of the year, Hua waged a relentless wall poster campaign and mobilized numerous rallies to denounce the "gang of four." At a mass demonstration in Tien An Men Square, Politburo member and Peking mayor Wu Teh announced that Mao personally had selected Hua as his successor by writing in his own hand: "with you in charge, I'm at ease."

The "anti-party clique" apparently had tried to seize power shortly after Mao's death but was denied support by the Peking military garrison, which quickly alerted Hua to the plan. Numerous wall posters revealed that divisiveness had existed within the Politburo during the last few years. The "gang of four" was alleged to have used its power and influence to denigrate Chou En-lai and obstruct party policy in key cities of central China. At the end of the year, violence erupted in Hupeh and Fukien provinces, around the major industrial center of Wuhan, in Szechwan, and only 100 miles south of Peking at Paoting. People's Liberation Army units were called upon to restore order, suggesting that "gang of four" supporters may have attempted to seize power in certain localities.

The turbulence that took place in China during the late fall has not yet influenced the Asian communist world. Thus far, other Commnist-ruled states have had to cope only with their own problems arising from local conditions and internal party difficulties. A notable example has been North Korea, one of the most secretive countries. Fragmentary information coming out of Pyongyang suggests that a serious leadership crisis may be under way. Kim Il-song's health could be deteriorating, and a number of high-ranking leaders have died recently: Nam Il on 7 March, Hong Won-kil on 16 May, Choe Yong-kon on 19 September. Others, like Choe Hyon and Kim Yong-chu, Kim Il-song's younger brother, are said to be gravely ill. The average age of North Korea's top leadership is estimated at around 66 years. As the old guard fades away and, when Kim Il-song passes from the scene, the mantle of leadership is expected to fall upon his son Kim Chong-il.

In Indochina, Communist control over Cambodia reportedly has begun to rely less on mass terror (at least 700,000 reportedly were killed in the aftermath of the takeover) and more on persuasion to mobilize the population to grow food. Premier Pol Pot has been quoted as saying that the regime is reconsidering its policy of total self-reliance and will import raw materials that would permit idle factories to resume production. However, all 300,000 Vietnamese living in Cambodia when the Communists seized power have been driven out of the country, which may have affected relations with Hanoi.

On 15 December the Vietnamese party's 4th Congress opened at Hanoi, the first since 1960. A major topic of discussion was the resettlement of people from larger cities to rural parts of the South. A plan is expected to receive approval that would convert large areas into a farm belt and involve the transfer of more than a million people from Ho Chi Minh City (Saigon) into this new economic region, which would be developed to supply sufficient foodstuffs for urban areas. The congress also discussed proposals that the North continue to develop heavy industry, whereas the South would specialize in light industry and handicrafts.

Communist insurgent activity in Malaysia, although considerably less than in previous years, has by no means disappeared. A Malaysian Air Force helicopter was shot down by guerrillas near the Thai border. Railway tracks in several areas, including the state of Perak, were blown up. An attempt was made to dynamite an electric power station in Kuala Lumpur, while other bombs went off at a construction site in the Malaysian capital and in the suburban village of Kepong. Kedah State chief minister Syed Ahmad Shahabudin announced that two Communist camps in the Ulu Muda forest had been destroyed.

In neighboring Indonesia, the Communist party continues to wage a clandestine struggle on Borneo, along the border with Malaysian Sarawak, but its guerrilla activity remains weak. The Communist party of the Philippines still operates underground, divided into a pro-Peking faction and a smaller one sympathetic to Moscow. Both groups claim national representation, but only the pro-Chinese party is waging armed resistance to the government. The visit by President Marcos to the USSR early in June and establishment of diplomatic relations with the Soviet Union have made the pro-Moscow faction less critical of the government.

In India, the pro-Moscow Communist party (CPI) until recently had supported Indira Gandhi's program. However, her son Sanjay has been attacked by the CPI, since he acquired considerable power after the state of emergency was declared. The government forced the resignation of the pro-Communist leader of Orissa on 17 December and placed the state under federal controls. The CPI then announced nationwide demonstrations for 1 January 1977 to demand price controls, nationalization of the texile, sugar, pharmaceutical, and jute industries, and a takeover by the state of the wholesale food trade. These were called off when the government cracked down by arresting 70 CPI organizers in the state of Uttar Pradesh.

Meanwhile, in Japan the Communist party (JCP) continued to expand its popular appeal by promulgating a "Manifesto of Freedom and Democracy" which professed to guarantee human rights and freedoms should the country come under its administration. The movement deleted from its constitution the term "Marxism-Leninism." It is seemingly moving toward policies similar to those of the Communist parties in France, Italy, and Spain. Yet in a public opinion poll, taken during October, only four percent of all respondents replied that the JCP was the party of their choice. Then, in early December national elections resulted in only 17 Communist seats (previously 39) in the expanded (from 491 to 511 members) lower chamber of parliament. Upper house elections in July 1977 should indicate whether JCP strength will grow.

CHECKLIST OF COMMUNIST PARTIES AND FRONTS

Eastern Europe and the Soviet Union (9)

Country	Population	Communist party membership	Percent of vote; seats in legislature	Status	Sino-Soviet dispute
Albania	2,440,000	101,500	99.9 (1974); all 250 Democratic Front	In power	Pro-Chinese
Bulgaria	8,803,000	789,796	99.9 (1976); 272 of 400 Fatherland Front	In power	Pro-Soviet
Czechoslovakia	14,928,000	1,382,860	99.9 (1976); all 200 National Front	In power	Pro-Soviet
East Germany (GDR)	16,849,000	2,043,697	99.9 (1976); 127 of 500 National Front	In power	Pro-Soviet
Hungary	10,603,000	754,353 (1975)	99.6 (1975); all 352 Patriotic People's Front	In power	Pro-Soviet
Poland	34,383,000	2,500,000	99.4 (1976); 255 of 460 Front of National Unity	In power	Pro-Soviet
Romania	21,452,000	2,577,434	99.9 (1975); all 349 Front of Socialist Unity	In power	Neutral
USSR	256,885,000	15,900,000	99.9 (1974); all 1,517 CPSU-approved	In power	– –
Yugoslavia	21,520,000	1,400,000	– – (1974); all 220 Socialist Alliance	In power	Independent
Total	387,863,000	27,449,640			

Western Europe (22)

Country	Population	Communist party membership	Percent of vote; seats in legislature	Status	Sino-Soviet dispute
Austria	7,539,000	25,000 est.	1.2 (1975); none	Legal	Pro-Soviet
Belgium	9,809,000	12,000 est.	3.2 (1974); 4 of 212	Legal	Pro-Soviet
Cyprus	647,000	12,000	30.0 (1976); 9 of 35 Greek Cypriot seats	Legal	Pro-Soviet
Denmark	5,080,000	9,500 est.	4.2 (1975); 7 of 179	Legal	Pro-Soviet
Finland	4,726,000	47,000	19.0 (1975); 36 of 200	Legal	Pro-Soviet
France	52,979,000	550,000	21.3 (1973); 73 of 490	Legal	Pro-Soviet
Germany (FRG)	61,929,000	42,500	0.3 (1976); none	Legal	Pro-Soviet
Germany (W. Berlin)	2,100,000	8,000	1.9 (1975); none	Legal	Pro-Soviet
Great Britain	54,421,000	29,000	0.5 (1974); none	Legal	Pro-Soviet
Greece	9,048,000	27,500 est.	3.6 (1974); 8 of 300	Legal	Split
Iceland	221,000	2,200 est.	18.3 (1974); 11 of 60	Legal	Independent
Ireland	4,525,000	500 est.	— (1973); none	Legal	Pro-Soviet
Italy	56,211,000	1,806,000	34.4 (1976); 228 of 630	Legal	Pro-Soviet
Luxembourg	360,000	500 (1974)	9.0 (1974); 5 of 59	Legal	Pro-Soviet
Netherlands	13,707,000	10,000	4.5 (1972); 7 of 150	Legal	Independent
Norway	4,040,000	2,500 est.	10.1 (1973); 16 of 155 (coalition of 3, incl. CP)	Legal	Pro-Soviet
Portugal	8,782,000	115,000	14.6 (1976); 40 of 263	Legal	Pro-Soviet
San Marino	19,000	300	23.7 (1974); 15 of 60	Legal	Pro-Soviet
Spain	35,972,000	150,000 claim	(1971)	Proscribed	Independent
Sweden	8,224,000	14,500	5.0 (1976); 17 of 349	Legal	Split
Switzerland	6,496,000	7,000	2.5 (1975); 5 of 200	Legal	Pro-Soviet
Turkey	40,988,000	2,000 est.	— — (1973)	Proscribed	Pro-Soviet
Total	387,823,000	2,873,000			

Asia and the Pacific (20)

Country	Population	Communist party membership	Percent of vote; seats in legislature	Status	Sino-Soviet dispute
Australia	12,756,000	2,500 est.	— (1975); none	Legal	Split
Bangladesh	75,529,000	2,500 est.	— (1973)	Proscribed	Pro-Soviet
Burma	31,140,000	7,700 est.	— (1974)	Proscribed	Pro-Chinese
Cambodia	7,000,000	10,000 est.	100.0 (1976); all 250	In power	Pro-Chinese
China	950,744,000	30,000,000 (1976)	No elections scheduled	In power	—
India	627,883,000	90,000 CPI	5.7 (1976); 14 of 244	Legal	Pro-Soviet
		85,000 CPI (M)		Legal	Neutral
Indonesia	134,294,000	1,000 est.	— (1971)	Proscribed	Split
Japan	112,818,000	380,000	10.4 (1976); 17 of 511	Legal	Independent
Korea (DPRK)	17,000,000	2,000,000	100.0 (1972); all 541	In power	Neutral
Laos	3,414,000	unknown	No elections scheduled	In power	Neutral
Malaysia	12,337,000	2,170 insurgents	— (1974)	Proscribed	Pro-Chinese
Mongolia	1,489,000	67,000	99.9 (1973); all 336	In power	Pro-Soviet
Nepal	12,866,000	6,500 est.	— (1959)	Proscribed	Split
New Zealand	3,149,000	400 est.	0.2 (1975); none SUP	Legal	Split
Pakistan	72,600,000	800 (1973)	— (1970)	Proscribed	Pro-Soviet
Philippines	43,948,000	1,600 insurgents	Elections suspended	Proscribed	Split
Singapore	2,281,000	350	— (1972)	Proscribed	Pro-Chinese
Sri Lanka	14,027,000	6,000	3.5 (1970); 19 of 187	Legal	Split
Thailand	43,569,000	8,000 insurgents	— (1976)	Proscribed	Pro-Chinese
Vietnam	49,633,000	1,533,500	99.0 (1976); all 492	In power	Neutral
Total	2,228,477,000	34,205,020			

The Americas (26)

Country	Population	Communist party membership	Percent of vote; seats in legislature	Status	Sino-Soviet dispute
Argentina	25,718,000	100,000 claimed	— — (1973); 2 of 243	Legal	Pro-Soviet
Bolivia	5,551,000	500	Elections postponed indef.	Proscribed	Split
Brazil	110,177,000	6,000	— — (1974)	Proscribed	Split
Canada	23,145,000	4,000 est.	— — (1974); none	Legal	Split
Chile	10,445,000	unknown	No elections	Proscribed	Pro-Soviet
Colombia	24,800,000	11,000 est.	— — (1974); 2 of 199	Legal	Split
Costa Rica	2,023,000	3,200	2.3 (1974); 2 of 57	Legal	Pro-Soviet
Cuba	9,492,000	200,000 est.	100.0 (1976); 441 of 481	In power	Pro-Soviet
Dominican Republic	4,835,000	1,650 est.	— — (1974)	Proscribed	Factions
Ecuador	7,014,000	800	No elections scheduled	Legal	Split
El Salvador	4,128,000	150 est.	— — (1976)	Proscribed	Pro-Soviet
Guadeloupe	350,000	3,000 est.	— — (1976); 7 of 36	Legal	Pro-Soviet
Guatemala	6,016,000	750 est.	— — (1974)	Proscribed	Pro-Soviet
Guyana	809,000	100	3.6 (1973); none	Legal	Pro-Soviet
Haiti	4,637,000	unknown	— — (1973)	Proscribed	Pro-Soviet
Honduras	2,823,000	650	No elections scheduled	Proscribed	Split
Martinique	359,000	1,000 est.	— — (1976); 3 of 36	Legal	Pro-Soviet
Mexico	62,159,000	5,000 est.	— — (1976); none	Legal	Pro-Soviet
Nicaragua	2,224,000	100 est.	— — (1974)	Proscribed	Split
Panama	1,719,000	600	— — (1972); no parties	Allowed	Pro-Soviet
Paraguay	2,622,000	3,500 est.	— — (1973)	Proscribed	Split
Peru	15,804,000	3,200	No elections scheduled	Legal	Split
Puerto Rico	3,200,000	125	— — (1976); none	Legal	Pro-Soviet
United States	215,700,000	15,000	0.2 (1976); none	Legal	Pro-Soviet
Uruguay	2,781,000	6,000 est.	(1971)	Proscribed	Pro-Soviet
Venezuela	12,366,000	5,000	9.0 (1973); 11 of 195	Legal	Factions
Total	560,897,000	371,325			

Middle East and Africa (15)

Country	Population	Communist party membership	Percent of vote; seats in legislature	Status	Sino-Soviet dispute
Egypt	38,150,000	1,000 est.	— (1976); 2 of 350	Proscribed	Pro-Soviet
Iran	33,955,000	1,500 est.	— (1975)	Proscribed	Pro-Soviet
Iraq	11,388,000	2,000 est.	no elections since 1958	Allowed	Pro-Soviet
Israel	3,499,000	1,500	1.4 (1973); 4 of 120	Legal	Pro-Soviet
Jordan	2,789,000	500 est.	no elections since 1967	Proscribed	Pro-Soviet
Lebanon	2,523,000	2,500	— (1972); none	Legal	Pro-Soviet
The Maghreb					
Algeria	17,301,000	300 est.	— (1976)	Proscribed	Pro-Soviet
Morocco	17,961,000	400 est.	— (1976); none	Allowed	Pro-Soviet
Tunisia	5,902,000	100 est.	— (1974)	Proscribed	Pro-Soviet
Réunion	497,000	1,000 est.	— (1973); none	Legal	Independent
Saudi Arabia	6,255,000	unknown	no elections scheduled	Proscribed	Pro-Soviet
Senegal	4,398,000	unknown	— (1973); none	Legal	Pro-Soviet
South Africa	26,244,000	300	— (1974)	Proscribed	Pro-Soviet
Sudan	18,202,000	3,500	— (1974); no parties	Proscribed	Pro-Soviet
Syria	7,597,000	5,000	no elections since 1961	Allowed	Pro-Soviet
Total	196,661,000	19,600			

International Communist Front Organizations

	Claimed Membership	Headquarters
Afro-Asian People's Solidarity Organization	No data	Cairo
Afro-Asian Writers' Permanent Bureau	No data	Cairo
International Association of Democratic Lawyers	25,000	Brussels
International Federation of Resistance Fighters	4,000,000	Vienna
International Organization of Journalists	150,000	Prague
International Union of Students	(Affiliates in 90 countries)	Prague
Women's International Democratic Federation	200,000,000	East Berlin
World Federation of Democratic Youth	40,000,000	Budapest
World Federation of Scientific Workers	300,000	London
World Federation of Trade Unions	170,000,000	Prague
World Peace Council	(Affiliates in 90 countries)	Helsinki

The Americas. Most pro-Soviet communist parties in Latin America continued to advocate participation in broad fronts to replace existing governments without armed struggle. They gave varying degrees of "critical support" to the governments in Argentina, Ecuador, Guyana, Peru, and several others but withdrew it from Honduras. Tension in Peru between the military regime and the communists increased throughout the year, particularly in the labor movement, as the Morales government continued to modify the radical reformist policies of the Velasco period (1968-1975). The Argentine communist movement, which had become increasingly disenchanted with the government of Isabel Peron, gave a measure of unenthusiastic support to the military regime since the coup in late March. However, tensions mounted as President Videla pushed his program against domestic subversion.

Jagan took the People's Progressive Party back into parliament in Guyana at mid-year, after a three-year boycott, professing to see an improvement in the Burnham government. The move caused important defections from his party, and Jagan maintained a critical attitude toward the People's National Congress for the remainder of the year. The Marxist Popular Socialist Party in Mexico supported the government (PRI) candidate, while the communists ran their own unofficial candidate in the presidential election. The Communist party of Chile, backed by a major international campaign, continued its denunciation of the Pinochet regime; the party's secretary general, arrested shortly after the 1973 coup which overthrew Allende, was released in mid-December 1976 in exchange for a Soviet political prisoner.

Marxist-Leninist guerrillas (not pro-Soviet) suffered losses in several Latin American countries — Argentina, Colombia, Mexico, and Nicaragua — although terrorist operations continued in these and several other countries. Guerrillas were particularly active and hit hard in Argentina after the March coup. By mid-year, they were unable to launch any major attacks against government or police installations. By the end of the year, they had concentrated on bombings, kidnappings, and assassinations of military, police, and business leaders as well as agitation (by "industrial guerrillas") among laborers.

Cuba experienced several important events during the year. A new "socialist" constitution replaced the former inactive one, several new provinces were established, and "people's power" elections were held throughout the country. Havana continued to maintain an estimated 12,000 to 20,000 troops and advisers in Africa, mostly in Angola. However, this Cuban-Soviet involvement in Africa caused a number of Hemisphere governments, particularly the military regimes in the southern part, to fear similar involvement in Latin American affairs. Nicaragua on 16 November officially accused Cuba of training Nicaraguan leftists and infiltrating them into the country for guerrilla warfare against the government.

In the United States, the Communists (CPUSA) and the Trotskyite Socialist Workers' Party (SWP) devoted their main attention to national elections. The CPUSA ran candidates in 19 states and the SWP in 26, and both tried to get on the ballot in more. The Communists claimed that President Ford had carried out reactionary policies, designed by former President Nixon, and that Democratic Party nominee Carter was a reactionary millionaire, a conservative, anti-labor cold-warrior and racist. Interestingly enough, SWP received some 70,000 votes, surpassing by 10,000 the CPUSA, whose general secretary, Gus Hall, ran as its presidential candidate.

Middle East and Africa. The Communist movements in the Middle East registered little success. The Tudeh Party of Iran largely operates outside the country. Its radio station in the USSR went off the air on 30 November. The left wing in Iran is badly divided, although terrorism on a minor scale continues. In August, three U.S. technicians were murdered in Tehran; near the end of December, eight guerrillas were killed and eleven captured in two gun battles. The Jordanian and Syrian parties are split. The Communist Party of Iraq has made little headway in comparison with the ruling Ba'thists. Ironically enough, one of the largest movements, and certainly the most freely active, is found in Israel, where Communists are allowed to operate a legal organization. In the absence of an Arab nationalist party, they have obtained substantial Arab support. The party held its 18th Congress in mid-December.

Above all, the Middle East movements have suffered severely as a result of the civil war in Lebanon, which introduced bitter disagreements. The Communist Party of Lebanon, through its paramilitary units, fought alongside the Lebanese left and the Palestinians. It condemned Syrian intervention as did "the Arab Communist parties," not further identified, which met on 16-17 October. The civil war presented the Lebanese leftist alliance, including the Communists, with a brief opportunity for setting up a possibly Soviet-oriented government. The USSR, however, appears to have hesitated in sponsoring a People's Democratic Republic of Lebanon.

Pro-Soviet movements failed to make headway also in Africa. The once powerful Sudanese Communist Party has continued in a state of disarray. The Communist Party of South Africa, primarily an organization of exiles, still remains an army of officers without mass support. The USSR has, however, extended its support to established governments of a leftist or ostensibly leftist type. Change has occurred most rapidly in the former Portuguese overseas territories, especially Angola. The MPLA, the only recognized party in that country, stands committed to a pro-Soviet policy. When founded in 1956 it absorbed the Partido Communista de Angola and derived its principal support in the cities from Portuguese-speaking African and Eurafrican *asimilados*; its rural backing came mainly from members of the Mbundu people. The MPLA owed its 1976 military victory to intervention by Cuban forces that were transported to Angola in large part by Soviet aircraft and ships. Cuban and MPLA forces continue to suppress armed opposition to the government, though fighting goes on in Cabinda and throughout southern Angola. They also lend support to the South-West African People's Movement (SWAPO).

USSR support for FRELIMO in Mozambique and ZAPU in Rhodesia has not been on the same scale as that given MPLA in Angola. China has been and still is involved in assistance to Mozambique, and to a part of the Rhodesian guerrilla movement. The Soviet Union supports an ostensibly more moderate group, led by Joshua Nkomo, but his forces are distinctly weaker than their rivals. Nkomo says he is committed to the Soviet Union. He has explained that Rhodesia, under black rule, would look to the USSR for aid and support.

Fronts. The international Communist front organizations continued through the year their multifaceted activities. Indeed there exists no political, economic, or social crisis of any importance in the non-Communist world upon which they do not seize with impressive unanimity. At meetings and conferences, through messages, protests, resolutions, or simple statements, these fronts loudly denounce "colonialism, neo-colonialism, racism and imperialism," under the umbrella of "peace, national liberation, democracy, liberty, disarmament and détente." Most vocal are the World Peace Council (WPC), the World Federation of Trade Unions (WFTU), and the World Federation of Democratic Youth.

The situation in the Middle East, the independence of Angola, the problem of apartheid in South Africa, the situation in Namibia (South-West Africa) and Zimbabwe (Rhodesia), the violation of human rights in Chile, and the struggles of national liberation movements throughout the so-called Third World were the main issues continuously brought up, discussed, and made the subject of "appeals" by the fronts, under the guidance of the USSR as well as other members of the Soviet bloc.

Certain among the fronts actively attempt to promote their cause with various United Nations agencies (e.g., the WPC has "Class A" status with UNESCO) and with non-Communist youth, workers', and journalist organizations. This implements a policy of developing intensive relationships with "progressive" sectors of the capitalist world. Fronts also advanced the principles of the Helsinki conference on security and cooperation in Europe and the New Stockholm (Peace) Appeal in order to "overcome the consequences of the cold war." It would appear that 1976 represented another active year for the international Communist front organizations, especially because of their astute propaganda in a number of developing countries. They have scheduled for 1977 a world forum of peace forces in mid-January at Moscow, a conference on the Indian Ocean as a "zone of peace" in April-May in Madagascar, a world conference of religious peace forces in June at Moscow, and a preparatory meeting on the Mediterranean as a "zone of peace" for the end of November at Athens.

*　　*　　*

Staff members and several of the associate editors were responsible for some of the writing, research, and most of the data-collecting effort that produced this *Yearbook*. Profiles were contributed by a total of 66 outside scholars, many of whom prepared more than one. Names and affiliations appear at the end of individual essays. Mrs. Ica Juilland and Mrs. Dorothy Grouse Fontana assisted in the processing and filing of research material as well as in assembling some of the data. Much of the final typing was done by Miss Nancy Dibble, who also handled correspondence with contributors. Special appreciation is due the curators and their staffs as well as members of the Readers' Services Department at the Hoover Institution for their response to emergency requests and for the bibliography. We are indebted particularly to the copy editor, Mr. Jesse M. Phillips, for putting the manuscript in its final form.

Sources are cited through the text, with news agencies normally identified by generally accepted initials. Abbreviations are also used for the following widely quoted publications:

FBIS	*Foreign Broadcast Information Service*
NYT	*New York Times*
WMR	*World Marxist Review*
IB	*Information Bulletin* (of the *WMR*)
YICA	*Yearbook on International Communist Affairs*

January 1977　　　　　　　　　　　　　　　　　　　　　　　　　　Richard F. Staar

EASTERN EUROPE AND THE SOVIET UNION

Albania

The Albanian Communist Party was founded on 8 November 1941. At its First Congress, November 1948, the name was changed to the Albanian Party of Labor (Partia e Punës e Shqipërisë; APL). As the only legal political party in Albania, the APL exercises a monopoly of power. Party members hold all key posts in the government and the mass organizations. All 250 seats in the national legislature, the People's Assembly, are held by members of the Democratic Front, the party-controlled mass organization to which all Albanian voters belong.

At the Seventh APL Congress (1-7 November 1976), it was announced that party membership totaled 101,500. Of these, 88,000 were full members and 13,500 candidate members. Party membership increased by 14,500 between the Sixth Congress (1971) and the Seventh Congress. In 1976, 37.5 percent of APL members were reportedly laborers, 29.0 percent were peasants, and 33.5 percent were white collar workers. Women in 1976 comprised 27 percent of the party's membership, an increase of 5 percent since 1971. Approximately 4 percent of the Albanian population are party members. (*Zëri i popullit*, 2 November.)

The population of Albania in early 1976 was approximately 2,440,000 (Tirana radio, 16 April). According to recent census data, peasants comprise 49.4 percent of the population; laborers, 36.2 percent; and white collar workers,14.4 percent. Approximately 42 percent of the population is under the age of 15. (Ibid., 28 May, 8 June 1975.)

Leadership and Organization. Enver Hoxha, leader of the APL since its founding, was reelected first secretary in 1976. Despite press reports concerning his alleged poor health (e.g., *Washington Post*, 1 January; *NYT*, 4 May), Hoxha delivered a thirteen-hour speech to the Congress and participated in the various social activities held in conjunction with it. The proceedings of the Seventh Congress confirmed that the APL first secretary continues to be the dominant personality within the ruling elite.

After some fifteen years (1956-71) of relative stability within the ranks of the APL leadership, there have been numerous changes in the composition of the party's Politburo and Central Committee since 1971. Of the 13 Politburo members elected at the Sixth Congress, three—Beqir Balluku, Abdyl Këllezi, and Koço Theodosi—were deposed during 1974-75. Three of the four Politburo candidates elected in 1971, Petrit Dume, Piro Dodbiba, and Xhafer Spahiu, were also ousted between 1974-76. The Politburo selected by the Seventh Congress consists of 12 full members: Enver Hoxha, Adil Çarçani, Haki Toska, Hekuran Isaj, Hysni Kapo, Kadri Hazbiu, Manush Myftiu, Mehmet Shehu, Pali Miska, Ramiz Alia, Rita Marko, and Spiro Koleka; and five candidates: Lenka Çuko, Llambi Gegprifti, Pilo Peristeri, Qirjako Mihali, and Simon Stefani (*Zëri i popullit*, 8 November).

Hekuran Isaj and Pali Miska, who had been named to full Politburo membership, and Llambi Gegprifti and Qirjako Mihali, who had been designated Politburo candidates, during 1975 (see *YICA, 1976*, p. 2) were formally elected to these posts at the Seventh Congress. Two additional Politburo candidates, Lenka Çuko and Simon Stefani, were also chosen at this time. Çuko is the first woman to sit on the Politburo since the ouster of Liri Belishova in 1960. She was elected a candidate Central Committee member in 1971 and in 1975 became first secretary of the party organization in the Lushnjë district (the nation's leading agricultural region). Stefani, who was first elected to the Central Committee at the Seventh Congress, had been first secretary of the Përmet district party organization since 1972. In October 1976, he became a secretary of the Tirana district party organization, where he serves as a deputy to his colleague Qirjako Mihali. The only sitting Politburo member not reelected was Xhafer Spahiu, who had served as a candidate member of that body since 1971. Spahiu, a deputy prime minister since 1970, was, however, reelected to the Central Committee.

There were also extensive changes in the makeup of the Central Committee. Of the 71 full Central Committee members elected at the Sixth Congress, three had since died, while 28 were ousted and seven demoted to candidate status at the Seventh Congress. Of the 39 Central Committee candidates chosen in 1971, seven were dropped, 13 retained their positions, and 18 were promoted to full membership. The Central Committee selected by the Seventh Congress consists of 77 members and 38 candidates (*Zëri i popullit*, 8 November). It includes 26 full members and 25 candidates who have not previously served on this body. A majority of the new Central Committee members and candidates are relatively young political unknowns who have apparently distinguished themselves by their loyalty to Hoxha and his associates in the political battles within the APL during the past five years. They all appear to have had at least some experience working outside Tirana. For the most part, those dropped from the Central Committee had served on that body since the mid-1950s or early 1960s. They had, with a few exceptions, been ousted between 1973 and 1976 from their high-level posts in the military, economic, and cultural sectors for either questioning the wisdom of Hoxha's domestic or foreign policies, or failing to carry out the responsibilities assigned them to the satisfaction of the party leadership (see below).

There was one change in the composition of the Central Committee Secretariat. Prokop Murra, a Central Committee member since 1956 and first secretary of the Shkodër district party organization in 1968-76, replaced Haki Toska (ibid.). Murra, an economist by training, had also served as a deputy chairman of the State Planning Commission in the 1960s. He will presumably take over Toska's responsibilities in the economic sector. Toska, a long-time associate of Hoxha's, retained his seat on the Politburo, and he was subsequently appointed minister of finance (ibid., 14 November). In addition to Hoxha, the secretaries of the Central Committee are Hysni Kapo, Ramiz Alia, Hekuran Isaj, and Prokop Murra (ibid., 8 November).

Pilo Peristeri, a Politburo candidate since 1952 and another Hoxha crony, was selected chairman of the party's Central Control and Auditing Commission in place of Ibrahim Sina. Only three of the 21 sitting members of the Commission were reelected (ibid.).

There have also been extensive changes in the leadership of the district party organizations since 1971. In November 1976, only two of the 26 district first secretaries in office at the time of the Sixth APL Congress remained in these positions. Of the 24 top leadership changes at the district level since 1971, at least 14 appear to have resulted in demotions for the 1971 incumbents, primarily for failing to carry out party directives dealing with the economy or culture. In October 1976, Politburo member Manush Myftiu, first secretary of the Tirana district party organization since 1969, relinquished this post to become a deputy prime minister (ibid., 11 October). He was succeeded by Politburo candidate Qirjako Mihali, who held the first secretary post in the Durrës district. At this time Politburo candidate Simon Stefani was also named to the secretariat of the Tirana district organization, and Central Committee member Xhelil Gjoni became the third person in three years to serve as district party secretary for propaganda and culture (Tirana radio, 10 November). This sweeping transformation of Tirana district party leadership seems to indicate that Hoxha is still not entirely pleased with the pace at which his policies are being implemented in the most populous and most politically sensitive of the nation's administrative units (*Zëri i popullit*, 7 October).

In his report to the Seventh Congress (ibid., 2 November), Hoxha shed little light on the circumstances that had prompted him to initiate his extensive purge of the APL elite. He did, however, single out for special condemnation eight of his erstwhile colleagues deposed between 1973 and 1976: Beqir Balluku (Politburo member, deputy prime minister, and defense minister); Petrit Dume (Politburo candidate, armed forces chief of staff, and deputy defense minister); Hito Çako (Central Committee member, head of the armed forces political directorate, and deputy defense minister); Abdyl Këllezi (Politburo member, chairman of the state planning commission, and deputy prime minister); Koço Theodosi (Politburo member and minister of industry and mining); Kiço Ngjela (Central Committee member and minister of trade); Fadil Paçrami (Central Committee member and secretary for propaganda and culture of the Tirana district party organization); and Todi Lubonja (Central Committee member and director of the Albanian radio-television service). This "anti-party group"of "traitors"allegedly conspired with "foreign enemies" to open Albania to "revisionist influences" and to "destroy the independence of the homeland." In April, Hoxha claimed that the APL had thwarted a move by "internal enemies" to disrupt the Sino-Albanian friendship and to "sabotage the construction of socialism in Albania" (ibid., 30 April).

On the basis of the available evidence, largely conjectural, there appear to be two primary explanations for Hoxha's actions (e.g., *Rruga e partisë*, January-October; *Zëri i popullit*, 1-9 November, 4, 12, 21 December). First, differences do appear to have arisen within the Albanian leadership during the early 1970s over such matters as the Albanian-Chinese relationship and related foreign policy issues, the regime's hard-line cultural policies, and the definition of the respective roles of the party and the state bureaucracy in the management of the economy and the military establishment. Confronted with what he viewed as a serious challenge to his authority and programs, Hoxha deposed and publicly denounced several of his oldest and closest associates, who apparently had not only disagreed with his stands on China, the economy, the armed forces, and culture, but had also argued that in the future the party give greater weight to the recommendations of the technocrats and professional managers in policy formulation. Second, the Albanian leader seems to have removed from high-level party and state posts individuals loyal to him, but unsuccessful in carrying out their assigned responsibilities, on the grounds that their ineffectiveness posed a danger to his regime. These persons have not as yet been publicly denounced.

Auxiliary and Mass Organizations. The Union of Albanian Labor Youth (UALY) celebrated its 35th anniversary in November 1976 (*Zëri i popullit*, 23 November). Lumturi Rexha, a member of the UALY Secretariat since 1972, was elected first secretary in place of Jovan Bardhi, who became first secretary of the Dibër district party organization. Rexha is the first woman to head the organization since the late 1940s, and her election reflects the policy of the party leadership to place more women in positions of responsibility. Unlike her immediate predecessors, however, Rexha was not elected to the Central Committee, a reflection of the fact that the APL leaders are still not wholly pleased with the performance of the organization. Rexha, presumably, will have to earn her seat on the Central Committee.

One of the major responsibilities assigned the UALY in 1976 was to encourage the nation's youth to "live and work where they are most needed." In this connection, it was revealed that during 1975-76 some 11,000 young Albanians had left the cities to work in the countryside as a consequence of the organization's efforts (*Rruga e partisë*, October). Another important task of the UALY is to improve the morale and discipline among young workers as well as to raise their "ideopolitical consciousness." Since approximately 40 percent of the Albanian work force is comprised of those eligible for UALY membership (ages 14-26), the organization is considered an important auxiliary of the United Trade Unions of Albania (UTUA) in the campaign to fulfill the goals of the 1976-80 Five-Year Plan (*Zëri i popullit*, 21 May).

A prime assignment of the UTUA in 1976 has been to develop an appreciation among the Albanian working class of the implications for the party, nation, and themselves that arise from Albania's "being forced" to live under an "imperialist-revisionist economic blockade" (*Puna*, 3 August).The two main projects of the Democratic Front were to rally mass support for the new constitution (see below) and to arouse enthusiasm for the APL's programs under the slogan, "Let us always and everywhere carry out the directives and policies of the party" (*Rruga e partisë*, October). All the mass organizations were exhorted to step up their efforts in combatting "liberal and alien bourgeois-revisionist ideas." It was observed that while some progress had been made in this latter campaign, the mass organizations "were a long way from realizing the expectations of the party" in this matter (*Puna*, 3 August).

Party Internal Affairs. The most notable party events in 1976 were the holding of the Seventh Congress and the commemoration of the 35th anniversary of the party's founding. Both Central Committee plenums dealt primarily with matters relating to the Congress. The Ninth Plenum, 19-20 July, set the date and approved the agenda for the Congress and established the procedure for electing delegates to it. The plenum also discussed the draft proposals for the Sixth Five-Year Plan (1976-80) (*Zëri i popullit*, 20, 21 July). At its Tenth Plenum, 12-14 October, the Central Committee approved the report on the activities of the APL Central Committee during 1971-76 that Hoxha would present to the Congress and the draft directives for the 1976-80 Five-Year Plan which Prime Minister Mehmet Shehu would submit (ibid., 15 October).

Domestic Attitudes and Activities. *Political Developments.* There were seven changes in the composition of the Council of Ministers during 1976. Between October 1974-December 1976 there have been a total of fourteen changes in the makeup of the cabinet. In April, Agriculture Minister Piro Dodbiba, who had served in this capacity since 1965, and Minister of Education and Culture Thoma Deljana, who assumed his post in 1966, were both fired for "grave errors in the implementation of the party line" (*Zëri i popullit*, 30 April). Dodbiba subsequently was dropped as a Politburo candidate and Central Committee member. Deljana also lost his Central Committee seat.

Both were succeeded in their cabinet posts by relatively young (both appear to be in their late 30s or early 40s) women with extensive experience at the local level. Themie Thomaj, the new agriculture minister, is a university graduate in agronomy and economics. She had worked her way up from farm hand to directress of the model Kemishtaj collective farm at the time of her appointment. Thomaj was elected to the APL Central Committee at the Seventh Congress. Minister of Education and Culture Tefta Cami, a university graduate in education, had been a school teacher and administrator before she became an APL *apparatchik*. In 1971 she was elected a Central Committee candidate, the following year was made a member of the secretariat of the Berat district party organization, and in 1973 she served in the same capacity in the Dibër district. Cami was promoted to Central Committee membership at the Seventh Congress.

In October, Manush Myftiu relinquished his post as first secretary of the Tirana district party organization to become a deputy prime minister. He retained his Politburo seat and apparently will oversee the execution of policies in the areas of education and culture. In mid-November, Spiro Koleka, who had been a member of virtually every Albanian cabinet since the end of World War II, was relieved of his post as deputy prime minister and assigned to other, unspecified "important duties." At this time Deputy Prime Minister Xhafer Spahiu and Minister of Industry and Mining Pali Miska switched positions. This move represented a further demotion for Spahiu, who had lost his candidate Politburo membership at the Seventh Congress. Spahiu, however, had been permitted to retain his Central Committee seat, and his appointment as minister of industry and mining indicates the APL leadership was willing to give him an opportunity to compensate for his past shortcomings. With the departure of Koleka from the cabinet and the demotion of Spahiu, Deputy Prime Minister Pali Miska will assume greater responsibility for the management of the industrial sector of the economy. The ouster of Finance Minister Lefter Goga, who was also demoted to Central Committee candidate membership, is attributable to his inability to exercise the "tight-fisted control over expenditures" he had pledged upon assuming office in October 1974. The appointment of Politburo member Haki Toska, a top-ranking party economic specialist and another of Hoxha's intimates, to succeed him underscores the seriousness with which the APL leadership views the problems that have plagued the finance ministry in recent years (ibid., 14 November).

The composition of the Council of Ministers in December was Mehmet Shehu, prime minister and defense minister; Adil Çarçani, first deputy prime minister; Manush Myftiu, deputy prime minister; Pali Miska, deputy prime minister; Petro Dode, deputy prime minister and chairman of the state planning commission; Kadri Hazbiu, minister of the interior; Nesti Nase, minister of foreign affairs; Xhafer Spahiu, minister of industry and mines; Myqerem Fuga, minister of light and food industry; Themi Thomaj, minister of agriculture; Tefta Cami, minister of education and culture; Rahman Hanku, minister of construction; Nedin Hoxha, minister of trade; Luan Babamento, minister of communications; Haki Toska, minister of finance, and Llambi Zicishti, minister of health.

In mid-January the draft of the new Albanian constitution was completed and presented to the people for study and reaction (ibid., 20, 21 January). The product of a 51-person committee headed by Hoxha, the draft constitution, according to the Albanian party leader, "reflects the true socialist society which is being constructed in accordance with the teachings of Marx, Engels, Lenin, and Stalin as these teachings have been embodied and verified in the revolutionary experiences of our country" (ibid., 2 November). A major purpose of the document, according to APL spokesmen, is to ensure that Albania will always follow the "correct Marxist-Leninist road" to the achievement of communism (ibid., 28 January; 6 February; 2, 5 November). In other words, the promulgation of the new Albanian constitution appears to represent an attempt on the part of Hoxha to make his policies binding on his eventual successors.

Upon adoption of the new constitution, Albania will be known as the People's Socialist Republic of Albania (Art. 1). Other clauses in the constitution sanction the political monopoly of the APL (Art. 3), proclaim Marxism-Leninism as the nation's official ideology (Art. 3), declare that economic development and the construction of socialism in Albania are based mainly on the principle of "self reliance" (Art. 26), prohibit the obtaining of credits from "bourgeois or capitalist monopolies or states" (Art. 26), exempt Albanian citizens from all "levies or taxes" (Art. 31), affirm state support for the development of literature and the arts "according to the tenets of socialist realism" (Art. 35), require the government to maintain a program of atheist propaganda to develop a "scientific-materialistic world outlook among the people" (Art. 36), designate the APL first secretary as commander in chief of the armed forces (Art. 90), and forbid the establishment of foreign military bases and the stationing of foreign troops on Albanian soil (Art. 94). Hoxha claimed, in his report to the Seventh Congress, that some 1,500,000 Albanians (virtually the nation's entire adult population) had attended the public meetings held throughout the country to explain and analyze the draft constitution and that some 300,000 had actually participated in the discussions at these sessions. In mid-December the constitution drafting committee voted to submit the document to the December session of the People's Assembly for final approval (ibid., 16 December).

The Ideological and Cultural Revolution. Perhaps the most significant development in Albania's continuing Ideological and Cultural Revolution during 1976 was the promulgation on 1 April of a series of new measures intended to further inhibit the emergence of a privileged class of intellectuals and bureaucrats, reduce the economic and social gaps between the nation's white- and blue-collar workers, and narrow the differences in the quality of life in the urban and rural areas. This new program calls for salary reductions for those earning more than 900 leks ($210 at the "official" exchange rate) per month, wage cuts for teachers and researchers employed in higher education, and pension reductions for highly compensated military personnel. It also provides for adjustment of individual or group salary inequities and requires that pension differentials between farmers and industrial laborers be eliminated. It further mandates the improvement of educational, health, and cultural facilities in the countryside and promises to increase the quantity and assortment of consumer goods in rural areas. In addition, the government has pledged to increase its investment and subsidy programs for collective farms situated in the upland regions of the country (ibid., 1 April). The regime emphasized that it did not consider these measures to be of a "purely routine administrative nature"; rather, they were viewed as having a "profound, ideological, political, and social significance" for the building of socialism in Albania (ibid., 2 April).

The APL persisted in its efforts to keep Albanian cultural life free of "harmful bourgeois influences." In this connection, there were renewed calls for the "further revolutionization" of the school system. Specifically, teachers were urged to become "social activists" so they might better serve as models for their students. Also, the schools were instructed to upgrade their vocational and physical-military training programs and to take the requisite steps to ensure their graduates are imbued with a "strong proletarian revolutionary outlook" (e.g., ibid., 5 July, 1 September). Since nearly a third of the Albanian population is enrolled in the various components of the school system, the regime has come to view the schools as the most important instrument for the ideological training of the nation's youth. The party leadership, however, is distressed that some younger-generation Albanians are still being influenced by "bourgeois and revisionist" ideas, and still very much resent efforts to dictate their clothing and hair styles. There also seems to be more than just token resistance to party directives obliging younger people to live in the countryside and to "perform those tasks required by society." Also alarming to the APL hierarchy is the fact that the nation's youth is not as well acquainted with the teachings of Hoxha as party officials would like (ibid., 15 August). These reported shortcomings undoubtedly contributed to the political demise of the ousted minister of education and culture, Thoma Deljana.

The educational and cultural sectors have become increasingly significant for the regime as a consequence of a quantitive development in these areas. In 1976 the educational system enrolled nearly 800,000 students, who were taught by 34,000 teachers. There were 24,000 graduates of various institutions of higher education and 60,000 secondary school graduates in the country. There were also 510 culture palaces in Albania, of which 460 were in rural areas. During 1971-75 there were published 3,214 books, with a circulation of more than 42 million copies, and 35 feature films and numerous documentaries were produced in the country (*Nentori*, September).

The Economy. In his report on the results of the Fifth Five-Year Plan (1971-75) to the party congress (*Zëri i popullit*, 5 November), Prime Minister Shehu announced that industrial production in 1975 was 52 percent greater than in 1971, somewhat below the 61-66 percent planned increase. Agricultural output in 1975 was 33 percent higher than in 1970, about half the 65-69 percent projected growth. National income rose by 38 percent during 1971-75, considerably less than the 55-60 percent increase foreseen by the Plan. The Albanian prime minister assigned the major portion of the blame for the difficulties encountered in realizing the Plan's goals to the "hostile activities" of the deposed chairman of the State Planning Commission, Abdyl Këllezi, and to "shortcomings in the administration of the Ministry of Agriculture." On the positive side, Shehu claimed that Albania in 1976 had achieved self-sufficiency in the production of bread grains and was able to supply 85 percent of its consumer goods requirements.

The Sixth Five-Year Plan (1976-80) establishes somewhat more modest targets than its predecessor. Industrial production in 1980 is expected to be 41-44 percent above the 1975 level. The projected increase in agricultural output for the current plan period is 38-41 percent, and national income is expected to rise by 38-40 percent. According to the Plan, heavy industry will continue to grow at about twice the rate of light industry (ibid., 10 November). Shehu indicated that by 1980 the APL leadership expected that Albanian industry would be able to fulfill 95 percent of the nation's spare parts needs and 90 percent of its consumer goods requirements. There was a further expectation the country would remain self-sufficient in the production of bread grains and that its balance of payments deficit would be markedly reduced (ibid., 5 November).

The Albanian prime minister thanked the Chinese for the "internationalist aid they had given and continued to give Albania for the construction of socialism and the strengthening of its defensive capabilities." At the same time, however, he stressed that during the Sixth Five-Year Plan, Albania would "*rely more heavily than ever before*" (emphasis in text) on its own efforts and resources to fulfill the Plan directives (ibid.). This observation, coupled with Shehu's failure to mention any specific new projects that would be initiated with Chinese support, would seem to confirm reports that the Albanians are not entirely pleased with the level of economic assistance they will be receiving from the Chinese during the current five-year plan (e.g., MTI, Budapest, 2 April; *Washington Post*, 2, 8 November).

Hoxha's comprehensive purge of the nation's economic and technical elites between 1974 and 1976 was in part intended to correct problems in the management of the economy. The party leadership is apparently sensitive to the need for developing improved techniques for planning and monitoring the economy, but it has emphasized that the economic experts must understand they are the servants rather than the masters of the party. There is further recognition that the ultimate success of the nation's economic programs depends on the training, motivation, and discipline of the work force both in the factories and on the farms (e.g., *Zëri i popullit*, 2, 5 November).

International Views and Policies. The People's Republic of Albania (PRA) during 1976 established diplomatic relations with the Malagasy Republic, Iceland, San Marino, Sierra Leone, and Burma, and at year's end had diplomatic ties with 77 countries. In February the Albanian government issued a decree extending its territorial waters in the Adriatic and Ionian seas to 15 nautical miles (*Zëri i popullit*, 26 February).

The speeches of the APL leaders at theCongress and at meetings celebrating the 35th anniversary of the party reveal no significant shifts in the PRA's international attitudes or policies. Hoxha repeated the standard Albanian line that all "genuine Marxist-Leninists must continue to wage a simultaneous two-front war against the forces of imperialism and revisionism." He reiterated that in Tirana's view the two "superpowers," the United States and the Soviet Union, posed the greatest danger to peace and to the freedom and independence of the nations of the world. The Albanian party leader scoffed at the "notion" that the PRA is isolated from the rest of the world, but did emphasize his country would remain off limits to "fascists," "spies," "foreign agents," and "others who wished to bring bourgeois or revisionist ideas into Albania." He further declared that Albania was interested in maintaining commercial relations with all countries except the United States, Soviet Union, Spain, Israel, and "several other states under the control of fascist regimes."

Hoxha appeared to adopt a tougher stance toward the "third world" countries, courted by him in recent years, when he ridiculed the "notion" that a people or nation could "wage a struggle for true national and social liberation outside the banner of Marxism-Leninism" (ibid., 2 November).

Shehu neatly summarized the position of the Albanian leadership for both friends and adversaries when he declared the PRA would continue to base its foreign policies on "Marxist-Leninist" principles "irrespective of whether others may agree or disagree with its views" (ibid., 9 November).

Albanian-Chinese Relations. The deaths of Chou En-lai and Mao Tse-tung coupled with ensuing political unrest in China undoubtedly complicated the ties between Tirana and Peking. It appeared, however, that the new Chinese leadership was desirous of maintaining a close, if not intimate, relationship with the Albanians despite the differences over foreign policy and, perhaps, economic issues that have arisen between them in recent years. Hoxha likewise did not appear eager to permit the PRA's ties with China, still Albania's major foreign aid donor as well as its closest ideological and diplomatic ally, to deteriorate. In April the Albanian party leader reaffirmed the primacy of Tirana's relationship with Peking and claimed he had "crushed" a plot fabricated by "domestic enemies and revisionists" to "disrupt" the Sino-Albanian friendship (ibid., 30 April). In his report to the APL Congress Hoxha attempted to refute rumors of growing tensions between Tirana and Peking (e.g., *Newsweek*, 10 May; *Chicago Daily News*, 12 August) by declaring:

> The Albanian Party of Labor and the Albanian people are the friends and faithful allies of the Chinese Communist Party and the Chinese people. . . . Neither the lies nor the fabrications of bourgeois-revisionist propagandists can besmirch the Marxist-Leninist character and vitality of the Albanian-Chinese friendship. Our party and people will work unceasingly to preserve the purity and strength of our fraternal friendship and cooperation with the great Chinese people, their glorious Communist Party, and with great People's China. (*Zëri i popullit*, 2 November.)

In keeping with recent practice, the Chinese did not dispatch a delegation to the Congress. They sent a warm message of greeting, hailing Albania as "the great citadel of revolution towering over Europe" and expressing a desire to strengthen the Sino-Albanian relationship (ibid., 4 November). Similar sentiments were contained in the Chinese Communist Party's congratulatory message on the occasion of the APL's 35th anniversary (ibid., 9 November). The Chinese press also published lengthy excerpts of Hoxha's address to the Congress (ibid., 17 November).

Albanian-Soviet Relations. Throughout 1976 the USSR continued to express a willingness to improve relations with Tirana (e.g., Moscow radio, 11 January, 17 July). In broadcasts beamed to Albania, the Soviets, hoping perhaps to capitalize on reported economic difficulties within the country, recalled the "generous aid" the USSR had provided the PRA in 1947-60 (e.g., ibid., 31 May, 1 August). In a speech to the October Central Committee plenum of the Communist Party of the Soviet Union (CPSU), party leader Leonid Brezhnev invited the Albanians to reestablish friendly relations with Moscow (*Washington Post*, 3 November). Hoxha spurned Brezhnev's overture with the declaration his regime had not changed its attitude toward "the revisionist Soviet Union, the enemy of Albania, of socialism, and of the freedom and independence of all peoples" (*Zéri i popullit*, 2 November). The negative Albanian attitude toward the USSR was reinforced by the publication of volumes 19-22 of Hoxha's *Works*, which focus on the events that culminated in the 1961 diplomatic break between Moscow and Tirana (e.g., ibid., 3 February, 22 March).

Relations with Eastern Europe. With the exception of Romania, the PRA displayed little interest in improving its relations with the East European Warsaw Pact countries. Hoxha was especially harsh in his denunciation of Bulgaria, which he branded an "instrument of Soviet imperialist policies in the Balkans and Eastern Europe" (ibid., 2 November). Although Albania boycotted the conference on Balkan cooperation hosted by the Greek government during January-February, it appeared both Tirana and Athens were anxious to expand their economic and cultural ties (ibid., 23 May, 8 December).

Hoxha again stressed Albania's desire to maintain diplomatic, economic, and cultural relations with Yugoslavia, and reaffirmed that the Albanians were prepared to fight "shoulder to shoulder" with the Yugoslavs to resist any "external threats" to Belgrade's independence. At the same time, however, the Albanian leader made it clear he would continue to speak out against what he viewed as Yugoslav deviations from "Marxist-Leninist principles" (ibid., 2 November). Albanian-Yugoslav relations were somewhat strained by Hoxha's criticism of Tito's domestic policies at the Seventh Congress, the conviction of 31 ethnic Albanian Yugoslav citizens from the autonomous province of Kosovo for allegedly advocating the unification of Kosovo with Albania, and the killing by the Yugoslavs of an Albanian fishing boat captain whose vessel was intercepted in Yugoslav territorial waters (*Washington Post*, 1 March).

Relations with Western Europe and the United States. Hoxha indicated that Albania enjoyed satisfactory relations with France, Belgium, Austria, Switzerland, and the Scandinavian countries, and expressed the hope that commercial and cultural relations with Italy could be improved. Prospects for better relations with West Germany were dependent upon Bonn's payment of $2 billion in World War II reparations. Similarly, normalization of relations with Great Britain hinged on London's return of the Albanian gold it was awarded by the World Court as a consequence of the 1947 Corfu Channel incident (*Zëri i poppulit*, 2 November).

There was no indication of any change in Tirana's attitude toward the United States. Hoxha characterized the USA as "the political and economic bastion of the exploiting capitalist system, the great defender of colonialism and neo-colonialism, the inspirer of racism, and the main enforcer of international reaction" (ibid). The Albanians expressed the view that the election of Jimmy Carter to the U.S. presidency would not result in any significant changes in American foreign or domestic programs, because there have been no discernible differences in the policies pursued by U.S. presidents since the Kennedy administration (ibid., 11 November).

International Activities and Contacts. The Seventh APL Congress provided an opportunity to assess the support enjoyed by Albania in the world Communist movement in 1976. Only three ruling parties—the North Korean, Vietnamese, and Laotian—were represented at the Congress. An additional 29 parties, mostly pro-Peking "Marxist-Leninist" organizations, were represented. (Ibid., 2 November.) In comparison with the Sixth APL Congress, two more ruling parties and seven additional non-ruling parties attended the Seventh Congress.

The Albanians published a declaration of the Communist Party of Germany (M-L) which claimed that a "section" of this party had been formed in the German Democratic Republic in late 1975 (ibid., 24 February). In July the second volume of Enver Hoxha's *Selected Works* was published in English, French, Spanish, and Russian editions (*Shqipëria e re*, July).

Publications. The APL daily newspaper (with a claimed circulation of 101,000) is *Zëri i popullit*. The party's monthly theoretical journal is *Rruga e partisë*. Another major publication is *Bashkimi*, the daily organ of the Democratic Front (claimed average circulation of 45,000). The newspapers of the Union of Albanian Labor Youth, *Zëri i rinsë*, and the United Trade Unions of Albania, *Puna*, are published twice weekly. The official news agency is the Albanian Telegraphic Agency (ATA).

Western Illinois University   Nicholas C. Pano

Bulgaria

The Bulgarian Communist Party (Bulgarska kommunisticheska partiya; BCP) has carried this name since 1919, but its separate identity dates from 1903, when it split from the Bulgarian Social Democratic Party as the "Workers Social Democratic Party (Narrow Socialists)." It took the name of "Workers Party" in 1927 and of "Bulgarian Workers Party (Communist)" in 1934, but reassumed the current name in 1948, after having consolidated its power. Its most famous leader, Georgi Dimitrov, one-time secretary-general of the Third Communist International (Comintern), was Bulgarian head of state until his death in 1949.

The BCP came to power in the wake of the unanticipated declaration of war on Bulgaria by the USSR and the entry of Soviet troops in September 1944, while the pro-Western Muraviev government was arranging for an armistice with the Western powers and had declared war on Nazi Germany. The confused situation was exploited by the Communist-dominated Fatherland Front coalition to stage a coup d'état and take over the government. In violation of its pledges and international obligations, the BCP split the coalition and subdued by violence its former allies, the United Opposition, in a monumental struggle lasting two years and ending with the hanging of the Agrarian leader Nikola Petkov in 1948. It has remained the only political force ever since, although nominally a splinter party assuming the name of the Bulgarian Agrarian People's Union is allowed to coexist, yet not to compete for power. Over the years, the BCP has been slavishly pro-Soviet, although some of its leaders, most notably Traycho Kostov (hanged as a Titoist), have tried unsuccessfully to moderate its course; domestically, the party has also been among the most repressive and centralistic, with its current leader Todor Zhivkov holding the helm since 1954 with increasing power.

The 11th Party Congress, held in 1976, reported a total membership of 789,795. This amounted to an increase of more than 90,000 in five years and represented about 9 percent of the population.

One in eight Bulgarians over the age of 18 is a party member. The proportion of workers has increased slowly to 41.4 percent (from 40.1 percent in 1971), while that of white-collar workers has grown faster, to 35.6 percent (from 33.8) and that of peasants has continued to fall, to 23.1 percent (from 26.1). Although the share of women members was reportedly on the increase, it has remained small—27.5 percent in a population with a majority of women. The fact that only 70 percent of the members work in material production underscores the bureaucratization of the party.

The BCP holds a dominant position in all governmental bodies, including the National Assembly (Parliament), where the Fatherland Front selects also some non-Communist deputies (Agrarians and Komsomol members) who run unopposed.

Bulgaria had a population of 8,729,720 according to the 1975 census, an increase of 501,854 over the 1965 figure.

Leadership and Organization. The 1976 Party Congress confirmed again the undisputed power position of Todor Zhivkov, who holds not only the top party post of first secretary (since 1954) but also the top government job of chairman of the State Council (equivalent to a head of state). The Congress reduced the number of Politburo members to 9 (from 12), dropping the 86-year-old dogmatist-philosopher Todor Pavlov, the technical expert Professor Ivan Popov, who had led a government delegation to Washington in 1974, and the once promising and potential rival of Zhivkov (his namesake, but no relation), Zhivko Zhivkov. The current members, besides Todor Zhivkov, are Tsola Dragoycheva, Grisha Filipov, Pencho Kubadinski, Aleksandur Lilov, Ivan Mikhaylov, Stanko Todorov (also premier), Tano Tsolov, and Boris Velchev. Todorov and Velchev are Zhivkov's closest and oldest collaborators. The 6-man candidate group remained the same.

The Secretariat was also streamlined, to 10 members (formerly 12), among whom the 6 secretaries were Zhivkov (first secretary), Ognyan Doynov, Grisha Filipov, Aleksandur Lilov, Ivan Prumov, and Boris Velchev. Doynov, a younger engineer-apparatchik, replaced Konstantin Tellalov, considered a potential contender for the top position. Penyu Kiratsov was dropped, as was Georgi Bokov, the editor of the party daily, *Rabotnichesko delo* (hereinafter abbreviated as *RD*).

The leadership changes, although relatively minor, can be interpreted as a new indication of Zhivkov's continued vigilance to thwart any challenge to his power by eliminating promising figures and filling responsible positions with his trusted lieutenants. Among the latter is also his daughter, Lyudmila, who was continued, with ministerial rank, as head of the Committee on Art and Culture, but also was made a member of the 11-man managing bureau of the 33-man Council of Ministers. Other changes affected the leadership of the Communist youth organization, Encho Moskov being replaced by Boycho Shteryanov, after serious criticisms, and Georgi Bokov losing also his chairmanship of the Journalists Association; both moves were symptomatic of shortcomings on the ideological front.

Mass Organizations. All mass organizations follow official ideology and policy and are headed by members of the BCP. The Fatherland Front, the largest "non-partisan mass organization" has some 3.5 million members and includes as collective members the Bulgarian Komsomol (Dimitrovski Kommunisticheski Mladezhki Suyuz; Dimitrov Communist Youth Union), with about 1.2 million members, the Agrarian Party (about 120,000), and the trade unions (about 2.5 million).

Party Internal Affairs. The major event of 1976 was the 11th Party Congress, held between 29 March and 2 April, about one month after the congress of the Communist Party of the Soviet Union (CPSU), as has become the custom. The major theme remained the protestation of complete loyalty to and identity with the USSR and its goals and policies. In his report to the Congress, Zhivkov reiterated that he could not visualize any other road than "shoulder to shoulder with our Soviet brothers and sisters, under conditions of the closest possible cooperation with the party of Lenin and of a fuller and more organic rapprochement between Bulgaria and the Soviet Union." (Proceedings in *RD*, 30 March-3 April.) The report dealt with foreign policy, economic and technical progress, the socialist way of life, the role of the BCP, and the future transition to communism. On the domestic front Zhivkov stressed the need for modernizatin of the economy, relying on scientific-technical progress; paid lip service to raising living standards; and identified several problems on the road to developed socialism and communism.

On internal party affairs, Zhivkov reported the increase in party membership, the leading share of blue-collar workers, and the increased share of young people among the new members. But he struck an ominous note when he announced that all party membership cards would be renewed, in order to recheck the degree of activism and responsibility of each member. Although he specifically denied an intention to conduct a purge, the implication of a purge was clear as he also stated that the exchange of cards offered an opportunity to "get rid of those members who violate the party program and statute, principles and norms, and socialist legality" and "undermine the political and moral prestige of the BCP." (Ibid., 30 March, p. 6.)

Touching on the conflict between old and young cadres, the party leader defended the merits of his generation (the average Politburo age was 62), but also criticized nepotism and personal patronage in promotion practices, and placed emphasis on ideological purity and "an uncompromising struggle against bourgeois ideology." In this connection, particular emphasis was laid on the performance of the youth. Zhivkov leveled an exceptionally strong criticism at the Komsomol leadership in its ideological-educational work and identified "consumerism, petty pursuit of material well-being, and a disdain for work" as spreading phenomena, alongside with the increased use of alcohol and tobacco. (Incidentally, legal efforts to restrict the use of alcohol were strengthened by an order of the Ministry of Domestic Trade. *Durzhaven vestnik*, no. 20, 9 March.)

In preparation for the Congress, the BCP issued several documents, called "theses," on economic, social, scientific-technical, and political goals and policies (details below).

The Congress approved all these documents and performed its usual task of electing the various levels of party officials, from First Secretary Zhivkov to the Central Committee, consisting of 154 full members and 121 candidates, a slight increase over the old Central Committee. The proportion of government officials was increased at the expense of local party personnel and agricultural experts, and of ethnic minorities which remained grossly underrepresented (for details see "The Central Committee after the 11th Party Congress," in Radio Free Europe Research, *Background Report/140 (Bulgaria)*, 16 June).

The BCP held several plenums during 1976: one on 27-28 January, dealing with the theses on living standards and the BCP; two, on 19 April and 15 June, devoted to the elections to the National Assembly and the composition of the state organs; a fourth, and seemingly the most important one, on 1-2 July, at which Zhivkov himself presented a detailed report on the implementation of the decisions of the 11th Congress, with the emphasis on social policy and the economical use of the country's scarce resources (editorial in *RD*, 26 July); and one on 27 October devoted to the 1976-80 five-year plan. All in all, the events of the year indicated that party life remained conventional and stagnant, despite outward appearances of activism and change.

Domestic Attitudes and Activities. The positions and activities surrounding the 11th Party Congress remained the major evidence of the BCP's views on key domestic issues and expressed the attitudes of the Zhivkov leadership, secure and comfortable in its power monopoly yet at the same time confronted with inertia and growing discrepancy between ambitious goals and lackluster performance. The Congress proceedings were further supplemented by the several lengthy "theses," by pronouncements by Zhivkov and other leaders, and by enactment of the new five-year plan and various measures to implement domestic policies.

The Central Committee's "Theses on the State and Development of the BCP and of the Public Organizations and Movements," approved by the plenum of 27-28 January 1976 (see *RD*, 5 February), called for continued raising of the Party's leading role in and control of society as the country moves toward "the construction of developed socialism." The theses extolled the need for an enhanced role of the primary party organizations in particular, but at the same time complained of the adverse effects of growing party membership (hence the need to "replace membership cards") and of general inefficiency of these basic organizations. The usual attacks on nepotism, careerism, and consumerism were coupled with demands for "militant and efficient ideological work," current performance of which was called unsatisfactory.

The many shortcomings in the ideological sphere applied not only to the party cadres but also to the mass media, literature and the arts, and to the mass organizations, especially the Komsomol. This criticism was followed, among others, by a resolution of the Politburo on the media (ibid., 9 August), the demotion of Georgi Bokov from the party Secretariat, his replacement as editor of the party daily, and his removal from the chairmanship of the Bulgarian Journalists Association, and the replacement of the first secretary of the Komsomol, Encho Moskov. Zhivkov, in his Congress report and elsewhere, continued to expose apathy, loose morals, and "admiration for anything foreign" among the young people. Serious self-criticism was exercised as well. In view of these phenomena, which seem to persist and deepen, it is hard to expect such marked improvements as those targeted by the leadership.

Long-term goals in the socio-economic and scientific fields were revealed in the set of theses on economic development, development of science and technology, and raising of living standards (ibid., 8, 22 January, 12 February), and especially the Seventh Five-Year Plan (ibid., 23 February, 7 April, 29 October).

In brief, these lengthy documents called basically for a continuation of the past policies aimed at building a developed socialist society and contained the usual contradictions between lofty intents and increasing difficulties in their implementation. Thus, the emphasis was on increased living standards, scientific-technological progress, and the building of the "new man," but at the same time the pattern called for heavy-industrial growth, and the goals of efficiency and of altruism appeared as elusive as before. Moreover, actual targets of real income growth were reduced (to 20 percent by 1980, as against a reported achievement of 32 percent for 1971-75) and most 1980 targets for per capita consumer goods, especially foodstuffs, were below the goals of the December 1972 Plenum on Living Standards, already missed for 1975. Housing (reported at 13.3 square meters per person by 1976) and the promised reduced work week (targeted in November 1962 for 40 hours by 1970 but reported as 42.5 hours in 1975 in most of industry), remained as other examples of unfulfilled promises.

The Party Congress itself placed large emphasis on the economy and on its intensive modernization, as the very motto of the Congress, used by Zhivkov, namely "effectiveness and quality" (borrowed from the Soviet Congress) indicated. But while the need for increased productivity was openly recognized and encouraged as the major road to success in view of the growing paucity of domestic material and human resources, the economic system remained highly centralized and based on larger and larger economic units, culminating in mammoth "national complexes." Thus, the national agro-industrial complex, formally set up in August 1976 (*Durzhaven vestnik*, nos. 75 and 76, 21, 24 September), as an organizational management form, similar to yet smaller than the complexes in construction, transport, and chemicals, unites all of the existing smaller agro-industrial complexes with many industrial trusts and includes the Ministry of Agriculture and Food Supply itself, which is given, however, the function of managerial leadership. The primary task is to ensure the supply of fresh and processed foods and agricultural raw materials for industry. According to official data, the national complex, as constituted in 1976, would account for 29 percent of the national income, 32 percent of all exports and 45 percent of the commodity stock on the domestic market (see *RD*, 23 September). The huge size of the complex raises the question of diseconomies of scale, including the ability of a single ministry to manage it effectively, although the efforts made in recent years to improve agricultural performance, and to make farm incomes and social benefits comparable to industry, have had a degree of success. (See also Radio Free Europe Research, *Bulgaria*, 30 September.)

The major balance sheet of the economy was to be the performance of the past five years as a basis for comparison with the Seventh Five-Year Plan, for 1976-80. Although not enough detail was available thus far, official accounts claimed an overall fulfillment of the Sixth Plan (national income grew by 46 percent, industry by 55 percent, agriculture by 17 percent), with per capita income and retail trade turnover showing over-fulfillment, though from modest levels. Foreign trade allegedly nad doubled its ambitious target, albeit in nominal terms: if the drastic increase in free-world prices and the upward adjustments of prices of Soviet oil and other commodities are taken into account, the increase in real terms is reduced substantially. But the new stresses and strains, added to the endogenous ones, were not expressed in the original targets for 1980. In fact, unlike the USSR, Bulgaria did not announce a slackening but a maintenance of the previous growth rates. However, as the plan neared and reached its legislative approval, some targets were gradually lowered: national income growth to 45 percent (from 52), real income to 20 percent (from 25), and retail trade to 40 percent (the achieved increases in 1976 were 46, 32, and 47 percent, respectively). A higher figure was provided for capital investments (nearly 31 billion leva, as against 21 for the Sixth Plan), but one should discount for inflation and also for the drop in the last two years of the Sixth Plan. Still industry retains the first priority, while agriculture is underfinanced and, despite the growth in output, consumption levels are low; also the fodder and livestock sectors remain serious problem areas. (See Professor V. Mishev's articles in *Ikonomicheski zhivot*, no. 4, 21 January, and *Novo vreme*, no. 2.)

The major stresses and strains were clearly evident from continued exhortations to rely more and more on "intensive" factors. In fact, the new plan calls for strict economies in materials, a six- and even seven-day utilization of machines and equipment, intensified production employment of students, and the training of most able-bodied citizens under 35 to drive tractors and trucks (Radio Free Europe Research, *Bulgaria*, 14 April). At the same time an attempt to streamline the bureaucracy and most notably its managerial level was announced in August (decree in *Durzhaven vestnik*, no. 66, 17 August) which authorized the dismissal, transfer, or downgrading of managerial-administrative personnel, accounting for 13.5 percent of the total labor force. Although rumors had it that up to 30 percent of these employees were to be affected and transferred to production jobs, this seems unlikely, as it would hurt the very group on which the regime bases its support.

The problems of the economy point to a still greater reliance on the USSR and the Soviet bloc, as Bulgarian exports remain largely uncompetitive in the West and the Soviets require Bulgarian loans and investments for the development of Soviet resources—a relatively recent occurrence. Zhivkov himself made an unusually critical reference to the low quality of Bulgarian goods and threatened penalties (*RD*, 29 May).

Finally, the year saw the election of deputies to the Seventh National Assembly (Parliament) and to the local government bodies. The election took place on 30 May, with the usual uncontested slate of officially designated candidates. This slate received 99.93 percent of the votes cast, with 99.92 percent of them for the single candidates. The distribution of the 400 seats, 272 went to members of the BCP, 100 to the Agrarian Union, and 28 to non-party people, showing a slight increase in the number of BCP deputies at the expense of non-party (mostly Komsomol) members. It is symptomatic that such potential rivals as Venelin Kotsev or Ivan Abadzhiev, now in disgrace, were not among the new deputies, while Zhivkov's daughter Lyudmila won a parliamentary seat.

The National Assembly convened on 15 June and elected the new government, supreme court, and chief prosecutor. Zhivkov was reelected as chairman of the State Council, consisting of 26 members, and Stanko Todorov as chairman of the Council of Ministers, consisting of 31 ministers, 11 of whom comprise the "bureau" of the Council. Another deputy chairman, Sava Dulbokov, was added to the list in September. Among the upcoming younger bureaucrats, aside from Zhivkova, are Andrey Lukanov, a well schooled foreign-trade expert and son of the former foreign minister Karlo Lukanov; Krustyu Trichkov and Ognyan Doynov (both typical aparatchiki); and Vladimir Velchev, (son of the number three man, Boris Velchev), who was nominated ambassador to Great Britain. The Assembly approved changes in government agencies, which by and large amounted to the usual periodical reshuffling of "musical chairs," except the enhancement of Zhivkova's role, whose committee absorbed the press, radio, and TV agencies.

The National Assembly met again in October to approve the actions of the Council of Ministers, including the five-year plan and a new law on the People's Militia (police). In his report, Premier Todorov reiterated the problems of shortages in raw materials and labor and stressed the impact on the country of the "unstable international economic situation." He called again for higher effectiveness and quality and an improved structure of the branches of material production as a pre-condition from meeting the goals of the plan. (*RD*, 28 October.) The Militia Act, superseding the 1955 Ukaze, devotes considerable attention to the struggle against "anti-social" activities, catch-all term for various actions and attitudes against the regime's policies, thus implying that restiveness is not a resolved phenomenon (see article by the Militia director, Major General Kostadin Iliev, in *Trud*, 30 October).

International Views and Policies. The Bulgarian leadership pursued its unswervingly loyal alignment with the Soviet Union in 1976, supporting Soviet views and policies without reservation. In view of the centrifugal tendencies in the Communist movement, most notably in Western Europe, the Bulgarian attachment to Moscow became even more obvious and slavish. In fact it was "personalized" to an extent reminiscent of Stalin's "personality cult," when Zhivkov engaged in an extensive eulogy of Brezhnev's qualities and merits in a lead article assessing the Communist achievements during 1976, and on the occasion of his visit to Moscow to honor the Soviet leader with the highest Bulgarian decoration (see *RD*, 1 and 3 December).

The Bulgarian support was verbalized on every suitable occasion but most noticeably at the 11th Party Congress, at the CPSU's 25th Congress, and at the conference of the European Communist and workers parties in East Berlin. In Sofia, Todor Zhivkov rejected "any other road" to socialism and communism than "the ever fuller and more organic rapprochment with the great Soviet Union" (*RD*, 30 March), and proclaimed in Moscow that "our love for Bulgaria and for the Soviet Union today is indivisible — it is a single love as our goal is single and our great and glorious road is one and the same" (ibid., 30 June). In East Berlin, Zhivkov supported both the Soviet leadership role and "proletarian internationalism." Earlier Foreign Minister Mladenov referred to a "monolithic system" within the Soviet bloc (ibid., 19 March). In an article in *World Marxist Review* (June) Zhivkov summarized the ideological position of the Bulgarian regime as follows:

> The ideological struggle is particularly important today. The 11th Congress stressed that a key task of central ideological bodies and every Party branch is to carry on an uncompromising ideological offensive against every manifestation of bourgeois ideology, against right and "left"-wing revisionism, Maoism and anti-Sovietism, bar them from our country, and cooperate on a growing scale and ever more fruitfully with the CPSU and the Communist parties of other fraternal socialist countries in the field of ideology.

Elaborating on these concepts in an interview with *Le Monde* (Paris, 4 August), Zhivkov fielded the question about the significance of the modifications in terminology in the document of the East Berlin conference by arguing that "words are of no significance," but suggested that a new such conference, if it were to take place, should be on a "world" and not a European scale, since at such a meeting, "90 to 95 percent of the parties would agree," thus undirectly admitting the disagreements in East Berlin.

Relations with the USSR and the Soviet Bloc. The year saw a further tightening of Bulgaria's integration with the bloc — especially with the USSR and most visibly in the economic field. More than 75 percent of Bulgaria's trade was with the CMEA countries in 1975 and about 53 percent with the Soviet Union alone, making Bulgaria its third largest trading partner. Coordination efforts in planning, forecasting, and joint production and exploitation were intensified, and Bulgaria increased its credits to Moscow to 280 million leva (U.S. $1.00=0.96 leva at the official exchange rate) in 1976 alone. These credits were used to help develop Soviet resources and are to be repaid in deliveries of fuel and other raw materials after 1979.

Besides the renewed trend of greater dependence on the USSR and the bloc, the country experienced unusual deficits in its CMEA trade, reaching 570 million leva in 1975, much of it caused by the revaluation of foreign-trade prices, favoring the USSR. Thus, the reported increase in Bulgarian-Soviet trade for the concluded five-year period must be deflated for the rise in Soviet oil (reported to be about $250 million by the *Christian Science Monitor*, 4 December 1975); the 1976-80 plan target of a 76 to 80 percent increase in that trade contains also an inflationary factor estimated at nearly 30 percent (Radio Free Europe Research, *Bulgaria*, 15 January 1976).

Bulgaria will continue to rely heavily on the USSR for supplies of oil, gas, coal, iron ore, and metals, and for complete plants and equipment for such enlarged projects as the Maritsa-East power plant and the Kozloduy atomic plant, and will export, aside from agricultural and consumer goods, machines and equipment, mainly from the electrical industry (*RD*, 14 August). In the field of "industrial cooperation" the Soviets contribute not only scientific-technical advice, but also the construction of industrial enterprises whose output goes substantially to the USSR.

The new element of Bulgaria's contribution to the development of Soviet resources, including the sending of hundreds of forestry workers to Siberia for the duration of four years (Sofia radio, 5 February), has generated resentment to such an extent that a noted Bulgarian expert and director of the Institute of Problems of Socialist Economic Integration saw fit to "dispel doubts" in the Moscow *Komsomolskaia Pravda* (17 July). The author, Professor Nesho Tsarevski, took issue with "bourgeois propaganda" that was "spreading lies" about the Soviet "exploitation of workers from East European countries," including Bulgaria, and argued that the Bulgarian contingents in the Komi Republic, along the Orenburg gas pipeline, in the Kursk fields and the Ust-Ilimsk pulp plant were in fact treated better than average workers in both Bulgaria and the USSR by receiving higher pay as an offset for relative discomforts. As to the accusation that the country had become an appendage to the USSR and especially that it was working on consignment for Soviet needs, the author extolled socialist specialization and praised Soviet assistance. Be this as it may, the growing Bulgarian dependence on trade with the USSR and CMEA would require the Bulgarians to produce more and better goods in order to pay for crucial and more expensive supplies, a difficult task to accomplish, and the Tsarevski article on a previously prohibited topic was symptomatic of the stresses resulting from the too close relationship between the "small" and the "big brother."

Relations with Balkan Neighbors. No noticeable changes occurred in attitudes and policies with regard to the Balkan neighbors during 1976, with the possible exception of an improvement of relations with Turkey, so as to even out the closer rapprochement with Greece of the year before. This was evident from Zhivkov's official visit to Ankara in June, the first postwar encounter between heads of state of the two countries. The communiqué referred to the increased trade volume (quadrupling between 1972 and 1975), but no specific agreements were announced on such active bilateral issues as visa-free travel or the repatriation of ethnic Turks residing in Bulgaria (Radio Free Europe Research, *Situation Report: Bulgaria*, 24 June, pp. 3-6).

In a surprise move, Zhivkov sent unpublicized personal messages to the prime ministers of both Greece and Turkey, possibly suggesting either the good offices of his country or a "neutral" site in Bulgaria for conversations between the two neighboring countries aimed at settling the Cyprus problem (Sofia radio, 3 September). This act in itself was viewed as "proof" of the "even-handed" Bulgarian attitude and is significant in that a Soviet-bloc country had deemed it appropriate to serve as an intermediary between two NATO allies. It is quite clear, however, that the Bulgarian regime did not act without Moscow's approval, as the goal remains the further alienation of Greece and Turkey from the Western alliance without raising the suspicion of Moscow's direct involvement.

Moscow's hand was seen also in Bulgaria's attitude toward the Balkan area as an entity. The conference of the five Balkan states held in Athens at the beginning of the year (26 January-5 February), initiated by Greek premier Karamanlis, saw the Bulgarian viewpoint of favoring bilateral to collective ties prevail, as has been the Soviet policy since the days of the attempted Bulgarian-Yugoslav federation; moreover, the conference remained purely consultative and without a sequel although Karamanlis has continued his efforts. (Radio Free Europe Research, "Bulgaria and the Balkan Conference in Athens," *Background Report*, 2 February).

Relations with Yugoslavia also remained "as usual," including occasional flare-ups of the Macedonian controversy, with the Yugoslav media in the typical role of accusers. In 1976 the Yugoslavs objected strongly to such Bulgarian manifestations as election speeches in Bulgarian Macedonia referring to the area as Bulgarian in character, the failure to list the majority of the area's population in the 1975 census as "Macedonians," and the reminder of the role of the Bulgarian armed forces, together with Soviet and Yugoslav troops, in the liberation of Yugoslavia (*Nova Makedonia*, 29 May 1976; *Komunist*, Belgrade, 13 December 1975; Tanyug, 15 September 1976).

Relations with the West. The Soviet line was detected in relations with the West as well. The regime paid lip service to "peaceful coexistence," the Helsinki Accord, and other cooperative ventures, and supported the convocation of a world disarmament conference. In more concrete terms, the major Bulgarian interest was in promoting trade and obtaining credits from the West, but success was mixed. The Federal Republic of Germany remained the country's leading Western partner, but trade deficits grew and reached serious proportions as trade with the West declined in relative terms in 1975 and Bulgaria reported deficits with the industrial West amounting to more than 1.4 billion leva for the five-year period, half of which (more than 770 million leva) was incurred in 1975 alone. Part of the reason was the world recession, but a more endemic explanation was the unattractiveness of Bulgarian goods and the growing Bulgarian integration with the USSR and the Soviet bloc, which would reduce the hard currency earnings available for much needed Western technology. International tourism remained a good source of revenue but the repeated revaluation of the Bulgarian currency, mandatory per diem expenses, and higher prices for largely inferior facilities seem to have peaked the increase in Western visitors at a time when foreign exchange is needed more than before.

Little change occurred in Bulgarian-U.S. relations, especially since Bulgaria refused to take advantage of the Trade Reform Act of 1974 and remained subject to higher tariffs and Export-Import Bank credit restraints.

International Activities and Contacts. As noted earlier, the BCP participated in the conference of European communist and workers parties held in June in East Berlin. Zhivkov attended the 25th CPSU congress in March-April; he also visited Bielorussia in October, and Moscow in December for a tête-à-tête with Brezhnev, whom he decorated as "hero of Socialist Bulgaria." Zhivkov's other foreign trips included Greece in April, Turkey in June, and India in November. Among foreign visitors to Bulgaria were Fidel Castro in March, Andrei Gromyko in November, and many dignitaries as honored guests at the 11th BCP Congress; however, it was Politburo member Fedor Kulakov and not Brezhnev who represented the CPSU.

Publications. The daily organ of the BCP is *Rabotnichesko delo* (Workers' Cause), the monthly is *Partien zhivot* (Party Life) and the theoretical journal is *Novo vreme* (New Times). Other mass party publications are *Politicheska prosveta* (Political Education) and *Ikonomicheski zhivot* (Economic Life). The official news agency is Bulgarska Telegrafna Agentsiya or BTA.

University of Vermont   L. A. D. Dellin

Czechoslovakia

The origins of the Communist Party of Czechoslovakia (Komunistická strana Československa; KSČ) date back to the First World War, when the Social Democratic Party was split by internal conflicts over policies and the impact of the Bolshevik revolution in Russia. The so-called Marxist Left which emerged from this split, advocating radical opposition to war and a revolutionary way to socialism, became later the basis of the Czechoslovak Communist movement. The KSČ was constituted at a merger congress of several ethnic Communist organizations, held in Prague in November 1921, and was shortly afterward admitted to the Third International.

Unlike other Communist parties now in power in Central and Eastern Europe, the KSČ did not acquire control in a gradual process but rather suddenly, through a coup d'état in February 1948 which signified the end of a pluralist system of a fairly long tradition. Three other political parties still exist in name in Czechoslovakia; however, they are integrated in the National Front of Working People, a formalized coalition whose statutes guarantee a two-thirds majority to the Communists. The president of the republic, Gustav Husák, and the prime minister of the federal government, Lubomír Štrougal, are both members of the KSČ.

In October 1968 Czechoslovakia, until then a centralist state, was transformed into a federation of two ethnic units: the Czech Socialist Republic and the Slovak Socialist Republic. This revision of the 1960 constitution is the only surviving part of a comprehensive reform program adopted by the liberal party leadership under Alexander Dubček during a short period, often referred to as the "Prague Spring." The implementation of other reforms was stopped by a Soviet-led military intervention of five member countries of the Warsaw Pact in August 1968. However, the federalist system of the government is not reflected in the Communist Party, where a kind of "asymmetric dualism" prevails, with an autonomous body of the Communist Party of Slovakia (Komunistická strana Slovenska; KSS) in the eastern part of the country, but no counterpart in the western provinces, inhabited by Czechs. This state of affairs makes Czechoslovakia a federal polity ruled by a centralist party.

The KSČ is one of the largest Communist parties of the world. After the Soviet intervention of 1968, many party members were expelled in a purge carried out in 1970, but the membership began to grow again after the 14th Congress in 1971. According to Secretary-General Husák, the KSČ in

June 1976 comprised 1,382,860 members and candidates, organized in 43,506 branches. Of the membership total, 333,952 were admitted between the 14th Congress in 1971 and the 15th Congress in 1976. More than half are 25 years of age and younger, 90 percent are under 35. About 62 percent of the membership is of working-class origin. In 1976, for the first time in 23 years, the steady decrease in the proportion of worker members was halted and reversed. (*WMR*, June.)

Czechoslovakia has a population of 14,928,000.

Organization and Leadership. The KSČ is governed by two top decision-making bodies: the Central Committee and the Presidium. In April 1976, the party held its 15th Congress. (Strictly speaking, it was the 16th if one counts the emergency congress called by the Dubček leadership in August 1968, immediately after the Soviet invasion; the present leaders, however, do not recognize the legitimacy of that congress.) The next Congress is to take place in 1981.

The changes in the membership of the Presidium made by the 15th Congress were not extensive; only the former president of the republic, Ludvík Svoboda, seriously ill at the time of the congress, was not reelected. The Presidium at present is composed of 11 members and 2 candidates. The Secretariat, headed by Husák as secretary-general, includes three other secretaries: Miloslav Hruškovič, Jan Janík, and Ludovít Pezlar, and one Secretariat member, Bohumil Trávníček. The Central Committee was expanded and comprises now 121 instead of 115 members and 52 instead of 45 candidates. The first secretary of the Communist Party of Slovakia remains Jozef Lenárt. (*Rudé právo*, 22 April; *Pravda*, Bratislava, 29 March.) Today's leadership and political course, imposed upon the party under Soviet pressure in 1969, are marked by unqualified obedience to the USSR, in both domestic and foreign matters.

Party Internal Affairs. The most important event in party life in 1976 was the 15th Congress, held in Prague on 12-16 April. It was preceded by a series of regional party conferences and a congress of the Communist Party of Slovakia in March. Some observers had anticipated that the KSČ Congress would become the scene of a clash, or even a showdown, between the actual leadership, which takes a centrist conservative position, and the extreme dogmatist wing, which calls for stern measures against all real and potential partisans of more independent policies. These observers based their expectation on the discussions at the regional party conferences, particularly on the speeches of two Presidium members, Vasil Biľák and Alois Indra, the former being considered a rival of Husák (Radio Prague, 13 March; this and the subsequent radio sources are in *FBIS*). The results of the congress, however, did not bear out these speculations. Husák and his group, strengthened in the previous year by Husák's election to the presidency of the republic, were reconfirmed by the Congress in their party posts. Significantly, neither Biľák nor Indra were included among the official speakers at the congress.

On the whole, the meeting seemed to mark further progress on the way to "normalization"—a term coined during the Soviet intervention of 1968 to denote return to the state of things existing before the "Prague Spring" and neutralization of all tendencies other than the unreservedly pro-Soviet. It was probably under the impetus of this advancing "normalization" that Husák expressed the willingness of the leadership to readmit to the party those among the expelled members who "had erred but recognized their errors" (ibid., 12, April). Husák also acknowledged that the party was facing a serious challenge in the increasingly difficult economic situation of Czechoslovakia. Economic problems, too, were the main topic at the first post-Congress plenary session of the Central Committee, 13-14 September. It can be assumed that the changes in the federal government, decided upon at this session, were motivated by the dissatisfaction with the performance of the economy (ibid., 14 September).

Domestic Affairs. The parliamentary and municipal (national committee) elections in October 1976 were treated as a very important political event in the party press, but, as in all Communist-controlled countries, their outcome was hardly a surprise.

The election campaign started at the September plenum of the party Central Committee. Economic issues dominated the campaign, indicating the awareness of the leadership of the urgency of these problems (ibid., 4 October). Next to the state of national economy, ideological questions and loyalty to the Soviet Union were in the foreground of the pre-election speeches (ČETEKA, 7 October). In all, 350 seats in the two main legislative bodies, the Chamber of the People and the Chamber of the Nations, and tens of thousands of seats on the various national committees throughout the country had to be filled. Although the constitution theoretically admits more than one candidate for every function, very little use was made of this provision, in 1976, as in all previous elections. The only ballot, that of the National Front, obtained more than 99 percent of all valid votes (*Rudé právo*, 24 October). The relatively very small turnover among the incumbents—especially in comparison with 1971, when more than 70 percent of the officeholders were dropped from the list of the candidates—was another sign of progressing "normalization."

The cautious hopes of the population that the agreement signed in Helsinki by the delegates of Communist Czechoslovakia in 1975 would bring some relaxation of the internal controls, censorship, and restrictions on travel abroad, did not materialize in 1976. In February, Czech writer Pavel Kohout complained in an open letter published in West European press that the authorities had denied him and other citizens the right to visit countries outside the Communist orbit. It was also reported, on the same occasion, that the government had resorted to new tactics in handling dissidents, obviously imitating the Soviet example: the dissidents are offered the possibility of leaving the country for a prolonged period or for good. (*Frankfurter Allgemeine Zeitung*, 29 January.)

In March, Czechoslovak Secret Service captain Pavel Minařík, who had been smuggled into the Czechoslovak desk of Radio Free Europe in Munich, returned to Prague and made headlines in the media (*Rudé právo*, 9 March). He could not, however, submit any convincing proof that the leaders of the "Prague Spring" of 1968 had been supported by Western agencies or Western funds. Several of these leaders—former Central Committee member František Kriegel, Minister of Foreign Affairs Jiří Hájek, and Central Committee secretary Zdeněk Mlynář—were interviewed by Western radio and newspaper editors in the spring. They insisted that the great majority of the Czechoslovak population rejects the present leadership and policies of the KSČ (*Dagens Nyheter*, Stockholm, 9 April; Vienna radio, domestic service, 21 May). Mlynář sent an "Open Letter to the European Socialists and Communists" in which he claimed that only crude force, deployed by the USSR, had stopped the widespread support of the policy of democratization in 1968 (*Sunday Times*, London, 11 April). These and other statements by the former liberal leaders of the KSČ were emphatically rejected, on many occasions, by spokesmen of the present course, thus confirming that the post-invasion regime had not, even by 1976, acquired sufficient legitimacy to be able to ignore the manifestations of dissent.

Culture, Education, Youth, and Religion. Culture in Czechoslovakia also continued to feel, in 1976, the pressure of the "normalization" politics. On the one hand, only carefully selected works of art and literature, in agreement with the Soviet concepts of esthetical values, were exhibited and published; on the other hand, the cultural production suffered from the loss of a great number of talented artists who had emigrated or who had been silenced. The principle of strict political control of literature was reconfirmed by an ideological-cultural seminar in Prague at the beginning of the year (Czechoslovak TV, 5 January). Yet, unofficial literary production was lively. "Edicepetlice," the Czech counterpart of the Soviet "samizdat," had published 50 volumes by 1976 (*Svědectví*, Paris, no. 50). Czechoslovak film production in 1976 was more politically "streamlined" than any other branch of the creative arts, but the movies imported from the West, about 35 percent of all those shown during the year, enjoyed very great popularity (*Záběr*, 2 January). Concerning the theater, the official press expressed satisfaction about the "definite disappearance . . . of all anti-socialist tendencies and traces of the theater of the absurd," meaning by the latter the satirical genre introduced in the sixties by Václav Havel (*Tvorba*, 21 January). Havel himself staged a kind of "samizdat" performance of his unpublished drama "Beggars' Opera" for a restricted circle of friends; this later became a subject of police investigation, and a letter of protest was sent by him to Prague municipal authorities and published in Western newspapers (*Christian Science Monitor*, 15 January). A cultural event of significance, but given little publicity, was the unveiling of a memorial plaque to the writer Franz Kafka, author of *The Castle*, at the U.S. Embassy in Prague (Reuters, 3 June). Kafka had been rediscovered by unorthodox Czechoslovak Communist intellectuals in the years immediately preceding the "Prague Spring," to become again politically objectionable after the Soviet invasion.

The educational system in Czechoslovakia, built to a large extent on the Soviet model but nevertheless retaining some significant elements of domestic traditions, faced in 1976 problems akin to those experienced at present by all educational institutions, particularly those of higher learning, such as large student populations and uneven distribution of choices of curricula and subjects (*Učitelské noviny*, 15 April). The authorities, however, felt that the main problem was to "assure that class and international aspects of education be accentuated" (*Nové slovo*, 29 January). This indicated concern about the right proportion of pupils with working-class background, as well as about successful indoctrination with orthodox Marxism of Soviet vintage. It is probably for these reasons that plans for a far-reaching reform of the entire school system have been developed. The new educational structure will be introduced during the next decade; the changes will affect all levels, beginning with kindergartens. Obligatory school attendance will be extended to ten years, and extramural activities are to become an integral part of the curriculum (*Učitelské noviny*, 23 September).

Atheistic propaganda among the students and youth in general continued all through 1976. Special attention was paid to atheistic education of adults. The antireligious legislation of the Stalinist era was positively appraised in the party media (*Tvorba*, 21 January; *Tribuna*, 26 April). Harassment of churches and their representatives went hand-in-hand with the promotion of politically subservient religious organizations such as "Pacem in Terris," which claims to be an organ of "progressive Catholic clergy willing to assist in every way possible the realization of the program of the National Front government" (*Katolícke noviny*, January). Before the October elections, the antireligious campaign subsided somewhat, in exchange for church support of the National Front ballot (*Svobodné slovo*, 16 September). The Greek Catholic Church, mercilessly persecuted during the era of Stalinism and restored in 1968, had considerable difficulties in recovering its property and was practically ignored by the political authorities. The situation of the Greek Catholics, and Catholics in general, had considerable influence on the negotiations between the Vatican and the Czechoslovak government, begun in December 1975 and pursued during 1976. The main issue of the talks has been the incumbency of eight vacant episcopal seats in Czechoslovakia. The negotiations appeared to be rather slow and tedious. (Radio Hvězda, 10 July.)

Economy. The national economy presented a fairly stable picture in 1976 although the growth rate did not meet the expectations of the planners. Sharp increases in prices of commodities (which had caused serious unrest in neighboring Poland) were avoided, and regime spokesmen on several occasions assured the population that no such increases were envisaged (Radio Prague, 5 September; *Rudé právo*, 15 October).

The appearance of stability, however, could not hide the fact that the economy had to deal with a number of problems. Among these the increasing deficit in the foreign trade balance, the insufficient food production, aggravated by a less-than-average harvest, the high prices of oil, and the labor force shortage caused particular concern to party economists. These constraints rendered difficult the meeting of the targets of the economic plan for 1976, the first year of the sixth Five-Year Plan (*Hospodářské noviny*, 18 June; *Rudé právo*, 27 July). Central Committee secretary Josef Kempný warned the public that the Czechoslovak economy may "be unable to maintain the growth rates of the past few years (ČETEKA, 4 September).

The shortage of hard currency, resulting from the decrease of the trade with the West, was an especially alarming feature of the adverse foreign trade balance. The possibility of at least a partial remedy through an increase in tourist visits from the West was ignored by the government because of apprehensions about eventual "contamination by hostile ideology." Thus political considerations prevailed over economic necessities. (*Plánované hospodářství*, June.) The unsatisfactory performance of the economy was most probably the reason why the minister of agriculture and two vice-premiers of the federal government were relieved of their functions and replaced in the fall (ČETEKA, 14 September).

Armed Forces. Czechoslovak army units participated in the military exercises "Shield '76" carried out by the forces of the Warsaw Pact in East Germany in September (*Rudé právo*, 16 September). Military education at the institutions of higher learning was reformed and extended in 1976 (*Učitelské noviny*, 5 February). Furthermore, the responsibility for the organization and maintenance of civil defense was transferred from the Ministry of Interior to the Ministry of Defense, for the purpose of "improving the system" (Radio Prague, 27 April).

Foreign Affairs. The visit to Prague in February 1976 of Austrian federal chancellor Bruno Kreisky symbolized an improvement in the relations between Czechoslovakia and its southwest neighbor, which had been considerably strained because of a series of border incidents since 1968 and the return to the "normal" Iron Curtain system. A joint communiqué pointed to a rapid expansion of the mutual trade in recent years (Radio Prague, 18 February).

Among the major European powers, Great Britain was host to Czechoslovak minister of foreign affairs Bohuslav Chňoupek, in late summer. This visit took place five years after an invitation to Chňoupek's predecessor was cancelled when British authorities discovered that Czechoslovakia had supplied arms to the Irish Republican Army. Some obstacles to Czechoslovak exports to Great Britain were eliminated in the course of Chňoupek's trip; others still remained in force (Reuter, 16 September). An improvement was also marked during 1976 in the relations with other countries of the British Commonwealth, particularly New Zealand. The volume of foreign trade in this area has been steadily rising (*Rudé právo*, 21 May).

In June, Chňoupek paid an official visit to Belgium, where he signed a consular agreement (Radio Prague, 17 June). In August he travelled to Copenhagen and was guest of the Danish foreign minister. At this occasion, in a manner somewhat unusual for governmental visitors on diplomatic missions, he vehemently attacked Alexander Dubček and other leaders of the "Prague Spring" (*Politiken*, Copenhagen, 31 August; UPI, 2 September). Relations with Norway were further developed by the visit of the Norwegian minister of foreign affairs to Prague and by the promotion of the diplomatic representations of the two countries to the status of embassies (*Svobodné Slovo*, 7 September). Shortly before the Norwegian minister, his Icelandic counterpart came to Prague for a four-day exchange of views with government officials (Radio Prague, 24 August).

South and Southeast Europe were represented in the calendar of diplomatic visits by a quasi-unexpected trip of Prime Minister Štrougal to Turkey in January (*Pravda*, Bratislava, 5 January), by a courtesy visit of the Portuguese foreign minister during his tour of Central and Eastern European countries (Radio Prague, 15 January), and by two-day consultations in Prague between the Greek minister of foreign affairs and Chňoupek concerning several open problems of the Czechoslovak-Greek relations (ČETEKA, 10 February).

Relations and economic cooperation with developing countries were given high priority in the Sixth Five-Year Plan (*Hospodářské noviny*, 13 February), but political factors at times had disturbing effects on the relations with some of these nations, such as Egypt, where Communist Czechoslovakia took a hostile position in accordance with the overall unqualified support given to Soviet foreign policies (*Rudé právo*, 31 March).

The Soviet line was followed by Czechoslovak spokesmen and mass media on many other occasions—as in the manner in which the U.S. Bicentennial celebrations were covered. Relatively little was reported about the anniversary festivities themselves, and Czechoslovak party and government leaders restricted their participation to an official congratulatory message sent in the name of Gustav Husák, president of the republic, to U.S. president Gerald Ford (Radio Hvězda, 2 July; *Rudé právo*, 3 July).

International Communist Movement. Czechoslovakia and the KSČ continued to be an important theme of the discussion within the international Communist movement during 1976, although this hardly was the desire of the KSČ leadership. The ongoing discussion dates back to the year 1968 and the Soviet military intervention against the reformist course of Alexander Dubček. As then, the opinions are sharply divided, with the great majority of the Communist parties condemning, or at least regretting, the action of the five Warsaw Pact nations, and the USSR and the present top officials of the KSČ justifying the intervention.

These differences of opinion came to the fore on several occasions, especially at national and international Communist meetings. The 15th Congress of the KSČ was one such occasion. In the pre-Congress campaign, party media stressed the correctness of the present policies of the Husák group and attacked "some Communist parties" for their "unwillingness to learn from the crisis of 1968" and their alleged "readiness to be manipulated by imperialist forces," obviously meaning the French and Italian parties, whose position on the August 1968 Soviet invasion has remained critical (*Nová svoboda*, 19 March). At the Congress itself, the representatives of the Yugoslav and Romanian parties reaffirmed their opposition to "setting one's own path and practice of socialist development as an absolute norm"—an allusion to Soviet claims to hegemony among Communist nations (*Rudé Právo*, 15 April), while neither the French nor the Italian delegation was given an opportunity to speak.

Another occasion when disagreement on the subject of Czechoslovakia became evident was the conference of European Communist and workers' parties in East Berlin, 29-30 June. Critical remarks by Italian party head Enrico Berlinguer about Soviet interference with Czechoslovak affairs were omitted from the text of his speech as it appeared in Czechoslovak media (ibid., 2 July), and the contributions of the other more independent Communist parties were heavily censored before they appeared in the Czechoslovak press. It was not by accident that precisely at the time of the East Berlin conference, the KSČ central daily *Rudé právo* (1 July) carried an article by Soviet party leader Leonid Brezhnev defending the principles of "proletarian internationalism," particularly the right of "socialist nations to defend the achievements in any socialist state."

Subservience to the USSR and the conspicuous endorsement by Czechoslovak authorities of the views of the most loyal Soviet satellite, Bulgaria, further exacerbated, at the end of the summer, the already tense relations between Czechoslovakia and Yugoslavia (ibid., 11 June; *Politika*, Belgrade, 30 April; Tanyug, 26 July). The ideological skirmishes with the French and Italian communists continued after the KSČ Congress and the East Berlin conference (*L'Unità*, Rome, 31 August; *Rudé právo*, 2 September). They were refueled by a series of articles in the Italian party organ commemorating the Soviet intervention of 1968.

Publications. The main daily party organ is *Rudé právo* in the Czech language, the Slovak edition of which was discontinued. The Communist Party of Slovakia publishes the daily *Pravda* in Bratislava.

The KSČ weekly *Tribuna* deals with questions of theory and general party policies. International problems and topics are approached by the weekly *Tvorba*. The Slovak counterpart of *Tribuna* is *Predvoj*. The fortnightly *Život strany* addresses issues concerning party work and questions of party organization. The Revolutionary Trade Union Movement publishes the daily *Práce* in the Czech republic and its Slovak version *Práca* in Bratislava. The Czech organ of the Socialist Youth Union is *Mladá fronta*, the Slovak counterpart being *Smena*. The official press agency is *Československá tisková kancelář*, often referred to by abbreviations ČTK or ČETEKA.

University of Pittsburgh   Zdenek L. Suda

Germany: German Democratic Republic

In contrast to the Western Allies, the Soviet Union had carefully planned the steps it would take to influence the political development in Germany after the termination of hostilities of World War II in Europe. About a month after the fighting had stopped and the Allied military occupation zones had been established, the Soviet Military Administration (SMA) issued its Order No. 2 on 10 June 1945 which allowed the founding of "anti-fascist" political parties in its zone. The Communist Party of Germany (Kommunistische Partei Deutschlands; KPD), an underground organization during the Third Reich, was the first party to be legally reactivated. The Social Democratic Party of Germany (Sozialdemokratische Partei Deutschlands; SPD) followed on 16 June, and the Christian Democratic Union of Germany (CDU) and Liberal Democratic Party of Germany (LDPD) also received permission to organize. In spite of substantial support provided by the SMA to the KPD, the Communists failed to gain the confidence of the population, which had experienced totalitarianism of the fascist brand as well as the cruel behavior of the Red Army. Thereupon the Soviet occupation authorities forced the merger of the KPD and SPD. A new party, the Socialist Unity Party of Germany (Sozialistische Einheitspartei Deutschlands; SED), was founded at a "Unity Party Congress" (21-22 April 1946) attended by delegates representing 680,000 Social Democrats and 620,000 Communists, who decided "unanimously" to combine their two parties. Many Social Democrats resisted the merger, with the result that many of them were incarcerated and some killed. Only in the Berlin sectors was it possible for the SPD to hold a plebiscite on the merger, and there 82 percent voted against it. Walter Ulbricht, Moscow's most trusted agent in Germany and deputy chairman of the SED, declared at the Unity Congress that from then on there were no longer Social Democrats and Communists, but only socialists. Thirty years later, SED Chief Erich Honecker recognized only the existence of Communists in the German Democratic Republic (Deutsche Demokratische Republik; GDR). He also declared on the anniversary of the merger that the SED had considered itself from the beginning "a part of the international Communist movement" (*Die Welt*, Hamburg, 22 April 1976). The objective of the SED was the creation of a "socialist Germany." The Communists, with the aid of the SMA, gained control of the party apparatus, and as early as July 1948 the SED had become a "party of the new type," following the model of the Communist Party of the Soviet Union (CPSU).

About a month after the establishment of the Federal Republic of Germany (FRG) in the three Western occupation zones, a "German People's Congress" unanimously adopted on 7 October 1949 a proposal to create the GDR. On 10 October 1949 the SMA transferred its administrative functions to the GDR government and on 15 October the USSR extended diplomatic recognition to it. From the very inception of the GDR, the SED leadership was in complete control of the "first German socialist state." In July 1950 the Third SED Party Congress approved the draft of the GDR's first Five-Year Plan.

Moscow believed that its occupation zone could serve as the nucleus of a reunited Germany under Soviet control, a view held during the immediate postwar years. This is the reason for a number of developments in the Soviet zone which are different from those in other areas under Soviet domination, where different tactics were used. For example, the first constitution of the GDR consciously followed in some respects the Weimar constitution, including a federal system and a multi-party arrangement, although the SED assumed complete control of the non-Communist parties which together with the SED and the mass organizations formed the "National Front." The federal system was eventually eliminated and replaced by a highly centralized order. In 1968 the GDR received a new "socialist constitution" for the "first socialist state of the German Nation." (In October 1976, Erich Honecker, probably referring to the FRG, stated that there is a possibility of the establishment of a "second socialist state on German territory" [ibid., 29 October].)

In September 1974, on the occasion of the 25th anniversary of the GDR, the People's Chamber unanimously adopted a number of significant amendments and additions to the 1968 constitution which became effective on 7 October. Any reference to the "German Nation" and to "German Reunification" was omitted.

An all-embracing program of socialization of the entire economy, including agriculture, was undertaken quite early. Elimination of the traditional professional civil service and of the trade unions commenced in 1946. The employment of terror and mass intimidation succeeded in creating in due time the political, economic, and social structure characteristic of a "people's democracy." About three million East Germans fled to the West before the erection of the Wall in Berlin and of the border fortifications along the demarcation line between East and West Germany.

Soviet economic exploitation of the GDR necessitated the establishment of effective controls. Only Moscow-loyal indigenous party functionaries were permitted to hold any significant office. Economic and military integration of the GDR with the Soviet Union and the other Communist-ruled countries of Eastern Europe were other means of maintaining control. The integration process has gained momentum through the years. In September 1950 the GDR joined the Council for Mutual Economic Aid (CMEA). In May 1955 it became a full member of the Warsaw Pact. Remilitarization started as early as 3 July 1948 when the SMA authorized the formation of armed and garrisoned units of the People's Police (Kasernierte Volkspolizei). These units were renamed National Armed Forces (Nationale Streitkraefte) in 1952. After the GDR joined the Warsaw Pact, they became known as the National People's Army (Nationale Volksarmee; NVA).

The SED in 1976 had 2,043,697 members and candidates (*Neues Deutschland*, 21 May). The population of the GDR is 16,850,125 (*Deutsche Zeitung*, 1 October).

Government and Party Structure. The SED leadership, one of the most Moscow-loyal of any group of Communist leaders, is in complete control of the GDR. The SED Politburo and the Central Committee are decision-making institutions which also select the key personnel within the party and governmental bureaucracy. The most important position, that of the secretary-general (known as first secretary until the party congress in 1976), has been held since 1971 by Erich Honecker. The other members of the Politburo or the Central Committee are in charge of the most important ministries and other governmental institutions.

The People's Chamber (Volkskammer) appoints the GDR government, consisting of the State Council (Staatsrat), comprised of 24 members plus one secretary, and the Council of Ministers (Ministerrat), whose 42 members head the various ministries and other top governmental institutions, such as the State Bank and the Planning Commission. Fifteen of them form the Presidium of the Council of Ministers, a kind of "inner cabinet." The chairman of the Council of Ministers, his two first deputies and the representatives of the National People's Army and State Security are full members of the Politburo, and two deputy chairmen are Politburo candidates. (Bundesminister fuer innerdeutsche Beziehungen, *Informationen*, no. 11, Bonn, 1976.) The State Council, like the Soviet Presidium, manages the business of the People's Chamber between its infrequent sessions. The Council chairman, since 29 October 1976, is SED secretary-general Honecker, who also holds the position of chairman of the National Defense Council (Nationaler Verteidigungsrat), a government organ with unlimited powers in case an emergency situation is brought about by domestic or external circumstances. Honecker follows the example set before by Walter Ulbricht, who also combined the 3 most significant power positions in his own person. The former chairman of the State Council, Willi Stoph, resumed his position as chairman of the Council of Ministers, a post he held between 1964 and 1973, replacing Horst Sindermann, who became president of the People's Chamber, a position previously held by Gerald Götting, a member of the CDU of the GDR. (*Die Welt*, 30 October 1976.) At the time of his appointment (29 October) by the People's Chamber, Willi Stoph was given the task to form a new Council of Ministers. The only change made was the replacement of first deputy chairman Günter Mittag with Werner Krolikowski. (Ibid., 2 November.)

The Council of Ministers consists of 38 SED members and one member each from the other "Block Parties," the CDU, the LDPG, the National Democratic Party of Germany, and the Democratic Peasant Party of Germany. The power of the State Council was reduced in favor of the Council of Ministers as of 1 April 1976 (Bundesminister fuer innerdeutsche Beziehungen, *Informationen*, no. 8, p. 4).

The latest election of the 500-member People's Chamber was held on 17 October 1976. The "National Front" (the Communist-controlled alliance of all political parties: the SED and the four "Block Parties"), the trade unions, and the "mass organizations," such as the Free German Youth (Freie Deutsche Jugend; FDJ) and the Democratic Women's League of Germany (Demokratischer Frauenbund Deutschlands; DFD), provided a single list of candidates. Before the elections, the 500 seats in the People's Chamber were allotted to the different components of the National Front and to the mass organizations. (The SED with its affiliated organizations hold the controlling number of seats, so that the other parties and organizations are completely dominated.) In the elections, 11,263,431 or 98.58 percent of the eligible 11,425,822 voters took part. Spoiled ballots accounted for 0.02 percent of all votes cast. The vote for the list of candidates "nominated" by the National Front was 11,245,243 or 99.86 percent. There were 15,432 votes against the list, or 0.14 percent. Because of the special status of East Berlin, its citizens voted for the list the National Front prepared for the 200-member "Greater Berlin Council," and here the list received 800,354 or 99.61 percent of all valid votes. (Panorama DDR, *The 1976 Elections in the GDR*, "Our Point of View" series, East Berlin, 1976, pp. 6-7. The East Berlin legislature at its constituent session appointed 66 delegates to the People's Chamber as provided for in the Four Power Agreement. Since its inception the People's Chamber has always voted unanimously on all issues with only one exception: with SED permission, a few deputies were allowed to vote against the bill concerning abortion in March 1972.

The purpose in allowing other political parties to exist, each with its own "party organ," is to appeal to specific segments of the population in an effort to integrate them into the socialist society.

However, with the alleged progress in achieving this objective, their significance as transmission belts is steadily decreasing. Only the CDU reported a membership increase in 1976, claiming 110,000 members, up from 100,000 in 1975 (*Die Welt*, 11 October). (In 1947, the CDU had as many as 220,000 members.) (For the membership of other political parties in 1975 see *YICA, 1976*, p. 26.)

The present SED Central Committee, elected at the 9th Party Congress in May 1976, has 145 full members and 57 candidates (*Neues Deutschland*, 24 May). The 19 full members of the Politburo are: Hermann Axen, Friedrich Ebert, Werner Felfe, Gerhard Grüneberg, Kurt Hager, Heinz Hoffmann, Erich Honecker, Werner Krolikowski, Werner Lamberz, Erich Mielke, Günter Mittag, Erich Mückenberger, Konrad Naumann, Alfred Neumann, Albert Norden, Horst Sindermann, Willi Stoph, Harry Tisch, and Paul Verner; the 9 candidate members are: Horst Dohlus, Joachim Herrmann, Werner Jarowinski, Günther Kleiber, Egon Krenz, Ingeburg Lange, Margarete Müller, Gerhard Schürer, and Werner Walde.

The Politburo is the real power center of the GDR. The 12 members of the Secretariat are assigned control functions within their respective areas of responsibility. The former members of the Secretariat were reelected at the 9th Party Congress and their previous assignments confirmed (see *YICA, 1976*, p. 26). The only changes were the addition of the editor in chief of the SED organ *Neues Deutschland*, Joachim Hermann, and the change in the name of Erich Honecker's Secretariat position from first secretary to secretary-general (*Neues Deutschland*, 24 May). Politburo member Erich Mückenberger was reelected chairman of the Central Party Control Commission (9 full members, 7 candidates). Kurt Seibt, a leading party official, was reappointed chairman of the Central Auditing Commission, which was enlarged to 30 full members and 6 candidates. ("Staats-und Parteiapparat der DDR, Personelle Besetzung, Stand: 15 August 1976," Beilage zu Bundesminister fuer innerdeutsche Beziehungen, *Informationen*, no. 17, 1976.)

Salaries of top party and government officials are very high by GDR standards. Willi Stoph received as chairman of the State Council 9,000 Marks per month. Expense accounts and representation funds are not included in this amount. A GDR minister gets 6,000 marks per month and a secretary of state about 4,500. In comparison, a worker earns between 500 and 800 marks and a nurse about 400 marks. High functionaries also enjoy many material advantages and privileges. (*Die Welt*, 20 July.)

For the SED total membership see below, "Party Internal Affairs."

Mass Organizations. The main task of the mass organizations of the National Front is to assist the SED in its work and control functions. Furthermore, they provide a mass basis for political indoctrination and pre-military training. They also serve as a recruiting ground for future party functionaries. This holds especially true for the Free German Youth, the most important of these organizations. The membership of the FDJ, as reported at the 10th FDJ Parliament (equivalent to a party congress), 1-5 June 1976, is 2,157,734. (Reported membership at the 9th Parliament in 1971 was 1.7 million.) The FDJ maintains 98,318 primary organizations and groups, which are run by 585,000 functionaries. The 10th Parliament reelected as first secretary of the Central Council (equivalent to the Central Committee of the SED) Egon Krenz, candidate member of the SED Politburo. The FDJ is, in the words of Erich Honecker, the "combat reserve (Kampfreserve) of the SED." (Bundesminister fuer innerdeutsche Beziehungen, *Informationen*, no. 12, 1976, pp. 12-14.) Since the 1971 Parliament the number of youth clubs has increased from 1,025 to about 4,000. One of the tasks of the FDJ is the supervision of the Ernst Thälmann Pioneers, a children's organization with 1.9 million members. Under the Party Congress initiative of the FDJ, 109,935 of the most active FDJ members were admitted to the SED (East Berlin, domestic TV, 1 June, in *FBIS*). In spite of its monopoly position, the FDJ has failed up to now to organize the entire youth of the GDR, about a third of which still remains outside its organizations (*Deutschland-Union-Dienst*, 30, no. 108, Bonn, 8 June).

The Free German Trade Union Federation (FDGB) has some 8 million members, of whom 2,261,970 are elected functionaries in various trade union committees or function as shop stewards (*Neuer Weg*, East Berlin, no. 11, 1976). Most useful for foreign propaganda purposes are the various solidarity committees and the Peace Council of the GDR. (For other mass organizations see *YICA, 1976*, p. 26.)

Party Internal Affairs. The most significant intra-party event in 1976 was the 9th SED Party Congress held on 18-22 May in East Berlin in the New Palace of the Republic. The Congress adopted a new Party Program and the 5th Party Statute. (Formally the program is the second; however, in reality it is the third; the first program was not designated as such but referred to as "Basic Principles and Objectives" of the SED.) Preparations for the Congress started early in 1975. The SED Central Committee session of 26 November 1975 dealt with the drafts of the new program and statute and decided to publish them in January 1976 together with the Congress directive for the development of the economy from 1976 until 1980 (*Neues Deutschland*, 27, 28 November). The first phase of the party elections went on from 1 December 1975 to 31 January 1976. Reports were rendered and elections of the executive organs in the SED primary units, numbering 74,306 basic and departmental party organizations, were held. (Ibid., 21 May.) Elections in the 269 SED district (*Kreis*) organizations were carried out during February, the second phase of the party elections; 227 of the 261 first secretaries were reelected. (There are 29 *Kreis*-level organizations of a functional nature, constituting the party organization in the most important industrial enterprises, in the universities, and in the central organs of the state apparatus and mass organizations. Eight of these held their elections in the third phase of the party elections with the regional organizations.) The 33 first secretaries who were not reelected either left for reason of age or because they were transferred to other positions in the party or government apparatus. (Bundesminister fuer innerdeutsche Beziehungen, *Informationen*, no. 7.) The elections in the 15 regional (*Bezirk*) organizations and in area headquarters at Wismut were held in March and April at the regional conferences of delegates, the third phase of the system. Ninety-two of the 95 regional secretaries—the real party leaders in the regions—were reelected. (Ibid., no. 8.) It is of interest to note that among the additional members of each of the regional organizations three officers are included: the Chief of the Command of the Military Region, the Chief of the Regional Administration of the Ministry of State Security, and the Chief of the Regional Office of the People's Police (ibid., no. 10).

At the 9th SED Party Congress, it was reported that the party had a membership of 2,043,697 (1,914,382 full members and 129,315 candidates). The social composition reflects the lasting effort of the leadership to build up the percentage of workers: 56.1 percent workers, 20.0 percent intelligentsia, 11.5 percent white collar workers, 5.2 percent cooperative farmers, and 7.2 percent members of other social categories. The age distribution indicated that 43.4 percent are younger than 40 years. Women amount to 31.3 percent. Graduates of universities and technical schools constitute 27.4 percent. Party members who received training in Marxism-Leninism in a party educational institution since the 8th Party Congress (1971) numbered 340,000. (Ibid., no. 15.)

Communist and workers' parties, national-democratic parties, and socialist parties from 92 countries were represented at the Congress by 103 delegations. Of the 2,519 delegates elected by secret ballot at the regional conferences of delegates on the basis of the Party Statute, 2,392 had voting rights (12, however, were absent for justified reasons) and 127 had a mandate with advisory vote. The social composition of the voting delegates strongly favored the workers' group (63.6 percent). The intelligentsia was also strongly represented (25.4 percennt; 8.2 percent were cooperative farmers, and 2.8 percent members of other social strata. Women delegates accounted for 28.6 percent. The composition of the advisory delegates was similar. (*Neues Deutschland*, 21 May.)

After the drafts of the Program and Statute were published, the Central Committee received numerous proposals for changes and supplements. Some of them were included in the final documents. The new Program and Statute received the unanimous approval of the Congress.

An important section of the Program deals with the further developing of the evolved socialist society in the GDR. The Program is supposed to provide the guidelines for the period of several five-year plans and to give the party a clearer orientation on the road toward communism—that is, to prepare the basic preconditions for the gradual transition to communism. One of the criteria for this development is the deepening of the alliance with the Soviet Union and the other countries of the community of socialist states. The integration of the CMEA countries is considered to be the basis for the collaboration. The constitutional changes of October 1974 which eliminated any references to the "German Nation" and German reunification required that the new Program also exclude these subjects. The new Statute introduces for the first time the term "communists" for the SED members and follows the Statute of the CPSU even more closely than its forerunners. The political contents also had to be changed in order to remain in line with the new Party Program, and therefore the Statute refrains from making any reference to the "German Nation." As mentioned earlier, it created the position of secretary-general in place of the first secretary.

The East German communists emphasized their loyalty to the traditional Marxist concept of the dictatorship of the proletariat. Erich Honecker declared at the Congress:

> It is the historic mandate of the working class to establish the socialist and communist society. To this end it must be in firm control of power. Power is primary. Without power the working class and its allies would have been unable to transfer the key means of production to public ownership or to lay the foundation of socialism. . . . Karl Marx formulated the principle that during the period of transition from the capitalist to communist society the state cannot be other than the dictatorship of the proletariat. Without it no socialist society has ever been built anywhere throughout history. The experience of the revolutionary working class and our own experience also bear out this Marxist-Leninist principle. That is why our new Party Program says: the policy of the SED is designed to further the continued all-round strengthening of the socialist state of workers and peasants as a form of the dictatorship of the proletariat representing the interest of all the people of the GDR; it is the main instrument of the working people, led by the working class, in shaping the advanced socialist society along the path to communism. (Ibid., 19 May.)

The SED apparently also heeded the warning of Soviet chief ideologist Mikhail A. Suslov, an important member of the CPSU delegation, who stated at the Congress: "any deviation from the principle of proletarian internationalism bears in itself the seeds of defeat and of losses" (*NYT*, 20 May). There was no indication of any attempts by the SED of challenging the central control of Moscow. Precisely the opposite—the complete subordination of East Berlin to Moscow—was repeatedly stressed. The Congress also approved unanimously the directives for the five-year plan for the GDR's economic development for the period 1976-80.

Other party activities concentrated on the elections to the People's Chamber and on the implementation of the decisions of the Congress. (See, e.g., the closing speech of Honecker to the Second Plenary Session of the SED Central Committee, 3 September 1976, in Panorama DDR, *Current Aspects of Our Domestic and Foreign Policy after the 9th Party Congress*, East Berlin, 1976.)

The ideological indoctrination of the members of the party and of mass organizations continued to be regarded as a high priority task. Honecker reported:

> The further extension and intensification of mass propaganda, of our Marxist-Leninist theory as well as the history and politics of the SED, have been an outstanding characteristic of the period under review. Leading officials, many scientists and specialists, tens of thousands of propagandists as well as press, radio, and television have taken an active part in this. The party indoctrination year gains in importance in the further adoption of Marxism-Leninism and the development of communist ways of thinking and behavior. The

comrades organized in the FDGB, FDJ, DFD, Urania, and other social organizations and, last but not least, in adult evening schools and enterprise academies attach great attention to the teaching of Marxism-Leninism which is close to life. The schools of social work, in which more than 1.8 million working people take part, make an especially great contribution to the propagation of our Weltanschauung. This also applies to universities and technical schools as well as to secondary schools, whose role in the teaching of Marxism-Leninism is further growing. (*Neues Deutschland*, 19 May.)

Among the individual party functionaries who were given special honors was Politburo member Hermann Axen, who on the occasion of his 60th birhday received the Karl Marx Order (*Die Welt*, 8 March). Late in 1975 the newly created title "Hero of the German Democratic Republic" was conferred by Erich Honecker on Politburo member and Minister of Defense Heinz Hoffmann, on Politburo member (then still candidate) and Minister for State Security Erich Mielke, and on Central Committee member, Minister of Interior, and Chief of the People's Police Friedrich Dickel (*Deutschland-Archiv*, 9, no. 1, Cologne, January 1976, p. 108.)

Domestic Affairs. *Elections.* Elections to the People's Chamber and to the East Berlin Legislature were held on 17 October (see results above). The People's Chamber at its 18th Session, 24 June, adopted a new election law which came into effect on 1 July and provides for elections to the People's Chamber and the regional and communal legislatures to be held every 5 years instead of 4 years as before. Also, the age when a GDR citizen can be elected to serve as deputy was reduced from 21 to 18 years. The new legal arrangement became necessary as a result of the changes contained in the constitution of 1968. (Bundesminister fuer innerdeutsche Beziehungen, *Informationen*, no. 14, 1976.)

At the Second Session of the SED Central Committee, 2-3 September, the candidates and substitute candidate members of the SED proposed for the National Front list for election to the People's Chamber was confirmed (East Berlin, ADN, international service in German, 3 September, in *FBIS*). On 17 September the president of the National Council of the National Front presented the joint election proposal list for the People's Chamber to Friedrich Ebert, chairman of the Election Commission of the Republic. Ebert commented that the process leading up to the compilation of the election proposal list was an expression of true socialist democracy (East Berlin, "Voice of the GDR," domestic service in German, 17 September, in *FBIS*).

Legal Reforms. The new Code of Civil Law, adopted by the People's Chamber in June 1975, came into effect on 1 January 1976, replacing one dating from the imperial past at the turn of the century. The new code with its 480 paragraphs governs matter such as buying, selling, rents and inheritance. It is designed to match the realities of life in a communist-ruled country. (*NYT*, 3 January.)

A seminar was held in Kleinmachnow for officials concerned with legal matters at regional and district levels in order to discuss the consequences for their work of the decisions of the 9th SED Party Congress—that is, the impact of the class nature of the socialist state upon legal affairs (East Berlin, domestic service in German, 5 September, in *FBIS*).

Youth Indoctrination. At the 9th Party Congress the significance of the indoctrination of the young with Marxism-Leninism was strongly emphasized. Honecker declared:

. . . it is a most important task of the youth to learn the doctrine of Marx, Engels, and Lenin and to act always with word and deed as socialist patriots and proletarian internationalists. This demands that all young people of the GDR always act with all their strength for the all round strengthening of the German Democratic Republic, the further strengthening of the fraternal alliance with the Soviet Union, the cooperation between countries and nations of the socialist community, the defence of socialism, and for the anti-imperialist solidarity. The Free German Youth has been, is, and will remain to be the active helper and fighting reserve of the party. The main task of the Free German Youth remains to be helping the party to educate steadfast fighters for the establishment of the communist society who will be acting in the spirit of Marxism-Leninism. (*Neues Deutschland*, 19 May.)

The GDR children's book publishing house announced 80 new books for 1976. They include for the first time an "introduction to the teaching of scientific communism" for 12-year-old readers. (*Die Welt*, 2 February.)

In 1976 some 282,000 students aged 14 years (99.6 percent of all students of the 8th grade) participated in the so-called Youth Consecration (*Jugendweihe*) and pledged their allegiance to socialism. In theory, the Youth Consecration is voluntary; however, those students who refuse to participate are excluded from higher education. (Ibid., 21 April.)

GDR Anniversaries. The National People's Army marked its 20th anniversary on 1 March with a military parade in East Berlin. This military display was in violation of the Four Power Agreement which prohibits the presence of military troops in all of Berlin. (Ibid., 2 March.)

Politburo member and Defense Minister General Heinz Hoffmann spoke at the occasion of this anniversary at the SED "Karl Marx" Party College and asserted that a nuclear war between East and West is a "just war" for the socialist forces and represents the "last and decisive retribution of imperialism" and the "continuation of the class struggle" (ibid., 28 April). The GDR issued a 10 mark coin in honor of this event displaying on one side the coat of arms and on the other side an NVA soldier with steel helmet (ibid., 10 February). Also a number of officers received promotions on the occasion of the anniversary. As of 1 March there were 125 officers on active service with the rank of general (Bundesminister fuer innerdeutsche Beziehungen, *Informationen*, no. 5).

The FDJ celebrated its 30th anniversary on 7 March. The Soviet Ambassador to the GDR transmitted greetings from the Komsomol to the FDJ (*Die Welt*, 9 March).

Also the 30th anniversary of the founding of the SED at the "Unity Congress" (21-22 April 1946) was celebrated (*Foreign Affairs Bulletin*, East Berlin, 16, no. 13, 4 May), as was the 27th year of the existence of the GDR. On this latter occasion, 7 October, units of the NVA paraded in East Berlin. Many "deserving workers," scientists, artists, and functionaries received various honors. (*Die Welt*, 8 October.)

State-Church Relations. The pressure of the SED regime against the churches was stated as the reasons for the suicide attempt of a Protestant clergyman, Oskar Brüsewitz, on 18 August 1976. He died as a result of his severe burns four days later. The self-immolation dramatized the difficulties under which the churches operate in the GDR. The SED regime reacted first by declaring that Parson Brüsewitz was an abnormal, sick person who frequently suffered from delusions, and by accusing Western news agencies of utilizing this incident for a slanderous campaign against the GDR. (*Neues Deutschland*, 21 August.) Concerned about the impact abroad, the propaganda office in East Berlin, Panorama DDR, published a brochure in the "Dokumentarische Information" series under the heading "Respect and Equality for Christians in the GDR" which it mailed to its foreign addressees. This brochure asserts that "churches and religious communities in the GDR have rich opportunities to avail themselves of their guaranteed rights and freedoms" (p. 4). It also provides statistical data about the strength of the Church organizations, although no indication as to the size of membership is given. The Federation of Evangelical Churches (formed by a union of 8 Protestant churches in 1966) is supposed to have altogether 4,235 ministers. In addition there are a number of Evangelical Free Churches and other religious communities. According to this report the Catholic church has more than 1,400 priests, serving more than 1,000 parishes. The Jewish community maintains 8 synagogues and a house of prayer. (pp. 4-5.) According to church estimates, the total number of Protestants is about 12.5 million and there are 1.28 million Catholics, served by 1,342 priests. The Jewish community counts about 800 members. (Bundesminister fuer innerdeutsche Beziehungen, *DDR Handbuch*, Cologne, 1975, p. 713.) The decline in participation in church activities is significant. The numbers of baptisms, confirmations, church weddings, and children attending religious instruction have substantially decreased. (For example, the Mecklenburger church newspaper reported that 19,064 children attended religious instruction in 1975, compared with 25,924 in 1973. *Die Welt*, 23 August 1976.) All churches receive considerable financial support from the West German churches (*NYT*, 4 April).

The Protestant church showed great concern about the determination of the SED leadership to indoctrinate all citizens of the GDR with Marxism-Leninism. Bishop Albrecht Schönherr requested in the name of the Federation of Churches that the SED should respect the fact that East German society includes people with a different Weltanschauung (*Die Welt*, 26 April). Because of existing vacancies in church communities, Bishop Schönherr also appealed to his clergy not to leave the GDR (ibid., 29 January). About 15,000 Protestants participated in a church-sponsored celebration (*Kirchentag*) in Halle in September (ibid., 23 September).

An important development of the Catholic church in the GDR was the decree of the Vatican which united the church within the GDR under the administration of the "Berlin Bishop Conference." It was pointed out, however, that this administrative move did not create an independent, national bishops' conference of the Catholic church within the territory of the GDR; therefore the name Berlin Bishop Conference was chosen. (Ibid., 26 October.) The Vatican apparently does not intend to recognize the permanency of the division of Germany.

There are several reasons for the SED-regime not to prohibit church activities altogether. One reason certainly is that there are still a considerable number of conscientious Christians in the GDR and forceful measures against them would probably have overall disrupting effects. Secondly, the churches maintain many hospitals and other social institutions. And thirdly, the churches are a convenient channel for obtaining hard currency from the West.

Military Affairs. The increase of the miitary budget by 6.99 percent for 1976, amounting to 10.233 billion marks, as compared with that of 1975, is one of the indications of the high priority military matters receive in the GDR. The actual spending for "defense" is considerably greater than the budget discloses because many expenditures are hidden under various "civilian" categories. (*Rheinischer Merkur*, 19 December 1975, 27 February 1976.) The GDR continued throughout 1976 with its build-up of military and paramilitary forces and with the improvement of their "combat readiness" and "ideological indoctrination and hatred of the class enemy." (See Eric Waldman, "The Military Policies of an Archetypal Soviet Satellite, The German Democratic Republic," *Canadian Defense Quarterly*, 5, no. 4, Toronto, Spring 1976, pp. 46-52.)

The increase of the combat readiness of the National People's Army is also directly related to the modernization of its weapons systems, the increase in military personnel, and the greater emphasis of pre-military training and utilization of the reservists of the NVA, numbering about 2 million men, and of the combat groups of the working class (Kampfgruppen der Arbeiterklasse), which have about 500,000 men. The East German Air Force (about 25,000 men) has 290 fighter planes (MIG 19, MIG 21, MIG 25), 25 transport planes, 120 helicopters, and more than 200 anti-aircraft guns in addition to a substantial number of anti-aircraft rockets (SAM 2). The Navy (about 17,000 men) has under its command 6 destroyers, 54 ships to protect the coast (Küstenschutzboote), 50 mine sweepers, 40 patrol boats, 25 landing craft, 75 torpedo boats, and many others. The Land Forces (at present, more than 95,000 men) replaced most of their T54 and T53 Soviet-made tanks with the new Soviet combat tank T62. The Land Forces possess 1,900 tanks, 140 amphibious tanks, 2,050 armored personnel carriers, 1,040 guns, and 420 anti-aircraft guns. There are apparently plans to increase the Land Forces by one third. (Four new cadre divisions have already been organized and form the nucleus for the planned 4th Assault Army.) The border troops have 54,000 men and are supported by units of the paramilitary organization of the Kampfgruppen of the working class. There are indications that the NVA has a special unit, trained on the Kola Peninsula in the USSR, which under Soviet supervision is guarding an underground nuclear weapons arsenal near Jägerbrück in Mecklenburg, located in the GDR Military District 5, headquarters at Neubrandenburg. (*Rheinischer Merkur*, 25 June.)

Almost every officer and officer candidate, every third noncommissioned officer, and every ninth soldier is a member of the SED. More than 90 percent of the noncommissioned officers and soldiers belong to the FDJ. (*Ostsee-Zeitung*, Rostock, 28/29 February.) The FDJ members entering the NVA in compliance with the universal military service law are well prepared. They have participated in the pre-military training provided by the Society for Sport and Technique (GST) and in so-called military sport activities (Wehrsport) provided by the FDJ, schools, and GST. (*Junge Welt*, East Berlin, 4 May; *Wochenpost*, East Berlin, 19 March.) The GST, headed by Lieutenant General Günter Teller, has up to now prepared 220,000 youths in training programs, lasting up to two years, for their service in the NVA. (*Die Welt*, 28 July; *Wochenpost*, 19 March.)

At the end of the training period for 1973-76, the combat groups of the working class were tested in fall maneuvers in order to prove their combat efficiency. Special emphasis was given to strengthen the political-moral motivation of these units. (*Die Welt*, 24 September.) Also civil defense programs received increased attention. In 1975/76 the civilian participants in civil defense have been subjected to more than 10 million training hours in order to improve their readiness for action (*Berliner Zeitung*, East Berlin, 11 May). The political indoctrination of the NVA soldiers is high on the priority list. "Socialist Military Education" (Wehrerziehung) has been given the task to educate every citizen of the GDR, especially the young citizens who must serve in the NVA, concerning their duties in protecting the republic from imperialist aggressors (ibid., 12 January). The noted increase of the combat strength of the NVA is attributed not only to the introduction of modern Soviet weapons systems but also to the leading role of the SED in developing the "socialist defense" and utilizing the knowledge of Marxist-Leninist military science (*Volksarmee*, East Berlin, no. 22). The NVA has the mission to protect the development of socialism and, together with the fraternal armies of the countries of the Warsaw Pact, to secure the peace strategy of the socialist states. "The National People's Army [has been] since its founding a military instrument of the contemporary class struggle. . ." (*Neue Zeit*, East Berlin, 11 February.)

The political importance of the NVA was also expressed in the address of General of the Army Heinz Hoffmann Politburo member and Minister of National Defense, at the SED Congress:

> It has never been as clear as in the last few years that the politically conscious actions of army members, their disciplined engagement in carrying out military assignments in the interest of the working class, are a decisive contribution to safeguarding socialism and peace and realizing international détente. (*Foreign Affairs Bulletin*, 16, no. 18, East Berlin, 14 June.)

Erich Honecker, at the Congress, stressed the significance of military preparedness:

> Any faltering vigilance and any unilateral reduction in the military strength of socialism would only encourage the aggressive designs of the imperialist adversary. The GDR's National People's Army, border troops, the organs of the Ministry of Interior and State Security, the civil defense forces and the fighting militia of the working class—all have the duty to secure under all conditions a high level of combat readiness for the protection of peace and socialism and to guarantee the GDR's territorial integrity and the inviolability of its borders and its security. (*Neues Deutschland*, 19 May.)

It appears, however, that the confidence of the SED in the effectiveness of its indoctrination is limited. According to the "rules for members of the NVA," soldiers whose relatives move to places abroad, including the FRG and West Berlin, must immediately report this fact to their superiors. They are prohibited from attending family reunions when West Germans are present. Any such contacts are to be avoided. Requests from West German relatives for visits in the GDR are to be reported, as well as unexpected meetings with them. (*Die Welt*, 22 June.)

As of March 1976, the GDR had 23 military attachés accredited at foreign capitals, including three NATO countries (Belgium, Italy, and Norway) (ibid., 10 March).

Security Matters. Throughout 1976 the SED regime continued to take measures designed to discourage the escape of its citizens to the West and to foil espionage efforts of the "class enemy," while employing thousands of agents in the FRG. "Military restricted areas" comprise 40.4 percent of the territory of the GDR. There are a total of 52 of these areas, including the belt along the border. (Ibid., 23 January.) In order to prevent the escape of its citizens, the border fortifications along the Western boundary are continually "improved." About two thirds of an additional elaborate barrier has been completed. More anti-personnel mines have been placed along the 900-mile-long border. The cost of this installation per kilometer (0.6 mile) is estimated at $415,000. (*NYT*, 3 October.) Also, the Wall and other fortifications surrounding West Berlin, guarded by about 14,000 border troops, have been further built up. Special "mobile task force commandos" (Mobile Einsatzkommandos) have been organized and placed under the Ministry for State Security and assigned to the border brigades. (*Rheinischer Merkur*, 23 July.)

The effectiveness of these measures is seen in the decrease of escapees to a small trickle, compared with the exodus of more than 3 million prior to the building of the Berlin Wall in August 1961. The cases of 171 persons who lost their lives while attempting to escape, since that time, are known to the West. Seventy were killed at the Wall (66 of them were shot) and 101 on the border between East and West Germany (21 of them by anti-personnel mines). (*Die Welt*, 10 August.) During the first nine months of 1976, nevertheless, 3,985 GDR citizens managed to escape, among them 482 who made their way through mine fields, death strip and automatic anti-personnel mines. There were 7,009 additional persons who obtained permission to leave the GDR, most of them in advanced age. (During the same period in 1975, 4,282 persons escaped, 539 of whom made it across the fortified border.) (Ibid., 12 October.) Individuals arrested while attempting to escape usually receive long-term prison sentences (ibid., 31 August). A growing number of GDR citizens—estimated between 50,000 and 120,000—have asked to be permitted to leave the country legally. Many of them refer to the Final Document of the Helsinki Conference, to which East Berlin gave its consent and which provides for freer movement of people and ideas. A group of 79 persons from the town of Riesa signed a petition complaining that their requests to emigrate were not granted. A number of them were arrested and a Soviet military unit marched through the town in an effort to intimidate the population. (Ibid., 28 September; *Christian Science Monitor*, 19 October.) East Berlin also is taking a firmer hand in dealing with dissidents among East German writers and artists. The most recent example of this crackdown is the decision to deprive poet and balladeer Wolf Biermann of his GDR citizenship while on a concert tour in West Germany allegedly because of his "hostile performance" on 13 November in Cologne. More than 90 leading figures of the artistic world signed a petition protesting the move and asking the communist rulers to reconsider and permit Biermann to return to the GDR where his family is residing. (*NYT*, 19, 20 November; *Die Welt*, 7 December).

Political Prisoners. The number of political prisoners in East German penal institutions remained the same as in 1975, about 7,000. One report asserts that between 6,300 and 7,800 persons are incarcerated for political offenses. About 60 percent of them were sentenced for attempted "flight from the republic" (*Republikflucht*). Others were found guilty of offenses such as "anti-state slander," "anti-state agitation," and "organization of groups hostile to the state." (*Die Welt*, 12 August.) A West German agency at Salzgitter registered 1,485 political sentences in the GDR courts, during 1975, 346 more than in the preceding year (ibid., 3 January). Professor Robert Havemann, who was dismissed from his university position because of his anti-party statements (he is presently held under house arrest in East Berlin), asserted that the SED regime is confining dissidents in psychiatric clinics, following the practice widely used in the Soviet Union (*Frankfurter Rundschau*, 26 June). It is believed that about 400 citizens of the FRG are in East German prisons (including five who received life sentences) for various political offenses, such as helping escapees or alleged espionage (Bundesminister fuer innerdeutsche Beziehungen, *Informationen*, no. 12), and 63 individuals from West Berlin (*Die Welt*, 19 July).

The FRG government continued in 1976 to buy the freedom of political prisoners confined in the GDR. During the first eight months of this year the freedom of 950 prisoners was achieved by this method. The minimum amount per "head" is 40,000 marks, and in some cases up to one million marks was paid. From 1962, when this program was started, up to October 1976, the West German government has paid 610.3 million marks for the freedom of several thousand political captives. The SED frequently prefers items such as gold bars and mercury, which East Berlin cannot obtain in the official intra-German trade, instead of cash. This type of transactions in shipment of goods is administered by an office of the Protestant church in the southern part of Germany. (Ibid., 20 October.) A number of cases of "forced adoption" of children whose parents had escaped to the West or were serving time for political offenses became known (Bundesminister fuer innerdeutsche Beziehungen, *Informationen*, no. 2; *Die Welt*, 13 March).

The Economy. The SED regime reported that the objectives of the 1975 Economic Plan were reached and that the national income rose to 141.6 billion marks, an increase of 5 percent over the year before. Industrial commodity production increased by 6.4 percent, and nine tenths of the growth in output was credited to higher labor productivity; investments went up only about 4 percent. (*Foreign Affairs Bulletin*, 16, no. 6, 25 February 1976.) However, the effect of high prices for raw material, including oil obtained from the USSR, created serious difficulties in foreign trade, the main source of hard currency. The GDR even attempted the use of "dumping" prices to improve its trade balance. For example, an export-import firm in the Netherlands offered British retailers 60,000 suits, produced in the GDR, for $10 apiece. (*Die Welt*, 7 February 1976.) By the end of 1975 the foreign debt had reached 2.4 billion dollars (ibid., 7 April). The foreign trade deficit in 1975 alone amounted to 4.2 billion Valuta Marks ($1 = 4.667 Valuta Marks of the GDR) (ibid., 15 September). A later report sets the estimated East German debt to Western countries at $4.4 to $4.8 billion, with interest payments of about $400 million annually (*NYT*, 24 September). The GDR debt to the FRG is about $1 billion (2.4 billion Deutsche Marks) (*Deutschland-Union-Dienst*, 30, no. 132, 13 July).

The necessity to obtain foreign credits continued in 1976. In June it was announced that the German Bank for Foreign Trade received a $175 million credit for five years from an international banking group led by the Bank of America (Bundesminister fuer innerdeutsche Beziehungen, *Informationen*, no. 12). The spring and fall trade fairs at Leipzig, attended by exhibitors and visitors from many countries, are regarded as important means for improving trade relations with the "capitalist" countries (*Foreign Affairs Bulletin*, 16, no. 7, 3 March). At the fall trade fair more than 2,800 GDR manufacturing enterprises offered their products for export sales (ibid., no. 28, 22 September). The GDR also planned to participate during 1976 in international trade fairs held in 31 countries (*Bauern-Echo*, East Berlin, 2 January).

The difficulties encountered by the economy of the GDR are first of all the result of the highly centralized and inflexible planning system. The situation became further aggravated by the price increases of raw material. The Soviet Union, which is the source of 90 percent of the oil required by the GDR, doubled the prices for oil and raw materials in 1975; the oil prices, however, were still 20 to 30 percent lower than world market prices (*Die Welt*, 2 December 1975, 17 April 1976). On that basis the new Five-Year Plan (1976-80) envisages an increase of 12 billion rubles in prices for raw materials supplied by the USSR (ibid., 2 December 1975). On the other hand, in its trade agreement for the next five years, Moscow insists on fixing prices for East German export goods destined for Soviet import at 1975 prices and for some items even at reductions up to 26 percent (*Bayernkurier*, Munich, 17 January 1976).

The GDR had a poor harvest in 1976 because of the summer drought and must import further grain from Western countries because the Soviet Union will not be able to supply all the grain needed. By September, East Berlin had already ordered about 2 million tons of grain from North America. (Hamburg, DPA in German, 30 September, in *FBIS*.)

The East German economic planners are also faced with the problem created by the increasing integration of the economies of the CMEA countries which has been ordered by Moscow. Already 75 percent of the GDR's "foreign" trade is with the community of socialist countries. The economic difficulties encountered by East Berlin might be one of the main reasons why, on 1 November, Günter Mittag was replaced by Werner Krolikowski as first deputy chairman of the Council of Ministers and put in charge of the implementation of the new SED economic directives. (*Die Welt*, 2 November.)

The Economic Plan for 1976, approved by the 14th Session of the People's Chamber on 5 December 1975, covers the first year of the new Five-Year Plan (1976-80) (*Neues Deutschland*, 8 December). The planned economic growth rate has been cautiously stated and great emphasis is placed upon the development of foreign trade. According to the "Draft of the Directive of the 9th SED-Party Congress for the Development of the Economy of the GDR 1976-1980" (published in *Neues Deutschland*, 15 January 1976), a growth rate of 27 to 30 percent is set for the entire duration of the plan. The increase in labor productivity is to be 30 to 32 percent (35 percent in previous plan). Industrial production is to increase by 34 to 36 percent and the gross national product by 27 to 30 percent. This means an annual increase of about 7 percent. For investments, 240 to 243 billion marks are to be used; this includes, however, 7 to 8 billion marks of investment participation in projects with the Soviet Union and other CMEA countries.

The presentation and approval of these economic directives was one of the main businesses of the Party Congress. *Neues Deutschland* (13 May) reported the result of the 1976 economic plan as of the end of April: industrial production had fulfilled its task by 101.1 percent and labor productivity had increased by 6.2 percent; also, the planned export to the USSR and the other socialist countries had been carried out. Honecker, in his address, stressed the achievements of the "interlinking of the GDR's economy with the national economies of the Soviet Union and the other countries of the socialist community" (ibid., 19 May). Priority was placed on exports to compensate for the higher prices of oil and raw material imports from the USSR; hence production of industrial export goods again took precedence over consumer goods. The deficiency in the service industry has forced the SED regime to promote private artisan enterprises by granting them tax reductions which were made retroactive to 1 January (*Die Welt*, 28 June).

During the first half of the year (according to *Neues Deutschland*, 16 July), the GNP rose by 5.0 percent (the target was 5.3 percent). Industrial production again reached 101.0 percent of its goal. Labor productivity moved up by 6 percent. Investments were to increase by 8.7 percent, but only 5.6 percent was achieved. This shortfall might in the long run impair foreign trade objectives. Total exports rose by 11 percent, but mostly with the CMEA (up 14 percent) and developing countries (up 13 percent) because of the higher cost of raw materials. Trade with the Western industrial states went up only by 4 percent.

In order to provide some incentive for the further increase of workers' productivity, the SED Central Committee together with the FDGB leadership and the Council of Ministers decided in May to raise the minimum income to 400 marks (from 350) and to make certain adjustments (between 15 to 40 marks) of incomes between 400 and 500 marks (ibid., 29/30 May). About one million of the total of 8.35 million employees are affected by this law, which became effective on 1 October. (*Die Welt*, 31 July.) Also, minimum pensions were to be raised on 1 December to 230 marks (from 200) and in the highest category to 300 marks (from 240). The GDR has 3.4 million old-age pensioners. (*Die Welt*, 31 May.) Almost 85 percent of the able-bodied women are employed. Also, every fifth pensioner finds it necessary to work. (Ibid., 10 March, 1 June.) The regime encourages these activities because of the constant shortage of labor.

Though the extent of "economic criminality" is kept secret, it is believed that theft of "socialist property" and various fraudulent activities of GDR citizens, not infrequently officials of the economy, are costing the entire economy several million marks per year (ibid., 13 July).

Foreign Affairs. *Relations with the Federal Republic of Germany.* As far as the SED is concerned, the so-called "German question"—that is, the issue of German reunification—has been settled once and for all. Erich Honecker at the SED Congress explained the only possible basis for the "normalization" of the relations between the GDR and the FRG:

> The GDR will continue to rebut all attempts by reactionary and revanchist forces in the FRG which cling to the thesis—as outdated as it is futile—of keeping open the German question. This question, dear comrades, is no longer open. History has long since given its verdict. With the socialist revolution and the creation of a socialist society in the GDR, the foundations, content, and forms of national life have been qualitatively altered. Led by the workers class, the people of the GDR, in keeping with the course of history, have through the construction of socialism realized their right to socioeconomic, political, and national self-determination.
>
> The socialist German nation is developing in the GDR. Its essential features are being molded by the workers class as the leading force in socialist society. The GDR, as a socialist national state, is an inseparable part of the community of socialist countries. It is a member of the world-embracing United Nations Organization. From this it naturally follows that the policy of peaceful coexistence forms the sole basis for the further normalization of relations with the FRG and all other capitalist states. We favor the continuation of this approach. If both German states act with regard for reality and in a spirit of reason, then it will serve peace, détente, and the happiness of the peoples. (*Neues Deutschland*, 19 May.)

He also affirmed that after the socio-political delineation and the various treaties concluded between East Berlin and Bonn, the division of Germany was finalized under international law. Politburo member Hermann Axen explained that the class-based economic and political foundation of the development of the socialist nation in the GDR excluded any "rapprochement" or "commonness" with the "socially opposed capitalist nation in the FRG." In this view, the relations between the two states are characterized by insoluble contradictions determined by the irreconcilable antagonism existing between socialism and capitalism. (Bundesminister fuer innerdeutsche Beziehungen, *Informationen*, no. 6.) GDR foreign minister Oskar Fischer declared that the reuniting of the two German states with opposite social systems is not possible because capitalism and socialism cannot be brought together. The Basic Treaty between the GDR and FRG makes it quite clear that the relations can only be developed on the basis of peaceful coexistence. There is no place for the "interventionist concept of an alleged special relationship." (*Horizont*, no. 3.) In further developments, according to official East German views, "the objective process of delineation of the socialist nation of the GDR from the capitalist nation of the FRG will become more far-reaching and will proceed irresistibly" (*Forum*, East Berlin, no. 8). The dissolution of the "West Germany" department within the Ministry of Foreign Trade and the assignment of its activities to the "Non-Socialist Economic Area" department is one example of the attempt to place relations with the FRG on the same level that the GDR maintains with other non-socialist countries (*Die Welt*, 19 December 1975). Also, as noted earlier, the new SED program, approved at the 1976 Party Congress, eliminated one of the important objectives of the 1963 program, the creation of a unified socialist Germany.

Among recent agreements between East Berlin and Bonn, the Traffic Agreement (19 December 1975) and the Agreements on Postal and Telecommunication (30 March 1976) have a certain significance (*Foreign Affairs Bulletin*, 16, no. 2, 16 January, and no. 12, 23 April). The GDR has consistently been able to obtain substantial financial concessions from the FRG which in the period from 1970 to 1975 amounted to 7.194 billion marks. In 1976, it is estimated that East Berlin will obtain about 900 million marks from the federal government in Bonn and the city government of West Berlin for various services and fees such as the compensation paid for the use of the roads leading to West Berlin, for improving these roads, fees for postal services and visas, and so on (*Die Welt*, 12 March; *Bayern-kurier*, 12 August). However, in spite of the existing agreements and the financial advantages, the SED regime has taken a number of actions which brought notes of protest from Bonn and in some cases from the Western Allies. For example, the Western Allies protested when 13 of 20 buses were turned back on the transit roads to West Berlin. Members of the youth organization of the Christian Democrats were the passengers on these buses and were on their way to participate in a demonstration at the occasion of the 15th anniversary of the erection of the Wall on 13 August. (*Die Welt*, 16 August.) It is of interest that on the same day 8,500 men of the "combat groups of the working class," together with border troops and police, paraded in East Berlin. SED Politburo member Konrad Naumann spoke at that occasion and referred to the increasing number of border provocations inspired by Bonn. He promised that all those who wish to continue this antagonistic policy against the GDR will fail in their attempts because East Berlin successfully terminated their efforts on 13 August 1961. *Neues Deutschland* published an "honor list" of the 18 members of the border troops who had been killed since 1949 at the borders with the FRG and West Berlin. (Bundesminister fuer innerdeutsche Beziehungen, *Informationen*, no. 17, 1976.) East Berlin rejected the protests made with regard to the interference on the transit road to West Berlin. Hermann Axen justified the obstruction with the "provocative character" of the would-be visitors to West Berlin and furthermore declared that there is no "free access" between the Federal Republic and West Berlin but only transit traffic on GDR roads regulated by agreements (*Die Welt*, 4 September). During the time since the transit agreement came into force on 4 June 1971 up to 30 June 1976, 511 persons, among them 301 from West Berlin, were arrested by GDR authorities. In the meantime 181 were released. (Bundesminister fuer innerdeutsche Beziehungen, *Informationen*, no. 16.)

East Berlin expelled an accredited reporter of the West German news magazine *Der Spiegel* because of "slanderous statements" against the GDR (*Berliner-Zeitung*, 17 December 1975). His "slanderous statements" were his report about forced adoption of children of parents who fled to the West or were apprehended in their attempts to escape from the GDR. East Berlin also barred three West German radio correspondents from going to the trade fair at Leipzig in violation of the Basic Treaty and subsequent arrangements. The Federal Ministry for Postal Affairs in Bonn reported that between 1 January and 30 September 1975 a total of 30,200 packages mailed from the FRG and West Berlin to people in the GDR have not reached their destinations (*Die Welt*, 1 April 1976).

There has been a marked increase of visitors from West Germany and West Berlin to the GDR; however, the authorities in East Berlin periodically threaten to cut down the number of visitors if the alleged systematic campaign against the GDR does not cease (ibid., 9 August). *Neues Deutschland* published on 9 August a long article about the relations between the two German states in which the actions of the FRG were equated with the "Nazis' notorious *Heim ins Reich* campaign" (i.e., the Nazi propaganda slogan alluding that all ethnic Germans should belong to one country):

It is to be hoped that common sense will prevail in the scramble for votes in the FRG | reference is made to the federal election on 3 October 1976| and that the electorate will not enable the CDU/CSU, the party which advocates "returning the fire" in a manufactured incident like the one the Nazis staged at Gleiwitz, to form the next federal government. Considering the immoderateness of Strauss, Kohl, Carstens and company this could result in the already tainted democratic image of the Federal Republic being tarnished still further.

As reported earlier, the intra-German trade continued to increase in 1976, as did the GDR debt to the FRG.

The year witnessed an increasing number of arrests in the FRG of East German intelligence agents, some of whom had managed to infiltrate various government agencies and political parties. The Federal Office concerned with Criminal Activities (Bundeskriminalamt) estimated that the GDR Ministry for State Security has 19,000 full-time employees. About 10,000 of them are operational. The number of agents in the FRG is not known but there are believed to be about 3,000. During the last five years 7,137 espionage missions have been recognized, among them 2,117 cases of military espionage. (*Die Welt*, 3 July.)

Relations with the Soviet Bloc. The integration process of the GDR with the Soviet Union and the other countries of the socialist community in the political, economic, and military spheres broadened its scope even further during 1976. The Treaty of Friendship, Cooperation and Mutual Assistance between the GDR and the USSR, signed by Honecker and Brezhnev in Moscow on 7 October 1975 and unanimously adopted by the People's Chamber on 5 December, is considered as the basis for the intensification of the integration process. According to GDR foreign minister Oskar Fischer, this treaty, based on Marxism-Leninism and socialist internationalism, "introduces a new phase in the fraternal relations between the GDR and the USSR" (*Foreign Affairs Bulletin*, 16, no. 1, 13 January 1976). Based on this treaty, an agreement on the extension of the exchange of goods between the two countries for the period of the next five-year plan (1976-80) and the annual protocol for 1976 were signed in Moscow on 7 January 1976. Under the agreement, mutual trade between the GDR and the Soviet Union will exceed 31.5 million rubles, taking into account price corrections. The Soviet Union will continue or increase the supply of raw materials including oil. The GDR will export complete plants, machinery, and equipment and will assist in the establishment and completion of joint projects of integration and other projects within the scope of the complex program of socialist economic integration. Furthermore, the GDR will participate in investment projects in the USSR. (Ibid., no. 4, 4 February.) Two other important agreements were signed on 2 February in Berlin. One of them will provide technical assistance to the GDR geological research and exploration activities for natural gas and mineral raw materials. The other contractual agreement is in regard to Soviet cooperation in building industrial plants and factories in the GDR for which the USSR will provide equipment for the power industry and technological production lines for the chemical and metallurgical industries and for housing construction. (Ibid., no. 6, 25 February.) It is apparent that with the planned deliveries to the Soviet Union which will almost double those of the last five-year plan, an extension of the production facilities has become mandatory. The SED regime attempts to explain this development as a new aspect of the intensification of socialist economic integration.

On 2 April, at a meeting of Erich Honecker with the deputy chairman of the Council of Ministers of the USSR, N. A. Tikhonov, it was emphasized that further strengthening of economic, scientific, and technological cooperation between the two countries is essential for their successfully accomplishing the task set out in the 1976-80 five-year plan. The Joint Government Commission for Economic, Scientific and Technical Cooperation between the GDR and USSR is primarily responsible for close cooperation between the economies of the two countries. (Ibid., no. 12, 23 April.) More than 100 government and ministerial agreements between the GDR and the Soviet Union give witness to the degree of integration achieved so far. These agreements have also led to an increase in the division of labor and specialization. (East Berlin, "Voice of the GDR," domestic service in German, 13 March, in *FBIS*.)

The deputy chairman of the USSR State Planning Commission, Nikolai Inozemtsev, confirmed that the GDR is the biggest partner of the Soviet Union. About half of all machine tools and instruments and more than a third of the total production of heavy engineering, agricultural hardware, construction, and road-making machinery which the Soviet Union will purchase in the CMEA countries during the five-year plan will come from the GDR. Inozemtsev also explained that in accordance with the comprehensive socialist economic integration program, the GDR together with a number of other CMEA countries participated in the construction of the gas pipeline from Orenburg to the Western borders of the Soviet Union, and Ust Ilimsk pipeline, the Kiembay asbestos enrichment combine, and the electricity supply line originating in Vinnitza, Ukraine. (TASS, international service in Russian, 1 October, in *FBIS*.)

The SED leaders are attempting to convince the East German population that the progressive integration in economic and military matters with the USSR and with other countries of the socialist community is in the best interest of the GDR. At the occasion of the 30th anniversary of the SED, Erich Honecker stated that the "fraternal alliance" with the USSR is the basis for all the achievements the GDR was able to accomplish.

Thirty years of SED — that is three decades of fraternal and unbreakable combat alliance with the CPSU on the basis of proletarian internationalism. It is a basic truth of our era: only in the closest alliance with the CPSU and the Soviet state can a people definitely liberate itself from capitalist exploitation and subjugation and shape the new social order. With the conclusion of the Treaty of Friendship, Cooperation and Mutual Assistance of 7 October 1975 our fraternal alliance was elevated to a new, qualitatively higher level. On a long-term basis the main directions of the development of our relations with the chief power of the socialist community have been staked out. We are jointly pursuing a further rapprochement of our peoples.

It is one of the greatest results of the ideological and educational activity of our party to have profoundly anchored in the people of the GDR the noble idea of unbreakable friendship with the Soviet Union. We will make this friendship and combat community ever closer and this includes our continuing determined opposition to anti-Sovietism in all its forms.

As a party holding high the banner of proletarian internationalism, the SED meets its responsibility to the international communist and workers movement and is one of its reliable combat units. We continue to follow the iron principle that the attitude toward the CPSU and the USSR is the touchstone for loyalty to Marxism-Leninism, to the revolutionary cause of the working class. (*Neues Deutschland*, 23 March.)

Politburo candidate Konrad Naumann declared at the 9th Party Congress:

The building of socialism and communism in the Soviet Union represents to the revolutionary world movement a topical and inexhaustible treasure of experience. We always abide by the words of Ernst Thälmann that the true criteria for judging an upright communist is his attitude towards the Soviet Union, towards proletarian internationalism. (East Berlin, domestic service in German, 19 May, in *FBIS*.

The meeting of Honecker with Brezhnev in the Crimea on 24 August was, according to the SED chief, "an event of national and international significance." Honecker declared that the friendship between the two countries provides "a firm foundation and guarantees the freedom and independence of the people of the GDR." (*Pravda*, 15 September.)

A plan for the exchange of delegations and experiences between the Central Committees of the SED and the CPSU for 1976-77, concluded in East Berlin on 12 January, provides for such consultative meetings not only of the Central Committees but also of the executives from the lower levels of the party hierarchy and between scientific institutions, universities, and newspapers (East Berlin, "Voice of the GDR," domestic service in German, 12 January, in *FBIS*). The meeting of Kurt Hager, member of the SED Politburo and Secretariat, with Michail Simianin, secretary of the Central Committee of the CPSU, in Moscow in June, at which "questions of ideological cooperation" between the two parties were discussed, came under the auspices of this arrangement (*Neue Zeit*, East Berlin, 14 June). Numerous exchange visits of SED officials and leaders of the Communist parties and governments of the USSR and the other states of the socialist community provided opportunities to coordinate their policies and demonstrate their fraternal relationship and unity of purpose to the population of the Soviet bloc. Among the most important events in this respect were the speeches made by Honecker at the party congresses of the CPSU, the Polish United Workers' Party (December 1975), the Bulgarian Communist Party (March 1976), and the Czechoslovakian Communist Party (April) (*Foreign Affairs Bulletin*, 15, no. 36, 17 December 1975; 16, no. 7, 3 March 1976; and no., 11, 12 April).

The Soviet Union indicated its appreciation of the loyalty of its East German ally. Erich Correns, chairman of the National Council of the GDR's National Front, was awarded on the occasion of his 80th birthday the Soviet Order of Peoples' Friendship for his contribution to the consolidation of the fraternal friendship and cooperation between the two countries. (Moscow domestic service in Russian, 11 May, in *FBIS*). More than 4,500 students from the GDR were attending institutions of higher learning in the Soviet Union during 1976 (*National-Zeitung*, 25 February).

At the CMEA session in East Berlin on 7-9 July, attended also by a Yugoslav delegation, it was pointed out that the national income of the CMEA countries had increased by 36 percent in the period 1971-75 and that the conditions for the further development of socialist economic integration and joint target programs were favorable (*Foreign Affairs Bulletin*, 16, no. 23, 27 July).

The military integration of the Warsaw Pact countries received further impetus during 1976. Werner Lamberz, member of the SED Politburo and Secretariat, stated: "As far as the military aspect of the alliance [of socialist states] is concerned, the entire world knows that there is no military coalition as strong and as solid as ours" (*Neues Deutschland*, 10/11 January).

Soviet ambassador Pjotr Abrassimov presented, in the name of the Soviet Presidium, high Soviet orders to high-ranking military officers of the GDR "in recognition and appreciation of their meritorious services for the consolidation of the German-Soviet class and military alliances." Among those decorated were GDR defense minister General Heinz Hoffmann and his deputy, Lieutenant General Heinz Kessler, who received the "Order of the October Revolution" (Bundesminister fuer innerdeutsche Beziehungen, *Informationen*, no. 7).

The "collaboration" in the intelligence field appears to be one-sided.The Soviet Committee of State Security (KGB) assigns missions to the GDR Ministry of State Security and by means of a Soviet-German liaison staff controls its flow of information. It is also known that the entire government and party apparatus has been permeated by KGB agents. (*Die Welt*, 27 December 1975.)

Other International Positions. The GDR continued during 1976 to consolidate and expand its contacts with the international community. In May, it was reported that East Berlin had established diplomatic relations with 121 states (*Neues Deutschland*, 19 May). The GDR also took an active part in the United Nations and its Specialized Agencies, and even played host to a UN ecological symposium which was attended by representatives from 33 countries (*Die Welt*, 21 September).

Mutual visits of government officials took place between the GDR and Great Britain, France, Belgium, Denmark, Austria, Portugal, Australia, and North Korea. A consular convention was signed with Great Britain on 4 May (*Foreign Affairs Bulletin*, 16, no. 14, 14 May).

The GDR showed special interest in maintaining close relations with the countries of the Middle East, for economic as well as political reasons. Following the Soviet lead, the SED regime supports the Arab cause and accuses Israel of pursuing a policy of aggression. (*Die Welt*, 22 January.) East Berlin provides diplomatic and material support to the PLO.

> For many years the Palestine Liberation Organization and the other progressive forces in the Middle East have received solidarity shipments from the GDR which in accordance with the concrete situation and wishes are sent by special plane and ship. Wounded liberation fighters have been nursed back to health in the most modern health institutions of the GDR or supplied with artificial limbs. Universities and vocational schools have permitted Palestinian students expelled from the FRG to study or have given them special training. (*Neues Deutschland*, 25/26 September.)

The GDR Peace Committee sent a telegram to Tawfig Toubi, a Communist member of the Israeli parliament, assuring him of its solidarity with the struggle of the Arabs and all democratic forces against the terror of the Israeli government and its soldiers (Peace Council of the GDR, *Information*, East Berlin, no. 7).

The visits of Dev Kant Barooah, president of the Indian National Congress, 25-29 April, and India's prime minister, Indira Gandhi, 1-4 July, were indicative of the good relations East Berlin has established with India. A number of East German delegations, among them a military group headed by National Defense minister General Heinz Hoffmann, visited India at the invitation of the Indian government. (*Foreign Affairs Bulletin*, 16, nos. 4 and 9, 4 February, 22 March.)

Trade union contacts accounted also for a number of exchange visits (e.g., with Great Britain and Finland).

The GDR utilizes every opportunity offered by its membership in the UN and in the various UN Specialized Agencies and Commissions to support the common foreign policy objectives of the Communist-ruled countries. The GDR, for example, advocates a convocation of a world disarmament conference. East Berlin also proposed a universal treaty on the renunciation of use of force and the complete and general prohibition of nuclear weapons tests at the Geneva Disarmament Committee (ibid., nos. 11 and 12, 12, 23 April.)

The SED regime closely follows Moscow's lead in its policy toward the non-aligned states. Erich Honecker assured them in a message to their 5th Conference of Heads of State and Governments at Colombo (August) of the GDR's support "in the just struggle for political and economic independence, for gaining and safeguarding complete sovereignty over the natural resources, for eliminating all forms of colonialist and neo-colonialist suppression, exploitation and discrimination, for equality-based international economic relations" (ibid., no. 26, 7 September).

The GDR also continued its support of the People's Republic of Angola. During the fighting, the SED regime maintained an airlift operation taking wounded soldiers and other African "freedom fighters" to East Germany (*Christian Science Monitor*, 13 February). It was reported that at least 700 "advisers" from the GDR participated in the civil war in Angola (*Die Welt*, 23 February). More recent reports state that soldiers of the NVA are training members of the South West African Liberation Movement, SWAPO, for guerrilla warfare (ibid., 8 October). Negotiations between the GDR and the People's Republic of Angola were concluded in June, and a number of agreements between the SED and the MPLA were reached concerning cooperation in 1976 and 1977. (East Berlin, ADN, international service in German, 25 June, in *FBIS*).

It appears that the GDR still has the task of attempting to improve the relations of the Soviet bloc with Yugoslavia. A delegation of the FDGB led by the SED Politburo member and FDGB chairman Harry Tisch visited Yugoslavia for several days in March. A Yugoslav delegation of "parliamentarians" returned the visit (31 May-5 June). (Bundesminister fuer innerdeutsche Beziehungen, *Informationen*, no. 7; *Foreign Affairs Bulletin*, 16, no. 19, 22 June.)

SED leaders also reflect Moscow's condemnation of the Chinese Communists. Peking is accused of anti-Sovietism and of attempting to split the community of socialist states (*Einheit*, East Berlin, no. 1). The Chinese leadership was strongly attacked because they referred to the Cubans in Angola ("who were following a request of the legitimate government of Angola" and came to the aid of "their Angolan brothers") as "satellite troops" of the Soviet Union (*Horizont*, East Berlin, no. 7).

The SED asserts that peace and détente not only improve the conditions for the development of socialism but also provides better circumstances for the revolutionary struggle in other parts of the world.

> The overthrow of fascism in Greece and Portugal, the end of the Portuguese colonial empire, the successes of the left parties in France, Italy, and Japan—these also are results of the process of détente with definite impact upon international relations. . . . The closer all revolutionary forces of the world work to-

gether, the better will be the conditions for revolutionary change and the development of socialism. Peaceful coexistence and proletarian internationalism are two sides of one and the same revolutionary policy. (*Forum*, East Berlin, no. 6.)

International Party Contacts. The Conference of European Communist and Workers' Parties finally met in East Berlin on 29-30 June 1976 after overcoming considerable difficulties encountered during its preparatory phase. The fact that the SED was entrusted by Moscow with the chairmanship of the working committee to draft in advance the final communiqué is one of the many indications of the high degree of confidence the Kremlin has in its East German ally.

The Yugoslav, French, Italian, Romanian, Spanish, British, and Swedish parties rejected the SED draft of the "final document" of the conference because they felt that the proposed unity of action—that is, Moscow's monopoly position as undisputed leader of the Communist world movement, would impair the freedom of action of the individual parties. Other differences of opinion, concerning the relations between fraternal parties, contacts with social-democratic parties, the role played by non-aligned states, and the evaluation of the contemporary "crisis of capitalism," were expressed in a number of "preparatory conferences" and caused the conference to be delayed for about 20 months. An "editorial conference," meeting in June, the same month in which the conference eventually took place, was able to find a formulation of the final document acceptable to all.

The conference was attended by the top leaders of 29 parties, including the Yugoslav party. Among them were party chiefs Brezhnev, Enrico Berlinguer, Georges Marchais, and Tito. Only the Communist Parties of Albania and Iceland did not participate. (*Die Welt*, 30 June.) The conference unanimously adopted the document "for peace, security, cooperation and social progress in Europe" which confirmed the "independence" of the individual parties (*Foreign Affairs Bulletin*, 16, nos. 20/21 and 23, 5, 27 July).

Brezhnev, while praising "proletarian internationalism," denied the existence of any intention to reinstitute an organizational center. "Proletarian internationalism" means, accordig to him, the solidarity of the working class and of the Communist parties of all countries in the fight for their common objectives. (*Die Welt*, 30 June.) *Neues Deutschland* (2 July) reported that the participating parties, representing 29 million Communists, declared their will to contribute to the achievements of their common objectives.

Among fraternal parties in the "capitalist" area, the SED's closest relationships were with the German Communist Party (DKP) and the Socialist Unity Party of West Berlin (SEW). A delegation of high SED functionaries attended the 9th DKP Party Congress (March 1976). Contacts were also encouraged between "mass organizations" in the FRG and in the GDR. For example, a delegation of the German Peace Society/United War Service Resisters from the FRG visited East Germany in April at the invitation of the Peace Council of the GDR (*Neues Deutschland*, 12 April).

The SED took it upon itself to criticize the French Communists, who for apparently tactical considerations had dropped the term "dictatorship of the proletariat" from their party program (*Die Welt*, 20 March).

Publications and Broadcast Media. Erich Honecker at the 9th SED Congress reported that the circulation of SED publications such as the daily *Neues Deutschland*, the monthlies *Einheit* and *Neuer Weg*, the district and factory newspapers, and the illustrated magazines had reached a total of 16.7 million during the last five years (*Neues Deutsche Press*, East Berlin, no. 12, 1976). The reported increase of the most important papers of the SED party press between 1971 and 1975 confirmed Honecker's claim.

Neues Deutschland	1971: 955,109	1975: 1,063,547
Einheit	1971: 197,429	1975: 238,571
Neuer Weg	1971: 196,169	1975: 202,187
15 SED district newspapers:	1971: 4,120,041	1975: 4,512,046

(Bundesminister fuer innerdeutsche Beziehungen, *Informationen*, no. 15, 1976.)

In addition to these national and regional party organs, 628 factory newspapers were published, with a total circulation of about 2 million (ibid.).

It also was reported that the daily official newspaper of the FDJ, *Junge Welt*, had increased its circulation from 400,000 in 1971 to more than 900,000 in 1976 and thereby had become (after *Neues Deutschland*) the second largest daily in the GDR (ibid., no. 12). The political parties of the National Front and the mass organizations have their own publications in order to reach specific sections of the population, and a number of publications, some in foreign languages, are produced in the GDR for propaganda purposes abroad. (See *YICA, 1976*, p. 38.)

The University of Calgary   Eric Waldman

Hungary

Hungarian communists formed a party in November 1918 and became the dominant force in the left-wing coalition that established the Republic of Councils the following March and ruled for four months. Subsequently proscribed, the party functioned sporadically in exile and illegality. With the Soviet occupation at the end of World War II the Hungarian Communist Party emerged as a partner in the coalition government and exercised an influence disproportionate to its limited electoral support. Communists gained effective control of the country in 1947, and the following year absorbed left-wing social-democrats into the newly named Hungarian Workers' Party. On 1 November 1956, during the popular revolt that momentarily restored a multiparty government, the name was changed to Hungarian Socialist Workers' Party (Magyar Szocialista Munkáspárt; HSWP).

The HSWP rules unchallenged as the sole political party, firmly aligned with the USSR. Its exclusive status is confirmed in the revised state constitution of 1972: "The Marxist-Leninist party of the working class is the leading force in society." Coordination of formal political activities, such as elections, is the function of the Patriotic People's Front (PPF). In the 1971-75 Parliament 71 percent of the deputies were party members. Of municipal and local council members 46.9 percent belong to the HSWP. In the police forces 90 percent of officer rank are HSWP members. Party membership (estimated mid-1976) stands at 765,700. At the time of the HSWP's 11th Congress (March 1975), by current occupation the membership was composed of 45.5 percent physical workers, 6.1 percent "immediate supervisors of production," 40.0 percent intellectual workers, and 8.4 percent dependents and others. By original occupation, 59.2 percent were workers, 13.0 percent peasants, 8.9 percent intellectual workers, 16.3 percent white-collar employees, and 2.6 percent others. Of current members, 8,212 joined the HSWP prior to the country's liberation in 1945.

The broadest umbrella organization for political mobilization is the PPF. It works through some 4,000 committees with 112,400 members. A related agency is the National Peace Council, with international responsibilities. Trade unions, directed by the National Council of Trade Unions (NCTU), comprise close to four million organized workers. The Communist Youth League (Kommunista Ifjusági Szövetség; KISZ) has more than 800,000 members, in 25,600 basic organizations. Thirty-one percent of working youths, 56 percent of secondary school students, and 96 percent of post-secondary students belong to the KISZ. In the Workers' Militia 81 percent are HSWP members. Other active mobilizing agents are the National Council of Hungarian Women and the Hungarian-Soviet Friendship Society.

Hungary has a population (estimated 1976) of 10,603,000.

Leadership and Organization. Ultimate political power in the HSWP, and therefore in Hungary, remains in the hands of the first secretary, János Kádár. Current Politburo members are Kádár, György Aczél, Antal Apró, Valéria Benke, Béla Biszku, Jenö Fock, Sándor Gáspár, István Huszár, György Lázár, Pál Losonczi, László Maróthy, Dezsö Nemes, Károly Németh, Miklós Óvári, and István Sarlós. In addition to Kádár the Central Committee Secretariat includes Biszku, Sándor Borbély, Németh, Óvári, András Gyénes, and Imre Györi. Chairman of the Central Control Committee is János Brutyó.

The most notable leadership change in 1976, announced at the 27 October Central Committee plenum, was the release of Árpád Pullai as secretary, an office he had held for nearly ten years. One of the more dogmatic HSWP leaders, Pullai (born 1925) had been charged with party and mass organizational affairs and most recently with the membership card exchange. His new assignment is as minister of transport and telecommunications. His replacement on the Secretariat is Sándor Borbély (born 1931). Unlike Pullai, Borbély is a graduate of the Komsomol academy and the Soviet party academy. Since July 1975 he had been head of the Central Committee's Department of Industry, Agriculture, and Communications.

The Central Committee elected at the party's 11th Congress (March 1975) has 125 members. County party committees, together with the Budapest Party Committee, number 24. There are also 97 district party committees, 104 city and Budapest district party committees, 1,033 plant and office party committees, and 24,450 primary party organizations. The leaders in the latter organizations number 106,692. Of these primary party organizations, 7,066 are active in industry and construction, 4,215 in agriculture, 1,473 in transportation, and 1,216 in commerce.

Auxiliary and Mass Organizations. The 23d Congress of Hungarian Trade Unions was held 8-12 December 1975, attended by 789 delegates representing 4 million trade union members. NCTU secretary-general Sándor Gáspár in his report said that the unions support stronger central economic direction as well as the development of enterprise independence, proclaimed the need for more economically rational allocation of labor, and emphasized that enterprise and shop floor democracy require clearer interpretation and implementation, as does union consultation with the higher state authorities.

The Congress was also addressed by Politburo member Béla Biszku, who declared that the proportion of enterprise income reverting to the state budget must be increased, that workers' views must be heard by management, and that "more just income proportions" and an end to "unearned income" are imperative in the coming period of slower increase in real wages. In general the stress at the Congress was on labor discipline, productivity, and on the primacy of social over group and individual interests.

The NCTU on 31 May 1976 approved new principles for expanding the prerogatives of shop stewards (who are elected by secret ballot), notably through greater participation in decisions on wages and other benefits. At a press conference on 22 September Gáspár said that representative democracy in trade union councils, the KISZ, and party organizations must be complemented by elements of direct democracy on the shop floor level, and he reported that "concrete experiments are being conducted in 50 factories and have already achieved concrete results and experiences." In half of the 50 enterprises the direct democracy experiment depends on elected shop stewards, in the other half on worker delegates. Results will determine which system will be applied in the future. The thrust of the campaign is to induce worker participation not only on issues of immediate benefit to them but also in the production sphere in the interest of greater labor discipline and productivity.

At the 8th Congress of the Federation of Art Workers' Unions, in October 1975, Politburo member Miklós Óvári delivered a reminder that artistic work requires not only talent but also a world outlook based on the proper ideological foundation. The general assembly of the 467-member Hungarian Writers' Union was held 17-18 May 1976. One topic of debate was nationalism, described by secretary-general Imre Dobozy as one of the most dangerous conservative inheritances. The related discussion on national minorities had as one implicit target the problems of the Hungarian minority in Romania. The difficulty of encouraging socialist realism without dogmatism was explored by Dobozy and Miklós Óvári. Their remarks testified to the existence of a certain pluralism in literary circles. The assembly elected Dobozy president and Gábor Garai secretary-general of the Writers' Union. Both are HSWP Central Committee members.

The 9th KISZ Congress was convened 8-11 May and attended by 907 delegates. Preparatory work was inspired by the "new obligation to strengthen the League's communist and political nature" (*Ifjukommunista*, January). In his address to the Congress, Politburo member and KISZ Central Committee first secretary László Maróthy called for more youth participation in "socialist work competition," stressed the need for better ideological and educational work while recognizing that it was impossible to "inoculate our youth against the petty-bourgeois and bourgeois ideologies and an idealist world outlook," and identified a fundamental task of KISZ as the preparation of members for admission to the HSWP (7.5 percent of KISZ members also belong to the HSWP). Kádár also spoke to the Congress, expounding on general economic problems, in the context of which he noted that while more intensive and rational use of manpower was necessary (see below, "Domestic Attitudes and Activities"), this was not tantamount to a return to the days of "sheer brute force." He criticized suggestions that religious youths and those involved with private plot farming ought to be excluded from the KISZ (*Népszabadság*, 11 May).

Preparations for the 6th Patriotic People's Front Congress began with the elections of PPF committees in February-May and the selection of delegates. This process provided for the airing of local problems, notably the situation of private plot farming and the inadequacy of facilities and services in the smaller villages. Concurrently special national minority conferences were held in manifestation of the HSWP's policy of exemplary treatment of these groups. Official statistics show 156,000 persons (1.5 percent of the population) belonging to minority groups, although a more broadly based Ministry of Culture survey identifies 220,000 Germans, 100,000 to 110,000 Southern Slavs, and 20,000 to 25,000 Romanians. In the context of a massive media campaign heralding the Congress, PPF National Council president Gyula Kállai stressed the need for ideological education in light of the fact that "there remain traces of the old system's ideology, and indeed in certain political and economic circumstances this harmful inheritance may and does reemerge. We must confront calmly but determinedly the fact that the philosophy of individualism and egoism is, under the ostensible veneer of socialism, spreading through not negligible strata of our society." (*Népszabadság*, 27 June.)

The Congress, held 18-19 September, was attended by 776 delegates as well as 200 other guests and numerous foreign delegations. The report of the National Council, presented by secretary-general

István Sarlós, adopted the resolutions of the HSWP's 11th Congress as a "national program": "An indispensable criterion of our social system is the widening of socialist democracy in every sphere of life. It is our task to strengthen this process. An essential element and method of socialist democratism is that the population participates in the elaboration of important enactments, in the preparation and constitution of laws." Said Sarlós: "Politically our people are unified. Of course, we understand it unmistakably that it is still not a perfect unity because there are citizens who hold views different from ours, but the actual picture of the whole country is formed by the overwhelming majority that approved our program at the time of elections." Sarlós endorsed the role of the private sector, the ancillary activities of agricultural cooperatives, and the importance of garden and private plots. The national minorities, he said, "are freely cultivating their national traditions, mother tongues, and customs." The role of the churches has been "developing favorably." He called for support for economic and cultural tasks, for labor discipline and for more voluntary work: "The People's Front not only inspires every layer of workers to fulfill national or local plans, but also seeks to bring to the surface the criticisms and proposals of the masses and to represent them in state and political organizations." Sarlós also stressed the virtues of socialist patriotism, which he defined as the amalgam of patriotism and internationalism. The latter "demands action, commitment to the Soviet Union, to the socialist community, and to the cause of international progress." (MTI, 18 September.)

The Congress reelected Kállai and Sarlós president and secretary-general. As the PPF's formal programmatic statement put it: "The Patriotic People's Front is the most comprehensive framework of the alliance policy of the Hungarian Socialist Workers' Party. The conscious cooperation of Hungarian social strata is embodied in it. The policy of alliance plays a conclusively determining role in the historical stage of the building of socialism as one of the basic prerequisites of our progress. It is our task to urge, in the name of this policy, the gathering together of our country's creative forces—party members and non-members, materialists and believers, people following different ideologies—and their conscious cooperation in the shaping and execution of this policy." (Ibid., 20 September.)

Party Internal Affairs. In the wake of the HSWP's 11th Congress (March 1975), which reiterated the "alliance policy," stressed the party's leading role in the construction of a developed socialist society, and emphasized economic objectives, the party's principal internal activity has been the membership card exchange anticipated by the Congress. At the Central Committee plenum of 23 October 1975, Pullai reported that the "fundamental political task" was to reinforce party unity, expand the activity of party organizations and members, and promote implementation of the congressional resolutions. It was anticipated that stiffer requirements would probably lead some people to decline the responsibilities a party member must face: "It is a voluntary association with the party, and anyone who wants to quit may do so without any harmful consequences." (*Társadalmi Szemle*, November 1975.)

At the Central Committee plenum of 21 July 1976 Pullai reported that the exchange was proceeding correctly and that the interviews, which had been "critical, self-critical, and sincere in character," had been completed. He observed that "the development of consciousness of a large part of the members falls short of the growing requirements. Religiousness, egotism, and petty-bourgeois materialism occur also among the members." As a result of the interviews 5,736 members announced their intention to resign. Their motives included ideological uncertainty, unwillingness to pay dues, and personal offendedness. A large proportion of them were pensioners. The leading party organs recommended that 2,528 members be struck off the rolls, mainly for "neglect of party duties." Many of those expelled were young and had joined the party within the past 5-6 years. Altogether 9,298 persons ceased to be members of the party, 1.2 percent of the total membership. (This compares with 7,133 expulsions, 7,478 resignations, and 15,474 cancellations of membership in the four-and-a-half years between the 10th and 11th HSWP Congresses.) A disproportionate two-thirds of those leaving the party were active or retired physical workers.

Pullai reported that "not all persons unsuitable for membership have left the party. In many cases concrete duties and demands were set to give members a probationary period for the improvement of their behavior and party work. The party's continual cleansing, which is a natural part of party life, does not end with the card exchange." Separation from the party, according to Pullai, did not carry a stigma or, in the main, give personal offense; nor did it affect working conditions. There have been few appeals. The report indicated widespread demand among the membership for more regular exchanges of views between leaders and ordinary members in the interest of party democracy. (*Pártélet*, August.) The interviews produced criticism of mistakes in the implementation of party policy, of leaders who did not maintain adequate contact with the working people, of insufficient support for leaders who imposed strict demands with regard to work and discipline, and of extraneous matters such as wage levels, inadequate workshop democracy, and high foodstuff prices. The official party daily concluded that "it has been proven that the exchange of party membership cards did not constitute a party purge." (*Népszabadság*, 25 July.)

In his report to the Central Committee plenum of 27 October on ideology and education in the HSWP, Imre Györi stressed the dangers of "both right- and left- distortions." Topical ideological questions requiring more attention were the "nature of state power" and "proletarian internationalism," the latter opposing anti-communism and "all varieties of anti-Sovietism." (Ibid., 28 October.)

Domestic Attitudes and Activities. As indicated by the programmatic statements of the 11th Congress, Hungary's economic problems and the tasks arising from them are the principal current preoccupation of party and government.

The Central Committee at its 26-27 November 1975 meeting approved the guiding principles of the fifth five-year plan (1976-80). The key targets are a 30 to 32 percent increase in national income (to be achieved solely by higher productivity and comprising a 33 to 35 percent growth in industrial production and a 15 to 18 percent growth in agricultural production); an 18 to 20 percent increase in real income, lower than for the preceding five-year period; and very high foreign trade levels. In view of the precipitous deterioration in the terms of trade, the plan anticipates a 40 percent rise in trade with the socialist sector, with exports having to increase more than imports. (Because of the commodity structure of Hungary's trade with CMEA, export prices in 1975 rose by an average of 12 percent, and import prices by 22 percent.) A similar priority is given to exports to the non-socialist sector.

Kádár himself has stressed the great difficulties in developing the five-year plan in the context of world-wide inflation and energy price increases, and has called for public understanding and sacrifice. He has also proclaimed the unity and mutual benefits of the socialist camp: "Our development is in harmony with the planned rate of growth of the socialist countries" (*Társadalmi Szemle*, March). In presenting the five-year plan and the 1976 budget to the National Assembly in December 1975, Politburo member Károly Németh cited such adverse factors as the excess of domestic consumption over national income, a budget deficit, unfavorable trade and payments balances, insufficient productivity, and unnecessarily slow progress in the transformation of the production structure toward more marketable commodities. The plan's official general objectives are greater productivity, better adaptation to changing economic conditions and improvement in the overall economic equilibrium, and an improvement in Hungary's defense capability. (*Magyar Közlöny*, 24 December.)

The November 1975 Central Committee meeting also approved a new price policy which, in the context of the five-year plan, is designed to be more responsive to production costs and international price changes. There followed a series of announcements on price increases for foodstuffs and other consumer goods, industrial goods, and services. Consumer prices of meat and meat products, which had not changed since 1966, were raised by an average of 30 percent on 5 July 1976. The immediate purpose was to slow down the growth of domestic consumption, increase exports, and reduce state subsidies. The increase was partly offset by wage and social benefit improvements, but the 1976 plan provides for only a 1.5 percent rise in per capita real wages.

The move to bring prices into closer approximation to production costs and world market prices is one aspect of the new system of economic regulators that are being introduced to provide tighter central control over the economy. In a related shift, the state will withhold a larger proportion of the profits of individual enterprises; as Kádár explained, "all we have done is to reinstate the original proportions in the name of the national economic interest" (*Társadalmi Szemle*, March).

Economic problems are also spurring the drive for improved quality. The general marketing practice has been to reserve the best quality for Western markets, medium quality for the socialist market, and the lowest quality for the domestic market. The current impetus is for the production of single-quality, "convertible" goods that are competitive on the Western market. The director of a large enterprise was dismissed for producing substandard goods and thereby losing the firm's most important (probably Soviet) customer.

The future course of the New Economic Mechanism is a subject of both public and expert debate. In GNP per capita Hungary (at $2,140) ranks fifth among socialist countries and 36th in the world; the ratio of highest to lowest personal real income is 5 to 1. Reflected the government's semi-official daily: "We reject what used to be called 'barracks communism,' but the capitalist road of a consumer society is of course not our ideal either. So let us seek a future socialist way of life. The question is urgent, as the high-income brackets of our society have by now reached, if not surpassed, the relative limits of their requirements." (*Magyar Hirlap*, 8 August.) Addressing the 15th "traveling economic congress," which was attended by party and government officials as well as leading enterprise managers, Károly Németh tried to dispel suspicions that the enterprise autonomy ushered in by the NEM was being phased out: "It is important, in order to ensure the successful completion of our tasks, to increase the efficiency of our central direction and simultaneously to uphold and develop the enterprises' independence, initiative, and incentives." Nevertheless, for the present the real stress appears to lie on the reassertion of central direction.

In agriculture, following the Soviet example, a process of consolidation of collective farms has been under way for several years, and through mergers the number of such farms has fallen to 1,600 from a peak of 4,500. Recognizing that this consolidation was not always inspired by economic rationality, Agriculture Minister Pál Romány has stated that "it is in general inexpedient to continue to increase the size of the farms, and what we must attend to now is not size, but better production and more efficient farming" (*Magyar Mezögazdaság*, 1 October 1975). There has been criticism that the large merged cooperatives promote alienation between management and members and between the membership and production.

Agricultural cooperative managers as well as the more dogmatic party members continue to show hostility toward private plot farming, but the regime regards the latter's contribution to agricultural output as vitally important, particularly at a time when consumers are plagued with acute shortages of certain vegetables. A Council of Ministers resolution in March 1976 directed large farms to support the agricultural work of household plots and auxiliary farms as a socially useful activity, and in October modifications were announced in the taxation of this activity to stimulate production.

The weakness of the private sector is visible in the numerical decline of private artisans reported by the National Association of Artisans. The most chronic shortages are in the service sector. A key disincentive is the complexity and level of taxation.

The problems of manpower and labor discipline have prompted a series of measures that add up to drastic government intervention in labor management. In 1966-70 Hungary's labor force increased by 345,000 and in the following five-year period by 100,000. In contrast, the estimated increase for 1976-80 is no more than 50,000 to 60,000. In December 1975 the Ministries of Labor and Finance issued a decree imposing a total or partial freeze on the hiring of white-collar workers, whose numbers have been expanding at a rapid pace while shortages of labor exist in other areas. A lively public debate ensued on this controversial measure, and the authorities explained that it was an unpleasant but necessary step to achieve a more efficient distribution of manpower. In a speech before the Budapest party organization on 4 February 1976, Kádár observed that "the really urgent need is to put a stop to the avalanche-like increase in administrative staffs," and he described a positive instance: "They had the guts in the Györ Wagon and Machine Works to transfer 450 office workers to the workshops. At the time these people showed their annoyance, but in a couple of months they were gladly accepting their new circumstances and were even earning more." (*Társadalmi Szemle*, March).

Even greater controversy was generated by the December 1975 announcement of the Ministries of Labor and Education calling for mandatory annual classification of schoolchildren by social origin. Following a storm of criticism that this represented a departure from the HSWP's "alliance policy," which had abandoned class discrimination in education, even party officials voiced reservations, and the ministries issued a clarification denying any intent of social categorization. The proposed instrument, Kádár explained, "was nothing but a simple instrument for assembling statistical data. In the ministry they wanted to know the percentage of workers' children in the kindergartens and in the primary and grammar schools. Statistics do have their uses, but the introduction of the form was clumsily handled and gave the impression that it presaged a return to a now discarded practice." (Ibid.)

The widespread practice of moonlighting (and a consequent neglect of primary employment responsibilities) has been a perennial subject of official and public criticism, and in January the Ministry of Labor issued a decree restricting the freedom to take on ancillary or secondary jobs. Said a government official, "The objective is to restore the prestige of the primary job" (*Magyar Hirlap*, 6 February). On 11 March the Council of Ministers issued a regulation tightening "sick pay discipline." A Ministry of Labor decree on 10 April set new guidelines for the recruitment and redirection of labor. At the June session of the National Assembly, labor minister László Karakas announced the preparation of a new complex manpower program to provide better wage incentives, particulary for mothers and pensioners to remain active and to expand the training of skilled labor.

Many of these measures clearly limit the freedom of both employers and job seekers, but they are a response to genuine inefficiencies. The administrative hiring freeze in particular has created public uncertainty regarding the future of new graduates.

Unpaid "social work," under the general guidance of the PPF, is an important contributor to the economy (valued at 2 billion forints in 1974), although in practice some of it is done during normal (paid) working hours. One form of it is an unpaid shift, "Communist Saturdays," which some enterprises have been accused of exploiting.

Determined efforts to improve the trade balance have begun to show some results. In the first half of 1976 exports increased 6 percent by value over the last corresponding period, while imports declined by 9 percent. In the ruble area, exports were up 9.8 percent, and imports up by 5.8 percent; in the non-ruble area exports rose by 3 percent but imports declined by 18.5 percent. A number of recent trade agreements indicate an intensification of Hungarian-Soviet economic relations and growing Hungarian dependence. A new basic trade agreement with the USSR provides for increased oil imports, in exchange for which Hungary will have to share in Soviet investments in crude oil production and provide machine industry products to cover the rising price of oil, which is now tied to a moving average of world market prices. Moreover, between 1976 and 1980 the number of Hungarian plants built with Soviet cooperation is expected to be 150 percent greater than in the preceding five-year period. Supplementing the normal intergovernmental agreement, a new type of Hungarian-Soviet agreement has also been concluded amounting to a major long-term commitment (to 1990) to the Soviet market. It provides for exports of wheat, maize, and beef and the import of oil and timber products and cotton, with settlement in Western currency at world market prices. One factor necessitating this reorientation is the European Economic Community's restrictions on Hungarian agricultural exports. Hungarian workers have been assigned to Soviet projects such as the Orenburg natural gas pipeline and a hotel in Uzhgorod, and will also aid in the building of a Siberian cellulose factory, a joint investment project arising from CMEA's comprehensive program.

At its March session the National Assembly passed a new law on national defense which prescribes the organization of defense and the responsibilities of a hypothetical National Defense Council, of the Council of Ministers, and of other state agencies down to the level of local councils. The law sets maximum compulsory military service at two years (which has been the recent practice), or 18 months in the case of students in post-secondary education. In October 1975 the Council of Ministers provided by decree for the organization of voluntary border guard auxiliaries to aid the regular security forces in apprehending frontier violators.

A July 1976 decree of the Ministry of Internal Trade imposes new restrictions on the sale of alcoholic beverages in the fight against alcoholism, a major and growing social problem in Hungary.

Following lengthy consultations between Hungary and the Vatican, the appointment was announced in February of László Lékai as archbishop of Esztergom, primate of Hungary, and president of the Bench of Bishops. His elevation to cardinal was proclaimed by the Pope on 27 April. In his sermon on the occasion of his ceremonial installation at Esztergom, Lékai referred to 6 million Hungarian Catholics and invited the respect for their belief guaranteed by the constitution (to which he swore allegiance). He has also alluded to persisting restrictions and difficulties in the teaching of catechism. Lékai's appointment is the latest step in the progressive normalization of relations between the Hungarian régime and the Vatican. HSWP and PPF policy is to praise the loyalty and tolerate the reduced activity of the various churches (Budapest has the only rabbinical school in the Soviet bloc) while maintaining, particularly through the KISZ, the necessity for peaceful ideological struggle against religion. Said Kádár in February: "Without exception the churches are loyal to our system. . . . Is it possible that by doing this the churches may be prolonging their existence? It may be so. . . . It could be said that this is a compromise. . . . But we learn from Lenin that any compromise which advances our revolutionary course is acceptable." (*Társadalmi Szemle*, March.)

The 20th anniversary of the October-November 1956 revolution passed unobserved. It coincided with joint Soviet-Hungarian military maneuvers.

International Views and Policies. The HSWP continues to follow faithfully the Soviet line in foreign and intra-party policies. In February 1976, Kádár hailed as milestones and successes of the world Communist movement the victory of the North Vietnamese, the Helsinki conference, and the independence of Angola. Regarding Helsinki, deputy foreign minister János Nagy declared that Hungary has favored "complete implementation" from the outset and was in most respects ahead of other signatories in fulfillment of the Final Act." On "Basket Three," he deplored selectivity in the Western demands, noted the need for reciprocity, including Western measures to liberalize visa regulations and encourage the distribution of Hungarian cultural products, and asserted that there was no demand in Hungary for Western publications that "slander our system" (*Társadalmi Szemle*, July). It was ostensibly in the spirit of Helsinki that authorization was given for two television programs in May and August in the "International Studio" series, in which a panel including Western journalists engaged in fairly open debate on aspects of détente and East-West relations. The debates were a significant innovation, although Western participants were requested to avoid certain sensitive topics, including any mention of Solzhenitsyn.

The HSWP has maintained a relatively low profile in the intra-party controversies that marked preparations for the conference of European communist and workers' parties in East Berlin, 29-30 June. On the occasion of his visit to the 25th Congress of the Communist Party of the Soviet Union (CPSU), in February, Kádár declared that the HSWP "has always supported, and will continue to support, conferences of fraternal parties, be they bilateral, regional, or world-wide. Accordingly, we are participating in the preparation of the conference of European communist and workers parties and will do our utmost to ensure its success." At the conference, Kádár voiced a moderate endorsement of the Soviet line: "Today, when the Communist world movement does not have a center or a leading party, when the fraternal parties determine their tactics and strategy independently, the safeguarding of the purity of Marxist-Leninist theory is of special significance, together with the theoretical application of experience gained in practice and the enforcement of the principle of proletarian internationalism" (*Népszabadság*, 1 July). The Budapest press also reported on the other participants' statements.

The issue of Eurocommunism subsequently sparked an ideological polemic between Politburo member Dezsö Nemes and French Communist Party Politburo member Jean Kanapa. In an article in *World Marxist Review* (September), Nemes denounced Western Communists who proclaimed abandonment of the dictatorship of the proletariat in favor of socialist-pluralist democracy. Kanapa in turn rejected theSoviet and East European model for having banned all political opposition. Said Nemes of the lessons of history: "Failure of the counterrevolution marked the end of attempts to revive the multiparty system. In 1956 it was strongly discredited in our country as a weapon of the enemies of working-class power, of the agents of Western imperialism."

The HSWP mirrors the CPSU's hostility toward China. According to one party commentator, "the Peking leadership is approaching the imperialist countries under the banner of anti-Sovietism, anti-socialism, and nationalism, and there is not a single international sphere in which it is prepared to cooperate, or at least pursue a parallel policy with the Soviet Union and other like-minded socialist countries" (*Társadalmi Szemle*, November 1975). Along with "extremist imperialist circles," the Maoist leadership is accused of impeding détente.

The HSWP has endorsed Comecon's February 1976 proposal to the European Economic Community for an institutional relationship between the two trading blocs.

International Activities and Contacts. Prime Minister György Lázár paid his first official visit to the Soviet Union 21-24 October 1975 and discussed economic issues. A delegation led by Soviet culture minister Pyotr N. Demichev visited Budapest in November 1975 for the conclusion of a five-year agreement on closer academic and ideological cooperation, including Russian language instruction. Demichev declared in an interview that there were two kinds of culture, democratic and revolutionary, and reactionary pseudo-culture, and that socialist countries must present a united front against the latter. First Secretary Kádár represented the HSWP at the CPSU's 25th Congress and delivered the ritualistic tribute to the Soviet party, along with a denunciation of Maoism.

Hungary participated in the 30th CMEA Council session, 7-9 July 1976, in East Berlin. Official statements professed unswerving loyalty to CMEA. The "road of socialist economic integration," said deputy premier Gyula Szekér, "corresponds to the interests of our nation and of the whole socialist community" (*Népszabadság*, 10 July). It has also been stressed, notably by deputy premier István Huszár, that "the CMEA institutional and decision-making system guarantees that expanding reciprocal relations will not lead to the violation of the national economic interests of any individual country" (ibid., 20 June). Hungary continues to press for currency and financial reform within CMEA, notably an increase in the role of the transferable ruble.

The visit to Budapest 8-11 December 1975 of Romanian foreign minister George Macovescu was one of infrequent high-level contacts between the two countries. The resulting communiqué lacked the customary fulsome references to "identity of views." Romanian minority policies were probably one topic of discussion in light of Romanian party chief and president Nicolae Ceauşescu's attack on nationalism before the Hungarian and German Nationality Councils of Romania on 3 December. Kádár attended the congresses of the Polish and Cuban parties in December 1975. Prime Minister Lázár paid an official visit to Poland, 2-3 August 1976. In October, Lázár made an "official friendly visit" to Yugoslavia to discuss mainly bilateral economic relations (Yugoslavia is the only socialist country with which Hungary's trade is cleared in dollars). The positive influence on cooperation of the two countries' respective minorities was noted, and Lázár also visited Novi Sad, capital of the Yugoslav autonomous province of Vojvodina, which has a large ethnic Hungarian population.

A Laotian party and government delegation headed by Kaysone Phomvihan, prime minister and secretary general of the Laotian Revolutionary People's Party, visited Budapest 23-27 September.

Identity of views on international issues was proclaimed and an agreement was signed for Hungarian economic aid. The visit of Iraqi Communist Party first secretary Aziz Muhammad produced an expression of "solidarity with the Lebanese progressive forces and the Palestine liberation movement."

Contacts with the West have been mainly in the realm of trade promotion to seek ways of ameliorating Hungary's deteriorating trade balance. U.S. secretary of commerce Rogers Morton visited Hungary 8-10 October 1975 and met with Prime Minister Lázár and other economic leaders. Morton endorsed Hungary's desire for most-favored-nation status, and the two countries' chambers of commerce have established an Hungarian-American Economic Council to promote trade, but no official trade agreement exists between Hungary and the United States. Earl Butz, U.S. secretary of agriculture, was in Hungary 23-25 November 1975 for discussions on the expansion of agricultural relations through joint enterprises and by scientific and technological exchanges. In recent years Hungary has adopted certain U.S. production technologies and has purchased U.S. farm machinery. Deputy Premier Szekér led an economic delegation to the USA and Canada in May 1976. In October, an Hungarian-American cultural and technological-scientific agreement received preliminary approval in Budapest. A delegation led by Pál Romány, minister of agriculture and food, visited the USA on 25 September-5 October and, in a meeting of the Hungarian-American Economic Council, discussed trade and industrial cooperation. Over the past four years Hungary has accumulated a trade deficit with the USA of approximately $300 million.

Portuguese foreign minister Ernesto Melo de Antunes' visit 12-15 January was marked by the signing of a cultural agreement. West German foreign minister Hans-Dietrich Genscher held talks in Budapest 28-30 April with the Hungarian foreign minister. West Germany is Hungary's most important Western trade partner; two-thirds of Hungary's inter-enterprise cooperation ventures are with West German firms. Relations with neighboring Austria remained harmonious. Lázár visited Austria in May, while Chancellor Bruno Kreisky paid a brief unofficial visit to Kádár and Lázár at Lake Balaton in September.

French Socialist Party leader François Mitterrand met Kádár during an official visit to Hungary in late May, and agreed on "practical steps to expand and deepen relations" between the two parties. On his return to Paris Mitterrand said that the Hungarian system was stable and had made great progress in freedom but could not be compared to the system proposed by France's Socialists and Communists. Negative trade balances were the main problems discussed during the visits of Lázár to France (13-16 June) and Szekér to Great Britain (19 July). The Belgian foreign minister held talks in Budapest on 8-10 July, in the wake of a visit by a Belgian Communist Party delegation.

Third World contacts included visits by the chairman of the Presidential Council, Pál Losonczi, to Somalia and South Yemen in October 1975 and to Libya and Tunisia in November. The purpose of the visits was to show solidarity against imperialism and colonialism and to conclude economic agreements, notably with Libya, Hungary's biggest trade partner in Africa, for food in exchange for oil through the nearly completed Adria pipeline. Politburo member Béla Biszku led a party delegation to Algeria in November 1975. Simultaneously, a delegation of the Palestine Liberation Organization led by Yasser Arafat visited Budapest and was assured by Kádár of support for the restoration of the legal national rights of the Palestinians. In February 1976 a Syrian Ba'th Party delegation was received by Biszku. Losonczi visited Venezuela, Peru, Panama, and Cuba between 7-19 October.

Publications. The HSWP's principal daily newspaper is *Népszabadság* (People's Freedom), with a circulation of 750,000. The theoretical monthly *Társadalmi Szemle* (Social Review), edited by Valéria Benke, has a circulation of 40,700. The monthly organizational journal *Pártélet* (Party Life) has a circulation of 130,000. The official news agency is Magyar Távirati Iroda (Hungarian Telegraphic Agency; MTI).

University of Toronto   Bennett Kovrig

Poland

The Polish United Workers' Party (Polska Zjednoczona Partia Robotnicza; PUWP) is the official name of the Communist party in power in the Polish People's Republic. Its origins date back to December 1918 when the Communist Workers' Party of Poland was founded. In early 1919 this party was outlawed by the Polish government and forced to operate underground. In 1925 it changed its name to the Communist Party of Poland. For reasons that are still not entirely clear the Comintern dissolved the party in 1938, and many of its leaders perished in the great Soviet purge. The party reappeared in January 1942 under the name of the Polish Workers' Party. Following the advance of the Red Army into Poland in 1944-45, the newly reconstituted party quickly achieved the dominant position in the "national unity" coalition government set up to appeal to the broad mass of the population. After consolidating its position and undermining the non-Communist parties in the coalition, the Polish Workers' Party in late 1948 engineered a merger with the left wing of the old Polish Socialist Party to form the Polish United Workers' Party. Ever since, the PUWP has been in firm control of all elections and other formal political activities in Poland, using the Front of National Unity (Front Jednosci Narodu; FNU) to create a solid bloc of support for what is ostensibly a coalition government consisting of the PUWP (which officially plays the leading and directing role), two Communist-controlled "independent" parties—the United Peasant Party (Zjednoczone Stronnictwo Ludowe; UPP) and the Democratic Party (Stronnictwo Demokratyczne; DP), officially representing the peasantry and the working intelligentsia and small entrepreneurs respectively—and representatives of "progressive" non-party organizations and individuals. In an attempt to make the government appear as broadly representative as possible, the PUWP has allowed several Catholic groups to include candidates in the preferred lists of the FNU since 1956.

These other parties, as well as various other mass and special-interest organizations, have been consulted by the PUWP and the government on economic and political questions of interest to their respective constituencies, especially in the period following the change of leadership in December 1970. Nevertheless, the PUWP clearly dominates the political life of Poland and expects all other parties and organizations to follow its lead and support its main policy lines. The constitution of 1952, in fact, was amended in February 1976 to include official legal recognition of the leading role of the PUWP.

The Front of National Unity had been chaired since June 1971 by non-party professor and former non-Communist wartime resistance member Janusz Groszkowski, who was appointed at a time when the PUWP was anxious to broaden its support following Gomułka's fall from power and the new leadership's attempt under Gierek to mobilize all groups in Polish society for the task of modernizing the economy. In February 1976 Groszkowski was replaced by Council of State chairman Henryk Jabłonski, returning to the traditional pattern of having the FNU chaired by the head of state and a high-ranking PUWP member.

Although Polish elections consist of a ballot with a single list of FNU candidates in each of the 70 multi-member districts (80 districts in the 1972 election, before the recent administrative reforms), ever since 1956 there have been about a third more candidates than seats on each list. In the latest election, for example, there were 631 candidates for the 460 Sejm (parliament) seats, and 9,618 candidates for the 6,740 seats on the 49 voivodship people's councils. Although all of the candidates are FNU nominees, they are placed on the ballot in a "preferred" order, without party labels, in such a way that the PUWP, UPP, DP, and independents all receive their quota of seats. To vote for the preferred candidates (i.e., those at the top of the list) a voter need only drop his ballot into the ballot box unmarked. If he wishes to vote against any of the preferred candidates (e.g., any of the top 6 on a list of 8, in a district with 6 seats), the voter may use a voting booth and cross out a name (or names) on the top part of the list, thereby automatically voting for the candidate (or candidates) immediately below the invisible line dividing the preferred candidates from the remainder.

The most recent elections were held on 21 March 1976 for both the Sejm and for the provincial people's councils. (Elections for the local "gmina" people's councils were held 9 December 1973.) In the March elections the FNU candidates received 99.43 percent of the valid votes cast for the 460 Sejm seats. For the first time since the 1961 elections there was a change in the share of the Sejm seats allocated to each of the parties (i.e., because of a change in the way in which they were placed on the ballot): The PUWP received 6 more seats than before, or a total of 261 (56.7 percent); the UPP, 4 fewer, or 113 (24.6 percent); the DP, 2 fewer, or 37 (8.0 percent); and the independents the same number as before, 49 (10.7 percent), including 13 seats for various Catholic groups (5 for Znak, 5 for PAX, 2 for the Christian Social Association, and one for Caritas). In early December the Sejm formally filled three Sejm vacancies caused by death. By law they were filled by the person who appeared next highest on the ballot (below the number of seats to be filled) in each constituency. Consequently three PUWP candidates replaced the two PUWP and one UPP deputies who died, thereby increasing the PUWP seats to 262 and reducing the UPP seats to 112.

The professional composition of the new Sejm also reflects a decision to give the parliament a more legislative and less of an administrative character, with the candidates including all the members of the PUWP Politburo and Central Committee Secretariat, a large number of PUWP aparatchiks, all the deputy premiers, and all the 49 voivodship first party secretaries (who also serve as chairmen of the provincial people's councils) and excluding most of the administrative personnel who formerly served as Sejm deputies.

The PUWP has about 2,500,000 members (December 1976 figures) out of a population of almost 34,500,000. The UPP has approximately 420,000 members and the DP about 94,500. (Both of these minor parties held their Seventh Congresses in early 1976.)

Organization and Leadership. The basic PUWP unit is the primary party organization, set up in places of work (factories, stores, offices, schools, military units, etc.) and in residential locations (villages and small towns in rural areas, streets or housing units in cities). There are about 72,600 civilian and 3,500 military primary units. The next level of the party hierarchy is the district unit, corresponding to the gmina level of government administration in the countryside and the urban district in the larger cities. The province (voivodship) or regional organizations comprise the next level. The highest PUWP authority is the party congress, which meets at least every four years according to PUWP statutes. (The party's Seventh Congress met 8-12 December 1975.) In 1973 for the first time a special national PUWP Conference was held to review developments since the Sixth Party Congress. A similar Conference is planned for 1977. The congress elects the Central Committee and the Central Party Control Commission. The Central Committee, composed of 140 full members and 111 candidate members (expanded from the previous 115 full and 93 candidate members at the Seventh Congress), is the supreme party authority between congresses. One additional Central Committee candidate member, Emil Wojtaszek, was promoted to full membership in December when he was appointed Minister of Foreign Affairs. The Central Committee elects the Politburo (currently 14 full members and 3 candidates, compared with 11 full and 5 candidate members before the Seventh Congress) and the Secretariat (currently 11 full secretaries and 1 regular member, expanded from 8 secretaries and 2 regular members before the Seventh Congress). The Politburo serves as the supreme policy-making body between Central Committee plenary meetings (plenums). The Secretariat functions as the executive organ of the Central Committee and the Politburo and supervises the work of the party bureaucracy. There are separate Central Committee departmens for various functions. The Central Party Control Commission oversees party discipline and maintains ideological correctness. There are corresponding simpler structures at lower levels.

Edward Gierek, Politburo member and first secretary, has headed the party since December 1970, when he replaced long-time leader Władysław Gomułka. Politburo members Piotr Jaroszewicz and Henryk Jabłoński are respectively premier and head of state of the Polish government.

The Politburo consists of full members Edward Babiuch,* Edward Gierek,* Zdzisław Grudzień, Henryk Jabłoński, Mieczysław Jagielski, Piotr Jaroszewicz, Wojciech Jaruzelski, Stanisław Kania,* Josef Kępa, Stanisław Kowalczyk, Władysław Kruczek, Stefan Olszowski* (appointed Central Committee Secretary at 5th plenum, 2 December), Jan Szydlak* and Józef Tejchma, and candidates Kazimierz Barcikowski, Jerzy Lukasiewicz,* and Tadeusz Wraszczyk. The Secretariat consists of eleven secretaries—the five marked by an asterisk and Ryszard Frelek, Alojzy Karkosza (replaced Wincenty Kraśko, who died in August; also appointed Warsaw Voivodship 1st Secretary in December), Józef Pinkowski, Andrzej Werblan, and Zdisław Żandarowski—and Secretariat member Zdzisław Kurowski. The chairman of the Party Control Commission is Stefan Misiaszek.

The PUWP relies heavily on mass membership and other smaller and more specialized organizations to (1) increase the legitimacy of the party and government, (2) disseminate propaganda and mobilize support for its political and economic objectives and policies, (3) mold socialist attitudes and control mass behavior, (4) provide a party-controlled substitute for every organization normally found in modern society and preempt the field for any potential opposition organizations, (5) undermine existing organizations not yet under party control (e.g., the Catholic church), and (6) mobilize the population for socially useful work over and above their regular employment. The publications, mass meetings, rallies, campaigns, activities, and social services of these organizations provide an important supplement to the direct work of the PUWP activists and press. They also provide channels through which those opposed to the PUWP can be induced to work for party objectives and can in turn be supervised by party members or those sympathetic to the PUWP. Moreover, they create the appearance of a more pluralist and complex society and provide outlets for the organizational energies of a great many citizens who would otherwise not be willing or able to work for the party's goals.

The most important of these mass organizations are the 23 trade unions, with a total of more than 12.3 million members. Their work is coordinated by the Central Council of Trade Unions, headed by Politburo member Kruczek. The trade unions play a particularly important role in mobilizing workers to fulfill the economic tasks set by the party and the planning commission. In addition, they perform various social welfare functions, such as administering pension funds, organizing day-care centers, canteens, and inexpensive vacation homes and summer camps for their workers, and carrying out work-safety campaigns. Despite their subservience to the party, there has been an increasing tendency for the unions to represent more actively the interests and demands of the workers. The new party leadership has continued to show an active interest in using the trade unions, the 7,600 workers' self-government conferences, and party organizations in places of work to provide channels of feedback to the top levels of the party. Thus they have an important role in the PUWP leadership's concept of expanded consultation with the workers and building socialist democracy in Poland.

Also very important are the youth organizations, united since 1973 in the Federation of the Socialist Unions of Polish Youth (FSUPY), headed by PUWP Secretariat member Kurowski. On 28 April 1976 a new "Union of Polish Socialist Youth" was formed within the framework of the FSUPY when three of its former constituent organizations merged: the Union of Socialist Youth (approximately 1,083,800 mostly young urban worker members), the Union of Socialist Rural Youth (about 928,500 mostly rural youth members), and the Union of Socialist Military Youth (exact membership unknown, but probably including a little more than half of the regular soldiers in uniform). The other constituents of the FSUPY—the Socialist Union of Polish Students (234,400 members) and Union of Polish Scouts (2,680,300)—retained their organizational autonomy within the federation.

Other important mass organizations include the League of Women (454,000 members), active in educating women in various problems of family life, practical economics, and socialist values; the Union of Fighters for Freedom and Democracy (ZBoWiD), a patriotic veterans' organization (422,000); the Volunteer Citizens' Militia Reserve (ORMO), whose approximately 332,000 members assist the regular militia in crowd control and other police work requiring extra manpower; the League for the Defense of the Country, a civil defense organization (1,847,000); the Polish Red Cross (4.5 million); the Polish Committee for Social Assistance (1,276,000), engaging in volunteer social work; the Polish Union of Retirees and Invalids (568,000); the Society of Children's Friends (871,000); the Social Committee Against Alcohol (113,000); the League for the Defense of Nature (1,125,000); and the Society for the Popularization of Knowledge.

Party Internal Affairs. There was continued stability in the PUWP leadership until December, and even then only minor changes in the leadership were made, even though the party in June faced its worst crisis since the riots over food price increases in December 1970 that brought about the fall of Gomułka and Gierek's elevation to power. The current crisis was precipitated by the announcement on 24 June of very sharp increases in the long-frozen prices of basic food items—hurriedly withdrawn the next day following widespread strikes and two major riots (see details below).

In December, two new PUWP Central Committee Secretaries were appointed: Politburo member (and former Foreign Minister) Stefan Olszowski and Alojzy Karkosza (who was also named 1st PUWP Secretary for Warsaw Voivodship) replacing Wincenty Kraśko and adding one additional Secretary for a total of 11. (Central Committee Secretary and Politburo member Jan Szydlak was also appointed deputy premier in December. A Central Committee Secretary normally is relieved of his position when appointed to a government post, but an exception was clearly made in this case. It is also unusual, though not so exceptional, for a person—in this case Karkosza—to be both a provincial 1st party secretary and a Central Committee Secretary.) Likewise there were relatively few changes in the government above the vice-ministerial level (where a number of changes occurred). In March a few changes were made in the ministerial structure. The Ministry of Heavy Industry was disbanded, the Ministry of Mining and Power was renamed the Ministry of Mining, and four new ministries were created: Energy and Nuclear Power, Iron and Steel, Heavy and Agricultural Machinery, and Raw Materials. Tadeusz Bejm became Minister of Transportation and was replaced as Minister of Administration, Local Economy and Protection of the Environment by Emil Wojtaszek. Professor Jerzy Bafia became Minister of Justice, and Jan Kaminski was appointed Minister without Portfolio. In early December Minister of Foreign Affairs Stefan Olszowski (who became Central Committee Secretary) was replaced by Emil Wojtaszek, who, in turn, was replaced as Minister of Administration, Local Economy and Protection of the Environment by Maria Milczarek. Antonin Kowalik replaced Jerzy Gawrysiak as Minister of Foreign Trade and the Maritime Economy. Henryk Konopacki replaced Maciej Wirowski as Minister of the Chemical Industry. The remaining 20 ministers were unchanged. It is also worth noting that in December the presidium of the government was expanded once again—to 11 members—by addition of three more deputy premiers: Jósef Kępa (Politburo member and former 1st Secretary for the Warsaw Voivodship), Kazimierz Secomski (1st deputy chairman, Planning Commission), and Jan Szydlak (Politburo member and Central Committee Secretary). The expansion of the presidium was explained by pointing out that the 5th plenum had "entrusted the government with increased tasks and duties connected with the development and management of the economy, intensification of its control and coordination functions, and the necessity to tighten up discipline throughout the country's economic and administrative management" (*Trybuna Ludu*, 3 December).

There was widespread speculation that the June crisis would lead to major changes in the PUWP and government leadership, including the replacement of Premier Piotr Jaroszewicz or even Gierek, but none took place—nor did it become clear just who was responsible for the decision to raise prices, why the increases were so sharp and sudden, and why there was so little consultation with the people in general, the workers in particular, or even with the party before the increases were proposed in the Sejm on 24 June (and tentatively approved the same day). Price increases on basic food items had long been expected and were in principle predicted by Jaroszewicz in his 27 March speech to the Sejm outlining government policy for the coming year. The need for the price increase was justified by the necessity of making "it possible to adapt market supply to the potential of the economy at its present stage of development." The press also carried a few articles supporting the need for a price increase. When the details of the increases were announced, however, there was widespread disbelief at their magnitude—a 69 percent average increase for meat with a 90 percent increase for the better cuts, a 30 percent increase for poultry, 50 percent for butter, 100 percent for sugar—especially in view of the consequences of the much smaller price increases in 1970 and Gierek's promise at the PUWP congress in December 1975 that the leadership would submit its price increase proposals only "after discussing the problem with the working people." It was clear that the promised widespread consultations had not taken place and that there had been little consultation even within the party. Moreover, local party and government officials seemed taken by surprise by the announcement.

The price increase proposals for food were also accompanied by proposals for increased procurement prices to be paid farmers for most agricultural products. At the same time, the prices farmers had to pay for seeds, fertilizers, and services were also scheduled to rise sharply (20 to 45 percent). To compensate for the price increases, plans were also announced for wage and pension supplements of from 240 to 600 zloties, depending on income and pension levels (with the greatest subsidies going to the highest paid).

By 25 June, the day after the price increases were announced, there were widespread strikes and work stoppages all across the country. Most serious, however, were the events in Ursus, in the western suburbs of Warsaw, where the workers in a large tractor factory ripped up rails and derailed the Paris-Moscow express, and in Radom, south of Warsaw, where there was widespread vandalism, looting, and burning of shops, and the local party headquarters and the villas of several local party leaders were set on fire. Plock, Wrocław, and Olsztyn were also reported to have had open protests. There was obviously a real danger that as news of the strikes and violence became more widely known the protests would spread rapidly to the rest of the country, and events would get totally out of hand, perhaps leading even to an intervention (recalling 1968 in Czechoslovakia) by Warsaw Pact troops. It is clear that there was little enthusiasm for the price increases, especially in the manner of their introduction, and it is questionable, given a nationwide protest strike, that the militia or army could have been counted on for effective intervention.

There seems to have been an almost unprecedented and near universal loss of support for the top leadership on this issue, even within the party. In the circumstances there was no real alternative but for Premier Jaroszewicz to announce the withdrawal of the price proposals the day after they were announced, arguing at the same time, however, that some form of price increase would still be necessary, but that it would come only after further consultation with the workers. In order to try to salvage the situation, the party organized rallies all across the country in support of Gierek, the party, and the government and its policies. There were rumors of widespread detention and firing of protesting workers, and of swift trials and stiff sentences of those most directly involved in the Ursus and Radom violence (3-5 years for the seven Ursus defendants and 4-10 years for the six in Radom). At least 40 others were reportedly tried or to be brought to trial. (The Polish Supreme Court in late September reduced the sentences of the Ursus seven to a one-year suspended sentence on the basis of their previous record as good workers, following widespread protests over government and police action and appeals for understanding and leniency, including appeals from the Church, the Italian Communist Party, and Polish intellectuals, 14 of whom formed a "Committee to Defend Workers" to collect funds for the families of those arrested.)

Tension remained high throughout the summer as the party and government began a more earnest campaign of consultation with the workers and a press campaign designed to explain the necessity of price increases. The major arguments were that real wages had increased more than 40 percent since 1970 while the price of basic food items had remained frozen (though hidden price increases and prices on the private market had boosted food prices considerably), requiring the government budget to provide subsidies for food amounting to 50 percent of the retail price. In such circumstances there was an excessive demand for food in comparison with other goods, causing an excessive strain on the supply of food, especially meat, at a time when two years of poor harvests in a row had created shortages and necessitated the importation of fodder, grain, meat, and other foodstuffs for scarce hard currency. Moreover, Poland's growing foreign debt—as a result of Gierek's crash program of investment and modernization of the economy—had to be paid, and meat and other agricultural products were important components of the export mix, thereby necessitating a reduction in the domestic demand for these items.

The public, however, must have remained unconvinced, as in mid-July Premier Jaroszewicz announced that the government had decided to raise only the prices of meat, meat products, and poultry, and then by only 35 percent. Finally at the September Central Committee plenum it was announced that the projected price increases would be further postponed until at least the summer of 1977, when five economic commissions, to be appointed and headed by Politburo members, would have had a chance to complete their work and report back to the mid-Congress Conference of the PUWP. The commissions are to deal with the following problems: (1) working out the principles that should guide price policy on food articles, including meat and meat products, (2) activization of market production, (3) investigation of the reserves (potential) in agriculture and the food economy, (4) preparation of a program of savings in the national economy, and (5) preparation of "suggestions within the sphere of implementing housing policy."

One of the minor, but symbolic, byproducts of the June price-increase announcement was a run on the sugar supply (a good investment in the face of a projected 100 percent price increase). It was impossible to keep sugar on the shelves or provide equitable distribution of the normal supply of sugar deliveries, so the government in August introduced sugar rationing (4.4 pounds per person per month at the old price, with unlimited quantities available at a little more than double the price) to deal with the problem.

The overall impact of the crisis precipitated by the decision to increase prices in June was far-reaching. The authority of the government was seriously undermined, and the party must have been badly split and weakened. The arrest and trial of the Ursus and Radom rioters and the dismissal of strike leaders led to a continuing and embarrassing wave of protest and unwelcome publicity from the Committee to Defend the Workers and protests and calls for amnesty and leniency by the Church, workers, and other groups. (Sixty-seven Radom workers, for example, wrote a letter demanding an investigation of alleged police brutality during the riots and subsequent investigations in Radom. In November 889 Ursus workers wrote Gierek demanding that the striking workers who had been fired be reinstated in their jobs.) Perhaps more important in the long run, the events of June further deepened the lack of confidence that even the Gierek leadership can do anything to bring about any significant and rapid improvement in the Polish standard of living.

One other development of major importance during 1976 was the approval by the Sejm in February of a series of amendments to the Polish constitution of 1952 which had been long discussed and were finally formally proposed after the Seventh PUWP Congress in December 1975. The proposed amendments created an unexpected amount of controversy, protest, and discussion, both inside and outside the party. The Polish Catholic church and a wide range of intellectuals vigorously protested some of the proposed amendments, and this together with opposition within the party helped bring about a significant modification of the wording before they were eventually approved. Most notable was an appeal to the Sejm (published in the London Polish exile paper *Tydzień Polski*) by 59 prominent Polish intellectuals, including Roman Catholic writer and politician Stefan Kisielewski, Marxist philosopher Leszek Kolakowski, poet and former Polish Writers' Union chairman Antoni Słonimski, and writer Jerzy Andrzejewski. It called for a constitution with much stronger civil liberties guarantees. Reportedly, a group of law professors from the Academy of Sciences sent a letter to the PUWP Central Committee and 300 university personnel and students sent an appeal to the Sejm.

The amendments as approved changed the description of Poland from a "people's democratic state" to a "socialist state," but retained the name of the Polish People's Republic, instead of changing it to the Polish Socialist Republic as originally proposed. The PUWP was recognized in the constitution for the first time as "the leading political force in the country," but the article referring to Poland's ties with the USSR and other socialist states was significantly weakened and is easily the weakest such reference of any of the constitutions of the Eastern European socialist states. The final version also dropped the proposed attempt to link citizens' rights with "their honest fulfillment of their duties to the socialist motherland," a point that had been particularly strongly opposed on the grounds that rights should be unconditional. Another amendment emphasized the goal of increased agricultural production and the socialist transformation of the village, while at the same time guaranteeing the individual peasant the protection of the state.

The problem of socialist democracy and consultation received a considerable amount of attention in the Polish press and in the speeches of party leaders, especially after the June crisis. Although considerable precedent was established after December 1970 for the idea of consultation of workers and party leaders in the 100 or so largest factories before the implementation of major decisions, in practice this had not been done on a regular basis, and clearly not immediately preceding the presentation of the food price-increase proposals to the Sejm for approval. In a speech to cooperative workers on 5 July and again at a session of the Politburo on 13 July Premier Jaroszewicz outlined a new procedure for consultations on legislative measures, as follows: (1) the government submits its draft of legislation to the Sejm for consideration by the pertinent committees, (2) from the Sejm committees the draft proposal is "directed by the government for consultations, first of all in work establishments," (3) "after the completion of consultations," the draft is submitted to the Sejm for consideration. Radio Warsaw commented: "This procedure may appear long and complicated, but the problem is important from both the economic and social points of view." Later in the summer interesting articles appeared in the August and September issues of *Nowe drogi* ("The Crucial Role of Consultation in the Activity of the PUWP," by Janusz Kubasiewicz and Stefan Gajda, and "Some of the Problems of Socialist Democracy," by Sylwester Zawadzki) and in the 25 September issue of *Polityka* ("Moods and Views," by Jacek Marziarski).

The Economy. Despite the unexpected setbacks in the area of price policy and continued problems with agriculture (with the notable exception of meat production), party policy in the economic field continued much as over the previous years, with the major objectives still modernization of the economy, attainment of higher living standards, provision of more housing, streamlining of the system of planning and enterprise management, improving of investment efficiency, achievement of greater economies in the use of material and human resources, uncovering of additional reserves, and increase of exports. In terms of capital investment the economic modernization drive seems to have been a great success, with more than 50 percent of current Polish industrial capacity having been built since 1970, much of it on the basis of imported Western technology, including both plant and equipment and licensing arrangements for production. It is estimated that in this period Poland's foreign debt increased from less than $2 billion to almost $8 billion, with most of the new debt in the West.

The Polish balance of trade continued its long-standing unfavorable balance of imports over exports and has been creating a growing concern both inside Poland and abroad—and is not unconnected with the need to raise domestic food prices. The balance of payments problem seems to have been compounded by increases in the international price of petroleum, falling copper prices, an unfavorable international market for coal, and a general decline in demand for Polish exports because of the recession in the West.

Domestically, the rate of investment continued at the very high level of the past five years. One of Poland's major problems, however, contnued to be how to translate high investment rates and imported technology into an efficient production system able to meet growing popular demands for abundant and varied consumer goods of high quality. Despite new investment in the most modern plants and equipment, these do not always seem to have been used most efficiently, owing to problems of mismanagement, overemployment, and low worker morale and on-the-job effectiveness.

In agriculture there were a number of developments related to the plan (announced at the PUWP Seventh Congress) to increase the share of land held by the socialized sector from 20 percent to more than 30 percent by 1980. The primary motive here seems to be the more effective use of privately held land that is producing lower-than-average yields—mostly land held by aging farmers and peasants who are now working primarily as industrial employees. This planned reduction of the private agricultural sector by 10 percent (about 2 million hectares) over the next five years compares with the 4 percent reduction during the five years before which came about largely when older farmers, who lacked heirs interested in taking over the family land, were either retiring because of age or exchanging their land for pensions offered in exchange by the state. Given the high proportion of farmers over 55, it seems likely that the goal can be reached. It is estimated that about 2,500,000 hectares of land produces below average crop yields.

Although the law allows land to be transferred to private individuals from the state land fund, it is clear that the current government policy favors turning the land over to state farms, collective farms, or agricultural circles to be farmed by collective production teams. One other development of interest was the decision announced at the fourth Central Committee plenum to extend the pension system to include private farmers.

At the fifth plenum and Sejm session immediately following in December, it was announced that a number of changes would be introduced into the plan and budget for the next 5-year period. Highest priority would be placed on readjusting the unfavorable balance of payments and bringing exports into line with imports by the end of the period. Priority would also be placed on housing (47 percent increase over the previous 5 years) and consumer goods in general (43 percent increase planned). Special emphasis is also to be placed on increasing food production, including additional investment allocations to the private sector. To facilitate these ends the investment rate is to be reduced to about 32 percent of national income and the growth rate is to fall from 10 to about 8 percent.

Relations with the Catholic Church. Compared with the relatively uneventful previous year, relations between the Polish state and the Catholic church were considerably more strained in 1976, beginning with the Church's expression of concern early in the year over the proposed amendments to the constitution and over the treatment of the intellectuals who spoke out in opposition to them. The Church also spoke out vigorously for more lenient treatment of the workers involved in the 25 June strikes and protests, though at the same time it condemned the use of violence and appealed to the Polish people to support the government in its search for a way out of the economic crisis.

Gierek on a number of occasions, most notably in Mielec in September, made conciliatory remarks about the Church, repeating his earlier views about the need for mutual tolerance and a recognition of the importance of "consolidating the patriotic unity of our nation." The Church continued its long-standing criticism of the government and party policy of encouraging atheism, the government's reluctance to issue building permits for new churches, the policy of encouraging people to give up their family farms, and the lack of rights of religious believers. Also noteworthy were the visits to Rome by Cracow Archbishop (and Cardinal) Woytyla in March and by the Polish Primate, Stefan Cardinal Wyszyński, in October. (Cardinal Wyszyński, who reached the obligatory retirement age of 75 in August, was asked to extend his term in office by the pope.) Archbishop Luigi Poggi, the Vatican's Nuncio for Special Tasks and delegate for working contacts with the Polish government spent 25 days in Poland in April and May.

The Znak group in the Sejm was purged of virtually all of its original members in the March election, and its present members seemed to be taking a more conciliatory stance toward government policies. The old Znak leaders, representing the Catholic Intelligentsia Clubs (KIK) in Warsaw, Cracow, Wroclaw, and Lódź, wrote a letter to the group's parliamentary spokesman in March, arguing that the new group could not be regarded as a lawful continuation of Znak, as its members had "neither been elected nor accepted" by the majority of the Catholic groupings represented by KIK. The letter asked the Sejm group to cease using the Znak name.

International Party Contacts. The PUWP's most important and extensive contacts with other parties in 1976 took place at the East Berlin Conference of Communist and Workers' Parties in June. The Polish delegation was headed by First Secretary Gierek and included Babiuch, Werblan, and the head of the Central Committee Secretariat office, Jerzy Waszczuk. The Polish press (*Trybuna ludu*, 29 June) noted that the PUWP and the Italian party had initially suggested convening the conference, and that the first consultative meeting had been organized by the PUWP in Warsaw in October 1974. Meetings were reported between Gierek and Leonid Brezhnev, Tito, and the Communist party leaders of Czechoslovakia, Bulgaria, Romania, and West Germany. The Polish press provided quite extensive coverage of the conference, including summaries of the most important controversial speeches. In light of the embarrassing recent events in Poland and Gierek's continued stress on building socialist democracy, some passages from his speech to the conference deserve quotation: "Through the development of its socialist democracy, the state of proletarian dictatorship is being transformed into a state of all people, a state whose main support is the working class and its alliance with the peasants and the intelligentsia. . . . On all matters important for the country and the nation, before taking a decision, we consult society about them."

In October Gierek visited Romania for the first time as first secretary. (He had already visited every other Eastern European socialist country, including Yugoslavia, and the Polish and Romanian premiers had exchanged visits in 1974 and 1975.)

Gierek met three times during 1976 with Brezhnev in addition to the meeting in Berlin: on 4 March in Moscow during a meeting of heads of delegations to the Soviet party congress, on 28 July in the Crimea during vacation, and, most important, in November during a longer combination party and state visit. It is worth noting the unusual composition of the delegation, which included, in addition to Gierek and Premier Jaroszewicz and the usual high-ranking party and government officials, the chairman of the UPP and Sejm speaker, Stanisław Gucwa; the new chairman of the DP and deputy chairman of the Council of State. Tadeusz Witold Młynczak; and the chairman of the Polish Writers' Union, Jarosław Iwaszkiewicz. The most important result of this trip was the announcement of about $1.3 billion in Soviet credits for the delivery of food, raw materials, capital equipment, and consumer goods to assist Poland in its current economic crisis.

Other visits of note during 1976 were Gierek's June visit to West Germany, Jaroszewicz's visit to France in May, and the unofficial visit of French president Giscard d'Estaing to Poland in October.

Publications. The daily organ of the PUWP is *Trybuna ludu* (People's Tribune); its monthly theoretical journal is *Nowe drogi* (New Roads). A monthly, *Zycie partii* (Party Life) is directed toward party activists, and a biweekly, *Chłopska droga* (The Peasant's Way) is aimed at rural readers. The Central Committee Department of Propaganda, Press, and Publications puts out a fortnightly, *Zagadnienia i materialy* (Problems and Materials), for the training of party members. In addition a party monthly, *Ideologia i polityka* (Ideology and Politics) has been published for several years. The voivodship party organizations also publish regional dailies. Two influential Warsaw weeklies, *Polityka* (Politics) and *Kultura* (Culture), also deserve notice though they are not official PUWP publications.

University of Florida   James F. Morrison

Romania

The Communist Party of Romania (*Partidul Comunist Român;* CPR) was founded, according to official histories, on 8 May 1921, after the splitting of the Social Democratic Party. The arrival of Soviet troops in 1944, accompanied by a coup d'état, brought the party into participation in the government. In February 1948 the CPR and what remained of the Social Democratic Party were merged to become the Romanian Workers' Party (Partidul Muncitoresc Romîn), but at its 9th Congress, in July 1965, the party reverted to its original name—a move concomitant with the elevation of Romania from the status of a people's republic to that of a socialist republic. Since 1948 the CPR has been the only political party in Romania.

As of 31 December 1975 party membership was officially said to be 2,577,434. The figure includes some 108,000 members who joined the party during that year. About 50 percent of the membership were classed as workers (up from 43 percent in 1969), 20 percent as peasants (down from 28 percent in 1969), and 22 percent as intellectuals and white-collar personnel. The party's ethnic composition remained approximately the same as that of the country as a whole—87.7 percent Romanian, 7.7 percent Hungarian, 1.9 percent German, and 2.7 percent other nationalities (*Scînteia*, 8 August 1969, 24 April 1976). Total population was estimated at 21,320,000 on 1 January 1976 (*Anuarul Statistic al RSR*, 1976.

Organization and Leadership. The CPR is organized into basic units or cells in factories, on farms, and in the smaller political subdivisions; in 1974 there were 70,000 such units. The next higher step is represented by the party organizations in communes (rural territorial subdivisions) and municipalities, in which there were 2,706 and 235 organizations, respectively. Finally, there are party organizations for each of the 39 counties and the municipality of Bucharest; these supervise the lower-level party organizations within their territories. (*Scînteia*, 25 July 1975; *WMR* no. 5, 1973.)

According to the party statutes, the supreme authority of the CPR is vested in the Congress, which is held every five years and to which delegates are elected by county party organizations. The 11th Congress, the most recent, was held in November 1974. In fact, however, it is the party's Secretariat, Political Executive Committee, Permanent Bureau, and Central Committee that wield the power.

CPR secretary-general Nicolae Ceauşescu has held this position since March 1965. According to the party statutes the secretary-general is chosen by the party congress, not by the Central Committee as with most Communist parties. At the end of 1976 the Secretariat was composed of nine secretaries in addition to the secretary-general: Ştefan Andrei, Iosif Banc, Emil Bobu, Cornel Burtică, Constantin Dăscălescu, Aurel Duma, Dumitriu Popescu, Iosif Uglar, and Ilie Verdeţ.

The CPR does not have a politburo, but two organizations, the Permanent Bureau and the Political Executive Committee, serve somewhat similar functions. The Permanent Bureau was created by the Central Committee in March 1974 and reduced in size at the 11th Congress. It is composed of five individuals whose primary concern is economics—and particularly foreign economic problems. They are the secretary-general, Ceauşescu; Central Committee secretary Ştefan Andrei, responsible for the party's international policies; the chairman of the Council of Ministers, Manea Mănescu; the deputy chairman of the Council of Ministers, Gheorghe Oprea, who has been active in promoting international economic cooperation; and the deputy chairman of the Council of Ministers, Ion Paţan, who is also minister of foreign trade and international economic cooperation. It is owing to its small membership and its orientation toward foreign economic problems that the Permanent Bureau does not function as a politburo.

The Political Executive Committee (PEC), on the other hand, is much larger than the average politburo (23 full and 15 alternate members), but it performs somewhat similar functions. As a result of organizational changes during 1974, the PEC became more prominent. It was originally created at the 9th Congress, in 1965, primarily to give Ceauşescu a leading party body in which his own supporters would predominate, since at that time the Permanent Presidium (Politburo) was composed largely of older party leaders not beholden to the new party head. The PEC meets frequently between plenary sessions of the Central Committee, and supervises party affairs. The full members include the secretary-general and most Central Committee secretaries, as well as leading members of the government and mass organizations.

The Central Committee is elected at a party congress to direct party affairs between congresses. It meets in plenary session two to six times a year to consider and approve programs and policies. The committee chosen in November 1974 has 205 full and 156 alternate members.

Auxiliary and Mass Organizations. In 1968, after having opposed the Soviet-led invasion of Czechoslovakia, the party sought to mobilize mass support and created the Front of Socialist Unity (FSU) to replace the largely inactive People's Democratic Front. (The latter was an outgrowth of the National Democratic Front, created in October 1944 to link the CPR, the Social Democrats, and other left-leaning political groups in order to achieve a consolidation of power.) The FSU includes trade union, youth, and women's front organizations, as well as associations representing the various national minorities living in Romania. The CPR is the only political party. The FSU provides the permanent organizational framework for mass participation in politics at all levels. The FSU plays a primary role in coordinating the activities of other front organizations and in the election process. The leadership of the FSU includes the leadership of the party. Nicolae Ceauşescu is chairman, 11 full and alternate members of the PEC sit on the 28-member FSU Executive Bureau, and all major party and government leaders and county party heads are on the 477-member National Council.

The trade unions represent one of the largest and most significant of the mass organizations that function under the CPR's guidance. The Union of Communist Youth (UCY), the Union of Communist Student Associations, and the Pioneers represent a second major group of mass organizations. The National Council of Women, headed by PEC member Lina Ciobanu, is the party's front organization for women.

Internal Party Affairs. The 11th Congress of the CPR was held on 25-28 November 1974, and party statutes call for the next to be convened five years from that time.

During 1976 four plenary sessions of the Central Committee were held. The first, on 3 February, had a two-point agenda—examining the results of the 1971-75 socio-economic plan and considering certain problems to be dealt with the following day at a conference of local government officials. The plenum adopted a decision on the fulfillment of the five-year plan (*Scînteia*, 4 February) which praised the fact that the plan targets adopted at the 10th party congress in 1969 were met 6 months ahead of schedule, while the higher targets approved subsequently were completed 2 months early. In 1972, Ceauşescu had supported a campaign to reach the higher targets 6 months early, and although he encountered resistance on that question his campaign did achieve some success; the overall targets were reached, but in several important areas plan goals were not achieved.

The second plenum was held on 14 April and its agenda was a long one. The following items were approved (ibid., 15 April): a long-term program for flood control and water use; plans to take a census of the population, housing,and domestic animals in January 1977; a report on the strength and composition of the party; a report on the party's cadre policy stressing the importance of "socialist ethics and equality"; a proposal to create a "legislative chamber" (actually a consultative body) representing local government officials; and a program for celebrating, in 1977, the 100th anniversary of Romanian independence and the 70th anniversary of the 1907 peasants' uprising.

The third Central Committee session, on 1 July, also had a long agenda (ibid., 2 July). A number of important economic issues were discussed, and the "improved" draft of the 1976-80 socio-economic plan was approved. It was subsequently enacted into law by the Grand National Assembly (ibid., 3 July). The "improvement" over the original draft adopted by the 11th party congress in November 1974 lay in the fact that certain targets (investment, social product, national income, industrial and agricultural production, labor productivity, etc.) were raised. Lower figures, however, were set for certain important industrial products, including steel and electric power. To emphasize official concern for the consumer, special programs for 1976-80 were adopted at this plenum regarding the production and sale of consumer goods (ibid., 13 July), the food industry, and livestock breeding. For the most part, these programs were propaganda measures designed to highlight certain aspects of the five-year plan; they added few resources beyond those envisioned in the original draft plan. The plenum also adopted a decision setting standards for dealing with proposals, suggestions, and requests from the population (ibid., 16 July). The purpose was not to encourage complaints but to prompt suggestions for increasing economic and social efficiency. The East Berlin conference of European Communist and workers' parties was reviewed and the Romanian stand taken there was approved.

The final item on the July plenum's agenda involved a number of personnel changes in the party, which complemented government changes made two weeks earlier. The former minister of national defense, General Ion Ioniţă, who had been made a deputy premier on June 15, was advanced from alternate to full member of the Political Executive Committee. The new minister of national defense, Colonel General Ion Coman, was elected an alternate member of the PEC, as was Ion Dincă, who had recently become the first secretary of the Bucharest municipal party committee and head of the Bucharest government. Other newly elected alternate members of the PEC were the minister of the interior, Teodor Coman, and two first secretaries of county party committees—Stefan Mocută (Cluj) and Ludovic Fazekas (Harghita). Two new party secretaries were also chosen—Constantin Dăscălescu and Aurel Duma. On 15 June, Dăscălescu was appointed chairman of the Union of Agricultural Production Cooperatives, and it was decided at that time that the position would carry with it ex officio party-secretary status. Duma was head of the Central Committee Chancellery and thus a close associate of party leader Ceauşescu. Presumably he retained this position.

The fourth and last plenary session of the Central Committee, 2-3 November, again had a lengthy agenda. An ideological program to implement decisions of the 11th party congress and the June 1976 "Congress on Political Education and Socialist Culture" was approved. A draft of the program had been published for popular discussion and amendment in September (ibid., 15 September). In a related move, it was decided to "improve the composition" of the Central Committee's Ideological Commission, which is headed by Ceauşescu. The draft socioeconomic plan and state budget for 1977 were also approved at the plenum and subsequently enacted into law by the Grand National Assembly (ibid., 6 November). A decision was adopted on supplies of food and consumer goods to the population for the fourth quarter of 1976 and the first half of 1977 (ibid., 9 November), as were provisions regarding reduction of the work week, which suggested a delay in the implementation of earlier pledges in this regard (ibid., 6 November). A new system of income taxation was also considered and a proposed basis for altering the current system was approved (ibid., 11 November). A few personnel changes were also made: Vasile Vîlcu was chosen chairman of the Central Auditing Commission and thus was required to resign as a member of the Central Committee and the PEC. Ion Dincă, who became an alternate member of the PEC in June, was promoted to full membership.

Domestic Attitudes and Activities. The CPR sees the economic development of the country as one of its main priorities, and to this end it has been concerned to mobilize the population to achieve its ambitious economic goals. With the new five-year plan period beginning in 1976, establishing the targets for 1976-80 was a central preoccupation of the party. In July, after a number of delays, the plan was approved by the Central Committee and the Grand National Assembly. Its final version (*Scînteia*, 3 July) contains some significant increases over the draft targets approved at the 11th party congress in November 1974. It calls for an average annual growth rate of 10.2 to 11.2 percent over the five years. For certain sectors the rate will be somewhat higher—11.8 to 12.6 percent for machine building, for example, and 15.2 to 16.6 percent for the chemical industry. The consumer sector received lower priority—the rate of growth in the food industry is to be 9.2 percent and in light industry 8.7 percent.

Plan targets in agriculture are ambitious, calling for an overall increase of 28 to 44 percent over the previous five-year period. These targets seem particularly highflown in view of the fact that the 1971-75 targets were not met, in part owing to natural causes, though shortfalls were also attributable to slow progress in expanding the amount of land under irrigation, inconsistency in the production of fertilizers, and administrative and organizational problems in the agricultural sector. The average annual output of cereals in 1971-75 was only 14,800,000 tons, despite the all-time record crop (16,900,000 tons) in 1972. The target for the next five-year period is an annual average of 20,000,000 to 22,400,000 tons.

In general, performance in the agricultural sector in the last five years, and during 1975 in particular, was not good. This prompted a number of high-level meetings involving Ceauşescu and other important leaders. At a special congress of local government officials in early February agricultural shortcomings and the responsibility of local officials for agriculture were given particular emphasis (ibid., 5, 7 February). Ceauşescu interrupted his attendance at the 25th Congress of the Communist Party of the Soviet Union to return to Bucharest for an important meeting with county party first-secretaries at which the situation of agriculture was discussed (ibid., 29 February).

Agricultural shortages exacerbated the problem of providing the population with adequate amounts of food products. A number of meetings were held to discuss the food supply and consumer goods, and in order to deal with the long-term aspects of the problem a number of bills to increase the production of food were introduced in the Romanian parliament. The plan for 1976, reflecting this concern, called for a greater investment in agriculture than was originally foreseen. Also, in mid-1976 a special council to coordinate the production of consumer goods was established under the chairmanship of a deputy premier (ibid., 2 June).

A second major concern of the CPR, and one that received particular attention in 1976, was the cultural-ideological sphere. The Congress on Political Education and Socialist Culture, held in Bucharest in early June, was the culmination of year-long preparations and in many respects was a continuation of the cultural-ideological policies instituted in 1971. Ceauşescu set the tone for the congress in a speech in which he again stressed Romanian history and bolstered the party's attempt to portray itself as the culmination of a long process of national historical development. He also included a catalogue of shortcomings in the cultural and ideological fields, including past distortions of Romania's history and the ethnic descent of its people. He called for greater emphasis on mass culture, and urged professional culture figures to adhere to party guidance in their creative work. (Ibid., 2-5 June.)

In September an "Ideological Action Program" was drawn up and approved by the PEC as the logical and practical consequence of the ideological program adopted in 1971 and amended at the 11th party congress and the June cultural congress (ibid., 15 September). This program represents an attempt to transform the entire spectrum of ideology and education, bringing all into line with the principle of "permanent revolution." It includes modification and intensification of political education, which will henceforth include the entire—party and nonparty—population, starting from the age of four years: a newly instituted political organization called the "Falcons of the Fatherland" will provide indoctrination for children between four and seven, and at all levels of elementary and high school education a fusion between manual and intellectual labor (and, on the higher level, research) is to be effected. Patriotic education, the dissemination of information on the history of Romania and of the party, will be stepped up considerably. Most important, a new system of "unified guidance" of the propaganda, educational, and cultural fields, based on a newly created system of Committees on Political Education and Socialist Culture, will be introduced from factory and institution up to county level. The program also stipulates the establishment of a "National Center for the Promotion of Friendship and Cooperation with Other Peoples," in order to enhance Romania's prestige abroad. The Action Program was approved by the November plenum of the Central Committee.

International Views and Policies. The year 1976 was one in which international relations received particular attention. A number of important gatherings were held during the year, including the conference of European Communist and workers' parties in East Berlin in June, a meeting of the Political Consultative Committee of the Warsaw Pact, and, among a number of lesser gatherings, a conference on Balkan cooperation. In general, Romania's foreign policy continued to follow much the same general pattern as in the past—relations with the USSR were the first priority, and improvement was apparent in this regard; the campaign to identify Romania with the developing countries made some progress; and the maintenance of good relations with Western states based on its own interests put Romania slightly out of step with the rest of the Warsaw Pact countries. This order of priorities and the general framework of Romanian foreign policy was set forth by Ceauşescu in a speech to the Grand National Assembly at the end of 1975 (*Scînteia*, 19 December).

In the summer of 1976 there were significant signs of improvement in ties with the USSR. Since the spring of 1975 an extensive debate had been going on between Soviet and Romanian historians over the history of Bessarabia and the ethnic descent of its inhabitants, and the moderation of this controversy was an important indication of better relations. In an implicit reference to Bessarabia in a speech in June, Ceauşescu expressed the hope that "certain problems inherited from the past . . . should not affect the cooperation and solidarity between our parties and peoples," and denied the existence of "territorial or other problems with the Soviet Union" (ibid., 3 June). To underline the point further he visited Soviet Moldavia (Bessarabia) in August—the first such visit by a Romanian leader. During this stay in the USSR Ceauşescu met with Soviet party leader Brezhnev, and reports on their talks noted "an even closer unity of views with regard to the problems discussed." The visit was preceded by high-level negotiations on economic exchanges in the coming five-year period.

The most definite indication of improved relations was the "friendly" visit paid by Brezhnev to Bucharest at the end of November—the first formal visit of the Soviet party leader to Romania in a decade. Despite the show of warmth toward Brezhnev, however, there were signs that all outstanding issues between the two countries have not been resolved. The joint statement expressed satisfaction, but there was no mention of unanimity of views, and in their speeches both Ceauşescu and Brezhnev admitted differences on "nonessential questions." Perhaps the key to the results of the visit is a statement made by the latter: "There are premises for broadening Soviet-Romanian collaboration. The decisive role is naturally played by strengthening the links between the Communist Party of the Soviet Union and the Romanian Communist Party." He also noted: "Our talks have broadened the understanding between our parties and strengthened the atmosphere of trust that is so important for further consolidation of our fraternal relations." (Ibid., 23, 25 November). In other words, conditions exist for expanding relations in many areas, including the economic field, but whether such expansion will in fact take place will be determined by political conditions. The Romanians have made some concessions in this regard, but the Soviets apparently wish to test their sincerity. Brezhnev's visit to Bucharest confirms the willingness of both sides to continue the dialogue, and the invitation he extended to Ceauşescu to visit Moscow will provide an opportunity to do this. At present it would seem that a new balance in relations is being negotiated, but much still remains uncertain.

Relations appeared to be improving not only with the USSR but also with the Warsaw Pact in general. A summit conference of this organization was held in Bucharest and agreement was reached to increase the political consultations among the member states by creating a joint secretariat and establishing a permanent framework for meetings of foreign ministers. The Warsaw Pact's joint appeal for a treaty that would prohibit initiating the use of nuclear weapons and other measures proposed relating to détente and disarmament were consistent with Romania's desires. On a bilateral level improvement was also apparent. Polish party leader Edward Giereck visited Bucharest in October, some six years after coming to power and long after he had visited all other East European states, including Yugoslavia (ibid., 11 October). Relations with Bulgaria were strengthened by two visits exchanged between Todor Zhivkov and Ceauşescu (ibid., 29 July, 5 October).

Ties with the non-Warsaw Pact socialist states were also a matter of concern. Ceauşescu met with President Tito of Yugoslavia in September for the latest in their long series of meetings (ibid., 12 September), and a number of high-level Romanian civilian and military leaders visited the People's Republic of China during the year. The latter visits take on particular significance in view of the leadership changes that have rocked China this year.

Second place in Romania's foreign policy goes to the developing countries, and a number of high-level visits were exchanged with them. In 1975 trade with the Third World amounted in volume to five times the 1970 figure, and trade with this group of states is planned to reach 30 percent of Romania's total foreign trade by 1980. The need for raw materials and for outlets for Romanian manufactured goods and preferential treatment for Romanian trade are only some of the reasons for this interest in the developing countries. By linking itself politically with them, and particularly with those that are nonaligned, Romania intends to bolster its foreign-policy autonomy and attain a greater role in world affairs. As a result of its efforts Romania secured an invitation to attend the Lima conference of foreign ministers of nonaligned countries as an invited guest in the summer of 1975. In 1976 a major effort was mounted to secure observer status at the Colombo nonaligned summit in August, but because of its Warsaw Pact membership Romania was given the status of permanent guest. Its efforts to be recognized as a developing country were given an important boost in January when the Group of 77 agreed to accept it as a member.

The developed industrial states rank third in importance in Romania's foreign policy. Since the Helsinki Conference on Security and Cooperation in Europe (August 1975), many elements in the relations with Western Europe and the USA have been related to that conference. Romania has insisted that détente must move from the political realm to the military, and there have been frequent calls for progress in the Vienna force-reduction talks. The Romanians have enthusiastically advocated increasing trade and scientific-technical exchanges, but on humanitarian questions they have been considerably more reserved. The West German and French foreign ministers raised the questions of family reunification and mixed marriages during visits to Bucharest, and the Romanian foreign minister canceled a visit to Sweden because officials there intended to raise similar questions. In a lengthy statement on such problems Ceauşescu expressed willingness to solve them "appropriately" as in the past, but was also critical of Western attitudes (ibid., 3 June).

Romania singled out three international problems for particular attention in 1976—eliminating under-development and establishing a new international economic order; achieving general, and particularly nuclear, disarmament; and improving the operations and effectiveness of the United Nations (ibid., 19 December 1975). Romania's action at the U.N. where it was a nonpermanent member of the Security Council, was concerned with these three issues.

Romania's desire to improve relations with its Balkan neighbors was reaffirmed in its response to the Athens conference on regional cooperation at the end of January. Romania has been one of the most consistent ɪdvocates of multilateral cooperation in the Balkans, and its conduct in Athens reflected this. During the year Ceauşescu visited both Greece and Turkey, and the heads of government of these two countries were his guests in Bucharest.

Publications. *Scînteia* is the official daily of the CPR Central Committee. *Era socialistă* is the party's popularized theoretical-political fortnightly, and *Munca de partid* the fortnightly that deals with questions of organization and methods of party activity. Other important publications include *Munca*, the weekly of the trade union confederaton; *Romania liberă*, the FSU's daily; *Romania literară*, the weekly of the Writers' Union; and *Scînteia tineretului*, the daily of the Union of Communist Youth. Agerpres is the Romanian news agency.

Radio Free Europe   Robert R. King
Munich

Union of Soviet Socialist Republics

The Communist Party of Soviet Union (Kommunisticheskaia Partiia Sovetskogo Soiuza; CPSU) traces its origins to the founding of the Russian Social Democratic Labor Party in 1898. The party split into Bolshevik ("majority") and Menshevik ("minority") factions at the Second Congress, held at Brussels and London in 1903. The Bolshevik faction, led by Vladimir I. Lenin, was actually a minority after 1904 and, unable to regain the policy-making dominance attained at the Second Congress, broke away from the Mensheviks in 1912 at the Prague conference to form a separate party. In March 1918, after the seizure of power, this party was renamed the "All-Russian Communist Party (Bolsheviks)."

When "Union of Soviet Socialist Republics" was adopted as the name of the country in 1925, the party's designation was changed to "All-Union Communist Party (Bolsheviks)." The party's present name was adopted in 1952 at the 19th Congress. The CPSU is the only legal political party in the USSR.

The CPSU at the beginning of 1976 had 15,694,187 members, including 636,170 candidate members (*Partiinaia zhizn'*, no. 10, May). This represents an increase of 1.92 percent over the announced total membership of 15,300,000 as of 1 January 1975 (TASS, 23 February 1975). According to General Secretary Leonid I. Brezhnev, in the exchange of party cards conducted between 1973 and 1975, 347,000 members failed to receive new cards (*Pravda*, 25 February). While the overall trend toward stabilization of party size continues, the figures reveal that, despite the exchange of cards, there has been a slight upsurge in rate of growth. Between 1961 and 1966, the average annual increase in CPSU membership was 6.0 percent, between 1966 and 1971, 3.16 percent, between 1971 and 1973, 1.28 percent, and between 1973 and 1976, 1.96 percent.

Reported distribution of CPSU membership by category is as follows: 41.6 percent workers, 13.9 percent collective farmers, 44.5 percent employees and others. Recent changes in membership have yielded a slight increment in the percentage of workers and a decline in the proportion of collective farmers; as of 1 January 1974, workers reportedly accounted for 41.0 percent of membership and collective farmers 14.4 percent. Workers accounted for 57.6 percent of the new candidate members since the 24th CPSU Congress and collective farmers 11.3 percent. During this period 65.1 percent of new candidate members came from the ranks of the Komsomol, and for 1975 the figure was 70.2 percent. Women constitute 24.3 percent of the membership in 1976, as against 20.6 percent in 1966 and 22.2 percent in 1971. The present CPSU membership is 9.3 percent of the adult population (*Partiinaia zhizn'*, no. 10, May) and 6.11 percent of the total USSR population of 256,700,000 (TASS, 23 July).

The most recent quadrennial elections for the Supreme Soviet, the country's nominal legislature, were held in June 1974. The Supreme Soviet has 1,517 members and is divided into two equal chambers—the Soviet of the Union, in which each deputy represents approximately 300,000 persons, and the Soviet of the Nationalities, in which deputies represent the republics, regions, and national areas of the USSR.   All candidates on the single slate supported by the CPSU were elected in the June 1974 balloting, with a total of 578,414 negative votes against nearly 161 million for the official slate (*Izvestiia*, 19 June 1974).

Organization and Leadership. The structure of the CPSU parallels the administrative organization of the Soviet state. There are 380,000 primary party organizations. Above this lowest level, there are 2,810 rural *raion* committees, 448 urban *raion* committees, 760 city committees, 10 *okrug* committees, 142 *oblast'* committees, six *krai* committees, and 14 union-republic committees. There is no separate subsidiary organization for the Russian republic (RSFSR), largest constituent unit of the Union. At the top, the All-Union Congress is, according to the party rules, the supreme policy-making body. The 24th Congress, in 1971, set the maximal interval between congresses at five years. Between congresses, the highest representative organ is the Central Committee. At this level, power is concentrated in the Politburo, the Secretariat, and the various departments of the Central Committee.

There were two plenums of the Central Committee during 1976. The first, held in conjunction with the 25th Party Congress in March, made several changes in Politburo and Secretariat membership (see below). The second, in October, featured a report on the 1976 harvest and a speech by Brezhnev on the international situation.

The 25th Congress met in Moscow, 24 February-5 March. The congress was preceded by a report and election campaign in all echelons of the party, which included congresses of 11 of the 15 union-republic party organizations. The preparatory meetings at each level of the party organization were devoted to a survey of the results of the work done to implement the decisions of the 24th Congress and to discussion of the draft "Main Directions for the Development of the USSR National Economy in 1976-80" approved by the Central Committee at its December 1975 plenum. The 4,998 delegates to the 25th Congress were said by Ivan V. Kapitonov, secretary for cadres in the Central Committee and chairman of the Credentials Commission, to include 3,672 who were elected to attend a congress for the first time (*Pravda*, 28 February). According to Kapitonov, the delegates included 1,310 workers, 1,114 members of the party apparatus, 1,255 women, 887 representatives of agriculture, and 314 military officers. 3,035 delegates, nearly 60 percent of the total, represented RSFSR party organizations.

Selection of the new Central Committee at the Congress was in accord with the general trend of the Brezhnev years toward stabilization and security for middle- and upper-level cadres. The Central Committee increased in size from 396 to 426 members, with the number of full members rising from 241 to 287 and candidate members dropping from 155 to 139. Of the surviving full members elected at the 24th Congress, 89 percent retained their memberships and the average age of members rose to about 60, continuing the tendency toward gerontocratic politics in the USSR. Notable personalities dropped from Central Committee ranks included Aleksandr N. Shelepin, Gennadi I. Voronov, and Piotr Y. Shelest, all of whom had lost their Politburo posts since the 24th Congress, and Vasily P. Mzhavanadze and Anton Y. Kochinyan, ousted as party chiefs of Georgia and Armenia during the same period. Anastas I. Mikoyan, a powerful party and government figure during the Stalin and Khrushchev eras, completed his political career at age 80 by yielding his seat (*Pravda*, 6 March; *NYT*, 7 March).

Dimitri S. Poliansky, whose political fortunes had been declining for some years, was excluded from the Politburo; he retained his membership on the Central Committee. Grigori V. Romanov, first secretary of the Leningrad *oblast'* party committee, and Dimitri F. Ustinov, Central Committee secretary for the armaments industry (named Defense Minister in April; see below), were promoted from candidate to full members of the Politburo (TASS, 5 March). Geidar A. Aliev, first secretary of the Azerbaidzhan party, was elected by the Central Committee to candidate membership on the Politburo. Konstantin U. Chernenko, head of the Central Committee General Department, and Mikhail V. Zimianin, editor of *Pravda*, were named members of the Secretariat. Other members of the Politburo and Secretariat were confirmed in their posts at the March Central Committee plenum.

A Politburo vacancy was created by the death of Marshal Andrei A. Grechko on 26 April (see below). The present composition of the Politburo is shown on page 72.

The present Central Committee Secretariat is composed of ten men: Brezhnev, Suslov, Kirilenko, Kulakov, Ponomarev, Vladimir I. Dolgikh, Ivan V. Kapitonov, Konstantin F. Katushev, Konstantin U. Chernenko, Mikhail V. Zimianin.

Republic first secretaries were as follows: Karen S. Demichyan (Armenia), Geidar A. Aliev (Azerbaidzhan), Piotr M. Masherov (Belorussia), Ivan G. Kebin (Estonia), Eduard A. Shevardnadze (Georgia), Dinmukhamed A. Kunaev (Kazakhstan), Turdakun U. Usubaliev (Kirghizia), August E. Voss (Latvia), Piatras P. Griskiavicus (Lithuania), Ivan I. Bodiul (Moldavia), Dzhabar R. Rasulov (Tadzhikistan), Mukhamednazar G. Gapurov (Turkmenia), Vladimor V. Shcherbitsky (Ukraine), Sharaf R. Rashidov (Uzbekistan).

Auxiliary and Mass Organizations. The most important of the many "voluntary" organizations allied with the CPSU is the Communist Youth League (Kommunisticheskiy Soyuz Molodezhi; Komsomol). Its membership of some 35 million young people is led by 48-year-old Yevgeny M. Tyazhelnikov, first secretary of the Komsomol Central Committee. Tyazhelnikov is the oldest first secretary in the Komsomol's history; the aging of the CPSU leadership extends even into its youth organization. The fifth plenum of the Komsomol, held in Moscow on 19 March 1976, heard a report by Tyazhelnikov on "the results of the 25th CPSU Congress and the tasks of further stepping up the Communist education of youth" and effected several changes in the composition of the Komsomol Secretariat and Central Committee Bureau (*Komsomolskaia Pravda*, 20 March).

POLITBURO

Members:

Brezhnev, Leonid I.	General Secretary, CPSU Central Committee
Podgorny, Nikolai V.	Chairman, Presidium of the USSR Supreme Soviet
Kosygin, Aleksei N.	Chairman, USSR Council of Ministers
Suslov, Mikhail A.	Secretary, CPSU Central Committee
Kirilenko, Andrei P.	Secretary, CPSU Central Committee
Pel'she, Arvid I.	Chaiman, Party Control Committee
Mazurov, Kiril T.	First Deputy Chairman, USSR Council of Ministers
Grishin, Victor V.	First Secretary, Moscow City Party Committee
Kunaev, Dinmukhamed A.	First Secretary, Kazakh Central Committee
Shcherbitsky, Vladimir V.	First Secretary, Ukrainian Central Committee
Kulakov, Fedor D.	Secretary, CPSU Central Committee
Andropov, Yuri V.	Chairman, Committee of State Security (KGB)
Gromyko, Andrei A.	Minister of Foreign Affairs, USSR Council of Ministers
Romanov, Grigori V.	First Secretary, Leningrad *oblast'* Party Committee
Ustinov, Dimitri F.	Minister of Defense, USSR Council of Ministers

Candidate Members:

Demichev, Piotr N.	Minister of Culture, USSR Council of Ministers
Rashidov, Sharaf R.	First Secretary, Uzbek Central Committee
Masherov, Piotr M.	First Secretary, Belorussian Central Committee
Solomentsev, Mikhail S.	Chairman, RSFSR Council of Ministers
Ponomarev, Boris N.	Secretary, CPSU Central Committee
Aliev, Geidar A.	First Secretary, Azerbaidzhan Central Committee

Other large mass organizations include the All-Union Central Council of Trade Unions (AUC CTU), which has 107 million members (*Pravda*, 4 June); the Soviet Voluntary Society for the Promotion of the Army, Aviation, and Navy (DOSAAF),whose 70 million members seek to "instill patriotism and pride" in the armed forces; the Union of Soviet Societies for Friendship and Cultural Relations with Foreign Countries; and the Soviet Committee of Women.

Party and Government Affairs. There was widespread speculation in the Western press at the outset of 1976 concerning the possible declining health of General Secretary Brezhnev. His absences from the party congresses in Bulgaria (March), Czechoslovakia (April), and the German Democratic Republic (May), where the CPSU was represented respectively by Party secretaries Fedor D. Kulakov, Andrei P. Kirilenko, and Mikhail A. Suslov, fanned these rumors. However, Brezhnev's delivery of the lengthy major speech at the 25th CPSU Congress, his address at the meeting of 29 Communist parties in East Berlin in June, his unusually demanding schedule of public appearances during the second half of the year, and the marked improvement in his physical appearance finally convinced most Western observers that his imminent retirement for reasons of health was unlikely.

Brezhnev was also reportedly enmeshed in domestic political difficulties at the beginning of the year. The unraveling of his détente policy, particularly the failure to achieve a breakthrough on SALT II and the apparently unexpected Western backfire on the Helsinki accords, produced a measure of tension within Soviet leadership ranks. The economic failures of 1972-75 and the CPSU's relations with other Communist parties, especially those of China, France, Italy, and Spain, also were troublesome. In the final quarter of 1975, there was an extensive debate in the upper echelons of party and government concerning détente and the allocation of resources between consumption and heavy industrial interests—a debate mainly carried on via esoteric articles in official ideological journals. This debate was resolved in favor of the military and economic planners, as evidenced by the downgrading of consumer interests in the Tenth Five-Year Plan. This outcome was not necessarily detrimental to Brezhnev's power position in the party, given his long-time close association with the "military-industrial complex," but it accorded poorly with earlier initiatives attributed to Brezhnev, particularly the projected 15-year plan, which was scheduled to feature a substantial reorientation toward satisfaction of consumer demands. While Soviet planners continued to speak of economic goals on a 15-year basis, the overall grandiose design for the economy to 1990 was not ready as expected prior to the 25th CPSU Congress, apparently blocked by internal party and government wrangling. Moreover, the projected new Soviet constitution, one of Brezhnev's pet projects for the past decade, was again delayed (*Christian Science Monitor*, 19 February). Nevertheless, the changes in party and governmental leadership made during the year appeared to leave Brezhnev, on balance, in an even stronger position than before. The composition of the new Central Committee appeared favorable to his interests, emphasizing the stability and security of upper cadres, which has been a major source of his popularity within the party. The striking tendency toward an aging leadership throughout the upper echelons of party and government also worked in Brezhnev's favor, discouraging any moves to unsettle the status quo. However, the general problem of renewal of leadership at varius levels remained and Brezhnev's success in holding together a broad coalition of aged *aparatchiki* compounded the systemic problem of preparing the new leadership which must inevitably appear within the next decade.

Whatever difficulties Brezhnev faced behind the scenes, the external manifestations of his "cult of personality" were more blatant than ever. The encomiums of praise accorded him at the 25th Party Congress were more lavish than any bestowed upon Khrushchev at the peak of his power. Uzbek first secretary Rashidov said that Brezhnev "is distinguished by supreme modesty and a brilliant talent, revolutionary optimism, proletarian solidarity and a firm class posture, spiritual beauty, and personal charm" (*Pravda*, 27 February). Rashidov also referred to him as "not only the most outstanding but also the most influential political figure of the present time" (Moscow domestic service, 25 February in *FBIS*, 1 March). Lithuanian first secretary Griskiavicus called Brezhnev "not only a wise, talented leader of our party and an outstanding figure of the international Communist and workers' movement" but "also a magnanimous person who embodies all the best qualities of man with a capital 'M' " (*Pravda*, 29 February). Georgian first secretary Shevardnadze credited him with helping to create a "clear and cloudless sky over our heads" (ibid., 27 February).

Brezhnev was named a Marshal of the Soviet Union on 8 May (ibid., 9 May) and the next day a bust of him was unveiled in his home town of Dneprodzerzhinsk (*Baltimore Sun*, 24 May). Brezhnev was the first living political figure to be honored with such a monument since the Stalin era; however, similar honors were accorded Party secretary Suslov and Supreme Soviet Presidium chairman Podgorny in September (AP, 4 October).

Several important changes in government positions were made during the year. Dimitri S. Poliansky, who earlier had been dropped from the Politburo, was dismissed as Minister of Agriculture on 5 March (*NYT*, 6 March) and was replaced by Valentin Mesiats (TASS, 16 March). Poliansky, who had been the "boy wonder" of Soviet politics during the Khrushchev era, attaining full Presidium (Politburo) membership in 1960 at the age of 43, was subsequently named ambassador to Japan (TASS, 17 April). The firing of Poliansky was the latest in the periodic reshufflings of governmental officials concerned with agriculture, which included his demotion from the post of First Deputy Prime Minister in 1973. Despite the agricultural crisis, Fedor D. Kulakov, party secretary in charge of agriculture since 1965, appeared to retain undiminished stature within the Party.

Marshal Andrei A. Grechko, Minister of Defense and full Politburo member, died on 26 April and was replaced by Dimitri F. Ustinov (*NYT*, 30 April). Ustinov, who had directed the Soviet armaments industry since 1941, became the first civilian to head the military since the ouster of Leon Trotsky as War Minister in January 1925. The appointment of Ustinov came as a surprise to most Western observers, who had expected the Defense Ministry to go to General Ivan I. Yakubovski, commander in chief of Warsaw Pact forces, or to General Viktor G. Kulikov, Army chief of staff. The naming of Ustinov to the position was widely viewed as an affirmation of civilian control of the military forces, without any fundamental change in policy or threat to basic military interests. The tradition of professional soldiers in the top defense post was formally continued when Ustinov, a reserve colonel general, was named a General of the Army upon his appointment to the Defense Ministry; later in the year he was promoted to Marshal of the Soviet Union (*Pravda*, 31 July).

Prime Minister Aleksei N. Kosygin was reported to have suffered a heart attack or stroke during the summer and was not seen in public for nearly three months after 22 July. Brezhnev confirmed the illness, without specifying its nature, when he told former U.S. ambassador W. Averell Harriman in September that Kosygin would be "back at his desk within a few weeks" (*Christian Science Monitor*, 21 September). Brezhnev's conversation with Harriman was fully reported in the Soviet press, leading to speculation that the public was being prepared for Kosygin's departure from the premiership. Meanwhile, Nikolai A. Tikhonov, 71, one of 11 deputy premiers, was promoted to First Deputy Prime Minister (*Pravda*, 3 September), to assume much of the work load of the absent Kosygin. Tikhonov was a factory director in Nikopol when Brezhnev headed Dnepropetrovsk *oblast* in the 1940s and was one of the original members of the "Dnieper Mafia," the informal group of Brezhnev associates during his days of provincial party leadership in the Ukraine who have risen through the ranks with him. The group includes, among many other top party and government officials, party secretary Kirilenko, Ukrainian first secretary Shcherbitsky, and Ministry of Internal Affairs head Nikolai A. Shchelekov.

Another member of the "Dnieper Mafia" was involved in a governmental shuffle during the year. Deputy Prime Minister Veniamin E. Dymshits was released from his duties as chairman of the State Committee for Material and Technical Supply (*Gossnab*) in connection with his transfer to work directly in the USSR Council of Ministers. The loss of his departmental portfolio was an apparent demotion for Dymshits, but its significance was not certain. This area of administration had received some sharp criticism in recent years and Dymshits may have been a scapegoat; it seemed more likely that the move simply represented one more round in the tug of war between Brezhnev and Kosygin for control of the governmental apparatus. Dymshits, who had been for some time the only Jew in the Soviet cabinet, was replaced in the *Gossnab* post by Nikolai V. Martynov, who was also named as a deputy prime minister (ibid., 28 June). A major shakeup also occurred in the corresponding union-republic ministry (*Glavsnab*) in Georgia. The republic's Minister for Material and Technical Supply, four of his main deputies, and several lesser officials were fired and "severely punished" for "unsatisfactory leadership," "crude violations" of proper administration, and "an intolerable situation" in the "safeguarding of socialist property," according to a July resolution of the Georgian Central Committee (*Zaria Vostoka*, 22 July, in *FBIS*, 9 August).

Matters of internal organization and shortcomings in the work of party cadres attracted much attention during the year. Union-republic congresses prior to the 25th CPSU Congress spotlighted cadre deficiencies, especially in Georgia, the Ukraine, and Turkmenistan; inadequate supervision of the economy was emphasized. Much of this criticism was repeated later in the year and the Belorussian party's Vitebsk *obkom* organization was singled out in July for scathing criticism of party work (*Sovetskaia Belorussia*, 16 July, in *FBIS*, 4 August). In addition to the fire directed at particular organizations, the top leadership vented its displeasure at inadequate cadres throughout the party. Gennadi F. Sizov, chairman of the Party's Central Auditing Commission, reported to the 25th CPSU Congress that some members were delaying and even cheating on their payments of dues and that some primary party organizations were slow in depositing collected dues in savings banks and were overspending on administrative expenses (*NYT*, 27 February). In his principal address to the Congress, Brezhnev spoke approvingly of the rising level of technical training of party cadres and the promotion of "popular initiatives" by the primary organizations, but called for more intensive ideological training of cadres and stressed the need for much stricter supervision of the fulfillment of decisions. The General Secretary restated his highly popular approach to cadres policy: "A solicitous, considerate attitude toward cadres has become firmly established in the Party. An end has been put to the unwarranted shuffling and frequent replacement of personnel, a question that was raised back at the 23rd Congress." However, Brezhnev pointedly noted that this general approach would not inhibit the leadership in dealing with the party's serious internal organizational problems:

> We cannot leave in leadership work people who display irresponsibility and live on their past glories, thinking that their position will in itself assure them prestige and respect. We cannot have Party leaders who have lost the ability to evaluate their own activity critically, who have lost touch with the masses, who engender flatterers and toadies, who have lost the trust of the Communists. (*Pravda* and *Izvestiia*, 25 February.)

Following Brezhnev's lead, the Central Committee passed a resolution in May on popular appeals and complaints (*Pravda*, 4 May). A time limit of one month was set for party, soviet, and economic organs to respond to letters of complaint, and unspecified "strict punishment measures" were directed for cadres who fail to follow established procedures or "display a formal-bureaucratic approach" in these matters.

Georgia remained a trouble spot for the Party throughout the year. At the 25th Georgian party Congress in January, First Secretary Shevardnadze noted improvement in party discipline but admitted lack of success in the struggle against nationalism and capitalistic mentality. "Unfortunately," he said, "no sphere of the republic's life has been unaffected by the negative tendencies of the private-ownership psychology"(*Zaria Vostoka*,23 January). The republic witnessed more than 100 arson and bombing incidents between 1973 and mid-1976; the authorities attributed this violence to opponents of Shevardnadze's campaign against corruption and private-ownership. The most serious incident was a bomb blast at the headquarters of the Georgian Council of Ministers in April 1976; shortly thereafter, the Georgian party newspaper directed criticism against the police for failing to maintain order (ibid., 29 April). A CPSU Central Committee resolution in June praised the Georgian Party's efforts under Shevardnadze's leadership, particularly in organizational matters, but stressed the need for intensifying the struggle against "the infiltration of bourgeois ideology" and "private-ownership tendencies" (*Pravda*, 27 June, in *FBIS*, 30 June). The resolution pointedly noted that only a beginning had been made "in the huge amount of work that has to be continued in the future in the ideological and political education of Communists and all workers." At the plenum of the Georgian Central Committee in July, Shevardnadze stated that both the committee and the republic's Council of Ministers were "doing poor work" in the supervision of agriculture, and pointed to "weak links" in primary party organizations and a general lack of coordination among party organizations (*Zaria Vostoka*, 25 July, in *FBIS*, 11 August).

Vladimir V. Shcherbitsky, first secretary of the Ukrainian party, has substantially enhanced his prestige in the CPSU hierarchy on the basis of his tough approach to the republic's problems. However, developments in the Ukraine during the year indicated that the party continues to be plagued by severe organizational problems. In January, Shcherbitsky criticized the Kiev city party leadership for "insufficient exactingness and a liberal and in several cases an unprincipled attitude toward persons who commit serious shortcomings in their work and even toward those who compromise themselves" (*Pravda Ukrainy*, 25 January). A. P. Botvin, Kiev city party first secretary, was singled out as one of the transgressors.Nevertheless, Botvin was reelected to the Ukrainian party Politburo at the party congress in February, where the Central Committee criticized five of the republic's province central and executive committees "for being slow to improve their style of work" (*Pravda*, 14 February). Earlier, Shcherbitsky had personally supervised a shakeup in the Donetsk province party organization, which included the firing of first secretary V. I. Degtyarev and his replacement by B. V. Kachura (*Pravda Ukrainy*, 7, 11 January). At the plenum of the Ukrainian party Central Committee in May, Shcherbitsky called for further improvement in personnel work (*Pravda*, 29 May). Ivan Grushetsky, 72, former president of the Ukraine and a holdover from the pre-Shcherbitsky leadership, retired from the Ukrainian party Politburo in October (AP, 12 October).

A prominent Moscow party official also lost his job during the year, possibly due to his role in a highly publicized incident in 1974 which had aroused much negative reaction in the West. Vladimir N, Yagodkin, the hard-line ideological and cultural chief of the Moscow city organization, was dismissed from his post in February (*NYT*, 7 February). Yagodkin's name was linked with the bulldozing of an exhibition of abstract art in early autumn 1974.

Police officials continued their steady incursion into the party's upper echelons during the year. At the party congresses in the Ukraine, Belorussia, Azerbaidzhan, and Tadzhikistan, the local Committee of State Security (KGB) chiefs were made full members of the union-republic Politburos. In Kazakhstan, Uzbekistan, and Lithuania, the local security police chairmen were made alternate Politburo members. The KGB chief in Moldavia is also a member of that republic's Politburo (*Christian Science Monitor*, 2 March). New Politburo candidate member Aliev was formerly KGB chief in Azerbaidzhan.

Domestic Policies. On the domestic front, party and government officials concentrated attention upon the economy throughout 1976. The preparatory meetings of party organizations in January and February, the 25th CPSU Congress, and most party conclaves during the remainder of the year all featured calls for improvement in economic performance. The Tenth Five-Year Plan was launched in January 1976 at a critical juncture in Soviet economic development. Sluggishness of the economy resulted from a blend of general long-run and specific short-run deficiencies. Growth rates slowed during the period of the Ninth Five-Year Plan, 1971-75, primarily because the USSR no longer had substantial surpluses of labor and capital and failed to compensate for this through increased productivity, efficiency being hampered by failures in management, technological adaptation, and labor discipline. The general problems of the economy were compounded by the second disastrous farm harvest in four years, the 1975 shortfall in grain production amounting to more than 75 million tons (*NYT*, 1 February).

The Soviet economy did account for a substantial quantitative expansion between 1971 and 1975 and, according to official figures, held world leadership at the end of 1975 in the production of steel, oil, mineral fertilizers, pig iron, coal, cement, tractors, cotton, and wool (ibid., 2 March). However, the major goals of the final Ninth Five-Year Plan draft were not realized. Of special importance was the fact that, although consumer goods had been given priority in the plan, heavy industry as in the past grew faster than consumer-oriented industry. Between 1971 and 1975, national income increased by 28 percent (as against the 40 percent planned), industrial output by 38.9 percent (instead of 41-45 percent), agricultural output by 13 percent (instead of 22 percent), and the output of consumer goods by 33.5 percent (instead of 44-48 percent). Industrial labor productivity was up by 23 percent over the five-year period, compared with a goal of 39 percent. (*Pravda*, 3 December 1975; 1 February, 2 March 1976.)

The government's report on 1975 economic results, released 31 January, showed that labor productivity grew by 5.9 percent, down from 6.5 percent in 1974. Industrial output was reported up by

7.5 percent compared with an 8 percent increase the previous year and a planned rise of 6.7 percent, a goal that had been revised downward. Agricultural output was 6 percent below 1974, which in turn was 3.7 percent below 1973. (*Pravda* and *NYT*, 1 February.)

The disastrous crop year of 1975 led to an expansion of the already massive grain imports from abroad and included orders for more than 16 million tons of U.S. grain for the first eight months of the 1975-76 marketing season, which began 1 October 1975 (BBC, 28 May). By July, the USSR had already ordered nearly 4.5 million tons of grain from the USA for the 1976-77 marketing year (*NYT*, 10 July) and was expected to meet the eight million ton annual ceiling imposed by the 1975 Soviet-U.S. grain agreement which came into force 1 October 1976 and possibly surpass that ceiling, with permission of the U.S. government. There were indications that the Soviet foreign trade deficit might run even higher than in 1975, when it had been $4.8 billion (*Le Monde*, Paris, 7 May). For the first quarter of 1976, the trade deficit was $1.7 billion (*NYT*, 5 June). Largely as a result of the grain sales, the trade balance with the United States for the first nine months of 1976 ran about 12 to 1 in favor of the United States (*NYT*, 1 December).

Despite the foreign grain purchases, there were reports of bread shortages in several regions of the country in the early months of 1976. Shortage of fodder led to the early slaughtering of cattle, which produced a temporary glut in meat supplies and subsequent shortages. By May, restaurants in Moscow, normally privileged in food distribution, were observing meatless Thursdays. Kiev was reportedly having two meatless days per week. Food riots were reported to have occurred in Rostov and Kiev, and there had been a docker's strike in Riga related to food shortages. (*Daily Telegraph*, London, 19 May.)

The seriousness of the situation was underscored by the sensitive reaction of *Pravda* in a 10 February article which charged that Western observers had distorted the Soviet agricultural situation and described the reports as the work of "bourgeois falsifiers." Soviet consumers could hardly have been cheered by the first-quarter plan fulfillment report which noted that food industry production was 99.5 percent of that for first quarter 1975 and meat and dairy industry production only 93 percent of quarterly production a year earlier (*Pravda* and *Izvestiia*, 26 April). At mid-year, food production reportedly had risen to 101 percent of the previous year's first half output but the meat and dairy industry had fallen further, to 91 percent (ibid., 24 July).

Meanwhile, the long-range problems of Soviet industry remained unresolved. Party and government meetings continued to regularly score management failures and certain branches of industry were particular trouble spots. Slowness in the completion of industrial projects posed a severe problem, especially in the Soviet north, Belorussia, and Kazakhstan (*Pravda*, 13, 18 June; *Christian Science Monitor*, 1 April; Moscow domestic service, 3 July, in *FBIS*, 4 August). Improved labor productivity had been scheduled to account for 87 percent of the projected increments in production under the Ninth Five-Year Plan but fell considerably short of that percentage for the actual increments, which were far below planned goals. Worker absenteeism has been a major factor in low productivity, and alcoholism has been identified as a significant reason for absenteeism. A 1975 study showed that in 1973, 52 million man-days were lost because of downtime and absenteeism, excused and unexcused; this works out to a rate of about 2 percent for the economy as a whole. The same study demonstrated that labor productivity at industrial enterprises is 20 to 30 percent lower on Mondays, days following holidays, and pay days; this was attributed to heavy drinking. (*Ekonomika i organizatsia promyshlennogo proizvodstva*, September-October 1975.) The "consumer revolt," the widespread rejection of shoddy merchandise leading to accumulation of huge unsold inventories, has apparently continued unabated. Despite the fact that Western observers estimate overall Soviet consumption levels as about one-third those in the USA, the increase in liquid savings has in recent years consistently run about double the rise in personal incomes.

The Tenth Five-Year Plan, released in draft form in December 1975 and approved in its finalized version at the 25th Party Congress, represented an attempt to cope with these and other economic problems, and was widely viewed by Western observers as more realistic in approach as well as more modest in goals than previous plans. The new plan provides for greater emphasis upon quality of production, lower industrial growth rates, stricter enforcement of labor discipline, and more extensive automation and use of computers. Heavy industry again takes priority, with a scheduled production rise of 38 to 42 percent against a 30 to 32 percent increase in consumer goods. For 1976, the projected rise in overall industrial output was 4.3 percent, the lowest planned growth rate since World War II. Investment in the agricultural sector was slated to account for 34 percent of all state investment through 1980. The first draft of the plan scheduled a 26 to 28 percent increase in food production; in the final version, this was scaled down to 23 to 25 percent. The plan calls for 85 to 90 percent of the planned increase in national income to be derived from a rise in labor productivity. Given the failure of the economy in the Ninth Five-Year Plan to meet approximately the same proportional increase in productivity, realization of this part of the plan appeared highly unlikely, despite the lower production goals. (*Pravda*, 3 December 1975, 1 February 1976; *Washington Post*, 11 January; TASS, 30 January; *Izvestiia*, 2 March.)

General Secretary Brezhnev, in his keynote address to the 25th CPSU Congress, gave highest priority to the emphasis upon efficiency and quality in the new plan. He promised a doubling of material and financial resources between 1976 and 1990, and stated that real income had doubled in the last 15 years. Brezhnev offered general criticism of planning and management in the economy and called attention to specific shortcomings of medical and health agencies (*Pravda*, 25 February). He also rebuked light industry for failing to adequately meet needs of consumers, as did Prime Minister Kosygin in his report for the government.

Kosygin asserted that the USSR had made important gains in its economic competition with capitalism. Since the second half of 1974, according to Kosygin, the capitalist world had been in the grip of "a profound economic crisis," "an organic disease of the capitalist system," marked by inflation and unemployment, in contrast to the USSR's full employment and stable retail prices. He said that between 1971 and 1976 Soviet industrial output had grown at an average annual rate of 7.4 percent, compared with a 1.2 percent annual rate in the USA and the European Common Market countries. However, his identification of severe problems in the Soviet economy tended to negate his optimistic assessment of Soviet strength in the competition between differing economic systems. In addition to inferior quality of consumer goods and the agricultural shortfall, which he attributed to bad weather and shortcomings in mechanization, Kosygin pointed out that in certain sectors of industry only 60 to 80 percent of the planned targets had been reached and that billions of rubles were lost each year through mismanagement. He emphasized the failure to "eradicate bottlenecks existing in the national economy," particularly in the area of capital construction. (Ibid., 2 March.) These criticisms were remarkably similar to those contained in a Central Committee statement in early 1975, indicating that little had changed during the year.

State Planning Committee (*Gosplan*) chairman Nikolai V. Baibakov spelled out graphically the crucial role of labor productivity in the new plan in a March interview. According to Baibakov, an increase of only one percent in output from existing fixed capital would insure a rise in the national production over the five-year plan sufficient for the construction of housing for 2-2.5 million families (*Sotsialisticheskaia Industriia*, 31 March, in *FBIS*, 7 April).

Planners and party leaders continued to pursue a middle course in the structural realignment of the economy but, as usual, the "centralizers" were somewhat favored by the very nature of the system in matters of organization. All major efforts at rationalization of the economy since Stalin's time, particularly the Liberman reforms of the mid-1960s, have stressed the wastefulness associated with excessive centralization; on the other hand, drastic decentralization measures tend to pose problems of political control for the party leadership. Consequently, the middle-level concentration envisioned in organizational reforms announced in 1973 continued to be stressed; this planning approach features industrial associations, which group related factories into large corporations, and the development of territorial-production complexes, or macroregions (ibid., 1 July, in *FBIS*, 9 July). According to V. Mozhin, director of the RSFSR *Gosplan* Central Economic Scientific Research Institute, "at the present stage of the country's development the national economy's production capacity has reached a level enabling us to resolve comprehensively tasks covering whole economic regions" (*Izvestiia*, 9 April).

On the agricultural front, the leadership took a major step toward middle-level concentration with a June Central Committee resolution that called for the transfer of agriculture to a "modern industrial base" and replacement of the mixed system of collective farming by "agro-industrial complexes," large specialized enterprises of an industrial type responsible for production, storing, processing, joint building schemes, land reclamation, and other work (*Pravda* and *Izvestiia*, 2 June). The shift had been under way in Moldavia and several other places on an experimental basis for more than a decade. Progress in this reform effort has been slowed by the reluctance of farm managers and agricultural bureaucrats to scrap traditional methods and start over; moreover, many regions, lacking the natural advantages of the fertile Moldavian countryside, have neither the funds nor the personnel to spare on reforms while struggling to maintain existing output. Nevertheless, party spokesmen have claimed that in the 6,000 farms where agro-industrial techniques have been applied, labor productivity has more than doubled and costs have been cut nearly in half (*Washington Post*, 22 July). One indication of less than total commitment to "agro-industry" and of continued experimentation in the agricultural sector is the fact that one of the key farming areas in the Soviet Union, the Stavropol region in the northern Caucasus, has decided to go over completely to the system of mechanized "link-farming" (*Ekonomicheskaia gazeta*, no. 20, May). Under this system, a team of peasants is assigned a specific area of farmland and given full responsibility for it, with pay according to production. Some links have reportedly grown yields four times as large as those produced by conventional collective farming (BBC, 2 July). However, the "link system" has been extremely controversial in the past and its ideologically suspect emphasis upon individual self-interest will no doubt continue to evoke opposition from hard-lining party leaders.

Despite continuing problems, the 1976 harvest surpassed the planned goal of 207 million tons production. At the beginning of the year, the main Soviet farmers' journal reported a lack of snow cover in the Baltic republics, the Western part of the Russian federation, and almost the whole Ukraine (*Selskaia Zhizn'*, 4 January). The RSFSR Central Statistical Administration reported in July that much less grain had been harvested than at the corresponding date a year earlier, but that grain had ripened much more slowly in 1976 (Moscow domestic service, 20 July, in *FBIS*, 21 July). It was reported at the same time that in the Ukraine's Nikolaev *oblast'* only 22 percent of the planned area had been seeded for the second time (Kiev domestic service, 20 July, in *FBIS*, 21 July). The usual party-government decree on harvesting, issued in May, conveyed an impression of urgency, calling for "round-the-clock" work by trucks transporting grain and other agricultural produce (*Pravda*, 22 May). Brezhnev expressed optimism about the harvest in a television interview in October, predicting that Soviet farmers would bring in "a very good grain crop" (*NYT*, 6 October). This optimism was not ill-founded; it was reported on 25 October that the harvest had already yielded 216 million tons and might reach a total of 222 million (*Pravda*, 26 October).

The Central Statistical Administration's mid-year economic report, issued in July, claimed an increment in industrial production of 5.0 percent in comparison with the corresponding period of 1975, against the planned figure of 4.3 percent. Production of consumer goods was less impressive, with a reported rise of 3.0 percent, compared with the planned increase of 2.7 percent. Labor productivity grew by 3.5 percent, with almost three-fourths of the increment in industrial volume accounted for by higher productivity; however, this proportion fell well short of the 85 to 90 percent productivity share of increased production envisioned in the plan. The machine tool industry, given special emphasis in the plan, reportedly increased production by 10 percent; however, other machinery production grew at a slower place. Among the union-republics, the lowest production increases were recorded by Kazakhstan, Tadzhikistan, and Turkmenistan. The poorest results of labor productivity were found in Kazakhstan, Moldavia, Turkmenistan, and Tadzhikistan. For Tadzhikistan, the government reported a decline in labor productivity (*Pravda* and *Izvestiia*, 24 July).

Increasing concern was displayed by the Soviet authorities during the year over the incidence of economic crime. Many cases of "theft of socialist property," fraud, and embezzlement were reported in the press, notably a vegetable produce swindle in Azerbaidzhan involving 64 people that cost the government nine million rubles and the diversion of more than 750,000 rubles' worth of fashionable fabric from a textile factory in Lithuania for bootleg resale in Georgia (*NYT*, 8 April). Violent crime is not widespread in the USSR, but has grown sufficiently in recent years to arouse alarm; much of this the authorities attribute to alcoholism (*Pravda*, 20 July). In January, Ukrainian first secretary Shcherbitsky denounced the "conciliatory attitude toward manifestations of hooliganism, alcoholism, grubbing practices, and profiteering" (Kiev domestic service, 25 January, in *FBIS*, 29 January). A Soviet youth journal reported a serious drinking problem among people and attributed it to the prevalence of boredom (*Znamia Iunosti*, May). Several articles in the military newspaper *Krasnaia Zvezda* cited the same reason for the alarming increase in alcoholism among the armed forces (*Christian Science Monitor*, 24 May). The average Russian consumes twice as much alcohol as the world's next biggest consumers, Americans and Frenchmen. The official concern with alcoholism is motivated primarily by the adverse effect on labor productivity, noted above. Measures initiated in 1972, including limitation on bar open hours and the raising of prices, have apparently had little effect on consumption. More stringent measures face obvious difficulties: drinking serves as an outlet for discontents and, perhaps more important, the sale of liquor provides about 12 percent of the state revenues.

Issuance of new internal passports began with much fanfare in January. Over a period of six years, Soviet citizens are to receive new identification documents as the USSR adopts a universal registration system reflecting what party spokesmen call "the profound democratization of our country" (*Baltimore Sun*, 10 January; *Kommunist*, April). The "democratization" of the passport system is its extension to all citizens 16 years old and older, including peasants who were previously generally excluded from the system, and the removal from the documents of any reference to occupational status.

Dissent. The democratic protest movement has persisted stubbornly in its opposition to regime policies, despite the monumental pressures brought to bear against it, and during 1976 even added some prominent personalities to its ranks, notably the historian Aleksandr Nekrich and the linguist I. A. Mel'cuk. However, the regime continued its inflexible hard line toward dissent and further contained the protest movement by arrests, trials, exiles, and other forms of pressure. Apparently satisfied with the results of the exiling of Aleksandr Solzhenitsyn in 1974, the regime applied the same punishment to two other major critics, Leonid Plyushch and Andrei Amalrik. At home, the dissidents have been unable to extend their influence beyond a rather limited circle of intellectuals. However, their activities have adversely affected the Soviet image abroad, and the year 1976 was marked by continuing protests in the West against Soviet internal repression, particularly in regard to the confinement of political dissidents in psychiatric institutions; objections were voiced even by some Western Communists.

At the beginning of the year, the USSR felt a Western backlash from the December 1975 sentencing of Sergei Kovalev to seven years of strict-regime labor camp and three years of Siberian exile. Kovalev, a biologist and member of the Soviet chapter of Amnesty International, had been charged with helping to compile the major *samizdat* publication, *The Chronicle of Current Events*, and with the distribution of copies of Solzhenitzyn's *Gulag Archipelago*. Two dissident priests, Fathers Dmitri Dudko and Gleb Yukinin, had been removed from their posts shortly after the Kovalev trial, arousing further Western concern about religious liberty in the USSR. (*Baltimore Sun* and *NYT*, 30 December 1975.)

Leonid Plyushch, formerly a member of the Committee for Human Rights headed by Andrei Sakharov, was exiled in early January after two and a half years of confinement in a mental hospital. The release and deportation of Plyushch followed a personal appeal from Georges Marchais, head of the French Communist Party, and a statement in *L'Humanité*, its newspaper, condemning the treatment of Plyushch (BBC, 10 January). Plyushch arrived in Vienna on 10 January, looking frail and trembling (*NYT*, 11 January); subsequently he was granted political asylum in France. Shortly after his arrival in France, Plyushch issued a statement confirming earlier reports about the perversion of psychiatric treatment for political purposes in the USSR. Plyushch said that he had been diagnosed as suffering from "sluggish schizophrenia" and had been subjected to injections of the drugs haloperidol and triftazin and to insulin therapy. He said that there had been 60 other political prisoners in the hospital where he was confined and these were mixed with criminally insane murderers and rapists and were harassed by doctors acting as political interrogators. "The savage persecution of dissidents in the Soviet Union," Plyushch declared, "is a shameful taint on the bright ideals of Communism." (Ibid., 4 February). Encouraged by the intervention of Marchais in the Plyushch case, the mother of Vladimir Bukovsky, prominent civil rights activist sentenced to 12 years of prison and internal exile in 1972, appealed to the French party chief for his assistance in attempts to obtain the release of her son (*Le Monde*, 8 January). Bukovsky was freed in mid-December in exchange for the release of the imprisoned general secretary of the Chilean Comunist Party, Luis Corvalan. The exchange, believed to be the first involving political prisoners, was proposed by Andrei Sakharov, while the United States acted as intermediary between the countries. Bukovsky and Corvalan were exchanged at Zurich airport (*NYT*, 18, 19 December).

Faced with mounting criticisms of Soviet violations of the human rights provisions of the 1975 Helsinki agreement and with possible discord in international Communist ranks as plans for the summer parley of Communist Parties in Berlin proceeded, the regime responded with two major statements of rebuttal. In an article in *Izvestiia* (31 January), Vladimir A. Kuroyedov, chairman of the government's Council for Religious Affairs, branded as "enemies of détente" those who circulated the "filthy fable" that freedom of conscience is restricted in the USSR. He specifically denied Soviet government responsibility for the sanctions against Fathers Dudko and Yakunin, although the dissident priests had been guilty of "antisocial sermons" and "unseemly activity." "All in all," said Kuroyedov, "our country is doing all it can to assure freedom of conscience and we have every right to state that our legislation on religious cults is the most humane and democratic in the world. It equally guarantees the interests of believers and nonbelievers." However, a few days after the Kuroyedov statement, the official press in Belorussia reported prison sentences for several Jehovah's Witnesses found guilty of copying articles from the Western publication *Watchtower* and maintaining secret chapels (*NYT*, 1 March).

On the eve of the 25th CPSU Congress, from which Marchais was conspicuously absent (see below), an article entitled "About Genuine and Imaginary Freedoms" appeared in *Pravda* (20 February), signed "I. Aleksandrov," understood to be a pseudonym used by the Central Committee for policy statements. The article conceded that some individuals in the USSR who oppose Communist ideology are prosecuted in the courts but only for "actions that break the law." It contended that the Soviet people oppose granting freedom of action to those who "damage socialist society and national security." Charges that dissidents are confined in psychiatric hospitals without medical cause were rejected as "slanderous" assertions: "Soviet medicine guarantees that only persons with psychiatric disorders are subjected to treatment, but it cannot guarantee that the so-called dissidents will not be among them." Responding to Western charges of Soviet stalling on the humanitarian provisions of the Helsinki agreement, the article said that 5,500 Soviet citizens who married foreigners in recent years had been allowed to depart to live in 110 different countries and that 98.4 of those who asked to emigrate between 1970 and 1975 had been allowed to leave.

At the height of the furor over human rights violations, General Secretary Brezhnev went out of his way at the 25th CPSU Congress to pay homage to the early Bolshevik Feliks Dzerzhinsky, founder of the Soviet secret police and first architect of state terror. The state security agencies reliably protect Soviet society against subversive actions, Brezhnev said, "on the basis of strict observance of constitutional norms and socialist legality." Further, "our Chekists cherish and develop the traditions started by the knight of the Revolution, Feliks Dzerzhinsky" (ibid., 25 February).

This signal was followed in April by the conviction of two prominent dissidents on charges of "anti-Soviet slander." Mustafa Dzhemilev—a long-time campaigner for rehabilitation of the Crimea Tatars persecuted and exiled by Stalin, and one of the founders of the Committee for Human Rights—was sentenced in Omsk to two and a half years in a labor camp. Andrei Tverdokhlebov, secretary of the Soviet branch of Amnesty International, was sentenced in Moscow to five years of internal exile; the prosecution's case reportedly mainly concerned public statements by the accused affirming the sanity of Leonid Plyushch (*NYT*, 15 April). Supporters of Tverdokhlebov expressed relief at the comparatively lenient sentence. More than 380 Soviet citizens signed appeals on behalf of Dzhemilev, to no avail. (Ibid., 21 April).

In July, Andrei Amalrik was exiled from the Soviet Union via the legal route of forced "emigration to Israel," although in fact the Soviet authorities agreed to a direct flight to the Netherlands by Amalrik and his wife. Neither Amalrik nor his wife are Jewish but, as he explained to reporters, emigration to Israel gives the appearance of a nationality problem rather than political protest. (Ibid., 16 July.) Amalrik had been imprisoned twice and had served two terms of exile in Siberia. During his lecture tour in the United States, Amalrik met on 23 December with the Secretary of State-designate, Cyrus R. Vance. He reportedly urged the incoming Carter administration to develop a toughned, long-term program of accommodation with Moscow that would gradually lead to a more democratic society in the Soviet Union (ibid., 23 December).

Nine Soviet dissidents announced in May the formation of a group to monitor Soviet compliance with the Helsinki declaration and to report human rights violations to other signatory countries. The organization, named the Public Group to Assist the Fulfillment of the Helsinki Accords in the USSR, was headed by Yuri Orlov, a scientist, and included among its members Yelena Sakharov, wife of Andrei Sakharov, and former Major-General Piotr Grigorenko. Sakharov was not a member but announced his support. (Ibid., 14 May.) Orlov was taken into brief custody by the KGB and warned that members of the group could face legal action for their "unconstitutional activity." The Soviet news agency TASS issued a statement calling formation of the group "another provocation aimed at hampering the process of relaxation of tension" and its actions "inadmissible." (*Daily Telegraph*, London, 17 May.) Despite the threats, the group continued its work and its third report, issued on 18 June, asserted that the Soviet government was inflicting "physical and moral torture" of hunger and cold on prisoners of conscience. The report also charged the Soviet government with blocking reunification of internationally split Jewish families and with depriving some religious parents of their children. (*Christian Science Monitor*, 21 June.)

Sakharov, the best-known dissident remaining in the USSR, continued to be harassed by the authorities. After the refusal of the government to allow him to travel to Oslo to receive his Nobel Peace Prize in late 1975, he encountered difficulties over his residence permit in Moscow (BBC, 19 January). He was regularly denounced by the Soviet press as a traitor and supporter of Western imperialism, and in April was arrested on a charge of striking a policeman outside the courtroom where Dzhemilev was tried in Omsk, but was shortly released (*NYT*, 15 April). Sakharov's son-in-law,

Efrem Yankelevich, has been denied permission to continue his studies at Moscow State University and reportedly has been threatened with jail (ibid., 8 August).

In an August interview with Western newsmen, Sakharov displayed pessimism about the future of human rights in the USSR. Sakharov charged that violence inspired by the KGB had been responsible for the deaths of several dissident intellectuals and for serious physical assaults upon others. He described the Soviet intelligentsia as broadly sympathetic to dissidents but too straitjacketed to show it, found no serious gap between the intelligentsia and the man in the street, and saw little hope that the next generation of political leaders might allow more freedom. (*Christian Science Monitor*, 10 August.) One minor hint of liberalization appeared in November when Eduard Fedotov, a religious activist who had been confined in a psychiatric institution, and three other dissidents were released from custody. (Associated Press, 22 November.)

The leadership appeared to have largely succeeded in one aspect of its anti-dissent policy that has been little publicized in the West, the strengthening of control over principal cultural organizations. The Writers Union has been rather thoroughly purged of dissidents, and at its Sixth Congress, in June, "anti-Soviet" writers were roundly denounced. Party supervision of literature was emphasized by the presence of practically the entire Politburo, led by Brezhnev, at the opening session of the Congress (BBC, 25 June). The USSR Academy of Sciences had been somewhat slow in purging dissidents from its ranks, and its 250th anniversary celebration, scheduled for 1974, was postponed for eighteen months. Under Anatoly P. Aleksandrov, a Central Committee member named to head the Academy in late 1975, the organization apparently regained its ideological "soundness" and its effectiveness as a "transmission belt" for the party. Aleksandrov gave one of the opening speeches at the 25th CPSU Congress and pledged full support by scientists for the party's program (TASS, 26 February, in *FBIS*, 2 March).

International Views and Policies. In the international arena, the Soviet Union suffered some setbacks during the year, notably in the Middle East, but displayed an increasingly aggressive posture in line with perceptions of Soviet movement toward the status of the world's number one superpower. While the Soviet leaders made some tactical concessions in relations with the USA and with the non-ruling Communist parties of Western Europe and offered tentative gestures of conciliation to the post-Mao leadership of China, the general approach to world affairs emphasized growing Soviet military power and an activist stance toward a number of international issues under the slogan of "proletarian internationalism." This included refinement and application of recently developed formulations concerning consolidation of the East European bloc and acceleration of support for national liberation movements.Soviet spokesmen explained the present USSR role in world affairs in terms of a further intensification of the struggle between capitalist and socialist systems and a continuing change in the "correlation of forces" in favor of the socialist system.

Détente continued to be the tactical centerpiece of Soviet world policy, but greater difficulties were encountered in its application than at any time since the Yom Kippur war of 1973. Specific problems arose over charges of Soviet violations of the strategic arms limitation (SALT I) agreements and the Helsinki Conference on Security and Cooperation in Europe (CSCE) accords, but the overriding reason for the slowing of processes of détente was the growing perception in the West, especially in the USA, that earlier agreements had been one-sidedly favorable to the USSR. Détente became a heated issue in the U.S. presidential primaries, leading U.S. President Gerald R. Ford to drop the word "détente" from his public statements (*NYT*, 2 March). Georgi A. Arbatov, director of the Institute for the United States and Canada, dismissed pronouncements made in political campaigns as "unreliable indicators" of U.S. policy. He said that attitudes expressed both in Congress and among the public indicated that "the cold war is quite an unacceptable alternative" for the USA. (Moscow domestic television service, 23 March, in *FBIS*, 2 April.) Arbatov had earlier denounced "fantasies" in the USA about a "Communist conspiracy" and a "Soviet menace," but said that prospects for improved relations were good if the USA would avoid "saber rattling" (*Pravda*, 2 April).

Other Soviet spokesmen painted U.S policy in darker colors, but Arbatov, who is reputed to be very close to Brezhnev, apparently reflected the General Secretary's interest in assuring that the tremendous political capital he had invested in the policy of détente would not be dissipated. Brezhnev clearly was eager for further agreements with the USA in the area of arms limitations, and Soviet leaders could not lightly discount the continuing need for U.S. food and technology. However, the USSR made it clear that concessions to the USA in the name of détente would not under any circumstances extend to sacrifice of its vital interests and its incessant drive for world leadership.

Soviet support for the Cuban intervention in Angola provided a clear demonstration of Moscow's disdain for the U.S. view of détente. The U.S. Congress refused President Ford's belated request for support for anti-Soviet factions, and on 5 January Ford announced that the USA would not use food as a weapon to pressure the Soviets on the Angolan intervention (*Los Angeles Times*, 6 January). Realistically appraising the situation as one of low risks and potentially major gains, the Soviet leadership stepped up aid to the pro-Soviet forces. By January 1976, more than 10,000 Cuban troops had been airlifted to Angola to assist the Popular Movement for the Liberation of Angola (MPLA), and both Cuban and MPLA forces were heavily armed with Soviet equipment. As the Soviet-backed forces rapidly completed the rout of their opponents, U.S. Secretary of State Henry Kissinger issued a stern warning to the USSR and Cuba in testimony before the Senate Foreign Relations Committee on 29 January (*NYT*, 30 January). On the same day, certain of success, the Soviet government blithely indicated its willingness to accept a political settlement in Angola (*Izvestiia*, 29 January). The Soviet leadership rejected Kissinger's warning and criticized it and his subsequent protests as inimical to détente (*Pravda*, 1, 5 February, 14 May).

As Cuban troops were gradually withdrawn and the MPLA established itself as a regular government, the USSR sought to consolidate its foothold in black Africa. On 31 May the Soviet government agreed to provide Angola with additional military assistance and Prime Minister Kosygin signed a "declaration of the principles of friendly cooperation between the USSR and the People's Republic of Angola" (ibid., 1 June). On 8 October a treaty of friendship and cooperation was signed by Brezhnev and Angolan President Agostinho Neto after two days of talks. This was the first treaty concluded by the Kremlin with a South African state. At the same time, a separate agreement was signed on cooperation between the CPSU and the MPLA. (*Washington Post*, 9 October.)

Acrimony over fulfillment of the Helsinki agreements and other issues interpreted by the USSR as tied to détente continued to color Soviet-U.S. relations. The Soviet record on the Helsinki accords was defended via a two-pronged counterattack. On the one hand, KGB head Yuri Andropov maintained that there was no agreement to "support efforts to harm socialism in support of the plans of reactionary circles" (*Pravda* and *Izvestiia*, 23 April). On the other hand, party chief Brezhnev claimed that the Soviet record on cultural exchanges was superior to that of the Western countries. In his speech at the Berlin meeting of Communist parties, Brezhnev maintained that the USSR's showing of Western films and TV programs and publication of Western books far exceeded the bourgeois countries' corresponding issuance of Soviet works (TASS, 29 June).

When U.S. Secretary of State Kissinger warned that the USA could not support a country in the NATO area that permits Communists in its government, *Pravda* charged that this violated the Helsinki agreement (*Pravda*, 18 April). When both U.S. presidential candidates opened fire on the Soviet pattern of control in Eastern Europe following a controversial remark by President Ford in the second campaign debate in October, Soviet spokesmen responded with arguments similar to those used against Kissinger in April. In addition to the Soviet linkage of Kissinger's approach on Angola with the deterioration of détente noted above, the Secretary's efforts to effect a peaceful transition to majority rule in Rhodesia were scored as manifestations of imperialism and neocolonialism, particularly when these efforts gave promise of an early settlement (*Izvestiia*, 14 August). Further, a warning containing the usual themes of the general foreign policy line indicated above was issued in April concerning possible military intervention by the USA in Lebanon (*Pravda*, 8 April). Soviet spokesmen reiterated on numerous occasions during the year the thesis that there is no co-existence in the ideological area or where a national liberation struggle breaks out. From these exchanges and pronouncements, a basic position on Soviet-U.S. relations clearly emerged: Soviet support for West European Communist parties and intervention to promote national liberation movements do not constitute violations of détente, but U.S. actions to sustain anti-Soviet or anti-"progressive" forces anywhere threaten the framework of détente and are viewed as "imperialist resistance to the restructuring of international relations" (*Sovetskaia Kultura*, 20 February). Eastern Europe is a special case. Here the Helsinki agreement is seen as legitimizing the status quo and ruling out of bounds any Western attempt to influence developments. This double standard fully accords with the Soviet reassertion of the "two camps" doctrine in recent years and the crediting of détente to Soviet success in the "diplomatic struggle of the two worlds."

A rather bizarre diplomatic episode added another source of friction in Soviet-U.S. relations early in the year. It was reported that for several years sophisticated Soviet electronic mechanisms had been directed against the U.S. Embassy in Moscow to disrupt communications equipment, causing unusually high levels of radiation on the upper floors and endangering the health of personnel. This report produced a brief sensation in the U.S. press, and there were indications of exceptionally low morale among Embassy staff members. An *Izvestiia* editorial on 19 February denounced the charge as a "fabrication" and claimed that the level of the ambient electromagnetic field in the U.S. Embassy was considerably lower than the minimum sanitary norm in effect in the USSR and several times lower than the allowable level of electromagnetic radiation in the USA. Although the U.S. press made a convincing case for the charge, the U.S. State Department played down the incident and sought to resolve the matter through quiet diplomacy.

The Soviet ambassador in Washington delivered a note to the State Department in early May expressing the USSR's displeasure over the 13 April unilateral declaration prohibiting foreign fishing within 200 miles of the U.S. coast. *Pravda* (6 May) said that the action "goes directly against efforts to reach mutually acceptable decisions" at the UN Conference on the Law of the Sea. The Soviet press also spoke out against U.S. handling of the Panama Canal issue. *Pravda* (5 May) reported that negotiations with Panama had been brought to the "verge of rupture" by a campaign of U.S. rightists to prevent concessions. According to *Pravda*, the USA sought "to impose on Panama a new variation of the one-sided treaty and thereby reaffirm its "right" to undivided rule over a part of the territory of an independent country."

Disarmament talks continued at various levels during the year, with minimal progress. When the 30-nation disarmament conference ended its spring session in Geneva in April, there had been no break in the deadlock on prohibition of all nuclear tests. The USSR continued to insist that "national means of verification" are adequate to monitor a ban of all nuclear tests, while the USA maintained its position that some on-site inspection is necessary (*Washington Star*, 23 April). However, the Soviet government had already sent out a strong signal that it was interested in arriving at an early agreement on the issue. When the date (31 March) for the entering into force of the 1974 treaty on underground tests, which banned all explosions for military purposes but contained no inspection provisions, passed without U.S. Senate ratification of the pact, Moscow announced that it would take no actions incompatible with the provisions of the draft treaty, "with the understanding that the United States will act in a similar manner." At the same time, *Pravda* (2 April) expressed the hope that "mutual energetic efforts will be made for the earliest possible conclusion of an agreement on underground nuclear explosions for peaceful purposes and for putting the treaty of 3 July 1974 into effect." Thereafter the pace of negotiations quickened and on 28 May, the USA and the USSR signed a treaty limiting underground nuclear explosions for peaceful purposes (*NYT*, 29 May).

The five-year treaty sets a ceiling of 150 kilotons for any single underground explosion or any series of explosions and allows a series of explosions up to 1,500 kilotons. A system of on-site inspection is provided for if the yield exceeds 150 kilotons. The Soviet agreement on the matter of on-site inspections appeared to be a substantial concession, but the U.S. Senate failed to take ratification action prior to its fall adjournment. A Soviet memorandum made public at the UN in late September hinted at Soviet willingness to compromise further on the issue of on-site inspection. However, U.S. spokesmen indicated that this matter was not discussed in the lengthy White House meeting between President Ford and Soviet Foreign Minister Andrei A. Gromyko on 1 October (*Washington Post*, 6 October).

In the matter of arms limitation in Europe, Brezhnev announced that the Soviet Union was prepared to accept in 1976 force reductions for the USSR and the USA only, while the level of the armed forces of the other participants in the disarmament talks would remain frozen and could not be cut until the second stage, in 1977-78. Brezhnev said that the USSR had also submitted very specific proposals on reductions by both sides in the number of tanks, planes carrying nuclear weapons, missile launchers, and specified amounts of nuclear ammunition for these delivery vehicles (*Pravda* 25 February). The two-stage Soviet approach was rejected and the ninth round of the Vienna talks on mutual reduction of armed forces and armaments in Central Europe ended in July with no agreement. The major stumbling block continued to be the Soviet insistence upon numerical parity and the understandable Western concern about the geographical proximity of massive Soviet forces outside the area covered in the talks. In a post-mortem on the Vienna conclave, *Izvestiia* (24 July) charged that the Western countries continued to seek unilateral military advantages, citing a Western proposal for the selective withdrawal of 29,000 military personnel of the NATO countries and a reduction three times as large in troops of the socialist countries. Moreover, *Izvestiia* said, "The Western participants, with the exception of the United States, do not want to commit themselves to the reduction of armed forces and armaments."

Progress on SALT II and efforts to achieve a follow-up agreement to the Vladivostok accord foundered on the issue of inclusion of the U.S. Cruise missile and the Soviet Backfire bomber in the ceiling of 2,400 delivery systems set at the November 1974 summit conference. During Kissinger's negotiating visit to Moscow in January, an understanding reportedly was reached that the Backfire would be excluded from the ceiling, provided that the bombers were not positioned within easy striking distance of the USA. Subsequently, U.S. intelligence reported that the Backfire had a longer unrefueled range than previously believed. The USA then moved to exclude both the Cruise missile and the Backfire from the ceiling on delivery systems, a proposal rejected by the Soviet government in a formal note in March. The USA did not reply to the Soviet note, and SALT II was allowed to languish during the spring and summer as President Ford came under heavy fire on détente policy in his bid for the Republican presidential nomination. On 21 September, the SALT II talks were resumed in Geneva, with no new U.S. proposals or concessions (*NYT*, 22 September).

CPSU chief Brezhnev, in his 20 September interview with W. Averell Harriman, expressed disappointment that a second agreement on limiting strategic nuclear arms had not been reached with the USA. Brezhnev said that he favored setting a fixed ceiling on strategic nuclear arms, then negotiating later to lower it; otherwise, he offered no specifics (*Christian Science Monitor*, 21 September). U.S. officials quickly seized upon this signal and, in conversations with Gromyko in New York and Washington within the following ten days, Kissinger and Ford offered a proposal almost identical to the one rejected in March. Under terms of the proposal, the Cruise missile and the Backfire would be excluded from the 2,400 ceiling, which would be extended to 1985 upon expiration of the interim agreement in October 1977; the negotiators in Geneva would be allowed to complete terms for agreement on issues already settled. Another Soviet turndown followed, but U.S. spokesmen said that both sides were actively pursuing agreement and that negotiations would continue (AP, 8 October). In the second presidential campaign debate, which followed his conversation with Gromyko by five days, President Ford said that the Cruise missile could be included in a treaty but that the USA must insist, at the same time, on limiting the Backfire bomber (*NYT*, 7 October).

At the October Central Committee plenum, Brezhnev accused capitalist "aggressive circles" of frantically building up armaments and charged the USA with dragging its feet in important arms-limitation negotiations. "Matters are actually at a standstill in such an important question of Soviet-U.S. relations as the drafting of a new long-term agreement on the limitation of offensive strategic weapons, although the main content of this document was agreed upon at summit level already late in 1974," Brezhnev told the plenum. "Having received our latest proposals on the remaining questions already in March of this year, the American side has not yet given an answer to them." (TASS, 25 October.) Following the American presidential elections, Brezhnev reiterated this appeal, directing it to the incoming Carter Administration at a Kremlin dinner for 150 American business and government executives. "We believe it is high time," Brezhnev said, "to put an end to the freeze imposed on this question by Washington almost a year ago." He appealed to the Democratic Administration "to act in the same spirit" (*NYT*, 1 December). An unsurprising rebuff from the outgoing Republican Administration followed in early December, when Secretary of State Kissinger in his farewell message to the North Atlantic Treaty Organization urged rejection of a Warsaw Pact proposal that the two blocs agree by treaty not to be the first to use nuclear weapons. Kissinger also said that growing Soviet military power is the "greatest long-term threat facing the West" (AP, 9 December).

Although Brezhnev's October and November speeches indicated urgent concern, the USSR could well afford from the military-strategic standpoint to wait for an agreement, considering its seemingly inexorable movement toward superiority in virtually every category of armament. Soviet military forces expanded their advantages in missile arms, especially in throw-weight, with the deployment of four new types of missiles and the Y-class ships carrying 16 SLBMs since 1974; moreover, ten additional ICBM systems and two more SLBMs were projected (*Air Force*, March 1976). When the aircraft carrier *Kiev*, the first of a projected fleet of six, took up station in the Mediterranean in May, a milestone was reached in the massive expansion of the Soviet navy. The military buildup went on at a near frantic pace in other categories of arms and was hardly compatible with a goal of mere parity with the USA. Brezhnev told the 25th CPSU Congress that the USSR was not increasing its military budget (*Pravda*, 25 February), a claim universally disputed by Western military analysts. U.S. Central Intelligence Agency director George Bush, in secret Congressional testimony of May 1976, made public in October, estimated that Soviet military spending during the period 1970-75 increased at a rate of 4 to 5 percent a year and that Soviet military spending was 11 to 13 percent of the USSR's GNP, against about 6 percent for the USA. For 1975, Bush said, Soviet defense spending was about 42 percent higher than U.S. defense authorizations. (*Washington Post* and AP, 6 October.)

There was obvious concern among the Soviet political leadership about this heavy burden of armaments upon an economy reeling from recent reverses. In his Lenin Anniversary speech in April, KGB chief Andropov said that it is easier for the new society to build under conditions of "a diminished arms burden" (*Pravda* and *Izvestiia*, 23 April). Amid widespread speculation that the military leaders were exerting pressure for a faster tempo of arms expansion than desired by the top political figures, it was in fact military men who frequently sounded the loudest calls for increased struggle against imperialism and the use of détente as a weapon in that struggle. Lieutenant General S. Bobylev, chief of the Political Directorate of the Air Defense Forces, said that "even with the new correlation of forces, the class nature of imperialism remains unchanged," and that the NATO countries were continuing the arms race and increasing their military expenditures. "Under these conditions," said Bobylev, "the CPSU Central Committee is doing everything necessary to consolidate the country's defense and further raise the combat might of the Soviet armed forces." (*Sovetskaia Kultura*, 20 February.) General A. Yepishev, head of the Soviet Army and Navy Main Political Directorate, said that the further intensification of the general crisis of capitalism meant that "the reactionary circles of imperialism are ready to resort to the most extreme means and are urging on the arms race by every method" (*Sovetskaia Rossiia*, 23 February, in *FBIS*, 27 February).

While military spokesmen usually dwelt upon the necessity for bigger and more effective armaments, there was also appreciation of the efficaciousness of political methods. A January article in *Krasnaia Zvezda* quoted approvingly a Western writer who maintained that the atmosphere of détente leads the West to underestimate the USSR, reduce arms budgets, and allow alliances to fall apart. "As a result," the Soviet Army paper said, "the balance of power will change further in favor of the Soviet Union," leading to "the demoralization of the West and to a Soviet victory." (*Christian Science Monitor*, 19 February.) If there was indeed a conflict between the military and political leaderships, it was clearly over the economy of means and not a difference on the goal of Soviet primacy. The clearest indication of the aim of primacy not parity indeed came from the political leadership. During the lengthy debate on allocation of resources in the latter part of 1975, Foreign Secretary Gromyko had written in *Kommunist* (September) that "the forces of peace and progress have a visibly increased preponderance" over their "imperialist" opponents and may soon be able to "lay down the direction of international politics."

As usual, long-time party secretary for ideology Mikhail A. Suslov was in the forefront of ideological reformulation related to Soviet world policies. It was Suslov whose July 1975 speech on the 40th anniversary of the Seventh Comintern Congress had marked a new phase in the ideological offensive under the banner of "proletarian internationalism." For the remainder of 1975 and throughout 1976, "proletarian internationalism" was the watchword of Soviet world revolutionary rhetoric. The phrase has in the past been taken to mean the solidarity of the world revolutionary movement, the absence of any distinction between particular party and national interests and those of international communism, and, at least implicitly, the primacy of the CPSU and the Soviet Union in the world movement. This usage was maintained in the pronouncements of Suslov and other Soviet spokesmen, and it was clear from Gromyko's September 1975 *Kommunist* article, from Brezhnev's negative response to French President Valery Giscard d'Estaing's call for a suspension of ideological conflict in October 1975, and from Suslov's remarks on 26 December 1975 reaffirming détente as a form of class struggle (*Le Monde*, 5 January) that a period of revolutionary flow under the leadership of the CPSU and the Soviet Union was envisaged. Détente and the crisis of capitalism had created favorable conditions for the construction of socialism, the success of national liberation movements, and the general expansion of Soviet power. There was confusion, however, on the specific tactics to be used in the application of "proletarian internationalism," whether it was to be the approach of "Popular Front" or "class against class," or some combination of the two.

Konstantin Zarodov's much publicized August 1975 *Pravda* article had criticized parliamentary methods and had called for direct revolutionary action among the masses (see *YICA, 1976*, p. 66). Meanwhile, Soviet analysts continued to emphasize the "two camps" classification that grouped imperialists, revisionists, and Maoists as enemies of socialism and made Soviet ideology the touchstone for identification of the polarized world social forces. At the same time, on the practical level, the CPSU continued to encourage flexible tactics and collaboration with non-Communist political forces, particularly through the activities of Boris N. Ponomarev, Central Committee secretary for relations with non-ruling Communist parties. In other words, the CPSU seemed torn between the "Popular Front" line pursued after the Seventh Comintern Congress and the approach of uncompromising class and ideological struggle associated with the Cominform.

Brezhnev, in his main address at the 25th CPSU Congress, only added to the ambiguity. He asserted that there would be "no compromise on matters of principle" with "right and left revisionism";

at the same time, he encouraged cooperation with other forces of the left, saying that ties with progressive non-Communist parties did not mean "ideological convergence with them" (*Pravda*, 25 February). Faced with simultaneous pressure from domestic ideological hard-liners, led by Suslov, and from recalcitrant Western Communist parties which threatened to scuttle the upcoming summer parley of European parties, Brezhnev was in no position to cut the Gordian knot.

In March, the hard-lining "two camps" ideologues appeared to have scored a decisive victory. P. Rodionov, deputy director of the Institute of Marxism-Leninism, and A. G. Yegerov, the Institute's director, both delivered lavish homages to Andrei A. Zhdanov on the 80th anniversary of his birth (ibid., 12 March). Such praise for the celebrated protagonist of the "two camps" doctrine in the Cominform period was an unmistakable signal. Rodionov particularly left little room for doubt about the relevance of Zhdanov's views for the current ideological debate: "A. A. Zhdanov resolutely opposed a neutral, objective attitude toward hostile, anti-Marxist views and himself set examples of militant party-mindedness, profound moral fiber and principledness in struggling against bourgeois ideology and against any deviations from creative Marxism-Leninism." Rodionov also cited approvingly statements by Zhdanov emphasizing Soviet leadership of the world proletarian movement (*Pravda*, 10 March, in *FBIS*, 15 March).

Suslov also returned to the fray with his clearest statement to date on the outlines of the contemporary ideological struggle. In his speech to the USSR Academy of Sciences, Suslov denounced a wide range of alleged adherents of the anti-Soviet "camp": "left-wing revisionists, Maoists, nationalists, and proponents of 'regional' or 'national' versions of Marxism." Pointedly stressing Soviet claims to leadership of the international movement, Suslov said that the countries building socialism and communism, primarily the Soviet Union, constitute "a powerful base for the development of the world revolutonary process." Further, he maintained that proletarian internationalism "permeates the entire content of the theory and practice of Communism" and that "the entire history of Marxism is a history of the rise and development of proletarian internationalism." (TASS, 17 March, in *FBIS*, 18 March).

Confronted with threats of non-participation in the long-sought European parties meeting by the Yugoslav, Italian, and French Communist parties, Brezhnev was forced to step back further from the extreme claims of the "two camps" analysts. Yugoslav spokesmen said that their party's participation was conditioned by Soviet agreement to drop emphasis on "proletarian internationalism" superseding independent national trends as a conference theme (*NYT*, 29 June). Brezhnev did offer a low-key endorsement of "proletarian internationalism" at the parley, and said that there is no separation of "the destinies of the Soviet Union from those of other countries of Europe and the world." However, the main thrust of his speech was aimed at appeasement of the independent parties. "Each Communist party is responsible first of all to the people of its own country," Brezhnev said, adding that relations among the fraternal parties were based on voluntary cooperation and the strict observance of "the equality and independence of each of them"; he denied that the CPSU aimed to establish an organizational center for the movement. (TASS, 29 June.)

While Brezhnev was unable to secure assent by major Communist parties outside the East European bloc for the more aggressive aspects of CPSU policy toward the world movement, Soviet spokesmen continued to emphasize "proletarian internationalism" and the main outlines of policy remained intact. Leonid M. Zamyatin, general director of TASS and a member of the Central Committee, summarized major priorities in a 23 March television interview. First, he said, was the "strengthening of the socialist community, the development of joint actions by socialist countries for strengthening peace, and for strengthening the unity of the communist and workers movement against both left and right opportunism." Other priority tasks included progress in nuclear arms limitations and central European disarmament, creation of a system of collective security for Asia and a "zone of peace" in the Middle East, "liquidation of all vestiges of the system of colonial oppression," and development of "wide international economic cooperation on a non-discriminatory foundation." (Moscow domestic television service, 23 March, in *FBIS*, 2 April.)

Whatever their differences on world revolutionary tactics, all Soviet spokesmen agreed upon the strategic importance of the East European bloc. Strengthening of the political, military, and economic cohesion of the bloc has often been cited as a major factor in the increasingly favorable "correlation of forces" in recent years, a point reiterated with special emphasis by Kirilenko in his April speech to the 15th Czechoslovak Party Congress (Prague domestic service, 13 April, in *FBIS*, 14 April).

Reflecting a general trend in Soviet ideological interpretation, Belorussian theoretician Yuri Organisyan in a June article pointed out several key manifestations of "proletarian internationalism": socialist economic integration, defensive organization of the Warsaw Pact, and coordination of the international activities of the socialist countries (*Sovetskaia Belorussia*, 8 June). The generalized term "proletarian internationalism" had, by 1976, largely displaced the specific term "socialist internationalism" in discussions of relations among the East European socialist countries. This terminological change reflects recognition of a qualitative change in relationships among these countries that has evolved since enunciation of the Brezhnev Doctrine in 1968. This is not merely a matter of objective processes of integration; as early as 1970, Soviet legal theorists had spoken of "socialist internationalism," i.e., the special relationship between the USSR and other socialist states, as having been recognized in general international law. The Conference on Security and Cooperation in Europe (CSCE) at Helsinki in 1975 was the culmination of a long Soviet drive to gain international legitimation for "limited sovereignty" in Eastern Europe. As Kirilenko told the Czechoslovak Party Congress, the Final Act of CSCE "enshrined the results of the war and of the postwar developments in our continent." The subcategory "socialist internationalism" apparently was no longer necessarily applicable to the East European bloc countries since their status as national states had been substantially eroded. The practical significance of these theoretical distinctions became clear with an apparent extension of the Brezhnev Doctrine in early 1976.

The U.S. State Department, obviously reluctant and embarrassed, released under pressure in April the text of a lecture given by Helmut Sonnenfeldt, counselor of the Department and "right-hand man" of Henry Kissinger, to U.S. ambassadors to Western European countries at a December 1975 meeting in London. Sonnenfeldt had called for U.S. support for a more natural and "organic" relationship between the USSR and the East European countries to replace the existing "inorganic, unnatural" relationship based upon "sheer power," which was unstable and dangerous, containing the potential for an explosion that would have the effect of "causing World War III." How the alleged threat of World War III arising from Soviet troubles in East Europe could be squared with the consistent U.S. refusal to intervene in the region was not explained. Sonnenfeldt pointed to Poland as an example of how autonomous existence satisfying needs for a national identity could be worked out "within the context of a strong Soviet geopolitical influence" (a view strikingly mirrored in President Ford's controversial remarks in the second presidential campaign debate on 6 October). Sonnenfeldt also warned the Yugoslavs to be "less obnoxious," since they could not count upon a "free ride" from the USA. (*NYT*, 6 April.) This staggering analysis by a prominent official of the need for the USA to support consolidation of East Europe under Soviet hegemony evoked a lively reaction in the USA and drew immediate protests from the press in Yugoslavia and Romania. Elsewhere in Eastern Europe, no sparks were kindled by this diplomatic spectacle, apparently because the Soviet version of the so-called "Sonnenfeldt Doctrine" had already been accepted.

Brezhnev had set out the Soviet doctrinal position on this matter at the 25th CPSU Congress in February. In a discussion of cooperation among the socialist countries, Brezhnev spoke of their mutual ties "becoming ever closer" and of the "gradual evening out of their development levels." "This process of the gradual drawing together (*sblizhenie*) of the socialist countries is now operating quite definitely as an objective law (*zakonomernost'*)." (*Pravda*, 25 April.) This process was elaborated by Brezhnev in a wider-ranging discussion of "proletarian internationalism."

Suslov's speech to the party congress of the German Democratic Republic (GDR), in May, with its emphases upon the "solidarity and united actions of the socialist countries" and "proletarian internationalism," seemed to echo Brezhnev's February speech (*Pravda* and *Izvestiia*, 20 May). In his June address to the conference of European parties, Brezhnev conceded the independence of other parties but in fact spelled out an exclusion of the East European bloc countries from the admitted polycentrism. Brezhnev linked "proletarian internationalism" and the "fraternal solidarity of socialist countries," and explicitly reaffirmed his February formulation, speaking of the "profound, organic, and ever-growing friendly ties" among the socialist countries. The integration of Eastern Europe was called "an absolutely new phenomenon," a "truly fraternal union of peoples." Marxist-Leninist parties are, Brezhnev said, "the cementing force of this union." (TASS, 29 June.)

The significance of Brezhnev's formulation lies in the fact that the concepts and terminology employed are identical to those used to describe the integration of nationalities within the USSR. In recent years, Soviet spokesmen have frequently compared Soviet national integration and the integration of Eastern Europe and have advanced Soviet nationalities policy as a model for the consolidation of the bloc. According to Soviet theoreticians, there are four stages in national integration, of which the third is the stage of rapprochement or drawing together (*sblizhenie*) and the ultimate stage is that of merger (*sliianie*). This design for assimilation has been applied to East European integration, and Brezhnev explicitly identified the current level of integration as that of the third stage. A. Viktorov, writing in *Pravda* on 27 March, again stressed that East European integration had reached the third stage, when he spoke of the "constant rapprochement of the socialist countries" as a "law-governed pattern." Further, Victorov said that "proletarian internationalism" makes it possible "to combine organically" the "international aims of the working class" with "national, patriotic interest."

By mid-summer, when Prime Minister Kosygin addressed the CMEA Council in Berlin and called for further economic integration and the establishing of common production goals for the 1980s (*Izvestiia*, 8 July), the Soviet leadership had clearly staked out a claim to a special "organic" relationship with East Europe under the general rubric of "proletarian internationalism" and left little doubt about the aim of the eventual merger of bloc countries with the Soviet Union. The Romanian, Yugoslav, French, and Italian Communist parties resisted this apparent extension of the Brezhnev Doctrine, but Bulgaria accepted it enthusiastically, with Bulgarian party leader Todor Zhivkov affirming the need for an "organic" relationship among socialist countries (see *Survey*, 22, 1 (98), 1976, p. 34). The USSR-GDR treaty of 1975 and the new Polish constitution both contain provisions evidently legalizing "limited sovereignty."

Another strong indication of the Soviet commitment to the Brezhnev Doctrine and its extension came in a posthumously published article by General Sergei Shtemenko, late commander of the Warsaw Pact forces, in the weekly magazine *Za Rubezhom*. According to General Shtemenko, the main military purpose of the alliance was the suppression of counterrevolutionary activity in the socialist countries (*NYT*, 8 May).

In the wake of these claims and controversies, the conference of 29 European Communist parties was held in East Berlin in late June. The outcome of the parley was a mixed bag of gains and losses for Moscow. Preconditions for the conference included renunciation of any attempt to anathematize China or to impose Soviet orthodoxy under the banner of "proletarian internationalism." The conference document was a bland, painstakingly composed compromise statement designed to ruffle no feathers among participants. Brezhnev was forced to listen to expressions of independent views and criticisms of Soviet policy from representatives of the Romanian, Yugoslav, French, and Italian parties. The strongest statement came from Spanish party leader Santiago Carrillo, who pointedly denied that Moscow was the center of the movement and said that "diversity must be accepted once and for all. There will be no schism if nobody puts his own position forward as dogma." Further, Carrillo argued not only that Western Communists required special leeway to succeed in capitalist countries but also that full democracy was essential for all "socialist societies." (*NYT*, 30 June.)

On the plus side, the Italian party seemed to be somewhat mollified by Soviet flexibility as PCI international secretary Sergio Segre indicated that Brezhnev's speech went "beyond expectations" on the issue of independence of parties. French party chief Georges Marchais, who had boycotted the 25th CPSU Congress and sent his deputy Gaston Plissonier instead, attended this time. The CPSU had indicated its strong concern for ties with the French party by dispatching party secretary Kirilenko to the PCF's 22d Congress in February, where Kirilenko delivered a speech very conciliatory in tone toward the French Communists (TASS, February 6). This, plus Moscow's compromising attitude on the issues involved in pre-conference planning, paid off in the presence of the PCF leader at the Berlin parley, although the PCF continued to pursue a very independent line, which included rejection of the concept of the dictatorship of the proletariat.

The fact that all the European parties except those of Iceland and Albania participated in the conference was something of a propaganda triumph for Moscow, showing as it did that the Soviet leadership could still rally international support, if only for limited objectives. Despite the specific rejections of Soviet doctrinal claims at the Berlin parley, *Pravda* (5 July) could still view the meeting as a success for "proletarian internationalism," and the CPSU Politburo issued a statement (*Izvestiia*, 4 July) claiming that "the conference was a factor in strengthening the interaction of the European continent's fraternal parties and the development of international cooperation among the fraternal parties on the basis of generally accepted norms of interparty relations." The conference did provide important contacts behind the scenes between the CPSU and independent-minded Communist parties, either through direct talks between Brezhnev and other party leaders or through the inter-mediation of Brezhnev's chief agent, GDR party leader Erich Honecker. Of special importance was the meeting between Brezhnev and Yugoslav president Josip Broz Tito. Marshal Tito had not attended an all-European conference in two decades. The official GDR press agency described the Tito-Brezhnev meeting as "friendly" and said that they "discussed several questions regarding the development of Soviet-Yugoslav cooperation on the party and state levels" (*NYT*, 28 June).

Tito's attendance had been obtained at the price of the concessions noted above, but was nevertheless rather remarkable in view of the fragile state of Soviet-Yugoslav relations. While regular cooperation in military matters was maintained, the April conversations at Dubrovnik between Soviet Army chief of staff General Viktor Kulikov and Yugoslav army chief General Stane Potočar being their third such meeting within two years (BBC, 28 May), relations otherwise were severely strained. In Yugoslavia, more than 100 pro-Russian dissidents arrested in 1975 had been sentenced to long prison terms and in May 1976 Mrs. Irina Požega, a Soviet citizen, was sentenced to five years in prison on a charge of spying for the USSR. Mrs. Požega was said to have acted as a contact between Yuri Sepelev, Soviet consul-general in Zagreb, and various anti-Tito dissident groups. Sepelev, who had been expelled from Britain as a Soviet spy in 1971, left Zagreb hurriedly after Mrs. Požega's arrest in early 1976. (*Daily Telegraph*, London, 27 May.) Tensions between the two countries led Brezhnev to cancel his trip to Yugoslavia scheduled for June (*Washington Post*, 2 June). Following the Berlin conference, the Yugoslavs remained uneasy over Soviet affirmation and extension of the Brezhnev Doctrine and over the continuing threat of some form of Soviet intervention upon Tito's departure from the political scene.

Yugoslav uneasiness was increased by USA President-elect Jimmy Carter's statement during the American political campaign that he would not send troops to Yugoslavia in case of a Soviet invasion. The Brezhnev visit to Belgrade was rescheduled for November and the Soviet leader sought to calm Yugoslav fears. At the outset of his three-day visit on 15 November, Brezhnev said that the "Soviet

Union abides by endeavors to strengthen and develop with Yugoslavia friendly relations based on complete equality, mutual respect and trust and absolute noninterference in internal affairs." At the conclusion of the visit, Tito described the talks with Brezhnev as "very successful" but a Yugoslav spokesman said that some major differences remained. The final communiqué of the meeting carefully avoided references to "proletarian internationalism" and stated that relations between the Yugoslav and the Soviet bloc parties would be based on "internationalist comradely voluntary cooperation" (AP, 15, 17 November).

The Berlin parley was followed by new approaches to Romania. Brezhnev met with Romanian president Nicolae Ceauşescu at the former's vacation retreat in the Crimea in early August (TASS, 3 August); major issues disturbing the countries' relations apparently remained unresolved. As with Yugoslavia, the Soviet doctrinal formulations on East European integration produced intense concern in Bucharest. The Romanians were also worried about the fact that, despite the Helsinki guarantee of frontiers, recent articles and books appearing in Hungary and Bulgaria appeared to revive old claims to Romanian territory (NYT, 31 May). If the old Bulgarian claims on Dobruja were to be satisfied today, Romania would lose access to the Black Sea and the USSR would have a land link to Bulgaria. Given Bulgarian leader Zhivkov's support for "organic relationships" and the persistent rumor that Bulgaria would eventually accept voluntary absorption into the Soviet Union, the Romanians had cause to consider this a real threat.

Brezhnev made another attempt to pacify the Romanians, when he traveled to Bucharest in November for talks with Ceauşescu and a Warsaw Pact summit meeting. Arriving one day after the signing of a ten-year USA-Romanian trade agreement, Brezhnev said that he hoped his first visit in a decade would be "a constructive forum of good will" rather than "an arena of propagandist wrangle." However, both sides appeared to hold fast to their respective positions. In a speech on 22 November, Ceauşescu repeated several times that Romania would reject any foreign attempts to interfere in its internal affairs. "The Berlin conference," Ceauşescu said, "powerfully confirmed the independence of all our parties." In his response, Brezhnev accepted the principle of "noninterference in home affairs" but said that the Soviet Union would still be a watchdog for "proletarian internationalism" in the Communist movement (NYT, 23, 25 November).

Moscow continued to press for closer relations with France, apparently undeterred by the French grant of political asylum to Leonid Plyushch. Foreign Minister Gromyko visited Paris, 27-30 April, and held talks with French Foreign Minister Jean Sauvagnargues and with French President Giscard d'Estaing on disarmament, the situation in the Middle East, and other matters. Pravda (1 May) characterized the talks as proceeding "in an atmosphere of friendship and mutual understanding characteristic of Soviet-French relations" and noted that "both sides hold close or similar views on many questions." Sauvagnargues returned Gromyko's visit in a July trip to Moscow, where a Franco-Soviet agreement on prevention of nuclear accidents was signed. Izvestiia (20 July) hailed the 16 July agreement as "an important contribution to international détente." Brezhnev called for friendship with France in a television interview broadcast simultaneously in France and the USSR in October. At the same time, in a move that was unusual since no formal invitation had been received, Soviet sources revealed that Brezhnev would probably travel to Paris in late 1976 or early 1977 (NYT, 6 October).

Relations with Japan contained no such cheerful prospects. In January, Gromyko warned that the USSR might "reconsider" its relations with Japan if that country signed a peace treaty with China (NYT, 13 January). Nevertheless, Japan proceeded with plans to include an "anti-hegemony clause" directed at the USSR in the Sino-Japanese treaty. Presumably, new ambassador Polyansky's assignment is the thawing out of Soviet-Japanese relations, a formidable task in view of the adamant Soviet refusal to follow the U.S. lead on the Okinawa issue by returning to Japan the four Kurile Islands seized at the end of World War II. Relations were further strained by an incident in September. When a defecting Soviet pilot landed his top-secret MIG-25 "Foxbat" jet-fighter in Japan, he was given political asylum and U.S. intelligence agents were given the opportunity to examine the plane. The USSR protested vigorously and Brezhnev told the Central Committee plenum in October that Japan's handling of the matter had clouded Soviet-Japanese relations (TASS, 25 October).

During the year, relations were strengthened with India and with three socialist countries bordering China. India Prime Minister Indira Gandhi visited Moscow in June. At the close of the visit, Brezhnev and Mme Gandhi signed a declaration of agreement on a number of matters, including the further development of trade and technical cooperation between the two countries and efforts to turn the Indian Ocean into a "zone of peace" (*Pravda*, 14 June). The USSR stepped up its aid to the Democratic Republic of Vietnam (*NYT*, 31 January) and in May several agreements on trade, cultural cooperation, and other matters were signed with the People's Democratic Republic of Laos (*Pravda*, 5 May). In October, Mongolia's leader Yumzhagin Tsedenbal journeyed to Moscow for several days of talks with Soviet leaders and was ceremoniously welcomed at Vnukovo Airport by Prime Minister Kosygin in the latter's first public appearance since July (*Washington Post*, 19 October).

In another flanking movement against China, the USSR succeeded in establishing diplomatic relations with the Philippines. This was announced during the visit of Philippine president Ferdinand E. Marcos to Moscow, 31 May-7 June. A trade agreement between the two countries was also signed. (*Pravda*, 1 June; *Izvestiia*, 2 June; *Pravda* and *Izvestiia*, 8 June.)

The USSR made one dramatic move to extend its influence into South America, where its profile generally was quite low. In October, Peru was reported to have accepted a Soviet offer of up to 36 Sukhsi-22 supersonic fighter bombers after attempting to buy similar planes from the USA. The USSR reportedly offered to make the planes available on more attractive terms than could be given by Western manufacturers. The Peruvian Army was also estimated to have acquired 200 Soviet T-55 tanks. (*NYT*, 13 October.)

In the Middle East, the USSR sought and failed to unify the Arab confrontation forces against Israel. When Egypt turned sharply toward a U.S. orientation and appeared to drop from the ranks of confrontation states, the Soviet leadership responded with a punitive tightening in its military and economic assistance. Egypt, meanwhile, was having difficulties with Libya, whose president, Muammar el-Qaddafi, posed threats of subversion against theEgyptian regime. According to Egyptian president Anwar Sadat, the USSR had accepted Libyan orders for Soviet arms worth $11 billion by early April (ibid., 5 April). Sadat's reply to this heavy-handed Soviet pressure was the abrogation of the 1971 Soviet-Egyptian treaty of friendship and cooperation on 14 March and cancellation of Soviet navy access to Egypt's Mediterranean ports on 4 April.

The Soviet government declared that the Egyptian government was responsible for the "consequences" of the treaty abrogation, but insisted that the Soviet Union "has conducted and will continue to conduct a principled, consistent policy aimed at developing friendly relations with the Arab Republic of Egypt and with the Egyptian people" (*Pravda*, 16 March). Further condemnation of Sadat followed in the Soviet press (*Izvestiia*, 18 March). On the matter of relations between Egypt and Libya, *Pravda* (18 March) quoted approvingly assertions in the Libyan press that Sadat's actions, particularly the expulsion of some Libyan citizens, resulted from the Egyptian leadership's "deeply reactionary domestic and foreign policy and their close ties with U.S. imperialism and Arab reaction." Despite the growing antagonism, Moscow did not burn all its bridges to Cairo. On 28 April a new Soviet-Egyptian trade agreement was signed (*Izvestiia*, 29 April), and the USSR continued to provide about 90 percent of Egyptian military hardware.

Faced with a check in the south, the Soviet Union turned to Israel's foes to the north and east, attempting to shore up that sector. In May and June, Kosygin traveled to Baghdad and Damascus in an unsuccessful effort to bring together the quarreling Iraqi and Syrian elements of the confrontation forces (*Pravda*, 1 June; *Izvestiia*, 2 June; *Pravda* and *Izvestiia*, 3 June). While Kosygin was in Damascus, Syria launched its major offensive in Lebanon to contain its erstwhile ally, the Palestine

Liberation Front (PLO). As the anti-Israeli coalition crumbled and Syria's intervention gained the tacit support of Israel and the USA, the USSR was forced to take sides. It predictably opted for radicalism and "national liberaton," giving strong verbal support for the PLO. On 8 June, *Pravda* stated that "a positive solution to the Lebanese crisis can be reached only by the Lebanese people themselves through the earliest possible termination of bloodshed and the strengthening of all forces opposing imperialist aggression, and through the preservation of Lebanon's integrity, sovereignty, and independence and the refusal to permit the subversion of the Palestinian resistance movement." On the following day, TASS issued a statement sharply critical of Syria: "The Syrian Arab Republic has repeatedly stated that the troops it has sent into Lebanon are there to help stop the bloodshed. It is obvious, however, that the bloodshed in Lebanon is not only continuing but is actually increasing." (*Pravda*, 10 June.) Soviet-Syrian friction continued throughout the year, with both sides stopping short of an open break. In August, the USSR issued a further call for Syrian forces to leave Lebanon and for Syria to collaborate with its "natural allies," the PLO and Lebanese leftists (*Pravda*, 29 August).

Another failure in Soviet policy toward the eastern Mediterranean came with the rejection of its April proposal for a resumption of the Geneva talks on the Middle East, with a two-stage schedule of negotiations (*Izvestiia*, 28 April). The only bright spot appeared to be an improvement in Soviet relations with Jordan. King Hussein of Jordan spent twelve days in Moscow in early July and negotiations proceeded on purchase of an SAM air-defense network for deployment against Israel.

In regard to Soviet relations with China, the year opened on an upbeat note but no substantive progress followed on normalization of relations. In late December 1975, the Chinese released the three-man crew of a Soviet helicopter that had been captured in northwest China on 14 March 1974 (*Washington Post*, 28 December 1975). However, this conciliatory gesture had no sequel as China was soon caught up in the swirl of dramatic changes and domestic turmoil occasioned by the death of Chou En-lai and the physical decline and demise of Mao Tse-tung. At the 25th CPSU Congress, Brezhnev said that "we shall continue the struggle against Maoism, a principled struggle, an uncompromising struggle," but reaffirmed the USSR's readiness to normalize relations with China in accordance with the principles of peaceful coexistence. However, he pointedly asserted that relations must be "consonant with the principles of 'proletarian internationalism.' " (*Pravda*, 25 February.)

An "I. Aleksandrov" article in *Pravda* on 28 April proposed resumption of border talks between the USSR and China, without "any preliminary conditions whatsoever" on the Soviet side. "Our Party and state have done everything possible," said *Pravda*, "to regulate and normalize Soviet-Chinese relations." However, the article contained language hardly calculated to encourage Chinese flexibility. It spoke of "truly monstrous territorial claims on the USSR" that pursued "far-reaching geopolitical aims that combine the fomenting of hostility among peoples and the pursuit of great-Han hegemony." Within one day an unofficial reply was forthcoming from Peking, when an explosion occurred at the gates of the Soviet Embassy in the Chinese capital (*Pravda*, 30 April, *Izvestiia*, 1 May).

Following the death of Mao in September, the CPSU leadership dispatched a message of condolence which was rejected by Peking on grounds that there were no "party-to-party relations" (*Washington Post*, 2 October). However, Moscow sent a formal message of greetings on the occasion of the 27th anniversary of the Peking regime on 1 October. On the same day, another "I. Aleksandrov" article appeared in *Pravda* indicating the USSR's willingness to resume ties. The article contained no mention of Mao, an omission that Western observers regarded as proof of Soviet interest in setting aside tension. "There are no problems that cannot be resolved," said *Pravda*, "provided there is a mutual desire and, in the spirit of good neighborliness, mutual benefit and consideration of each other's interests." The article further maintained that "the fundamental interests of the Soviet and Chinese people do not clash but coincide" and that "the Soviet Union has never had and does not now have economic, territorial, or other grievances against China."

Meanwhile, in a speech on disarmament to the UN General Assembly, Foreign Minister Gromyko had spoken favorably of the "positive impact" that normalization of Soviet-Chinese relations would have. These overtures were brutally repulsed by Chinese foreign minister Chiao Kuan-hua in a speech to the General Assembly on 5 October. Chiao scornfully dismissed Gromyko's disarmament proposals and said that "Soviet social-imperialism is the biggest peace swindler and the most dangerous source of war today" (*NYT*, 6 October).

The Soviet press responded to Chiao's tirade with dire warnings about future Sino-Soviet relations; China's official press continued to depict the USSR as the likely source of a new world war (AP, 24 October). Another overture from Moscow came in the form of a joint Soviet-Mongolian communiqué at the end of the Tsedenbal visit in October. The statement said that the USSR and Mongolia "stand for restoring equal, good neighborly relations with China" (TASS, 24 October).

Speaking to the Central Committee plenum in late October, Brezhnev said that "it is still difficult to say what will be the future political course of the People's Republic." "However," he added, "it is clear already today that the foreign policy line Peking pursued for a decade and a half has been greatly discredited throughout the world." (TASS, 25 October.)

Some thawing of Sino-Soviet relations was indicated by events at the 59th anniversary celebration of the Bolshevik Revolution in Moscow, 5-7 November. Chinese chargé d'affaires Wang Chin-Ching remained impassively in his seat throughout the major speech by Fedor D. Kulakov at the Palace of Congresses, 5 November. This was the first time since 1970 that the Chinese representative had not walked out of the celebration when the anniversary speaker's remarks touched upon China. Kulakov's references to China were much milder than those of other major speakers in recent years and offered a marked contrast to the anti-Maoist harangue delivered by Arvid I. Pel'she at the 1975 celebration (*NYT*, 6, 7 November).

A brief Chinese message of greeting delivered on 7 November stopped short of a clearcut proposal for reconciliation but included a note of "friendship for the Soviet people" not found in the 1975 message (TASS, 7 November).

Publications. The main CPSU organs are the daily newspaper *Pravda*, the theoretical and ideological journal *Kommunist* (appearing 18 times a year), and the twice-monthly (*Partiinaia zhizn'*, journal on internal party affairs and party organizational matters. *Kommunist vooruzhennikh sil* is the party theoretical journal for the armed forces, and *Agitator* is the journal for party propagandists, both appearing twice a month. The Komsomol has a newspaper, *Komsomolskaia pravda* (published six days a week); a monthly theoretical journal, *Molodoi kommunist*; and a monthly literary journal, *Molodaia gvardia*. Each USSR republic prints similar party newspapers and journals in local languages, and usually also in Russian.

University of New Orleans   R. Judson Mitchell

Yugoslavia

The Communist Party of Yugoslavia was created in June 1920, although the Yugoslav Communists put the beginning of their party in April 1919, when a unification congress in Belgrade established a "Socialist Workers' Party of Yugoslavia (Communists)" including both Communist and non-Communist elements, but which was disbanded 14 months later. In November 1952, at its Sixth Congress, the name was changed to the League of Communists of Yugoslavia (Savez komunista Jugoslavije; LCY). As the only political party in the Socialist Federative Republic of Yugoslavia (SFRY), the LCY exercises power through its leading role in the Socialist Alliance of the Working People of Yugoslavija (Socijalistički savez radnog naroda Jugoslavije; SAWPY), a front organization which includes all mass political organizations as well as individuals representing various social groups.

The LCY claims a membership of 1,400,000 (*Borba*, 10 November 1976). According to an official estimation, on 1 July 1976 Yugoslavia had 21,520,000 inhabitants. The breakdown of the party membership (*Večernje novosti*, 12 June) when there were 1,302,843 members, was as follows:

Structure	Numerical strength	Percent
White-collar workers	542,248	41.8
Blue-collar workers	366,272	28.1
Private peasants	65,910	5.1
Students and pupils	96,139	7.5
Others	232,274	17.5
Total	1,302,843	100.00

Despite the fact that the 1976 membership was the highest in the party's 57-year history, the leaders are not satisfied, and one reason for their dissatisfaction is the rather weak representation of blue-collar workers. The figure of 366,272 (see table) "is 0.2 per cent less than in the previous years" (*Komunist*, 14 June). Between 1971 and 1975 the number of blue-collar workers in the LCY remained virtually unchanged, ranging from 28.4 percent in 1971 to 28.1 percent in 1975. Approximately every eighth worker in Yugoslavia has joined the party, but every fourth white-collar worker is a member of the LCY, and every 50th private peasant (ibid.).

Leadership and Organization. The supreme bodies of the LCY are its 166-member Central Committee and the Central Committee Presidium of 48 members (47 plus Tito). At the 10th LCY Congress, in May 1974, the Presidium elected the 12-member Executive Committee (for details see *YICA, 1975*, pp. 112-14; also *YICA, 1976*, p. 91-92).

The only two personnel changes in the LCY's top echelons in 1976 were the elections of Veljko Milatović (born 1921) and Nijaz Dizdarević (1920) to the Central Committee of the LCY. Both were delegated by their respective republican central committees (CC), Milatović by the Montenegrin CC and Dizdarević by the CC of Bosnia-Hercegovina. At the third plenary session of the LCY Central Committee which took place in Belgrade on 17 April, Milatović, who is president of the Presidency of the Socialist Republic of Montenegro, was in addition elected to the Yugoslav CC's Presidium to replace his countryman Veljko Vlahović who died in 1975. (*Politika*, 18 April.) No reason was given why Dizdarević, who until the autumn 1975 was Yugoslavia's ambassador in France, was elected to the CC to replace his Moslem fellow-countryman Kemal Karačić (1934), a worker from Sarajevo.

Party Internal Affairs. The third plenary session of the LCY Central Committee (17 April) was held in the absence of President Tito and with Stane Dolanc, secretary of the CC Presidium's Executive Committee, in chair. Roman Albreht (1921), a member of the CC's Presidium, submitted the main report on the new draft Law on Associated Labor (see below) and attacked what he called "Stalinist concepts of state ownership centralism linked both directly and indirectly with so-called Cominformist tendencies." Albreht also attacked "ultra-leftist theories" that were trying to weaken self-management.

Another speaker at the CC plenum, Yugoslavia's number two man, Edvard Kardelj (1910), admitted that there were serious weaknesses in the Yugoslav system, but said that the new Law on Associated Labor would equip workers "with the necessary resources for the construction of a free community of producers in which they can become free creative personalities." Kardelj warned, however, that this was "a historical process rather than something to be achieved from one day to the next." He stressed that the Yugoslav "self-managing socialist society cannot accept either the system of multiparty democracy, a product of the bourgeois political state, or the one-party system which came into being under special conditions of the transitional period between bourgeois and socialist democracy." No "multiparty system" is possible in Yugoslavia, Kardelj said, because under it only "counter-revolutionary forces" would benefit. He repeatedly attacked those who advocated "absolute freedom" and the "dogmatic-conservative critics of self-managing democracy who would like to replace the authority of the working class by a monopoly of narrow-minded groups, i.e., by a bureaucratic one-party system." (*Politika*, 18 April.)

During 1976 there were ten sessions of the Presidium of the LCY Central Committee: the 16th (20 February-ideological problems, foreign trade, Yugoslavia's international cooperation); the 17th (30 March—agenda for the third CC plenum, foreign trade, cadre policy, a commission for party history formed); the 18th (26 April—internal political situation in the country and the party's ideological activities); the 19th (no date of this session was revealed but one may assume that it was held in connection with Tito's 84th birthday on 25 May); the 20th (10 June—the LCY's relations with socialist countries and Western social-democratic parties as well as the situation in the international Communist movement); the 21st (22 June-the preparation for the conference of European Communist and workers' parties in East Berlin); the 22nd (14 July—the work of the LCY delegation at the East Berlin conference approved, preparations for the fifth non-aligned summit in Colombo, ideological aspects of the new penal code discussed); the 23rd (4 October—ideological-political aspects of the current economic situation in the country discussed); the 24th (3 November—foreign policy, situation within the international workers' movement; the LCY international activities); the 25th (9 December—discussion of a report about the visit to Yugoslavia of Leonid Brezhnev). It should be noted that the Presidium's June session "unequivocally requested that the Marxist way of thinking and practical action be established in all the spheres of our social life" (*NIN*, Belgrade, 21 November, article under the title "Marx Has Returned").

An interview of President Tito (*Vjesnik*, 1 February) revealed a series of weaknesses plaguing the Yugoslav party and state although he described himself as optimistic concerning the country's and party's future after his departure from the political stage. He said that the nine-man collective leadership, officially called the Presidency of the Socialist Federative Republic of Yugoslavia, has proved itself "very efficient" (the Presidency is composed of one member from each of the six constituent republics and two autonomous provinces, plus Tito). Tito listed a number of weaknesses both inside and outside the party, and said he was not satisfied "with what has so far been achieved, because there are still those in the League of Communists who cannot be said to be Communists or to deserve a place in the organization." He admitted that there was "a considerable lack of discipline" and that the decisions made at the 10th LCY Congress in May 1974 "are being implemented only slowly or even disregarded." He also admitted that quite a few people in the party have enriched themselves. This interview of Tito was later used as an official document referred to by other party functionaries in their criticism of the current weaknesses.

On 11 September it was announced that Tito was suffering from "acute liver trouble" and had to interrupt all public activities; he reassumed them by chairing the 3 November session of the Presidium of the LCY Central Committee.

Domestic Affairs. *The Law On Associated Labor.* After more than a year's discussion the SFRY Assembly adopted on 25 November the 671-article Law on Associated Labor. The first version of the draft law was published in October 1975 with 557 articles; the second version appeared in April 1976 with 646 articles. The law is in Yugoslavia popularly called "the little constitution" although the currently valid constitution (promulgated on 21 February 1974) has only 406 articles—265 fewer than the Law on Associated Labor. Edvard Kardelj praised the new law as a historic document with which "Yugoslavia has entered into a rather mature phase of the development of the self-management socialist society, thus creating a new type of democracy—self-management democracy" (*Borba*, 28, 29, 30 November 1976). The reason why the new law had to be passed has obviously not been to grant the workers "greater rights" but rather to discipline both them and the managers, so that the party line be strictly observed.

The problem of Yugoslavia's self-management system has remained the same since June 1950, when the law on the workers' councils was introduced: whether the system of workers' self-management, that requires a *broad democratic basis*, is at all possible in a *one-party dictatorship* essentially hostile to any real democratization. This contradiction could only lead to conflict not only between two completely different systems (self-management vs. one-party dictatorship), but also to the conflict between the workers and their party-inspired managers. This duality, in which the workers have been required to observe all legal norms but to forget about them whenever ideological goals have been in question, has created many difficulties and deficiencies, which in the long run made the new Law on Associated Labor necessary, as a sort of "super-law."

The law has six parts. Part One, "Basic Provisions," contains 44 articles dealing with the principles of self-management socialism. Part Two (Articles 45 through 319), "Socioeconomic Relations among Workers in Associated Labor," is divided in seven chapters. Part Three (Articles 320 through 460), "The Self-Managing Organization of Associated Labor," has two chapters. Part Four (Articles 461 through 646), "The Realization of Workers' Self-Management in Associated Labor," is composed of seven chapters. Part Five (Articles 647 through 659), "Penal Provisions," has three chapters. Part Six (Articles 660 through 671) is called "Transitional and Final Provisions." (*Borba*, 13 December, special supplement.)

Articles 211 through 219 have attracted the workers' special attention, for they deal—for the first time—with the right of enterprises to dismiss workers who perform poorly. Workers in Yugoslavia have, of course, been dismissed also in the past, but usually when an enterprise was closed down owing to economic unprofitability ("political factories"). There was until now no law in Yugoslavia covering dismissal for poor performance. According to Article 211 a worker can cease to work in a factory (1) on the basis of his free volition, (2) following an agreement with competent organs, (3) for having refused to take a job he was offered, (4) for having given "untruthful data" to the enterprise while applying for job, and (5) for not having fulfilled his obligations, thus "seriously violating working obligations." Among other things, "unjustified absenteeism from work for at least five days in succession" is considered to be a "serious violation of working obligations" (Art. 195). The law differentiates clearly between "good" and "bad" workers and advises "good" workers to dismiss their "bad" colleagues. Article 216 provides other reasons why a worker could cease to work in an enterprise: (1) if he refused to sign a statement to accept the "self-management agreement" in the enterprise, (2) if it was proven that he was "totally incapable for work," (3) because of retirement, (4) if a court decision prohibited him to work in certain fields and no other working fields were available, (5) if he had to spend more than six months in prison, and (6) if he was, for security reasons, deprived of the right to work for a period longer than six months.

Article 220, on the other hand, provides for the worker to protect his rights through self-managing organs, associated labor courts, and other competent authorities.

Report of the Presidency of the SFRY. At its session on 26 November the Assembly of the SFRY discussed a report by the Presidency of the SFRY, the nine-man collective leadership of Yugoslavia. The report was distributed several weeks in advance and President Tito made only a brief survey of the country's internal and external policies. (*Borba,* 27 November.) Article 318 of Yugoslavia's constitution provides that the Presidency of the SFRY must keep the Assembly of the SFRY informed on the state and problems of internal and foreign policy. Along with the praise for the country's self-management system, the Presidency report criticized the "slowness in the process of the reorganization of the associated labor and self-management in general." Such a development leads to "techno-burocratic and other resistances." As far as the country's agriculture was concerned, the report said that private farmers should join agricultural collectives only on the basis of the "full voluntariness." The report hailed successes in the solution of the nationality problem, especially the struggle against "bourgeois and bureaucratic nationalism and separatism," and stressed also that "about two million persons" were involved in the system of delegations (about the latter, see *YICA, 1975,* pp. 116-17).

Discussing the problem of the country's nationwide defense system [opštenarodna odbrana], the report stated that the "military political situation in the world is still complex, especially because of the armament race, not only the conventional but also nuclear rearmament." It was further claimed that "pressure, various forms of interference in other countries' internal affairs, threats and even military interventions against nonaligned and other independent countries have become frequent." Even "local wars" were organized by various "imperialist, neo-colonialist, and hegemonistic forces." The report said that Yugoslavia "considers the possibility of a new war an objective reality," because of which it has strengthened its defense system and armed forces. Yugoslavia has 156 diplomatic representations throughout the world.

In the concluding part of the report the Presidency warned against privileges in society which "have provoked justified dissatisfaction of the working people." It admitted that "within the working class ideological and political differences [had] appeared which in everyday practice might become a stronghold of foreign infuences." (*Komunist,* 29 November).

In commenting on the Presidency report Tito said that the "nationalist forces" had been successfully countered, regardless of whether they advocated unitarism, separatism, or irredentism (*Borba,* 27 November).

Political Opponents and Dissidents; Arrests and Trials. As in the previous year, the Yugoslav regime in 1976 was confronted by a variety of groups and individuals who, in one way or another, were opposed to, or critical of, the existing political system. Groups and individuals in question may be divided into two broad categories: one relating to attempts and intentions (real or alleged) to violently change the existing conditions in the country, the other dealing with the problems of civil rights and the judicial process.

In a statement made on 20 July before the Federal Assembly, General Franjo Herljević, the secretary for internal affairs, asserted that 13 "subversive" groups with 237 members had been uncovered and sentenced during the past two years. He specified that 105 of them were "Cominformists"; 19 persons were convicted of espionage and 22 were suspected of it. (*Borba,* 21 July.) In fact, a series of trials of "Cominformists" (i.e., pro-Soviet groups) took place during 1976. With the sole exception of Slovenia, all parts of the country witnessed these trials. Although the public authorities and media insisted on the domestic character of the Cominformist "counter-revolutionaries and plotters," it is obvious that the affair had foreign ramifications, especially since the discovery that in April 1974, at an underground congress in the Montenegrin town of Bar, a pro-Soviet Communist party of Yugoslavia was established (see *YICA, 1975*, pp. 118-19, 121-22; see also a special section on that party at the end of this profile).

Early in the year, between February and April, *in camera* trials of "Cominformists" took place in Priština (Kosovo), Belgrade, Novi Sad (Vojvodina), and Banja Luka (Bosnia). The Priština trial ended on 7 February, when an announcement was made that 19 "Albanian irredentists" were given long prison sentences, ranging from 4 to 12 years. The verdict stated that the accused tried to create a so-called "People's Liberation Movement of Kosovo" based on "dogmatic-Stalinist ideology" (*Borba*, 8 February). The Belgrade trial was significant because of the political past of four individuals who on 12 March were sentenced to prison terms ranging from 7½ to 10 years. The convicted "Stalinists" were Dušan Brkić, 63, deputy prime minister of Croatia until 1950; Radovan Žigić, 55, once Croatia's minister for the processing industry; Milivoje Stefanović, 64, once editor of Yugoslavia's Tanjug news agency; and Ljubomir Radulović, 58, who is said to have traveled to Moscow, Kiev, and Budapest to make contacts with the Cominformist exiles abroad. The group is alleged to have asked Yugoslav Stalinist émigrés outside the country whether, when Tito was no longer in power, the Soviet army would intervene in Yugoslavia if requested to do so by anyone inside the country (*NYT*, 13 March). The 10 "Cominformists" (seven men and three women) who on 16 March were sentenced in Novi Sad to prison terms ranging from 18 months to 15 years, were charged with setting up an "illegal Cominformist group" which "mimeographed and disseminated leaflets with inimical contents" after "having established links with Cominformist exiles" (*Politika*, 9 January; *Keesing's Contemporary Archives*, 28 May). A court in Banja Luka imposed on 14 April prison sentences from 3 to 12 years on nine people accused of "anti-state activities" practiced from "counterrevolutionary Cominformist positions" (*Borba*, 30 January; *Keesing's Contemporary Archives*, 28 May). Finally, at a trial which drew the most attention abroad, Vlado Dapčević, 62, a former Yugoslav army colonel, was in July initially sentenced to death for high treason, but the sentence was commuted to 20 years imprisonment (*Borba*, 6 July). Dapčević had opted for the USSR during the 1948 Tito-Stalin conflict. When he tried to flee the country, he was arrested and sentenced to 20 years' imprisonment. Amnestied in 1956, he fled in 1959 first to Albania and then to the USSR. He had lived in Brussels since 1967 and had acquired Belgian citizenship. In August 1975 he traveled to Romania, where he was allegedly kidnaped by Yugoslav secret police. Brought to Yugoslavia, he was accused of being an organizer of the above-mentioned Bar congress of the illegal Yugoslav Communist party, with the aim of overthrowing Tito's government and seeking to divide the country. He claimed at his closed trial that the proceedings were staged, and asserted that he had long since broken with the USSR. He also charged that he was seized in Bucharest and brought by force to Yugoslavia. The prosecutors never mentioned the circumstances of his arrest. (*NYT*, 6 July.)

While the majority of those brought to trial during 1976 were charged as "Stalinist elements," groups of different political colorations were also the targets of persecution. Thus "Croatian nationalists," "Serbian Chetniks" (the followers of the World War II guerrilla leader General Drazha Mihailović, who was captured and executed by the new Communist regime in July 1946), "Albanian irredentists," and pro-Western people in general were tried and sent to prison (for details see *Keesing's Contemporary Archives*, 19 March, 28 May, 10 September). It should be added that a sort of underground war was waged outside Yugoslavia during the year, particularly between groups of Croatian terrorists favoring separation of Croatia from Yugoslavia and organs of the UDB, the Yugoslav secret police. On 7 June, a Croat fatally wounded the Uruguayan ambassador to Paraguay, whom he had mistaken for the newly appointed Yugoslav ambassador to that country. On 9 June, the Yugoslav Embassy in Washington, D.C., was bombed, though the identity of the perpetrators was not ascertained. In mid-September the hijacking of a passenger jet in the USA by a group of Croatian terrorists made news around the world and contributed to the worsening of the Yugoslav-U.S. official relations (see below). Agents of the UDB are believed to have murdered Croatian and Serbian anti-Tito activists in France, West Germany, and Belgium.

The Yugoslav judicial system has been widely criticized in the West in several cases related to persons arrested or sentenced for activities of a different, civil rights, kind. A prominent Belgrade lawyer, Srdja M. Popović, 39, known for his defense of political dissidents (and legal adviser to some of the American companies doing business in Yugoslavia, as well as to the Netherlands and Japanese embassies) was sentenced on 10 March to a year in prison for having given a courtroom speech in which he agreed with the views of a political dissident he was defending. The sentence drew protests from 106 prominent American lawyers and from international legal groups and civil rights organizations. On 25 May, the appeals court in Belgrade suspended the sentence but barred Popović from practicing law in Yugoslavia for a year (*NYT*, 2, 11, 24, 26, 27 March). In a somewhat similar case, a Slovenian district judge, Franc Miklavčič, was arrested in May and convicted on 15 October of treason and other crimes and sentenced to six years' imprisonment. Judge Miklavčič, a Christian Socialist who fought with Tito's partisans during the war, was accused of advocating the separation of his native republic of Slovenia from Yugoslavia, a charge he denied. Most of the evidence supporting the accusation was drawn from a private diary seized by the secret police in a raid (ibid., 16 October). The prominent dissident Mihajlo Mihajlov, 41, sentenced in February 1975 to 7 years in jail on charges arising from articles published in the West, went on a hunger strike twice during the year (the last time in November) in trying to gain some concessions such as better heating in his cell and the right to read foreign-language books, as well as protesting a new Yugoslav penal code (ibid., 24, 26, February, 30 November).

To sum up, what was going on in Yugoslavia during 1976 in the field of internal security was not strictly an anti-Soviet campaign, but rather a series of moves designed to deter any would-be troublemakers of tomorrow (i.e., after Tito disappears from the political scene). At the 14th session of the LCY's Presidium, October 1975, it was decided that greater severity had to be applied in prosecuting "foreign" and "internal" enemies of the regime. Yugoslav information media avoided any one-sidedness and were most careful not to confirm the impression gained in the West that only the followers of Moscow had been prosecuted.

Economy. To achieve the perennial and elusive goal of the Yugoslav economy, stabilization, limited state intervention and controls were introduced in 1976 in order to reduce the rate of inflation and the foreign trade deficit. The Presidium of the LCY Central Committee devoted its 23rd session (4 October) almost entirely to the economic situation. Main speakers were the prime minister, Džemal Bijedić, and the country's leading economic expert, Kiro Gligorov, the president of the SFRY's Assembly. According to Bijedić, in the first nine months of 1976 exports increased by 22 percent and imports dropped by 85 percent in comparison with the same period in 1975. (*Borba*, 5 October). Exports amounted to 60,563 million dinars (about $3,600 million) and imports to 89,656 million dinars (about $5,300 million) (*Indeks*, Belgrade, no. 11, November). A deficit of $1,700 million ensued. As far as the deficit of the balance of payments was concerned, Bijedić said that in the past two years (1974 and 1975) it amounted to about $1,000 million annually, but "now it is balanced while the situation of foreign currency reserves is very favorable." (Ibid.) It amounted to $2,700 million and was the result not only of "good exports and imports" and foreign currency earned by Yugoslavs working abroad, but also of foreign currency credits "our banks have obtained from other countries." (*Nedeljne novosti*, 21 November.) Yugoslavia's foreign debts amounted in 1976 to "almost $7,000 million" (ibid.).

Besides the improvement in the foreign trade exchange, an impressive slowing down of inflation was registered (from about 30 percent at the beginning of 1975 to 9 percent by the end of June 1976), although the level of prices remained uncomfortably high (*NIN*, 7 November). The chronic illiquidity of enterprises was considerably eased (*Komunist*, 11 October).

The reverse side of favorable economic trends in 1976 was a slowdown in industrial production, resulting in low accumulation capacity of the economy, and the stagnation or deterioration of the quality of services in general. The low labor productivity remained the most worrisome aspect of the economy (*NIN*, 7 November). The return of at least 200,000 Yugoslav emigrant workers created supplementary problems, in view of the fact that 10 to 11 percent of the registered Yugoslav labor force was unemployed (*Quarterly Economic Review*, "Yugoslavia," no. 3, London, p. 5). There were still some 860,000 Yugoslav workers employed abroad (*Politika*, 25 October). Another weak point of the Yugoslav economy was absenteeism: on average, 65 million working hours are annually lost because of sick leaves (*NIN*, 21 November). In 1975, 24,700,675 working days (or 187,605,400 working hours) were lost because of the same reason (*Politika*, 17 November). In Serbia alone, 80,000 workers were on sick leave every day (ibid.).

As for agriculture, the very good wheat harvest of 1976 amounted to 5,979,000 tons (2,457,000 tons in the socialist sector and 3,522,000 tons on private farms) (*Indeks*, no. 11). The corn harvest amounted to 9,112,000 tons, three percent less than in 1975 (*Borba*, 8 October). Private farmers in Yugoslavia hold about 8,500,000 hectares, accounting for 85 percent of the country's arable land; they also raise some 91.3 percent of its livestock. The socialist farms work 1,509,000 hectares, accounting for 15 percent of the country's arable acreage, and raise 8.7 percent of the livestock. (*Yugoslav Survey*, no. 1, February.)

On 20 July the Federal Assembly adopted an ambitious five-year economic plan for 1976-80. An average overall growth rate of 7 percent is anticipated (below the 7.3 of the original draft). The 1971-75 target had been 7.5 percent per annum, and the outcome 6 percent. (*Quarterly Economic Review*, no. 3, p. 11.) On 28 May the new 296-mile rail link between Belgrade and Bar (which took 20 years to build and will require further ameliorative works) was inaugurated. Cooperative ventures with foreign firms and foreign loans will also benefit the Yugoslav economy. On 26 March an agreement was signed by the Dow Chemical Company, of Midland, Minnesota, USA, and the largest Yugoslav oil and petrochemical company (Industrija Nafte, INA) for the joint construction and operation of a $700 million petrochemical complex on Krk Island (near Rijeka) in Dalmatia. World Bank loans to Yugoslavia, contracted in May and June, and amounting to $153 million, will be used for water development in Serbia, air-pollution control, and various industrial projects in the less developed regions of the country.

Personal Income. The most important characteristic of the Yugoslav system of remuneration is that persons employed in the so-called nonproductive enterprises (banks, insurance companies, schools, party and state administration) make more money than those in the productive enterprises (industry, agriculture). According to the official Yugoslav statistics, the average monthly personal income in nonproductive enterprises was 3,734 dinars (about $207), while in productive enterprises it was 3,106 dinars (about $172). Personal income was lowest in forestry (2,899 dinars, or about $161 and highest in the state administration (4,014 dinars, or $223) (*Ekonomska politika*, 17 May). In May 1976 the accompanying table of personal monthly salaries for March 1975 was published.

Personal Monthly Salaries, March 1975
($1 = 18 dinars)

Monthly salary, in dinars, from previous figure up to	Total number of employed persons in socialist sector	Percentage of all employed persons in socialist sector
1,200	28,185	0.6
1,400	61,068	1.3
1,600	150,321	3.2
1,800	263,060	5.6
2,000	371,103	7.9
2,500	930,107	19.8
3,000	930,107	19.8
3,500	690,534	14.7
4,000	455,658	9.7
4,500	286,548	6.1
5,000	187,900	4.0
6,000	187,900	4.0
over 6,000	155,017	3.3
Total	4,697,508	100.0

Source: *Politika*, 11 May 1976.

For the purpose of comparison, the president of the Belgrade City Party Committee in 1976 earned 11,340 dinars ($630) per month, the secretary of the same party committee 10,385 dinars ($577), and members of the party secretariat 9,365 dinars each ($520) (*Večernje novosti*, 29 May).

Foreign Affairs. *The Soviet Union.* Yugoslav-Soviet relations seem to have been strained in the first six months of 1976 due to differences concerning the convocation of the conference of European Communist and workers' parties (see below). After the conference Yugoslav suspicion vis-à-vis Moscow did not automatically disappear because of the one-sided—in Yugoslav opinion—Soviet interpretation of the conference's resolution. The Russians had, namely, continued to talk of "proletarian internationalism," a term the Yugoslav Communists have always identified with Moscow's plans designed to dominate other parties and countries and restore the Soviet party's hegemony within the world Communist movement.

Leonid Brezhnev's 48-hour visit to Belgrade (15-17 November) seems to have led to some improvement in the relations between the two parties. In the U.S. presidential election campaign, Governor Carter's statement in his third TV debate with President Ford, 23 October, that, as president he would not send U.S. troops into Yugoslavia to counter a Soviet invasion certainly contributed to Tito's efforts to improve his relations with Moscow. Thus far Brezhnev has traveled to Yugoslavia four times: in September-October 1962, as President of the Supreme Soviet (i.e., state president), in September 1966 (on his way from Sofia to Budapest), in September 1971, and in November of 1976. Since the May 1955 reconciliation between Tito and Nikita Khrushchev, the Yugoslav president has visited the USSR eight times, most recently in November 1973.

The joint communiqué signed on 17 November 1976, included almost all the points which were component parts of earlier declarations and statements, especially Yugoslavia's insistence on independence, sovereignty, responsibility "to one's own working class," and mutual respect for equality and noninterference in internal affairs. "Comradely voluntary cooperation" was mentioned twice, as was the concept of "the freedom to choose different ways of socialist development" coupled with internationalism. The communiqué avoided the term "Marxism-Leninism" in stating that cooperation should develop "in the spirit of the teachings and the great ideals of Marx, Engels, and Lenin." In the section dealing with situation within the international Communist movement it was said that "the working class, the communist and workers' parties, and other progressive forces act in different conditions, which give rise to the differences in the forms in the paths of the struggle for socialism and for the construction of socialism." Nevertheless, "these objective differences should not be an obstacle to the development of all-round mutual cooperation between communist and workers' parties, and between all revolutionary and progressive forces, in the struggle for social progress and peace throughout the world." "Strict respect" for the equality and sovereign independence of every party was mentioned twice.

Several paragraphs dealing specifically with the Yugoslav-Soviet relations stressed the "particular significance [of the] expansion of party ties in the future" and agreed on "constant development of contacts between the governments," from the highest state assemblies to "the republics and the cities of the two countries." The strengthening of the economic cooperation in the future should include "a more extensive use of modern forms of the international division of labor and the development of production cooperation on a long-term basis." Another sentence of the communiqué (reflecting a major Yugoslav concern) insisted that the information media of both countries should "objectively inform on the totality of socio-economic developments" in both countries.

Finally, on the foreign political issues, covering the largest part of the communiqué, both sides expressed full agreement: struggle for the further relaxation of international tension (mentioned seven times in the text); denunciation of imperialism, colonialism, and neo-colonialism; halting of the arms race and attaining, ultimately, general and complete disarmament; support of the UN General Assembly in aiming at a change in international economic relations; high evaluation of the final act of the 1975 Helsinki conference; a request that the Israeli troops fully withdraw from all Arab territories; praise for the nonaligned countries' movement — "one of the most important factors in world affairs"; and favorable assessment of the East Berlin conference of European Communist and workers' parties. (Tanjug, 17 November; *Borba*, 18 November; *FBIS*, 19 November.)

Brezhnev's obvious efforts to improve Moscow's image in Yugoslavia, especially in preparation for the post-Tito era, and Tito's eagerness to appear as equal partner in dealing with Moscow, were reflected in the communiqué statement that both sides shared "complete satisfaction with the results of their talks in Belgrade." To affirm that the Soviet Union and the Soviet party did not harbor any hostile feelings to Yugoslavia and the LCY, Brezhnev at a state banquet went as far as to denounce the "absurd fabrication," concocted by the West, of the "terrible and bloodthirsty wolf" (USSR) about to devour a "helpless Little Red Riding Hood" (Yugoslavia). (*NYT*, 16 November.)

Despite Tito's winning a new pledge of independence from the Soviet leader, hints started to filter soon after the Belgrade meeting that Tito had dismissed a wide range of Soviet overtures for closer ties with Belgrade and had rejected the Kremlin's request to increase the servicing of Soviet warships at Adriatic ports and to permit Soviet warplanes to enter Yugoslav airspace unless a third country friendly to Belgrade asked for it (as was the case during the 1973 Middle East war) (ibid., 14 December).

Yugoslavia has again run into difficulties with the utilization of Soviet credits promised to it in November 1972. The first installment for the period 1973-76, amounting to $540 million, appears now to be inadequate for the reconstruction and expansion of almost 40 industrial facilities in Yugoslavia. The solution of this problem was on the agenda of the Yugoslav-Soviet Committee for Economic and Scientific-Technical Cooperation, meeting in Moscow in December. As for the trade between the two countries, it had reached, in the last five-year plan, almost $6 billion. In the new five-year plan, it will increase another 240 percent. With its 25 percent share of Yugoslav exports, the USSR is Yugoslavia's largest foreign trade partner. (Radio Moscow, 7 November.)

A final note for the record: just as was the case in September 1971, the LCY delegation that met with Brezhnev and his group did not include any Croatian leader (with the exception of Tito himself, who is a Croat by birth, but a "Yugoslav" by political conviction). This time, the LCY delegation included, with Tito, three Slovenians (Edvard Kardelj, Stane Dolanc, and Jože Smole, SFRY ambassador to the USSR), one Moslem (Džemal Bijedić), one Serb (Miloš Minić, federal secretary for foreign affairs), and one Macedonian (Aleksandar Grličkov, secretary of the Executive Committee of the Presidium of the LCY Central Committee and chief LCY representative in the preparatory discussions for the East Berlin conference.

The United States. Yugoslavia's relations with the United States in 1976 were characterized by a special dualism: the Yugoslav Communist leaders expected to receive major economic and other support from Washington, yet they continued to wage an intensive anti-American campaign, almost on a daily basis. This is why the relations between the two countries fell to the lowest point in 30 years, causing concern in many parts of Europe. Yugoslav declarations regularly associated Washington's policies with "neo-colonialism," "imperialism," or worse (*NYT*, 26 July). The U.S. ambassador in Belgrade, Laurence H. Silberman, was proclaimed persona non grata by Tito personally (*Politika*, 1 August). Tito claimed Silberman had "initiated a campaign against Yugoslavia" by having insisted that an innocently sentenced U.S. citizen, Laszlo Toth, should be freed. Toth, a Yugoslav-born U.S. citizen, was convicted in 1975 of "industrial espionage" and sentenced to 7 years imprisonment. Following Silberman's intervention, he was released in July. On the day of Leonid Brezhnev's leaving Belgrade, 17 November, the U.S. State Department announced Silberman's resignation.

Another matter which generated heat in Yugoslav-U.S. relations was the so-called Sonnenfeldt doctrine, which the Yugoslavs interpreted as "the revival of Yalta" (Radio Zagreb, 14 May). Despite all U.S. denials, the Yugoslav information media for several weeks dealt with Helmut Sonnelfeldt's ideas, especially criticizing his alleged advice to the Yugoslav Communists that they should be "less obnoxious to Moscow" (*Politika*, 2 April). During a press conference in Stockholm in March, Tito said that "if Yugoslavia is in question, no statements, including Sonnenfeldt's, could scare us and make us deviate from our road which we are going to follow also in the future" (*Dagens Nyheter*, 30 March).

If, however, Sonnenfeldt's warnings did not scare the Yugoslav Communists, the 23 October TV statement of Governor Carter certainly did. They were consequently relieved when in his press conference on 4 November, President-elect Carter rectified his position: "If the Soviet Union should invade Yugoslavia, this would be an extremely serious breach of peace; it would be a threat to the entire world, as far as a peaceful world is concerned. It would make it almost impossible for us to continue under the broad generic sense of détente. And whether or not we actually committed troops to Yugoslavia would be conjectural. My opinion is that would be unlikely, but I would have to make a decision on a final basis at that point." (USIS transcript of the remarks, 6 November.) Tito echoed parts of President-elect Carter's statement when he said during a visit of the French president Valéry Giscard d'Estaing: "I can't say whether Yugoslavia would be attacked in the future and, at the moment, I don't know where such an attack might come from. For the time being, there is no danger to Yugoslavia's independence." (*Borba*, 8 December.)

Back to the usual anti-U.S. backbiting, a top Yugoslav party functionary, Jure Bilić, the Croatian representative in the LCY Executive Committee, claimed that former President Nixon "was deeply involved in the policy of Yugoslavia's disintegration." During his October 1970 visit in Zagreb, Nixon was said to have exerted pressure upon Yugoslavia by "riding the nationalist-separatist horse" and by promising Yugoslavia economic aid with the aim "to interfere in our internal affairs." (*Politika*, 3 December.) This claim is believed to have been made as an attempt to influence the trial of a group of five Croatian terrorists and an American woman, the wife of one of the Croatians, who on 11 September hijacked a TWA jetliner on its routine flight from New York to Chicago, with more than 90 people on the plane. On 12 September the Croatian hijackers surrendered in Paris and were taken back to New York, where a policeman was killed by a hidden terrorist bomb. (*NYT*, 13 September.) The demand of the hijackers that their "declaration" issued by "Headquarters of Croatian National Liberation Forces" be printed in the *New York Times, Los Angeles Times, Chicago Tribune, Washington Post,* and *International Herald-Tribune* was fulfilled on 11 September. The Yugoslav information media attacked "reactionary circles" in the USA as having been behind the hijackers. Even the negotiations with the hijackers in order to rescue the hostages were criticized as being in contradiction with the officially proclaimed policy of the U.S. government. (Tanjug, 12 September.) In a commentary a day after the U.S. ambassador ended his tour of duty, *Borba* attacked the U.S. attitude toward the non-aligned movement, claiming that Washington was attempting to disrupt its unity and commitment" (*NYT*, 28 December).

During a visit to Yugoslavia by U.S. secretary of commerce Elliot Richardson (25-28 November) it was reported that the United States was investigating Yugoslav diversion to the USSR of sophisticated American equipment imported by Yugoslavia. At least six Yugoslav companies were suspected of diverting civilian strategic materials, including weaponry, to the USSR during the 1960s, and their permits to obtain these goods from the USA had been suspended. But export licenses for strategic materials, including computers, had been reissued to another 10 Yugoslav companies. Still there is no way for the United States to monitor what happens to strategic materials once they enter Yugoslavia. The six Yugoslav enterprises suspected of having acted for Soviet intelligence interests were not publicly identified (UPI, 29 November). The resumption of U.S. arms sales to Yugoslavia, including advanced military equipment, in what would have been the first major purchase since 1961, was announced in mid-January 1976 and was indefinitely postponed in mid-May (*NYT*, 14 January, 14 May).

The U.S.-Yugoslav trade was developing favorably, particularly from the Yugoslav standpoint. According to the official data in the first ten months of 1976, Yugoslavia's exports to the USA amounted to $310 million, while its imports from the USA amounted to $305.6 million (*Ekonomska politika*, 6 December). During his visit to Yugoslavia, Elliot Richardson "restated American support for independence, territorial unity, integrity and non-alignment of Yugoslavia" (Reuter, 27 November.)

Non-Aligned Summit in Colombo. The 5th non-aligned summit took place on 16-19 August in Colombo, Sri Lanka, with 112 countries represented (86 full members and 26 with the status of "observers" or "permanent guests"). Yugoslavia's delegation was headed by President Tito, who delivered his speech on 17 August urging the non-aligned world to press for global détente in all spheres. He regretted that little had been achieved in implementing Helsinki conference decision on cooperation and security, and attacked Israel, which he said was the main cause for the dangerous Middle East situation. He also condemned "some forces" which, he said, claimed to have the right to intervene in the internal affairs of other countries. He did not, however, identify them. These forces, according to Tito, were attempting to destroy the unity of the non-aligned nations or to subordinate some of them to their policies by resorting to pressure and interference and even to the use of force. He also said that attempts at undermining the internal stability of individual countries had become more frequent. Finally he insisted that a "new economic order" in the world had to be created. (*Borba*, 18 August.) The non-aligned summit adopted a Political Declaration, a Program of Action, an Economic Declaration, and 16 special resolutions dealing with the main problems discussed in Colombo. The assembled non-aligned leaders decided that the sixth summit should take place in Havana in 1979.

A short historical background to nonalignment may be in order. The first non-aligned summit took place in Belgrade on 1-6 September 1961 with 28 countries participating (25 full members and 3 observers); the second, in Cairo, on 5-8 October 1964, with 57 countries (47 full members and 10 observers); the third, in Lusaka (Zambia) on 8-10 September 1970, with 64 countries (54 full members and 10 observers), and the fourth in Algiers on 2-8 September 1973, with 87 countries (75 full members, 9 observers, and 3 guests). In Algeria the representatives of 15 liberation movements were also present—these were given the status of observers—plus 4 international organizations.

Tito's role among the non-aligned countries has been very important from the beginning. Yugoslavia has been the only European Communist country in the group, and the newly independent countries have from the start of their nationhood been troubled by weaknesses resulting from the schism between the forces advocating socialism and those opposing it. External freedom has often not been matched by the growth of domestic liberties, and these emergent countries have also been involved in disputes about whether they should remain neutral or not. In addition, the Yugoslav Communist leaders presented non-alignment as a path leading ultimately to socialism. In his speech at the East Berlin conference in June, Tito said that by defending the policy of non-alignment the Yugoslav Communists were also fulfilling their "international Communist obligations" (ibid., 1 July). In a critical appraisal of Yugoslavia's non-aligned policy Milovan Djilas said in an interview: "It is an illusion to think Yugoslavia could be leader of a large portion of humanity, though this doesn't mean we should not have relations with these countries. But I am against this ideological talk within the non-aligned that it is a class struggle for the world." (UPI, 26 October.)

The Balkans. Between 26 January and 5 February a conference of five Balkan countries (Greece, Turkey, Yugoslavia, Romania, and Bulgaria) took place in Athens. The sixth Balkan country, Albania, refused to come with the explanation that it has been against any type of multilateral meetings. There were 74 delegates from the five countries and the Yugoslav delegation was headed by Kazimir Vidas, under-secretary in the Finance Ministry. The conference was opened by Greek prime minister Karamanlis. Despite great words the communiqué published on 6 February showed that nothing substantial was achieved. It suggested that another conference should be held in the future. In a critical appraisal the Yugoslavs said the Bulgarian delegates did their utmost to prevent "any continuity in the cooperation" among the Balkan countries. In contrast to this the Romanians were hailed by the Yugoslavs for having been interested in "all-round co-operation." The Turks were said to have maintained a reasonable attitude, but they rejected an idea concerning the creation of a "permanent secretariat" advanced by the Greeks. The latter were full of "discreet feelings" about a new Balkan pact, such as these five countries originally created in 1934. As far as Yugoslavia is concerned, it was said to have "no problems" such as those plaguing the four other countries, two of which belong to the Warsaw Pact, and two to NATO. (*Vjesnik*, 8 February.)

On 10 May President Tito arrived in Athens for an official visit until 13 May. The Yugoslav leader had last been to Greece in March 1959. After Romanian leader Ceauşescu's visit to Athens (26-29 March 1976), followed by that of Bulgaria's Todor Zhivkov (9-11 April), Tito's visit was made in order to straighten out some issues which have created a certain degree of dissonance in the relations between Athens and Belgrade. One of them was the existence of the "Macedonian nation," negated by both the Bulgarians and the Greeks. Another issue on which two sides were differing was Karamanlis's attitude to the policy of nonalignment, as expressed in a speech before the Greek National Assembly in answer to the Greek leftist opposition which insisted Greece should become a non-aligned country. Karamanlis answered that non-alignment would be "the worst policy," designed "to keep Greece at remove from the democratic West, and, in a subsequent stage, to include Greece in the Communist East." (*Politika*, 23 April.) In the joint Greek-Yugoslav communiqué this problem was not mentioned. Instead the two sides hailed the "peaceful activities" of non-aligned countries. (*Vjesnik*, 14 May.)

Two days after Todor Zhivkov left Ankara and 10 days before Ceauşescu arrived, President Tito spent four days (8-11 June) in the Turkish capital on an official visit. This was his second official visit to Ankara, the first having taken place 22 years before, in April 1954. The reason why so much time elapsed between visits was explained by Yugoslav information media as the result of the fact that "no problems" have ever existed in Yugoslav-Turkish relations. In Belgrade satisfaction was voiced over the fact that while Tito was driven from the airport to Ankara in a motorcade, Bulgarian party and state chief Zhivkov had to be transported by means of a helicopter "because of organized demonstrations protesting the treatment of the Turkish minority in Bulgaria" (*Politika*, 8 June). Generally speaking, the Yugoslav-Turkish meetings appeared to have been devoted more to international problems, including the Greek-Turkish conflict over Cyprus, than to mutual relations between the two countries.

The 13th meeting between Tito and Ceauşescu, the Romanian party and state chief—not counting those at international conferences—took place on 8-11 September at the Slovenian mountain resort of Brdo. The Romanian leader was the last foreign visitor before Tito fell ill, ordering the cancellation of a number of scheduled visits. The main topics discussed appear to have been the June conference of European Communist and workers' parties in East Berlin, Ceauşescu's August "vacation" in the Soviet Union, the follow-up of the Helsinki conference scheduled to be held in Belgrade in June 1977, and the Balkan problems (*Review of International Affairs*, 20 September). The news media of the two countries made no reference to the Soviet Union and its post-East Berlin ideological campaign or to the Brezhnev-Ceauşescu talks. Both Tito and Ceauşescu praised the non-aligned movement for its "open character" and as a factor of peace. Ceauşescu expressed "warm gratitude" to Tito "for Yugoslavia's active support in connection with Romania's admission to the group of 77 and for its participation as a guest in the Colombo conference of non-aligned countries." (*Borba*, 10 September.) The joint declaration spoke of identity and closeness of views, and the two leaders agreed on the importance of calling a special session of the UN General Assembly to discuss disarmament. With regard to the Balkans, the two presidents stressed the significance of the Balkan conference in Athens (see above), and said that multilateral co-operation was in the interest of all countries in the region. (*Politika*, 11 September.)

Relations between Yugoslavia and Bulgaria remained unsettled by the problems of Macedonians living in Bulgaria, predominantly Pirin Macedonia, or as it is locally called, the Blagoevgrad Okrug (county). Exhaustive Yugoslav-Bulgarian consultations held in Sofia in early October brought no positive results, with the positions of both countries remaining diametrically opposed. Consequently, on 11 November, Yugoslavia officially informed the United Nations that the Macedonian national minority in Bulgaria has been deprived of its rights, and that its existence is being totally denied. A Yugoslav representative at the UN claimed that 178,862 individuals declared themselves Macedonian during the 1956 census in Bulgaria. Subsequent pressures on the Macedonian minority led, according to the Yugoslav speaker, to decreasing the number to fewer than 10,000 Macedonians in the census of 1965. Thereafter, official Bulgarian statements repeated that the Macedonian national minority does not exist in Bulgaria. (Tanjug, 11 November.) The visit of Todor Zhivkov to Byelorussia at the end of October was criticized in the Yugoslav press, especially a speech he made in Minsk together with Piotr Masherov, the first secretary of the Byelorussian party's Central Committee. A prominent Yugoslav newspaperman objected to some "new forms of contact" between individual East European countries and individual Soviet republics. He quoted Masherov's words on the "unification" and "fraternal rapprochement among socialist nations," and noted that Zhivkov expressed himself in similar terms. (*Politika*, 5 November.) Dispute over the Macedonian issue and press polemics did not hinder, however, trade relations between the two countries or circulation of their citizens in both directions.

Yugoslav-Albanian relations, relaxed during the past few years, turned sour again when in his opening speech at the 7th Congress of the Albanian Workers' Party, on 2 November, Enver Hoxha used harsher anti-Titoist terms than had been heard in years. After expressing his "respect and trust for the peoples of Yugoslavia" he said of Tito's regime: "Yugoslav revisionism remains a favorable weapon in the hands of the international imperialist bourgeoisie in the struggle against socialism and the liberation movements" (*NYT*, 5 November; Tanjug, 2 November).

Other Contacts and Problems—West and East. During his extensive diplomatic trips in the first part of 1976, Tito in March visited Mexico, Panama, and Venezuela, and then Portugal and Sweden. Before leaving for these trips he was host to Cuban premier Fidel Castro, who made his first visit to Yugoslavia on 6-8 March. Castro, who visited Yugoslav President on the island of Brioni, obtained Tito's full approval of armed Cuban intervention in Angola (*NYT*, 9 March). Egyptian president Anwar Sadat visited Yugoslavia on 8-9 April. At the end of the year, Yasir Arafat, the Palestinian guerrilla leader, visited Yugoslavia for two days, receiving assurances that Yugoslavia would give full backing to the organization he heads (ibid., 6 December). On 6 December, French president Valéry Giscard d'Estaing arrived in Yugoslavia for a two-day official visit, the first of its kind by a French head of state. He said that he wanted to get Tito's views on the political and economic future of the Third World and declared that "Yugoslavia's independence is a factor for peace and stability in Europe" (ibid, 7 December).

Austria was the country with which Yugoslavia had a most heatedly debated problem in 1976. It centered on the census, held on 14 November, asking each Austrian citizen to declare his mother tongue. The controversy focused on Carinthia, Austria's southernmost province, with a sizable minority of Slovenes. The Austrian authorities insisted that the census was held in furtherance of minority rights, and was intended to determine exactly how many Austrian citizens speak languages other than German, thus fixing the legal requirement for bilingual road-signs and other bilingual facilities in some areas. Slovenian local leaders, strongly supported by the Yugoslav government, denounced the census as leading to a restriction on the rights of minorities and as an attempt to assimilate and Germanize the Slovenes, Croats, and other ethnic Yugoslav citizens of Austria. Throughout the year, Yugoslav media were scoring the Austrian "anti-minority campaign" and the Slovenes in Carinthia were encouraged to boycott the census. There were reports that some Slovenes who took part in the census had written "Hebrew" or "Chinese" as their response to a question about their native tongue (ibid., 15 November). As in the case of the Macedonian minority in Bulgaria, Yugoslavia raised the issue of the Slovene and Croat minorities in Austria at the United Nations.

Yugoslav-Czechoslovak relations were also less than friendly in 1976. An article in a Zagreb daily criticized an article in a Czechoslovak newspaper which made a distinction between "real" Communist parties (i.e., those obedient to Moscow) and the others (*Vjesnik*, 11 January). Belgrade's *Politika* in its 22 April issue carried a report by its Prague correspondent complaining about the suppression of Yugoslav newspapers in Czechoslovakia during the recent congress of the Czechoslovak Communist Party. Finally, on 30 April *Politika* announced that it would close its office in Czechoslovakia because of "obstacles repeatedly placed in the way of fulfillment of professional obligations."

Conference of European Communist and Workers' Parties. After 20 preparatory conferences (two in 1974, in Warsaw and Budapest; 14 in 1975 and 4 in 1976, all in East Berlin), the representatives of 29 European Communist and workers' parties gathered in East Berlin on 29-30 June. The LCY delegation was headed by President Tito, who delivered a low-key speech on 30 June avoiding anything that might have offended Moscow. Having been convinced that he had already won the game as far as the preparations for the conference were concerned, he let Berlinguer of Italy and Marchais of France be more critical. Still, the Yugoslav leader did not hesitate to stress once again that his country and party would continue to stick firmly to their independence and non-alignment. (*Vjesnik*, 1 July.) All of this, however, did not leave the impression that the Yugoslav Communists were quite sure that Moscow would stick firmly to all its promises—in the past many similar promises have been made only to be broken. Even though the joint document passed at the East Berlin conference was also approved by the LCY, its real meaning must be sought in the statement of an unnamed senior Yugoslav delegate, who was quoted as having said privately that no document could defend his country and that its only effective guarantee was preparedness for "a total war of self-defense" (ibid.).

The fact that Tito created a sensation by personally attending the East Berlin meeting, rather than by what was in his speech, is quite understandable. His stubborn oppositon over the past two years, during the preparations for the conference, when he rejected the mention of the only "leading center" in the world Communist movement and also any final document of the conference which would be obligatory for all participating parties, was interpreted in the West as meaning that Tito went to East Berlin as a "victorious heretic." It was a symbolic gesture when, on 28 June, one day before the conference was to start, Brezhnev and Tito met for a private talk in East Berlin. June 28 is a historic date: on that day, in 1948, Tito and the Yugoslav Communist Party were expelled from the Cominform as "revisionists" and "traitors." A year later (in November 1949), they were even called "fascist murderers" (in the so-called second Cominform resolution).

After the East Berlin conference the Yugoslavs did not show any exaggerated enthusiasm about the conference's results. As a quid pro quo for the alleged concessions Moscow gave in East Berlin, the Yugoslav leaders stressed that they belong to the "Communist world" (Aleksandar Grličkov) and share the general Communist view about "the deep crisis of the capitalist system" (Tito). While the "Communist world" to which the Yugoslav Communists believe they belong is certainly different from the Communist world Brezhnev has in mind, the "strategic aims" of both have remained identical: a classless communist society.

Not long after the East Berlin conference the Yugoslav leaders were again involved in an ideological controversy with Moscow: the Soviet interpretation of "proletarian internationalism" appeared to have not changed after the conference. A round-table discussion in September at Titograd, the capital of the Socialist Republic of Montenegro, criticized the Soviet views on "proletarian internationalism" as completely ignoring the East Berlin conference. The text of the speeches delivered at the Titograd meeting by 13 party theoreticians from all six Yugoslav republics revealed that the Soviet views were attacked at least as sharply as before the East Berlin conference. Soviet ideological or other supremacy within the international Communist movement was resolutely rejected, and several speakers insisted that "proletarian internationalism" must not be interpreted as meaning simply unqualified loyalty to the USSR and the Communist Party of the Soviet Union (*Borba*, 21 August-13 September). On the other hand, Yugoslav information media revealed a secret talk between Tito and Khrushchev in November 1956, only one day before the Soviet invasion of Hungary, in which the Yugoslav president agreed with the Soviet military intervention to save socialism (*Vjesnik*, 27 April).

Publications. The chief publications of the LCY are *Komunist* (weekly) and *Socijalizam* (monthly). The most important daily newspapers are *Borba* (with Belgrade and Zagreb editions), *Politika* (Belgrade), *Vjesnik* (Zagreb), *Nova Makedonija* (Skoplje), *Oslobodjenje* (Sarajevo), and *Delo* (Ljubljana). The most important weeklies are *NIN (Nedeljne informativne novine)*, Belgrade, *Vus* (Zagreb), and *Ekonomska politika* (Belgrade). *Tanjug* is the official news agency.

Radio Free Europe   Slobodan Stanković
Munich

The (illegal) Communist Party of Yugoslavia (Komunistička Partija Jugoslavije; CPY). Never since the late 1940s and early 1950s—the period of the Tito-Stalin conflict—have the anti-Titoist Communist groups, in and outside of Yugoslavia, been more active than in the last couple of years. As revealed by Tito himself (*Borba*, 13 September 1974), the Yugoslav "Cominformists," i.e., people advocating Yugoslavia's return to the "Communist family" headed by Moscow, held in the spring of 1974 a clandestine congress in Montenegro's Adriatic port Bar. At that occasion they proclaimed themselves, in contradistinction to the "treason" of Tito and his League of Communists of Yugoslavia, the standard bearers of the genuine Communist Party of Yugoslavia. They dubbed their meeting "The Fifth Congress of the CPY," indicating in this way that all the subsequent congresses of the LCY were in their eyes null and void. For them the official CPY Fifth Congress in July 1948, at which the party leadership defended itself against the Cominform-Stalin accusations, took the party on a wrong path leading to total severance of ties with the CPSU and, in 1952, to the change of the party name and character.

Following Stalin's death and the Khrushchev-Tito reconciliation, Yugoslav "Cominformists" were reduced to prison confinement or elimination from any positions of public responsibility, or to the status of political refugees in other Communist countries. It is therefore even more remarkable that just at the time when Tito and Brezhnev exchanged "friendly" visits and the relations between the two countries and parties seemed to be at least correct, the Cominformist activities came again to the surface, with greater acuity than at any time in more than two decades. It should immediately be added that no *public* trials of the Cominformists were staged, and that the Yugoslav information media never made an accusation or implied that the Soviet Union was directly supporting the prosecuted people who claimed to be the sole faithful Soviet followers in Yugoslavia. Likewise, Soviet media never lent public support to the Yugoslav Cominformists. In an article published on 27 November 1975, and frequently quoted in the Yugoslav press, *Pravda* dissociated the Soviet Union and the CPSU from "conspiratorial sectarian groups" in Yugoslavia (i.e., the Cominformists) "who represent no one but themselves." At the same time, however, the Soviets have not publicly dissociated themselves from the anti-Titoist Cominformist exiles living in the Soviet Union and the other East European countries.

It has been no secret that two main anti-Titoist (Cominformist) groups have been active outside Yugoslavia: the first, and smaller, in Prague; the second, stronger and more important, in Kiev, the capital of the Ukraine. Two leaders of the Kiev group, Dr. Mileta Perović and Professor Bogdan Jovović, left Kiev in the beginning of October 1975 and, according to at least two Western reports (AFP dispatch, Belgrade, 27 January 1976; *Daily Telegraph*, London, 24 February), went to Paris to wage anti-Titoist propaganda. They brought with them from Kiev the "Party Program" of a "new" pro-Soviet CPY, whose creation was proclaimed at the "Fifth Congress" in Bar.

London's *Daily Telegraph* of 24 February gave the gist of that Program, designed to provide the basis for a transitional regime between "Tito's dictatorship" and a "genuine people's democracy." In its wake, the Swedish liberal daily *Dagens Nyheter* (24 May) carried an article by its Belgrade correspondent under the title "Soviet-Loyal Communists: It Is Time to Overthrow Tito." The article summarized also the new 150-pages-long CPY program and hinted (quoting Yugoslav sources) that the rival CPY, though not called by name, was represented at the 25th Congress of the CPSU in February.

In Yugoslavia itself, as mentioned in the preceding LCY profile, the authorities sentenced harshly the apprehended Cominformists, for in the words of a leading Montenegrin Communist, "Cominformism is not ideology but treason" (*Borba*, 10 January). Still, despite the official insistence that the Cominformist affair should not be exaggerated, thousands of meetings and symposia took place throughout Yugoslavia to discuss the problem of Cominformism, which a member of the LCY Presidium's Executive Committee viewed as "an expression and instrument of dogmatist-Stalinist ideology which is still present within the international workers' movement, as well as an embodiment of an idea cherished by some people in our country" (ibid., 5 February).

While the Yugoslav authorities, in their understandable nervousness about the course which international and domestic events might take after Tito leaves the stage, are vigilant about Cominformist activities, it is impossible to judge how strong the Cominformists in Yugoslavia really are and especially who might be their "sleepers" still exercising high functions in the LCY, the Army, secret police, and other public bodies. No less predictable is the role of the Cominformists in contingency plans which the Kremlin policy makers undoubtedly have for post-Tito Yugoslavia.

Without entering into any speculation on these matters, it is interesting to note that Dr. Mileta Perović gave an interview to a Brussels weekly, *Notre Temps* (22 January), in which he was introduced to the readers as the secretary-general of the clandestine Communist Party of Yugoslavia and a brief biographical sketch was provided. He was born in 1923, was a member of the Alliance of Communist Youth of Yugoslavia (SKOJ), joined Tito's partisans in 1941, and became the commandant of a brigade. After the war he served in the diplomatic corps and was a military attaché in Albania. In 1948, as stated in the biographical notice, he "criticized the positions of the Central Committee, the lack of democracy in the party and the state" (i.e., opted for Stalin against Tito). He was arrested, sentenced to forced labor, and kept until 1956 at the Goli Otok, the best-known Adriatic island camp for Cominformist prisoners. In 1958 he fled to Albania and in 1960 went to the USSR. He obtained his doctoral degree in economics, and became a professor at the University of Kiev, specializing in capitalist economy. He is said to be writing an analysis of present-day Yugoslavia, comparing constitutions of Salazar's Portugal, Franco's Spain, Nazi Germany, and Tito's Yugoslavia.

The interview reiterated the harshest overall condemnation of Tito's Yugoslavia contained in the new Program of the CPY, of which Perović is presumably the author. There are no other indications in the interview about the strength of the Yugoslav Cominformists, with the exception of a remark that there are at present 3,000 Yugoslav political refugees living in the USSR. The main target of the clandestine CPY, in Perović's words, is "the liquidation of the personal counterrevolutionary dictatorship of Tito," whom he accuses of using yearly for his own and his closest entourage's services a sum which is two-and-a-half times larger than the budget of the Republic of Montenegro. Insisting that the CPY is "a democratic alternative to Titoism," Perović concluded that "the final aim of the Communist Party of Yugoslavia is the construction of a communist society which will be an inseparable organic part of the world communist system."

Moscow has thus far not tried to deny anything Dr. Perović and Professor Jovović have propagated while in Western Europe. In the meantime, after Belgrade's strong protest in Paris, the French authorities have ordered the two Cominformist leders to leave France; Dr. Perović departed for Israel, while Professor Jovović went to London.

The length of the new CPY Program prevents its full reproduction here. It appeared, however, advisable that the most significant passages be excerpted in English translation. The text corresponds very closely with the second Cominform denunciation of Tito's Yugoslavia of November 1949; its presumed author taught until recently at a Soviet university, and might have been encouraged if not helped to pen the program and bring it personally to the West; its violent polemical tone may be found inspirational, once in the hands of other Yugoslav Cominformists. And even if the Marxist-Leninist-Stalinist jargon of the document does not rhyme with the détente phraseology of the present Kremlin leadership (one may detect deeply veiled criticism of the Brezhnev line here and there in the text), the historical importance of the "new" CPY Program remains: either as a last vestige of a violent phase in Yugoslav-Soviet relations, or as a harbinger of one possible post-Tito alternative.

Central Committee of the Communist
Party of Yugoslavia

THE PROGRAM OF THE COMMUNIST PARTY OF YUGOSLAVIA
(1976)

PART ONE

THE COMMUNIST PARTY OF YUGOSLAVIA AND THE SO-CALLED "LEAGUE OF COMMUNISTS"

[The first several pages of this part of the Program are highly laudatory of the past of the Communist Party of Yugoslavia, including the inter-war period and the Party's armed struggle during the Second World War. The only discordant notes, in comparison with the official Yugoslav historiography, here, would be the omission of the term "people's liberation struggle," the reference to the Soviet Union as "the only fatherland of the workers and peasants," and the insistence on the "unselfish help given by the great Soviet Union and the fraternal armies of Albania and Bulgaria" for the final liberation of the country. High marks are also given to the Party for its radical post-war policies. Then the tone changes and the leadership of the CPY is charged with inability to wage the "great battle for socialism."]

. . . The difficulties that had cropped up during the reconstruction of the country after a four-year war and the fascist occupation, the strong resistance shown by the class enemies in the country, and a mixture of pressure and promises from the international imperialist *bourgeoisie* combined to demoralize the top party leaders, headed by Josip Broz [Tito], who became imbued with nationalism and infected with Austro-Marxism. Frightened by objective difficulties during the period of socialist construction, amazed by the postwar boom in the capitalist economies, dazzled with glory and burdened with various weaknesses, the top party leaders gradually deviated from Marxism-Leninism and sank ever deeper into the swamp of opportunism and bourgeois nationalism, until the logic of class struggle led them to a complete capitulation before the class enemies, thus pushing them into open treason to the working class, socialism, and Yugoslavia. That is how these leaders came to join the camp of the world reactionary forces and counterrevolution.

Their policy encountered mass resistance, and Tito actually carried out a *coup d'état*, opening the way to counterrevolutionary terror and establishing a regime of personal dictatorship. More than 200,000 party members, mostly Communists of long standing, were expelled and arrested. In the process of counterrevolution the Marxist-Leninist party was destroyed and from its remnants the so-called "League of Communists of Yugoslavia" was created which, both by its program and practice, has nothing in common with its name. This was publicly admitted by its initiator and organizer, Milovan Djilas, who was politically liquidated by Tito precisely because of his openness, after the latter had adopted all Djilas's ideas; these ideas were put into practice by Tito in the economic and cultural programs of the "League of Communists of Yugoslavia." This "League" is an anticommunist, reactionary, nationalist organization, whose main object is to secure Marshall Tito's personal power by relentless hostility to Yugoslavia's internationalist Communists and democrats, and to the international communist movement.

Conscious of this fact, the Yugoslav Communists, who have remained faithful to the teachings of Marxism-Leninism and to the glorious revolutionary and internationalist traditions of the Yugoslav workers' movement, have—after years of persecution, displacement, and dispersal—clandestinely renewed the work of the Communist Party of Yugoslavia. By serving the working class, the working peasantry, the progressive intelligentsia, the people, and the country in general, the Communist Party of Yugoslavia believes it possible under present conditions to oust Marshal Tito and the worthless minority of the leading bureaucratic clique from power, because this clique subjugates and misinforms the public. This ouster can be carried out with a minimum of disruption and harm to Yugoslavia's peoples, but if it is to be achieved, it is indispensably necessary to gather all sociopolitical forces with a socialist and democratically anti-Titoist orientation around the Communist Party of Yugoslavia.

The Communist Party of Yugoslavia is a revolutionary Marxist-Leninist party of the Yugoslav working class. It resolutely and logically defends its class character and has opposed every deviation from Marxism-Leninism, in particular revisionism and an alliance with the *bourgeoisie*. By resolutely defending its workers' class character, it has become the main revolutionary force of the working people and all the peoples of Yugoslavia. The Communist Party of Yugoslavia is deeply internationalist and at the same time a truly patriotic party. Its practice has been determined by Marxist-Leninist doctrine, cleansed of all revisionistic perversions and dogmatic simplifications, and it has stuck strictly to the principles of proletarian internationalism. It has been faithful to the revolutionary and internationalist traditions of the working class of Yugoslavia and has continued to develop these progressive traditions among our peoples.

The Communist Party of Yugoslavia is an organic part of the international communist movement from which it draws knowledge, experience, and inspiration. In its work the party has been led by the teaching of the great Lenin that the most important thing in proletarian internationalism has been the subordination of the interests of the working class of a single country to the interests of the struggle of the proletariat throughout the world. "Proletarians of all countries unite!" Under this great battle cry the Communist Party of Yugoslavia was born in 1919 in Belgrade; it lived and fought for two full decades under the conditions of a monarchico-fascist dictatorship, inspired Yugoslavia's peoples to an armed uprising against the fascist invaders, won the victory and created a worker-peasant state—the Federative People's Republic of Yugoslavia. With this cry it rose again like a phoenix from the ashes at the Bar Congress of the CPY, and is today conducting a remorseless battle against a counterrevolutionary regime based on personal dictatorship. With this cry it will carry through the socialist transformation of Yugoslav society and build communism.

The Communist Party of Yugoslavia is a truly patriotic party because it has been the inheritor and sustainer of the great revolutionary and democratic traditions of Yugoslavia's peoples. By its heroic struggle it saved Yugoslavia's peoples from annihilation, freed the country from fascist slavery, and increased its reputation throughout the world. By its unparalleled struggle against the counterrevolutionary personal dictatorship of Marshal Tito and his unprincipled careerist aides, the Communist Party of Yugoslavia will rescue Yugoslavia's peoples from under the bloody boots of Tito and wipe from the face of its natural and frank allies the dirt of treason. . . .

PART TWO

THE LEAGUE OF COMMUNISTS OF YUGOSLAVIA—A
REACTIONARY NATIONALISTIC PARTY

[This part begins by another description of how the LCY, "the Tito's clique," landed into "the camp of counterrevolution." It goes on then to explain how the "antagonist contradictions" in Yugoslav society forced the LCY leadership to look for new ways to strengthen its rule.]

. . . The socioeconomic circumstances that have secured the temporary and relative victory of Titoism and have directly contributed to the development of the "LCY" are: a military-inflationary boom in the capitalist countries; the huge economic and military help given to the Titoists by international imperialism; and the enrichment of the *bourgeoisie*, the kulaks, and one section of the middle class. These economic circumstances, which have temporarily and relatively contributed to an increase in support accorded by the popular masses to the "LCY," have been accompanied by certain specific features of the social scene. A specially important role has been played by the total militarization of social life, the activities of the Titoist organizations, the inadequate influence exerted by the communists and democrats on the middle class because of the absence of a Communist Party of Yugoslavia formed organizationally and politically, as well as the disappearance of other democratic parties forced by means of political terrorism "voluntarily" to carry out their own liquidation. . . .

. . . Both from the Statutes and practice of the "LCY" one can see that its organizational principles are identical with those of fascist parties. It is constructed on the principles of bureaucratic centralism embodied in a form of hierarchy that excludes any control of the activities of the higher party organs by the basic organizations and ordinary members. The supreme ruling authority is the President of the League, in whose hands all power rests, who does not have to account to anyone, who is elected for life, and is not a member of any organization or "forum"; he is not even a member of the Central Committee or of the

Presidium. The construction of the "LCY" on these organizational principles has made it an obedient operational instrument of Marshal Tito's personal dictatorship. Its main task in the sphere of domestic policy has been the militarization of the socioeconomic, sociopolitical, and cultural life of the country by introducing the so-called "nationwide defense" system coupled with a total espionage system masquerading under the name of "self-protection." In international relations its goal has been to destroy the unity of the communist, workers', and national liberation movement under the label of "nonalignment.". . .

. . . The "LCY" program has been greatly influenced by the modern bourgeois sociological ideas of the "industrial society," "convergency," "deproletarization," and "deideologization," and through the philosophical concept of abstract humanism and the fascist notions of "solidarism," the economic doctrine of "market socialism," and corporatism. The basic line of both the "LCY" program and its practical activities has been the struggle against Leninism which it has expressed in criticism of what it calls "Stalinism." The negation of Leninism actually means a direct negation of the ideological foundation of the whole communist movement, because Leninism—the Marxism of the contemporary era—has provided that foundation.

Therefore the "League of Communists of Yugoslavia," both in its practical behavior and in its Statutes and program, is not a Marxist-Leninist party but a reactionary anticommunist nationalistic party whose chief aim has been the securing of the counterrevolutionary personal dictatorship of Marshal Tito, the sabotage of the construction of a developed socialist society and communism in the socialist countries, the slowing down of the revolutionary process in the capitalist states and in the developing countries, the destruction of the unity of the communist and workers' movement, and prevention of the coming together of all freedom-loving and peaceful forces throughout the world.

Because of all this, but especially because of a particularly vigorous antidemocratism which is the basic norm of the whole internal policy of the "League of Communists of Yugoslavia," the Communist Party of Yugoslavia considers that the "LCY" should be dissolved. In this connection the CPY declares before the working class and the working peasantry, before all the peoples of Yugoslavia, and before all the national minorities living on its territory, that if the Marxist and democratic forces within the "LCY" do not replace Marshal Tito as president and do not democratize their party, the CPY will struggle resolutely for its dissolution. If, however, the democratic forces replace Tito and reform the "LCY" in a democratic spirit, the Communist Party of Yugoslavia declares its readiness to co-operate with the "LCY" within the framework of a Popular Front whose aim will be to transform Yugoslavia in a democratic and socialist manner. If the democratic forces within the "LCY" are not capable of carrying out a democratic transformation of their party, the Communist Party of Yugoslavia is ready to accept into its ranks all "LCY" members who express their desire to join it by giving proof of their readiness to accept the CPY's program and policy line. . . .

PART THREE

[This part is divided in two sections, each of which contains several sub-sections. The two sections are entitled "The Socioeconomic System of Market Self-Management Socialism" and "Marshal Tito's Personal Counterrevolutionary Regime Threatens Yugoslavia's Existence." A sub-section of the first section, called "The Situation of the Working People in Yugoslavia" paints in darkest colors "the most brutal exploitation" of workers in a system whose methods of remuneration (premiums) force the workers to exhaust themselves maximally, using antiquated machinery and obtaining the lowest wages in Europe. The main target of attack is, however, the existence of unemployment, "the highest in the world."]

. . . The reserve army of labor is the most essential and most characteristic feature of the "Market Self-Management System of Socialism" in Yugoslavia. The state policy of noninterference into economic relations has made it impossible for the working class to realize its demand that all citizens have the right to work. In such a situation, the working people in Yugoslavia have been continually threatened by a rise in unemployment and by the possibility that it might acquire a mass character. The basic reason for such a development is to be sought in the internal contradictions of the "Market Self-Management System of Socialism," because the system of private and group ownership over the means of production, motivated by profit making, has made it impossible to guarantee everyone the right to work. The Titoist authorities have not taken any serious steps to solve this problem. The only way in which the state has regulated the labor market has been to allow manpower to be exported.

The geographic flow of the manpower "surplus," i.e., its migration to the capitalistic labor market, is the best evidence proving the bourgeois class character of the economic policy of the counterrevolutionary regime of personal power in Yugoslavia. This has resulted in such a waste of the country's main social production forces that it endangers the country's independence, and even leads to a degeneration of the country's people. It is possible that the Titoist bureaucratic leaders, under the pressure of popular demand, might even be forced to introduce "etatistic" measures in order to reduce unemployment. Thus far, however, they have been trying to solve the problem of unemployment by simply exporting to the capitalistic states. Such an approach to the problem of unemployment has been contrary to the interests of the working people, but in the current situation it serves the regime. The export of manpower has, on the one hand, reduced the danger of social unrest; but, on the other hand, it has made possible a huge inflow of foreign currency into the Titoist state. The counterrevolutionary regime of personal power, in the years of its existence, has exported 1,500,000 slave laborers to the capitalist states, including a great number of LCY members and veterans of the War of National Liberation. This has been done by no other regime that has ever existed. In ancient times, the owners of slaves were obliged to feed their vassals even after they grew old and ceased to work. Old Plutarch was disgusted by the lack of morals displayed by Cato when the latter sold his aged slaves, but the Titoist opponents of "etatism" try to justify their sale of veterans of the National Liberation War to their old Nazi enemies.

[The remaining part of the same sub-section enumerates with an abundance of examples the other unmitigated evils of "the counterrevolutionary regime of personal power": the lack of socio-medical protection of the workers; the building of villas and summer houses for "the bourgeois and Titoist bureaucracy" while "hundreds of thousands of workers have no apartments"; the capitalist development of villages, which is favorable to the kulaks and most harmful for the broad working masses; "the unbearable conditions for the people's intelligentsia," which is faced by "unemployment, insecurity, and an insecure future"; the conditions of women, which is worse than that of males, "a most horrible phenomenon never noted before in the modern history of Europe—the selling of one's own children"; "the complete neglect of young people's physical and spiritual education"; the absence of any organization to protect the interests of state officials; and, last but not least, "brutal military discipline."]

. . . the Yugoslav People's Army has been the target of constant attacks by the Titoist police, which has introduced the most brutal terrorism in the army, in order to make it its most obedient instrument in the struggle against Yugoslavia's own peoples. In the course of bloody Titoist purges, about 20,000 officers have either been arrested or expelled from the army. . . .

[The second section of the Program's part three has four sub-sections: (1) "The Political Regime," (2) "The Nationality Policy," (3) "The Sphere of Culture," and (4) "Foreign Policy." The first long subsection on the political regime is a vitriolic attack on Tito, his "personality cult," and his transformation from a "fighter for popular rights" into "Yugoslavia's Fuehrer" who has introduced a regime of "political gangsterism." In his persecution of "internationalist communists, friends of the Soviet Union," and in the creation of concentration camps Tito's regime is accused of being much worse than that of Nazi Germany. After a long enumeration of names and geographical locations of these extermination camps, here is how their victims are described.]

. . . Among them have been hundreds of famous war commanders and political commissars of battalions, brigades, divisions, corps, and armies; high army officers, generals, secretaries of CPY committees and SKOJ (CP youth organizations), ministers and deputy ministers, fighters from the Spanish Civil War, and participants in the Great October socialist revolution. In these camps and prisons several thousand communists, democrats, patriots, and heroes of the national liberation struggle have been killed in the most brutal way, hitherto unexampled in the history of mankind; the methods used included trampling by heavy boots, stoning, beating, and starvation. Their only sin was that they remained loyal to the great teachings of Marxism-Leninism and to the high revolutionary, democratic, and internationalist traditions of the Yugoslav communist, workers', and progressive movement; they were guilty of loving their people and their country and of wishing to see it a democratic community of fraternal peoples, an inseparable part of the powerful camp of peace, socialism, and democracy; they wanted their party to form an organic part of the international communist and workers' movement; they were found guilty of having remained loyal to their ally from the darkest days—the great Soviet Union, which liberated them from the Hitlerite yoke.

[This infernal description of the recent past is then matched by an analysis of the present situation, which is hardly an improvement: "The secret police has penetrated the whole fabric of social life"; Tito has vitiated all political institutions and state functions, accumulating in his hands powers matching those of "the absolute monarchs and dictators of ancient Rome." The latest Constitution, of 1974, by introducing the "system of delegation" has virtually put an end to equal and direct balloting.

The nationality policy of the Titoist regime is said to be based on "hypocrisy and naked lie"; it has fostered the appearance of "bourgeois nationalism and the spreading of chauvinistic passions"; the old principle of divide and rule has become a trade-mark of Titoism. The result has been the shattering of the working-class unity and the destruction of the Yugoslav peoples' brotherhood and unity. The reprivatization of socialist ownership over the means of production has destroyed the material foundations of the self-identity, equality, and self-determination of Yugoslavia's peoples.]

> . . . This process has especially gained momentum since the system of state management in the sphere of production, trade, and other economic relations was abolished. This is why management over the means of production by the "working collectives," i.e., the nationalistic disintegration of production, the private distribution of the labor surplus (which is, in fact, the private appropriation of the result of social labor), the feudalistic "Turkish" type of self-management in communes, the parceling of social funds in communes and republics, as well as the inequity in distributing the national income are unequal and unjust for objective reasons. . . .

[The landmark of Titoism—workers' self-management—is interpreted as a fountain of the chief evil.]

> The introduction of so-called "self-management" and free competition represents a merciless struggle of everyone against everyone else for the distribution of profit. This struggle could not remain confined within the framework of enterprises and communes, but has infected the republics and the whole social community. This has led to the appearance of bourgeois nationalism of a special kind; this nationalism is now being turned by the top bureaucratic leadership into a struggle among the nations and national minorities of Yugoslavia, a struggle that at any time could turn into fratricidal war.

[Tito has again been selected as a villain who has kindled an open struggle among the republican nationalistic leadership of the LCY. He is accused of having at first, in 1971, taken the side of the nationalists among the Croatian Communists, people who "wanted to create a new [Utasha-type] Independent State of Croatia" [which existed between 1941 and 1945 under the leadership of Ante Pavelić]. He had then turned against them, as well as against the other republican leaderships, blaming them for his own errors.

Several pages of the Program are used to depict the Titoist "rule of darkness" in all the spheres of culture—arts, education, journalism, and so on.

The gist of the long sub-section on foreign policy is that domestic terrorism has forced Titoism "to make a satellite-like subjugation to American imperialism the basis of its foreign policy." The list of proofs follows page after page: reception of Western "aid" worth about $10,000 million, of which the Americans have contributed more than two thirds, and a series of agreements starting in 1951 with the United States, and later economic arrangements with capitalist firms, in particular American, which have "sold Yugoslavia's national sovereignty and integrity *en détail* and *en gros*." The Balkan

Pact of 1954 was another chain in the same link, confirming Tito's role in the scheme of American imperialism.]

> . . . Yugoslavia has not only become the main U.S. base for its "extension to the East" but has also been given the task of undermining the socialist camp and the world communist and workers' movement, of opposing the national liberation struggle and of working against all peaceful forces and states. Such a foreign policy, along with the strengthening of Yugoslavia's dependence on international capitalism, could have led to the complete loss of its national sovereignty, to a new and bloody civil war, but for the burgeoning of the policy of *détente* in international relations and the complete dissolution of the Balkan Pact because of clashes between monarcho-fascist Greece and bourgeois Turkey. . . .

[Two basic tenets of Yugoslavia's foreign policy — non-alignment and active peaceful coexistence — are seen as means of the Titoist clique to "undermine the national liberation movements in Asia, Africa, and Latin America, [serving] as an instrument of American imperialism." Other "crimes" of Titoism in the realm of foreign policy have been: aggressiveness and intrigues against socialist neighbors: Bulgaria and Albania; the betrayal (in 1949) of "the Greek people's revolution"; most active support to the Hungarian counterrevolution in 1956; sympathy for the counterrevolutionary coup in Czechoslovakia [i.e., the Dubček regime], or in the case of antisocialist activities in Poland and the German Democratic Republic; solidarity with the renegades from the fraternal Communist parties; "smearing of the glorious struggle of the people of Indochina," by glorifying Emperor Bao Dai and attacking Ho Chi Minh; support to the Americans in the Korean and Laos wars, as well as on the rostrum of the United Nations. Despite the fact that all these instances of treason have isolated Tito's Yugoslavia from all the progressive forces in the world, the Program perceives an ultimate Titoist perfidy.]

> The Titoist state and the League of Communists of Yugoslavia, completely isolated from the socialist world, from the international communist and workers' movements, and from the forces of national liberation and anti-imperialism, and abandoned by imperialism because of its incompetence, have begun to make overtures to the socialist countries, the Marxist-Leninist parties, and the national liberation movements. The majority of socialist countries and fraternal parties are prepared to meet the Titoists' wishes in order to prevent them from "finally" siding with imperialism; they do not, however, believe that a Titoist return to the Marxist-Leninist line is possible.
>
> In this connection the Communist Party of Yugoslavia affirms here openly that a return by the Titoists to the Marxist-Leninist road is nothing but an illusion; this is not a matter of Tito's subjective wishes and the wishes of his aides, who have definitely and irreversibly accepted the road of treason to the revolution. As for their "finally" taking sides with imperialism, the international communist and workers' movement would lose nothing if this were to happen. On the contrary, they could only benefit because the traitors would then leave the communist ranks and join those of our class enemies.

PART FOUR

HISTORICAL TASKS OF THE COMMUNIST PARTY OF YUGOSLAVIA
Liquidation of the Counterrevolutionary Regime Based
on Personal Power and Construction of a Communist Society

[This final part of the Program, after a long introduction which reiterates all the previous anti-Titoist assertions, enumerates at the end 12 points as a "minimal program."]

> 1.   The creation of a united People's Front of all socialist, democratic, and progressive parties, groups, and currents with an anti-Titoist orientation; the carrying on of a common struggle against the counterrevolutionary regime based on personal authority, until it is overthrown;
>
> 2.   The formation of a provisional government composed of parties, organizations, groups, and currents taking part in the overthrow of Tito's dictatorship;

3. The abolition of all laws and other regulatory acts depriving groups of citizens and organizations of the working people, as well as their avant-garde—the Communist Party of Yugoslavia—of their rights; one should introduce standards guaranteeing a stable legal order, ones that would reflect the qualities generally accepted by mankind and achieved by democratic means: democratic freedoms must really be introduced: freedom of assembly, speech, and press, freedom of association, freedom to demonstrate, freedom to strike, freedom of creative endeavor, and freedom for socialist, democratic, and progressive parties and organizations;

4. The introduction of a regime of strict legality, one that would preclude any judicial or administrative arbitrariness by state officials; the freeing of all political prisoners and exiles, the rehabilitation of all citizens dismissed from their jobs or pensioned because of their political convictions; all of them must be returned to their former jobs; the death sentence must be abolished as must administrative punishment;

5. Abolition of the federal, republican, provincial, and communal national assemblies and formation of commissariats of a provisional government and the democratization of the state apparatus; the most important functions in the state apparatus must be entrusted to loyal and politically educated cadres: workers, peasants, activists, and democratic people from other strata of the population, tried and tested in the struggle against the counterrevolutionary regime based on personal authority;

6. Disbandment of the State Security Service and the counter-intelligence organizations of the Yugoslav People's Army, as well as the counterintelligence service of the People's Militia; the abolition of all concentration camps and political prisons;

7. Abolition of all corporative organizations of the fascist type, abolition of all laws and other regulatory acts which, directly or indirectly, have discriminated against individual groups of the working people, and proclamation of new laws expressing the will of the broadest spectrum of the population and guaranteeing their real participation in the management of production and distribution;

8. Abolition of the post of President of the Republic, dismissal of Marshal Tito from all ruling functions, prohibiting him from engaging in any political activity whatsoever, and confiscation of the property he has obtained illegally;

9. Abolition of all reactionary laws and other regulatory acts which, directly or indirectly, have strengthened the privileges of the *bourgeoisie*, the top bureaucratic technocratic leaders, and urgent solution of the most important socioeconomic problems; the dinar must be made truly stable, and conditions producing inflation must be overcome; all able citizens must be guaranteed work and working conditions must be significantly improved, as must be the living conditions of all working people; all laws and other regulatory acts promoting the interests of the working people in any given period must be systematically and strictly applied;

10. Transitional measures must be urgently introduced in order to permit nationalization of the principal means of production; state control over the distribution of raw materials, equipment, and auxiliary materials must be introduced, as must be control over trade, prices, and credits; state monopoly over foreign trade and foreign currency operations must be introduced;

11. A new provisional electoral law giving every adult the right to vote, irrespective of his political views, should be introduced, and elections for a constitutional assembly should be carried out within 12 months;

12. Yugoslavia must leave the Balkan Pact, which is a part of the aggressive Atlantic Pact, and all obligations stemming from Yugoslavia's membership in the pact must be annulled as must be all other international agreements concluded with imperialist countries by the Titoist government, including all secret agreements and secret clauses linking Yugoslavia with aggressive, anticommunist, and imperialist groups; sincere fraternal relations with the socialist countries on the basis of proletarian internationalism must be inaugurated; relations and co-operation with the developed countries should be significantly improved and extended, relations with the capitalist states must be made normal, especially with neighboring countries, on the basis of peaceful coexistence; Yugoslavia should make a maximal contribution to the relaxation of international tensions.

The Communist Party of Yugoslavia is of the opinion that the realization of the above-mentioned demands is the indispensable precondition for the introduction of a regime of a transitional character between the counterrevolutionary personal dictatorship of Marshal Tito, and a socialist, truly people's democracy. That is why the CPY solemnly declares before Yugoslavia's people, before the international workers' movement, before all people throughout the world fighting for socialism, democracy, and social progress, that it would totally abide by the spirit and the text of the agreement signed by all socialist, democratic, and progressive forces; it further declares that it would respect and submit itself to the will of Yugoslavia's peoples, expressed by them in free elections, and that it would resolutely and consistently fight to carry out the popular will.

WESTERN EUROPE

Austria

The Communist Party of Austria (Kommunistische Partei Österreichs; KPÖ) was founded on 3 November 1918. The party has enjoyed legal status during the entire democratic history of the Austrian Republic, from 1918 to 1933, and since 1945. The partial occupation of Austria by the USSR (1945-55) is no doubt the basis of the party's insignificance, both political and otherwise. This insignificance increased as a consequence of armed Soviet intervention in neighboring Hungary (1956) and Czechoslovakia (1968).

Estimates as to KPÖ membership differ, but the number appears to be between 20,000 and 25,000. The party does not unite all of Austria's Communists. Trotskyists compete in a few elections, and Maoists are active in student affairs. The population of Austria is 7,575,000.

Much of the electoral constraint on the KPÖ, from the beginning, has been a strong Socialist Party. That party's postwar history has proved that there is no need for a doctrinaire socialist stand to keep the KPÖ in check. Recent elections have indicated that continued strength of the Socialist Party (SPÖ) goes along with even increasing insignificance of the KPÖ.

Flattened by Chancellor Kreisky's (SPÖ) electoral steamroller in 1975—there were 55,000 Communist votes cast—the KPÖ spent an almost totally inactive year and could not take advantage of the interesting developments in international socialism and communism. Franz Muhri, the KPÖ Chairman, aptly characterized the party's situation in 1976 when he referred to "the presence of a strong Socialist Party which has a decisive influence on the working class, which has formed the government for the last six years, which has an absolute majority in parliament, and which exerts a determining influence on the association of Austrian trade unions" (speech to the conference of European Communist and workers' parties, East Berlin, 29 June, in *Pravda*, 1 July).

There were no public elections anywhere in Austria during 1976, for the party to show its strength or rather its weakness. The only—very minor—success of various extreme left groups in the "minor" student elections of early June occurred at the philosophic faculty of the University of Vienna (*Wiener Zeitung*, 4 June). The shop steward election in VOESt-Alpine, Austria's largest (nationalized) steel plant, cut Communist representation from six to three on a body with 51 members (*Die Presse*, Vienna, 29 January).

Party Internal Affairs. The KPÖ's Central Committee met in Vienna on 4-5 December 1975, two months after the federal election. In addition to conducting a post-election assessment, the meeting decided to carry out a fund-raising campaign for the party press in 1976. The Central Committee met again in March, July, and September.

Early in 1976, Muhri discussed the issuance of new membership cards to all party members. He explained the purpose in terms of revitalized recruitment as well as the need for an increase in membership fees. His appeal culminated in these words: "The new membership card does not only serve the purpose of orderly receipts of membership fees and of money for the election and press funds; with its red covers, the new membership card at the same time is a political symbol of membership in the KPÖ, of being wedded to the great ideals of the communist movement" (*Volksstimme*, 10 January).

Domestic Attitudes and Activities. Muhri's keynote on domestic policy (in 1976) was sounded in a speech in Moscow on 27 February (*Pravda*, 29 February): "Today, the KPÖ sees its main intrapolitical task as the development of a broad campaign against the attempts of the bourgeoisie and the social-democratic government to shift the burdens of the crisis unto the shoulders of the working people." Two weeks later, at the Central Committee meeting in Vienna, he called for Socialist-Communist cooperation "against the crisis burden" (*Volksstimme*, 13 March). That same call for cooperation, this time extended to include Catholic workers, formed an important part of Muhri's speech before the Conference of European Communist and workers' parties in East Berlin (*Pravda*, 1 July).

Early in the year, Muhri claimed that the continuation of compulsory military service in Austria would run counter to the maintenance of peace and neutrality in Central Europe (TASS, 7 May).

One domestic issue cannot be dealt with fully at the time of writing: the question of the secret-ballot head count to determine the size of the Slovene minority population in the province of Carinthia, scheduled for November. All three parties represented in the Austrian parliament sided with Carinthia's German nationalists to support the head count, which the Slovenes claim is designed to decimate their official number, and thus to affect their language rights. As the Socialist *Neue Zeit* (Graz, 11 April) commented sadly, the KPÖ was given the opportunity by the other parties to move into a vacuum and present itself as the only country-wide party to take the side of the Slovene minority.

There was one more domestic issue the KPÖ took up. As one of Austria's antiquated coal mines, in Fohnsdorf, Styria, was about to be closed, Muhri appeared to be the politician most solicitous to maintain the mine (*Wiener Zeitung*, 14 October).

International Views and Positions. Late in 1975, *Pravda* (4 December) published a lengthy article by Hans Kalt, KPÖ Central Committee member and *Volksstimme* editor, extolling the benefits Austria would derive from the Helsinki conference.

In mid-1976, Kreisky was strongly criticized for his suggestion that European democracies, the USA, and Canada hold a summit conference prior to the 1977 European Conference in Belgrade (*Volksstimme*, 20 June). Around the same time, however, Muhri welcomed Kreisky's appeal for a continuation of détente, made at the SPÖ's biennial congress in March (*WMR*, July, p. 8); for details of Kreisky's remarks see *Wiener Zeitung*, 13 March.

International Activities and Contacts. There were two aspects to the KPÖ's international activities in 1976: the usual international visits and, more important, the party's attitude toward the Berlin Conference's stand on mutual relations among Communist parties.

In late December 1975, Hans Kalt, *Volksstimme*, and several KPÖ press workers, visited Moscow, Vilnius, Kaunas, and Minsk as guests of the Central Committee of the Communist Party of the Soviet Union (CPSU), (*FBIS*, 7 January).

Franz Muhri was the Austrian delegate to the 25th Congress of the CPSU. In this connection, he made routine statements about the CPSU and the KPÖ (*Pravda*, 29 February; *FBIS*, 1, 10 March).

In May and June, there was an exchange of visits with Hungary. Premier Lazar met with the KPÖ Politburo in Vienna during a visit to Austria (*Volksstimme*, 20 May), and Muhri visited Hungarian party chief Kádár in Budapest (*FBIS*, 7 June). Also in June, three KPÖ delegations visited the USSR (ibid., 11, 18 June). At the same time, a different KPÖ delegation visited Romania (*Scînteia*, Bucharest, 16 June). Later in the year, a delegation of the Central Committee of the Hungarian party visited Vienna (*FBIS*, 4 October).

A more unusual visit took place in Vienna in February: a delegation of the National Council of the Socialist Unity Front of Romania visited Austria not at the invitation of the KPÖ, but of the Austrian People's Party.

Austria's member of the drafting commission to prepare the East Berlin conference of European Communist and workers' parties was the KPÖ veteran Erwin Scharf (*Volksstimme*, 15 June). Muhri expressed the Austrian version of the conference's major resolution on diversity:

> In the opinion of the KPÖ, proletarian internationalism, independence, equality and non-interference as the basis of relations among Communist parties do not contradict one another but are most closely interconnected.
>
> Our independence and the principle of equality include acknowledgment of the objective fact that the Soviet Union is the strongest socialist country and the CPSU as the strongest and most experienced party of the international Communist movement play a particularly important and positive role in the international class struggle and in the struggle against imperialism, for the liberation of the peoples, and for peace and social progress.
>
> There is no longer a leading center . . . of the Communist movement. The KPÖ independently works out its own policy from the conditions of its own country. It was on this basis that we worked out our program tenets of Austria's pull to socialism, which were adopted at the 22d KPÖ Congress. A socialist society cannot be imposed from outside, it cannot be built by a minority, it can be built only on the basis of voluntary, deliberate, and active support by the working class in alliance with the peasants, small manufacturers, and the intelligentsia. (*Pravda*, 1 July.)

Bruno Kreisky, Austria's Socialist chancellor, when asked about cooperation with the KPÖ by some young socialists, had this to say when interviewed on 14 July (not 14 June as reported in *FBIS*, 15 July):

> . . . there is one real limit [to the activities of these young Socialists]: namely cooperation with the Communists. The Austrian Communists are a party that is very far, say, from the Italian Communist Party. The Austrian Communists are the most subservient, the most undignified species of communist party which I have ever come across in a long political career. They defend every Soviet intervention. . . . To cooperate with Austrian Communists is exceedingly undignified, and is utterly pointless politically.

Publications. The KPÖ publishes the daily *Volksstimme* (People's Voice) in Vienna. A circulation of about 70,000 is claimed. The party monthly is *Weg und Ziel* (Path and Goal).

*   *   *

Austria's splinter groups of the extreme left reported only one newsworthy event in 1976. On 6 August, Maoists formed the Communist League of Austria by a merger of groups from Vienna, Graz, Klagenfurt, Linz, Salzburg-Hallein, and Tyrol (NCNA, 12 August). The League's publications are the biweekly newspaper *Klassenkampf* and the theoretical journal *Kommunist*.

The University of Alberta   F. C. Engelmann

Belgium

The Communist Party of Belgium (Parti Communiste de Belgique; PCB) was founded in 1921. It is firmly pro-Soviet and is estimated to have 12,000 members among Belgium's population of 10 million.

In 1976 the PCB continued to be only of marginal importance in Belgian politics. In the 1974 elections to the Chamber of Representatives the party received 169,668 votes (3.2 percent) and four seats out of 212. It has one seat in the 181-member Senate, and 9 seats out of 720 in provincial councils.

The PCB does not control any part of the labor movement, but rather exercises some influence in the General Workers Federation of Belgium (FGTB), the nation's largest labor group, in which the Belgian Socialist Party (PSB) predominates. The PCB's strategy, of necessity, has aimed at closer ties with the much larger PSB and with "progressive forces" within the generally conservative Christian Social Party (PSC/CVP). In 1976 the PCB believed it had the best chance in a quarter-century to transcend its lowly status (*Pravda*, 2 July).

Leadership and Organization. The PCB's 22nd Congress, in Ghent on 9-11 April 1976 (the previous congress was held in December 1973), reelected Louis Van Geyt as chairman and Jean Terfve, Joseph Turf, and Claude Renard as vice-chairmen. Renard is responsible for the Wallonian federations—the majority of the party. Turf is responsible for the Flemish federations. Terfve is the second-ranking person in the party. The chairman's report was adopted unanimously, but with 31 abstentions (*Drapeau Rouge*, 12 April). This may point to some struggles over leadership or policy.

The PCB's auxiliary organizations are limited to the Communist Youth of Belgium (Jeunesse Communiste de Belgique; JCB) which held its 6th Congress on 24-26 April; the National Union of Communist Students (UNEC); and a children's organization, the Union of Pioneers. These are not "mass organizations." Rather they serve primarily to socialize the children of Communists and to train young recruits.

The 22nd Congress was meant to emphasize the importance of five tasks: (1) "to mobilize the workers' movement in support of the demands advanced by the FGTB and the General Trade Union Front," (2) to struggle "against the government's policy of harsh economies at the expense of the working people," (3) to struggle "against the anti-Soviet propaganda of reactionary circles in the country," (4) to struggle against the reactionary resistance to détente and the Helsinki accords, (5) to strengthen "solidarity with the Socialist countries and in particular with the Soviet Union" (*Drapeau Rouge*, 7 February).

Domestic Views and Activities. Given its minuscule size, the PCB can affect national affairs only by infuencing political groups larger than itself. Thus Terfve's formulation of the alliance strategy common to Europe's Moscow-line parties is particularly appropriate to the PCB: "In the present situation [Communists] must not say they can do everything themselves; . . . they must strive to create alliances . . . with all forces which, for various reasons and proceeding from various viewpoints, are calling into question the ability of the existing system to find effective solutions to the most urgent problems" (*Pravda*, 2 July 1976). The PCB's strategy has therefore aimed, first of all, at persuading the PSB to ally with it.

The PCB believes that at the present time a prerequisite for unity with the PSB is that the latter remain in opposition to the Christian Social cabinet of Leo Tindemans. The PCB considers the PSB's decision to go into opposition in 1974 a watershed in Belgian politics, and it carefully avoids polemics with the Socialists in order not to diminish prospects for unity. In 1976 it was not as worried as in previous years that the PSB might return to its moderate ways. (Claude Renard, interview, *L'Unità*, Rome, 23 March.)

But the PCB realizes that a mere Communist-Socialist coalition cannot hope to take power in Belgium. It considers "an alliance between Socialist and Catholic forces" essential for the accomplishment of the hoped-for "left-wing alternative." The party resolves the contradiction in the foregoing by specifying that the *conditio sine qua non* of a Catholic-Socialist alliance be the acceptance of the Communists "because of what they represent not only in terms of influence but in terms of ideas and the ability to make strategic choices" (ibid.). Thus it appears that the PCB's long-range outlook depends as much on the internal affairs of the Christian Social Party as on those of the PSB.

The prototype of the alliance for which the PCB is working is the front already formed by the FTGB and the Confederation of Christian Trade Unins (CSC). The latter has broken its ties with the Christian Social Party and, according to the PCB, "is developing toward class positions." The PCB is trying to provide CSC activists—who operate a variety of insurance, cooperative, youth, and women's organizations—with "a political outlet for their action." That is, not having "many organizations" of its own, the PCB hopes to co-opt others'. The party judges it important that those groups of CSC activists which have taken "left-wing action" have not been expelled from the Christian workers' movement. (Ibid.) The PCB does not believe it is on the verge of power in Belgium, but it is enormously heartened by how, despite occasional setbacks (*Le Soir*, Brussels, 11 February), so important a constituent of the Social Christian Party's strength has lent itself to the PCB's strategy (*IB*, no. 7).

The party continued to oppose wholeheartedly any effort by the government to cut public spending, reduce its deficit, or hold down inflationary wage increases. Here, the very-short-range interests of union members indeed coincide with the long-range ones of the PCB.

International Views and Activities. PCB statements depict the USSR and all its allies as the forces of goodness and peace in the world, and the USA as the world's greatest, though diminishing, danger to peace. China is seen as "giving political and even practical support to the most zealous defenders of Imperialism." (*IB*, no. 7, 1976.)

On 23 January, *Drapeau Rouge* published a lengthy statement to reaffirm the party's support of the USSR and at the same time to make it possible to argue that the PCB does not want to bring Belgium the way of life prevalent in the Soviet homeland.

The party stated it "disapproves of recourse to administrative and judiciary methods in the area of ideological struggle," but suggested that any closer attention to the disagreeable aspects of Soviet life was a sign of enmity to socialism and progress. Those aspects, it went on, derive from the burden of the struggle against Czarism and world reaction, and the Soviets too have denounced them. Hence it is up to Soviets "alone, now, to determine in what manner and at what pace should be pursued the extension of socialist democracy, which in many respects is superior to Western political systems." The statement then went on to criticize sharply the coverage of Soviet life by Belgian radio and television.

The PCB "observed with satisfaction" favorable trends in the international balance of power which it attributed to the efforts of the Socialist countries, the international workers' movement, and progressive world opinion. Détente must be made "irreversible." By this is meant that the world's peoples will make progress toward socialism. (Report on visit by Louis Van Geyt to Hungary, *FBIS*, 8 July.)

According to the PCB, U.S. foreign policy, as formulated by Henry Kissinger, is based on a realistic assessment of the USSR's inevitably growing importance, whereby the USA is "condemned" to coexistence by the changing balance of forces. By this very token the party deems vain Kissinger's hopes that the "pro-Western orientations of the Western European countries" may be preserved within the framework of détente. The changes in the balance of forces "must be used to the maximum to create irreversible trends." (Jean Terfve, *Le Soir*, 12 May.)

While the PCB supports greater cooperation among the nations of Western Europe, it does so on condition that this imply greater detachment from the USA, greater cooperation with Eastern Europe, and under no circumstance an increase in military potential. Thus it opposes the plan of Belgian premier Tindemans for a military-political alliance within the Common Market framework. This, in the opinion of the PCB, "would help to create conditions for a counter-offensive of the reactionary forces," "restrain the influence of the working class and the democratic movement of Western Europe," and "put the EEC countries under U.S. control" (TASS, 29 March). Therefore also the PCB takes every opportunity to brand as interference in Belgian affairs suggestions by Americans that West European nations arm or beware of growing Communist influence within them.

International Party Contacts. At the conference of European Communist and Workers' parties in East Berlin, in June, 1976, the PCB's Terfve said that "cooperation and internationalist solidarity" is of an importance "difficult to overestimate," that it is "irreplaceable," and that to undermine it at all "would mean a victory for our class enemy." The PCB urged simultaneously that each Communist party make decisions independently, and that all parties "preserve and develop" their "international solidarity." (*Pravda*, 2 July.) Indeed, according to Terfve, who served on the planning committee, the need to stress equally these two contrasting themes had been the cause for the long postponement of the conference (*Drapeau Rouge*, 30 December 1975).

At the 25th Congress of the Communist Party of the Soviet Union (CPSU), Louis Van Geyt portrayed the USSR as a society progressing on all fronts, while the West, including Belgium, was gripped by systemic crisis. He ended his address by praising "the profound solidarity between our parties." (*Pravda*, 29 February 1976.) After the congress, the PCB delegation stayed in Moscow for working meetings with B. N. Ponomarev and V. V. Zagladin (ibid., 7 March). Van Geyt, in an interview on Soviet radio, praised every aspect of the Brezhnev administration (*FBIS*, 3 March). At the PCB's 22d Congress the place of honor was held by the Soviet delegation, headed by Zagladin and the Chairman of the CPSU Central Auditing Commission.

On 24 May Van Geyt was in Paris for talks with French Communist Party leader Georges Marchais. These took place "in an atmosphere of warm friendship and fraternal solidarity." (*L'Humanité*, Paris, 26 May.) On 6 August a PCB delegation visited Budapest and met with Hungarian party chief János Kádár; no details were given out (*FBIS*, 6, 7 July).

Publications. The PCB's daily organ is *Le Drapeau Rouge*. Like other European Moscow-line parties, the PCB holds an annual festival to raise money for the newspaper and to foster "closer ties with the masses." In 1976 the festival featured displays by *Pravda* and other Communist papers, and track and field contests by athletes from Belgium, the USSR, and East European countries. The party also publishes a weekly for the smaller Flemish community, *Rote Vaan*. *Cahiers Marxistes* is the theoretical journal. The youth group publishes a bimonthly, *L'Offensive*.

Competing Communist Groups. The Marxist-Leninist Communist Party of Belgium (Parti Communiste Marxiste-Leniniste de Belgique; PCMLB) is the official Peking-line party. It publishes *Clarté et L'Exploité*, and is sharply critical of the Soviet Union. A Flanders-based Maoist organization, All Power to the Workers (Alle Macht an de Arbeiders; AMADA) is not recognized by China. The Trotskyite organization in Belgium is the Revolutionary Workers' League (Ligue Revolutionaire des Travailleurs/Revolutionaire Arbeiders Liga; LTR/RAL). These groups are not politically significant.

Stanford University   Angelo Codevilla

Cyprus

The original Communist Party of Cyprus (Kommounistikon Komma Kiprou), secretly founded through Greek-trained Cypriots, held its first party congress in August 1926 while the island was a British crown colony. Outlawed in 1933, it survived underground and in April 1941 emerged as the Progressive Party of the Working People of Cyprus (Anorthotikon Komma Ergazomenou Laou Tis Kiprou; AKEL). It was outlawed again in 1955, when all political organizations were proscribed by the British, but has had legal status since the proclamation of the Cypriot Republic in 1960. As the oldest and best-organized political party in Cyprus, AKEL commands a following far in excess of its estimated 11,000 to 12,000 members. In 1976 the Communist Party of the Soviet Union (CPSU) sent the following message to AKEL on the occasion of the golden anniversary of its founding: "In the 50 years of its revolutionary activity your party has been transformed from a small group of Marxists into a mass political party of the working class enjoying deserved authority among the broad popular masses of Cyprus" (*Pravda*, 15 August).

Virtually all AKEL support comes from among the Greek Cypriot majority, about 80 percent of the island's estimated 647,000 total population. The proportion of party members to national adult populace possibly ranks AKEL second only to its Italian counterpart among non-ruling Communist parties. One recent report even went further by claiming that AKEL is "proportionately the world's strongest communist party not in power" (*Washington Post*, 7 September). Despite the party's overall potential, AKEL has played down its strength in past parliamentary elections and has never held any cabinet posts.

Since July 1974 the socio-political setting in Cyprus has been a fragile calm because of the Turkish occupation of 40 percent of the northern part of the island. The Turkish Cypriots once held a constitutional share of the power in the government of the Republic, but they now have a separate Turkish Federated State of Cyprus and hold elections within their own community. On 5 September 1976 the Republic of Cyprus held its first parliamentary elections since 1970, and AKEL contested only nine previously secured seats, winning all handily with the same incumbents.

The Greek Cypriot elections saw a three-party coalition win 34 of the 35 seats in the House of Representatives. It was composed of the Communists (AKEL), the Socialists (EDEK), and the Democratic Front (DF), a new center-right party which supported President Makarios. The former speaker of the House, Glafkos Clerides, had a falling out with Makarios, and his Democratic Rally (DR) did not capture a single seat, though it received some 26 percent of the vote. To exploit Cyprus's winner-take-all electoral system, each party in the coalition had agreed to direct its supporters to cast their ballots for the candidates of the other two parties for those seats it was not contesting. This arrangement creates difficulty in determining the actual strength of each party. The Communists and the DF probably each received between 30 to 35 percent of the vote; the Socialists, 5 to 10 percent. (See table.)

It cannot be known for sure what is the political persuasion of each of the 21 DF members of the House, but the USSR grouped them with the AKEL and Socialist members under the "left-wing" banner: "... the coalition of left-wing forces of Cyprus [has won] an absolute majority of votes at the parliamentary elections. The front, supporting the foreign and home policy of the government of President Makarios, upholds the independence, sovereignty and territorial integrity of the island state." (TASS, 6 September.)

AKEL's reluctance to show its true potential acknowledges two realities; first, the fact that the 1959 Zurich and London agreements—which gave Cyprus independence—provide a rationale for the three

1976 Election Results

Registered voters	273,516
Actual ballots cast	234,196
Abstention rate	14.8 percent

81 Candidates, four parties for 35 seats:

	Contested	Won
AKEL	9	9
EDEK	6	4
DF	21	21
DR	34	None
Independents	11	1

(*Nicosia Domestic Service*, 6 September 1976.)

guarantor powers (Greece, Turkey, and England) to intervene against an internal subversion of the government; and second, the probability that a legal push for power by AKEL would unite the nationalist parties against the leftists. Thus, AKEL says it does not seek "partisan predominance" in the government (Nicosia domestic service, 6 June). While AKEL continues to have friction with the non-Communist Greek Cypriots, its one consistent tactic in recent years has been open support of the domestic and foreign policies of Archbishop Makarios. AKEL supported Makarios for a third consecutive term as president in 1973 and has played down its many differences with the Church of Cyprus. The autocephalous church has traditionally been most influential in secular politics, and AKEL cannot appeal to the Greek Cypriots by attacking their Orthodox faith.

AKEL is the only professed Marxist-Leninist party, but there seems to be less and less competition, and more convergence on issues, with the active Socialist Party (EDEK), headed by a 56-year-old physician, Vassos Lyssarides. In a 1975 radio interview Dr. Lyssarides summarized his party's position:

Our party is a socialist party and is based on scientific socialism. It was formed approximately 6 years ago and it has very good relations with all national liberation movements in the world, particularly in this Middle East area. . . . The party membership is composed of the workers class, peasants, and scientific workers, who in Cyprus are a part of the workers class. . . .

Our primary concern is the national liberation of Cyprus, the struggle against imperialism and the struggle aimed at not allowing Cyprus to deviate from the policy of non-alignment. Our foreign policy has always been based on non-alignment and on non-interference in the internal affairs of other countries. Within the local framework we are fighting for a socialist transformation within the Cyprus reality. (Belgrade domestic service, 10 January 1975.)

The Socialists increased their seats in the House from two to four as a result of the last elections, in which they doubtless received much support from the Communists. EDEK and AKEL have had differences, "but as they are both parties of the left a feud between the two parties is to be avoided at all costs" (personal correspondence from George Cacoyannis, EDEK Central Committee member, 31 April 1976). An AKEL spokesman said before the election that the collaboration between his party, the Socialists, and the DF "might develop into a permanent one" (*Cyprus Mail*, 29 August). One point where there seems to be an obvious divergence is that the Socialists are much more militant than the peace-loving Communists. Reportedly Dr. Lyssarides sponsors a private band of armed fighters which has been in forefront of much of the blood-letting that has characterized Cypriot life in recent years. AKEL has repeatedly called for "drastic measures" to "disband all illegal armed groups and collect all illegal arms" (*Kharavyi*, 27 January).

Leadership and Organization. The leading figures in AKEL are the general secretary, Ezekias Papaioannou, in office since 1949, and his deputy, Andreas Fantis. Both were reelected in April 1974 at the party's Thirteenth Congress. The leadership structure follows the usual pattern of Communist party organization. The party leadership is notable for its stability and the comparatively advanced age of each individual, most of whom are 60 and older. (For other names see *YICA, 1975*, p. 142).

Auxiliary and Mass Organizations. The total membership of the AKEL apparatus, including various fronts and allowing for overlapping memberships, is estimated at some 60,000. Official government figures in 1974 showed that AKEL controlled the largest trade union organization, the Pan-Cypriot Workers' Confederation (Pankiprios Ergatiki Omospondia; PEO), which has 44,454 members—45.7 percent of all those holding membership in labor unions—and is an affiliate of the Communist-front World Federation of Trade Unions (*Kharavyi*, 12 February). Andreas Ziartides, a labor leader since 1943, was reelected PEO general secretary in April 1975, with Pavlos Dinglis as his deputy. Influential in AKEL's decision-making structure, Ziartides professes that he is a self-taught Marxist. He has been rumored as a choice to be the first Communist to join the cabinet, as minister of labor. Possibly Papaioannou was thinking of Ziartides when he tried to secure one ministry in an abortive attempt at forming a "government of national unity" in 1975. Eighteen months later, Papaioannou recalled: "We had then asked only for one ministry, any ministry that the president of the republic would allow, and we accepted that the candidate should be neither the general secretary nor the assistant general secretary of AKEL." (*Cyprus Mail*, 23 June 1976.)

The AKEL-sponsored United Democratic Youth Organization (Eniaia Dimokratiki Organosis Neolaias; EDON), is headed by a 29-year-old London-trained lawyer, Mikhail Papapetrou, elected in 1975. EDON claims to have 10,000 members and is believed also to operate a branch in England. Through sport and social programs, EDON extends its influence to more than thrice its young membership. The Communist organization of secondary school students, PEOM, is thought to have some 2,000 members, indoctrinated with anti-imperialist slogans (*Kharavyi*, 10 September 1975). POFNE (Pan-Cyprian Federation of Students and Young Professionals) is also a Communist-front group. During the 1974-75 academic year 986 Cypriot students were enrolled in institutions of higher learning in the USSR and other East European countries, about 8 percent of the total number of Greek Cypriot students outside the country (ibid., 11 September 1975).

Other AKEL-dominated organizations include the Pan-Cypriot Confederation of Women's Organizations (POGO), the Pan-Cypriot Peace Council (PEI), the Cypriot-Soviet Association, and the Cyprus-East German Friendship Society. The Communists continually work on strengthening their front groups, "with special emphasis on the party's activities among the intellectuals, professionals, the youth, and women" (ibid., 21 May), a priority listing that may be important, since AKEL has been less effective in organizing the first two groups, compared with its success among the latter two. In 1970 the USSR opened a cultural pavilion in Nicosia which is regularly used for Communist-front group activities.

The AKEL-sponsored Union of Greek Cypriots in England has an estimated 1,250 members. Of the estimated 40,000 Turkish Cypriots who reside in England, a few are open members of the Communist Party of Great Britain and some others are undoubtedly crypto-Communists. Some of the leftist tension in mainland Turkey is thought to be abetted by Turkish Cypriot Communists in London, who are also allied with representatives of the "progressive forces of Turkey," which are underground groups on the European mainland.

While professed Communists are unknown within the Turkish community on Cyprus, some of its young people, especially those enrolled in Turkish universities, are Marxist-influenced. AKEL has made continual overtures for membership among the Turks on the island (as has EDEK), and also has tried to infiltrate the one Turkish Cypriot labor union.

The Communists are usually critical of the Turkish Cypriot leader, Rauf Denktash, because he is allegedly under control of political forces in Turkey and is "chauvinistic" in all his proposals toward a settlement (ibid., 5 May 1976). They also draw a distinction between the Turkish Cypriot masses and the Turkish troops on the island:

> We view the Turkish Cypriots in a way completely different from the way the Turkish occupation troops view them. There can be no conciliation with the Turkish troops. These troops, as well as all other foreign troops in our country, must go. But we shall live together with the Turkish cypriots in the future. (Ibid., 29 January.)

AKEL is often embarrassed in trying to explain the friendly moves the USSR makes toward Turkey. While the Soviets did find it necessary to condemn the Turkish Cypriots in 1975 for their threatened unilateral declaration of independence, they have never officially condemned the Turkish invasion of Cyprus. With regard to Turkey, the USSR consistently expresses the wish to "facilitate a further improvement of good neighborly relations between the two countries" (TASS, 14 April). AKEL seldom, if ever, comments on such statements.

Party Internal Affairs. AKEL's Central Committee and Central Control Committee (or Auditing Commission) meet in plenary session every two or three months to discuss both domestic and international developments. In addition the two committees often meet in "extraordinary" sessions, as was the case in late January 1976 when they met to review plans for the party's 50th-anniversary "jubilee" on 15 August. The meeting resulted in AKEL's lauding itself for "consistently defending the interests of the working class" as a consequence of "being guided by scientific socialism" and believing in the 'ultimate triumph of socialist ideals" (*IB*, no. 3, 1976). The plenary meeting in February issued a formal declaration which glorified the progress of the Communists in Cyprus over the past half century (ibid., no. 5-6). A more contemporary report came out of the third regular plenum, in May, dealing with developments that "have made necessary the proclamation of parliamentary elections." (*Kharavyi*, 5 May.)

Each September AKEL has an "annual Pan-Cyprian fund drive," organized by the Central Committee, and generally sets a goal of some 25,000 Cypriot pounds which it has no difficulty raising. On meeting the goal in 1975 AKEL noted that its success "proves the political appreciation and trust the party enjoys among the Cypriot working people" (ibid., 12 September). Where the rest of the money for AKEL's many activities comes from is something of a mystery.

Party Congresses are held every four years, the last on 25-28 April 1974. At this Congress "900 delegates and representatives from 400 Party organizations took part, as well as delegations from 16 Communist and workers' parties of other countries incuding a delegation from the Soviet Communist Party" (*IB*, May).

Domestic Attitudes and Activities. AKEL has consistently exploited anti-colonialist sentiment in its protests against the restrictions placed on Cyprus by the 1959 Zurich and London agreements, and has opposed the continuing presence of the two sovereign British bases on the island. Furthermore, because as a mass party it seeks to attract the Turkish minority, AKEL has openly shown little favor for the purely Greek objective of enosis—the union of Cyprus and Greece. Prior to the 1967 coup in Greece, AKEL's strength as a national party was for some time precarious; unable to advocate enosis openly, it instead used the vague term "self-determination" in its slogans. The conflicting positions of Greek and Turk on Cyprus comprise the most perplexing domestic issue that the Communists have faced. That they have not resolved the dilemma was shown early in 1976 by an editorial in a Turkish Cypriot newspaper which again raised the old problem:

> We ask the leader of AKEL: Does AKEL favor or does it not favor the union of Cyprus with Greece? We ask Papaioannou: In statements issued during the years 1964, 1968 and 1974, AKEL kept declaring that it was for the union of Cyprus and Greece, even under the junta regime. Does AKEL still maintain the same view? If not, when did it change its view? Can it explain the reasons?

> We ask Papaioannou: What does he understand by the term "democratic, independent Cyprus"? What are the rights to be accorded to the Turks in such a regime, which means domination of Cyprus by the Greek Cypriots? We ask Papaioannou: Does he or does he not accept Turkey's guarantees of independence? If he does not accept them, can he explain the reasons why he is against these guarantees, which have been preserving the independence of Cyprus for the last 12 years? (*Zaman*, 10 February.)

The issue of enosis is kept alive by the efforts of a reactionary political group called ESEA (Coordination Committee for the Enosis Struggle), in conjunction with remnants of the guerrilla force EOKA-B (National Organization of Cypriot Struggle). Papaioannou continually states that a "purge in our internal front and a cleansing of our state machinery" is necessitated by the presence of "unrepentant coupists" in the police and National Guard (*Kharavyi*, 7 January). He claims there are still some 14,000 illegal automatic weapons among these die-hards. In a move to bring unity among the Greek Cypriots, President Makarios granted a full amnesty and pardon for all those who participated in the July 1974 coup d'état against his government. The pardon was also extended to Nicos Sampson, who served as president of the Republic for eight days; but for Sampson this good fortune was not to last, and he was eventually to have the prison fate of the mainland Greek junta leader General Ioannidis, who originally put him in power.

After months of unrelenting efforts by the leftist forces in Cyprus Sampson was finally arrested in March 1976 and committed to trial. The Socialists were in full agreement with the Communists on this development, as indicated by an editorial in the EDEK daily:

> The coupists, being used to the defective behavior of the state, thought that by employing threats and by spreading rumors they would prevent the arrest of Sampson and his commitment for trial. Finally, the arrest gave the impression—even though late, even though after an unjustifiably long procedure—that there is a state that means what it says. For this reason we are certain that for the first time since the coup the juntaist-fascists will begin to feel uneasy because their past or future unlawful actions will be decisively dealt with by the state.

> The arrest of Sampson and the hearing of his case will not be of importance to Cyprus and Greece alone but also to the world.

> In Greece it will deprive of any arguments all those who refuse to open the Cyprus dossier in order to establish who is responsible for the national crime and punish them in accordance with the law. (*Ta Nea*, 18 March.)

The trial ended in August with Sampson pleading guilty to one of the two charges that "he aided in the carrying out of warlike undertakings and illegally usurping the office of the president" (Nicosia domestic service, 23 August). The supreme court, taking into account the amnesty announced by

President Makarios, sentenced the one-time terrorist turned newspaper editor to 20 years in prison. The trial did not reveal the extent of Greek or U.S. complicity in the coup and, according to Sampson's newspaper, "The Cyprus dossier will not be opened." (*I Mahki*, 24 August.) Since the trial ended in the last days before the parliamentary elections, the comments of the leftist press were muted, apparently so as not to offend any Sampson supporters who might be inclined to vote for the nationalist coalition.

The election campaign provided AKEL with a prime opportunity to outline its basic aims. The May plenum listed the extant domestic issues and the principles upon which AKEL would run its campaign:

> It will be based on a solution insuring the independence, sovereignty, and territorial integrity of Cyprus, removal of Turkish and all foreign troops from Cyprus territory, return of the refugees to their homes and properties, tracing and release of all missing persons who are still alive, solution of the constitutional aspect of the Cyprus issue on the basis of the Greek Cypriot proposals within the framework and basis of the UN resolutions, purge and cleansing, equal distribution of economic burdens, a more just distribution and redistribution of national income and resources, and the formation of a national unity government from all the parties that basically agree with our stance on the solution of the Cyprus issue. We must insist on the policy of getting close to our true friends, particularly the Soviet Union. (*Kharavyi*, 5 May.)

The tactic used by AKEL during the campaign was to support President Makarios by joining in with other left-wing and patriotic groups to "deal a blow to the forces of reaction and the extreme right wing." The "extreme" right was represented by the former speaker of the House, Clerides, whom the Communists denounced as "the slave of the policies of Kissinger and NATO" (ibid., 20 August). The attack followed an editorial in a pro-Clerides newspaper which described AKEL's call for a "pan-democratic front" as a "Trojan horse driven inside the ideological walls of the democratic right wing" which was causing former rightists to "surrender numbly to the political embrace of the Communists" (*Dimokratiko Vima*, 13 July). The editorial further accused AKEL of compelling the leaders of the DF to "accept the line of internationalization through an international conference," which it said was against "the salvation of Cyprus."

AKEL's plea for an international conference to consider the Cyprus problem is a carryover from the USSR proposal to the United Nations in 1974. The proposal never got anywhere in diplomatic circles, but AKEL has never stopped pushing for broadening the Cyprus talks beyond the context of a purely bilateral issue between Greece and Turkey, two NATO allies. In one of his final speeches before the campaign, Papaioannou extolled the USSR for standing on the "side of Cyprus and its elected President, Archbishop Makarios, from the first moment of the treacherous coup." He then concluded: "Instead of insulting and slandering the Soviet Union, we should move closer toward it, prepare a summit meeting in Moscow through diplomatic channels; and we can be certain that we shall acquire still greater gains and support from such an action." (Nicosia domestic service, 3 September.)

This call for a "summit meeting" in Moscow was a new twist on the internationalization theme, and it was obviously well received by the USSR. After the election victory, the CPSU Central Committee sent a warm fraternal message, which ended with this thought: "We wish you further successes in the struggle against foreign imperialist interference and also against the forces of domestic reaction" (*Sovetskaya Rossiya*, 11 September).

Cyprus's trade to the Eastern bloc countries has flourished, with the USSR in particular importing large quantities of copper concentrate and vine products, two staple items of the Republic's national export. The once ravaged, now prospering economy of divided Cyprus is, however, still "the basis of the political struggle." Papaioannou has called for a "greater state role in the investment sector and in economic planning and for radical measures to solve the problems facing the refugees" (Nicosia domestic service, 13 August). The Communists have also insisted upon a "proper use of such strategic instruments of economic development as goal-oriented trade, a proper financial policy and 'active' state intervention in the economy." In their view, a comprehensive solution of Cyprus's economic problems "will only become possible when political issues have been settled within the framework of an independent, sovereign and territorially integral state, with the Greeks and Turks living in it like brothers." (*WMR*, July.)

The fifth round of the inter-communal talks, at Vienna in February, did not achieve any notable results. In April the Greek Cypriot representative Clerides was forced to resign when he allegedly acted beyond his authority in agreeing to submit draft proposals to the Turkish side. The Communists claimed that this action raised "an issue of moral order" which "leaves us embarrassed and makes us a laughingstock" (*Kharavyi*, 1 April). Clerides was replaced and the talks were moved down to a lower governmental level, which did little to inspire confidence. When the UN Secretary General invited the two new negotiators to meet him in New York in September, AKEL saw in this an effort by theWest, particularly U.S. secretary of state Kissinger, to "deceive [the U.S.] Congress with the argument that there has been progress on the Cyprus problem and thus have the military agreement with Turkey approved prior to the presidential elections" (ibid., 12 September). This is yet another example of how difficult it is to separate the purely domestic problems of Cyprus from the larger international context, a phenomenon which has affected Cypriot affairs for centuries.

International Views and Policies. "The distinguishing feature of the international situation today is the further development of the policy of relaxation of tension and peaceful coexistence"—so began a resolution adopted at the third regular plenum of AKEL, May 1976. The relaxation of tension, it went on, is "spearheaded against attempts by the most reactionary imperialist quarters to revive the 'cold war' policy to retain hotbeds of tension in their strategic interests." (TASS, 6 May.)

In a speech at the 25th Congress of the CPSU, Papaioannu hailed the USSR's "unrivaled achievements in all fields of human endeavor" and declared:

> There are no people in any part of the world who have struggled or who are still struggling against imperialism for their liberation from imperialist oppression and influence and who have not enjoyed the generous help and support of the Soviet country, the Soviet Union. The people of Angola, Vietnam, Cuba, of the Arab countries, of Cyprus as well as the people of dozens of other countries are the most indisputable witnesses of this truth.

The AKEL leader also mentioned the Conference on Security and Cooperation in Europe (Helsinki, 1975), and termed the signing of its Final Act a "landmark in the peoples' struggle for international détente, peace, and cooperation." (*Kharavyi*, 2 March.)

The conference was seen by AKEL as a great victory for "all peace forces." However, the aggressive imperialist forces, instead of "accepting their defeat in Helsinki," were "intensifying the arms race and aggravating the situation in the Middle East, the Mediterranean and Southern Africa." It was therefore "necessary to make détente a code of conduct for all countries." (*WMR*, March.)

Throughout the year, AKEL kept up its attacks on U.S. foreign policy toward Cyprus, particularly "Kissinger's secret diplomacy" (*Kharavyi*, 3 August). Papaioannou warned "Washington, Bonn, and political circles in Greece andTurkey [who] are now promoting double enosis" that the USSR would "avert the annexation of Cyprus" by diplomatic measures. He also implored the Cyprus government to "proceed without hesitation with the proper utilization of this Soviet support and solidarity." (Ibid., 25 June.) "It is thanks to the Soviet Union," he said, "that Cyprus continued to exist as a separate state" (TASS, 17 July).

AKEL was highly critical of the arms deals that the USA made with Turkey and Grece in March and April respectively. In addition to arms aid, the Turkish people would get the "continuation of the American yoke of 27 military bases on their necks," and Greece would continue to be a "prisoner in the gears of NATO" (*Kharavyi*, 30 March, 16 April).

At the CPSU Congress Papaioannou made his yearly attack on the Peking leadership. "The Maoists in their anti-Sovietism and war psychosis," he said, had become "imperialism's and neofascism's allies." He concluded that they had "betrayed the principles of Marxism-Leninism and proletarian internationalism and disgracefully moved into the camp of sworn enemies of Communism." (TASS, 4 March.)

International Activities and Contacts. AKEL's policy on international solidarity and its relations with other Communist parties has been dictated by Moscow. Accordingly, numerous AKEL delegations visit Eastern bloc countries for ceremonial purposes, and individual members go for vacations and health treatments. Because of its good air service and location, Cyprus has been a favorite stopover for Communists from abroad. After its international airport was closed following the Turkish invasion there was an interruption of the direct services, but as of 1 April 1976 the Soviet, East German, Bulgarian, and Czechoslovak lines were to commence use of a smaller airport (*Kharavyi*, 1 January).

The two-member AKEL delegation to the 25th CPSU Congress was made up of General Secretary Papaioannou and Politburo member Michael Poumbouris.

A World Federation of Trade Unions (WFTU) delegation, headed by Enrique Pastorino, arrived in Cyprus for a seven-day visit inMay. The visit was highlighted by an official reception with President Makarios, meetings with cabinet members and PEO trade union leaders, and visits to refugee camps. The joint communiqué stressed that "the WFTU will do everything possible toward constant and increasing solidarity with Cyprus" (ibid., 18 May). The WFTU later sent a cable to Turkish prime minister Demirel demanding "the implementation of the UN resolutions on Cyprus" (Nicosia domestic service, 20 July).

At the June conference of 29 European Communist and workers' parties in East Berlin, AKEL was represented by Khristos Petas, a member of the Politburo. Papaioannou apologized for being unable to attend "because of very serious political developments in Cyprus that required his presence" (*Kharavyi*, 29 June). Peta's speech, extolling the USSR and denouncing "imperialism," contained an allusion to the "gigantic force" of proletarian internationalism "to which the Arab fraternal people, the fraternal people of Ireland, Spain, Portugal and the FRG, of Turkey and Greee are looking." His claim that this same force was also "aiding the fighting people of Cyprus" (East Berlin, ADN international service, 29 June) was omitted in *Pravda*'s version of the speech (1 July).

In August President Makarios went to Colombo to attend the summit conference of the non-aligned nations. AKEL commented that "His Beatitude may visit Moscow either on his way or on his return" (*Kharavyi*, 22 June). This stopover never took place, and an Athens paper editorialized that the reason was that "the Soviets are currently flirting openly with Ankara, offering to help it in many ways in various fields, and consequently are not prepared to sacrifice the Soviet Union's national interest for the sake of the Cyprus problem" (*Elevtheros Kosmos*, 29 September).

In March there was an unusual meeting of delegations from AKEL, the Communist Party of Turkey, and the Communist Party of Greece (presumably the party of the exterior). The AKEL newspaper carried the joint statement, but did not disclose where the meeting was held, nor did it give the exact date or name the personalities involved. "In a spirit of brotherly friendship," the three parties agreed on, among other things, "the restoration of the Cypriot peoples' unity through the development and strengthening of the bonds between the Greek and Turkish Cypriots." (*Kharavyi*. 11 March.) In August, the Greek Communist Party of the interior sent two representatives who met with President Makarios and expressed support for his policies (*I Ayvi*, Athens, 25 August). The story was apparently not highlighted by AKEL's newspaper.

Politburo members of AKEL and the Lebanese Communist Party in June issued a communiqué appealing "to Syria to withdraw its troops in Lebanon" (*Kharavyi*, 5 June). Later, the PEO met in

Nicosia with Lebanese and Palestinian trade union leaders (ibid., 1 July). AKEL greeted the arrival of the first Cuban ambassador to Cyprus with "warm congratulations" on the anniversary of the Cuban Revolution (ibid., 27 July). AKEL sent "warm fraternal greetings" to the Workers' Party of North Korea in a seemingly belated reply to the congratulations received on its 50th anniversary (Pyongyang, Korean Central News Agency, 6 October).

Publications. AKEL's central organ is the large-circulation daily newspaper *Kharavyi* (Dawn), but there are also sympathetic writers and editors on most of the island's periodicals. AKEL issues an occasional theoretical journal, *Theoritikos Dimokratis* (Theoretical Democrat) and a weeky magazine, *Neoi Kairoi* (New Times). PEO publishes a weekly newspaper, *Ergatiko Vima* (Workers' Stride). EDON publishes a newspaper, *Dimokratia* (Democracy) and a monthly, *Neolaia* (Youth). In London a weekly called *To Vima* (The Stride) has been published by Greek Cypriot Communists for the past 36 years.

Washington, D.C.   T. W. Adams

Denmark

The Communist Party of Denmark (Danmarks Kommunistiske Parti; DKP) sprang from the left-wing faction of the Social Democratic Party (SDP) in the turbulent aftermath of World War I. It was organized on 9 November 1919, and exept for the German occupation during World War II, it has always been a legal party.

The DKP draws most of its support from among urban industrial workers, together with some leftist intellectuals in Copenhagen and other urban centers. Membership has edged upward during the 1970s after a decade of stagnation and is now estimated between 9,000 and 10,000. The population of Denmark is about 5,080,000.

The DKP continues to capitalize on the rising discontent of Danish workers and taxpayers—first expressed by a high protest vote in the national election of 4 December 1973. The last parliamentary election, on 9 January 1975, with ten parties vying for representation and none winning more than a third of the seats, reflected a continuing trend of political turmoil in this normally tranquil country. The Communists gained 0.6 percent in the popular vote, for a total of 4.2 percent. This tally represented the highest percentage achieved by the DKP since the September 1953 election, when it won 4.3 percent. With the gain of one seat, the party now holds seven seats in the 179-member Folketing (Parliament). Frequent public opinion surveys during 1976 showed DKP support fluctuating between 3.5 and 6.1 percent.

The DKP would appear to be the strongest of several socialist parties to the left of the reformist governing Social Democrats. The Left Socialists (Venstresocialister; VS), who had fallen below the 2 percent threshold for parliamentary representation in the 1971 and 1973 elections, cleared the barrier in 1975 and got the minimum of 4 seats. The Socialist People's Party (Socialistisk Folkeparti; SF) received 5.0 percent of the vote and 9 seats in 1975. Continuing intraparty strife in the SF during 1976 has at least temporarily weakened that party's popular appeal. A recent Gallup poll gave the SF only 3.5 percent of the electorate.

Recent Communist advances contrast sharply with what had been a fairly consistent decline in voter support. Party power peaked in 1945-47, owing in large part to the DKP's effective role in the Danish resistance. The party's unswerving loyalty to Moscow eroded support, and starting in 1956 after Khruschev's secret speech denouncing Stalin and the uprising in Hungary, the DKP faced a series of severe internal crises. The expulsion of the late Aksel Larsen (party chairman 1932-58) for "Titoist revision" in 1958, the formation of the SF in 1959, the emergence of the VF in 1967 and other radical socialist factions in the late 1960s all contributed to the DKP's eclipse. Even during the lean years, however, the DKP held a base of power in some industrial trade unions, and the party's press and headquarters have always seemed to be adequately financed. In recent years its political base has gained significantly, partly as a result of the large protest votes in Denmark to the left as well as right of the established major parties. After some fifteen years of strong economic advances, Denmark has been hit hard in the past three years by burgeoning inflation, unemployment, and severe deficits on current accounts occasioned, in part, by the country's total dependence on imported energy resources.

Leadership and Organization. Supreme party authority is the DKP's triennial congress, which held its 25th meeting in September 1976. It discusses the report of the Central Committee, adopts the Party Program and Rules, and elects the leading party bodies, consisting of the Central Committee (41 members, 11 alternates), a five-member Control Commission, and two party auditors. The Central Committee elects the party Chairman, the Executive Committee (15 members), and the Secretariat (5).

Knud Jespersen is DKP chairman, a post to which he was first elected in 1958 and to which he was re-elected in October 1976, just after the 25th Party Congress. Poul Emanuel is party secretary. The DKP is unique among the several Marxist parties in Denmark in that personality conflicts and policy differences, if any, are not discussed in public (since 1958). Hanne Reintoft, a prominent Communist member of Parliament, resigned from the Folketing to pursue her professional career. She was replaed by Margit Hansen, who was also elected to the DKP Executive Committee. The party has a youth affiliate, Communist Youth of Denmark (Danmarks Kommunistiske Ungdom; DKU). In 1975, Faroese Communists formed the Communist Party of the Faroe Islands (FKP). FKP chairman Egon Thomsen has stressed both the independence of the DKP and FKP from each other and the need for close cooperation between them.

Domestic Attitudes and Activities. Although the economic recession in Denmark was stabilized by early winter 1975-76, the Danish economy still suffers from idle capacity, low rate of investment, and high unemployment. These issues remained the focus of the DKP's domestic policy comments. No longer distracted by the stunning growth of the 1960s and early 1970s, Chairman Jespersen stressed that "facts have forced everyone to admit that capitalism has been struck by a crisis" (*Land og Folk*, 7 October 1975). During the opening debate in Parliament, Jespersen called on the minority Social Democratic government of Anker Jorgensen to attack real estate speculation and monopolies, and to remove the Value Added Tax (VAT) from food, building materials, and medicines. The DKP along with the two other left socialist parliamentary groups (SF and VS) faced a dilemma. The SDP government was anxious to find solutions to the economic crisis, but its policies required support from several non-socialist parties in order to receive parliamentary approval. The Communists and the People's Socialists called upon Jorgensen to reject non-socialist proposals and turn his government leftward. These appeals, which were repeated frequently during 1976, lacked specific policy pro-posals and neglected the basic truth that even with solid leftist support, the SDP would still be many votes shy of a parliamentary majority.

Much of 1976 was taken up by the preparations for the DKP's 25th Congress, which met in Copenhagen on 23-26 September. The Party Program, issued in draft form several months before the Congress, contained few significant changes from the program adopted at the 24th Congress in 1973. It reflected the party's two electoral advances and the rapid deterioration of the Danish economy during the interval. Although the DKP continues to extol the political, economic, and social achieve-ments of ruling Communist parties in Eastern Europe and especially the USSR, it was possible to detect a recognition of the necessity to adapt general Marxist-Leninist principles to Danish conditions. Longtime DKP spokesman Ib Nørlund stressed that "Communists do not recognize any 'model of socialism,' any copying of the methods of the building of socialism in one or another country." Moreover, "each Communist Party is independent . . . in shaping its policy to conform to the concrete conditions of its country, and bears full responsibility for the methods of struggle it has chosen." (*WMR*, January 1976.)

The draft program gave some attention to constitutional matters, incuding a proposal to amend the constitution to require that members of Parliament be responsible to their electorate on the basis of their party programs rather than their conscience, which is currently the case. The program also reflects the current antipathy toward excessive bureaucracy, but focuses upon monopolistic banks and large industry as the real domestic sources of public discontent. Danish membership in the European Community (EC) is frequently denounced, as are the military expenditures occasioned by Danish membership in NATO.

At the Congress itself, in September, the increased self-confidence of the DKP was evident. Some 600 delegates gathered to ratify the new program and to renew their confidence in the DKP leadership. The program demands an end to real estate speculation and calls for public ownership of the banks, heavy industry, and the energy sector. Addressing the delegates and guests on 23 Sep-tember, Chairman Jespersen recounted the party's progress since the previous congress. Party membership had grown by 5,000; the DKP had done well in two parliamentary elections and in municipal and county elections as well; the daily newspaper *Land og Folk* had received nearly 5 million kroner ($833,330) over three years; finally, the party's influence in key trade unions had improved. Despite these gains within the system, Jespersen exhorted his comrades to remember that "we are the revolutionary party of the Danish working class. Therefore, we have never been confined to the narrow framework of parliamentarianism." (*Pravda*, 24 September.)

The DKP has always been stronger in the trade union movement than in electoral politics. Al-though the Trade Union Confederation (Landsorganisationen; LO) is firmly controlled by unionists loyal to the SDP, some Communists and other Marxist activists are prominent in union locals. Preben Møller Hansen, a member of the DKP Executive Committee, is head of the Seamen's Union, and several other prominent Communists have high union positions. The Seaman's Union has been the stage of bitter struggles. Other unions saw increased unrest during the year. A small extremist group calling itself the Communist League of Marxist-Leninists (Kommunist Forbund-Marxister-Leninister; KFML) gained some attention because its members instigated wildcat strikes in the Postal Service and at various enterprises. The KFML is headed by Roskilde University lecturer Benito Scocozza and is frequently referred to by Social Democratic unionists as "Maoist" or "Chinese." The KFML has been critical of other left groups in Denmark, including the DKP, and is quite open in its hostility toward the Soviet Union.

As mentioned above, the Socialist People's Party suffered from internal party discords during 1976. Among the major points of contention is the degree to which the SF should support the minority SDP government on specific domestic policy questions. The SF was a tacit coalition partner of the SDP in 1966-67 and 1971-73, but such policies have been unpopular with the party's rank and file, electorate, and some members of Parliament. The SF is not exclusively a Marxist party in its ideology and is quite definitely non-Leninist in its political tactics. Its delegate to the Assembly of the EC in Strasbourg, Jens Maigaard, works closely with French and Italian Communist delegates.

International Views and Positions. The 25th DKP Congress and statements of DKP leaders reaffirmed the party's international views. Primary attention is given to denouncing Danish participation in the EC, NATO, and other organizations for cooperation among the Western nations. A foreign policy statement in the Folketing by Communist Ib Nørlund in January 1976 summarized the DKP position. Nørlund stressed that "the most important issue in the area of Danish foreign policy is removing the blinders of EC." The Tindemans Report calling for progress toward a European political union was denounced. In addition considerable attention was given to the strife in Angola and defense was made of Soviet support for the Popular Movement for the Liberation of Angola. (*Land og Folk*, 20 January.)

The Helsinki Conference of 1975 continued to receive attention in the DKP foreign policy perspective. Chairman Jespersen declared that despite the achievements of the Helsinki Accords, "imperialism" was continuing to spread anti-Soviet propaganda and to threaten intervention in the domestic affairs of European states (*WMR*, December 1975). Jespersen praised the foreign policy leadership of the USSR in his speech at the 25th Congress of the Communist Party of the Soviet Union (CPSU) in March 1976 (TASS, 2 March).

Danish foreign relations with Communist nations indirectly affect the DKP. In early January confirmation was given that four KGB agents connected with theSoviet Embassy in Copenhagen had been expelled for industrial espionage among Danish subcontractors in the multi-nation F-16 aircraft project. Soviet and Warsaw Pact military activity in the Baltic attracted considerable comment in both press and parliament throughout the year. Finally, in October it was revealed that the North Korean Embassy was heavily involved in the many violations of Danish law. Several senior Embassy personnel were expelled or recalled.

Other Marxist socialist groups in Denmark also express opposition to Danish membership in NATO and the EC, along with the concomitant defense and economic policies. The VS, SF, and KFML are critical of Soviet imperialism, but such statements tend to be less frequent.

International Party Contacts. Danish Communists continue to participate in frequent exchanges with their counterparts in other European Communist parties, and loyalty to the Soviet party remains the *sine qua non* of DKP international activity. This latter point was demonstrated on several occasions during 1976. DKP chairman Jespersen led a delegation to Moscow in late February to participate in the 25th Congress of the CPSU, where he praised the foreign and domestic achievements of the USSR (TASS, 2 March). The DKP practiced their traditional bilateral visiting, particularly in anticipation of the conference in East Berlin in June. On 20-23 May Polish party secretary Jozef Pinkowski was a guest of the DKP Central Committee. A five-member DKP delegation led by party secretary Poul Emanuel visited Romania a month later. DKP Chairman Jespersen led the Danish delegation to the Conference of Communist and Workers' Parties of Europe, held in East Berlin on 29-30 June. In a speech to the Conference on 29 June, Jespersen stressed the importance of proletarian internationalism and went on to denounce Danish membership in NATO and the EC. His talk did not touch directly upon the question of "Eurocommunism" which was raised by several West European Communist delegations (*Pravda*, 1 July). Jespersen met with Soviet general secretary Leonid Brezhnev just prior to the Conference (TASS, 28 June).

At the DKP Congress in September, 21 foreign Communist delegations were represented, and six of these (from the USSR, Cuba, the German Democratic Republic, France, Italy, and Finland) addressed the congress. Soviet Central Committee secretary Konstantin Chernenko praised DKP loyalty "to the principles of proletarian internationalism." (TASS, 24 September.)

Publications. *Land og Folk* (Nation and People), a daily newspaper, is the DKP central organ. Its circulation of some 8,000 increases on weekends to about 11,500. *Tiden-Verden Rund* (Time round the World) is the party's theoretical journal. The DKU publication is *Fremad* (Forward).

There are several left socialist publications not connected with the DKP. Among the more prominent are the SF's *Minavisen* (Mini-newspaper); the independent radical socialist, *Politisk Revy*; and the KFML's *Kommunist*.

University of Massachusetts　　　　　　　　　　　　　　　　　　　　　Eric S. Einhorn
Amherst

Finland

Consistently appealing to nearly a fifth of the Finnish voters, the Communist Party of Finland (Suomen Kommunistinen Puolue; SKP) again in 1976 had the distinction of being the only European Communist party participating in a democratic parliamentary government. Given the strains and problems facing any Finnish government, the SKP's distinction was surely a mixed pleasure. Finns are, however, used to rough sledding, and such has certainly been the history of the country's Communist movement. The SKP was established in Moscow on 29 August 1918 by "reds"—dissident Social Democrats—escaping from Finland's bloody civil war. Until 1930, the SKP operated through a variety of front organizations. The party was forced underground in the 1930s because of its own internal division and the government's ban on its operations. It became legal in 1944, as stipulated by the Finnish-Soviet armistice that year.

The SKP draws most of its members from either the industrialized urban areas of southern Finland or the small farming communities of the northern and eastern districts, where a "northland" radical tradition thrives. SKP members number an estimated 48,000. Finland's population is just over 4,700,000.

After the party's dual triumphs of 1975—gains in the September parliamentary elections and four of the eighteen portfolios in the new coalition government—1976 has been a year of strain and frustration. Finland's 58th government in as many years was sworn in on 30 November 1975 after President Kekkonen had appealed to five parties of the center and left to form a "national emergency" government to meet the country's serious economic problems. Although the SKP had originally been opposed to participation through its electoral and parliamentary front organization, the Finnish People's Democratic League (Suomen Kansan Demokraatinen Liitto; SKDL), SKP chairman Aarne Saarinen and SKDL chairman Ele Alenius were finally persuaded by Kekkonen's appeals. The SKP

Central Committee approved joining the coalition by 20 to 14, the SKDL Executive Committee approved 16 to 4, and the SKDL Parliamentary Group followed suit 23 to 10 with 7 not voting. The new government headed by Centrist Martti Miettunen was composed of representatives of the Social Democratic Center, Swedish People's, Liberal, and Communist parties (through the SKDL) and had the support of 140 to 152 members of the Parliament (the difference being the 12 Stalinist-faction Communists who were not expected to support the Miettunen government consistently). SKDL members holding portfolios in the new government included Olavi Hänninen (second minister of the interior for housing), Kauko Hjerppe (minister of transportation and communications) Kalevi Kivisto (second minister of education), and Paavo Aitio (minister of labor). Hänninen and Hjerppe are members of the SKP as well as the SKDL. Arno Hautala succeeded Hänninen in the cabinet on 29 June when the former became vice-chairman of the Confederation of Finnish Trade Unions (SAK).

Communist participation in the government was a condition for Social Democratic support and participation because the new government faced difficult decisions on Finland's economic problems. Inflation was running at an annual rate of 17 percent, unemployment approached 80,000 (3.5 percent of the labor force), and the country's current accounts were in severe deficit. When the new government's economic program was presented in March, the SKDL objected to the proposed increase in sales taxes. Among the alternatives suggested by the SKDL/SKP were surtaxes on high incomes, a company capital tax, employer wage taxes, better collection of business taxes, and foreign and domestic loans. Nevertheless, a majority of the SKP accepted the necessity of some restrictive measures. Within the SKP, government responsibility worsened tensions between the liberal majority wing led by Chairman Saarinen and the "orthodox" or "Stalinist" wing headed by Vice-Chairman Taisto Sinisalo.

Communist rejection of sale tax increases brought the government to a stalemate in May, and on 13 May Premier Miettunen submitted his government's resignation. This was rejected by President Kekkonen, who suggested that the government grant the SKDL a "dispensation on the tax issue since their votes were not strictly necessary for a parliamentary majority. The SKDL accepted Kekkonen's strategem, and the finance package passed in June. Problems in economic policy remained, and on 17 September Miettunen again tendered his resignation when the Social Democrats balked at Communist refusal to support major government policies. This time President Kekkonen was forced to accept the failure of the five-party government, and after negotiations Premier Miettunen formed a three-party minority government on 29 September. His coalition was now composed of the Center, Swedish People's, and Liberal parties, but only 58 of the parliament's 200 mandates were formally committed to the government. Thus ended the second attempt within a decade to include the Finnish Communists in a left-center government.

Nationwide municipal elections on 17-18 October give a partial judgment of how the several parties fared in the nine-month coalition experiment. The Center party gained significantly while the Social Democrats held their own as Finland's largest party. The SKDL slipped back to 18.5 percent, which was a slight decline from their 19.0 percent in the 1975 parliamentary elections.

Leadership and Organization. Aarne Saarinen, "liberal" Communist and former union leader, was reelected SKP chairman at the party's 17th Congress, in Helsinki in May 1975. He has been chairman since 1966, and he has supported SKDL participation in center-left governments. The Congress also reelected the so-called Stalinist (hard-line, particularly in parliamentary and government issues) Taisto Sinisalo and liberal Olavi Hänninen as vice-chairmen, and liberal Arvo Aalto as general secretary. The relative strength of the two factions of the SKP has remained more or less constant since 1970: a ratio of liberals to Stalinists of 20-15 in the Central Committee, 9-6 in the Politburo, and 5-3 in the Secretariat. Between the triennial congresses, the Central Committee is the highest decision-making organ of the party.

Party Internal Affairs. The SKDL/SKP's nine-month term in the five-party government fueled the continuing intraparty strife. The conflict between the "liberal" majority and the Stalinist minority harked back to the ideological turmoil following the 1956 "de-Stalinization" congress of the Communist Party of the Soviet Union (CPSU). Among the issues widening the split have been different reactions to the Warsaw Pact invasion of Czechoslovakia in 1968, domestic political tactics, and interpretations of seemingly ambiguous signals from Moscow.

During 1976 the principal source of contention was SKP attitudes toward Finland's economic difficulties and, more specifically, the role of the SKDL/SKP in the five-party coalition government of Miettunen. Vice-Chairman Sinisalo, on behalf of the orthodox faction, had stated before the government was formed that "[e]veryone can be sure Communists will prove their ability for cooperation in all its forms when the issue is defending the rights and interests of our nation and its working people" (*Tiedonantaja*, 3 September 1975). His faction was unwilling, however, to support the majority decision to accept a formal role in the center-left government, and in 1976 it remained a vocal critic of the government's policies in party forums and in its press. When Saarinen defended the government's difficult decisions in April, he went on to warn against "leftist opportunism" and accused the minority Stalinists of "left sectarianism, dishonesty, uncomradely behavior, and backwardness" (*Nordisk Kontakt*, no. 8). Sinisalo referred sarcastically to Saarinen's "blue-white" (Finland's national colors) national Communism. Previously, at the SKP Central Committee meeting on 31 January, Sinisalo noted that even the SKP majority had only agreed to participate for a "trial period." After the Miettunen government's economic policies were announced, in the Stalinist view it was clear that the government was "not a result of a demand by the working people, of the will and desire of workers' organization," but "a result of bourgeois pressure," and that the government solution was "an effort to weaken the force of the battle against capitalism" (*Tiedonantaja*, 3 February). An editorial in the Stalinist paper a few days later warned that the bourgeoisie was hoping that the tensions caused by the majority's support for the coalition would split the SKP (ibid., 6 February).

As mentioned above, by September the SKDL/SKP could no longer support the government, and the coalition ended. Strife and contention within the SKP can be expected to continue. Despite the tensions generated by SKP factionalism, both groups seem anxious to coexist within the same party structure. The complex relationship between the SKP and the SKDL probably facilitates nominal party unit, as does pressure from Moscow. An advantage to the SKDL/SKP of this tenuous unity is the avoidance of significant left socialist splinter parties and organizations.

Domestic Attitudes and Activities. The preoccupation of the SKP during 1976 was the issue of participation in and support of the two Miettunen coalitions as discussed above. Both party factions expressed concern for short- as well as long-term consequences of government participation. Much of the medicine administered to the ailing Finnish economy by the Miettunen government has been bitter. Advocates of direct responsibility in shaping these policies, such as SKP chairman Saarinen and SKDL chairman Alenius, claimed that the interests of worker required participation in government. Several prominent Communists have criticized the weakness of minority governments due to frequent cabinet changes and parliamentary elections. SKP general secretary Arvo Aalto commented: "The bourgeois parliamentary system is in crisis in Finland. This is seen in the weakness and instability of the government, a parliament which is powerless to exert decisive influence on national policy, the fact that midterm elections are becoming something of a rule, and the decline of parliamentary ethics. More and more, parliament is becoming a debating club instead of functioning as the highest authority responsible for the fundamental content of national politics." (*WMR*, December 1975.) This observation would not provoke strenuous objections from most Finnish politicians today. Aalto went on to invite the Social Democratic and Center parties to join with the Communist Party to find acceptable solutions to the country's political and economic problems.

The theme of the "popular front" was also echoed by Paavo Aitio, who served as SKP minister of labor in the Miettunen government and who is also a liberal Communist veteran of the left-center coalition of the late 1960s. Aitio emphasized that "fundamental social change could only be brought about by a popular front, backed by a majority of the workers and peasants and a united trade union movement" (Hella Pick, *Manchester Guardian Weekly*, 14 March 1976). Aitio went on to assert that although revolutionary change remained the Communist goal, such change was to come about without violence and in cooperation with other progressive groups. SKP chairman Saarinen commented that "Marxist-Leninism must be flexibly applied according to the condition of each country," and that in Finland, where the SKP is recognized by other parties as an equal partner, change would be peaceful and tolerant of the "plurality of parties" (ibid.).

In the perspective of modern Finnish politics, the SKP/SKDL has become part of the political establishment. The first center-left government which included the SKP/SKDL, in 1966, was headed by the Social Democrats, who have traditionally been the bitter rivals of the SKP in both electoral and trade union politics. The partial rapprochement between the Socialists and Communists was encouraged by the former's hope that SKP participation in government decisions would allow necessary economic reforms and controls without excessive labor protest. Communists in the government would protect the Social Democrats from having to face a disappointed electorate alone in difficult economic times. Finally, the coalition of the Communist, Socialist, and Center parties would assure Moscow of continuity in Finland's foreign and domestic politics. Leaders of both Social Democratic and Center parties are aware that a major threat to continuing cooperation with the SKP is the orthodox minority's strong objections to Communist participation in governments led by non-Communists.

The Finnish trade unions remain an important theater of Communist activity. The reverberations of the hard-fought and scandal-punctuated Metalworkers Union election of November 1975 were still felt in 1976. The Social Democrats kept their control of the largest Finnish union, but with a reduced majority. Efforts to reduce the soaring rate of inflation inevitably brought proposals for income/wage controls. Such measures were opposed by Communist, Socialist, and other trade union leaders, but were deemed to be crucial to the five-party government's economic plans. There were several strikes in industrial and service unions during the winter and spring of 1976.

A final element in the complex position of the SKP in current domestic politics is the role of Finnish president Urho Kekkonen. After 20 years of incumbency, Kekkonen is a rather unique institution in Finnish politics. The SKP/SKDL generally falls into line with most other factions in Finland in supporting Kekkonen's active foreign policy, which has satisfied the ever-vigilant Soviet neighbor for two decades. In domestic politics, Kekkonen's measures are often respected but occasionally thwarted. The liberal majority in the SKP has been more cooperative, and their decision to join the five-party coalition was principally the result of Kekkonen's pressure. The Stalinist minority, while rarely directly critical of the President, has pushed for a non-conciliatory line. Both factions support Kekkonen's reelection in 1978 despite his advanced age.

International Views and Positions. The intraparty schism of the SKP is least evident in foreign and international policy. The Conference on Security and Cooperation in Europe (CSCE), which placed Helsinki and President Kekkonen in the international limelight during the summer of 1975, remains the keystone of Communist Party foreign policy. Other principal issues include opposition to Finland's special arrangement with the EC, denunciation of NATO encroachment in the Nordic region, support for the Communists in Portugal and Spain, and solidarity with the USSR.

The SKP statement—"For Peace, Security, and Progress"—at the 1975 Congress summarized the international views of Finnish Communists. The party welcomed the defeat of "U.S. imperialism" in Indochina and political developments in southern Europe. The SKP remained resolutely in the pro-

Soviet camp—whether in advocacy of specific economic programs or general loyalty in the international Communist movement. The basic principles of Finnish foreign policy, especially neutrality and good relations with the USSR, is not contested by any significant political party. The SKP frequently detects signs of "reactionary plots" to change this profile, but such references are usually vague. The Communist emphasis is one of explicit verbal support for pro-Communist (Moscow-oriented) movements in various countries around the globe. This posture was reiterated in a declaration following a meeting of the SKP Central Committee in September 1976 (TASS, 19 September).

The SKP was represented by its leaders at the June 1976 conference of European Communist and workers' parties in East Berlin. The Finnish delegation joined in warning against anti-Communist forces in Europe and elsewhere which threatened to weaken the Helsinki Accords. (*Pravda*, 13 August).

International Party Contacts. In addition to the East Berlin conference, the SKP maintained its usual contacts with Communist parties in both East and West Europe. The SKP attended the 25th Party Congress of the Communist Party of the Soviet Union (CPSU) in Moscow, February 1976. Both at the Congress and upon his return home, SKP chairman Saarinen stressed the close ties between the SKP and the CPSU and their agreement in perceptions of international developments.

SKP secretary Aalto visited Czech Communist Party leader Gustav Husák in August (Prague domestic radio service, 11 August). During the same month French Communist Party leader Georges Marchais paid a six-day visit to Finland at the invitation of SKP chairman Saarinen. Following Marchais's visit a year earlier, the Finnish Communist press emphasized the growing strength of the French party and the analogous domestic challenges confronting both parties. In August, Marchais also visited Finnish Social Democratic leader and foreign minister Kalevi Sorsa (Helsinki domestic radio service, 19 August).

Vice-Chairman Sinisalo also maintained contacts abroad. In September he visited Hermann Axen, East German Politburo and Secretariat member (ADN, 8 September).

Publications. The SKP's *Kansan Uutiset* (People's News), published daily in Helsinki, is the principal organ of the liberal majority of the SKP. *Kommunisti* is the monthly theoretical journal. *Tiedonantaja* and *Hämeen Yhteistyö* speak for the SKP's Stalinist faction. The weekly *Folktidningen* (People's News) is the Communist newspaper for Finland's small Swedish-speaking minority. Finnish Maoists, who are outside of both SKP factions, circulate several publications, such as *Lakakuu* (October) and *Punalippu* (Red Guard), which are perhaps the only violently anti-Soviet publications in the country.

University of Massachusetts   Eric S. Einhorn
Amherst

France

The French Communist Party (Parti communiste français; PCF) was founded in December 1920. Except for a short period of illegality (1939-40) following its support of the Nazi-Soviet pact and the clandestine period (1941-44) of the Resistance, the PCF has operated publicly and legally, a record unique among major non-ruling Communist parties. The PCF membership remains by far the largest and the most militant of all French parties. It is probably larger than the membership of all other parties combined, most important among them the French Socialist Party (Parti socialiste; PS), with which the PCF has been allied both electorally and, since 1972, programmatically. Despite this, the PS has, since the 1973 elections, changed the face of French politics by reversing the previous PCF electoral dominance on the French left. According to 1974-76 legislative by-elections and the 1976 cantonal elections, the PS is in fact now the dominant electoral party in France, although the measure of this superiority, vis-à-vis the Gaullists as well as the Communists, cannot be determined at the national level before the next legislative elections, scheduled for spring 1978. A serious flanking challenge to the PCF from the *gauchistes*, or extreme leftists, lasted only briefly after the 1968 "events of May." Today the gauchistes are largely marginal, although their political support could conceivably balloon once again should a left-wing government come to power. The small Unified Socialist Party (Parti socialiste unifié; PSU) split at the end of 1974, with its major leaders joining the PS. The rump extreme-left wing of the PSU has since generally allied itself with the Trotskyist Communist League (Ligue communiste; LC).

The PCF electorate today continues its post-1958 stagnation at more or less a fifth of the total vote, despite the "Union of the Left" (Union de la gauche) alliance with the PS and the Movement of Left-Wing Radicals (Mouvement des Radicaux de gauche; MRG). The latter is a center-left splinter wing formerly joined to the moderate Radical Party, which in 1974 joined the governmental majority in the National Assembly. The most recent legislative elections, March 1973, gave the PCF 21.3 percent (5,026,417 votes), as opposed to 20 percent in 1968, 22.5 percent in 1967, and 21.7 percent in 1962. The PCF has not been able to recover its losses in the 1958 elections, which created the Gaullist Fifth Republic — it had 25.6 percent in 1951, 25.7 percent in 1956, and 18.9 percent in 1958. The stagnation was confirmed in the 7-14 March 1976 cantonal elections — 22.8 percent at the first ballot, 17.3 percent at the second. The lack of significant momentum and the sectorial regression are in contrast with the extraordinary Socialist Party gains in the past few years: the PS won 18.9 percent in the 1973 legislative elections and 26.5 percent in the 1976 cantonal elections (30.8 percent at the second ballot). The PS continued to progress, partly at Communist expense, in seven by-elections in November 1976. Most of the Socialist gains, however, came from centrist voters moving to the opposition. Opinion polls in the past two years have given the PS anywhere between 25 and 38 percent of the intentions to vote in the next legislative elections.

In the 490-seat National Assembly, the Union of the Left electoral alliance for mutual second-round withdrawals has benefited all three constituent groups. The PCF in December 1976 had 74 seats (including that held by the Guadeloupe Communist Party) as opposed to 34 in 1968, while the PS had 93 and the MRG 13. In the 283-seat Senate, there were 20 PCF, 52 PS, and 38 Left Radical and Radical Senators (the two Radical groups in the Senate are allied in the "Democratic Left").

In presidential elections, the PCF tactic in 1969 was, for the first time, to present a Communist candidate at the first ballot. Jacques Duclos's 21.5 percent total indicated the PCF could muster its legislative electorate in a presidential election. In 1974 (as in 1965), the Union of the Left parties presented a joint first-ballot candidate, PS first secretary François Mitterrand, who nearly won (49.3 percent) against Valéry Giscard d'Estaing. This result indicated that the Communist electorate complied more or less totally with the party's electoral instructions. The next major elections, the municipal elections of 13-20 March 1977, are expected to show further Union of the Left gains, and there is at least a reasonable chance that it can win the 1978 legislative elections. The next presidential election is normally to be held in 1981, and President Giscard d'Estaing has said he will remain in office even should the left alliance win in 1978. However, it is generally agreed that a left victory in 1978 would likely provoke a constitutional crisis—opposing the powers of the Presidency to those of Parliament—whose outcome cannot be predicted. The Fifth Republic institutions after de Gaulle remain therefore problematic and contested.

The Union of the Left parties are committed to the Common Program (Programme Commun de gouvernement) signed in June 1972, the aim of which is to move France toward socialism. The PCF, which was last a governmental partner in the Tripartite governments of 1944-47, at present refuses to consider any other possibility of national governmental participation, and no other has been offered. It has relatively little influence in regional administrative institutions and in the Departmental Councils (Conseils généraux), which are in any case relatively powerless. At the local level, the PCF after the 1971 municipal elections had 787 mayors, in a total of nearly 38,000. Altogether it controls or participates in approximately 1,100 municipal governments comprising more than 5 million people (about 10 percent of the population, estimated at 51,915,000 in 1973) and including many sizable cities, such as Le Havre, Nîmes, and Saint-Denis.

PCF membership has grown significantly in absolute terms in the past few years. After stagnating around 300,000 to 350,000 in the 1960s, the total at the end of 1975 was 491,000. PCF organizational secretary Paul Laurent said on 30 November 1976 that the total was approaching 550,000 and that more than 100,000 new members had been added during the year (L'Humanité, 1 December). In February 1976, at the party congress, a short-term goal of 600,000 members was announced.

The intensification of PCF recruitment has been essentially a process of increasing membership within the Communist "world" itself: that is, mainly it involves getting voters and "sympathizers" to take out a party card. The counterpart of this is no doubt a reduced level of militant activities on a relative scale and serious problems of organizational integration—both of which are indicated by constant articles in the party press. Moreover, the total new membership figure is ambiguous, in that some who sign a membership form never get a party card or buy only one or a few of the monthly dues stamps. Most importantly, the fact that new recruitment has occurred essentially within the already Communist "world" is no doubt the major reason why membership increases have not, or at least not yet, increased the Communist electorate.

As to social composition, PCF doctrine still insists on the absolute priority of workers in all party activities, although there has been for the past few years an attempt to shade the most dogmatic aspects of the party's traditional ouvriériste ideology in order to attract more electoral and organizational support from other classes and groups. In 1966-67 the PCF claimed to be about 60 percent working class in its membership, including housewives of workers and retired workers without which the figure was closer to 40 percent. No global statistics have been given since 1966-67, although the party's social composition has changed considerably. At the 1976 congress, André Vieuguet said the 1975 recruits were 45 percent workers and about 20 percent salaried employees.

The percentage of women, 11 percent in 1946 and 25.5 percent in 1966, has risen further still in recent years. In L'Humanité of 29 September 1976, Politburo member Madeleine Vincent spoke of 150,000 women members, or approximately 30 percent of the total. She said the present goal was to increase female membership to 40 percent.

The PCF electorate in 1973 was slightly over 50 percent working class (workers make up about 32 percent of the total active work force; the PCF got 31 percent of the working class vote in 1967 and 37 percent in 1973) and about 15 percent salaried employees. It is dominantly male (58 percent) and younger than other large party electorates in France.

The setting for French Communist strategy is a continuing bipolarization of French party and electoral politics; on one side the present governmental majority (the Gaullists—now known as the RPR, the Giscardist Independent Republicans, and a "Reformer" coalition of the Social Democratic Center and the Radical Party), and on the other side the Union of the Left. Other organizations are politically marginal. Despite continuing historical and policy disagreements within the Communist-Socialist alliance (see below, "Domestic Attitudes and Activities"), observers generally agree that the PCF-PS coalition will last at least through the legislative elections of 1978. Beyond this, in the case of either a victory or a defeat, it is quite possible the two parties will not be able, or will not choose, to remain partners. In the meantime, a small organization of opposition Gaullists may join the left-wing alliance as a fourth partner.

Leadership and Organization. The national leadership of the PCF was elected at the party's 22d Congress, 4-8 February 1976. The Central Committee numbers 97 full and 24 candidate members. The Politburo's 18 full members are: Gustave Ansart, Mireille Bertrand, Guy Besse, Jacques Chambaz, Jean Colpin, Etienne Fajon, Guy Hermier, Jean Kanapa, Henri Krasuki, Paul Laurent, Roland Leroy, Georges Marchais, René Piquet, Gaston Plissonier, Claude Poperen, Georges Séguy, André Vieuguet, and Madeleine Vincent; the three candidate members are: Charles Fiterman, Maxime Gremetz, and André Lajoinie. The Secretariat of the Central Committee consists of Colpin, Charles Fiterman, Laurent, Leroy, Piquet, and Plissonier. Georges Marchais remained secretary-general.

With a total of 21 members, the Politburo is larger than ever before. In 1972 there were 19 members. Chambaz was added to take charge of party intellectuals when Roland Leroy was shifted to become director of *L'Humanité*, and Kanapa was elected after the death of Jacques Duclos. Of the 1972 Politburo, Duclos and former CGT leader Benoît Frachon died in 1975, and Georges Frischmann retired. The changes in the 1972 Secretariat are that Fajon and Vieuguet have been replaced with Colpin, Laurent, and Fiterman. Speculation about a possible successor to Marchais has settled on Paul Laurent, who at the Congress was named both organizational secretary and "coordinator" of the several Paris federations.

The cell structure of the PCF continued to show significant development along with the rise in membership. In January 1975 there were 21,340 cells in the 97 federations, and by December 1976 this had increased to approximately 24,000. A strong emphasis in the past few years on increasing the number and relative percentage of workplace cells continued in 1976—partly to overwhelm the rather minor efforts of other parties (in particular the PS), partly to foster the membership increase, and partly to reinforce PCF mobilization capacities for the prospect of a left-wing government. The 1975 target of raising the total from 6,500 to 8,000 was achieved (*L'Humanité*, 31 December 1975), and at the 1976 congress Marchais announced a goal of 10,000 (ibid., 5 February). On 30 November, Laurent said the total was well over 9,000 (ibid., 1 December). At the end of 1975 there were 5,457 rural cells and 9,649 neighborhood or local cells. The percentage of enterprise cells was 20 percent in 1945, 26 percent in 1970, and about 37 percent in 1976.

Auxiliary and Mass Organizations. The Communist Youth Movement (Mouvement de la jeunesse communiste; MJC) has made significant membership gains recently. The MJC claimed 65,000 members in 1971 and 70,000 in 1975; in 1976 the claim was 94,417 (*L'Humanité*), 5 October). Hermier is the Politburo member supervising youth organizations. Jean-Michel Catala is the MJC secretary-general and also a member of the Central Committee. The MJC held a special convention, 9-12 December on the theme "Socialism and Freedom."

The Union of French Communist Students (Union des étudiants communistes de France; UECF), part of the umbrella MJC organization, is the PCF university student movement. It claims 15,000 members and is the dominant tendency in the National French Student Union (Union nationale des étudiants de France; UNEF), which claims 49,000 members (*Le Monde*, Paris, 9 November). The minority in the UNEF is made up largely of students favorable to CERES, an organization on the left wing of the Socialist Party. This organization is countered principally by another, Trotskyist-led UNEF, claiming 26,000 members. In fall 1976 the student union movement as a whole remained fragmented, unrepresentative, and relatively quiescent after a series of strikes in the spring. Communist influence also is strong in the National Union of High School Action Committees (Union nationale des comités d'action lycéenne; UNCAL).

In keeping with the relative feminization of the PCF membership in recent years, the Union of French Women (Union des femmes françaises; UFF) also has increased its membership, from 80,000 in 1935 to about 100,000 in 1976 (ibid., 12 November). But the UFF seems to have little public impact, despite an attempt to modernize by speaking directly to women about their problems rather than organizing them within explicitly class orientations. At the May Day parade, CGT union marshals physically excluded non-Communist feminist groups of the Paris area who sought to join the march.

The major mass movement controlled by Communist influence continues to be the General Confederation of Labor (Confédération générale du Travail; CGT), whose secretary-general, Georges Séguy, and second leading figure, Henri Krasuki, are both members of the PCF Politburo. Still by far the largest union organization in France (between 1.5 and 2.5 million members), the CGT is, according to the results of professional elections and mobilization capacities, the dominant union in all three sectors of the French economy—private, nationalized, and public. In the public sector, however, this dominance is mitigated by the large impact of the autonomous Federation of National Education (Fédération de l'Education Nationale; FEN), the union of teachers and professors, which is the third largest French union after the CGT and the Socialist-oriented CFDT. Communist elements in the FEN comprise the second strongest of five main factions.

In rural areas, a Communist-influenced agricultural syndicate, the Movement for the Coordination and Defense of Agricultural Enterprises (Mouvement de coordination et de défense des exploitations agricoles; MODEF), formed in 1959, occupies a rather distant second place, behind the autonomous FNSEA organization. Other Communist mass organizations—such as the Peace Movement (Mouvement de la paix), which had great importance two decades ago—are of relatively little consequence today, although they may still be the vehicle for gestures of international solidarity, such as sending a relief boat to Lebanon in the wake of the Syrian military offensive against the Palestinians in the fall, or underwriting public appeals and petitions for "peace" in the Middle East.

Party Internal Affairs. The PCF Congress in February 1976 adopted the slogan "Socialism in French colors," a new wording of the two-decades-old "French Road to Socialism." In general, the Congress marked a consolidation of the left-wing alliance option and an elaboration of the French Communist version of the peaceful, pluralist, and democratic strategy for a transition to socialism and for socialism itself. Therein, the Congress also marked a personal triumph for Marchais, whose leadership in this direction had been questioned in 1973-75 because the alliance with the PS clearly benefited the Socialists electorally much more than the Communists. The leadership today appears on the whole unified in the belief that the PCF has no interesting alternative to a strategy of broadened political and social alliances, and a parliamentary conquest of power, although, to be sure, differences may arise over tactical questions (as when Séguy and Marchais disagreed publicly in late October—see below, "International Views and Policies"). Socialist electoral superiority is accepted for the time being as the necessary price for alliance with the PS, the only likely PCF access to national government. Furthermore, in the Common Program the PS accepted an essential demand of Communist political economy, a "rupture" with the capitalist system through a "minimum threshold" of nationalizations. The PS has also gone far toward a foreign policy of less intensive alignment with the United States.

The major innovations at the Congress were an elaboration of the PCF doctrinal commitment to a pluralist and democratic form of socialism, and an extension of explicit and implicit criticism of the USSR (see, here and in what follows, *Cahiers du communisme*, February-March). In particular, the Congress voted with considerable fanfare to drop the "dictatorship of the proletariat" doctrine, saying it no longer expresses the French Communist conception of political and social power in either the transition phase of "advanced democracy" or in socialism itself. Though the vote was unanimous, this proposal had been opposed by some members in earlier cell, section, and federation votes: Kanapa said at the Congress that "of 22,705 delegates to the 98 federal conferences, only 113 voted against dropping the dictatorship of the proletariat, and 216 abstained." In addition to the inner-party debate, the party leadership displayed a certain limited openness of a new kind toward intellectuals, permitting Etienne Balibar, a PCF theorist and professor of philosophy (and a protégé of Louis Althusser) to publish a book, *Sur la dictature du prolétariat* (Paris, Maspéro, 1976), which argues that in true Leninism the dictatorship of the proletariat is in a sense socialism itself, and that the party decision is hence radically revisionist. An opposing book by PCF historial Jean Elleinstein, called *Le P.C.*, appeared in late spring (Grasset, 1976). Elleinstein, whose position in the PCF today is broadly similar to that of Roger Garaudy a decade ago (before his exclusion) and who in 1975 published a controversial and critical *Histoire du phénomène stalinien*, speaks for the current "democratic" evolution in the PCF in its most advanced form. He asserts for example that *Le P.C.* was written without any party authorization or pre-publication scrutiny (p. 9), and both his recent books are extremely critical of the Soviet regime (past and present), going so far as to say that no socialist country today is a democracy.

During the past year the leadership group has also become more united and reconciled with a foreign policy of critical relations with the Communist Party of the Soviet Union (CPSU). The most striking example is the Politburo foreign policy specialist Jean Kanapa, long one of the most pro-Soviet of the PCF leaders, who in the past year has become one of the leading spokesmen for the Marchais-style criticisms and provocations of the Soviet leadership. In addition, many of the old pro-Soviet leaders are gone, and Etienne Fajon, now the only Politburo member elected before 1956, has been removed from the center of party decision-making. René Andrieu, editor-in-chief of *L'Humanité*, is one of the remaining important leaders espousing traditional views.

Laurent has become in the past two years more or less clearly the number two man in the PCF. His views are considered to be if anything more open and more consistent than those of Marchais. Leroy, director of *L'Humanité*, earlier had seemed Marchais's chief rival, but has health problems and is now much less influential than he was a few years ago. Marchais's health has also been questioned since a slight coronary in January 1975. The three Politburo candidate members named in 1976—Fiterman, Gremetz, and Lajoinie—are all close to Marchais. Fiterman has quickly become a leading party figure and public spokesman.

Domestic Attitudes and Activities. The PCF analysis of domestic conditions during 1976 was hardened by the disappointing French attempts to surmount the economic recession, marked by the change of premier in August (Jacques Chirac giving way to Raymond Barre) and by the austerity measures introduced by the new government.

The general line was given at the party congress (see *Cahiers*, February-March): The concentration of power and wealth in "state monopoly capitalism" continues, and France today is ruled by 25 large financial and industrial groups. The French crisis is neither a vague and general "crisis of a civilization" nor a limited problem of economic and financial policy (i.e., inflation and unemployment). Rather it is a new stage in the general crisis of capitalism, a global crisis—economic, political, ideological, moral. Yet despite the increasingly international character of contemporary capitalism, it is possible, the PCF argues, to achieve a national French solution, to "get out of the crisis in one capitalist country," so to speak.

The strategy offered is to combine the "Union of the French People," a proposed grand alliance of all social groups whose "objective" interest is "anti-monopolist"—a "crushing majority of the people"—with the PCF-PS-left-wing Radical "Union of the Left" political alliance. The PCF asserts the present electoral bipolarization in two nearly equal forces is a "subjective" phenomenon which does not reflect the objective interest of nearly all French people in a coalition against "big capital." The focus of the "Union of the Left" coalition is the 1972 Common Program, which a left-wing government would seek to enact. The working class still has the historic role of vanguard in the social struggle, and the PCF, because it is the political vanguard of the working class, is thus also the political vanguard of the left-wing coalition and of the struggle for socialism as a whole. The conclusion is that the "possibiliity of building socialism in France is linked to the Communist Party's capacity to exercise a directing influence in the popular movement." The strategic problem, as the Communists see it, is thus to expand the social bases of the "Union of the Left" and to increase PCF political influence, so that the "Union of the French People," the left-wing alliance, and Communist influence coincide as much as possible.

Apart from the small ruling stratum, all the other classes, groups, and parties in the proposed "Union of the French People" are said to express legitimate interests and to have "nothing to fear" from the PCF and working-class directing influence in socialism. These others "play a useful role and will therefore have [their] place in the kind of socialism we want." As Marchais put it:

> We do not propose to other social groups that they melt into the working class. . . . We understand that they struggle to remain what they are and we help them. In return, we tell them their struggles will not be efficacious and victorious unless they join the working class struggle. We tell them it is the refusal to give the working class its place in national life, and in the government of the nation, which is the primary cause of the evils of French society.

Within the Left-Wing party coalition, on the other hand, "union is combat." This means, above all, PCF vigilance vis-à-vis the Socialist Party, to forestall a PS return to "class collaboration," to an alliance with bourgeois forces. According to Marchais, "It is true that the Socialist Party is still a reformist party," but alliance with the PS is "indispensable," given the French situation. Moreover, the PCF must become dominant in the alliance, or at least avoid Socialist dominance, because the PS "would return to the policy of class collaboration . . . if the left were disequilibrated in its favor. . . . This is only a lesson from past experience. . . . It is not an ad hominum argument."

PCF strategy requires that it become more important electorally, and Marchais has suggested a goal of 25 percent for the next legislative elections (more or less what the PCF had during the Fourth Republic). The tactic is to fabricate a "convergence of struggles" among the widely different sectors of society included in the "Union of the French People" analysis. The most important potential clienteles are said to exist among Gaullists and Catholics.

For one thing, the French Communist criticism of the USSR has the advantage of playing to the Gaullist theme of national independence, and is combined with policies against further integration in the European Community and the Atlantic Alliance (e.g., during 1976 the PCF took positions against direct election of the European Parliament, as decided by the European Council in September, and against the "forward defense strategy" envisaged by President Giscard d'Estaing, which would commit French military power—including the Pluto tactical nuclear missiles—to defense of West German borders against an attack from the East, thus abandoning the Gaullist doctrine of a "national sanctuary" defense *tous azimuts*). The Communists also renewed the "extended hand" to Catholics. On 10 June, in Lyons, Marchais made a speech recalling Maurice Thorez's first overture to Catholics (April 1936). In October the Communist-Catholic contact was given considerable publicity with the simultaneous publication and joint public presentation of a Communist book, *Communistes et chrétiens* (Editions sociales), edited by candidate Politburo member Maxime Gremetz, and a book *Communistes et chrétiens, communistes ou chrétiens*, by Georges Hourdin, founder of *La vie catholique*, published by the Catholic-oriented firm (Editions Desclée).

A third and more general Communist campaign for new support spoke to the wide variety of social categories who fear an attack on private property. The PCF Congress attempted to refute charges of "collectivist" intentions (1) by saying that French socialism would avoid the deficiencies of Soviet socialism, and (2) by introducing a new threefold elaboration of property categories: "personal property," including a house or apartment and the right of heritage; "small private property" in artisan, commercial, industrial, or small agricultural form; and "social property," divided into diverse forms—nationalized, cooperative, municipal, departmental, regional.

The need to justify the party on the question of civil and political liberties leads to attacks on current French practice in addition to "defensive" criticism of existing socialist regimes. Disparate attempts all during the year to gain greater media exposure were turned into an explicit campaign against bias and a "lack of pluralism" in the news media with a Central Committee report in September by Georges Gosnat (*L'Humanité*, 28 September). The PCF focused in particular on French television, pointing out that there is no Communist newscaster, and alleging a consistent bias against reporting Communist activities on the basis of equality with other parties. For example, after the 7 October general strike, the GCT protested that Séguy's interview had been deliberately excluded from the news programs in favor of that of Edmond Maire, the CFDT leader. On 22 September *L'Humanité* protested that *Le Monde* had deliberately omitted the article in *L'Humanité dimanche* from a 21-article summary of commentary on the death of Mao Tse-tung. (Among other things, the PCF wanted to insist on the fact that its weekend paper had run a very favorable 5-page article and had adopted conciliatory positions toward the possibiliity of a PCF-Chinese rapprochement). Communist criticism of the media caught more public notice when President Giscard's book *Démocratie française*, which appeared in the middle of October, received almost unprecedented media attention. Jacques Chambaz published an "Open Letter to the Directors and Broadcasters" of the French radio-television system (ibid., 16 October) calling for a dialogue about more equitable news presentation, and an opinion poll at this time indicated the French public agreed that Giscard's book had received "too much" attention. In November the PCF raised another issue of political liberty by criticizing the practice of anti-Communist loyalty oaths in the European Community bureaucracy.

Vis-à-vis the Socialist Party, the ideological polemics of 1974-75 were somewhat quieted in 1976, although a major disagreement was provoked over the PCF--MRG agreement for joint lists in the March 1977 municipal elections, signed on 28 June. PS leader Mitterrand publicly accused the Communists of disloyalty, of attempting to present the agreement as a blanket, binding national contract, when it in fact stopped at "encouraging" departmental and local party organs to negotiate, taking into account local conditions and thus allowing for exceptions. The Communists implicitly recognized the Socialist grievance (ibid., 18 September), but, in any case, the local level negotiations have not gone smoothly and have been a constant test of strength.

The conflict regarding the municipal elections was related to another over political-party competition in the workplace. The municipal electoral agreement will undoubtedly work to increase Communist strength considerably, in that the rather localized PCF municipal presence will now gain access to the very extensive Socialist local governments. Furthermore, the PS is committed to breaking most of its centrist local coalitions throughout the country, a potentially historic change in the fabric of French municipal politics which could have serious repercussions at higher levels. The Socialist leaders, as a quid pro quo, have demanded joint PCF-PS actions in the workplace, but the Communists, not surprisingly, are extremely reluctant to dilute their major organizational influence.

After failing to impose the argument that only the PCF has a "serious structure" of workplace organizations (e.g., *L'Humanité*, 2 October), Fiterman in a late October press conference indicated that the PCF would compromise (ibid., 27 October). The PCF's successful campaign over the past few years to increase enterprise cells has been in part designed to forestall this very development, and the question now is how much the limited PS workplace organizational structure will permit it to achieve.

On medium-term strategy (i.e., when, and if, a left-wing government comes to power), Marchais's Congress report cited two lessons from the failure of the "peaceful transition to socialism" strategy in Chile and of Leninism in Portugal: (1) "the danger of not going fast enough, once conditions are adequate," to create an irreversible situation, and (2) "the danger of adventurist slogans and actions" which sabotage the movement toward socialism. The "decisive condition for success," he said, was the support of "a large majority of the people":

> In the struggle for socialism in our epoch and in a country like ours, nothing—absolutely nothing—can be substituted for majority popular will as expressed democratically in the social struggle and through universal suffrage.... One must admit that at every stage the political and arithmetical |i.e., electoral—Marchais is replying to the arguments of Zarodov and other "hard-liners" in the international movement| majorities must coincide. And this is possible.

The French Communist strategy, though now wed to electoral legitimacy and parliamentary action, continues to foresee a sudden radical break with capitalist economic structures (i.e., rapid large-scale nationalizations) when a left-wing government takes power. The PCF analysis is (1) that Giscard's narrow victory in 1974 shows the left is quite near a majority, (2) that the present governing coalition has no other potential allies to convert, and (3) that in France a radical policy is therefore possible, given the necessary political will. Communist commentary on the Swedish Social Democrat defeat in 1976 followed from this logic. Marcel Veyrier wrote in *L'Humanité* (22 September) that it was "not the natural erosion of power that brought down Olof Palme and his colleagues, but rather their incapacity to transform the system durably and irreversibly."

Such a conception is contrary to the strategy of the Italian Communist Party (PCI) for a progressive takeover of government power and explains why the PCI could cooperate with the Andreotti government's plan for economic recovery, whereas at almost the same moment the PCF rejected totally and *a priori* the austerity measures proposed by the new Raymond Barre government (see especially Marchais's Central Committee report, ibid., 7 September). Yet the *L'Humanité* coverage of the Italian situation during the fall showed a striking tolerance of diversity, arguing that the PCI choice was correct under Italian conditions. Its correspondent David Laurent wrote: "Let us continue to resist the temptation to transfer the Eiffel Tower to the Piazza del Popolo" (ibid., 20 October). He also tended to play down disagreements within the PCI leadership and, on the contrary, to praise the openness of PCI debates.

Some major Communist domestic political initiatives came in reaction to the Barre government and its austerity plan. The CGT initiated a strike on 7 October, which rallied the CFDT, FEN, and other unions, resulting in the largest general strike since 1968. The PCF-PS-MRG coalition introduced a motion of censure in the National Assembly (defeated on 20 October). The Communist attack on the government plan was continued with an only partly successful day of demonstrations on 23 October, keyed to the problem of unemployment among young people.

International Views and Policies. As always, it is necessary to distinguish two PCF foreign policies, that of a "government party" dealing with relations between nation-states, and that of a Communist party dealing with other parties in the international movement. Again, the general line was given at the PCF Congress (*Cahiers*, February-March 1976).

At the nation-state level, according to the Congress, "a new relation of forces is being established in the world" in favor of socialism. The socialist bloc has imposed détente and the abandonment of military conquest on the capitalist nations, and it is now necessary to make détente "irreversible" and to complete political détente with military détente. The capitalist governments are seen as trying to pretend that "peaceful coexistence implies a separation of the world into zones of influence" and the "renunciation of social and national liberation struggles." The USA, the leading imperialist power, is attempting to further the integration of a bloc of advanced capitalist countries. In Europe this means further consolidation of the European Community under West German leadership, and the submission of French national independence to West German and U.S. leadership generally. President Giscard d'Estaing's renewal of an Atlanticist orientation, said Marchais, is a "criminal policy." The PCF foreign policy for France is, on the contrary, said to be a policy of national independence, which furthermore rejects the idea that détente and peaceful coexistence imply a social status quo: "Far from being an idea whose time is past, national independence is a great rallying cry of our time." Thus the PCF opposes further integration of the European Community, including direct election of the European Parliament (although Marchais has already said the PCF would participate). According to Jean Kanapa, the "real objective" of such elections would be "to extend the European Parliament's powers. A foreign majority, reactionary to boot, could thus dictate its law to the French people and to their elected representatives." (*L'Humanité*, 22 September.) In this nationalist vein, the PCF opposed the recent sale of French nuclear energy and computer industries to U.S. interests, French cooperation with the International Energy Agency, widening of the French trade deficit with the USA and West Germany, "submission" of the French franc to the dollar and Deutschmark, and the "de facto reintegration of NATO."

French Communist reaction to the election of Jimmy Carter was unusually careful, saying essentially that, while the new U.S. President could hardly escape the capitalist system, he would be judged on his acts. In *L'Humanité* of 27 October, Kanapa hinted at a policy of formal non-alignment for the future. On 4 November, Marchais envisaged the possibility of contacts with the new Administration, the central question so far as the PCF is concerned being obviously the U.S. attitude toward Communist governmental participation.

In general, the PCF continued to agree with Soviet policy regarding trouble spots in world politics, such as the Middle East and southern Africa. The major PCF-Soviet disagreement in foreign policy continued to be over Soviet conciliation of conservative French governments and toward the West in general; the French Communists have demanded a more aggressive Soviet posture. This disagreement has always been refracted into foreign policy among the Communist parties, and in 1976 the PCF took a decisive turn toward autonomy from the Communist Party of the Soviet Union (CPSU).

In February, the decision of the Congress to drop the "dictatorship of the proletariat" doctrine capped several years of criticism of Soviet practice. One such criticism concerns the definition of socialism itself, for which the Soviet example is no longer said to be a model. Another concerns the practice of "proletarian internationalism," on which PCF criticism cuts in several directions. First the PCF in 1976 decisively rejected Communist solidarity conceived as a one-way street running from Paris to Moscow, and the most significant consequence was the French Communist adoption of an "autonomist" position in preparatory meetings for the June 1976 conference of European Communist and workers' parties in East Berlin. At the Congress, Marchais criticized the Soviets for having created a hierarchy among kinds of solidarity among Communist parties, and Kanapa drew the argument out more explicitly in the 29 March issue of *France nouvelle*:

> . . . it wasn't we who invented this notion of "socialist internationalism" which appeared in 1968 to designate the internationalist solidarity which was supposed to unite the Communist parties of socialist countries particularly, and which was supposed to be "superior" to the type of internationalist relations which link the other Communist parties . . . [The French Communists] have never accepted this variation of proletarian internationalism.

Marchais turned the question of internationalism in still a third direction at the Congress by asserting that the universal character of Communist solidarity would not admit privileged regional solidarities, an implicit rejection of the "Eurocommunism" concept. This rejection of Eurocommunism was repeated several times during the year, though discussion of it is increasingly difficult to resist, as is shown in Jacques Denis's participation in a formal debate about Eurocommunism at the Italian Communist Party's *L'Unità* festival on 11 September. The PCF argument is that the term is inaccurate, not that the French Communists are against the doctrines of socialism with freedom and pluralism: for example, the PCF objects that the Japan Communist Party might be included with the French, Italian, and Spanish parties, and that Eurocommunism generally refers only to West European communism. Regarding the question of international Communist organization at the June conference in East Berlin Marchais said that such meetings "no longer correspond to the requirements of the epoch," considering that "any elaboration of a strategy common to all our parties [is] excluded." He later added that relations among the Communist parties today ought to be essentially bilateral.

There are indications beyond the PCF-CPSU organizational struggle of a personal antagonism between Marchais and CPSU chief Leonid Brezhnev. Despite the growing hostility, however, the PCF leadership did not seem interested in a total rupture. At the PCF Congress, for example, Marchais praised the USSR for having been the first country to end class exploitation and said that, despite all disagreements, the PCF remained in solidarity with the USSR against imperialism and in the struggle for "our great common objectives," defined as "peace, collective security, disarmament, and international cooperation."

Nonetheless, criticisms of the USSR and other Eastern bloc countries continue regularly, most often in the form of *L'Humanité* news stories. For example, in a series of articles in September-October, *L'Humanité* correspondent Serge Leyrac reported interviews documenting the fictions employed by Soviet factory managers to meet quota impositions or to overfulfill them (23 September). He also criticized Soviet foreign policy for failing to pressure the Syrians to abandon their invasion of Lebanon, and for failing to support the Palestinians (19 October; see further the strongly worded editorial by *L'Humanité* foreign editor Yves Moreau on 16 October). Commenting on a two-day visit by President Giscard d'Estaing to Polish leader Edward Giereck in October, *L'Humanité* criticized the Polish party weekly *Polityka* for effusive attitudes toward Giscard and in particular for publishing large excerpts from his book accompanied by favorable commentary. In another vein, the same article noted that a "mother of three children," under sentence to five years in prison for taking part in the 25 June riots against the Polish government's decision to raise food prices, had been given 30 months' parole (18 October). Another item (16 October) reported that a Slovenian judge had been sentenced to 5 years and 8 months in prison for "allegedly" calling for Slovenian secession from the Socialist Federative Republic of Yugoslavia and for "the creation in Slovenia of a Western-type democracy." In a very significant action, the PCF took part in a Paris meeting on 21 October of the "Committee of Mathematicians" (organized two years ago to support the imprisoned Soviet mathematician Leonid Plyush, who is now in France and who spoke at this meeting) to call for the liberation of two Soviet political prisoners (Bukovsky and Gluzman), one Czech, and three Latin American. (The Communist CGT leadership, in an unusual public disagreement with party policy, refused to take part in the meeting, arguing it was "scandalous" to equate socialist countries with fascist dictatorships in any way. The party leadership said the same, but chose to participate for other reasons. This provoked commentary about the possible existence of a "Séguy-CGT" tendency opposed to the "Marchais-Party" leadership). When a TASS dispatch criticized the PCF for having joined such a "dirty operation," *L'Humanité* (23 October) published the TASS article, replying that "To make criticisms of this or that criticizable aspect of Soviet reality is not to be anti-Soviet." Next to this article was an item reporting a demonstration of Soviet Jews in Moscow, noting that "administrative measures" had been used against them, a practice the PCF has criticized often in the past few years. In *France nouvelle* (18 October) Jean Kanapa concluded as follows:

Writers from socialist countries generally think only the worst of the concept of "democratic socialism." In fact, one regrets that it is necessary to add the adjective "democratic," since the very word socialism itself should normally imply it. But the serious distortions in the past, as well as the persistent insufficiencies of democratic progress in several socialist countries, make this necessary. . . . What "weakens the attraction of socialism" is not . . . the criticisms we make of these deficiencies, but rather their existence. . . . One must say that, unfortunately, the reasoning of our foreign comrades is still often impregnated with the idea that the methods of one socialist country are the model of socialism itself . . .

The PCF attitude regarding the Sino-Soviet dispute, and toward China generally, evolved somewhat during 1976. At the February Congress the earlier extremely pro-Soviet line had persisted, although, in contrast to the usual blanket condemnation, Marchais referred mainly to the "reactionary" character of Chinese foreign policy and did not criticize the regime itself. The death of Mao Tse-tung was the occasion for proposals of better relations with the Chinese, much beyond the cautious, if persistent, Soviet calls for "normalization" of Sino-Soviet relations. On 10 September, L'Humanité headlined: "One of the Greatest Figures in History Is Gone," and a Central Committee declaration saluted "the memory of President Mao Tse-tung with emotion and respect." The declaration added: "It is true that serious disagreements have grown up between our two parties . . . regarding international problems as well as regarding the conception of socialism itself. We have profoundly regretted that the disagreements changed our relations. It was not our fault and it is not our wish." PCF publications devoted an extraordinary amount of space to the event, and a minute of silence was observed at the "Fête de l'Humanité." The Chinese party, however, rejected PCF messages of condolence, with those of all parties who in the past had followed the Soviet line on China.

The potentially Gaullist-style autonomy building in the PCF over the year was symbolized laconically by a note which appeared above the table of contents in La nouvelle revue internationale (the French edition of WMR) for the first time in April and has since been a regular insert: "The articles of foreign writers . . . do not in any way engage the responsibility of the French Communist Party."

International Activities and Contacts. The major French Communist international contacts in the early part of 1976 were at the PCF congress in early February and at the CPSU congress later in the month, both of which indicated deteriorating relations between the two parties. The Soviet delegation to the PCF congress was led by André Kirilenko, and for the first time in 20 years neither Mikhail Suslov nor Boris Ponomarev was present (Ponomarev was replaced by Vadim Zagladin). As noted above, Marchais did not attend the CPSU congress, a serious breach of Communist protocol. The PCF delegation was led by Plissonier. The PCF (unlike the Italian party) sent a delegation to the Czechoslovak party congress in May, however, and made a point of avoiding serious criticism.

The first international trip for Marchais in 1976 was his visit (with Kanapa) to Japan, 4-10 April. This was significant in that the Japan Communist Party had not sent a delegation to the CPSU congress and was preparing to drop its reference to Marxism-Leninism as the party ideology. The PCF-JCP talks allowed Marchais to emphasize both the French party's distance from Soviet influence and its resistance to the Eurocommunism concept. The joint declaration published by Marchais and JCP president Miyamoto Kenji insisted on the identification of socialism and freedom: "[The PCF and JCP] affirm their desire to assure . . . the guarantee and extension of individual rights and liberties, to respect universal suffrage and a multiplicity of parties . . . in the stage of democratic transformation as well as in the stage of socialism. They reject the imposition or interdiction by the State of any ideology or belief . . ." (Cahiers, May.) The other major PCF international contact was the series of preparatory meetings and final 29-30 June meeting of the conference of European Communist and Workers' parties in East Berlin.

The PCF also participated in several meetings of non-ruling European parties, including the Stockholm conference on inflation and wage-price policies, the 7 July Strasbourg meeting against

West German political restrictions on the right to work, the 11-12 October meeting in Ferrara on the European Community's Common Agricultural Policy, and the 6 November meeting against the "new cartel" in the European steel industry. The PCF also signed a joint declaration of 17 non-ruling European parties, "Solidarity with the Democratic Lebanese and Palestinian Forces" (*L'Humanité*, 27 July).

There were several noteworthy bilateral party contacts. Most importantly, 3 June, Italian party leader Enrico Berlinguer appeared with Marchais at a mass rally in Paris, the first time the two leaders had done so in France. In early August, a PCF delegation went to the Middle East, meeting with Yassir Arafat on 2 August. On 6 August, in Paris, Marchais met with the Lebanese Communist Party's secretary-general. Marchais, with Jacques Denis, led a PCF delegation to Finland, 19-24 August, and signed a joint declaration with Aarne Saarinen, chairman of the Communist Party of Finland (*Cahiers*, October). Marchais met also with Social Democratic Party chairman and Finnish foreign minister Kalevi Sorsa.

Publications. The main publications of the PCF in 1976 were: the daily newspaper *L'Humanité* (circulation 150,000 to 200,000), whose director is Roland Leroy and editor in chief is René Andrieu; the weekly *France nouvelle*; the Central Committee's monthly theoretical journal, *Cahiers du communisme*; a popular weekend magazine, *L'Humanité dimanche* (450,000 to 500,000); a rural weekly, *La Terre* (200,000); an intellectual monthly, *La nouvelle critique*; a literary monthly, *Europe*; a bimonthly economic journal, *Economie et politique*; a philosophically oriented bimonthly, *La Pensée*; a historical bimonthly, *Cahiers d'histoire de l'Institut Maurice Thorez*; a monthly review for teachers, *L'école et la nation*. The party has a number of provincial newspapers and journals as well. In October the Paris federation of the PCF began to publish a new weekly popular magazine, *Paris-Hebdo*. For intraparty communication, the Central Committee publishes *La vie du parti*. In the early 1970s there were approximately 5,000 cell newspapers or periodicals, about a tenth printed, the others mimeographed. For young people, the MJC publishes the bimonthly *Avant-Garde*, and the UECF the bimonthly *Le nouveau clarté*. The major Communist publishing houses, Editions sociales and Editeurs français reunis, put out a considerable number and variety of books and pamphlets.

Amherst College   Ronald Tiersky

Germany: Federal Republic of Germany

The earliest forerunner of the present German Communist Party (Deutsche Kommunistische Partei; DKP) was the Spartacist League, a revolutionary group which emerged within the Social Democratic Party of Germany (Sozialdemokratische Partei Deutschlands; SPD) during World War I. The Spartacist League was under the leadership of Rosa Luxemburg and Karl Liebknecht, who were highly critical of the SPD leaders' support of the war effort. After the November Revolution of 1918, the Spartacist League founded the Communist Party of Germany (Kommunistische Partei Deutschlands; KDP) on 31 December of the same year. The young KPD participated actively in the abortive revolt of the Revolutionary Shop Stewards in January 1919, known erroneously as the Spartacist Uprising, which attempted to replace the moderate socialist provisional government with a council system modeled on the Russian example. Luxemburg and Liebknecht were brutally murdered in the process of the suppression of the revolt, the work of the remnants of the German Army and the so-called Free Corps.

The lasting hostility of the Communists toward the SPD goes back to this time; in their view, the Social Democrats saved the bourgeois society and the capitalist system from destruction by revolutionary elements of the working class. The severe economic depression which marked most of the years of the short-lived Weimar Republic was one of the main causes for the steadily increasing influence of the KPD. In the November 1932 elections, the last free elections prior to the appointment of Adolf Hitler as Reich Chancellor, the party received almost six million votes out of a total of about 35 million valid votes. During the "Third Reich" (1933-45) the KPD was outlawed, but it continued its activities as an underground party. In contrast to underground Communist parties in other European countries, its impact was negligible with the possible exception of the party's support of Soviet espionage.

At the end of World War II, in 1945, the KPD was reconstituted in the four Allied occupation zones of Germany and the area of Greater Berlin. The Soviet Military Administration (SMA) was the first occupation authority which gave permission for the reestablishment of anti-Nazi political parties. When the KPD failed to obtain support from the population in spite of substantial Soviet material assistance, the SMA forced the merger of the SPD with the smaller KPD as early as 1946. However, only in the Soviet Zone and the Soviet Sector of Berlin could this merger be enforced. The product of the merger is the Socialist Unity Party of Germany (Sozialistische Einheitspartei Deutschlands; SED). In the Federal Republic of Germany (FRG), which emerged from the three Western zones of occupation, the KPD was outlawed as an unconstitutional party on 17 August 1956 by the Federal Constitutional Court, which found the party's objectives and methods to be in violation of Article 21/2 of the Basic Law of the FRG.

In the first federal elections in the FRG, in 1949, the KPD received 5.7 percent of the vote, entitling the party to 15 seats in the Bundestag. In 1953, at the next election, the Communist vote went down to 2.2 percent, considerably below the 5 percent required for representation in the legislature.

After being outlawed, the KPD operated underground, directed from East Berlin by Max Reimann, the party chairman. The German Peace Union (Deutsche Friedensunion; DFU) was organized in 1965 by Communists, former Socialists, and pacifists as a Communist front organization. The DFU participated in the federal electi. ns in the same year and obtained only 1.3 percent of the vote. The DFU is still active, but in spite of its merger with the International of War Resisters (Internationale der Kriegsdienstgegner; IDK) and the Association of War Service Resisters (Verband der Kriegsdienstgegner; VK) it has remained ineffective in the Communist effort to organize unity-of-action activities.

The German Communists in 1969 started a campaign to legalize the outlawed KPD, notwithstanding the fact that the present DKP had been founded meanwhile on 22 September 1968. Two reasons might be responsible for this campaign: (1) to demonstrate that the DKP is not a successor organization of the prohibited KPD, in order to forestall any move to outlaw the DKP as an unconstitutional party, and (2) to unite "progressive forces" in the fight against the "undemocratic" practice of outlawing any left-wing political party. In August 1976 a "Central Working Group" (Zentraler Arbeitskreis) demanded in a letter addressed to Federal Chancellor Helmut Schmidt that the prohibition of the KPD be revoked and a law be passed to provide that the outlawing of a political party may not exceed 10 years. The demand was signed by a number of teachers, physicians, clergymen, and journalists. (*Die Welt*, Hamburg, 13 August.)

At the time of the founding of the DKP, the underground KDP had about 7,000 members. Almost the entire leadership of the new party was comprised of KPD members, proving beyond doubt that the DKP is a successor of the outlawed KPD (see *YICA, 1975*, p. 174). DKP deputy chairman Hermann Gautier admitted this fact quite openly on 15 March 1976 in an inteview broadcast in German by Radio Moscow in which he referred to the KPD as "our party" which the Communists "newly organized in 1968 as the DKP" (*Die Welt*, 14 April).

The DKP regards itself as part of the international Communist and anti-imperialist movement and maintains close contacts with fraternal parties throughout the world.

According to the Federal Security Service (*Bundesverfassungsschutz*; BVS) membership in the various Communist and left-extremist organizations in 1975 was as follows:

Type of organization	Number of organizations	Membership
Orthodox and pro-Communist	105	119,000
Maoist	64	15,000
Trotskyist	10	1,200
Anarchist	26	500
Organizations of the "New Left"	74	4,500
TOTAL	279	140,200
Deduction for membership in more than one organization		35,200
Total Membership		105,000

(Bundesminister der Innern, *Verfassungsschutz '75*, Bonn, July 1976, p. 44.)

Leadership and Organization. The illegal KPD is still in existence, with about 6,000 members although its importance to Moscow has markedly declined as a result of the activities of the DKP. Nevertheless, there are at least two reasons for the continuation of the KDP. First, it is generally recognized that underground organizations provide fertile recruiting grounds for the massive Soviet espionage effort. Secondly, the KPD can provide the organization for underground activities in case the

DKP should be outlawed as an unconstitutional party or successor to the KPD. However, at present as well as in the near future the chances that the DKP might follow the fate of the KDP are rather remote. In spite of occasional statements by government officials concerning the unconstitutional character of the DKP, it is most unlikely that the socialist-liberal government will outlaw the party, especially since former chancellor Willy Brandt while in office assured Soviet party chief Brezhnev at their Crimea meeting that the DKP is a constitutional party.

The DKP was reported at the Fourth Party Congress, March 1976, as having 42,453 members (an increase of some 3,000 over the membership of 39,344 reported at the Third Congress, in November 1973). Neither the relatively small number of members nor the poor election results reflect the actual influence the DKP has among trade unions and institutions of higher learning. Its headquarters in Düsseldorf directs a closely knit organization which has the structure of a typical Communist party. At the lowest level are the industrial and residential primary party organizations. Above them are the approximately 200 district (*Kreis*) organizations and the 12 regional (*Bezirk*) headquarters.

The Fourth Party Congress, held on 19-21 March 1976 in Bonn, elected the leading party organs. Party chairman Herbert Mies and deputy chairman Hermann Gautier were reelected. The composition of the ten-man Secretariat is: Mies, Gautier, Jupp Angenfort, Werner Cieslak, Gerd Deumlich, Kurt Fritsch, Willi Gerns, Ludwig Müller, Rolf Priemer, and Karl Heinz Schröder. (*Deutscher Informationsdienst*, 27, no. 1428, Bonn, 29 March.) The Party Directorate (Parteivorstand), the equivalent of a central committee, has 91 members; the Presidium, the equivalent of a politburo, 16; the Central Auditing Commission, nine; and the Central Arbitration Commission also nine. The following party officials were elected by the Party Directorate to comprise the Presidium: Mies, Gautier, Angenfort, Jurt Bachmann, Martha Buschmann, Deumlich, Kurt Erleback, Fritsch, Gerns, Manfred Kapluk, Heinz Land, Müller, Georg Polikeit, Priemer, Max Reimann, and Max Schäfer. (*IB*, no. 5-6, 31 March, pp. 12-13; *Deutscher Informationsdienst*, 27, no. 1428, 29 March).

Close cooperation between the DKP and the ruling SED in the German Democratic Republic (GDR) continued throughout 1976 with the SED providing the major financial support of the DKP direct supervision of its activities, and schooling of Communists from the FRG in SED party institutions. Every one of the 12 regions of the DKP is supervised by one or two regions (*Bezirke*) of the SED, which refers to the DKP regions as *Paten-Bezirke*, (sponsor regions) (*Die Welt*, 19 February).

The Socialist German Workers' Youth (Sozialistische Deutsche Arbeiterjugend; SDAJ), founded prior to the DKP on 4 May 1968, is the official youth organization of the senior party in spite of its claim of "independence." The SDAJ held on 4-5 December 1976 its Fifth Federal Congress at Frankfurt/Main and elected the 65 members of the Federal Directorate (*Bundesvorstand*). The Federal Directorate elected at its constituent session as the chairman of the SDAJ Wolfgang Gehrcke and as his deputy Dieter Gautier, the son of the deputy chairman of the DKP Hermann Gautier. It was reported that the 793 delegates and guest delegates at the congress represented 33,000 SDAJ members who are organized in about 600 groups and directed by 12 *Land* organizations. (*Deutscher Informationsdienst*, 27, no. 1446, 20 December 1976.) Cooperation with the SED youth organization in the GDR and the Soviet Komsomol continued throughout 1976. The "election" of the longtime former SDAJ chairman Rolf Priemer into the DKP Secretariat at the Fourth Party Congress might be an indication of increased Communist attention to work among the young.

The Marxist Student Union-Spartakus (Marxistischer Studentbund-Spartakus; MSB-Spartakus) celebrated its fifth anniversary in Cologne on 22 October (*Deutscher Informationsdienst*, 27, no. 1441, 12 October). There have been no changes in leadership and organization as of 1975 (see *YICA, 1976*, p. 146). The MSB-Spartakus was able during 1976 to hold or increase its percentage of the vote for student governments and continued to control them in many institutions of higher learning in coalition with the Socialist Student League (Sozialistischer Hochschulbund; SHB), the former official SPD student organization, and in several instances also in cooperation with the Young Socialist University

Groups (Jungsozialistische Hochschulgruppen; Juso-Hochschulgruppen). The Juso-Hochschulgruppen are part of the "Jusos" which form an intricate part of the SPD and are comprised of SPD members up to the age of 35. (*Deutscher Informationsdienst*, 27, no. 1435, 12 July.) In addition to the MSB-Spartakus, the DKP maintains DKP University Groups (DKP-Hochschulgruppen) which have a total of about 3,500 members.

The Young Pioneers (Junge Pioniere; JP), the children's organization founded by the DKP in 1974, was able to strengthen its organization and intensify its activities during 1976. The high point of the work of the JP is the organization of summer camps in the GDR and other East European countries. In 1975, it was reported, 4,500 children from the FRG participated in this program (*Das Parlament*, 26, no. 3, Bonn, 17 January 1976). Also the SDAJ made propaganda for an "International Friendship Camp in the GDR," scheduled from 17 to 31 July at Bogensee near Berlin, and encouraged young people from the FRG to participate in this event (*Deutscher Informationsdienst*, 27, no. 1435, 12 July).

The Communists' emphasis on attempts to influence the young was also evident in the efforts of the August Bebel Society (headquartered in Frankfurt/Main in the same building as the DKP publishing house, Marxistische Blätter), to induce 14- and 15-year-olds to participate in the "Youth Consecration" (Jugendweihe) on 9 May. In this secular ceremony, used in the GDR to replace the Christian confirmation, young people pledge themselves to serve the cause of socialism. The Society organized between January and April eight instructional sessions in preparation for the Youth Consecration and scheduled one trip to Erfurt, in the GDR, in April. (Ibid., 27, no. 1423, 12 January.)

A number of affiliated groups, such as the DFU, VK, and the League of Persons Persecuted under National Socialism (Vereinigung Verfolgter des Nationalsozialismus; VVN) participate in the Communist effort to obtain a stronger foothold among the population and to support the activities of the DKP (ibid., 27, nos. 1436, 1437, 26 July, 12 August). The Nature Friend Youth publicly declared the necessity of working with the Communists (ibid., 27, no. 1431, 12 May).

Also the "friendship societies," such as the Society FRG-USSR Hamburg (Gesellschaft BRD-UdSSR Hamburg e.V.), are utilized (ibid., 27, no. 1430, 27 April). The DKP also exerts a marked influence over the German Young Democrats (Deutsche Jungdemokraten; DJD) and a number of left extremist "professional" organizations among lawyers, artists, and scientists.

The membership of other left extremist organizations in the FRG in 1976 remained at about 102,000 (*Die Welt*, 6 April). The population of the FRG (excluding West Berlin) is about 61.6 million.

Party Internal Affairs. The major event of 1976 in the DKP was the Fourth Congress, 19-21 March. As stated before, the Congress elected, in most cases reelected, the party leadership. It was preceded by the election of delegates at 12 regional conferences (*Deutscher Informationsdienst*, 26, no. 1422, 15 December 1975, and 27, no. 1423, 12 January 1976).

The session of the DKP Presidium on 7 January dealt almost entirely with the preparation of the Congress. Chairman Mies stressed the necessity of the "unity of action of Communists and Social Democrats in the struggle against big capital and against the reactionary [forces] and for the protection of democratic rights and freedoms" (ibid., 27, no. 1424, 30 January).

Of the 770 elected delegates to the Congress (three did not attend because of illness), 629 had voting rights and 138 were guest delegates. The emphasis on the work among trade unions was borne out by the fact that 702 delegates belonged to trade unions; among them were 189 shop stewards and 335 trade union officials. The social composition indicated the predominance of the working class. Blue- and white-collar workers (including three apprentices) accounted for 590 delegates, while 57 were intellectuals, 13 farmers and professionals, and 37 housewives and pensioners. The average age of the delegates was 36 years, in keeping with the stress laid upon involving the younger generation.

Party offices at various levels were held by 715 delegates, and 603 were also members of "mass organizations," in which 155 were functionaries. There were 185 women delegates.

Forty-five delegations from Communist parties from all parts of the world attended the Congress, the most important among them the delegation of the Communist Party of the Soviet Union (CPSU), led by Central Committee secretary W. J. Dolgikh. The Soviet Delegation included also W. W. Sagladin, who as deputy department chief of the International Department of the Central Committee is in charge of the non-governing Communist parties in the "capitalist" countries. The 80-man strong delegation of the SED was led by Politburo and Secretariat member Paul Verner, the close collaborator of Erich Honecker, and included high-ranking party functionaries, among them Professor Herbert Häber, chief of the West Department of the SED Central Committee. Nine ambassadors or high embassy officials attended, including Soviet ambassador V. M. Falin and the "permanent representative" of the GDR, Michael Kohl. Also Sami Musallam, the representative of the Palestine Liberation Organization (PLO) in the FRG was present. (Ibid., no. 1428, 29 March; *Political Affairs*, East Berlin, June, pp. 24-25; *Die Welt*, 20 March.)

The "Action Program" of the DKP for the federal elections on 3 October was one of the main subjects of the Congress, although its content had been determined at a meeting of Chairman Mies and Herbert Häber in East Berlin in February. A communiqué signed at that time by Erich Honecker and Mies referred to the close political, ideological, and material bond of the DKP with the SED. (*Die Welt*, 17 March.)

The report presented by Mies emphasized the "alliance policy," calling for the establishment of "unity of action of Communists and Social Democrats in the interest of the working class" and the creation of a "broad front of all left forces" and of an "anti-monopolistic alliance." (*Deutscher Informationsdienst*, 27, no. 1428, 29 March.) Other topics discussed during the three-day Congress reflected the other main efforts of the party, such as intensification of the work in industrial enterprises, the activities of the DKP in "citizen initiatives," and membership recruitment among young people and students. It also was quite evident that every opportunity was utilized during the Congress to emphasize the complete adherence to Moscow's leadership and strategy. There was absolute avoidance of any reference to an independent German road toward socialism. (*Die Welt*, 22 March.)

Party organizations had submitted 234 resolutions and one initiative. Of these the Resolutions Committee recommended the rejection of 8 and the adoption of 136, which thereupon were unanimously approved. The rest were referred to party organs. (*Foreign Affairs*, June, p. 25.)

Simultaneously with the Party Congress, the DKP organized mass rallies in a number of cities such as Cologne, Frankfurt/Main, and Dortmund (ibid., p. 26).

Prior to the Congress, the industrial and residential primary party organizations and the DKP University Groups held their annual main meetings (*Jahreshauptversammlungen*). At these meetings, representatives of the Party Presidium demanded the intensification of the "work among the masses" in order to "strengthen the struggle for the protection of the democratic rights and freedoms, for co-determination, against the prohibition to carry on one's profession (*Berufsverbot*), and to achieve the common democratic action of everyone who is ready to defend the Basic Law." (*Deutscher Informationsdienst*, 27, no. 1424, 30 January.)

According to the DKP's own financial statement, the total income of the party for 1974 was 11.43 million marks of which 1.7 million derived from membership fees and 7.1 million from donations (*Die Welt*, 6 April). Other sources of income are revenues derived from publications and from some 30 so-called "collective bookshops" in the FRG which apparently are connected with the DKP. The Interior Minister of North Rhine-Westphalia reported that the SED provides the main financial support of the DKP and that this money comes from the "West Department" of the SED Central Committee. His report states that the SED and DKP have organized a "special financial machinery which is separate from the DKP organization and operates secretly. It is through this machinery that the DKP receives annually about 30 million marks, of which 12 million marks goes to the party organization in North Rhine-Westphalia." Part of the money is brought by couriers who take it to secret drops in the FRG, or it is passed on to the party via pro-Communist trading firms. (*FBIS*, 26 March.) However, this constitutes only a part of the 100 million marks supplied by the SED when the cost of printed material, trips of delegations, training courses, and vacations of party officials are included. (*Die Welt*, 6 April.)

In addition to the traditional 1 May demonstrations and rallies, the DKP organized a number of other events such as the "Week of the DKP" (17-25 January), held in many cities of the FRG. The purpose was to broaden the party's contact with the masses. (*Deutscher Informationsdienst*, 27, no. 1425, 16 February.) The "UZ-Press Festival" (10-12 September) was, as in the preceding year, a marked success. The "Festival of Youth" co-sponsored by the SDAJ and the MSB-Spartakus on 24 April in Dortmund was attended by more than 7,000 people (*Die Welt*, 26 April).

The year 1976 witnessed an increased emphasis upon the ideological schooling of the party members. An "analysis of the situation" in late 1975 found that the stagnation of recruitment for the industrial primary organizations was caused by the members' lack of "political-ideological qualifications" (ibid., 29 December). Robert Steigerwald, DKP Directorate member and chairman of the "Marxist Worker's Education" (Marxistische Arbeiterbildung; MAB) reported in February 1976 that about 90 active MAB groups had been organized. Thirty-one of them operate at the level of "Marxist Evening Schools" (Marxistische Abendschulen; MASCH). The MASCH in Munich has been functioning for about a year and is exclusively for factory workers. In a number of other cities work has been started to build the same kind of schools. Fees are minimal and amount as a rule to 10 marks. (*Deutscher Informationsdienst*, 27, no. 1426, 26 February.) The "Karl Liebknecht School" in Essen, which can accommodate about 50 students at a time, organizes annually about 35 courses lasting one or two weeks; during 1975 about 1,400 DKP and SDAJ members attended these courses (ibid., 27, no. 1430, 27 April). There are 39 courses planned for 1977, among them ten basic courses, three for public relation work, one for workers' correspondence in the party organ *Unsere Zeit*, and one for alliance policy (ibid., 27, no. 1441, 12 October). During the 1976-77 "education year" of the DKP the topics "freedom under capitalism" and "freedom under socialism" are being stressed (ibid., 27, no. 1437, 12 August).

In addition to the ideological schooling provided by the DKP, many leading functionaries have been trained in the USSR at the "Institute for Social Sciences" of the CPSU Central Committee in courses lasting three months and one year. Since the founding of the DKP about 100 party officials have attended these courses. The "Karl Marx University" in East Berlin, established in 1969, has "educated" up to now about 850 selected DKP and SDAJ members. In 1975 about 260 West German Communists graduated from this institution. (Ibid., 27, no. 1430, 27 April.)

Domestic Attitudes and Activities. DKP chairman Mies announced in his "New Year's Message" that in 1976 his party intended to make a contribution "to the opening of the road of the Federal Republic toward socialism, toward the unity of action of the working class and the alliance of all democratic forces" (*Deutscher Informationsdienst*, 27, no. 1423, 10 January). The session of the DKP Presidium on 22 January dealt with the preparations for the federal elections, scheduled for 3 October, and announced that the party would participate actively and aggressively in the election campaign, which would provide opportunity for the primary party organizations to establish contacts with the masses. Additional local and factory newspapers were to be produced, as well as leaflets, in order to challenge the parties represented in the Bundestag. (Ibid., 27, no. 1424, 30 January.) On 30 April, *Unsere Zeit* published the party's proclamation on the federal elections. The proclamation, which was adopted by the Party Congress, attacks all other political parties either for representing big capital or for failing to live up to their promises to initiate reforms.

By the middle of May membership meetings in all the Länder had elected DKP candidates for the Land lists in the federal elections. The second session of the party Directorate, 12 June, was almost entirely devoted to the preparation of the DKP election campaign (ibid., 27, no. 1435, 12 July). Special efforts were exerted to obtain donations from party members and sympathizers to finance the campaign. By the beginning of July some 380,000 marks allegedly had been collected (ibid., 27, no. 1436, 26 July).

The DKP presented direct candidates in all 248 election districts and on all 10 *Land* lists, a total of 571 Bundestag candidates. Among them, according to information supplied by the DKP, were 270 workers and 192 white-collar workers. During the final phase of the campaign the party planned to hold more than 1,000 meetings, primarily in industrial centers. A number of "election initiatives" among writers, actors, and various professional groups were organized. Appeals signed by soldiers asking the military personnel to elect Communists were distributed in front of military installations. (Ibid., 27, no. 1439, 9 September.)

The outcome of the federal elections brought a slight increase of the Communist vote as compared with the elections in 1972. (See Table.)

Final Official Results of the Elections to the 8th German Bundestag on 3 October 1976
Valid Second-Ballot Votes: 37,822,500

	Second-ballot votes			First-ballot votes		
	Total 1976	Percent of vote 1976	Percent of vote 1972	Total 1976	Percent of vote 1976	Percent of vote 1972
DKP	118,581	0.3	(0.3)	170,855	0.5	(0.4)
EAP[a]	6,811	0.0	(--)	3,177	0.0	(--)
GIM[b]	4,759	0.0	(--)	2,037	0.0	(--)
KPD[c]	22,714	0.1	(--)	8,822	0.0	(--)
KBW[d]	20,018	0.1	(--)	21,414	0.1	(--)
VL[e]	701	0.0	(--)	217	0.0	(--)

[a] European Worker's Party (Europäische Arbeiterpartei). [b] Group of International Marxists (Gruppe Internationaler Marxisten). [c] Communist Party of Germany (Kommunistische Partei Deutschland—not identical with the underground and Moscow-loyal KPD). [d] Communist League West Germany (Kommunistischer Bund Westdeutschlands). [e] United Left (Vereinigte Linke).

Based on "Countdown," *Relay from Bonn*, VII, no. 126, Ottawa, 21 October 1976.

Note: The German election system provides two votes for every voter. His first ballot is cast for a candidate in the 248 election districts. However, the second ballot determines the percentage of representation in the Bundestag provided that the party obtains at least 5 percent of the total valid vote or 3 seats by direct vote (first ballot).

The DKP in 1976 obtained 170,855 first-ballot votes or 0.5 percent (1972: 146,258 or 0.4 percent) and 118,581 second-ballot votes or 0.3 percent (1972: 113,891 or 0.3 percent). It is of interest to note that 52,274 voters who cast their choice for a specific Communist candidate either voted for another political party with their second ballot or abstained altogether.

Municipal elections were held in Lower Saxony and in some regions in North Rhine-Westphalia also on 3 October. The DKP succeeded in having a few of its candidates elected in a number of communities. The best results were achieved in Bottrop, where the DKP obtained 6,561 votes or 8.41 percent and 5 seats (on the same day the Communist vote for the federal elections was only 0.4 percent). The DKP announced that the party is now represented in 25 city and local parliaments (ibid., 27, no. 1441, 12 October).

These local results were considerably better than those of the Land elections in Baden-Württemberg on 4 April. The DKP obtained 18,760 or 0.4 percent as compared to 21,973 or 0.5 percent in 1972 (*Die Welt*, 6 April).

The DKP in its effort to establish contact with the masses continued to organize "unity of action" activities. The most successful campaign is the struggle against the so-called *Berufsverbot*, the prohibition of carrying on one's profession, which even succeeded in receiving support from left-wing groups in other European countries. Numerous personalities known in public life lent their names or actively supported the DKP actions to remove the legal barriers for employment of Communists in the public service. The citizen initiative "Remove the Berufsverbot" led by the SPD Professor Gerhard Stuby planned, in cooperation with local committees, for rallies in November throughout the FRG. (*Deutscher Informationsdienst*, 27, no. 1441, 12 October.) The Communist-inspired actions against the exclusion of DKP and other Moscow-loyal Communists from civil service positions have been very successful in those Länder with SPD/FDP coalition governments and on the federal level. (See Eric Waldman, *Deutschlands Weg in den Sozialismus*, Mainz, 1976, pp. 112 f.)

Just prior to the Party Congress in March, the DKP published a 50-page brochure "The DKP and the Basic Law" in which the Communists claim to be the defenders and protectors of the Basic Law, the West German constitution (*Deutscher Informationsdienst*, 27, no. 1427, 10 March).

Unity of action activities were also carried on in the area of disarmament, initiated as a rule by Communist-led peace organizations and committees. For example, on 22 May the Committee for Peace, Disarmament, and Cooperation organized a demonstration (ibid., 27, no. 1435, 12 July). The combined organizations of the "German Peace Society" and "United War Service Resistors" were equally active in promoting disarmament actions throughout the FRG (ibid., 27, no. 1425, 16 February).

The major effort of the DKP to penetrate the German Trade Unions (DGB) continued during 1976 with considerable success. The DKP requests that all of its eligible members join the trade unions and fully support all trade union objectives. Up to 99 percent of the Moscow-loyal Communists employed in industry are trade union members. It is reported that the DKP and its auxiliary organizations provide about 10,000 shop stewards, or about 6 percent of the total numbers of shop stewards elected in the past year. The Communists' tactic is to place their candidates on the trade union election slates. The Institute of the German Economy (Cologne) prepared an analysis of the Communist influence in industry and found that during the past six years the impact of the "Old Left" (i.e., the DKP, SDAJ, MSB-Spartakus, and other Moscow-loyal auxiliary organizations) has strongly increased, with their combined membership going from 38,000 to 119,000. The number of orthodox Communist newspapers has quadrupled during the same period and has now reached 1,420. Every week about 800,000 copies are distributed in factories and residential areas, as compared with 212,000 in 1970. (*Die Welt*, 18 August.) The number of DKP members who are trade union officials is also continually increasing. The membership policy of the "nonpartisan" DGB, which accepts Moscow-loyal Communists, bars members of the right-wing National Democratic Party of Germany (NPD) and of the various Maoist- or anarchist-oriented political organizations.

International Views and Party Contacts. The complete dependency of the DKP upon East Berlin and Moscow does not permit the party to hold any other international views than those of the SED and CPSU. Chairman Mies in an interview with the *World MarxistReview*, published in February 1976, asserted that there is no contradiction between the "defense of West Germany's national interest and our friendly relations with the Soviet Union, the GDR and other socialist countries." He also endorsed the Communist evaluation of the world situation, in which allegedly the international balance of forces continues to change "in favor of peace, democracy and socialism." With regard to the Helsinki Conference, Mies follows the optimistic interpretation of Moscow and regards the conference as a "historic gain of the forces which for decades have championed détente and peace in Europe and the world." He pledged that his party will insist that the FRG contribute its share to disarmament by reducing its record military budget by 15 percent annually because "no one threatens our country today." He also stated:

> The decisions adopted at Helsinki have created more favorable conditions for a campaign of international solidarity with the peoples fighting for freedom, against imperialist intervention. We identify ourselves with the anti-fascists and democrats of Portugal and Spain and emphatically condemn the crimes of the Chilean Fascist Junta, which is making a mockery of human rights. We support the Arab peoples and the progressive forces of Angola. We hail the heroic people of Vietnam, who have moved on to peaceful construction. We see this anti-imperialist solidarity as part of the struggle for the Helsinki decisions. (*WMR*, no. 2, February, pp. 31-32.)

In keeping with the especially DKP-SED relations, Mies and SED chief Honecker met in February and decided on the collaboration of their respective parties for 1976 (*Deutscher Informationsdienst*, 27,no. 1426, 26 February).

At the Party Congress Mies made an unequivocal declaration of the loyalty to the course pursued by the USSR and the GDR, and clearly denounced any divergent tendencies (Hamburg DPA, in German, 19 March 1976, in *FBIS*). On returning from the 25th Congress of the CPSU, the DKP chairman ordered the functionaries of his party not to discuss among the membership the qualified independence which the French and Italian Communists claimed for their parties (*Die Welt*, 8 March).

DKP delegations attended the 9th Congress of the SED (May) and the 22nd Congress of the French Communist Party (February). The DKP participated in a number of international meetings, such as the conference of representatives from several Communist parties of European capitalist countries in Brussels on 15 March dealing with current social and economic problems. A DKP delegation took part in a three-day conference of West European Communist parties in Stockholm in early March concerned with "inflation and income policy." DKP representatives attended at the same time a conference of 45 communist parties sponsored by the Central Committee of the Hungarian Socialist Workers' Party at Tihany, Hungary, discussing the interrelation of the world situation and the international Communist movement. On 7 July the DKP was one of 15 European Communist parties holding a conference in Strasbourg for the purpose of condemning the *Berufsverbot* and the "anti-democratic" developments in the FRG (*Unsere Zeit*, 9 July).

The most important international conference in which the DKP participated, also in its preparatory phase, was the conference of 29 European Communist and workers' parties on 29-30 June in East Berlin. Following the report of Chairman Mies abut this conference at the session of the DKP Directorate on 3 July, a resolution was adopted which stressed the alliance policy of Communist and other "democratic forces" and the spirit of proletarian internationalism (Moscow TASS, in English, 4 July, in *FBIS*).

A delegation of the Hungarian Socialist Workers' Party visited the German Communists in early March (ibid., 1505 GMT, 3 March). A "Solidarity with Portugal" committee continued its activities and sent a delegation to Portugal (*Deutscher Informationsdienst*, 27, no. 1426, 26 February).

Even though DKP pronouncements carry hardly any weight within the FRG, they are hailed for propaganda purposes in Communist-ruled countries. For example, *Pravda* (6 July) reported about a DKP pronouncement condemning a West German government statement regarding East-West relations. Also a joint communiqué of the DKP and the French Communist Party protesting against the latest plans for stationing French troops in the FRG was publicized by TASS (Moscow TASS, in English, 1219 GMT 6 July).

SDAJ, MSB-Spartakus, the Young Pioneers, and the other "mass organizations" affiliated with the DKP continued their contacts with fraternal organizations abroad.

Publications. The official DKP organ is the daily *Unsere Zeit*, which has a circulation of more than 50,000 and issues a number of local supplements. Other DKP publications are *DKP-Pressedienst, Marxistische Blätter*, the quarterly *Marxismus Digest*, the Party Directorate magazine *Praxis*, the illustrated *Sozialismus Konkret-DKP Report*, and the cultural journal *Kürbiskern*. (For publications of related youth organizations see *YICA, 1976*, pp. 153-54.) Among other leftist periodicals are *Sozialistische Korrespondenz* (Hamburg), *Express* (Offenbach), and Links-Sozialistische Zeitung, (Offenbach).

As a result of the emphasis placed upon the work in industrial enterprises, the number of factory papers is continually increasing, including those intended for "guest workers," such as Turkish laborers. The *Deutscher Informationsdienst* (27, no. 1433/34, 16 June 1976) published a list of 743 titles of factory, residential, apprentice, and student newspapers produced by the DKP, SDAJ, and MSB-Spartakus. The listing does not claim to be a complete compilation of all Moscow-loyal publications now circulated in the FRG. As noted earlier, a report of the Institute of the German Economy gave the number of orthodox Communist papers as 1,420 with a weekly total of 800,000 copies.

A compilation of orthodox-Communist and pro-Communist periodical publications by the Federal Security Service (BVS) revealed 1,420 publications with a weekly edition of 801,500 copies for 1975. The "new Left" was credited with 417 periodical publications with a weekly edition of 389,000. The total of Communist and left-extremist periodical publications was 1,837 with a total of 1,190,500 copies distributed weekly. (*Bundesminister des Innern, Verfassungsschutz '75*, Bonn, July 1976, p. 45.)

Other Leftist Groups — Rival Communists. In addition to the orthodox, Moscow-loyal Communist organizations, there are a number of other leftist groups, some of which consider themselves to be political parties and participated as such during 1976 in federal, Land and municipal elections. In the federal elections on 3 October the "political parties" of the extreme left obtained a combined vote of 55,003. The more significant of these organizations are Maoist-oriented, following a dogmatic Marxist-Leninist line. There are also a number of Trotskyist and anarchist groups. It is most difficult to keep track of these organizations because they are in a continual state of flux. They emerge, sometimes combine with other groups, more frequently break up into splinter groups, and, often, disappear as rapidly as they were formed.

In spite of Peking's pressure for the Maoist parties and organizations to combine, they usually insist upon their separate identity and maintain a rather hostile relationship toward one another. On specific occasions, such as a May 1 demonstration, some of them agree to work together. All of the Maoist parties demand from their members complete subordination, iron discipline, and considerable material sacrifices. Members may on command change their places of residence and employment regardless of financial disadvantages. Members in academic professions are known to contribute frequently up to 1,000 marks monthly to the party coffers.

The most important Maoist "party" is the KPD, which has the same name as the Moscow-loyal underground KPD but is not to be taken as a successor organization (for background see *YICA, 1975*, pp. 183-84, and *1976*, p. 154). The KPD maintains six regional committees which coordinate the activities of 18 local headquarters with about 75 cells (1974: 65 cells). Members and candidates number about 900 (1974: 700). In spite of this relatively small membership the KPD is capable of mobilizing up to 5,000 sympathizers. (*Deutsche Zeitung*, Bonn, 10 September 1976.) At the federal elections on 3 October 1976, the party obtained 22,714 votes or 0.1 percent. The KPD also participated in Land and municipal elections and submitted candidates in 70 factory elections of shop stewards. KPD candidates were elected in 30 industrial enterprises. (*Deutscher Informationsdienst*, 27, no. 1423, 12 January.) The official organ of the KPD, *Rote Fahne*, is published in Cologne.

The KPD has an active youth organization, the Communist Youth League of Germany (Kommunistischer Jugendverband Deutschlands; KJVD). During the summer of 1976 the KJVD organized three youth camps in the FRG dedicated to ideological and practical training for the revolutionary struggle (ibid., 27, no. 1431, 12 May). Two KPD-affiliated student organizations, the Communist Student League (Kommunistischer Studentenverband: KSV) and the Communist High School Student League (Kommunistischer Oberschüler-Verband; KOV), are very active in many universities and high schools, respectively. The KPD has also organized a number of "mass organizations," such as the Rote Hilfe (see *YICA, 1976*, p. 155).

The KPD and other political organizations of the extreme left, including the anarchists, are most active in the field of publication, considering publications and their sporadic actions as the main instruments for winning sympathizers and members. Especially the number of their factory and local newspapers is increasing.

The Communist Party of Germany/Marxist-Leninist (Kommunistische Partei Deutschlands/ML; KPD/ML), founded 31 December 1968, is the oldest Maoist party. The estimated membership is about 700. The official organ is the *Rotor Morgen* and there is also a theoretical periodical, *Der Weg der Partei*. Its youth organization is the Rote Garde (see *YICA, 1976*, p. 155).

A third Maoist party is the Communist League of West Germany (Kommunistischer Bund Westdeutschlands; KBW), which publishes the *Kommunistische Volkszeitung*. The KBW participated in the 1976 elections at various levels. In the federal election the party obtained 20,018 votes or 0.1 percent. The KBW candidates receivd 21,414 first-ballot votes.

Other Maoist organizations are the Communist Workers' League of Germany (Kommunistischer Arbeiterbund Deutschlands; KABD) and the Communist League Hamburg (Kommunistischer Bund Hamburg; KB). The KAB's organ is *Rote Fahne* and the magazine of its youth organization, Revolutionary Youth League of Germany (Revolutionärer Jugendverband Deutschlands) is the *Stachel*.

Of interest are the different attitudes of the various Maoist organizations with regard to the German armed forces (Bundeswehr). The KPD intends to support the Bundeswehr in view of the existing danger of Soviet aggression. The KPD/ML does not believe that the Bundeswehr, an "imperialist army," can defend the FRG: only the armed people themselves can achieve this, and therefore the party demands that a people's army be formed now because of the possibility of an attack by Soviet "social imperialism." The KBW supports universal military training because it ensures that the workers will learn how to handle weapons and thereby obtain the capability to free themselves from capitalist suppression. The slogan about "turning the guns around" in case of war expresses the attitude of the KBW. The KABD maintains that the task of the working class is to overthrow the indigenous bourgeoisie. In the opinion of the KABD only a revolution can prevent the outbreak of a war; hence it completely rejects the Bundeswehr. (*Deutscher Informationsdienst*, 27, nos. 1426, 1427, 26 February and 10 March 1976.)

The hostilities between the Maoists and the DKP are deep-seated. The KPD considers the Soviet Union the most dangerous superpower and the DKP as the "worst enemy" of the German worker (*Deutsche Zeitung*, 10 September). DKP Chairman Mies in his post-mortem on the federal election stated: "Maoist groupings, calling themselves Communists, have waged their campaign exclusively against the DKP and proved themselves once more to be henchmen of reaction who contribute to confusing the people" (East Berlin, ADN international service in German, 4 October, in *FBIS*).

The KPD/ML claimed in early 1976 that it had formed an underground section in the GDR whose task is to lead the working class to "overthrow with force the bourgeois dictatorship in the

GDR" (*Die Welt*, 9 February). Also the KPD intends to enlighten the population in the GDR, "where fascism has been established" (*Deutscher Informationsdienst*, 27, no. 1435, 12 July).

The Trotskyists are represented by several small groups, among them the Group of International Marxists (Gruppe Internationaler Marxisten; GIM). The GIM has a centralized apparatus and a weekly paper, *Was tun*, and is the German section of the Fourth International. It has about 1,000 members, organized in about 45 city and factory groups. There are also some units at universities. The publication of factory newspapers continues to be one of its major efforts. In the federal elections the GIM received 4,759 votes.

The Spartacus League (Spartacusbund; Spabu), with about 600 members and 35 local groups, believes that the situation in the FRG is ripe for revolution. The monthly publication is called *Spartacus*. A third organization is the Trotskyist League of Germany (Trotzkistische Liga Deutschlands; TLD), started in 1974; it has about 150 to 200 members. Other Trotskyist organizations are the League of Socialist Workers (Bund Sozialistischer Arbeiter; BSA) and the Socialist Workers' Group (Sozialistischer Arbeitergruppe; SAG), each with about 250 to 300 members. The official monthly SAG organ *Klassenkampf* was superseded as of 1 May 1976 by the biweekly *Sozialistische Arbeiterzeitung* (ibid., 27, no. 1438, 23 August).

Terrorist activities in the FRG were less numerous in 1976 than in 1975 primarily because of the fact that several of the terrorist leaders have been arrested and committed to trial. Ulrike Meinhof, one of the apprehended leaders of the notorious Baader-Meinhof gang, committed suicide in her prison cell. This in turn caused a number of bombing incidents. (*Die Welt*, 15 May.) A group calling itself the "Revolutionary Cell Brigade Ulrike Meinhof" assumed responsibility for two time-bombs that exploded in the headquarters area of the U.S. Fifth Corps at Frankfurt/Main (*NYT*, 3 June).

In the beginning of 1976 it was estimated that there were at least 100 terrorists in the FRG with about 300 active assistants and 3,000 or more general sympathizers (*Die Welt*, 16 January).

*   *   *

West Berlin. West Berlin is comprised of the three Western "Occupation" sectors and is not a part of the Federal Republic of Germany. The U.S., British, and French troop contingents stationed in Berlin are not under NATO. The "special status" of the former German capital is the outcome of Allied agreements of 1944 and 1945, restated as recently as the Quadripartite Agreement concerning Berlin on 3 September 1971. In spite of the fact that all of these arrangements were to apply to the area of Greater Berlin which includes the Soviet sector in the eastern part of the city, the German Democratic Republic has for all practical purposes incorporated East Berlin with Moscow's approval. The GDR declared "Berlin" as its capital and appears entirely unconcerned about its violation of the various provisions of the Allied agreements, such as the demilitarization of the entire city. However, at the elections for the People's Chamber on 17 October 1976, East Berliners did not elect their 66 deputies directly. The deputies were "delegated" to the People's Chamber at the constituent session of the East Berlin City Parliament as required by the Four-Power Agreements concerning all of Berlin. (*Die Welt*, 27 October.) Apparently, the Soviet Union did not wish at this time to challenge the Western Allies. On the other hand, both Moscow and East Berlin have pursued a consistent policy designed to isolate West Berlin from the FRG as the first phase of the eventual absorption of the three Western sectors into East Germany. One significant aspect of this policy is their insistence that West Berlin is an "independent political entity." (See Eric Waldman, *Die Sozialistische Einheitspartei Westberlins und die sowjetische Berlinpolitik,* Boppard am Rhein, 1972.)

The FRG maintains close ties with West Berlin, with the Western Allies' encouragement, a situation which has been reaffirmed by the Quadripartite Agreement of 1971.

The special status of Berlin, though only implemented in its entirety in the Western sectors, enabled the Socialist Unity Party of Germany (SED) to establish a West Berlin subsidiary. Thus the present Socialist Unity Party of West Berlin (Sozialistische Einheitspartei Westberlins; SEW) is the product of the East German SED and was not founded by Communists in West Berlin. In its early stage it was nothing more than the SED organization in the three Western Sectors of Berlin. Therefore, up to the time of the "separation" from the "mother party," it has the same history as the SED.

Khrushchev's demand in the spring of 1959 that West Berlin be made a "free city" necessitated the appointment of a separate leadership of the SED in the Western sectors. This was done in order to give the impression of the existence of an independent and indigenous Communist party. The next step was taken in November 1962 when a "Conference of Delegates" changed the name of the party to Socialist Unity Party of Germany-West Berlin (Sozialistische Einheitspartei Deutschlands-Westberlin; SED-W). The reason for this move was the erection of the Wall (13 August 1961) which separated East and West Berlin. In February 1969 one more name change was accomplished at a special congress. In line with the notion of the "independent political entity" of West Berlin, "Germany" had to disappear from the name of the party and the present designation SEW was adopted. It is of interest to note that only the ruling Communist party in the GDR carries "Germany" in its name, implying that the other German Communist parties (DKP and SEW) are merely carrying out the task given to them by the SED.

Leadership, Organization, and Domestic Activities. The year 1976 did not bring any changes in leadership and organization for the SEW, nor was it able to increase its membership of about 8,000 members. (West Berlin's population is close to 2 million.) (For a discussion of the organization, structure, and leadership personnel and the affiliated organizations such as the Free German Youth-West Berlin—Freie Deutsche Jugend Westberlins; FDJ-W—and other "mass organizations" see *YICA, 1976*, p. 157.)

The SEW chairman is still Gerhard Denelius, who was unanimously reelected at the Fourth Party Congress in November 1974. There have been reports that because of the very poor results the SEW achieved in the West Berlin elections in March 1975, when the party obtained 1.9 percent of the vote (1971: 2.3 percent), Danelius is attempting to give the impression that his party is no longer a subsidiary of East Berlin (*Die Zeit*, 27 February 1976). This, however, is a most difficult task because the SEW's declarations dealing with the position of West Berlin and its relations with both East and West Germany are completely in harmony with the view expounded by the SED.

Nevertheless, the SEW was able to increase its influence at the universities, both among faculty and student body, as well as among academicians, professionals, actors, and writers who frequently are willing to sign their names to SEW resolutions (ibid). The SEW not only improved its position at the institutions of higher learning but also made good use of its penetration of the trade unions as part of its concerted effort to better its contact with the masses.

International Views and Party Contacts. The SEW's statements on West Berlin in relation to East and West Germany are identical with the positions expressed by Moscow and East Berlin. Early in 1976 Danelius stated that the Four-Power Agreement made it absolutely clear that West Berlin is not a part of the FRG and must not be governed by it. Hence, he maintained, West Berlin has now the opportunity to establish good all-around relations with socialist as well as capitalist countries. (Moscow TASS in German, 26 February 1976, in *FBIS*.) According to the SEW, one of the party's tasks is to work for relaxation of tension and draw attention to

the constant attacks of the SPD leadership on the concluded treaties and agreements, as well as their attacks on the Soviet Union and the German Democratic Republic, [because] the anti-Communist attitude of the West Berlin SPD leaders, along with their deficient understanding of democracy, is not only hurting our party but the SPD as well. (*Die Wahrheit*, 17 February.)

The SEW maintains close contacts with fraternal Communist parties. Relations with the SED, from which the party receives most of its financial support as well as political direction, are very close. Its complete submission to Moscow is borne out by numerous declarations in which the CPSU is given unlimited praise "for its experience and leadership of the world Communist movement, for its vigorous implementation of the policy of peaceful coexistence and the results of the Helsinki conference." (See, e.g., the greeting sent to the 25th CPSU Congress, in *Pravda*, 1 March.) From 10 to 14 May a SEW delegation led by Danelius visited Hungary at the invitation of the Central Committee of the Hungarian party. (Budapest MTI domestic service, 14 May, in *FBIS*.) Another SEW delegation visited the Soviet Union from 26 May to 1 June (*Pravda*, 3 June).

The SEW also participated in the Conference of European Communist and Workers' Parties in East Berlin. Erich Ziegler, deputy chairman, addressed the 29 June session and declared his party's full agreement with the conference document for peace, security, cooperation, and social progress in Europe: "Our party is resolved, in accordance with its responsibility to the West Berlin working class and spirit of proletarian internationalism, to contribute toward realizing our common noble aims." (East Berlin, ADN, international service in German, 29 June, in *FBIS*.)

Publications. The official organ of the SEW, *Die Wahrheit*, celebrated its 20th anniversary in November 1975. It appears six times weekly in about 16,000 copies. (For publications of the "mass organizations" affiiated with the SEW such as the FDJ-W see *YICA, 1975*, p. 191.)

Other Leftist Groups — Rival Communists. The "left extremists" maintain numerous groups and organizations in West Berlin, each of them claiming to possess the only correct interpretation of Marxism-Leninism. The Free University and the other institutions of higher learning provide the most fertile ground for the activities of the various Maoist-Trotskyists, anarchists, and left communist groups. Many of them emerged from the once influential Extra-Parliamentary Opposition, the so-called APO.

The Maoist KPD and KBW are the most significant Maoist "parties" among these left extremist organizations. They participated in the March 1975 elections for the West Berlin legislature and obtained 10,277 and 802 votes respectively. The Maoist Communist Student Union (Kommunistischer Studenten-Verband; KSV) continued in 1976 its activities at the various post-secondary institutions with considerable success. The year also witnessed the emergence of at least two additional Maoist groups in West Berlin. The first issue of the bulletin "Westberliner Kommunist" claimed to be the organ of the new KPD/Marxist-Leninist Party (KPD/ML) in West Berlin. It characterized the SED regime as a "military government of the Russian social imperialism." At the same time the Liebknecht Association (Liebknecht Vereinigung) was formed in opposition to the KPD/ML, which it accused of belittling the danger of West German imperialism, revanchism, and militarism. (*Deutscher Informationsdienst*, 27, no. 1429, 12 April.)

Like other Moscow-loyal Communist parties, the SEW is strongly opposed to these "left extremists" and accuses them of petty-bourgeois tendencies.

University of Calgary — Eric Waldman

Great Britain

The Communist Party of Great Britain (CPGB) was founded in 1920 and was a subsection of the Communist International from 1920 until the dissolution of the International in 1943. The CPGB confines its activities to Great Britain and is not operative in Ireland. It continues to be Great Britain's largest and most significant Marxist party although in recent years it has faced increased competition from other ultra-leftist groups.

The CPGB is a recognized political party and contests local and national elections. It has, however, had no Members of Parliament since 1950 when it had two. There is one Communist member of the House of Lords, and at present it has about 15 council members at various levels of local government.

Current membership of the CPGB is 28,519. The population of Great Britain is 54,421,000 (Annual Abstract of Statistics, 1975).

Leadership and Organization. The CPGB has four levels: the National Congress, the Executive and its departments, the Districts, and the Branches which are both local and factory based.

Constitutionally, the National Congress is the supreme authority of the party. It meets biennially to elect a new 42-member executive, hears reports on the activities since the last meeting, and considers documents on future policy and activity. The delegates comprise representatives from districts and branches. The Congress serves as a rubber stamp for the party leadership and opposition is unusual.

The Executive Committee meets every two months and directs party activities on particular issues. It also chooses the members of specialist committees and full-time heads of departments, and selects the 16-member Political Committee which is the party's effective controlling body. The Political Committee meets once a week or when the occasion arises.

During 1976 the leading officers and heads of department were Gordon McLennan (general secretary), Reuben Falber (assistant secretary), Mick McGahey (chairman), Dave Cook (national organizer), Bert Ramelson (industrial organizer), George Matthews (press and publicity chief), Jack Woddis (head of international department), Betty Matthews (head of education department), Dennis Ellward (national treasurer), and Malcolm Cowle (national election agent).

The Young Communist League (YCL) has been affiliated to the CPGB since the latter's foundation. Despite a determined campaign to expand YCL membership, which included a Red Festival on 22-23 May 1976, the YCL's membership fell significantly from 2,300 in September 1975 to 1,950 twelve months later (*Comment*, 2 October). Most YCL members are students and there are 50 Communist organizations in the universities.

The CPGB exercises its greatest influence through the trade union movement. This influence is considerable and although the CPGB does not control any individual union it has played a prominent role in nearly all the union-Government confrontations of recent years. This is partly attributable to the fact that the Communists are the only effective organization within the trade union movement seeking to control the outcome of elections. Its success, partly due to the very low poll in most trade union elections, has been outstanding and there is a party member on nearly every union executive in Great Britain.

Toward the end of 1976 there were some indications that the Communists were beginning to reverse the trend of the previous year, in trade union elections, which had been toward the right. Whereas formerly the CPGB had been most influential in the Amalgamated Union of Engineering Workers (AUEW), elections to the union executive in 1975 had produced a massive victory for the moderates. However, in elections for the union executive in November 1976 a prominent left-winger, Bob Wright, running with Communist support, became assistant general secretary.

In 1976 the CPGB continued to sponsor the Liaison Committee for the Defence of Trade Unions (LCDTU), a Communist-dominated umbrella organization found in 1966. With a membership embracing many shades of ultra-left opinion, the LCDTU remains the party's chosen instrument for the promotion of industrial campaigns and propaganda. In addition to this, in 1976, the party had 185 workplace branches, a net gain of 23 over the 1975 figure, and 2,172 members (2,014 in 1975) (*Comment*, 30 October). At the party's national conference of workplace branches, held in Birmingham on 2-3 October and attended by 116 delegates, the CPGB placed its emphasis on the enlargement of the number of workplace branches and the strengthening of existing ones.

Party Internal Affairs. The 34th Congress, 5-18 November 1975, was not controversial (see *YICA, 1976*). However, in 1976 the appearance of unanimity was disturbed by two currents, one industrial and the other ideological, which questioned the rigidity of the party's attitudes toward Stalinism and the USSR.

In industry the most alarming development for the CPGB in 1976 was the defection of Jimmy Reid, whose resignation was announced on 11 February. An executive member with 26 years of party membership behind him, Reid had become a nationally known figure when he directed the work-in by employees of the bankrupt UpperClyde Shipbuilders group in 1971-72. His criticisms of the party were not specific, but he attacked its general tendencies toward dogmatism and sectarianism. A reply by Gordon McLennan, party general secretary, made clear by its length what a blow Reid's defection was. It was widely believed that Reid had felt that party membership had been a hindrance to him in elections to official posts in the AUEW (see *YICA, 1976*). This suspicion gained in credibility when John Tocher, North-West England organizer of the AUEW and former national chairman of the CPGB, also resigned from the party in August.

Ideologically, an intimation of divergent party opinions came in the wake of a 20,000-word article which appeared in the January issue of *Marxism Today*. Written by former party general secretary John Gollan, the article, "Socialist Democracy/Some Problems Today," was part of the CPGB's efforts to demonstrate its independence from Moscow. Gollan took issue with the Soviet leadership over the persecution of dissidents and franky admitted that the CPGB had been "insufficiently critical" of the Soviets in the 1930s. Although endorsed by the party executive, the article was evidently too powerful a critique for many Communists and it provoked a lively correspondence in the following issues. There was also a report that the Communist Party of the Soviet Union (CPSU) sent a private message of protest to the British party (*Guardian*, 13 February).

The CPGB, in common with other British political parties, is having its funds adversely affected by inflation and would appear to be living beyond its means. In March the party launched a national fund campaign with the aim of raising £60,000 — twice as much as 1975's achievement. Apart from such special appeals the main source of income, the Communists say, is from private donations and legacies. In the latest figures available, 1974-75, the party received £90,000 from this source. Sales of literature bring in about £20,000 a year. Here there is a discreet subsidy in operation as many of the publications are produced in the USSR and Czechoslovakia and clearly marketed below cost price. Membership fees are 25p. a month per member (5p. for old age pensioners), but many members are reported to be behind in their dues.

The Communist daily newspaper, the *Morning Star*, is financially independent of the party organization, and has been struggling to support itself with a daily sale of 50 to 60,000 copies, of which about 18,000 are sold behind the Iron Curtain.

The party has a wide range of business interests, many of which are nominally independent organizations. Such enterprises include Central Books Ltd; Lawrence and Wishart, publishers; Fasleigh Press and London Caledonian, printers; Rodell Properties Ltd; the Labour Research Department; and the Marx Memorial Library.

The CPGB is aware of its abysmal performance in national elections and continues to campaign for a much expanded party membership, hoping that it will, like a lizard's tail, regenerate itself. In recent years its electoral fortunes have been as follows:

Election	CPGB votes	Percent of vote	Candidates	MPs	Out of
Oct. 1959	30,896	0.1	18	None	630
Oct. 1964	45,086	0.2	36	None	630
Nov. 1966	62,112	0,2	57	None	630
Jun. 1970	38,431	0.1	58	None	630
Feb. 1974	32,741	0.1	44	None	635
Oct. 1974	17,008	0.05	29	None	635

Domestic Attitudes and Activities. The national economic crisis remained the central theme of British politics in 1976. As the gravity of the country's plight deepened, the rift between the ruling Labour Party's left and right wings became more pronounced. Rising unemployment, public spending cuts, industrial closures, high interest rates, and wage restraint served to convince the left wing that the Labour Party had departed from its principles.

This development gave a new impetus to the CPGB's drive for "left unity" which it has been pursuing since 1956. Traditionally, cooperation with other left bodies has largely been restricted to single-issue campaigns such as industrial relations, Vietnam, Northern Ireland, Chile, the EEC, and the Shrewsbury Pickets. The CPGB has, however, always been more interested in attching itself to the Labour movement. The current rift in the Labour Party therefore has helped the CPGB to present itself as a leading force for left-wing unity. In 1976 many Labour Members of Parliament, including National Executive members, have written in the *Morning Star* or attended party rallies. Among the most prominent are Sydney Bidwell, Renée Short, Joan Maynard, and Frank Allaun.

The CPGB attacked the Labour government's economic strategy, claiming that it could only lead to the return of a Conservative government and that it must therefore adopt an alternative left-wing strategy embracing much of the Communists' own economic policies. Thus the main goal of Communist activities was clear enough: "To force the Labour government off its present disastrous course and secure the implementation of a counter-crisis programme, such as the Communists and Left demand, requires the unity of all Socialists and Communists in the labour movement" (*MorningStar*, 2 March). The "counter-crisis" program remains unchanged: a rent and prices freeze; the restoration of free collective bargaining; an improvement in the social services; import controls; selling of overseas investments; a wealth tax; nationalization of major business enterprises; increased investment; a 50 percent cut in military expenditure; expanded trade with Eastern Europe and the Third World.

More humbly, the most successful application of the Communist strategy of the "Broad Left" alliance of Communists, Labour Marxists, and unattached Marxists has been in the National Union of Students (NUS). Here the Communists are extremely influential and the party nominees continue to hold most important NUS positions, including the key post of secretary held by Susan Slipman.

Attempts to extend this influence in the academic field have been made through a series of "Communist Universities." In 1976 at its eighth annual session the Communist University of London, which lasted for nine days, again increased its membership, which has grown from a figure just over 1,100 in 1968 to 1,940 in 1976. There were 200 speakers at the 1976 course.

The CPGB campaigned on a number of issues in 1976: opposition to public spending cuts, unemployment, race relations, devolution, and Northern Ireland. Policy statements on domestic affairs differed little from previous years. The Communists played a prominent part in organizing a nationwide day of action on 26 May protesting against unemployment. At the largest demonstrations, in London and Liverpool, there were about 10,000 participants. In the course of the year there were occasional clashes with members of the extreme right National Front (NF), but the party was careful not to let these escalate, in sharp contrast to the attitudes of the ultra left.

Even though the CPGB has always supported a large measure of devolution, and has area branches for Scotland and Wales, it remains fundamentally unitarist and therefore continues to be unsettled by the upsurge of regional nationalism. This is particularly true in Scotland, a traditional area of Communist support, where there is evidence that many Marxists are turning to the newly founded Scottish Labour Party and even to the Nationalists.

The Communists were active in sponsoring or supporting various conferences in the course of the year. These included the Scottish Festival of Marxism, the North-West Festival of Marxism, and the International Forum to End the Arms Race and for World Disarmament (held in York University).

International Views and Party Contacts. In international terms the most significant event in 1976 for the CPGB was the Conference of European Communist and Workers' Parties, held in East Berlin on 29-30 June. The British party took the opportunity to emphasize the independent nature of its policies, which it has been espousing since 1968. Commenting on the effectiveness of such meetings, the Executive Committee stated: "Last month's conference in Berlin and the preparations for it, indicated that some methods utilized hitherto in the international Communist movement were no longer appropriate" (*Morning Star*, 12 July). Such criticism reflected a growing awareness within the CPGB that its fortunes would be best served by distancing its policies from those of the Soviets.

This tendency toward an ideological posture independent of Moscow was underlined when party General Secretary McLennan at the CPSU Congress in March, reiterated his faith in a British type of socialism distinct from the Russian version: "Our aim is the construction of socialism in Britain in forms which would guarantee personal freedom, the plurality of political parties, the independence of the trade unions, religious freedom, freedom of research, cultural, artistic and scientific activities" (ibid., 2 March).

However, in its attitudes to international affairs the CPGB continued to give unstinting support to Soviet foreign policy objectives. It called for an end to NATO and "neo-colonialism" in southern Africa, and termed Soviet naval expansion a force for peace in the world. Its obituaries of Mao Tsetung were couched in terms of a highly qualified respect clearly acceptable to the Soviet Union. On southern Europe, the party campaigned for the legalization of the Spanish Communist Party and attempted to gather some refracted prestige from the Italian party's increased prestige by giving special publicity to talks by its leader, Enrico Berlinguer, with McLennan and Woddis. Developments in southern Africa were seen as marking a decisive movement against imperialism. The Cuban-led victory of the MPLA in Angola was hailed as a "body blow to imperialism"; invective against Rhodesia and South Africa remained high. Much attention was given to the alleged atrocities of the Rhodesian army and to the rioting in South Africa.

Solidarity with Chile remained a stable feature of Communist propaganda though the CPGB's attitudes differ significantly from its ultra-left rivals. While the latter believe the Chilean experience points to the impossibility of a peaceful revolution, the Communists believe the Allende strategy to have been the right one.

The CPGB continued its anti-EEC campaign unabated during 1976, undisturbed by the massive vote in favor of the EEC in the referendum of the previous year. The party tries to present itself as the custodian of British sovereignty, opposed to any transfer of power from Westminster to Brussels. It is therefore bitterly opposed to the introduction of direct elections to a European parliament and warns that "the government intends to go along with the fraud and deception of direct elections to lull the people into thinking the Market is the opposite of what it really is" (ibid., 17 January).

Foreign visits by CPGB members included those of Cook to the French party's congress in February; McLennan to Moscow for the CPSU congress in March; McLennan and Woddis to Rome, where they had talks with Berlinguer in April; Ashton to the East German party's congress in May; and McLennan and Woddis to the conference of European parties in East Berlin in July.

Publications. The principal organ of the CPGB is the daily *Morning Star*. Its other principal publications are *Comment* (fortnightly) and *Marxism Today* (a monthly theoretical journal). The YCL publishes *Challenge* and *Cogito*.

*   *   *

Other Marxist Groups. Numerous other Marxist groups compete with the orthodox Communists for leadership of left-wing militancy in Great Britain. Of these, the most significant in industry is the Workers' Revolutionary Party (WRP). Founded on 4 November 1973, it was reconstituted from the Socialist Labour League (SLL), which had existed since 1959. The WRP is a Trotskyite organization and an affiliate of the Fourth International (International Secretariat).

The WRP is estimated at just over 1,000 members. It is active in docks, engineering, mining, the theater, and most major motor groups. It also controls the All Trade Union Alliance (ATUA), an organization similar to the Communist-controlled LCDTU. The ATUA campaigns for nationalization of industry and guarantees of full employment and incomes.

The WRP used to boast the world's first Trotskyite daily newspaper, *Workers' Press*, but this ceased publication on 14 February. A successor, *Newsline*, was successfully launched on 1 May. The WRP also publishes an irregular journal, *Fourth International*.

Its youth movement, the Young Socialists, claims to have 20,000 members, and certainly it has had some success in attracting young working people, particularly colored immigrants. The WRP's youth policies attracted some notoriety in 1976 by offering courses for teenagers on smashing capitalism.

In the more esoteric Trotskyite circles, the WRP caused a controversy in August by charging the American Socialist Workers' Party with implication in the murder of Leon Trotsky.

Mike Banda (real name: van der Poorten) was appointed general secretary of the party in April, replacing Gerry Healy, who had been secretary for 27 years. Among the more prominent members is the actress Vanessa Redgrave.

The largest Trotskyite organization in Great Britain is the International Socialists (IS), with a membership of about 2,900. For what used to be one of the country's fastest growing ultra-left groups, 1976 was a bad year. Membership dropped by 600 and the print order for the party's weekly paper, *Socialist Worker*, continued to fall. It is now 2,400 with a paid sale of only 1,200. Leading personalities include Tony Cliff (real name: Ygael Gluckstein) and Paul Foot. IS has 38 branches but has generally been confined to white-color workers, though in 1976 the party had hoped to enroll at least 2,000 manual workers. At the grass-roots level its activities are coordinated by the Rank and File Movement, founded in 1974. The party was badly damaged in 1976 by the defection of many prominent members (including John Palmer, European editor of the *Guardian*, and Jim Higgins) who objected to the rigid control of the Central Committee and therefore formed their own organization, the Socialist League.

The main IS achievement in 1976 was the "Right to Work" march from Manchester to London in March which culminated in a violent clash with police. It has also been involved in scuffles with NF demonstrators. In November IS took what was for it the unprecedented step of putting up two Parliamentary candidates in by-elections under the name Socialist Workers' Party. Both were soundly defeated. IS is considering fielding 50 to 60 candidates at the next general election.

The International Marxist Group (IMG) is the British section of the United Secretariat of the Fourth International. Membership is about 1,200. Prominent members include Tariq Ali, Robin Blackburn, Fred Halliday, and Pat Jordan. It publishes *Red Weekly* and *International*. In 1976 the IMG was involved in many single-issue campaigns, polemics against other ultra-left groups, and demonstrations. Issues of particular concern were public spending cuts, unemployment, Chile, southern Africa, and Northern Ireland.

The IMG's highlight of the year was its surprising strength in Scotland. In November, during the first national conference of the Scottish Labour Party (a breakaway movement from the Labour Party with three sitting MPs) some 25 percent of the membership had to be expelled largely because of their association with the IMG.

In addition the IMG was involved in violent altercations with the NF. The IMG has a history of being involved in violent street scuffles and would appear to be making a determined effort to introduce violence into British political life.

In 1976 eight pro-Chinese Marxist parties were identified as still operative in Britain though all were very small. The largest, with a membership of 300-400, is the Communist Party of Britain Marxist-Leninist. Its significance resides in the fact that its head, Reg Birch, is a member of the General Council of the TUC.

London   Richard Sim

Greece

There were no dramatic or spectacular developments during 1976 in the policies, relationships activities, or leading personalities of the Greek left. The two Communist parties, KKE and KKE (interior), continued their separate existence without any indication that the split was to be healed soon. A third political party with Marxist orientation, the United Democratic Left (EDA)—the party which had served as KKE's front from 1951 to 1967—continued to pursue a moderate leftist line. A fourth political party, the Pan-Hellenic Socialist Movement (PASOK), though not formally a section of the Greek Communist Left, advocated positions which were often similar to those supported by KKE.

The Communist Party of Greece (Kommounistikon Komma Ellados; KKE) evolved from the Socialist Workers' Party of Greece, which was formed in November 1918. The party remained a marginal force in Greek politics for several years, undergoing repeated splits and intra-party convulsions till the 1931 intervention of the Comintern which installed a Stalin-supported leadership under Nikos Zakhariades. With the economic depression of the early thirties and the internal instability in Greee, the party grew in membership and popular influence. Its progress was disrupted by the Metaxas dictatorship, imposed in August 1936. During the country's World War II occupation by the Axis, the party succeeded in organizing a strong resistance movement but its attempt to seize power by force in December 1944 was thwarted by the intervention of the British. In 1946-49 the party organized a guerrilla campaign which failed to win broad popular support. The rebellion was crushed in August 1949. In the 1950s and 1960s the party, outlawed since 1947, operated through a front organization, the United Democratic Left (EDA). The military dictatorship imposed in April 1967 banned EDA together with all other political parties. During the years of the dictatorial rule, KKE leaders divided into two basic factions, known as KKE (exterior), composed of the party's leaders residing in Eastern Europe and the Soviet Union since the collapse of the 1946-49 guerrilla campaign, and KKE (interior), led by some of those who had remained in Greece and had spent several years in jail.

Following the collapse of the dictatorship in July 1974 and the return of all parties, including the Communists, to a legitimate status, the two factions of KKE appeared as two distinct organizations with separate leaderships and identifiable policies. KKE (exterior), which enjoys Moscow's support, has now dropped the added reference "(exterior)" and uses the plain title KKE. Its policies are in keeping with basic Marxist-Leninist principles and totally in line with whatever policies Moscow may be favoring at the moment. In contrast, KKE (interior), which tries to display moderation and independence, is not accorded any legitimacy by the Soviet Union or the other East European Communist parties, with the exception of that of Romania.

In addition to the principal political parties of the Greek left—KKE, KKE (interior), EDA, and PASOK—several other Marxist-oriented organizations have made their appearance since 1974. Most of these organizations have a rather limited number of members, mostly young. The most noteworthy among them are the following:

(1)   Organization of Marxist-Leninists of Greece (OMLE). It has been active among the university students through its Pan-Student Progressive Syndicalist Camp (Parataxis), and among young workers through its Progressive Workers Syndicalist Camp.

(2)   Revolutionary Communist Movement of Greece (EKKE). It has a "radical" Maoist orientation and is active among students and young workers through its Anti-Imperialist, Anti-Fascist Student Camp of Greece (AASPE) and Anti-Imperialist, Anti-Fascist Student Camp of Working Technicians (AASPET).

(3)   Greek Revolutionary Liberation Front (EEAM). Opposed to the "opportunism of KKE," it favors a Stalinist and Maoist line. It, too, is active among the students with its Union of Struggle of Leftist Students (EPAS).

(4)   Greek Communist Party/Marxist Leninist (KKE/ML). Stalinist in its orientation, this organization operates through "militant" groups within existing student organizations.

(5)   Several small groups with Trotskyist leanings continue to operate, especially among university students and young workers, but their appeal remains limited. Most important among them are the Revolutionary Communist League (EKS), the Socialist Revolutionary Organization (OSE), the Greek Internationalist Union (EDE), and the Socialist Revolutionary Union (SEE).

(6)   "Socialist March" (Sosialistiki Poreia) aspires to appeal to the intelligentsia.

(7)   Particularly noteworthy because of their partisan affiliations are the workers' organizations known as Anti-Dictatorial Workers Front (AEM), associated with KKE (interior); the United Syndicalist Anti-Dictatorial Movement (ESAK), an offshoot of KKE/ and the Pan-Hellenic Socialist Workers Movement (PASKE), affiliated with PASOK.

At the present time there is no accurate estimate as to the KKE's strength. There may be approximately 25,000 to 30,000 persons, in Greece and abroad, who could be labeled as communist party members or followers; but this estimate would also include members and supporters of the numerous small Leftist groups and should be regarded with caution. The population of Greece is just over 9 million (see *YICA, 1976,* p. 167).

Internal Affairs. In the elections held by university student organizations in December 1975, Communists, Socialists, and other leftists won 260 out of 329 seats in student councils. Candidates supported by student organizations affiliated with KKE, KKE (interior), and more extreme left-wing organizations such as those mentioned in earlier paragraphs won 179 of these 260 seats. The success of the leftist candidates may be partly attributed to the low participation of moderate students in the voting.

Just before the end of the year, the "Socialist March" held its first conference, which discussed internal developments and the dispute between Greece and Turkey over the Aegean. The main theme of the conference was the "continuing subservience" to the United States and a call to end "all ties of dependence." In spite of its grandiloquent pronouncements, this organization remains a marginal force.

In January 1976, KKE held its first Pan-Thessalian Conference, which took a strong stand against suggestions from other parties of the left that the opposition parties form a "democratic alliance." KKE first secretary Kharilaos Florakis, speaking at the conference, rejected any such alliance with center or center-left parties because, as he put it, their views on "democracy" differ from those of KKE. As expected, Florakis called for a complete withdrawal from NATO, dissolution of the American bases in Greece, and "an end to the privileges of domestic and foreign monopolies."

Florakis reaffirmed these positions in his address to the First Congreess of the Communist Youth Organization (KNE), which was held in February. In an obvious rebuke to the more moderate pronouncement of EDA and KKE (interior), Florakis added that there can be no socialism with only Marxism, without Leninism. In spite of this emphasis on ideological purity, KKE's Central Committee responded to the call for a "democratic alliance" with a call of its own to "the people, the democratic parties, organizations, and personalities" to join in a common "minimum program." Such a minimum program, it specified, should include an agreement to press for a plebiscite to abolish the U.S.-NATO bases; abrogation of the 12 October 1953 treaty between Greece and the United States; Greece's withdrawal from NATO; and a settlement of the Cyprus problem through an agreement between Greek and Turk Cypriots "without outside interference."

In May a wave of strikes supported by KKE, KKE (interior), PASOK, and their worker organizations led to some violent clashes with the police, but worker participation was not as wide as their sponsors anticipated.

On 6-12 June, KKE (interior) held its First Congress in Athens. The fact that it did not consider the Congress to be KKE's Tenth (or Ninth) Congress underscored the party's inability to claim effectively that it is indeed the Communist Party of Greece. Although the Congress received the moral support of the major center party ED.I.K.—with the unlikely sight of a bourgeois personality such as I. Pesmatzoglou addressing the gathering—the speeches and the resolutions approved by the participants revealed the party's major handicap. KKE (interior) aspires to attract the 20 percent of voters that EDA was able to influence in the late 1950s. But to do so, it must disassociate itself from its Marxist-Leninist heritage. By so doing, however, it leaves itself exposed to the attacks of KKE. Thus, as it tries to compete with both EDA and KKE, the KKE (interior) loses its appeal on both sides. As an additional indication of the party's weakness, one may cite the financial difficulties of its newspaper *Avgi,* which almost suspended publication in early 1976 due to inadequate circulation.

EDA also faces a similar handicap. This was shown during the Fourth Conference of its Administrative Committee, 28-29 February. Several of the Committee's 60 members come from the Communist ranks and many of them find it difficult to accept the moderate line advocated by the party's chairman, Ilias Iliou. Diametrically opposed views were voiced during the Conference by the moderate and the more doctrinaire members as to whether EDA must accept the leaderhip of Premier Karamanlis in the effort to safeguard democracy, or should undertake a decisive struggle against his government, which in the opinion of many EDA members "represents the interests of the domestic and foreign monopolies." There were similar differences on Greece's induction into the European Economic Community and on the demand of the left for a complete withdrawal from NATO. Moreover, EDA still finds it difficult to establish a separate identity from KKE (interior) since their views on key questions are often similar.

The issue of the repatriation of pro-Communist refugees from Eastern Europe and the Soviet Union remained unresolved. All parties of the left support a massive repatriation of the approximately 56,000 persons involved. The Karamanlis government has agreed that they may return after individual screening. So far, approximately 6,600 have returned to Greece. In addition to the legal problems that such a massive repatriation would entail, there is official uneasiness over the fact that two-thirds of the refugees are under forty years of age and many of them may be dedicated Communists.

In November 1976, Andreas Papandreou called for a united front of the "democratic forces" of the Opposition in a "framework of democratic unity, cooperation, and coordination of activity" to promote their positions "inside and outside of Parliament." Papandreou stressed that the proposed cooperation did not mean the formation of an "electoral front." KKE (interior) first secretary Kharalambos (Babis) Drakopoulos, in a letter to Papandreou, applauded the proposal. EDA's Iliou also took a positive view. The center party ED.I.K. took a negative stand, as did KKE.

A minor tempest was caused in November by a statement issued by Mikis Theodorakis, the celebrated leftist composer, voicing his "disgust" at the behavior of certain circles of the left toward himself and his family. The implication of the Theodorakis allegations was that members of KKE and its Youth Organization (KNE) engaged in harassment tactics because of his criticism leveled against KKE and its continuing dogmatism and subservience to the Soviet Union... KKE (interior) and EDA rose in defense of Theodorakis. Ironically, so did the governing party of the "New Democracy." Capitalizing on the unlikely support Theodorakis received from the Karamanlis government, KKE and PASOK spoke of a deliberate ruse of the "right" in using the celebrated composer and his squabbles with his former associates in the Communist party as a means of "striking a blow against the genuine forces of the left."

The continuing disunity and fragmentation of the Greek left would seem to imply weakness and ineffectiveness. However, the anti-Americanism resulting from the popular conviction that Washington is favoring and even encouraging Turkey's pressures on Greece and the continuing Turkish occupation on Cyprus amply serves the propaganda objectives of the extreme left. This anti-Americanism and the anti-NATO stand finds support even among bourgeois politicians and hence legitimizes the positions held by the extreme left for many years. The young people in particular are exposed to a constant barrage which comes not only from the traditional anti-Western quarters but from almost every corner of the political arena. In fact, the non-Communist parties, including the governing party of the "New Democracy," find it necessary to either condone or avoid strong criticism of the anti-American and anti-NATO pronouncements of the opposition parties or the press. The left has not been able to capitalize on these advantages largely because of its fragmentation and the stabilizing influence exercised by Premier Karamanlis. However, ther true extent of left influence will not be ascertained till the next parliamentary election, which should take place sometime before November 1978.

International Views and Policies. Three major issues preoccupied the Communist left during 1976: the Greek-Turkish dispute over Cyprus and particularly over the Turkish claims in the Aegean, Greece's induction into the European Economic Community, and the fate of U.S.-NATO bases on Greek soil.

The exploratory trips of the Turkish special vessel *Sismik* into the Aegean in search of oil deposits in the summer of 1976 heated up the political climate in the area to the point that many predicted that a military confrontation between Greece and Turkey was inevitable. In the face of the crisis, KKE (interior) asked the government to call a broad conference of all political parties to chart a common position. A similar demand was voiced by PASOK. EDA, on its part, called for national unity. KKE by contrast was forced into an unpopular stand when the Soviet Union, through its ambassador in Athens, advised Greece to exercise self-retraint and abstain from the use or the threat of force. Moreover, Moscow noted its support for free navigation and for the settlement of disputes through negotiations—admonitions which appeared to be too much in accord with what Turkey was also advocating. The fact that a similar démarche was also undertaken by the Soviet ambassador in Ankara did not lessen the Greek displeasure with the Soviet stand. KKE (interior), through its *Avgi*, openly criticized the Soviet position. In contrast, KKE's daily newspaper, *Rizospastis*, praised Moscow's action as being in keeping with the Soviet Union's "declared peace-loving policies." Moreover, KKE had to revise its previous view on Cyprus (that there should be direct negotiations between the two communities on the island without outside interference) when in late June Moscow came out in favor of an international conference. The Soviet proposal was obviously designed to forestall any solution within the "Western framework." Such a solution, involving a compromise over the size of the Turkish sector in Cyprus and the constitutional arrangements, was rumored at the time. It must be noted that KKE was not the only political party welcoming the Soviet initiative. The Soviet proposal for an international conference on Cyprus received the support of PASOK and ED.I.K.

With regard to Greece's induction into the European Common Market, KKE is unequivocally opposed. To quote a proclamation of the Central Committee's Fourth Plenin, 1-2 August, Greece's induction into the EEC will lead to the "total subjugation of the Greek economy to the international monopolies, and will increase the dependence of our country on imperialism." PASOK's stand on this issue is equally negative. KKE (interior) and EDA take a more moderate, somewhat ambivalent position since their ties are mostly with the Communist parties of Western Europe.

The opposition to NATO and the continuing U.S. presence in Greece flared up once again in late summer when press accounts disclosed that units of the U.S. Sixth Fleet had received permission from the Greek government to conduct landing exercises in the southeastern Peloponnese. The parties of the left, especially KKE and PASOK, launched a virulent campaign, but the Karamanlis government stood its ground and the landing exercises took place in the middle of August as planned.

The victory of Jimmy Carter in the U.S. Presidential election was welcomed by most segments of the Greek people, including the parties of the moderate left. PASOK and KKE, however, warned the Greek people against unwarranted expectations since "the basic lines of foreign policy are determined by the American Establishment."

Publications. The major Communist dailies are KKE's *Rizospastis* and KKE (interior)'s *Avgi* ("Dawn"). KKE also publishes a theoretical magazine, *Kommunistiki Epitheorisi* (Communist Review). The other leftist organizations intermittently publish tabloids such as *Laikos Dromos* (affiliated with OMLE), *Laikoi Agones* (EKKE), *Kokkini Simaia* (KKE/ML), and *Ergatiki Pali*, (an organ of the Trotskyist OKDE). Greek bookstores continue to carry a large number of Marxist-oriented volumes in Greek translation. Moreover, non-Communist newspapers and periodicals such as *Ta Nea, Athinaiki, Eleutherotypia, Politika Themata, Epikaira,* and *Oikonomikos Takhydromos* often publish articles and feature stories with a pro-socialist, anti-Western slant. Open criticism of Communist views and principles is rare. This is a legacy of the 1967-74 military dictatorship, which discredited most anti-Communist arguments and legitimized the Communist left.

Howard University   D. George Kousoulas

Iceland

Iceland's political culture, with its emphasis on egalitarianism and fervent nationalism, has produced various left-socialist and Communist movements over the years. As is so often the case with Icelandic politics, analogies can be drawn to events in other western European countries, but there inevitably emerge unique national characteristics. In recent decades the main party of the socialist left has been the People's Alliance (Altydubandalagid; PA) which while advocating fairly radical alternatives to current domestic and foreign policy, nevertheless does so without any reference to Communist pronouncements and cliches from abroad. The PA is supported by a heterogenous collection of trade union members, radical teachers and students, die-hard nationalists, and disenchanted Social Democrats. It has an estimated 2,500 members, out of a total population of about 221,000. Its main strength rests in the Reykjavik area (where half of Iceland's population lives) and in the smaller fishing and processing towns along the eastern and northern coasts.

Communism has had a rather confusing and maverick history in Iceland. Its first organizational form was a secessionist left-wing splinter from the Social Democratic Party (Altyduflokkurinn; SDP) in 1930. There have never been any legal prohibitions against the Communists. In 1938—now considered its birth year—the Communist party withdrew from the Third International (Comintern), reconstituted itself to include more radical Social Democrats, and took the name of United People's Party-Socialist Party (Sameiningarflokkur altydu-Sosialistaflokkurinn/ UPP-SP). Even before this realignment the Icelandic Communist Party (Kommunistaflokkur Islands; ICP) had actively sought a "Popular front" with the Social Democrats. The new UPP-SP based their ideology on "scientific socialism-Marxism," and although there were no longer organizational ties to Moscow, the UPP-SP generally echoed Moscow's viewpoint on international affairs. In 1956 an electoral alliance was formed between most of the UPP-SP, members of the National Preservation Party, and dissident Social Democrats. This "People's Alliance" of 1956 strengthened the electoral position of the socialist left, while the merger with the National Preservation Party (formed in 1953 to protest Iceland's NATO membership and the NATO air base at Keflavik, and to promote a return to neutrality in foreign policy) made the PA the principal opponent of NATO membership. The People's Alliance became an openly avowed "Marxist political party" in November 1968 and so replaced the UPP-SP. Several elements in the National Preservation Party objected and, under the leadership of Hannibal Valdimarsson, formed the Organization of Liberals and Leftists (Samtök frjalslyndra og vinstri manna; OLL). In domestic policy the OLL is more pragmatically socialist than the PA's leading elements. There is also a pro-Soviet Marxist faction, the Organization of Icelandic Socialists (OIS), and a Trotskyite Revolutionary Communist League (Fylking Bytingarsinnadhra Kommunista; FBK), but both groups are without political significance. In April 1976 still another leftist group, the Icelandic Communist Party-Marxist-Leninist, was established by 30 delegates. Its chairman, Gunnar Andresson, claimed that the new party was the rightful heir to the original ICP, and the new group's program was to lead Icelandic workers against modern revisionism and the greatest danger of all, Soviet "social imperialism" (*Nordisk Kontakt*, no. 10).

The principal left-socialist/Communist group, currently represented by the PA, has consistently done well in Icelandic elections. Since World War II it has polled between 12 and 20 percent of the popular vote. In the 1971 parliamentary elections, the PA received 17.1 percent of the vote and won 10 of the 60 seats in the Althing (pariament). A coalition government was formed by Progressive (agrarian centrist) Olafur Johannesson, including the PA and the OLL. The PA became one of the few West European Communist parties to participate in a democratically elected government when two PA leaders, Ludvik Josefsson and Magnus Kjartansson, became minister of commerce and fisheries and minister of health, social security, and industries in the seven-man Johannesson government.

The June 1974 parliamentary elections brought the PA electoral gains (18.3 percent of the vote and 11 seats), but the OLL lost both votes and seats (down from 8.9 percent to 4.7, and from 5 mandates to 2). This brought a 30-30 tie in the Althing and two months of intense political negotiations. The election's biggest winner, the Independents, persuaded the Progressives to join a new majority coalition under Prime Minister Geir Hallgrímsson. The PA was thus forced back into the opposition.

Leadership and Organization. Ragnar Arnalds, former leader of the anti-NATO campaign, remains PA chairman, and Adda Bara Sigfusdottir is vice-chairman. Parliamentary leader of the PA Althing group is Ludvik Jósefsson, and Steingrimur Hermansson is second vice-president of the parliament. The Management Council is the party's highest authority between meetings of the 32-member Central Committee.

Party Internal Affairs. As related above, the recent history of Iceland's leftist and Communist movements has been one of factionalism, splits, and realignments. This has been especially true of the PA, whose parliamentary strength has fluctuated more because of intra-party disagreement than from lost popular support. The struggle between Hannibal Valdimarsson and the Communists for control of the PA in 1968 resulted in the forming of the OLL, which has captured seats in parliament which might otherwise have gone to the PA.

There have also been personality clashes within the remainder of the PA, such as that between the PA's two most influential members, Jóseffson and Kjartansson. During 1976, however, with Icelandic attention focused on the dramatic diplomatic crisis with Great Britain over the extension of fishing limits, the PA's internal politics were relatively calm.

The OLL would seem to be in the process of disintegrating after years of factionalism and eroding electoral support. The party's Reykjavik section is intent on continuing as a distinct party organization while the rural groups are anxious to cooperate closely with the Social Democrats. In October 1976 the OLL Executive Committee decided to cancel the party's National Congress and dissolve itself in favor of the small OLL parliamentary group. One of the OLL members of parliament has already announced his intention to join the PA. (*Nordisk Kontakt*, no. 15.)

Domestic Attitudes and Activities. Iceland continued to be buffeted by a severe economic crisis during 1976. In announcing his government's economic program to parliament in October 1975, Premier Geir Hallgrimsson warned that per capita national income was expected to fall by 9 percent during 1976, the largest reduction since national independence (*Nordisk Kontakt*, no. 13, 1975). Preliminary indications are that the fall was not quite so severe, but problems remained enormous. Iceland's chronic inflation, which had soared at 40 percent in 1974 and 50 percent in 1975, was expected to decline to 25-30 percent in 1976. These economic issues provided the PA with substantial ammunition for continuing attacks on the Independence-Progressive coalition.

During 1976 the problems of the economy were partly displaced by the even more critical question of Iceland's fishing limits, which returned as the main domestic and international concern. Iceland derives about 75 percent of its export earnings from the sales of fish and fish by-products. The fishing and fish processing industries are the country's largest employers. During the past decade, Iceland's economic prosperity has been increasingly threatened by the expanded operations of foreign fishermen, tougher competition for foreign markets, and declining fish resources. No other Western society is so dependent on a single commodity.

Iceland has for some years tried to control foreign access to its fishing grounds. A four-mile fishing limit, declared in 1952, was extended to 12 miles in 1958, and to 50 miles in 1972. Although each extension has provoked a "Cod War" with foreign, principally British, fishing fleets, these fleets still catch more than half of the fish netted around Iceland. Early in 1975, Iceland announced that it was unilaterally extending its fishing limits to 200 miles on 15 October, a month before the expiration of its 1973 two-year pact with Britain.

All political parties supported this measure as essential to the country's survival, but the Communists have been especially vehement in pushing for an extended limit. In December 1975 there were frequent clashes between the Icelandic Coast Guard and British trawlers and naval vessels. Mediation efforts by the NATO secretary-general were only partly successful, but after Britain withdrew its naval vessels Premier Hallgrímsson went to London for negotiations in late January 1976. These talks were inconclusive, and former PA fisheries minister Josefsson called for threats to the NATO base at Keflavik (ibid., no. 2). On 19 February diplomatic relations between Iceland and the United Kingdom were severed, and a few weeks later the PA proposed a 25 percent tariff surcharge on British goods.

Fortunately the Norwegian government, itself concerned about fishing limits, offered to mediate, and on 1 June a British-Icelandic agreement was announced in Oslo. The 200-mile limit prevailed, but Britain was to be granted limited fishing rights 20-30 miles off the Icelandic coast at least until 1 December 1976. On 11 November the Althing ratified the Oslo agreement by 39 to 17 with the PA voting against. PA spokesmen protested the delay in parliamentary consideration of the fishing agreement and stated that an agreement with Britain was superfluous since British capitulation was near. The role of the British navy had demonstrated the worthlessness of Icelandic NATO membership, the PA spokesmen concluded. (Ibid., no. 15.) Diplomatic relations between the two countries had been restored after the signing of the Oslo agreement.

International Views and Positions. As demonstrated during the latest fisheries dispute, the PA has consistently voiced a strong nationalist line. This has meant consistent opposition to Icelandic membership in NATO and to retention of the U.S. Icelandic Defense Force (the Keflavik base) in any form. The Communists' long-term objective has been and is an unarmed (except for the Coast Guard) and neutral Iceland.

The PA brought that sentiment to bear with its hard line in the 1974 Icelandic negotiations with the United States over the Keflavik NATO base. The PA advance in the 1974 elections may have been promoted by anti-NATO feelings, but the even larger gains of the Independence Party and the mass "Defend Our Land" petition campaign indicated that many Icelanders favor a more moderate security policy. The NATO base continues, however, to allow Icelandic governments to gain considerable leverage in political and economic dealings with other Western states. During the recent "Cod Wars" the Keflavik base agreement has always been Iceland's ultimate weapon.

Iceland has consistently had substantial trade with the USSR, and the PA has been among the most vociferous in extolling the advantages of trade with non-Western nations. In late October 1975, Iceland signed a five-year trade agreement with the USSR calling for the exchange of fishing products for Soviet raw materials and machinery. About 10 percent of Iceland's foreign trade is to be composed of Soviet-Icelandic trade.

International Party Contacts. The Icelandic Communists have consistently been absent from international Communist meetings and avoided contacts with foreign Communist movements. In fact, no other Western European Communist party has maintained such an isolationist position.

The PA does not maintain formal ties with the Communist Party of the Soviet Union, and it has condemned the Warsaw Pact invasion of Czechoslovakia in 1968. Accordingly, no PA representatives attended either the 25th Congress of the Soviet party in February 1976 or the conference of European Communist and workers' parties in East Berlin in June. In the past the PA has offered moral support for Communist parties, most notably those of the Romanians and the Yugoslavs, which are known for their independent or nationalistic views.

The PA strengthened its ties with another Communist center when Chairman Arnalds visited Italy as a guest of the Italian Communist Party (PCI) between 30 August and 5 September. (*L'Unità*, Rome, 5 September.)

Publications. The PA's central organ is *Thjodviljinn* (Will of the Nation), a daily newspaper in Reykjavik with a circulation of 8,400. The party also publishes a biweekly theoretical journal, *Ny Utsyn*. Outside the capital, there are at least two pro-Communist weeklies, *Verkamadhurinn* in Akureyri and *Mjolnir* in Siglufjördhur. The Trotskyite FBK publishes a monthly, *Neisti*, with a circulation of some 2,000. The publication of the fledgling Maoist organization is *Stettabarattan* (Class Struggle).

University of Massachusetts   Eric S. Einhorn
Amherst

Ireland

The Communist Party of Ireland (CPI) was founded on 14 October 1921 when the Socialist Party of Ireland decided to expel all dissenters and adhere to the Communist International. However, the party's initial existence was shortlived and was conditioned by the Civil War. The CPI was refounded in June 1933, the date now adopted by Irish Communists for its origin. The organizational structure of the CPI was disrupted during the Second World War largely as a result of the belligerent status of Northern Ireland and the neutrality of the South. In 1948 the southern Communists founded the Irish Workers' Party (IWP) and those in the North the Communist Party of Northern Ireland (CPNI). At a "Unity Congress" in Belfast on 15 March 1970 the two groups reunited, forming a united Communist Party of Ireland.

The CPI has about 500 members and has its main support among northern Protestants. Catholic Marxists in the South usually join the Official Sinn Fein or any one of about 20 tiny ultra-left parties.

The population of the Republic of Ireland is 2,978,248 and that of Northern Ireland 1,547,000.

Leadership and Organization. The CPI is divided into two branches, northern and southern. Overall direction is in the charge of a 23-member National Executive. The CPI's innermost conclave is the National Political Committee: Andrew Barr (chairman), Hugh Moore (secretary of the northern area), Sean Nolan, Michael O'Riordan (general secretary), Tom Redmond, and James Stewart (assistant general secretary).

In 1975 the CPI won official recognition in the South, thus enabling it to be registered as a political party. This means that its candidates' party membership is now officially recognized in parliamentary and local elections. The initial application had been turned down by the Registrar of Political Parties on the grounds that the CPI was not a genuinely national organization. However, the party won out when the Appeal Board announced on 12 December 1975 that they were satisfied that the CPI had a visible organization and was organized to contest Dail and local elections.

The CPI is not a significant party in either North or South and holds no seats in any legislative assembly. However, it is reputed to have a degree of influence within the Official Sinn Fein. In the South the party is a key component of the so-called Left Alternative which includes the Liaison Committee of the Labour Left, the Official Sinn Fein, the Socialist Party of Ireland, and the Union of Students in Ireland.

The Communists control a small youth organization, the Connolly Youth Movement (CYM).

Party Internal Affairs. The 16th Congress of the CPI was held in March 1975 in Dublin. The Congress adopted a resolution of 65 clauses which covered party attitudes on the political situation generally, the economic crisis, the EEC, Northern Ireland, and the nature of the Labour Party's participation in the government of the Republic.

The resolution stated CPI attitudes succinctly: "There is only one force and one movement in Ireland with the potential for bringing about the end of violence, the provision of jobs and the long term power to transform our country into a place where the interests of the working people are paramount: that is the organized working-class in the Irish labour and trade union movement" (Congress document).

Moreover the resolution called on the Labour Party to leave the government and instead to form an alliance with the CPI, the Official Sinn Fein, and such groups as tenants', small farmers' and students' organizations, the Irish Sovereignty Movement, and the Resources Protection Campaign. The resolution also called for a new secular constitution for the Republic, the introduction of inter-denominational education, and democratic rights in the fields of family planning and divorce.

The Connolly Youth Movement held a congress of its northern branch on 1 June 1975. The main preoccupation was with the perfecting of propaganda; the principal result was the launching of a new paper in the North called *Young Worker*.

A disturbing feature for the CPI in 1976 was the defection of many prominent members. In January four Dublin-based members of the National Executive resigned from the party. They were Patrick Carmody, George Jeffares, Michael O'Reilly, and Samuel Nolan. In the North many CPI members were known to have left the party and held talks with former members of the Irish Republican Socialist Party and the Peoples' Democracy. Little appears to have emerged from these discussions.

Domestic Attitudes and Activities. The fundamental objective of the CPI is the establishment of a united socialist republic in Ireland. In order to accomplish this the party is trying, by basing itself on the trade unions, to establish as broad a left-wing front as possible. Tactically, therefore, the CPI campaigns on the basis of fighting repression and sectarianism in the North, combating Labour's involvement in the Republic's coalition government, opposition to the rising unemployment rates of both the North and South, and fighting for equal pay and a halt to the deterioration of living standards.

In the North the CPI insists that prime responsibility for the conflict rests with the Unionists because of the latter's intransigence on the issue of democratic rights and also with the British government for pursuing what the CPI considers to be a policy of repression. According to the Communists, British Army involvement in the North constitutes a fundamental error in policy and has only served to escalate violence in the province. The CPI was particularly virulent in its detestation of the deployment of troops from the Special Air Service in January 1976: "The SAS is notorious throughout Britain's ex-colonies as the terror unit of the British Army. The announcement that it is being openly brought into Northern Ireland on active service will in itself act as a recruiting agent for the paramilitary, particularly for the Provisionals." (*Unity*, 10 January.) The CPI's hostility to the security forces is not confined to the Army: the Royal Ulster Constabulary is also seen as a repressive agency.

The CIP itself, however, eschews violence and is therefore opposed to all sectarian tendencies, preferring to seek a broadly based trade union orientated front embracing both Catholics and Protestants. It is accordingly antipathetic to the Provisional IRA, which it considers a promoter of sectarian strife. Similarly the CPI believes the Protestant paramilitary forces to be inherently anti-working class and spawned merely by the bigotry of the United Ulster Unionist Council.

The CPI seeks the immediate implementation of a bill of rights to guarantee fundamental liberties. In addition it endorses the program of the Northern Ireland Committee of the Irish Congress of Trade Unions as expounded in the NICTU's "Better Life for All" campaign. The objectives of this campaign are sixfold: security of employment and well-paid work, the right to live free from threats of intimidation, free association to secure peaceful change, good housing accommodation, equal educational opportunity, and adequate social services to protect the socially deprived.

The CPI claims to have been subjected to harassment by the British Army. In January, James Stewart, assistant secretary of the CPI, wrote to the then secretary of state for Northern Ireland, Merlyn Rees, complaining of military interference. His protests referred specifically to visits by soldiers of the 17/21st Lancers to the party's Belfast headquarters on 13, 23, and 31 December 1975 and 14 January 1976. He also requested the Northern Ireland Secretary to meet a CPI deputation and listen to their views on how to end the crisis.

In August 1975 the Protestant extremist organization, the Ulster Voluneer Force, named the CPI as a legitimate target for their murder squads, but little appears to have come of this.

The CPI fielded two candidates in the elections to the Northern Ireland Constitutional Convention, 1 May 1975. Both were unsuccessful.

In the South the CPI's policy statements differed little from previous years. It continues its campaign of opposition to the government on most issues, including state ownership, education, health, women's rights, civil liberties, unemployment, and the new emergency powers legislation. The CPI continues to base its hopes on a broad left-wing alliance though it acknowledges that it has no popular support for its policies. "The economic programme of the Left Alternative has shown how this is not a Utopian illusion, but, given the balance of political weight, can charter a way out which will benefit the vast majority of people" (*Irish Times*, 3 May 1976). The CPI's economic proposals include the setting up of a national development corporation, public ownership of banks, and the establishment of state oil and mineral companies.

The CPI was vehement in its opposition to the Irish government's stringent anti-terrorist laws, introduced in August. Party general-secretary O'Riordan denounced these measures as being both unnecessary and dangerous. He could see no signs of an impending terrorist offensive in the Republic and commented: "A more effective way to defeat the bombers and assassins has been shown by the women in Belfast who have organised a mass movement of protest in the streets" (quoted in *Morning Star*, London, 26 August).

A notable success for the CPI in 1975 was the election of Andrew Barr, its national chairman, to be president of the Irish Congress of Trade Unions and then to be the first Communist on the Executive Committee of the European Confederation of Trade Unions.

Another small success for the CPI was in the Union of Students of Ireland, which, with the cooperation of the Official Sinn Fein, it is alleged to dominate. The USI is pro-Moscow and generally devotes more attention to endorsing the foreign policies of the Kremlin than discussing the problems of students. The USI is linked to the International Union of Students in Prague.

There was a brief diversion in February 1976 when Gaeltacht councillors alleged that Communists had been acting subversively in the planning office of the Donegal County Council. In addition, the Gaeltacht councillors alleged that Communists had "played havoc" with Donegal planning schemes because of their disruptive work in housing organizations,language movements, and parents' groups. (*Irish Press*, 9 February.0

International Views and Party Contacts. The CPI is not associated with the phenomenon of Eurocommunism which was a characteristic feature of many West European parties in 1976. It does not hesitate to use phrases associated with Soviet hegemony of the Communist movement. Accordingly CPI statements and declarations on international affairs tended to be simply endorsements of Soviet foreign policy. For example, during the Angolan civil war the CPI completely supported the MPLA and urged China, the USA, Zaire, and Southern Africa to "leave Angola," but made no condemnation of the dramatic Soviet intervention in the war.

The CPI continued to call for Irish withdrawal from the EEC, which is deemed to have no remedy to offer for ameliorating the current economic crisis.

Among foreign contacts made by the CPI in recent times has been the visit of Michael O'Riordan to the 25th Congress of the Communist Party of the Soviet Union in March 1976. Vasil Bilák, a member of the Czechoslovak Communist party Presidium, received a CPI delegation on 2 August 1975. The delegation was headed by James Stewart and National Executive members Edwina Stewart and Samuel Sean. Stewart visited East Germany on 1-10 December 1975 and met members of the Central Committee of the Socialist Unity Party of Germany.

Publications. The CPI publishes the monthly *Irish Socialist* in Dublin; the *Irish Socialist Review*, a theoretical journal; and a weekly, *Unity*, published by the northern branch. The CYM publishes *Young Worker.*

London   Richard Sim

Italy

The Italian Communist Party (Partito Comunista Italiano; PCI) was founded in 1921 out of that faction of the Italian Socialist Party (PSI) which voted to accept the 21 conditions for membership in the Comintern.

In the 1976 general elections the PCI received 34.4 percent of the vote and 228 out of 630 seats in the Chamber of Deputies, and 116 out of 315 in the Senate. It numbered 1,806,000 members (TASS, 6 September) out of a national population of 56.2 million.

In 1976 the PCI was in a category by itself among Communist parties. Not a ruling party, it nevertheless could no longer be thought of as a party without state power. It took part directly in the government of six of the country's twenty regions, and indirectly in four more. Without counting the instances where it exercises indirect influence, the PCI ruled in 2,715 of the country's 7,900 municipalities. Among these were 40 out of 93 provincial or regional capitals, including Rome itself. In sum, the party held some official power over about half of Italy's population. Moreover, it controls a network of "mass organizations," labor unions, and cooperatives which are in themselves political and economic forces in Italian life. From the neighborhood to the factory, the Parliament, the board room, the judicial chambers, or the diplomatic conference room, the PCI's representatives make their influence felt. Thus, certain questions traditionally asked concerning political parties lose their value in the case of the PCI. For example, it does little good any more to ask what the PCI's budget is. The party can pay for services rendered by placing people in the state bureaucracy or in any of hundreds of firms. It also has a great deal to say about who gets what loans or contracts from government agencies. The desire not to run afoul of the PCI is doubtless one of the principal motives in Italian politics.

In 1976 the PCI was unquestionably the most important of Italy's political forces, despite the fact that the elections confirmed the place of the Christian Democratic Party (DC) as the top vote getter. But in 1976 all of the moderate parties traditionally allied with the DC in government coalitions withheld their support and, like the PCI, abstained on parliamentary votes of confidence. Thus DC governments became dependent on the PCI's sufferance.

The PCI's climb to its 1976 position began during the period 1931-43 when its then general secretary, Palmiro Togliatti, served in the Moscow offices of the Comintern (where he worked his way up to the post of secretary). During those years of exile the PCI lived on the resources of the Comintern, and the Italian Socialist Party (PSI) lived on those of the PCI. The bonds which grew between the PSI and PCI in those years—joint administration of labor, financial, and "mass" organizations—have never been broken. In 1948 the PCI and PSI, joined in an electoral front, directly confronted the Italian electorate with the choice between a Communist regime or a Western-style democracy. They suffered a crushing defeat. Since 1953 the two parties have touted their autonomy, but their policies have tended to be complementary. In 1953 the PSI's secretary, Pietro Nenni, received the Stalin Peace Prize, placed his party in the framework of Stalin's policy of "peaceful coexistence," and set its sights on entry into partnership with the governing Christian Democrats. In 1956 Khrushchev's denunciation of Stalin's activities during the years Togliatti had been secretary of the Comintern confronted Togliatti with new problems. But the PCI supported the PSI's campaign to convince the DC that there would be no social peace in Italy until the PSI's entry into the government. This event, known as the "Opening to the Left" was accomplished informally in 1960, and formally in 1963. Its principal feature was a "closing to the right." That is, the DC could no longer receive the support of Italian conservatives on pain of a resumption of pressure from the left. In exchange, the DC hoped the PSI would cut its ties with the PCI. But the PSI never did so. Moreover, in every presidential election in the Italian Parliament the PSI has voted with the PCI. (The PSI has a half million members and received 9.2 percent of the vote in 1976.) Since 1975 the PSI has refused to support any government—even by parliamentary abstention—unless that government earned the support of the PCI. Thus the PSI and PCI have effectively restricted the DC's use of its electoral superiority, and have forced it to bargain with them, in effect, on the PCI's terms.

The PCI's immediate aim, whether expressed in the formula "historic compromise" or "government of national unity," is the erasure of the distinction between "majority" and "opposition." But the party is less interested in cabinet posts than in two objectives: the acquisition of great numbers of key posts in the bureaucracy, police, military, and economy, and the "conditioning" of the major non-Communist parties.

The party's greatest difficulties stem from its being perceived by many Italians as dangerous. Hence, it has spared no effort to convince Italians that it would not institute a regime such as the USSR's, that it is not anti-religious, and that its greater infuence would not alter Italy's status as protégé and beneficiary of the USA. Indeed, the PCI currently claims that its aims are quite compatible with those of the most up-to-date elements of the Church and of the USA. It has eagerly cited any hint that either the Church or the U.S. government might agree with it, and deplored manifestations of the contrary.

The PCI is well aware that, since Italy is neither an island (as is Cuba) nor accessible to Soviet troops, the party's quest for power has had to be gradual and tenuous. Mindful of what befell the Allende government in Chile, the PCI wants to advance so that each step does not raise more opposition, but rather makes opposition less likely. Hence it is wary of taking governmental responsibility except as part of the broadest possible coalition of parties. It trusts that each of its advances will be accompanied by changes within the other coalition partners. To this end the PCI wants to put its own people in key posts without displacing so many people from other parties as to worsen relations with them. Also, while it must continue to keep the labor unions hostile to "the system," the PCI wants to keep the unions from plunging the nation into economic chaos. The continued pursuit of this strategy can be accomplished only if the Italian economy continues to be supported by foreign loans.

Leadership and Organization. The basic unit of the PCI is the section. There are 11,000 sections in localities and places of work throughout Italy. Party statutes call for them to hold annual conferences. These meetings are to be "open," so that members of other parties may be drawn into the discussion (*WMR*, July 1976). But meetings are orchestrated (*NYT*, 28 June). Candidates and resolutions are voted unanimusly. Sections elect representatives to plant, town, and area committees, and to 93 provincial and 17 other federations. All officials above the section level are full-time career employees of the PCI or of one of its affiliated organizations.

The federation committees and the 20 regional committees into which they are organized hold biennial congresses. They elect delegates to the quadrennial national congress (*WMR*, July). The Congress in turn elects a 177-member Central Committee, 53-member Central Control Commission, six-member Central Auditing Committee, 33-member Directorate, and eight-member Secretariat. Enrico Berlinguer is general secretary, and Luigi Longo is party president. In practice the general secretary rules the Secretariat, and superior bodies rule inferior ones according to invariably orthodox democratic centralism. The PCI has never dissimulated its attachment to this norm. Berlinguer has called it "the system which guarantees greater efficiency and greater democracy" (*Corriere Della Sera*, Milan, 15 June).

To join the PCI, according to Berlinguer, means "to make a choice entailing sacrifice and commitment, a choice that cannot be made lightheartedly," for those who join belong to a "political organization dedicated to struggle" (*L'Unità*, 28 March). This public emphasis on the burdens of membership coincides with the precipitous rise in the number of applications. Between 1 January and 1 September 1976 the PCI accepted a record 170,000 new members as reported by TASS (6 September). Indeed, just over half the 1.8 million members have joined since 1968. The party is aware that people seek it out to further their immediate interests, and encourages this (*WMR*, July). If they wish to advance, members must attend one year of cadre training at the party school, the purpose of which, according to Berlinguer, is "to develop our theoretical political activity . . . and to understand the party line in changing situations" (ibid., 28 March). The first principle of this line is party unanimity. Dissent is extremely rare, and is punished by expulsion. Berlinguer contends, however, that the party cannot afford expulsions, and that therefore, even if the party wanted to do authoritarian things, "then the first to desert us would be our members and voters" (*La Stampa*, Turin, 25 June).

The party headquarters in Rome contains 17 working sections, meant to resemble shadow ministries. Over and probably above these are "institutes" for international policy, state reform, and economic policy (headed by Giancarlo Pajetta, Pietro Ingrao, and Giorgio Amendola). On the same level are the committees on local government (Armando Cossuta) and labor (Giorgio Napolitano). This suggests that the PCI continues to employ much of its talent in areas not specified in the scheme, and that it has not altered the traditional pattern of assigning overlapping tasks to several party bureaucracies in competition with one another.

The party's leading personalities are Enrico Berlinguer (biographical note in *YICA, 1976*, pp. 601-2); Giorgio Napolitano, who may be in charge of most mass organizations in addition to the labor unions; Armando Cossuta, who in addition to local government is in charge of commercial relations with Eastern Europe, and is particularly close to the Soviet leadership; Giancarlo Pajetta, who is Sergio Segre's superior in foreign affairs; Pietro Ingrao, who from his post as president of the Chamber of Deputies is in charge of legislative matters; Paolo Buffalini, the party's expert on the Church and the DC; Ugo Pecchioli, in charge of relations with sympathizers in the armed forces; Sergio Flamigni, concerned with police matters; Ugo Spagnoli the party's chief lawyer, vice-president of the Judiciary and Investigative Committee of the Chamber, who supervises the defense of ultra-leftists in trouble; Eugenio Peggio, an exceptionally ambitious but polished political economist who shares with Luciano Barca the task of representing the party on economic matters; and Giovanni Cervetti, who heads the party's organization section, once headed by Berlinguer. In addition there are Giovanni Berlinguer (physician, Enrico's brother), Nilde Jotti, Giuseppe d'Alema, Giorgio Chiaromonte, Guido Cappellone, and Tullio Vecchietti.

The PCI's published final balance sheet for 1975 (*L'Unità*, 18 January 1976) showed total expenditures of 27 billion lire—about $35 million at current rates of exchange, up from 23.8 billion lire in 1974. Forty percent of the sum was from state financing, the rest from members' dues, festivals, and contributions from the salaries of its members of Parliament. But this budget, both on the revenue and the expenditure side, covers only between half and a fourth of the party's activities (see Michael Ledeen and Clare Sterling, *New Republic*, New York, 3 April). On the revenue side, the practice of turning over one's paycheck to the party and receiving a lesser amount is not limited to members of Parliament, but extends to all party officials placed in important positions. This benefits the party treasury and reminds the officials in question that their real employer is the PCI. The PCI openly collects money from the people it places on jobs.

The budget specifies that "there have been no contributions from companies, other organizations or trade union or other associations." Thus the party claims "clean hands" (*L'Unità*, 18 January). It has always pointed with pride to the economic strength of the National League of Cooperatives (annual turnover $4 billion in 1974) and other auxiliaries engaged in trade with the Soviet bloc. But in 1976 the PCI felt obliged to deny publicly that it benefited financially from them, though it could not deny they were "a valuable contribution to the consolidation of democracy which coincides with workers' interests" (ibid., 11 April).

The PCI's economic activities have taken many forms. Immediately after World War II the PCI formed a company called SIMES to exploit a monopoly, granted by Stalin himself, on the supplying of Italian citrus to the USSR. The PCI also purchased meat in Hungary for sale in Italy. Because it was allowed to buy low and sell high behind the Iron Curtain, the party made money. It also established a company, "Falchimex," to act as middleman for Western businessmen who wanted to sell strategic materials to the USSR, and other companies to facilitate various kinds of trade with the East. By 1976 it appeared probable that about half the one billion dollars' worth of meat imported into Italy came from behind the Iron Curtain, and that the PCI gained something above 5 percent of the total value of the transaction. "Restital" was the foremost of five companies in this trade. Restital itself acted as a holding company for export-import ventures. It was headed by Enzo Gemma, former secretary of the PCI's Alessandria provincial federation and Luigi Longo's trusted man. Other companies were dealing in products such as lumber (LASA, URE) and petroleum equipment (COIN, CLERICI). Although extensive lists of companies controlled by the PCI have been published (*Borghese*, Milan, 28 March), these are not exhaustive.

In February-March 1976 the PCI began to restructure its participation in business. Restital (whose connection on the one hand with the PCI and the USSR and on the other with such renowned and corrupt DC figures as Camillo Crociani had embarrassed the party) was closed, as were several other companies. Their assets were bought by individuals friendly to the party. This seems to indicate that the new pattern of PCI participation in business is that set by the conglomerate "GI and GI." This is a partnership owned by two Communist businessmen, Pietro Gibertoni and Nelson Giovanardi. It includes 10 companies in the food and food processing field, three textile mills, a building company, two real estate companies, and a development company. The whole is probably worth not less than a billion dollars. Such obligations as the owners may be under to the PCI are partisan, not legal arrangements. The party certainly provides these businessmen with labor peace, with influence in local and national governments, and with contacts in Eastern Europe. But the PCI cannot be held responsible for what such "independent" businessmen do. Hence this is the kind of operation toward which the party is moving.

The financial link between the PCI and its cooperatives, which are engaged in everything from making salami and television sets to insurance, house construction, and retail sales, is not clear. The SIEM real estate cooperative in Parma, and its cashier, Renato Corsini (who was also the PCI's representative on the local government's home loan board), have been implicated in an attempt to profit from the rezoning of land. After a series of complicated transactions, from which leading local Communists profited, it appears that the company received payment for one more apartment than it had built. Double payments may well be the means by which the PCI's affiliated cooperatives pay their dues. (*New Republic*, 3 April.)

Another type of transaction also involves the cooperatives. Gino Sferza, president of the department store chain "Standa," is accused of making political payoffs to expand his business. He confessed publicly that one such payoff was to the Communist local government of Casoria (Naples province) in the form of a building put up by Standa for a retail cooperative affiliated with the PCI (*Il Tempo*, Rome, 21 March).

In 1976 there was no public confirmation of the persistent rumors that the PCI receives direct cash grants from the USSR to cover the subsidies the PCI gives to Communist parties like Spain's. No such evidence has come to light since Giulio Seniga defected with such moneys in the 1950s.

Auxiliary Organizations. The PCI has not changed its evauation (14th Party Congress, 1975) of its network of auxiliary organizations as one of the greatest achievements of the "popular movement." Of these, only the Italian Communist Youth Federation (FGCI) is formally affiliated with the party. It has 140,000 members. Its expenses in 1975 cost the party 350 million lire ($425 thousand) (*L'Unità*, 18 January 1976). The FGCI continued in 1976 to recoup the membership losses it suffered in the late 1960s and early 1970s. It did so by advertising the party's commitment to the proposition that every Italian youth has the right to a job. This was particularly evident at the FGCI National Congress in Ravenna (ibid., 31 July; TASS, 1 August). The party is encouraging young people to come to it to be placed.

The largest and most important auxiliary is the General Confederation of Italian Labor (CGIL), with 3,827,000 members. It is the largest element in an alliance which also includes the other two major labor federations, the CISL (formerly Christian Democratic) and the UIL (formerly Social Democratic). The CGIL's importance within the new unit continued to increase. The only threat to PCI influence in the three confederations comes from the ultra left (see below).

As the PCI edged closer to power in 1976, one of its biggest tasks was to control the labor movement's dynamism. This had served both the party and the unions well. The political system was forced to its knees by political strikes. Despite the raging inflation, union members who were employed were prosperous as never before. But unemployment was causing strains within the unions and "bourgeois radicals" continued to push for higher wages regardless of inflation. Hence the PCI sought to turn the labor movement's attention to the political goals of control over hiring and investment. For example, the metalworkers union (FIOM) in Milan province alone held 225 factory council meetings in which the following motto was agreed to: "Collective bargaining, power, and employment are most important aspects of united strategy" (*WMR*, February, p. 138). When one counts all unions and provinces, one realizes the size of the effort. The PCI claims it "has committed all its forces" (ibid., p. 139) to the achievement of the labor movement's goals—and implicitly of its own goals within the labor movement. Despite talk of a revolt by the labor movement after the PCI agreed to support the government's austerity program in October, the CGIL, CISL, and UIL held their organizations firmly behind the plan.

The PCI continued to emphasize the labor movement's autonomy (see *YICA, 1976*, p. 179). The CGIL's secretary, Luciano Lama, a member of the PCI's Central Committee, declared its official neutrality in the 1976 election campaign. But the PCI's representatives in the organization, as usual, worked for the party, not in the role of leaders of the CGIL, but as members of the PCI. On the other hand, the PCI continued to promise none too subtly that if it were granted power, its influence over the labor movement could bring "order and discipline" to the factories (*Corriere Della Serra*, 4 June). TheCGIL continued to strengthen its action squads, the Proletarian Police, as well as its participation in anti-Fascist committees. It continued also its role in Moscow's World Federation of Trade Unions.

The city, provincial, and regional administrations in which the PCI plays either the major or a minor role are not, strictly speaking, organs of the party. But, given that the Communists in these governments, with few exceptions, are employees of the PCI, it is not surprising that they tend to turn these holdings to the party's account. The coordination of the party's actions in local, provincial, and regional government continued to be entrusted to a central party working section. All Communist-controlled cities instituted—semiofficially, until the Italian government recognized the fait accompli in law on 8 April—*comitati de quartiere* or "neighborhood committees" to establish contact between citizens and city hall (*Economist*, 28 February). But these are almost everywhere run by the PCI and play an important role in its strategy (*YICA, 1976*, p. 180). The party uses local governments as founts of patronage. In Naples the outstanding act of the administration of Mayor Maurizio Valenzi was the creation of 2,000 new city jobs. They went either to leftists or to key defectors from the opposition. In Turin the administration of Diego Novelli purchased 250 houses for leftists. Milan's Aniasi (PSI), who runs an administration of which the PCI is the largest component, has done similar things on a larger scale. In Florence the administration was able to secure bank financing for a public works project dear to the unions. Of course, the PCI, its operatives, the unions, and mass organizations do not make trouble for Communist-run administrations (*Wall Street Journal*, 2 March). But more significantly, the local governments matter to the PCI because under their aegis the growth of the entire gamut of mass organizations may be fostered.

The following regions are administered by PCI-PSI coalitions: Piemonte, Liguria, Emila-Romagna, Toscana, Umbria, Lazio. The PCI also exercises substantial influence in the administrations of Lombardia, Marche, Campania, Sicilia. The following provincial capitals are administered by PSI-PCI coalitions (occasionally with the help of the Social Democrats and the Republicans): Aosta, Turin (population 1.3 million), Vercelli, Asti, Alessandria, Milan (2 million), Pavia, Cremona, Mantua, Venice (0.5 million), Imperia, Savona, Genoa (1 million), La Spezia, Piacenza, Parma, Reggio, Modena, Bologna, Forli, Ravenna, Ferrara, Massa, Pisa, Leghorn, Grossetto, Siena, Arezzo, Florence (0.5 million), Pistoia, Pesaro, Urbino, Perugia, Terni, Rieti, Rome (3 million), Naples (1.5 million), Cosenza, and Sassari.

The PCI's most spectacular acquisition in 1976 was Rome. It received 35.5 percent of the city's vote to the DC's 33.1 percent. But even with the help of both the PSI and the Social Democrats, the DC's erstwhile partners, the PCI only mustered 39 out of 80 council seats. Its election of a mayor was made possible by the benevolent abstention of the Republicans (PRI). Just as in Naples, Milan, Asti, and elsewhere, the PCI was able to achieve a majority by purchasing the necessary edge. This has greater significance for national politics than the fact that Giulio Argan is mayor of Rome.

The National League of Cooperatives (2,412,000 members, $4 billion annual turnover) increased in importance because of the aforementioned change in the party's financial arrangements. The Association of Democratic Lawyers registered a significant increase in importance. The adoption in 1976 of proportional representation for the election of the Superior Council of the Italian judiciary meant that after the elections of 13 October the two factions of the judiciary friendliest to the PCI—Magistratura Democratica and Impegno Costituzionale (combined strength about 30 percent of Italian judges)—were able to exercise greater influence in Italian law. In the Italian bureaucracy, each ministry contains an organized faction of officials friendly to the PCI. In the Foreign Ministry, for example, this faction calls itself "Farnesina Democratica."

The PCI's traditional auxiliaries, associated with their respective Moscow-line international organizations, continued to operate as in 1975. These include, for example, the Union of Italian Women, Association of Democratic Journalists, and Union of Popular Sport. So did the anti-fascist committees (see *YICA, 1976*, pp. 183-84).

Party Internal Affairs. The only publicly known, significant developments within the PCI in 1976 centered on a plenum of the Central Committee held in Rome on 20 October. On this occasion Berlinguer reduced the size of the party's top body, the Secretariat, and replaced two of the members elected at the 14th Congress. The new appointee is Giovanni Cervetti, who replaced Ugo Pecchioli, and is in charge of the Party's organizational section, once headed by Berlinguer. All votes at the plenum were unanimous.

The meeting was held against a background of dissatisfaction on the part of some members with the party's passive support of the government's relatively austere economic program. The *New York Times* and *Washington Post* (21 October) referred to "a rare display of public disunity" in the Central Committee. They cited Luigi Longo's statement of the obvious truth that "the great mass of the working class" did not clearly understand the Party's position, as well as Giorgio Amendola's statement that the Party's course is the best under the circumstances, and that it would be in the interest of the working class to clarify this. The complementarity of the two positions is highlighted by the fact that the same Amendola, also responding to the same dissatisfaction in the ranks, had earlier suggested the party would soon demand more from the DC in exchange for its cooperation. But the *New York Times* (30 September) took this statement also as "dissent," despite its acknowledgment of Amendola's denial of "a conflict between Amendola's hurry and Berlinguer's caution."

There is no doubt, however, that the process of applying the brakes on the unions is causing difficulties within the party. But the official acts of the three labor confederations against the policy of austerity have been incomparably milder than previous anti-government efforts.

Domestic Views and Activities. In 1976 the PCI worked to eliminate the DC's insistence that the rules of democracy demand that the party with the greatest number of votes should govern and the runner-up be in opposition. The PCI sought to convince the DC that it would allow only government by agreement between the "anti-Fascist" parties of the "constitutional arc" (the DC, PCI, PSI, Social Democrats, Republicans, and Liberals). Thus, as the PCI sought the erasure of one political distinction, it sought to establish another—that between the "legitimate" political forces, whose consensus would be Italy's only law, and all other political forces which now exist or might spring up in the future.

In 1976 the PCI explained that its strategy results directly from the nature of the Italian polity. Thus it cited Antonio Gramsci's judgment that capturing control of a Western government will not give one control over its society. In the West, social institutions are independent of government. Each is a bastion from which oppositon to socialist government may sally forth. Thus Berlinguer argued in 1973 that the Chilean workers' movement took control of the government unmindful that the bastions of civil society remained unconquered and posed a mortal danger. The PCI contends that on this Gramscian basis Togliatti worked out the party's "position warfare strategy, i.e., the Italian road to Socialism: a powerful and united mass movement attacks and besieges all the 'bastions' of Italian civil society, and develops democracy to its ultimate, Socialism" (*WMR*, July 1976). Hence party spokesmen stressed the continuity of the party's emphasis on alliances with "all popular forces" in all forums, including the U.S. journal *Foreign Affairs* (July).

Occasionally, however, the PCI has sought to represent its alliance strategy as "a new and different thing." Thus Giancarlo Pajetta, in an important article in *Rinascita* (28 November 1975), wrote that the party bases its actions on the recognition that society is composed of various interest groups, each of which, however, is moved by "similar needs." The party must place them all within the framework of the "democratic movement." The party's role here seems to be the coordination of interest groups. Thus the working class' hegemony is exercised through a "much different process." According to Pajetta, the "dictatorship of the proletariat" may be achieved just as the "dictatorship of the bourgeoisie" once was—by means which vary from place to place. Therefore, dictatorship should not be confused with tyranny. Even though, according to Pajetta, the complex articulation of Western society "represents an obstacle to the construction of a society whose aim would be a class-less society," he promises that the PCI would permit "an articulation, let us even say a social, pluralism." Regarding personal rights, Pajetta stated that they are "[in our situation] the most appropriate instruments for socialist change."

The PCI affirmed on countless occasions that its distinctive raison d'être remained unchanged. The two most prominent were Berlinguer's interview with the *Corriere Della Sera* (15 June), in which he stated that though the party might propound social-democratic policies, it differs from the Social Democratic Party in that it sees these policies not as ends in themselves, but as means for the overcoming of bourgeois society; and his speech at the *Unità* festival on 20 September. There he said, "It is being asked whether we Communists are taking the road to becoming a social-democratic party. Our party has remained, remains, and will remain a Communist party. To be and remain such means first of all that in whatever circumstance (even when one must demonstrate realism and flexibility), one must not lose sight, not even for a single moment, of the seeds for which we are fighting: the emancipation of workers and of all society, the construction of a society superior to the bourgeois society in everything and for everything." (*L'Unità*, 21 September.)

The PCI believes that, in order to change society, it must have access to it. It says the current crisis dates back to the break which occurred between the PCI and the nation's other "anti-Fascist forces" shortly after World War II. That break made contact difficult between the PCI and the economic, labor, religious, and social organizations affiliated with other parties. "From that rupture, which led to the discrimination against the PCI, derived a method of government" in which the Christian Democrats were able to form majorities and govern while the PCI was relegated to sterile opposition. (PCI leadership statement, ANSA, 24 April.) Now the strength of the workers movement is forcing the "anti-Fascist" parties to realize that the breach must be repaired and that, once again, one cannot govern Italy exept with the concurrence of all six "anti-Fascist" parties of the "constitutional arc." On one level, the meaning of the terms "historic compromise" and "emergency government" is rule by the "constitutional arc."

According to the PCI, the historic compromise-emergency government would be a dynamic arrangement. Since its very establishment is opposed by elements of the parties within the "arc," that establishment would tend to transform those parties. The case of the DC is clear: a party formed largely to keep the Communists out of power in Italy can hardly bring the PCI into the government without losing adherents. But there would be no place for these to go except out of the "constitutional arc," and out of the new definition of legitimacy in Italian politics. Presumably all of the party organizations within the arc would have an incentive to maintain their joint hold on power against those outside.

The PCI sees the DC as composed of a variety of groups, only some of which are not disposed to working with it. The PCI is not generally disposed toward simply wooing away the DC's left wing. This would lead to the formation of a classical-type conservative party, "purged of the 'pollution of the peoples' problems.' " People who vote for theDC and are used to working through DC organizations should not be given an incentive to "rancor and plans for revenge." Rather, the PCI should aim at making those very organizations incapable of anti-Communism. The PCI prefers "making use of the contradiction existing within the DC in order to avoid counterpositions and to ease relations with moderate forces." This is because "where poltical alignments are in fact 'simplified,' the capacity for social transformation by the working class is reduced to the minimum." (*L'Unità*, 21 January.) Clearly the PCI sees alliance as a means of transforming the DC. Thus Buffalini said: "We have never imagined that the historic compromise could be implemented without a profound change in the policies of and the political balances within the DC" (*L'Espresso*, Rome, 18 April). Other party spokesmen regularly say that the purpose of the historic compromise is the liquidation of the DC power structure. In sum, the PCI's strategy regarding the DC is not to provoke it to a frontal encounter (Nilde Jotti, *Il Settimanale*, Milan, 12 November 1975), but to offer cooperation in all fields (Pajetta, *L'Unità*, 23 September 1976), and to make alliance attractive to those many Christian Democrats used to "sailing with the wind" (Pajetta, ibid., 27 March).

As its strategy toward the DC has unfolded, the PCI has had to maintain its ties with the PSI. In 1976 perhaps even more than in 1975, the PSI voiced misgivings about following the PCI's lead. But despite these, its adherence was thoroughgoing. Polls at the beginning of the year showed that PSI voters distrusted the Communists (*L'Espresso*, 9 November 1975). The then party secretary Francesco de Martino expressed mistrust of the PCI's commitment to liberty, and of its connections with the authoritarian power structure in Eastern Europe. Above all, he was fearful that, as the PCI dealt with the larger DC organization, the PSI would lose its place as the PCI's foremost ally. (Ibid.) This fear, combined with its long tradition of "Massimalismo" ("Maximalism"), overcame its mistrust and led the PSI to express preference for a government based on the PSI-PCI alliance and incuding whatever bourgeois leftist elements might care to join. The PSI, at its 40th Congress, went so far as to brand the PCI's proposal for a "historic compromise" an obstacle to an otherwise thoroughgoing cooperation among left-wing forces (ANSA, 8 March). In 1976 the PCI continued its earlier assurances to the PSI that the latter was "essential and irreplaceable" in the common struggle for socialism. At the PSI Congress, Buffalini, member of the PCI Politburo, said that the search for alliances with Catholics is only meant to avoid a repetition of Allende's fate, and "not only does not hinder, but in fact stimulates and contributes to stronger unity within the working class and among its parties" (*L'Unitá*, 5 March). This, he added, was the "only correct" interpretation of the historic compromise. Despite its misgivings, however, the PSI throughout 1976 did not waver from its position that it would deal with the DC only if the DC simultaneously dealt with the PCI. The PSI Central Committee, in a rare and impressive show of unity, approved the notion of a joint DC-PCI-PSI government (*Il Giornale*, Milan, 17 November).

Two of the minor parties held congresses which radically changed their previous opposition to cooperation with the PCI. In the PSDI (the Social Democratic Party), leftist factions unseated party secretary Mario Tanassi. The PLI (Liberals), by electing Valerio Zanone party secretary, shifted from the right of the DC to a position "somewhere between the Christian Democrats and the Communists." (ANSA, 16 March, 13 April.) The attitude of the PRI (Republicans) remained ambiguous (*Corriere Della Sera*, 18 February). Hence the PCI singled out the PRI from among the minor parties for criticism and threat.

The political context in which the PCI pursued its strategy in 1976 may be divided into four periods: (1) the period preceding the calling of national elections, (2) the election campaign, (3) the negotiations for the formation of a post-election government, and (4) the difficulties with economic austerity.

(1) On 7 January the Moro-La Malfa (DC-PRI) cabinet, which had governed Italy since the 15 June 1975 local elections, resigned because the PSI had withdrawn its "benevolent abstention." Although it was arithmetically possible for the DC to build majority coalitions with the MSI and the liberals or with the center-left, the former course was ruled out by the experience of leftist violence in recent years (especially against the centrist coalition of 1972-73). The latter was impossible because the PSI would support the government only if the PCI did so (cf. Berlinguer's speech in Parliament, ANSA, 20 February). On the other hand, the PCI emphatically did not want the government to call new elections (TASS, 8 January). Indeed it judged the PSI imprudent for starting the crisis (*L'Unità*, 8 January; *L'Espresso*, 11 January). Elections, according to the PCI, work directly against the party's alliance strategy because they give the leaders of other parties the incentive to emphasize the differences between themselves and the PCI. The party especially warned the PSI not to shun compromise on issues like abortion, which involve principle.

On 10 February, Aldo Moro formed a one-party (DC) cabinet, Italy's 38th since Fascism. The PCI encouraged the PSI's abstention in its favor. On the same day the PCI Directorate issued a call for "all democratic forces and especially the DC, to come to terms seriously with the Communist question" and not allow themselves to split over the question of abortion (*L'Unità*, 11 February). But in the following two months the PSI continued to press for the DC's capitulation on that issue. The DC refused to give in, and with the votes of the rightist Italian Social Movement (MSI), beat the entire united Left. In retaliation the PSI announced it would cease its benevolent abstention, which had upheld the DC cabinet. (It went so far as to say it would welcome a referendum on abortion, for which the PCI called it irresponsible. (ANSA, 3 April.) There were then but two practical possibilities. When the DC rejected an arrangement with the PCI (ibid., 8 April), new elections became inevitable. They were set for 20 June.

(2) The abortion issue was barely touched on in the campaign. The PCI sees it strictly in political terms as something which can make difficult the rapprochement of "progressives of Christian and Socialist provenance." Given its "progressivist" constituency, the PCI supports abortion-on-demand. But it is not averse to compromise with the DC, and did not mention the subject during the campaign. Rather, both the PCI and the DC, following recent practice, campaigned by attacking each other's general "image" with the general public and by trying to marshal their clienteles. In this regard, the PCI's well-publicized and growing ability to dispense jobs was a strong asset (*NYT*, 13 June).

The PCI's major strategic objective was the blurring of the old distinction between majority and opposition and the establishment of a new distinction. Therefore, at the outset of the campaign, it made clear that, regardless of how it did at the polls, even if it and the PSI won a relative majority, it would still seek an arrangement with the DC, being "convinced that the DC's conservative and anti-unitary forces can be hit more effectively in this way" (*L'Unità*, 24 April). Therefore, the PCI tried not to campaign so hard as to complicate the post-election negotiations. The PCI had feared that the DC, to appeal to its largely anti-Communist electorate, would commit itself "never" to consider a coalition with the PCI. It did this on 20 May. But the PCI repeatedly warned the DC not to let the election atmosphere make it unmindful of the political realities—that is, the PCI's power—it would have to face whatever the outcome.

Hence the PCI spent most of its campaign countering the DC's charges that the PCI would take away Italy's liberties, its religion, and its good relations with the munificent West. In sum, in all but the party press, it sought to convey the impression of itself as a highly professional, highly moral group of reformists who happened to be encumbered with the name "Communist." Its commitment to socialism would not endanger private property, its commitment to atheism would pose no danger to the Holy See, its ties to the USSR would not adversely affect Italy's love affair with the USA, and its monolithic internal structure would not seek to change Italy's political pluralism. To bolster these points, the PCI included in its lists of candidates men not previously known by the public to be associated with the party. Here are the most prominent: Altiero Spinelli had been in charge of the Common Market's industrial and technological policies since 1970. He had formally left the PCI in 1937. Raniero La Valle had been editor of the DC daily newspaper *Il Popolo*, and Mario Gozzini of the newspaper of the Italian Bishops' Conference. Both had been raised to their posts by Pope Paul VI, but both had also urged and practiced a rapprochement with the PCI. Nino Pasti, until 1969 a four-star general in the Italian Air Force and member of the NATO military committee, had not been known as a friend of the PCI.

In the 1976 campaign the PCI had to face stronger opposition from the Catholic Church than in the previous fifteen years. Beginning in November 1975, the Church tentatively reversed the policy of accommodation with the left which had led it to drop its customary appeal to Catholics prior to the 1975 elections. This might have been due to the left's pressure for abortion, or to the moves by thousands of leftist city administrations to cut off public funds for Church-run schools and social welfare activities (*Washington Post*, 17 December 1975). In December, Cardinal Poletti, speaking for the Italian Conference of Bishops, declared that Marxism and Christianity are incompatible, and that Marxism leads to slavery. During the campaign the Holy See reaffirmed Pope Pius XII's warning that Catholics who vote for the PCI are making themselves liable to excommunicatin. The PCI's answer to this was to name La Valle and the others to its electoral lists. The Pope expressed his anger at their treason (*NYT*, 18 May 1976), but did not excommunicate any of them, much less PCI voters.Indeed, even Don Luigi Franzoni, a priest who had actually taken a membership card in the PCI (ibid., 5 August), was merely defrocked. The PCI made much of this.

The 1976 election campaign occurred in an atmosphere of violence. However, the threats of the minuscule self-styled Fascist organization "New Order-Black Order" (ANSA), 13 May) were followed by only one shooting. The shooting of a left-wing disrupter at an MSI election rally, in which MSI deputy Sandro Saccucci was implicated, was highly publicized. Otherwise, with minor exceptions, the violence was perpetrated by leftist groups which claim to be Communist (see below, "Competing Communist Organizations"). The PCI itself maintains a capability for violent action in the CGIL's Proletarian Police and in the anti-Fascist committees. During 1976 these committees prevented dozens of MSI campaign appearances.

Moreover, since the violence usually strikes those the PCI has labeled enemies of the people—conservative politicians, journalists, and businessmen—it provides incentive against running afoul of the "popular forces." The PCI presents itself to the public as the party whose presence in power will calm he people's legitimate anger. But the PCI blames violence—even that against Fascists—on Fascist provocateurs. Thus, after the murder of Enrico Pedenovi, MSI provincial counselor for Milan, the PCI-PSI administration said, "The goal of the current wave of violence was that of national and international Fascism—the overthrow of the government" (ANSA, 30 April). The party routinely speaks of a "strategy of tension" by means of which unknown powers are attempting to lay the groundwork for a rightist coup d'état. If the perpetrators of violent acts are not outright agents provocateurs, they are "groups notorious for their adventurism." The PCI has repeatedly appealed to its members to forego spontaneous violence and to "isolate the forces and groups of provocation and disorder." (*L'Unità*, 9 April.)

At the end of the campaign a national poll by "Demoskopea" showed that the electorate by very wide margins considered the PCI superior to the DC in every category, from honesty to organization. Nonetheless, the same poll showed that, when asked if they would rather be governed by the PCI or the DC, only 35 percent of Italian people chose the former (*L'Espresso*, 13 June).

On 20 June the PCI received 12.6 million votes for the Chamber of Deputies—34.4 percent of the total—and 227 seats, for an increase of 3.5 million votes, 7 percentage points, and 48 seats over its performance in 1972. The DC recouped the losses it had suffered in 1975 and, as in 1972, received 38.7 percent of the vote and 263 seats. Its success was at the expense of the right, and of the center parties which had moved left. The PCI's gains also came at the expense of its kindred party, the PSI However, as a whole, the PCI-PSI coalition increased its strength from 37 to 44 percent of the vote. Giacomo Sani (drawing from the research of Giovanni Sartori) shows convincingly that the left's gains were due in about equal proportions on the one hand to its greater success in recruiting first-time voters, while a smaller proportion of its electorate was reduced by death, and on the other to a net shift of voters from the center parties to the left. (Sani, "The PCI on the Threshold," *Problems of Communism*, November-December 1976, pp. 27-51.)

(3) The election did not change the DC's status as the party of relative majority. But it added to the PCI's political influence. Thus, while arithmetically options were available to the DC for the formation of a government without leave of the PCI, the latter's influence upon the DC's possible partners foreclosed them (ANSA, 1 July). In its formal post-election statement, the PCI directorate declared there coud be "no stable and secure way out of this crisis without resolving the problem of participation of the entire workers' and popular movement in the political leadership of the country" (*L'Unità*, 25 June).

The PCI's primary objective in the negotiations leading to a new government was to bring home to the DC that, regardless of its promises to stand on its rights as the majority party (*NYT*, 1 July; ANSA, 24 June), in the new situation the PCI could not be relegated to opposition, and that therefore the DC could not govern against the wishes of the Communists. Hence, for the PCI, the form of the official negotiations was as important as their outcome. The first stage involved the organization of Parliament. The PCI successfully insisted not only on a number of posts, but, more important, that the decisions be made by the unanimous consent of the six parties of the "constitutional arc." This resulted in election of Pietro Ingrao to the presidency of the Chamber of Deputies, and of other Communists to the chairmanship of the Finance, Public Works, Constitutional Affairs, and Transport committees.

As premier-designate Giulio Andreotti sought support for a new cabinet, he faced the demand for "official" negotiations. For the PCI all other considerations were subordinate to this one.

The agreement to establish the new government, formally announced on 4 August, provided for a "monochrome" DC government, whose existence would depend on the joint abstention of the other five parties of the "constitutional arc." During the debate on the vote of confidence, Berlinguer declared the cabinet would stay in office only so long as the PCI deemed it useful, and that the joint abstention of the five parties was the first step in the achievement of a government of national unity (AP, 11 August). Giorgio Amendola said the significant fact about the new government was that it marked "a recognition of the relationship of powers and a shift away from the old discrimination against the Communists" (*L'Unità*, 4 August). On another occasion the PCI organ exulted that the DC's policy—stated as recently as 15 July—of distinguishing between the roles of the majority and opposition had been broken (ibid., 30 July).

(4) After the installation of the Andreotti government, the PCI continued to explain—to what extent in order to pacify internal recalcitrance, one cannot say—that it would continue to exact compensation for its abstention, and that this price would have to include participation in the government. In this vein Longo said: "This compensation can only be the certainty for all Italians that the efforts and discomforts which will have to be made and suffered will serve not only to extract us from these straits, but to create the conditions for moving on from an economic and government system which has brought us to the present difficulties" (ibid., 10 October).

The most pressing difficulties which the new government faced stemmed from the state of the Italian economy—inflation was about 20 percent, unemployment 5 percent, the lira dwindling, and the balance of payments highly unbalanced. Actually, the situation had been managed only on the basis of massive foreign loans. In the first half of 1976 the lira lost a third of its exchange vaue. These conditions were due primarily to high labor costs due to high union wage scales indexed to the cost of living, and to high absenteeism. The PCI officially recognized that unit labor costs in Italy should be competitive. But this goal, said Eugenio Peggio, can be attained "only at the cost of improving the political and social climate" (*Frankfurter Allgemeine*, 25 March); that is, by giving greater power to the PCI. As the PCI came to grips with these in September-November, it did not refer to the detailed economic proposals its spokesmen had outlined earlier in the year. These—virtually identical to those of the year before (*YICA, 1976*, p. 184)—had been based on the principle of socialization of demand. (In 1976, however, the PCI would have had local and regional governments place the orders on the bases of which manufacturers and farmers would work [*L'Unità*, 15 February]. The PCI's economic statements also contained references to a gradual reduction of the public debt, and economy in public spending as well as to an increase in public consumption [ANSA, 23 March]. The PCI, however, has been thoroughly consistent in its opposition to a freeze on wages.) Yet the massive awareness in Italy that the essence of the economic crisis lay in the inflated cost of production led the government to attempt to reduce it. The PCI agreed to go along to some extent with this course because (a) it has no interest in economic catastrophe in the foreseeable future, (b) not to have gone along would have meant thoroughly sabotaging the government and facing new elections as the party which had made impossible any anti-inflationary action, and (c) by some kind of cooperation in lowering the cost of production, the PCI could collect a political price.

The government's austerity package included new taxes, increases in railroad rates and the price of gasoline (25 percent), abolition of five religious holidays, and the promise of a crackdown on tax evasion. But its heart was the proposal to suspend the workings of the so-called "sliding scale," which raises wages to keep up with inflation. The PCI added provisions for reimbursing the poor for the gasoline increase and limiting the sliding scale's suspension to wages above 8 million lire per year. Immediately after the government's announcement on 8 October, the PCI's Giorgio Napolitano charged it with being serious only about cutting down the workers' standard of living, and not about the other parts of the program (*Corriere Della Sera*, 10 October). But the party's criticism of a government which survives at its pleasure did not sound sincere to many union members. The PCI's operatives in the labor movement found it more difficult to counter the extremist groups' calls for violent action.

The discontent was mentioned at the Central Committee meeting of 18 October described above (see "Party Internal Affairs"). As the year ended, the party seemed to have found at least a temporary means of supporting both the government and the trade unions. On the key issue of the "sliding scale" the PCI continued to support its suspension for higher incomes, but took most of the teeth out by getting Andreotti to withdraw his proposal that these higher incomes themselves be frozen, thus allowing for increases, even if not automatic ones (*Il Giornale*, 24 November).

As the year ended, the PCI made a change in its policy toward the *comitati di quartiere* (neighborhood committees) which reflected the advances it had made. On 8 April the Parliament passed a law sponsored by the PCI instituting the committees and calling for the direct election of their members. The elections began on 28 November. On 19-20 November the PCI held a colloquium on the situation, in which both Marcello Stefanini, mayor of Pesaro and Armando Cossuta, propounding a new party line, warned that the committees ought not to be given deliberative powers. They cited the fact that since the PCI has come to power in so many city halls, the direct election of the committees—even though the party can influence many—still provides political bases and legitimacy for the party's opponents, especially the Catholic group "Communion and Liberation" (ibid., 19, 20 November).

International Views and Activities. During 1976 the PCI continued to conduct its foreign policy as much as possible on a party-to-party level (see below, "International Party Contacts"). The following international subjects drew substantial public comments from the PCI: the unwillingness of foreigners to extend loans to a Communist-led Italy, Italy's commitment to NATO, the state of democracy in, and of relations with, both the USA and the USSR.

The PCI's position on the foreign loans by means of which the Italian government has maintained its level of spending without even greater inflation (e.g., the EEC's $1 billion loan in March) is that they have threatened Italy's "autonomy and independence," and that future loans should be "without any conditions being imposed by the creditors" (Eugenio Peggio in *Frankfurter Allgemeine*, 25 March). The party has taken the position that the warning issued to Italy by the governments of the USA, West Germany, France, and England that loans would stop were the PCI to enter the government is an insult to national pride and "economic blackmail" (TASS, 22 July). By this means the PCI portrayed itself as truly patriotic and the true defender of Italy's independence, and the Christian Democrats who represented Italy at the Puerto Rico "financial summit" as unfit to govern because unable to muster "any national pride" (Giancarlo Pajetta, *Der Spiegel*, Hamburg, 26 July). The PCI implied that nations have the right to foreign credit, that foreign leaders need the Italian market, and that they would come to terms with a Communist-run Italy.

During 1976 the PCI further explained, but did not alter, its position on NATO. In an interview with the London *Times* (4 February), Berlinguer restated that "the Communist Party does not want Italy to withdraw from NATO, because such action would prejudice détente." That is, Italy's withdrawal would arouse fears in both the USA and Italy that the world's balance of power had tipped toward the Soviet bloc, and would therefore cause both Italy and the USA to abandon détente. The PCI had made clear at its 14th Congress that it considers détente the *conditio sine qua non* of its own advancement as well as of the strengthening of "progressive" forces throughout the world (*YICA, 1976*, pp. 188-89).

The PCI does not suggest that it accepts NATO as it is. The party spokesman on U.S. and NATO matters, Alberto Jacoviello, holds it "unthinkable" to do so, and claims that PCI participation in a NATO government would raise problems for the alliance. But these problems would be resolved by making changes in the alliance which are, at any rate, inevitable. (*L'Unità*, 1 March). Liberal groups in the USA, although they "advance all kinds of reservations on our account," are ready to accept as inevitable the changes in the relationship between the USA and Europe proposed by European Communists (ibid., 25 March). Led by the PCI, Italy would press NATO to greater cooperation with Eastern Europe, and to take the lead in banning nuclear weapons in Eastern and Western Europe. (*Washington Post*, 18 April.) The PCI would not immediately demand the evacuation of U.S. bases in Italy, but would insist, on the basis of the Helsinki agreement, on "full sovereignty" over them (*L'Unità*, 4 December 1975). For example, on 21 April 1976 a group of PCI deputies questioned the environmental impact of the U.S. submarine base on La Maddalena island, off Sardinia, and supported a local environmental commission's demand for curtailment of activities there (TASS, 21 April).

On 15 June the *Corriere Della Sera* printed an interview with Berlinguer in which he said that the PCI feels more comfortable on the Western side of the Iron Curtain, implying that Italy's membership in NATO gives the PCI an opportunity to develop the sort of communism that the Soviet Union did not allow in Czechoslovakia. Neither *L'Unità* nor *Paese Sera* reprinted this part of his remarks, but they reported his other comments to the effect that whereas in the East there might be restrictions on the kind of socialism one could develop, in the West there were barriers to developing socialism at all.

In sum, the PCI is actively, and successfully, pursuing good relations with NATO Europe (*Economist*, 20 March), as well as with the USA, but its purposes are substantially different from theirs. Giancarlo Pajetta pointed out that whereas the USA (and even China) promotes European unity with a view to countering the USSR, the PCI is urging Western Europe's "full autonomy, above all from the United States" (*L'Espresso*, 15 August).

The PCI presents the USA to its members and to the Italian public as the perfect example of what Lenin meant when he said that imperialism is the last stage of capitalism: because it has become an imperial power, the USA now regularly bypasses even the decision-making organs of bourgeois democracy. For example, it is said to have ordered South Africa to intervene in Angola not to "check Soviet penetration," but to prevent the formation of anti-imperialist, independent states. Toward Italy it is shown as having behaved as a contemptuous owner, and to have given aid to create the conditions for thwarting the peoples' will, and for further exploitation (*L'Unità*, 11, 12 March). But the USA is also "a society which is anything but static," and the nomination of Jimmy Carter as president was taken as evidence of a desire for change (ibid., 20 August). The PCI openly wished for Carter's victory because three men who were considered likely appointees to high policy-making posts in any Democratic administration expressed not unfriendly feelings toward communism in Western Europe (*NYT*, 14 April). The PCI also appreciated the attitude of newspapers associated with the Democratic Party(e.g., *Los Angeles Times*, 16 July). Said Giorgio Amendola, "The new fact is not condemnation from the American government. It is new that this is not the only voice we hear from America." (*Washington Post*, 19 April).

In 1976, as in 1975, the PCI took every possible occasion to declare itself wholly autonomous and hence independent from Moscow. When the news media reported Soviet actions repugnant to the average Italian, the PCI disassociated itself from them. For example, when Andrei Sakharov was refused permission to go to Oslo to receive the Nobel prize, the PCI said that although Sakharov's taking sides with "unprogressive or openly reactionary forces ... prompts the expression of a negative judgment on his work," he should be allowed to go (*L'Unità*, 3 Decemer 1975). But in the same article, the PCI equated the Soviets' limitation of liberties with U.S. immigration laws. The party did not volunteer opinions in the less publicized case of the Soviet mathematician Plyushch, who had been imprisoned in mental hospitals as an "anti-Soviet psychopath," but when asked, Giorgio Napolitano expressed the party's disapproval of the Soviet action (*Corriere Della Sera*, 20 February). In the same interview, Napolitano explained that the PCI was planning to depart from the Soviet model in that the seizure of power by the Italian working class would not demand "recourse to a revolutionary dictatorship." But he said the PCI was reluctant to abandon the formula "dictatorship of the proletariat" lest it signify "a renunciation of the aim of working class hegemony." As to this and other contradictions in PCI statements about the USSR, Napolitano acknowledged there had been duplicity in the past, but ascribed it to a long process of liberation. Nonetheless, he refused to say that the USSR is not a socialist country according to the PCI's understanding of socialism, and praised it for social progress, equality, and achievement of Roosevelt's Four Freedoms.

International Party Contacts. In 1976 the PCI continued its practice of exchanging as many visits as possible with the Communist Party of the Soviet Union (CPSU). These were carried out by thousands of rank-and-file party members (through the party's travel agency Italturist) as well as by working-level delegations and by top leaders. The following are some examples. A Soviet delegation led by Lev Tolkunov, editor of *Izvestia*, attended the annual "festival of the Soviet Union" in Emilia-Romagna and remained in Italy a month for "candid talks" (*L'Unità*, 10 December 1975). On 27 January 1976, Giovanni Cervetti led a high-ranking delegation to Moscow. On 23 February another high-ranking delegation, led by Berlinguer, left for the 25th Congress of the CPSU. On 28 July a delegation of federation secretaries spent a month with the leaders of local Soviets and talked about party organization (TASS, 28 July). On 15 September a delegation of Communist local officials met with their Soviet counterparts in Lithuania and the Leningrad area (ibid., 15 September). Meanwhile, Armando Cossuta was in Tashkent for talks with S. R. Rachidov.

In 1976 the CPSU continued its policy of support for the PCI's strategy. Articles by PCI spokesmen continued to be published in *World Marxist Review* and *Pravda*. Interviews with them continued to be carried by TASS. In addition, the CPSU had the proceedings of the PCI's 15th Congress translated and published in Russian (ibid., 19 March). The PCI's 55th anniversary brought a comment on Moscow radio which ascribed the party's successes to its "responsible stances" and praised it as a "consistent and firm defender" of the Italian working people (*FBIS*, 22 January). On 30 March, *Pravda* reported the following remark by Berlinguer: "The constant growth in the ranks of the Italian Communist Party is proof of the correctness of the policy being pursued by the Communists." The PCI's electoral victory and its post-election maneuvers were reported without comment.

Although the PCI presented itself to the Italian electorate as the harbinger of something other than what the CPSU has brought to its country, the CPSU never explicitly criticized it. The PCI explicitly contradicted the belief frequently expressed in the bourgeois press abroad as well as in Italy that the CPSU was sending "messages" by means of certain articles as a "warning not to bypass certain supposed canons of Marxist-Leninist orthodoxy" (*L'Unità*, 9 December 1975). While Berlinguer's speech to the 25th Congress of the CPSU was cited by the *New York Times* (28 February) as evidence that an "ideological rift grows" within the world Comunist movement, TASS (27 February) quoted the same passages as evidence of PCI's good Marxism.

In March, a Soviet graduate student published a pamphlet on revisionism which, among other things, attacked PCI ideologist Luciano Gruppi for having said the USSR is not as free as it should be. The *Corriere Della Sera* (18 March) reported "Soviets attack PCI Ideologist." But an accompanying story reported that copies of the pamphlet had been withdrawn from circulation in Moscow. *L'Unità* (19 April) ridiculed the insignificant author, and stated that he did not represent the views of the CPSU.

Of a more serius nature was the PCI's publication in *Rinascita* (20 February) of four articles on the 20th Congress of the CPSU. These generally contend that Khrushchev's explanation of what happened under Stalin by the term "cult of personality" was superficial and misleading. They suggest that had the CPSU searched more thoroughly for what had gone wrong in the 1920s, its answer would have made for a more democratic society. The articles themselves do not offer an explanation, and thus do not depart from orthodoxy. But from the standpoint of Leninism the question was a dangerous one.

At the conference of European Communist and Workers' parties, East Berlin, 28 June-1 July, Berlinguer began his speech (*L'Unità*, 1 July) by noting that the conferees were addressing a worldwide public. He made several references to the different viewpoints held by the parties, to what he termed the absolute equality, autonomy, and independence of all the parties present, and to the proposition that there was no leading party or leading state. He said that, under present conditions, it is possible for Communist parties to work within collections of "political and social forces of differing ideological inspirations," and that the "prevalent tendency in this very broad and diversified movement is that which motivates the solution of the problems of today's society along a road toward socialism." According to Berlinguer, the image of the movement's openness "helps to increase the appeal of socialism." The PCI, he said, was sruggling for a society "based on the assertion of the significance" of the traditional liberal norms. But he especially stressed that this did "not at all signify concessions to the ruling groups." Rather, it afforded "the most effective means of struggling [for the primacy] of the working class and its allies."

In 1976 the PCI maintained its usual relations with East European Communist parties, characterized by mutual visits, greetings, and awards. The only exception was the Czechoslovak party. On 12 March *L'Unità* reported that eight Italians working for Radio Prague's foreign broadcasts section had been fired after refusing to reveal all their foreign contacts. The PCI, which had placed them, supported them. It has long had men at Radio Prague. The best known and most typical, Francesco Moranino, a former partisan, was sent to Czechoslovakia after having been convicted of murder in 1946. He returned to Italy in 1968 after he had been elected to the Chamber of Deputies on the PCI list. Recently, members of the extremist Red Brigades sought by the police have found safe haven in the Italian contingent in Prague and Karlovy Vary. (Il Tempo, 12 March).

On the occasion of the 8th anniversary of the Soviet invasion of Czechoslovakia, *L'Unità* (21 August) for the first time praised the Dubcek government for having "created a positive relationship among citizens, the party and the socialist state." It said that under Dubcek "the Communist Party's executive role was in no way undermined," and that the invasion had "opened a wound which is very far from being healed." Prague's *Rudé pravo* replied by charging the PCI was soft on anti-social elements" and was interfering in Czechoslovak party affairs. The PCI organ then (3 September) backed off a bit and moved closer to its previous stand, objecting primarily to "the way in which the new course was blocked and interrupted."

PCI relations with the Communist parties of Western Europe improved further, especially with regard to the French and Spanish parties. On 18 November 1975 the PCI and the French party released a declaration which recognized the essentially common problems faced by the two parties and committed them to respect all the procedural norms of bourgeois democracy, including "the freedom of formation and the possibility of democratic alternation between majorities and minorities." The two parties rejected the intervention of foreigners in internal affairs, and extended an invitation to Catholic progressives to join them in creating a new society. (Ibid., 19 November.)

On the eve of the French party's congress, which decided that the term "dictatorship of the proletariat" was no longer operative, the PCI's Luciano Gruppi published an ideological justification for that action. The hegemony of the proletariat, he said, is to be exercised through a diverse bloc of social and political forces, and the working class exercises "the ruling function within the bloc, which in turn exercises coercion within the framework of state legality against reactionaries" (ibid., 3 February 1976.

The PCI has long acted as the big brother of the Spanish Communist Party (PCE). On 15 December 1975, the PCI held a rally in Rome in honor of the 80th birthday of Dolores Ibarruri, "La Pasionaria" of the Spanish Civil War and elder statesperson of the PCE. Enrico Berlinguer and Santiago Carillo, chairman of the PCE, joined Ibarruri on the platform. The crowd of 20,000 which shouted "Si, si, si Dolores" was provided by the Italy-Spain committee, which has grown far beyond the normal dimensions of similar front activities. Its chairman is the octogenarian Pietro Nenni (PSI president and a member of the International Brigade in the Civil War). Its leading members are high-ranking politicians from all the parties of the "constitutional arc," including Christian Democrats anxious to earn "anti-Fascist" credentials. The committee exists to support the efforts of the two umbrella Spanish political organizations in exile. The top leaders of these organizations had working meetings in Rome beginning 24 February with virtually every major Italian politician and trade union leader (ibid., 24, 25 February). Giancarlo Pajetta has described willingness to help the Spanish opposition as a test of anti-Fascism. On 28 July, in Rome, the PCE Central Committee held its first public meeting since 1939 and was addressed by Berlinguer, who cited the presence at the meeting of Spanish non-Communists and Italian non-Communist anti-Fascists as proof of the invincibility of the PCI-PCE political strategy. (Ibid., 28, 30 July.)

The PCI took the occasion of the death of Mao Tse-tung to praise him and to attempt to open communications with Peking by a warm message of condolence (ibid., 10 September). But the party carefully limited its new-found sinophilia. It branded as a "distortion of Communist Party policy" an article in Le Monde, Paris, in which Alberto Jacoviello said Mao had anticipated a historic process when he rejected Soviet predominance (ibid., 13 September). Soon it was clear that the Chinese Communists had rejected the PCI condolences along with those of all Moscow-line parties (ANSA, 16 September). Berlinguer then spoke wistfully about the PCI's vain attempts to reestablish relations with China, and stated that China's foreign policy is diametrically opposed to that of the PCI (L'Unità, 20 September).

On the Middle East the PCI expressed wholehearted support for the forces backed by the USSR. For example, in February, a PCI delegation visited Syria's Ba'th Party, the Syrian Communist Party, and the National Council of the Palestine Liberation Organization (PLO). During its stay in Beirut the delegation met with Yasir Arafat and with the Lebanese Communist Party directorate (ibid., 10 February). In August the secretary of the Lebanese party met with Berlinguer in Rome and heard him announce an effort to enlist Italy's "democratic forces" in the cause of the Lebanese left and the PLO (ibid., 11 August). In September the PCI received a PLO delegation, introduced the members to labor organizers, and expressed support for the PLO's desire once again to operate in Lebanon independently of Lebanese authority (ibid., 18 September). The PCI continued to support the PLO's demands for an independent Palestinian state (TASS, 22 January) and to blame Israeli rule over Arabs as the cause of the region's troubles (*L'Unità*, 25 March). When Israel rescued some hundred hijacked passengers from Uganda, the PCI called on the Italian government to condemn the violation of Uganda's sovereignty (ANSA, 8 July).

During the Angolan civil war, the PCI received a delegation from the Popular Movement for the Liberation of Angola (MPLA) and reaffirmed its desire to contribute to the eventual success of the People's Republic of Angola (*L'Unità*, 12 February). In October the MPLA prime minister visited the PCI and the Italian government. He thanked both for substantial help his party received during the fighting (ANSA, 1 October).

In April the Italian National League of Cooperatives signed an agreement with the Marxist government of Mozambique. Although no information was given as to its economic substance, the agreement was said to "allow cooperation between the progressive forces of Italy and Mozambique to continue" (*FBIS*, 31 March).

The PCI continued to support the decision taken by India's Indira Gandhi to outlaw all political opposition. In December 1975 a PCI delegation led by Tullio Vecchietti and Giovanni Berlinguer was received both by the Communist Party of India and by the Indian National Congress party (*L'Unità*, 16 December).

Publications. The PCI's official organ is *L'Unità*, a daily published in both Milan and Rome, circulation 400,000. Its editor, Luca Pavolini, is a member of the Central Committee. The festivals held annually in nearly every city to raise money for *L'Unità* provide competition for the traditional patron saint feasts. In 1976 they raised $7.5 million (TASS, 12 September). The PCI evening newspaper *Paese Sera*, published in Rome, has a circulation of 180,000. The other major PCI daily is Palermo's *L'Ora*, circulation 35,000. The party's two publishing houses, Editori Riuniti and Il Rinnovamento, are under the supervision of Renato Zangheri, mayor of Bologna. The major periodicals issued by these houses are *Rinascita, Critica Marxista, Politica e Economia, Riforma Della Scuola, Donne e Politica, La Nuova Rivista Internazionale,* and *Studi Storici*.

Competing Communist Groups. The following groups also claim to be acting on behalf of communism.

The Party of Proletarian Unity for Communism (Partito di Unita Proletaria; PDUP), founded in Rome in 1974, is an uneasy alliance between the "Manifesto" group, expelled from the PCI in 1969, and that part of the Party of Proletarian Unity (PSIUP, an offshoot of the PSI) which did not merge with the PCI in 1972. It has 15,000 members, mostly intellectuals and labor organizers who retain some of the influence in the labor movement they had gained while working for the PSI or PCI. Its leaders are Rosanna Rossanda, Lucio Magri, Luigi Pintor, and Vittorio Foa. Its daily *Il Manifesto* has a circulation of 25,000. For the 1976 elections the PDUP allied with Workers Vanguard (AO) and other grous under the label Proletarian Democracy (DP). These slates received 550,000 votes (1.5 percent). Beginning in late 1975 the PDUP stopped attacking the PCI and pledged to cooperate with it on all levels. It now participates in local administrations with the PCI and has a seat on the directorate of the United Labor Confederations.

Continuous Struggle (Lotta Continua; LC) has been organized on a national scale since 1972. It publishes a daily by the same name, with a circulation of 20,000. The 12,000 members, drawn from various backgrounds, are mostly young and violent. In 1976 LC was led by Adriano Sofri, who enjoys good relations with the PCI, and Lionello Massobrio, who is a protégé of the PSI's Giacomo Mancini (*Il Settimanale*, 31 March). Beginning in late 1975 the LC improved what had been very poor relations with the PDUP. Despite its Trotskyist origins, it does not attack "Stalinism." It has contact with the Irish Republican Army and its members travel to Czechoslovakia. The LC is very powerful in Italy's secondary schools and has had considerable success in organizing draftees and junior NCO's in the Italian armed forces. The LC is the principal author of a pamphlet, *Pagherete Tutto*, ("You Will Pay All"), which lists the names of prominent conservative business, professional, and political figures and threatens them with the people's wrath. A number of these have been killed. The LC also acts as political guide and possibly as supplier to two other even more violent groups: The Collectives (I Collettivi) and Workers Autonomy (Autonomia Operaia, AO).

Workers Autonomy was formed by a group which split from the LC in 1969 and the remains of the defunct Workers Power. It is a clandestine terrorist organization active in northern Italy. Like AO, the Collectives have no identifiable central organization, but serve as foci for the violent activities of leftists in universities, hospitals, and factories.

The Red Brigades (BR) and the Armed Proletarian Nuclei (NAP) are almost indistinguishable. Allegedly founded by the publisher Giangiacomo Feltrinelli in 1968, they are responsible for the most spectacular acts of murder and arson in Italy. Their targets are always conservatives, never leftists. Some members have found refuge in Czechoslovakia. In 1976 they were so feared that it was difficult to find jurors for their trials (*Il Giornale*, 25 November).

Workers Vanguard, founded in Milan in 1968 by Trotskyist labor organizers, claims 25,000 members. It publishes the daily *Quotidiaro dei Lavoratori* and the weekly *Politica Comunista*. It is the one group with both the inclination and the wherewithal to challenge the PCI's influence in the labor movement, at least in the Milan area. It was responsible for the October riots in Milan against the PCI's support of the government's austerity program.

The Communist Party of Italy, Marxist-Leninist has been led by Fosco Dinucci since 1966. It is the largest Maoist group. In 1976 it continued to exchange messages with China (January, September) and delegations with Albania (July, August). Its daily *Nuova Unità* and periodical *Voce Della Cella* continued to appear. But the party has not been active.

The Italian Communist Party (Marxist-Leninist), led by Aldo Brandirali, publishes a journal, *Servire Il Popolo*, and expounds an anti-Soviet, anti-PCI, pro-Chinese line. It is ignored by China.

The Communist Revolutionary Groups (GCR) is the official representative of the Trotskyist Fourth International in Italy. It is isolated.

Stanford University   Angelo Codevilla

Luxembourg

The Communist Party of Luxembourg (Parti Communiste de Luxembourg; PCL) was founded in January 1921. Before World War II it played an insignificant role in Luxembourg politics. After the war the party increased its influence to some extent, in part because of the enhanced prestige of the Soviet Union. Since 1945 the PCL has been represented in parliament and in the town councils of Luxembourg city and several industrial centers of the South. During 1945-47 the cabinet included one Communist minister. The party's influence decreased thereafter, but increased again following the elections of 1964. It reached a new climax in the elections of 1968 and decreased again in the elections of 1974.

PCL members are estimated to number between 500 and 600. The population of Luxembourg is about 357,000 (estimated 1974).

For many years the PCL recruited its members mainly among industrial workers; gradually it has been able to extend its influence to other segments of the population. In the latest parliamentary elections, 26 May 1974, the PCL received approximately 9 percent of the vote and won five of the 59 seats (six of 56 seats in 1968). The next elections are scheduled for May 1979.

On the municipal level, the PCL increased its influence as a result of the decision of the Luxembourg Socialist Workers' Party (Parti Ouvrier Socialiste Luxembourgeois; LSAP) to form a coalition government with the PCL after the municipal elections of October 1969. This occurred in Esch-sur-Alzette, the second-largest town of the country, where PCL Secretariat member Arthur Useldinger, who is also a member of parliament, continued as mayor following the municipal elections of 12 October 1975.

The policy of the LSAP to cooperate more and more with the PCL engendered strong tensions among LSAP members and resulted in a party split in 1970. In 1945 the PCL formed its own trade union, which merged in 1965 with the far stronger LSAP-oriented workers association. This merger permitted the PCL to significantly influence the association in a Marxist direction and paved the way for its opening of relations with East European labor unions.

Leadership and Organization. The PCL, strongly pro-Soviet, presents the image of a united party. Differences of opinion are not made public. Party members vote as a bloc in parliament. The decisions of the party's congress and of its leading bodies are usually passed unanimously. The Congress itself meets every three years, most recently at Rumelange on 24-25 March 1973. At that time the Central Committee was reduced to 28 members (formerly 35). The Executive Committee remained at 10 members. The three-member Secretariat consists of party chairman Dominque Urbany, party secretary René Urbany, and treasurer Arthur Useldinger. The next congress is scheduled for 26-27 December 1976, and will be discussed in the next edition of the *YICA*.

The PCL leadership is strongly centralized. This point is emphasized by the complete absence of regional party organizations, although local party sections do exist. The party leads the League of Luxembourg Women (Union des Femmes Luxembourgeoises) and has a youth auxiliary (Jeunesse Progressiste). In addition it dominates a group of former resistance members (Le Réveil de la Résistance) and various societies which cultivate good relations with East European organizations.

Members of the Urbany family occupy key party positions. René Urbany, son of the party chairman, is party secretary and director of the party press. The "Réveil de la Résistance" is directed by François Frisch, son-in-law of the chairman and member of the PCL Central Committee. René Urbany's father-in-law, Jacques Hoffmann, is a member of the Central Committee and the Executive Committee of the PCL, and his brother-in-law, François Hoffmann, is a member of the editorial staff of the party press.

Domestic Attitudes and Activities. At the party congress in March 1973 the delegates approved the following declaration: "In view of the strong democratic and parliamentary tradition of our people, the democratic-parliamentary form of government can be the appropriate foundation from which the worker class can rise to power and construct socialism." As "a national party" the PCL advocates the establishment of "a socialist regime" to defend the "total national independence of Luxembourg." At the same time the PCL emphasizes the principle of "proletarian internationalism" and therefore pursues "its own path toward socialism." It condemns "the idea of a one-party system" as being incompatible with "the Luxembourg circumstances and traditions. (*Zeitung vum Letzeburger Vollek [ZVLV]*, 26 March 1973.)

Major discussion at the party congress was devoted to the creation of a "unité d'action" with the LSAP with the object of achieving a "socialist order" by unifying all leftist forces of the country "on the basis of a common program" (*ZVLV*, 26 March 1973). In its "appeal to the working population of our country," the congress pointed to the "positive results for the working class" of the close cooperation between Socialists and Communists on the labor union level and in some town councils. Shortly after the congress, however, the LSAP leadership disavowed any movement of "unité d'action" until after the national elections scheduled for 1974 (*ZVLV*, 3 April 1973) and confirmed its anti-PCL attitude following the elections of 1974.

In the past several years the activities of the PCL have been partly disrupted by Maoist and Trotskyist splinter groups. Initially these groups consisted of high school and university students. In the past two years, however, some industrial laborers have joined the Trotskyists. Thus the PCL has to contend with "leftist" competition. The Trotskyist group presented incomplete lists of candidates in two districts for the parliamentary elections of 1974, with negligible results.

International Views and Positions. The foreign policy positions of the PCL closely reflect those of the Communist Party of the Soviet Union (CPSU). The 1968 military intervention of the Warsaw Pact states in Czechoslovakia was approved by the PCL without reservation, and seldom, if ever, has the PCL criticized the policy of the Soviet government. The Soviet Union's diplomatic representation in Luxembourg far exceeds the number of persons normally assigned to a small country. There also exist strong indications that the PCL is financially dependent on Moscow. Its leading members travel frequently in the Soviet Union and Eastern Europe, and often attend CPSU meetings and congresses or spend their vacations in the Soviet Union. In 1973, on his seventieth birthday, party chairman Urbany was decorated by the Supreme Soviet with the Order of the October Revolution (*ZVLV*, March 1973).

As "essential tasks of every communist party," Urbany in his speech to the party congress stressed stabilization of "the international solidarity of the working class" and "the unity of the communist world movement and the fight against imperialism and reaction." The PCL, he said, rejects any moves against "proletarian internationalism" and "especially the Soviet Union" (*ZVLV*, 31 March 1973).

Publications. The party organ of the PCL is the *Zeitung vum Letzeburger Vollek*, which has a daily distribution of 1,200 copies. The PCL also publishes a weekly, *Wechenzeitung*. Both are printed by the party's publishing company, Coopérative Ouvrière de Presse et d'Editions, which also handles the sale and distribution of foreign Communist publications. The PCL distributes its publications periodically to households and also participates in the political programs of Radio Luxembourg. The value it places on the remarks of PCL members in parliament is underscored by the gratis door-to-door distribution of the parliamentary reports. During 1976 the PCL began construction of a new building on the outskirts of Luxembourg City which will house the party headquarters, the party's printing company, and the offices of the party publications.

Netherlands

The Communist Party of the Netherlands (Communistische Partij van Nederland; CPN) was founded as the Communist Party of Holland in 1918. The official founding date, however, is that of affiliation to the Comintern, 10 April 1919. The present name was chosen at the party congress in December 1935. The party has always been legal (with the exception of the period 1939-1945).

CPN policy is based on the "new orientation" proclaimed at its 1964 congress, which gives primary importance to the realization of domestic political goals: relations with the international Communist movement are subordinated to the realization of a united front of which Communists and Socialists form the pivot. In 1975, however, more involvement of the CPN in the international Communist movement was noticeable, a tendency which increased in 1976. The autonomous attitude of the CPN to the Sino-Soviet dispute has led to the formation of both pro-Soviet and pro-Chinese groups outside the party. Their influence on CPN politics is small.

The number of CPN votes received in elections has been increasing since the low point of 2.4 percent in 1959, when the party was split. In the November 1972 general elections the CPN received 4.5 percent of the votes, which means 7 seats out of 150 in the Lower House of the parliament. In the provincial governing bodies the CPN has 19 seats out of 670, in the municipal governing bodies 130 seats out of 12,000. In 16 out of more than 800 municipalities the CPN has aldermen.

The CPN does not publish figures, but the number of members is estimated at 10,000 and the number of subscribers to its daily paper, *De Waarheid*, at 16,000. CPN followers are irregularly spread over the country, with centers of activity in Amsterdam, the highly industrialized "Zaanstreek," and the province of Groningen. The population of the Netherlands is about 13,707,000.

Leadership and Organization. The CPN's 25th Congress, in June 1975, elected a new Central Committee which does not differ much from the previous one. The principal policy-making body is the 14-member Executive Committee of the Central Committee, including H. J. Hoekstra (chairman), M. Bakker (chairman of the CPN fraction in parliament), G. Hoogenberg (charged with work in industry), and J. IJisberg (administrative secretary). During 1976 the Executive Committee was expanded from 12 members to 14 (the two new members are J. de Leeuw and A. van Kooten). The Secretariat, consisting of 5 or 6 members of the Executive Committee, is the organizational and administrative center of the party. The Central Committee, consisting of 37 members and 3 deputy members, only meets a few times per year. Former leader P. de Groot still has a strong influence on CPN politics.

The significance of the CPN front organizations has decreased considerably since the breaking of their ties with the international front organizations because of the party's autonomous policy. The most active is the General Netherlands Youth Organization (Algemeen Nederlands Jeugd Verbond; ANJV). The activities of the Netherlands Women's Movement (Nederlandse Vroouwen Beweging; NVB), like those of the ANJV, supported CPN demands. The organization of former resistants, "Verenigd Verzet 1940-1945," is politically of no importance.

Party Internal Affairs. The CPN Central Committee meeting on 10-11 September 1976 focused preparations for the general elections in May 1977. In the beginning of 1977 a special national party conference is to present clearly to the people the national and international policy of the CPN.

During the election campaign the CPN will try to start a discussion with the Labor Party and other progressive parties toward effecting a change in government policy, The Labor Party (Partij van de Arbeid), however, has already made it clear that it does not want to cooperate with the CPN in a new left-wing government. As usual, much attention was paid to the role of the trade union movement, which would also seek a change, on the basis of a unity of "progressive" elements.

The year 1976 was rather satisfactory for the CPN as far as organization and activities were concerned. The number of members increased, as did the number of subscribers to the party's daily paper, *De Waarheid*. However, one of the problems of the CPN party is that new members are often not industrial workers, and this might affect the proletarian character of the party.

A special financial campaign was a success. Training activities were stepped up. As already noted, the Executive Committee of the Central Committee was extended by two members. A special party coordinator was appointed. Meetings of party functionaries were held more regularly. There was increased activity in the field of political and social research at the CPN's Instituut voor Politiek en Sociaal Onderzoek (IPSO). Increasing activity in student circles met with some success. Student membership in the CPN grew, and these students exert a strong influence in representative bodies at the universities, particularly in Amsterdam, where they also often dominate the editorial staff of influential student papers.

Domestic Attitudes and Activities. The CPN in 1973 adopted a policy of "constructive" opposition to the present Den Uyl coalition government. Since the end of 1974 its policy has been directed toward replacement of this government by a "really progressive" one.

In order to promote this policy the CPN made efforts to drive wedges between the leadership of the Labour Party and the Labour Trade Union Movement, between that leadership and the Labour Party followers. The social-economic situation in the Netherlands, particularly the government's policy of limiting wage increases, favored these CPN efforts. It has been made increasingly clear by CPN leaders that in the present situation the party does not strive for a revolutionary overthrow of the existing order, but for a policy which, within the framework of the capitalist system, seeks to avoid violation of the position of the majority of the people.

Former CPN chairman de Groot confirmed this in an article in *De Waarheid* (6 August 1976). According to him, there was a need for a "positive, realistic, Communist policy in coordination with all those who are of good will," for a "purposeful general action" against immediate deterioration, and for a new government of "progressive unity."

The CPN realizes that it can attain its goals only if it uses the bourgeois system. Therefore it intends to seek united front efforts with social-democratic forces, particularly political parties and trade unions, in the campaign leading up to elections in May 1977.

On the basis of its action against the "crisis" which started in the autumn of 1975, the CPN launched a series of activities which were continued in 1976, and which were directed against government plans to reduce expenses in social and cultural fields. Other actions were launched against unemployment and the closing down of certain factories. Special activities were pushed inside the trade unions to promote opposition in those organizations. These efforts were rather successful and contributed to tougher trade union policies. Some strikes were organized in the harbors of Amsterdam and Rotterdam. The split between the government and the trade union movement over wage policy stimulated the CPN to extend its activities. A special strategy was worked out, discussed with cadres, and carried out in practice.

International Views and Positions. The "new orientation" adopted at the CPN's 21st Congress, in 1964, affirmed that international policy is determined more by the domestic political situation than by the internationalist Communist line. A turn in this policy, begun in the course of 1975 and continued in 1976, was caused by the wish of the party leaders to normalize relations with the Communist Party of the Soviet Union (CPSU). This means that CPN foreign policy is again based on the principles of "proletarian internationalism."

This process has been rather slow, and sometimes the statements of CPN leaders remind one of the old situation of strained relations with the CPSU. On the whole, it looks as if better relations are really wanted, but this does not imply abandonment of an autonomous policy and the right to criticize the international Communist movement or the Communist parties of other countries. The party leaders hope that the CPSU will recognize its wrong judgment of CPN policy in the past and will cease its support of pro-Soviet groups in the Netherlands.

That the CPN still reserves the right to criticize the CPSU was shown in utterances of party leaders Hoekstra and de Groot at the conference of European Communist and workers' parties at East Berlin in June 1976. Leonid Brezhnev was criticized for his attack on Chinese communism, and the CPSU for its exaggeration of the significance of the conference. Occasion was also taken to criticize the CPSU for its hostile attitude toward the CPN and its former chairman, de Groot.

The CPN regards better relations with the CPSU as a condition for better relations with the other Communist parties. In consequence of this, the party made several efforts to improve its relations with other Communist parties, particularly in Western Europe.

International Party Contacts. As results of the improving relations between CPN and the CPSU in 1976 there were increasing contacts of the CPN with the Soviet Embassy in the Netherlands, exchanges of journalists, participation in the conference of European Communist and workers' parties at East Berlin and attendance at the 25th Congress of the CPSU by a CPN journalist who is also a member of the party's Central Committee.

Results of better relations with other Communist parties were seen in a common declaration of the CPN and the French Communist Party in June against the supply of nuclear power technology to South Africa; participation in a meeting of West European Communist parties in Strassburg in July against the "Berufsverbote" in West Germany (see *Federal Republic of Germany*), and participation in a meeting of the Central Committee of the Spanish Communist Party in Rome in July.

The CPN is particularly interested in contacts with the French and Italian Communist parties. Former chairman de Groot visited the Italian party in September. One problem in the relations between the CPN and these parties concerns its different view on the European Economic Community.

The CPN still regards the EEC as "an EEC of the big monopolies, of the most perfect exploitation of the workers and of the working masses in general" (*De Waarheid*, 23 July).

Publications. The main CPN organ is its daily, *De Waarheid* (The Truth). The paper is in constant financial trouble, which the party tries to overcome by collections from time to time. The bimonthly *Politiek en Cultuur*, devoted to the theory and practice of Marxism-Leninism, is used for training purposes. The ANJV and NVB have their own monthly papers. The CPN institute for political and social reseach, IPSO, issues a quarterly, *Info*, which draws attention to articles published by other parties on problems of present-day communism. The CPN has its own publishing house and bookshop,"Pegasus." In the importation of Russian publications, the pro-Soviet bookshop "Sterboek" competes with "Pegasus." The CPN has two commercial printing plants, one for *De Waarheid* and one for other printed matter.

Dissident Groups. Pro-Soviet Communists in the Netherlands do not have organizational unity. Most are members of the "Nederland-USSR" friendship society, which is not engaged in domestic politics; it promotes cultural relations between the Netherlands and the USSR, hoping to foster appreciation for the socialist system. Its monthly paper is *NU* (standing for "Netherlands-USSR"). An important part is played by the "Vernu BV" travel agency, which organizes an increasing number of tourist visits to the USSR. The chairman of the friendship society, who is also director of the travel agency, is W. Hulst. He has been awarded the Soviet "Order of the Friendship of the Peoples" for "his promotion of better relations between the peoples of the Netherlands and the Soviet Union" over many years. Highlights in the life of this society are the annual "Month of the Soviet Union" and the signing of the yearly cultural plan. Improving CPN-CPSU relations have already affected the activity of Nederland-USSR, which was less in 1976 than in previous years.

Similar activities, but on a smaller scale and directed at the Balkan states and the German Democratic Republic, are fostered by a society for cultural exchange, "Vereniging voor Culturele Uitwisseling" (VCU) which seeks to coordinate its activities with those of the Nederlands-GDR friendship society.

Young members of Nederland-USSR founded in 1973 a new organization, Jongeren Kontakt voor Internationale Solidariteit en Uitwisseling (Youth Contact for International Solidarity and Exchange; JKU). It issues a paper, *Solidair*. In cooperation with Vernu BV, travels to Eastern Europe are organized with the principal aim to learn more about the system of socialist society. The JKU maintains contacts with similar organizations in other West European countries and with the coordinating Soviet youth organization. JKU is a member of the Communist-front World Federation of Democratic Youth.

As a rival of the CPN-oriented organization of former resistants, "Verenigd Verzet 1940-1945," pro-Soviet Communists have founded an organization of anti-fascist resistants, Anti-Fascistische Oud-Verzetsstrijders Nederland" (AFVN). It issues a paper, *Antifascist*. The AFVN is a member of the Communist-front International Federation of Resistance Fighters.

Soviet views are also presented by the "Nederlands Comité voor Europese Veiligheid en Samenwerking" (Dutch Committee for European Security and Cooperation) and by a monthly paper, *Communistische Notities* (Communist Notes), edited by a former CPN Executive Committee member, F. Baruch. As the unofficial mouthpiece of the CPSU, this paper played a role in the rapprochement between the CPN and the CPSU.

Although originally splinter groups of the CPN, the pro-Chinese groups find their followers among students and young workers who have no past or present connection with the CPN. There are six competing pro-Chinese groups. The two main groups are the Netherlands Communist Unity Movement-Marxist-Leninist (Kommunistische Eenheidsbeweging Nederland-marxistisch-leninistisch;

KEN-ml) and the Socialist Party (SP). Both are small. The SP issues a monthly, *De Tribune*, and the KEN-ml a fortnightly, *De Rode Tribune*. The SP took part in the municipal elections in May 1974, for the first time, and received a total of 15,000 votes in 12 municipalities.

Oost-West Instituut   C. C. van den Heuvel
The Hague

Norway

The Norwegian Communist Party (Norges Kommunistiske Parti; NKP) remains small and isolated following its decision not to merge with several left socialist parties. This decision, taken at the NKP's 15th Congress in November 1975, split the party and caused the chairman and several other leaders to leave the NKP for the new Socialist Left Party (Sosialistisk Venstreparti; SV). Although the NKP remains intact, initial surveys indicate that it has lost much of its traditional constituency among industrial workers in Oslo and low-income groups in the northern province of Finnmark and the eastern region of Hedmark. Prior to the schism, estimates of NKP membership estimates ranged from 2,000 to 5,000. The lower figure is probably currently the most accurate. The population of Norway is just over 4 million.

The NKP was organized on 4 November 1923, when a few radical politicians and trade unionists split from the Norwegian Labor Party (Det Norske Arbeiderparti; DNA). The NKP, which adhered to Comintern principles, was initially stronger than its Danish and Swedish counterparts, but its strength deteriorated quickly except for a brief revival in 1945 as a consequence of Communist participation during World War II in the Norwegian resistance and Soviet liberation of northern Norway. NKP representation in the 150-seat Parliament (Storting) fell from 12 in 1945 to one in 1957, and with the rise of the Socialist People's Party (Sosialistisk Folkeparti; SF) in 1961, the NKP lost its last mandate.

The Communists have clearly suffered from being sandwiched between the powerful DNA and the Socialist People's Party, which was a splinter from the DNA combined with a motley collection of tiny extremist groups. The SF itself suffered internal dissension in the late 1960s, and in 1969 lost its two parliamentary seats. Norwegian politics was churned up considerably by the intense agitation in 1971-72 over whether Norway should join the European Economic Community (EEC). A national referendum rejected membership in September 1972, and when the dust began to settle, it was clear that the socialist left wing had gained at the expense of the DNA. In the 1973 parliamentary elections, the NKP joined with the SF and a new DNA splinter group, the Workers' Information Committee (Arbeidernes Informasjon Komite; AIK) to form the Socialist Electoral Alliance (Sosialistisk Valgforbund; SV). The alliance did quite well, receiving 11.2 percent of the vote and 16 seats in the now 155-seat Storting. The then NKP chairman, Reidar T. Larsen, was elected to Parliament on the common list. It appeared as if the NKP had come in from the cold.

The SV was thus initially an electoral alliance with a common platform, and not a party. It held the balance of power between the minority Labor government and the combined rightist and centrist opposition. Both DNA and SV, however, did poorly in the September 1975 municipal and county elections, with the SV losing nearly half of its 1973 percentage of the votes. In the course of 1976 the Labor party was able to reverse its fortunes. With the NKP-SV split and improving economic conditions in Norway, most pundits were predicting a sizable DNA advance in the September 1977 parliamentary elections, perhaps enough to win an outright majority.

Leadership and Organization. Despite efforts at unification since 1972, the Norwegian left remains fragmented into a large number of small and hostile groups. Besides the NKP, one can identify the Norwegian Communist Youth League, which split from the NKP in the late 1960s; Communist Youth, the NKP's new youth affiliate; the Socialist Youth League/Marxist-Leninist; the Socialist Youth League; the Norwegian Communist Workers Party—Marxist-Leninist (Arbeidernes Kommunistparti—Marxist-Leninist; AKP-ml); and several special discussion groups attracting intellectuals.

It was against this fragmentation that the efforts to transform the Social Electoral Alliance into a new amalgamation, the Socialist Left Party, were directed. By mid-1975 the leaders of the Socialist People's Party, including Finn Gustavsen and Berit Aas, as well as the leadership of the Workers' Information Committee (AIK), agreed on the formation of a party and the dissolution of the three old factions in early 1976. The then NKP chairman, Larsen, strongly supported this decision at the Trondheim conference of March 1975, but from the start there were dissident voices in the NKP. Months of debate in the pages of the NKP weekly *Friheten* and elsewhere failed to bring about party unity. At its 15th Congress, held in Oslo on 1-2 November 1975, the NKP delegates voted 117 to 30 against the policy of the chairman and several other leaders that the party should merge totally into the new SV (*Nordisk Kontakt*, no. 15, 1975). Larsen publicly defied the Congress's decision, and he was replaced as chairman by Martin Gunnar Knutsen, who had led the anti-merger forces as vice-chairman (see Per Egil Hegge, " 'Disunited' Front in Norway," *Problems of Communism*, May-June 1976). In a post-Congress interview, Chairman Knutsen emphasized that the new NKP leadership wished emphatically to continue electoral cooperation with SV (*Friheten*, 3-8 November 1975).

In the weeks after the NKP Congress and schism, the new leadership sought to avoid a final break with the former electoral allies. Nevertheless, when the SV held a conference in Oslo on 22 February 1976 they reaffirmed their decision of a year earlier against dual party membership and set 1 May as the deadline for enforcing party preference. The SV elected simultaneously historian and Storting member Berge Furre as its party chairman, Berit Aas and Steinar Stjerno as vice-chairmen, and former NKP chairman Reidar Larsen as parliamentary leader. Former NKP secretary Rune Fredh joined the SV, as did another prominent Communist, Aud Gustad, who several months previously had succeeded to a seat in Parliament on the death of an SV member. In addition to Martin Gunnar Knutsen, other prominent leaders of the rump NKP included Rolf Nettum, organizational vice-chairman; Hans Kleven, political vice-chairman; and Arne Jorgensen, editor of *Friheten.*

Domestic Attitudes and Activities. Despite the NKP's sectarian preoccupations during most of 1976, some energy remained for consideration of issues beyond the left socialist ghetto. No longer represented in the Storting, the NKP had only its weekly paper and other press coverage to let its views be known. Following a meeting in early February, the National Board (Executive Committee) of the NKP published the party's new program. Emphasis was upon the necessity for working class unity at a time of severe crisis for capitalism. Other points were: protection must be given to all workers from the effects of unemployment and inflation; Norway's economic resources must remain in Norwegian hands; the government must exercise greater direction over the economy. (*Friheten*, 16-21 February.)

Despite warnings of dire crisis from the NKP and SV, Norway's economy remained the most prosperous in Western Europe during 1976. Although demand for traditional Norwegian industrial exports and the services of the large Norwegian merchant marine was hit hard by the international recession, Norway's economy and labor force was spared most of the hardships felt elsewhere. During 1976 the rich Norwegian oil resources of the North Sea contributed significantly to domestic economic activity. Not only did oil provide offshore and coastal jobs, but the expectations of future earnings allowed the government to tolerate large domestic and international payments deficits. The government provided special support for employment in early 1976 when unemployment reached 2.1 percent of the labor force. The most severe economic problem was inflation, which remained at 10 to 12 percent. The leftist parties were anxious to protect wage earners from harsh wage and income controls. Although some Norwegians feel guilty about their country's current affluence and future prospects of being the wealthiest country in Europe, such concerns have not been as prominent in discussions within the NKP as in the SV, DNA, and several non-socialist parties.

Norwegian Communists have traditionally been stronger in the trade union movement than in electoral politics, but at no time have they been able to challenge the close ties between the leadership of the social-democratic DNA and the Norwegian Federation of Trade Unions (Landsorganisasjonen; LO). Neither the Communists nor the Left Socialists (SV) have representation in the National Executive of the LO or control any national labor union. At the local level, the NKP is most significant in the construction workers' union and, to some extent, in the metal, wood, transport, and electro-chemical fields. As is generally the case in Scandinavia, the election of individual Communists to positions of responsibility results from particular personal and union issues and is quite independent of the Communist party's ideology or national policies.

International Views and Positions. The change in leadership at the NKP Congress has not changed the party's views on international issues. The 1975 Helsinki Accords of the Conference on Security and Cooperation in Europe (CSCE) still form the basis of NKP views on European relations. Emphasis on "peace" remains a vague cliché in most party statements (*WMR*, January 1976). The NKP and the SV are firmly opposed to continued Norwegian membership in NATO and to such policies as the acquisition of the F-16 fighter in consortium with other Western European NATO states.

As mentioned, the new NKP Program of February 1976 stressed the importance of Norwegian economic independence and guarantees that Norwegian resource development would be guided by Norwegian and not foreign economic interests (*Friheten*, 16-21 February). Since the DNA government has assured majority Norwegian state control of petroleum drilling and a substantial state sector in petroleum refining and distribution, neither NKP nor SV have been able to make political capital on these important issues.

Norwegian relations with the USSR, although amicable, remain sensitive because of Soviet military concentrations in the Kola Peninsula along the Soviet-Norwegian border. The complex treaty arrangements for the Norwegian Arctic islands of Svalbard (Spitzbergen) and the disputed economic zone in Arctic territorial waters were the subject of inconclusive Soviet-Norwegian negotiations during 1976. NKP and SV statements on these issues were cautious, but the two parties denied that the situation demanded increased defense preparations. The pro-Peking AKP-ml protested Soviet encroachments on the occasion of an official Soviet visit to Oslo in late August, but neither the government nor the other left socialist groups have sought to stimulate public discussion of the sensitive matter (*Aftenposten*, 13 September; NCNA, 31 August).

International Party Contacts. Internal divisions and conflicts did not prevent the NKP from maintaining contacts with other European Communist parties. Just after the NKP Congress in November 1975, several East European party organs stressed the importance of maintaining the Leninist identity of the NKP (*Neues Deutschland*, East Berlin, 5 November). Visits to Eastern Europe and the USSR brought Chairman Knutsen into contact with other Communist party personalities. Knutsen visited East Germany on 20-23 February and was received by the ruling party's first secretary Erich Honecker and other party and government officials. The resulting communiqué stressed NKP support for the international views of the Soviet bloc nations (ibid., 24 February).

Knutsen represented the NKP at the 25th Congress of the Communist Party of the Soviet Union in Moscow in late February. In his statement to assembled Communist activists, Knutsen lavished praise on the CPSU, under whose leadership "the Soviet people surmounted all obstacles in its path and created a socialist society — the most progressive society of our time" (TASS, 27 February). In response to domestic criticism of his extensive praise of the USSR, Knutsen stressed party independence on several occasions. In the wake of the conference of European Communist and workers' parties in East Berlin in late June, where he had led the NKP delegation, Knutsen emphasized that his party's tactics were based on Norwegian conditions and traditions. Although the "class struggle continues," he said, "the conference did not concern itself with elaborating any single model for waging this struggle" (*Pravda*, 16 July). In an address to the conference on 30 June, Knutsen warned against anti-Communist and anti-Soviet propaganda, which he said was being stepped up by rightists as well as ultra-leftists (ibid., 3 July).

Additional summer excursions brought the NKNP chairman to Poland for talks with Polish party officials and to Bulgaria for a meeting with Bulgarian party chief Todor Zhivkov (PAP, 5 July; BTA, 26 July). Return hospitality was shown to East German foreign minister Oskar Fischer who met with NKP deputy chairmen Kleven and Mettum during an official visit to Oslo (*Neues Deutschland*, 28 July).

Different interests were evident when a delegation of the Italian Communist Party visited Oslo in February. Their principal talks were with Reiulf Steen, the new chairman of the DNA, and were reportedly focused on the importance attached by the Italian Communists to national independence (*Aftenposten*, Oslo, 28 February).

Publications. The main NKP organ is *Friheten* (Freedom). First published as an underground paper during World War II, *Friheten* reached a peak circulation of 100,000 in 1945. Financial hard times and dwindling demand caused its transition from daily to weekly publication in 1967. Fund raising to keep the paper going is a continuous NKP preoccupation. The KU publishes a youth bulletin, *Fremad* (Forward). The primary voice of the AKP (m-l) is *Klassekampen* (Class Struggle). The new SV newspaper is *Ny Tid* (New Times), intended to absorb much of the readership of the SF publication, *Orientering*, which was admired by many outside the SF party circle. Initially, *Ny Tid* has had staff and circulation problems, and it is reported to be in financial difficulties. (Hegge, " 'Disunited' Front in Norway.")

University of Massachusetts
Amherst

Eric S. Einhorn

Portugal

The Portuguese Communist Party (Partido Comunista Português; PCP) celebrated its 55th anniversary in March 1976. Illegal from 1927 to 1974, the PCP nonetheless has assembled the largest, best organized, and most powerful left-wing apparatus in the country. It claims to have more than 100,000 militants, especially among industrial and farm workers in southern Portugal, and makes a special effort to appeal to young people through three Communist youth organizations.

The PCP lost support in popular elections during 1976 and also saw its influence eroded among officers of the Armed Forces Movement (AFM), the government bureaucracy, and the news media. Party backing in labor unions, on the other hand, appeared to be growing by the end of the year, particularly among printers, metallurgists, electricians, and insurance workers of Lisbon and Setúbal. The PCP also retained its power base among farm workers of the Alentejo area.

The Portuguese Democratic Movement (Movimento Democrático Português; MDP) is a front group for the PCP. In an effort to avoid dividing the Communist vote, as in the 1975 elections when it received 4 percent of the ballots, the MDP decided not to offer candidates in 1976 (*Diário de Notícias*, 28 February).

Much more militant than the PCP or the MDP are some 14 organizations of the revolutionary "new left." (For a list of 13 minor parties, see *YICA, 1976*, p. 201; an additional group was the Trotskyite Workers Revolutionary Party—Partido Revolucionário dos Trabalhadores, or PRT.) They are variously identified as Maoist, Marxist, or Trotskyite. Eight of these participated in the April 1976 elections for the National Assembly, drawing 5 percent of the votes, compared with 4 percent in the 1975 elections for the Constituent Assembly. Only one, the Maoist People's Democratic Union (União Democrática do Povo; UDP), received enough votes, as in the 1975 elections, to qualify for a seat.

Most of the far-left parties, especially the Maoists, view the "revisionist" PCP as just as dangerous as the ultra-right, if not more so. Their dogma is distinguished from that of the PCP primarily by their insistence that power should flow upward from a grass-roots level toward a central authority rather than in reverse (*Intercontinental Press*, New York, 14 June).

Portugal's population is about 8,820,000.

Leadership and Organization. The PCP's Eighth Congress met in Lisbon in November 1976. Some 1,200 party members gathered to fix policy guidelines and to elect the Central Committee; attendance at the Seventh Congress in 1974 had only totaled 1,000 (see *YICA, 1975*, p. 228). Alvaro Cunhal was reelected secretary-general, a post he has held since 1961. There had been speculation that Cunhal might be replaced as party leader by Octávio Pato, the PCP candidate for president in June. Pato and fellow Central Committee member Carlos Aboim Inglés have long been viewed as heirs-apparent to Cunhal. Pato reportedly favors abandoning the party's rigid Stalinism in favor of a more flexible strategy akin to that of the Italian and Spanish Communist parties (*Washington Post*, 19 May).

The Congress assailed the "rightward drift" of the Socialist government of Mário Soares and warned that wage demands, demonstrations, and strikes were "legitimate weapons of the working masses" if their interests were threatened (*Christian Science Monitor [CSM]*, 15 November).

Domestic Attitudes and Activities. A steady weakening of PCP leverage in national affairs followed the aborted coup attempt of November 1975 (see *YICA, 1976*, p. 208), which the PCP and other leftist groups were charged with engineering. Returned to original owners were many factories, farms, and mass media outlets that had been seized by Communist-influenced workers (*CSM*, 9 February 1976). Many revolutionary leftists were ousted from the state-owned press, radio, and television networks (*NYT*, 7 January). Austerity measures were introduced and attempts made to restore labor discipline and to wrest union control from Communists. Anti-Communist right-wing politicians and groups were able to act more openly than during the previous two years, most political prisoners jailed between April 1974 and November 1975 were released, and former president General António Spínola was able to return from exile to Lisbon, where he was only briefly detained for questioning about his role in a March 1975 coup attempt. (See *YICA, 1976*, p. 204; *NYT*, 24, 25 January, 1, 11, 13 August 1976; *CSM*, 9 February, 31 March).

The AFM's Council of the Revolution purged itself of its own Communist supporters and far-leftists; it also agreed to give up its tutelary role in government in favor of a merely "consultative" one. It thereby deprived the Communists of a key potential springboard to power. Elections in April brought Portugal an all-Socialist government, the first without Communist participation since the April 1974 revolution that toppled the Caetano dictatorship. In June, an anti-Communist military president, dedicated to assuring "law and order" and respect for the "will of the majority," was elected with 61 percent of the vote and with the support of the three major parties. The PCP fielded its own candidate, Octávio Pato, who received a scant 8 percent of the ballots (*Washington Star*, 29 June).

The new chief executive, General António Ramalho Eanes, had, as chief of staff, led the crushing of the November uprising. Little had been known publicly about his views, but he did emerge as the leader of the "operational" wing of the Council of the Revolution, which favored the depoliticization of the armed forces and the restoration of discipline. By February this policy had prevailed over that of the "political" wing, which sought a continuing central role in politics for the military in order to "guarantee the revolution." The Constituent Assembly was then able to approve a new constitution, effective on 25 April, which gave full power to a freely elected president and legislature. The Council of the Revolution was to retain an advisory position to the president. (*NYT*, 18 January, 15 February, 28 March, 25 April.)

As president, General Eanes further sought to separate military and political functions by requiring members of the Council of the Revolution to resign either from that body or from their military commands (ibid., 17 August). Major Ernesto Melo Antunes, who as foreign minister in the provisional coalition cabinet had led the "military politicians," again spoke publicly in November of the need for a "primary role" for the military, but the president responded sharply that "the formation of states within the state" would not be accepted. Melo Antunes was an anti-Communist who professed strong Marxist sympathies. (*CSM*, 9 November.)

Even though the new constitution permitted the election of a non-military president, the Socialist, Popular Democrat, and Social Democratic Center parties felt that Eanes's broad military support offered the best guarantee of democratic stability and insurance against a leftist or rightist coup (*NYT*, 13 June). The PCP appeared to be wary of Eanes, but did not abandon efforts to make him more receptive to cooperation with it. In announcing its own candidate in May, the party had to retreat from a position publicly stated a month earlier that a military man should be president. It then hedged by saying that its own campaign would not prejudice the support it might give to an elected military man. (Ibid., 22 April, 11 May; *Washington Post*, 19 May; *Intercontinental Press*, 31 May.)

Lacking the military contacts that had helped to propel it in 1974-75 to a position of decisive influence, the PCP veered to the tactic of seeking accommodation with the Socialists. Before and after the legislative elections, Secretary-General Cunhal doggedly urged Soares's party, which he had previously denounced as "reactionary," to ally itself with the PCP in order to save the country from the "reactionary right." Victory by the latter, he predicted, would lead to dictatorship and a military bloodbath (*NYT*, 6 February, 16 March; *Diário de Notícias*, 16 February). After elections gave the Socialists no more than 41 percent of the seats in the National Assembly (and only 35 percent of the popular vote), the PCP warned that to exclude the Communists from the next government would be to take no account of the election results. The election, it claimed, represented a "victory of the left" since the combined vote of the Socialists and the Communists gave them a majority of 146 deputies, compared with a total of 112 for the Popular Democrats and the Social Democratic Center. The PCP also pointed to its own increased popular vote count, 15 percent versus 12.5 percent in the April 1975 elections, and to Socialist losses, down to 35 percent from 38 percent in 1975 (*NYT*, 28 April; *Washington Post*, 19 May). In the 1975 election, the Communists had actually attracted 16.5 percent of the vote, which was divided between the PCP and its front organization, the MDP. The latter offered no candidate in 1976. Incidentally, PCP strength increased to 17 percent of the popular vote in December municipal elections, versus 33 percent for the Socialists, a slight decline from April (*CSM*, 15 December).

Though calling for "national reconciliation," the victorious Soares adamantly rebuffed overtures from all parties to form a coalition government. He insisted that his government had to be cohesive to prevent a continuing paralysis by internal bickering that had characterized the six previous governments (*NYT*, 18, 24 July). He refused an alliance with the Communists because they had "not given sufficient proof that they are ready to abide by the rules of democracy." Coalition with the Popular Democrats and the Social Democratic Center would allow the Communists to "polarize the left" and to wean away much of the Socialists' working class support. Some observers thought this possibility was confirmed by the results of the presidential election in June. The Socialists lost a sizable percentage of their voters to the independent and populist candidates, Major Otelo Saraiva de Carvalho (16 percent of the total vote) and Admiral José Pinheiro de Azevedo (14 percent). A contributing factor may have been the Socialist alliance with the center parties in supporting General Eanes. (Ibid., 6 February, 3 July/ *Washington Post*, 9 March, 8 July.)

In the face of Soares's refusal to cooperate, the PCP warned that it would reject any government that did not allow it to participate in policy making. An exclusively Socialist government, it said, would "open the way to a capitalist recovery" and "inevitably would provoke the opposition and resistance of the masses" (*NYT*, 22 April, 8 July, 15 August; *Washington Post*, 19 May).

Undeterred by the Communist "blackmail" threats, the outgoing Socialist-dominated cabinet launched an austere program of tax increases, energy cuts, and limits on worker participation in business management (*Manchester Guardian*, 18 July). Then the new Socialist government tackled the more critical and sensitive issue of trying to raise labor productivity. It revoked the 1975 law recognizing the Communist-dominated union confederation, Intersindical (*CSM*, 19 October). It also submitted to the National Assembly measures to allow employers to dismiss workers for such causes as unjustified absenteeism, refusal to obey instructions, and acts of violence against people and goods. The latter was aimed in part at correcting the practice of workers in many plants of holding managers hostage in their offices. Curbs on strikes and other union rights were likewise called for. (*NYT*, 2 October; *CSM*, 19 October; *Wall Street Journal*, 19 November.

The PCP vigorously protested against the "anti-worker" policies, but refrained from mobilizing the unions they controlled into a massive strike action. The party appeared to be holding back to allow worker discontent to feed on further Socialist "mistakes," thereby strengthening Communist support in the unions (*CSM*, 15, 30 November). Earlier in the year, when they held a cabinet post, the Communists had also been restrained in their opposition. Reportedly, they had been allowed to remain in the government coalition—in spite of their alleged participation in the November putsch attempt—as a form of insurance to keep down labor agitation. However, they had pointedly refused to share responsibility for austerity measures and for the offensive launched by "reactionary and conservative" forces to "restore the positions lost by big capital. (*NYT*, 7, 11, January; TASS, 6 February; *Visión*, New York, 15 May.)

The Socialist government was also faced with a continuing decline in agricultural production, especially in the southern Alentejo region. That Communist stronghold was the only area in the country where land had been occupied, much of it illegally, under the agrarian reform law of 1975. António Lopes Cardoso, minister of agriculture in both the coalition and Socialist cabinets, condemned the illegal occupations—though many said he was actually tolerant of them—and set new guidelines in January for a more orderly transfer of land. The PCP agreed to the new procedures and to the dismissal of the much criticized Communist administrator of the agrarian reform program, on condition that he be succeeded by another Communist (*NYT*, 6, 10 January). His replacement was also relieved of the post in March, accused of having incited farm workers to violence. Such "slanderous" charges, said the PCP, were part of the right-wing offensive against agrarian reform. (*WMR*, May.)

In October, Cardoso ordered 101 small and medium-sized farms that had been illegally seized to be returned to their owners (*CSM*, 19 October). The Communist-dominated farm unions indicated they would accede to the law provided the original plan for the expropriation of all large properties was carried out. Evictions of squatters took place without violence, but late in November squads of National Republican Guards reportedly had to act as bodyguards for the returning owners (*NYT*, 28 September, 2 October; *CSM*, 30 November). The Soares government announced that it would go ahead with the expropriation of another one million acres in the South, the only area of the country with huge landholdings (*CSM*, 19 October).

A rift in the cabinet between moderates headed by Soares and Marxists led by Cardoso forced the latter's resignation in November (ibid., 9 November). His dismissal had long been demanded by farmers who accused him of "consciously or unconsciously" communizing agriculture and of providing the southern collective farms with the bulk of financial aid available for agriculture. Some accused him of being a Communist agent in the Socialist party. Communists, on the other hand, labeled him a "fascist" (*NYT*, 13 January). Soares said that under the new minister of agriculture, António Barreto, there would be no policy changes on agrarian reform except to try to save the program "from being corrupted by totalitarianism" and to prevent new "overlords" from replacing the old estate owners (*CSM*, 9 November).

International Views and Policies. During the 1976 campaign for the legislative elections, the PCP and other parties assailed the Socialist party for exploiting for electoral advantage a two-day March meeting of European Socialists in Oporto. Soares campaigned after the meeting that "Europe is with us," and suggested that a victorious Socialist party would be in the strongest position to secure financial aid from abroad (*NYT*, 16 March). Then and later, as negotiations proceeded for heavy loans from the United States and some European countries, the PCP denounced the reinforcement of "ties of dependence" with the United States and "privileged relations" with capitalist Europe. Alvaro Cunhal criticized Portugal's entry in September into the Council of Europe and its plan to seek full membership in the Common Market. While continuing to accept Portuguese participation in NATO, the Communist leader opposed creation of NATO-type army brigades in Portugal. U.S. and West German assistance in planning the latter was requested by President Eanes. Cunhal called it "bad taste" to have scheduled NATO air-sea maneuvers off Portugal to begin the day after the April elections. (Ibid., 22 April, 6 August, 23 September; *CSM*, 28 July; *Wall Street Journal*, 19 November.)

Hostile press reaction in Portugal followed a comment by U.S. President Gerald Ford in an October television debate that seemed to suggest a U.S. success in preventing a Communist takeover in Portugal. This was cited by Communists as confirmation of CIA intervention; others insisted it was the "Portuguese people" who saved democracy in 1975 (*CSM*, 18 October).

The PCP led the fight in Portugal early in the year to win support for Portuguese recognition of the Luanda government of the Popular Movement for the Liberation of Angola (MPLA). The pro-Communist *Diário de Notícias* warned that further delay could jeopardize all of the Portuguese government's $4.6 billion investment in Angola since recognition had to precede discussion of the problem. The Socialist party finally withdrew its opposition, thereby making possible recognition on 22 February. Prior to the legislative elections in March, Cunhal said that friendly relations with all independent African states could be guaranteed only by a victory of the "left." He said Portugal had to set aside "once and for all the idea of being superior and paternal" (ANSA, Buenos Aires, 31 March).

Between May and September, diplomatic relations between Portugal and Angola were suspended when Angola took offense at hostile articles in the Portuguese press and a bomb explosion in its mission at Oporto (*NYT*, 1 October).

International Activities and Contacts. The PCP sent a delegation to Luanda early in February 1976 for a meeting sponsored by the Afro-Asian People's Solidarity Organization (AAPSO). The objective was to rally international support for the immediate withdrawal of foreign troops from Angola and for the prompt international recognition of the MPLA government (IPS, Buenos Aires, 3 February). In March, Cunhal led a PCP group on a visit to Angola and Mozambique. He joined local officials in expressing support for the evacuation of South African troops from Angola and for African struggles against colonialism, racism, and apartheid (TASS, 24 March).

PCP delegations also visited Moscow and several East European countries. In February, the Portuguese Communist Youth Union, the Portuguese Union of Communist Students, and the youth section of the "Portugal-USSR" Society visited the Soviet Union. They discussed problems of the international youth movement with the Komsomol Central Committee and the USSR Youth Organizations Committee (*Komsomolskaya Pravda*, Moscow, 22 May).

Also in February, Cunhal headed a group that visited with Communist parties in Czechoslovakia, Yugoslavia, Romania, and Bulgaria. The group then attended the 25th Congress of the Soviet party in Moscow. In Sofia, Cunhal receifed the "International Dimitrov Price" that had been awarded him in 1974 in honor of his struggle for "peace, democracy and socialism" (Bulgarian Telegraphic Agency, BTA, 20 February; TASS, 28 February, 1 March; *Diário de Notícias*, 1 March).

In June, Cunhal attended the conference of European Communist and workers' parties in East Berlin. Questioned on his return to Lisbon regarding possible splits among the parties assembled there, he acknowledged that there were "differences of opinion" but insisted that "common solutions" were reached (Lisbon radio, 1 July; *Neues Deutschland*, East Berlin, 1 July). In this connection, Cunhal had stressed at a Lisbon rally during the previous month that the PCP was determined to "remain in solidarity" with the Soviet Union in spite of efforts of "imperialists and reactionaries" to divide the "progressive forces." The rally was held in honor of visiting leaders of the Chilean, Uruguayan, and Brazilian Communist parties (Lisbon radio, 16 May).

Publications. The PCP's principal publication is the daily *Avante*. Except for a two-year hiatus under the Salazar dictatorship, it has been publishing continuously — though mostly underground — since 1931 (Avante, 4 March). Pro-Communist views are also expressed in *Diário de Notícias*. The Socialist newspaper, *República*, which had been seized by its Communist printers in May 1975 (see *YICA, 1976*, p. 206), had to cease publication in December of that year because its publisher, a leftist military officer, resigned and because of a drastic drop in circulation. In January 1976 it was returned by the Azevedo government to its owner (*NYT*, 29 January).

Rival Communist Organizations. Left-wing violence was relatively subdued during 1976, apparently inhibited by the disciplined hand of General Eanes as chief of staff and later as president. The first test of his declared determination to brook no defiance of legal authority came on New Year's Day when a crowd of leftists, many of them allegedly armed, attempted to storm a prison in Oporto. They were protesting the continued detention of 150 military men and civilians implicated in the November 1975 uprising. When the demonstrators began to throw stones at guardsmen, the latter opened fire, killing three and seriously wounding 15. The general staff of the AFM charged that the rioters were seeking to discredit the authorities with their provocations. (*NYT*, 2 January.)

The PCP joined Marxist-Leninist and Maoist groups in condemning the "repressive acts" but at the same time it warned that such was the fruit of "pseudo-revolutionary leftist provocations" (ibid., 4 January). The party also condemned as "divisive" a rash of anti-government demonstrations held later in the month as well as a one-day "people's market" organized by far-leftists in downtown Lisbon to offer food at cut-rate prices. The intent was to show that the government and "capitalist intermediaries" rather than farmers were responsible for high food prices; actually the project failed because very little food could be provided for the market. (Ibid., 17, 19 January.) Such "futile adventurism" showed, said Alvaro Cunhal, that inflexible "leftism" could not give correct guidance to the "people's" movement, as it could never understand the need for an occasional orderly and disciplined retreat or for collaborating with allies in order to broaden the battle front, but instead always advocated attack even when it was "in full retreat" (*Diário de Notícias*, 16 January).

Presumably Cunhal was suggesting, in effect, that the crushing of the November revolt necessitated a strategic retrenchment. A few days after his advice to the far left, a military commission released a preliminary report fixing responsibility for the revolt on the radical Major Otelo Saraiva de Carvalho, former AFM chief of security, and on the PCP, the PCP-dominated labor confederation, and several far-leftist organizations. Carvalho was arrested, and reduced in rank from general to major, though released shortly afterward pending trial on charges of military conspiracy. He was specifically accused of having provided arms and the go-ahead for the mutiny. (*NYT*, 21, 24 January.)

A ban on participation by Carvalho in political activities was lifted to permit him to take part in the presidential race in June. He won second place with 16 percent of the votes. His populist campaign, calling for a revolutionary front of leftist forces, apparently enabled him to attract a sizable number of voters who had previously supported the Socialists and Communists. Carvalho professed to see himself as a potential "Fidel Castro of Europe" had the circumstances been right. (Ibid., 13, 29 June, 8 July; *Intercontinental Press*, 5 July.)

Following the elections, leftist groups that had supported Carvalho organized a "Movement for Popular Unity" and applied in July for legal status as a party. Defying orders of the general staff not to make political statements, Carvalho told members that the movement was prepared to propose a revolutionary "grass-roots alternative" to the "bourgeois" Socialist government (*NYT*, 5 October).

Elbert Covell College
University of the Pacific

H. Leslie Robinson

San Marino

Politics in this tiny (19,000 population) republic entirely surrounded by Italy are an extension of Italian politics. The Communist Party of San Marino (Partito Comunista di San Marino; PCS) is a branch of the Italian Communist Party (PCI). The PCS is estimated to have about 300 members. In the most recent general election it gained 15 seats in the 60-member General Council.

Unlike the PCI, the PCS and its Socialist allies were unable to force San Marino's ruling Christian Democrats to abandon the concept of majority and opposition. But the PCS feels that the changes taking place in Italy and the world will make for the success of its "policy of unity" between "all democratic and anti-fascist forces" (*Pravda*, 6 March 1976). At its Ninth Congress, held in December 1976, the PCS again stressed that it aims to unite "all left-wing, democratic forces" and that it believes "conditions are ripe for establishing a government on a broad popular basis, including the Communists" (TASS, 11 December).

The party president is Ermenegildo Gasperoni; Umberto Barulli is general secretary. Gasperoni delivered the PCS's address at the conference of European Communist and workers' parties in East Berlin (*Pravda*, 3 July). Barulli delivered the main address at the Ninth Congress of the PCS, in which he termed the USSR "the bulwark of peace and freedom" (TASS, 11 December). He also addressed the 25th Congress of the Soviet Party in March (ibid., 6 March), where his speech cited the successes of the USSR as proof of "the decisive supremacy of the Socialist system." ascribed to the Soviet party the "main role" in the common struggle for socialism, and praised L. I. Brezhnev.

The PCS maintains excellent relations with Moscow-line parties around the world. The Soviet party sent Vadim Zagladin, first deputy of the Central Committee's International Department, to carry its greetings to the PCS's Ninth Congress. European parties sent representatives of similar rank, and Asian parties, such as the Vietnam Workers' Party (*FBIS*, 9 December) and the Workers' Party of Korea (*FBIS*, 14 December 1976) sent messages of congratulations. The PCS probably remains as staunch a Moscow-line party as ever.

Stanford University   Angelo Codevilla

Spain

The largest and most influential Communist organization in Spain, and the third largest in Western Europe, is the Communist Party of Spain (Partido Comunista de España; PCE). Founded in 1920, it has been illegal since 1939. It claims that its membership of 100,000, which it announced in mid-1976 that it was going to triple, is the largest of any illegal party in history. Polls taken in 1976 indicated that in free elections the PCE might attract up to 12 percent of the votes, mostly in the big cities and highly industrial areas. Some analysts speculated that in Andalusia the party would probably win up to 35 percent of the votes (*NYT*, 29 January). The PCE's independent stance toward the Soviet Union has deprived it of financial support from that source, but it has attracted ample contributions from others, especially the Italian Communist Party (*Washington Post*, 22 September).

A rival group that splintered from the PCE in 1970 is known as the Spanish Communist Workers' Party (Partido Comunista de Obreros Españoles, PCOE). Led by Enrique Líster, it favored continued close alignment with policies of the Soviet Union. It has been ineffectual and not very active, especially since 1974 when the Soviets sought to appease the PCE by withdrawing support from Líster (see *YICA, 1975*, p. 243).

Though there are semi-autonomous PCE branches that exploit the separatist sentiments of various regions, such as the Catalan United Socialist Party and the Basque (Euzkadi) Communist Party, the principal separatist movements are rival factions of the ETA (Euzkadi ta Askatasuna, "Basque Homeland and Liberty"). The ETA has been active since 1959 as a guerrilla group seeking "national liberation" for the Basque region. In 1970 the movement separated into a terrorist wing called ETA-V and a military-political wing called ETA-VI. The latter was an outgrowth of ETA's Sixth Assembly, which opposed the Fifth Assembly's resolutions calling for violence. A Marxist ideology is said to inspire about a third of the ETA militants, with the ETA-VI having merged in 1974 with a Trotskyist organization to become the Revolutionary Communist League-ETA-VI (Liga Comunista Revolucionaria-ETA-VI; LCR-ETA-VI). This league was itself a rival of the Trotskyist Communist League of Spain (Liga Comunista de España; LCE). In September the LCR-ETA-VI announced that henceforth it would be known as the Revolutionary Communist League except in the Basque provinces, where it would continue with the name ETA-VI. The party announced that it currently has 3,500 members, 60 percent of whom are workers. (*FBIS*, 20 September; EFE, Madrid, 25 September.)

The principal terrorist groups in Spain are the ETA-V and a Maoist urban guerrilla group called the Patriotic and Revolutionary Anti-Fascist Front (Frente Revolucionario Antifascista y Patriótico, FRAP).

Leadership and Organization. The PCE is headed by a 7-member Secretariat, 35-member Executive Committee, and 142-member Central Committee. Secretary-General Santiago Carrillo claimed in 1976 to have directed party activities while living illegally in Spain during most of the year; Chairman Dolores Ibarruri, whose position was largely honorary, continued to live abroad. Carrillo claimed that Ibarruri was the only member of the Executive Committee not now living underground within Spain. (*NYT*, 7 August.)

223

The Central Committee decided in July at a meeting in Rome to transform its hitherto clandestine cell organization to an "open" system of labor, school, and neighborhood branches. These would hold public assemblies in which political and organizational questions could be debated and resolved. The Central Committee refused to accept an offer by Spanish authorities to allow it to meet discreetly in Madrid if Carrillo and Ibarruri did not participate. (Ibid., 1 August.)

Carrillo led his party in forming an alliance in 1974 with various leftist-to-rightist opponents of the government in a "Democratic Junta of Spain." In March 1976, the Junta joined with the Socialist-dominated "Democratic Convergence Platform" to organize the "Democratic Coordination" to pressure the government into making an immediate break with the past in favor of a coalition government. The new organization, which embraced 13 major opposition groups, was branded subversive and illegal by the government because it included various illegal parties such as the PCE.

Party workers also occupied positions of leadership in the underground trade unions called Workers' Commissions (Comisiones Obreras, or "CC OO"), which are organized in small cells and are used to promote strikes and other labor agitation. The PCE claims a CC OO membership of 1 million. The chairman of the Workers' Commissions is Marcelino Camacho, who is also a member of the PCE Executive Committee.

Communists also manipulated their way, through 1975 elections, into key positions within the government-sponsored National Confederation of Trade Unions (Central Nacional Sindicalista; CNS) "in order to wreck" the latter from within. Employers were said to estimate that at least 50 percent of official union leaders in big companies were at the same time militants playing dual roles as CC OO leaders (*Wall Street Journal*, 30 August). Communists claimed election of 80 percent of the shop stewards in the CNS (*NYT*, 14 July).

Domestic Attitudes and Activities. Under King Juan Carlos, democratic reforms gradually introduced during 1976 brought increasing freedoms for all non-Communist and non-violent political groups. Most political prisoners and exiles—except for some 100 terrorists, PCE leaders Santiago Carrillo and Dolores Ibarruri, and the PCOE's Enrique Líster—were pardoned. Among the more than 6,000 prisoners granted amnesty between November 1975 and July 1976 were 60 PCE leaders, including CC OO chairman Marcelino Camacho.

Political meetings and demonstrations—with some exceptions—were legalized, and strikes and other disturbances were generally handled by police with restraint. The government partly repealed the 1975 decree that called for summary trials and mandatory death sentences for terrorists. The censorship office interfered little with an increasingly critical press. Opposition spokesmen were even permitted late in the year to express themselves on the state-run radio and television. (*Christian Science Monitor* [CSM], 9 February; U.S. News & World Report, 7 June; *New Orleans Times-Picayune*, 27 September; *NYT*, 13 November.)

A division within the government between conservatives and reformists resulted in a cautious approach to innovation. During the first half of the year, Premier Carlos Arias Navarro and his cabinet sought a delicate blend of "continuity" and modest liberalization, trying to balance rightist resistance to change against opposition demands for an immediate and total dismantling of the entire Francoist apparatus (*NYT*, 9 May). As the year progressed, the King's growing popularity with Spaniards strengthened his personal leverage and that of his cabinet. However, even after he succeeded in replacing the Arias government in July with the more aggressively reformist one of Premier Adolfo Suárez González, army and other right-wing apprehension about making concessions to Communists inhibited government negotiations with opposition forces (ibid., 2 July).

The Franco-fashioned Cortes (parliament) was persuaded in June to legalize all political parties exept the PCE and violent separatist groups (ibid., 10 June). Then it accepted the government's proposal for general elections to be held in the spring of 1977 for a bicameral legislature. The latter would be empowered to devise a new constitution (ibid., 19 November). The plan was also approved by an overwhelming 94 percent of Spanish voters in a December referendum. The turnout at the polls was over 77 percent. The vote was dismissed by extreme leftists as a "Francoist, rigged one" (*CMS*, 17 December).

Abstention from the voting had been urged by a left-of-center opposition to the "democratic masquerade." It was protested that a political solution had to be negotiated among all parties—including the PCE—instead of being "bestowed" (*NYT*, 3 July; *CSM*, 17 November). The opposition concensus was expressed through the "Democratic Coordination," the alliance forged between the Communist-led Democratic Junta and the Democratic Convergence Platform. The latter group included the Spanish Socialist Workers Party (Partido Socialista de Obreros Españoles; PSOE)—the main Socialist force in Spain—and the Christian Democrats (see *YICA, 1976*, p. 213). These two parties had previously refused to cooperate with the Communists; they put aside their misgivings in March to join with them in demanding formation of a provisional government embracing all political parties (*CSM*, 29 March; *Washington Post*, 30 March). Even so, PSOE's moderate leader, Felipe González, spoke out in September against any possible coalition government with the Communists—that, he said, could provoke a civil war and coup d'état. He expressed doubts about the sincerity of the Communists: they were not "believable as democrats" because their internal power structure was not democratic (*Washington Post*, 22 September).

The exclusion of Communists and terrorists from the political process was secured by two provisions of a penal code promulgated in July. Illegal parties would be those that engaged in violent subversion or sought "the destruction of the juridical, political, social, and economic system," and those that, "subject to international discipline, seek to implant a totalitarian system" (*NYT*, 15 July). Interior Minister Manuel Fraga Iribarne was understood to convey the notion that Communists might be legalized after 1977 elections if they "behaved themselves," but that such a step would not be acceptable to the army any earlier. Theoretically, the delay would allow time for the "respectable" parties of the center and non-Communist left to gain strength so that Spain would not "make Italy's mistake" (*Washington Post*, 8 June; *CSM*, 24 June, 2 August; *NYT*, 4 September). Some secret service authorities were said to fear there would not be sufficient resources to confront a wave of Russian spies supposedly preparing to "invade" Spain (*CSM*, 17 August).

As proof that the PCE did not take orders from abroad, Communist leaders called attention to the party's record of fierce defiance of Moscow. They insisted that parties in Spain, Italy, and France were trying to bring Marxism up to date. CC OO leader Camacho said that Secretary-General Carrillo was "even more reasonable" than Italian Communist leader Enrico Berlinguer. A jailed Communist wrote in a Madrid daily that banning the party in the name of democracy was "as impossible as squaring the circle." At a press conference to which the Soviet news agency TASS was not invited, Carrillo warned that if Spain's left were not admitted to parliament a grave economic crisis would result. This was not a threat, he said, but a "logical deduction." (Ibid., 13 December.)

Spokesmen of other parties in the Democratic Coordination agreed that the PCE's new liberal stands had earned it the right to be legalized so that its conversion to democracy could be tested (*Washington Post*, 22 September). They downgraded fears that experiences in Italy and Portugal could be duplicated in Spain. It was said that the Italian Communist Party had grown recently in power through default because of 20 years of bad government by other parties, and that the Portuguese Communist Party had waned in influence after free elections proved how weak it really was. Polls were cited showing that the PCE could muster only 12 percent or less of the votes in free Spanish elections. (*NYT*, 14 June; *CSM*, 2 August.)

A more significant concern of the PSOE and the Christian Democrats was that they could alienate much working-class support by participating in elections from which the Communists were banned. The PCE might gain a major advantage, it was felt, by charging them with "cooperating with Franco's

successors" while it maintained its clandestine "purity." It was even argued that this was a "clever trap" set by Interior Minister Fraga Imbarne to assure a center-right victory in the election—as a vehicle for his own personal ambition—since leftist parties would be sufficiently weakened because of abstentions by those who might otherwise support them (*Washington Post*, 8 June; *CSM*, 24 June). Since pressure on the government to legalize the PCE failed to have any effect, the PSOE decided at a party congress in early December to leave the door open for possible participation in 1977 elections, even while continuing to boycott the December referendum (*CSM*, 10 December). Incidentally, Fraga Imbarne, who did not join the Suárez cabinet, formally announced in October the formation of a new conservative party called Popular Alliance (*NYT*, 10 October).
Popular Alliance (*NYT*, 10 October).

In spite of its outlawed status and continued police harassment, the PCE circulated much more openly than it had ever dared under the Franco government. Party members were periodically detained during the year, but later relesed, for taking part in illegal meetings or press conferences. Five were arrested in November for openly recruiting members in Madrid, handing out "the first of 200,000 membership cards" (*CMS*, 23 November). Carrillo was arrested in December and later released on bail after he held a press conference in Madrid. He mocked the government's refusal to allow him in Spain by saying he had lived there anyhow clandestinely since February, except for a few trips abroad, and that he intended to remain (ibid., 13 December). His return to Spain was prompted, it was said, by the expectation of amnesty and by concern that if he stayed abroad he might be pushed aside by younger leaders openly operating within Spain. Premier Suárez seemed to be encouraging his displacement by newer leadership unassociated with civil war memories when he said that the return of Carrillo and Ibarruri would make conciliation difficult. There was an apparent implication that a transformed party might be more acceptable to the government and the army (ibid., 27 August). Carrillo was arrested, but was released 30 December on bail, in effect gaining the right to reside legally in Spain (*NYT*, 31 December).

One consequence of the official attempt to ostracize the PCE from national politics, according to some analysts, was that the party had little or no incentive to try to contain a labor backlash over wage freezes. The Finance Minister suggested in January 1976 that Spain had manufactured its 17 percent inflation in 1975 with 28 percent wage increases. He appealed for a social pact in which labor would agree to moderate its demands. Communist labor organizers in the CC OO denounced government austerity measures, charging that labor was being made to pay for the economic crisis (ibid., 2 January). During the first three months, a massive labor offensive was launched, with strikes in Madrid alone affecting more than 150,000 workers in a two-week period in January. This was said to be the biggest show of labor strength since Franco had come to power (ibid., 13, 18 January, 5 March). In November a nationwide strike brought out between 500,000 workers—estimated by the government— and 2 million—claimed by the unions (*Wall Street Journal*, 15 November). The Spanish labor force totals 8 million."

Police reaction was relatively subdued, following government orders to replace Franco-era harshness with internationally accepted crowd-control techniques (*CSM*, 5 March). Arrests and the use of tear gas, truncheons, and rubber bullets generally were resorted to just as a last resort. Striking rail and post office employees were conscripted into the army to force them back to work, but subway strikers were not (*NYT*, 15, 25 January, 26 September). Police in the Basque town of Vitoria panicked in a mob situation in March, when they fired on strikers, killing two and injuring 30. The incident was exploited by leftists as additional "proof" that the government's "controlled advance" was merely Francoism with a good public relations agent (*CSM*, 5, 9 March).

The authorities charged that most of the labor conflicts were orchestrated by the Communists with the intent of bringing down the government (*NYT*, 14 January). Certainly the strongest union force in Spain continued to be the workers' commissions, in which the Communists appeared to have the dominant influence. Some West German analysts were said to think that should Spain be overtaken by a political disruption similar to the recent one in Portugal, the Spanish Communists would find it much easier to take over the government than had their Portuguese counterparts. This was allegedly because the PCE has a higher percentage of party members in the CC OO and in the press (*CSM*, 12 January). On the other hand, others pointed out that rank-and-file worker support for the PCE is not measured and may be unimpressive. There were reports in January that many workers ignored Communist pleas to continue striking after settlements were reached (*NYT*, 14 January).

The chief rivals of the Communists for influence on workers were the Socialists, through their General Union of Workers (Unión General de Trabajadores; UGT). The latter surfaced in April with its first congress within Spain in 44 years. Hopes were expressed of rebuilding its pre-civil war strength of a million members—compared with 6,700 at present—so as to displace the Communists as the dominant force in the labor movement. The UGT demanded that the government discontinue the state-controlled syndicate organizations that join labor and management. It feared the Communists would retain their advantage over the Socialists if the government followed its own suggestion of merely overhauling and giving freedom to the existing syndicates. While Socialists were boycotting syndicate elections in 1975, the Communists infiltrated the organization and claimed to have secured election of 80 percent of the shop stewards (*CSM*, 28 January; *NYT*, 19 April).

To head off possible Socialist advances, CC OO leader Camacho announced plans in July for setting up a new single labor organization "containing all shades of public opinion." The central leadership would act not on the basis of its own interpretation of workers' wishes but on the basis of decisions of factory assemblies. All workers, whether dues-paying members or not, would have a voice and vote in such decisions. Camacho's proposal was interpreted by the UGT as a Communist effort to monopolize Spanish labor. (*NYT*, 14 July).

International Views and Positions. In 1976 a major concern of Santiago Carrillo and his party continued to be the projection of an image of a democratic, nationalist PCE independent of the Soviet Union. The image was not helped by an alleged Moscow offer, passed along to Interior Minister Fraga Imbarne, to have Carrillo and Ibarruri removed from their positions of leadership if that would facilitate official recognition of the party (*Intercontinental Press*, New York, 19 April). PCE leaders were said to be increasingly irritated by stepped-up overt contacts that Soviet officials based in Spain made with opposition leaders, including PCE members. They also condemned theSoviet Union's trade with Spain because it helped bolster the anti-Communist Spanish monarchy. (*Washington Post*, 23 August.)

The PCE especially emphasized its alignment with the independent "Euro-Communist" parties of Italy and France in opposition to Moscow's call for "solidarity." At the two-day conference of European Communist and workers' parties in East Berlin, in late June, Carrillo publicly declared, "Today we are adults. . . . We have no center that gives us directions." He compared the new resistance to Moscow's dominance to the heretic Martin Luther's rejection of Rome: "We also had our pope, our Vatican . . . but as we mature and become less of a church, we must become more rational, closer to reality." He could not have said these things at a Communist meeting two years ago, he said, but now the Russians had to "resign themselves" to such views. (*CSM*, 13 January; *NYT*, 7 July, 22 September.)

Carrillo said it was too bad that the United States was also opposing the development of "Euro-Communism." He blamed U.S. secretary of state Henry Kissinger for provoking the "political crisis" that forced the June resignation of the Arias cabinet. Carrillo indicated that he regretted the departure, not of Arias himself, "a relic of Franco," but of the more progressive Foreign Minister Areilza and Interior Minister Fraga Imbarne, (*NYT*, 7 July, 7 August). Presumably the "provocation" was a reference to advice said to have been given by Kissinger to King Juan Carlos against immediate legalization of the PCE. Areilza and Fraga Imbarne were said to have pushed within the Arias government for such legalization. Washington's ambassador in Madrid also reportedly warned liberals in the government, as well as opposition leaders, that recognition of such a "non-democratic" party would be dangerous for Spain (*Washington Post*, 8 June).

In spite of the American attitude toward the PCE, Carrillo said he endorsed continuation of the U.S. bases in Spain for the present and a bilateral alliance as a counter to the Warsaw Pact. Americans should realize, he said, that the West European Communist parties do not want to change the strategic balance, but really want both blocs to take away their foreign bases simultaneously. He also indicated that he favored Spain's application for NATO membership, on condition that organization did not try to veto Communist participation in the Spanish government or otherwise interfere in the country's internal affairs. Carrillo likewise expressed support for Spain's admission into the European Common Market. Spain belongs to Western Europe, he asserted, and cannot join COMECON, "Russia's mirror image." (*NYT*, 7 July, 7 August; *EFE*, Madrid, 18 August.)

International Party Contacts. Santiago Carrillo made "friendly visits" to Romania and Yugoslavia in January and May 1976. His five-day visit to Japan in February to meet with Japan Communist Party leaders marked the first time the Spanish and Japanese parties had conferred since 1971 (Kyodo News Service, Tokyo, 28 March). Carrillo was in Rome in February for consultations with Italian parties and in July for a three-day PCE Central Committee meeting. He was asked in February if there was any political significance in the fact that he was in Rome instead of attending the 25th Congress of the Communist Party of the Soviet Union in Moscow. He replied that the PCE delegation there was headed by Dolores Ibarruri; it was more important, he asserted, for him to be in Rome with delegations of the Democratic Junta and the Democratic Convergence Platform seeking the support of Italian democratic parties for Spain's struggle for full democracy (*Corriere della Sera*, Milan, 26 February).

Dolores Ibarruri also attended the Central Committee meeting in Rome, where she told cheering delegates that "all the facts indicate this will be the last session held outside Spain" (Belgrade radio, 28 July). Ibarruri visited Romania in January, where she received the "Victory of Socialism" award on her 80th birthday, and Yugoslavia in August.

In February, Marcelino Camacho addressed a conference of British trade unionists in London and conferred with party leaders in France. In August he spent two weeks in the USSR, stopping off in Yugoslavia on the way there. He was warmly received in Moscow, where he remarked that perhaps no capitalist country could compare with the Soviet Union in giving its people such opportunities for education, recreation, and care of children (TASS, 30 August).

Two other members of the PCE Central Committee, Marcos Lana and Ramón Mendezona, visited Yugoslavia in May, the latter to attend the Fifth Congress of Yugoslav Volunteers in the Spanish Republican Army. Juan Gómez, a member of the PCE Executive Committee, made a visit to Hungary in September.

PCE Media. The PCE publishes abroad the quarterly theoretical journal, *Nuestra Bandera*, and the weekly official organ, *Mundo Obrero*, "Radio Independent Spain" also broadcasts short-wave party messages to Spain from facilities in Bucharest.

Activities of Basque and Rival Communist Organizations. ETA-V terrorists, unimpressed by the government's moves toward political liberalization, continued their campaign of violence in 1976. They allegedly theorized that terrorism would foment divisions within the government and provoke repression, thereby sparking a leftist revolution. With their top leaders in prison and unlikely to be favored with amnesty, the remaining militants were said to be bankrupt and rent by internal quarrels (*CSM*, 20 February, 13 April, 6 October). In a desperate move to collect ransom money, one subfaction kidnaped the son of a Basque industrialist in January and a popular Basque industrialist in

April, and murdered them when it was unable to collect. It also sought to extort a heavy "revolutionary tax" out of 50 other Basque industrialists. In an effort to halt ETA fund raising, the government threatened stiff penalties against anyone paying or negotiating with kidnappers (ibid., 5 April; *NYT*, 9 April).

Also slain in February was the mayor of a Bilbao suburb, though ETA apologized for this "involuntary crime" (Madrid radio, 13 February). In October, ETA terrorists assassinated a Basque member of the Spanish Council of the Realm, Juan María de Araluce y Villar, along with his chauffeur and three police bodyguards (*NYT*, 5 October). The killers then held a press conference in France to boast of their "act of revolutionary justice" (*CSM*, 16 October).

The government responded to these incidents with a big mobilization of security forces, but there was reportedly no heavy-handed over-reaction as in previous years. In April, Interior Minister Fraga Imbarne promised to wage war on the terrorists "in a civilized way" but "implacably." In October, Fraga Imbarne's successor, Rodolfo Martín Villa, pledged "firmness" and "serenity." Both vowed that terrorism would not slow down the evolution toward democracy. Following each murder, more than 100 alleged ETA members were arrested, including three who were said to have confessed to the first killing (ibid., 19 April, 6 October). Basques repudiated the ETA for the killings and were indignant at this "enormous step backward" for the regional freedom struggle. Most of Spain's political groups, including the PCE, also condemned the killings (ibid., 6 October).

Another abduction took place in December, though credit was claimed by an unknown radical group that called itself the October First Anti-Fascist Resistance Group (Grupo de Resistencia Anti-fascista del Primero de Octubre; GRAPO). The victim was Antonio María de Oriol, a wealthy Basque industrialist and president of the Council of State, an advisory body to the King. The kidnappers threatened to kill Oriol if 15 leftist political prisoners were not released and flown to Algeria. Many Spaniards suggested that GRAPO might actually be a right-wing group seeking to promote a revulsion among Spaniards toward the left, thereby encouraging support for "law and order" and a vote against the December 15 referendum (ibid., 15 December).

GRAPO also claimed responsibility for a series of bomb explosions that rocked eight Spanish cities on 18 July. The organization declared that the date, the 40th anniversary of the start of the civil war, had been chosen for "numerous acts against monuments and centers of the fascists." Damaged were buildings of the government, of official labor syndicates, and of rightist organizations. A possible connection between GRAPO and the ETA and FRAPO groups was suggested (*NYT*, 19, 20 July).

Other violence during the year was attributed to right-wing extremist vigilantes, who attacked and threatened numerous leftists and fatally shot a student. Some charged that the July bombings were also a provocation by the right rather than by leftists. There was bitterness because the government was "soft" on rightist violence, promising investigations but scarcely ever making an arrest, while left-wing extremists were swiftly apprehended and dealt with much more rigorously. (*CSM*, 13 May, 5 October, 1, 24 November.)

Elbert Covell College
University of the Pacific

H. Leslie Robinson

Sweden

The forerunner of Sweden's Communist Party (Sveriges Kommunistiska Parti; SKP) was founded in May 1917. It joined the Communist International in July 1919. It originated from a split with the Social Democrats, and today's party and the name dates from another split in 1921. Inner tensions continued to plague the Communists during the 1920s and the 1930s.

After a period of relative insignificance during the 1950s the party profited from the rise of the New Left in Sweden and in 1967 changed its name to Left Party-Communists (Vänsterpartiet Kommunisterna; VPK). A large minority within the party criticized it for being "reformist" and founded Communist League, Marxist Leninists (Kommunistiska Förbundet Marxist-Leninisterna; KFML). The KFML was under the influence of Chinese Communism (Maoism). In 1973 the KFML appropriated the name SKP.

During the period 1970-76 the VPK has exerted an influence on Swedish politics disproportionate to its number of seats in the parliament. In 1970, Prime Minister Olof Palme and the Social Democrats, with 163 seats in the 350-seat parliament, had to rely on the VPK's 17 members for the survival of the Palme government. When the Social Democrats in the parliamentary elections of 16 September 1973 dropped to 156 seats and the VPK gained two, the importance of the party increased even more. During 1970-73 the VPK was admitted to such important parliamentary committees as defense and taxes, but after 1973 Palme compromised to the right with the liberals, thus putting a stop to a real Communist breakthrough in Swedish parliamentary life. With the fall of the Social Democratic government in the elections of 19 September 1976, the VPK seems once more to be threatened by political insignificance. In the 1973 parliamentary elections the VPK received 274,929 votes, or 5.3 percent of the electorate, a rise of 0.5 percent since 1970. In 1976 it received 252,898 votes, or 4.7 percent, a loss of 0.6 percent since 1973. The party is strongest in Stockholm, Göteborg, and the northernmost electoral region, with between 8 and 11 percent of the votes, and weakest in the southernmost region with 1.4 percent of the votes.

The latest VPK membership figures are from 1972, when the party was reported to have 14,500 members. The figures may be higher in 1976. The population of Sweden is about 8,143,000.

Organization and Internal Affairs. The party congress is theoretically the all-important organ of the VPK. It elects the 35-member Central Commiittee, since 1964 known as the Party Board. The Board selects an eight-member Executive Committee (Politburo), which directs the party work. There are 28 party districts, corresponding to Sweden's electoral regions, and 395 local organizations. Communist Youth (Kommunistisk Ungdom) is the party's youth organization.

Lars Werner is the new VPK chairman. He has been less successful than his predecessor Carl-Henrick Hermansson in keeping the party united. Dissension troubled VPK the whole year of 1976. One of the main points of debate seems to have been the VPK stand on nuclear energy. The party majority is opposed to nuclear energy, but the Västernorrland and Norrbotten party districts, along with some VPK members of parliament, are in favor of it.

The situation had worsened in October 1975 when two ombudsmen and a Västernorrland district chairman of the party were reprimanded and threatened with expulsion. All were later expelled. The main accusation seems to have been that the district was opposed to distributing the party's central organ, *Ny Dag*, in favor of *Norrskensflamman*, the Stalinist daily published in Luleå. Another accusation against the expelled was that they supported the USSR openly.

New local party organizations in Västernorrland were founded in January 1976 in opposition to the local district administration. At the Västernorrland annual party district conference, 14-15 February, the party district split in two and a rival district committee for Västernorrland was formed. The new committee criticized VPK for being anti-Soviet.

Dissension spread during the spring to Göteborg, where Stalinist, Rolf Hagel, ousted loyal VPK parliament member Gunvor Ryding. Alf Löwenborg, the Norrbotten Stalinist, ousted Eivor Marklund, the party's deputy chairman, from first place on the parliamentary election ticket.

Dissension also deeply split the party youth organization. In November 1975, 21 members were expelled for taking a pro-Moscow line.

The party's ideological and tactical fight with SKP continued during 1976. During the election campaign the SKP attacked the VPK for being the mouthpiece of the Soviet Union in Sweden.

Domestic Activities and Attitudes. In parliament the Communists concentrated during 1976 on a number of domestic and international issues. A seven-point economic program was put forward: "1. A wage struggle of solidarity, where different groups support each other in a struggle for higher wages and better working conditions with the aim to increase the share of workers in the production result. 2. An active price policy which interferes with monopolistic pricing through a price stoppage on food, measures for rent stoppage, etc. 3. A democratic tax policy whereby taxes of wage earners and low-income groups are reduced through higher taxation on big incomes, on property, profits, legacies, and gifts, and on company profits. 4. An active regional policy and investment policy by the government. . . . 5. A determined fight to reduce military expenditure and other costly, useless, and unproductive activities. 6. Nationalization of big companies—banks, steel industries, building corporations, etc. 7. An active struggle against big international monopolies, their speculation in currency, and their attempts to control the economy." (*Kommunisterna i riksdagen*: Motioner 1976.)

The VPK also demanded a working day of seven hours by 1977 and six hours by 1980, a cut in defense expenditures of about U.S. $500 million, a new defense force of local "guerrilla units" and the scrapping of Sweden's new, nationally constructed 37 Viggen aircraft.

Most of the domestic activities of the party were concentrated on the September elections. At an electoral conference on 12-13 June Lars Werner stressed the VPK's anti-nuclear energy stand and commented on the "Swedish road to socialism": "We are willing to discuss problems of democracy with Olof Palme and others. We say along with, for instance, our French and Italian comrades that our road to socialism is the road of democracy. . . . The socialism we are working for is not a transcribed model from other countries." (*Socialistisk Debatt* No. 3/1976.)

The results of the parliamentary and communal elections on 19 September were not encouraging for VPK. From having exerted a considerable influence on the ruling Social Democrat Party through its decisive 19 seats in parliament, the party lost its influence completely after the victory of the nonsocialist parties. With 252,902 votes, the party went from 5.3 to 4.7 percent of the electorate and from 19 to 17 seats in parliament. It was deserted by 22,027 voters who probably supported the Social Democrats, fearing a bourgeois victory. (The Maoist SKP lost 2,135 voters and was reduced from 0.4 to 0.3 percent.) Locally the Communist strongholds in northern Sweden were hit hardest. (There, two bitter enemies now represent the party in parliament, the aforementioned Löwenberg and Marklund.) The internal struggle in Västernorrland also hurt the VPK. In the town of Kramfors, a center of the dissidents, only one representative was elected to the town council.

Lars Werner's comment on the election result reflected disappointment: "It means working harder outside the parliament than inside" (*Svenska Dagbladet*, 22 September). He also noted that the election was a sign, as he expressed it, that the rightists were starting to do well in Sweden.

International Views and Activities. In foreign policy the VPK asked the government to recognize and give foreign aid to the "Democratic Republic of East Timor," and to support liberation movements in Eritrea, Oman, South Africa, South West Africa, and Rhodesia. Sweden's withdrawal from the World Bank was also demanded. Cambodia, Laos, South Yemen, Cape Verde, and Somalia were suggested as recipients of Swedish foreign aid. Chile, Portugal, and Spain, and also Indochina continued to be in the VPK focus.

Policies of the Italian and French parties were discussed after analysis by Olof Palme in February, comparing their situation with that of the VPK. The major parties, he said, had abandoned proletarian internationalism, and must soon abandon democratic centralism; he called the VPK a mere dogmatic sect. In a speech at Tyresö, Lars Werner angrily answered Palme. The internationalism of the proletariat was increasing, he said, but the VPK did not endorse the dictatorship of the proletariat: "We have actually not advocated the dictatorship of the proletariat since 1944 when we wrote our own program for the first time. It is only with the aid of the workers and with their support that a socialist government can function in this country . . . (*Ny Dag*, 27 February-2 March.) Werner admitted that there was a "sectarian current" in VPK ranks, but added: "It is a misuse of words to call a party that is supported by 300,000 voters a sect." In August the VPK Board called for an end to the arms race. "An arms race, whose rate is still high, is continuing in Europe and all over the world. Military bases are strengthening, new systems of weapons that threaten the existence of the whole world are being designed." (TASS, 24 August.)

Maoist journals in Sweden carried a number of articles to mark the 8th anniversary of the Soviet occupation of Czechoslovakia. The SKP's *Gnistan* said: "The Soviet social-imperialists have established strict control across the land of Czechoslovakia. However, there is still resistance. The Soviet leaders are doomed to head for the end Hitler came to."

An article in the same journal (13 August) attacked détente, accusing the two superpowers, the USSR and the USA, of "preparing a war to redivide the world," and added: "Russian social-imperialism is the biggest menace to peace today. It has increasingly undertaken shameless acts of aggression against other countries. For instance, Russian mercenary troops are still in Angola."

International Activities and Contacts. Lars Werner headed a delegation to the 25th Congress of the Communist Party of the Soviet Union (CPSU). During a meeting of foreign guests and party activists in Moscow he stressed the importance of "proletarian internationalism." He also lauded the USSR for building "a developed socialist society" and went on to say that "the Soviet people have proved in practice the superiority of socialism in the matter of raising the working people's material, social and cultural standard. This fact is all the more obvious today, when a general crisis is deepening in the capitalist world and mass unemployment is growing." (TASS, 28 February 1976.)

At the end of May a Czechoslovak trade union delegation visited Sweden. The delegation met with Werner and other VPK representatives and also visited a state enterprise in northern Sweden.

A delegation from the VPK Göteborg district led by Rolf Hagel visited Leningrad in June and met with G. V. Romanov, first secretary of the Leningrad *oblast'* committee of the Soviet. Later in June, Werner visited Hungary as guest of the Hungarian ruling party and met with its first secretary, János Kádár. Also in June a group of VPK officials working in state and municipal institutions, headed by Party Board member S. Henriksson, visited party and trade organizations in the USSR.

A VPK delegation took part in the East Berlin Conference of European Communist and Workers' Parties on 29-30 June.

Other Leftist Groups—Rival Communists. There are a number of extreme leftist groups in Sweden. Among these, the Maoists are split into two "parties" each claiming to have the true interpretation of Marxism-Leninism.

The SKP, as noted earlier, grew out of KFML. Membership is secret, but is believed to be around 2,000. In 1973 party chairman Gunnar Bylin claimed SKP had 100 local organizations. In January an SKP delegation visited Albania at the invitation of the Central Committee of the Albanian Workers' Party (AWP). In late January the delegation was followed by one from the SKP's youth and student organization. When the SKP held its Second Congress, in April, the AWP sent a telegram expressing unity in the "struggle against U.S. imperialism, Soviet social imperialism, the monopolistic bourgeoisie, and all the various reactionaries" (Tirana Domestic Service, 25 April).

The Communist Association of Marxist-Leninist Revolutionaries—Kommunistiska Förbundet Marxist-Leninisterna; KFML(r)—broke away in October 1970 from the KFML (as the SKP was then named)). It has been riddled by internal conflicts but is a well organized cadre party claiming "cells" within Swedish industry and in the defense forces. It did not take part in the 1976 elections, but in 1973 received 8,014 votes or 0.2 percent. Membership is believed to be somewhat under 2,000.

The Trotskyites are weak in Sweden. The Communist Workers League (Kommunistiska Arbetarförbundet; KAF) is the Swedish section of the Fourth International. It ran candidates in a number of districts in the parliamentary 19 September elections. The World Congress of the Fourth International was held in Sweden in February 1974.

Publications. *Ny Dag* (New Day) is the VPK's twice-weekly central organ. It appears under the name *Arbetare-Tidningen* (Worker News) in Göteborg. The only daily of the party is *Norrskensflamman* (Blaze of the Northern Lights), published in Luleå. The VPK theoretical organ is *Socialistisk Debatt*. The central organ of the SKP is the weekly *Gnistan* (Spark). KFML(r)'s main voice is *Proletären* (The Proletarian). The Trotskyite KAF publishes *Internationalen* (The International).

Ängelholm, Sweden   Bertil Häggmann

Switzerland

The Swiss Labor Party—Partei der Arbeit (PdA), Parti du Travail (PdT), Partito del Lavoro (PdL), here referred to as PdA—is the oldest and main Moscow-oriented Communist party in Switzerland. It was founded as the Swiss Communist Party on 5-6 March 1921, banned by emergency decree (wartime legislation) on 27 November 1940, and re-formed under its present name on 14 October 1944.

Two other Communist organizations of later origin have acquired increasing prominence. The Marxist Revolutionary League—Ligue marxiste révolutionnaire (LMR), Marxistische Revolutionäre Liga (MRL), here referred to as LMR—was founded in 1969 by some 100 young intellectuals in Geneva and Lausanne who had been excluded from the PdA. It advocates violent overthrow of the system and is a member of the Trotskyite Fourth International. The Progressive Organizations, Switzerland (Progressive Organisationen, Schweiz; POCH, the CH being the car number-plate letters for Switzerland) was founded in 1972 by a congress of local and cantonal groups, with the oldest one, POB (Progressive Organisationen, Basel) dating back to a congress of extraparliamentary leftist opponents in 1968. It comprises young people who are dissatisfied with overcareful, rigid PdA leadership; some are below voting age—the POB makes a point of recruiting high-school students and apprentices in their teens. It follows the general Soviet line internationally; it has avoided so far a full-fledged commitment for or against "Eurocommunism," arguing that this is a tactical question concerning overage, top-heavy parties. It disagrees with the PdA on tactics and time tables in the field of domestic policy. The POCH concentrates almost totally on local, regional, and national questions, in that order, dealing with foreign policy only marginally. A third group, although older than the above two, is only intermittently active: the Swiss Popular Party (Parti populaire suisse; PPS), founded by dissident pro-Chinese in 1963 as Communist Party, Switzerland, renamed PPS in 1967.

Close to fifty groups and grouplets, some local, some regional, and most of them shifting into and out of more or less ephemeral alliances or roof organizations with equally variable names are enlivening the scene of what used to be called the "New Left" some years ago; today this associative-dissociative pattern of groups inspired by an endless range of leftist thinkers from Spartacus to Marx to Fanon to Dutschke, that ranges from anarchists to the left wing of Second International Socialists to social-minded elements in religious movements, has become the actual aspect of the Left, a Left that is in a state of flux which becomes more pronounced, in Western Europe anyway, year after year.

The PdA keeps spreading somewhat (see *YICA, 1976*, p. 223) in formerly conservative regions. Its total membership is given by party sources as close to 7,000 now, but it has lost votes to radical groups in its former strongholds of Geneva, Lausanne, Basel, and Zurich; its average loss in 15 of 22 cantons where PdA members ran for office in the national elections of October 1975 (see *YICA, 1976*, pp. 225-26) was 0.2 percent, falling from 2.6 percent of the national vote to 2.4. But the POCH gained 0.9 percent of the national vote, totaling 1.3 percent in eleven cantons, while the LMR, running for the first time, obtained 0.4 percent of the national vote in eleven cantons (only in six of these cantons did the LMR and the POCH run simultaneously). Although this competition (the PdA had suggested an alliance which was rejected by almost all cantonal POCH and LMR groups) limited the number of National Councillors (Representatives) of the Left to its previous 5 (see *YICA, 1976*, p. 226), the total voting strength of PdA, POCH, and LMR together rose by 1.1 percent to a national level of 4.1 (2.4 + 1.3 + 0.4).

The total population of Switzerland is 6.3 million. As it is, and until 1979, the PdA has four seats in the 200-member National Council and claims a fifth, a maverick New Left Socialist from the Italian-speaking Ticino canton. It has no seat in the Senate of 44. It is not, and has never been, represented in the seven-member Executive (Federal Council), which consists of the "traditional coalition" of two Liberal-Democrats, two Catholics, two Socialists, and one Popular Party (former Artisans' and Farmers' Party) member.

The LMR, the most disciplined of the militant groups of the Left, appears to have a core of some 600 full-fledged members and some 1,100 sympathizers. The LMR was disappointed by its showing in the 1975 elections, it was learned from party sources. Although they had practically no hope of having a candidate elected, they seem to have hoped to draw even with the POCH. The LMR came up pretty fast among radical intellectuals of the Left and its main influence lies with the newly developing Soldiers' Committees (Soldatenkomitees, Comités de soldats) which united in 1976 (date unknown) in a "national coordinating action." Soldiers' Committees are the spearhead of anti-militarist activities, and their personnel changes constantly, as they are formed among draftees of the militia system who do 17 to 19 weeks' basic training at age 20. In annual refresher courses lasting up to one month for cadres and three weeks for soldiers, agitation has not had meaningful results, so the aim of the Left is to recruit a sufficient number of draftees during basic training over many years to wind up with an "osmotic" influence among older reservists. The LMR also influences, especially since 1973, the militant teachers union, Gewerkschaft Kultur, Erziehung und Wissenschaft (GKEW). POCH, by the way, reacted by establishing its own Gewerkschaft Erziehung (GE) to fight LMR influence, but has so far only succeeded in forming six groups, while the GKEW numbers about a dozen. However, LMR groups tend to encapsulate themselves in their theoretically pure militancy and seem to remain somewhat stagnant, while the activities of the POCH are spreading.

POCH has been on the rise in several off-year local elections in 1976. In Basel (legislature of Basel half-canton and city), in March, it captured 5.3 percent of the vote (last time: 3.7 percent) and gained two seats at the expense of the PdA. In the Ticino (communal elections), acting through its occasional ally, the Partito socialista autonomo (PSA), it agreed to a common front with the PdA and the Socialists (SP). The coalition gained two seats in communal executives and holds now three seats, one each in Chiasso, Mendrisio, and Minusio. The PdA said it would "develop this successful election unity in everyday politics" (*Lavoratore*, 10 April), but experts pointed out that without POCH the common front of the left would have been decisively weaker and that it isn't so much the PdA as rather New Left circles around the Ticino PSA who are calling the shots. In the newly emerging half-canton of the Jura (see *YICA, 1976*, p. 225), where a constituent assembly was elected on 20-21 March, the PdA ran alone with 18 candidates and failed to have a single one elected.It put the blame squarely on the refusal of "leftist" groups like the LMR to cooperate (*Vorwärts*, 6, 15, 27 March). Also in Lausanne, a city of 120,000, where the PdA ran alone during a by-election for the city executive, its candidate collected an incredibly low 24 votes, because neither groups to its left nor socialists cooperated.

The POCH has now 14 seats in cantonal parliaments: 7 in Basel, where it gained 2 in the spring of 1976, 2 in Basel-Countryside, 2 in Zurich, one each in Lucerne, Solothurn, and Bern. It adds in its own statistics the 6 seats of the PSA in the Italian-speaking canton of Ticino (see *YICA, 1976*, p. 223) for a total of 20. It also has now 10 seats in the municipal councils of nine cities, among them Basel, Lucerne, and Zurich.POCH representatives have a single aim in legislative assemblies: to make their voice heard and be on the record. One seat is quite enough for this.

The inroads of extreme leftist trends into the Swiss Socialist Party (Second International), mentioned in *YICA, 1976*, p. 226), have come to a temporary standstill after almost creating a schism in the party during cantonal elections in Basel in March. National party president Helmut Hubacher, who held a seat in the cantonal parliament, had urged a "common electoral alliance of the Left" with the PdA, thus voicing the logical conclusion of many noises heard since the November 1975 national elections, but the Socialists rejected his idea, both nationally and locally. This had two consequences: Hubacher did not get the quorum in a first ballot. For the second ballot, the PdA withdrew its candidate in his favor, but he failed again, while a rank-and-file Socialist, proposed by the moderate party center, was elected; second consequence, the PdA lost one of its 9 seats in the city and half-canton's legislature. The POCH gained two seats and increased its vote percentage (see above).

The elections in Basel illustrated the actual situation: Some cadres and a militant wing try to push the Socialist Party to the left; however, if the pushing becomes too crude, as was the case with Hubbacher's cut-and-dried appeal, the majority of the party balks. This is the more remarkable as Basel is a city with strong leftist influences among the young and many working-class people.

PdA Leadership and Organization. Determined at the party's Tenth Congress in Basel, 1-3 June 1974, the PdA has a 50-member Central Committee whose composition of 32 French-speaking, 15 German-speaking, and 3 Italian-speaking members shows its unequal strength in the linguistic regions, which consist of 4.5 million German-speaking Swiss, barely one million French-speaking, and under 500,000 Italian-speaking. The 14-member Political Bureau has a 5-member Secretariat led by Jean Vincent (Geneva) as chairman; the others: Andrew Muret (Lausanne), Jakob Lechleitner (Zurich), who was given some prominence in Moscow publications recently, Hansjörg Hofer (Basel), and Armand Magnin (Geneva).

The PdA is the traditional, Soviet-style "party of cadres" that comprises an "avant garde" of the working class. Its membership (about 7,000) does not reflect its voting strength. It goes on trying to be respectable and to cooperate within the parliamentary system, although its hopes of catching disillusioned militants of the left when they get older have totally failed to materialize so far.

Domestic Affairs. The domestic scene in Switzerland in 1976 was dominated, as it was in 1975, by the economy. The recession flattened out, unemployment went down slowly (see below), and anti-inflation measures by the "National Bank" (bank of issue) were particularly successful—toward the end of the year Switzerland led the industrialized world with an inflation rate below 2 percent. The negative effect was that confidence in Swiss money management rose steeply, the Swiss franc was under extraordinary demand pressure all through the year, and the exchange rate showed the franc on a level with the German mark most of the time, with the U.S. dollar at times below Sfr. 2.50. In spite of this unfavorable basis for a country dependent on exports, employment rose slightly. The number of fully unemployed, around 30,000 early in the year, dipped below 20,000 in autumn. Strict measures against hasty hiring of new workers from other countries remained in force. Experts pointed out that Switzerland has lost close to 300,000 jobs since 1973; but with the departure of foreign workers ("exporting Swiss unemployment") and with many second earners—women, teen-agers—never registering as unemployed, the official statistical figure of unemployed represents some 10 to 20 percent of the actual loss of jobs.

The political climate remained relatively quiet: the physical disappearance of most of the unemployed abroad gave the angry Left no leverage on the streets.

Other important events were three national votes (with a fourth one coming in December) and two scandals—one an espionage case, the other a "Watergate"-type case of reciprocal political spying.

On 21 March Swiss voters rejected both a proposal to introduce extensive participatory rights for workers in private enterprise, supported by all parties with a leftist trend, and a counterproposal in a milder form, which had been put forward by the government. Interpretations varied, but it seemed that a majority of the 39.3 percent of Swiss eligible to vote who went to the ballot box (a normal proportion for this unemotional country) had confidence enough in the existing system to want to keep their relations with employers as they were. The proposal from the Left was defeated by 968,000 against 472,000 votes, the government counterproposal by 973,000 against 434,000.

In retrospect, it would seem that the government was needlessly afraid that unless it gave in to loud cries for participation coming from the vocal Left, and offered a milder package of its own, the Left might carry the day. The double rejection left both camps somewhat shamefaced and groping for explanations. There was talk of a "silent majority" that had been forgotten both by the militants and by the government.

On 13 June, among other questions (the principle of a compulsory unemployment insurance was overwhelmingly approved), Swiss voters, with a turnout of 34.5 percent, showed their displeasure at present Third World trends in the UN and UNESCO by rejecting, 714,000 to 551,000, the financial package of Sfr. 200 million for the International Development Association (IDA), thus leaving Switzerland's official percentage of development aid in terms of GNP at a lowly 0.2 percent. Almost all parties, which had sensed the cool reaction against development aid, had launched a last-minute campaign for the IDA contribution, but in vain. On 26 September, Swiss voters rejected — by 695,000 votes to 531,000 — a complex and poorly balanced constitutional amendment that would have introduced a simulacrum of competition to the semi-public monopoly of TV and radio, the whole show still to be tightly run by the government and the existing monopoly. Rejection was due mainly to two factors — first that the debate had been so deformed by political interests that there was a general feeling of not being fully informed of what was going on, and second that the electronic media, already more important than the written press for immediate news, were going to be given even more attention and money by the government, while a plan was under discussion, at the same time, to subsidize the written press with public funds too. The feeling was that more and more tax money was going to be spent on the media without changing fundamentally a situation which was felt to be unsatisfactory, exept for one thing: free competition was about to be stifled. Here the Left agreed with the majority. Although its aim was not to allow free competition per se, it feared that leftist opinions would be throttled by a public authority that is still largely middle-of-the-road. In October, a militant leftist group in Zurich, in the wake of the rejection, made a first attempt to request a license for an avowedly militant "New Left" radio station. The request, together with half a dozen other, non-political requests, is still under consideration.

On the same "voting Sunday" of 26 September, voters also rejected massively — 939,000 to 301,760 — a proposal by the Union of Public Service Employees (Verband des Personals der öffentlichen Dienste; VPOD) to nationalize all motor-car insurance, now in the hands of competing — but largely cartelized — private companies. Motor-car insurance practices are usually the target of quite a bit of criticism. The massive rejection, however, showed that two out of three Swiss who cared to vote prefer the unsatisfactory situation of a more or less free enterprise to state ownership; and the turnout on that day of 32.5 percent showed that two out of three Swiss don't even care to utter an opinion. This is one of those typical results that show why groundswells of opinion, political and otherwise, are difficult to unleash in Switzerland: when it comes to the test, most Swiss are grumblingly satisfied with things as they are.

On 5 December, Swiss voters have to vote on a constitutional initiative, launched by the POCH, which would introduce the 40-hour week immediately, without loss of salary. Present working hours, subject to various covenants according to industries, vary from somewhat over 40 hours to 48. Under pressure that has been mounting since the recession forced many industries to cut working time, the government has agreed basically to aim progressively at a 40-hour week — probably in a couple of years. The POCH, by its own admission, would prefer to withdraw the initiative, because the lead time from launching to collecting signatures to voting has meant in this case that the idea, hatched at a time when most futurologists foresaw a massive accumulation of petrodollars in the hands of oil states and a steadily worsening crisis in the industrial world, comes to the vote at a time when people are getting used to the sawtooth movements of an unpleasant but bearable economic uncertainty. On the same 5 December voters will also have to decide whether to extend present price controls and credit supervision.

The spy scandal—Switzerland's biggest so far—has hardly drawn any comment on the Left, for a good reason. A brigadier general, Jean-Louis Jeanmaire, who retired at the end of 1975 as commander of Switzerland's nationwide and complex civil defense, confessed after arrest that he had spied for the USSR for some thirteen years. An infantry instructor (professional officer), he had been promoted to this one-star command in 1969, after years of frustration because he was thought unfit for promotion — and because the job, regarded as a lowly semi-civilian administrative post by many military, was all he could get through political pressure. Frustrated ambition was thus thought to be his main motive, but Swiss counterintelligence was caught with its pants down, as it dawned on most citizens that the chief of the civil defense system knows, among other things, the most detailed war mobilization plans. The impact of the Jeanmaire case, still under investigation, on the public's attitude toward the pro-Soviet Left will be felt sometime in 1977 as the full extent of the damage done becomes known.

The aforementioned "little Watergate" broke in November 1976. The offices of a right-of-center publisher of information letters about the Left, Ernst Cincera, were broken into and a leftist organization, Democratisches Manifest, displayed some of the booty at a press conference. The authors of the break-in were arrested, but it turned out that some of Cincera's material could only have been leaked to him by officials who, in doing so, are supposed to have been at least indiscreet and, at worst, guilty of betraying confidential files. Cincera's files are said to contain information about some 4,000 leftists.

Publications. The proliferation of leftist groups has brought about a number of new pamphlets and irregular and regular periodicals. Details about financing, circulation and periodicity are practically unobtainable and a complete list would be hardly meaningful. Anarchists are publishing a periodical, *Akratie*, in collaboration with a West German anarchist periodical, *Zeitgeist*. Young Socialists (Junge Sozialisten; Juso), a group which the Socialist Party does not recognize, publishes *infrarot*, (in French: infrarouge). The Kommunistischer Jugendverband der Schweiz (KJVS), a communist youth movement started in 1974 (see *YICA, 1975*, p. 253), publishes a new periodical in French, *L'Unité*. A young printers' group (Jungdrucker Zürich) has a periodical called *Zündstoff* (Flammable Matter).

The POCH is now overtaking the PdA in the publishing field. In addition to the *POCH-Zeitung*, weekly, circulation about 6,000, it also publishes *Emanzipation*, for progressive women's groups, *Tribune ouvrière*, weekly, French counterpart of the German-language *POCH-Zeitung*, and *positionen*, a periodical for university groups. The LMR publishes *Bresche* (The Breach) fortnightly; it follows a Trotskyite line.

Publications of the PdA have remained unchanged, their circulation figures are PdA-given estimates, but their impact is clearly diminishing, faced with a flood of publications from the left that are, if nothing else, full of lively invective, preposterous ideas, and irreverent writing, while PdA journals are as stodgily dignified as a retired peoples' commissar.

The PdA publishes journals in three languages: *Vorwärts*, Basel, weekly (circulation 12,000) in German; *Voix Ouvrière*, Geneva, daily (8,000), in French; and *Il Lavoratore*, Lugano, weekly (under 1,000), in Italian. (All circulation figures are estimates.)

Martigny   Richard Anderegg

Turkey

The year 1976 brought no basic changes either in the position of the left in Turkey or in political conditions in general. It was essentially a year in which trends evident in 1975 continued without any major resolution. Nor was there any change in the legal provisions which ban not only the Communist party, but the propagation or advocacy of its ideology as well. The conservative four-party National Front coalition government led by the Justice Party (JP) and Prime Minister Süleyman Demirel remained in power throughout the year.

Perhaps the best means of summarizing the events of 1976 is to point up three major themes which seemed to dominate the political scene. First, there were continued clashes among students at universities and other institutions of higher education, as well as at some secondary schools. These clashes almost invariably took the form of conflict between leftists and rightists. Arms were frequently used, and death and serious injury were commonly among the outcomes. Many institutions closed for varying periods of time as a result. All of this had occurred before. A possible new development was increasing evidence that, with some exceptions, these clashes seemed to have less impact on public opinion than in the past. A prominent exception was a major incident early in June in the southeastern provincial capital of Gaziantep. On this occasion, a 25-hour siege ensued when the authorities attempted to raid a house suspected of harboring members of the underground Turkish People's Liberation Army. Armor, machine guns, and grenades were used, and there were six killed (including two police officials) and nine wounded. Generally, the government appeared no more able to bring this type of political violence under control than had been the case during 1975.

A second major theme in the political developments of the year was an intensification of the level of conflict between the two major parties, the Justice Party at the head of the coalition government and the Republican People's Party (RPP) as the major opposition party. The two parties exchanged sharp accusations concerning the continuing violence outlined above. The JP charged that the RPP was responsible because of its alleged encouragement of Communists and anarchists, while the RPP accused the JP and the government of aiding and abetting right-wing extremists by selectively enforcing the law only against leftists. The RPP reiterated the charge of earlier years that law enforcement officials were all but cooperating with the violence-prone hoodlums associated with Deputy Prime Minister Alparslan Türkeş's National Movement Party.

The two major parties also traded bitter charges on other issues, such as Cyprus, contention with Greece over control of the Aegean Sea, the U.S. arms embargo, continuing negotiations on the status of U.S. bases in Turkey, and so on. Each claimed to be a more effective defender of national interests and national honor than the other. Nor was the partisan bickering limited to the level of policy questions. There was also considerable personal animosity expressed directly between the two party leaders, and by each of the parties against the person of the other party's leader. Thus, Bülent Ecevit and the RPP accused Süleyman Demirel personally of corruption by virtue of the involvement of his nephew in an apparently fraudulent and illegal import operation. Demirel and his associates in turn accused Ecevit of harboring an unrestrained lust for power which led him to stop at nothing in his efforts to undermine the legitimate government of Turkey. No doubt much of this bickering could be explained as part of the preparations for the next Parliamentary elections, due no later than October 1977.

A third theme which permeated the political atmosphere in Turkey throughout 1976 was continued tension on the international sene, specifically involving Cyprus, the Aegean, and relations between Turkey and the great powers, especially the USA. The tensions generated by these issues were not relieved during 1976, undoubtedly at least in part because the National Front coalition government was too weak domestically to launch major diplomatic initiatives or to respond boldy to thrusts or challenges from abroad.

In connection with each of these three major issue-areas, climactic events did occur during the year, however. Proceeding in reverse order, the activities of the geophysical research vessel *Sismik I* during the summer may be singled out. The ship engaged in several sweeps of the Aegean continental shelf in an ostensible search for oil deposits. These "scientific" missions became occasions for tense confrontations with Greek air, naval, and land forces, for the issue of rights to the Aegean continental shelf remains in dispute between the two countries. Indeed, late in the summer, these tensions were sufficiently high to generate a meeting of the UN Security Council—which did not contribute visibly to a reduction of tensions. Nor did the activities of the *Sismik* lower the political fever charts in Turkey. On the contrary, for perhaps the first time, the status of the Greek-owned Dodecanese Islands entered political discussion in a major way, to the dismay of some moderate observers and spokesmen. This development was probably due to a desire to strike ultra-nationalist poses for purposes of partisan advantage on the part of minor partners in the governing coalition, who appeared to be responsible for bringing this issue into the political arena.

The issues of political violence and partisan bickering also passed through a form of climax during the months of September and October. The government, responding to a decision of the Constitutional Court outlawing the special tribunals which had been established in 1973 to deal with anarchism and other perceived threats to national security, introduced a bill into the Parliament which was designed to reestablish these tribunals. In deference to the religious proclivities of one of the participating parties in the coalition—the National Salvation Party—the government's bill conspicuously proposed to omit from the purview of these tribunals cases involving advocacy of a theocracy or other forms of opposition to the constitutionally declared secular character of the Turkish state. The result was a storm of opposition from the RPP and supporting groups. RPP parliamentarians resorted to obstructionist tactics within the Parliament itself. Such organizations as the left-wing labor federation, DISK, and the major organization of teachers, TÖB-DER, swung into action. DISK, in particular, actively encouraged its members to stage protest work stoppages and strikes, and large numbers of them did so. These strikes were forcefully countered by the government, leading to violent confrontations between workers and the police, and to the arrest of some thousands. The government also declared the teachers' organization illegal and sealed its offices throughout the country (a move which reportedly was later declared invalid by the judiciary). Meanwhile, as a sort of by-play to all this, the government removed the RPP mayor of Ankara (elected in late 1973) from office, following strikes by municipal workers, particularly sanitation men. The municipality was unable to pay their wages because of the government's failure to subsidize the city. This move, too, was reportedly later invalidated by the courts. The level of political tension thus seemed to be rising, with direct involvement of masses of workers and teachers, as well as the judiciary.

The outlawed Turkish Communist Party (TKP), speaking primarily through the clandestine "Our Radio" (Bizim Radyo) from East Germany, maintained a running commentary on these developments. Three themes dominated these commentaries. First, there was continued denunciation of the National Front government, which was characterized as serving the interests of fascism at home and U.S.

imperialism internationally. Second, the Communist radio continued to echo Moscow's line on Cyprus and the Aegean Sea. Moscow's interest in these conflicts were clear enough: to avoid offending both Greece and Turkey while seeking to capitalize on the disillusion with the USA which has surfaced in both countries. Thus, it made perfect sense for the Soviet government to advocate the withdrawal of all foreign (read Turkish) troops from Cyprus, and bilateral negotiations directly between Greece and Turkey to resolve both disputes. However, as so often in the past, what served Moscow's interests flew directly in the face of popular demands which domestic politicians must take into consideration. The proposal to withdraw foreign (Turkish) troops from Cyprus bore this character, and the frequent reiteration of this theme on the Communist radio is but one more indication of the basis underlying the failure of Moscow-oriented leftism in particular to gain any visible political support within Turkey. Finally, on the other side of this ledger, the Communist radio enthusiastically welcomed the work stoppages inspired by DISK in September 1976. Indeed, the Communists urged the workers to expand their efforts and to organize a nationwide general strike. Although the work stoppages were successfully nipped in the bud by the government, the Communists could claim that on this issue at least they stood with a significant body of Turkish public opinion.

University of Illinois at Chicago Circle   Frank Tachau

ASIA AND THE PACIFIC

Australia

The Communist Party of Australia (CPA) was founded in October 1920. It reached its peak of influence in 1944 when its membership reached 23,000. By 1976 this figure had dropped to about 1,500 and the party had split twice. The pro-Peking Communist Party of Australia (Marxist-Leninist) — CPA (M-L) — was established in 1964 in response to the CPA's abandonment of China in the Sino-Soviet dispute. Similarly, the pro-Moscow Socialist Party of Australia (SPA) was formed in 1971 after the CPA adopted a critical attitude to the Soviet Union. The CPA(M-L) and SPA have current memberships of about 100 and 700 respectively. (Australian population: 12,755,638.)

The 25th Congress of the CPA, in June 1976, adopted a new policy. Firstly, it called for a "united mass movement" involving members and supporters of the Australian Labor Party (ALP). National Executive members Bernie Taft and Mavis Robertson had long advocated (and in the case of Taft, Victorian state secretary, practiced) such a strategy. However, they had been unable to make headway at the previous Congress, in 1974, against opposition of the national secretary, Laurie Aarons, his brother Eric Aarons, and a Left Tendency of mainly young members from the Glebe-Balmain (Sydney), Carlton (Victoria), and South Australian branches of the party. Eric Aarons had derogatorily characterized this strategy as one of seeking out lowest-common-denominator demands which might be progressive but were certainly not radical, let alone revolutionary. The Left Tendency was opposed to united front policies in principle.

Secondly, the Congress made no reference to the USSR, and thus backed away from its previously hostile and outspoken stance. Again, Bernie Taft and Mavis Robertson had fought for such a retreat prior to and during the 1974 Congress and lost out to the Aarons group and the Left Tendency. At that time, Laurie Aarons felt obliged to criticize the Communist Party of the Soviet Union (CPSU) in order to underline the independence of the CPA, and the Left Tendency flatly denied that the USSR was a socialist country.

Finally, the 1976 Congress passed a number of resolutions designed to enhance the organizational coherence of the Party. As early as November 1973, John Sendy, the Party president and an ally of Taft, had deplored the ad hoc manner in which the party conducted its affairs. However, the 24th Congress was unreceptive to his implicit call for reform in this area.

Thus, the Taft group, thwarted in 1974, succeeded two years later in having its policies substantially adopted. This growth in its influence can be explained by a shift in outlook and alignment of the Aarons group, which adopted a more favorable stance toward united-front activities and consequently moved closer to Taft, whom it joined in condemning the Left Tendency.

One factor in this change was the collapse of Laurie Aarons' industrial strategy. It was in accordance with his wishes that the 24th Congress had specifically endorsed the green-banning, go-it-alone, confrontation style of the New South Wales (N.S.W.) branch of the Australian Building Construction Employees and Builders Labourers' Federation (BLF) as a means of breaking out of the reformist tradition of the trade union movement. However, no sooner was the Congress over than the Australian Industrial Court ordered the cancellation of the BLF's registration. Moreover, the judges took particular exception to the N.S.W. green bans.

Therefore, as the first step back on the road to reregistration, BLF federal secretary Norm Gallagher, a member of the pro-Peking Communist Party of Australia (Marxist-Leninist), decided to take over the N.S.W. branch. If Gallagher and the builders, some of whom had been brought to their knees by the green bans, could agree on little else, at least they recognized their common interest in overthrowing the N.S.W. leadership. In March 1975, when Gallagher persuaded the Master Builders' Associaton (MBA) to give employment preference to laborers he had been successful in enrolling in a new, rival federal branch of the BLF, the N.S.W. leadership capitulated and recommended that its members join the new branch. Then, on 17 April, Gallagher expelled from the union N.S.W. secretary Joe Owens (a member of the CPA), his predecessor Jack Mundey (also a CPA member), N.S.W. president Bob Pringle, (a member of the ALP), the other eight members of the N.S.W. Executive, and fifteen full and temporary organizers.

Thus, the fruit of the policy which Laurie Aarons hailed for showing the way to overcome reformism proved very bitter indeed. Not only did the CPA lose its influence in the N.S.W. BLF; it lost this influence to the rival CPA(M-L). But Laurie Aarons remained unrepentant, blaming others—the MBA, the Maoists, and an unholy alliance between them—for the debacle. However, he was due to resign as CPA national secretary at the 25th Congress in keeping with a six-year tenure rule passed in 1970, and it may be that his resignation enabled the "Aarons" group to recognize the shortcomings of the N.S.W. BLF's industrial policy of confrontation and see merit in the united front strategy advocated by Taft.

Also, the unprecedented step taken by the Governor General in dismissing the Whitlam Labor Government on 11 November 1975 and the subsequent defeat of the Labor Party at the polls on 13 December by a conservative Liberal-National Country Party coalition, alerted the Aarons group to the futility of pressing revolutionary demands when even the moderate reforms of the former Labor Government were under threat.

Finally, success of the *Daily Tribune*—which the CPA published in the last three weeks of the election campaign in the hope of making inroads into the tens of thousands of radical and radicalized supporters turning up at Labor Party rallies—encouraged the leadership to think in terms of the long-term viability of such broadly based activity.

Accordingly, after the electoral defeat, which left Labor Party supporters angry and embittered at having had their party forced into an election under unfavorable circumstances by what they regarded as unconstitutional methods, the CPA issued a clarion call which anticipated the new policy adopted by the 25th Congress: "Unity in struggle around immediate issues, and projection of a socialist alternative for Australia—are the basic concerns of the Communist Party. . . . The struggle is not over; it is just beginning!" (*Tribune*, 15 December 1975.)

The 25th CPA Congress, 1976. The Congress, convened in June, called for a "united mass action of all anti-[Prime Minister] Fraser forces." (*For a Left and Democratic Advance for Socialism*, p. 6.) Although casting its net very widely it repeatedly stressed the important role which militant rank-and-file workers, the organized working class, and trade union activities would play in this broad coalition. Indeed, for the first time since the 20th Congress, in 1964, the CPA unequivocally asserted the centrality of the working class to its political strategy. The political resolution stated: "We see the working class as the core of the anti-Fraser, anti-capitalist coalition and the potential leader of the struggle for socialist change" (ibid., p. 10). Students and members of the radical middle class, women, and homosexuals, championed by recent Congresses, received only brief and passing reference.

CPA National Committee Members and Party Membership, 1976

State or District	Names of National Committee Members Elected	Number of National Committee Members	Ratio of National Committee to Party Members	State or District Membership
Queensland	H. Ergas G. Goullet C. Gifford H. Hamilton	4	1:40 - 80	160 - 320
Newcastle (N.S.W.)	P. Barrack D. Dawson	2	,,	80 - 160
Sydney (N.S.W.)	E. Aarons L. Aarons A. Beaver L. Carmichael D. Freney Jack Mundey Judy Mundey J. Palmada P. Pierisi M. Robertson J. Stevens R. Walsham	12	,,	480 - 960
South Coast (N.S.W.)	M. Nixon	1	,,	40 - 80
Victoria	D. Davies L. Ebbels J. Frazer P. Herington M. Ogden B. Taft M. Taft	7	,,	280 - 560
Tasmania	P. Slicer	1	,,	40 - 80
South Australia	R. Durbridge	1	,,	40 - 80
Western Australia	V. Slater	1	,,	40 - 80
Total		29		1,160 - 2,320

In striking contrast to 1974, when the party only showed interest in revolutionary demands, but again in keeping with the policies of the middle sixties, the 1976 Congress reverted to a two-stage theory of revolution, declaring that within the anti-Fraser coalition the CPA would advance "demands which, though not socialist in themselves, are transitional to the struggle for socialism" (ibid).

The CPA position now resembled that of the Socialist Party of Australia. This is not surprisng, as the SPA looked like nothing so much as the CPA frozen in its 1964 mold. The two parties still differed over their attitudes to the CPSU. But even on this point the CPA narrowed the gap, however slightly, between the SPA and itself. The 1974 Congress confirmed the party's definition of the USSR as a "socialist-based" country and, in a historical allusion, made reference to the "Russian Revolution" (*The Socialist Alternative: Documents of CPA 24th National Congress 1974*, p. 4). The 1976 Congress made no direct reference to the USSR and referred to the "Russian *Socialist* Revolution." (*For a Left and Democratic Advance for Socialism*, p. 13; author's italics.)

Finally, the 25th Congress devoted considerable attention to problems of organization. It substituted democratic centralism for the ad hoc practices which had characterized party administration for the last three or four years (ibid., p. 22). Also, it outlawed "tendencies." (See *Constitution and Rules Adopted at the 25th National Congress*, p. 7.) This step was made possible by the fact that the Aarons group had now moved to a more moderate position and was, therefore, no longer dependent on the Left Tendency, as it had been in 1974, to maintain its ascendancy within the party.

As in 1974, State and District Conferences elected one National Committee member for each 80 members (or part thereof greater than 40). The number elected and the numerical strength of each district or state, based on this ratio, are given in the accompanying table. As in 1974 also, the conferences elected one Congress delegate for each 30 members (or part thereof greater than 15).

But at this point the similarity with 1974 ends. At that Congress, the 103 delegates—based upon a party membership between 1,545 and 3,090—elected a president, a national secretary and eight other National Executive members from the National Committee. At the 25th Congress, on the other hand, the Aarons and Taft groups agreed that there should be five national officeholders—a president, vice-president, and three secretaries—and five other Executive members. Rather than battle it out for each position as in 1974, they agreed upon who should occupy the various offices. What must have been an extraordinarily docile Congress of 100 delegates—based upon membership between 1,500 and 3,000—endorsed this top-level agreement and accordingly elected Laurie Carmichael (Sydney district) as president, Bernie Taft (Victoria) as vice-president, and Mavis Robertson, Eric Aarons, and Joe Palmada (all of Sydney) as national secretaries. The Congress also elected Dave Davies (Sydney), Rob Durbridge (South Australia), Joyce Stevens (Sydney), Charlie Gifford (Queensland), and Darrell Dawson (Newcastle) to the remaining positions on the Executive.

If things should come to the crunch between the national officers, then Taft could in all likelihood rely on the support of Carmichael and Robertson while Aarons could rely on Palmada. Among the other Executive members, Davies and Gifford are clearly identifiable as Taft and Aarons supporters respectively. The remaining three—Stevens, Dawson, and Durbridge—probably incline toward Eric Aarons.

Congress greetings came for the most part from Communist Parties which have, like the CPA, adopted a more or less independent stance within the international Communist movement. They included the Italian and French Communist Parties (both now exponents of the "Eurocommunist" doctrines of "national communism" and party independence), the League of Communists of Yugoslavia, the Romanian Communist Party, the Vietnamese Workers' Party, the Japan Communist Party, the Titoist Communist Party of Great Britain, the Communist Party of Belgium, and the anti-Soviet Communist Party of Greece (Interior). Greetings were also received from the Popular Movement for the Liberation of Angola (MPLA), the Socialist Workers' Party of Papua New Guinea, the Mauritius People's Progressive Party, the Anti-Imperialist Front of Malta, the Communist Party of Chile in the

Exterior, which thanked the CPA for its solidarity in opposing the military junta in Chile, and the Portuguese Communist Party. Finally, the Fretelin movement in East Timor sent "fraternal and revolutionary greetings to the militants of the independent Australian Communist Party." (*Tribune*, 16, 23 June.)

Political Strikes. On numerous occasions in 1976, trade unionists withheld or continued to withhold their labor as a way of expressing a political viewpoint or making political demands on the Government, Federal or State. These non-industrial or political strikes can be divided into two categories. The first are those which, one may surmise, would have occurred or continued to occur even if the Labor Party had remained in federal office. Strikes and bans of this category include the boycott of Indonesian shipping by the Waterside Workers' Federation in support for the beleaguered Fretelin movement in East Timor. (Thirty years before, the Federation placed a similar ban on Dutch shipping in order to protect the nascent Republic of Indonesia.) The Victorian Trades Hall Council's long-standing green ban on the construction of the Newport Power Station and the Building Workers' Industrial Union (BWIU) ban in May 1976 on the construction of an Omega navigation base in Australia are other examples. In a radio statement, Pat Clancy, federal secretary of BWIU and president of the pro-Moscow SPA, declared that Omega was connected with nuclear warfare and its construction would make Australia a "prime target" in the event of war. He added that he would seek support for this ban from the Australian Council of Trade Unions (ACTU). (*Socialist*, 31 March; *Tribune*, 31 March.)

The Australian Railways Union ban in May on shipments to and from the Mary Kathleen Uranium Mine is also of this type. The ACTU, which passed a resolution at its biennial Congress in 1975 calling for a halt to uranium mining pending the completion of an inquiry, convened a meeting of federal unions to discuss the ban. The meeting, fearful of jeopardizing the jobs of workers at the mine, decided that uranium mining at Mary Kathleen would continue. However, it declared that the product must be stockpiled and cannot be removed. Apart from Mary Kathleen, the meeting resolved that there will be a complete union ban on the mining, manufacture, and export of uranium in Australia "until such time as satisfactory investigation is concluded." (*Tribune*, 9 June 1976.)

Secondly, there are those political strikes which took place because Communist and left-wing ALP trade union leaders, who regard the Fraser government as illegitimate, had resolved to veto its actions wherever possible, and even to bring it down. The clearest examples are the Victorian and national Medibank strikes of June and July. These were triggered off by the Government's decison of 20 May to force approximately half the adult population out of the previous Government's national health insurance scheme (Medibank) by imposing a 2.5 percent levy on participants' taxable income. On 27 May, the Victorian Trades Hall Council (THC) voted for a half-day (four hour) strike on 16 June to protest the Government's action.

On 9 June, a shop stewards' rally, convened presumably by John Halfpenny, state secretary of the Amalgamated Metal Workers' Union (AMWU) and a member of the Victorian State Committee of the CPA, attempted to push the THC into a more extreme position by calling for a full-day strike instead. Speaking at the rally, Halfpenny struck a very radical note indeed. He said:

> We don't want to do deals with Fraser. We don't want any social contracts. What we want is to get rid of this government. (Ibid., 16 June.)

The motion passed by the rally was equally radical. After calling for a full day stoppage, it continued:

> Should this stoppage fail to produce a withdrawal of Fraser's economic measures and attacks on Medibank, etc., we call on the ACTU to organize 24 hour general stoppages, state by state, for four weeks; and if still no withdrawal, national meetings to consider firmer action and possibly a general strike. (Ibid.)

On 10 June, moderate and right-wing delegates used procedural methods to prevent the THC from discussing the shop stewards' motion of the previous day. Subsequently, 24 union leaders condemned a section of the THC Executive for adopting such tactics (*Socialist*, 23 June).

During the half-day strike on 16 June another meeting was held at which Halfpenny moved a resolution, sponsored by the left-wing leaders of 22 unions, calling for a state-wide 24-hour stoppage—to be held on 30 June. While speaking to the motion, Halfpenny appealed to unionists to "bring the Fraser government down on its scabby knees. . . . Now is the appropriate time to act. Since December 13 we have seen the worst 160 days of misery in this country. We cannot stand by and wait." (*Tribune*, 23 June.) The resolution was passed overwhelmingly.

Two days later, the THC, unable to resist this kind of pressure further, officially requested the ACTU Executive to call a 24-hour stoppage for 30 June besides declaring its own intention to strike on that date. A similar call was made by the Commonwealth Council of the AMWU, whose assistant federal secretary is Laurie Carmichael, president of the CPA. (*Socialist*, 23 June.)

Then, on 21 June, the ACTU Executive met to hear reports by ACTU officers concerning their talks with government officials on the state of the economy. Almost immediately after the Executive had heard the reports, one of its members, SPA president Pat Clancy, apparently unmoved by their content and determined to press the Medibank issue, moved a resolution calling for a 24-hour national stoppage. (*Australian Financial Review*, 22 June.)

The following day, the ACTU president Bob Hawke succeeded in having this resolution defeated in the Executive by 12 votes to 5. Instead, it decided, presumably on the prompting of Hawke, to call a national unions conference—at which each union, irrespective of size, would have two votes, thereby ensuring moderate control—to be held on 5-6 July, after ACTU officers had held further talks with the Government. The ACTU president's success in at least delaying a national stoppage angered Joe Palmada, perhaps the most radical of the CPA national officers, who wrote a bitter attack on the Executive's decision under the headline: "Shame, Hawke, Shame!" (*Tribune*, 30 June).

On 24 June, however, the Victorian THC voted to go ahead with its strike on Wednesday 30 June. But as it turned out, it was, in the words of one trade union official, a "fizzer." The Australian Workers' Union, the Federated Clerks' Union, the Australian Telecommunication Employees' Association, and the Shop Assistants' Association did not take part. (*Herald*, Melbourne, 25 June; *Tribune*, 30 June.) Also a sizable number of people in other unions did not obey their leaders' instructions to strike.

These gaps in the trade union ranks did not go unnoticed. Indeed, by revealing the weakness of the unions' hand, the Victorian THC undermined Hawke's bargaining position with the Government. It is not surprising, therefore, that the Federal Cabinet, meeting on 2 July, rejected out of hand all the ACTU's proposals for changes in the Government's Medibank scheme (*Australian Financial Review*, 5 July).

This action left Hawke with no alternative but to propose a national 24-hour stoppage to the ACTU Executive in order to maintain his authority in the face of the left-wing challenge. The Executive endorsed his proposal and placed it before the federal unions conference on Monday 5 July. It, in turn, declared its support. Only five of the 207 delegates abstained from voting for the proposal. (Ibid., 5, 6 July.)

In light of this vote, the strike appeared to enjoy widespread backing. However, the date for the stoppage—from midnight on Sunday till midnight on Monday 12 July—clearly indicated that trade union leaders were less than confident of carrying their memberships with them. For, by giving only one week's notice of the strike, they ensured that there would be no time for the rank and file to vote on—and possibly against—the issue. Also, by holding the stoppage on a Monday, they hoped that if their memberships' dubious loyalty wouldn't keep them away from work, then the attraction of a long weekend would. (The writer is indebted to Professor Ross M. Martin for the above two points.)

The following day, Mr. Fraser stated: "This is not a Hawke strike . . . it is a Halfpenny, Carmichael, left wing union strike . . ." (*Herald*, 6 July). The statement is true as far as it goes. The Prime Minister might have added, however, that it was also a Clancy strike.

It proceeded as scheduled, but, like the Victorian strike, this first national general strike in Australia's history was, as the Government had hoped and the left-wing union leaders had feared, a failure. Five unions affiliated to the ACTU did not instruct their members to strike and the Tasmanian Trades and Labour Council refused to endorse it. Also, large numbers of workers disobeyed their unions' strike orders. Over all, it appears that 40 percent of trade union members did not participate in the national stoppage. (*Industrial Disputes*, Australian Bureau of Statistics, July.)

Thus, the national stoppage, far from demonstrating working class unity in opposition to the Fraser Government, highlighted instead the division between leaders—especially left-wing leaders— and members of the trade union movement. A 1976 survey of attitudes to trade unions, based on a sample of 4,046 men and women aged 14 and over and a sub-sample of 1,003 trade union members, suggests some reasons for this division. It shows that 95 percent of unionists support their unions' attempts to negotiate better working conditions. On the other hand, only 22 percent support strikes called because of disagreement with Government economic policy. (*Bulletin*, Sydney, 12 June.) Unionists, it appears, regard their unions as instrumental in their quest for improved wages and conditions but not as agencies of economic or social change (D. Aitken, *National Times*, 19-24 July).

John Halfpenny, apparently undaunted by the Medibank failure, tried next to wring political gain out of the budget. Three days before the Treasurer, Mr. Lynch, brought down the federal budget in Parliament, Halfpenny, speaking "on behalf of seventeen unions and a dozen welfare, ethnic and community groups," brought down a "People's Budget" at the headquarters of the AMWU (*Tribune*, 28 July). The CPA organ supported him with a call for the development of a mass movement "around the People's Budget" (ibid.). But nothing came of it. Evidently, the idea of a strike was floated briefly at the Victorian THC only to be rejected (*Bulletin*, 4 September).

A similar pattern of events marked the visit to Melbourne of the U.S. nuclear-powered warship *Truxtun*. Port and maritime union leaders, including Ted Bull, a vice-chairman of the CPA(M-L) and secretary of the Melbourne branch of the Waterside Workers' Federation, claimed that the ship was an environmental hazard and called for a six-day shutdown of the entire port as a protest. The Prime Minister condemned the proposed strike as an attack upon the ANZUS alliance. The Minister for Defense implied that if the strike went ahead the government would use troops to break it. The Premier of Victoria declared that the strike was "politically motivated by a small group of Communist leaders of unions who are opposed to America" (ABC Radio, 2 September). ACTU president Hawke indicated his displeasure in more temperate language: "I can understand the concern of the unions involved, but I doubt whether it's right that the whole port of Melbourne should be brought to a standstill for the whole of the period that the Truxtun is here" (*Australian*, Southern edition, 4 September). In the face of this pressure, not to mention the rumblings of other unionists who would be adversely affected by the strike and the lack of public support for their stand, Bull and company backed down, advocating a 24-hour stoppage instead (*Herald*, 7 September). Apparently the lesson of the Medibank strikes had not been entirely lost on left-wing trade union leaders.

Trade Union Election Legislation. Prime Minister Fraser blamed the national general strike on Carmichael and Halfpenny. Also, in a television broadcast on the eve of the strike, he appealed over the heads of the trade union leaders to the rank and file. "Ask yourselves," he said, "why you have not been given a say in whether or not you want to go on strike" (*The Age*, Melbourne, 12 July). This two-pronged approach neatly characterizes his attitude to the trade union movement. He believes (correctly) that blue-collar workers are turning in growing numbers to the Liberal Party (David Kemp, "Social Change and Future of Political Parties: The Australian Case," In *The Future of Politi-*

cal Parties, edited by L. Maisel, Sage Publications, 1975). Consequently, he views Communist and left-wing union leaders as increasingly unrepresentative of their memberships; they maintain their positions, he believes, only through the active support of the militant few. In this connection, the Minister for Employment and Industrial Relations, Mr. Street, is fond of citing the fact that Dick Scott was elected Commonwealth chairman of the AMWU in a ballot in which less than 2 percent of the membership exercised their right to vote.

In order to rectify this situation, the Liberal-National Country Party Government declared its intention of legislating for secret postal ballots, conducted by the Commonwealth Electoral Office, to be held for all organizations registered under the Conciliation and Arbitration Act.

On 5 May the ACTU, in a meeting with Mr. Street, expressed its objection to this proposal that union elections be removed from union control (Australia, House of Representatives, *Debates*, 1976, p. 2325). Two weeks later, the Government conceded this point to the unions. They could choose, it decided, either to conduct the secret postal ballots themselves or allow the Commonwealth Electoral Office to hold them on their behalf. By making this concession the Government hoped to win union support for wage restraint. (*The Age*, 19 May.) It was also anxious, however, as part of its campaign to cut Government expenditure, to save itself the $1.5 million a year it would cost the Electoral Office to conduct the ballots.

The legislation, amended accordingly, passed both Houses of Parliament on 8 July and was proclaimed on 9 August. It remains to be seen whether it will be successful, as it is intended to be, in toppling left-wing and Communist trade union leaders.

Industrial Relations. One reason, it was suggested above, for the failure of the Medibank stoppages was the hostility of trade unionists to political strikes. Even in the pursuit of improved wages and conditions—widely regarded as legitimate activities, as the survey noted above makes clear—trade union leaders found themselves constantly thwarted by a rank and file unwilling to use strike action. For example, the AMWU has found it almost impossible to persuade its members to strike for their February 1975 claim of $20 for tradesmen and $18 for non-tradesmen (*Bulletin*, 12 June).

The contrast with 1974-75 could not be more marked. In that period, through ruthless and effective use of the strike weapon, there was an increase of 25.5 percent in average weekly earnings, compared with an increase of 16.7 percent in consumer prices. The resulting real increase in wages of 7.5 percent was the highest annual increase in the postwar period. Consequently, the share of national income going to wages and salaries showed a marked increase also. The labor share of Gross Domestic Product in June 1973 stood at 60.0 percent. In June 1975 it stood at 66.7 percent. Almost all of this increase is accounted for by a fall in the percentage of gross operating surplus going to companies and unincorporated enterprises. (Bob Carr, "Australian Trade Unionism in 1975" *Journal of Industrial Relations*, December 1975, p. 415; Christopher Jay in *Australian Financial Review*, 11 March 1976.)

However, the rapid rise in unemployment during the same period—from about 125,000 to 300,000—evidently encouraged the belief among employees that if there were any more wage victories of that order then they would all become unemployed.

Another factor which may have stayed the hand of the unionists was the adoption of a wage indexation policy by the Australian Conciliation and Arbitration Commission. Accordingly, the 3.6 percent rise in the Consumer Price Index (CPI) for the March quarter 1975, the 3.5 percent rise for the June quarter, and the combined 6.4 percent rise for the September and December quarters were passed on to wage earners. Indeed, as many employees probably realized, indexation guaranteed them larger wage increases than they could otherwise have won in a period of recession.

The other side of the picture, of course, is that indexation has served to perpetuate price inflation by canceling out the price rises by means of which companies and enterprises hope to regain their previous share of Gross Domestic Product (*Australian Financial Review*, 11 March 1976). Presumably this factor led the Fraser Government to oppose pay raises based on the 6.4 percent CPI increase for the September and December quarters of 1975; instead, it argued before the Commission for a 3.2 percent increase in wages.

This step immediately produced a reaction on the left. Pat Clancy, who wrote at the end of 1975 that "wage indexation without strings" was the issue to be "fought out in the early part of 1976" (*Socialist*, 17 December), called for an emergency meeting of the ACTU Executive. He proposed an ultimatum that unless the full increase was paid by 15 February, rolling strikes would be organized, industry by industry. (*Tribune*, 4 February 1976.)

The Arbitration Commission took the wind out of the left's sails by deciding, on 13 February, to award the 6.4 percent pay raise. The president of the Commission said that there had been substantial compliance with the indexation guidelines, and that the general expectation of the increase was "a matter deserving weight." (*Australian Economic Review*, 1st Quarter, 1976, p. 65.)

For the March quarter, the Commission adopted what became known as "plateau" indexation. This was in accordance with government submissions. It passed on the 3 percent rise in the CPI only to those earning up to $125 a week. Those earning more, received a flat rate adjustment of $3.80 based on the application of the full percentage rise to $125.

Before this decision was handed down, the SPA newspaper declared: "Any tampering with wage indexation will open the flood-gates to wage demands as the denial of workers' wage rights will be plain for all to see. A confrontation with the Government on the wage issues will then be only a matter of time." (*Socialist*, 14 April.) Afterward, the CPA organ stated that the decision "robs sixty per cent of wage and salary earners of full cost of living adjustments. It will force unions to ignore indexation guidelines and take the struggle outside the courts and into the workplaces and factories." (*Tribune*, 2 June.)

Both predictions of industrial upheaval fell flat. For the Commission was able to report at the end of the June quarter, as at the end of the March quarter, that there had been substantial compliance with the indexation guidelines (*Sydney Morning Herald*, 13 August). Evidently, employees' fears of pricing themselves out of a job led them to reject the calls of the SPA and CPA for militant industrial action and to continue to support even a watered-down indexation wage policy.

For the June quarter, the Commission decided to apply the full 2.5 percent rise in the CPI to the lowest wage in the Metal Industry Award for Melbourne, namely $98 a week, and to make the resulting $2.50 payable to those receiving up to and including $166 per week. In order to rectify the compression in relativities which had occurred as a result of the previous decision, the Commission also decided to award an increase of 1.5 percent to those earning more than $166 a week. (Ibid., 13 August.)

Responding to this decision, Pat Clancy declared: "We will not accept the lowering of real wages." He also said that he would put a resolution to the ACTU Executive condemning the indexation decision as a deliberate move to cut workers' wages. (*Australian*, 14 August.) This step fell a long way short of his February proposal for an ultimatum by the ACTU executive that rolling strikes would be organized, industry by industry, unless the full CPI increase were granted. Evidently, Clancy finally realized that the militant pursuit of higher wages would only further alienate unionists from the leadership, and especially left-wing leadership, of the trade union movement. Moreover, it is hard to imagine a change in this state of affairs until there is a significant drop in the level of unemployment.

The BLF. All three Communist Parties were represented in the building industry until N. Gallagher, the federal secretary of the BLF and a member of the CPA(M-L), disbanded the N.S.W. branch led by CPA member Joe Owens. This left Gallagher with only one other prominent Communist protagonist in the industry, namely, Pat Clancy, federal secretary of the Building Workers Industrial Union and president of the SPA. In addition to their rivalry based on membership of different Communist Parties, the relationship between these two men has been characterized by considerable personal competition as well. For example, Gallagher displaced Clancy as Building Group representative on the ACTU Executive at the 1973 ACTU Congress, only to be defeated by Clancy at the 1975 Congress. This personal and politically competitive relationship between the two union secretaries helped cause the dispute which took place between the BLF and BWIU in 1976.

To understand this dispute, it is first necessary to go back to 8 July 1974, one month after the BLF's registration was canceled. On that date building industry unions, in accordance with a decision of the ACTU Building Unions meeting, later endorsed by the ACTU Executive, agreed not to intrude on work normally performed by builders' laborers and the Builders Labourers' Federation. They also agreed to regard the BLF, despite deregistration, as an integral part of the trade union movement. (K. D. Marshall, in the matter of an application for the registration of an association called the Australian Building Construction Employees and Builders Labourers' Federation as an organization of employees, pp. 9-10; unpublished.)

On 26 November 1974, the Federal Council of the BLF voted unanimously to seek registration (ibid.,p. 4). The CPA and pro-CPA N.S.W. delegates did not attend as Gallagher had suspended, and was later to cancel, their membership.

On 4 December, the BWIU, having accused the BLF of failing to respect the rights of other building unions, informed the ACTU: "We regard the ACTU agreement which was embodied in the July 8 resolution as being repudiated by the BLF and thus becoming void" (*Socialist*, 17 March 1976).

Then, on 27 February 1976, a Federal councillor for and secretary of the Australian Capital Territory (A.C.T.) branch of the BLF, Mr. D. McHugh, met with officers of the BWIU. He proposed an amalgamation of the A.C.T. branches of the two organizations. An amalgamation agreement was concluded about 10 March. (Marshall, op. cit., p. 7.) Clancy, now unencumbered by the building unions agreement, gave it his full support.

McHugh, with other BLF branch officers, then visited most of the building sites in the A.C.T. and encouraged between 180 and 380 members of the BLF to resign from that organization and join the new amalgamated body called the "BWIU, A.C.T. Branch" (ibid.).

To clinch this takeover of the A.C.T. branch of the BLF, the BWIU filed applications on 23 March seeking the consent of the Industrial Registrar to alterations of its industry and eligibility rules to enable it to cover builders' laborers in the A.C.T. (ibid., p. 8). Clearly, the BWIU was taking advantage of the BLF's deregistered status in order to swell its own ranks with builders' laborers.

Gallagher reacted swiftly. He secured an order from the Australian Industrial Court restraining BWIU officials from admitting builders' laborers to membership (*Tribune*, 21 April).

Also, he entered an agreement with the Master Builders' Federations of Australian, Victoria and N.S.W., the Australian Federation of Construction Contractors, and the National Industrial Executive of the Building andConstruction Industry whereby they would not oppose the BLF's application for registration. Of course, Gallagher's anxiety to gain registration in order to head off Clancy's attempt to "white ant" his union in the A.C.T. gave the employers the whip hand in negotiating this agreement. Accordingly, it provided for the forfeiting of wage claims, the lifting of work bans, and the establishment of a restrictive disputes-settlement procedure. (Marshall, op. cit., Annexure 2.) The only bright spot so far as the BLF was concerned was an undertaking by the employers not to stand in the way of the union's application for a paid Picnic Day (ibid.).

Finally, for good measure, Gallagher or one of his colleagues took action which led to the ransacking of BWIU offices in Sydney and Melbourne (*Socialist*, 17 March; *Tribune*, 17 March).

The bitterness of the conflict, of which the above incident is one example, was also given expression in the polemical language of the Sino-Soviet dispute. *Vanguard*, the official organ of the CPA(M-L), stated: "Through the BWIU, Clancy is trying to bring all building workers under the Soviet social-imperialist aegis" (22 April). To which the SPA newpaper responded. "The fact that Maoism objectively serves the bosses stands nakedly exposed in the continuing fight by officials of the

Gallagher-led Builders Labourers' Federation to block builders laborers' moves to strengthen their union by amalgamation with the BWIU" (The *Socialist*, 28 April).

Gallagher himself told the press that Clancy's "move [to poach BLF members] is part of a plan to widen the Soviet sphere of influence in the building industry." Asked about Chinese influence in Australia, Gallagher replied: "All you can see around are dim sims and chiko rolls." (*The Age*, 29 April.)

On 16 July the Industrial Registrar granted the BLF's application for registration, thereby enabling Gallagher to shore up his membership on that new front in the Sino-Soviet dispute—the building industry in A.C.T.

International Relations and the International Communist Movement. The CPA maintains contact with the more independently minded parties in the international Communist movement. Philip Herington, a National Committee member, attended the 80th-birthday celebration of Dolores Ibarruri ("La Pasionara"), which the Communist Party of Italy held in Rome on 13 December 1975. In February 1976, Bernie Taft met high-ranking officials of the League of Communists of Yugoslavia (*FBIS*, 16-17 February). He went on to Paris to attend the Congress of the French Communist Party (*Tribune*, 17 March). In July, Mavis Robertson and two others visited Romania at the invitation of the Central Committee of the Romanian Communist Party (*FBIS*, 30 July). The following month, they, too, had discussions with the Yugoslav Communists (*FBIS*, 6 August).

The failure of the CPSU to invite the CPA to its Congress proved the occasion of one more argument between the CPA and the SPA as to which is the "real" Communist Party. The CPA newspaper declared: "The CPSU obviously intends to carry on its campaign against parties which adopt independent positions. . . . [One] method is inviting a breakaway group like the Socialist Party of Australia while ignoring the real Communist Party." (*Tribune*, 17 March.) The SPA replied: "There is more to being a Communist Party than just having that name. The CPA's abandonment . . . of the ideology of Marxism-Leninism . . . its contempt for the International Communist Movement as a whole . . . its abandonment of democratic centralism (witness current 'tendencies') . . . disqualified it from that title." (*Socialist*, 14 April.) The last criticism was rendered obsolete when the CPA Congress in June restored democratic centralism.

Peter Symon, SPA general secretary, represented his Party at the CPSU Congress and addressed the gathering (ibid., 17 March).

Besides the CPSU, a number of Soviet-bloc Communist Parties held congresses in 1976. This resulted in a heavy itinerary for the delegates of the pro-Soviet SPA. Jack McPhillips, a national organizer, attended the Eleventh Congress of the Bulgarian Communist Party (ibid., 31 March). Barbara Curthoys, vice-president, and Ron Hearn, Central Committee Executive member, attended the Ninth Congress of the Socialist Unity Party of the German Democratic Republic (ibid., 26 May). Another Central Committee Executive member, Alan Miller, attended the 17th Congress of the Mongolian People's Revolutionary Party in mid-June (ibid., 23 June, 7 July). The SPA played host in Australia to Stelios Jacovides, a member of the Central Committee of AKEL, the pro-Soviet Reconstruction Party of the Working People of Cyprus (ibid., 1 September).

The CPA(M-L) continued its close relationship with the Albanian and Chinese Communist Parties. In November-December 1975, its chairman, E. F. Hill, visited Enver Hoxha, head of the Albanian Party of Labor (*FBIS*, 7 December 1975; *Vanguard*, 5 February 1976).

On 9 January, Hill sent a message of condolence to Chairman Mao Tse-tung and the Central Committee of the Chinese Communist Party (CCP) upon the death of Chou En-lai (*Peking Review*, 16 January).

In February, a delegation composed of Hill and A. E. Bull, a new vice-chairman who has apparently replaced Norm Gallagher, visited China at the invitation of the Central Committee of the

CCP (*Vanguard*, 11 March). Two of the Chinese leaders whom they met, Wang Hung-wen and Chang Chun-chiao, have since been purged by the new chairman of the CCP, Hua Kuo-feng.

On 12 April, Hill, Bull, and the other vice-chairman, Clarrie O'Shea, cabled the CCP to declare the support of the CPA(M-L) for the dismissal of Teng Hsiao-ping. They also welcomed the appointment of Hua Kuo-feng as first vice-chairman of the Central Committee and premier of the State Council. (Ibid., 22 April.)

In June, the Australian Prime Minister paid an official visit to China. The anti-Soviet stance which he adopted before and during the visit delighted his Chinese hosts and (therefore) the CPA(M-L). The SPA, on the other hand, was appalled (*Socialist*, 7 July). The CPA's national officers used the occasion to reiterate party policy. Australia should, they said, adopt "a non-aligned, independent . . . foreign policy" (*Tribune*, 30 June).

Hill, O'Shea, and Bull sent another message of condolence to Peking, this time upon the death of Mao. They wrote: "In deep grief we extend to you [the Central Committee] and through you to all the Chinese people our deepest sympathy on the death of Comrade Mao Tse-tung. . . . His name is correctly ranked with the names of Marx, Engels, Lenin and Stalin." (Vanguard, 10 September.)

The SPA Central Committee Secretariat expressed the hope that now China would reestablish good relations with the USSR (*Socialist*, 15 September). And with the subsequent accession of Hua Kuo-feng to the chairmanship of the CCP this appeared to be a distinct possibility.

Publications. The CPA publishes a weekly newspaper, *Tribune*, a monthly theoretical journal, the *Australian Left Review*, and an occasional internal publication, *Praxis*. The SPA publishes a fortnightly newspaper, the *Socialist*, and a monthly digest, *Survey*. The CPA(M-L) publishes a weekly newspaper, *Vanguard*, and a monthly theoretical journal, *The Australian Communist*.

La Trobe University   Angus McIntyre
Bundoora, Victoria, Australia

Burma

The Burma Communist Party (BCP) was established on 15 August 1939 with probably 13 members and Thakin Soe as secretary-general. After participating in the struggle for the liberation of Burma under the leadership of the "Anti-Fascist People's Freedom League" (AFPFL), the Communists more and more disagreed with the Socialists in the AFPFL. In March 1946, Thakin Soe and some followers split from the BCP, where Thakin Than Tun had taken over the leadership, and founded the Communist Party of Burma, also known as the "Red Flag." The Red Flag soon went underground, and in January 1947 was declared an unlawful association. The BCP or "White Flag" Communists under Thakin Than Tun also went underground at the end of March 1948, and in October 1953 they too were declared illegal.

Except for the years 1948 to 1950 when the government of Prime Minister U Nu nearly collapsed, Communist activities were confined to certain areas (especially the Irrawaddy delta, the Pegu Yoma highlands, and the Shan State) and therefore were a local, but constant, harassment to the Union government. Large-scale counterinsurgency operations of the Burmese army, undertaken in cooperation with local "People's Militia," together with internal party struggles and purges of "revisionists," critically weakened the BCP after 1967-68. After the death of Thakin Than Tun in September 1968, leadership was taken over at most levels by men subservient to Peking. With Communist Chinese aid given openly after June 1967 and continued secretly after the resumption of full diplomatic relations between Burma and China in 1971, the BCP stepped up its guerrilla activities in the Shan State, first north of Lashio and about 1971 in the Kunlong area east of the Salween River, which it has controlled since the end of 1973.

The Red Flags, whose main base was in the Arakan region and for some time also in the Irrawaddy delta, did not reach any major importance. The capture of their leader Thakin Soe and the loss of other leaders at the end of 1970 critically weakened the group. Thus, the Red Flag and its splinter group, the Arakan Communist Party, have lost even the small local importance they were able to claim during the mid-1960s. As there is hardly any information on them any more, they are not noted further in the following survey.

Reliable figures on the membership of the BCP are not available. However, it seems to have grown over the last year or two from a strength of at least 6,000 men under arms in 1974 to a "well-armed guerrilla force of more than 10,000 troops," a figure given by rightist minority leaders, but probably still an accurate estimate (*The Nation*, Bangkok, 6 June 1976, p. 2; *FBIS*, 7 June). The strength of the government troops is estimated at 130,000. Burma's population is just over 30 million.

Leadership and Organization. Since the reshuffle following the deaths of Chairman Thakin Zin and Secretary Thakin Chit in March 1975, no changes in the top ranks of the BCP have become known. Thus, the Politburo should consist, as in May 1975, of Thakin Ba Thein Tin (probably still residing in Peking) as chairman, Thakin Pe Tint as vice-chairman, Khin Maung Kyi, Myo Myint, Kyaw Mya, Kyin Maung, and Ne Win. The Central Committee comprises, in addition to these men, Soe Kyi, Saw Han, Zaw Myaing, Taik Aung, Pe Thaung, Fran Gan, Ye Tuni, Thet Tun, Than Shwe, and two unidentified persons, one each from the northwest command and the delta region. There are also 14 candidate members to the Central Committee. On 3 November ex-Brigadier Kyaw Zaw, who went underground in July (see "Domestic Activities"), was appointed to the Central Military Commission (*FBIS*, 15 November).

The organizational structure extends from the Politburo and the Central Committee through divisional and district committees down to township and, in some areas, even village committees. Divisional committees exist, as the elections to the Central Committee revealed, for all parts of Burma, though sometimes only in name, and other committees only in regions where the BCP is active. Since the Central Committee meeting in May 1975 there is also a "border area people's administrative body," of whose activities nothing is known. The BCP's "People's Army" is structured along traditional communist lines with party political cadres superior to military commanders at all levels.

Party Internal Affairs. Since the re-establishment of the BCP's top committees in May 1975, the party organization appears to have come to a rest after nearly ten years of internal struggles and purges. Only in a broadcast of 21 December 1975 were internal difficulties mentioned:

> The problems the BCP and the People's Army are encountering today are temporary. They are not problems that cannot be solved because of basic [word indistinct] contradictions, but are natural occurrences during revolutions and during the expansion of revolutions. The BCP and the People's Army are not only

certain to solve these problems but also will surely achieve a revolutionary victory in the end. This will be done through a united one-party effort by relying on all Burmese nationals and the people, through the maximum organizational work, through persistently following a correct policy politically and ideologically, through self-reliance and regeneration via our own efforts, through the will to endure hardships, and through gallant, resolute and indomitable spirit in battle. (*FBIS*, 30 December 1975.)

There have been no further references to internal difficulties or to general policies regarding internal affairs of the BCP.

Domestic Activities. Although the BCP's continuing armed struggle against the Rangoon government (see below) is restricted mainly to the eastern and northern areas, the propaganda broadcasts of its clandestine "Voice of the People of Burma" (VPB) radio are aimed at the population of Burma as a whole. Reports of military activities, including summaries of successes of past years (e.g., VPB, 11 December 1975; *FBIS*, 16 December) are a minor but nevertheless important part of the propaganda because they are supposed to document the strength of the "People's Army" and the weakness of the government troops. With a similar intention, a radio broadcast marking the 28th anniversary of the "people's democratic armed revolution in Burma" on 28 March—the day the BCP in 1948 went underground to escape arrest—took the occasion to justify armed struggle:

The only way for the people [?to gain their rights] is through armed struggle. [The government] is violently struggling against the BCP and the revolutionary people. [The] military government will never give way willingly; it will vehemently oppose the revolution until its last dying breath. That is why the main duty of the people is to destroy the mercenary troops of the enemy. (VPB, 28 March 1976; *FBIS*, 31 March.)

In such broadcasts the BCP tries to connect itself—as does the ruling "Burma Socialist Programme Party" (BSPP)—with the liberation movement during and after World War II. Thus it points to the "military government's reactionary policies of imperialism, feudalism, landlordism and bureaucratic capitalism (ibid.) as main cause of the country's more and more declining economy, which affects the whole population, and presents itself as the only remedy for this continually worsening situation. The government—for example, in a speech of General San Yu in Kengtung (*The Guardian*, Rangoon, 24 December 1975)—accuses the Communist insurgents of having "no political policy and principles of their own that would really benefit the indigenous working people" and "recklessly giving trouble to the people, persecuting them and killing them." The rightist insurgents, on the other hand, point out the similarity of the government's and the BCP's policies: "While Ne Win practices Burmese chauvinism, the BCP also practices Burmese chauvinism.While Ne Win suppresses the people, so the BCP also suppresses the people." (*FBIS*, 11 May 1976.)

BCP broadcasts also publicize the "growing factional power struggle within the military clique" reflected by "the recent loss of chief of staff and Defense Ministry posts by Tin Oo," and try to instigate general envy of the privileges and the "luxurious life" of the "high-ranking members of the military clique" (VPB, 20 April; *FBIS*, 22 April). By these means the BCP hopes to isolate the government generally from the people, and particularly to work up the dissatisfaction existing in some lower ranks of the army to eventual defection:

Officers and troops of the lower echelon, who are being tricked and deceived by reactionary, wrong lines and policies, will one day see the truth and turn down the gun now trained at the workers, peasants and working people toward the common enemy—the Ne Win-San Yu military government—and join hands with the oppressed working people in the struggle. (Ibid.)

A special event for the BCP was the disappearance of Kyaw Zaw from Rangoon and his escape to the Communists. Kyaw Zaw is one of the "30 comrades," a group of young Burmese patriots (including national hero Aung San and present president U Ne Win) who fought alongside Japanese occupation troops against British troops in Burma at the start of World War II. He was a member of the BCP Central Committee in 1945, but was expelled in 1948 for refusing to give up his military career and go underground. In the army Kyaw Zaw rose to the rank of brigadier, but was pensioned off in 1957 because of his strong Communist leanings, which prompted him to betray the government. Now once again with the BCP, he stated in a lengthy broadcast speech that increasing numbers of people ate only boiled rice with salt, and that the middle class had to sell their property in order to eat:

> From a political point of view, there is no democracy and no freedom of speech. Economically, we have become impoverished and are starving; socially speaking, our people, who at one time proudly upheld moral principles, have been corrupted by Ne Win and his men. (*Far Eastern Economic Review*, Hong Kong, 3 September 1976, p. 24.)

Altogether the Communist propaganda seemed to direct itself in 1976 more than before at special groups in the population which are also wooed by the ruling BSPP. Besides the active soldiers, it addressed the veterans (for whom the BSPP founded a special "Central Council of Burma War Veterans Associations" on 17 December 1975), and also the students:

> Why is the military clique, which neglected the veterans for such a long time, now in a frenzy to organize them? Why is the military clique saying that it will solve their problems and |words indistinct| them? There are reasons for this. The veterans are not isolated from society. Most of them, like the working people, are poor and have problems. They have lost their rights. They realize that their interests are inseparable from the interests of the workers, peasants and working people. That is why they begin to detest and oppose the military government. So the military government has tried to appease some of them, separating them from the others and using them as they see fit. (VPB, 15 January 1976; *FBIS*, 21 January.)

> The students and youths never create disturbances nor are they instigators. They are simply fighting for their rights and for a just cause. Why were all the universities and colleges closed down in such a hurry if it was just a case of a handful of students rioting? It was because of the |word indistinct| movement and not just a small group of students protesting. There would be no reason to be afraid nor would the universities have to be closed down if it was just a movement by a small group of students. This is the seventh time during the military government's 14-year rule that the universities have been closed down with the excuse of "a small group of students rioting"—but this excuse is like a phonograph needle stuck in one place on a record, playing the same tune repeatedly. (VPB, 6 April; *FBIS*, 7 April.)

Armed Struggle. The Burmese Communists continued their armed struggle against the "Ne Win-San Yu military government" (referring to President U Ne Win and to General San Yu, secretary of the Council of State and also of the BSPP). Compared with the years before, the struggle in 1976 seems to have been limited more and more to concentrated and quite effective guerrilla activities in the northern and eastern parts of the Shan State.

With the exception of a few towns such as Kunlong, Hopan, and Panglong, and of bigger villages with army outposts, the BCP controls in the Shan State the mountainous area east of the Salween River up to approximately 30 or 40 miles north of Kengtung. Thus, the BCP aimed at expanding their area of direct influence southward and especially toward the Laotian and also the Thai border. In November-December 1975 the BCP undertook a greater offensive to occupy the area of Mong Hpayak and Mong Yawng in the triangle of adjoining China and Laos:

> Fighting 46 battles including four big ones, the Tatmadaw |regular army| has dealt crushing blows on CPB |ie., BCP| insurgents and their followers, SSA (Shan State Army) rebels, who had perpetrated military activities in northern, southern and most eastern Shan State . . . in November and December last year.

> In these engagements the Tatmadaw captured 216 insurgents dead and ten alive. . . . There were 46 killed, 13 missing and 157 wounded on Tatmadaw side. (*The Guardian*, Rangoon, 6 January 1976.)

The fact that the government troops were obviously able to repulse the offensive was due not only to the use of artillery and airplanes, but also to the circumstance that this area, to the great displeasure of the Rangoon government, has been controlled for many years now by Kuomintang (KMT) remnants protecting the smuggling of opium. Having great influence on the local population, they were probably more effective in defending the area against the BCP than were the government troops. This explains, on the other hand, why the BCP's "Voice of the People of Burma," in its account of the 1975 combat actions, could claim that the "People's Army of the Northern Division," in more than 1,300 small- and large-scale battles, had killed "a Kuomintang military adviser" along with 900 soldiers (VPB, 23 January 1976; FBIS, 28 January), thus insinuating that the KMT troops were "accomplices of the military government" (VPB, 20 February; FBIS, 24 February) and that they were not fought by the government (cf. "Opium smuggling KMT remnants suffer heavy casualties—The Guardian, 4 January).

The Communist activities from January 1976 onward concentrated more on the area around, especially north of, Kengtung. They were evidently combined with efforts to cross the Salween River to its western bank (e.g., VPB, 1 February; FBIS, 4 February). In their guerrilla attacks the BCP troops were supported by the "Shan State Army," a force of 600 to 700 Shan rebels who had joined forces with the BCP in the course of 1975 (Bangkok Post, 28 April, p. 5; FBIS, 28 April). More big battles were fought when, at the same time, 1,200 BCP troops (a probably exaggerated figure) were said to have attacked an army outpost and "a 300-strong force of BCP rebels shelled a column of the No 4 Chin rifles" near Mong Yang (BBS, 26 March; FBIS, 29 March). The government's counterattack was supported by "airstrikes of the Burma Air Force and artillery barrages." According to official statements, "over 100 BCP rebels were killed and 150 wounded in the 5 days of fighting, while government forces suffered 26 dead and 48 wounded." (Ibid.) Although the BCP is emphasizing guerrilla activities more than ever before, since Thakin Ba Thein Tin became chairman, these figures concerning the Communists appear to be considerably if not highly exaggerated. The Communist activities in Kengtung area, nevertheless, caused the Rangoon government to close down Thailand's consulate in Kengtung because it could not guarantee enough security for it.

Other areas where Communist military activities of light or moderate intensity occurred were, as in earlier years, the northern Shan State between Lashio and the Chinese border and the northern Kachin State (Lauhkaung area). General San Yu mentioned in a speech at Haka, Chin State, that "it was learnt that some CPBs based in Arakan State had come into southern part of Chin State; these CPBs, he said, were divided among themselves" (The Guardian, 29 February). They probably, however, belong to remnants of the Red Flags and therefore need not be regarded as a dangerous spark which could light a new fire in the near future.

Militarily the overall situation is characterized by the fact that the BCP through its guerrilla activities tries to expand its "liberated areas," which supposedly comprise already a third of the Shan State. In this attempt to infiltrate into new areas it is confronted not only with the government troops, but also with insurgents of several minority groups who are in name separatist and in fact quite often connected with smuggling and who have regarded those areas up to now as their territories. After a meeting where leaders of nine such rebel ethnic minorities formed a new alliance, the "Federal National Democratic Front" (FNDF), the Karen Mahn Ba Zan as spokesman indicated to Western journalists their desire to reach agreement with the better-armed BCP. He added, however, that "it is quite likely that we will have to fight the BCP soon and it will be the biggest encounter against the communists ever carried out in Burma" (The Nation, Bangkok, 30 May, p. 1; FBIS, 1 June). As Mahn Ba Zan's propaganda has exceeded his military successes by far during recent years, such a three-party war, which would surely devastate Burma, is, nevertheless, not very likely to occur soon.

International Views and Contacts. The BCP remains firmly aligned with the People's Republic of China in spite of the officially good diplomatic relations between the governments in Rangoon and Peking. The BCP leaders probably still reside in China and the BCP broadcasting station may also be located there. Furthermore, the People's Republic continued to be the glorious example to be followed:

> In China production has always developed. There is no contradiction between production and consumption. There is no economic hardship. Ever since the Chinese Communist Party took over, production has continuously increased and the various difficulties of the Chinese people have been overcome in a very short time. (VPB, 29 January 1976; *FBIS*, 4 February.)

President U Ne Win's visit to Peking in November 1975 evidently resulted in much less open relations between the Chinese and the Burmese Communist parties, at least up to Mao Tse-tung's death. Reports state, nevertheless, even for this period, that the armament of the Burmese Communists has improved so that they are able now to use heavier weapons than they had in the past, including artillery. Even according to Burmese newspapers these weapons came from "across the border of South Vietnam, Cambodia and Laos when the old regimes there collapsed." And circumstances suggest that they passed through China on their way to the BCP because "observers here [in Rangoon] doubted that the weapons could have come directly from Vietnam or Cambodia as they had no common border with Burma. As for Laos, they thought it unlikely that artillery could be brought across the Mekong River and the heavily guarded Kengtung area. (*NYT*, 1 April 1976.)

The BCP sent a condolence message celebrating Chou En-lai as a leader who "made a great contribution to the relationship between the Communist Party of China and the Communist Party of Burma and thus won the wholehearted love, respect and admiration of the Communist Party of Burma" (*Peking Review*, 16 January, p. 25). On 9 September, the VPB announced as "important news" in its regular service the death of Mao Tse-tung (*FBIS*, 10 September). In a message sent the following day the Central Committee of the BCP paid reverence to Mao Tse-tung as "the great leader of the Chinese people and the great teacher of the international proletariat and the oppressed nations and oppressed people." After praising his merits in the proletarian revolution and in the establishment and consolidation of the People's Republic of China, "the reliable bulwark of the world proletarian revolution," the message emphasized that the BCP will further follow his teaching and with it the example of the Communist Party of China:

> We will turn grief into strength with determination. To mourn forever Comrade Mao Tsetung we will apply ourselves to the study of Marxism-Leninism-Mao Tsetung thought and make efforts to integrate it more correctly with the practice of the Burmese revolution. (NCNA, Peking, in English, 13 September; *FBIS* 14 September.)

In the reports on the mourning festivities, the BCP figured first among the underground Communist parties of southeast Asia (e.g., *FBIS*, 15 September). And a 10-minute film on "Comrades of Foreign Marxist-Leninist Parties and Organizations and Foreign Friends and Experts" paying respect to Chairman Mao's remains showed BCP chairman Thakin Ba Thein Tin in a long sequence "approaching Hua Kuo-feng and immediately shaking hands with and embracing Hua" and other Chinese leaders, and finally "bowing and remaining for a while in that position" in front of the catafalque (*FBIS*, 21 September).

On 18 November, Thakin Ba Thein Tin and Thakin Pe Tint were officially received by the new Party Chairman Hua Kuo-feng who afterward hosted a banquet for them. This could mean nothing else but a sort of duty gesture toward international communism. In view of the mourning reports, it can, however, be suspected that the BCP leaders were not chosen by pure accident, but carefully selected for this occasion. And this then could perhaps indicate that Peking intends to tighten the contact with the BCP again and thus begin once more a harder and rather conflict-provoking policy toward Burma.

As in earlier years, Moscow criticized China for supporting the BCP, and more, "Peking's support does not end there. Regular units of the Chinese Army have operated on Burmese territory with the rebels more than once" ("Radio Peace and Progress," in French, 15 January; *FBIS*, 23 January). It cannot be presumed that Moscow's wooing will really cause the Burmese government to give up its policy of neutrality and non-alignment. It should, however, be noted that contacts between Burma and Vietnam, Laos, Cambodia, and the Democratic People's Republic of Korea increased in 1976. Whether this can be regarded as the beginning of a reorientation of Burma's foreign policy, and hence as an answer to Peking's support for the BCP, can only be decided in the light of future developments.

Publications. The only first-hand information on the BCP comes from the broadcasts of its clandestine radio station, the "Voice of the People of Burma," inaugurated on 28 March 1971 and supposedly located in southwest Yunnan Province in China. According to the *Bangkok Post* (28 February 1976; *FBIS*, 5 March) this or another radio station has been set up in Mong Pulong (southwest of Kengtung) "to broadcast propaganda in the various dialects of the area."

Köln-Weiss   Klaus Fleischmann
Federal Republic of Germany

Cambodia

The second year of communist rule in Cambodia, 1976, offered some interesting contrasts with the chaotic and bloody first year. During 1975, systematic executions of former civil and military officials of the Lon Nol regime and harsh forced migrations and forced labor drove thousands of Khmers to seek refuge in Thailand and Vietnam. But by mid-1976, the regime no longer seemed to face a major problem of food supply or internal dissidence—and a diminishing number of refugees reported that mass executions seemed to have ended or at least become more selective.

Perhaps to demonstrate that they had consolidated their hold, the regime produced a new constitution in December 1975, held elections in April 1976, reshuffled the government (though the question of who holds power remained hazy), and changed the name of the country to "Democratic Cambodia."

In July, Vietnam News Agency conducted a long interview with a senior Khmer leader in which he gave a surprisingly candid assessment of the regime's achievements and of its problems.

Just after that, in August, Cambodia established relations with a number of non-Communist nations. Then, in September, the Khmer leadership publicly acknowledged, for the first time, that their regime is "Marxist-Leninist." They also described themselves as the "Cambodian Revolutionary Organization," although messages from the communist regime in Laos have twice referred to the Communist Party of Kampuchea (KCP). (See *FBIS*, 19 April and 16 October 1976; and Timothy M.

Carney, *Communist Party Power in Kampuchea (Cambodia): Documents and Discussion*, Ithaca, N.Y.: Cornell University Southeast Asia Program Data Paper, December 1976.)

This took place in a carefully arranged memorial ceremony for Mao Tse-tung in Phnom Penh. The Chinese ambassador, who was present, also stated that the Cambodian Revolutionary Organization was Marxist-Leninist and a "fraternal" party to the Chinese Communist Party. This is as close as the present regime in Phnom Penh has come to publicly acknowledging they are communist. One reason for their long reluctance to do so may be the fact that "Communist" and "Vietnamese" probably remain synonymous in the minds of many Cambodians.

KCP membership may be on the order of 10,000. Cambodia's present population may be 6 million.

History. The KCP traces its lineage to Ho Chi Minh's pre-World War II Indochina Communist Party, which was reconstituted as the Lao Dong (Workers) Party in 1951. Vietnamese communists continued to dominate the communist movements in Cambodia and Laos; but an effort was made to disguise their unpopular presence by giving the Cambodian and Lao organizations separate names. Until 1962, Prince Norodom Sihanouk, who ruled Cambodia, allowed the Khmer communists some leeway to take part in the political process, though there were periodic crackdowns by his police. In this period, the legal and semi-open communist movement in Cambodia was known by the Khmer name Pracheachon—loosely translated as "People's Revolutionary Party." The communist and fellow-traveler *maquis* was dubbed *Khmer rouge* by Sihanouk.

In 1962, Sihanouk denounced the Pracheachon and forced it underground. However, in the same year, he appointed Khieu Samphan, Hou Yuon, Hu Nim, and several other prominent young leftists to key positions in the government. In 1966 he allowed the rightists to force them out, and they fled to the maquis.

Sihanouk's overthrow in March 1970 and his formation of an avowedly pro-communist exile regime based in Perking (in May 1970), coincided with the beginning of a rapid increase of communist influence in Cambodia. Scattered bands of dissidents gradually coalesced into an army under strong Vietnamese communist tutelage. In 1972, most Vietnamese communist forces left Cambodia for the final stages of the Vietnam war. Thereafter, traditional Khmer-Vietnamese hostility rapidly asserted itself between the Khmer guerrilla forces and their Vietnamese communist neighbors.

The main indigenous elements comprising the leftist camp in Cambodia during the 1970-75 war were probably: (1) the Khmer rouge dissidents, who during the 1960s opted out of a society tightly controlled by Sihanouk; (2) a few thousand Khmers who went to North Vietnam in the 1950s, received military and political training, and reentered Cambodia after Sihanouk's overthrow; and (3) peasants recruited by these more highly motivated and indoctrinated groups during the 1970-75 war.

At the end of the five-year war, the KCP immediately began to carry out one of the most comprehensive and brutal social transformations ever attempted. Their revolutionary measures in liberated areas during the war had caused mass flight to the towns controlled by Lon Nol. With no other administrative machinery than their army of peasant youths, the KCP immediately emptied the cities and forced all inhabitants to begin clearing land and planting rice. Tens of thousands are believed to have died from the rigors inflicted on them by teen-age cadres of the KCP. Other tens of thousands who had served the Lon Nol regime were summarily executed. In all, perhaps a million Cambodians lost their lives during the war and in the first year of communist rule.

Meanwhile, all non-Asian foreigners were ordered out of Cambodia, and nearly all contacts ended with the outside world, except for Radio Phnom Penh, weekly plane flights connecting Phnom Penh and Peking, and thousands of fleeing refugees.

Prince Sihanouk returned for a brief visit in October 1975, was appalled by what he saw and by the treatment he received from the new leaders (according to his retinue), but returned again after making a tour of Third World countries on behalf of the new regime. In April 1976, Radio Phnom

Penh announced his retirement, in Cambodia, on an $8,000 pension. Since then, some visiting communist diplomats have said, he has dropped out of sight completely; others say he grows his own food under armed guard.

Leadership and Organization. The KCP is run by a Central Committee which acts as the collective leadership of Cambodia. Although its membership is secret (and its existence not even acknowledged by the regime), press speculation has focused on a few individuals long active in Cambodian left-wing political circles. Saloth Sar has been variously described as "chairman," "secretary-general," and "secretary" of the KCP. "Pol Pot," who was named premier in April 1976 and granted sick leave in October, may be a pseudonym for Saloth Sar.

Saloth Sar probably played an important organizing role in the buildup of KCP membership during the war. He was born in 1928, took a radio technicians' course in France, married one of the elite Khieu sisters (the other married Ieng Sary), and entered the maquis in 1963. Despite these credentials, he has been described by Cambodians who knew him as an unimpressive personality. The July VNA interview attributed to him is discussed separately below.

Khieu Samphan, Ieng Sary, and Son Sen—who were named as deputy premiers in August 1975—are believed to be members of the KCP Central Committee and dominant political personalities in Phnom Penh. All are in their early forties, French-educated, and have been pro-communist or communist all their adult lives. They have shared the rigors of life in the maquis for a number of years, and they probably feel that their personal survival, as well as that of their party and country, depends on their close collaboration. However, there are differences in the backgrounds—and perhaps in the political orientations—of these three leaders.

Khieu Samphan was named chief of the state praesidium (hence chief of state) in the April 1976 government reshuffle. He was always one of the most outstanding members of his age group, since working his way through school and helping support his widowed mother in Kompong Cham. Physically slight, morally ascetic, and brilliant, he earned scholarships that led to a doctorate in economics at the Sorbonne. In 1962 he was one of the young leftist deputies in the National Assembly to whom Sihanouk entrusted the government (to stifle their criticism and harness their energies). By 1966 their radical experiments with state control had brought the economy to a virtual standstill, and Sihanouk allowed older rightist elite members to regain control. He probably also approved police intimidation of the most prominent leftist intellectuals. Khieu Samphan and others (including Hou Yuon and Hu Nim, who may be members of the KCP Central Committee) were believed at the time to have been secretly executed. But they fled to the maquis and played a well-publicized role as leaders of it during the war.

In late spring 1974, Khieu Samphan made an extended tour of friendly nations, beginning with a lavish reception by Mao in Peking that seemed to put him on terms at least of equality with Sihanouk. This produced speculation that he was being groomed by the Chinese to replace or supplement Sihanouk as the focus for Chinese influence in Cambodia.

Khieu Samphan was favorably regarded, even by prominent officials of the Lon Nol regime, as a Khmer nationalist and a man of rare integrity. His doctoral dissertation spells out his fanatical determination to make Cambodia independent of foreign economic influence. Since 17 April 1975 Khieu Samphan has played a prominent but not preeminent role in the very limited public activity of the new regime. In the April 1976 reshuffle, he was named head of the state praesidium, replacing Sihanouk as chief of state.

Ieng Sary, who retained his post as vice-premier for foreign affairs in the April 1976 reshuffle, has made several visits to Peking and to non-aligned nations' conferences. He attended the 1975 and 1976 UN General Assembly sessions. In November 1975 he led a group to Bangkok to negotiate the reestablishment of bilateral economic and diplomatic relations. (Ambassadors had not been exchanged as of the end of 1976.)

Son Sen also retained his post as deputy premier for defense affairs in the April 1976 reshuffle. Son Sen was born in South Vietnam in 1930. (Ieng Sary was born the same year but in southeastern Cambodia.) Both are of "Khmer Krom" families (Khmers long domiciled in South Vietnam). They both received some education in France. Ieng Sary probably owes his political affiliation and much of his prominence to his marriage to Khieu Thirith, daughter of a wealthy, leftist Phnom Penh family. She is now minister of social affairs. Her sister married Saloth Sar, as noted above, and probably shaped his career as well.

Ieng Sary and Son Sen took to the maquis together in 1963. Ieng Sary subsequently visited Hanoi and formed close ties with Vietnamese communists. He went to Peking early in the 1970-75 war to "represent" the Khmer guerrillas and probably to watch Sihanouk on behalf of the pro-Vietnam faction (or simply on behalf of Hanoi).

If Ieng Sary is, or has been, pro-Vietnam, this has not prevented him from making a number of official visits to Peking since 1970; nor did it prevent him from negotiating the terms of Cambodia's diplomatic and economic rapprochement with Bangkok in 1975. This action was fostered by Peking, which had just normalized its own relations with Thailand in an obvious effort to limit or counter Hanoi's influence in Southeast Asia.

The complete list of appointments announced in April 1976 is as follows:

Chairman, praesidium of state	Khieu Samphan
First deputy chairman	So Phim
Second deputy chairman	Nhim Ros

Standing Committee of the Cambodian People's Representative Assembly:

Chairman	Nuon Chea (named acting premier in September 1976)
First deputy chairman	Nguon Kang
Second deputy chairman	Peou Sou

Members, Ros Nim, Sor Sean, Mey Chham, Kheng Sok, Mat Ly, Thang Si, and Ros Preap

Government of Democratic Cambodia:

Premier	Pol Pot (granted sick leave in September 1976)
Deputy premier, Foreign Affairs	Ieng Sary
Deputy premier, National Defense	Son Sen
Deputy premier, Economy	Vorn vet
Minister, Information and Propaganda	Hu Nim
Minister, Public Health	Thiounn Thioeunn
Minister, Social Affairs	Ieng Thirith
Minister, Public Works	Toch Phoeun
Minister, Culture, Education and Learning	Yun Yat
High counselor	Penn Nouth

Peoples Representative Assembly Committee chairmen (with personal rank of minister):

Communications Committee, chairman	Mey Prang
Agriculture Committee, chairman	Chey Suon
Industry Committee, chairman	Cheng An
Commerce Committee, chairman	Prom Nhem

Auxiliary and Mass Organizations. During the 1970-75 war, refugee reports indicated that the usual range of mass organizations (e.g., for peasants, women, students, and Buddhist monks) was created by the KCP to aid in the reconstruction of Cambodian society. This was the central nonmilitary goal of the KCP during the war and has been its main concern since military victory. It is not known how important a role mass organizations have actually played in the process of reconstruction. Many refugees have reported that virtually their only contact with the new regime was with gun-wielding guerrillas and anonymous cadres, who lectured them on political subjects or on practical matters such as farming.

Domestic Attitudes and Activities. In July 1976 the Vietnam News Agency broadcast what it described as the English translation of an interview with Premier Pol Pot (a possible pseudonym for Saloth Sar). (See *FBIS, Daily Report, Asia and Pacific*, vol. IV, no. 146, annex no. 124, 28 July, pp. 2-6.) Ieng Sary, deputy premier for foreign affairs, was reportedly present. "Pol Pot" is said to have told the VNA that his government scored few noteworthy achievements during its first year in power, except to mobilize the people to produce enough food for domestic needs. Though he referred in passing to dissidence (which he claimed was U.S.-sponsored), he said such "dark schemes and plans of the U.S. imperialists and their lackeys have been successively brought to failure."

Pursuing the subject of food production, Pol Pot told VNA that an ambitious water control scheme to supply 1.5 million hectares of rice fields was one-third complete and was being constructed entirely by hand labor. However, he added the shocking comment that "eighty percent of the people's labor were exhausted by malaria." He indicated that imported medical supplies were inadequate for general needs and that locally produced medicines were ineffective. This seems to represent a softening of the regime's former position that the long-term good of the people justifies a policy of total self-reliance—which in practice has involved the rupture of most normal trade contacts. Indeed, it could well be interpreted as a plea to foreign countries to provide medical supplies on an emergency basis.

Pol Pot provided several other hints that the regime was rethinking its policy of total self-reliance. He said that factories destroyed in the war are being repaired, although no new ones are being built. Some repaired factories are evidently standing idle, because (he said) they depend on imported raw materials, which are still unavailable. However, Pol Pot predicted that crepe rubber exports would reach 200,000 tons in 1976; he said that half that amount had been shipped by mid-1976. (Though he did not say where, China seems a good possibility.) He also implied a hope that more sophisticated transportation systems would be developed to permit shipment of liquid latex, as was done by the French before the war.

Technical training centers were being opened, Pol Pot said, and the regime was struggling to eliminate illiteracy among the peasants. Emphasis was also being given to hand production of simple consumer goods, such as towels, blankets, textiles, mosquito nets, and fish sauce, a basic source of protein in the traditional Cambodian diet. In the past, most small-scale manufacturing operations of this kind were performed by the Vietnamese and Chinese minorities. The Vietnamese have nearly all fled Cambodia; the fate of the Chinese is unknown, though they were surely forced to leave the urban areas with the rest of the population. Peking's large technical assistance mission in Cambodia may provide them some protection.

When prompted by his Vietnamese interviewers to comment on the "fraternal friendship and militant solidarity between the peoples of Cambodia and Vietnam," Pol Pot answered bluntly that this was a "problem of strategy and sacred feelings." He said it was essential to "strengthen" friendly relations and solidarity. He hinted that relations between Cambodian and Vietnamese leaders were better than between ordinary citizens of the two countries.

International Views and Policies. Avoiding economic dependence on foreign powers—and particularly avoiding any form of domination by Vietnam—seem to comprise the foreign policy goals of the new Khmer regime. In 1975 they established close relations with China and correct relations with Thailand. In mid-1976 they began to improve or expand their relations with a number of non-communist countries (having meanwhile allowed several pro-Peking communist countries to set up embassies in Phnom Penh, though under extremely tight restrictions). With the non-communist countries (including Japan, Great Britain, and most ASEAN states), they issued joint communiqués expressing the intention to establish relations at the ambassadorial level and repeating the five principles of peaceful coexistence. Some non-communist ambassadors accredited in Peking have flown to Phnom Penh for this ceremony.

Party Internal Affairs. On 18 September 1976, two days before he was granted temporary leave from his post for health reasons, Pol Pot delivered a long eulogy for Mao Tse-tung. Nuon Chea replaced Pol Pot, who does not seem to be in disgrace. In his speech, Pot linked the Chinese Communist Party and the "Cambodian revolutional organization" as "fraternal" and "Marxist-Leninist." The Chinese ambassador responded with the same terminology. This was the closest the Cambodian leaders have ever come to admitting being communist. A few days later, they signed messages to Peking repeating the terms. In April, by contrast, a message of "fraternal" greetings from the Lao Communist Party was corrected (to delete any implication that the Cambodian organization was communist) very quickly after it was initially sent over Radio Vientiane. Thus, the KCP seems to have been unwilling to acknowledge its communist character in April (the anniversary of their victory), but was willing by September.

Publications. Radio broadcasts, by the two relatively weak transmitters of Radio Phnom Penh, are virtually the only means the KCP has of communicating news and comments on internal developments to the outside world—and indeed to the Khmer people (though batteries for transistor radios are probably in short supply in Cambodia). No printed publications are known to circulate in the country.

Washington, D.C.

Peter A. Poole

China

The First Congress of the Chinese Communist Party (Chung-kuo kung-ch'an tang; CCP) was held in Shanghai in July 1921. The Tenth and latest CCP Congress was held in Peking in August 1973. The party celebrates its anniversary each 1 July.

The People's Republic of China(PRC)was established 1 October 1949. State organs and all other organizations of society are in all important respects provided leadership by the CCP, which is the sole legal party. The Tenth Party Constitution, adopted in 1973, makes this clear: "State organs, the

People's Liberation Army and the militia, labour unions, poor and lower-middle peasant associations, women's federations, the Communist Youth League, the Red Guards, the Little Red Guards and other revolutionary mass organizations must all accept the centralized leadership of the Party" (Chap. II, Art. 7).

The CCP is the largest Communist party in the world. In October 1976 it was reported to have a membership of 30 million (*Peking Review*, 29 October, p. 7). The population of China is generally estimated to be well over 800 million. The latest officially given Chinese figure in 1976 was 811 million, but the under-reporting of deaths was conceded (AFP, Peking, 3 November). Analysts using provincial statistics made available in the fall of 1976 estimated the population to be between 853 and 890 million (Fox Butterfield, *NYT*, 9 October). The U.S. Central Intelligence Agency estimated the figure already to have been 920 million by mid-1974 (*NYT*, 16 July 1975). A private group in Washington, D.C., the Environmental Fund, has estimated the population to be 964.4 million (NYT Service, 13 October 1976).

Organization and Leadership. According to the party constitution, the "highest leading body" of the CCP is the national party congress, which is to be convened every five years, although under often-invoked "special circumstances" the congress may be convened early or postponed. The party congress elects the Central Committee, which leads when the congress is not in session and which elects the Politburo, the Standing Committee of the Politburo, and the chairman and the vice-chairmen of the Central Committee. Membership in these high offices is said to embody the combination of the old, the middle-aged, and the young. This is meant to reflect a determination to have the three generations of leaders work together in a way that shows that while experience is still respected and utilized, there is in China "no lack of successors."

The Tenth Central Committee, elected at the most recent party congress, in August 1973, consists of 195 members and 124 alternate members (319 total). This compares with the 170 members and 109 alternates (279 total) of the previous Ninth Central Committee, elected in 1969. Only 115 members of the Tenth Central Committee were newly seated; 204 were continued from the previous committee. About 100 seats are said to be assigned to representatives of the masses, that is, outstanding workers, peasants, soldiers, and leaders of the recently reconstructed mass organizations.

The chairman of the Central Committee is Hua Kuo-feng, who was appointed to this position on 7 October, following the death of Mao Tse-tung on 9 September. Since 7 April Hua had been first vice-chairman.

By late 1976 only Yeh Chien-ying remained of the five vice-chairmen (Chou En-lai, Wang Hung-wen, Kang Sheng, Yeh Chien-ying, and Li Teh-sheng) elected at the party congress in August 1973. An additional one, Teng Hsiao-ping, was added in January 1975, but was purged in April 1976. Chou En-lai died in January; Kang Sheng died in December 1975. Li Teh-sheng was demoted and transferred in late 1973 or early 1974. Wang Hung-wen was purged in October.

Effective policy-making power within the party rests with the Central Committee and at higher levels, particularly the Politburo and its Standing Committee, both of which are elected by the Central Committee. There appeared to be in late 1976 only two remaining members of the Politburo's Standing Committee: Hua Kuo-feng and Yeh Chien-ying. (Of the erstwhile members of the Standing Committee, Mao Tse-tung, Chu Teh, Chou En-lai, Kang Sheng, and Tung Pi-wu were deceased; Wang Hung-wen, Chang Chun-chiao, and Teng Hsiao-ping had been purged; and Li Teh-sheng had been demoted.) Other members of the Politburo were Wei Kuo-ching, Liu Po-cheng, Hsu Shih-yu, Chi Teng-kuei, Wu Teh, Wang Tung-hsing, Chen Yung-kuei, Chen Hsi-lien, and Li Hsien-nien (Chiang Ching and Yao Wen-yuan having been purged.) Alternate members of the Politburo were Wu Kuei-hsien, Su Chen-hua, Ni Chih-fu, and Saifudin.

Below the Central Committee there is a network of party committees at the provincial, special district, county, and municipal levels. A similar network of party committees exists within the People's Liberation Army (PLA), from the level of the military region down to that of the regiment. According to the party constitution, primary organizations of the party, or party branches, are located in factories, mines, and other enterprises, people's communes, offices, schools, shops, neighborhoods, PLA companies, and elsewhere as required.

Except within the PLA, the national structure of party organization was shattered in the course of the Great Proletarian Cultural Revolution (GPCR). Reconstruction began in late 1969 and by mid-August 1971 the last of the provincial-level party committees was reestablished. Reconstruction at the lower and intermediate levels was probably completed during 1973. The "revolutionary committees," which were created at all levels during the GPCR in order to provide leadership in the temporary absence of regular party and government organizations, have been confirmed as "permanent organs" of local government at various levels (and officially replace the people's councils) in the 1975 PRC constitution. However, the revolutionary committees are now clearly subordinate to reconstituted party committees.

The long-overdue Fourth National People's Congress (NPC) met in Peking on 13-17 January 1975. While the Third NPC was held with great fanfare and lasted for three weeks in the winter of 1964-65, the Fourth NPC came unheralded (not mentioned even in the 1975 New Year's Day message two weeks earlier) and its session was short and secret. The meeting was preceded by the Second Plenary Session of the Tenth Central Committee, 8-10 January, which dealt with the final preparatory work of the NPC and submitted to it the draft revised text of the PRC constitution, a report on the revision of the constitution, a report on the work of the government, and lists of nominees for membership on the Standing Committee of the NPC and the State Council. There were 2,864 delegates at the Fourth NPC.

Mao Tse-tung did not attend either the plenary session or the NPC. It is not known that he had ever missed such meetings previously. The reason for his absence remains a matter of speculation.

The Fourth NPC terminated the anomalous constitutional situation which prevailed for so long after the GPCR. The 1954 PRC constitution had long been a dead document although it had never been officially rescinded or supplanted, which could only be done by a new NPC. The constitutional-stipulation that annual sessions of the NPC be held was ignored for ten years, as was the stipulation that a new NPC be elected every four years. In the meanwhile, a number of actions had been taken which were clearly extraconstitutional. Only the NPC was empowered to elect and remove the chairman of the PRC and confirm the members of the State Council as recommended by the premier. Nevertheless, after the GPCR there were many personnel changes in government that did not receive the NPC's approval, although the Standing Committee of the Third NPC might have performed the necessary formalities despite the fact that its legal term had expired. However, Liu Shao-chi was removed from all posts by the Twelfth Plenum of the party's Eighth Central Committee in October 1968 and not by the NPC. Thus, the Fourth NPC in January 1975 did clear the air in a number of respects and conferred for a time a new aura of legitimacy in Chinese government.

According to the 1975 PRC constitution the powers of the NPC are exercised contingent upon recommendation by the party's Central Committee. The NPC's enumerated powers are "to amend the Constitution; make laws; appoint and remove the Premier and members of the State Council on the proposal of the Central Committee of the CCP; approve the national economic plan, the state budget and the final state accounts; and exercise such other functions and powers as the NPC deems necessary." The term of the NPC was increased from four years to five. It is to be convened annually.

The NPC reaffirmed Chu Teh as chairman of the NPC Standing Committee, a post he had held since the Second NPC in 1959. However, Chu Teh died 6 July 1976 and no replacement had been announced by late November. Of the 22 original vice-chairmen, all of whom were on the Tenth Central Committee, two have died.

The Fourth NPC Standing Committee

Chairman: Chu Teh (deceased 6 July 1976)

Vice-Chairmen:

Tung Pi-wu (deceased 2 April 1975)	Tan Chen-lin
Soong Ching Ling	Li Ching-chuan
Kang Sheng (deceased 16 December 1975)	Chang Ting-cheng
Liu Po-cheng	Tsai Chang
Wu Teh	Ulanfu
Wei Kuo-ching	Ngapo Ngawang-Jigme
Saifudin	Chou Chien-jen
Kuo Mo-jo	Hsu Teh-heng
Hsu Hsiang-chien	Hu Chueh-wen
Nieh Jung-chen	Li Su-wen
Chen Yun	Yao Lien-wei
Teng Ying-chao (nominated December 1976)	

The Fourth NPC in January 1975 confirmed a new State Council which reflected many changes from before the GPCR. Chou En-lai was re-elected premier, but following his death in January 1976 the position was filled by Hua Kuo-feng. Twelve vice-premiers were named at the Fourth NPC, four less than the number approved by the Third NPC in 1965. Of the 16 pre-GPCR vice-premiers, only two were retained—Teng Hsiao-ping and Li Hsien-nien, but Teng was removed from office in April 1976. All but four of the vice-premiers were members or alternates of the Politburo. The only military man is Chen Hsi-lien, the Peking regional military commander, who is also a member of the Politburo.

The Standing Committee of the Fourth NPC held its third session on 1-3 December 1976. Vice-Chairman Soon Ching Ling presided. The Standing Committee confirmed the ouster of Chiao Kuan-hua as foreign minister, replacing him with Huang Hua. Chiao was said to have been too closely associated with the "gang of four." The Standing Committee also endorsed the nomination of Teng Ying-chao, the widow of Chou En-lai, as one of its vice-chairmen (UPI, Hong Kong, 3 December).

The 26 ministries and 3 commissions of the new State Council listed above reflect the simplification and streamlining of administration that has taken place in the several years since the GPCR. Some of the streamlining came about as the result of combining ministries. Thus the Ministry of Petroleum and Chemical Industries (known for a while after the GPCR as the Ministry of Fuel and Chemical Industries) represents a merging of the three earlier ministries of Chemicals, Coal, and Petroleum. Among the pre-GPCR ministries which were not revived are those of Labor, Internal Affairs, and Allocation of Materials. The erstwhile Overseas Chinese Affairs Commission was not resuscitated. The Second through Seventh Machine Building Ministries and the Ministries of Culture and of Education reemerged at the Fourth NPC.

According to the 1975 PRC constitution the specific functions of the State Council are as follows: to formulate administrative measures and issue decrees and orders; exercise leadership over ministries and commissions and local state organs; draft and implement the national economic plan and the state budget; and direct state administrative affairs. It is also to exercise such other functions and powers as are vested in it by the NPC or its Standing Committee.

The new constitution, adopted by the Fourth NPC in January 1976, is shorter than the one adopted in 1954 which it replaces, containing only 30 articles as against 106. It reflects many of the great changes that took place in the intervening 20 years. To begin with, it redefines the PRC as a "socialist state of the dictatorship of the proletariat" rather than a "people's democratic state." (This constitution is analyzed and compared with the 1954 one in *YICA, 1976*, pp. 262-64.)

The State Council

Premier: Hua Kuo-feng (acting premier 8 January to 7 April when appointed premier)
                Chou En-lai (until death on 8 January)

Vice-Premiers: Li Hsien-nien   Yu Chiu-li
                Chen Hsi-lien   Ku Mu
                Chi Teng-kuei   Sun Chien
                Chen Yung-kuei   Teng Hsiao-ping (purged April 1976)
                Wu Kuei-hsien   Chang Chun-chiao (purged October 1976)
                Wang Chen   Hua Kuo-feng (promoted April 1976)

Ministers	*Ministries and Commissions*
Huang Hua (from 2 December)	Foreign Affairs
Chiao Kuan-hua (to 2 December)	
Yeh Chien-ying	National Defense
Hua Kuo-Feng	Public Security
Li Chiang	Foreign Trade
Fang Yi	Economic Relations with Foreign Countries
Sha Feng	Agriculture and Forestry
Chen Shao-kun	Metallurgical Industry
Li Shui-ching	First Ministry of Machine Building
Liu Hsi-yao	Second Ministry of Machine Building
Li Chi-tai	Third Ministry of Machine Building
Wang Cheng	Fourth Ministry of Machine Building
Li Cheng-fang	Fifth Ministry of Machine Building
Pien Chiang	Sixth Ministry of Machine Building
Wang Yang	Seventh Ministry of Machine Building
Hsu Chin-chiang (died 21 July)	Coal Industry
Kang Shih-en	Petroleum and Chemical Industries
Chien Cheng-ying	Water Conservancy and Power
Chien Chih-kuang	Light Industry
Wan Li	Railways
Yeh Fei	Communications
Chung Fu-hsiang	Posts and Telecommunications
Chang Ching-fu	Finance
Fan Tzu-yu	Commerce
Yu Hui-yung	Culture
Chou Jung-hsin	Education
Liu Hsiang-ping	Public Health
Chuang Tse-tung	Physical Culture and Sports Commission
Yu Chiu-li	State Planning Commission
Ku Mu	State Capital Construction Commission

The constitution states (Chap. 1, Art. 15), that "The Chinese People's Liberation Army and the people's militia are the workers' and peasants' own armed forces led by the Communist Party of China; they are the armed forces of the people of all nationalities." It also gives command of the armed forces to the chairman of the CCP Central Committee, in contrast to the 1954 constitution which invested command in the chairman of the PRC, a post which was eliminated. There is a well-established Communist tradition in China that although "political power grows out of the barrel of a gun," the "party commands the gun, and the gun shall never be allowed to command the party."

The PLA played an important role in stabilizing the situation during the GPCR and for many months afterward the military were prominent on the revolutionary committees. Following the Lin Piao Incident in 1971 the party reasserted its dominance, and in late 1973 there was an unprecedented series of transfers of top military regional commanders. By the fall of 1976 more than 200 such transfers had taken place, apparently as part of an effort to weaken old alliances and to make the PLA more responsive to civilian party command (see Jay Matthews, Washington Post Service, 18 September; *Taipei Central Daily News*, 2 June, in *FBIS*.

This party dominance, particularly under the influence of Maoist or radical priorities, has resulted in greatly reduced investment in conventional arms and equipment in recent years. Defense spending in 1972-74 dropped about 25 percent lower than that of the 1970-71 peak period. This reduced attention to military needs continued with few exceptions into 1976. While the procurement of British Spey aircraft engines, German helicopters, and American computers with possible military usage represented a tentative departure from this pattern, most of China's military equipment is 10 to 20 years out of date, as U.S. deputy assistant defense secretary Morton Abramowitz reported (Stephen Barber, *Far Eastern Economic Review*, Hong Kong, 7 May). However, China's nuclear and missile program continues to develop. China exploded its 21st nuclear device, a four-megaton hydrogen bomb, on 17 November, the fourth such explosion in 1976 and the largest yet detected (UPI, Hong Kong, 18 November). On 30 August, China launched its sixth earth satellite in as many years (UPI, Hong Kong, 2 September), and on 7 December it launched a seventh (UPI, Tokyo, 8 December). Nevertheless, despite such continuing successes the Chinese military have probably been greatly concerned over the relative inattention given to the need for conventional weaponry. Hence it is very likely that key military leaders would support Hua Kuo-feng in his bid for power, in the expectation that the regime would opt for a more rapid modernization program which would provide greater investment in conventional military hardware as well.

The PRC militia consists of three organizations: the armed militia, numbering about five million men and women; the "backbone militia" of about 20 million loyal party members and "positive elements," including PLA veterans; and the "ordinary militia," a national force numbering about 75 million, mostly younger able-bodied peasants and urban workers. The urban militia units have received the greater share of publicity in the past two or three years, but the rural militia remains important, particularly units in areas near the Soviet border. While regular PLA commanders may have mixed feelings about the responsibility of training the militia, they probably have approved of tasks assigned the militia in helping to combat increasing "hooliganism" in many places (see David Bonavia, "New Role for the Militia," *Far Eastern Economic Review*, 30 July, and Clare Hollingsworth, *Daily Telegraph*, London, 2 August). If the urban militia was becoming a base of support for Maoists, the effort in that direction proved to be unsuccessful, as the militia did not protect the radicals during the October crunch.

Mass organizations are a significant component of sociopolitical life in China, though they have not figured prominently in the news from 1974 through 1976. Mass organizations had been very important from 1949 to the GPCR. They were dismantled during that great upheaval. Largely reconstructed in 1973, they now again play important roles. The Communist Youth League is involved in the educational system. The Women's Federation is active in the recurrent criticism campaigns. The trade unions are the most important of the mass organizations, evidenced by the large trade union representation in the Tenth Central Committee, in which they have a ninth of the regular and a sixth of the alternate membership. Twenty-two of the chairmen and vice-chairmen of the 28 known trade union committees are members of the Central Committee, and 19 are alternate members. This representation contrasts with that of the Women's Federation, which has only three top officers among its local committees who are members of the Central Committee, and only eight who are alternates. Of top officers from Communist Youth League local committees, seven are members of the Central Committee, and only one is an alternate.

It appears that there is a concerted effort to bring women into junior leadership positions. This is seen in CCP recruitment, cadre promotion, and trade union and Communist Youth League leadership changes. As the aging leadership is replaced, these junior-level women cadres will probably play an increasingly larger role (see Joan Maloney, "Women Cadres and Junior-Level Leadership in China," *Current Scene*, March-April 1975). However, as a result of the purge of Chiang Ching in October, only one woman remains on the Politburo—Wu Kuei-hsien (an alternate member who is a textile worker from Sian).

The mass organizations also were regarded as a principal source of support for the radical faction in the Politburo. Celebrations of the tenth anniversary of the founding of the Red Guards were held throughout China in August. However, when the radical leadership was purged in October there appears to have been little response or assistance from the mass organizations. In fact, these organizations quickly joined in the widespread public condemnation of the radical leadership.

Domestic Party Affairs. The year 1976 was one of the most important and decisive in the history of the PRC. It was marked by the death of the three most senior party leaders—Chou En-lai, Chu Teh and Mao Tse-tung. It was a year of intensive political struggle that saw the surprisingly sudden second decline of Teng Hsiao-ping and the even more surprisingly meteoric emergence to power of Hua Kuo-feng. Most important of all, the internal power struggle was dramatically, and perhaps fundamentally, resolved with the eclipse of the radical faction which as late as the time of Mao's death appeared to be in a relatively good position. The year traversed a great distance, from the shrill struggle-campaign atmosphere in the early months to the beginnings of what may be a relatively more relaxed "hundred flowers" ethos at year's end. There was the expectation as the year closed that henceforth governmental plans and policies would basically be more in accord with the thinking of the late Chou En-lai than with that of the late Mao Tse-tung, rhetoric notwithstanding.

Premier Chou En-lai died 8 January at the age of 78. The death of this capable leader came as no surprise for he had been seriously ill and bedridden for months. His passing was widely and genuinely mourned. It was generally expected that First Vice-Premier Teng Hsiao-ping, whom Chou had engineered to the pinnacles of power from 1973 to 1975 after Teng had been one of the two primary targets of the GPCR, would be formally installed as Chou's successor. However, in a surprise move Hua Kuo-feng was appointed acting premier on 8 January (although this startling fact was not made known until February), and Teng's funeral oration for Chou on 11 January proved to be his last known public act. Teng immediately disappeared from view, and an intensive campaign against him was mounted.

This anti-Teng Hsiao-ping campaign was an extension of the Criticize Confucius, Criticize Lin Piao and the Water Margin campaigns which had been under way intermittently for months. These campaigns were the work of the radical faction, which dominated the news media and the mass organizations and which undoubtedly had Mao Tse-tung's support. Teng Hsiao-ping was not immediately identified by name in the new 1976 campaign, but it was soon apparent that he was the accused "unrepentant capitalist roader" because of the repeated quotations of his well-known statement: "Any cat that can catch mice is a good cat, whether it is black or white." Finally, a 21 March *People's Daily* lead article quoted Mao himself to the effect that Teng was the symbol of everything wrong in the party. The article also reassured all that the campaign would confined itself to Teng Hsiao-ping alone; there would be no widespread purges despite the radical protestations against the "reversal of verdicts" which had allowed so many rehabilitated moderates such as Teng back into the government and party machinery.

Thus Teng Hsiao-ping, no longer protected by Chou En-lai, became in effect the lightning rod to absorb the ire and the attacks of the radicals. However, the program of promoting the "four modernizations" (in agriculture, industry, national defense, and science and technology) which had been outlined by Chou in January 1975 and rather successfully adhered to by Teng throughout 1975, continued under Hua Kuo-feng, who had already basically supported Teng's policies in the past year (see Victor Zorza, *Washington Post*, 12 April).

A riot erupted on Tien An Men Square on 5 April when large crowds protested what was regarded as a premature removal of wreaths dedicated to the memory of Chou En-lai which had been placed there during the Ching Ming Festival. Some of the demonstrators' placards indicated criticism of Chiang Ching and indirectly of Mao Tse-tung himself. Demonstrators set fire to three vehicles and a building near the Great Hall of the People. The mayor of Peking, Wu Teh, broadcast an appeal to the crowd and three hours later tens of thousands of worker-militiamen, police, and PLA guards who had encircled the Square mounted an attack and the rioters were soon dispersed. Many were arrested. The riot appeared to be on behalf of Teng Hsiao-ping, but his actual connection to this event was not clarified. Similar disturbances were reported elsewhere. In Chengchow rioters killed one person (AP, Tokyo, 11 April).

On 7 April Hua Kuo-feng was named first vice-chairman of the CCP and premier of the State Council "on the proposal of" Mao Tse-tung. These appointments made Hua the likely successor to Mao. The anti-Teng campaign continued with further demands by radicals to "defend the victorious fruits" of the GPCR, to root out "class enemies," and to prevent sabotage. It does not appear that Hua Kuo-feng encouraged this campaign, and this surely aroused the radicals. Perhaps Hua, who had been minister of public security for more than a year, was concerned about the deterioration of public order during this period. Reports of spreading crime in China, including armed bank robbery (e.g., see Fox Butterfield, NYT Service, 25 August), reached the outside world in 1976. The new premier was not anxious to promote the kind of instability which would encourage social disorder and further detract from the ambitious national economic development program which was already under way. Hence the passive resistance throughout the bureaucracy to the radicals' cries for class struggle was not dealt with resolutely.

On 15 June it was announced briefly (although not publicly in China) that the Central Committee would no longer make arrangements for foreign visitors to meet with Chairman Mao (NYT Service, 17 June). That Mao had become increasingly feeble physically was clearly seen during visits with Prime Ministers Robert Muldoon of New Zealand, Lee Kuan Yew of Singapore, and Ali Bhutto of Pakistan in May. That this decision was made by the Central Committee and not by Mao himself seemed significant.

On 6 July, 90-year-old Chu Teh, who together with Mao had founded the Red Army and also with Mao had led the Communists to military victory in China, died. Interestingly, although his death could not have been entirely unexpected at his age, Chu Teh had been well enough to meet with visiting Prime Minister Malcolm Fraser of Australia on 21 June (*after* Chairman Mao was no longer seeing foreigners).

As if to underscore the significant changes in political leadership, the intensive political struggle, and the basic policy decisions that were being affirmed during 1976, China was shaken by a series of devastating earthquakes. Early in the morning of 28 July a tremor measuring 8.2 on the Richter scale struck near the large North China industrial and coal mining city of Tangshan. A second shock registering 7.9 followed 16 hours later. This earthquake, the strongest on record anywhere since 1964, caught the Chinese by surprise, despite their recent claims of success in earthquake prediction. Although information was not released abut the extent of damage or the number of casualties, it is believed that the destruction and losses must have been enormous. Within a month another quake hit Kansu Province. Aside from the economic ramifications of the earthquake was the possibility that they may have been taken as portents by many Chinese, particularly in the older age groups. However, if this is true and such portents were read as an indication of supernatural displeasure at the radicals who would subsequently be purged, the earthquake of mid-November, after the purge, must have seemed a puzzlement. It is likely, however, that the severe earthquakes of 28 July gave new Premier Hua an opportunity to demonstrate and to consolidate his leadership in the crisis and to emphasize the need for political stability and national unity in order to cope with the disaster.

At ten minutes after midnight on 9 September, Mao Tse-tung, chairman of the CCP, at the age of 82, died "as a result of the worsening of his illness and despite all treatment, although meticulous medical care was given him in every way after he fell ill." Because of the central role that Chairman Mao played in the history of the Chinese Revolution it is worth quoting at some length from the "Message to the Whole Party, the Whole Army and the People of All Nationalities Throughout the Country" of 9 September by the Central Committee, the Standing Committee of the NPC, the State Council, and the Military Commission of the Central Committee (*Peking Review*, 13 September):

> . . . Chairman Mao Tse-tung was the founder and wise leader of the Communist Party of China, the Chinese People's Liberation Army and the People's Republic of China. Chairman Mao led our Party in waging a protracted, acute and complex struggle against the Right and "Left" opportunist lines in the Party, defeating the opportunist lines pursued by Chen Tu-hsiu, Chu Chiu-pai, Li Li-san, Lo Chang-lung, Wang Ming, Chang Kuo-tao, Kao Kang-Jao Shu-Shih and Peng Teh-huai and again during the Great Proletarian Cultural Revolution, triumphing over the counter-revolutionary revisionist line of Liu Shao-chi, Lin Piao and Teng Hsiao-ping, thus enabling our Party to develop and grow in strength steadily in class struggle between the two lines. Led by Chairman Mao, the Communist Party of China has developed through a tortuous path into a great, glorious and correct Marxist-Leninist Party which is today exercising leadership over the People's Republic of China.
>
> During the period of the new-democratic revolution, Chairman Mao, in accordance with the universal truth of Marxism-Leninism and by combining it with the concrete practice of the Chinese revolution, creatively laid down the general line and general policy of the new-democratic revolution, founded the Chinese People's Liberation Army and pointed out that the seizure of political power by armed force in China could be achieved only by following the road of building rural base areas, using the countryside to encircle the cities and finally seizing the cities, and not by any other road. He led our Party, our army and the people of our country in using people's war to overthrow the reactionary rule of imperialism, feudalism, and bureaucrat-capitalism, winning the great victory of the new-democratic revolution and founding the People's Republic of China. The victory of the Chinese people's revolution led by Chairman Mao changed the situation in the East and the world and blazed a new trail for the cause of liberation of the oppressed nations and oppressed people.
>
> In the period of the socialist revolution, Chairman Mao comprehensively summed up the positive as well as the negative experience of the international communist movement, penetratingly analyzed the class relations in socialist society and for the first time in the history of the development of Marxism, unequivocally pointed out that there are still classes and class struggle after the socialist transformation of the ownership of the means of production has in the main been completed, drew the scientific conclusion that the bourgeoisie is right in the Communist Party, put forth the great theory of continuing the revolution under the dictatorship of the proletariat, and laid down the Party's basic line for the entire historical period of socialism. Guided by Chairman Mao's proletarian revolutionary line, our Party, our army and the people of our country have continued their triumphant advance and seized great victories in the socialist revolution and socialist construction, particularly in the Great Proletarian Cultural Revolution, in criticizing Lin Piao and Confucius, in criticizing Teng Hsiao-ping and repulsing the Right deviationist attempt at reversing correct verdicts. Upholding socialism and consolidating the dictatorship of the proletariat in the People's Republic of China, a country with a vast territory and a large population, is a great contribution of world historic significance which Chairman Mao Tse-tung made to the present era; at the same time, it has

provided fresh experience for the international communist movement in combating and preventing revisionism, consolidating the dictatorship of the proletariat, preventing capitalist restoration and building socialism.

All the victories of the Chinese people have been achieved under the leadership of Chairman Mao; they are all great victories for Mao Tse-tung Thought. The radiance of Mao Tse-tung Thought will forever illuminate the road of advance of the Chinese people.

Chairman Mao Tse-tung summed up the revolutionary practice in the international communist movement, put forward a series of scientific theses, enriched the theoretical treasury of Marxism and pointed out the orientation of struggle for the Chinese people and the revolutionary people throughout the world. With the great boldness and vision of a proletarian revolutionary, he initiated in the international communist movement the great struggle to criticize modern revisionism with the Soviet revisionist renegade clique at the core, promoted the vigorous development of the cause of the world proletarian revolution and the cause of the people of all countries against imperialism and hegemonism, and pushed the history of mankind forward.

Chairman Mao Tse-tung was the greatest Marxist of the contemporary era. For more than half a century, basing himself on the principle of integrating the universal truth of Marxism-Leninism with the concrete practice of the revolution, he inherited, defended and developed Marxism-Leninism in the protracted struggle against the class enemies at home and abroad, both inside and outside the Party, and wrote a most brilliant chapter in the history of the movement of proletarian revolution. He dedicated all his energies throughout his life to the liberation of the Chinese people, to the emancipation of the oppressed nations and oppressed people the world over, and to the cause of communism. With the great resolve of a proletarian revolutionary, he waged a tenacious struggle against his illness, continued to lead the work of the whole Party, the whole army and the whole nation during his illness and fought till he breathed his last. The magnificent contributions he made to the Chinese people, the international proletariat and the revolutionary people of the whole world are immortal. The Chinese people and the revolutionary people the world over love him from the bottom of their hearts and have boundless admiration and respect for him. . . .

Mao's body lay in state in the Great Hall of the People for eight days, during which time more than 300,000 persons, including foreigners in the capital at the time, filed by the glass-encased bier. On 18 September a solemn half-hour ceremony was held at Tien An Men Square. It was opened with a three-minute silent standing tribute in which the entire nation participated while watching the event on TV or listening to the radio. More than a million persons jammed Tien An Men Square and the broad Avenue of Eternal Peace which leads into it. Foreigners were not allowed to take part in the event. Premier Hua Kuo-feng gave the only speech, which followed the lines in the "Message" quoted from above, but which was much more explicit in commenting upon "class struggle" in China. He repeated Mao's last public warning, used against Teng Hsiao-ping, that the bourgeoisie was "right in the Communist Party." (Ibid., 24 September.)

On 8 October, two decisions were adopted by the Chinese authorities and given prominent publicity. The first was that there would be established a memorial hall in which Mao's body will be kept on perpetual display. The second was that a new edition of Mao's selected works would be published under Hua's editorship and preparations would begin for the publication of his "collected works." (Ibid., 15 October.) In the light of subsequent developments it would appear that these decisions represent an effort by Hua Kuo-feng and his "moderate" supporters to appropriate the remains of Mao and edit Mao's writings in order to promote their objectives as opposed to those of the Maoists or radical adherents of Mao's basic line (see Victor Zorza, *Manchester Guardian*, 31 October).

The significance of the above two decisions and the heavy publicity they received was made clearer when the surprising news began to leak over the next few days that Mao's widow, Chiang Ching, and her three radical associates in the Politburo, Wang Hung-wen, Chang Chun-chiao and Yao Wen-yuan, were under arrest, along with a number of their supporters. The arrests appear to have taken place on either 6 or 7 October (Fox Butterfield, *NYT*, 22 October). That there would be an intensification of struggle between this radical faction and the so-called moderates following Mao's death was expected. What was surprising was the timing—so soon after Mao's death—and the swiftness and thoroughness with which the coup by Hua was carried out. Hua and his supporters in swift succession took over the erstwhile strongholds of the radicals, including the capital itself, the Shanghai party organization, and the urban militia.

The campaign against the arrested radicals, now labeled the "gang of four," was initiated in Shanghai, where wall posters condemning their alleged crimes appeared. Festive parades were staged from 21 to 23 October throughout the country in which a reported 50 million people (*Peking Review*, 29 October) participated.

On 24 October, a million "jubilant and ecstatic armymen and people" participated in a mass rally at Tien An Men Square to celebrate the appointment of Hua Kuo-feng as the new chairman of the Central Committee of the CCP, and as chairman of the Military Commission of the Central Committee (ibid.). These appointments had been made by the Central Committee on 7 October, but the news had been withheld from public announcement, with mixed success, for days. Hua retained his position, at least for the time being, as premier of the State Council, and perhaps as minister of public security as well. Thus, in one fell swoop, Hua managed to concentrate more power (at least titular) into his own hands than Mao Tse-tung ever chose to do.

With the exception of the deposed radicals and Liu Po-cheng, who is very old and probably ill, all other members of the Politburo were present at the celebration. Wu Teh, Politburo member and "mayor" of Peking (i.e., first secretary of the Peking CCP Municipal Committee and chairman of the Peking Municipal Revolutionary Committee) gave the principal address.

Wu Teh explained to the throng that it was Mao himself who selected Hua as his successor. It was Mao, he said, who personally proposed Hua for the posts of first vice-chairman of the CCP and premier in April 1976. Then, according to Wu, on 30 April Mao wrote to Hua "in his own handwriting, 'With you in charge, I'm at ease,' " which "expressed his boundless trust" in Hua.

Wu said that "At the critical moment of the Chinese revolution after Chairman Mao had passed away, the Party Central Committee headed by Comrade Hua Kuo-feng took resolute measures to expose the anti-Party clique of Wang Hung-wen, Chang Chun-chiao, Chiang Ching and Yao Wen-yuan, thus saving the revolution and the Party, consolidating the dictatorship of the proletariat in our country and enabling our Party, our army and the people of all nationalities in our country to continue their victorious advance along the socialist and communist course charted by Chairman Mao."

Wu catalogued the crimes of the radicals: "This anti-Party clique refused to heed what Chairman Mao said, wantonly tampered with Marxism-Leninism-Mao Tse-tung Thought, opposed Chairman Mao's proletarian revolutionary line, and practiced revisionism in the guise of Marxism. They formed a 'gang of four' and carried out sectarian activities to split the Party. They plotted and conspired tirelessly to overthrow a large number of leading Party, government and army comrades in the central organs and various localities and usurp Party and state leadership. During the period when Chairman Mao was seriously ill and after he passed away, they launched even more frantic attacks on the Party, in a hasty attempt to usurp the supreme leadership of the Party and state. They worshipped things foreign, fawned on foreigners and maintained illicit foreign relations, engaging in flagrant activities of capitulationism and national betrayal. The essence of their line is outright betrayal of Marxism-Leninism-Mao Tse-tung Thought—internally, changing the proletarian nature of our Party, subverting the dictatorship of the proletariat in our country and restoring capitalism and, externally, renouncing the principles of proletarian internationalism and capitulating to imperialism. Chairman Mao pointed out: 'You are making the socialist revolution, and yet don't know where the bourgeoisie is. It is right in the Communist Party—those in power taking the capitalist road. The capitalist-roaders are still on the capitalist road.' The actions of the Wang-Chang-Chiang-Yao anti-Party clique prove that they are typical representatives of the bourgeoisie inside the Party, unrepentant capitalist-roaders still travelling on the capitalist road and a gang of bourgeois conspirators and careerists. . . ." (Ibid.)

On the next day, 25 October, a joint editorial by the *People's Daily, Red Flag*, and the *Liberation Army Daily* added further explanations and charges. It noted that the "gang of four" had long formed a cabal, and that Mao "was aware of this long ago and severely criticized and tried to educate them again and again. And he made some arrangements to solve this problem." The editorial recounted that on 17 July 1974 Mao criticized them, saying: "You'd better be careful; don't let yourselves become a small faction of four." And on 24 December 1974 Mao reportedly criticized them again: Don't form factions. Those who do so will fall." In November and December of 1974, during preparations for the Fourth NPC, Mao reportedly said: "Chiang Ching has wild ambitions. She wants Wang Hung-wen to be Chairman of the Standing Committee of the Party Central Committee." On 3 May 1975, at a Politburo meeting, Mao reiterated the basic principles of "three do's and three don'ts" and warned the radicals: "Practice Marxism-Leninism, and not revisionism; unite and don't split; be open and aboveboard, and don't intrigue and conspire. Don't function as a gang of four, don't do it any more, why do you keep doing it?" The editorial continued: "That very day Chairman Mao, on this question, gave the instruction that "If this is not settled in the first half of this year, it should be settled in the second half; if not this year, then next year; if not next year, then the year after."

The editorial claimed that the response of the radicals toward Mao's criticism and education was to take the attitude of "counter-revolutionary double-dealers who comply in public but oppose in private. Not only did they not show the slightest sign of repentance, but on the contrary they went from bad to worse, further and further down the wrong path." The editorial restated and embroidered upon the alleged crimes listed by Wu Teh the preceding day: "The 'gang of four,' a bane to the country and the people, committed heinous crimes. They completely betrayed the basic principles of 'three do's and three don'ts' that Chairman Mao had earnestly taught, wantonly tampered with Marxism-Leninism-Mao Tse-tung Thought, tampered with Chairman Mao's directives, opposed Chairman Mao's proletarian revolutionary line on a whole series of domestic and international questions, and practiced revisionism under the signboard of Marxism. They carried out criminal activities to split the Party, forming a factional group, going their own way, establishing their own system inside the Party, doing as they wished, lording it over others, and placing themselves above Chairman Mao and the Party Central Committee. They were busy intriguing and conspiring and stuck their noses into everything to stir up trouble everywhere, interfere with Chairman Mao's revolutionary line and strategic plans and undermine the socialist revolution and socialist construction. They confounded right and wrong, made rumors, worked in a big way to create counter-revolutionary opinion, fabricated accusations against others and labelled people at will, and attempted to overthrow a large number of leading Party, government and army comrades in the central organs and various localities and seize Party and state leadership. They worshipped things foreign and fawned on foreigners, maintained illicit foreign relations, betrayed important Party and state secrets and unscrupulously practiced capitulationism and national betrayal. Resorting to various manoeuvres, they pursued a counter-revolutionary revisionist line, an ultra-Right line. . . ."

In the days and weeks that followed, further charges were made against the radicals. Chiang Ching was accused of having tried to establish a "cult of herself." This, ostensibly, was one of her motives in granting an extensive interview to Professor Roxane Witke, during which she allegedly betrayed party secrets, and which reportedly greatly angered Mao (*NYT*, 28 October). Chiang Ching allegedly removed several of Mao's documents from the party's special archives soon after his death and reworded them. For example, Mao had supposedly written one directive in Hua Kuo-feng's presence on 30 April, an altered version of which was then published in a major joint editorial on 16 September. In the changed form, the directive read: "Act according to the principles laid down." Apparently, the point of the revised quotation was that Mao's policies were to be followed, under the stewardship of his closest followers. However, two days later Hua himself did not use the quotation in his eulogy for Mao, and it has not been used since the arrest of the radicals (Fox Butterfield, *NYT*, 27

October). The four radicals have also been charged in wall posters in Peking with complicity in an alleged assassination attempt against Hua Kuo-feng which was supposed to have taken place on 6 October (ibid., 31 October). The radicals have been accused of disrupting industrial production and interfering with the management of the economy (ibid., 3 November). Chiang Ching allegedly had to be coaxed away from a poker game to go to the bedside of her dying husband (UPI, Hong Kong, 20 November). The four radicals were accused of indulgently viewing foreign pornographic movies (AP, Tokyo, 17 November).

It was well known that Chiang Ching was unpopular and that collectively the radicals had alienated many Chinese leaders. Nevertheless, even though the downfall of the group seems to have been greeted with widespread enthusiasm and relief, many of the charges against them strain credulity (see for example, John Gittings, *Manchester Guardian*, 24 October). An investigation commission under Yeh Chien-ying is reportedly examining the activities of the purged radicals. On 4 November a visiting delegation of Finns in Peking was told that a trial was planned for the purged leftist (Reuters dispatch, *NYT*, 5 November). In late November army propaganda teams were being sent into government offices, schools, and factories in Fukien Province in order to "enthusiastically propagate the instructions of the party central committee" (UPI, Hong Kong, 26 November). Reportedly the PLA was used to put down a veritable rebellion in Fukien as well, and instances of unrest and support for the deposed radicals were noted in Hupei, Hunan, Honan, and Kiangsi too (Washington Post Service, Hong Kong, 29 November).

By early November there were already indications of the likelihood of a more relaxed policy in various areas of cultural expression. The deposed radicals were rebuked for having imposed severe restrictions on writers and artists.One New China News Agency dispatch featured Lu Hsun's comments on the significance of translating foreign literature, pointing out that about half of the work of this prolific popular writer had been such translations. It pointed out too, that Lu Hsun "was attracted to the powerful graphic arts being produced by progressive artists in other lands." (Hsinhua *Daily News Release*, 27 October.) Other dispatches have criticized the "gang of four" for undue criticism and suppression of the film "Pioneers" and the Hunan opera "Song of a Gardener" (ibid., 9, 12 November). On 10 November, for the first time in years, the *People's Daily* carried the slogan: "Let a Hundred Flowers Blossom; Let a Hundred Schools of Thought Contend" (Rene Flipo, AFP, Peking, 11 November).

Hence, the year which began with the *People's Daily* featuring two of Mao's poems which suggested another restrictive cultural revolution in the offing actually evolved in quite a different direction after all.

International Views and Positions. "Chairman Mao's revolutionary line in diplomacy" continued to be implemented successfully in 1976, the year of his death. This outwardly oriented policy began in May 1969, and contrasts with the diplomacy of the GPCR period, in the course of which ambassadors were withdrawn from all posts except Cairo. Diplomatic relations were established with five more countries in 1976. Thus, there were diplomatic ties with 110 countries by the end of 1976. The accompanying three tables provide a comprehensive overview of China's diplomatic relationships (I am indebted to Professor Peter Van Ness for helpful suggestions regarding this information):

I. Countries which established diplomatic relations with China before 1970, exclusive of those which later suspended relations (45):

Afghanistan	India	Somalia
Albania	Iraq	Southern Yemen (PDR)
Algeria	Kenya	Sri Lanka
Bulgaria	Korea (North)	Sudan
Burma	Laos	Sweden
Congo	Mali	Switzerland
Cuba	Mauritania	Syria
Czechoslovakia	Mongolia	Tanzania
Denmark	Morocco	Uganda
Egypt	Nepal	USSR
Finland	Netherlands	United Kingdom
France	Norway	Vietnam (North)
Germany (East)	Pakistan	Yemen Arab Republic
Guinea	Poland	Yugoslavia
Hungary	Romania	Zambia

II. Countries which have established or resumed diplomatic relations with China since 1970, listed chronologically with date of establishment of diplomatic relatons (65):

Canada	13 October 1970	Australia	21 December 1972
Equatorial Guinea	15 October 1970	New Zealand	22 December 1972
Italy	6 November 1970	Dahomey (resumed)	29 December 1972
Ethiopia	3 December 1970	Spain	9 March 1973
Chile	15 December 1970	Upper Volta	15 September 1973
Nigeria	10 February 1971	Guinea-Bissau	15 March 1974
Kuwait	22 March 1971	Gabon Republic	20 April 1974
Cameroon	26 March 1971	Malaysia	31 May 1974
Austria	26 May 1971	Trinidad and Tobago	20 June 1974
Sierra Leone	29 July 1971	Venezuela	28 June 1974
Turkey	4 August 1971	Niger	20 July 1974
Iran	16 August 1971	Brazil	15 August 1974
Tunisia (resumed)	5 October 1971	Gambia	17 December 1974
Burundi (resumed)	13 October 1971	Botswana	6 January 1975
Belgium	25 October 1971	*Cambodia	17 April 1975
Peru	2 November 1971		(capture of Phnom
Lebanon	9 November 1971		Penh)
Rwanda	12 November 1971	Philippines	9 June 1975
Senegal	7 December 1971	Mozambique	25 June 1975
Iceland	8 December 1971	Thailand	1 July 1975
Cyprus	14 December 1971	Sao Tome and Principe	12 July 1975
Mexico	14 February 1972	Bangladesh	4 October 1975
Argentina	19 February 1972	Fiji	5 November 1975
Malta	25 February 1972	Comoros	13 November 1975
Ghana (resumed)	29 February 1972	Western Samoa	15 November 1975
Mauritius	15 April 1972	Cape Verde	25 April 1976
Greece	5 June 1972	Surinam	28 May 1976
Guyana	27 June 1972	Seychelles	30 June 1976
Togo	19 September 1972	Central African Republic	20 August 1976
Japan	29 September 1972	Papua New Guinea	12 October 1976
Germany (West)	11 October 1972		
Maldives	14 October 1972		
Malagasy Republic	6 November 1972		
Luxembourg	16 November 1972		
Zaire	19 November 1972		
Jamaica	21 November 1972		
Chad	28 November 1972		

* Relations with Cambodia had been broken in the spring of 1970.

III. Countries which have diplomatic relations with Taiwan (24):

Barbados	Honduras	Nicaragua
Bolivia	Ivory Coast	Panama
Colombia	Jordan	Paraguay
Costa Rica	Korea (South)	Saudi Arabia
Dominican Republic	Lesotho	South Africa
El Salvador	Liberia	Swaziland
Guatemala	Libya	United States
Haiti	Malawi	Uruguay

Despite the political upheavals and the natural catastrophes of 1976 a continuing stream of important foreign dignitaries visited the PRC. Before his final illness and death Mao Tse-tung met with the following foreign visitors: Mr. and Mrs. David Eisenhower on 31 December 1975, former President and Mrs. Richard Nixon in February 1976, a delegation of Lao party and government leaders and the vice-president of Egypt in April, and the prime ministers of New Zealand, Singapore, and Pakistan in May. From 15 May the ailing Mao no longer received visitors. Subsequent visitors of note were the king of Nepal, the president of the Malagasy Republic, and the prime minister of Australia in June, the presidents of Benin and Botswana in July, the head of state of Western Samoa and former U.S. secretary of defense James Schlesinger in September, the prime minister of Papua New Guinea in October, and the president of the Central African Republic in November.

China's international trading pattern continued to be active, although because of the usual delay in receiving statistics we shift our focus to the previous year. In 1975, the PRC's trade rose only modestly to U.S. $14,090 million, from $13,975 million in 1974. However, the trade deficit which had burgeoned in 1974 was brought under control in 1975, falling by half to $400 million. This was made possible by reducing imports and promoting exports. There was a slight shift in the direction of trade away from the USA and Canada and toward Japan and Western Europe. Agricultural imports declined, while machinery imports increased. Petroleum continued to become an even more important part of the export program. Crude oil exports doubled to an estimated U.S. $1 billion in 1975, which helped compensate for a decline in such traditional exports as foodstuffs, arts and handicrafts, and textiles. Overall, exports increased only slightly in 1975. Japan was the major export market, purchasing $750 million from the PRC (*Current Scene*, vol. XIV,, No. 9, September 1976). For an excellent analysis of the commodity composition of China's trade in 1975 see *Current Scene*, Vol. XIV, No. 10, 1976.

In 1975 the PRC reduced its participation in international trade fairs by one-fourth, reversing an upward trend that began in 1970. This was probably attributable to the economic recession which has weakened foreign markets. However, the number of solo exhibitions staged abroad was the same as in 1974. See Table VII below.

The following tables (drawn from *Current Scene*, September 1976) give a comprehensive picture of the direction and pattern of PRC trade, and of PRC trade fair participation from 1970 to 1975:

Table I

PRC Trade by Area[a]
(US$ Million)

	1975[b]				1974			
	Total	Exports	Imports	Balance	Total	Exports	Imports	Balance
Total	14,090	6,845	7,245	−400	13,975	6,560	7,415	−855
Non-Communist countries	11,760	5,485	6,275	−790	11,535	5,130	6,405	−1,275
Developed countries	8,015	3,610	5,405	−2,795	7,745	2,405	5,340	−2,935
Less-developed countries	2,690	1,825	865	960	2,860	1,815	1,045	770
Hong Kong and Macao	1,055	1,050	5	1,045	930	910	20	890
Communist countries	2,330	1,360	970	390	2,440	1,430	1,010	420

[a]Data are rounded to the nearest $5 million. The statistics are adjusted to show China's exports FOB and imports CIF. [b]Preliminary.

Table II

China's Major Trading Partners
(US$ Million)

Country	Total Two-Way Trade			Rank		
	1975	1974	1973	1975	1974	1973
Japan	3,790	3,330	2,021	1	1	1
Hong Kong	1,035	895	796	2	3	3
West Germany	750	650	487	3	4	4
France	550	345	231	4	8	11
Malaysia/Singapore	530	550	460	5	6	5
United States	460	1,070	876	6	2	2
Romania	440	300	265	7	10	9
Canada	430	575	409	8	5	6
Australia	410	465	247	9	7	10
United Kingdom	310	330	340	10	9	7
Soviet Union	280	280	272	11	11	8
Italy	275	220	196	12	12	12

Table III

PRC Trade with North America and Oceania
(US$ Million)

	1975 Exports	1975 Imports	1975 Balance	1974 Exports	1974 Imports	1974 Balance
Total (adjusted)[a]	310	1,120	−810	325	1,850	−1,525
of which (unadjusted)[b]						
Australia	85	325	−240	120	320	−200
Canada	55	375	−320	60	435	−375
New Zealand	10	10	0	7	14	−7
United States	160	300	−140	115	820	−705

[a] Adjusted for shipping costs to show PRC exports FOB Chinese ports, and PRC imports CIF Chinese ports. [b] Unadjusted data obtained from trading partner customs statistics. The United States, Australia, and Canada all value their imports FOB port of origin, so no shipping adjustment is necessary for that category.

Table IV

PRC Trade with Western Europe
(US$ Million)

	1975 Exports	1975 Imports	1975 Balance	1974 Exports	1974 Imports	1974 Balance
Grand total (adjusted)[a]	840	1,915	−1,075	840	1,405	−565
EEC total (adjusted)[a]	705	1,640	−935	720	1,110	−390
of which[b]						
West Germany	225	525	−300	195	420	−225
France	175	375	−200	185	160	+25
United Kingdom	130	180	−50	155	170	−15
Italy	130	145	−15	115	105	+10
Netherlands	80	135	−55	100	60	+40
Belgium/Luxembourg	45	45	0	45	35	+10
Denmark	25	25	0	30	15	+15
Other Europe	135	275	−140	120	295	−175
of which[b]						
Austria	15	30	−15	15	5	+10
Finland	20	15	+5	20	20	0
Iceland	0.5	10	−10	0.5	0.2	0
Norway	10	65	−55	10	110	−100
Sweden	45	40	+5	35	55	−20
Switzerland	30	55	−25	35	55	−20
Spain	35	25	+10	20	10	+10

[a] Adjusted for shipping costs to show PRC exports FOB Chinese ports, PRC imports CIF Chinese ports. [b] Unadjusted data obtained from trading partner customs statistics.

Table V

PRC Trade with East Asia
(US$ Million)

	1975			1974		
	Exports	Imports	Balance	Exports	Imports	Balance
Total (estimated) (adjusted)[a] of which (unadjusted)[b]	3,335	2,550	+785	2,960	2,305	+655
Japan	1,530	2,260	−730	1,305	1,985	−680
Hong Kong[c]	1,030	5	+1,025	875	20	+855
Singapore	290	40	+250	265	50	+215
Malaysia	150	50	+100	195	90	+105
Philippines	50	25	+20	25	15	+10
Macao	30	Negl.	+30	35	Negl.	+35
Thailand (estimated)	10	3	+7	5	Negl.	+5

[a]Adjusted for shipping costs to show PRC exports FOB Chinese ports and PRC inports CIF Chinese ports. [b]Unadjusted data obtained from PRC trading partner customs statistics. [c]Excludes PRC-originated goods imported into Hong Kong and later reexported, and third-country-originated goods imported into Hong Kong and later reexported to China.

Table VI

PRC Trade with Communist Countries
(US$ Million)

	1975			1974		
	Exports	Imports	Balance	Exports	Imports	Balance
Total (estimated)[a] of which	1,360	970	+390[b]	1,430	1,010	+420[b]
Romania	220	220	—	180	165	+15
Soviet Union	140	140	—	140	145	−5
East Germany	95	85	+10	80	75	+5
Czechoslovakia	74	72	+2	50	55	−5
Poland	50	42	+8	44	44	—
Hungary	34	35	−1	30	30	—
Yugoslavia	20	10	+10	30	120	−90
Bulgaria	10	13	−3	10	10	—

[a]Communist country figures are not adjusted for shipping costs. [b]Includes sizable PRC surpluses in trade with Albania and the Asian Communist countries.

Table VII
PRC Trade Fair Participation by Region, 1970-75

Region	1975	1974	1973	1972	1971	1970
Communist Countries	3	3	4	5	2	2
Europe	3	8	4	3	0	0
Africa	3	4	5	1	2	0
Near East	2	3	4	3	1	1
East Asia	2	1	0	0	0	0
North America	1	0	0	0	0	0
Latin America	0	0	0	0	1	0
Total	14	19	17	12	6	3

The Fifth Five-Year Plan, which was supposed to have begun in January 1976, is expected to begin in early 1977. Its delay is said to have been largely caused by the campaign against Teng Hsiao-ping and rightists. Minister of Foreign Trade Li Chiang gave this information to foreign diplomats and businessmen in Peking in October. Minister Li also disclosed that China would resume large-scale foreign trade, particularly purchases of whole plants, in 1978. He said that foreign trade in 1976 was expected to show only a small increase over 1975, and that this was another result of the anti-rightist campaign (Fox Butterfield, *NYT*, 28 October).

Following the purge of the "gang of four" the Peking authorities made clear that they would return to the ambitious two-stage economic development and modernization program enunciated by Chou En-lai at the Fourth NPC in January 1975. In the first stage of this program an independent and relatively comprehensive industrial and economic system is to be built in 15 years (from the Third Five-Year Plan), "that is, before 1980." The second stage "is to accomplish the comprehensive modernization of agriculture, industry, national defense and science and technology before the end of the century, so that our economy will be advancing in the front ranks of the world," to quote Chou's own words.

In 1975 the Chinese economy performed well, and the Fourth Five-Year Plan ended on an upbeat. The value of industrial output rose an estimated 10 or 11 percent over 1974, during which year industrial production had risen only 4 to 5 percent. However, 1974 had been a record year in agricultural production, and, despite bad weather, 1975 also saw agricultural output increase from 2 to 4 percent. (*Current Scene*, June 1976.)

Relations with the USSR. Despite Peking's surprise release in December 1975 of a Soviet helicopter crew that had been incarcerated for 21 months, the chilly relationship between the two countries did not abate much in 1976. The USSR did not respond positively to the late 1975 gesture. For their part, the Chinese continued an almost unremitting verbal offensive against the USSR. Peking quickly seized the opportunity to score against Moscow, when, following the abrogation of the Sino-Egyptian friendship treaty in May, it took the initiative in soliciting the visit of Vice-President Hosny Mobarak to China. The Egyptians had few illusions about China's motives, regardless of the aid now pledged, and there is no apparent desire by the Chinese to get deeply involved in the Middle East (Thomas Lippman, Cairo, *Washington Post*, 2 May). The charges of "capitulationism" in the anti-Teng campaign also were taken as a rebuke by Mao of any sentiment for improving Sino-Soviet ties.

On 28 April the USSR proposed that the border talks be resumed. The proposal—in the form of an article in *Pravda* signed by the pseudonym I. Alexandrov—was notable because it conceded that the Chinese territorial claim involved about 13,000 square miles. This contrasts with the claim made in the

Soviet press as recently as December 1975 that the figure was 600,000 square miles. The article made no other concessions and continued to refer to China's "groundless claims." It also made clear that Moscow would not accept Peking's prior conditions for negotiations—that is, an acknowledgment that the territory was in dispute and a mutual withdrawal of troops from both sides of the frontier. The article also made the familiar condemnations of Mao's policies (*NYT*, 29 April). Border talks began in 1969 and have continued periodically. They were again suspended in May 1975, and were resumed once more in December 1976 (AFP, Peking, 4 December).

On 29 April there was an explosion at the gates of the Soviet Embassy in Peking. Two Chinese guards were killed in the blast, but unfortunately no member of the Soviet mission (which numbers about 300 and is the largest diplomatic contingent in Peking) was injured. Chinese authorities blamed the act on a lone "counter-revolutionary," although Soviet officials maintained it was done by a small group of terrorists (UPI, Hong Kong, 1 May). Despite the circumstances and a formal Soviet protest, Premier Hua Kuo-feng at a reception for the New Zealand prime minister on the following evening sharply criticized the USSR, with the Soviet ambassador present. Hua repeated a familiar refrain: "The superpower that is most vociferous in selling 'detente' is the most dangerous source of war." He also condemned the USSR's "expansionist ambitions in the Asian-Pacific region." (AP, Tokyo, 30 April.)

In its commentary on the Fifth Conference of the Non-Aligned Countries, which concluded on 20 August in Colombo, Sri Lanka, Peking noted that the conference was able to brush aside the obstacles set by the USSR, which tried "its utmost to pass itself off as the "natural ally' of the non-aligned countries," but which "resorted to a variety of underhand means to sabotage their unity, reverse the political orientation of the non-aligned movement and place the movement under its hegemonic control." Peking stressed this last point: "A series of international events in the past few years show that the hegemonic ambition of the Soviet Union is exceptionally frenzied and its tactics for aggression and expansion unusually sinister. Today, Soviet social-imperialism is the most dangerous enemy of the people of all nations." The United States came in for its share of such criticism but in any comparison of the two superpowers in this as in other contexts. Peking usually singled out the USSR "in particular." (*Peking Review*, 27 August.)

Despite Peking's unrelenting verbal attacks, Moscow, sensing Mao's imminent passing, increasingly focused its own attacks on Mao and his policies alone. This signaled Moscow's desire for a rapprochement with Peking once the obstacles the aged chairman represented were removed. When Mao died on 9 September, the Central Committee of the Communist Party of the Soviet Union sent a brief telegram of "deep condolences" (Peter Osnos, Moscow, *Washington Post*, 10 September). However, Peking rejected this message of condolence, and similar ones from other Soviet-bloc countries, on the grounds that the CCP does not have relations with the Communist parties of these countries (Reuter, Peking, *Christian Science Monitor*, 15 September).

Nevertheless, the USSR continued to explore possible opportunities presented by Mao's death. On 1 October, Moscow issued its first authoritative statement on Sino-Soviet relations since that event. A lengthy *Pravda* article, again signed I. Alexandrov, marked the 27th anniversary of the PRC without mentioning Mao's name. It said that there are no problems which cannot be resolved, "provided there is a mutual desire, and in the spirit of good neighborliness, mutual benefit and consideration of each other's interests" (Peter Osnos, Moscow, *Washington Post*, 2 October).

With the fall of the radical leadership in Peking in October, the prospects of a thaw in Sino-Soviet relations seemed to improve. The same emphasis on more pragmatic rather than ideological considerations that might lead the PRC into more extended trade involvement elsewhere in the world is likely to lead to a relationship with the USSR that would reduce the national threat from that direction. The threat has been a very real one, and for years seems to have been the linchpin of Chinese foreign policy.

While Chinese troops are reported to outnumber Soviet troops along their common border by 618,000 to 475,000, the Chinese forces, with their obsolete weapons, are no match for the nuclear-equipped Soviet forces (UPI, Washington, 11 August). The Chinese have reason to be wary too over Soviet naval expansion in the Pacific and South and Southeast Asia. Peking accused the USSR in July of staging military maneuvers around the islands of Japan (*Japan Times*, Tokyo, 10 July). Peking is especially concerned about the possibility of Soviet use of the U.S.-developed facilities at Cam Ranh Bay in Vietnam, which could severely limit Chinese maritime freedom in the South China Sea. Such concern is heightened by the reported completion of a fourth Soviet naval yard at Sovetskaya Gavan in Far Eastern Siberia (Drew Middleton, *NYT*, 20 July).

Relations with the United States. Both the PRC and the USA were greatly preoccupied with questions of the transfer and consolidation of leadership in 1976, which did not affect the direction of Sino-American relations but neither did it facilitate a quickened pace toward "normalization." In fact, early in the year there were a series of apparent signals that the Chinese were dissatisfied with the sluggish implementation of the terms of the 1972 Shanghai Communiqué. The most dramatic such indicator was the Chinese invitation to Richard M. Nixon to visit China in February in order to celebrate the fourth anniversary of that historic document. The Chinese provided the plane that transported the disgraced former president, and in their continuing admiration for the man and gratitude to him, seemed unmindful or unconcerned about the embarrassment of the event to President Ford. However, despite U.S. reticence to discuss China policy during the election year, there is reason to believe that the issue has increasingly become a bipartisan one, aiming in the direction of full diplomatic recognition, the vexing Taiwan problem notwithstanding.

Hence, a number of other significant American visitors traveled to China during the year. These included twelve congresswomen in January, nine Republican representatives in April, Senate minority leader Hugh Scott in July, Democratic senators Mike Mansfield and John Glenn and former secretary of defense James Schlesinger in September. On his return from China the latter gave a lengthy debriefing session to Democratic presidential candidate Jimmy Carter at his home in Plains, Georgia.

Earlier, in June, Governor Carter had told the Foreign Policy Association that the United States should establish full relations with China, yet keep the trading relationship with Taiwan (*NYT*, 21 June). Following his return from China, Senator Scott counseled President Ford to normalize relations early in 1977 (ibid., 12 August). Senator Mansfield also urged normalization upon his return. The U.S. ambassador to the UN, William Scranton, also said that the United States should recognize the PRC (UPI, Washington, 5 November). A prominent dissenting voice was that of Ray Cline, former CIA deputy director and director of intelligence at the Department of State, who said that the USA should recognize two Chinas (UPI, Washington, 23 August).

In addition to rhetorical statements some concrete steps continued to be taken toward normalization. In March, it was announced that the United States would continue to reduce its military personnel in Taiwan and that there would be a sharp cutback in military credit sales to Taiwan (AP, Washington, 11 March). In May, the new head of the U.S. Liaison Office in Peking, Thomas Gates, announced that his main objective was to work toward normalization. In June it was announced that the last of the U.S. military advisers on Quemoy and Matsu were being removed (Washington Post Service, 24 June).

There was much talk during the year of possible U.S. military assistance to the PRC. However, the Chinese expressed no interest in either a formal defense arrangement with the United States or the acquisition of U.S. weapons or military technology. This was made clear to the U.S. congressional delegation which visited with Vice-Premier (at the time) Chang Chun-chiao and Foreign Minister Chiao Kuan-hua in April (AP, Washington, 26 April).

Nevertheless, the talk persisted throughout the year, and a number of actions indicated the possibility of such a relationship at least on an informal basis. Senior CIA analyst Roger Brown advocated such military ties in the May issue of *Foreign Policy*, and Professor Jerome Cohen, an adviser on China to President-elect Jimmy Carter, supported the idea of some military support to China in the August issue of *Foreign Affairs*. The United States did not interfere with sales by its allies to the PRC, it was announced (in the Cohen article). There was speculation that James Schlesinger may have discussed the subject during his September visit. Schlesinger was appreciated for his known hard line on Soviet-U.S. détente, and was the first American to visit Tibet. He also visited Sinkiang and Inner Mongolia, and paid last respects to the deceased Mao in the Great Hall of the People. There have been unconfirmed press reports that the United States has been providing the PRC with intelligence reports on the Soviet Union (*International Bulletin*, 8 October). In late October it was announced that the Ford administration allowed the sale of two relatively advanced computer systems "as a symbol of support for the new government consolidating its power in Peking" (AP, Washington, 29 October).

Christopher Phillips, president of the National Council for U.S.-China Trade, following a two-week visit to China in October with a top American business delegation, said that Sino-U.S. trade is likely to expand in the wake of the purge of Peking's leading radicals. Comments of Foreign Trade Minister Li Chiang, who met with the American group only four days after the purge, were noted earlier, but to this can be added here his comment that "China was interested in buying American fully-constructed plants, machinery, technical information, lumber products and possibly cotton." Li said that China would continue to seek U.S. buyers for its non-ferrous metals, light industrial products, textiles, pharmaceuticals and chemicals. (Washington Post Service, Hong Kong, 27 October.)

Relations with Japan. Sino-Japanese relations improved in 1976, at the expense of Russo-Japanese relations. Soviet foreign minister Andrei Gromyko's visit to Tokyo in early January was a failure. Following this visit, the Japanese agreed to the inclusion of an anti-hegemony clause in the proposed Sino-Japanese peace treaty (*Japan Times*, 14 January). However, the Japanese and Chinese were unable to agree on the exact meaning and wording of the controversial clause. The Chinese intend the clause to be aimed at the USSR, an implication which the Japanese wish to avoid. The matter remained unsettled at year's end. The Japanese foreign minister objected, in July, to Peking's repeated public statements in support of Japan's claim to the disputed northern islands held by the USSR. However, any Soviet wish to follow up on this minor Sino-Japanese disagreement was set aside by the landing in Japan in September of a Soviet defector in a highly sophisticated MIG-25, and the Japanese decision to study the plane with Americans. Also, in September, there was appointed a new Japanese foreign minister, Zentaro Kosaka, a known Sinophile.

China's trade with Japan began to correct the massive 1975 imbalance in early 1976. In the first quarter of 1976 Japan purchased 10.6 percent more Chinese goods, while the PRC reduced its imports from Japan by 26 percent. The PRC expects to pay for the Japanese imports with oil, but refinery problems and an oil glut in Japan resulted in lower first quarter 1976 exports than expected. Peking promised to more than double oil exports to Japan by the fourth quarter of 1976 (Susumu Awanohara, *Far Eastern Economic Review*, 28 May).

Relations Elsewhere. In South Asia, relations between India and the PRC became normalized for the first time since the 1962 border war. Diplomatic relations were never formally broken off in the fourteen-year interval, but only in 1976 did the two countries once again exchange ambassadors (*Current Scene*, August, October). This important development took place apparently without adversely affecting the PRC's relationship with Pakistan, which remained strong in 1976. Prime Minister Zulfikar Ali Butto visited Peking in May and, as it turned out, was to have the distinction of being the last foreign guest in China to see Chairman Mao. Bangladesh and the PRC exchanged ambassadors in 1976 (ibid., April, June). The warm Sino-Nepalese ties were underscored by King Birendra's visits to Szechuan and Tibet in June. Sri Lanka's minister of cultural affairs and deputy ministers of defense and foreign affairs made separate trips to the PRC in May, and the PRC enjoyed reflected status through the August meeting of the Fifth Nonaligned Summit Conference in Colombo at the Bandar-anaike memorial hall which had been built by the Chinese.

There were no dramatic developments in relations with Southeast Asia in 1976. Prime Minister Lee Kuan Yew of Singapore met Chairman Mao in May, but the visit did not result in the establishment of diplomatic relations. Singapore may be deferring such a move until Indonesia restores its PRC relations. In this regard, it appeared that Indonesian president Suharto relaxed his anti-PRC posture in an Indonesian national day address (*Far Eastern Economic Review*, 1 October). However, the PRC sharply criticized Indonesia for its role in East Timor, recounting reports of atrocities committed there by the Indonesians (e.g., *Peking Review*, 9 January). On the other hand, Peking remained silent about the Thai government's attack on Thammasat University until that government was toppled by a military coup. Then Peking criticized the fallen government's "savage suppression" (ibid., 22 October). The new Thai government has pledged to maintain the Thai-PRC relationship (*Far Eastern Economic Review*, 19 November).

The PRC's relationship with Vietnam and Laos have been tempered somewhat by the friendship of these two countries with the Soviet Union. China continues its aid program in Vietnam, which includes oil, medicine, textiles, and rice. Also the Chinese completed construction of a nitrogen fertilizer plant, a thermal power station, and a medical equipment factory in 1976 (ibid., 1 October). It is believed that the Russians have more than 500 personnel involved in their aid program in Laos. Nevertheless, during Laotian prime minister Kaysone Phomvihan's visit to China, in March, the PRC agreed to provide economic and technical aid (*NYT*, 19 March).

In the United Nations, the PRC followed its well-established policies, generally supportive of Third World interests as it interprets them and condemnatory of the two superpowers, especially the USSR. On 2 January it supported the General Assembly and Security Council in calling for the withdrawal of Indonesian troops from East Timor (*Peking Review*, 2 January). On 13 February it condemned South Africa for its "illegal occupation" of Namibia (ibid., 13 February). On 19 March it demanded the withdrawal of all U.S. and UN troops from South Korea (ibid., 19 March). The PRC supported the Security Council resolution of 17 March denouncing Rhodesian aggression against Mozambique (ibid., 26 March). On 26 March the PRC joined 41 other nations in calling for revision of the UN Charter to strengthen the position of the Third World vis-à-vis the superpowers (ibid., 26 March). On 31 March it chose not to participate in the Security Council resolution on the Angola question. Ambassador Huang Hua explained that the Angolan people "have the full right to solve their own problems free from outside interference." He said: "We are duty bound to stress that the aggression by Soviet social-imperialism and its mercenary troops against Angola is a serious event unprecedented in the history of African national-liberation movement (*sic*) since World War II." (Ibid., 9 April.)

At the 25 March meeting of the 32d Session of the UN Economic and Social Commission for Asia and the Pacific, in Bangkok, the Chinese representative again pointed out that the situation was "complex" and the struggle "acute," and that unity against hegemony was necessary (ibid., 16 April). At the UN Conference on Trade and Development, in Kenya during May, Peking agreed with the call for a "new international economic order," and said that its establishment was "a protracted, sharp and complicated struggle" (ibid., 21 May). The *Peking Review* (21 May) discussed the fourth session of the Third UN Law of the Sea Conference, held in New York on 15 March to 7 May, almost exclusively in terms of the opposition of the two superpowers. At the 13th Regional Conference in Asia and the Far East of the UN Food and Agricultural Organization, in Manila on 9-13 August, the PRC had a delegation for the first time. Its head counseled that the question of rural development is not isolated, but that it is part of the struggle of the developing countries for the development of their national economies. Such development "must be integrated with their struggle to oppose imperialist, colonial-ist and hegemonic oppression and exploitation and to actively set up a new international economic order" (ibid., 27 August). The PRC vetoed the first ballot effort to reelect UN secretary-general Kurt Waldheim on 7 December, in support of Mexico's Luis Echeverría, but voted for Waldheim on the second ballot (UPI, United Nations, 7 December).

Foreign Minister Chiao Kuan-hua summarized the Chinese world view and stand on UN issues in his speech to the UN General Assembly on 5 October in commemoration of Mao Tse-tung. Chiao recalled Mao's assessment: "The current situation is characterized by great disorder under heaven and it is excellent." Chiao warned that global war between the USA and the USSR was inevitable and "independent of man's will." (*NYT*, 6 October.)

Completion of the PRC's principal aid project in Africa, the Tanzam Railroad, came in July. After six years of construction the line was finally opened to traffic.

Publications. The official and most authoritative publication of the CCP is the newspaper *Jen-min jih-pao* (People's Daily), published in Peking. The theoretical journal of the Central Committee, Hung chi (Red Flag) is published approximately once a month. The daily paper of the PLA is *Chieh-fang-chun pao* (Liberation Army Daily). The weekly *Peking Review* is published in English and several other languages. It carries translations of important articles, editorials, and documents from the three aforementioned publications. The official news agency of the party and government is the New China News Agency (Hsinhua; NCNA).

University of Hawaii   Stephen Uhalley, Jr.

India

The Communist Party of India, since its formation in 1928, has been divided in social character, base of support, and ideological stance. These factional cleavages were difficult to contain, and the party split in 1964. As a consequence, two antagonistic organizations emerged, the Communist Party of India (CPI) and the more militant Communist Party of India-Marxist (CPM). In part, the dispute was about domestic strategy, separating those who thought the best way forward was in alliance with the leftist elements within the dominant Congress Party, and those who wanted one or another of the more radical alternatives.

But, what made it impossible to hold the party together was the Sino-Soviet split, and more immediately the border clash between India and China in 1962. The CPI remained loyal to the international goals of the Soviet Union while the CPM tended towards a more critical stance. The CPI, the smaller fragment of the split, retained the bulk of the party bureaucracy, the members of central and state assemblies, and the trade unions; the larger group (CPM) carried off the main geographic areas of the party's strength—West Bengal, Kerala, and Andhra Pradesh. The radical left of the CPM later scattered into a number of groups which protested against the CPM's participation in united-front ministries in Bengal and Kerala during 1967-71. Most of these radicals, avowedly opposed to parliamentary democracy, were committed to the Maoist conception of guerrilla warfare and armed revolution. Some met in March 1969 at Calcutta to proclaim the formation of the Communist Party of India (Marxist-Leninist), the CPML.

The two major Communist parties each won about 4 percent of the vote in India's last general elections, 1971. The CPI won 24 of the 525 parliamentary seats, and the CPM 25 (the ruling Congress Party, 364). State assembly elections were held the next year. The CPI, which had an alliance with the Congress Party in some states, won more than three times as many seats as the CPM. Neither party, however, held a large bloc of seats in any state.

The CPI and CPM took divergent stands on the national Emergency, declared by the government on 26 June 1975 after several months of protest of corruption, inflation, and the scarcity of essential commodities. The CPI, which supported the government, clearly hoped to increase its influence with the government. It anticipated that Prime Minister Indira Gandhi would be inclined to support socialist economic and social policies, a pro-Soviet foreign policy, and the institutionalized ties between itself and the Congress Party. Of course, the Emergency also represented a potential danger to CPI influence, for it gave the government vast discretionary power that could be used to suppress the "left." The CPM, on the other hand, claimed that the Emergency was a tactical move to shore up the position of the "big bourgeoisie," and its leaders expected that the CPM would become a special target.

The population of India is perhaps 570 million.

The CPI. Organization and Tactics. The CPI is an all-India organization based on the principle of "democratic centralism." Its structure, however, has been essentially regional in orientation. Tactics and election strategy have been frequently determined more by local circumstances than by directives from the top.

The party's major decision-making unit is the nine-member Central Secretariat led by party chairman Sripat Amrit Dange and general secretary C. Rajeswara Rao. Other national CPI bodies are the 31-member National Executive Committee and the 138-member National Council. The party claimed in July 1976 that its membership had increased by 130,000 since 1975, which would put the total at about 480,000. Some 70 percent of the membership is in five states: Bihar (135,000), Andhra Pradesh (102,000), Kerala (69,000), Uttar Pradesh (44,000) and Tamilnadu (43,000). (*Link*, 18 July.) The CPI, unlike the CPM, has been able to establish a base of support in the Hindi-speaking heartland of India.

The major auxiliary organizations of the CPI are the All-India Student' Federation (AISF) (105,000 members); the All-India Trade Union Conference (AITUC) (2,600,000), and a peasant organization, the All-India Kisan Samiti (AIKS) (175,000). The Jan Seva Dal, the party's "educational" auxiliary, organizes camps to train its cadres.

Since the Emergency, the CPI has pursued a three-pronged strategy: (1) support Prime Minister Indira Gandhi and thus strengthen links with the ruling Congress Party; (2) organize mass conferences to build popular support; and (3) unify the urban working class and establish links between it and the poor peasantry. In line with this strategy, the CPI general secretary placed an ideological stamp of approval on the Emergency, stating that it had preempted "the imperialist threat from the outside and the reactionary bandwagon" from within (ibid., 27 June 1976).

Despite the expectation of increased influence over policy-making, CPI leaders and publications have become increasingly apprehensive over the trend of events since the Emergency. The propaganda impact of the party, moreover, has diminished owing to the decline in the influence of parliament and the press, and to the party's self-imposed restraint on agitational activities. A CPI M.P. declared on the floor of parliament in August 1976 that local authorities used Emergency powers to detain CPI cadres in at least seven states (*New Age*, 15 August). One of his colleagues stated that even some CPI state assembly members had been arrested (*Link*, 29 August). During the same month, speakers at the AISF annual conference said that university authorities had expelled AISF student leaders for speaking openly on economic and political affairs (ibid., 22 August).

Further, a primer prepared by the Congress Party for its workers noted that the CPI and the Jana Sangh (a militantly Hindu revivalist party) were "two opposing and deviant trends in the otherwise composite polity of India" (reported in *Link*, 10 October). Despite this, Mohit Sen, a CPI Central Executive Committee member, had stated in an article published two months before: "[The CPI] has never had so many friends, never had so much influence. . . . All that is the finest proof that we chose the correct road." (*WMR*, August.) There is considerable hyperbole in this statement, and CPI influence would surely decline significantly if it opposed the Prime Minister, for the severe constraints placed on other parties would be imposed on it, and the party has too thin a base of support to resist effectively.

The Congress connection has facilitated mass contact, the party's second broad tactical objective. Even before the Emergency, it had organized a series of anti-fascist conferences and rallies, often with Congress cooperation. It went on to intensify its anti-fascist campaign, which was often used as a vehicle to praise the Prime Minister. In Uttar Pradesh alone, it organized 225 rallies within a four-month period (*Link*, 24 August). This publicity aroused antagonism from some state units of the Congress Party. The president of the Bihar Congress, for example, issued an order forbidding the use of Congress forums by "other political parties," and he reportedly criticized the CPI for not permitting Congress representatives to participate fully in the "World Anti-Fascist Rally" held in Patna in December 1975 (*Searchlight*, 14 August).

The CPI National Council in February directed the party to launch a *padyayatra* (walking pilgrimage) campaign to "educate the masses" about the 20-point set of economic goals announced by the Prime Minister soon after the declaration of Emergency and to "collect information about its implementation" (*Economic and Political Weekly*, 2 October). This campaign was the party's most intensive effort to date to establish a support base among the rural masses. In Uttar Pradesh, for example, some 10,000 cadres in 300 groups visited about 3,000 villages. (*New Age*, 25 July.) The information gained during these visits confirmed the party's suspicion that local authorities were not enforcing the social and economic reforms spelled out in the Prime Minister's 20-point program. The Uttar Pradesh state executive committee issued a statement that official reports of land distribution to the rural poor "appear[ed] to be unjustified." Party leaderes laid the blame on corrupt police and revenue officials. (Ibid.)

To facilitate the third general objective, the party's labor affiliate moved quickly to support the Emergency. Indeed, AITUC leaders met on the day it was declared and pledged to cooperate with the government (*Link*, 10 October). The government's initial moves toward AITUC seemed to augur well. AITUC and unions supporting the Congress Party (INTUC, the country's largest labor organization, and HMS) were included on national and state committees to advise the government on labor/management issues. The government, moreover, promised increased labor influence on internal plant policy-making. Communist publications in late 1975, however, had begun to report increased layoffs and lockouts, wage freezes, and the government's virtual prohibition of strikes. Communists, moreover, were alarmed over attempts of INTUC unions to take control of local AITUC affiliates. This apprehension revealed itself at the 30th AITUC session, which met in October 1976. The delegates passed a resolution describing the "acute discontent" caused by intensified attacks on "basic democratic and trade union rights," while union leaders called on workers to observe 15-22 November as a "Week of Workers' Fundamental Rights." (*New Age*, 24 October.) Despite this call to register disapproval over the labor situation, AITUC leaders gave no indication that they would engage in agitational tactics. Rather, observation of this special week was probably a public call on INTUC to close ranks with AITUC to put joint pressure on the government to honor past commitments to labor. A pro-CPI publication speculated that labor unity would improve if the "healthy section" of INTUC would assert itself against its "entrenched anti-communist section" (Link, 17 October).

Domestic and International Attitudes. The economic initiatives proposed by the Prime Minister soon after the Emergency promised a number of reforms, but represented no radical changes of the economic structure. Indeed, the Prime Minister assured business that no major nationalization schemes were contemplated. Industrial peace was stressed as an essential condition for further economic growth. Nevertheless, the CPI welcomed the 20-point program as a constructive first step of more comprehensive reform.

Yet, even here, the party was disturbed by the record of implementation. Early in the Emergency, the party proposed the formation of local vigilance committees to monitor its implementation, but nothing has come of this scheme. Even more alarming to the CPI has been a series of policies designed to encourage the expansion of private industry, including measures easing restrictions against foreign investment. Six months after the Emergency, the Central Executive Committee met in New Delhi, where the General Secretary complained publicly about the reduction in the annual bonus to workers, the introduction of the seven-day work week, the dropping of the plan to nationalize the wholesale trade of food grain, and the delay in setting up a public distribution system (Link, 7 December 1975). Yet, both he and other CPI officials have been careful not to link the Prime Minister to these developments. Rather, blame is placed on the bureaucracy and on a resurgence of "reactionary" influence within the Congress. Prime Minister Indira Gandhi has reacted negatively to such charges and on December 23 she told a group of Congress Party workers that these charges are an indirect attack on her leadership. (FBIS, December 23, 1976.) Three days earlier, she said that the CPI's criticism of her politically influential son, Sanjay Gandhi, who has publicly condemned communist philosophy, was an attack against her policies. (Associated Press, December 23, 1976.) Relations between the two parties have become increasingly strained, but it is not yet clear if the central leadership of either will permit a full confrontation to occur.

On the internal political front, the party welcomed restrictions on "rightist" parties and their publications, and the laws designed to restrict the powers of the judicial system. It applauded the suspension of opposition governments in Tamilnadu and Gujarat in early 1976. However, it too has begun to complain about restrictions on CPI activities. Since at least mid-1976, party leaders have made public statements advocating a loosening of the Emergency and the holding of elections at the earliest convenient time.

Prime Minister Indira Gandhi called for a "national debate" on the constitution at the annual session of the Congress Party in late December 1975. The congress President in February chose a committee, chaired by former minister Swaran Singh, to formulate a set of constitutional revisions. The recommendations were incorporated in the 44th Amendment Bill which passed both parliamentary houses during the 1976 special fall session. CPI leaders in private discussions with government spokesmen on 13 August suggested a further reduction in the powers of the judiciary, the deletion of the property guarantee from the Fundamental Rights provision of the constitution, an opposed penal restriction attached to proposed Fundamental Duties (New Age, 15 November). Bhupesh Gupta, the party's chief spokesman in parliament, wrote that the constitutional committee's "conception of the fundamental rights seems to have inspired by adminstrative considerations that suit the status quo" (ibid., 11 July). The property clause was not removed and the judiciary retained a substantial part of its powers. Party leaders are apprehensive that a new clause in the constitution providing the government with the right to ban "anti-national" organizations could be used to curb trade union activities. The party also had misgivings about extending the term of parliament and empowering the center to deploy security forces in the states. (India Today, 16-30 November.) Nevertheless, the CPI voted for the Amendment Bill. Indeed, it was the only opposition party to do so; the others boycotted the debates.

During the debates, India's Law Minister announced that elections would be further delayed to at least March 1978. CPI MP's protested that this extension would undermine the country's democratic system, and the party's official publication predicted that a postponement would "provide opportunities to the anti-democratic forces to cash in on the resultant frustration" (ibid., 5 September).

On the international front, the party has generally approved the government's initiatives. Mrs. Gandhi visited the USSR and the German Democratic Republic during June and July, the first time she has traveled abroad since the Emergency. Moreover there has been a steady stream of Communist bloc officials to India since early 1976 and they have lauded the Prime Minister and her policies. The USSR came closer to endorsing India's stand on an Indian Ocean Peace Zone proposal in the joint statement issued at the conclusion of Mrs. Gandhi's June visit, and it subsequently responded favorably to the political declaration issued at the August non-aligned conference in Colombo. The CPI press exploited these developments as evidence of the compatibility of Soviet foreign policy with the goals of the developing countries generally and with India specifically.

India's decision to reestablish diplomatic relations with Pakistan and the People's Republic of China in mid-1976 was officially welcomed by the CPI, though its propaganda line would be undermined if there were a significant improvement in Sino-Indian relations while Sino-Soviet relations remained strained. The CPI, however, has expressed dissatisfaction with the establishment of the Indo-American Joint Commission in 1975 and with the government's easing of restrictions on foreign investment.

The CPM. Organization and Strategy. The Emergency has probably weakened the organization structure of the CPM. Indian newspapers report large-scale defection of members, and CPM publications complain about the arrest of low-level cadres, though the major leaders have not been arrested under the detention laws. The Emergency has prevented the CPM and its auxiliaries from engaging in mass agitation to regain the support it lost during the 1970-72 resurgence of the ruling Congress Party.

The CPM, with an organizational structure roughly parallel to that of the CPI, reported some 120,000 members in 1974, concentrated in Andhra Pradesh, West Bengal, and Kerala. While official membership figures are considerably below those of the CPI, the active membership of the CPM is probably comparable. Because the bulk of the pre-1964 CPI organization went with the new CPI, the CPM has had to build up a separate set of auxiliary organizations. The Centre of Indian Trade Unions (CITU) was formed in 1970. It has some 900,000 members. Unions affiliated to the CITU have been excluded from the advisory bodies established by the government since the Emergency. Also in 1970 the CPM established the Student's Federation of India (160,000 members). The CPM has been far more successful than the CPI in organizing the peasantry. The CPM peasant organization, the All-India Kisan Sabha, claimed some 1,100,000 members in 1974.

The 9th Party Congress, 1972, set the CPM firmly in opposition to the ruling Congress Party. To undermine the ruling party's support, the CPM has been willing to cooperate with other opposition parties. The CPM had already participated with opposition forces in united front ministries in Kerala and West Bengal during 1967-71. It demonstrated its commitment to cooperation by participating with several opposition groups on the National Coordination Committee that directed the massive May 1974 railway strike. In Kerala it assumed unofficial leadership of a nine-party alliance of leftist parties. In Bihar it decided to participate in Jaya Prakash Narayan's anti-government movement, and it extended its support similarly to his national campaign against the Congress during late 1974 and 1975.

In January 1976, the CPM Central Committee proposed a 10-point minimum program which might be acceptable to those who seek "left and democratic unity," including the CPI. This program included confiscation of foreign capital, a total ban on multi-national corporations, nationalization of large business enterprises and foreign trade, the right to work as a constitutional right, confiscation of land and its distribution to the landless, and reduction of prices of essential articles and their distribution through local popular committees (*Link*, 25 July). This was a signal for talks with the CPI, but Pramode Das Gupta, West Bengal CPM leader, cautioned that cooperation with the "right communists" was impossible "as long as they do not give up their class collaboration and their close alliance with the Congress (ibid.).

Subsequently, discussion were held with CPI leaders. That talks were held at all is notable and undoubtedly demonstrates a certain apprehension over the fate of communism in post-Emergency India. Nevertheless, the talks were unsuccessful and the CPI's Rajeswara Rao announced that the talks failed because: (1) the CPM did not appreciate "the tremendous role of the Soviet Union and the shameful role of Maoist China" in international affairs, and (2) left unity between the CPI and CPM was not sufficient to defeat "reaction"—such an objective required the cooperation of "progressive" elements with the Congress Party. In response, the CPM maintained that the real danger to the country came from the Prime Minister herself (*New Age*, 15 August). The failure to develop a leftist front has probably strengthened the position of the CPM radicals who tend to reject constitutional politics. Yet, the decision of a subsequent Politburo meeting to press for elections indicates that the moderates are still in command. (*India Today*, 16-30 November.)

Attitudes on Internal and External Issues. While there is considerable agreement between the CPI and CPM on specific economic policies, the two differ fundamentally on how to achieve the "people's democracy." The CPM maintains that the immediate objective of the "people's front" must be to eliminate "bourgeois-landlord government" (i.e., the Congress regime). Consequently, it not only attacks those economic policies which benefit the "bourgeois-landlord" classes, as does the CPI, but it goes further and labels the Emergency an attempt to suppress the working class. Indeed, the disagreement with the CPI is largely over political tactics. Since the Emergency, the CPM has become increasingly involved in a loosely organized opposition front, composed of the Jana Sangh, the Socialist Party, the Organization Congress, and the Bharatiya Lok Dal. Along with them, it boycotted the special parliamentary session debating the constitutional amendments and voted with the other major opposition parties (with the exception of the CPI) in opposing parliamentary sanction of the Emergency, the extension of parliament, and the preventive detention activities of the executive. It has not, however, directly participated in talks aimed at unifying the opposition into a single party.

After the 1964 split, the CPM praised the Chinese Comunist Party (CCP) for its fight against revisionism. But after the CPM opted to participate in united front ministries in 1967, the CCP accused the CPM itself of revisionism. The CCP mantle of approval was then transferred to the revolutionary CPML. Since then, the CPM has had a policy of equidistance between the two major Communist powers, condemning with equal intensity "left sectarianism" and Soviet "revisionism."

The support of the USSR and other Communist countries for the Emergency moved the CPM's Politburo in September 1976 to criticize them for subordinating the class struggle to government-to-government relations. The party did, however, welcome New Delhi's decision to exchange ambassadors with Peking, as did the CPI. It has opposed foreign investments and the USA in even stronger terms than the CPI.

The CPML. The government on 4 July 1975, just eight days after imposing the Emergency, banned 15 revolutionary Communist groups, including both the pro- and anti-Lin Pao factions of the CPML. It is difficult to assess the government's success in diminishing this group's potential for violent activity. The CPML, like other revolutinary Communist groups, operates secretly and has made almost no provisions for building mass organizations. This policy is based on the premise that mass organizations would result in domination by rich peasants and the "bourgeois," thus leading inevitably to "revisionism." The CPML has remained an elitist group with little mass support. (Its members, along with those of other numerous but smaller Maoist organizations, continue to be referred to popularly as Naxalites, a name taken from Naxalbari, West Bengal, where the PCML instigated a peasant revolt in 1967.)

The group adopted the "Annihilation Tactic" in February 1969, and organized squads of cadres launched an attack on large landlords. This line enabled the police to close in on CPML cadres whenever the cadres undertook any action, since these roving bands of urban students were easy to identify in rural areas. In 1970, CPML leader Charu Mazumdar unleashed a "Red Terror" in Calcutta which involved the murder of policemen, military personnel, and "capitalists." A massive response by the government in 1970-72 decimated its urban cadres. As its ranks thinned in the confrontation with the authorities, the CPML movement collapsed. Since then, there have been periodic newspaper reports of "Naxalite" terror, but these accounts probably refer to violence set off by long-standing rural rivalries rather than to organized "Naxalite" activities.

Washington, D.C.   Walter K. Andersen

Indonesia

Indonesian Communism today consists of the activities of a handful of refugees outside Indonesia, and of underground members and sympathizers inside the country belonging either to the Peking-1 or the Moscow-oriented wing of the Communist Party of Indonesia (Partai Komunis Indonesia; PKI). In the aftermath of an abortive coup attempt in Djakarta and parts of Central Java on 30 September 1965 by some PKI leaders and front members, and a few Indonesian Army and Air Force officers and their units, the PKI, until then perhaps the most influential party in Indonesia, went into a steep decline, being formally banned in 1966. The party has remained illegal and organizationally shattered since then. The PKI underground supports the North Kalimantan Communist Party in its guerrilla struggle in Sarawak (see Malaysia), but this guerrilla activity is sporadic, on a minimal scale, and wholly ineffective.

History. The PKI, founded on 23 May 1920 during the closing decades of the Dutch colonial period, is the oldest Communist party in Asia. Dutch Marxists, like the Comintern agent Hendrik Sneevliet (alias "Maring"), were prominent in laying the groundwork, in 1914, of the Indies Social Democratic Association, the PKI's forerunner. After the PKI's founding, Indonesians assumed leadership and directed the party into trade union organizing and ineffectual strike activity. In 1926-27, despite internal leadership opposition and partly because of poor policy relationships with the Comintern, the PKI attempted a coup in West Java and West Sumatra, which the Dutch colonial authorities had little difficulty in putting down. Scores of party cadres were confined in prisons and camps, notably in the Upper Digul region of West Irian (New Guinea). During the 1930s a few underground cadres continued to proselytize in East Java among lower naval and dock personnel at Surabaya and among sugar estate workers, but it was not until the proclamation of Indonesian independence on 17 August 1945 that the PKI became a legal party again and could begin rebuilding itself.

In contrast to Malaya, Burma, the Philippines, and Vietnam, where Communists played a major role in organizing resistance to the Japanese occupation of Southeast Asia during World War II, there was little PKI-led or -organized resistance in Indonesia. Although prominent Communists like Tan Malaka had little love for the Japanese, influential Indonesian nationalists like Sukarno, who "promised Japan his support," actively collaborated with them (Harry A. Poeze, *Tan Malaka*, The Hague, 1976, p. 498).

In the early years of the revolution against returning Dutch colonial authority (1945-49) the PKI assumed a significant role in the Indonesian Republic's fledgling parliament, and party members held cabinet offices. But relations with other political factions soon tended to polarize, and the Communist armed units were feared. Moscow's new, hard-line "two camp doctrine," heralding a more aggressive confrontation of the West, and the Communist Youth Conference in Calcutta (February 1948) probably acted as catalysts of a PKI line of tighter organizational discipline and militant policy toward the revolutionary government. On 18 September 1948 a number of second-echelon PKI and front group leaders, with support from local Army personnel, attempted a coup d'état at Madiun, East Java. It is doubtful that this action had been approved by top PKI leaders, but as the Indonesian Army swiftly overcame the coup, the party was once again discredited, although not banned.

When Indonesia formally won independence from the Dutch in December 1949, the PKI lay in ruin, enveloped in popular mistrust. Yet within six years, under younger leaders, among whom the Sumatra-born future party chairman Dipa Nusantara Aidit was the most important, it was able to regain respectability and influence. In the first national parliamentary elections, in 1955, the party won about 16 percent of the popular vote and the fourth-largest number of seats. Identifying itself with a militantly nationalistic program to "Indonesianize" the economy, culture, and all aspects of policy, and allying itself as far as possible with President Sukarno, the PKI became virtually indispensable to Sukarno in his developing power struggle with the Army.

By early 1965, having greatly expanded its network of front organizations, the PKI had about 3 million members (in a population of perhaps 120 million), with additional thousands of supporters in all walks of life, and Aidit and other top party figures held minor cabinet posts. In the Sino-Soviet dispute, the PKI under Aidit followed formally an independent policy, but, in accord with the government's foreign policy at this time, seemed to fall in with Peking's line more and more.

Within a few months, a debacle overtook the party through the involvement of a number of its top officials, Aidit among them, in a plot with a handful of left-leaning dissident Army and Air Force officers to establish a new, presumably more radical government, although Sukarno's status as president was to be preserved. The extent to which Sukarno was aware of the plot, and the degree of encouragement given by People's China to the plotters, remains controversial. In a number of areas throughout Indonesia, it was subsequently discovered, lists of suspected or real enemies of the PKI, and others desired out of the way, had been compiled by local party cadres. Those on the lists were presumably marked for liquidation if the plot should succeed. In the night of 30 September 1965, at the direction of Aidit and other PKI leaders, and of representatives from the dissident officers' group, specially trained members of the party's women's and youth fronts, supported by a few Army and Air Force units, attempted a coup d'état by assassinating six prominent Army generals and seizing a number of government buildings. Loyal Army units, led by the commander of the Strategic Reserve, General Suharto, isolated the insurgents, and even though the coup had a following in Central Java, where fighting flared briefly, the expected popular support for the coup failed to materialize.

In subsequent weeks, as the Army under Suharto and the defense minister, General A. H. Nasution (who had escaped the coup assassins sent against him), established their authority, an extensive anti-Communist pogrom took place throughout the country, mainly led by Army-supported Muslim youth groups. Several tens of thousands of Communists, suspected party sympathizers, and, it is to be feared, innocents were killed. The total number of those massacred has never been exactly established. On 12 March 1966, as President Sukarno, who had been trying to protect the PKI, was rapidly losing his power, the PKI was formally banned. On 5 July the Provisional People's Constituent Assembly, chief policy-making body for the country, banned the dissemination or propagation of Marxism-Leninism, including public discussion except for purposes of academic study.

In the past decade a handful of exiled PKI spokesmen, divided along pro-Soviet or pro-Chinese lines, have issued statements condemning the alleged evils of the regime of President Suharto, who succeeded Sukarno in 1967, and each other. Early in 1968 underground PKI cadres organized a short-lived "Indonesian People's Republic" in Blitar, East Java. A number of underground pro-Peking party *kompros* ("project committees") functioned briefly in the mountain areas of Central Java. Military action quickly nipped all PKI activity in the bud. However, a continuing domestic anti-Communist campaign in the years since 1965 has seen tens of thousands arrested on charges of PKI connections or alleged complicity in the coup attempt. In West Kalimantan (Borneo), some cadres have been assisting Communist guerrillas across the border in Sarawak (see *Malaysia*).

Organization and Tactics. Little is known of the reportedly persisting attempts at deep-cover penetration, proselytizing, and other objectives by PKI cadres, mainly of the pro-Peking faction, in Indonesia itself. Over the years the government has made announcements of such Communist activity (see, for example, *YICA, 1976*, p. 293, and *1975*, pp. 339-41), but in 1976 there were very few reports, although general warnings against the "latent" problem of subversion routinely continued.

The Maoist-oriented PKI consists—apart from an undetermined number of supporters in Indonesia, mostly in West Kalimantan—of perhaps three score Indonesian exiles, resident mostly in Peking, Tokyo, and Tirana (Albania). They are led by former PKI Politburo member Jusuf Adjitorop, who was in China at the time of the 1965 coup attempt for medical treatment. The group usually refers to itself as "The Delegation" of the PKI, or as "The Delegation of the Central Committee" of the PKI. In 1966 the group's Politburo issued statements and an *otokritik* (self-criticism) which have remained the faction's basic policy principles. The otokritik sees the 1965 debacle primarily as the result of the party's too close accommodation of the Sukarno regime. To get itself on the right track again the PKI must raise and follow "three banners": first, the building of a Marxist-Leninist party free from "subjectivism, opportunism, and modern revisionism"; second, the development of the "armed people's struggle," specifically that of the peasantry; third, the building of a new "revolutionary united front," led by the working class and based on the unity of workers and peasants (*Build the PKI along the Marxist-Leninist Line to Lead the People's Democratic Revolution in Indonesia*, published by the Delegation of the Central Committee of the PKI, Tirana, 1971, pp. 148-49, 199). Major political objectives of the party program adopted in November 1967 by the "Delegation" are to "destroy completely the entire state machine of the Suharto-Nasution fascist dictatorship," which is considered to be "the general representative of U.S. imperialism," and to establish in its place a "people's democratic dictatorship" (ibid., p. 269).

In its 1 January 1976 New Year's Message (broadcast on 27 January by the clandestine radio transmitter of the Communist Party of Malaya, "Voice of the Malayan Revolution") much attention is paid to revolutionary developments outside Indonesia, such as to the recent "brilliant victory" of the peoples of Vietnam, Laos and Cambodia, and the alleged rivalry "between imperialism and socio-imperialism" in the Middle East. The "two superpowers," the USA and the USSR, are charged with attempting to "rule the world" and suppress the peoples' revolutionary cause. The message also continues the group's sharp criticism of the present government of President Suharto in Indonesia. The government's "aggression" against the "Democratic Republic of East Timor" is viewed as an attempt to expand Indonesian power and dominate the other countries in Southeast Asia. Indonesia's oil production is said to have been put under the control of "foreign monopolies" while the vast majority of Indonesians continue to live in misery. Recent Suharto-sponsored legislation providing for control of the operations of political parties is said to further tighten the regime's grip on the people. Soviet "social imperialism" is charged with exploiting a "handful of Indonesian renegades" for its own ends (a reference to the rival pro-Moscow faction of the PKI), but this "act of betrayal" inevitably will meet with opposition and "be smashed." The message concludes with the expectation that during 1976 the "domestic and international situations will gradually develop in favor of the people's revolutionary forces in Indonesia and throughout the world."

A claim that the "Suharto fascist regime," appearing to be strong, is actually weakening daily, was made in a statement issued by "Delegation" on 3 May, the 56th anniversary of the founding of PKI. (This too was broadcast by the "Voice of the Malayan Revolution.") According to the statement, "imperialist" and monopoly capitalist control over the Indonesian economy, allegedly coming particularly from the USA and Japan, is increasingly adversely affecting the lives of Indonesians; "more and more" of them, specifically workers and peasants, fishermen and "poor people in the towns," pedicab drivers and intellectuals and students, are said to be rising up against the Suharto government, while mismanagement and "large-scale corruption" in the government oil company, Pertamina, have produced more than $10 billion in foreign and domestic debts. The statement predicts that despite extensive political suppression a general election (considered but a "farce") will be staged again in the near future to "deceive the people about democracy in Indonesia." Yet "objective factors," both at home and abroad, are claimed to be highly favorable to the revolutionary struggle, and therefore the PKI must work hard, especially in the rural areas, to arouse and lead the masses. (Broadcast in Malay to Malaysia and Singapore, 10 June; *FBIS*, 14 June.)

The Soviet-oriented wing of the PKI, known during the late sixties as the "Marxist-Leninist Group of the PKI," has in recent years referred to itself as the "Committee Abroad of the Communist Party of Indonesia," or simply "the PKI." It consists now of about three dozen Indonesian exiles, former students, diplomats, and journalists, mostly resident in Prague, Moscow, and other East European capitals and in Colombo (Sri Lanka). These serve primarily in publicity and public relations functions, supported by the host government except for Sri Lanka, and form a nucleus from which a leadership could be recruited in the unlikely event that the party should be relegitimized, or if it should find an organizational front at home in the near future. Their deep-cover following in Indonesia itself is minimal, though the faction has the relative advantage of the existence of a functioning Soviet embassy in Djakarta (Sino-Indonesian diplomatic relations were frozen, though not formally broken, in 1967, in the aftermath of the 1965 coup attempt), and of continuing interest by both Djakarta and Moscow in furthering Soviet technical aid relations in Indonesia.

The Moscow wing's February 1969 statement, "Urgent Tasks of the Communist Movement in Indonesia," authoritatively spelled out basic policy. While not rejecting the possibility of armed struggle, it declared such struggle to be premature so long as careful preparation of the population had not been completed by means of a rehabilitated and popularly accepted PKI in Indonesia (*IB*, no. 7, 1969, pp. 27, 33-37). In a 1975 statement on the PKI's 55th anniversary, "For Democracy, Social Justice and the People's Welfare" (ibid., no. 11, pp. 26-36), briefly summarized in theSoviet press (*Pravda*, 23 May; *FBIS*, 29 May), the Moscow wing declared that the Suharto regime "depends entirely" for its existence on "bayonets and foreign imperialism," and that "imperialists" are allowed to plunder Indonesia's wealth: "hundreds of thousands of Communists and democrats" remain in jails and concentration camps throughout the country, and workers, peasants, fishermen, national entrepreneurs, civil servants, and intelligentsia are all suffering badly, while the "new big-compradore bourgeoisie," the speculators, and the "village exploiters" are thriving. The statement affirms generally the principles of the "Urgent Tasks" document, and cautions that though popular discontent is rising in Indonesia, "there is no force as yet capable of overthrowing the military regime." This is said to be so not least because the "democratic forces" are "still divided," and feelings of mistrust and enmity still exist among them, as the result of the "terror and slander campaign" against the "patriots" who were involved in the "September 30 movement" (i.e., the 1965 coup attempt). Urging that it is time to realize that "the main enemies of the Indonesian people" are "the regime in power and imperialism," the statement calls for the formation of a "National United Front" against the Suharto regime. Also proposed is a "program of struggle" for "abolition of the dictatorship," restoration of free political activity and of a free trade union movement, abolition of anti-Communist laws, adoption of a "progressive labor code," guarantees of academic freedom, more effective state controls on the operations of foreign capital, implementation of the basic agrarian law, and so on.

A subsequent publication by a "Member of Leadership, CP of Indonesia," noted some of the characteristics of the proposed "National Unity Front." There must be voluntary cooperation by "patriots" of different political and ideological backgrounds, and hence "organisational and ideological independence" within the front must be preserved. Also, "the question of leadership" should not be a condition for joining the front, as that question must be settled "in the course of the struggle." (Satiadjaja Sudiman, "The Key to Victory over Reaction," *WMR*, April 1976, p. 104.) In other words, the PKI does not propose to be wholly merged with the national front it proposes, nor to accept its leadership in advance. Noteworthy for the position in PKI thought of the late President Sukarno, currently held in rather low esteem by the Indonesian government, is the reiteration of a demand also made in the 55th anniversary statement. "Sukarnoism" is defined as "the anti-imperialist, patriotic system of views" of the late President, and therefore it, as well as "scientific socialism" (i.e., Marxism and Leninism), should not be banned in Indonesia (ibid., p. 105).

The Moscow faction's call for the building of an anti-Suharto front runs parallel with occasional statements by Indonesian military and civil officials in recent years that the PKI underground is seeking to infiltrate and win adherents in various groups, from Muslim associations to students. But no specifics on the extent or organization of such underground infiltration have thus far been revealed. Nor is there definite information on the present organizational structure of the Indonesian Maoist underground, whose members, at least operationally, have been absorbed by the North Kalimantan People's Guerrilla Force along the Sarawak border.

The continuing trials of former PKI members and alleged 1965 coup participants, and the detention of thousands of political prisoners suspected of coup involvement, re-enforce in the public's mind the Suharto government's general and unrelenting domestic anti-Communist policy. Popular fear of being identified with the Communists, or with anything resembling political radicalism, is pervasive in Indonesia today, although this has not prevented protest actions, mostly by students in Djakarta. Only furtive, deep-cover attempts at proselytizing, in an environment of slowing rising public discontent, especially over bureaucratic mismanagement and corruption, and over the economic plight of the mass of Indonesians, are tactically open to the PKI. Neither "People's War," advocated by the Maoist faction, nor the building of a broad "National Unity Front," called for by the Moscow faction, seems likely to bear significant fruit in the near future.

In September 1976 (exact date unspecified), the Maoist Delegation of the PKI Central Committee, over the signature of its chairman, Jusuf Adjitorop, issued a statement commemorating the anniversary of the Delegation's "self-criticism" of 1966. The statement declared that the self-criticism of ten years ago had put the PKI on the "correct revolutionary path," and that the Indonesian working class, peasants and fishermen, youth, students, women, urban poor, and other groups, were now all rising up and developing "various resistance activities." (VMR, 4 November, in *FBIS*, 8 November.)

Domestic Developments. As in years past, government spokesmen in 1976 stressed the potential or actual dangers posed by Communist and other sources of subversion. It is difficult to gauge whether officials take their own warnings seriously, or whether such warnings serve primarily as a means to maintain the power of the Suharto government (The Economist Intelligence Unit, London, *Quarterly Economic Review, Indonesia*, 1975, no. 2, p. 2). In early February, Admiral Sudomo, chief of staff of the nation's principal counterintelligence and security agency, the Command for the Restoration of Order and Security, declared that the Command continued to be necessary in light of "various threats and tensions that could endanger national security." Sudomo gave no details as to these alleged threats, but conceded that his Command was only temporary in nature (*FBIS*, 6 February). In mid-May, the territorial defense commander for Java, Lieutenant General Widodo, declared that security conditions within his command generally were good, although certain underground PKI elements had been exploiting various religious-mystic organizations (ibid., 14 May). One of Indonesia's most influential military figures, Lieutenant General Ali Murtopo, deputy chairman of the National Intelligence Coordinating Board, declared in June that while the recent uncovering of Communist subversive activity in Singapore had "not yet" prompted the need to take new special precautions in Indonesia, it was evident that Communists still had their eye on Indonesia, which "should therefore always build up its national resilience with strong infrastructures and potentials to reject Communist movements within the country and to ward off Communist movements from outside" (Antara news agency dispatch, Djakarta, 11 June; *FBIS*, 11 June).

Speculation that some attempt would be made to sabotage the forthcoming 1977 general elections increased in official statements and the press. Also, in May, Attorney General Ali Said said that although all those detained after the mid-January 1974 Djakarta riots touched off by the visit of then Japanese premier Kakuei Tanaka had now been released (save three persons who had been convicted), he still could not yet reveal the real "masterminds" behind the riots (*Antara Daily News Bulletin*, 13 May, vol. 27, no. 660, p. 1). On 28 April the government inaugurated the "Satgas Atbara," comprising sharpshooters and special troops, as a special task force against future terrorists and hijackers using Indonesian territory. Air Force Colonel Umar Safiuddin, commandant of the Halim Perdana-kusuma Airbase near Djakarta, was appointed to head the task force (*FBIS*, 29 April).

Official references to PKI activity, as distinct from general warnings about threats of subversion, were few in late 1975 and most of 1976. According to Admiral Sudomo, in an address to Indonesian diplomatic personnel, "remnants" of the PKI and the 1965 coup movement remain active abroad. In mid-November 1975, the Indonesian armed forces news agency reported that two recently formed farmers' associations in Central Java, one in Pati, the other at Semarang, had been discovered to be "disguised Communist tools" and had been outlawed. The exact "Communist" functions of the proscribed associations were not then disclosed. In early 1976, however, there were official allegations that they had been part of a broader underground PKI effort throughout Central and Eastern Java to infiltrate rural associations of a religious and mystical nature.

Official allegations were made also, as in the past, that a segment of the 1965 Communist leadership still remains at large in the country and is being sought. According to Army spokesmen, for example, "two percent of the PKI leaders" in the Madiun area of East Java (exact number not further specified) who fled after the 1965 coup attempt are still being searched for by the authorities (*FBIS*, 13, 26 November 1975; *Angkatan Bersenjata*, Djakarta, 1 October; *Indonesian Current Affairs Translation Service Bulletin*, Djakarta, October, p. 785).

Trials of alleged PKI activists, or of those said to have been involved in the coup attempt, also continued. The former police commander in chief of Djakarta, Brigadier General Sawarno Tjokro-diningrat, on 30 December 1975 was sentenced to 13 years in prison for having taken part in the coup plot and promoted rebellion (*Antara Daily News Bulletin*, 30 December, vol. 27, no. 549, p. ii). In the January 1976 trials of the former East Java PKI provincial committee chairman, Gatot Sutarjo, and his post-1965 underground successor, Djoko Untung, on charges of participation in the "prologue" as well as the "epilogue" of the coup attempt, the death penalty was demanded (*Indonesian Times*, Djakarta, 8 January). On 30 March, former minister of state Oei Tjoe Tat was sentenced to 13 years in prison for conspiracy in the coup attempt, including the spreading of "feelings of enmity, splits, conflicts, and upheavals, so that disturbances occurred in wide circles of society" (*Berita Yudha*, Djakarta, 31

March; *Indonesian Current Affairs Translation Service Bulletin*, Djakarta, March, p. 215). Oei had held offices in a prominent association of Indonesian Chinese and in the small left-wing Partindo party, believed PKI-infiltrated, before the attempt. On 13 July a former Air Force sergeant, Marsudi, was sentenced to death for his involvement in it.

The Suharto government has continued to be extremely sensitive to any criticism, overt or implied, of state policies, and has reacted by suggesting or asserting that such criticism is a threat to national security. An illustration is what befell B. Diah, publisher of one of Djakarta's leading dailies, *Merdeka*. In three articles in Merdeka, on 13-15 January, Diah criticized Indonesian foreign policy and Foreign Minister Adam Malik for alleged shortcomings in the East Timor crisis (*YICA, 1976*, pp. 297-98), which had led to criticism by members of the United Nations of Indonesian intervention. Sharp government reaction included an allegation by Malik that Diah really wanted "a Communist government" and a warning by Admiral Sudomo to Diah that his articles "could endanger the national stability and jeopardize security and order" (*Indonesia Times*, 27 January; *Suara Karya*, Djakarta, 15 January; *Indonesian Current Affairs Translation Service Bulletin*, January, p. 23). Diah apologized for the articles and no further overt official action was taken.

The government has remained equally sensitive about the issue of the so-called *tabanan politik* ("political prisoners"), of whom some 55,000 remain (official estimates vary between 20,000 and 35,000) (*YICA, 1976*, pp. 291-92; Amnesty International, *Annual Report, 1974-75*, London, 1975, p. 91). About 10,000 prisoners, most of them active in PKI fronts before the coup attempts or suspected of PKI sympathies, remain confined on the small East Indonesian island of Buru. They face indefinite detention without trial. According to the government, about 1,745 detainees, comprising the group against whom there is sufficient evidence for a trial, are still awaiting their day in court (Hamish McDonald, "The Ghosts from 'Gestapu'," *Far Eastern Economic Review*, 28 May, p. 10). Contradictory government statements made over the years as to the number of political prisoners being held, as well as allegations of very poor prison conditions and torture of some detainees, have added to the international controversy over Indonesia's prisoner problem and have raised doubts as to the credibility of official assurances that the government is accelerating release procedures (Justus M. van der Kroef, "Indonesia's Political Prisoners," *Pacific Affairs*, Winter, 1976-77). On 22 September it was officially announced that an attempt to overthrow the Suharto government and to replace Suharto with former Vice-President Muhammad Hatta, one of Indonesia's most revered nationalist leaders, had been foiled. According to the government, the attempt was plotted by four prominent religious leaders who apparently through deceit had obtained Hatta's written support. (*NYT*, 23 September.) The plot suggested increasing dissatisfaction in broad segments of society with the Suharto regime, particularly with its increasingly more stringent controls over all organized political activity.

During the year, Indonesia and Malaysia agreed to implement new procedures to meet their common-border guerrilla problem in West Kalimantan. A joint communiqué on 21 November 1975, after consultations by the "General Border Committee," an Indonesian-Malaysian military agency that supervises the counter-insurgency effort, declared that operations against the 200 or so border guerrillas "would be further intensified." Recent joint naval patrol operations around Borneo waters, it was said in the same communiqué, had prevented "the infiltration of undesirable elements and illegal activities" in the "sea region." A military spokesman for the Indonesian West Kalimantan command said in mid-January 1976 that the two countries hoped to "eliminate Communist terrorists in their common frontiers" by the end of the year, and in mid-April a "coordination meeting" of commanders of the joint counter-insurgency operations concluded that the "security situation" along the border was now "quite stable," with "no longer any disturbances" being caused by either "small or large units" of the guerrillas. On 29 May, however, after a meeting of Indonesian and Malaysian military commanders in Djakarta, it was announced that still another scheme for joint anti-guerrilla operations "on land, sea, and in the air" along the common border had been developed and would be submitted for final approval. (Antara news agency dispatch, Kuala Lumpur, 25 November 1975; *Asia Research Bulletin*, Singapore,Political Supplement, 30 June, p. 220; *FBIS*, 13, 25 November 1975, 15 January, 15, 21 April 1976.)

Announcements of new joint Indonesian and Malaysian military and border counter-insurgency plans have been frequent in the past five years, as have announcements that the border guerrillas had been virtually wiped out. According to a statement by Indonesian Army chief of staff at the beginning of 1976, the "most effective strategy" against the West Kalimantan insurgents would be to segregate them from the surrounding populace (*Indonesian Times*, 2 January). But while the government of Indonesia, like that of Malaysia, has periodically attempted to move border villagers suspected of assisting guerrillas to new, more closely supervised settlements, and to limit guerrilla contact with frontier inhabitants, there is little question that on both sides of the border in West Kalimantan the Communist insurgents continue to find those ready to supply them.

International Aspects. On 18 November 1975, the Indonesian Information Minister announced that the USSR had agreed to provide aid in building two hydroelectric power plants, of 400 to 600 and of 180 megawatt capacity, respectively, and to be located at Saguling, West Java, and Mrica, Central Java (*Indonesia Times*, 19 November 1975). During the previous three years the USSR, through its readiness to renegotiate Indonesia's remaining $450 million debt and discuss new trade and credit programs, had already periodically indicated that the hostile and critical attitude it displayed toward the Suharto regime during the first few years after the 1965 coup attempt was no longer policy. The hydro power agreement was widely seen as a sign that the Soviet-Indonesian "normalization" process was now complete (Dan Coggin, "Indonesia: A Soviet Fund Package," *Far Eastern Economic Review*, 12 December, 1975, p. 48). In mid-May 1976 an Indonesian mission went to Moscow to seek further Soviet assistance, this time in connection with exploitation of bauxite resources on Bintang Island, between Sumatra and Singapore. Radio Moscow, in a comment on the activities of this mission, declared that "there are indications that Soviet-Indonesian relations are improving," evidenced by recent increases in Indonesian rubber exports to the USSR and "the growing export to Indonesia" of Soviet textile machinery and mineral fertilizer (*FBIS*, 24 May). Subsequently new $300 million Soviet credit in order to exploit Bintang's bauxite was made available. An annual production of 600,000 tons was anticipated, of which 150,000 would be shipped to the USSR and the rest to the aluminum smelting plant in Asahan, North Sumatra. (*Neue Zürcher Zeitung*, 17 June.)

These positive developments did not preclude a continuation of earlier Soviet warnings and implied criticism with respect to the Indonesian government's relations with the USA and People's China and in the crisis over Eastern Timor. Radio Moscow charged that "foreign monopoly capital," much of it coming from U.S. investors, was continuing to flood Indonesia, with "very small" benefit to the mass of Indonesians, and that U.S. military aid under President Gerald Ford's "Pacific Doctrine" would not benefit anybody except the Americans, whose objective was to turn Indonesia into a "warmongering anti-Communist bulwark in Southeast Asia" (*FBIS*, 2, 25 June). Radio Moscow in July said that foreign oil companies, in the wake of the Pertamina oil company scandal, allegedly had threatened to curtail or even totally end their investments in Indonesia. The commentary added that Indonesia's problem with the foreign oil companies was part of the larger problem of establishing a more just "new world economic order" in which developing countries would receive a fair return for their resources. (Ibid., 28 July.)

Citing the Indonesian press, Moscow radio commentators have also continued to warn the Suharto government as to any future improvement of its currently suspended relations with People's China, because "the latest facts show that the Maoist leadership continues to interfere in the domestic affairs of its neighbors" and to further "subversive activities" by "numerous pro-Peking elements" (ibid., 10 May). The Soviet reaction to Indonesian intervention in East Timor has been more restrained than that of Peking, generally confining itself to citing the international concern such intervention has aroused, and emphasizing that the USSR supports the position of "all people" to decide their own future without outside interference (ibid., 11 December 1975).

These Soviet criticisms, at this point, seem much less representative of Soviet attitudes toward Indonesia than the assurances of the Soviet ambassador to Djakarta, A. V. Kuznetsov, at the close of February 1976, that while historically Soviet-Indonesian relations have had ups and downs, during the past two years both countries have sought improvements, and that the USSR is ready to hold talks to further the expansion of relations. In 1975, according to Kuznetsov, the USSR imported more than 30,000 tons of rubber, spices, and other commodities from Indonesia and in turn supplied such Soviet goods as automobiles (which have been assembled in Djakarta by a local firm since last year) and equipment for textile factories. (Ibid., 1 March; *Antara Daily News Bulletin*, 3 March, vol. 27, no. 603, p. i.)

Relations with a number of other Communist nations also improved. Plans were implemented for the construction of four electric power projects and the building of a shipyard under the $80 million Yugoslav aid program to Indonesia, agreed to during President Suharto's visit to Yugoslavia in July 1975 (Antara dispatch, Djakarta, 10 July). On 9 April 1976, at the conclusion of the four-day visit by the foreign minister of Mongolia, both countries agreed in a communiqué that: (1) return of peaceful conditions in Indochina greatly improved the political climate in Asia, (2) relations between Asian states should be based on respect for territorial sovereignty, renunciation of force, and mutual cooperation, and (3) a just settlement of the Middle East conflict could only be achieved through the withdrawal of Israeli troops from all Arab territories occupied since the 1967 war (Antara dispatch, Djakarta, 20 April).

In July, a delegation of the newly unified Socialist Republic of Vietnam, headed by deputy foreign minister Phan Hien, visited Djakarta for the general purpose of "laying the foundation of goodwill . . . understanding and cooperation" between the two countries and for extensive discussions on diplomatic questions, and navigation, trade, agricultural development, and industrial affairs (*Antara Daily News Bulletin*, 21 July, vol. 27, no. 717, p. ii). Phan Hien declared upon arrival that he was very pleased to be able to visit a country which had been a "strong fighter against imperialism, colonialism and neo-colonialism" and had helped Vietnam's struggle against imperialism (ibid., p. iii). These friendly sentiments, indeed the visit itself, seemed in marked contrast to the Hanoi media's sharply critical comments on Indonesian policies in recent months, particularly in the context of the Hanoi government's announced hostile position toward ASEAN, the five-member Association of Southeast Asian Nations, of which Indonesia is a leading member. Although Indonesian foreign minister Malik had asserted on 20 May that Hanoi was seeking to become independent of both the USSR and People's China, and that the ASEAN countries should encourage this desire, the government-controlled Indonesian Antara news agency as late as 29 May asserted in a commentary that there was no evidence that Hanoi, "which has the ambition to control the whole of Indochina," would "be friendly towards ASEAN" (ibid., vol. 27, no. 668, p. i; *FBIS*, 1 June).

After Phan Hien's visit, Malik issued a statement welcoming the promise reportedly made by Phan Hien in Djakarta that the Socialist Republic of Vietnam "will not export its revolution to other Southeast Asian countries" (Antara dispatch, Djakarta, 23 July). Hanoi has continued its criticism of Indonesian policies in East Timor, however. An article in Hanoi's daily *Nhan Dan* on 2 June repeated the charge that Indonesia was guilty of armed aggression by its intervention in East Timor (on this intervention see *YICA, 1976*, pp. 297-98), and urged that the East Timor people's "just struggle" for independence be respected (*FBIS*, 2 June). With the parliament's formally passing a law on 15 July annexing East Timor into Indonesian territory, and the signing of the measure by President Suharto two days later, the Djakarta government (already in de facto control over most East Timorese territory since January) completed its carefully phased takeover of the former Portuguese territory, despite condemnation by the United Nations and the opposition of leftist guerrillas still seeking the territory's independence (Justus M. van der Kroef, "The Problem of Portuguese Timor," *Asian Affairs*, November-December 1975, pp. 83-98). While this annexation is likely to lead to continuing periodic verbal attacks from Hanoi, particularly if the leftist nationalist Timorese insurgents are able to persist in their struggle, it would not seem that the East Timor question, in and of itself, would make impossible in the Indonesian case Hanoi's new general policy of officially seeking better relations with its Southeast Asian neighbors while moderately and/or covertly providing assistance to Communist and other rebel guerrilla forces now operating in these countries.

Relations with People's China remained formally suspended, although talk and speculation of an impending normalization continued to be heard. In a television interview in Hong Kong on 23 June (as reported in *Antara Daily News Bulletin*, 1 July, vol. 27, no. 700, p. i) Indonesian foreign minister Malik declared that agreement in principle had already been reached some time ago to normalize diplomatic relations, but that time was still needed to "reeducate" the people in China and Indonesia about the matter. Earlier Malik had expressed appreciation for what he termed China's support of ASEAN and for the concept of Southeast Asian neutralization formulated by ASEAN (Antara dispatch, Djakarta, 22 May 1976).

President Suharto and the Indonesian press meanwhile were a good deal less sanguine. Suharto declared in an interview with the Japan Broadcasting Corporation in March that Indonesia cannot restore relations with China "so long as that country continues to give support to the banned Indonesian Communist Party" (*FBIS*, 24 March). Press editorials reflected continuing official suspicions of Peking's policy intentions among its Asian neighbors, and the view that China is to blame for the current freeze of diplomatic relations (because of its support for the 1965 coup conspirators) also continues to be met with in the Indonesian media (ibid., 14 April).

China, moreover, remains the principal foreign supporter of the Leftist "East Timorese Liberation Front," known as Fretilin, whose delegates abroad have found a sympathetic reception there, as well as in the Socialist Republic of Vietnam. The Peking *People's Daily* and the New China News Agency in the course of 1976, frequently carried reports of ongoing Fretilin resistance against the Indonesian-installed and -backed provisional government in Dili, the capital of East Timor, which by mid-July had succeeded in bringing about the formal annexation of the territory. Fretilin denunciations of Indonesian control over East Timor, carried by the Chinese news media, may be taken as reflecting Peking's official position (ibid., 3 June). During the UN Security Council debate on the question in April, Chinese ambassador Huang Hua declared that Indonesia's alleged defiance of the Security Council's decision last December calling for withdrawal of its forces from East Timor could not be tolerated. The Chinese on 22 April voted for a new resolution that passed the Council, again calling on Indonesia to withdraw and urging all states to respect East Timorese self-determination. But although China supported this resolution, Huang Hua said that it was not altogether satisfactory since it failed to condemn Indonesia explicitly for continuing defiance of the Security Council (*Peking Review*, 30 April, p. 29). In late 1975 the Peking-oriented PKI faction issued a statement over the signature of Jusuf Adjitorop, its principal spokesman, strongly denouncing Indonesian "armed aggression" against the "Democratic Republic of East Timor" which had been proclaimed by Fretilin. Adjitorop's statement was carried in the Chinese media (ibid., 26 December, p. 20).

Since the international criticism of the annexation has also been echoed, if briefly, in the Indonesian press, the Suharto regime has become particularly sensitive to it, and since it appears that China will continue to give some kind of forum for the statements of the ongoing Fretilin resistance movement, a new and significant obstacle to diplomatic normalization may be developing.

The specter of potential Chinese subversion in Indonesia itself continues to be raised. In April 1976 the Indonesian attorney general, Ali Said, reported that the possibility existed of "subversive activities by illegal Chinese immigrants." In February the minister of Justice, Professor Mochter

Kusumaatmaja, had reported that 346 Chinese former residents had been arrested for illegally reentering the country and were under investigation. Already in mid-1975 Said had declared that while official precautions had been stepped up, the "whole people" of Indonesia should take part in the effort to prevent illegal immigration (*Antara Daily News Bulletin*, 12 July 1975, vol. 27, no. 410, p. ii). Demands by various officials that Indonesian Chinese stop self-ghettoizing themselves, accelerate their assimilation, and intermarry with native Indonesians have been common for some time (see, e.g., *Empat Lima*, Djakarta, 10 November 1975; *Indonesian Current Affairs Translation Service Bulletin*, November 1975, p. 865). These exhortations, symptomatic of lingering official suspicions toward the 3 million Chinese minority in Indonesia, in turn afffect relations with People's China.

Publications. The pro-Peking PKI faction's principal publication, *Indonesian Tribune*, appears every two months or so and, like the faction's irregularly appearing four-page youth front paper API (*Api Pemuda Indonesia*—"Fire [or Flame] of Indonesian Youth"), is issued from Tirana, Albania. The "Indonesian Organization for Afro-Asian Solidarity," headquartered in Peking, has been little heard from during the past two years, and its publication, *Suara Rakjat Indonesia*, has appeared only rarely.

The Moscow faction of the PKI seems to rely principally on the Prague-based *Information Bulletin* and *World Marxist Review* for major statements. The Indonesian-language *Tekad Rakjat* ("Will of the People"), edited by PKI émigrés in Moscow, has appeared infrequently during the past three years.

Although in principle Peking remains supportive of the pro-Mao PKI "Delegation," Chinese media now only occasionally carry reports on statements of the "Delegation," compared with their coverage five to ten years ago. At the same time, the clandestine radio transmitter of the Peking-oriented Communist Party of Malaya, the "Voice of the Malayan Revolution," is increasingly being used to disseminate policy statements or congratulatory messages of this faction. In Indonesia itself, officials periodically claim discovery of PKI printed materials, such as mimeographed leaflets, but neither PKI faction now issues any regularly appearing publication.

University of Bridgeport   Justus M. van der Kroef

Japan

The Japan Communist Party (Nihon Kyosanto; JCP), founded in July 1922, operated illegally until the Allied Occupation restored freedom to all political parties in October 1945. The original postwar membership was estimated at less than 1,000. In the first postwar elections, April 1946, the JCP captured five seats in the House of Representatives. The party's parliamentary success of 1949 (35 seats) was surpassed only in 1972 when 40 candidates supporting the JCP were elected. From 1950, when it suffered condemnation by the Cominform and a "red purge" by the Occupation, until 1955, the party was moribund. After reorganization in 1955 the JCP began a steady growth in membership and representation in national and local parliamentary bodies.

Party officials stated that membership was 380,000 in 1976, nearing the goal of 400,000 set for the next Congress to be held in 1977. The party holds 20 seats (out of 252) in the (upper) House of Councillors and 19 (out of 511), in the (lower) House of Representatives, the latter as a result of general elections on 5 December 1976.

Although numerous dissident leftist groups exist, the only ones who claim status as political parties are one pro-Soviet splinter organization, Voice of Japan (Nihon no Koe), with an estimated 400 members, and three pro-Chinese parties: the Japan Communist Party (Left), with an estimated 1,000 members, split into two factions; Japan Labor Party (Nihon Rodo-to), 900; and Japan Workers' Party (Nihon, Rodosa-ha), 400.

The population of Japan in 1976 was estimated at 112,818,000.

After the elections of 1972 and 1974, the JCP became the second opposition party in the national Diet, with a total of 59 seats. In 1976 its strength in Japan's 3,324 prefectural, city, town, and village assemblies amounted to 3,215 out of a total 72,900 seats (*Koan Joho*, July 1976). The party claims that the number of women members (305) in both national and local assemblies is greater than that of any other party—three times that of the Japan Socialist Party (JSP) and seven times that of the governing Liberal Democratic Party (LDP). JCP-supported executives are in office in 200 local administrations (including the governors of Tokyo, Kyoto, Osaka, and six other prefectures) which embrace 47.8 million people, or nearly 43 percent of Japan's total population. (*Report to 13th Extraordinary Congress* by Kaneko Mitsuhiro, *Akahata*, 29 July.)

The JCP has, with some success, cultivated the image of a benign, "democratic" party, abjuring revolution by violence and abandoning the classic communist nomenclature of Marxism-Leninism and of "dictatorship of the proletariat." It has publicly clung to the principle of power through parliamentary means and in 1976 went even further to expand its popular appeal by promulgating a "Manifesto of Freedom and Democracy" which professed to guarantee human rights and freedoms should Japan become a socialist country. The party has erased from its constitution the words "Marxism-Leninism" and "regency" (*shikken*), the word chosen in 1973 to replace "dictatorship" (*dokusai*). Having broken with the Communist parties of both the Soviet Union (1964) and the People's Republic of China (1966), the JCP can effectively claim to be independent and "Japanese." It asserts affinity with West European Communist parties, such as those of France, Italy, and Spain, which have been following similar "democratic" lines. The JCP must contend, however, with an innate suspicion of communism which has long been a characteristic of the Japanese people. In a public opinion poll taken in October 1976, only four percent of the respondents replied that the JCP was the political party of their choice (*Asahi*, Tokyo, 9 October). In a separate poll taken about the same time, 61 percent opposed Japan's becoming a socialist state and ony five percent supported the JCP's brand of socialism (*Sankei*, 8 October).

Organization and Leadership. The affairs of the JCP are directed by a Central Committee of 165 members (122 regular and 43 alternate). In addition there are two honorary members of the Central Committee and nine advisers. The chairman of the Central Committee is Nosaka Sanzo, the "grand old man of the party," now 84 years of age and a member of the House of Councillors. The following personnel changes were made by the 11th plenum of the Central Committee on 31 July 1976: membership in the Presidium, headed by Miyamoto Kenji, effective leader of the party, was increased from 39 to 43 and a new post of deputy chairman was established, to which Fuwa Tetsuzo, chief of the Secretariat, was appointed; three new vice-chairmen of the Presidium were added, making six in all; membership in the Standing Committee of the Presidium, the party's actual control organ, was augmented by three, from 14 to 17. Present members of the Standing Committee of the Presidium are:

Miyamoto Kenji, chairman; Oka Masayoshi, Murakami Hiroshi, vice-chairmen; and Fuwa Tetsuzo, Kurahara Korehito, Matsushima Harushige, Ichikawa Shoichi, Iwabayashi Toranosuke, Kaitani Harumatsu, Kaneko Mitsuhiro, Okamoto Hiroyuki, Suwa Shigeru, and Takahara Shinichi, the latter three newly appointed. Among the most important party organs are the 15-member Secretariat, headed by Fuwa Tetsuzo, the third-ranking party official after Nosaka and Miyamoto, the Control Committee, the Audit Committee, and the Publications Committee. Some 22 other special committees are charged with such varied responsibilities as international affairs, policy, theory, intellectual activities, propaganda, mass movements, education, legal matters, elections, environmental problems, finances and management, united front, advertising, and sports. A special research institute for social and scientific problems is maintained, and a center for "defense of human rights" concerns itself with acts of violence and discrimination against party members. JCP Diet members are organized in each of the parliamentary houses. Local party headquarters can be found in all prefectures, and in many districts and municipalities. Branches (the word "cell" has been abolished) are often formed within factories and other organizations.

Auxiliary and Mass Organizations. The JCP controls or receives the support of some 40 principal national organizations. These include peace movements, cultural societies, professional groups, and international friendship associations, and relate to youth, labor, students, women, businessmen, doctors and nurses, lawyers, consumers, writers, journalists, scientists, athletes, and many other professions and interests. The youth movement receives most attention and is regarded by the JCP as the most important of its affiliates.

The Youth Movement. The Democratic Youth League (Minseido) was organized a year after the JCP (1923) and is regarded as the training school for future leaders of the party. In spite of strenuous efforts at expansion, Minseido's membership remains at approximately 200,000, restricted in principle to youths between the ages of 15 and 25. Its purposes are as defined in the latest JCP publication designed to attract new members as: (1) to protect the livelihood and raise the social position of youth, (2) to improve the health and happiness of youth, (3) to defend and strengthen democracy, and (4) to aim for an independent, peaceful, neutral Japan (*Nihon Kyosanto Shokai* [Introduction to JCP], Tokyo, 1976, pp. 191-92).

Minseido's 14th Congress was held 24-27 March 1976 with 1,000 delegates in attendance. Fuwa Tetsuzo, chairman of the JCP Secretariat, and seven members of the Presidium attended. Delegates were also present from the North Korean Ho Chi Minh Young Workers' Alliance and from communist youth organizations in Vietnam and France. A membership goal of 300,000 was set for the next Congress. Fuwa in his address to the meeting spoke of the crisis of the present age in which the LDP was taking advantage of the disunity in the progressive camp. He identified three goals for Minseido: (1) mobilization against Trotskyism, political indifference, and decadence; (2) expansion of Minseido, but with control over spies and "splitters"; and (3) preparation for elections not only in the 1970s but in the 1980s.

The Congress resolution called for joint efforts with the JSP's Socialist Youth Alliance for a united youth front and placed special emphasis on young workers, said to make up half the youth of the country. It appealed for the activation of youth sections in trade unions, aggressive action in the work place against discrimination by monopoly capitalism, and establishment of Minseido as the "defender of youth." Special attention was given to the fight against decadence, reflecting Miyamoto's call in January for the abolition of pornography, at which time he defined the "four sins" as violence, sex, drugs, and gambling (*Akahata*, 8, 9 January). Much was made of the proposed changes in the party constitution which were being discussed in meetings of the JCP's Central Committee and would be formalized in the party's 13th Extraordinary Congress to be held in July. These changes included the substitution of the term "scientific socialism" for "Marxism-Leninism." Another addition to Minseido regulations was assertion of the right to question, express opinions, and demand answers from the Central Committee. An example had been cited of leaders at Tokyo headquarters who had refused to listen to complaints and suggestions from a member in Aichi Prefecture.

Education was proclaimed indispensable for the young adherents to Minseido, "heir of the JCP." Leaders at the Congress exhorted the rank and file to realize the necessity for erasing the "dark image" of the past which had hindered party expansion, and to pay attention to the new emphasis on the autonomy of workers, freedom of religion, abandonment of outdated terminology, and riddance of pornography.

A meeting of Minseido's Central Committee on 15-16 June reflected the discussions and decisions of the 9th plenum of the party's Central Committe held earlier in the month. Under the slogan "Minseido and the JCP must together save Japan," speakers called for the wiping out of the "three evils" (plutocracy, war criminality, national betrayal) and exhorted the members to expand the youth movement and work for victory in the general elections under the banner of freedom and democracy. A special appeal was made for 30,000 new members in 1976.

Labor. Since the JCP claims that 71 percent of its members are workers, the labor movement receives priority attention. Miyamoto Kenji, in a New Year's interview, said that while 1975 had been a year in which the party had tackled dialogues with religious organizations (the ten-year pact between the JCP and the Buddhist Soka Gakkai—see *YICA, 1976*), during 1976 the JCP would focus on the labor movement as part of its design to "create a consensus" in the country. (*Kanagawa Shimbun*, Yokohama, 3 January). In spite of strenuous efforts, however, the party has not significantly improved its position with labor. Party literature has stressed the importance of aggressive activities in the "work place" to enlist support for the JCP, but has complained that such activities have been hampered by employers' discriminatory practices obstructing the freedom of members to pursue the party's aims.

While the JCP has preponderant influence in certain individual labor unions, it has never been able to make much headway in Japan's largest labor federation, the General Council of Trade Unions (Sohyo), which has some 4.5 million members. (A second labor federation, Domei Kaigi, with a membership of 2.2 million, is supported by the Democratic Socialist Party (DSP)). To increase the labor vote for JCP candidates in elections, the party has persistently sought rejection of the principle of "support for a designated party" which has obligated Sohyo members to vote for the JSP. Annually the JCP submits to the Sohyo congress a resolution to reject this principle and guarantee "freedom of choice" to the Sohyo voter; annually the resolution is turned down. It received fewer votes at the 1976 congress than at any time since 1970.

During 1976 the JCP launched an aggressive campaign against "discrimination in the work place," charging that large companies have subjected JCP members or sympathizers to observation, shadowing, discrimination in status, promotions, and salary, and have harassed and pressured them to renounce affiliation with the JCP. The party newspaper *Akahata* denounced "suppression of liberties by big companies" repeatedly during May and June. One specific allegation was that the Hitachi Company separated four women workers—JCP members—from their co-workers and placed them in a glass-enclosed room where they could be observed. This became known, in JCP parlance, as the "glass cage incident." A special month-long campaign was organized from 20 June to 19 July, during which some 45 articles in *Akahata* took up the subject and "struggle committees" were formed by 1,500 party members in some 80 trade unions. The commentaries emphasized that the protests were a matter of concern for the whole party and should not be left to branches within companies. Workers were invited to write, telephone, or inform in person the "Headquarters for Policy for Defense of Human Rights" which had been established by the Central Committee in 1974.

On 13 July *Akahata*, under the heading "Freedom and Democracy in the Work Place," presented "Ten Articles for Workers' Freedom." Among other items, the articles called for the abolition of all forms of discrimination, oppression, and anti-communist propaganda; for guarantees of the right of assembly during rest periods *without* being photographed or tape-recorded, freedom to distribute party publications, and freedom from inspection of private lockers; and for elimination of the principle of "support for a designated party." Party officials, who had named offending companies (Matsushita, Ishikawajima, Hitachi), announced success in two instances: both Japan Tube Steel (Nihon Kokan) and Mitsubishi Paper Company (Kyoto factory) had redressed grievances and apologized. The JSP organ *Shakai Shimpo* attacked the ten articles, especially the one rejecting the principle of support for a designated party, stating such a proposal confused the goals of trade unions and could only delight the LDP. *Akahata* defended its proposals, as expected. (*Akahata*, 24 July.)

In October, 142 employees of the Tokyo Electric Power Company, all members or supporters of the JCP, filed suits demanding 630 million yen in damages for infringement of human rights and discrimination in wages, work allocation, and welfare measures (*Japan Times*, 15 October).

Sohyo leaders have made strenuous efforts to stop feuding with the Komeito (Clean Government Party) in order to present a joint opposition front against the LDP in the coming elections. Miyamoto Kenji pointed out that Komeito had declared it could not trust the JCP; in mid-October, JCP officials stated a reconciliation depended on moves by the Komeito, while the latter put it the other way. Each side agreed that if there was a move by the other, some form of rapprochement was not impossible. Sohyo's demarche was not likely to bear significant fruit. (Ibid., 22 September; *Asahi*, 15 October.)

The JCP paid particular attention to the 634,000-member Japan Teachers' Union (Nikkyoso), in which it has traditionally exerted substantial influence. The union held its national congress on 1-4 June. In contrast with the year before, the Nikkyoso chairman omitted criticism of the JCP in his principal address. JSP general secretary Narita Tomomi, a special guest, attacked the JCP indirectly by attacking the charge that the principle of "support for a designated party" hampered the unity of the progressive movement. A representative of the JCP responded vigorously and, according to a non-communist account, the "war by proxy" between the JSP and JCP developed sharply over the issues of the united front, strike tactics, the "Dowa problem" (rival policies toward the *burakumin* or outcast communities), and the principle of support for a designated party. The pro-JCP anti-mainstream delegates to this year's Nikkyoso congress were fewer in number than those in attendance the previous year. The "freedom of party choice" resolution won the same number of votes as in 1975, although its percentage of the vote was smaller because total attendance was greater.

Peace Movement. Japan's unique position as the only country to have suffered atomic bombing gives a special character to its peace movement. The Japan Council Against Atomic and Hydrogen Bombs (Gensuikyo), organized in 1955, split in 1963 over the partial nuclear test ban treaty. Three groups have existed since that time, differentiated according to political orientation. Gensuikyo, which claims to be the original body, is supported by the JCP, Gensuikin by the JSP and Sohyo, and Kakkin Kaigi by the DSP and Domei. Continuing efforts have been made to reunite the three groups but without success; in fact, there was little discussion of unity at the 1976 convocations.

Gensuikyo announced its meeting as the "22nd World Congress for the Abolition of Atomic and Hydrogen Weapons" and, as usual, held its principal assembly at Hiroshima (4-6 August), with separate gatherings in Tokyo, (31 July) and Nagasaki (8-9 August). A local committee sponsored a rally in Okinawa. Attendance this year was smaller in both Hiroshima (7,000) and Nagasaki (3,700) than in 1975. JCP's delegation to the Gensuikyo meetings was Kaneko Mitsuhiro, member of the Standing Committee of the Presidium.

Gensuikyo is now emphasizing its "international" character and has sponsored a group of seven Japanese professors of international law to prepare a draft international treaty for a total ban on the use of nuclear weapons. The draft treaty was to be submitted to all nations and in special appeals to the United Nations and to the Conference of Non-aligned Nations. It was announced that 65 foreigners from 19 countries (13 from the USA) and representatives from eight international organizations attended the congress (*Akahata*, 2 August). At a press conference, the sponsors announced the receipt of congratulatory telegrams from seven members of the U.S. Congress—Senators McGovern, Gravel, Abourezk, Cranston, Clark, and Mathias, and Representative Abzug. Messages were also sent by the presidents of Iraq, Cuba, Yugoslavia, and Laos and the prime ministers of Vietnam and Mauritius. (Ibid., 3 August.)

In consonance with Gensuikyo's decision to take the ban-the-bomb movement to the UN, a delegation of 39 pacifists, including representatives of Gensuikyo, left on 9 October to meet with the UN Secretary General, staff members of appropriate UN committees, and representatives of non-aligned countries, and to join American and Japanese pacifists on a transcontinental trek across the USA to publicize disarmament (*Asahi Evening News*, Tokyo, 6 October).

The JSP-supported Gensuikin held mass meetings in Hiroshima (5-6 August), Nagasaki (7-8 August), and Okinawa (16-19 August) with estimated attendance of 7,000 in Hiroshima, 6,000 in Nagasaki, and 900 in Okinawa. The much smaller DSP-oriented Kakkin Kaigi drew only 200 in Hiroshima and 800 in Nagasaki.

Although no progress has been made toward unity in the ban-the-bomb movement, leaders of Sohyo are particularly anxious to pursue the question, believing that a thaw is possible, since all groups favor unity in principle (*Koan Joho*, August).

Other JCP-affiliated Organizations. The estimated membership of other important organizations supported by the JCP are as follows: All Japan Students Federation (Zengakuren-JCP wing), 520,000; New Japan Women's Association (Shin Fujin), 160,000; All Japan Merchants Federation (Zenshoren), 331,000; Democratic Federation of Doctors (Min-i-ren), 240,000; Japan Council of Scientists (10,000); and Japan Peace Committee (Nihon Heiwa Iin Kai), 14,000 (*Koan Joho*, July).

Party Affairs. In 1976 the JCP leadership emphasized party growth and preparation for elections (held 5 December) to the House of Representatives. Although party spokesmen continually referred to 380,000 members, non-communist observers believe that the number of active ones is much smaller. Many among the total have not paid dues for six months or more and have failed to participate in party activities. According to party rules, these inactive members—estimated to be as numerous as 60,000—should be expelled. Party practice has been, however, to retain them on the rolls and endeavor to win them back to active status. The total circulation of the party organ *Akahata* (combined daily and Sunday) is usually put at 2.8 or "about 3 million" in public statements by party officers; actual circulation is believed to be less. Difficulties have been encountered in distribution (*Akahata* is delivered house-to-house by party members) and in efforts to make the newspaper competitive with Japan's metropolitan dailies. Circulation increases at the time of party congresses and special campaigns but falls thereafter. As of the end of 1976, circulation may in actuality reach approximately 2.2 million.

In the fiscal year ending 31 March 1976 the JCP received and disbursed more funds than any other Japanese political party. According to JCP figures, total revenues amounted to 11.9 billion yen (approximately $41 million), with 93.4 percent from publications and 5.8 percent from party dues, and disbursements were 11.7 billion yen ($40 million), leaving a surplus of 221 million yen ($762 thousand). The nearest in revenues to the JCP was the LDP, with total receipts in the same period of 11.4 billion yen ($39 million). (*Shinten Tokuho*, Tokyo, 20 August.)

The Central Committee held more than the usual number of meetings during 1976, six by November. This activity denoted major decisions to institute an "image change" and to mobilize total party resources in a crucial election year.

Central Committee Meetings. On 11-12 May the Central Committee of the JCP held its 8th plenum (numbered from the party Congress of November 1973) and, after hearing reports from Miyamoto Kenji and Fuwa Tetsuzo, passed a resolution convening an extraordinary party congress for the latter part of July. The next regular congress was postponed until 1977, to precede the scheduled House of Councillors elections. The rationale of the 8th plenum was to prepare the party for the extraordinary congress, the first to be held since the end of World War II, and for the general elections required before the end of the year.

The principal issues discussed in the speeches and in the resolution were the status of the "united front," projected changes of wording in the party constitution, and party expansion on the eve of elections. Miyamoto shattered the concept of a united front embracing the JSP, Komeito, and JCP, which had been advocated by the general secretary of the General Council of Trade Unions, but approved continuing cooperation and consultation with the JSP on differing policy-making levels. He welcomed the shift in the JSP's position from support of a united front of all *opposition* parties to one of all *progressive* parties. Reserving his most bitter language for the Democratic Socialist Party, Miyamoto referred to it as a "second LDP," "the LDP's Fifth Column," and "LDP's 'Kasuga faction' " (Kasuga is general secretary of the DSP). He avowed that the Komeito was *not* a progressive party.

Both Miyamoto and Fuwa spent much time in explaining the need further to revise the classic Communist expression "dictatorship of the proletariat." The previous party congress substituted the word "regency" for "dictatorship," but the party leaders had now concluded that even "regency" would confuse the public and incite anti-Communist elements. Furthermore, a modern party should not be saddled with the term "Marxism-Leninism" when what was truly meant was "scientific socialism." Miyamoto asserted that the distinguished service of Marx, Engels, and Lenin was ineradicable but that scientific socialism in the present day lies not only within the writings of these three men but has become enriched through later experience and teachings. He concluded that the party must study whether the use of the term "Marxism-Leninism" was not too simple a way to describe scientific socialism. Fuwa had published in *Akahata* an 11-part essay entitled "Scientific Socialism and the Regency Question: A Study of Marx and Engels," running from 27 April through 8 May. In the course of this lengthy treatise, Fuwa stated that even in a future socialist Japan, the JCP envisaged a democratic political system, including freedom for more than one party. He called it an error to term such a system inseparable from violent revolution.

Miyamoto then discussed "freedom and democracy," emphasizing the party's support of the "three freedoms": existence, civil liberties, and nationality. He denied that such a policy was concocted merely as a defense against anti-Communist attacks. "The JCP is the battleground for the fight for the freedoms and rights of the great majority of the people." (*Akahata*, 13 May.)

In his report to the Committee, Fuwa boasted that membership in party supporters' associations had increased more than 500,000 and that party membership at that time had reached 370,000. *Akahata* subscriptions had not increased, however, due to distribution and collection problems. Future tasks for the party were to increase membership by at least 10 percent, prevent a decrease in the circulation of *Akahata*, and prepare assiduously for the extraordinary party congress and the coming election campaign. (*Akahata*, 18 May.)

Only two weeks later, the 9th plenum of the Central Committee was held on 2 June, with the object of preparing for the extraordinary party congress, set for 28-30 July. Besides the main Resolution, two other proposals were passed unanimously for submission for final approval to the Congress: concerning (1) partial revision of the constitution and regulations, and (2) the Manifesto on Freedom and Democracy. In addition, an "Appeal" outlined the "urgent duties and tasks for the coming extraordinary party congress."

Miyamoto in his "greetings" laid stress on the intra-party crisis of the LDP and called for a settlement of the "Lockheed scandal" (see below, "Domestic Attitudes and Activities") before an overthrow of the Miki Cabinet and dissolution of the Diet. He castigated the LDP for its "three political evils": plutocracy, war criminality, and national betrayal. He avoided criticism of the JSP but admitted that the absence of a united front had precluded progressive politics from taking advantage of the internal crisis within the LDP; furthermore the number of voters refusing to support any political party had increased. Miyamoto announced that the JCP was now in the "home stretch" before the general elections and had created a special campaign headquarters with Fuwa Tetsuzo as its director.

The immediate objective of the main resolution to be presented to the extraordinary congress was the general election. It repeated previous statements that the only way out of the Japanese crisis was the establishment of a united front and a democratic coalition government, but clearly confined "joint struggles" to those with the JSP. The coming election would be a "great political battle," with a confrontation between the JCP and Komeito for the place of second opposition party after the JSP. Party members were enjoined not to underestimate the force of anti-Communist attacks and to respond vigorously. They were urged to work untiringly for increased party membership (each party member should recruit one new one) and expanded readership of *Akahata* and other party publications.

The more controversial resolutions concerned changes in the party constitution and regulations and the Manifesto on Freedom and Democracy. The former proposed to substitute "national power" (*kokka kenryoku*) for "regency" (*shikken*), and to replace "Marxism-Leninism" by "scientific socialism."

The Manifesto on Freedom and Democracy had been germinating for some time. As early as 2 June 1974, Miyamoto, in a speech at Sapporo, had brought forth the "three freedoms." He discussed these and the "regency" question in a press conference on 26 March 1976, in a television interview on 6 April, and in a joint press conference with Georges Marchais, the secretary general of the French Communist Party, on 10 April. The Manifesto, when published in *Akahata* on 3 June, drew national and international attention. It specified what appeared to be, for a Communist party, a remarkable series of policies. The document promised support for a multiparty system, with changes of government dependent on elections; called for continuing and strengthening the principle of separation of powers; and affirmed guarantees of human rights, freedoms of speech, press, reporting, assembly, thought, belief, conscience, scholarship, research, travel, and change of domicile. The Manifesto also pledged respect for the rights of women and called for the wiping out of discrimination against the burakumin (former outlawed class) and the Ainu (indigenous tribes in Hokkaido). Other guaranteed freedoms would be liberty to leave the country, freedom of choice of nationality, and freedoms of taste, hobbies, dress, fashion, and sports. The Manifesto cited limitations on national freedom which should be removed: the U.S.-Japan military alliance based on the San Francisco peace treaty and the mutual security pact, the U.S.-Japan mutual security aid agreement, and the economic dependence of Japan upon the United States. The Manifesto further decreed that in a socialist Japan, nationalization would be confined to key industries, and ownership of private property and housing by individuals would be guaranteed.

Predictably, non-Communist press comment on the "freedom declaration" was adverse. The *Mainichi* on 4 June editorialized that many people would see the JCP as a "wolf in sheep's clothing," noting that "existing socialist nations contain too many features which make it impossible to eliminate the image of dictatorship." *Sankei* on the same day wrote that unless the JCP changed its party name, the freedoms mentioned in the declaration remain only "manufactured" freedoms, and that the "high declaration stems only from the JCP's 'strategy and tactics' to approach political power." *Asahi*, also on 4 June, opined that the JCP has a sense of crisis and intends to use the declaration as a powerful prop to win more votes in the coming elections. Pointing out that parliamentary democracy had set down roots in Japan, a highly developed capitalist country, the editorial continued: "The Communist

Party has probably started to think that unless it uses the 'freedom' desired by the people as the foundation, it cannot formulate a revolutionary strategy. This change is worth noting, but there still remain doubts."

In the document "Urgent Duties and Tasks for the Coming Extraordinary Party Congress," the 9th plenum urged that every party member participate in discussions of the draft resolutions and further the solidarity and advancement of the party. The same admonishments for party expansion expressed at the 8th plenum of the Central Committee were repeated.

Between the 9th plenum and the 13th Extraordinary Party Coingress, the JCP attempted to promote the image of an "open party" by encouraging discussion of the documents presented at the plenum. Comments reportedly received from members throughout the country were published in a series called "Party Reports." The first, appearing on 14 July, contained a total of 51 letters, the majority of which opposed the proposed changes in the party line. The new revisions were criticized for undercutting the teachings of Marxist-Leninist literature, long instilled in the minds of party members. A second report, 19 July, contained 40 letters, all favorable, and incuded rebuttals by party leaders of the previous critical comments. Succeeding reports contained no dissents and were devoted overwhelmingly to defense of the new proposals. Japanese government internal security officials believe that the criticisms in the first report actually represented large segments of the party, although Miyamoto in a press conference disparaged the dissenting views as originating with young student party members with a "half-baked" understanding of party publications and declared that only "some tens" of critical letters had been received. Some observers believe that there is considerable confusion, anxiety, and lack of confidence in the party leadership among the members, indicative of a serious split over the "Miyamoto line."

In response to internal disagreements and to the storm of adverse comment in the mass media, the JCP mounted an aggressive campaign to meet the attacks. Fuwa and his brother, Ueda Koichiro, wrote defensive theses in the August issues of *Bunka Hyoron* and *Zenei* respectively. Many of the JCP critics were former party members or orthodox Marxism-Leninists who found the "new" JCP "revisionist." To meet this challenge, JCP leaders found it necessary to repeat endlessly that "the fundamental line of the party has not changed." Fuwa insisted that the term "scientific socialism" embraces all of the teachings of Marx, Engels, and Lenin, and that, therefore, the party had not changed in character or policy. The contradiction between this statement and the galaxy of freedoms promised in the documents presented at the 9th Central Committee plenum has not been lost on non-communist observers. (*Koan Joho*, August.)

At the 10th plenum, 25 July, just before the meeting of the extraordinary party congress, the proposals of the 9th plenum, presumably revised after wide discussion among the party members, were approved unanimously by the Central Committee for presentation to the congress.

The principal purpose of the 11th plenum, 31 July, the day following the close of the extraordinary congress, was to confirm certain personnel changes. Fuwa Tetsuzo, in addition to his responsibility as chief of the Secretariat, was appointed to a newly established post, deputy chairman of the Presidium. This action confirmed his position as second to Miyamoto in the party leadership. Three additional vice-chairmen of the Presidium were named and the Standing Committee of the Presidium was enlarged by three. Thus the Presidium, with a membership of 42, now has a deputy chairman and six vice-chairmen; the Standing Committee consists of 17 members.

A one-day plenum of the Central Committee on 22 October adopted a platform for the forthcoming elections. The principal points called for a cleanup of politics following the Lockheed scandals, "democratization" of the economy, opposition to LDP-advocated reforms in the Japanese electoral system and "detrimental" (in JCP eyes) revision of the national constitution, improvement of morals and culture, abolition of the U.S.-Japan security treaty, opposition to increases in the Self Defense

Forces, and establishment of a democratic coalition government. The purpose was again to instill zeal into the party membership for the election campaign.

The 13th Extraordinary Party Congress. The principal purposes in convening an extraordinary party congress were to push for victory in the general elections, make certain revisions in the party's program and constitution, and present the Manifesto on Freedom and Democracy—probably the most controversial and most widely discussed JCP document in recent history. The congress lasted three days, 28-30 July, and was attended by 1,127 delegates. It approved unanimously documents which had been presented to both the 9th and 10th sessions of the Central Committee, discussed above.

The Extraordinary Congress (the first such in 53 years, according to party statements) met in an atmosphere of near panic over the future political status of the party. Not only had the JCP lost some seats in mid-term local elections but it had been badgered by the revival of a 1933 scandal involving the chairman of the Presidium, Miyamoto Kenji (see below, "Domestic Attitudes and Activities"). The "democratic coalition government" so loudly proclaimed over the last few years, had become an impossible dream. The so-called united front had been reduced to a shaky collaboration on certain issues and in certain elections by the JCP and JSP, and relations with the two other opposition parties, the Komeito and DSP, had deteriorated from friction to enmity. The party had tried to make much of the Lockheed scandals, which temporarily diverted public attention from the "lynch incident" involving Miyamoto, but could only with difficulty claim special merit among other opposition parties who likewise pursued the government to clear up the Lockheed affair definitively.

Miyamoto, in his "greetings" to the Congress, tried to implicate the DSP, the Eda faction of the JSP, and the Komeito in the Lockheed scandals by charging that they had accepted money from monopoly capitalists and thereby disqualified themselves from protesting LDP financial entanglements. "These parties," said Miyamoto, "talk of an alliance of 'clean progressive forces' but only help the LDP by becoming a 'second LDP'."

On the united front, Miyamoto could say only that, since the DSP regarded the JCP as "the enemy," the Komeito called the JCP "dangerous" and the JSP's Eda faction was "anti-Communist," all the JCP could do was try to combat this threatening "anti-Communism." Furthermore, he could not ignore the fact that the JSP constitution still contained a phrase which advocated the "overcoming of Communism." He admitted that the 1975 Soka Gakkai-JCP pact was stagnant. On the defensive against charges of isolation, he touted the JCP's close relations with the Communist parties of Italy, France, and Spain.

Miyamoto reminded the membership that JCP votes in elections to the lower house had jumped by five times between 1960 and 1972 and by four times in upper elections in 1962-74. He went on, however, to cite the anti-Communist attacks which had developed after the JCP's spectacular rise and warned against complacency or underestimation of the force of these attacks.

Obviously sensitive to the charge that democracy did not exist within the party, Miyamoto described the submission to open party discussion of the proposed changes in the constitution and by-laws. This action was evidence that "we respect the right of small minorities." Members were naturally guaranteed the right to varying opinions on various subjects, but when discussion had been exhausted, he said the "objective truth is one," and it was from this premise that unanimity of opinion on important questions followed.

The Congress resolution propounded the slogans "National Salvation and Progressive Change" and "Save Japan together with the JCP," and proclaimed as a major task of the party the elimination of the "three evils": plutocracy, war criminality, and national betrayal. The text of the resoution did not differ essentially from the one approved by the 9th plenum, described above.

Kaneko Mitsuhiro, member of the Standing Committee of the Presidium, presented a report on the resolution which went into more detail about the party's policies and programs. Repeating

Miyamoto's attacks on the DSP and Komeito, Kaneko was less charitable than the resolution toward the JSP. He noted that the agreement of 8 April between Miyamoto and Narita of the JSP "has not been realized due to the anti-Communist current existing in the Socialist Party." Kaneko argued that the JCP must work for a "possible united front and must strengthen its driving force for a united front."

The text of the controversial revisions reiterated that the elimination of the terms "regency" and "Marxism-Leninism" represented no fundamental change in the party's line but rather its "progressive development." The term *shikken* (regency) did not express the essence of scientific socialism, which is concerned, rather, with the obtaining of political power by the working classes. The resolution argued that the party program had never tied the concept of a "proletarian regency" to "revolution by force": it demanded a democratic process through a stable parliamentary majority which would guarantee human rights. "In a future Japan there will be no discrimination in political rights along class lines; political rights of cpaitalists will not be restricted because they are capitalists; all people of whatever class to which they belong will be extended equal rights as sovereign citizens. The character of people's power is power for the majority in a society."

The Extraordinary Congress approved unanimously all the resolutions and reports that were presented.

Domestic Attitudes and Activities. During 1976 two "incidents" produced strong repercussions within the JCP, placing the party on the defensive in one case and on the offensive in the other. These were the revival of the 1933 "spy lynch case" implicating Chairman Miyamoto in murder charges and the "Lockheed scandal" arising out of congressional testimony in the USA regarding the payment of bribes by the Lockheed Corporation to Japanese industrialists and politicians.

Although the murder case was well known and had been frequently aired by journalists and denied by the JCP (*Akahata*, 9 March, 15 April 1972), its introduction into proceedings of the House of Representatives by Kasuga Ikko, secretary-general of the DSP on 27 January 1976 put the case in a new perspective. Kasuga's statement was inspired by a long article in the January issue of *Bungei Shunju*, a leading monthly magazine, by the journalist who had won fame by exposing the financial machinations of former prime minister Tanaka Kakuei, leading to the latter's resignation in December 1974.

The outline of the "spy" incident was as follows: Miyamoto was arrested on 26 December 1933 on the charge of murdering a member of the JCP Central Committee who wa under interrogation by the committee as a suspected government spy. Hakamada Satomi, a member of the present Standing Committee of the Presidium, was later arrested on the same charge. Reflecting the glacier-like movement of Japanese justice, Miyamoto's sentence to life imprisonment was handed down only on 5 December 1944, to be sustained by a higher court in May 1945. Hakamada was sentenced to 13 years' imprisonment in December 1942. Both had been under detention since the time of their arrests. Although Miyamoto was not a political prisoner, since he had been convicted of a crime, he was permitted to leave Abashiri prison in Hokkaido on 9 October 1945 at the time all political prisoners were freed under the civil rights directive issued by General Douglas MacArthur on 4 October. A forged medical certificate allegedly was presented to the court in Hokkaido to facilitate Miyamoto's release. As convicted criminals, Miyamoto and Hakamada had lost their civil rights; they appealed for restoration of these rights in both 1946 and 1947. The Justice Ministry requested an opinion from MacArthur's headquarters and, after discussions within the appropriate sections of GHQ, approval was given. The Justice Ministry by special decree restored civil rights to both men on 29 May 1947.

Kasuga's point was that both Miyamoto's release and the restoration of rights were illegal since he was not a political prisoner but a convicted criminal. He asserted that Miyamoto, under a legal sentence to life imprisonment, was not fit to head a recognized political party and should resign forthwith. The case became a "cause célèbre," received columns of attention in the daily press, and was the subject of numerous press conferences by JCP leaders and pages of commentary in *Akahata*. The JCP position was that the victim and an accomplice were clearly government spies, that the former's death was due to heart failure during the interrogation (he may have banged his head against the wall during an attempt to escape), and that Miyamoto had applied artificial respiration but without success. *Akahata* contended that Miyamoto's trial and conviction were carried out under abusive prewar laws removed from the statute books by the Occupation. His release and restoration of rights were legal acts and the case therefore was long since closed. ("Attempts to Distort Relationship between Release of Political Criminals and Restoration of Rights—Careless Sticking to Sense of Old Constitution," *Akahata*, 25, 26, and 27 January 1976.)

After prolonged discussions in the Diet, massive press play, and investigation by the Justice Ministry, including searches of GHQ records, the government on 28 September published its official view, namely, that the judgment against Miyamoto was valid, that his recovery of rights was directed by Allied Headquarters ("Miyamoto was really saved by the Allied Forces") and was therefore of a "supra-legal and supra-constitutional" nature, and that the right of the Diet to investigate national administration, including trials and court judgments, was not in violation of the constitution (*Mainichi*, 29 September).

Both the LDP and the DSP set up special committees to investigate the "spy incident." The other opposition parties, the JSP and the Komeito, took somewhat equivocal attitudes. Both deplored the fact that joint struggles among the opposition parties were no longer possible. The JSP agreed that facts had to be investigated but regretted that the case was distracting the Diet from consideration of more urgent matters.

The public reminders of the "black past" of the JCP undoubtedly inspired the party to greater efforts to present itself as a champion of freedom and democracy. Consequently, the emphasis on "image change" was greatly intensified in JCP publicity surrounding what it called the "spy provocation incident."

If Miyamoto had been "saved" by GHQ, so the JCP was to a degree "saved" by the revelations made before the U.S. Senate's subcommittee on multinational corporations on 4 February. The "Lockheed incident" quickly superceded the so-called "lynch incident" in its attraction for the media. The allegations that more than $12 million had been paid to high-ranking government officials and industrialists by Lockheed officials brought the JCP immediately to the attack. Following up its previous charges against the LDP for its "money politics," the party decided at once to send JCP Diet members to conduct investigations in Washington. On 10 February two JCP members of the upper and lower houses respectively traveled to the USA, the first JCP Diet men to receive U.S. visas. They interviewed U.S. government officials and representatives of Lockheed, including a company vice-president who had become a key figure in the controversy, and sent back a stream of reports prominently played up in *Akahata*.

The Lockheed incident occupied the attention of the media and the politicians throughout the year. The JCP accused the governments of both countries of trying to cover up the scandal by withholding vital evidence. In March the JCP sent another emissary to Washington to request the publication of all documents. The opposition parties brought all business of the Diet to a halt from 8 to 28 March. *Akahata* charged the CIA with having recruited Kodama Yoshio, one of the most notorious figures allegedly involved in Lockheed payoffs and claimed that the CIA had funneled funds to prominent LDP politicians for many years. By April the JSP, Komeito, and JCP unitedly demanded new negotiations between the two governments. On 11 April *Akahata* published a list of 28 former and present high government officials whom they accused of involvement in the Lockheed scandal. These included former prime ministers Kishi, Sato, and Tanaka, finance minister Ohira, and LDP secretary-general Nakasone. As a result the LDP filed suit against *Akahata*. The JCP constantly claimed to be the only "clean" party in the Japanese political spectrum.

Meanwhile the Tokyo Public Prosecutor's Office had set up a special investigation office and assigned 105 persons, including prosecutors and administrative officials, to look into the case. By October, 18 persons had been arrested: executives of Marubeni Trading Corporation and All Nippon Airways, and government officials, including three Diet members, one of whom was former prime minister Tanaka Kakuei. The JCP put the Lockheed case high on its list of issues which featured the campaign for the December elections to the House of Representatives.

Relations with Other Parties. Except for a well-publicized and, as *Akahata* called it, "historic" meeting between the JCP and JSP leaders on 8 April, there were few signs of agreement between the JCP and any of the three other opposition parties. In spite of the ten-year pact signed in 1975 between Miyamoto and Ikeda Daisuke, president of the Soka Gakkai and founder of the Komeito, relations between the JCP and the "Clean Government" party reached new lows. Even worse, in Communist eyes, was the DSP, which had revived the "spy incident" and which was termed by JCP spokesmen a "faction of the LDP." In January, Miyamoto characterized the Komeito and DSP as "Trojan horses" and "reinforcement units to prop up the conservative party line at a time when the strength of the LDP was in decline" (*Kanagawa Shimbun*, 3 January).

At their meeting in April, Miyamoto and Narita Tomomi of the JSP proclaimed joint support of a united front and determination to pursue to the end in coordination the investigation, exposure, and punishment of those guilty of implication in the Lockheed scandals (*Akahata*, 9 April). Miyamoto shortly afterward appealed for joint action by the JSP and JCP. However, in actuality, cooperation developed in words rather than action. Miyamoto himself stated in July that the JSP displayed slogans calling for joint struggles but had been in no position to promote a united front in real earnest (*Kanagawa Shimbun*, 14 July). The JCP continued to espouse a "united front of all opposition parties" which was obviously impossible in view of the mutual antagonism between the JCP and the Komeito and DSP, whose top leaders had been accused by the JCP of having taken bribes from large enterprises. In an attempt to prove itself the only "clean" party in the Japanese political arena, the JCP succeeded only in isolating itself. Failure even to join with the JSP in supporting candidates for local by-elections drew denunciation from "progressive" sympathizers (letter to the editor, *Asahi Evening News*, 12 October). As the elections approached, it became clear that, except for isolated instances, no coalition of significance which would include the JCP would develop. What chances remained for united action among opposition parties would be confined to cooperation among the JSP, Komeito, and, possibly, the DSP.

During the fall, confrontation between the JCP and the Komeito was intensified by the fact that both expected to be fighting for second place among opposition parties, a position lost by the Komeito to the JCP in 1972. The rivalry between the two thus became increasingly bitter. On 28 September, Komeito secretary-general Yano Junya took up in the Diet the famous "spy incident" which the DSP had introduced in January. During the Diet deliberations a JCP member called Yano an "anti-Communist dog," which, with other provocations, caused the Komeito to file two libel suits against the JCP. The latter, fearful of stagnation in party membership and electoral strength, staged an increasingly vituperative struggle to besmirch the Komeito and the DSP in order to gain additional Diet seats and retain its number two position in the opposition ranks. Consequently, even if the LDP were to lose its absolute majority in the House of Representatives, the opposition was in no position to unite to form an alternative government.

At the same time, in a contradictory propaganda move designed to take advantage of the internal troubles then besieging the LDP, the JCP proposed in September that a coalition government should be formed to include "all reformist forces, including dissidents of the LDP." The *Japan Times* (9 September) called this step "particularly noteworthy" as an indication of the "soft line" which the JCP had been attempting to promote in order to broaden its popular appeal.

International Views and Policies. While the JCP continued to condemn American imperialism and to express hostility toward the Communist parties of both the Soviet Union and the People's Republic of China, the thrust of its international concerns in 1976 was concentrated on a growing affinity with the so-called "democratic" Communist parties of Western Europe. Visits to Japan by the secretaries-general of the Spanish and French parties in March and April were greeted with fanfare and unusually wide publicity not only in *Akahata* but in Japan's general mass media. Renunciaton by the Spanish and French parties of the phrase "dictatorship of the proletariat" strengthened Miyamoto's campaign to alter further the vocabulary of the JCP, which was officially done at the extraordinary congress in July. Commentators in the non-Communist press debated vigorously whether the "new Communism" being propagated by Western Europe parties and by the JCP represented in reality a fundamental change in principles and policy or was merely a tactical move to win popular support in highly industrialized, capitalist countries. The parties' pronouncements emphasized independence and a moving away from Soviet influence.

For example, Spanish secretary-general Santiago Carrillo, during his visit on 27-31 March, spoke thus to his Japanese comrades: "Marxism-Leninism is not a dogma, not a religious sect. . . . Scientific socialism is incompatible with unchanging commandments and worn-out incantations, which some people are eagerly trying to force on us. The Japanese and Spanish Communist parties are fighting for a socialist society in which there will be a plural number of democratic political parties and which will completely respect freedom, including the freedom of religion and human rights in the same way as the members of the Italian, French, British, and other Communist parties. (applause)." (*Akahata*, 1 April.) The joint statement signed by Miyamoto and Georges Marchais, secretary-general of the French party, who visited Japan on 4-10 April, contained this passage: "The JCP and the PCF once again confirm their intention of guaranteeing and expanding freedom and human rights, of respecting the outcomes of universal elections, of respecting the system of plural political parties and the guaranteeing of continuing development of democracy, whether at the stage of democratic reforms or at the stage of socialism. Neither party will recognize the forcing of any special ideology by the state or the banning of any ideology or religion by the state. They will cope with ideology by ideology and they will receive the support of a wide range of people." (*Akahata*, 11 April.)

The non-Communist press welcomed the statements by the Western European and Japanese Communist leaders as indicating a new principle for non-ruling Communist parties, but professed skepticism that words would be translated into action. The "new image" could not but help JCP candidates to win votes in the forthcoming elections, but the traditional wariness of the Japanese people toward anything "Communistic" could not easily be swept away. The *Mainichii* (13 April) editorialized: "In the end, the problem for the Communist Party is how to answer faithfully the doubts deep-rooted in the minds of the people, and win the hearts of the people by practical activities. . . . The people are watching what the Communist Party is thinking and what it will do, at this time when both the ruling and opposition parties are faced with the serious necessity of studying the way to be followed by the system of parliamentary democracy."

Recognizing solidarity with the Italian Communist Party, the JCP, after the June elections in Italy, issued a statement hailing the result as of "important international significance, even for the advance of reformism in other developed capitalist countries." Nishizawa Tomio, author of the statement, noted that, as in Japan, the Italian ruling class had propagated the slogan of anti-Communism in order to scare the electorate into believing that Communist participation in national administration meant dictatorship. Nishizawa concluded: "The results of the election showed the collapse of anti-Communist middle-of-the-roadism and advance by the Italian Communist Party." (*Nihon Keizai*, 22 June.)

In July, following the meeting of representatives of seven industrialized nations in Puerto Rico, and statements by Western leaders expressing dismay over the possibility of Communist participation in the Italian government, the JCP sounded an alarm over "four-power intervention" (U.S., U.K.,

French, and West German) in the internal political affairs of another country. Announcements emanated from Bonn and Washington to the effect that loans and aid might be withheld from the Italian government should Communists enter the Cabinet. An *Akahata* editorial (23 July) called such "intervention" a blatant attack on the right of self-determination of another people, a challenge to parliamentary democracy based on the will of the people expressed in open elections, and a crisis for all peoples looking for a democratic road to the future.

Relations with the Chinese Communist Party. There was no apparent improvement during the year in the relations of the JCP and the Chinese party. The latter continued to recognize splinter parties which had broken from the JCP as the "true" representatives of Japanese Communism. Miyamoto had at the end of 1975 denounced the proposed peace and friendship treaty which was being sporadically negotiated between Japan and China because of Chinese insistence on the inclusion of a "hegemony" clause. This would have pledged the two governments to oppose hegemony by any other nation but was interpreted by the JCP as a hostile reference to the USSR. Miyamoto stated that the incorporation of such a clause, making opposition to the USSR obligatory and regarding it as the world's greatest enemy, would restrict the autonomous nature of Japanese diplomacy. "We will oppose it," he announced. (*Akahata*, 24 December.)

At the time of the death of Premier Chou En-lai, the JCP contented itself with an oral statement by the chief of its Information Division which, while expressing condolences over the death of "an individual, especially of a politician who belonged to the international communist movement," mentioned that since 1966 Chou En-lai had played an important role in the Chinese policy of intervention in the affairs of the JCP (*Mainichi*, 9 January).

When Chairman Mao Tse-tung died, *Akahata* gave front-page space to a statement by JCP Central Committee chairman Nosaka Sanzo, who had associated closely with Mao during the war years in Yenan from 1940 to 1945. Nosaka pointed out that the history of friendship and solidarity between the Japanese and Chinese parties was much longer than the period of present temporary abnormal relations. Nosaka expressed the hope that the present unfriendly relations between the parties caused by Chinese "big-powerist interference" could be improved in the future. (*Akahata*, 10 September.)

Relations with the Communist Party of the Soviet Union. Relations between the CPSU and the JCP remained unchanged in 1976, although there were signs that each might like to restore formal relations with the other. The Soviet party dispatched a delegation to Japan in early February to seek reconciliation and to invite the JCP to send representatives to its 25th Congress. The stumbling block to normalization of relations between the two parties is still the encouragement and support given by the CPSU to the splinter party, Voice of Japan, led by Shiga Yoshio, who was expelled from the JCP in 1964. Although talks were held for three days, 4-6 February, no progress was made and the JCP Central Committee rejected an invitation to send a delegate to the CPSU congress. Instead a congratulatory message, published in *Pravda* on 6 March, expressed the hope that obstacles impeding normalization could be overcome and party relations reestablished on a positive basis.

Although the CPSU was not invited to be represented at the JCP's 13th Extraordinary Congress in July, the meeting was given extensive coverage in the Soviet press and cabled congratulations conveyed "solidarity with the struggle of the JCP members who . . . are striving to create a Japan founded on peace, democracy and social progress" (Moscow radio, in Japanese, 28 July). Full details of the discussions and decisions of the Congress were published in *Pravda* (31 July), written by the newspaper's Tokyo correspondent.

The landing in September of a Soviet MIG-25 fighter plane in Hokkaido and the application of its pilot for asylum led the JCP to criticize the actions of the Japanese government in allowing examination of the plane, particularly by U.S. specialists. The Moscow press immediately picked up and made prominent use of *Akahata*'s statements, particularly its assertion that the Japanese government, by its actions in regard to the plane, was "directly being drawn into the system of U.S. military strategy" (TASS, 16 September).

In late November the JCP announced that Nishizawa Tomio, member of the Presidium, would proceed to Moscow following his attendance at the congress of the Vietnam Labor Party in Hanoi in December, and probe with officers of the CPSU the possibilities of normalizing relations between the JCP and the CPSU. It was hoped that, if all went well, reconciliation between the two parties could be effected in 1977.

The United States. Exploiting Lockheed scandals, the JCP found ample material for attacks on the USA as dominating Japan's diplomacy and defense through U.S.-controlled multinational corporations and the Counter Intelligence Agency. The keynote was set by *Akahata*'s comment (21 January) which found in President Ford's "State of the Union" message proof that "the arrogant U.S. ruling clique still intends to play its self-conceited role of 'leader of the world'." Yet, JCP leaders cannot ignore the reservoir of good will for the USA which exists in Japan. An October public opinion poll revealed that U.S. popularity had risen ten points in six months since April, reaching 35 percent, one percent below that of Switzerland (*Sankai*, 1 November). JCP Secretariat chief Fuwa Tetsuzo took occasion in February to remark that the party would try to promote friendly relations based on equality between the two countries and that opposition to the U.S.-Japan security treaty did not mean hostility to the USA (Kyodo News Service, 27 February).

In 1976 the JCP had more personal contacts with the USA than ever before. As previously noted, three Diet members visited Washington in connection with the Lockheed investigation and a second reporter from *Akahata* (*YICA, 1976*) was sent on an extensive 35-day tour which included Washington, New York, San Francisco, Los Angeles, and Hawaii. The result was a ten-part series in *Akahata* which began with the reporter's attendance at a rally in New York's Carnegie Hall for the rehabilitation of the Rosenbergs, executed as espionage agents, and ended in Hawaii, "land of everlasting summer," which he found to resemble a "Japanese colony" with half of its foreign capital ($6 billion) originating in Japan, manipulated largely by the entrepreneur Osano Kenji, who was under investigation in connection with the Lockheed case. (*Akahata*, 4-13 July.)

Early in the year *Akahata* (24 January) accused the CIA of carrying on clandestine activities in Japan and in April mounted a campaign which filled full pages in the party organ for several days. These articles followed extensive coverage of purported CIA activities in Italy, Chile, and other countries. *Akahata* related CIA activities to the Lockheed revelations amid charges that CIA had in the postwar period suborned the notorious Kodama Yoshio, one of the central figures in the Lockheed case. In mid-April its columns were filled with reports of CIA involvement in Japanese politics from the days of the Occupation. On 15 April a double-page spread, with a photograph of the U.S. Embassy prominently displayed alongside a chart of the "spy network," listed the names of 196 U.S. officials who had served in Japan and who were branded as "CIA agents." Among those named were former ambassadors Edwin O. Reischauer and U. Alexis Johnson, along with numerous foreign service officers posted to Japan in the past or at present. Needless to say, reports of CIA activities emanating from congressional investigations in Washington received prominent display in the JCP paper.

On the 25th anniversary of the signing of the U.S.-Japan security treaty, 8 September, *Akahata* editorialized that Japan was still under the yoke of U.S. imperialism, dating from the imposition of the treaty on Japan when the country was in a state of virtual martial law. It concluded that only the JSP and the JCP were boldly taking a stand for the abrogation of the security treaty, one of Japan's increasingly urgent problems, since other opposition parties either openly supported it (DSP) or called for consultations with the USA to bring it gradually to an end (Komeito).

Although the JCP continued to denounce the security treaty and to criticize U.S. use of Japanese military bases, both in Okinawa and in the main islands, its attitude toward national defense began to show subtle change. Although for some years the JCP had declared that even under socialism Japan would require some "democratic" armed forces, it consistently maintained that the present Self-Defense Forces were unconstitutional and subordinate to the USA. In a press conference in January, Miyamoto for the first time referred to the possibility of a constitutional change: "The party will not push for disbandment of the SDF if a renovationist coalition government is established in the future and may propose constitutional revision to make it possible for Japan to possess military strength based on a national consensus." The chairman emphasized the importance of avoiding antagonizing SDF personnel who had joined the military for patriotic motives and for self-defense only. "They must not be turned into enemies meaninglessly. . . . Self-defense and neutrality will be more easily understood by the SDF personnel than unarmed neutrality." (*Mainichi*, 20 January.) The *Yomiuri* (20 January) concluded that if the JCP continues to pursue its present line toward the defense problem, it will sooner or later come into collision with the constitutional issue. Thus far, the JCP has maintained unflinching support for the "peace constitution" and has vigorously attacked those who would attempt to revise it "for the worse," meaning the elimination of Article 9 which prohibits Japan from possessing a true military establishment.

The JCP interpreted the election of Jimmy Carter as a manifestation of popular reaction against the "corruption and deterioration of American politics, economy, and society, as symbolized by the Watergate case, the exposure of CIA crimes at home and abroad, and the Lockheed case." Party spokesmen saw no change, however, in U.S. imperialist policies and affirmed that Carter's quoted intention to attach more importance to Japan meant nothing more than maintenance of the long-time subordinate relationship of Japan with the United States. (*Asahi*, 4 November.)

Elections. On 5 December, in the first lower house election to be held since 1972, termed by some commentators as the "most significant poll since the war" (*The Japan Times Weekly*, 11 December), the JCP won 17 seats, less than half of its pre-election strength. With the addition of two elected "reformist" candidates who will vote with the JCP, the party's total membership in the House of Representatives is now 19 and its position among the four opposition parties has receded from second to fourth. Just as the heavy losses suffered by the LDP were surprising to prognosticators, the poor showing of the JCP was unexpected. On the eve of the election, the predictions by Tokyo's six leading dailies of JCP seats to be won varied from 33 to 39. (*Sankei*, 4 December). The addition of 20 new seats (from 491 to 511) and the balloting of four million new voters (total votes in 1976 were 56 million, in 1972, 52 million) changed the character of the election from that of 1972. Voter turn-out was 73.45 percent as compared to 71.76 in 1972. The JCP captured 5.8 million votes (5.5 million in 1972) or 10.4 percent of the total vote (10.5 in 1972). The disparity between votes and seats won is explained by the fact that the JCP dispersed its support by running candidates in each of Japan's 130 electoral districts. Thus, while the communist vote-pulling power was higher in numbers, the percentage was slightly lower and individual candidates were unable to compete successfully in districts which counted.

Various factors explained the JCP's "defeat." In 1972 the party captured much of the "floating vote" which in 1976 went to middle-of-the-road candidates from the Komeito, DSP, and the newly formed New Liberal Club. The "spy incident" involving the Party's chairman, obviously hurt the JCP and, in spite of strenuous efforts to effect a new image and expand membership, the party failed to overcome the basic Japanese wariness of communism. JCP success in 1972 had intensified this sense of wariness and spurred the other parties to greater efforts to defeat communist candidates.

The party suffered a severe blow in the defeat of ten of its outstanding Diet representatives: two members of the Standing Committee of the Presidium, three members of the Presidium, four members of the Central Committee, and one alternate member of the Central Committee.

International Activities and Contacts. As described above, the JCP's most important international meetings during 1976 were those held at the time of visits to Japan of the secretaries-general of the Spanish and French Communist parties. Other international contacts included the following:

A meeting was held in Tokyo on 10 January to establish a "Japan Committee for the Solidarity of Palestine." The purposes of the committee were to recognize the Palestine Liberation Organization as the sole legitimate representative of Palestine and to lend support to the establishment of a Palestine state.

On 8-25 February Nishizawa Tomio led a delegation to Romania, Yugoslavia, and Algeria for conversations with top-ranking officials and Communist leaders.

On 20 June a three-man delegation from the Communist Party of Cuba arrived in Tokyo for a week's visit at the invitation of the JCP.

In August the JCP sent an observer to attend the conference of non-aligned nations in Colombo, Sri Lanka.

On 19-21 August Nishizawa Tomio again visited Yugoslavia.

In mid-December Nishizawa and Fuwa attended the Vietnam party congress in Hanoi.

JCP Publications. The publishing empire of the JCP issues a stream of books, magazines, pamphlets, and tracts, in addition to the principal party organ, *Akahata*. As stated above, while the latter's combined Sunday and daily circulation is frequently estimated by party leaders as "about three million" its actual distribution may more nearly approximate 2.2 million. Other periodicals are as follows:

Party organs: *Zenei* (Vanguard), principal monthly magazine, has a circulation of more than 100,000. *Gekkan Gakushu* (Studies Monthly), offers guidance for new members. *Gikai to Jichitai* (Parliament and Autonomous Organizations), monthly founded 1959 as "Parliament and the JCP," treats matters pending in the Diet, laws and regulations, and parliamentary politics. *Seikai Seiji Shiryo* (Documents of World Politics), founded 1956, bimonthly, deals with international affairs. *Riron Seisaku* (Theories and Policies), founded 1967, monthly, publishes JCP resolutions, essays, press conferences, and reprints of articles from *Akahata*. *Akahata Shukusatsuban* (Akahata reduced edition), founded 1961, published monthly, is principally for reference libraries. *Akahata* in Braille, founded 1975, claims to be the only party publication of its kind; it is sent postage free to blind subscribers and is expected to become a weekly in the future. *Gakusei Shumbun* (Students' News), founded 1961, newspaper format, 4-6 pages, is a "weekly to point the way for modern students." *Bulletin*, published in English ten to twenty times per year, includes translations of important texts of resolutions, essays, and party declarations.

Semi-party organs: The following, while not formally party publications, are issued by the "New Japan Publishing Company," an obvious affiliate of the JCP. *Keizai* (Economics), founded 1962, is advertised as the only monthly magazine specializing in economics from the standpoint of scientific socialism. *Rodo Undo* (Labor Movement), monthly, founded 1966, presents easily understood articles on labor and trade union matters. *Asu no Noson* (Tomorrow's Farm Village), monthly, founded 1974, treats agriculture, management, technology, village life and culture. *Kagaku to Shiso* (Science and Thought), quarterly, founded 1971, dealing in philosophy, sociology, natural science, includes reports of criticism and discussions. *Minshu Bungaku* (Democratic Literature), monthly, founded 1967 as the organ of the Japan Democratic Literary Alliance, includes novels, reportage, essays. *Shonen Shojo Shimbun* (Boys' and Girls' Newspaper), founded 1969, published weeky in tabloid size, is aimed at primary and middle school children.

The JCP publishing enterprises also supply films, tapes, and slides. The Sunday *Akahata*, for example, is available on tape. (Above information on publications is from *Nihon Kyosanto no Shokai* [Introduction to the JCP], published by the JCP Central Committee, 10 July 1976, pp. 164-70.)

Splinter Parties. Splinter parties which have broken away from the JCP are generally either pro-Soviet or pro-Chinese. The Nihon no Koe (Voice of Japan) was founded in 1964 by Shiga Yoshio, one of the founders of the postwar JCP. Shiga's adherence to a pro-Soviet stance and the continuing benign attitude of the CPSU toward his party have been the principal obstacles to normalization of relations between the JCP and the CPSU. The membership has never exceeded 400.

The pro-Chinese splinter parties now number four. The Japanese Communist Party (Left) has split into two groups, the so-called "Yamaguchi faction" (named after Yamaguchi Prefecture), with 600 members, and the "Kanto faction" (denoting the area around Tokyo), with 400. The Japanese Labor Party (Nihon Rodo-to) seems to have gained some respect from China and is mentioned frequently in Peking publications; its membership is estimated at 900. A fourth party, the Japan Workers' Party (Nihon Rodosha-ha), with 400 members, has also attracted some attention from the Chinese. At the time of Chou En-lai's death, messages of condolence were printed in the *Peking Review* from the central committees of the JCP (left) and the Japan Workers' Party.

Hoover Institution
Stanford University

John K. Emmerson

Korea: Democratic People's Republic of Korea

The Korean Communist Party (Choson Kongsan-dang; KCP) was formed at Seoul in 1925 during the time of the Japanese rule; in 1928, due chiefly to suppression, it ceased to function. Shortly after World War II, a revived KCP appeared briefly in Seoul. Control of the communist movement in Korea soon shifted to the northern part of the country, then occupied by Soviet forces, where the "North Korean Central Bureau of the KCP" was formed in October 1945 under Soviet auspices. The three major factions of the movement—comprising Korean communists who during the Japanese period had gone to China, or to the Soviet Union, or had remained in Korea—subsequently merged, and on 23 June 1949 the Korean Workers' Party (Choson Nodon-dang; KWP) was established. The KWP is today the ruling party of the Democratic People's Republic of Korea (DPRK).

Kim Il-song, Korean-born but Soviet-trained, who had been an anti-Japanese communist guerrilla leader in southern Manchuria in the 1930s, consolidated his dictatorial power by eliminating rival factions, and today his Manchurian partisan group (the Kapsan faction) holds unassailable supremacy in the North Korean leadership.

The number of the KWP members was estimated in 1972 at 2,000,000 by the party newspaper, *Nodong Shinmun* (editorial, 29 August). A recent outside estimate is 1.6 million. The estimated population of the DPRK is 17 million.

Leadership and Organization. North Korea has a typical communist administrative structure. The center of the decision making is in theKWP, and the government merely executes party policy. All important leaders hold concurrent positions in the party and government.

The present top leaders of the DPRK, most of whom were elected at the KWP's fifth Congress on 13 November 1970, include the following (note: since the 1970 congress, the DPRK has not announced the membership of the KWP Political Committee, and this list is based on an analysis of fragmentary information):

KWP Political Committee	Other Positions Held Concurrently
	Regular (Voting) Members
Kim Il-song	KWP secretary-general; DPRK president; supreme commander of armed forces; chairman of KWP Military Committee; marshal
Kim Il	KWP CC (Central Committee) secretary; 1st DPRK vice-president; member of Central People's Committee
Kim Tong-kyu	KWP CC secretary; DPRK vice-president; member of Central People's Committee
Choe Hyon	Colonel general; vice-chairman of DPRK National Defense Commission; member of Central People's Committee
O Chin-u	Colonel general; KWP CC secretary; minister of People's Armed Forces; vice-chairman of DPRK National Defense Commission; member of Central People's Committee
So Chol	Colonel general; member of Standing Committee of Supreme People's Assembly
Pak Song-chol	Premier of State Administration Council; member of Central People's Committee
Im Chun-chu	Secretary and member of Central People's Committee
Yi Kun-mo	Deputy premier of State Administration Council (machinery and heavy industry expert); member of Central People's Committee
Yon Hyung-muk	KWP CC secretary; member of Central People's Committee
Kim Yong-chu	Kim Il-song's younger brother; director of KWP CC Organization and Guidance Department; KWP CC secretary; deputy premier of State Administration Council; member of Central People's Committee; co-chairman of South-North Coordinating Committee
Yi Yong-mu	Colonel general; chief of Political Bureau of (North) Korean People's Army
Yang Hyong-sop	KWP CC secretary; director of KWP Inspection (Control) Committee; member of Central People's Committee
Kim Chun-nin	KWP CC secretary; director of KWP Liaison Bureau (General Bureau of South Korea); member of Central People's Committee

Candidate (Non-Voting) Members

Yu Chang-sik	KWP CC secretary; director of KWP CC External Affairs Department; member of Central People's Committee
Kim Yong-nam	KWP CC secretary; director of KWP CC International Department; member of Standing Committee of Supreme People's Assembly
Hyon Mu-kwang	KWP CC secretary; member of Central People's Committee
Pak Su-tong	Deputy director of KWP CC Organization and Guidance Department
Han Ik-su	KWP CC secretary; colonel general; member of Standing Committee of Supreme People's Assembly
Chong Chung-ki	Deputy premier of State Administration Council; member of Standing Committee of Supreme People's Assembly
Kang Song-san	Chief secretary of KWP Pyongyang Municipal Committee; member of Standing Committee of Supreme People's Assembly; chairman of Transport and Communications Committee of State Administration Council
Chon Mun-sop	Colonel general; director of Escort Bureau (for Kim Il-song)
Choe Chae-u	Deputy premier of State Administration Council; member of Central People's Committee
Chong Kyong-hui	— — —

The 25-member KWP Political Committee (one vacancy in 1976) and the 15-member Secretariat constitute the core of important decision-makers in the DPRK and act as a controlling nucleus for the Central Committee (123 regular and 60 alternate members at the Fifth Congress, November 1970; about 20 of these seats were vacant in 1976 due to either death or retirement).

The present central government structure consists of three pillars of power: the 25-member Central People's Committee (basically a policy-making and supervisory body under KWP guidance), the 29-member State Administration Council (an organ to execute policies already made by the Central People's Committee), and the 19-member Standing Committee of the Supreme People's Assembly (a symbolic and honorific body which functions as a legislative branch).

The KWP controls the following mass organizations: the 2-million-member General Federation of Trade Unions of Korea (GFTUK), the 2.7-million-member League of Socialist Working Youth of Korea (LSWY), the Union of Agricultural Working People, the Korean Democratic Women's Union, and the General Federation of Korean Residents in Japan (Chongnyon, or Chosen Soren).

At least two subordinate political movements under the tight KWP control exist in North Korea: the Korean Democratic Party (Choson Minju-dang) and Young Friends' Party of the Chondogyo Sect (the sect being the Society of the Heavenly Way—Chondogyo Chong-u-dang). No membership figures are available on these movements. Their function is to enhance acceptance of the United Democratic Fatherland Front (Choguk Tongil Minjujuui Chonson), created by 71 political and social organizations in June 1949, which is assigned the task of uniting "all the revolutionary forces of North and South Korea" under the leadership of the KWP, in order to implement the "peaceful unification and complete independence of the country." The KWP also controls the "Committee for Peaceful Unification of the Fatherland," established in May 1961 and consisting of representatives from the KWP, the subordinate "democratic" parties, and the mass organizations.

Death and illness among veteran DPRK leaders during 1976 soon caused a change in the country's top political lineup in several years.

Nam Il, member of the KWP Central Committee, deputy to the DPRK Supreme People's Assembly, member of the Central People's Committee, and vice-premier of the State Administration Council, died as the result of an automobile accident on 7 March, at the age of 64.

Hong Won-kil, member of the KWP Central Committee, deputy of the DPRK Supreme People's Assembly, member of the Central People's Committee and vice-premier of the State Administration Council, died on 16 May at the age of 52, due to a long illness.

On 14 May, Choe Hyon was released from the post of Minister of the People's Armed forces for health reasons and appointed vice-chairman of the DPRK National Defense Commission. (O Chin-u, member of the KWP Political Committee and chief of the KPA General Staff, succeeded him.)

On 29 April, Kim Il, a member of both the KWP Political Committee and Secretariat, resigned from the premiership for health reasons; however, he did accept the post of the first vice-president of the DPRK, a newly created post ranking immediately after Kim Il-song. (Pak Song-chol succeeded him.)

Choe Yon-kon, member of the KWP Political Committee, member of the Central People's Committee and DPRK Vice-President, died after a long illness on 19 September at the age of 76.

Kim Yong-chu, Kim Il-song's younger brother, once believed slated eventually to succeed to his brother's position, has not been seen in public since April 1975. He is believed to have taken ill with an incurable disease in late 1973.

The above events indicate that Kim Il-song is today surrounded by an aging team of loyal aides who have helped him run the country since their return from Russia in 1945. The average age of North Korea's top leaders in 1976 was 66.4 years. As the aging "old guard" or first-generation leaders are expected to fade away from the North Korean scene gradually due to normal attrition, a critical process of transition in the party-government leadership is in the offing. The convening of the overdue Sixth Congress of the KWP is likely in the near future. The Fifth Party Congress of 1970 merely reconfirmed the existing leadership pattern. But the forthcoming congress is likely to be highlighted by a new overall, or major, reshuffle of the North Korean power structure and thus signal the start of the generation shift in leadership.

The personality cult of Kim Il-song continued, ever increasing in scale and intensity, during 1976. The DPRK media constantly stressed that the loyalty to Kim and his ideology of *chuche'* (self-identity or national identity) should continue from generation to generation, and the program of perpetuating his ideology and policies was given further institutional muscle during the year.

This cult of the North Korean dictator has been extended recently to embrace almost all of his family members—ranging from his great-grandfather, grandfather, grandmother, and uncle on his father's side, his father, mother, younger brothers, and deceased first wife, to his grandfather and uncle on his mother's side. All of them are hailed as "ardent, brilliant, and foremost revolutionary fighters and patriots."

During 1976 there were increasing foreign press reports that Kim Il-song was quietly laying the groundwork for a Communist dynasty with his son, Kim Chong-il, as heir-apparent, although the role and activities of Chong-il remained unpublicized and his name did not appear in North Korean announcements.

Kim Chong-il is reportedly holding an important position in the DPRK power structure—possibly as a candidate member of the KWP Political Committee, a secretary of the KWP Central Committee, and a member of the party's propaganda division. According to a recent North Korean defector, with a rank equal to a vice-cabinet minister in Pyongyang, who previously made two espionage trips to South Korea, Kim Chong-il has been in charge of North Korea's operations toward the South and Japan.

The increasing speculatons about Kim Chong-il's succession to his father's leadership position coincided with Kim Il-song's reportedly deteriorating health, coupled with the forthcoming generation shift in the top echelons of the country's power structure.

Kim Il-song has a fist-sized tumor on the back of his neck. The tumor is rumored to be malignant, and might soon incapacitate him or cause his death. He was said to have made a secret visit to Romania in recent months for the treatment of what was known as cervical cancer. The suspicions of illness were fortified in December 1975 when the DPRK president, who was known to make daily appearances, suddenly disappeared. It was not until 7-8 February 1976 that he appeared again, at the 28th-anniversary celebrations of the North Korean Army. On both days the official news agency emphasized his health and vigorous appearance. Ten days later, *Nodong Shinmun* said that it was the North Korean people's "most sacred duty to ensure the longevity of the Great Leader [Kim Il-song]" and exhorted efforts to "lessen, even a little, his concern for the country."

In connection with the speculations about Kim Chong-il's succession, the deification of his real mother, Kim Jung-sook, who was Kim Il-song's first wife and died in 1949 of tuberculosis, became increasingly intensive as well as extensive during 1976. For example, portraits and bronze busts or statues of her were set up in many places with the designation of "unparalleled Communist revolutionary fighter," "an independence (*chuche*')-oriented woman revolutionary who devoted her life to both the Great Leader [Kim Il-song] and the goal of Communist construction," and so on. (During 1975 a song was composed to praise her with the title, "Mother Kim Jung-sook, A Star of Loyalty." On the occasion of the commemoration of International Women's Day in March 1975, Kim Song-ae, Kim Il-song's present second wife, eulogized her predecessor as an "indomitable Communist revolutionary fighter and outstanding woman activist," who "fought for the sake of the Great Leader, sacrificing her youth and life," through many years of anti-Japanese resistance.) Undoubtedly, the intent is to strengthen the status and image of Kim Chong-il.

Several changes of position in the high party leadership in 1976 were noteworthy. Lieutenant General Chon Mun-sop, who appeared in April 1975 as a candidate member of the KWP Political Committee, jumped to 13th in rank (from 21st). O Paek-yong, also an army general, was elevated to the 15th in rank (from 26th), and Lieutenant General Kim Chol-man to the 18th (from 56th).

During 1975-76 there were some indications that Kim Chun-nin, member of the KWP Political Committee, who was in overall charge of anti-Seoul operations, had suffered some loss in status, while Im Chun-chu had been elevated.Im, who was previously listed 31st in rank, was not listed immediately following Pak Song-chol and preceded KWP Political Committee members Yi Kun-mo and Yon Hyung-muk.

Domestic Attitudes and Activities. The DPRK media constantly stressed during 1976 that the "three revolutions—ideological, technical and cultural—are the main content of the revolution the working-class party must carry out after the establishment of the socialist system; they are the tasks of the continued revolution to be carried on until communism has been built."

The sixth session of the 5th Supreme People's Assembly, 27-29 April, discussed two items: the state budgets for 1975 and 1976, and the "nursing and education of the children" in the DPRK.

It was reported to the meeting that the government had completed its Six-Year Economic Plan a year and four months ahead of its deadline with the exception of the two industrial fields of cement and steel. (The six-year plan officially ended in 1975.) The session stressed the remark made by Kim Il-song at the November 1975 meeting of the KWP Central Committee that the country should launch a drive this year to complete those unfinished tasks.

The 1975 state budgetary revenues amounted to 11,586,300,000 *won* and the expenditures to 11,376,480,000 *won*, according to Vice-Premier Choe Jae-u's report to the session. The 1976 revenues and expenditures envisaged in the budget amounted to 12,513,210,000 *won* each (about US $5,422 million based on an official exchange rate of about 43 U.S. cents to one *won*). The report presented by Finance Minister Kim Gyong-ryon said that the government's defense expenditure would amount to 16.5 percent of its total budget (about US $895 million). (The actual defense budget would be higher because the Pyongyang regime makes it a rule to hide defense expenditures in other sectors.) Total armed forces in 1976 were believed to number around 470,000 actives and 1,600,000 civilian militia.

The same session enacted a law making it mandatory that all children up to the age of five years be brought up at public nurseries and kindergartens with their parents allowed to take them to their homes only once a week or month (up to the age of three years at public nurseries and then at kindergartens). This law was apparently designed to indoctrinate children with the Kim Il-song ideology and to enable women to render more labor service by saving hours spent with their children. (In 1976 the DPRK had 60,000 nurseries and kindergartens capable of rearing and educating all the 3,500,000 preschool chihldren at state and public expense.)

On the last day of the session (29 April), Pak Song-chol was chosen as premier of the DPRK, replacing Kim Il who resigned for reasons of health. Pak pledged before Kim Il-song: "I will thoroughly defend and fulfill the ideology and instructions of the Leader [Kim Il-song] and the lines and policies of the party and firmly put the Leader's leadership into practice in order to accomplish the cause of our revolution."

The 12th plenum of the 5th Central Committee of the KWP was held in Pyongyang on 11-14 October under the chairmanship of Kim Il-song. Secretaries of the provincial party committees reported a harvest of more than 8 million tons of grain, the largest since the founding of the DPRK. The meeting discussed achieving 10 million tons through implementation of a five-point policy — construction of non-paddy irrigation works, land adjustment and land amelioration, construction of terraced fields, afforestation and water conservancy, and reclamation of tideland.

Foreign observers detected various symptoms of unusual developments inside North Korea shortly after the Panmunjom incident of 18 August in which two U.S. officers were murdered by North Korean guards in a tree-cutting dispute. Among these developments were: (1) officials of Japanese trade missions and technicians were ordered to leave North Korea; (2) all requests for the extension of visas by foreigners now staying in the DPRK were refused; (3) Pyongyang abruptly announced the cancellation of a projected visit by a delegation of Chongnyon, a pro-Communist federation of Korean residents in Japan, to attend a ceremony marking the 28th founding anniversary of the Communist regime; (4) a Communist Chinese basketball team was asked to leave the country in early September, although there were more games scheduled.

On 9 September, North Korea held a subdued national celebraton of the 28th founding anniversary of its Communist regime, even without the appearance of Kim Il-song. For the first time in years, the government-controlled (North) Korean Central News Agency (KCNA) failed to list the DPRK leaders who attended the mass meeting held in Pyongyang to honor the anniversary. (Normally, VIPs attending the ceremony are ranked in order of their importance, always starting with Kim Il-song.) KCNA's report gave the names of only two leaders attending,Vice-President Kang Ryang-uk and Yang Hyong-sop, a member of the KWP Political Committee.

Informed diplomatic sources and analysts said that "serious internal problems" were the main factor that had led the DPRK regime to close its doors to access to and from outside. The internal developments were assessed to be so serious as to make the North Korean Communists "extremely reluctant" to let them be divulged outside. The problems were considered to be related both to economic difficulties, as exemplified by Pyongyang's defaulting on foreign debts in the hundreds of millions of dollars, and to political tensions involving the succession problem of Kim Il-sung's son, Kim Chong-il, and the responsibility for the 18 August incident at Panmunjom, which only resulted in the strengthening of U.S. determination to defend South Korea and in Kim Il-song's official expression of "regret" over the bloodshed.

South Korea. During 1976, more than four years after a limited dialogue between North and South Korea started, relations between them continued to deteriorate. Talks on rapprochement between the two Koreas have been suspended for more than three years. Meanwhile, the DPRK in the North resumed violent propaganda attacks on the Republic of Korea in the South, and the tension between the North and the South was at its highest level since the end of the Korean War, following the bloody incident of 18 August at Panmunjom. In late June two North Korean infiltrators and two South Korean soldiers were killed in clashes just below the Demilitarized Zone. The Japanese daily *Sankei Shimbun* in Tokyo reported on 25 July that the DPRK had recently deployed 24 ground-to-ground missiles in Kaesong, about 60 kilometers northwest of Seoul. It also said that the North Koreans had concentrated about 200 amphibious vehicles and 120 high-speed landing craft on the lower part of the Yesung River, near Kaesong. A 17.3-ton South Korean fishing boat with 23 crewmen aboard was abducted to North Korea after it made a navigational error in bad weather and apparently crossed the eastern extension of the Military Demarcation Line on the morning of 30 August. (This boat and all crewmen returned to South Korea on 14 October after 45 days' captivity.) On 1 September some of the special communications lines installed in 1971-72, when the two Koreas agreed to forsake war and start political and other negotiations toward eventual reunification, stopped functioning. South Koreans believed that they were purposely cut by the DPRK regime.

Since the collapse of the rapprochement talks, the North Korean line has been that the road to unification lies through a revolution in the South. On 1 February, for example, a *Nodong Shinmum* editorial said that Republic of Korea president Park Chung-hee was an agent directly protected by the U.S. Central Intelligence Agency, and called upon South Koreans to overthrow the Park regime in Seoul.

During 1976 the DPRK launched propaganda campaigns on the theme that the danger of war between North and South Korea was steadily increasing and that a situation had been created by the U.S. and South Korean governments in which "a war might break out at any moment."

To many observers, after the end of the Indochina conflict in 1975, the principal danger spot in Asia seemed to be the Korean peninsula. Indeed, the military situation in Korea in 1976 was potentially as explosive as ever, as witnessed by the Panmunjom incident of 18 August. More than a million men were under arms in the divided peninsula, each side possessing the most sophisticated modern weapons short of the nuclear variety. South of the Demilitarized Zone, which became the de facto boundary after the 1953 truce which ended the Korean War, were the last U.S. combat troops committed on the Asian mainland, equipped with a frightening array of tactical nuclear weapons. While none of the great powers was encouraging either Pyongyang or Seoul to attempt to reunify the peninsula by force, Korea represented at least as great a threat to world peace as did the Middle East.

International Views and Positions. During 1976 Pyongyang supplemented its efforts on the reunification issue by becoming active on the foreign policy front, partly to undermine the international position of its rival regime in South Korea and partly to develop world support for North Korean policies. Parliamentary, trade, and other good-will missions were dispatched abroad and invited to North Korea, and friendly diplomatic gestures were made to every corner of the earth, especially the "Third World" countries whose bloc has increasingly dominated actions at the United Nations. In particular, the DPRK's foreign policy sought (a) to prevent recognition of "the two Koreas" concept by the world community, (b) to isolate South Korea from both the Third World and the Communist bloc, and (c) to drum up diplomatic support for the annual UN debate on the withdrawal of UN (actually U.S.) forces from South Korea.

Premier Pak Song-chol led the DPRK delegation to the fifth summit meeting of the nonaligned countries, at Colombo, Sri Lanka, in mid-August. (The general lack of warmth with which the Sri Lankans received the North Koreans was one important reason why DPRK President Kim Il-song decided not to attend the meeting, a decision not made public until the last minute. Sri Lanka expelled the North Koreans and closed their Embassy there five years ago because of a strong suspicion that they were helping to finance and train a young group of terrorists bent on overthrowing the government of this island reublic, which used to be called Ceylon.) With a view to getting diplomatic support from the nonaligned nations for its position on the Korean question at the United Nations, North Korea concentrated its efforts on a campaign for a strong anti-U.S. stand at the nonaligned summit meeting. (It is to be remembered that the incident of 18 August at Panmunjom coincided with this meeting.)

The nonaligned summit ended on the morning of 20 August in unexpected turmoil as it passed, over the objections of 15 of the 85 member nations, a resolution condemning "American imperialist maneuvers for aggression against Korea." (The nations voicing objections to the resolution included Jordan, Saudi Arabia, Singapore, Indonesia, Central African Republic, Gambia, Kenya, Ivory Coast, Zaire, Morocco, Mauritania, and Sierra Leone.) In one of the sharpest public disagreements in the nonaligned movement's 15-year history, the conference noted the objections but accepted the resolution of its drafting committee, which was much more critical of the USA and favorable to North Korea, a member of the nonaligned group. The drafting committee, composed of Zambia, Senegal, Nigeria, Algeria, India, Kuwait, Vietnam, Guyana, Cuba and Yugoslavia, concluded: "Today the American imperialists have turned South Korea into a military base for aggression and a base for nuclear attack . . . and have created a threat of aggression against the DPRK."

North Korea's relations with Vietnam, Cambodia, and Laos continued to be warm and cordial. For example, an agreement on trade payments between North Korea and Cambodia was signed on 29 April in Phnom Penh. On 5 July the DPRK leaders sent a message of greetings to the Vietnamese Communist leaders for the successful conclusion of the first session of the 6th National Assembly of the Socialist Republic of Vietnam. The next day the DPRK warmly hailed the reunification of Vietnam.

On 23 February, Jack Anderson and Les Whitten reported in the *Washington Post* that, according to secret Pentagon documents, North Korea was sending weapons and groups of army instructors to the Middle East, Africa, and other parts of the Third World. The DPRK media called the report "ridiculous." It was reported in mid-1976 that a large North Korean military advisory team that trained Zaire's best divisions had returned home after one year.

Newspapers in Finland and Sweden reported in late October that two members of the North Korean diplomatic missions in those countries had sought political asylum in the West in April. The two North Korean defectors were living in the Federal Republic of Germany, according to dispatches from South Korean correspondents in Paris.

Between 15 and 22 October, Sweden, Denmark, Norway, and Finland expelled 17 North Korean diplomats, including the ambassador to Denmark, on suspicion of illegal trafficking in liquor, cigarettes, and drugs. Shortly thereafter more DPRK diplomats, including the ambassadors to Sweden, Norway, and Finland, left the Nordic countries to avoid expulsion for smuggling and black market dealings. A grave shortage of foreign exchange was apparently in the background of the alleged contraband sales by North Korean diplomats, with the purpose of raising badly needed foreign currency to help finance the day-to-day needs and propaganda activities of DPRK embassies.

During 1976 Western and other creditors were miffed by North Korea's inability to honor contracts and finance its own growing trade deficits, and there was much talk of "bad faith." The figures of Pyongyang's external debts vary according to the source, but according to South Korean and other reliable sources, the DPRK owed a total of US $2,140 million to the Communist bloc (U.S. $900 million), Western Europe, and Japan at the end of 1975. Of this, according to the same sources, U.S. $244,470,000 was already overdue in delinquent payments to non-Communist creditors alone as of February 1976. (*Far Eastern Economic Review*, 9 April, and Seoul's *Korea Herald*, 4 May, 7 September.) Many of them — France, West Germany, Austria, Sweden, Finland, Italy, Switzerland, and Denmark — were demanding repayment of overdue debts and either cutting off or threatening to cut off government guarantees for trade deficits.

The above-mentioned difficulties in the DPRK's balance of payments indicated a serious bottleneck in North Korea's economy. They appeared to contradict claims made in April 1976 by the Pyongyang regime that its Six-Year Economic Plan had been completed a year and four months ahead of schedule.

North Korea's balance of payments, and therefore its ability to pay off its external debts, was in trouble for several reasons. Firstly, Pyongyang made its ambitious decision in late 1970, before the start of the Six-Year Economic Plan, to push economic development too quickly by importing industrial plants and other heavy machinery in greater quantities than the nation could pay for. Secondly, the North Koreans, like everyone else, were hit by a rise in the price of imported oil. Thirdly, the DPRK suffered from a fall in the price of its main exports, minerals and ores.

During 1976 North Korea drastically reduced the size of staff, facilities, and equipment of its overseas diplomatic and trade missions due to the increasing difficulty of financing them. (This cutback started in June.) Kim Il-song also ordered an end to all but the most essential imports to curtail his country's rising trade debts.

Since mid-1976 there have been signs that North Korea's courtship of the Third World has not been going well. When it got what it wanted at the fifth summit conference of the nonaligned countries in Colombo in August — a pro-North Korean resolution denouncing the U.S. presence in South Korea, Pyongyang apparently thought that this would be translated into 80 automatic votes for North Korea in the United Nations, but its aggressive tactics alienated several Third World countries. (As already noted, 15 nonaligned countries registered their objections to the resolution, indicating that they would not be bound by it.) An ominous signal came at the United Nations in late September. North Korea's allies in the Unitd Nations for several weeks had been preparing for debate in the General Assembly on a pro-Pyongyang resolution demanding withdrawal of the 40,000 U.S. troops in South Korea. Without advance warning, they notified the UN Secretary General that the resolution would be shelved for 1976 (see "United Nations," below).

Relations with China and the Soviet Union. During 1976 the DPRK continued to pursue a nationalistic, independent, and self-reliant foreign policy in Communist-bloc affairs by playing off the Soviet Union against China. But relations with the two major Communist powers remained equally warm and cordial.

A Korea-China friendship oil pipeline built between the two countries was opened on 7 January. Early in the year Pyongyang and Peking signed (a) an agreement on cooperation in the field of posts and telecommunications (18 January), (b) an agreement for the 15th meeting of the Korea-China committee for cooperation in border river navigation (21 January), and (c) a protocol on commodity exchange (9 February).

The DPRK sent messages of condolence to the People's Republic of China when Chairman Mao Tse-tung, Premier Chou En-lai, and Marshal Chu Teh passed away. On 29 July the Pyongyang regime sent a telegram of sympathy to the Chinese in connection with the very great damage caused by a strong earthquake in the Tangshan-Fengnan area in eastern Hopei Province. On 24 October Kim Il-song sent greetings to Hua Kuo-feng upon his election as chairman of the Central Committee of the Chinese Communist Party and chairman of the Military Commission of the party's Central Committee.

Chinese foreign minister Chiao Kuan-hua, in his 5 October speech to the UN General Assembly, reiterated his country's long-held position on Korea in requesting withdrawal of U.S. forces from South Korea and dissolution of the UN Command. He was known to have shown a "very lukewarm" reaction to the latest U.S. proposal of a phased conference on Korea in the recent U.S.-China foreign minsterial meeting

During 1976 China continued to send the USA signals that it wanted the U.S. troops to remain in South Korea. A number of U.S. congressional visitors to China, who held long talks with top Chinese leaders, got the impression that "on the surface, China was for a unified Korea," but the Chinese leaders "had no real objection" to the U.S. military presence in South Korea. (*Washington Post*, 28 February.)

British foreign secretary Anthony Crosland said on 11May that he was told by Chinese leaders that renewal of the 1950-53 Korean War was "out of the question." Crosland said that the statement was made to him by Chinese foreign minister Chiao Kuan-hua.

A U.S. congressional delegation to China, led by Representative Melvin Price, chairman of the House Armed Services Committee, was told in Peking in April that China would not send its troops to North Korea even in the case of a renewed conflict on the Korean peninsula.

The Soviet Union charged in an official TASS report of late July that China's "double-faced position on the Korean issue betrayed North Korean interests," stating that the Peking regime was paying only lip service to Korean reunification while encouraging in every way the maintenance of the U.S. forces in South Korea.

Premier Pak Song-chol led a delegation of the KWP to the 25th Congress of the Communist Party of the Soviet Union, and made a congratulatory speech at the congress on 27 February.

The trde volume between the Soviet Union and the DPRK has reportedly been increased by three times since they concluded a treaty of mutual friendship and cooperation and aid in 1961. In early July 1976 the Russo-North Korean mutual assistance pact was automatically extended for another five years until 1981. The extension was implied in a message sent by Soviet Communist Party leader Leonid Brezhnev and Premier Alexei Kosygin to DPRK President Kim Il-song on 5 July.

But, according to informed economic sources in Paris, North Korea was denied further loans by the Soviet Union from the beginning of 1976 because of its failure to pay interest (*Korea Herald*, 13 October). (The Soviet Union disbursed a total of US $724,900,000 in economic aid to North Korea during the period of 1969-74, according to the April 1976 issue of "International Policy Report" released by the Institute for International Policy in Washington, D.C.)

Relations with Japan. Relations between North Korea and Japan, never warm, were described by some Japanese observers as being at their coolest during 1976. Pyongyang viewed Tokyo as being excessively partial to Seoul, pursuing a policy of "two Koreas" and hostility toward the DPRK. The North Korean media continued to denounce the growing Japanese "imperialistic" stakes in South Korea and the alleged collusion of Japan and the USA to preserve their mutual "colonial interests" in the Korean peninsula.

During 1976 Japan was stuck with about US $260 million worth of outstanding trade loans to North Korea. Of this amount, US $67 million already was overdue for repayment. On 14 October, Japanese foreign minister Zentaro Kosaka denounced as a "breach of faith" North Korea's failure to pay its trade debts to Japan.

The DPRK asked Japanese trading companies for a two-year moratorium on its unpaid trade bills, with interest fixed at 7.5 percent a year. (Pyongyang reportedly made similar requests to France, West Germany, Sweden, and other European nations.)

The North Korean request raised the delicate problem of export insurance, a Japanese government program under which trading concerns could claim compensation for default on foreign trade bill payments. If Japanese traders asked for the compensation and were paid, the government would be forced to stop underwriting exports to North Korea, an action tantamount to an official declaration of Pyongyang's inability as a trading partner. The Japanese traders feared that this would possibly result in suspending totally the bilateral trade which was the only channel linking the two countries in the absence of diplomatic ties.

Negotiations with North Korea were continuing slowly, and in a counter-proposal for presentation to the DPRK, Japanese traders were expected to accept the North Korean request for the moratorium but they would ask for an interest rate closer to the Japanese open-market rate (9.5 percent) and a North Korean guarantee for its payment after the two-year deferment.

Delays in North Korea's repayments, stemming from its deteriorating foreign exchange earnings, slowed its imports from Japan. The DPRK's imports from Japan in the first three months of 1976 totaled US $30,244,000, (down 6.1 percent from the already depressed level of a year ago). Its exports to Japan in the same period amounted to US $12,337,000 (up 17 percent).

Relations with the United States. During 1976 the DPRK conducted a policy of increasing hostility toward the USA. North Korea kept charging that Washington was planning another war in Korea in which it would use nuclear weapons. It also condemned the alleged U.S. germ tests in South Korea. (Pyongyang domestic service, in Korean, 24 July.) Pyongyang's increasing antagonism culminated in the slaying on 18 August of two U.S. army officers by North Korean soldiers at Panmunjom, the truce village.

The most unexpected result of the Panmunjom incident was a statement by DPRK President Kim Il-song. He expressed "regret" in language that was far more moderate, and conciliatory, than his usual belligerent anti-U.S. pronouncements. (Many foreign observers interpreted Kim's term of "regret" as an "apology" for the incident.) It was also the first time since the end of the Korean War that he had communicated directly with the UN Command.

Some commentators suggested that Kim timed the incident to the opening of the fifth summit meeting of the nonaligned nations in Sri Lanka the next day—to demonstrate the danger of the U.S. military presence in South Korea. More likely, according to others who used Kim's apology as the basis for their argument, a local North Korean miitary commander overacted in the context of a continuous DPRK effort to intimidate the USA and South Korea.

Foreign analysts believed that Kim appeared to have backed down in August because he miscalculated the U.S. reaction. President Ford responded with a show of force that was supported by Jimmy Carter, the Democratic Presidential candidate, and by political leaders and editorial comments across the country.

Moreover, the DPRK failed to arouse support from its Communist allies or from the Third World nations then meeting in Sri Lanka. Nor did Japan object when the show of force was mounted from U.S. bases there.

Beyond short-run tactical considerations, however, the Pyongyang regime was constrained by domestic political problems involving Kim Il-song's succession and by economic troubles that had apparently delayed its plans for long-term industrial, and therefore military, expansion.

Shortly after the 18 August incident, the USA and North Korea agreed to a meeting of the Military Armistice Commission to discuss a DPRK proposal for partitioning the Panmunjom truce village to avoid further bloody incidents there. The new security arrangements, reached between the two sides on 6 September, included the following major points: (1) The joint security area, about 800 yards in diameter, will be split into halves along the military demarcation line that separates North and South Korea. (2) Guards will stay on their own side of the line. (Under the military armistice agreement that ended the Korean War, personnel from both sides were allowed to move freely throughout the security area.) (3) North Korea will withdraw its four guard posts now located south of the demarcation line in the area that will come under control of the U.S.-led UN Command. (4) Both sides would guarantee free movement of journalists and other civilians throughout the joint security area.

During 1976 the DPRK was vigorous and a good bit more shrill in demanding (a) the end of all UN involvement in Korea, (b) the withdrawal of the 40,000 U.S. troops in South Korea, with their nuclear arms, and (c) the replacement of the current armistice, signed at the end of the Korean War in 1953, with a bilateral "peace agreement" with the USA, without the participation of Seoul.

On 27 September U.S. secretary of state Henry Kissinger assured his South Korean counterpart Park Tong-jin that the USA would never have direct bilateral talks with North Korea. Speaking in Seattle on 22 July, Kissinger called for a four-power (Seoul, Pyongyang, Peking, and Washington) conference to reduce tensions on the Korean peninsula.

Simultaneously, DPRK President Kim Il-song renewed his own call for the opposite approach to divided Korea. From Pyongyang, he reiterated his proposal for "a great national congress" of Koreans from North and South "to drive the U.S. imperialist aggression troops out of Korea at an early date" and overthrow the government of Park Chung-hee.

On 30 September, Kissinger proposed "phased approaches" to settle the conflict in Korea. In a speech to the UN General Assembly, he called for a preliminary phase of talks between North and South Korea, including discussions on the place and scope of the conference. In this phase, Kissinger said, the USA and China could participate as observers or in an advisory role. If discussions yielded concrete results, the United States and China could join the talks formally, he added.

This, in turn, could set the stage for a wider conference in which other countries, presumably Japan and the Soviet Union, could associate themselves with arrangements that guaranteed a durable peace on the Korean peninsula, Kissinger added.

So far, there has been no positive response to the Kissinger proposal of 30 September from the DPRK.

United Nations. Daniel Patrick Moynihan, the former U.S. ambassador to the United Nations, said in late May that some members of the world organization had been selling their votes, in some cases for as little as US $600. Moynihan made the allegation in an interview with Columbia Broadcasting System (CBS) correspondent Eric Sevareid. The former ambassador, who said that he had never actually seen money exhanged, refused to identify the parties involved in the exchange.

An excerpt from the interview was shown on "CBS Evening News" on 28 May. At that time, CBS also reported that it had been told that on two occasions late in 1975 representatives from North Korea offered money to UN delegates from other nations. CBS said that it had learned of the above news from conversations with UN diplomats. It also said that the money was refused in both cases. A spokesman for the DPRK observer mission at the United Nations in New York denied the allegation.

The Korean question—a Cold War issue that has plagued the United Nations for more than two decades—disappeared from the agenda of the 1976 fall session of the UN General Assembly. Acting at North Korea's request in late September, 34 supporters of the DPRK at the United Nations withdrew their annual resolution calling for the dissolution of the UN Command in South Korea and the withdrawal of the 40,000 UN troops there.

Moments later, Japan, the USA, and 19 other allies of South Korea, who had been hoping to avoid another futile debate, withdrew their rival pro-Seoul resolution, and the issue was thus dropped until next year.

Western sources, although unsure of the North Korean motive, said that Pyongyang's backers at the United Nations had reached the conclusion that the pro-North Korean resolution would win less support at the world organization this year than it did last year, and persuaded the North Koreans to pull back. They cited the reaction to the North Korean attack on U.S. soldiers at Panmunjom on 18 August and the reservation expressed by some 15 nations on a pro-Pyongyang resolution adopted at the fifth summit conference of the nonaligned countries in Sri Lanka in August.

East European diplomats speculated that a peace offensive from the DPRK might be coming, possibly after the U.S. Presidential election.

Publications. The KWP publishes a daily organ, *Nodong Shinmun*, and a journal, *Kulloja*. The DPRK government publishes *Minju Choson*, the organ of the Supreme People's Assembly and the cabinet. The *Pyongyang Times, People's Korea*, and *Korea Today* are weekly English-language publications. The official news agency is the Korean Central News Agency.

Washington College Tai Sung An

Laos

Official organs of the ruling Communist party of Laos emphasized during 1976 the common root of Laotian and Vietnamese communism in the Indochinese Communist Party founded by Nguyen Ai Quoc, who became Ho Chi Minh. An important joint declaration issued by the parties of the two countries stressed their "special relationship." The gist of these statements reflected the predominant role of Hanoi in the late 1975 Communist seizure of power in Laos and in the subsequent realignment of politics throughout former Indochina.

The Lao People's Revolutionary Party (Phak Pasason Pativat Lao; PPPL) emerged in February 1972 from the Second Congress of the Lao People's Party (Phak Pasason Lao; PPL), which had been established with 300 members on March 22, 1955. Party membership was estimated in 1975 at 15,000 (*NYT*, 5 October 1975). The population of Laos is approximately 3.4 million.

Leadership and Organization. The following members of the PPPL Political Bureau were identified during 1976 by organs of the party and the government of the Lao People's Democratic Republic (LPDR), which was founded on 2 December 1975: Kaysone Phomvihan, secretary-general; Nouhak Phoumsavan, deputy secretary-general; Phoumi Vongvichit; Phoun Sipaseut; Sisomphon Lovansai; Khamtai Siphandon; and Prince Souphanouvong, who is described simply as a "member," although he holds the title of LPDR president.

Beyond these names, little is known to the outside world concerning PPPL leadership and organization. On 19 December 1975, however, the Pathet Lao News Agency issued a "summarized biography" of Kaysone containing the following details: born 13 December 1920 in Na Seng hamlet, Khanthaboury district, Savannakhet province, in a civil servant's family; studied law at Hanoi University in the 1940s and took part in the brief seizure of power by the Viet Minh and their Lao allies in Savannakhet during August 1945; formed a guerrilla unit in 1949 and held various posts in the resistance governments of the 1950s; became prime minister of the LPDR government on 2 December 1975; has held the post of secretary-general since the founding of the PPL (Pathet Lao News Agency, 19 December 1975; *FBIS*, 23 December).

Auxiliary and Mass Organizations. The Lao Patriotic Front (Neo Lao Hak Xat; NLHX—sometimes NLHS) was founded on 6 January 1956. It served as the PPPL's principal mass-mobilizing instrument during the long years of warfare and for the successful seizure of power. Little has been heard from the NLHX since its participation in the National Congress of People's Representatives which met on 1-2 December 1975 and established the new organs of state power.

Party Internal Affairs. The fact that the PPL held its Second Congress during February 1972 became public knowledge only in 1976. Up to this writing the party has revealed few other details of its internal affairs.

Domestic Attitudes and Activities. These have been authoritatively summed up in the concluding paragraph of an official PPPL history, released to mark the party's 21st founding anniversary:

> At present, the Lao People's Revolutionary Party is actively leading the Lao people to enhance their unity, bring into full play their revolutionary offensive position, strengthen the revolutionary forces in all fields, and consolidate the revolutionary administration at all levels in order to safeguard the fatherland, ensure social order and security, smash all counterrevolutionary schemes of the enemy, stabilize and constantly improve the people's livelihood, thoroughly complete the national democratic revolution, consolidate and build grassroots organizations in all fields so as to advance, step by step, to socialism without going through the stage of capitalist development, to build a peaceful, independent, democratic, unified and socialist Laos, thus pushing ahead the national liberation movement and contributing to the maintenance of peace in Indochina, Southeast Asia and the rest of the world. (Pathet Lao News Agency, 23 March 1976; *FBIS*, 24 March.)

Peace, independence, democracy, unity, and socialism have long been standard slogans of the PPPL and its front organizations, but the exact meaning of these terms was spelled out in greater detail by Kaysone in the political report he delivered on 1 December 1975 to the National congress. Peace is defined in accordance with the viewpoint of those in power as became evident from the following:

> Peace means that our country can completely wipe out domestic and external enemies, and that no reactionary influence is allowed to remain to sabotage peace, public order and efforts to build the country in peacetime. (Radio Vientiane, 4 December 1975; *FBIS*, 18 December.)

As for democracy, lest anybody confuse the meaning of this term with the notion of democracy prevalent in non-Communist countries where the people have the right to vote out government, Kaysone gave this definition:

> Democracy means that all our nationalities are the genuine masters of their own country and society, are earnestly participating in all facets of life of the nation, and act as the sacred support for the popular democratic administration. (Ibid.)

During 1976 the PPPL organs made increasingly frequent references to activities of "counter-revolutionaries," and certain indications of tighter security precautions became evident. On 21 March, e.g., Pathet Lao News Agency reported the arrest of a group of spies on the southern outskirts of Vientiane, the capital (*FBIS*, 24 March). On 16 April, Radio Vientiane broadcast a 92-minute program complete with sound effects, from a session of the "people's court" of Vientiane municipality during which six "rebel-saboteurs" were sentenced to death (ibid., 19 April). Such proceedings appear unusual for Laos, where the people are easy-going and the authorities in the past generally had been distinguished by their leniency.

On a less violent level, reports from Laos spoke about officials of the former regime attending "re-education seminars" in the vicinity of Viengsai, the former Pathet Lao "capital" in the northeast of the country. A former mayor of Vientiane was even quoted as expressing gratitude for the opportunity to perceive the error of his former ways and promising an interviewer "everything for the nation and people" (Radio Vientiane, 12 May; *FBIS*, 13 May).

International Views and Policies. The continued dependence of the PPPL on the Vietnam Workers' Party (VWP), established in the past and dictated by current geopolitical realities, could be seen during 1976 in the form of an early meeting of the highest-ranking leaders of the two parties which emphasized their "special relationship" by pledges on both sides to preserve this relationship, dispatch of Lao students to study in the Democratic Republic of Vietnam, and other signs. As a consequence, the PPPL adopted Hanoi's viewpoint on major foreign policy matters and followed its lead in leaning more toward Moscow than Peking.

A high-level party-government delegation, led by Kaysone, visited Hanoi from 5 to 11 February. This event was described by a Radio Vientiane editorial as "the most significant . . . in Lao international relations since the founding of the LPDR" (Radio Vientiane, 5 February; *FBIS*, 6 February). In a joint statement signed by Le Duan and Kaysone, the two parties noted the "special relationship" binding them by virtue of their common origin in the Indochinese Communist Party, a bond solidified by "the blood of tens of thousands of outstanding sons and daughters of the two peoples." The statement furthermore expressed the gratitude of the Lao side for Vietnam's "assistance in blood for the Lao revolution," and pledged both parties to "endeavor to educate the present generation as well as the generations to come to respect and defend this special Viet-Lao relationship like the apple of the eye." (Vietnam News Agency, 11 February; *FBIS*, 12 February.) During its visit the Lao delegation conferred with top Vietnamese leaders and inspected the Nguyen Ai Quoc school for high-ranking party cadres.

State-to-state relations witnessed Vietnamese assistance to Laos in the form of road-building and supplying scarce commodities. The joint statement, however, contained no mention of outstanding Vietnamese claims on border territories in Laos nor did it suggest any negotiations to settle them now that the war in Vietnam, which Pham Van Dong cited as a cause for postponement of such negotiations, had ended.

Deference to Hanoi also appeared to be written into a new history of the PPPL, published in 1976. Whereas a documentary article published by the NLHX Central Committee in 1975 had referred to the founding of a separate "Lao Restoration Party" in the 1930s (Radio Pathet Lao, 26 September 1975; *FBIS*, 2 October), the 1976 history mentioned only establishment in 1936 of "the party committee of Laos" under the old Indochinese Communist Party (Pathet Lao News Agency, 23 March 1976; *FBIS*, 24 March).

Prince Souphanouvong, who was not a member of the delegation to Hanoi in February, delivered a speech commemorating Lenin's 106th birthday anniversary which was remarkable for the fact that the speaker attributed all the successes of the revolution in Laos to the PPPL and did not mention the Indochinese Communist Party or the VWP even once.

In accordance with the special position occupied by Hanoi in PPPL affairs, the party gave voice in its official organs to pro-Soviet positions. These incuded a pledge of support for the Popular Movement for the Liberation of Angola (contained in the joint PPPL-VWP statement). The government of Laos also severed relations with Israel and expressed solidarity with the Palestine Liberation Organization.

A government delegation of the Socialist Republic of Vietnam led by Vice-Premier Le Thanh Nghi visited Laos from 29 August to 1 September. An agreement on gratuitous aid and interest-free loans from Vietnam to Laos in 1976 and 1977 was signed, and an agreement on economic, scientific, and technical cooperation, together with a transit freight agreement.

Unconfirmed reports circulated during 1976 in Southeast Asia that the USSR had established an electronic listening post in Laos for purposes of monitoring communications in southern China (*The Nation*, Bangkok, 3 May). If this is true, it may well be that Hanoi, anxious not to offend China, has persuaded the USSR to establish this listening post across the border inside Laos rather than on its own territory where its presence would be construed by Peking as an unfriendly act.

International Activities and Contacts. It appears that the PPPL was eager to establish relations with a number of other Communist parties, particularly those friendly toward Moscow. During 1976 it sent delegations, in sequence, to the following capitals for party-government discussions, apart from Hanoi: to Moscow and Havana in January (headed by Phoumi Vongvichit); again to Moscow for the 25th CPSU Congress in February and March (headed by Kaysone); to Peking in March (headed by Kaysone); to Czechoslovakia and East Germany during April and May (headed by Phoumi Vongvichit); to Moscow in April and May (headed by Kaysone); and to Ulan Bator in June (headed by Phoumi Vongvichit). It may be significant that after the visit to Peking, no joint statement or communiqué appeared.

A delegation from Laos led by Prince Souphanouvong and Phoun Sipaseut attended the non-aligned nations summit conference in Colombo in August.

A party-government delegation headed by Kaysone visited Moscow and held talks with Leonid Brezhnev between 5 and 7 September. Between 8 September and 11 October the delegation went on to visit Cuba, Czechoslovakia, Hungary, Bulgaria, Poland, Moscow again, and Mongolia. A party delegation headed by Phoun Sipaseut attended the congress of the Albanian Party of Labor in November.

Publications. The central organ of the PPPL is the newspaper *Siang Pasason*, published in Vientiane. Official news is released by the Pathet Lao News Agency.

Silver Spring, Maryland

Arthur J. Dommen

Malaysia

Communism in Malaysia mainly consists of guerrilla activity in West Malaysia along the border with Thailand and, in much lesser degree, also in the East Malaysian state of Sarawak, on the island of Borneo, where its operational focus is often, but not always, along or near the border with Indonesia.

In the Thai-Malaysian area the guerrillas are coordinated by the Communist Party of Malaya

(CPM), or by its two offshoots: the Communist Party of Malaya (Marxist-Leninist) or CPM(ML), and the Communist party of Malaya (Revolutionary Faction) or CPM(RF).

In East Malaysia the poorly organized guerrilla groups and underground cells are collectively known by various names, most commonly the North Kalimantan Communist Party (NKCP) and/or North Kalimantan People's Guerrilla Force (NKPGF). An earlier term, Sarawak Communist Organization (SCO), is occasionally still used, mostly by the government, to designate collectively the Communist guerrilla force and those youth, farmers, and other organizations which historically have been identified with Sarawak Communism.

Although the overwhelming majority of Communists in Malaysia are local ethnic Chinese, and although the Communist organizations in both parts of the country must be considered as pro-Peking in their international orientation, as well as being commited to Maoist tactical and doctrinal positions, there is no single, overcapping leadership body. The reason is that the formation of the state of Malaysia in 1963 is considered by Communists and their sympathizers in both parts of the country to have occurred illegally, undemocratically, and primarily in response to the demands of British and U.S. "imperialism."

The CPM and its offshoots today remain committed to the formation of a new state, a "Democratic Republic of Malaya," consisting of the states of peninsular Malaya and Singapore. The NKCP and NKPGF have as their aim an independent "Republic of North Borneo," which would presumably comprise not only the present East Malaysian states of Sarawak and Sabah, but also the oil-rich Sultanate of Brunei, a British protectorate. In their appeals over the years, the NKCP-NKPGF have tended to address themselves primarily to the inhabitants of Sarawak, creating the impression that the hoped-for republic would encompass Sarawak alone. This focus may be due to the fact that Communism in Sabah and Brunei at present is of negligible significance, and that the NKCP has no known following there. On occasion too the NKCP downplays its ultimate objective of a "North Borneo" republic, preferring to stress its intermediate tactical concern with the need of Sarawakians merely to express themselves "freely and democratically," e.g., in a plebiscite on their state's constitutional position. The Malaysian national government in Kuala Lumpur has repeatedly emphasized that it will not tolerate any secession of the state of Sarawak. The Sarawak United People's Party (SUPP), during much of the sixties, tended to reflect SCO demands and was, generally, considered to be a Communist front. In the present decade, however, the SUPP no longer has a discernible Communist-front role and, in fact, has become a party identified with ruling government coalitions at both state and national levels.

History. The Communist Party of Malaya was founded on 30 April 1930 (some sources claim 26 April) in Singapore, the culmination of nearly a decade of underground dispersed Communist activity among Chinese labor organizations, private school associations, and cultural and other interest groups in a number of major Malayan towns, particularly Penang and Singapore, the latter being then considered a part of Malaya (K. S. Pillai, "Communist Insurgency in Malaysia," *Pacific Community*, July 1976, pp. 588-89). During the 1920s the Comintern sought to coordinate Communist activity throughout Southeast Asia, but the CPM's direct precursor, the Nanyang (South Seas) Communist Party, founded in 1928, failed to provide much regional leadership. The birth of the CPM came in response to the dissatisfaction of local Malayan Communists and some expatriate Indonesian colleagues (who had fled after the failure of a Communist coup attempt in West Java and West Sumatra in 1926-27) with not having an organization of their own. During the 1930s the CPM gained some support from workers' organizations in the tin mining and rubber estate industries, but was unable to bring about political unity among radical Chinese and nationalistic, but generally more moderate, Malays, while effective police surveillance further limited operational effectiveness.

During World War II, CPM initiatives in organizing a broad-based multiracial resistance movement against the Japanese provided the Malayan Communists with prestige and a significant following. The advantage thus gained, however, was dissipated by 1948, as Britain effectively had begun to undercut the nationalist aspirations stirring many in the peninsula by unfolding its own plans of decolonization and eventual independence (Malaya formally acquired freedom from Britain on 31 August 1957, but chose to stay in the Commonwealth), and as moderate and conservative Chinese business and political interests in Malaya joined in a successful political alliance with the leading Malay nationalists, thus isolating the radical Chinese element in and around the CPM. Between 1948 and 1960 there existed what came to be known as the "Emergency" in Malaya, as CPM guerrillas launched a fluid "people's war" and terrorist campaign in the jungles as well as the towns. But already by the mid-fifties the insurgency was a demonstrable failure, and by the early sixties the guerrillas—numbering no more than a hundred or so, compared with some 3,000 in a "Malayan People's Liberation Army" (MPLA) in 1949—sought refuge in the jungles along the border between Thailand and Malaya. (Anthony Short, *The Communist Insurrection in Malaya, 1948-1960*, Crane Russak, New York, 1975; Noel Barber, *The War of the Running Dogs*, William Collins, London, 1975.)

From this nadir began the CPM's organization of the Malayan National Liberation Army (MNLA). It dropped the "Malayan People's" part of its "Emergency" period MPLA label, since taken up by the CPM(ML). Less frequently, the name Malayan Revolutionary Liberation Army (MRLA) is also used. It established new covert border training-camps, launched hit-and-run attacks on Malaysian police patrols and convoys, ingratiated itself with the population of Betong (a portion of Thailand's Yala Province that juts into Malayan territory) and with other border villagers, won supporters through intimidation or ideological appeals among Chinese rubber estate and logging industry workers on both sides of the border, and even was able to recruit a few score Malays for one of its guerrilla "regiments." The insecure Thai-Malayan frontier region—where also Muslim secessionists in Thailand's southern provinces, dissatisfied with the alleged neglect of a distant Bangkok, private armies of Thai tin mining and rubber magnates, and bands of mere brigands are active—has been an ideal environment for the CPM's reorganization (Justus M. van der Kroef, *Communism in Malaysia and Singapore: A Contemporary Survey*, The Hague, Nijhoff, 1967).

But the long-drawn-out "people's war" strategy of the MNLA, and the relentless counter-intelligence and counter-insurgency campaigns of the Malaysian government, marked by a number of instances of successful penetration and infiltration of the MNLA by government agents, inevitably contributed to serious leadership rifts and to attacks on Chin Peng, the longtime CPM secretary-general. Twenty recent recruits of allegedly doubtful loyalty were assassinated by party leaders in 1967. During January 1970, new fears of extensive infiltration by young Chinese recruits reportedly led to a Draconian order by the CPM Central Committee that commanders of MNLA units should kill all members thirteen years or older who had joined since 1962. Amid accusations that the Central Committee was betraying the MNLA, most of the "Eighth Regiment," which operates near the border in the upper part of Kedah State, seceded from the party. Led by former CPM Kedah state committee member Yat Kong, the secessionists established a rival party calling itself the Communist Party of Malaya (Revolutionary Faction), or CPM(RF). Undaunted, the CPM continued to press for new purges in other MNLA "regiments," and an even more serious secessionist movement developed in the "second district" unit of the MNLA's "Twelfth Regiment," which operates around Grik and Kroh in the northern part of Perak State, a movement in which some elements of the "Eighth Regiment" joined. This second secessionist movement culminated in the establishment of the Communist Party of Malaya (Marxist-Leninist), or CPM(ML), on 1 August 1974, with its own fighting force, the MPLA. Confusingly, the name was also adopted by the CPM(RF) for its combat units. (On the origins of the three-way split see *YICA, 1976*, pp. 334-36.)

More than the original purge order appears to be involved in the continuing split of West Malaysian Communist ranks. Even before the emergence of the splinter parties, younger MNLA activists had become impatient with what were viewed as failures of the CPM's aging leadership to pursue more aggressive terrorist policies and to carry them from rural areas into the cities through attacks there on government facilities and police posts. The increased frequency of such urban terror-ism, including daring daylight assassinations of police officials in the past two years, has been attributed to demands from younger MNLA cadres, as well as to CPM(ML) operatives. Disagreement also appears to exist over the extent to which the radicalized but not necessarily Marxist Malay and Chinese "New Left" student community and their sympathizers can be mobilized for the CPM and the MNLA. Meanwhile the government has been reporting increasingly frequent armed clashes between CPM and CPM(ML) members, in which both sides have sustained dead and wounded (*FBIS*, 18 March 1976). The "Voice of the Malayan Revolution" radio, which has remained in CPM hands, has repeatedly called for "a resolute counterattack in self-defense" against what it terms the *Chiu Chen* or anti-Party clique, presumably a reference to the CPM(ML) (*FBIS*, 2 August).

Communism in Sarawak primarily had its focus, before World War II, in the Chinese schools and school associations of such towns as Sibu and Miri (see Government of Sarawak, Information Service, *The Danger Within: A History of the Clandestine Communist Organisation in Sarawak*, Kuching, 1963). The Sarawak Advanced Youths Association (SAYA)—a major recruiting ground for Communist proselytizers from the Chinese mainland, who often posed as schoolteachers—and under-ground resistance groups like the "Sarawak Liberation League" participated in the local anti-Japanese resistance during World War II. By 1951 a new Communist coordinating body, the "Sarawak Overseas Democratic Youth League," had been formed to give direction to Communist "self-study" classes and cells in Chinese private schools and among young shop assistants and planters. The "Sarawak Farmers' Association" (SFA) became the principal front among Chinese planters in the interior. Com-munist appeals among other major population groups in Sarawak, like the Iban and the Malays, were generally negligible. The SCO played a major role in vainly opposing Sarawak's entry into the Malaysian Federation in 1963. Even before the formation of Malaysia, young Sarawak Chinese, with the aid of Indonesian Communists and Communist-sympathizing military commanders in neighboring Indonesian Borneo, began organizing a "people's war" similar to though smaller in scale than that being waged by the MNLA in West Malaysia. (Harold James and Denis Sheil-Small, *The Undeclared War: The Story of the Indonesian Confrontation 1962-1966*, Roman and Littlefield, Totowa, N.J., 1971.) Initially, the Sarawak United People's Party also served as an informal SCO front, but by the early 1970s, as noted above, the SUPP had divested itself of radical influences and become a partner in government coalitions.

Increasingly battered and isolated by improved joint Indonesian-Malaysian security operations, the guerrillas of the NKPGF sustained an even more serius blow when, in October 1973, the Malaysian government's so-called Sri Aman ("Lasting Peace") program of amnesty was launched. This program afforded rehabilitation to those who laid down their arms, and by June 1974, when it ended, an estimated 560 guerrillas, mostly Chinese men and women in their twenties and comprising more than two-thirds of the NKPGF, had come out of the jungle and surrendered. Nevertheless, resistance continued, though scattered and diminished, as some former guerrillas who had surrendered under the Sri Aman provisions redefected to the remaining insurgent force. Indonesian authorities claim that the Indonesian Communist underground near the Sarawak border is assisting the NKPGF remnant. Government sources have tended to exaggerate the extent of current guerrilla activity along the border and its effects on the sometimes uncertain loyalties of younger Chinese in both Sarawak and Indonesian Borneo.

No overt Communist activity has been reported in Sabah in recent years, though government sources claim there is some recruiting by the NKPGF among Chinese school-age and unemployed older youth in the towns. In previous years there was occasional official concern over the illegal entry of Chinese aliens with alleged Communist sympathies from Indonesia, the Philippines, and mainland China.

Organization and Tactics. According to the Malaysian government, the total number of Communist guerrillas is now around 2,500 (up from 2,000 figure in 1971), but this is generally regarded as too low (*The Economist*, London, 8 May 1976, p. 62). Another recent estimate puts the number inside peninsular Malaysia as not exceeding 500, divided into operational units of from three to twelve, with an additional 2,000 to 3,000 in jungle training camps in southern Thailand (David Andelman, *NYT*, 9 July). Most observers believe that the combined following of the CPM and the MNLA on both sides of the border is now well above 3,000 and that there are also probably 4,000 scattered sympathizers, with varying and fluctuating sentiments of commitment, among Chinese- and "New Left"-oriented Malays and Indians.

Malaysian officials tend to stress that the CPM and MNLA are primarily based across the frontier in Thailand, e.g. in the Betong salient. In early Apri 1976, for example, home affairs minister Ghazali Shafie told the Dewan Rakyat, Malaysia's parliament, that "only about 250 to 300 members" of the CPM's "assault unit" had "infiltrated" into peninsular Malaysia. He added that although the CPM allegedly had declared 1975 a "year of combat," its actions and those by the rival splinter factions had been limited. Ghazali said that thirty-one members of Malaysian security forces had been killed during the year in fighting against the insurgents, and an additional eighty-seven injured. Only seven Communists were known to have been killed in armed clashes, he reported, but their casualties likely had been more, since the insurgents took away the bodies of slain comrades. Security forces during 1975 also destroyed "30 Communist camps and 125 resting places." (*New Straits Times*, Kuala Lumpur, 8 April; *FBIS*, 9 April.)

Earlier in the year Ghazali tried to pinpoint the composition of the Communist guerrilla force with great accuracy. There were 2,054 Communists involved in operations against Malaysia from "within and without (i.e., from southern Thailand)," he said. Of this number, there were 732 Malaysians of Chinese origin, 107 of Malay origin, and two of Indian origin, together with 661 Thais of Chinese origin, 509 Thai Muslims, 23 Malaysian Chinese "claiming to be Muslim converts," and a remainder of other backgrounds, including "two Japanese." (*Malaysian Digest*, Kuala Lumpur, 15 February, p. 8; Ghazali's figures are at variance with other, official estimates.)

The basic structure of the CPM and MNLA and its satellite organizations remained unchanged. Led by a Central Committee of about forty-five persons headed by the veteran party leader Chin Peng, the CPM's membership and informal following overlaps with its principal affiliates (some of which are little more than paper organizations): the Malayan Communist Youth League, Malayan Peasant Front, Malayan National Liberation Front, Malayan National Liberation League, and Malayan Patriotic Front. The MNLA is the CPM's chief "mass" organization, however, and its main focus is on party recruiting efforts. The Islamic Solidarity Party (Parti Persuadaraan Islami; usually called by its acronym "Paperi") was established in 1965 by the MNLA's "Tenth Regiment" for the purpose of winning a following among Muslim, ethnic Malay villagers and peasants living on both sides of the Thai-Malaysian border. Tactical and leadership problems rendered Paperi relatively insignificant until late in 1973, when it began to urge a more militant and religiously exclusivist line, including advocacy of establishment of a wholly Muslim religious state in Malaysia (*New Straits Times*, 12 May 1976; *FBIS*, 13 May). This tactic evidently sought a connection with secessionist sentiments long apparent among some orthodox Muslims of ethnic Malay extraction living in Thailand's southern provinces. But the extent to which the CPM and MNLA have been able to exploit Islamic orthodoxy among Malays remains controversial.

The Malayan National Liberation Front (MNLF), Malayan National Liberation League, and Malayan Patriotic Front are all virtually identical with each other (indeed the last two groups are de facto arms of the MNLF), and serve primarily as a deep-cover political propaganda and recruitment mechanism for the CPM (as distinguished from a fighting force like the MNLA) in Malaysia's town and in Singapore (see *Singapore*). The Malayan Communist Youth League has its own executive committee and acts as the CPM's principal link to restive or radicalized Chinese youth in the country. The Malayan Peasant Front is a much more shadowy organization, reportedly concerned with radicalizing Malay rubber smallholders badly squeezed by fluctuations in world market prices.

Statements broadcast during 1976 by the CPM over its clandestine radio transmitter, "Voice of the Malayan Revolution" (VOMR), believed to be located in China's southern Yunnan Province, reiterated basic policy perceptions and positions of the past. A New Year's message viewed the "revolutionary armed struggle" in Malaya as being carried forward by "workers, peasants, poor urban residents, students" and other "oppressed people." Workers are reportedly continuing their struggle to "improve living standards," peasants have demonstrated to "demand free development of land and an increase in the prices of farm products," and students have been "increasingly integrating themselves" with peasants and workers in their own struggle "for freedom and justice," while "poor urban residents and rural working people" are described as resisting official efforts to drive them off their property and "force them to leave their homes" (the latter is a reference to periodic attempts by the government to remove illegal squatters from public lands). The same message excoriated the government for its "anti-people" policy (e.g., the increase of police force by 20,000) and for permitting inflation and failing to combat the rise in unemployment.

The message also stressed, however, that, internationally, the world's "revolutionary people," and "socialist China" in particular, have been winning important victories, such as the victory of the "three Indochinese peoples," which not only marked the failure of "U.S. imperialism" but also "exposed the features of Soviet social-imperialism pretending to support the national liberation movement." As the crisis of international capitalism deepens, according to the New Year's message, the "revolutionary armed struggles" of the people of other Southeast Asian countries like Burma, Thailand, the Philippines, North Kalimantan, and Indonesia are becoming mutually supportive and are winning one victory after another, and the "Palestinian and African people's armed revolutionary struggle" is forging ahead. (VOMR, in Mandarin to Malaysia and Singapore, 3 December 1975; *FBIS*, 6 January 1976.)

A broadcast on 29 April 1976, commemorating the CPM's 46th anniversary on the next day, emphasized the long-time fraternal unity between the CPM and the Communist Party of China. "Armed with Marxist-Leninist—Mao Tse-tung Thought," according to the VOMR, the CPM remains committed to the principle of not taking the road of parliamentary democracy, and not launching armed risings in the towns, but, instead of "using the countryside to encircle the cities, and seizing state power by means of waging armed struggle." The 1972 CPM constitution (*YICA, 1974*, pp. 495-96) was reaffirmed as the basic organizational guide for the party. Credit was claimed for an increasingly successful armed struggle ("new areas for guerrilla warfare are being expanded"), particularly in Perak, Southern Kedah, Kelantan, Wellesley Province, and Pahang, and for a widening "revolutionary mass movement" through Malaysia. The importance of simultaneously waging armed struggle and "all kinds of mass movements" is related, in the statement, to the need to mobilize rural people, particularly agricultural workers, in keeping with the principle that "we must continue to regard the countryside as the center of our tasks." (*FBIS*, 4 May.)

In this connection, the anniversary statement also urged implementation of the CPM's new land program, adopted by the Central Committee on 20 Deember 1975, charges that "large numbers of peasants are landless or have little land to farm" while large arable areas are in the hands of "big landlords, bureaucrats, plantation owners, and foreign monopoly capitalists"; when peasants claim jungle land in order to "make a living," the "reactionary government" charges them with illegal occupation. The "new democratic" reform program of the CPM provides for confiscatin and nationalization of the land of the big owners and "bureaucrats" and, in principle, for its distribution among the peasantry. However, the program suggests that such distribution will not necessarily be applied to all land that is nationalized. Large plantations, for example, will remain intact and be owned by the new "Republic of Malaya," to be operated with farm workers' participation in their management. Rice-producing lands held by the "bureaucratic organs" (i.e., the state or national Malaysian governments), capitalists, or (unspecified) "national traitors" will be distributed free of charge to landless or poor peasants; such free distribution also applies to "waste lands," presumably uncultivated lands under state control. (VOMR, in Mandarin to Malaysia and Singapore, 27 December 1975; *FBIS*, 31 December.)

On the other hand, plantations of "the middle and small nation capitalists would not be nationalized, though the living and working conditions of laborers on these estates would be improved through "consultation." A distinction is also to be made, however, in keeping with Chinese Communist doctrine, between "tyrannical" and "enlightened" landlords. The land of the former would be confiscated, whereas only the "surplus" lands of the latter would be "requisitioned and purchased through consultation." This "suplus" land would then be distributed free to the landless or peasants. Protected (i.e., free from confiscation) also is all land owned by religious organizations, schools, public welfare organizations, and religious teachers. The influential political and social role of the popularly venerated Muslim *kiajih* or *ulema* (scholar of the Islamic writ) in rural Malayan society, many of whom own or control considerable land, is thus explicitly recognized in the CPM program. There are also categorical assurances that "all usurious debts" are to be invalidated, that tenant farmers will be protected in their particular rights to the land they are now farming, that "poor" farmers will be safeguarded in their "legitimate" ownership of the lands on which their dwellings now stand, their vegetable plots, and rice fields, and that rents and taxes will be cut. (Ibid.)

A United front of peasants and farm workers must be formed in order to achieve all these objectives, and the CPM's general agrarian line is summarized as follows: ". . . to rely fully on the poor peasants and farm workers; to unite closely with the middle peasants; to win over the rich peasants; to abolish the neocolonialist and feudalist land system step by step; to liberate the productive forces in the countryside; and to develop agricultural production" (ibid.).

As in the past, CPM tactics are designed to enlist the support of ethnically or religiously self-conscious groups in the pluralistic Malaysian society. Thus, the party has been engaged in fostering Chinese cultural pride, and in projecting an image of being the champion of private Chinese language schools, frequently the target of Malayan and later Malaysian government suspicion and regulatory controls in the past. In April 1976 the VOMR charged the "reactionary" government with "frantically" attempting to eliminate Chinese-language education in the country, and with forcing the closing down of Chinese schools. The VOMR noted the closing down by the Negri Sembilan state government in February of a Chinese-language primary school in the Bahau district, an action which it said had aroused "unparalleled indignation" among the inhabitants of the area. (Broadcast in Mandarin to Malaysia and Singapore, 17 April; *FBIS*, 19 April.) A month later, the VOMR quoted a leader of the Malayan Chinese Association (the conservative Chinese government-support group of the Alliance Party, now in power in Malaysia) and Deputy Education Minister to the effect that graduates of private Chinese primary schools in Malaysia were disinclined to continue their education in the state-owned Chinese secondary schools, preferring to attend a private Chinese secondary school. This, the Deputy Minister allegedly said, was an "unhealthy development" which the parents should rectify. The broadcast, inquiring as to why the "reactionary" government seemed to "hate" the private Chinese schools so much, declared that the answer lay in the fact that these schools had remained staunch defenders of Chinese-language education, whereas the "national" or state Chinese secondary schools had become tools for the elimination of Chinese-language education. (VOMR, in Malay to Malaysia and Singapore, 15 May; *FBIS*, 20 May.)

Correlatively, CPM tactics play on the Islamic identity of the Malays in Malaysian society, and CPM media naturally have served as a megaphone for the policy announcements of its front, the aforementioned Paperi or "Islamic Solidarity Party." The CPM relayed the message of the Paperi's

Central Committee of 13 March 1976, which not only attacked the new Malaysian premier—Hussein Onn, who succeeded Tun Abdul Razak upon the latter's death in mid-January 1976, but also, and more importantly, addressed itself to the problems of the conservative Muslim peasant and village dweller, often economically hard-pressed by falling rubber prices and alarmed over secular and modernizing influences in his environment. On the one hand the message excoriated the "big bureaucrats" of the Hussein Onn regime for allegedly oppressing and exploiting the farmer:

> More and more peasants in the country have gone bankrupt and tens of thousands of them have been deprived of their land under the fabricated accusation of illegal occupation. Several hundreds of thousands of acres of their land have been seized and controlled by the "Federal Land Development Bureau" and other bureaucratic organisations (VOMR, in Mandarin to Malaysia and Singapore, 16 March; *FBIS*, 18 March).

On the other hand, it asserted that "Socialist China is becoming stronger" and China's prestige is increasing, while "Soviet social imperialism has met condemnation everywhere." The "struggle of the Islamic believers," whether in the Arab countries, southern Thailand, or the southern Philippines, was said to be steadily developing, with "new victories" being won in these areas. (Ibid.)

In keeping with its tactics of promoting recognition of ethnic identity, the VOMR, as in the past, commemorated the bloody events of 13 May 1969, when a post-election demonstration erupted into serious Sino-Malay racial disturbances in and around Kuala Lumpur, in which hundreds of Chinese fell victim. According to a VOMR commemorative broadcast in mid-May 1976, the "reactionary" nature of the government's "nationality policy" has been fully exposed, and "all nationalities" (ethnic groups) in Malaysia now realize that "only by implementing" the CPM's program will they be able to attain equal rights. (Broadcast in Malay to Malaysia and Singapore, 15 May; *FBIS*, 25 May.)

There is little certainty about the organization and size of the CPM's two offshoots, although early in 1976 government sources, claiming information gathered from defectors, asserted that the CPM(ML) had a following of about 200 and the CPM(RF) about 100, an increase for the former and a drop for the latter, compared with 1975 (*YICA, 1976*, p. 333). Each has its Politburo and Central Committee, but the names of current party leaders have not been published. Each faction has a "Malayan People's Liberation Army." The CPM(MF)'s MPLA is active along the border between Kedah and Perlis, and that of the CPM(ML) in Eastern Kedah along the Thai border and in and around the capital, Kuala Lumpur. According to government sources, units of the parent CPM's MNLA and the CMP(ML)'s MPLA met in bloody clashes during 1975-76 as they contested for territorial control; the clashes appear to have intensified as CPM(ML) forces attempted to take over the principal border infiltration routes leading from Thailand into Malaya. (Radio Kuala Lumpur, domestic service in English, 1 March; *FBIS*, 2 March.)

Branding the CPM(ML)'s MPLA as "controlled by Soviet Revisionism," the CPM radio has also accused the "so-called Marxist-Leninist Faction"—the CPM(ML)—with encroaching on the territory of the MNLA, imposing "a fascist rule in areas under its control," and "ruthlessly intimidating and blackmailing the people" (VOMR, in Mandarin to Malaysia and Singapore, 3 April; *FBIS*, 7 April). The reported relative increase in CPM(ML) strength and the VOMR's admission that its "Marxist-Leninist" rival actually has come into "control" of some of the CPM's operational areas suggest that the CPM(ML) may be more than holding its own in the struggle for hegemony of the West Malaysian Communist guerrilla movement. The CPM's major MNLA combat units, consisting of three regiments, have remained formally operational: the "Eighth Regiment" in upper Kedah State; the "Twelfth Regiment," including the MNLA command and CPM central secretariat, reportedly operating around Kroh in Northern Perak and into the Thai Betong salient; and a "Tenth Regiment," said to consist in part of Malays, in northern Kelantan State between Tanah Merah and Pasir Mas.

In Sarawak the NKCP and NKPGF have continued an intermittent, weak guerrilla struggle, under the NKCP chairman, Wen Ming-chuan; but the party clearly has not yet recovered from the hundreds of defections suffered in the Sri Aman amnesty and rehabilitation campaign. The NKPGF is estimated to have been between 150 and 200 members, mostly Sarawak—or West Indonesia—born ethnic Chinese, mostly men and women in their twenties, who were educated in Chinese private schools in Malaysia. Once-active NKCP front groups, like SFA and SAYA, are currently little more than paper organizations. Other than Wen Ming-chuan, and Lei Hai-ching, information officer, the names of Central Committee members have not been published. The NKPGF appears to have been reduced to small, furtive jungle-guerrilla units, with a few deep-cover supporters in the Sarawak towns and among the Chinese border population. Yet a trickle of recruits, mostly unemployed young Chinese, is continuing to flow to the NKCP.

Occasional NKCP policy statements, broadcast by the VOMR, have usually been concerned with denouncing the "Right Opportunist Capitulationist line" followed by those in the NKPGF who accented amnesty. There is also emphasis on the NKCP's general line of holding "still higher" the "great red banner of Marxism-Leninism—Mao Tse-tung Thought" and persisting "along the revolutionary road of encircling the cities from the countryside and seizing political power by armed struggle" (VOMR, in Mandarin to Malaysia and Singapore, 8 June 1976; FBIS, 10 June). On 22 July the VOMR broadcast an article by NKCP theoretician Ma Li, urging "conscientious study" and a "firm grasp" of "Marxism-Leninism—Mao Tse-tung Thought." Ignoring the study of revolutionary theory is viewed as a great danger to the party. (FBIS, 28 July.)

Over the years the social base of support for Communism in Malaysia has remained much the same, according to an analysis by the government's Department of Psychological Warfare. In remote rural areas the rubber tappers, loggers, and farmers are easily intimidated into giving food and money to the Communist guerrillas, some of whom have friends or relatives in certain villages who can be persuaded to provide covert support. Economic grievances or threats of exposure of past affiliation with the CPM during the "Emergency" of the fifties may impel others to give assistance. However, the psywar analyses indicate that it is not the poorest segment of the populace that usually provides the Malaysian Communists with their followers; rather, supporters are generally from among the more educated and skilled. Also, in the rural areas it is the *literate* small farmer, hard pressed by fluctuating rubber prices, who may be sympathetic to the Communist cause, whereas in the towns the skilled and semiskilled, ranging from carpenters and automobile mechanics to taxi drivers and shop employees, provide a source not so much of in-the-field party recruits, but rather of sympathizers and occasional agitators. The same may be said of hawkers and slum dwellers. Western-educated Chinese, or others in the modernized urban Malaysian intelligentsia, rarely are CPM supporters; it is rather the Chinese-language-educated group, with a stronger and allegedly more "parochial" Chinese identity, and feelings of having been slighted in advanced educational and/or employment opportunities, that is likely to fall in with Communist appeals. (Denzil Peiris, "Faceless Enemy," *Far Eastern Economic Review*, 13 February 1976, pp. 11-12.) According to Malaysian prime minister Datuk Hussein Onn, the Communists are "also trying to weaken the people's spirit through drugs and immoral activities" (FBIS, 7 September).

Domestic Developments. There were relatively fewer terrorist attacks and guerrilla clashes with security forces in 1976 than in the previous year, when August and September brought a spate of ambushes, bomb and grenade attacks, booby trap explosions, and armed skirmishes with the MNLA and the CPM(ML)'s MPLA (*YICA, 1976*, pp. 341-42; *Asia Research Bulletin*, 30 September 1975, pp. 124-25). On 13 November 1975, the chief police officer of Perak was gunned down, along with his driver, at noon in the town of Ipoh, and ten days later a deputy police superintendent was shot and seriously wounded in Kuala Lumpur. A nearly simultaneous spate of armed robberies in the capital, like the ongoing chain of assassinations of senior police officials, has been seen as part of a terrorist and "urban guerrilla" campaign directed possibly by the CPM(ML) (K. Das, "Malaysia Prepares for

Total War," *Far Eastern Economic Review*, 26 December, pp. 23-25). The new violence prompted an announcement by then premier Tun Abdul Razak of severe new surveillance and security control measures, as well as an announcement that Communist terrorists had also been discovered in attempting to gain a foothold in the state of Pahang, not previously thought of as a focus of Communist activity (*Sarawak Tribune*, Kuching, 10, 18 November).

By early February 1976, police officials in Perak State asserted, however, that recent tactics in ferreting out Communist subversives in the state had been successful, and that the public had come forward to provide essential information. At the same time, the Malaysian deputy inspector general of police announced that "Communist subversive activities throughout peninsular Malaysia" had been "seriously disrupted" because of "high pressure police operations in the last few months." (*FBIS*, 6, 11 February.) While a comparative lull in incidents was quite apparent during 1976, Malaysian officials, including the new premier, Datuk Hussein Onn, warned of the need for continuing vigilance and for public cooperation with the government in defeating the Communists. Hussein in particular made it a point, in an address in mid-March, to say that Communist ideology was totally in conflict with the teachings of Islam because it denied that the universe was created by God (*New Sunday Times*, Kuala Lumpur, 14 March).

Insurgent activity, however, had by no means vanished. During April, for example, a Malaysian Air Force helicopter was shot down by guerrillas along the Thai border, railway tracks in several areas, including Perak State, were blown up, and an attempt was made to blow up an electric power station in Kuala Lumpur, while other bombs went off there at a construction site and in the suburban village of Kepong. In the last incident two Chinese youths reportedly were arrested as they tried to place another bomb and "Communist flags" near the village. (*FBIS*, 28, 30 April.) On 30 April also, as various explosive devices went off in different parts of the capital and in nearby Petaling Jaya, two "suspected Communist agents" were arrested while planting booby-trapped red flags in Kuala Lumpur; there were no casualties and it was speculated that the explosions were in commemoration of the 46th anniversary of the MNLA (*New Straits Times*, 1 May; *FBIS*, 3 May). The Kedah State chief minister said on 23 April that in the continuing anti-insurgency operations in his state, two Communist camps in the Ulu Muda forest reserve, near the Thai border, had been captured (*FBIS*, 27 April).

The VOMR, meanwhile, hailed MNLA victories against security forces, and claimed success in the laying of mines in northeastern Kedah and other areas which, allegedly, "badly demoralized" Malaysian troops. A VOMR report relayed in mid-May by the Thai Communist radio transmitter claimed "many victories" over "local reactionary troops" in the border region of Kelantan State, although no details of these encounters were provided (VOMR, in Mandarin to Malaysia and Singapore, 28 February, and "Voice of the People of Thailand," clandestine in Thai to Thailand, 18 May; *FBIS*, 2 March, 24 May). On 3 July the government announced that new security units were being formed so as to enable citizen volunteers to "participate directly" in encountering Communist subversion. Some 220 persons from Perlis, Kedah, Perah, and other areas had already been selected for the new force. (*FBIS*, 7 July.)

On 22 June two of Malaysia's leading journalists, Abdul Samad bin Ismail, a prominent literary figure and managing editor of Kuala Lumpur's *New Straits Times*, and Samani Muhamad Amin, news editor of the Malay-language *Berita Harian*, were arrested under the Internal Security Act. Ismail was charged by the Malaysian government with "direct involvement in activities in support of the Communist struggle for power in this country," and Amin with being his accomplice. In an informational release the Home Affairs Ministry said that Samad had been a member of the CPM in Singapore, and had been arrested and held by the British there in 1951-53. Samad had risen to considerable prominence as a writer in Malaysia, it was said, but his activities were "subtly designed to blur the public fear of and antagonism towards a possible Communist take-over" of both peninsular Malaya and Singapore. Samad was also said to have created friction by "denigrating Islam" so as to reduce

Malay resistance against the Communist ideology. The arrest of Samad and Amin appeared to stem from the arrests on 16 June of two prominent journalists in Singapore who, according to a 22 June press statement of the Singapore government, had "revealed that since 1972 they were involved in a Communist scheme masterminded and directed" by Samad. (K. Das, "Malaysia the Enemies Within," *Far Eastern Economic Review*, 2 July, pp. 8-9; *NYT*, 23 June.) In an interview over Radio Television Malaysia on 1 September, Samad said that as an undercover Communist activist he had been "directed to penetrate" the United Malays National Organization (UMNO), the dominant Malay party in the government, and "to obtain Malay support." Samad declared that he had been a member of the CPM since 1949. (*FBIS*, 3 September.)

Both in Singapore and Malaysia there were questions about the validity of the charges against the arrested journalists, particularly since the Malaysian government's charges against Samad and Amin were lacking in the specifics of the subversive acts alleged. Observers believed the arrests to be an outgrowth of a government policy position, buttressed by alarmed and more conservative Islamic elements in the UMNO, that national consciousness in the country needed to be raised ever higher in the struggle against the CPM and its allies, in view of the potentially dangerously eroding effect on public morale and opinion of a seemingly interminable guerrilla struggle.

Frequent waves of arrests add to raising the national sense of crisis. In mid-June in two major sweeps in Perak and Kelantan 37 suspected "Communist agents" were arrested, and a month later the chief minister of the state of Johore announced that 205 had been arrested for "subversive activities" in that state alone in 1975, and 115 thus far in 1976 (*New Straits Times*, Singapore, 18 June, 31 July).

Insurgent activity in Sarawak was by comparison far less. Occasional clashes were reported in the Sankei district, in Lundu, in the Matang area, and in the Nonok Peninsula. The results of the announced "big-scale" government security operation against about two score guerrillas operating in the Lundu region (*Sarawak Tribune*, 21 November 1975) remained inconclusive, as most of the NKPGF force was apparently able to slip away. Former guerrillas who had surrendered under the Sri Aman program assisted the Sarawak government in issuing appeals to their former comrades to come out of the jungle. In January 1976, thirty such "self-renewed" former guerrillas signed a joint letter to the NKPGF, expressing appreciation to the government for its "generous and liberal policy" which had enabled them to be reunited with their families and to begin a new life (ibid., 10 January). Joint Indonesian-Malaysian border patrols have continued, occasionally making brief contact with and flushing out guerrillas from frontier hamlets (*Angkatan Bersenjata*, Djakarta, 14 January) and, unlike the Thai-Malaysian joint border patrol system, encountering few operational problems. Speculation is growing that some NKPGF elements have transferred their operations to Sabah. A number of bomb explosions in the Sabah towns of Kota, Kinabalu, Sandakan, and Kudat, and the arrest of 32 persons allegedly involved (*New Straits Times*, 10 May; *FBIS*, 11 May), have been attributed in some circles to Communist terrorists, while others blamed current tensions among rival Sabah political factions. The Sabah government has, thus far, declined to reveal the causes of the bombings. On 3 September the Malaysian national news agency Bernama reported that Sarawak authorities want "dead or alive" six NKPGF leaders, among them NKCP Central Committee member Hung Cho Ting, age 39, described as the NKPGF's "overall commander" of the insurgents' "special task force."

International Developments. During the first half of 1976 a serious strain developed between the Thai and Malaysian governments over border security. Increasing Malaysian concern that Thai officials were permitting CPM-MNLA elements to find a kind of informal sanctuary in the Betong district of Thailand's southern Yala Province, whence they could strike at will into Malaysia, had already produced a discussion between Thai premier Kukrit Pramoj and Malaysian premier Hussein Onn, during the latter's visit to Thailand on 10-12 February. The two then agreed in principle to revise and, according to Malaysian sources, "give more muscle" to their system of joint operations against the insurgents, with details to be worked out later by lower ranking officials (*Malaysian Digest*, Kuala Lumpur, 15 February, p. 8).

Meanwhile, the Thai population in the Betong salient had reportedly become increasingly dissatisfied with the forceful, across-the-border anti-guerrilla operations of Malaysian security forces, which were said to have led to kidnapings of Thai citizens and otherwise to jeopardizing the safety of those in the Betong district. On 21 April and again on 27 April, Malaysian jets reportedly bombed and strafed suspected terrorist positions on what they believed to be Malaysian territory but which turned out to be inside the Thai border. Betong residents who claimed destruction of property staged protest demonstrations, which the Malaysian press termed "Communist inspired and Communist directed" (*New Straits Times*, 7 May). On 4 May some 10,000 demonstrators in the town of Betong, capital of the district, demanded withdrawal of the Malaysian security forces stationed there under the joint border agreement.

In Malaysian circles, meanwhile, resentment mounted that the MNLA was being supplied by its Thai agents across the border, and that Malaysian military operations against CPM insurgents even inside the border were allegedly being frustrated by intelligence given to the insurgents by their Thai contacts (K. Das, "Border Breaking Point," *Far Eastern Economic Review*, 14 May, pp. 10-11). Thai officials, on the other hand, expressed concern that Thai Muslims in Yala and other areas were covertly being encouraged in their anti-Bangkok secessionist aspirations by orthodox Muslims and their political leaders in the northern Malaysian states. Thai Communists, reportedly, have encouraged such secessionist sentiments, as has the CPM. As the Thai press published complaints of Betong demonstration leaders that Malaysian forces on Thai soil "acted as if Thailand belonged to them," at least one leading Bangkok daily admitted editorially that "It is true that for 20 years Thailand has taken a lukewarm view of Communist insurgents in South Thailand, mainly because it was clearly known that the intention of the CPM was to attack Malaysia and not Thailand" (*Voice of the Nation*, Bangkok, 8 June; *FBIS*, 8 June). The allegedly friendly relations between the inhabitants of the Betong district and the MNLA and CPM personnel living in de facto sanctuary in their midst (the latter was referred to in Betong as "Chinese Border Guerrillas") — a state of affairs which local Thai officials, concerned with Communist insurgents elsewhere in their country, reportedly see no reason to change ("Why Thailand Wants Malaysia to Leave Communist Sanctuary," *Asia Research Bulletin*, Supplement, 31 May, pp. 204-5) — hardened the attitude of the security-conscious Malaysian government.

Yet Kuala Lumpur appeared to have few options in the face of the Betong demonstrations. After Thai foreign minister Phichai Rattakun and Malaysian home affairs minister Ghazali Shafie conferred on the problem in Kuala Lumpur, a new "understanding" was reportedly reached on 26 May between the two governments. After a formal Thai request, Malaysian forces were withdrawn from the Betong district, and Thai police units began replacing them on 17 June. Still, though the Malaysian government had agreed to the withdrawl, it made its deep concern abundantly clear to Bangkok authorities, indicating that it might become necessary for Kuala Lumpur to regard the district as "hostile territory" and to close the border with Thailand (Harvey Stockwin, "Troubled Border," *Far Eastern Economic Review*, 18 June, p. 8; *NYT*, 18 June). The Kuala Lumpur daily *New Straits Times*, on 9 June, commenting on the "Betong Vacuum" resulting from the agreed-to withdrawal of Malaysian forces, editorially contrasted this with the "more effective scheme for joint military operations" along the Borneo border agreed to by Indonesia and Malaysia only a week earlier.

In the weeks after the withdrawal from Betong, Malaysian authorities began restricting the flow of Thai trade to the Malaysian border town of Kroh, and in turn Thai traders in Betong began clamping down on the informal border trade coming from Malaysia. Malaysia insisted that henceforth all Betong taxis and buses would have to carry insurance before they could cross the border into Malaysia, and the Kuala Lumpur government now also asserts that Thai peasants have illegally been cultivating some 7000 acres of land in the northern part of the Malaysian state of Perak. (*Asia*

Research Bulletin, Supplement, 30 June, p. 215.) Malaysia's National Security Council, according to a government statement on 28 June, authorized still further but unspecified tightening of security measures along the border, in order to "check infiltration of Communist and subversive elements into the country." Also approved by the Council was an amendment to the internal security regulations, providing for the registration of workers in certain sensitive industries (*FBIS*, 29 June).

The VOMR, continuing to articulate the CPM's foreign policy outlook, praised the appointment of Hua Kuo-feng as premier of the People's Republic of China as marking a victory in the struggle to defend the "Great Proletarian Revolution" and beating back "the right deviationist wind" of Teng Hsiao-ping, the "revisionist" and "capitalist roader" (VOMR, in Malay to Malaysia and Singapore, 10 April, *FBIS*, 13 April). Earlier broadcasts extolled Mao Tse-tung's doctrines as a model for the MNLA and excoriated "Soviet social imperialism," which, it was alleged, had been following "in Hitler's footsteps" and thus had now become "the main source of a new world war" (VOMR, in Mandarin to Malaysia and Singapore, 31 January; *FBIS*, 5 February).

Malaysia's official relations with both the USSR and People's China underwent no change during the year, although the Hussein Onn government's continuing emphasis on the domestic Communist threat by implication raises questions in the public mind—and particularly in circles of the United Malays National Organization, the government's parliamentary mainstay—about the prudence of such relations. Formally, however, the Kuala Lumpur government remains committed to establishment of friendly relations and diplomatic ties with most Communist powers. On 3 July it said that an agreement had been signed to sell People's China an unspecified quantity of Malaysian rubber directly through a Malaysian company. On 28 May seven Vietnamese officials arrived in Kuala Lumpur to establish the embassy of the new Socialist Republic of Vietnam. (Malaysia and the then Democratic Republic of Vietnam in Hanoi had established diplomatic relations on 30 March 1973, but did not agree on an exchange of ambassadors until 15 October 1975. The Hanoi government's embassy in Kuala Lumpur will be housed in the building of the former South Vietnamese embassy, which had been taken over by the Malaysian government after the Provisional Revolutionary Government came to power in Saigon last year. The PRG subsequently informed the Malaysian government that the building should be transferred to the DRV, a directive with which the Malaysian government complied (Agence France Presse dispatch, Kuala Lumpur, 27 May; *FBIS*, 1 June). During a visit of the deputy foreign minister of the Socialist Republic of Vietnam, Phan Hien, to Kuala Lumpur in June, the Malaysian government announced its readiness to provide Hanoi with technical aid to rehabilitate its rubber and develop its palm oil industry. Phan Hien, in a Kuala Lumpur interview, declared that removal of all foreign bases was a precondition for Hanoi's acceptance of the neutralization of Southeast Asia, a concept pioneered by Malaysia (*FBIS*, 9 July).

Whether relations between Hanoi and Kuala Lumpur may be caught up in the present pattern of Sino-Soviet rivalry and whether the longer-term insurgency problem may become more serious are questions that have figured in recent speculations about Malaysia's future position toward the Communist world (see, e.g., "Leapfrog in Asia," *The Economist*, London, 24 Januaary, pp. 13-14).

Publications. On 4 May 1976 a transmitter identifying itself as "Suara Rakyat Malaya" (Voice of the People of Malaya) was heard on 7084 KHZ, with a very weak signal. It announced that future broadcasts would occur twice daily in Malay and Chinese. (*FBIS*, 12 May.) As yet it is not possible to determine which CPM faction the new transmitter belongs to. The clandestine VOMR remains the chief external communications medium of the CPM, broadcasting in Mandarin and Malay. The VOMR occasionally relays statements by the Maoist faction of the underground Indonesian Communist Party and of the NKCP.

The Malaysian Communist groups, having now no regularly appearing printed media, all rely in varying degrees of frequency on mimeographed leaflets, primarily for limited domestic distribution.

The *Malayan Monitor & General News*, the principal mimeographed publication of CPM supporters in London, has since 1974 appeared infrequently. One-time organs of the NKCP, like *Masses News* and *Liberation News*, have not appeared in the past three years. Those media of People's China, addressed to foreign audiences, which at one time gave frequent coverage fo NKCP and CPM activities, have in recent years paid only limited attention to them, although the domestic Chinese press is somewhat more frequent in its reports on Malaysian developments.

University of Bridgeport

Justus M. van der Kroef

Mongolia

A fusion of two revolutionary groups produced the Mongolian People's Party in 1921. The party held its First Congress in March of that year at Kyakhta, on Soviet territory. It became known as the Mongolian People's Revolutionary Party (MPRP) in 1924. Fiftieth-anniversary celebrations in November 1924 commemorated the shift to "socialism" in 1924, but Russian dominance had already been established in 1921. The designation of the country as the Mongolian People's Republic (MPR) was adopted in 1924, as was the name of the capital, Ulan Bator (formerly Urga). At that same time a non-capitalist and anti-bourgeois line was announced by the party's Third Congress and the first Great Khural (the structural equivalent of the USSR Supreme Soviet).

In 1976 the MPRP claimed 70,000 members (compared with some 58,000 in recent years). The population of the MPR is perhaps 1.5 million.

Organization and Leadership. The MPRP is organized along the lines of the Communist Party of the Soviet Union (CPSU). The party's longtime first secretary, Tsedenbal, continued in office in 1976. The 17th Party Congress, 14-18 June, elected a somewhat larger Central Committee consisting of 91 full members and 61 candidates. There were a few personnel changes in the Politburo (8 full members, two candidates) and the Secretariat (6 members), but without any public denunciation or signs of purge. Politburo member S. Luvsan was retired and replaced by Ragcha (first deputy prime minister and former chairman of Gosplan), who was raised from candidate to full member. Deputy prime minister Gombojav, former commercial counselor in the Embassy at Moscow and also former minister of foreign trade, became a candidate member.

The Politburo consists of Tsedenbal, Batmunkh, Molomjamts, Maidar, Luvsanravdan, Jagvaral, L Jalan-ajav, and Ragcha as full members, Altangerel and Gombojav as candidates. The Secretariat consists of Sosorbaram, Tsedenbal, Molomjamts, Jagvaral, Jalan-ajav, and Gombojav.

Heading the MPR government as prime minister is Batmunkh. The first deputy prime ministers are Maidar and Ragcha; deputy prime ministers are Tsevegmid, Sodnom, Gombojav, Luvsangombo, Suren, and Pelje. Party secretary Sosorbaram serves concurrently as minister of culture. Pelje was formerly minister of geology and mining. In August, M. Dugersuren became minister of foreign affairs (replacing L. Rinchin).

Military presence and participation in the Party Congress, and in life of the country generally during the year, remained steady, with General Dorj (minister of defense), Lieutenant-General Dejid (minister of security), Lieutenant-General Yondonduichir (head of the army's Political Administration), and S. Bata (defense specialist on the Central Committee) all serving in conspicuous executive positions for the congress. There has been announced the intention to construct a new Army Museum in Ulan Bator and also a 70-foot-high monument in the center of the capital to commemorate joint Mongolian-Soviet military cooperation.

A distinct escalation in the dimensions of Tsedenbal's personality cult occurred in 1976, involving celebrations on his 60th birthday accompanied by extensive press attention and adulation. In an elaborate ceremony, a bronze bust of him was unveiled at his birthplace, Ulangom, in September. That event plainly copied the unveiling of the bust of Brezhnev at Dneprodzerzhinsk in the USSR in May. This kind of special attention, along with press photographs and general media coverage, clearly fixed Tsedenbal's ascendance over Batmunkh, the prime minister, who had shown signs of challenging Tsedenbal's leading position in 1975. Tsedenbal's Russian wife received some press attention also, but markedly less than in 1975.

Domestic Activities. The new Five-Year Plan (1976-80) confirms the already announced intention to increase exports to the USSR, particularly of mining products, with the new gigantic copper-molybdenum project at Erdenet the centerpiece of the effort. But until the mine goes into production, scheduled for 1978 or 1979, and as the USSR increases its shipments of machinery and equipment, the trade imbalance can be expected to grow, having risen from 166 million rubles in 1974 to 230 million in 1975. Mining products comprised less than 7 percent of Mongolian exports to the USSR in 1975, and the plan calls for them to attain 30 percent of the total by 1980. The city of Erdenet continues to grow, with a 1976 population of 16,000 and a newly proclaimed separate status as a "republic city." (The MPRP has 18 aimak committees; three separate city committees—for Ulan Bator, Darkhan, and Erdenet; and a committee for the Ulan Bator Railroad Administration.)

The plan calls for substantially increased production of coal; new mines at Baganur are to provide 2 million tons of the 4.5 million total aimed for by 1980. Mongolia has developed further its role as substitute supplier of fluorspar to the USSR, replacing China: its exports increased to 302,000 tons in 1974/75 (from 250,000) while Chinese exports decreased to 55,000 tons (from 85,000). The plan includes reference to private livestock holdings, with no indication of any intention to restrict or eliminate them, but most of the animals continue to be collectively held. The herds total just over 23 million head, almost 2 million head more than in 1971, but 100,000 fewer than in 1973. The decades-old goal of 25 million head remained unattained. A Central Committee meeting in January called for a large New Lands program, involving 230,000 hectares (568,000 acres) added for grain farming and for the establishment of eleven new state farms. The Five-Year Plan confirmed the commitment, with 38,000 hectares representing the 1976 share of the total to be attained by 1980.

Two short-distance rail lines connect the Erdenet copper-molybdenum mine and the new Baganur coal mine to the Trans-Mongolian Railroad. Some high-voltage power lines in north-central Mongolia already are linked to a new Soviet power complex near Lake Gusinoe, and the Mongolian Five-Year Plan postulates integration of a major Mongolian power-grid with the USSR's East Siberian one. Most mining, industrial, and manufacturing development in Mongolia is located near the Siberian border in the valley of the Selenga River, north of Ulan Bator, and the Selenga feeds into Lake Baikal. Pulp and cellulose plants in Mongolia threaten pollution of the famed East Siberian Lake, and members of a

Mongolian "Society for the Protection of the Environment" now participate in a Joint Soviet-Mongolian Working Group to control such pollution.

Education continues to get high priority, with full middle schools at most state and collective farms. More boarding schools now serve the many rural pupils. The Ulan Bator Medical Institute graduated 300 doctors in 1976, and most of them were sent to work in rural areas. The "Ulan Bator Medical Technicum named Salvador Allende" graduated about 500 paramedics, midwives, X-ray and laboratory technicians, and nurses. Stress on Russian-language proficiency continues everywhere, with three to five hours a week devoted to it in all schools from the third grade on. Physical education and sports, aimed partly at Olympics participation, are the focus of more attention than ever. Television programming increases in quantity as availability extends via more cable and relay lines. Ulan Bator TV presented live coverage of the Party Congress, and a recent late movie was a documentary on Erdenet. Satellite transmission provides Moscow programming in Mongolia.

International Views and Activities. Tsedenbal led a large party-state delegation to Moscow in mid-October 1976. Brezhnev's reception of the Mongols was publicized as a major event in the USSR and Mongolia. The speeches of the two leaders on that occasion, as well as Tsedenbal's report to the Party Congress in June and specific reference in the new Mongolian Five-Year Plan, called for ever closer ties of the MPR to the Soviet Union in "politics, economics, culture, science, ideology, and society." Already existing strands of the infrastructural web binding Mongolia to the USSR were strengthened, and significant new ones were added. A "Soviet House" was opened in Ulan Bator, offering lectures, library facilities, exhibits, and Russian-language lessons, and the staff traveled around the country giving lectures and showing films, "acquainting the populace with Soviet achievements."

In the USSR there are 25 branches of the Soviet-Mongolian Friendship Society, operating at republic, *oblast'*, and city levels. Evidence of symbolic symbiosis of the two countries appeared when all the foreign delegates to the MPRP congress in Ulan Bator were taken to the principal monuments: the statue of Lenin, the memorial to the Soviet Army on Ziasan Mountain, and the Red Square-inspired Sukhe Bator-Choibalsan Mausoleum. Politburo member Molomjamts pointed out that the 25th Congress of the CPSU provided the model for the MPRP congress.

The new Five-Year Plan calls for closer integration of the Mongolian economy with the Soviet economy, and implementation is supervised by the Mongolian-Soviet Intergovernmental Commission for Economic, Scientific, and Technological Cooperation. The 60-year-old Maidar, a Politburo member for thirteen years and one of Mongolia's two first deputy prime ministers (he was also chairman of the Mongolian State Planning Commission in 1951), heads his country's side of the Intergovernmental Commission. His Soviet counterpart is a deputy prime minister of the USSR, I. T. Novikov. Educational connections are also even closer than before. A special dormitory was opened at Irkutsk University for 450 Mongols. They spend a year there in preparation for attendance at other Soviet higher educational institutions. It was reported that of 444 foreign students in higher education in the city of Volgograd, 61 are Mongols.

The special East Siberian and Soviet Central Asian connection to Mongolia was illustrated in the membership of the Soviet delegation to the MPRP congress: it included the Party first secretaries of the Buryat Autonomous Republic, of the Krasnoyarsk *krai*, and of the Tajik Republic. The current Soviet ambassador to the MPR was for many years party first secretary of the Chita *oblast'*. The concentration of new projects and developments in that part of Mongolia from Ulan Bator north to the Soviet border continues to develop the role of the MPR as a political and economic extension of East Siberia.

The death of Mao Tse-tung in September caused immediate cessation of the violent attacks on Maoism and the People's Republic of China which had been customary in the Mongolian media up to that time. Joint statements of Tsedenbal and Brezhnev in Moscow in October omitted any but bland references to China, whereas Tsedenbal's report to the MPRP congress in June rejected "reactionary Maoism" and accused the Maoists of joining with "racist-Fascist cliques" and imperialism against world socialism. One lower Party official's report at the congress repeated earlier Mongolian accusations that the Chinese were conducting a kind of germ warfare by deliberately sending infected livestock across the border into the MPR. However, leading Mongolian officials, including a candidate member of the Politburo and the minister of foreign affairs, paid their respects to the deceased leader at the Chinese Embassy on 10 September and a telegram of condolence was sent to Peking on 14 September (and was rejected by the Chinese).

The parties of China, Cambodia, and Albania did not send delegations to the MPRP congress. The many countries whose parties did so included Vietnam, Laos, North Korea, Cuba, and Yugoslavia. The visit in October of Laotian leader Kaysone Phomvihan, more specifically and clearly than in any previous case, was a textbook propaganda presentation—in the speeches, joint communiqué, and media coverage. The MPR offered its example to Laos as an object lesson in advancing from feudalism to socialism, skipping capitalism, made possible through the political and economic assistance of the USSR, and the Laotian guests unqualifiedly acknowledged and endorsed the idea.

The Third Congress of Mongolists, held in Ulan Bator on 28 August-4 September drew 200 delegates from twenty countries, including the United States. One of the Mongolian participants who delivered a report was B. Rinchen, who had been vigorously attacked as a liar and an opponent of socialism in the Mongolian press in March. This outstanding scholar, now over 70 years old, has many times before been vigorously attacked, yet he has survived and participated in scholarly meetings. Many conferences and meetings of various groups and organizations in Communist bloc countries were held in Mongolia during 1976, for example, the 8th Conference of Ministers of Culture of the Socialist Countries, and a meeting of the directors of youth publishing houses (Komsomol and Young Pioneers). The Asian Peace Conference met in Ulan Bator in mid-October, with delegates from some twenty countries. The declaration it issued particularly condemned the USA and its plans for developing Diego Garcia in the Indian Ocean. China, which did not send a delegation, was ignored except for a mild reprimand for its failure to adhere to the nuclear nonproliferation treaty. Diplomatic recognition was extended to the MPR by an additional six countries, bringing the total to 80, but that number still does not include the USA.

A representative from Mongolia serves as president of the Asian Buddhists, who held their Fourth Congress in Tokyo in July. The organization expressed its opposition to military bases in the Indian Ocean and called for a zone of neutrality there. United Nations projects continue in Mongolia, including the first moves to establish a computer center, and the opening of a trainees' communications center with equipment supplied by Japan and several other countries.

Publications. The MPRP issues *Unen* (Truth), *Namyn Amdral* (Party Life), the Russian-language *Novosti Mongolii* (News of Mongolia), and a Chinese-language weekly, *Meng-ku Hsiao-hsi Pao* (News of Mongolia). *Ediyn Dzasag* (Economics) is issued by the party Central Committee, and *Shine Hodoo* (New Countryside) by the Ministry of Agriculture. The MPR assigns a representative to the editorial board of *Problems of Peace and Socialism*. There are radio broadcasts in Mongolian, Russian, English, Chinese, and Kazakh. Television broadcasting was begun in 1970.

University of North Carolina   Robert A. Rupen
Chapel Hill

Nepal

The Communist Party of Nepal (CPN) was formed in 1949, and its membership is estimated at about 5,000. All political parties have been banned in Nepal since 1960 when the late King Mahendra dissolved the Nepali Congress party (NC) government. A "partyless' panchayat (assembly) system of government was later established. The CPN's major competitor among active political groups is the democratic-socialist NC. Nepal's population is approximately 12,600,000.

Leadership and Organization. The CPN has been openly split since 1960 when the King's actions exacerbated internal ideological and personal disagreements. The moderate faction led by Keshar Jung Raimajhi, the general secretary, has retained party control. Through its pro-monarchy stance and support of "progressive" government measures such as land reform, the Raimajhi CPN and its sympathizers have gained positions in government and officially sponsored political organizations.

Revolutionaries Pushpa Lal Shrestha, Tulsi Lal Amatya, and their supporters, militantly opposed to the monarchy, fled to India where they formed a parallel CPN organization at the "Third Party Congress" in May 1962. Further factionalization has developed in the revolutionary CPN. Pushpa Lal remains in India, but the less militant Man Mohan Adhikar, a CPN founder who was imprisoned for several years, now leads an extremist faction in Nepal.

Both CPN organizations operate within Nepal, concentrating their activities in the Kathmandu Valley and in the Tarai, the southern plains adjoining India, but in general their influence appears limited. Communist sympathizers appear most numerous among students, educators, and urban elements.

Among student groups, the pro-revolutionary CPN All Nepal National Independent Students' Union (ANNISU) competes with the National Student Union, sponsored by the moderate CPN. Their major non-Communist rival is the NC student organization, the Nepal Students' Union.

Domestic Attitudes and Activities. Although the moderate CPN has supported the monarchy, its policies and views as outlined at Raimajhi's own "Third Party Congress' in 1968 were critical of the present political system. The congress criticized the ban on parties, demanded the release of all political prisoners, and proclaimed the need for restoring democratic rights. Working with the system, the moderate faction's ultimate aim was establishment of a national democracy. Immediate targets in this task were "workers, peasants, students, youth, traders, and professionals." (*New Age*, New Delhi, 12 January 1969.)

The extremist CPN has called for reinstatement of political parties, restoration of parliamentary democracy, and distribution of surplus land among the peasants. Pushpa Lal and Adhikari differ over strategy: while Pushpa Lal has advocated overthrow of the King, Adhikari has been working for domestic political reforms.

Terrorist activity in Nepal, allegedly involving CPN extremists and NC dissidents, has declined since 1974. Those arrested during that year for subversive activities included a number of revolutionary CPN members, including Adhikari's nephew and members of its student affiliate, the ANNISU (*YICA,*

1975, p. 392). Periodic arrests of "extremists" and "Naxalites," however, continued in 1976 (*Gorkhapatra*, Kathmandu, 4 February; *Rastra Dhwani*, Kathmandu, 27 February). Several were arrested for smuggling literature from Pushpa Lal Shrestha in India (*Naya Sandesh*, Kathmandu, 2 July). Meanwhile, nevertheless, a number of his supporters have reportedly been seeking government permission to return from exile (*Rastra Dhwani*, 11 February).

The limited constitutional reforms of the panchayat system announced by King Birendra in December 1975 were the focus of political activity during 1976. Throughout 1975 there had been widespread political debate on the type and extent of reforms desired, and both the moderate and extremist CPN factions proposed liberalization measures.

The constitutional revisions included opening of the National Panchayat sessions to the public and increasing the membership of this assembly. One of the new National Panchayat members is D. P. Adhikari, associated with the extremist CPN. In addition, the "Back to the Village" campaign, originally formed to encourage national development, was given constitutional status. The campaign has been authorized to interpret panchayat ideology, aid in formulating political programs, and evaluate panchayat workers.

Various Nepalese politicians have welcomed the changes, but most CPN figures have not reacted publicly. Since the reforms fell short of their proposals, they are presumably dissatisfied. D. P. Adhikari did comment on the new policy of consensus in panchayat elections; while welcoming the "atmosphere of consensus," he thought that more time was needed for the selection of candidates (*Gorkhapatra*, 30 June).

Additional political prisoners were released during the year. According to an official statement in April, 266 out of 316 detainees under the Public Security Act had been released thus far (*Rising Nepal*, Kathmandu, 17 April). Some of the newspapers banned in 1975 to control the activity of "irresponsible elements" remained closed, however, including the *Raimajhi* and Soviet-oriented *Samiksha* (*YICA*, *1976*, p. 351).

International Views and Policies. The moderate CPN is recognized and given financial assistance by the USSR, which the party Congress in 1968 praised as a "bulwark of peace, Socialism and national liberation," while criticizing China's views (*New Age*, 12 January 1969). The moderate faction would prefer closer Nepal-Soviet relations, and the pro-Raimajhi *Samiksha* has previously criticized the state of these relations (*YICA*, *1976*, p. 351). During 1976 a delegation from the World Peace Council visited Kathmandu.

Competing factions of the revolutionary CPN have appealed to China for closer working relationships, but Chinese involvement appears limited to some financial support. In September, the Nepal-China Friendship Association and the Nepal-China Cultural Association sponsored one of the memorial meetings held in Nepal for Mao Tse-tung (*Peking Review*, 15 October). During the same month, extremist leader Man Mohan Adhikari called on the Nepalese to give "concrete support" to the liberation forces in southern Africa (*Matribhumi*, Kathmandu, 28 September).

Publications. The now banned weekly *Samiksha* has reflected the view of the moderate CPN. The Pushpa Lal Shrestha revolutionary faction reportedly publishes *Nepal Patra.*

Alexandria, Virginia   Barbara Reid

New Zealand

The Communist Party of New Zealand (CPNZ) was founded in 1921. For some time it functioned as a section of the Communist Party of Australia, but in 1927 it gained its independence and in the following year it affiliated with the Communist International. At the time of the Sino-Soviet split it took the Chinese side, which led to defections and expulsions of the pro-Soviet minority. In 1966 the latter formed a rival party, the New Zealand Socialist Unity Party (SUP). The third major Marxist group is a Trotskyist organization, the Socialist Action League (SAL), founded in 1969. In addition there exist several minor groups, some of them very small in numbers, such as the Communist Party of Aotearoa, the Wellington Marxist-Leninist Organization, the "Struggle" group, the South Auckland Marxist-Leninist Group, and, on the Trotskyist side, a Wellington Marxist group and a youth group in Auckland sponsored by the Australian Socialist Labour League.

These organizations are all legal, and they publish their points of view in pamphlets and leaflets, but only the three major groups are able to produce regular journals. Total membership is small, perhaps 400 altogether with an estimated 100 for the CPNZ, 160 for the SUP, and 50 for the SAL. The population of New Zealand is 3,100,000.

CPNZ and SUP membership is predominantly working class—in the case of the SUP, 80 percent are claimed to be wage earners, the rest salary earners, students, and housewives, with women making up 26 percent of the total (*WMR*, August 1976). The SAL had its origin among university students, and its average age is therefore considerably lower than that of the older Communist parties.

After a long period of decline there is again some evidence of growth of the extreme left, due to the deteriorating economic situation and the intensification of industrial conflict. The main beneficiary of this trend seems to have been the SUP, which is strongly anchored in the trade union movement.

Leadership and Organization. The general secretary of the CPNZ is V. G. Wilcox, who has held this office since 1951. Other national leaders are R. C. Wolf, described as secretary of the CPNZ (*Peking Review*, 30 September 1976), R. J. Taylor (who returned to New Zealand from Albania in 1976), and A. J. Rait. Leadership and membership are aging and the party, according to the rival SUP, is "in a state of fragmentation" and "plays an insignificant part" (*Socialist Politics*, March 1976).

The CPNZ Rules provide for a triennial national conference which elects the National Committee, which in turn elects the Political Committee and the general secretary. No national conference has been held for the last ten years and there has therefore been no opportunity to replenish the leadership constitutionally. The refusal of the party leaders to call a conference in accordance with the Rules, their opposition to secret ballots, and their preference for co-optation to higher bodies have caused internal dissension, which led to the most recent split in the South Auckland area.

The SUP is similarly constituted, with triennial conferences which elect a national president, national secretary, and the remainder of the National Committee. The current national secretary, G. E. Jackson, has held this office since the party's foundation. The fourth national conference of the SUP, at Auckland in October 1976, also marked the party's tenth anniversary. During the year the SUP restructured its organization in Auckland, where the bulk of its membership is concentrated, and held a regional conference in May which elected an Auckland Regional Committee. "Whereas formerly we operated mainly through neighbourhood branches," said the SUP national secretary, "now we are concentrating on the organisation of viable branches in industry" (*WMR*, August).

The SAL constitution provides for a national conference every two years, and its fourth conference is set for Christmas 1976. The League dissolved its Christchurch branch and is concentrating on strengthening its two branches in Wellington (where it is the strongest Marxist organization) and Auckland. The most prominent SAL leaders are G. A. Fyson, K. Locke, and R. Johnson.

Auxiliary Organizations. The three major groups each sponsor a youth organization, though the SUP's Democratic Youth Front (DYF) appears to be little more than a name. The Progressive Youth Movement (PYM), associated with the CPNZ, is the oldest. It celebrated its tenth anniversary with a function in Auckland in February 1976 which was addressed by CPNZ general secretary V. G. Wilcox. It continues to publish an irregular newsletter, *Rebel.*

Both PYM and DYF are confined to Auckland. The only nationwide Marxist youth organization is the SAL's Young Socialists, who held their second national conference in Auckland in April, with an attendance of some 150 people. The Young Socialists contested the student elections in Wellington and Auckland during the year, with minor successes in Auckland. They continued publication of their quarterly journal, *Young Socialist*, which reached a circulation of 700 to 800 copies.

Party Internal Affairs. Internal warfare continued to rend the CPNZ. The plenum of August 1975 was intended to unite the party around a new active policy and to help it break out of its self-imposed isolation. It is now clear that the plenum was also the signal for a new round of internal "two-line struggles" over the question of inner-party democracy. In October 1976 the CPNZ announced the expulsion of one of its leading members, S. H. Hieatt, who had joined the party more than 35 years earlier and had served on the National and Political Committees.

Hieatt was denounced as a "capitalist roader" and "revisionist," as well as an informer for the Security Intelligence Service (*People's Voice*, 4 October), but his real crime was having insisted on implementation of the party constitution, the holding of the long-postponed national conference, and the election of party officials by secret ballot. The leadership's view was that "The extent of democracy practised by our party is determined by objective and subjective factors. We do not practise 'full publicity' for the obvious reason that we are living in a class society dominated by the class enemy. Nor do we practise election to all offices. Certainly election of leading committees at all levels is practised. But if all offices include specialist workers or members being given increased responsibility under the guidance of elected committees, then election to all offices is not practised." (*N.Z. Communist Review*, June 1976).

Hieatt and the party members who left with him formed the South Auckland Marxist-Leninist Group and issued a statement setting out their fundamental organizational differences with the party. They continue to support the Chinese Communist Party and claim to have no political differences with the CPNZ.

Domestic Attitudes and Activities. The change of government following the election defeat of the Labour Party in November 1975 brought a sharp turn to the right in New Zealand politics. The USSR has been proclaimed the main external threat to New Zealand, and the SUP the major enemy within. With China, on the other hand, the new government is anxious to establish friendly relations, and the Prime Minister visited and praised Mao Tse-tung. There is rarely any official mention of the CPNZ unless it be disparaging, such as the comment by the retiring head of the Security Intelligence Service that the CPNZ was largely moribund, without much popular appeal, and torn apart by quarreling and internal dissension (*New Zealand Herald*, 17 July 1976).

The same interview expressed concern, however, over the high percentage of SUP members in trade union positions, while the Prime Minister has repeatedly attacked the SUP—for example, accusing it of orchestrating an attempt to destroy the government's economic stabilization policy, and calling it the "most disruptive element in New Zealand society" (*Auckland Star*, 26 November). In October the Minister of Labour joined the chorus by releasing "Red Rules of Revolution," allegedly found in 1919 in Düsseldorf on the body of a Communist courier. These were soon shown to be a long-exposed hoax of American origin, but when asked for his source the Minister next provided a telegram which claimed confirmation in another well-known forgery, the "Protocols of the Learned Elders of Zion."

The SUP has probably benefited from these attacks which gave it nationwide publicity. The party conducted an intensive recruiting drive during the year and claimed considerable growth. It certainly widened its influence in the trade unions, and its president, G. H. Andersen, was elected president of the influential Auckland Trades Council in October. Strains in the economy caused an unprecedented increase in strike activity, in which SUP trade union leaders have been to the fore. The repressive attitude of the new government has also brought about a revival of the protest movement around such issues as racism and sporting contacts with South Africa, abortion and women's rights, and visits by nuclear warships. In all these campaigns members of the various Marxist groups have been active.

Even the CPNZ, which in the past has been inclined to sit on the sidelines and refuse cooperation with other groups, has now joined these protests, though without lessening its attacks on the USSR and the SUP. It no doubt finds it embarrassing that Hua Kuo-feng urged the New Zealand prime minister to maintain the military alliance with the U.S. and Australia; but in line with Chinese policy the CPNZ regards the USSR not just as a country where capitalism has been restored, but as an imperialist power—moreover, the "major world imperialism" and the "major threat of world war" (*N.Z. Communist Review*, April). In New Zealand, on the other hand, the party sees—"whilst capitalism remains"—an irreversible trend toward fascism with no possible return to bourgeois democracy (ibid., November).

The SAL has little foothold in the trade unions and has been most active in the various protest campaigns. In February it released copies of files relating to CIA surveillance activities in New Zealand, which had been turned over to the Socialist Workers' Party in the U.S. by court order. G. A. Fyson, who was named in these files, toured New Zealand in March to speak on the CIA disclosures.

International Activities and Contacts. As in 1975, no CPNZ visits to China have been reported in 1976. The party has, however, maintained its unquestioning support for the Chinese leadership, sent messages of congratulations and condolence when appropriate, and denounced the "vile crimes" of both Teng Hsiao-peng and the "Gang of Four." Similar messages of support went to the Albanian Party of Labor.

The SUP greatly increased its overseas contacts during the year. National secretary G. E. Jackson attended the 22d Congress of the French Communist Party and the 25th Congress of the Soviet Party, and also visited Mongolia. A. B. Skilton attended Bulgarian and Czechoslovak party congresses, and F. E. McNulty the 9th congress of the East German party. In addition a small delegation led by P. Cross visited the USSR and East Germany, Denmark, and Britain in June at the invitation of the Communist parties of these countries.

Early in the year a statement of the SUP National Executive renewed the call for an international Communist meeting (*Socialist Politics*, March). The national conference of the SUP, in October, resolved to support "the calling of a world meeting of communist and workers' parties, in view of the changed conditions and new perspectives facing the world communist movement" (*New Zealand Tribune*, 1 November).

The SAL sent three delegates to the 4th national conference of the Australian Socialist Workers' League (now the Socialist Workers' Party) in Sydney in January. Jim Percy, the national secretary of that party, visited New Zealand in October, and the SAL also organized a tour in July with Willie Mae Reid, vice-presidential candidate of the Socialist Workers' Party of the USA.

Publications. The official organs of the three major groups are the *People's Voice* (CPNZ), published weekly in Auckland; the *New Zealand Tribune* (SUP), published fortnightly in Auckland, and *Socialist Action* (SAL), published fortnightly in Wellington. A fourth radical journal, *The Paper*, with which expelled CPNZ members in Wellington were associated, ceased publication in November 1975. Format, size, and distribution of these journals are all very similar: eight-page tabloids with an estimated circulation of between 2,000 and 2,500 copies within New Zealand. *Socialist Action*, which has probably the largest circulation, plans to increase its size to twelve pages from the beginning of 1977.

The CPNZ also publishes a monthly theoretical journal, *N.Z. Communist Review*, in Auckland. The SUP equivalent, *Socialist Politics*, appears quarterly. A third theoretical journal, which made its appearance in October 1975, is *Struggle*, subtitled "For the Study and Application of Marxism-Leninism-Mao Tse-tung Thought in New Zealand." This is published at irregular intervals by former CPNZ members in Porirua, near Wellington.

University of Auckland   H. Roth

Pakistan

In 1976 the illegal and virtually non-existent Communist Party of Pakistan (CPP) continued to pose no discernible threat to the government of Pakistan. The CPP, an offshoot of the Communist Party of India, was formed shortly after Pakistan became independent with the partitioning of British India in August 1947. In 1954 the GOP banned the CPP as a subversive and illegal organization under the provisions of the Criminal Law (Amendment) Act of 1908. The CPP continues to be proscribed under the Political Parties Act of 1962, which as amended prohibits the formation or functioning of any party that the government identifies as detrimental to "Islamic ideology" or to the "integrity and security of Pakistan."

Foreign observers speculate that in 1976 the CPP had between 500 and 1,500 members, a tiny fraction of the country's 70 million population. The identity of most of the members presumably was known to the government's various police and security organizations. In addition to the intelligence and investigative units within the Police Service of Pakistan (PSP), the Special Police Establishment, and the Federal Security Establishment, and to the Inter-Services Intelligence Board, another organization—the Intelligence Bureau of the Cabinet Division—reports directly to the prime minister and conducts intelligence and surveillance functions for him. These pervasive and at times competing organizations reportedly use networks of paid informants to infiltrate anti-government and other groups.

Until it was banned in February 1975 the National Awami Party (NAP) was the most prominent and effective opposition party. The government of Prime Minister Zulfikar Ali Bhutto has continued to imply—particularly to foreign government officials and foreign journalists—that the NAP was a subversive front organization for the illegal CPP and that the party's best known leader, Khan Abdul Wali Khan, was pro-Soviet as well as pro-Afghanistan and pro-Indian. This latter charge was linked to allegations that the NAP received support from Afghanistan and India, which states in turn depend upon Soviet economic and military assistance. There no doubt have been Communists in the NAP, but most of the leaders have been ideologically much closer to West European socialism than to the Soviet or Chinese models. NAP and other opposition leaders who have fled Pakistan have taken refuge in the United States or the United Kingdom; as of late 1976 no prominent NAP refugee was known to have gone either to the Soviet Union or the People's Republic of China after fleeing Pakistan.

In 1973 Prime Minister Bhutto dismissed the popularly elected NAP government of Baluchistan Province and forced the resignation of the NAP-coalition government in the North West Frontier Province. Hundreds of NAP leaders from the two provinces were subsequently arrested. On 15 April 1976 the government placed 44 NAP leaders on trial before a special tribunal on charges of high treason and of waging war on Pakistan. The special court was convened under the terms of an amendment to the 1908 Criminal Law Act. The amendment, passed on 13 April 1976, grants the government and the special court sweeping powers to suppress dissident groups and individuals.

With the banning of the NAP and the imprisonment of its leaders, some members of the NAP joined the National Democratic Party, which was formed in late 1975 by Sher Baz Mazari, Baluch chief or Sardar. Others sought a more militant organization. In Baluchistan—where during the 1973-76 period four or more Army divisions, elements of the paramilitary Frontier Corps, and detachments of the Pakistan Air Force were heavily engaged with tribal guerrilla forces—a self-described Marxist-Leninist organization emerged under the name of the Baluch People's Liberation Front (Baluch Awami Azadi Mahaiz). The leader of the front's military arm was Mir Hazar Khan, who reportedly views autonomy for Baluchistan—the front's initial aim—as a prelude to "socialist revolution" throughout Pakistan. The front either absorbed or was allied with a group of former students who had formed the Popular Front for Armed Resistance, which described itself as pro-Soviet.

Socialist issues and slogans have become blurred and confusing in Pakistan. The Baluch People's Liberation Front calls for a socialist revolution, whereas Bhutto's Pakistan People's Party (PPP) espouses Islamic socialism under the slogan of "Islam our Faith, Democracy our Policy, and Socialism our Economy." The constitution, which was drafted under Bhutto's close supervision, asserts that "the State should ensure . . . the gradual fulfillment of the fundamental principle, from each according to his ability, to each according to his work." Prime Minister Bhutto frequently asserted that the NAP in Baluchistan was the tool of the Sardars—the tribal chiefs—and on 8 April 1976 a government decree abolished the Sardar system. Yet Bhutto's agents in Baluchistan are Sardars, and in 1976 Bhutto ruled the area through his appointed governor, the Khan of Kalat, the hereditary titular head of the Baluch people and Sardars. And despite the government's firm stance against communism in domestic affairs. Bhutto's cultural adviser was Faiz Ahmad Faiz, who is the country's sole Lenin Peace Prize winner and in 1951 was involved in an abortive coup attempt known as the Rawalpindi Conspiracy.

Prime Minister Bhutto's flexibility and political dexterity continued to be apparent on the international scene. On the one hand, Pakistan during 1976 maintained its close diplomatic relations with China and expanded those with North Korea. On the other hand, it has used extensive military and economic assistance from monarchical and anti-Communist Iran in suppressing the uprisings in

Baluchistan. Furthermore, Pakistan continues to solicit and receive financial aid from such oil-rich and fervently anti-Communist Arab monarchies as Kuwait and Saudi Arabia.

Nationwide elections are scheduled to be held in the spring of 1977.By late 1976 most of the opponents of Bhutto's PPP were either in jail, in exile, or disbarred from standing for public office. Foreign observers feared that the government's rigorous suppression of those agitating for increased provincial autonomy in Baluchistan and the North West Frontier Province and Bhutto's willingness to use the police power of the state against his political adversaries were creating a situation in which opponents of government policy—particularly students and other dissidents in those two provinces and in Sind—might conclude that clandestine, illegal, and violent activity in such organizations as the Baluch People's Liberation Front was the only option available to them.

The American University   Richard F. Nyrop
Washington, D.C.

Philippines

Two formally outlawed, underground party organizations—one pro-Peking, with an active guerrilla force operating in most major areas of the country, the other smaller and oriented toward Moscow, with virtually no fighting units left—form the matrix of Communist activity in the Philippines today. Despite their foreign ideological and policy orientations, both Philippne Communist parties claim to be genuinely national organizations, addressing themselves primarily to national needs. The pro-Chinese faction is continuing its armed resistance and "people's war" against the government, and its units, on occasion, appear to be meshing their tactics with those of the Muslim insurgents in the southern part of the country, although Muslim leaders have rejected government allegations that their movement is Communist-infiltrated. The visit of Philippine president Ferdinand Marcos to Moscow, during the first week of June 1976, and the establishment of Soviet-Philippine diplomatic relations have accentuated the pro-Moscow faction's policy of seeking a cautious and critical collaboration with the government, stressing a commitment to "peaceful" change and with the probable aim of eventually obtaining a relegitimization of the party.

History. The Philippine Communist Party (Partido Komunista ng Pilipinas; PKP) was not formally established until 7 November 1930, although Chinese and Indonesian Communists, as well as Philippine trade unionists, had been disseminating Marxist-Leninist doctrine in the country for several years. This relatively late official founding reflected the low priority which the Comintern assigned to the Philippines and its position that the Philippines, then a possession of the United States, were a primary responsibility of the distant Communist Party, USA (CPUSA). Philippine Communist sources hold that the party had already organized itself on 26 August 1930, and that this is its true founding date.

Early party cadres were heavily dependent on CPUSA directives, and were drawn primarily from lower-middle-class white-collar workers and from the more radical trade union leaderships, like that of the Marxist labor federation Katipunan ng mga Angkpawis sa Pilipinas ("Association of the Sons of Sweat of the Philippines") or KAP. Crisanto Evangelista, a KAP leader, became the PKP's first secretary-general, and the party, after a series of poorly planned strike ventures and anti-government demonstrations, quickly ran into repressive government action. Both the PKP and KAP were officially banned on 14 September 1931, and on Comintern instructions the underground remnant of the party (some PKP leaders, Evangelista among them, had been arrested and given lengthy jail terms for sedition) began developing a number of front organizations in the hope of building radical ideological influence in the accelerating Philippine movement for complete national independence.

After the decision of the Seventh Comintern Congress, in 1935, to mobilize a global united-front struggle against fascism, a CPUSA functionary named Sol Auerbach (traveling under the name of James S. Allen) secured the release of Evangelista on 31 December 1936 by approaching the Philippine Commonwealth president, Manuel Quezon. Auerbach also brought about a merger of the PKP (by then relegalized to a degree by Quezon, who was concerned to unite all Philippine political groups behind a national demand for independence) with the small Socialist Party of the Philippines. The merger was formally announced at the PKP's third national congress in Manila on 29-31 October 1938, which also marked a new high in the party's respectability in the Philippine political system (Alfredo B. Saulo, *Communism in the Philippines*, Manila, Ateneo Publications, 1969, pp. 33-34).

The Japanese invasion during World War II provided Philippine Communists with additional opportunities to expand their influence, and the party played a major role in mobilizing the anti-Japanese resistance movement in the country, particularly the "Anti-Japanese National United Front," whose military committee on 29 March 1942 organized the "Anti-Japanese People's Army" (Hukbo ng Bayan Laban sa Hapon, or Hukbalahap—"Huks" in everyday parlance). A separate "squadron" of Communist-oriented Philippine Chinese operated alongside the Huks, but remained organizationally independent. When the war ended, PKP leaders expected that the HUK movement would assure them and their leftist associates a commanding political position, but the new government of the Philippines (which became an independent republic on 4 July 1946) soon arrayed itself against the PKP and the Huks. Having refused to surrender their arms, the Huks were outlawed on 6 March 1948. On 29 August of that year, a prominent Huk leader, Luis Taruc, who earlier had been expected to lead a new Huk accommodation with government policies, launched a vigorous criticism of President Elpidio Quirino's failure to keep his alleged promises to release imprisoned Huks and implement various agrarian and social reforms. According to the government, Taruc's attack marked the beginning of a new phase of organized armed Huk resistance (*The Communist Movement in the Philippines*, SEATO Short Paper, no. 46, Bangkok, March 1970, p. 23).

The new Huk organization, Communist-directed almost from its inception, but increasingly having to cope with undisciplined local commanders more concerned with enriching themselves than with the furtherance of political causes, called itself the "People's Liberation Army" (Hukbo ng Mapagpalaya ng Bayan; HMB). It was formally established on 7 November 1948 under the nominal leadership of Luis Taruc. Taruc, who, though legally elected to the post-war Philippine House of Representatives, was in effect denied his seat by the government because of his Huk affiliation, later emphasized in conversation with the author that he never had been a Communist. The PKP directing the HMB in an extended "people's war" of guerrilla-style hit-and-run attacks and creating a "counter-government," hoped to generate enough combined political and military pressure to cause the government in Manila to fall by 1 May 1952. But an extensive economic aid and counter-insurgency program developed by U.S. and Philippine officials, and the land resettlement and reform policies of Philippine defense secretary and later president Ramon Magsaysay, eventually turned the tide against the HMB, which numbered some 25,000 at the end of 1950 but never recovered from the capture of PKP secretary-general José Lava and most of the party's Politburo on 18 October 1952. By 17 June 1957, when the passage of Philippine Republic Act No. 1700 formally outlawed both the PKP and the HMB, the Communist party had already been shattered and the Huks' activities were rapidly degenerating into mere brigandage, extortion rackets, and other crimes, although some Huk leaders continued to profess lofty social-reformist goals.

During the 1960s unfocused but militantly Leftist and nationalist sentiments among students, intellectuals, labor leaders, and in some peasant groups provided impetus for a new more disciplined and ideologically "purer" organization than the discredited and disorganized HMB, or the shattered PKP. Groups such as the national youth front Kabatang Makabayan, or the Malayang Samahang Magsasaka (Free Peasants Union) performed a radicalizing function as informal PKP fronts. Maoist doctrines also acquired popularity among students convinced that a new program of revolutionary violence was the only way that the Philippines would be able to shed its dependence on U.S. military and economic supports. On 26 December 1968 (Mao Tse-tung's seventy-fifth birthday), after months of internal bickering within the scattered remnant of the PKP leadership (on 12 May 1964 the PKP's last major underground leader, Dr. Jesús Lava, who had succeeded his brother José as party secretary-general, had also been arrested), Philippine Maoists opened their "Congress of Re-Establishment of the Communist Party of the Philippines" near the town of Capas, in Southern Tarlac Province, Luzon. At the conclusion of the congress, on 7 January 1969, a new Communist Party had been established, calling itself the "Communist Party of the Philippines-Marxist-Leninist" (CPP-ML) or "Communist Party of the Philippines-Mao Tse-tung Thought"). (On these developments see Eduardo Lachica, *Huk! Philippine Agrarian Society in Revolt*, Manila, Solidaridad Publishing House, 1971, and Justus M. van der Kroef, "The Philippine Maoists," *Orbis*, Winter 1973, pp. 892-926). On 29 March 1969, again at a meeting near Capas, CPP-ML cadres and followers, some with HMB or old Huk ties and experiences, formed a "New People's Army" (NPA). A campaign of guerrilla attacks on government posts and units was begun in Central Luzon and by 1974 had been extended to the island of Mindanao and the Sulu archipelago in the southern Philippines, where an uneasy tactical alliance was established with the Muslim rebel movement against the Manila government.

PKP spokesmen denounced the founding of the CPP-ML and its alleged "cowboy ideology" of violence, but after severing some party connections with the most disreputable Huk leaders, the PKP also began developing a small fighting organization of its own, called the "Army ng Bayan" or National Army. The "Army ng Bayan" remained small, ineffectual, and poorly organized, probably as a matter of party strategy. Unlike the NPA, it has made little or no name for itself as a guerrilla force.

The advent of the CPP-MN and the NPA coincided with a deepening political and constitutional crisis in the Philippines, and during 1970-72 alleged NPA terrorism and violent student demonstrations in Manila were linked by some Philippine officials to an impending Comunist-inspired coup attempt. Blaming the NPA for a widespread state of rebellion, President Marcos, himself increasingly the target of various political attacks, on 22 September 1972 proclaimed martial law throughout the Philippines. Marcos said that the Maoist insurgents were in control of "33 municipalities" and that they had established communal farms and production bases. But it has been widely felt that Marcos unduly accentuated the NPA threat, and the danger of allegedly Communist-inspired demonstrations and terrorism in Manila generally, in order to legitimize sweeping measures with which to maintain himself in power. From the start, the top leadership of the Philippine armed forces and prominent business circles, alarmed over the political instability occasioned by the demand for thorough constitutional and social reforms being heard from many—not just leftist—quarters, supported with little question the proclamation of the martial law regime. Marcos's new authoritarian structure of government suspended operations of the Philippine Congress and sharply curtailed all partisan political activities and media freedoms. It was, however, repeatedly upheld by the Philippine courts and in various popular nationwide referenda.

Clashes with NPA guerrillas meanwhile continued, but at an apparently lessened rate, and from 1973 onward the Marcos regime claimed that the NPA was attempting to infiltrate and establish a common strategy with Muslim dissidents in the southern Philippine islands, especially on Mindanao and in the Sulu archipelago. Here a "Moro National Liberation Front" (MNLF) even today seeks greater autonomy (some sources claim complete independence) for Philippine Muslims. While the CPP-ML and NPA remain dedicated to "people's war," PKP seems to favor a process of "peaceful revolutionary change," including support for the Marcos government's "progressive policies." This is in line with an attempt to win a new legitimacy for the Soviet-oriented party now that Manila has completed establishing diplomatic relations with Moscow, Peking, and a number of other major Communist nations.

Program, Organization, and Tactics. A statement issued by the CPP-ML on 26 December 1975, marking its seventh anniversary, claims that the party has established nine regional party organizations throughout the country, as well as mass organizations, "professional guerrilla units," local armed forces, local political organizations, and various "underground agencies" (*FBIS*, 5 April). Earlier, in a 1972 statement, the social base of the CPP-ML's various organizations was described as comprising (1) "poor and lower middle peasants," (2) workers from the "revolutionary trade unions," (3) students and "other sections of the intelligentsia," (4) elements of the "petty bourgeoisie," (5) those members of the "national bourgeoisie" who can be persuaded to "support in cash or kind or allow use of their facilities," (6) the "national minorities," such as the Southern Muslims whose struggle for "self determination or autonomy" the CPP-ML says should be supported (though this does not mean that the CPP-ML, or for that matter the PKP, supports secession and political independence for the Philippine Muslims in a new state), (7) clergy and religious groups opposed to the Marcos government, (8) elements of the Nacionalista and Liberal parties and other "political groups and figures" who want a change, (9) the Filipinos resident abroad, including students, immigrant workers, and intellectuals, especially in the United States, where they number half a million, and (10) officers and troops of the "reactonary" Philippine armed forces establishment, among whom there are claimed to be opponents of the Marcos government (*Ang Bayan*, English edition, 12 October 1972, pp. 10-13).

In the writings of CPP-ML chairman José Maria Sison, who uses the pen name Amado Guerrero ("Beloved Warrior"), and in the party program, the CPP-ML's principal aims are said to be the liberation of the Philippines from the hold of "U.S. imperialism" and "feudal oppression" and the founding of a "people's democratic state" or "new democratic republic." The new Philippine state, according to Sison, would be neither a "bourgeois dictatorship nor a dictatorship of the proletariat," but rather a "joint dictatorship of all revolutionary classes" under the leadership of the proletariat. Specific characteristics of the desired new state include elimination of all "bureaucrat capital"; severance of all bonds that tie the economy to "U.S. imperialism"; development of a "national scientific and mass culture" that meets the needs of the people; opposition to ASEAN (the Association of Southeast Asian Nations), SEATO (Southeast Asia Treaty Organization), and other "long-standing instruments of U.S. imperialism in the region"; and, in keeping with the spirit of "proletarian internationalism," development of strong relations with People's China, Albania, and "all revolutionary governments and peoples." All "unequal treaties" with the "international bourgeoisie" led by "U.S. imperialism" would be immediately abrogated. (Amado Guerrero, *Philippine Society and Revolution*, Manila, Pulang Tala Publications, 1971, esp. pp. 286-87, 294; also, *The Maoist Communist Party of the Philippines*, SEATO Short Paper, no. 52, Bangkok, 1974, pp. 14-17.)

Committed to the path of "people's war," the CPP-ML's operational focus is the New People's Army (NPA). CPP-ML and NPA memberships tend to overlap, but there appear to be different levels of commitment among members and supporters, and estimates of total strength tend to fluctuate considerably. The hardcore CPP-ML, including NPA cadres, numbers probably between 700 and 800 nationwide. But in the second half of 1975, after informal and "part-time supporters" had slumped rapidly on Luzon, the number of sympathizers and adherents began increasing on Mindanao, probably in conjunction with the Muslim insurgency which NPA units have supported. In October 1975, according to one authoritative report, in the three Davao provinces around Davao city on Mindanao alone, CPP-ML-NPA full-time cadres were estimated as "several hundred," with, additionally, "about 10,000 peasant members" (Bernard Wideman, "Stepping Up Terror Mindanao," *Far Eastern Economic Review*, 10 October, p. 16). What degree of commitment to the party these peasant members have is a matter of conjecture, however.

A CPP-ML Central Committee statement on 29 March 1976, congratulating the NPA on its seventh anniversary, said: "Conditions for us to take the road of armed revolution are better now than ever before." It is claimed that the NPA now has its guerrilla forces operating in eight areas of the country: in the northeast, northwest, and central parts of Luzon; in Southern Tuguegarao; in Bicol; in the Eastern and Western Visayas; and on Mindanao. The NPA, according to the statement, should be aware of the tactics of the "Marcos fascist dictatorship," including the forced resettlement of people, rebuilding population centers, and the "slaughter, assassination, mass arrest, arson, robbery and wanton bombing" allegedly being perpetrated in connection with the regime's "long-term operations" against the NPA. The NPA should make full use of "ambush and surprise," according to the statement, which repeatedly stresses that the war being waged against the Marcos government is a "protracted" one. The CPP-ML Central Committee also cautions against "adventurism," and urges "painstaking mass work" as the foundation of a successful NPA campaign. This work includes the organization of "peasant committees," with core groups to be formed in all the villages and rural areas so that, especially, poor peasants and agricultural workers can be effectively mobilized. (*FBIS*, 28 June.)

In 1973 the CPP-ML organized a "National Democratic Front" (NDF) as the vehicle of mass organizational coordination, but this has largely remained a paper organization in the Philippines and its principal supporters seem to come, rather, from the more militant anti-Marcos Filipinos residing abroad. Various Communist or Communist-infiltrated fronts operating in the later 1960s, before the CPP-ML was organized, like the industrial workers' "self-help" organization, "Brotherhood for our Development" (Ang Kapatrian sa Ikauunlad Natin; AKSIUN), or radical student groups like the Democratic Union of Filipino Youth (Malayan Pagkakaisa ng Kabataang Pilipino; MKPK) have gone out of existence, some of their supporters ultimately entering the ranks of the NPA. Although, according to its constitution, the CPP-ML has a central committee and politburo, and although the constitution provides that the party's national congress is the ultimate originator and legitimizer of all announced party policies, the names and activities of party leaders other than party chairman Sison are virtually never publicized, giving the impression that both central committee, and politburo are rather ephemeral bodies, while the CPP-ML national congress has not met since the party's founding at the close of 1968. Apart from winning support among Filipino dissidents abroad through the NDF, and continuing efforts to recruit peasant supporters, CPP-ML operations appear to be wholly focused on the NPA's "people's war." In January 1976 a number of leading NPA cadres fell into government hands, among them Antonio Zumel and Satur Ocampo, Politburo members, and José Luneta, a Central Committee member. The backgrounds of some of those arrested suggest that the leadership continues to come from intellectual rather than peasant/worker ranks. Luneta is a University of the Philippines graduate in political science, and Ocampo is a former business editor of the now defunct daily *Manila Times*. (FBIS, 26 January; see also Tillman Dardin, "Philippine Communism," *Problems of Communism*, May-June, p. 46.)

The Moscow-oriented PKP is a much smaller organization (one Philippine military intelligence source claimed to the author in early March 1976 that the PKP now numbered more than "about 70" known cadres and members), and its direction, still dominated by older party leaders, continues to be in disarray. This is in part because the PKP formally takes a more positive line toward the Marcos regime, in accordance with Soviet policy toward the Philippines today, than does the CPP-ML. This more moderate position is known to have caused disagreement among younger party members, who believe that it is less essential for the party to legitimize itself, and more important to capture and unify as much as possible the scattered, cowed, but still protesting anti-Marcos groups both in the nation itself and abroad.

PKP policy statements continue, however, to view the Marcos regime as moving gradually toward closer links with the Moscow-oriented bloc of nations, a process which, it is anticipated, will bring much greater benefit to the PKP underground in the long run than would militant opposition. In a message to the Central Committee of the Communist Party of the Soviet Union in early March 1976, on the occasion of the CPSU's 25th Congress, the PKP Central Committee summed up its position this way:

> The Philippines are one of the countries which have been favorably affected by the changes now taking place in the world in international relations. Under the leadership of the present government of President Marcos, the Philippines are freeing themselves from the fetters with which the United States has bound our country for decades, and they are implementing an independent and more self-reliant foreign policy, establishing, in particular, friendly relations with the socialist countries. This process is accelerating, because of the adverse consequences for the Philippines of the present crisis of capitalism which is making President Marcos' government more and more inclined towards the idea of the necessity for the establishment of stable trade and economic links, and of relations of mutual assistance with the socialist countries. (*Pravda*, 7 March; *FBIS*, 12 March.)

The PKP, according to a November 1974 statement, "does not aim to overthrow by force of arms the present government," but rather seeks to make that government serve better the interests of the Philippine workers, and this position "necessarily implies that PKP cadres shall be free to conduct the party's political activities" (*IB*, 1975, no. 3, p. 24). Thus, in return for the abandonment of armed opposition, the PKP expects the Marcos government to allow it to operate legally. There is no indication that this will happen anytime soon, however. The government seems to prefer to concentrate its anti-Communist suppressive activities against the NPA, while permitting key PKP members a kind of unincarcerated, peripheral, but not wholly legitimate, political and civil existence. Some PKP cadres who came out of hiding last year and surrendered are reportedly working as advisers in the government's land reform program.

The current program of the PKP was adopted at its Fifth Congress, held "somewhere in Luzon" on 10-11 February 1973, according to PKP sources. At about the same time a set of "immediate demands" was formulated (for details see *YICA, 1976*, pp. 362-63). Restoration of political liberties, an end to the martial law state of emergency, release of political prisoners, abrogation of all "unequal treaties" with the USA, and nationalization of banks, insurance companies, and the mining industry are among the major "immediate" demands. The PKP program warns that the party cannot be dragged "into left adventurist policy by infantile revolutionary phrasemongering"—a slap at the CPP-ML (*IB*, 1973, no. 11, pp. 35-36).

Domestic Developments. During 1976 there were frequent arrests and/or captures of NPA and CPP-ML members, and fighting also continued intermittently against Muslim dissidents in the southern islands with whom, according to government sources, the NPA is in tactical alliance. On 22 and 24 January, Philippine authorities announced the arrest of four prominent CPP-ML leaders, among them the previously mentioned José Luneta, who was identified as "no. 3" in CPP-ML hierarchy. The arrests had come "in the wake of military disclosures" that the "Communist movement" after a period of relative quiet, had "surfaced anew as a major threat to President Ferdinand Marcos' regime." (*FBIS*, 26 January.) Luneta was said to have revealed in interrogation that some CPP-ML Central Committee members were now operating in the greater Manila area to monitor anti-government activities there.

He was also said to have coordinated a party meeting the previous month which discussed plans for the expansion of party activities and the "assassination of high government leaders." (Ibid.)

On 21 February a band of NPA guerrillas ambushed a convoy at Cha village, Ifugao Province, killing eight army officers and men, and just missing the Ifugao governor and a general (ibid., 24 February). The day before, the NPA had burned down the headquarters of a construction company in a nearby village. In May, prominent NPA leaders Degongino Gonzáles and Domingo Ortiz were killed in skirmishes with government troops in Agusan del Sur and Davao del Norte, respectively, suggesting heightened Communist guerrilla insurgency in these areas. Luzon remained a major NPA theater of operations also, as indicated by the clash with NPA elements in Labo town, Camarines Sur Province, southern Luzon, on 6 June in which five guerrillas were killed. (Ibid., 14 May, 9 June). On 1 May some 3,000 workers and a few student sympathizers who attempted to march on the Presidential Palace in Manila, demanding higher wages and protesting the martial law were turned back by police (ibid., 3 May). Speculation that underground CPP-ML activists were stirring up workers and slum dwellers in Manila found new credence when on 5 June some 2,000 slum dwellers demonstrated at the Plaza Gomburza, staging a "People's Academy on Human Settlements" which was meant as a corollary to the United Nations' Habitat Conference then taking place in Vancouver, Canada. Hundreds of them were arrested, but most, save a handful of leaders, were released in a few days. (*Ang Katipunan*, Oakland, Calif., 28 June-26 July, p. 12.) At the close of May, in the wake of more frequent rallies and meetings of students on various secondary school and college campuses, Education Secretary Juan Manuel ordered school officials in the nation to "take steps to prevent the resurgence of student activism on school campuses" since, the government alleged, these student activities were aimed at undermining "the faith of the students in the duly constituted authority" (*FBIS*, 1 June).

Concern over increased Communist activity in an urban united-front context, as distinct from rural guerrilla war, was voiced by Defense Secretary Juan Ponce Enrile, who accused Communists of attempting to forge an alliance between students, intellectuals, workers, squatters, and clerical personnel in order to stir up unrest (*Indonesia Times*, Djakarta, 3 February). On 25 July the Marcos government announced severer penalties (up to 20 years in prison) for incitement to rebellion or sedition, or for activities which "undermine the confidence of the people in the government and its duly constituted authorities" (*FBIS*, 26 July). The new penalties, announced under prevailing martial law powers of the president, were widely seen as counterattack on various opponents of the government, particularly elements of the Roman Catholic clergy which have long been widely critical of Marcos. Two weeks before, Justice Secretary Vicente Abad Santos had described such members of the clergy as "dilettantes pursuing an amateur interest in political science," and the 25 July announcement appeared to be aimed particularly at them.

Relations between the government and the Roman Catholic hierarchy in the Philippines have been strained for some time (*YICA, 1976*, p. 366), and matters did not improve with the publication, at the close of April, of a 100-page pamphlet by the Association of Major Religious Superiors in the Philippines (AMRSP), which consists of the heads of eight Roman Catholic religious orders. The AMRSP pamphlet provides case studies of the torture and disappearance of political prisoners arrested by the Marcos government. Generally harrowing conditions of detention, as well as systematic violation of prisoners' legal and civil rights by Marcos officials and the military, are also alleged. Instances of torture by beatings, electrical shock, burning with lighted cigarettes, and sexual abuse, as detailed in the pamphlet, elicited a comment from a Philippine military spokesman that there had been a "few" individuals who had abused prisoners, but that such persons had been disciplined. (*Ang Katipunan*, 23 May, p. 5; *NYT*, 30 April.)

At the end of July, Defense Undersecretary Carmelo Barbero announced that the government was reviewing the records of the 4,600 or so political prisoners being held, in preparation for granting temporary releases to all but those charged with serious crimes; reservists with law degrees had been called up, Barbero said, in order to help evaluate the cases of the detainees (*NYT*, 1 August). His announcement may have come as a result of a report issued at the end of June by Amnesty International, the London-based human rights organization, which said that torture of martial law prisoners (i.e., those arrested for political offenses) was widespread in the Philippines and indeed was part of a "general approach" by the government to intimidate suspected political offenders (ibid., 27 June). According to anti-Marcos sources, assaults by the military on hunger-striking political prisoners have continued at Camp Bicutan, in Taguig town, Rizal Province. Beatings reportedly inflicted severe injuries on the prisoners. (*Ang Katipunan*, 15-31 August, p. 1.) On 7 September, Undersecretary Barbero announced that from 1 July to 6 September a total of 929 "martial law detainees' had been released. The military administration of detainees announced at the same time that 4,172 persons remained under martial law detention. (*FBIS*, 15 September.) On 28 September, Barbero announced an official, "no holds barred" investigation of charges that prisoners had been tortured by military personnel (*NYT*, 29 September).

Meanwhile the government-supervised press has, from time to time, lashed back at critics. The Manila *Evening Post* on 7 February in a front-page editorial, charged that the clerical leadership in the Philippines refused to accept the principles of Marcos's "New Society" despite the overwhelming endorsement by the majority of Filipinos. The government seems to have become increasingly concerned over the Roman Catholic Church's involvement with destitute squatters and laborers, and particularly the activity of some allegedly radical priests in social reform work. (Bernard Wideman,"The Christian Party," *Far Eastern Economic Review*, 5 March, p. 26.) In the course of 1976 it appeared that the polarization of the Philippine political climate was pitting opponents and supporters of the Marcos regime across a broad spectrum of society—in the church, in the press, among urban workers, students, and intellectuals, in rural areas, and in such infuential minorities as the Chinese—ever more sharply against each other. This polarization process, unless quickly undercut, is likely to offer both wings of the Philippine Communist movement significant new tactical opportunities in the future.

On 26 August, NPA commander Bernabe Buscayno, ("Commander Dante") fell into government hands with nine of his followers, and President Marcos announced that as a result the Communist rebellion in the country was now virtually eliminated (*NYT*, 27 August). The next day Marcos also announced the capture of former Army lieutenant Victor Corpuz, who had defected to the NPA and become one of its top leaders. Marcos's claims may be premature, however. Buscayno had long been reported to be at odds with Sison, while there is suspicion that Corpuz was actually a government spy who at last succeeded in delivering Buscayno into government hands. Current CPP-ML emphasis on education and organizational development is expected to continue, unaffected by Buscayno's capture, nor is the present level of insurgent activity likely to be greatly affected. (Peter Bathurst, "Communist Threat Lingers On," *Far Eastern Economic Review*, 17 September, p. 33.) In August there were new clashes with the NPA in the provinces of Tarlac and Abra in Luzon, and Defense Secretary Enrile warned that a new "united front" of leftists and rightists, backed by unnamed Western sources, was attempting to overthrow the Marcos government (*FBIS*, 19 August and 2 September).

As NPA guerrilla units seemed as active as ever before, the government's struggle to subdue the Muslim insurrection in the southern islands (*YICA, 1976*, pp. 367-68) also went on, with but intermittent success. The Philippine Army now has about 35,000 troops, supported by an additional 49,000 armed militia, committed to destroying the 5,000-man Muslim rebel force, and in some operational areas (e.g., the Zamboanga provinces) the Philippine armed forces in the early months of 1976 were gaining the upper hand. In other sections (e.g., on Jolo), the Moro National Liberation Front appeared to be more than holding its own, inflicting severe losses on government forces in various ambushes. The amnesty-mass surrender policy promoted by the government seemed at first to have good results (according to the government some 10,000 MNLF troops surrendered during 1975). But officials now fear that the *balikbayans* (returnees)—the amnesty-seeking Muslim insurgents, many of whom were allowed to keep their weapons—have used the amnesty policy to infiltrate urban areas of the South in readiness for future attacks. (*Far Eastern Economic Review*, 9 January 1976, p. 8; 23 April, p. 10; 7 May, p. 21.)

On 3 June, led by a former police chief of Marawi city, who had joined the MNFL, Muslim rebels staged a spectacular attack with hand grenades on a power station in Marawi, aggravating the already existing power shortage and paralyzing commerce (*FBIS*, 14 June). In April and May there were new hijackings of Philippine planes by Muslim rebels, and the spate of kidnappings, a serious problem for several months, began to accelerate. Muslim rebels have been accused of kidnapping, since 1975, thirty-five Japanese (some of them employed in the pearl industry in the southern islands), four other foreigners, and an undetermined number of Filipinos. In early August the chief of the Southern Philippine military command ordered that wealthy businessmen and other prospective kidnap victims on Mindanao be given arms and military guard protection (Associated Press, Manila, 4 August).

Both factions of the Philippine Communist movement support autonomy for the Muslims, and the NPA units in Jolo, according to government sources, have for some time had a de facto tactical alliance with the MNLF. Leaders of the MNLF have repeatedly rejected charges that it is Communist-infiltrated, however, and neither the CPP-ML nor the PKP favors a formal Muslim secession and establishment of a separate Moro republic, the dream of some Muslim rebels. On the other hand, both Communist parties endorse extensive self-rule for the southern Muslim communities, including local application of Muslim law in family and other social relationships. On 6 September a new report issued in Manila by the Philippine military claimed that "the tide" had "turned" in the government's struggle against the Muslim rebels, claiming that 18,362 had surrendered in the past four years, of whom nearly 17,000 had been "processed" and returned to "a peaceful livelihood" (*FBIS*, 8 September).

In the closing months of 1976 there was little indication that the polarization in Filipino public life was abating. On 10 October riots erupted at the close of an anti-martial law rally, involving some 3,000 protesters, in downtown Manila. There were injuries and arrests as police remonstrated with demonstration leaders that the mass protest was in violation of martial law provisons (*FBIS*, 12 October). On 24 November, NPA guerrillas, led by Juanito Rivera, reportedly the successor to captured NPA chieftain Bernabe Buscayno, staged a daring raid on the town of Mabalacat, near Clark Air Force Base, disarming local guards and making good their escape with a quantity of firearms (*NYT*, 25 November). Toward the close of November, it was revealed that in an effort to combat what it called the "Christian Left," the government had arrested a number of professional workers connected with two Roman Catholic radio stations on Mindanao. The stations allegedly had been sending messages to the Communist underground. Bishop Francisco Claver, a Filipino Jesuit, in whose diocese one of the radio stations is located, leads a group of 17 bishops critical of the Marcos government. The action underscored the apparent division in the leadership of the Roman Catholic Church in the Philippines, some of whose bishops have attacked publicly the martial law regime, while others have been less vocal or silent. (Ibid., 28 November.)

International Aspects. On 30 May 1976, President Ferdinand Marcos and his wife, at the invitation of the Presidium of the USSR, arrived in the Soviet Union for a week's visit. The Soviet media meanwhile declared that the positions of the Philippines and the USSR "on the key issues of our time" were "identical or close" (*FBIS*, 1 June). At a Kremlin dinner on 31 May, Marcos said: "On the basis of our joint adherence to peaceful coexistence and international cooperation, we must open a new era in Philippine-Soviet relations during this visit." On 1 June, Soviet party leader Leonid I. Brezhnev and Marcos reportedly reached agreement to establish formal diplomatic relations between their two countries. A joint statement released in Moscow on 8 June, at the close of the visit, made reference to the signing of a joint communiqué establishing diplomatic relations and to a new trade agreement, and also agreements to promote scientific and technical cooperation and develop contacts "in the spheres of culture, education and sport." According to the statement, the USSR and the Philippines attached "great importance to the strengthening of peace and stability in Asia" and agreed to transform the Asian area into a continent of "peace, freedom and constructible international cooperation" whose states should be guided by "renunciation of the use of force, respect for national sovereignty, non-interference in international affairs, and international cooperation, based on equality and mutual advantage in accordance with the UN charter." (*Pravda*, 8 June; *FBIS*, 10 June.)

These last phrases, it might be noted, constitute something of a blend of the 1971 ASEAN (Association of Southest Asian Nations) Kuala Lumpur declaration on neutrality and the Soviet proposal for a new collective security arrangement in Asia, first announced by Brezhnev in 1969. After his return home, however, Marcos made a point of noting that "this new-found friendship" with the USSR "does not in any way diminish ties that already exist with any country, any ally or any partner," a remark widely understood to refer to the USA. He added that the trip had made him "more confident that we are insured within our territory much more than before I left." (*FBIS*, 8 June.) The USSR-Philippines diplomatic rapprochement had been long expected, and it had been evident for some time that, as Soviet media in the past three years were generally approving of Marcos's policies, it would be but a matter of time before this "last bastion of opposition to Russian diplomatic expansion in Southeast Asia" would also be overcome (Robert Evans in *Indonesian Times*, Djakarta, 16 December 1975).

Soviet media continued to praise the Marcos regime, with one commentator declaring, for example, that its land reform, anti-corruption, and foreign policies—the latter designed to achieve greater independence from U.S. influences—reflected the "real demands of the time" and relied on public support in the Philippines for their implementaton (N. Romanov in *Selskaya Zhizn*, Moscow, 16 June; *FBIS*, 18 June). Conversely, José Lava—the long-incarcerated former PKP secretary-general, still a member of the PKP Central Committee, who after his release three years ago went to live in Czechoslovakia—still found much to praise, especially in the extent and quality of various public and social services, in a number of East European countries which he had visited ("What I Have Seen in Socialist Countries," *WMR*, February 1976, pp. 100-108). Lava's reportedly current employment in Prague as a member of the *World Marxist Review*'s editorial council has been viewed as yet another indication of the significance of the Philippines in current Soviet-bloc calculations.

As was the case with other Southeast Asian countries, the Philippines too was visited by the deputy foreign minister of the newly unified Socialist Republic of Vietnam, Phan Hien, during his tour of the region in June and July. On 12 July it was announced in connection with his visit that formal diplomatic relations between Vietnam and the Philippines were "opened" as of that day. According to a joint communiqué issued in Manila, the relations were established on the basis of four principles, (1) respect for each other's independence, sovereignty, and territorial integrity, non-aggression and non-interference in each other's internal affairs, equality, mutual benefit, and peaceful co-existence, (2) not allowing any foreign country to use either's territory for "direct or indirect" aggression against any other country, (3) establishment of friendly and neighborly relations and cooperation, and settlement of disputes through negotiations, and (4) development of regional cooperation for the benefit of a "genuine independence, peace and neutrality" in Southeast Asia (*FBIS*, 12 June).

Phan Hien said on 9 July that his government would be a member of the Manila-based Asian Development Bank, even though only South Vietnam had been a member of the bank before the unification of the two Vietnams (ibid., 13 July). There were no details, however, of any discussion of the status of the Paracel Islands in the South China Sea (ownership of which is in contention among the Philippines, Vietnam, People's China, and the Republic of China on Taiwan), although Phan Hien had said when he came to the Philippine capital that that question would be taken up. The visit was generally, if cautiously, appreciated in Manila press and political circles, particularly so since President Marcos, as recently as March, in view of recent anti-ASEAN comments in the Vietnamese media, had urged Hanoi to eliminate its "bias" against ASEAN (ibid., 2 March).

Relations with People's China developed slowly in the aftermath of Sino-Philippine diplomatic recognition in June 1975 (*YICA, 1976*, p. 369). On 10 April 1976 a Chinese trade delegation, headed by Hai Yeh-sheng, a bureau director in China's Ministry of Foreign Trade,concluded a visit to Manila. Three days later, a Philippine economic delegation, headed by Finance Secretary Cesar Virata, arrived in Peking. Steady expansion of direct trade, including new Chinese oil deliveries to the Philippines, is expected to result. Philippine oil needs are increasingly becoming a matter of Chinese concern. In mid-June the Chinese Foreign Ministry issued a statement reacting to Philippine reports that a Swedish-Philippine oil consortium had started drilling operations in the area of the Reed Bank in the Nansha Islands. It said that the islands "have always been part of China's territory," and that any oil exploration there by a foreign group would be considered an encroachment on China's sovereignty. (*FBIS*, 15 June.) Current increased offshore oil-drilling activity in the South China Sea region by several international, including Philippine consortia, has brought the danger of a confrontation appreciably nearer. Philippine Foreign Secretary Carlos Romulo reacted sharply to the Chinese warning, saying that the "Reed Bank is within the continental shelf of the Philippines" and that Philippine oil exploitation of the area is "in accordance with the United Nations' convention on continental shelves in 1958" (*FBIS*, 16 June).

Diplomatic recognition of People's China has had a sharply divisive effect on the 400,000-member Philippine Chinese community, particularly as the Republic of China (Taiwan) retains an economic and cultural affairs office in Manila, though it has given up its embassy. Pro-Taiwan and pro-Peking factions in the community have become sharper in their attacks on each other, raising anew the age-old question of the adjustment and civil/political status of the Chinese in the Philippines. On 21 April, in an address to the pro-Taiwan Federation of Filipino-Chinese Chambers of Commerce in Manila, the director of the National Intelligence and Security Agency, Major General Fabian Ver, said that current ideological differences in the Philippine Chinese community were threatening national security. He declared that assimilation was perhaps the only solution and urged the Philippine Chinese to "achieve unity immediately" so as to avoid future conflict. After his address Ver was presented with a plaque carrying the national flag of the Republic of China. (*Asian Student*, San Francisco, 8 May; Bernard Wideman, "Conflict in Chinatown," *Far Eastern Economic Review*, 4 June, pp. 24-25.)

A foreign policy question impinging directly on Manila's relations with Communist countries concerns the status of the USA's miitary bases in the Philippines, in particular the 36,000-acre naval facility at Subic Bay, which provides jobs to some 44,000 residents of nearby Olongapo City (Bernard Wideman in *Far Eastern Economic Review*, 25 June, p. 26). Manila radio stations anounced on 29 April that the presidents of the two countries had reached agreement that "all military installations being used by U.S. forces in the Philippines are now Philippine bases" (*FBIS*, 30 April). Continued U.S. use of the bases would be permitted but, reportedly, under "closer Philippine supervision." The extent of the planned "supervision," and the nature of the de facto extraterritoriality enjoyed by U.S. military personnel while on the bases have not been detailed, however. Meanwhile discussions continue on the future format of U.S.-Philippine economic relations. With the lapsing of the Laurel-Langley Agreement in 1975 (providing for special treatment for U.S. investors in the Philippines) and the abandonment of the Sugar Act in 1974 (which had provided a special place for Philippine sugar on U.S. markets), the structure of these relations has been subjected to possibly deep changes and the future status of the estimated one to two billion U.S. dollars in American investments now in the Philippines has become potentially more uncertain (Bernard Wideman in *Far Eastern Economic Review*, 2 July, p. 50, and Laura J. Henze, "U.S.-Philippine Economic Relations and Trade Negotiations," *Asian Survey*, March, pp. 319-37).

Communist nations generally are appreciative of the Philippines' attempts to become militarily and economically more independent of the USA. Manila's diplomatic and increasing commercial and cultural contacts in recent years with the Communist powers tend to be described in the press of many Communist nations as indications of a significant shift in Philippine foreign policies. It should be noted, however, that proclaiming the need for such greater independence has been the Philippine politician's favorite theme for many years. The economic and strategic advantages of the relationship with the USA are recognized more quietly and are permitted to persist, be it in frequently shifting forms. Hence it remains to be seen whether the major communist powers will continue to find praise for Marcos's policies, in these circumstances. Manila's recent rapprochement with both Peking and Moscow appears to reflect more a pragmatic policy ploy necessitated by the changed post-Vietnam war environment of Asia than the beginning of a genuine, thorough alteration in U.S.-Philippine relations.

Publications. The CPP-ML's chief journal is *Ang Bayan* ("The Nation"), in English and Tagalog editions. In 1976 only three issues appeared. CPP-ML statements are now much more rarely relayed in the major Chinese media than was the case four years ago, and it is primarily the "Voice of the Malayan Revolution," the clandestine transmitter of the Communist Party of Malaya (see *Malaysia*), and also, though less frequently, *Indonesian Tribune*, the Tirana-based publication of the Maoist wing of the Indonesian Communist Party (see *Indonesia*), which among foreign media today primarily transmit CPP-ML messages. The PKP's principal organ, *Ang Kommunista* ("The Communist"), appeared only once in 1976, and, as in previous years, party cadres seemed to rely usually on stenciled materials for internal party communication. The international media of the Moscow-oriented parties, *World Marxist Review* and *Information Bulletin* occasionally carry major PKP statements and messages.

University of Bridgeport   Justus M. van der Kroef

Singapore

Communists in Singapore have no distinctive party of their own in the island state, and those arrested in recent years under the Singapore government's Internal Security Act, have usually been described by government sources as members or followers of the Communist Party of Malaya (CPM), its factional splinter groups, or their respective political fronts and guerrilla satellite organizations (see *Malaysia*). The creation of Malaysia out of the states on the Malayan Peninsula and Singapore, together with Sarawak and Sabah on Borneo, in 1963, and the subsequent secession of Singapore from Malaysia in 1965, are both considered to have occurred illegally and undemocratically by Communists and sympathizers in Malaysia and Singapore. What has been and is favored is a "merger" of the states on the peninsula with Singapore; formally, therefore, Communists in Singapore today fall under the jurisdiction of the CPM or its satellites. But stringent government security surveillance, as well as the weakening effect of a three-way split in the ranks of Malayan Communists, leaves Singapore

Communism with only limited continuous and direct organizational or leadership linkages with the CPM or its factional rivals, despite occasional intimations to the contrary in Singapore government statements.

The Barisan Sosialis Malaya (Malayan Socialist Front), usually called Barisan Sosialis, is a legal party in Singapore. Since its establishment on 26 July 1961 it has served as the principal above-ground organization for Singapore Communists and their sympathizers. But its activities have been severely circumscribed, and in recent years Barisan spokesmen, in conversation with this author, have claimed that government "repression," including inability to obtain publishing permits, and arrests and harassment of party organizers, are to blame for the party's ineffectual condition. According to the Singapore government, however, the charge of "repression" is false, and the Barisan's lack of popularity is attributed to the party's history of Communist infiltration and to the Singapore voters' repudiation of the Barisan's program, which in most essential points (e.g., the call for a "merger" of Singapore with the peninsula states into a "democratic Malaya") has long dovetailed with that of the CPM.

While there is generally broad public support for the Singapore government of Premier Lee Kuan Yew, which is wholly dominated by the People's Action Party (PAP), opposition to the government may be estimated to comprise from 20 to 30 percent of the electorate, and has on occasion been particularly apparent among university student and in some trade union circles. The Lee Kuan Yew government's major concern with a continuing flow of foreign capital, and with industrial and commercial development by multinational corporations to meet the needs of Singapore's population of some 2.3 million, crowded on 225 square miles and growing at a rate of 1.5 percent per year (*World Population Growth and Response, 1965-1975*, Population Reference Bureau, Washington, April 1976, p. 98), is believed to be interlocked with the necessity of depicting conditions as maximally stable and free from "subversion."

History. In 1925, Fu Ta-ching, Comintern agent and member of the Chinese Communist Party, arrived in Singapore to organize scattered Chinese, Malayan, and Indonesian Communists in the area. Three years later, the Nanyang (South Seas) Communist Party was founded in Singapore, designed by the Comintern's Far Eastern Bureau as a control and proselytizing mechanism for Communist activity not only in peninsular Malaya and Singapore, but in neighboring Southeast Asian countries as well. Operating through Chinese youth and trade union fronts, Singapore Communists soon ran afoul of British colonial police surveillance, while Communist cadres in Thailand, Indochina, Burma, and Indonesia generally went their own way. In 1930 the Nanyang Communist Party changed its name to the Communist Party of Malaya (CPM), which dedicated itself to establishment of an independent "Republic of Malaya," including Singapore. The CPM proved as little effective as its predecessor. Singapore party cadres, overwhelmingly Chinese, were limited to stirring up periodic labor unrest during the 1930s, and to recruiting and radicalizing among students of the private Chinese schools. Thus they did succeed, however, in developing a base of youthful activists who, during the Japanese occupation of Singapore (1942-45) and in the period after World War II, assumed some key positions in the Singapore Chinese-language press, trade unions, schools, and, supposedly, philanthropic organizations.

Neither in new waves of anti-British labor unrest after the war, nor in attempts to seize control of the presumably Socialist PAP (founded in 1954 and soon the main channel of independence aspirations in Singapore), was the CPM successful. The more moderate, English-educated and -oriented Chinese leadership in PAP, led by Lee Kuan Yew, increasingly divided itself from what Lee was to call "the Chinese educated world—a world teeming with vitality, dynamism and revolution, a world in which the Communists had been working for over the last thirty years with considerable success" (Lee Kuan Yew, *The Battle for Merger*, Government Printing House, Singapore, 1961, p. 17). This division proved fatal for the chances of Singapore Communism in successive elections in the 1950s and afterward as the PAP moderates won control of the government, repeatedly broke up strikes and student riots (notably in 1956), arrested Chinese-educated radicals, and ultimately, in effect, forced the latter to withdraw from the PAP and establish their own party, the Barisan Sosialis, in 1961.

Barisan agitation in 1963 against Singapore's entry into the new state of Malaysia failed. In that year and subsequently, as Lee Kuan Yew solidified his hold on the prime minister's office, the PAP gradually began to shut out virtually all competitors in national Legislative Assembly elections. The PAP-dominated Singapore government also remained ever ready to arrest scores of persons because of allegedly Communist or subversive activites, including trade unionists and student leaders at Nanyang University, a private Chinese-language oriented institution. (On these developments see *The Communist Movement in West Malaysia and Singapore*, Southeast Asia Treaty Organization Short Paper, no. 54, Bangkok, SEATO, 1972; J. M. van der Kroef, *Communism in Malaysia and Singapore: A Contemporary Survey*, Martinus Nijhoff, The Hague, 1967; Richard Clutterbuck, *Riot and Revolution in Singapore and Malaya 1945-1963*, Faber and Faber, London, 1973.)

Though the CPM continued as much as possible to use the Barisan as its above-ground organizational vehicle, the Lee Kuan Yew government's effective security policies provoked repeated leadership crises in the Barisan as well as among its greatly reduced trade union following. In the early 1970s periodic terrorist bomb explosions were attributed by the government to Singapore followers of the "Malayan National Liberation Army" (MNLA), a CPM affiliate, and official fears were expressed that—in conjunction with the agitation by "New Left" activists in the University of Singapore, ostensibly on behalf of unemployed or poorly paid workers—Singapore Communism might be entering a new phase of urban guerrilla warfare. Thus far these concerns have not been justified, however.

Over the past half-century much of the pattern of Singapore Communism has remained the same. As in the racial composition of the city state, ethnic Chinese have continued to wholly predominate the Barisan and the Communist underground (about 76 percent of Singapore's 2.3 million people are Chinese, 15 percent are Malays, and about 8 percent are of Indian, Pakistani, or other South Asian backgrounds). Students, shop assistants, hawkers, and workers have tended to be the Communists' most favorable recruiting ground, similarly in terms of appeals to Chinese ethnic and cultural pride, although there is some recent evidence that attempts are being made to win underground supporters among the better-situated Chinese business and professional circles.

Aims, Organization, and Tactics. During 1976 there were no significant changes in the established structure and objectives of the Barisan Sosialis, and party representatives in June emphasized to the author that, despite the Lee Kuan Yew government's persistent "repression," the Barisan would continue to compete with the PAP in as many future elections as possible. Party spokesmen claim that the government's refusal to issue publishing permits has made it difficult if not impossible to disseminate more widely the Barisan's policy positions on current issues (Singapore Home Affairs Ministry officials, however, claim that shortage of funds and lack of public donations impede Barisan program distribution).

Generally, the Barisan is committed to (1) establishment of "democratic" and socialist state, composed of a merger of Singapore with peninsular Malaya, (2) to "peace" and "independence" from "imperialist" encroachments, including those of the multinational corporations in the island state, (3) reaffirmation of workers' rights, including the right to strike for higher wages, and for improvements in working conditions and social services, and (4) the release of all political prisoners in Singapore, estimated at about 60 in number. Implicit in these general objectives are a reorientation of Singapore's foreign policy in the direction of the "Socialist countries," particularly toward People's China, and a fundamental restructuring of the private enterprise sector of the island state's economy. The report of Barisan chairman Dr. Lee Siew Choh to the party's Third Congress, in August 1969, continues to be distributed as an authoritative document embodying the main contours of policy. This report views U.S. and British "imperialism," in collusion with Soviet "revisionism," as the main obstacle to a "Malaya" merger and the formation of a new "democratic" state, and also as the principal support of the Lee Kuan Yew government. The latter, it charges, has turned Singapore into a total "police state." The need to form a "united front" of workers, peasants, and petty bourgeoisie is held to be paramount for the attainment of "national democracy" in a "unitary" multiracial state. The united front would be led by a single political party, which would also assist the "struggle for democracy" in countries like Thailand, Burma, and Indonesia. (*YICA, 1976*, pp. 373-74.)

Barisan spokesmen during 1976 particularly stressed two themes. First, persistently rising prices and inflationary pressures continue to deepen the plight of workers, and primarily benefit the big foreign corporations and investors linked to U.S. and British "imperialism." Secondly, the criticism of the Lee Kuan Yew government by the executive committees of the British and Dutch Labor parties and the resulting PAP withdrawal on 30 May from membership in the Socialist International (see "International Developments," below), demonstrates, according to Barisan spokesmen, the growing isolation of the Lee Kuan Yew government in the world's socialist and democratic community. The government's "fascist character," they assert, has been accentuated in the past year.

A Central Executive Committee of about a dozen members, headed by the Barisan's principal founder, Dr. Lee Siew Choh (who trained as a physician), formally directs the party's day-to-day affairs. Little is known of other recent or current principal party functionaries, in part because of concern over police surveillance and perhaps also because of reported persistent leadership conflicts between Barisan chairman Lee Siew Choh and officers of the Industrial Workers Union (IWU), the principal remaining trade-union supporter of the party. Barisan leaders claim that their party has about 6,000 members, but non-party sources believe that 400 to 500 is nearer the mark. On paper there is a Barisan executive in almost every electoral district, and a sufficient following to muster parliamentary candidates. Non-party sources claim that the last official Barisan party congress was that in 1969, and no significant congress documents beyond that date appear to be available. Barisan spokesmen assert that party "conferences" occurred prior to the September 1972 general elections.

The increased activity attributed during 1974-76 by the Singapore government to cells of the "liberation" underground, affiliated either with the CPM or with its factional offshoots operating in the island state, has underscored the declining significance of the Barisan Sosialis as the cutting edge of Singapore Communism. The Barisan's ineffectiveness and internal leadership problems also continue to aggravate its loss of prestige among the general public as a major opposition leftist party capable of rallying non-Communist votes. Reportedly, some within the Barisan and among its sympathizers recognize the need to devise a broad-based "common denominator" united front against the PAP, led by or embodied in a new leftist party with a different name, which would reflect a more distinctive Singapore rather than "Malayan" (the merger of Singapore with peninsular Malaya being now advocated by the Barisan) identity, but this new approach has been rejected by Lee Siew Choh and other older leaders as impractical and likely to lead to a swallowing up of the Barisan's distinctive position by less radical groups.

Domestic Developments. On 27 May 1976, three days before the PAP withdrew from the Socialist International, the Singapore Home Affairs Ministry announced that since January about fifty persons had been arrested under the provisions of the Internal Security Act, which, in effect, permits preventive detention and incarceration without trial. At the same time it was announced that the government had discovered a "plan" by two rival factions of Malayan Communists, the CPM and the equally Maoist-oriented CPM (Marxist-Leninist), for a "regrouping in Singapore" to carry forward a "new phase of subversion and terrorism." Twenty-three of those arrested were released after being questioned and warned against engaging in further "subversive activities"; another ten, who were citizens of Malaysia, were handed over to Kuala Lumpur authorities; the rest have remained imprisoned, according to the government statement.

Apart from its timing (which was widely interpreted as an effort by the government to counter growing international criticism of Singapore's domestic security policies by demonstrating the reality of subversive threats) the 27 May statement has other significant aspects. One is the allegedly international character of the Communist "plan." Along with documents, the police were said to have captured "photographs of communist guerrillas in a training camp at the Thai-Malaysian border," and "links" were said to have been traced between "Communist agents in Singapore" and a "cadre control post in Kuala Lumpur, a "training camp in the Johore jungle" (in the southern part of peninsular Malaysia), a "guerrilla coup in southern Thailand," various "contact points" in Bangkok and Hong Kong, and, not least, a "recruitment, propaganda and fund-raising center" in Sydney, established in order to "subvert Singaporeans and Malaysians" in Australia. An Australian-trained ballet teacher was among those arrested (she was released on 9 June). The statement alleged further that the Sydney branch of the 'Malayan People's Liberation Leage" (MPLL), a satellite of the CPM (Marxist-Leninist), had as its function the recruitment and indoctrination of Singaporean and Malaysian students and professional people studying in Australia, who were slated to return to important positions in their home countries. (Radio Singapore, domestic service in English, 27 May; *FBIS*, 28 May.)

As in previous statements since early 1975, the government emphasized that the allegedly new dangers posed by external sources of subversion were related to the Communist successes in Indochina:

> The fall of the anticommunist regimes in Indochina a year ago, has encouraged the Communist underground in the region. Although there has been an upsurge in terrorism in West Malaysia and Thailand, Singapore has remained relatively peaceful and apparently unaffected.

> But [the] latest security operations in Singapore [show] that beneath the surface calm, extensive clandestine activities have been going on. Only timely action by the ISD (Internal Security Department) has foiled the Communists before any real damage is done. (Ibid.)

Another important aspect of the 27 May statement concerns the new recruiting tactics attributed to the Singapore Communist underground. For the first time, the government reported that the Singapore armed forces had been infiltrated: among the arrested were a naval-officer engineer, who "apparently acted as a conduit for communist funds," and some lower-ranking uniformed military personnel, both male and female (Harvey Stockwin, "Lee Reveals His Ace in the Hole," *Far Eastern Economic Review*, 11 June, p. 12). Significantly too, the backgrounds and occupations of many of those arrested, as revealed by the government, suggest that recruits are being won in the relatively well-to-do middle strata of Singapore society (a school principal, a sales manager of a flour mill, an electrical subcontractor, a trading firm proprietor, and so on) as well as through the "classical infiltration route" of the trade unions and student organizations.

Finally, the underground Communist recruiting function today, as revealed in the captured documents described by the government, appears to have a twofold purpose: (1) to supply funds and followers from Singapore to the MPLL and to the CPM's satellite "political action" organization, the Malayan National Liberation Front (MNLF), and to their respective guerrilla "armies" the "Malayan People's Liberation Army" and the "Malayan National Liberation Army") operating in the Thai-Malaysian border zone, and (2) to penetrate and provide information on a broad range of institutions and groups in Singapore itself, as a basis for future political and terrorist action. This second function of the underground is detailed in the 27 May statement as involving infiltration of government departments and regulatory boards, labor organizations, civic and cultural groups, political parties, and schools in order to develop "united front" action; establishment of factories and businesses, "such as shops and contractor firms," as a screen for underground Communist activities; gathering of intelligence on military and police, and making "sketches" of government and other important buildings; working with and where appropriate recruiting "secret society gangsters," and promoting their acts of terrorism, including the robbing of "both local and foreign capitalists"; and storing covert arms caches and learning the various skills needed to put together grenades, mines, and ammunition.

On 16 June 1976 the government arrested Hussein Dahidin and Azmi Mahmud, respectively the editor and former assistant editor of the Malay-language paper *Berita Harian*, a sister paper of the Kuala Lumpur daily of the same name. The two were charged with reporting news "so as to put Communism in a favorable light," while allegedly also slighting Islamic beliefs. The arrests subsequently were linked to the arrest on 22 June of two prominent journalists in Kuala Lumpur (see Malaysia). In a television appearance on 28 June, Dahidin said that he had attempted to propagandize Malayan inhabitants of Singapore toward a rejection of Islam.

The chain of arrests of alleged subversives has over the years given the Singapore government occasion for warning the public that it continues to be a target of CPM blandishments. For example, an announcement on 4 November 1975 that three persons had been arrested for "communist activities"—a construction worker, a poultry farmer, and a business executive (Barisan Sosialis cadre), all of them alleged to be active in the CPM or its political front—was accompanied by an official warning that the CPM intended to stage "a resurgence of armed revolution," and that the public should be careful of being approached by "subversives" and should "exercise vigilance." The possibility that "terrorist acts" in Singapore similar to those in peninsular Malaysia was also indicated. (Radio Singapore, domestic service in English, 4 November; *FBIS*, 5 November; *Asia Research Bulletin*, 30 November, pp. 144-45).

In the previously noted 27 May 1976 statement the government declared that despite the arrests and the disruption of the plans of MNLF and MPLL activists, new agents could be expected to launch disruptive "united front" agitation similar to that seen in Singapore in previous decades. They would also "attempt sabotage and assassination to add terror to their political bid to try and destroy Singapore's stability and retard economic and social programs."

Despite such warnings and the periodic arrests of alleged communists, sources of opposition to the Lee Kuan Yew government remained alive, such as some elements of the volatile Singapore student community, which the government only recently had attempted to identify in subversive "New Left" terms (*YICA, 1976*, pp. 377-79). On 20 November 1975 the parliament passed the University of Singapore (Amendment) Bill, which compelled the University of Singapore Student Union (USSU) to register under the republic's Societies Act, thereby giving the government broad supervisory powers over its operations. The USSU, whose leaders have been frequent critics of government policies and have organized anti-government demonstrations in the past, would now, according to Singapore home affairs minister Chua Sian Chin, be required to assume responsibility for its political activities in the same way as other bodies and citizens "without the protective camouflage of academic autonomy and student exuberance." The new bill would also restrict membership in the USSU to Singapore citizens (in the past, according to the government, some of the more vocal USSU leaders came from Malaysia and Hong Kong). Chua added that the unwarranted domination of the USSU leadership by non-Singapore citizens had contributed to the impression that the entire university student body was behind them "in their activities of espousing the causes of Communist political detainees, interfering in labor disputes and trade union affairs, and generally taking up anti-establishment political issues." (*Asia Research Bulletin*, December 1975, p.159.)

If the Singapore government believed that the new bill would cow the student community, it was mistaken. In February 1976, hundreds of students in vocational institutes began demonstrating and agitating against the government because of an announced elimination of reduced bus fares for students. The government suspected that the Singapore Polytechnic Students Union (SPSU), the only student union still outside government control, was behind the agitation. During a demonstration before the City Hall, an SPSU student, who subsequently claimed to have been present only to investigate the news aspect of the event, was arrested. Though he was released again within twenty-four hours, the SPSU subsequently charged that he had been physically assaulted by police, that his dwelling had been ransacked, and that he had been denied access to an attorney. Meanwhile police began a close investigation of the vocational institutes. At the end of February, the bus company rescinded its decision to eliminate the reduced fares. (Ho Kwon Ping, "Students Rally Again and Win the Day," *Far Eastern Economic Review*, 5 March, p. 18.)

The incident sparked concern in government circles, however, that "New Left" student radicalism would continue to seek opportunities for agitation, especially in such problem areas as freedom of political expression and the rising cost of living. It is in these areas that significant opposition to the government can also be aroused outside the volatile student community, thus affording the Communist underground a range of tactical opportunities. On 27 February the secretary-general of the Workers Party, J. B. Jeyaretnam, pledged to restore the "rule of law" and to curb the government's wide powers if the party were successful in the next general election, which must be held before September 1977, when the term of the present parliament ends. The Workers Party polled 12 percent of the total votes cast in the 1972 election but did not win any seats. Jeyaretnam noted that in Singapore today political parties may not hold rallies except during an election campaign, and he lashed out repeatedly against what he asserted are the government's arbitrary and wide discretionary authority. (Agence France Presse dispatch, Singapore, 27 February; *FBIS*, 4 March.)

Perhaps no aspect of the government's policies remains so controversial, and is so frequently a source of criticism by Communists and many non-communists as well, as that relating to political prisoners. There are no official figures on political detainees as such, but according to one authoritative estimate about 60 men and women, arrested under the Internal Security Act for alleged political offenses, are currently in prison, some having been held without trial as long as twelve years (Amnesty International, *Annual Report 1974/75*, London, Amnesty International Publications, 1975, p. 101). In December 1975 eight political prisoners, arrested in June 1974 in an island-wide sweep of alleged CPM and MNLF members (*YICA, 1975*, p. 418, were released. Charges that political prisoners were being tortured were repeated by prisoner sources on this occasion (Ho Kwon Ping, "Allegations of Torture," *Far Eastern Economic Review*, 9 January 1976, p. 13). Among the eight released prisoners was T. T. Rajah, former legal adviser to the Barisan Sosialis, who asserted upon gaining his freedom that his political convictions had been strengthened "as a result of the years of inhuman treatment and detention in prison" (ibid.). On 4 June the government announced that Dr. Poh Soo Kai had once again been arrested under the Internal Security Act. Poh, a former assistant secretary-general of the Barisan Sosialis, had been released from a ten-year detention period on 13 December 1975, and upon his release Poh had joined a number of former fellow prisoners in condemning the government's allegedly brutal treatment of prisoners (*YICA, 1975*, p. 415).

Although its detention policies have made Singapore, and particularly the ruling PAP, increasingly anathema among influential Labor parties in the world (see "International Developments," below), Premier Lee Kuan Yew has taken the position that international criticism of political imprisonment under the internal security regulations is the result of the "distorted picture of the PAP" being disseminated abroad by "Communist front groups in Singapore," and that this campaign has as its objective "the release of some tough Communist political detainees" (Radio Singapore, domestic service in English, 8 April 1976; *FBIS*, 29 April). Lee has rejected allegations of prisoner maltreatment, noting that no action for "battery and assault" has been brought by anyone, and he has claimed because the political prisoners "are out to recreate an atmosphere of turmoil and tension conducive to Communist agitation, chaos, and terrorism," "the overwhelming majority of people in Singapore" are not in favor of setting them free. (Ibid.) On 4 August, Singapore foreign minister S. Rajaratnam warned that the Communists were "making a comeback" in Singapore; because Communists had achieved power in Vietnam, he said, they believed that rebellion (presumably in Singapore) also would be forthcoming (*FBIS*, 9 August). On 6 September, it was announced that police had arrested a number of students of the Ngee Ann Technical College and of Singapore Polytechnic. Acting on information supplied by the Malaysian Special Branch, Singapore authorities had moved against the underground Malayan New Democratic Youth League in June and July, arresting leaders and seizing office equipment, propaganda materials, and allegedly incriminating documents, such as a detailed directive on the tasks of the Communist underground in Singapore, including cadre recruitment and training, infiltration of low-ranking military and government employees, and manufacture of lethal weapons. Those arrested subsequently gave detailed statements, admitting to efforts in behalf of Communists fighting in the Malaysian jungle border area near Thailand, and to "stoking up" popular agitation against the Singapore government. (Ibid., 7, 8 September.)

International Developments. On 10 May 1976 premier Lee Kuan Yew arrived in Peking for a two-week visit during which he met briefly with Chairman Mao Tse-tung. In a banquet address on 11 May, Lee, though not in so many words, reaffirmed Singapore's basic policy position toward People's China: no diplomatic exchanges or recognition, for the time being, but a strengthening of trade, industrial, and cultural relations, in keeping with the "new phase begun for Southeast Asia." Lee, on this occasion, pointedly repeated statements by Chinese premier Hua Kuo-feng to the effect that "China does not interfere in the internal matters of other countries" and that how the Singapore government chooses to deal with its domestic Communists is Singapore's affair; he then said: "Based on non-interference I believe that we can develop our relations." At the end of the visit Lee said in a speech at Canton that he carried a "great experience" back with him, but added that he had also "become more conscious of Singapore's very different situation and different way of life." (*Asia Research Bulletin*, 31 May, p. 202; Harvey Stockwin, "Lee Lays It on the Line," *Far Eastern Economic Review*, 4 June, p. 14.)

Although Chinese media had previously expressed approval of ASEAN (the Association of Southeast Asian Nations, founded in 1967, of which Indonesia, Malaysia, Singapore, Thailand, and the Philippines are members), the first public indication of support by a Chinese premier came during Lee's visit. In response to Lee's banquet address on 11 May, Hua Kuo-feng noted that the ASEAN nations had reaffirmed their 1971 "positive proposal" to establish a "zone of peace and neutrality" in Southeast Asia, and he declared further that ASEAN had "achieved significant results" in advancing economic cooperation in the region.

Even before Lee visited Peking, Singapore foreign minister Rajaratnam had said on 14 April that the visit was "unlikely" to see the establishment of diplomatic relations with China, and he reportedly reiterated that Singapore "would be the last ASEAN country" to normalize relations with People's China. It must be noted that Lee's goodwill visit and an encouragement of increased Sino-Singaporean trade and cultural contacts are the limits at present to which Singapore, not least in deference to the current reluctance of neighboring Indonesia to normalize relations with China, is prepared to go on improving its own position vis-à-vis Peking. Singapore's reported practice of sending its troops to Taiwan for training (a practice soon to end) may also be preventing formal diplomatic recognition. (Harvey Stockwin, "Lee: Pathfinding in the Forbidden City," *Far Eastern Economic Review*. 14 May, p. 22.)

Rajaratnam's 14 April statement came shortly after his week-long visit to the USSR. According to Rajaratnam, during this visit a "deeper understanding" of the problems of Southeast Asia had been reached by the Soviets, and "possibilities of increased trade" between the USSR and Singapore had been discussed. Rajaratnam said further that Soviet foreign minister Andrei Gromyko had expressed concern about ASEAN becoming a military arrangement, but that he, Rajaratnam, had sought to explain ASEAN's primary economic purpose and concern, and Gromyko had "understood" his explanation. According to the Singapore foreign minister, "They (the Russians) have nothing against ASEAN, but they may not support it." Agence France Presse dispatch, Singapore, 14 April; *FBIS*, 14 April.)

On 30 May the People's Action Party formally resigned from the London-headquartered Socialist International (SI). The action came after nearly a year of criticism of the PAP by the Dutch and British Labor parties, with the less open encouragement of several other European socialist parties. A report submitted by the Dutch Labor Party criticized the alleged political repression in Singapore and the plight of political prisoners there. In reply, Premier Lee Kuan Yew charged that the SI had "wittingly or unwittingly become a vehicle to further the communist cause in Singapore," and blamed a "Communist front group in Singapore" for providing a caricature on the PAP to the front group's sympathizers abroad, who in turn, "working via Marxists and Liberal intellectuals," had been able to influence the SI. Even before the PAP's formal withdrawal, the Dutch Labor Party's international affairs secretary had said that the PAP's resignation would be considered substantiation of the truth of the charges against it. (Ho Kwon Ping, "Countering the Communist 'Sinister Conspiracy,'" *Far Eastern Economic Review*, 14 May, pp. 21-22.) The PAP's withdrawal from the SI has probably facilitated further the Communist tactics both within the island state and abroad to project the need for a broad "democratic" united front that can oust the Lee Kuan Yew regime. On 14 July, the deputy foreign minister of the Socialist Republic of Vietnam, Phan Hien, visited Singapore and held talks with Premier Lee Kuan Yew. No details of the meeting were published but it was believed that Phan had communicated a message from the Hanoi government to Lee expressing the wish for friendly relations between the Socialist Republic of Vietnam and Singapore (*FBIS*, 15 July).

Publications. According to Barisan spokesmen, it remains virtually impossible to obtain permits from the government in order to print partisan political publications, except at the time of general elections. Neither the Barisan's one time biweekly *Plebeian*, nor its Chinese-language mouthpiece, *Chern Siau Pau*, have therefore been able to appear with any regularity during the past four years, and the Barisan has relied primarily on a few stenciled leaflets of limited circulation.

In the past, reports on Singapore developments were on occasion broadcast by the CPM's clandestine radio transmitter, "Voice of the Malayan Revolution," but these have virtually ceased since 1974. The CPM's principal international publication, the London based *Malayan Monitor and General News*, which sometimes used to carry items critical of Singapore government policies, has begun to appear less and less frequently during the past three years. Leaflets attributed by Singapore police sources to the MPLL and the MNLF are occasionally discovered, but their circulation must be considered quite small and confined to deep-cover proselytizing efforts. Reportedly, the CPM transmitter broadcasts from the southern part of China's Yunnan Province. The Chinese government disclaims any official connection with or responsibility for it, and has stated that the broadcasts are the work of "Malayan friends."

University of Bridgeport   Justus M. van der Kroef

Sri Lanka

Sri Lanka's oldest Marxist party, the Lanka Sama Samaja Party (Ceylon Equal Society Party; LSSP), was formed in 1935. From the original LSSP, a number of parties and groups have emerged. The present LSSP, generally referred to as Trotskyist although it was expelled from the Fourth International, is the country's major Marxist party.

The Ceylon Communist Party was formed in 1943 by an LSSP founder, S. A. Wickremasinghe. In 1963 it split into pro-Soviet and pro-Chinese factions led by Wickremasinghe and N. Sanmugathasan, respectively. Membership in the pro-Soviet Sri Lanka Communist Party (SLCP) is estimated at 5,000. That in the now divided pro-Chinese groups is probably less than 1,000.

In 1968 the LSSP and the SLCP subordinated their mutual antagonism and joined in the "United Front" (UF) with the social-democratic Sri Lanka Freedom Party (SLFP). Following the May 1970 general elections, the three parties formed a coalition government headed by the SLFP leader, Mrs. Sirimavo Bandaranaike. In September 1975,the LSSP was ousted from the coalition.

In the 1970 elections the LSSP had won 19 of the 151 seats contested and 8.7 percent of the popular vote. The SLCP won 6 seats and 3.4 percent of the vote. Sri Lanka's population is estimated at 14,000,000.

Leadership and Organization. *The LSSP.* The Trotskyist party's most prominent leaders are N. M. Perera, Colvin de Silva, and Leslie Goonewardena, who were cabinet ministers until September 1975. Bernard Soysa is general secretary.

The labor movement has long been identified politically with the Marxists, and the LSSP is a major influence in trade unionism. The party controls the Ceylon Federation of Labor and receives support from the Government Workers' Trade Union Federation and the Government Clerical Service Union (*YICA, 1974*, p. 543). The Ceylon Students Federation also supports the party.

The Pro-Soviet SLCP. In 1975 elections to the Politburo and Secretariat, Pieter Keuneman was chosen general secretary, S. A. Wickremasinghe president, and K. P. Silva secretary for organizational matters (*Pravda*, 16 September 1975). Keuneman is also minister of housing.

Party affiliates include its Youth League, Women's Organization, and the Ceylon Federation of Trade Unions. Keuneman has claimed that the party has leadership in unions with memberships totaling 250,000 and that youth leagues supporting the party have nearly 30,000 members (*Ceylon Daily News*, Colombo, 20 August 1975).

The Pro-Chinese Communist Parties. In 1972 Central Committee member Watson Fernando broke away from N. Sanmugathasan's pro-Chinese SLCP to establish the Communist Party of Sri Lanka (Marxist-Leninist). Sanmugathasan's faction is now called the Ceylon Communist Party (CCP) and has retained support of the Ceylon Trade Union Federation.

The Revolutionary JVP. In April 1971 the traditional Marxist parties found themselves challenged by a young radical movement—the Janatha Vimukthi Peramuna (JVP), or People's Liberation Front.

Rohana Wijeweera and other JVP leaders had been members of the orthodox Communist parties. Although their armed attempt in 1971 to overthrow the government failed, sporadic violence has continued. In early 1976, a spate of robberies prompted a warning from Prime Minister Bandaranaike of a new insurgency. This has not materialized, however, and the government later lifted various restrictions on activities of thousands of those involved in the rebellion. Wijeweera, meanwhile, is serving a life sentence.

Party Internal Affairs. During the SLCP's Ninth Congress, August 1975, a program for the period preceding the 1977 general elections was adopted. According to General Secretary Keuneman, this includes "nationalization of foreign-owned plantations and banks and of branches of transnational corporations; extension of democratic rights and a higher living standard; expansion of food production and improvement of economic management, especially in the state sector" (*WMR*, December 1975).

Keuneman also stated that the Congress had stressed the importance of restoring unity "following elimination of the temporary differences" which had arisen. He claimed that members of the pro-Chinese groups were returning to the SLCP. (Ibid.) Internal differences over the SLCP's attitude toward participation in the coalition government apparently persist, however. The struggle between Keunemann's "soft-line" faction and Wickremasinghe's "hard-line" opposition to participation had led to a nine-month-long open split which was finally resolved in the 1974 reunification (*YICA, 1975*, p. 423).

Domestic Attitudes and Activities. *The LSSP.* Following the parliamentary path to power, the LSSP seeks extensive political and economic reforms, some of which have been achieved in government actions such as land reform, an income ceiling, greater press regulation, and the 1972 constitution. The younger, more militant party members consider the UF's progress toward socialism too slow, and their pressure probably contributed to the coalition's breakup in 1975.

Since the breakup, the LSSP has increased its criticism and non-violent harassment of Mrs. Bandaranaike's government. The party has sponsored an unsuccessful no-confidence motion against the Prime Minister, mounted an anti-government wall poster campaign for which several party members were briefly detained, has been involved in the limited labor unrest, and has called for termination of the state of emergency declared in 1971.

The LSSP suffered setbacks during 1976, including the outcome of the first by-election contested independently of the coalition; it obtained only 4 percent of the popular vote. In addition, publication of its daily newspaper, *Janadina*, was suspended, reportedly for financial reasons, and its efforts to form a new "socialist United Front" apparently have not been very successful.

Elections scheduled for 1977 have been the subject of increasing political debate, including speculation on their possible postponement. The LSSP was among the opposition parties warning the government against postponement, and N. M. Perera called on "all progressive forces" to unite in preventing such action (*Far Eastern Economic Review*, Hong Kong, 24 September).

The SLCP. The pro-Soviet SLCP has also followed the parliamentary strategy and officially continues to support the UF. The Wickremasinghe faction, however, has long criticized the government's failure to take over all foreign banks, industries, and plantations, and opposes Keuneman's participation in the cabinet. In late 1975 the party did welcome the government's decision to nationalize plantations.

The SLCP has also opposed proposals by senior SLFP figures to postpone elections. The SLCP reportedly told its coalition partner that the pro-Soviet Communists were not inclined to support postponement, and criticized any assumption that they would blindly follow the dominant SLFP's proposals (*Far Eastern Economic Review*, 22 October).

The Pro-Chinese Communist Parties. Sanmugathasan has consistently advocated violent overthrow of the government, but Fernando's faction is apparently willing to support the UF's "progressive" measures.

International Views and Policies. *The LSSP.* Although the LSSP rejects Soviet domination (for example, it condemned the Soviet-led invasion of Czechoslovakia), it has supported the "socialist" USSR against "imperialism" and "capitalism." It has accused the USA of subversive activities in Sri Lanka and called the U.S. military presence in the Indian Ocean a threat to littoral states.

The SLCP. At its 1975 Congress, the party approved the proposal for another international conference of communist and workers' parties, and favored relaxation of tensions between states. Noting the need for a collective security system in Asia, it criticized China's "anti-Sovietism and cooperation with imperialism." The Congress also discussed the "devastating effects" of the "international capitalist crisis" on the Third World and Sri Lanka as well as the USSR's "numerous peace initiatives." (*YICA, 1976*, pp. 383-84.)

In commenting on the 25th Congress of the Communist Party of the Soviet Union, which he attended, Pieter Keuneman stated that the SLCP and the CPSU had "complete unanimity of views" on international politics and the problems of the Communist movement (TASS, 27 February 1976). Keuneman also visited East Germany and Hungary during the year.

The Pro-Chinese Communist Parties. Both pro-Chinese parties sent messages of condolence on the death of Mao Tse-tung (*Peking Review*, 24 September, 5 November 1976). Ceylon Communist Party leader Sanmugathasan visited Albania in late 1975.

Party Publications. SLCP publications include *Aththa* and *Forward.* The current orientation of pro-Chinese publications, such as *Kamkaruwa, Tolilali*, and *Red Flag*, is not clear, but at least *Kamkaruwa* and *Tolilali* may favor the Ceylon Communist Party. LSSP newspapers include *Samasamajaya* and *Janadina.*

Alexandria, Virginia   Barbara Reid

Thailand

Clearly, the most important political event in Thailand in 1976 was the 6 October coup d' état which overthrew the elected government of Prime Minister Seni Pramoj. On that day a group of high-level military officers calling itself the Administrative Reform Council (ARC) seized power "to forestall a communist plot backed by the Vietnamese." The ARC moved quickly to consolidate their power and to proclaim anti-communist policies. Suspected communists and leftists were arrested, Marxist books were confiscated and burned, and an ultra-rightist government was established under the leadership of Prime Minister Thanin Kraivichien, a militant anti-communist judge. The new cabinet reflected the conservative nature of the new regime and the important role of the military.

At the time this essay was written, the new government had not yet declared specific policies that affect the communist movement in Thailand. The ARC did announce that the previous government's move to improve relations with Hanoi would be suspended, all "left-wing" student groups banned, communist documents, pamphlets, and books seized, newspapers censored, re-education camps established for those persons considered dangerous to the national security, and relations with the USA improved. The past policy follows a period when relations between the USA and Thailand were cool due to the Thai demand that U.S. military forces be withdrawn from Thailand and that U.S. Air Force bases be shut down.

Leaders of student groups considered leftist by the new regime as well as certain bureaucrats, politicians, and intellectuals fled to Laos, went into exile in the West, or went underground following the coup. There is not yet reliable evidence whether these persons will join with the communist movement. It is also not yet clear whether Hanoi will respond to the coup by stepping up support for insurgency in the Northeast. Malaysian officials, long concerned over what they see as Bangkok's ineffectiveness in barring insurgents from northern Malaysia from crossing the border to sanctuary in southern Thailand, are reported hopeful the new government will step up joint action on both sides of the border (Christian Science Monitor, 12 October 1976).

Communist Insurgency Strength. Communist insurgency strength in Thailand is difficult to judge accurately. The Internal Operations Security Command (ISOC) tends to exaggerate the number of insurgents, and banditry is sometimes included as insurgent activity. In the South, non-communist separatists who seek to form a separate state or to join with Malaysia are often referred to in insurgent counts.

According to U.S. official sources, the current (1976) strength of *armed* insurgents is approximately 8,720. These include three categories of communist military forces: village militia, local forces, and main force units, the latter two comprising the "Thai People's Liberation Army." Additionally, it is estimated that there is a 10 to 1 ratio of infrastructure supporters to the armed insurgents or a total of approximately 80,000 supporters. The population of Thailand is estimated at about 40 million.

The Communist Party of Thailand (CPT) increased the tempo of the insurgency in 1976. Incident and casualty levels for the first six months of 1976 were higher than the same period in 1975 by as much as 40 to 50 percent. This growth rate was carried out without an equivalent rise in the number of CPT casualties. In 1974 and 1975 there was a 4 percent yearly growth rate in armed communist insurgent strength, according to official U.S. sources, but in 1976 the growth rate was double that figure.

The CPT military forces are now capable of operating in multi-company strength, and even in provinces where there has not been much expansion there is now a company. In other more active provinces there is a platoon or a company in each district. In Na Kae District of Nakorn Phanom Province in the Northeast, for example, a CPT battalion has been formed, and in Nan Province the communist armed forces may have reached battalion level.

As for weaponry, in former years the armed insurgents used World War II firearms; now they are equipped with more modern weapons such as AK rifles, SKS automatic carbines, and B-40 rocket launchers. Government battle casualties, including those inflicted by CPT mines, have averaged thirty killed per month during the first half of 1976. Confirmed CPT casualties averaged about fourteen each month.

According to Thai government sources, a total of 412 Thai villages were either under strong communist terrorist (CT) influence or wholly under terrorists' control in January 1975. Some 6,000 villages with a population of approximately 3.9 million are said to be subject to some degree of CT influence. (*Investor*, October 1975, p. 9.)

In September 1976, the Seni Pramoj government issued a White Paper detailing communist activity in Thailand and the support of Vietnam, Laos, and China to the insurgency. The report puts the government's total death toll in the past ten years at 2,746 as against 1,979 deaths on the insurgents' side during the same period. A total of 5,893 government personnel were wounded in clashes with insurgents in the past ten years, the report says, adding that 605 insurgents were injured during the same period. While 99 government personnel were captured by CTs from 1966 to 1976, a total of 6,543 CTs were taken by government authorities. The report states that since 1966 more than 1,100 Thai insurgents have undergone political and military training in Vietnam, Laos, and China before returning to take up "key positions in the CPT." The White Paper dismisses the theory that the CPT is a strictly indigenous organization without outside support. (*The Nation*, Bangkok, 3 September 1976, p. 1.) General Saiyud Kerdpol, the ISOC commander, stated: "My estimate is that we have about three years to put our house in order. If not, the combination of internal and external pressures will make the future of this country very uncertain indeed."

Leadership and Organization. The CPT follows the classic organizational pattern of Communist organizations. It has a Central Committee still composed principally of Sino-Thais in leadership roles. Under Party leadership committees are organized clandestinely among the masses in villages, factories, and perhaps among the Royal Thai Government's armed forces. In the CPT armed forces, party military committees are now established at company and battalion levels.

It is difficult to identify the major leaders of the CPT. The emphasis is on "Thai-izing" the leadership of the CPT-led insurgency, particularly at county, district, and province levels, and de-emphasizing the Sino-Thai historical leadership. According to official U.S. sources, the current leaders of the three regional insurgencies are Song Nopakon in the North, Udom Sisawan in the Northeast, and Prasit Thiansiri in the South. All three are said to be members of the Central Committee of the CPT, with Song and Udom being two of the original Sino-Thai leaders of the Party.

ISOC has reported that Charoen Wanngam, alias Boosaba, a Thai in his mid-50's who is said to have fought at Dien Bien Phu and to have once been the senior CPT representative in the Nakorn Phanom region of northeast Thailand, is currently chairman of the CPT's Central Committee. ISOC reports that the Central Committee is probably based in the Chien Khong area bordering Laos in the North, but little else seems to be known about it, the Politburo policy debates, or the relationship with other communist forces. (*Far Eastern Economic Review*, 9 July 1976, p. 8-9.)

Some observers have reported factionalism within the CPT based on Thai and Sino-Thai differences as well as on the proper ideological program to be followed. In particular, these debates concern the Sino-Soviet split and whether or not tactics should be pure Maoist or based more on local conditions. In its message of sympathy to the People's Republic of China on the death of Mao Tse-tung the CPT noted that Mao "resolutely fought the new revisionism led by the traitorous Soviet revisionist clique." Most analysts agree that the Central Committee is Maoist. The Party radio station (thought to operate from Kunming in South China) never varies from the Peking line. The pro-China stand of the CPT is reported to have kept Hanoi's leadership from exercising more influence in the CPT.

Counter-Insurgency Response. The 6 October coup will no doubt change the Counter-Insurgency (CI) policies of the Thai government. The new deputy prime minister, General Boonchai

Bamroongphong, the former army commander in chief and one of the major powers in the ARC, has long criticized CI activities in Thailand. The basic CI strategy has been to contain the CPT forces in their current base areas, particularly in the North and Northeast. The containment strategy has been basically defensive in nature. However, analysis of recent incidents indicates increased willingness by the Royal Thai Government forces to engage the CT. Prime Minister Seni Pramoj gave increasing attention to insurgency and before the overthrow of his government suggested the need to reorganize CI policies. The major CI program is called "Aw Paw Paw," a Thai acronym for "Volunteers for Self-Development and Security," and all villagers are required to participate.

The combined military police-civilian response to the CT has been coordinated by the Communist Suppression Operation Command, which later became the Internal Security Operations Command. The arrangement suffers from the disadvantage that the only function of the Command is coordination; no operational forces are under its authority. The new coup leaders may strengthen ISOC's role in counterinsurgency efforts. (*Investor*, October, 1975, p. 13.)

Domestic Activities. Communist insurgency in Thailand continued in 1976 to be focused in the northern, northeastern, and southern regions of the country. In the South the policy of cooperation between Thailand and Malaysia with respect to the CT's was substantially reduced. In April and May 1976, Malaysian government forces conducted several operations within Thai territory. In Betong town near the Thai-Malaysian border, an organization called the Thai Sovereignty Protection Group protested the Malaysian actions and demanded the removal of all Malaysian Police Field Forces. It is not clear if the leadership of the Protection Group is in the hands of, or included, communists. The Seni Pramoj government asked Malaysia to withdraw all its Police Field Force units by early June and insisted on the termination of the right of "hot pursuit." Existing agreements for joint cooperation against the CT's were terminated, and discussions started on a new agreement. The new military government may give Malaysia the right to enter Thai territory once again. (See *Malaysia.*)

In 1976 a major battle between the CT and the government in the northern region began on 11 June when the son of Major General Yuthasorn Kaysornsuk crashed his F5A jet fighter in the mountains of Petchabun Province. An immediate operation was launched to find the pilot and plane. The paratroop unit which was called in became engaged in a heavy battle and called for reinforcements. An estimated 200 communist troops were killed. (*Los Angeles Times*, 2 September, p. 3, part 1A.) The incident took place in a remote and mountainous area where some 75 "violent incidents," such as ambushes using land mines, occurred in the first three months of 1976 as compared with 96 incidents in the entire North during 1975.

In the Northeast the principal problems concerned border incidents with Laos and violent anti-Vietnamese incidents in Nakhon Phanom Province. The Thai government told Vietnam that the latter incidents were isolated acts of local hoodlums and criminals. The statement, made through the Thai Embassy in Vientiane, was an official reply to the Vietnamese charges that Thai authorities were persecuting Vietnamese refugees.

The presence of tens of thousands of Vietnamese refugees—including both those who came to Thailand during the Indochina war and those who came following the Communist takeover in 1975—has caused grave concern among Thai officials. It is alleged that the original refugees retain loyalty to the late Ho Chi Minh and that they are held under the control of about 1,000 hardcore Communist cadres (*Bangkok Post*, 30 August, p. 8). The Thai and Vietnamese governments agreed in August to make arrangements for repatriation of the refugees.

Thailand-Vietnam Relations. On 6 August 1976 the Thai and Vietnamese governments established diplomatic relations on the basis of four principles:

(1) respect for each other's independence, sovereignty, territorial integrity, non-aggression, non-interference in each other's internal affairs, equality, mutual benefit and peaceful coexistence; (2) not to allow any foreign country to use one's territory as a base for aggression against any other country; (3) establishment of friendly relations, economic cooperation and cultural exchanges; (4) development of regional cooperation for the benefit of genuine independence, peace, and neutrality in Southest Asia (Office of the Public Relations Attaché, Royal Thai Embassy, no. 6).

Following the 6 October coup Hanoi and Vientiane bitterly attacked the new government. Hanoi radio accused the Thai leaders of having rounded up several thousand Vietnamese citizens and herded them into "disguised concentration camps" in northestern Thailand. Radio Thailand denied the allegations that the military-dominated government was trying to destroy the new relationship with Vietnam established during the previous democratic regime of Prime Minister Seni Pramoj. (*NYT*, 18 October.) However, the new government spokesmen accused "left-wing" students at Thammasat University of fighting "with deadly weapons of war in league with the Vietnamese Communist terrorists." Some diplomatic observers fear that anti-Vietnamese hysteria might again grip the Northeast resulting in repression against the estimated 40,000 Vietnamese in Thailand. (*Far Eastern Economic Review*, 22 October, p. 23.)

At the end of 1976 the potential role of the CPT remained unpredictable and in flux. It is not yet clear whether the new right-wing anti-democratic, anti-communist government will effectively counter the internal communist movement or, on the other hand, whether it will rally anti-government forces, strengthen the CPT's role, and give the insurgent movement a shot in the arm.

The CPT Central Committee issued a statement on 7 October condemning the coup and expressing sympathy to the bereaved families. The statement repeated the Maoist principle that the main strategy to be adopted must be based on the rural areas, while cooperating with workers in the towns. It described the "white danger" (U.S. imperialism) as "the most cruel power in the world" and said that the "red zones" (liberated areas) are the only reliable areas for the people. The statement ended with the declaration that "state power comes from the barrel of a gun and blood will only be washed out with blood." (Ibid.)

Northern Illinois University   Clark D. Neher

Socialist Republic of Vietnam

Communist thought and organization came to Vietnam, then part of French Indochina, in the mid-1920s. It was, in those infant years, a factionalized movement of three parts: the Stalinist movement which was destined to become the dominant one; the Trotskyite stream which was powerful until its leadership was emasculated by the French with some help from the Stalinists at the beginning of World War II; and an internationally unaligned group of intellectuals and gentry. The entire Communist movement was not large, numbering abut 1,000 activists in the late 1920s, according to French police records.

Seeking unity the Comintern ordered the man the world came to know as Ho Chi Minh, at the time chief of the Comintern's Eastern Department Southern Branch, to effect a merger of the disparate elements. The result was formation on 3 February 1930, in Hong Kong, of the Indochinese Communist Party. This was the first of a series of Stalinist Communist organizations in Indochina. The Vietnamese Workers Party (Dang Lao Dong; Lao Dong Party) was officially formed in March 1951. It was renamed the Vietnamese Communist Party in December 1976.

Functionally the Indochinese Communist Party, through much of the 1930s, was part of the French Communist Party and was under Comintern orders to effect the popular front—the stop-Hitler effort—which perhaps made sense to the Party in France but in Indochina meant cooperation with the hated *colon*. As a result militant anti-French activity during the period was in the hands of those called the nationalists, that is, anti-French, non-Communist Indochinese. The two main groups were the Dai Viet (Greater Vietnam) and the Viet-Nam Quoc Dan Dang (VNQDD), which had close associations with the Chinese Nationalists. The nationalists were the main challengers to communism at the time.

The subsequent organizational format used by Ho Chi Minh and his Stalinist Communists was the united front, one of the great political inventions of the 20th century. Ho was an organizational genius and used the united front to attack the opposition nationalist forces too large or too powerful to destroy frontally. Time and again he smothered his enemies in the front's encompassing arms. The most important of these was the League for Vietnamese Independence (Viet Nam Doc Lap Dong Minh Hoi), usually called the Viet Minh. It was created among anti-French, anti-Japanese militants early in World War II. The Viet Minh was incorporated into an even larger front, the Lien Viet (Mat Tran Lien Hiep Quoc Dan Viet Nam), at the end of the war, which pulled in more orthodox Vietnamese political groups. In 1955 the Fatherland Front (Mat Tran To Quoc Viet Nam) absorbed the Lien Viet and then, in 1976, absorbed the front which had been operating in South Vietnam, the National Liberation Front.

The Communists, as the Lao Dong Party, led the newly formed (1946) Democratic Republic of Vietnam (DRV) through the Viet Minh war and emancipation from French rule. In 1959 it embarked on a new and venturesome course: liberation of the South and unification of the country. After a long and bloody struggle—one which exacted a high toll, perhaps 10 percent of the male adults of the DRV—victory was achieved. Vietnam in mid-1976 became the Socialist Republic of Vietnam, run by the newly renamed Vietnamese Communist Party.

Position in 1976. The much postponed Fourth Lao Dong Party Congress was convened in 1976 and was by far the most important official event of the year.

A total of 1,008 delegates, representing 1,553,500 Party members from all parts of Vietnam, together with observers from 29 foreign Communist parties, met in Hanoi, 14-20 December. Delegates of ruling Communist parties came from Albania, Bulgaria, Cuba, Czechoslovakia, the German Democratic Republic, Hungary, Laos, Mongolia, North Korea, Poland, Romania, and the USSR. Communist party representatives also came from Angola, Canada, Chile, Finland, France, Great Britain, Italy, Japan, Mexico, Mozambique, the Palestine Liberation Organization, Portugal, South Africa, Spain, Sweden, the USA (Henry Winston), and West Germany. Out of the Congress came a new leadership list, a series of Party organizational and structural changes, and a new Party line or ideological directive.

It was the first Congress since 1960, although Party By-laws stipulate a national congress every four years. Even during 1976 there was uncertainty that the Congress would convene. The Party's 24th Plenum (Dalat, July 1975) decided that a Congress would be held in 1976 but left it to the Politburo to fix the date. Several dates were set and abandoned. Finally, in August or September, the 25th Plenum met and fixed the December date. The decision meant that Party officials and cadres had to move briskly to meet the early deadline. Some 16,000 basic-level Party meetings across the country were hastily called and representatives named or elected to district/precinct Party Congresses. These then met in late October and elected representatives to 38 provincial/municipal congresses which, in turn, met in November and elected delegates to the Fourth Congress. At the same time PAVN 2 units were naming 495 representatives to an All-Army Party Congress, staged by Lieutenant General Le Quang Hoa's General Political Department, which met in mid-November in Hanoi and elected 118 delegates to the Fourth Congress. (The PAVN, People's Army of Vietnam, is the North Vietnamese armed forces. In 1975 it absorbed the so-called Viet Cong, the People's Liberation Armed Force, or PLAF.)

These lower congresses, particularly at the province/municipal level, were accompanied by much panoply. Most were graced by the appearance of Politburo members, and the general sense communicated was that merely to attend such a gathering was to be regarded as a high honor. The lower congresses had before them various documents, including a draft of Party By-law amendments and a draft political report by Party Secretary Le Duan, all of which were studied, explained, and discussed. Voting for delegates at the province/municipal congress was complex. The number of delegates to be chosen from each region was determined by a complicated formula which attempted to balance various elements (and perhaps factions) such as technocrats, military, managerial personnel, and others. Also taken into consideration in the formula were age, ethnic minority status, and sex. Certain economic areas, such as industrial concentrations, were given additional representation with the result that the Fourth Congress had in attendance a disproportionate number of delegates from the economic sector.

The Congress was a festive affair. A great nationwide emulation campaign was launched in its name. Hanoi was cleaned up for the week and some 300,000 flowering trees planted. The six official slogans of the Congress convey the thrust of the session:

> Let the Party, Soldiers and People Greet the 4th Congress With a Revolutionary Heroism Emulation Campaign That Scores New Achievements.
> All for Production. All for Building Socialism. All for Prosperity, Strength, and Happiness of the Fatherland.
> Long Live Invincible Marxism-Leninism.
> Long Live the Glorious Lao Dong Party.
> Long Live a Peaceful, Independent, Unified, and Socialist Vietnam.
> Great President Ho Chi Minh Will Live Forever in Our Cause.

The tone of the Congress, once delegates were gathered, was generally congratulatory, the mood one of self-satisfaction. Said one speaker: "We have come to summarize the experience of victory."

There was a certain tidying up of history, to make it more neat, as in Le Duan's explanation that in the First Congress (1935) the Party was forged into the major political force in Vietnam; in the Second Congress (1951) the Party assumed direct leadership of the war against France; and in the Third Congress (1960) the Party mapped plans to build socialism in the North and liberate the South and unify the country. Now the Fourth Congress had met to chart plans to build the brave new world.

On balance, the Congress was neither major landmark in terms of new direction, new leadership, or new doctrine, nor was it simply a morale-boosting celebration to put the frosting on the cake of victory. Rather it was something in between. It offered no new programs or policies, but it did sharpen the focus on those which existed. It moved a few personalities, already important, into roles of even greater importance, but made no generational transfer of power. It defused but did not eliminate a variety of doctrinal disputes. Above all the Congress was, by the fact of its being, a clear declaration that the Party intended to remain not just number one but the only one: Vietnam's dominant institution, fundamental source of all inspiration, fountain of all wisdom, monopolizer of all power. As Le Duan indicated in his closing remarks, the Party is Vietnam's link with destiny. It alone can, and will, arm the Vietnamese people with necessary political views and guidance for action. Each Party member is a vanguard combatant. Each basic Party organization is to be a fortress from whence issues the orders to build socialism. Each Party committee must stimulate the masses so that they seethe constantly, advance unceasingly. The Party is the center of all unity. There will not be in Vietnam, as is a whispered suggestion in Eastern Europe, any "irrelevancy" of the Party.

Leadership. The Party's ruling organ—the Central Committee and its Politburo—was enlarged by the Congress, a reflection of the absorption of the southern *apparat*, and existing vacancies filled. Beyond numerical changes there was no significant socio-political alteration, no shifting of authority to the next generation, for example. The average age of the Politburo dropped by only one year, from 66 to 65 years.

The Politburo was enlarged to 17 seats (14 plus three alternates) from the previous 13 (11 plus two alternates). There were two vacancies due to death (Ho Chi Minh and Nguyen Chi Thanh) and one due to retirement (Hoang Van Hoan) thus seven persons have joined the Politburo.

The Politburo (asterisk indicates Fourth Congress appointment):

1. Le Duan, party Central Committee secretary-general
2. Truong Chinh
3. Pham Van Dong
4. Pham Hung
5. Le Duc Tho
6. Vo Nguyen Giap
7. Nguyen Duy Trinh
8. Le Thanh
9. Tran Quoc Hoan
10. Van Tien Dung
11. Le Van Luong*
12. Nguyen Van Cuc, alias Nguyen Van Linh*
13. Vo Toan, alias Vo Chi Cong*
14. Chu Huy Man*

Politburo alternate members:
1. To Huu*
2. Vo Van Kiet, alias Sau Dan*
3. Do Muoi*

The Party Secretariat membership was changed considerably when five of the nine previous members were dropped:

Previous Secretariat	**New Secretariat**
Le Duan (first secretary)	Le Duan (secretary-general)
Pham Hung	—
Le Duc Tho	Le Duc Tho
Le Van Luong	—
To Huu	To Huu
Hoang Anh	—
Nguyen Van Tran	—
Nguyen Con	—
Xuan Thuy	Xuan Thuy
	Nguyen Duy Trinh
	Nguyen Van Cuc
	Nguyen Lam
	Song Hao
	Le Quang Dao

The new and enlarged Control Committee appears to be a Party instrument which has been accorded new importance. Apparently this is the result of consultations with the Communist Party of the Soviet Union. Earlier in the year a team of Party officials arrived from Moscow billed as experts on Party control and auditing techniques. Probably this committee will play a major role in the promised crackdown on Party cadre misbehavior and inadequate performance. The new Control Committee:

1. Song Hao, chairman
2. Tran Van Som
3. Nguyen Van Chi
4. Ngo Thuyen
5. Pham Van So
6. Nguyen Thanh
7. Hoang Nguyen Cuong
8. Pham Chanh
9. Nguyen Thi Thanh
10. Phan Thi Tot
11. Duong Thi Hong Phuong

The Party's Central Committee was nearly doubled in size, again a reflection of absorbing the Party in the South. Although exact size of the 1960 Central Committee was not known, it had been reliably estimated at about 47 members plus an additional ten "hidden" members, those from the South whose names were withheld to protect them, and about 25 alternates. This has now been enlarged to 133 members (101 plus 32 alternates).

Publication of the full Central Committee list, together with previous aliases, will permit a far more detailed analysis of the composition and nature of Party leadership than was possible in the past. The average age remains high, either in the low 60s or high 50s (compared with the average age of the outgoing Central Committee, 65). At least 30 former Central Committee members are not on the new list; they may have been dropped, or may have retired or died. There is an increase in the number of members whose occupational tasks are in the economic sector, as well as an increase in military representation. There appears to have been an effort to balance the committee in terms of geographic regionalism although northerners still far outnumber southerners and centerites combined.

The new Central Committee:

1. Le Duan
2. Truong Chinh
3. Pham Van Dong
4. Pham Hung
5. Le Duc Tho
6. Vo Nguyen Giap
7. Nguyen Duy Trinh
8. Le Thanh Nghi
9. Tran Quoc Hoan
10. Van Tien Dung
11. LeVan Luong
12. To Huu
13. Xuan Thuy
14. Hoang Anh
15. Ton Duc Thang
16. Nguyen Luong Bang
17. Koang Quoc Viet
18. Nguyen Thi Thap
19. Nguyen Lam
20. Nguyen Van Cuc,
    alias Nguyen Van Linh
21. Bui Quang Tao
22. Phan Van Dang,
    alias Hai Van
23. Tran Do
24. Tran Quang Huy
25. Hoang Tung
26. Ha Thi Que
27. Tran Huu Duc
28. Tran Luong,
    alias Tran Nam Trung
29. Le Quoc Than
30. Vo Van Kiet,
    alias Sau Dan
31. Vo Toan,
    alias Vo Chi Cong
32. Do Huoi
33. Vo Thuc Dong
34. Nguyen Thanh Binh
35. Hoang Van Kieu
36. Nguyen Con
37. Phan Trong Tue
38. Dinh Duc Thien

39. Nguyen Huu Mai
40. Ha Ke Tan
41. Nguyen Huu Khieu
42. Duong Quoc Chinh
43. Chu Huy Man
44. Song Hao
45. Hoang Van Thai
46. Le Quang Dao
47. Tran Van Tra
48. Tran Van Som
49. Nguyen Van Chi,
    alias Sau Chi
50. Dang Huu Khiem
51. Pham Van Kiet,
    alias Nam Van
52. Nguyen Vinh
53. Nguyen Thanh Le
54. Nguyen Duc Thuan
55. Nguyen Thi Dinh,
    alias Ba Dinh
56. Nguyen Thi Nhu
57. Dang Thi
58. Tran Quyet
59. Nguyen Co Thach
60. Vu Tuan
61. La Lam Gia,
    alias Bay May
62. Nguyen Quang Lam,
    alias Tam Tu
63. Tran Sam
64. Tran Van Hien
65. Dang Quoc Bao
66. Tran Quynh
67. Dong Sy Nguyen
68. Le Quang Hoa
69. Le Trong Tan
70. Le Duc Anh
71. Bui Phung
72. Nguyen Quyet
73. Dam Quang Trung
74. Vu Lap
75. Doan Khue
76. Vo Van Thanh

77. Hoang Minh Thi
78. Hoang Cam
79. Tran Dong
80. Nguyen Duc Tam
81. Ngo Duy Dong
82. Nguyen Ngoc Triu
83. Bui San
84. Nguyen Ngoc Linh,
    alias Vu Ngoc Linh
85. Truong Minh
86. Ta Hong Thanh
87. Vu Dinh Lieu,
    alias Tu Binh
88. Mai Chi Tho,
    alias Nam Xuan
89. Tran Ngoc Ban,
    alias Muoi On
90. Nguyen Thanh Tho,
    alias Muoi So
91. Tran Van Long,
    alias Muoi Dai
92. Le Van Nhung,
    alias Tu Viet Thang
93. Phan Ngoc Sen,
    alias Muoi Chi
94. Le Van Pham,
    alias Chin Hai
95. Do Van Nuong,
    alias Tu Nguyen
96. Nguyen Nhu Y,
    alias Nam Chu
97. Nguyen Thi Bach Tuyet,
    alias Sau Tuyet
98. Tran Le,
    alias Nam Hoa
99. Le Van Hien,
    alias Tam Hien
100. Nguyen Xuan Huu,
    alias Bay Huu
101. Nguyen Tuan Tai,
    alias Tran Kien

Alternate members of the new Central Committee:

1. Vu Oanh
2. Nguyen Van Chinh, alias Chin Cam
3. Dao Duy Tung
4. Luong Van Nghia
5. Tran Hanh
6. Vu Thi Hong
7. Cao Dang Chiem, alias Sau Hoang
8. Nguyen Chan
9. Nguyen Tuong Lan
10. Tran Huu Du

11. Tran Phuong
12. Le Khac
13. Nguyen Dinh Tu
14. Tran Lam
15. Hoang Minh Thao
16. Le Ngoc Hien
17. Le Van Tri
18. Hoang The Thien
19. Dang Vu Hiep
20. Do Chinh

21. Tran Vy
22. Nguyen Ngoc Cu
23. Nguyen Huu Thu
24. Hoang Van Hieu
25. Truong Van Kien
26. Bui Thanh Khiet
27. Nguyen Dang, alias Nam Trung
28. Le Phuoc Tho, alias Sau Hao
29. Ho Nghinh, alias Dong Quoc
30. Nguyen Van Sy, alias Ksor Kron
31. Ms Y Mot
32. Y Ngong Niek-dam, alias Y Ngong

Party Internal Developments. The Fourth Congress ordered a revision of the Party apparat. This involved amending Party By-laws, creating a single all-Vietnam Communist party, and launching still another campaign to improve the quality of cadres and members.

Amended Party By-laws were not released immediately, hence the exact nature of the changes is not yet known. However, the thrust and purposes of the changes were outlined by Le Duc Tho in his "Statement on Party Building" at the 17 December meeting of the Fourth Congress. He listed seven:

—Fixing tougher standards of knowledge and mastery of Party ideology for both cadres and members.

—Creating a more complete Party apparat within the State's economic sector.

—Maintaining stricter Party discipline aimed at increasing unity and reducing factionalism.

—Overhauling the Party chain of command and incorporating the southern Party.

—Insuring that entrance requirements for Party membership are adhered to, and generally raising those requirements.

—Amendments on cadre performance.

The major consideration, obviously, was incorporating the previously separate southern element of the Party. Initially there was one Party in all of Vietnam. A southern branch arrangement developed during the Viet Minh war, largely for administrative reasons. This was changed in 1963, again partly for administrative and partly for cosmetic reasons, to a more distinct institution, the People's Revolutionary Party (PRP). At the same time, the Central Office for South Vietnam (COSVN), which had been around in one form or another over the previous decade, developed increased authority and by the mid-1960s COSVN and the PRP Central Committee were virtually synonymous. Gradually the PRP as a separate entity began to fade and the Party in the South simply became the Southern Organization (Dang Bo Mien Nam), a usage which became formal after the takeover of the South.

The new By-laws will now systematize such matters as Party age, Party hierarchy, and administration for the entire country. They also change the Party name—from Vietnam Workers Party to Vietnam Communist Party—ending a usage which began in 1951 and which, although useful externally, long has given trouble to Party theoreticians.

The title of the leading Party official was changed from first secretary to secretary-general, also a return to an earlier usage. It has been suggested that, in deference to the memory of Ho Chi Minh, no one again would hold the title "chairman" and that secretary-general, therefore, was a more appropriate designation for the leading official than first secretary. Within the Party, the switch may be considered to have anti-Chinese overtones since secretary-general usually is associated with Soviet communism while chairman/first secretary is regarded as more Chinese. But there may be other explanations for the title change.

The Party in recent years must have been bigger than outsiders believed. Previous estimates of about a million members (the range was from 950,000 to 1.2 million), plus at the most 180,000 members in the Southern Organization, appear to have been low. According to Le Duc Tho's "Statement on Party Building," the official membership total was 1,553,500 as of December 1976, representing 3.13 percent of the population (which means the official population of Vietnam now is about 49,633,000). Apparently earlier estimates were low because observers underestimated the Southern Organization. The one million figure for the North often came from Politburo-level statements and thus can be considered firm. This means that the Party in the South during the 1970s was at least 350,000 strong and may have had as many as 500,000 members.

In any event, the total number of 1.5 million is to be cut by what in effect is a mini-purge. Substandard personnel, particularly cadres, are to be weeded out—possibly as many as 10 percent—leaving a more competent, efficient, and dedicated membership. At the same time, a recruitment drive was ordered; hence the total membership figure may not change much during 1977.

For the Party cadre none of this will be new. Frequently in the past three decades he has been made the scapegoat for the Party's and regime's troubles. Le Duan, for a period in the late 1960s, acted like a man obsessed in his determination to achieve a quantum jump in cadre quality. This year in a National Assembly speech on 25 June, he returned to the attack, castigating cadres for bribery, corruption, misappropriation of public property, economic waste, and various bad personal habits such as "loafing, callousness, irresponsibility, arrogance, authoritarianism, and bureaucratism." However, the main campaign against cadre performance during the year was led by Nguyen Duy Trinh, the foreign minister, who appears to be moving into a new role as czar of economic cadres. During the year Trinh wrote a lengthy assessment of economic cadres and chaired several cadre conferences. He particularly criticized individualism (self-serving behavior) in cadres, and singled out what he called "carte blanche" or "free pass" cadres who regard their position as "a ticket to the easy life." He said bad cadre behavior damaged the prestige of the Party, and he condemned what he called "subjectivism by superiors" — manifested, for example, by promotions based on personal relationships or geographic regionalism. Such subjectivism, he added, was moving the Party in the direction of factionalism and must be strongly opposed by all-through development of a greater spirit of unity and solidarity. Within the PAVN, meanwhile, a similar anti-cadre campaign was under way. Here the major sins were "loss of fighting will, individualism, and [in the South] being bewitched by material life-style." Trinh again addressed himself to the matter at the Fourth Congress, referring to removing "blemishes in the Party" — members with "low political and revolutionary consciousness."

Increasingly during the year the anti-cadre campaign was directed at those on duty in the South, a corps estimated to number as high as 250,000. One charge made was that of ignorant performance, primarily in the economic sector, although in fairness to these northern cadres it should be noted that they never were trained and were totally unprepared to run the southern economy, or even to understand it. A second, more serious charge was dereliction of duty. Apparently among cadres in the South the earlier attitude of reformist occupier has given way to a carpet-bagger mentality. Not only the relative luxury of the South, but also the enormous opportunity tempts the newcomers. As was said of some of the early New England missionaries in the Hawaiian Islands, "they came to do good and they stayed to do well." The official name of this sin is "money guzzling," the seductive urge to buy things when one is able to do so. Even the highly trusted Public Security Force cadres are not immune to the lure. Sent south to halt the flow of persons fleeing the country with their scarf-wrapped gold, several of the PSF cadres themselves have absconded with impounded gold and fled to Thailand in fishing boats.

The Party's youth organization — now renamed the Ho Chi Minh Communist Youth Group — was extended into the South this year after a massive organizational reshuffle of the southern apparat, accompanied by an intensive recruitment drive. The Youth Group has an estimated membership of three million (800,000 in 1971), of whom 280,000 have "cadre" status, meaning they have met certain requirements in behavior and performance. The full-time cadre corps, that is, Party cadres working on youth affairs within the Party, is estimated at about 13,500. Of these, about 10,000 are in the North and 3,500 in the South.

Youth in general is being courted, even if this is not reflected in Central Committee appointments or other generational transfers of power. Nearly all company-grade PAVN officers are Youth Group members. Most new Party members are former Youth Group members — for example, 71 percent of the new members in Hanoi, and 89 percent of all new members in Hai Hung Province.

The Communist Youth Group is called the "reserve army of the Party." It is headed, in its overall organization, by veteran youth affairs official Vu Quang as first secretary, plus a central committee. This is largely a headquarters unit. Under it, extending to the villages, are three Party youth organizations in which membership is by age: the Ho Chi Minh Communist Youth Group (17-30), the Ho Chi

Minh Vanguard Teen-ager Group (10-16), and the Ho Chi Minh Children's Group (under 10). In the South in recent years, the two Party youth organizations were the PRP Youth Group and the paramilitary Youth Assault Group (which was associated with the PLAF but in effect was a Party organ). The PRP Youth Group was absorbed at the 22d Ho Chi Minh Lao Dong Youth Union Congress held 2-5 June in Ho Chi Minh City (which was followed by the Ho Chi Minh Vanguard Teen-Ager Congress on 8-11 June). Vu Quang was renamed first secretary and apparently will continue to be the Party's principal official for youth. He heads the now expanded Youth Group's 92-member Central Committee, which includes a 26-member Standing Committee and a 10-member Secretariat. The executive secretary of the Standing Committee is Phan Minh Tanh, formerly secretary-general of the Youth Liberation Association in the South.

Under Vu Quang are nine deputy secretaries of whom these appear to be the most important: Nguyen Van De, whom Tanh replaced as executive secretary but who stays on as a member; Pham Cong Khanh, who also is assigned to the Secretariat; Nguyen Duc Toan, chief of the Ho Chi Minh Vanguard Teen-Ager Group; Nguyen Tien Phong, chief of the Ho Chi Minh Children's Group; Le Cong Giau, who helped organize the 1976 Youth Group Congress. Five members of the Youth Group's parent organization, the Lao Dong Party Central Committee, also appear active in youth affairs: Hoang Quoc Viet, Tran Van Tra, and Ha Thi Que, all northerners, and Tran Nam Trung and Phan Van Dan, both southerners.

Domestic Developments. The Vietnamese society during 1976 moved rapidly, vigorously, and steadily toward a full-scale socialist/communist system. But it was at uneven pace, more rapidly in organizational, communicational, and ideological sectors, less so in the economic sphere. Overall, new goals were fixed for the society, revolutionary goals, which all must accept and work for, without any freedom of choice. All of Vietnam became a closed society, disciplined and praetorian.

Economics moved to the forefront, in policy making and public consciousness, to a degree never experienced in the past. Activity centered on the all-encompassing plan for 1976 through 1980, which was ambitious by design and comprehensive in scope.

The "economic leveling" of the South, with its steady northward flow of food, raw materials, and consumer goods, increasingly made life difficult for the average southerner, but with little indication that the "pauperization plan" (as it guardedly is labeled in the South) actually was enriching the North very much. Economic conditions in the North remained threadbare, essential commodities still difficult to obtain. The euphoria of victory evaporated in Hanoi, according to travelers, and there was during the year a return to the grim reality of a stagnant economy, marked by a decline in morale. Economic life in the South continued to deteriorate. On the all-important question of collectivization of southern agriculture, it appeared that the decision for the moment that there would be no immediate decision.

In the revised Five-Year Plan, as it emerged at year's end, are found the best indicators of future Vietnam, at least as its leaders intend it to be. The general thrust of the plan is this:

— Rationalize and modernize agriculture and attempt to become self-sufficient in food production by the end of 1980. Shift the major burden of food production out of the North, making the South the nation's pastureland. Develop production of industrial agricultural crops. Increase protein production, both meat and fish. "Leap Forward in Agriculture."

— Industrialize, with emphasis on heavy industry, but always remaining conscious of the need to keep a developmental balance between industry and agriculture.

— Effect a massive relocation of the labor force throughout the country but chiefly in the South. The goal here appears to be to move some eight million persons during the life of the plan (about 7.5 million in the South and 500,000 in the North) with about 90 percent of these moving from urban to rural areas. Use manpower more efficiently. Utilize PAVN manpower in the economic sector.

—Restructure the nation's various agricultural and industrial production units, combining small-sized units into more efficient large-sized ones (a continuing effort that began in the 1950s). Eventually create giant agro-factories.

—Develop the economic infrastructure, concentrating on the communication and transportation matrices.

—Reorganize the economic managerial system and train a new and better generation of economic cadres.

—Continue centralized planning but regionalize management operations. This is the so-called modified dual central-regional economic system, and is marked by the syndrome: don't dump it all on Hanoi. The idea is for centrally planned but semi-self-contained regionally operated economic activity.

—Establish new (or improved) economic production relationships (that is, ways of doing things) which are based on the criterion of productivity. (This is the heart of the pragmatist-versus-ideologue doctrinal dispute.)

—Develop a better consumer goods (light industry) production and distribution system; also, an improved and more advanced fiscal and banking system.

—Serve the national defense requirements. This is called for, but is not publicly detailed.

—Increase trade/aid solicitation with bloc countries and others.

Out of this, say the planners, will come a Vietnam with a modern industrial plant, a highly productive agricultural sector, a labor force which has advanced scientific and technological skills, a powerful defense establishment, and a happy and abundant life for the people.

Under the principle of rigorous centralism, amalgamation of the North and South proceeded apace during the year. This involved "state unification" which at midyear created the new Socialist Republic of Vietnam. It also involved the merger of all other major socio-political institutions: the Party, the mass organizations, the legal system, the communication matrix, and education. Each case consisted largely of the North's annexing its southern counterpart. In the South, the Party established its primacy at all levels and began to systematize and tighten control. State cadres from the North now occupy virtually all important positions (especially in the security organs), leaving remnant Provisional Revolutionary Government figures with little authority.

A massive population relocation program, partly economic and partly sociological in purpose, developed speed in the South (it also exists in the North) during the year. Although in no way as bloody-handed as the one in Cambodia, this "redistribution of labor power program," as it officially is called, has ominous overtones and quite clearly will have a profound and far-reaching effect on the whole society. Eventually it will require half the adult population to move somewhere else to live, either to newly built New Economic Zones or, in population switches, to new geographic areas. For example, southern villagers could move to northern villages and northern urbanites could move to southern cities. In the South this will amount to destruction of the former social order through the process of de-urbanization. It falls heaviest on the middle and upper classes and on professionals, particularly that ill-defined group known as intellectuals. The target for the New Economic Zone program, to be completed by mid-1977, is five million persons who are to move from the cities. This is 25 percent of the adult population of the South. People are to be moved by family but not by group; thus each must settle in among strangers. In the shuffle, networks of friendships and associations vanish, and the society of the South will obviously undergo a fundamental change.

Social reconstruction, accompanied by ever more stringent social controls, continued last year to emasculate the former southern culture. The new mass movements and social organizations, formed after takeover, sought to mobilize the population, control it politically, and foster an all-out class struggle in which 95 percent of the population is pitted against the remaining 5 percent. Re-education and labor reform camps became institutionalized, with three- and five-year "sentences" being fixed for the intransigent and the potentially dangerous. Camp conditions were reported poor, with little food, no medicine, and a high death rate. Churches (Catholic, Buddhist, the sects) were open, but churchmen were harassed and attendance was discouraged by social pressure. Public attitudes remained widely anti-Communist, but there was less hope of successful resistance than there was pessimism, bitterness, and resignation. Social change was being brought to the South, but at a near-maximum price in terms of civil liberties and human rights.

Mobilization of Vietnamese young continued in the form of universal compulsory military service and recruitment. Vietnam now has the fourth-largest armed forces in the world. The official explanation offered outsiders as to why Vietnam was not demobilizing was that the economy could not absorb the manpower. This, however, did not explain why intensive military recruitment continued. Little was said publicly, but it appeared that the continued drafting of men was something of a test of power, at the Politburo level, between the leaders of the economic sector advocating wholesale demobilization of military personnel and transfer into the civilian labor market on the one hand, and on the other the generals with their new-found status and political power, arguing that the internal and external security situation would not permit a stand-down and offering as compromise greater economic activity by their troops (running state farms, building roads, digging irrigation ditches, etc.). Apparently the generals won the test, for in October a major new military enlistment campaign with quotas for all villages was under way both in the North and the South.

Foreign Relations. The bamboo curtain continued to lower between Vietnam and the outside world. The last of the foreign journalists was expelled during the year and news reporting was curtailed. The diplomatic community was moved out of Saigon, renamed Ho Chi Minh City. Foreigners were sent home from the South in an exodus that was expected to be complete by mid-1977.

Relations with the external world during the year were measured in pace, conservative in terms of risk taking, and highly correlated to Vietnam's economic interests. Much foreign policy was tentative, the pursuit of limited political objectives while working out long-term policies.

In ideological terms, the orientation continued to be hard line: the world proletariat's attack on capitalist countries must continue and eventually it will eliminate capitalism from the globe. Delegates of the Socialist Republic of Vietnam went to the Colombo conference of non-aligned nations in August and deliberately injected division. Malaysia, acting with other Association of Southeast Asian Nations (ASEAN) members, proposed that Southeast Asia be declared a zone of peace, freedom, and neutrality. Hanoi denounced the proposal—and ASEAN nations as "not fully independent" lackeys—and called instead for Southeast Asia to be a zone of independence, peace, and neutrality. There was speculation that in this move the Vietnamese were mapping out a long-range foreign policy: polarize the world economic scene by offering a new ideological construct. This thesis would reject the doctrine of two forces now pulling on non-aligned, developing nations (Marxism and traditionalism), and offer instead of an either-or choice of values, a new synthesis of nationalism and collectivism. Thus, Vietnam would transfer to the international arena, to serve as foreign policy, the Party line that had delivered victory: forward under the banner of national independence and socialism. While a nation cannot be neutral in the battle between communism and capitalism, the Vietnamese argued, choosing the former need not mean embrace of Marxism, nor siding with one of the two Communist superpowers. The rule can be collectivism at home, nationalism abroad. But this will succeed, they argued, only if the non-aligned nations also are non-aligned economically (hence the great irritation with ASEAN's economic interdependence) and are united in their determination to bring the developed (capitalist) nations to their knees. Such was the view of emerging Vietnamese foreign policy. If it proves correct, there still remains the test of action, when radicalism faces reality.

With developed nations, Vietnam's behavior was marked by systematic efforts to solicit funds, an integral part of its economic development strategy. Vietnamese representatives fanned out over the world during the year in search of aid. They were successful, garnering an estimated total pledge of $3.5 billion from non-Communist countries, primarily Japan, France, and Sweden. Even as officials drummed up more money, the Vietnamese economy experienced difficulty absorbing that vast flow already arriving. For years there was a generous flow of assistance, but this went almost entirely into the war effort in the South. The Vietnamese economy's capacity to absorb, like a body long starved, has atrophied. Goods pile up on Haiphong docks. Well-intentioned foreign aid projects founder. Although the Vietnamese, in relative terms, are moving ahead with speed, the narrowness of their economic base—the economic infrastructure—means that by outside standards progress is at snail's pace and characterized by enormous inefficiency and wasted motion.

Vietnamese relations with Thailand—most important of all relations in Southeast Asia—were thrown off track late in the year by the sudden and unexpected change in the Thai government. Thailand's political swing to the right was termed privately, by Vietnamese officials speaking to visitors in Hanoi, as "an act of political suicide." Vietnamese reaction, at year's end, was not clear. Vietnamese pronouncements on Thailand grew increasingly stern and verbal support for Thai insurgents grew more lavish. There were ominous but unsubstantiated reports of PAVN troop movements through Laos toward Thailand, of USSR missile silos being dug in Laos (whose range included Bangkok), even of troops (in civilian clothes) making incursions into Thailand from Laos. The meaning of all this was not clear, but it appeared that prospects for a stable peace in Indochina at the moment were not good.

Vietnamese relations with its two major allies—the USSR and the People's Republic of China—continued to be demanding and bristly independent. The relationship with the USSR was as warm as it had ever been, but probably not as warm as was portrayed. Hanoi-Peking relations were frosty. The Chinese did not attend the Fourth Lao Dong Congress, sending a congratulatory note saying they did not attend foreign Communist party congresses. There was verbal sparring over the offshore islands, but this issue continued to be held in abeyance, apparently by tacit mutual consent. How much interest the Chinese actually have in Vietnam at the moment is problematical.

The U.S.-Vietnamese relationship during the year was developmental and measured in pace. Neither was much concerned by the affairs of the other. Despite the U.S. veto of Vietnam's UN membership, the Vietnamese met with the Americans at the deputy-chief-of-mission level in November in Paris. It was a pro forma session at which each side stated its concerns and interests (the U.S. concern being the resolution of casualties issue, the Vietnamese interest being money). There was no negotiation and the meeting ended with the tacit understanding that substantive negotiations, if they are to come at all, will take place after the new administration of U.S. president-elect Jimmy Carter has settled itself in office.

Publications. Major newspapers are the Hanoi and Ho Chi Minh City editions of *Nhan Dan* (The People), which is the official Party newspaper, and *Quan Doi Nhan Dan* (People's Army), the daily organ of the PAVN. The two major periodicals are *Hoc Tap* (Studies) and Tap Chi Quan Doi Nhan Dan, the theoretical journals of the Party and the PAVN respectively. Other publications include *Tien Phong* (Youth), the Party youth publication; *Lao Dong* (Worker), the weekly publication of the Vietnam General Confederaton of Trade Unions; *Cuu Quoc* (National Salvation), organ of the Vietnam Fatherland Front; and *Nghien Cuu Kinh Te* (Economic Studies), which contains material on national economic planning and economic development.

The Voice of Vietnam ("Radio Hanoi") broadcasts in 12 languages on both medium- and short-wave frequencies. The Foreign Language Publishing House, Hanoi, issues books and pamphlets in English, French, Chinese, Russian, Spanish, and Esperanto, for distribution abroad.

Washington, D.C.   Douglas Pike

THE AMERICAS

Argentina

The Communist Party of Argentina (Partido Comunista de Argentina; PGA) had its founding in 1918 and the PCA name was taken in 1920. The party is pro-Soviet and its membership in 1976 can be estimated at 85,000 to 100,000. The Revolutionary Communist Party (Partido Comunista Revolucionario; PCR) is pro-Chinese in tendency and may have about 20,000 members. The Socialist Workers' Party (Partido Socialista de los Trabajadores; PST) has links with the Fourth (Trotskyist) International and claims up to 50,000 members, but may have about 15,000.

Other parties on the Marxist left include the Socialist Democratic Party (Partido Socialista Democrático; PSD), with an estimated 20,000 members, and the Revolutionary Workers' Party (Partido Revolucionario de los Trabajadores; PRT), with an estimated membership of 10,000 exclusive of the guerrillas discussed below.

It will be most useful to examine all these parties in terms of three basic sectors— the Communists, the socialists, and the guerrillas. The PCA and the PCR belong to the Communist sector; the PST and the PSD are predominantly socialist; and the PRT is the political arm of the People's Revolutionary Army. (Ejércitor Revolucionario del Pueblo; ERP.) The PRT has had occasional ties with the Peronist "Montoneros," guerrillas of the far left who have in turn occasionally collaborated with the ERP.

Argentina's population is nearly 26 million, with about half concentrated in the city and province of Buenos Aires.

The Setting. The year 1976 began with an unaccustomed political openness in Argentina allowing many political parties to participate widely in national affairs. There was also enormous inter-party violence, some of which was officially sponsored by the Peronists within the ruling coalition party FREJULI (Frente Justicialista de Liberación, or Justicialist Liberation Front). Much of the preoccupation of Marxist groups during the first months of the year was with keeping the FREJULI government from collapsing. Many of the Marxists enjoyed some measure of political participation under FREJULI and feared, correctly in most cases, that this would be lost if the long-expected military coup occurred— which it did on 24 March. The coup ended the unique and politically violent period of political pluralism herein referred to as the second Perón era (May 1973-March 1976).

In June, the new military government's decree law (No. 21323, Art. 1) banned all political activities under threat of severe prison terms. The meaning of "activities" went so far as to include the use of insignia and the issuing of public declarations (*La Prensa,* Buenes Aires, 5 June). Traditionally conservative parties like the Radical Civic Union enjoyed a de facto exemption from the stiffer aspects of this decree, but it fell heavily upon all the Peronist groups and upon nearly all of the Marxists. Party offices and properties were confiscated in many cases. Under these conditions, the functioning of most of the Argentine Marxist political spectrum became clandestine and field interviews conducted by this author were valuable. It should be noted also that the military refrained from intervening in the civilian political process until Argentina reached the point of near collapse internally, suffered one of the world's worst inflation rates (during 1975), had the hemisphere's highest death toll from guerrilla insurgency (much of which was conducted by Marxist groups), and faced default on its international obligations.

The PCA. Leadership, Organization, and Attitudes. It has been traditional to refer to the Communist Party of Argentina as the principal Communist organization in the country. Said to be the oldest Communist party in South America, the PCA has sustained an erratic history of legal and clandestine operations. At present there are informed observers in Argentina who doubt that the PCA is the most significant organization in the entire Argentine Marxist spectrum if one's chief concern is the ability of a given group to influence events and/or elicit a threat-reaction behavior sequence from an incumbent government. It is assumed here that the PCA is still the principal party within the Communist sector of the overall Marxist spectrum. The PCA remains tied to Moscow.

Rudolfo Ghioldi is the titular leader of the PCA, but due to his advanced age (80 plus) the majority of the party's internal affairs are directed by Gerónimo Arnedo Alvarez. The latter signs most formal pronouncements under his title of secretary-general but all major ideological statements are cleared through Ghioldi, and occasionally are issued in his name. A brother, Orestes Ghioldi, also advanced in age, is the treasurer of the PCA. None of these could perform his traditional functions formally after the June decree law. The youth sectors and neighborhood cell committee structures of the PCA were largely inactive during 1976 due to the military decrees, but limited clandestine communication took place through handbills and bulletins. (Much the same can be said for most of the parties in the Marxist spectrum.)

At its 8th National Congress, November 1975, the PCA explicitly rejected the idea that Argentina could be governed effectively by a single (monolithic) party, an obvious reference to the crumbling Peronist movement. The PCA then called for the creation of a civilian-military government—they used the word "cabinet." The party made it clear that the military sector should be considered a "parallel power" to the civilian power; that is, the military sector should not be the "master of all power" (*Visión,* Mexico City, 1 February 1976; *WMR,* December 1975). The PCA was anticipating what was one of the most widely publicized coups in Argentina's history of military takeovers of civilian government. Importantly, the PCA sought to play a double game of obliquely endorsing the military's political participation before the coup, saying that a coup was not desirable but rather the resignation of President Isabel Perón so as to allow the "genuine" forces of the nation to coalesce in the national interest; following the coup the PCA said the action was regrettable but perhaps something good might come of it.

The PCA recognized that a coup was inevitable as Argentina's finances approached scandalous bankruptcy due to corruption, and as violence rent the nation. But also the PCA knew that Argentina was depending upon the sale of grain to the USSR to alleviate some of its economic deficit, so it took a conciliatory position, hoping for something like a Portuguese outcome in which the PCA would have a meaningful role.

Immediately prior to the military coup, the PCA sought to persuade Isabel Perón to resign peacefully under parliamentary pressure, making use of its two spokesmen in the federal Chamber of Deputies. After 24 March 1976 the PCA reluctantly endorsed the coup. TASS (27 March) reported a PCA statement to the effect that fortunately the Argentine generals had not taken Pinochet of Chile as their model. Informed sources reported to this writer that the PCA collaborated secretly with the military government of President Jorge Videla toward the end of 1976. (Since Argentina needed to sell wheat to the USSR, and the Soviets had a major trade fair going during October and November in Buenos Aires, open persecution of the pro-Moscow Communist party would have been poor diplomacy.)

An example of PCA collaboration with the military regime was the SEGBA (light and power) conflict of October and November. Strikes and sabotage resulted from the government's intervention in the electrical workers' union and the firing of some 200 employees deemed unnecessary, including 18 union leaders. The PCA secretly agreed to oppose the strike and to keep its people on the job in exchange for relaxed government control of the PCA's informal political activities, including the circulation of party publications. Overall, while condemning the coup, the PCA seemed to accept it as an unavoidable evil and maintained its basic collaborationist posture throughout 1976. A possible weakening of this position was evident in the October edition of *Fundamentos*, which accused the military junta directly of allowing the right-wing terrorism to go unchecked while carrying out its campaign against the left. The journal also criticized the government for allowing the left-wing terrorists to drive foreign companies out of Argentina and into Brazil, suggesting that Brazilian interests may have been behind some of the allegedly left-wing terrorism.

Despite its early conciliatory attitude, the offices of the PCA were raided during the first weeks of the new government and several Communist functionaries who resisted were kiled. The irony of this was captured by the *Intercontinental Press* (New York), which commented on 12 April: ". . . obviously the Stalinists [the PCA] thought that the way to prevent the junta from taking Pinochet as their model was to get down on all fours and lick their jackboots." The Soviet publication *Izvestiia* (27 March) supported the PCA's posture vis-á-vis the military junta. The PCA was understandably bitter toward the Peronists for having precipitated the situation which spawned the coup. One PCA article accused the Peronists of having collaborated with "the CIA, fascists, and imperialists" in plotting the coup, and claimed a drift of Peronists into PCA ranks, stating that 90 percent of those joining the PCA came from Peronist organizations with which they had become disillusioned (*WMR*, April).

The PCA position on terrorism was stated by Arnedo Alvarez in his 1 March address before the 25th Congress of the Communist Party of the Soviet Union (CPSU) in Moscow. He charged that "last year terrorist gangs killed more than 500 members of the democratic movement, including many Communists." He further deplored the terrorism of fascist gangs against the Communist youth federation and the incarceration of workers and union activists. He omitted mention of the fact that easily as many atrocities had been committed by Marxist gangs. Arnedo charged that the terrorism (implying that there was only one terrorism) was being financed by the USA so as to bring about a Pinochet-type coup, as in Chile, and went on to denounce "Maoist provocateurs" for carrying out anti-Communist and anti-Soviet activities. He did not charge the Maoists directly with terrorism. As noted above, the PCA challenged the government directly on the terrorist issue at the end of the year.

Before the June banning of political pronouncements, the titular leader of the PCA, Rodolfo Ghioldi, issued a statement criticizing Economy Minister José Martínez de Hoz for abolition of price ceilings and resulting rises in consumer prices, for freezing wages and labor negotiations, and for holding up the "Brazilian model" as a goal, saying this was a sure recipe for enormous poverty and skewed income distribution in favor of the rich. The PCA spokesman opposed the return of much state-owned enterprise to private hands, calling this the old formula of previous military dictatorships. He charged Martinez de Hoz with inviting an "economic onslaught" by foreign monopolies. (Ibid., June.) In October, *Fundamentos* denounced Martínez de Hoz for not taking advantage of the opportunities to increase trade with the USSR and other socialist nations, saying that these countries hold the real future for Argentine exports.

Close relations between the PCA and the Soviet government were evident in the PCA's failure to report Soviet repression of its own minorities and political critics or Soviet support for guerrillas in the Middle East and Africa. In his March speech to the CPSU congress, Arnedo Alvarez lauded the "moral-political unity of Soviet society" and declared that the tradition of Lenin and the Bolsheviks continued to inspire trust and respect among the peoples of Latin America. He praised the USSR's "genuine democracy of the working people" as providing a society more humane and free than any other in the world, and affirmed that the Communists of Argentina (without specifying which ones) were making efforts to emulate Soviet successes. He added, however, that Argentina presented a complex bourgeois-dominated atmosphere in which the PCA's efforts were fraught with great difficulties.

Publications. The PCA's organ, *Nuestra Palabra,* banned after the March 1976 coup, began circulation on a very limited basis (though not on newsstands) toward the end of the year as a result of PCA collaboration with the government. The unofficial PCA-subsidized weeky *Propósitos* was banned shortly after the coup, and it did not reappear during 1976. *Fundamentos,* an irregular monthly PCA organ, carries articles by Argentine, Soviet, and other Communists. Allegedly front publications, like the artistic review *Pluma y Pincel,* continued to circulate publicly, but their Marxist content was severely limited.

The Revolutionary Communist Party. Some accounts have contended that the PCR is pro-Maoist and violence-oriented. A part of this designation may be traced to the splintering from the PCR in 1967-70 of elements which later formed the guerrilla Revolutionary Armed Forces (FAR) and received military training and political indoctrination in Cuba (*La Opinión,* Buenos Aires, 25 July 1976). However, the consensus of informants during 1976 was that whereas the PCR might be termed a Chinese "fellow traveler," it should not be considered Maoist nor was it in 1976 the principal party of this tendency.

The PCR broke off from the PCA in the late 1960s and was composed of younger radical dissidents who wanted a firmer populist stance against bourgeois interests and, particularly, hoped to attract proletarian masses away from the Peronist movement. In this way the PCR thought that in the event of a coup against Isabel Perón it could emerge as a leading element in the post-coup resistance toward the establishment of Marxian-style "democracy." This logic led the PCR to support Isabel and her controversial adviser, López Rega, minister of social welfare and organizer of right-wing death squads, considered by most of the left (indeed by most Argentines) as the epitome of fascist authoritarianism. However, with López Rega forced into exile in July 1975, the PCR focused its defense principally upon Isabel. A handbill in this author's possession issued by the PCR in December 1975, called upon the workers of all factories to "take to the streets to defend Isabel against the coupmakers." That was the party's posture until the coup became a reality in March 1976. Thus, the PCR endorsed the principle of armed class sturggle, often in a vague theoretical context, but specifically condemned the guerrilla aspect of the violence. PCR leaders recognized their inability to control the insurgency and the impossibility of forming a mass following on the basis of terrorism.

The PCR and the PCA exchanged insults during 1976, using the terms "Stalinist" and "Maoist" pejoratively. The Videla government was aparently more concerned about the potential threat from the PCR, which was specifically included in Military Communiqué No. 45 banning a series of Marxist parties two days following the coup. Ascertaining the leadership of the PCR was a problem. The pre-coup leaders were said to be either exiled, or to have "disappeared"—the plight of a number of Argentine political figures following 24 March. A few clandestine handbills of the PCR circulated, but the party's offices and properties had been seized and the PCR remained virtually inert. One version given this writer was that some bulletins were being signed with the pseudonyms "Córdoba" and "Teitelbaum." The PCR is hardly a major political force at the moment of this writing.

The Socialist Vanguard Party. The Partido Socialista de Vanguardia (PSV) is a small party headed by a man named Semán (which is believed to be a pseudonym). It split off from the classic Partido Socialista in the 1960s. In the early 1970s it reconstituted itself as the Partido Comunista Marxista-Leninista but is still called the PSV by many. It is believed to have fewer than a thousand members and has significance only in that it was the true Maoist party of Argentina in 1976. At the moment the PSV has no political force, no bargaining power. It has been outlawed by the government and has no known publication at this time. The PSV has in the past advocated class struggle and while not formally condemning the guerrilla insurgency has remained aloof from it. Its current activity is nil.

The Socialist Workers' Party. The PST, proscribed by the military regime, competed electorially in the second Perón era and had limited political influence. Its leaders in 1976 were Juan Carlos Coral and Nahuel Moreno (a pseudonym for a man named Brezzano). The PST has links with the Fourth International, headquartered in Paris, but does not have recognition as the official Trotskyist party of Argentina, this being reserved for the PRT (see below). The PST circulates clandestine handbills reaffirming its 1975 opposition to the guerrilla warfare as well as to the officially sponsored violence of the right-wing death squads. The PST is vociferously anti-USA. It is considered to have a chance at regaining political relevance in the future should the current ban on political activism be lifted. However, in November 1976 the government accused the PST of having fortified its headquarters in preparation for armed conflict, thereby confusing future prospects (*La Opinión,* 7 November).

The Socialist Democratic Party. Out of the original Socialist Party, the party of Américo Ghioldi and Alfredo Palacios, a series of splinter groups emerged in 1957-58 and proliferated after 1970. Some of these have been discussed above. The most significant such group was probably the PSD. It claimed Américo Ghioldi as titular head. At the same time, Ghioldi was honored by the military regime by being appointed Argentina's ambassador to Portugal. The PSD appears to have worked out an even stronger rapprochement with the regime than was the case with the PCA, the tie with the PSD serving to give the military regime a bridge to some of the socialist Third World. The official party organ of the PSD, *La Vanguardia,* was the most open publication within the Marxist sector during 1976 and could be purchased freely at select newsstands. Examples from two post-coup editions of *La Vanguardia* serve to illustrate the domestic and international attitudes of the PSD.

Its 9 June issue contains a series of indictments against the ousted Peronist regime for its moral corruption and complicity in the officially sponsored violence. Another article scores violations of human rights in Chile, but then carefully does the same for Castro's Cuba. The principal editorial is devoted to the assassinations by rightist death squads during 1976 of the exiled Uruguyan politicans Zelmar Michelini and Héctor Gutiérrez Ruis plus the murder of former Bolivian president Juan José Torres, also exiled in Buenos Aires (whose death is still surrounded in mystery). The editorial also referred to the assassination of exiled Chilean general Carlos Prats in 1974 (another mysterious incident) and claimed that "death has found new life" in Argentina. The newspaper argues that orders from "external sources" have brought notoriety upon Argentina, and it places the blame on the political right while not making specific accusations. This is balanced by its denouncing the Kremlin for persecutions of critics and ethnic minorities. *La Vanguardia* condemns the Argentine guerrilla movement, arguing that the guerrillas want to produce a fascist state so as to better justify their own continued existence, citing Communist complicity in the collapse of the Weimar Republic as a case in point, that is, Communists prefer a repressive right-wing regime to a moderate and reformist socialist government. *La Vanguardia* blames the existence of police states squarely on Marxist guerrillas but is careful not to cite the incumbent Argentine regime as a police state. *La Vanguardia* appears as an intellectual socialist publication, not a party publication.

Later in the year, the 11 November issue of *La Vanguardia* was circulating openly but in very limited supply. Its criticism of "anti-democracy" was more subtle in word usage, but was there nonetheless. The front cover treated a series of injustices which the Ministry of Social Welfare was trying to solve (in terms complimentary to the regime). It condemned recent revelations of corruption involving union leaders and supported the military government's intervention in the General

Confederation of Labor and its various syndicates. Another article denounced lack of press freedom in the USSR. The editorial space was devoted to an elevated theoretic consideration of demagoguery versus democracy. It said that in the ideal democracy freedom of speech, union organization, and political assembly could be accomplished without fear of reprisal, but did not go beyond this to indict the military junta. Peronism was branded as demagoguery disguised and sold to the masses as democracy. Education of youth for exercise of a true civic spirit was offered in conclusion as Argentina's only alternative to continued atrophy and chaos.

In these two selections from *La Vanguardia* one does not have to be skilled at reading between the lines to detect the criticism of the military regime, yet the attack is muted to the point of tolerable politeness. Other evil characters in the cast, principally the Peronists, are scored openly. The party activity of the PSD was limited to the publication of *La Vanguardia* during nearly all of 1976. Its leader, Américo Ghioldi, had effectively been co-opted by the regime and his party's limited functioning made it possible for the junta to point to a measure of pluralism in Argentina's restricted political life.

The Revolutionary Workers' Party and Its Guerrilla Ties. Some observers consider the violent ultra-left guerrillas of Marxist persuasion the principal Communist force in Argentina during 1976 (in terms of the threat-response behavior they elicited from the government). Certainly the PCA was docile compared with the guerrilla sector. The guerrillas of the left did most to provoke the collapse of the second Perón era. In the military junta's initial communiqués of 24 and 25 March the need to eliminate guerrilla subversion figured most prominently in statements of defense for the coup. Also, at least initially, the leftist guerrillas provided a raison d'être for the right-wing terrorist gangs.

The Revolutionary Workers' Party — PRT — was founded during the 1960s. It gained prominence especially in the early 1970s when it became the political arm of the ERP guerrillas. The PRT-ERP had a brief truce with the original Peronist regime of Héctor Campora in 1973, but soon declared war on the government, saying it had betrayed its revolutionary promises. The flamboyant PRT-ERP leader, Mario Roberto Santucho, even arranged a daring televised press conference during June 1973 to issue his challenge to the regime. Later a complicated set of negotiations and events brought the PRT-ERP into close working relationships with the Montoneros, one-time Peronist guerrillas of the left who opted for Marxism by merging with the Revolutionary Armed Forces in 1973. By 1975 the Montoneros had been expelled from the Peronist movement and were declared illegal along with the PRT-ERP.

During much of 1975 the various guerrilla organizations tried to repeat the Che Guevara guerrilla *foco* idea of ruralizing the violence, declaring in their publications an affinity for the "Cuban model." (Interestingly, many of the guerrilla leaders in both the Montoneros and the PRT-ERP have come from right-wing backgrounds.) They suffered severe defeats at the hands of the Argentine security forces, especially in the mountains of Tucumán and near Córdoba. Toward the end of 1975 the guerrillas decided to return to the urban areas and sought a particular daring feat with which to launch their "urbanization campaign," namely the assault in December on the military arsenal at Monte Chingolo, in Buenos Aires Province. This attack, which failed, was planned by a former military officer who is currently in prison. Perhaps as many as 100 guerrillas died in the encounter. The security forces captured documents and extracted testimony which led to the detention of a high Montonero leader a few days later. It is believed that this leader divulged information which enabled the security forces to inflict serious defeats on the guerrillas during 1976, including the discovery and death of ERP leader Santucho in July.

The PRT-ERP (which some observers alleged had undergone an internal split) was thus left without a leader except for a lesser figure known as Enrique Merlo. The charismatic and at times Guevara-like Santucho was the leading force behind the PRT-ERP, and his passing was a serious blow to the entire Argentine guerrilla sector. The killing of Santucho relieved some right-wing pressure on President Videla which had grown out of an earlier incident the same month when Montoneros succeeded in placing a bomb in the dining room of the police intelligence headquarters in Buenos Aires (and thereby killing some 30 persons). It is reliably reported that the bomb was placed by a police officer who was working for the guerrillas, and that he was subsequently executed publicly in front of the obelisk landmark in downtown Buenos Aires by a death squad of "off duty" police officers. Such events were legion throughout 1976 and showed that in many cases personal hatreds and bureaucratic rivalries had replaced the original political goals of the violence and that the guerrillas and the security forces had successfully infiltrated each other.

Despite the loss of Santucho the PRT-ERP continued to try to create an impression of force and solidarity through its clandestine publications *El Combatiente* and *La Estrella Roja,* as did the Montoneros with several publications, including *La Causa Montonera.* Persons found with such periodicals in their possession were jailed, often indefinitely. The security forces continued to announce nearly daily the capture of large quantities of subversive materials, the discovery of "people's jails," and the killing of guerrillas, but at the same time they admitted the continuation of guerrilla attacks and bombings of military and police facilities.

One must interpret these reports with some caution, given the press censorship the military regime has imposed. Some events were reported many days later. A bomb which nearly killed President Videla in early October was never reported in the Argentine press, although the news was carried in Uruguay. Campaigns against the Marxist guerrillas received ample publicity; right-wing campaigns against, for instance, the Third World Priests, received much less attention. Much information had to be obtained by word of mouth. Censorship was not so strict, however, as that in Uruguary during the height of the Tupamaro guerrilla activities in the early 1970s, when the Uruguayan government forbade the use in print of that name plus a series of other words. For instance, on 10 November the Buenos Aires press carried extensive photos and a long story about a weapons and explosive factory belonging to the Montoneros (mentioned by name) that had been captured and was equipped to make bombs of all sorts, bazookas, and machine guns (*La Prensa*, 10 November). The security forces also carried out "clean sweeps" of entire university faculties, weeding out professors and students of alleged Marxist persuasion (ibid., 13 November). Undoubtedly this reduced the overall effectiveness of the Marxist guerrilla sector, yet the terrorism continued and showed no signs of abating as the end of 1976 approached.

In order to communicate the complexity of the environment within which the Marxist guerrilla activity took place it is essential to indicate the emotive state in which much of *la guerrilla* developed. The PRT-ERP and Montoneros often embraced the theory requiring that one discredit established bourgeois authority by attacking directly its physical symbols, especially human ones. Probably no event during 1976 illustrated this commitment more than the assassination of the head of Argentina's federal police, General César Cardozo.

The perpetrator of this act became one of Argentina's most wanted criminals. Eighteen-year-old Ana María Gonzáles told secretly to the Spanish publication *Cambio 16* (now prohibited in Argentina) how she had made personal friends with the general's daughter through a school relationship and eventually succeeded in placing a time bomb disguised as a Father's Day gift under his bed. The Montoneros' military tactician Horacio Mendizábal allowed himself, Miss González, and a weapons arsenal to be photographed. She related her personal anguish at sitting at the same table and taking meals with the enemy she was pledged to kill. Significantly, the authorities had originally tried to blame the Cardozo killing on the ERP, but a Montoneros spokesman offered an explanation of this that reflects upon the differences that are perceived between the ERP and the Montoneros: "It was more convenient to attribute the death of Cardozo to the ERP because they have international symbols; they can be called Marxists under international discipline; we [the Montoneros], in contrast, have no known relations with the Soviet Union. We are 'the boys' [los muchachos] who are part of the national folklore." (*Cambio 16,* 16 August, p. 42.) The Montoneros thus sought to enhance their claim to nationalism, but nonetheless they admitted in the same interview, and with pride, that they had placed the bomb in the police dining room.

Mendizábal pledged that the Montoneros would continue operations, using funds from their various kidnapping ransoms (such as that of the brothers Born which netted them $60 million in 1975). He predicted that the Montoneros would join the Palestinians in becoming one of the most powerful nationalistic guerrilla movements in the world. Their strategy, he said, would be to perpetually disturb the enemy's "power center of gravity" and to dwindle away its public support. Both the ERP and Montoneros had operations that were concentrated in Buenos Aires Province and the federal capital, but unlike the other groups in the Marxist sector, the ERP and the Montoneros had also cell-type subsidiaries in every Argentine province. Because of heavy losses inflicted upon both guerrilla organizations that were claimed by the security forces, and also in view of the possible exaggeration of such claims, it is nearly impossible to estimate membership figures for these groups during 1976.

It is difficult also to predict the future of the guerrilla sector of the Argentine Marxist spectrum. A clandestine edition of *El Combatiente* (dated only as 1976) carried a detailed formula for solidarity and group consciousness among the PRT and the ERP; this article formally carried the name of Santucho as author, but it is not clear whether the article was written by or attributed to the deceased guerrilla leader. It would seem to be an effort to give the PRT-ERP a unified image at a time when the Montoneros were suffering heavy defeats at the hands of the security forces. Internal fights among the guerrillas themselves have led to uncertainty as to whether this sector of the Marxist spectrum will survive 1976 as a political force to be reckoned with thereafter.

There is also the international dimension to the Argentine guerrilla struggle that is clearly Marxist and involves all of the countries contiguous to Argentina. It is well known that in 1974 and 1975 a "Joint Coordination Command" was established to integrate activities of the ERP (Argentina), the MLN-Tupamaros (Uruguay), the ELN (Bolivia), and the MIR (Chile). PRT-ERP publications like *El Combatiente* featured joint declarations of these armed Marxist groups. Because of the suppression inflicted by the Argentine security forces on the ERP, which served as "international host" to the other groups during the chaos of the Peronist epoch, it became impossible to continue using Argentina as a meeting place. One reliable report alleged that the Marxist guerrillas had gone as far north as Costa Rica for regrouping and "rehabilitation."

It was reported in September 1976 that Costa Rica had been used as a place of refuge by Montoneros, Tupamaros, the ERP, and other guerrilla organizations. Costa Rican authorities reported evidence of ERP activity in their nation, including a movement calling itself "Revolutionary Command in Solidarity with Mario Roberto Santucho." They alleged that this group placed a bomb in the Argentine Embassy shortly after Santucho's death in July, and they expressed the belief that the ERP and the Montoneros were tied in with a guerrilla organization of hemispheric scope that was being formed to replace unitary organizations, like the ERP and Tupamaros, which had suffered severe defeats in their home countries. Costa Rican authorities claimed no absolute proof, but said highly convincing evidence was being collected to support charges of such international guerrilla activity. (*La Nación,* San José, 19 September.)

University of Missouri, St. Louis   Kenneth F. Johnson

Bolivia

The Communist Party of Bolivia (Partido Comunista de Bolivia; PCB) was founded in 1950 and is pro-Soviet in orientation. A pro-Chinese splinter group became the Communist Party of Bolivia Marxist-Leninist (Partido Comunista de Bolivia, Marxista-Leninista; PCB-ML) in 1965. The Trotskyist Revolutionary Workers' Party (Partido Obrero Revolucionario; POR) is split into three factions. The National Liberation Army (Ejército de Liberación Nacional; ELN), founded in 1966, formed the Bolivian Workers' Revolutionary Party (Partido Revolucionario de los Trabajadores de Bolivia; PRT-B in March 1975. The Movement of the Revolutionary Left (Movimiento de Izquierda Revolucionaria; MIR) was formed in mid-1971 and reorganized after the 21 August 1971 coup in which rightist Colonel Hugo Banzer overthrew the government of leftist General Juan José Torres and seized the presidency for himself. Other revolutionary groups include the Union of Poor Peasants (Unión de Campesinos Pobres; UCP), the Tupac Katari, and other peasant-oriented organizations.

All of these parties were illegal during 1975. The PCB and PCB-ML are estimated to have 300 and 150 members, respectively. The population of Bolivia is 5,500,000 (estimated 1976).

The Setting. Disruptions in Santa Cruz department in November 1974 led to the establishment of a "new order" in Bolivia which proscribed political parties as well as activities by existing associations of businessmen, professionals, workers, and students, pending government reorganization of their associations. The new order was challenged in early 1975 by tin miners, students, and the Roman Catholic Commission of Justice and Peace, all of which were put down by the government. In mid-December 1975 the Bolivian minister of the interior announced the detention of Antonio Peredo Leigue and a small band of Bolivian and foreign comrades of the PRT-B. In the months that followed the government repeatedly charged that this and other similarly-intentioned ultra-leftist groups, part of an "international conspiracy," intended to bring down the Banzer government by fomenting strikes, acts of sabotage, and terrorism. (See, for example, the government communiqué in *El Diario*, La Paz, 10 June.) After the 24 March coup in Argentina, which overthrew the government of Isabel Perón, border security was tightened to prevent (or at least retard) the anticipated movement of guerrillas from Argentina to Bolivia. After bombings in Cochabamba early in the year, one departmental Prefect charged that extremists were trying to turn Bolivia into another Argentina, alluding to the extensive guerrilla activities then underway in the latter country. The body of former president Torres—who was assassinated in Argentina in early June—was not returned to Bolivia for burial since, according to President Banzer, its arrival was to have activated a massive subversive plot against the Bolivian government. During the year student and labor groups around the country engaged in strikes and other acts against the government, creating some of the most unstable conditions President Banzer has had to face since assuming office. The Federación Sindical de Trabajadores Mineros de Bolivia (FSTMB) defied the "new order" restrictions and held its 16th congress in early May, the government giving last-minute authorization in order to prevent a major showdown. A number of labor leaders were subsequently arrested and sent into forced exile in Chile. Numerous leftists were arrested during the year and "security houses" were uncovered in La Paz, Cochabamba, and other cities.

The PCB. Leadership and Organization. The first secretary of the PCB is Jorge Kolle Cueto. Others prominent in the party include Mario Monje Molina, a former first secretary, and Central Committee members Simón Reyes, Arturo Lanza, and Carlos Alba. Luis Padilla, a member of the Central Committee as well, is a frequent international spokesman.

The basic organization of the PCB is the cell, which consists of no fewer than three party members. District committees, elected at national congresses (the most recent of which was in June 1971), exist in each department and in most mining centers. The national congress of the party elects the Central Committee, the latter guiding the party between congresses. The Central Committee elects the Political and Control-Auditing Commissions and the first secretary, and convenes National Conferences to discuss current organizational and political affairs not requiring the convocation of the national congress. District committees may hold district conferences with the approval of the Central Committee. (According to *WMR*, September 1973.)

The PCB's youth organization, the Communist Youth of Bolivia (Juventud Comunista de Bolivia; JCB), is illegal. Among its leaders in recent years have been Jorge Escalera and Carlos Soría Galvarro. Simón Reyes, the head of the PCB's mining activities, in exile during 1976, was reelected in absentia to a top leadership position in the FSTMB at the May congress.

PCB. Domestic and International Views. First Secretary Kolle Cueto told an East German reporter that the omnipotence of the capitalist state and suppression are felt everywhere in Bolivia and that President Banzer's doctrine is geared entirely to the interests of the multinational monopolies and the domestic bourgeoisie. The regime's anti-national policy particularly favors Brazilian finance capital, according to the PCB leader, which has seized important positions in banking, agriculture, and transport. While the Bolivian workers must shoulder the burden of this economic policy, the Brazilian industrialists use Bolivia as a base for penetrating other countries of the Andean Pact. Kolle Cueto concluded that the PCB regards workers unity and the establishment of a broad front of all anti-imperialist forces as the prerequisite for political transformations in the country. However, although some general agreements and joint actions of the left have occurred, still the national democratic front in the country lacks stability.

Addressing the 25th congress of the Communist Party of the Soviet Union in Moscow on 1 March, Kolle Cueto asserted that despite the "new order" restrictions, and despite permanent imprisonment of many political and union activists, the national crisis in Bolivia is shaking the foundations of capitalism. In this situation, he added, the Bolivian people, headed by the working class and above all the workers in factories and the mines, are waging a constant struggle to regain the freedom and democracy they lost with the overthrow of President Torres in 1971. (*Pravda*, 3 March.) The Bolivian communists considered the assassination of Torres a "fascist crime" carried out (as in other similar instances) by "CIA-trained gangs of killers" (*WMR*, September 1976).

The PCB firmly supports the Soviet Union and the latter's struggle to achieve "international unity for the advancement of peace and freedom" in all countries. At the 25th CPSU Congress, Kolle Cueto directed pointed criticism at the leadership of the Chinese Communist Party. (*Pravda*, 3 March.)

Publication. The PCB paper is the irregular, clandestine *Unidad*.

*   *   *

The PCB-ML. The PCB-ML has long been torn by internal dissension. The section led by Oscar Zamora, for years the leading Maoist in Bolivia, sent condolences to China in September on the death of Mao Tse-tung. According to reports from La Paz, a large dissident faction, led by Rodolfo Sinani, split with Zamora due to disapproval of a variety of Chinese Communist activities since the visit of U.S. President Richard Nixon to China in 1972. The most recent Chinese Communist action to cause trouble within party ranks was the Chinese opposition to the MPLA in the Angolan civil war. (LATIN, Buenos Aires, 10 April.)

*   *   *

The ELN and the PRT-B. The ELN was formed in 1966 and under the leadership of Che Guevara issued its first communiqué in March-April 1967. It has had several leaders since Guevara's death in 1967, mostly brothers of the Peredo Leigue family. On several occasions during 1976 Rubén Sánchez was reported to be at the head of the ELN. Early in 1974 the ELN joined an international Junta of Revolutionary Coordination (Junta de Coordinación Revolucinaria; JCR) with guerrilla-oriented groups of Argentina, Chile, and Uruguay. In 1975 the JCR announced that the ELN had formed the PRT-B to grow into the vanguard of the Bolivian revolution. The ELN would not disappear but be the "armed fist" or military force of the Bolivian people under the "Marxist-Leninist leadership" of the new party. Contacts are maintained with guerrillas from Argentina, Chile, Colombia, Peru and Uruguay. Bolivian sources report that the ELN has long received substantial aid from the Argentine ERP in particular. According to the Bolivian government, the ELN as a major instigator of dissension within Bolivia during the year and the group was forcibly repressed.

Palo Alto, California   Lynn Ratliff

Brazil

The fortunes of organized Marxist-Leninist groups in Brazil appear to be at their lowest ebb in forty years. Several small organizations have dropped completely out of sight as the result of the government's intensified campaign of repression, while those that have survived face enormous difficulties in efforts to preserve their leaders and to attract new members and sympathizers. According to Brazilian security organs, Communist subversion still exists on a scale to require continuing surveillance and countermeasures, but that for the near future the Communists present no greater danger than that of a "localized endemic disease" (*FBIS*, 13 February 1976).

The original Communist Party of Brazil (Partido Comunista do Brasil), founded in March 1922, remains the most important Marxist-Leninist organization in the nation. Several small groups that broke away or were expelled in the first decade formed a Trotskyist movement which subsequently split into separate factions. At least one of these factions still maintains a precarious existence. In 1960, in a bid for legal recognition, the original pro-Soviet party dropped all international slogans from its statutes and changed its name to Brazilian Communist Party (Partido Comunista Brasileiro; PCB). A pro-Chinese element broke away the following year and in February 1962 adopted the original party name, Communist Party of Brazil (Partido Comunista do Brasil; PCdoB). Another source of far-leftist groups was the popular action (Ação Popular; AP), which originated in the Catholic student movement in the late 1950s. In the following decade a segment of AP identified itself as the Marxist-Leninist Popular Action (Ação Popular Marxista Leninista; APML).

Dissidence within these parties after the military coup of 1964 led to the formation of numerous splinter groups, predominantly of Castroite tendency, who strongly advocated the use of armed violence to overthrow the regime. There may have been as many as sixteen such organizations at one point. Some of them, employing urban guerrilla or terrorist tactics, gained considerable notoriety for a time, but between 1969 and 1972 the death of their most prominent leaders, the wholesale arrest of militants, and continued public apathy or hostility drastically reduced their number and effectiveness.

In February 1973 four extremist organizations issued a joint statement calling for a long "people's war" in the interior, but acknowledging the defeat of the guerrilla movement in the short run. In 1976 the PCdoB announced that the last organized armed resistance to the government—carried out since 1972 by the Guerrilla Forces of Araguaia (Forças Guerrilheiras do Araguaia; FGA) in the state of Pará—had been disbanded (*Latin America*, 9 July).

The Communist movement has been illegal in Brazil throughout most of its existence. Although the original party was outlawed in 1947 (when its membership reached about 150,000), it was allowed to function and its members ran in elections on the tickets of other parties. During the presidency of João Goulart (1961-64) the PCB succeeded in infiltrating and controlling important labor, student, political, and bureaucratic bodies. At that time its membership was estimated at 30,000. In this period other far-left groups, though denied legal recognition, were also able to operate freely.

The military regime which came to power in March 1964 drove the PCB and other far-left groups underground and banned the existing Communist-influenced organizations. Since 1969 certain acts of subversion have been punishable by banishment or death. In practice the death penalty has not been applied by the courts, but several dozen Brazilian terrorists have been exiled and others have died in prison or have been killed in clashes with the police and military.

PCB membership in 1976 was probably well below the 1974 estimate of about 6,000. The PCdoB was said to have some 1,000 members in 1974; no later estimates are available. Little is known of the strength of other Marxist-Leninist groups. The population of Brazil is estimated at 110,000,000.

The PCB. Organization and Leadership. The PCB apparatus includes a 21-member Executive Commission (some of whose members are resident abroad), a Central Committee (which functions chiefly in Brazil, although some of its members also reside abroad), state committees, municipal committees, and local cells in residential districts and places of employment. The Sixth Congress of the PCB, its latest, took place in December 1967. Occasional plenary sessions of the Central Committee have been held since, most recently in December 1975. Party secretary-general Luiz Carlos Prestes has resided in the USSR since 1971; his second in command, Giocondo Alves Dias, has reportedly now followed him into exile (*Latin America*, 27 February 1976).

A report of November 1975 by the commander of the Fifth Military Region (which embraces the states of Paraná and Santa Catarina) provides a description of the recently destroyed PCB state and municipal committee structure in Paraná. The organizational pattern was presumably similar to that in other states of Brazil. The state committee—five members and two alternates—was the highest body, responsible for carrying out directives from the Central Committee. Within the state committee a three-member secretariat acted for the full committee between plenary sessions and directed four sections, dealing with agitation and propaganda, finances, political understandings, and trade union affairs. All but the last were headed by members of the state committee. A comparable structure existed in the four municipal committees in Paraná, which were responsible for organizing and supervising base organizations (cells) within their areas of jurisdiction. The officers of each of these committees were arrested in 1975. (*Jornal do Brasil*, Rio de Janeiro, 15 November.)

News reports by other Latin American Communist parties, republished in the Cuban press, indicate that the Brazilian Communist Youth organization suffered the loss of two key leaders in 1976. These were its secretary-general, José Montenegro de Lima, and Jaime Rodrigues Estrella, of São Paulo. The "kidnaping" of the two men early in the year was denounced by the Communist Party of Ecuador (*Internacionales*, Havana, 6 February). The torture and subsequent "assassination" of Montenegro de Lima was condemned by the national youth section of the People's Party of Panama (*Granma*, Havana, 16 September).

The overriding problem of the PCB continues to be the decimation of its leadership and the dismantling of major organizational units as a result of repression by Brazilian security forces. Protests against the assaults on the party's leadership were a persistent theme in official PCB statements circulated internationally during the year. The introduction to the published account of the Plenum of the Central Committee stated:

> Before commencing discussions the participants endorsed a special message addressed to the prominent Party leaders who had been arrested recently, or had disappeared in the dungeons of the dictatorship.
> The plenum marked an important stage in reorganizing the Party, which had come under brutal attack by the dictatorship during 1974 and 1975.

The Central Committee document added that "the fascist regime increasingly resorts to atrocious repressions of the Communist Party and other anti-fascist forces." (*IB*, no. 4.) Prestes denounced the persecution of the party and its leaders in a series of statements. The Cuban press reported his call for international solidarity on behalf of the missing Communist Youth leaders (*Internacionales*, 6 February). In March he informed the 25th Congress of the Communist Party of the Soviet Union (CPSU) that the government in Brazil was "brutally persecuting" the PCB and "trying to carry out reprisals against its leaders." According to Prestes, "hundreds" of communists had been jailed and in the preceding twenty months the PCB had "lost one-third of its Central Committee members, ten of whom were murdered." (*FBIS*, 9, 10 March.) In a "Manifesto to the Brazilian People," published in Portugal in May, he again lashed out against "the fascist regime which makes our party . . . the main target of its policy of repression. Innumerable communist leaders and members have already died heroically in the struggle against tyranny." (*Avante*, Lisbon, 20 May.)

Brazilian press reports and military claims not only confirm these charges but suggest that the PCB spokesman may have understated the devastation in the ranks of party leaders. Early in the year military security agencies alleged that no fewer than 36 members of the Central Committee had been taken into custody (*Latin America*, 27 February). A partial gleaning of press accounts of the arrest of persons accused of trying to reorganize the PCB indicates that well over 400 were jailed between September 1975 and July 1976. During that period fewer than 10 percent were released for lack of evidence. The full toll of PCB leaders and militants was doubtless much higher, for mass arrests occurred from Ceará in the north to Santa Catarina in the south, and there was no indication of a respite in the anti-Communist campaign in the second half of the year.

In these circumstances the PCB's chief concern has been to rebuild its committee structures and to attract new adherents. The party draws its leadership and members from the ranks of students, intellectuals, and organized labor. Consistently there has been a substantial turnover in membership, especially among white collar elements, as individuals become inactive because of boredom, fear of arrest, or—in the past decade—impatience with the non-violent policies of the PCB. Information released by military authorities about persons arrested for subversive activities in 1976 reveals that the PCB has made a considerable effort to win back former members and to gain new recruits among students, teachers, and professionals. According to a purported Central Committee directive made public by the government in August, the press and television are the most promising areas for recruitment and infiltration at this time. The same directive, however, also pointed to the long-term need for deep infiltration among army lieutenants and captains, "who for many reasons, including their age, are sensitive to revolutionary indoctrination." (*FBIS*, 17 August.)

Domestic Activities and Attitudes. The PCB is an orthodox pro-Soviet party which upholds the role of the masses in obtaining power. It has long since recognized the impossibility of achieving power in Brazil by violence, and thus consistently advocates popular front tactics. Within its limited capabilities the PCB seeks to identify with—and to claim responsibility for articulating—the legitimate grievances and aspirations of broad sectors of Brazilian society. The total failure of the "reckless adventures" of extremist left-wing guerrilla organizations has reinforced the belief of PCB leaders in the correctness of the party's domestic policies.

The Central Committee plenum in December 1975 recapitulated the political line the party has followed in recent years and called for the formation of an "anti-fascist patriotic front" (*IB*, no.4, 1976). This policy statement, which was widely circulated in the Communist press outside Brazil (see, for example, *Granma Weekly Review*. Havana, 11 April), attributed all of the nation's present ills to the military regimes in power since 1964. In its review of the current situation the committee asserted that the failure of the so-called Brazilian economic miracle has revealed "the inability of the fascist dictatorship to solve the basic problems of the national economy when the country has entered a period of economic crisis" (*Granma Weekly Review*, 11 April). It characterized the Geisel administration as a "military terroristic dictatorship in the service of local and foreign monopolies, primarily of the most reactionary circles of North American finance capital," and as a "system of domination relying on brutal repression and serving anti-national interests" (*IB*, no. 4, 1976).

Among the actions of the Geisel regime singled out for special denunciation were the cooperative agreement on nuclear energy signed with the Federal Republic of Germany, and the decision to permit foreign corporations under contract with the state petroleum monopoly, Petrobrás, to explore for oil in Brazil. The PCB attacked the former as "opening the way to the production of atomic bombs," and the latter as "another crime against national sovereignty" (ibid.).

The party leaders insisted that opposition to the government was becoming nationwide, and implied that Communist influence was increasing, pointing to the defeat of administration candidates in the 1974 elections: "The slogans of our party met with response among the broad popular masses [which] shows that elections may play an important part in building up an anti-fascist front and in the struggle to overthrow the dictatorship" (ibid.). Predicting greater isolation of the regime and a sharpening of the political crisis, the Central Committee did not entirely rule out the possibility of action against the government by the military. It stressed, however, the need and opportunities for political activity by the masses. In its view,

> The possibility of political and class struggles becoming more acute obliges the Communists, whose basic target is democratic freedoms, not only to mobilize the main anti-fascist forces (the working class, the peasantry and the middle urban strata), but to bring about a broad system of alliances embracing all the forces discontented with the fascist regime. This will intensify its isolation and lead to its defeat. (Ibid.)

To achieve its primary goal—the undermining and eventual replacement of the present regime by a more open political system in which communists have greater freedom of action—the Central Committee set forth a series of tasks for the party. The first of these was to use all means available, including legal political activity by the masses, to expose and exploit the weaknesses of the government. Every party militant, moreover, should work to hasten the establishment and consolidation of an "anti-fascist patriotic front," whose platform was to include: abrogation of the extra-constitutional powers of the regime, amnesty for all political prisoners, a new constitution, and punishment of crimes and corruption by men in office since 1964; defense of the demands of the working class, of the interests of the "middle urban strata and non-monopoly bourgeoisie," and of national interests against "imperialist monopolies"; conversion of the armed forces into participants in the campaign for national development and democracy; and, an independent and peaceful foreign policy. In anticipation that the Geisel administration might deprive the people of the opportunity to express their opposition at the polls, the Central Committee directed the party to fight for the holding of municipal and national elections on the dates specified in 1976 and 1978. To attract outside attention to Brazil and isolate its government in the international arena, the party was to expose the "expansionism" of the regime, intensify solidarity with "the struggles of fraternal peoples" of Latin America, Africa, and elsewhere, and "launch an international movement of solidarity with the Brazilian people's anti-fascist and democratic struggle." (Ibid.) In order to assure the success of these projects, the Central Committee "stressed the need to strengthen the communist organization, maintaining strong links with the masses, working for unity and security and stepping up vigilance against internal and external enemy threats" (*Granma Weekly Review*, 11 April).

It is perhaps a measure of the weakness of the party, and of the dim prospects for creation of an effective "anti-fascist" front, that the Central Committee also instructed the communists to publicize the PCB's long-term goal in Brazil:

> The Communists must make it clear to the people that the defeat of the fascist dictatorship will only be the first step toward their genuine national and social emancipation. Full emancipation requires abolition of the power of the local and foreign monopolies, and the subsequent establishment of a national democratic government which would pave the way for the victory of socialist revolution in Brazil. (*IB*, no. 4, 1976.)

In the past, when PCB hopes were brighter, Communist militants were always instructed not to risk alienating potential allies by mentioning the party's ultimate objective of total and exclusive power in Brazil.

Several themes of the program announced by the PCB Central Committee were further elaborated by Prestes in articles, speeches, and interviews during the year. His views were given wide coverage in the international Communist press, and some, picked up by non-Communist wire services, were also reported by the press and radio in Brazil. Even before the Central Committee plenum, Prestes lashed out against the oil and nuclear energy policies of the Geisel administration. In a strong published statement he flatly denounced the decision on risk contracts for foreign oil companies as

> an affront to our national dignity, to all those who fought and in many cases sacrificed their lives in defense of our oil. . . . Undermining state monopoly on oil—a gain inscribed in the Constitution—is a crime against national security committed by those who proclaim themselves its defenders. . . . More topical than ever today is the slogan under which our people brought about the state monopoly: "The oil is ours!" (*IB*, no. 24, 1975.)

In an article published at the end of 1975 Prestes dealt at greater length with the Brazilian-West German nuclear agreement and the alleged expansionist ambitions of the Brazilian military regime (*WMR*, December 1975). He reiterated the attack in a speech before the 22d Congress of the French Communist Party and in talks with East German leaders, both in February 1976 (*FBIS*, 19 February). The Communist position, as expounded by Prestes, held that

> The fascist military regime today in control of Brazil does not threaten only the peace and security of the neighboring countries of Latin America and Africa; it represents a dangerous focal point of war and serves as a support for the most backward forces on our continent. . . . The Brazilian dictatorship also wants to possess nuclear weapons and to develop conditions to build the atomic bomb. That is the principal significance of the nuclear agreement it recently signed with West Germany. (*Estado de São Paulo*, 13 February.)

Prestes caused an uproar in Brazilian political circles in February by reasserting the claim that the Communists had contributed importantly to the 1974 electoral victories of the opposition Brazilian Democratic Movement (MDB) (ibid.; *Latin America*, 27 February). All leading officers of the MDB and some prominent members of the pro-government National Renovating Alliance (ARENA) rushed into print to deny the allegations—attributed to Prestes in his remarks to the French Communist Party congress and in interviews with French journalists—that the Communists had influenced the MDB program, the voters had gone to the polls at PCB urging, and, therefore, 16 MDB senators owed their election to Communist support. Some observers interpreted Prestes's statements as an effort to discredit the opposition party in the 1976 electoral campaign, while others saw them as part of a Machiavellian plot to goad the regime into suppressing all political freedoms in Brazil, thereby creating a revolutionary situation the PCB might exploit. (*FBIS*, 12-19 February.) It seems more likely that Prestes was merely seeking to implement Central Committee directives to portray the Brazilian government abroad as a beleaguered dictatorship and to promote a broad opposition front by publicizing and linking the PCB with mounting anti-government sentiment. He continued to hammer on these points after leaving Paris, telling reporters in East Germany:

> We must form an anti-fascist patriotic front which will fight for basic democratic rights. In the elections to the national congress in November 1974, 62 percent of the registered voters voted against the dictatorship; in industrial cities it was 80-90 percent. That was a great encouragement for us because the voters followed our advice and used their votes as weapons of protest. . . . All in all, the resistance against the dictatorship is growing (*Neuer Tag*, Frankfurt/Oder, 13 February.)

Whatever his primary motives, the excitement generated in Brazil by Prestes's widely quoted—and misquoted—remarks brought the PCB program to the attention of a much larger audience than the party could have reached with its own resources.

International Views and Positions. PCB views on international issues were expressed by Luiz Carlos Prestes at a series of Communist party meetings and congresses in December 1975 and the early months of 1976. In each instance he was the only member of the PCB delegation to be identified in the international communist press. On 11 December he met with Boris Ponomarev and Vitaliy Shaposnikov of the CPSU Central Committee to discuss relations between the two parties (*FBIS*, 16 December). Later that month Prestes headed the PCB delegation to the First Congress of the Communist Party of Cuba, which he hailed as a "demonstration of what a brave and determined people can accomplish when they join the forces of socialism" (*Granma*, 20 December). Early in 1976, Prestes attended the French party's congress in Paris (see above). After that he and the PCB delegation were guests of the East German government for a week. In joint statements issued during the visit, Prestes and Erich Honecker, first secretary of the East German party, denounced the nuclear agreement between West Germany and Brazil, lauded the "peace-loving and progressive" policies of the USSR, praised the results of the June 1975 conference of Communist parties of Latin America and the Caribbean region "an important contribution to [the] unity and cohesion of the world communist movement"), called for the immediate quashing of the trial of Luis Corvalán and other Chileans, and for the freedom of "all Communists and democrats" being persecuted in Latin America, proclaimed solidarity with the Popular Movement for the Liberation of Angola and with the People's Republic of Angola, and condemned the "big-power chauvinistic policy of the Peking leaders which is directed against peace [and] is playing into the hands of imperialism" (*Estado de São Paulo*, 13 February; *FBIS*, 19 February). At the CPSU congress, Prestes paid tribute to the material accomplishments of the USSR and to the "Leninist peace policy which found its expression in the peace program adopted by the 24th Congress," as important advances for Communists everywhere. In the case of Brazil,

Thanks to your successes we, Brazilian revolutionaries and communists, are receiving a powerful new weapon which helps us in our daily explanatory work. . . . It is now considerably easier to do this work thanks to the successes of international détente, which takes the last arguments away from the Brazilian reactionaries and makes their anticommunist cries about a "Soviet threat" and international communism an anachronism and fruitless.

Prestes was even more extreme than usual in identifying the Communist movement in Brazil with the USSR:

Our party educates its members and all working people in the spirit of love for the Soviet Union. We shall never stop fighting against those who defame the motherland of the great Lenin or slander it, whatever they are called—imperialists, reactionaries, fascists or Maoists. To the Brazilian working class the anti-Soviet is a counterrevolutionary and the enemy of freedom and progress. (*FBIS*, 9 March.)

This theme was emphasized again in an article Prestes prepared for publication in *World Marxist Review* late in the year:

The Brazilian communists see and set great store by the fact that the CPSU shows unflinching solidarity with all the forces of peace coming out for the liberation of nations from exploitation and national suppression. This stand of the CPSU enables all the revolutionary forces to be constantly aware that they are not alone in their struggle and that they have the vast international prestige and political weight of the Soviet Union on their side. (*FBIS*, 7 October.)

Publications. In January 1975 the Brazilian government seized the PCB's two principal printing facilities. The PCB daily, *Voz Operária*, reportedly has not circulated since May 1975 (*Latin America*, 27 February 1976). Testimony obtained by security forces indicated that the PCB state committee in Paraná was unable to distribute the two issues of the newspaper it managed to print in 1975 (*Jornal do Brasil*, 15 November 1975). Although papers for various interest groups had been claimed (*YICA, 1976*, p. 445), there were no reports of any PCB publications circulating in Brazil during 1976.

The PCdoB. The organizational structure of the PCdoB, which was founded by men who had long held leadership positions in the PCB, is believed to be patterned after that of the parent party. Little is known about the number or distribution of currently functioning units. Over the past few years PCdoB activities have been reported in São Paulo, Rio de Janeiro, Espirito Santo, Bahia, and the Northeast. An undated document, attributed to the PCdoB and published abroad in July 1976, asserted that the party had also been active in rural Pará (*Latin America*, 9 July). This item, which recounts the failure and dissolution of the Guerrilla Forces of Araguaia, is the only recent indication of the domestic activities and views of the PCdoB. According to the published account, the FGA began operations in the jungles of Pará in 1972. By the beginning of 1974, following four assaults by the Brazilian army, half the guerrillas had been killed. Subsequently the area was sealed off by the military, making the position of the survivors untenable. Early in 1976, Brazilian security forces announced the death of Augusto Frutuoso, a member of the central committee of the FGA and, presumably, of the PCdoB as well (ibid.). The absence of police reports of the death or arrest of other PCdoB militants suggests that the party has now gone far underground, virtually ceasing to function. There have been no recent reports on the circulation of the party's occasional publications, *A Classe Operária* and *Resistência Popular*. On the international scene the PCdoB reaffirmed its pro-Chinese position, presenting a wreath at the funeral of Mao Tse-tung (*FBIS*, 15 September).

Other organizations. Of the numerous extremist and terrorist organizations operating in Brazil in the late 1960s and early 1970s, only a few appear to have survived into 1976. The MR-8, a terrorist group of Castroite persuasion, was said to have been effectively smashed late in 1975 (*Latin America*, 27 August). Preventive arrest orders were issued in São Paulo for three Marxist-Leninist Popular Action members who were accused of traveling with false passports to other Latin American countries to contact subversive organizations and raise funds for APML activities (*FBIS*, 24 February 1976). There was no evidence of activity during 1976 by the Trotskyist Revolutionary Workers Party—(Partido Operário Revolucionário (Trotskista); POR(T). It is affiliated with the International Secretariat of the Fourth International headed by J. Posadas. According to *Intercontinental Press* (New York, 16 February), an underground newspaper known as *Independência Operária* is published in Brazil by an unidentified Trotskyist party. Presumably this is the Communist Workers Party (Partido Operário Comunista; POC), which is more or less aligned with the United Secretariat of the Fourth International.

University of California, Davis   Rollie E. Poppino

Canada

The Communist Party of Canada (CPC) was founded in 1921. It functions legally and has an estimated membership of 4,000 or more. The population of Canada is estimated at 23,145,000.

There are several other Communist parties or groups, of unascertainable membership, but all small. The following have some prominence. The Communist Party of Canada (Marxist-Leninist), or CPC (M-L), which is Maoist, is especially active in the province of Quebec and has its headquarters in Montreal. There is also a Canadian Communist League (ML) which apparently enjoys a better relationship with Peking. The League for Socialist Action/Ligue Socialist Ouvriere (LSA/LSO) is the most important Trotskyist organization in Canada. It has a youth wing, the Young Socialists. The Revolutionary Marxist Group (RMG) was founded in 1973 by LSA/LSO breakaways, the Red Circle group, composed of some left-wing members of the New Democratic Party, and the Old Mole, a student group at the University of Toronto. The Groupe Marxiste Révolutionnaire (GMR) is the RMG's "sister organization in Quebec," its founders being French-Canadian Trotskyists who broke away from the LSA/LSO in the summer of 1972. The Workers League of Canada, which is the Canadian section of the International Committee of the Fourth International in Paris, confines its activities to Montreal. The Canadian Party of Labour (CPL) was founded by breakaways from the Progressive Workers Movement, the first pro-Maoist organization in Canada. Like the Progressive Labor Party in the USA, the CPL followed a pro-Maoist line until the improvement in Sino-U.S. relations.

While most CPC members are thought to be elderly, there has been active recruitment of younger ones. In the provincial election in Ontario, 18 September 1975, there were 33 CPC candidates, more than half of whom were under 40 years old; none was elected, though altogether the candidates won

9,600 votes. The general membership continues to be composed of old-age pensioners, manual and white-collar workers, and many persons of East European extraction. In the most recent federal election (8 July 1974), the CPC nominated 69 candidates of 264 constituencies, who won some 12,000 votes altogether, some 0.13 percent of the total. Thus the CPC has no representation in federal parliament in Ottawa nor in any of the ten provincial legislatures. In the 15 November 1976 election in Quebec there were some 14 CPC candidates, none of them successful. There are some Communist members or sympathizers on municipal councils and local school boards.

The United Fishermen and the Allied Workers Union, on the West Coast, and the United Electrical, Radio, and Allied Workers Union are unions in which Communists are part of the leadership; also a number of CPC members are officers in union locals, and regional labor councils. Communists are influential on several district and town labor councils and in the British Columbia Federation of Labour. The CPC controls a half-dozen ethnic organizations of Canadians of East European origin.

CPC Leadership and Organization. William Kashtan continues as the CPC's national secretary. Alfred Dewhurst, the editor of *Communist Viewpoint,* is a member of the party's Central Executive Committee and director of its ideological work. Bruce Magnusson serves as labor secretary. Richard Orlandini was appointed central organizer for the CPC in 1976, with John Bizzel as the organizer in the metropolitan Toronto area. William Stewart is CPC leader in Ontario and Sam Walsh is the president of the Parti Communiste du Quebec; Jack Phillips is organizer in the province of British Columbia. The Parti Communiste du Quebec (PCQ) as before, enjoys certain autonomy within the CPC.

In the context of more difficult economic conditions in Canada there has been a special drive to increase the membership of the Young Communist League (YCL).

Domestic Attitudes and Activities. In the face of double-digit inflation and a great number of strikes for higher wages to keep ahead of the cost of living, Prime Minister Pierre Trudeau's Liberal government imposed anti-inflation controls in October 1975. This was taken by the Canadian Labour Congress as a blow to collective bargaining; and much of the CPC domestic activity was directed toward building the protest among the workers on the wage-control aspects of federal bill C73, as the legislation is designated. The anniversary of the controls, 14 October 1976 was the occasion for a national Day of Protest in which more than a million (out of a work-force of 9 million) stayed off their jobs to join in parades and rallies. It was an unprecedented show of unity in Canadian labor history and the CPC weekly, *Canadian Tribune,* spoke of it as a "triumphant Day of Protest carried out by Canada's labor movement from coast to coast."

Also during October the CPC held its 23d Convention, at Toronto. Party national secretary Kashtan described the economic situation as a crisis for monopoly capitalism. He attacked the "so-called anti-inflation program which aims to increase corporation profits at the expense of the living standards and jobs of working Canadians." In a note-worthy departure from some past practice, the CPC made an appeal to the New Democratic Party (which has usually been castigated as "reformist" rather than revolutionary) for cooperation to "bring into being a democratic alternative to the crisis policies of monopoly, and a democratic alliance powerful enough to stop the drive to the right." The NDP, a party of moderate socialist objectives, forms the government in Manitoba and Saskatchewan and is the official opposition in British Columbia and Ontario; it generally repudiates CPC support, but does have its own left/right divisions. The CPC argued at its convention that "the working class and democratic forces cannot afford to be disunited" in the face of what was termed a reactionary drive to the right.

While opposing the Parti Quebecois program for outright separatism in the November election in Quebec, the CPC supported the notion that the British North America Act of 1867 (in effect Canada's constitution) be scrapped, and a new constitution be written. It proposed the objective of "a bi-national state with language and culture guaranteed to the English and French Canadian people," in contrast to Trudeau's policy of affirming a bilingual system of services within a federally unified country.

John Boychuk, one of the founding members of the CPC in 1921, died in October 1976, age 84; he had been imprisoned in 1919 for possession of seditious literature and again in the 1930s for unlawful assembly; in World War II he was interned for two years. For a time he was the assistant editor of the *Canadian Tribune.*

During the summer Olympic Games at Montreal the CPC supported Canada's exclusion of the athletes from Taiwan as representing the Republic of China. It was critical of the commemorative services for the Israeli victims at the Munich games. Great attention was given by the CPC to the success of the USSR athletes in their winning of gold medals, and there was also positive CPC response to the participation of the USSR in the Canada Cup international hockey series.

The CPC began a "Norman Bethune School of Social Sciences" in Toronto as a center for Marxist education, and generally campaigned to better the détente between Canada and the USSR. At the same time Canada was encouraged to withdraw from NATO and NORAD, and the influence of the USA on Canadian affairs was deplored.

International Views and Policies. The CPC generally supports positions taken by the Communist Party of the Soviet Union (CPSU) on international issues. During 1976 the German Democratic Republic, Poland, and Angola received much favorable attention in the CPC press, whereas Chile, Uruguay, South Korea, and the USA were subject to much criticism. At Chairman Mao's death a distinction was made between the "harmful policies pursued by Mao on the one hand, and the real voice of the Chinese people and the fraternity of the Chinese Communists and working masses on the other" (*Canadian Tribune,* 20 September). An effort was made to discredit Soviet critics such as Andrei Sakharov, Leonid Plyusch, and Yuri Shukevitch, as well as Alexander Solzhenitsyn. The Brussels Conference of Jewish communities on Soviet Jewry came under attack. The British presence in Northern Ireland and the apartheid policy of South Africa were subject to criticism.

The Israili raid on the Entebbe airport was treated negatively by the CPC. In a news story reporting the Toronto Labor Council's resolution of approval, a delegate was quoted: "By applauding this act . . . we are supporting naked aggression and invasion of a country's sovereignty" (ibid., 26 July).

International Activities and Contacts. In December 1975, a four-member delegation led by Kashtan attended the First Congress of the Communist Party of Cuba. In February 1976 Kashtan, Dewhurst, and Walsh were welcomed at the 25th congress of the CPSU in Moscow. Magnusson represented the CPC at the 7th Congress of the Polish ruling party, and Mel Doig, a member of the Central Executive Committee, attended meetings of the French and Italian Communist parties. After a stay in Prague in July, Kashtan was greeted in Moscow by Boris Ponomarev of the CPSU Central Committee. In October a delegation of the Supreme Soviet of the USSR visited Ottawa, led by the chairman of the Soviet of Nationalities, who was received by members of Parliament. Also in October another Soviet delegation, led by P.T. Pimenov, secretary of the all-union Central Council of Trade Unions, visited Ottawa, Montreal, Vancouver, and Toronto at the invitation of the Canadian Labor Congress.

Communist Publications. The CPC publishes a theoretical journal, *Communist Viewpoint,* six times a year, and two weeklies, *Canadian Tribune* (Toronto) and *Pacific Tribune* (Vancouver). The PCQ issues the fortnightly *Combat* (Montreal). The organ of the YCL, *Young Worker* (Toronto) appears irregularly and has a circulation of 5,000. Party members edit pro-Communist weeklies in eight languages other than English and French.

The North American edition of the Prague-based *Problems of Peace and Socialism* is printed in Toronto as the *World Marxist Review.* The fortnightly *Information Bulletin* is its companion publication.

The (M-L) theoretical organ, *Mass Line,* continues to appear irregularly. The party's *People's Canada Daily News* appears regularly and republishes items supplied by the New China News Agency; the labor troubles of Quebec are given full attention.

The LSA/LSO publishes the bi-weekly *Labor Challenge* (Toronto). In 1976 it supported the New Democratic Party and worked with the Canadian Labour Congress in the protest against wage controls; much attention was given to Leonid Plyushch's criticism of the USSR. In French, the monthly *Libération* (Montreal) followed the labor strife in Quebec and the separatist movement. The *Young Socialist* (Toronto) is the organ of the LSA/LSO's youth wing.

The Workers League of Canada has a monthly, *Labor Press,* in English and French, printed in the USA.

The CPL monthly, *Worker* (Toronto), publishes articles in English, French, and Italian.

University of San Francisco   Desmond J. FitzGerald

Chile

The only success that the Communist Party of Chile was able to chalk up in 1976 was the release of its secretary-general, Luis Corvalán, who had been a prisoner since the military coup on 11 September 1973. However, the circumstances of his release were hardly propitious for a party whose activities are increasingly centered on propaganda campaigns mounted from abroad. At the suggestion of the Chilean government, Corvalán was freed in December in exchange for the release of one of the most celebrated Soviet political prisoners, Vladimir Bukovsky. Corvalán's declarations from Moscow on the plight of political prisoners in Chile were swamped in the media coverage of Bukovsky.

The Communist Party of Chile (Partido Comunista de Chile; PCCh) is one of the most doggedly pro-Moscow parties in the non-Communist world. Before the 1973 coup, it was also the largest and best-organized Communist party in the Western Hemisphere and one of the world pioneers of popular front tactics. It was founded by Luis Emilio Recabarrén in 1912 as the Socialist Workers' Party. It adopted its present name in January 1922, after its leadership had decided in 1921 to join the Communist International. It was declared illegal by President Gabriel González Videla in 1948, and operated clandestinely for a decade. It was again banned after the overthrow of President Allende.

Its rivals on the Marxist left include a pro-Chinese party, the Revolutionary Communist Party of Chile (Partido Comunista de Chile; PCRCh) which was founded in May 1966, primarily by dissidents expelled from the PCCh in 1963. The PCRCh is currently dormant, and its leaders have had difficulty in adjusting to the blossoming relations between President Pinochet and the Chinese government—as exemplified by the Chilean government's offer of aid to China after the serious earthquakes early in 1976.

More significant is the Castroite Movement of the Revolutionary Left (Movimiento de Izquierda Revolucionaria; MIR) which was founded in 1965. But the MIR virtually ceased to exist as an armed guerrilla movement inside Chile in 1976, as the result of successful actions by the security forces and its own internal feuds.

The parties that remained allied to the PCCh in the Popular Unity alliance (Unidad Popular; UP) included the Socialist Party (Partido Socialista de Chile; PSCh), always Marxist in its philosophy, and containing a significant Trotskyist wing; the Radical Party; the Movement of United Popular Action (MAPU), also predominantly Marxist; a MAPU splinter group calling itself the Worker-Peasant MAPU (MAPU-OC); and the Christian Left (IC).

Popular Front Tactics. The PCCh was a driving force in the Popular Front that brought President Aguirre Cerda to power in 1938, as in the Democratic Alliance that supported Gabriel González Videla—the man who was later to ban the PCCh—in 1945. Between 1956 and 1959, the PCCh allied itself for electoral purposes with the Socialists in the Popular Action Front (Frente de Acción Popular; FRAP). Realizing that a still broader front had to be established to secure victory at the polls, the PCCh engineered the UP alliance at the end of 1969, which enabled Salvador Allende to win a narrow plurality in the elections of September 1970.

All the parties represented in the UP were banned after the coup in 1973. Despite mutual recriminations and incessant self-criticism, the UP leaders in exile have managed to maintain a semblance of unity, and the Communists in particular have pressed for the widening of the UP into a broad "anti-fascist" alliance, to be built on the basis of the slogan in the PCCh's November 1975 manifesto: "The Dividing Line Runs between Fascism and Anti-Fascism" (*WMR*, 31 January 1976). But not all the parties represented in the UP share the Communists' enthusiasm for a "democratic" front with the Christian Democratic Party (PDC). In 1976 the differences came to a head at the UP conference that was held in Mexico in April, when the PCCh's proposals for public overtures to the PDC were opposed by the MAPU leader, Oscar Garreton, and (after heated internal debate) by the Socialists as well. At this meeting, Clodomiro Almeyda, a member of the Central Committee of the PSCh and a former minister under Allende, was elected secretary-general of the UP.

The UP had reached broad agreement on tactics at an important UP meeting in East Berlin in 1975 when Orlando Millas, a member of the PCCh's Political Commission, drew hope from the supposed isolation of the junta and from the country's economic difficulties:

> The junta is completely isolated and maintains itself in power only by force. There are more visible signs of unease within the armed forces. Servicemen are beginning to realize that they are but tools of an outright terrorist dictatorship, the U.S. monopolies and a handful of plutocrats who are robbing the country. (*WMR*, October.)

It was agreed that servicemen and priests should be special targets for UP propaganda. But Millas expressed rather more enthusiasm than other delegates for the formation of an alliance with the Christian Democrats. He warned (in contradiction to the position of the MAPU and PSCh delegates) that "an anti-fascist front cannot be formed unilaterally"—that is, without bringing in the PDC from the very beginning.

However, the PCCh had little success in pursuing this tactic in the course of 1976, despite the deepening conflict in Chile between the Christian Democrats and the military government that was symbolized in January by former president Eduardo Frei's decison to publish a booklet in which he attacked the junta's economic policies and its allegedly "fascist" tendencies. Still, Frei, as leader of the PDC's conservative wing, remained vigorously opposed to any idea of a common front with the Marxist left. Some of the most interesting efforts to bring the UP and the PDC closer together took place under church auspices, as in a little-publicized meeting in New York in September, which was organized by the U.S. National Council of Churches. It was ostensibly a gathering of "Christian politicians," and PDC delegates met—apparently with the approval of the party leadership—with members of the IC and MAPU-OC.

The PCCh's general line on the "anti-fascist alliance" was set out in an article by Sebastián González (*WMR*, March). He stressed the need to achieve an understanding with the PDC and to exploit the conflict between church and state and the divisions within the armed forces which, he believed, would become increasingly overt as it became plain to all that the government intended to make itself a permanent dictatorship in which politics would be outlawed:

> In Chile fascism is acting with ruthless consistency, does not tolerate the activity of reformist elements, does not want co-operation with any democratic forces, even with representatives of some sections of the bourgeoisie. Its aim is simply to make the whole of society subservient to local and foreign big capital. It is out to destroy the Christian Democrat Party. . . . Some Demochristian leaders are not aware of that, but others, and the Christian masses, are very much alive to what is happening in the country. And it is with these forces that a dialogue is beginning, and also joint action and agreement on concrete issues.

Within the UP itself, there was little divergence on foreign policy. The Socialist leader, Carlos Altamirano, attended the 25th Congress of the Communist Party of the Soviet Union (CPSU) in February (in company with a PCCh leader, Américo Zorrilla) and launched a bitter attack on the Chinese for allegedly providing $100 million in aid to the Pinochet regime (TASS, 28 February). The Central Committee of the PCCh, determined, as always, not to be outdone in the expression of pro-Moscow loyalty, sent a message to the CPSU congress which described China's position in world affairs as "further to the right than that of American imperialism" (*Pravda*, 1 March).

The PCCh in Exile. Before the overthrow of Allende, the leadership of the Communist Party of Chile was organized as a 75-member Central Committee, with a nine-member Political Commission and a seven-member Secretariat. Although this formal structure was disrupted by deaths, exile, and imprisonment after the coup, there is evidence that the PCCh's clandestine structures remained virtually intact. In 1976, the most prominent Chilean Communists abroad were former senator Volodia Teitelboim, Orlando Millas, and former trade union leader Luis Figueroa. The wife of Luis Corvalán, Viviana, was also wheeled into action at a number of international gatherings, following the example of Allende's widow, Beatriz, who continued to be a regular guest of honor at anti-junta rallies. Thus Viviana Corvalán addressed the "red festival" organized by Britain's Young Communist League on 22-23 May.

The PCCh in exile sustained the momentum of one of the most intensive propaganda campaigns ever mounted by the Marxist left, a campaign designed to isolate the Pinochet government from its potential Western backers and to deny it economic support. Many of the activities were focused on international occasions when the junta was in the spotlight, such as the Geneva meeting of the UN Human Rights Commission, the U.S. Senate debate on the Kennedy amendment cutting off arms to Chile (approved by 48 votes to 39 on 18 February), the visit of U.S. treasury secretary William Simon on 6 May, or the summit conference of the Organization of American States (OAS) in June.

The government blamed the PCCh and its alleged supporters in the Catholic human rights organization, the Vicarate of Solidarity (Vicaria de Solidaridad), for incidents during the OAS summit that appeared to be designed to damage the image of the junta. During the conference, for example, a group of 14 left-wing Chileans sought asylum in the Bulgarian Embassy in Santiago.

The Soviet bloc kept up the battle of the sound waves. Besides Moscow radio's five daily programs in Spanish on different wave lengths, the former PCCh radio station in Santiago, Magallanes, has been resurrected as a short-wave station broadcasting from Moscow. There was also a continued flow of well-produced pamphlets, newsletters, and posters.

Foreign Support Groups. The military coup in Argentina on 23 March 1976 deprived the Chilean left of one of its most useful bases abroad, and meant that (apart from Cuba) exiled UP leaders could look for support to only two significant countries in the Western hemisphere: Venezuela and Mexico. The shift to the right in Portugal after the failed leftist coup attempt in November 1975 had removed another important, if more remote, base for Chilean leftists—notably the MIR and its allies in the Junta de Coordinación Revolucionaria (JCR).

But Chile's Marxist parties could still count on effective support from "solidarity committees" in many Western countries, some of which had assembled impressive political and trade union support, and displayed considerable propaganda skills. Among the more notable of these groups was the Chile Solidarity Campaign in Britain. Its co-chairmen were George Anthony, a Communist official in the engineers' union (AUEW) and Brian Nicholson, a left-winger on the executive of the powerful Transport and General Workers' Union (TGWU). Many of the biggest British trade unions are affiliated to the Campaign, as are the Labour Party, the Communist Party, the Young Communist League, and British Trotskyist groups such as the International Socialists and the International Marxist Group.

The main activities of the Campaign in 1976 were to keep up a constant propaganda barrage against the Chilean junta, to provide British forums for exiled UP leaders, and to lobby within the ruling Labour Party and the trade union movement for a boycott of arms deliveries to Chile and of "non-essential" trade. A key Chilean figure in the Campaign was Pedro Cornejo, the former president of the peasants' Federation, Ranquil, who was named official delegate in London of the Chilean Central Unica de Trabajadores, or CUTCh (*Morning Star*, London, 9 April). At the Campaign's annual general meeting on 5 February, Angel Parra, an exiled Radical Party leader, called for a boycott of non-traditional imports from Chile. A signal triumph for the Campaign was the Labour Government's decision not to approve new arms contracts for Chile.

The UP parties could also look for support to influential organizations in the United States. In the course of the year, Orlando Letelier, formerly Allende's defense minister, was appointed president of the Transnational Institute, an offshoot of the Washington-based Institute for Policy Studies. Letelier was murdered under mysterious circumstances in September. Although it was instantly claimed that he had been killed by the junta's intelligence service (the DINA), no evidence was found to establish such a link. Still more intriguing, documents found in Letelier's car and later published in the American press suggested a connection between him and the Cuban intelligence service (the DGI).

Domestic Attitudes and Activities. At the end of 1975, the PCCh amplified its conception of an "anti-fascist" front in its clandestine publications. "We repeat once again," declared a leader of the PCCh in the interior, "that the anti-fascist front cannot be made up only of the Popular Unity parties. It must involve other political forces, including the Christian Democratic Party." (*Unidad Antifascista*, December 1975; *IB*, 15 February 1976.)

The church and the trades unions were particular targets for PCCh cadres inside Chile. There were bitter clashes between Cardinal Raúl Silva Henriquez and President Pinochet, involving the treatment of the Vicarate of Solidarity (the purely Catholic group set up after the ecumenical Committee for Peace was dissolved on the president's orders). The Vicarate's key organizer, a lawyer called Hernán Montealegre, was arrested in May. In a list of official charges that was subsequently published on 14 July, he was accused of being a covert member of the PCCh and of having worked with "Communists and subversives"—for example, by allowing his house to be used as a dead-letter drop.

The Vicarate's bulletin, *Solidaridad*, was bitterly criticized by government officials. The government and the church clashed again after 13 August, when three Chilean bishops were expelled from Ecuador—together with bishops from other countries—where they had been attending a conference. The Chilean bishops were all known as critics of the government. On their arrival at Pudahuel airport, they were greeted by noisy anti-Communist demonstrators. The Cardinal promptly excommunicated some of those who had taken part, and accused the secret police of having stage-managed the affair.

Again, the PCCh hoped to exploit the rising tension between the government and the officially tolerated trade union bodies. The Communist-dominated trade union federation, the CUTCh, was banned in 1973, but many non-Communist union officials had been confirmed in their posts and informed that they would be replaced, as necessary, on the basis of seniority—that is, older workers would take precedence. But in early September, the PDC-oriented leadership of the copper workers' union was dismissed *en bloc*, provoking protests from the other unions in the so-called "group of ten." But there was no significant industrial unrest; all strikes remained illegal under decree law-198 of 1973.

Meanwhile, the PCCh inside Chile continued to be eroded by arrests and "disappearances." According to defectors and captured internal party documents, the PCCh's advice to its cadres was essentially: keep your heads down and hold on to your jobs by working harder and more efficiently than your fellow employees. By comparison with other opposition groups, the PCCh's internal communications and private intelligence network remained impressive. There was a period of alarm, for example, when it was discovered that the PCCh had covertly taken control of the news vendors' union (gremio de suplementarios) and was using newsboys—who have a perfect excuse for strolling through anyone's gate—to collect information.

The MIR. The Movement of the Revolutionary Left seemed to be on its last legs in 1976. The only significant terrorist incidents appeared to be the work of other groups, such as "Red September" (including members, or former members, of the MIR, the IC, and the PCCh), which mounted a series of attacks on branches of the state electricity service, a tobacco company, and a telecommunications office. There were other incidents involving disaffected conscripts: on 28 July, four soldiers in Antofagasta hijacked a bus and took 13 passengers hostage, apparently with the aim of demanding a plane to seek refuge abroad. But one was killed and the other three were taken prisoner in a shootout with security forces. Although this episode was cited by the authorities as an example of the need to maintain internal vigilance, it was plain that "armed struggle" had failed as a left-wing tactic in Chile.

The MIR has never really recovered from the death of its leader, Miguel Enriquez, in a gun battle with the police in October 1974. Reports of splits among his successors at the end of 1975—including a decision by the executive of MIR to condemn Andrés Pascal Allende and Nelson Gutiérrez to death as "traitors" (*El Mercurio*, Santiago, 30 November)—were subsequently denied by spokesmen for the movement, but it was clear that MIR's leadership had been gravely weakened. In February 1976, Pascal Allende and his girl companion, Marie Anne Beausire, who had taken refuge in the Costa Rican Embassy, were given asylum in Costa Rica. Later that month, Nelson Gutiérrez reached Stockholm after three months in hiding in the papal nunciature in Santiago. In a sobering statement on his arrival, he warned MIR sympathizers that it was a grave mistake to imagine that the military government was about to collapse. He drew encouragement, however, from the argument that it had become seriously "isolated" from two important middle-class groups: the "lower middle-class wage earners" who identified with former president Frei, and the "owners of small industries and craftsmen" who gravitated toward a spokesman like Orlando Sáenz, the former head of the industrialists' association, SOFOFA, who has become an outspoken critic of the government's economic program. In Gutiérrez's view, the government was now wholly dependent on the support of "foreign and domestic capitalists" and this could be used to widen the breach between it and Chilean society as a whole.

The MIR suffered another setback in February when five *miristas* were killed when security forces attacked a hideout in Santiago. Among the dead were the brother and sister of Dagoberto Pérez, a MIR leader killed the previous October.

London   Robert Moss

Colombia

The Communist movement in Colombia began within the ranks of the Socialist Revolutionary Party (Partido Socialista Revolucionario; PSR) shortly after the party's formation in December 1926. Contacts between the PSR and the Communist International during 1929 and 1930 inspired a group of PSR members to proclaim publicly the creation of the Communist Party of Colombia (Partido Comunista de Colombia; PCC) on 17 July 1930. The party has retained this designation ever since except for a short period (1944-47) during which it was called the Social Democratic Party (Partido Social Democrático). In July 1965 a schism within the PCC between pro-Soviet and pro-Chinese factions resulted in the latter's becoming the Communist Party of Colombia, Marxist-Leninist (Partido Comunista de Colombia, Marxista-Leninista; PCC-ML). Only the PCC has legal status. It has been allowed to participate in elections under its own banners since 1972.

The PCC participated in the 1974 general elections as a member of the leftist coalition National Opposition Union (Unión de Oposición Nacional; UNO), founded in September 1972. The coalition won two seats in the 112-member Senate and 5 seats in the 199-member Lower Chamber. Of these, PCC members occupy one of the Lower Chamber seats from Cundinamarca and the seat from Cauca.

In the 1976 midterm elections for state assemblies and municipal corporations, the UNO coalition was severely weakened by the defection of the pro-Chinese Independent Revolutionary Workers Movement (MOIR), which offered a separate slate of candidates. Despite intensive pre-election publicity, only about 30 percent of the eligible electorate voted. The Liberals obtained roughly 51 percent of the vote, the Conservatives 40 percent, and the opposition parties of the left 9 percent. The PCC-dominated UNO won less than 4 percent of the nationwide vote, concentrated for the most part in urban areas. The MOIR secured approximately 1.5 percent, while the other major opposition party, the National Popular Alliance (ANAPO), obtained the balance. The concentration of UNO support in Bogotá was sufficient to elect two deputies to the Cundinamarca Assembly, both of whom are members of the PCC's Central Committee.

The PCC is estimated to have 11,000 members and exercises only marginal influence in national affairs. The population of Colombia is 24,800,000 (estimated 1976).

Guerrilla warfare, although not a serious threat to the government, has been a feature of Colombian life since the late 1940s, the current wave beginning in 1964. The three main guerrilla organizations are the Revolutionary Armed Forces of Colombia (FARC), long controlled by the PCC;

the pro-Chinese People's Liberation Army (EPL), which is the guerrilla arm of the PCC-ML; and the Castroite National Liberation Army (ELN). Estimates of membership vary considerably. The FARC and the ELN have between 250 to 300 guerrillas each, along with an undetermined number of urban supporters. The EPL is believed to have fewer than 100 members. All three guerrilla groups were active in 1976.

Urban guerrilla warfare took on a new dimension in Colombia with the reappearance of the group known as "M-19." The M-19 first appeared in January 1974 as the self-proclaimed armed branch of the opposition wing of ANAPO. It takes its name from the contested presidential election of 19 April 1970, although ANAPO leaders have disavowed any connection with the movement. Up to 1976, the group's first and most spectacular action was the theft of Bolívar's sword from the Liberator's finca in Bogotá. On 18 February 1976 the M-19 claimed responsibility for the kidnapping of José Rafael Mercado, president of the powerful Confederation of Workers of Colombia (CTC). During the week prior to the 18 April elections, the M-19 announced that Mercado would be executed as a "traitor to the interests of the popular classes" if the government failed to accept a series of conditions. The demands included the rehiring of workers "unjustly" laid off in several companies, the abolition of decrees against job stability, and the publication of the movement's newspaper in the major press (*El Tiempo*, Bogotá, 20 April). Mercado's body was found at a Bogotá intersection on the morning following the elections. In a declaration released on 29 April, the M-19 attempted to justify Mercado's assassination by stating that he had been tried "by mandate of the people and found guilty of betraying the fatherland and the working class" (ibid., 30 April). Prior to Mercado's abduction and assassination the M-19 was treated lightly by the media and security agencies. However, on 1 May an army commander likened the group's discipline and methods of operation to those of the Uruguayan Tupamaros and the Argentinian Montoneros (*Diario Las Américas*, Bogotá, 2 May). As of 3 August, the government's investigation into the murder of Mercado had been completely frustrated. Everyone being held at that time on suspicion of belonging to the M-19, including four persons who had been arrested on 19 April, was released for insufficient evidence. Also released were four university students who had been arrested on 26 July for alleged participation in terrorist activities attributed to the M-19 (*El Tiempo*, 4 August).

The political climate in Colombia during the first half of the year was characterized by widespread protest and strikes by student and labor groups. On 22 June the state of siege was lifted, almost one year to the date of its imposition on 27 June 1975. Government minister Cornelio Reyes announced that "the strikes, general commotion, and kidnappings, which were everyday events in the country, have practically disppeared." He admitted the continued existence of rural guerrillas, but stated that the military forces had adopted an adequate strategy to combat them (ibid., 29 June). However, the ensuing months witnessed an unexpected resurgence of public disorders and political violence. Student and labor unrest resumed in July in protest over the continued high cost of living and the government's announcement of an increase in bus fares in several major cities. The militant National Secondary Students' Union (UNES) denounced the "repressive persecution and arrest of Colombian student and labor sectors" (ibid., 16 July). Defense minister General Abrahám Varón Valencia charged the UNO, MOIR, and ANAPO with the organization of protest demonstrations and warned subversive groups that the government would not hesitate to use the "full force of the law" in combating public disorder (ibid., 31 July).

On 6 September some 12,000 physicians and paramedical personnel affiliated with the Colombian Social Security Institute went on strike for higher wages and improved working conditions. Student protests in support of the strike resulted in a renewal of campus and street confrontations with security forces (*El Espectador*, Bogotá, 17 September). The continuation of the strike, along with an escalation of political violence on varied social fronts, caused the government to reinstitute a state of siege on 7 October. In early November, violence again erupted at the National University in Bogotá, despite an announced resolution of the strike on 27 October. Student dormitories were ordered closed indefinitely and the university placed under police control after the government discovered they were being used as hideouts by urban guerrilla groups and common criminals (EFE, Madrid, 3 November.)

The PCC. Leadership and Organization. The PCC is headed by its 12-member Executive Committee and 54-member Central Committee. The highest party authority is the Congress, convened by the Central Committee at four-year intervals. The PCC held its 12th Congress on 5-9 December 1975 in Bogotá. The meeting, presided over by the general secretary, Gilberto Vieira, was attended by 235 delegates and representatives of 19 Communist parties, mainly from the socialist countries and Latin America (including Chile, Costa Rica, Cuba, Ecuador, Guyana, Peru, Uruguay, and Venezuela). According to one party source, 36 percent of the delegates were reportedly factory workers and 29 percent peasants. This was considered a fairly accurate reflection of the class composition of the PCC's membership at the present time. Three-fourths of the delegates were said to be leaders of mass organizations. Although party membership has presumably grown since the previous Congress, the leadership admits to deficiencies in recruitment. Membership is not growing fast enough to enable the PCC to become a mass Lenin-type party in the foreseeable future (*WMR*, March). The party's political positions, which served as the basis of discussions at the Congress, had reportedly been discussed during the preceding four months by party militants in more than 20,000 cell meetings and 30 regional meetings throughout the country (*Alternativa*, Bogotá, 15-22 December 1975). The Congress reelected the main nucleus of the previous Central Committee and endorsed the members of the incumbent Executive Committee and National Secretariat. Members of the Executive Committee include, besides Vieira: Alvaro Vásquez, Jesús Villegas, Joaquín Moreno, Roso Osorio, Hernando Hurtado, Julio Posada, Gustavo Castro, Teodosio Varela, Gustavo Osorio, Juan Viana, Manlio Lafont, and Manuel Cepeda Vargas. The first four named are also members of the National Executive Secretariat.

A major source of the PCC's influence lies in its control over the Trade Union Confederation of Workers of Colombia (CSTC), which claims an estimated membership of 300,000. The CSTC was granted legal status by the Colombian government in August 1974 and is a member of the World Federation of Trade Unions (WFTU). Sectarian disputes involving the MOIR and the PCC surfaced at the CSTC's national meeting in March 1975 and continued to weaken the organization during 1976 (see *YICA*, 1976, p. 457). In February the CSTC called on all working people to combat divisiveness within the labor movement. It proposed a program to serve as the basis for joint discussions with independent labor organizations, "regardless of ideology" (WFTU *Flashes*, 11 February). On 19 March the MOIR, in a joint statement with a portion of the Broad Colombian Movement (MAC) leadership, reaffirmed its contention that the UNO had become the hegemonic arm of the PCC and thereby "lost its unitarian meaning" (*El Tiempo*, 20 March). On 22 March, the president of UNO, Manuel Bayona Carrascal, and PCC member Carlos Romero signed a declaration affirming the expulsion of MOIR from UNO for the "divisionist campaign" it had undertaken within the CSTC (ibid., 23 March). The possible separation of additional labor unions from the CSTC would obviously weaken further the PCC's organizational efforts in the labor sector. On 27 June the PCC announced that the CSTC would not participate in the National Wage Council as a result of a ruling by the Labor Minister which apparently rescinded an earlier invitation for CSTC officials to attend. In a document referring to the state of the national economy, the CSTC charged that "in spite of the government's stated policy of favoring the nation's poorest percent, the living conditions of the Colombian workers continue to deteriorate" (*Voz Proletaria*, 28 June). The president of the CSTC is Pástor Pérez. Other prominent members are general secretary, Roso Osorio, and Hernán Sabogal, Luis Carlos Pérez, Julio Poveda, and Alcibiades Aguirre.

The PCC continued in 1976 its efforts to expand its influence within the one-million-member National Peasant Association of Land Users (ANUC). Although founded by the government in 1968 to encourage peasant participation in the development and implementation of agrarian reform, the

"Sincelejo" faction of ANUC soon established a militantly independent policy. The organization has retained an autonomous position under Carlos Almeciga, who was installed as president at the September 1975 meeting of the Executive Committee. The government's reformist offensive for development of the rural sector has coincided with a decline of political direction within ANUC's leadership hierarchy. Strong differences of opinion surfaced in late 1975 exposing serious internal contradictions with regard to ANUC's political orientation (*Alternativa*, 17-24 November).

In March 1976 the ANUC leadership denounced the intensification of reprisals against peasants by armed groups supported by large landowners. Beatings, arrests, and alleged death threats were reportedly directed against local ANUC leaders and peasants in rural areas of Córdoba, Sucre, Cundinamarca, Antioquia, and Magdalena (ibid., 29 March). On 16 April ANUC spokesmen denounced the military's repression against the rural inhabitants of the middle Magdalena region as part of the government's campaign to put an end to the guerrilla organizations operating in the area. In addition to the death of several peasants, the ANUC protested the mass arrest of 50 residents of the region as alleged "aides" to the guerrillas. (*Excelsior*, Mexico City, 17 April.)

The political resolution adopted by the PCC's 12th Congress, admitting that the party must pay more attention to organizing the peasants, cited insufficient resolve in combating "ultra-left adventurism" and the government's "splitting policy" within ANUC. The resolution called for more effective party leadership in the peasants' struggle for land and the creation of a national agrarian federation. (*IB*, 31 January.) The PCC's principal agrarian leaders affiliated with ANUC are Víctor Merchán and Gerardo González.

The PCC's youth organization, the Communist Youth of Columbia (Juventud Comunista de Colombia; JUCO), has an estimated membership of 2,000. JUCO has its own national directorate, executive committee, and central committee. The general secretary is Jaime Caicedo. JUCO's most effective work has been carried out at the secondary level, operating through the National Union of Secondary Students. It has yet to overcome serious organizational shortcomings in its attempt to influence the National Union of University Students. The MOIR and other anti-Soviet groups have seriously hampered the JUCO's efforts to establish any unified action at the university level. The PCC Congress's political resolution recognized the necessity for greater attention on the student front and specifically called upon JUCO to concentrate its activity in the larger state universities, and the technical and industrial schools (ibid.). JUCO is among the youth organizations in Colombia that are to participate in the preparatory work for the 11th World Youth Festival, to be held in Havana in 1978 (*Granma*, Havana, English edition, 23 May). In September, JUCO announced plans to hold its 4th National Congress in Bogotá on 10-14 November. The purpose of the meeting would be to "draft a struggle platform, modify the organization's statutes, and reorganize the JUCO commands in the university and other sectors of Colombia" (*Voz Proletaria*, 15 September).

The PCC has controlled a peasant guerrilla group since 1966. The Revolutionary Armed Forces of Colombia (FARC). Party leaders have maintained an ambivalent attitude in recent years toward the use of armed struggle in furthering the revolutionary process. Although the political resolution adopted at the 12th Congress affirmed that "the guerrilla movement in the rural area [has] always been a notable factor in the general popular struggle [and] is a component of the tactics of correctly combining all forms of action," the general position of the party is that armed struggle cannot yet be the chief means of resistance (*IB*, 31 January).

Speculation existed in late 1975 that a break between the PCC and the FARC was imminent. According to one report, PCC leaders allegedly accused the FARC of being "counterrevolutionary" and promised to support the EPL and the masses against the movement (EFE, Madrid, 3 December 1975). There was no evidence of an open split during 1976, but the PCC may well be moving toward a less compromising position. The party does not wish to jeopardize its quest to achieve power through an electoral coalition of opposition groups.

With or without the PCC's endorsement, the FARC was the most active of Colombia's guerrilla movements during 1976. In its news bulletin, *Resistencia,* the FARC reaffirmed its resolve to continue the guerrilla struggle "in spite of the relentless reactionary pressures against the popular guerrilla movement." It claimed that the existence of FARC units in 11 of Colombia's 22 departments was "proof" that the military high command had "failed in its campaign to hide the existence of the guerrilla movement from the eyes of national and international public opinion." (*Alternativa,* 8-15 December 1975.) On 25 March 1976 three FARC guerrillas were killed in a clash with regular army troops who failed in an attempt to rescue an industrialist kidnapped six days earlier in Santander (*El Tiempo,* 26 March). On 29 March it was reported that two wealthy cattlemen were murdered in an aborted extortion plot by alleged FARC members (*El Espectador,* 30 March). In May it was confirmed that FARC's principal leader and one-time recognized member of the PCC's Central Committee, Manuel Marulanda Vélez, had not succumbed to tuberculosis, as had been reported previously by the armed forces. The confirmation was made by an individual reportedly acting as a liaison between the FARC and the government to negotiate an amnesty (EFE, Madrid, 4 May).

In response to continued FARC attacks against army troops in the jurisdiction of Cimitarra, the government adamantly stated that no negotiations for amnesty would be possible for subversive organizations (*El Tiempo,* 11 May). The official rejection of amnesty for rebel groups was followed by a series of spectacular guerrilla operations between late May and September. FARC units occupied towns in remote areas of Santander, Chocó, and Antioquia departments. In each instance they seized money, drugs, clothes, and general supplies, including arms and communication equipment. A FARC pamphlet distributed in Bogotá in August reported that 30 peasants had been executed in the previous two months in Antioquia, Córdoba, and Santander for having served as army informants. It also claimed that guerrilla units had carried out 35 assaults in the departments of Antioquia, Chocó, and Caldas (RCN, Bogotá, 13 August). The attack on San Pedro de Uraba in September by an estimated 100 guerrillas was the first of its type to be carried out in broad daylight.

The increased guerrilla activity in the Uraba region, which borders the departments of Antioquia and Chocó, was duplicated in the resurgence of FARC assults in the Cimitarra and southern regions of Santander. Individual FARC units are operating on at least two fronts and possibly as many as five. Individual leaders associated with FARC besides Marulanda Vélez are Ricardo Franco, Arias Robledo, and Ciro Trujillo.

Domestic Attitudes and Activities. The political resolution adopted by the PCC's 12th Congress reaffirmed that the party's strategic aim is to "unite" the revolutionary forces in the struggle against imperialism and the oligarchy." In his political report to the Congress, general secretary Gilberto Vieira announced that the PCC would take part in the April 1976 elections under the banner of the National Opposition Union "in alliance with all those who seek popular and democratic unity." He added that the party's electoral program would place emphasis on the repeal of the state of siege, improving the lot of the working classes, the repeal of repressive legislation, the abolition of military tribunals, the release of all political prisoners, the nationalization of the country's natural resources without indemnity, the safeguarding of rural workers from the "tyranny" of the landowners, and the ensuring of university autonomy (*Pravda,* 8 December 1975; *El Espectador,* 9 December).

The basic document adopted by the Congress specified certain weaknesses that need to be overcome if the UNO is to become a model of successful alliance for achieving the party's political and organizational objectives. Foremost among the weaknesses cited are the split in the workers' movement, the lack of coordination with other opposition groups, and the weakness of the workers and peasants alliance (*Pravda,* 11 December 1975). These shortcomings are attributed in large measure to "petty bourgeois" tendencies in the guise of Maoism, Trotskyism, and anarchism. The PCC has noted both the factionalism within "the motley collection of Maoist groups and their "vicious anti-Sovietism, systematic attacks on the PCC, and repeated attempts to undermine the class trade unions" (*WMR*, January 1976). In waging ideological battle against such groups, the PCC called for intensification of political activity and broader contacts among workers, peasants, and students, representatives of the middle sectors, intellectuals, and women (*IB*, 31 January).

In a February communiqué the PCC criticized the "discriminatory nature" of the state of siege. The party also condemned the abduction of José Rafael Mercado, "an isolated and adventurous act that is not helping in the necessary process of unity and cohesion of the mass movement" (*Voz Proletaria*, 19 Febraury). Vieira asserted in a letter to the editor of *El Tiempo* (28 April) that allegations of PCC involvement in the kidnapping and murder of industrialist Octavio Echavarría were "false and of a provocative nature," and added that the party was "against terrorist acts as a matter of ideological principle." In May a PCC editorial denounced "a campaign by rightist sectors of the government against our party and other democratic organizations in the country," alleging that a special governmental commission had been established to study the manner in which other countries had succeeded in illegalizing the activities of communist parties. The further charge was made that reactionary sectors within the government, including the military, had escalated their repressive activities in response to the PCC's "strong showing" in the April elections. (*Voz Proletaria*, 19 May.) As an example of repression, the PCC accused the military of establishing a concentration camp for the torture of alleged guerrillas rounded up after the ambush of an army convoy on 7 May (*El Tiempo*, 19 May).

An article entitled "On Socialism and the Ways of Reaching It" reaffirmed the PCC's fundamental belief in an alliance of political unity as "the revolution's strategic line" in Colombia. In pursuing this goal through its participation in UNO, the party believes that it has already achieved a broader base of organization and leadership on a national level, and continues to view UNO as "the beginnings of a patriotic, national-liberation front." (*WMR*, August.) However, the party experienced only marginal gains in its efforts at mass organization in 1976. The PCC's relatively moderate political stance has contributed to mounting criticism by more radical groups for whom the PCC's leaders are simply "salaried bureaucrats on Moscow's payroll." The MOIR is the best organized and most vocal of the groups seeking to assume the leadership of the disparate forces representing the Colombian left.

International Views and Positions. The PCC faithfully follows the Soviet line in its international positions. The final resolution of the PCC's 12th Congress found "a considerable change in the world arena in favor of socialism" (*Voz Proletaria*, 11 December 1975) and party leader Vieira declared: "Proletarian internationalism serves as the backbone of the international workers' and communist movement. It is precisely proletarian internationalism that the international reaction is seeking to undermine with the aid of the ideology of bourgeois nationalism . . . and the splittist policy of the Maoists and Trotskyites." (*Pravda*, 7 December.)

The Congress report expressed concern that circles linked with the USA had hampered the consistent development of trade with the socialist countries. However, it should be noted that during the course of 1976 official Colombian trade and financial agreements were signed for varying amounts with the Soviet Union, the German Democratic Republic, Romania, Hungary, Poland, and Cuba.

Vieira manifested the PCC's solidarity with the position of Venezuela and Ecuador in their struggle to abolish the trade discrimination law adopted by the U.S. Congress. Support was also expressed for the struggle of the people and government of Panama "for the liquidation of imperialist domination in the Panama Canal Zone." (Ibid.). The final political resolution called for continued support for the progressive positions adopted by the governments of Peru, Panama, and Ecuador; repudiation of the OAS; and recognition of the historic advance represented by the triumph and consolidation of the Cuban Revolution (*Voz Proletaria*, 11 December). In a special resolution the Congress expressed fraternal solidarity with the working class and Communist Party of Chile. The

PCC subsequently called for renewed signs of support for Uruguay's political prisoners and repudiation of the "inhumane practices" of the Uruguayan government. (Ibid., 19 December.)

Vieira described the 25th Congress of the Communist Party of the Soviet Union (CPSU) as "an event of enormous significance to all forces of peace, democracy, and progress" (TASS, 21 February 1976). At the PCC's celebration on 17 July marking the 46th anniversary of its founding, Vieira reiterated the party's solidarity with the Cuban Revolution and hailed the victory achieved by the Popular Movement for the Liberation of Angola. He also spoke of the "tenacious struggle" carried out by the CPSU in favor of world peace, détente, and disarmament. (*Granma*, English edition, 8 August.)

Party Contacts. A PCC delegation headed by Vieira attended the First Congress of the Cuban Communist Party in December 1975. A delegation led by Alvaro Delgado visited Poland in February for the purpose of broadening contacts and cooperation with officials of the Polish ruling party. Vieira headed the PCC delegation to the CPSU Congress in March. In a speech on 2 March, he condemned all forms of anti-communism and particularly its "grossest form—senseless, systematic anti-Sovietism by the Peking leaders" (*Pravda*, 4 March). In April Vieira was awarded the Order of the October Revolution by the Supreme Soviet Presidium. A PCC delegation headed by Alvaro Vásquez visited Hungary in late May. The PCC sent a congratulatory message to the Central Committee of the CPSU on the occasion of the 59th anniversary of the October Revolution (*Pravda*, 12 November).

Publications. The PCC publishes a weekly newspaper, *Voz Proletaria* (reported circulation 25,000), a theoretical journal, *Documentos Políticos* (5,000), and a Colombian edition of *World Marxist Review* (7,500). The FARC publishes a clandestine bulletin, *Resistencia.*

The PCC-ML. The Communist Party of Colombia, Marxist-Leninist, is firmly pro-Chinese. Its present leadership hierarchy is not clearly known. However, the party has not recovered from the serious setback it received in July 1975 when its general secretary, Pedro León Arboleda, was killed by police in Cali. The previous general secretary was killed in combat in 1968. The PCC-ML has an estimated membership of 1,000. Its impact in terms of national political life is insignificant. Unlike the PCC, it has not attempted to obtain legal status. Within the labor movement, the party has exercised some influence in the past over the Bloque Independiente, a small trade union organization with an estimated membership of 20,000.

The PCC-ML's guerrilla arm, the EPL, was the first attempt to stage a revolutionary "people's war" in Latin America. Although its rural guerrilla operations have been virtually eliminated, in 1976 one attack on a town in Córdoba was attributed to members of the EPL (AFP, Paris, 10 March). The EPL has limited its operations largely to urban areas. In February it took credit for a series of terrorist bombings, mainly in Bogotá, carried out by an urban support group named after Pedro León Arboleda (*El Tiempo*, 12 February). On 24 July the group distributed a leaflet in Bogotá claiming responsibility for the murder of labor leader Nicolás Santana on 4 July (EFE, Madrid, 24 July). An EPL pamphlet sent to various media sources took credit for a wave of bomb attacks in Bogotá over a period of weeks in late July and early August, and also announced that a summit meeting of guerrilla and subversive groups from various Latin American countries would be held in Bogotá before the end of the year. The EPL asserted that it maintains ideological and technical training centers for the formation of subversive units operating in Latin America. (*El Espectador*, 13 August.)

The official organ of the PCC-ML is *Revolución*. PCC-ML statements are sometimes found in Chinese Communist publications and those/of pro-Chinese parties in Europe and Latin America.

The Independent Revolutionary Worker's Movement (MOIR), established in 1971, also follows a pro-Chinese orientation, although its leadership and organization are independent from those of the PCC-ML. The general secretary is Francisco Mosquera. The MOIR opted to run its own slate of candidates in the 1976 elections. It has also been active in supporting the formation of an independent labor movement free from PCC domination.

MOIR leaders were among the principal organizers of demonstrations to protest the visit of U.S. Secretary of State Henry Kissinger to Colombia in February 1976. Official sources blamed much of the student unrest in 1976 on the disruptive influence of the MOIR, which they claimed had "turned the National University into a hotbed of communism" (*El Siglo*, Bogotá, 6 April).

The ELN. The National Liberation Army was formed in Santander in 1964 under the inspiration of the Cuban Revolution. It undertook its first military action in January 1965.

The toll exacted on its leadership and urban network in recent years has left the ELN in a state of confusion. However, individual units continued to carry out operations on a limited scale in 1976. The largest ELN faction contains units that operate primarily in the departments of Antioquia and Bolívar; minor actions were also reported in César, Santander, and Córdoba. In March, military sources in Bogotá announced that guerrilla units in Colombia were "entering their final phase leading to total extinction," following operations in Córdoba that resulted in the death of four guerrillas from units belonging to the ELN and the EPL. The death of Orlando David Garciá on 20 March was said to have deprived the ELN of one of its few remaining leaders in that part of the country. (*El Tiempo*, 25 March). An ELN message sent to *El Tiempo* (18 April) blamed the FARC for the kidnapping and murder of industrialist Octavio Echavarría, and also accused the FARC and its "patrons" within the PCC of "mixing common delinquency with the ideology of revolutionary sentiments," suggesting that the PCC was seeking funds to support its electoral campaign.

In a letter published in *Alternativa* (21-28 April), the ELN's principal founder and surviving leader, Fabio Vásquez Castaño, was denounced by several ELN members for his arbitrary authority. They accused him of being responsible for a number of murders within the guerrilla ranks, for anarchy in the urban networks, and for "the mediocrity corroding the structure of our forces." In July a unit commanded by Germán Sarmiento rebelled against the leadership of Vásquez, charging that he had abandoned the ELN more than a year ago and had absconded with ELN funds to finance his travels abroad (*El Tiempo*, 11 July). A subsequent article reported that Nicolás Rodríguez Bautista also had rebelled and had proclaimed himself the new leader. In a message intended for the ELN's urban networks, Rodríguez declared that the movement would begin seeking closer cooperation with the FARC and the EPL. Although military authorities declined comment, it was widely believed that the principal members of Vásquez's command supported Rodríguez's position, including the Spanish priest Manuel Pérez who is now considered to be second in command. (Ibid., 8 August.)

In September the ELN's propaganda organ, *Insurrección*, confirmed that Fabio Vásquez had been deposed as the movement's top leader for having "alienated himself from the revolutionary struggle," and that activities would continue under the leadership of Rodríguez. A member of the ELN since 1967, he became second in command to Vásquez following the deaths of the latter's two brothers and Domingo Laín. In condemning the dissident group operating under Sarmiento, Rodríguez confirmed that a serious division existed within the ELN's top leadership. (*El Tiempo*, 12 September.)

In late October, Ricardo Lara Parada, former ELN leader and ideologue, was reportedly on the verge of being released from prison by order of the Supreme Court, which declared that procedural irregularities had occurred during his trial in 1974. If released, Lana almost certainly faces a death sentence from his former comrades for having provided authorities with information about the movement's operations (AFP, Paris, 30 October).

Press sources in Bucaramanga reported on 7 November that Fabio Vásquez was in Panama or Mexico. Although it has yet to be confirmed, speculation exists that he will attempt to reorganize the ELN by seeking a reconciliation with Nicolás Rodríguez and several alleged leaders of urban cells who recently were granted political asylum in Mexico (EFE, Madrid, 7 November).

Washington College   Daniel L. Premo

Costa Rica

The Communist Party of Costa Rica (Partido Comunista de Costa Rica) was founded in 1931 and accepted as a full member of the Communist International in 1935. In 1943, following the wartime policy of many Latin American Communist parties. it was reorganized under a new name, the Popular Vanguard Party (Partido Vanguardia Popular; PVP). The PVP and its youth and labor affiliates basically follow Soviet-line policies.

Essentially as a result of backing the losing side in Costa Rica's 1948 revolution, the PVP was illegal from that year until 1974, when Article 98 of the nation's constitution, which in effect proscribed the party, was rescinded. Despite the proscription the PVP had operated with some freedom in the early 1970s and in the 1974 elections it ran party members as candidates of the legal Partido de Acción Socialista (PASO), a leftist coalition of splinter groups. Two PASO candidates were elected to the 57-seat National Assembly: Eduardo Mora Valverde, brother of PVP founder and secretary-general Manuel Mora Valverde, and Antonio Ferreto Segura, a full-time worker in PVP affairs for many years with under secretary-general Humberto Vargas Carbonell. The PASO representatives have enjoyed more influence than their numbers would imply by frequently coalescing with the ruling National Liberation Party, which in 1974 (for the first time since 1948) did not gain an absolute majority in the elections. The combination has thrived despite the fact the two parties were on oppostie sides in the 1948 fighting and that it was the National Liberation Party which proscribed the PVP in the first place. With the legitimization of the PVP, the PASO appears to be fading. The PASO deputies in the Assembly now call themselves the PVP faction.

It is difficult to estimate the size of the PVP membership. Approximately 500 delegates attended the party's Twelfth Congress, in 1976. It probably has at least 500 members and not more than 1,500. The party received 29,310 popular votes in the 1974 elections, out of a total of 664,963 cast. Of course, voting statistics do not coincide with membership. The population of Costa Rica is 2,040,000 (estimated 1976).

Although the PVP may be the best organized and most sophisticated Communist party in Central America, it has not become a significant force in Costa Rican politics. Due to its small size and aging leadership, as well as general conditions in the country, it has faced an uphill struggle and little evidence of change is apparent.

Leadership and Organization. Manuel Mora Valverde has been secretary-general of the PVP since its founding. His brother Eduardo is assistant secretary-general and Ferreto Segura is organizational secretary.

The PVP-controlled General Confederation of Costa Rican Workers (Confederación General de Trabajadores Costarricenses; CGTC), one of four national labor confederations, is believed to enroll in its affiliates about 3,600 among the estimated 30,000 unionized workers in the country. The CGTC is strongest in the banana-growing coastal regions which also happen to be the areas where the PVP receives the largest share of the votes in national elections. A new thrust of the CGTC is toward the organization of employees in the semi-autonomous agencies of the government. Alvaro Montero Vega continues as secretary-general.

431

The PVP affiliate for work among young persons is the Vanguard Youth of Costa Rica (Juventud Vanguardia de Costa Rica; JVCR). The JVCR suffered a reverse in 1976 when its candidates lost the elections for the presidency of the University of Costa Rica Student Federation (Federación Estudiantil Universidad de Costa Rica; FEUCR) after effectively controlling that body for two years. The PVP-ticket was defeated largely by a backlash against what has been regarded as a do-nothing attitude on campus issues despite promises for new dormitories and dining rooms and more scholarships. At the National University of Costa Rica in Heredia the JVCR candidates remained in control.

Domestic and International Attitudes. The PVP has a threefold domestic aim of enlisting worker support through the CGTC, influencing and enrolling young persons at the universities, and improving its standing in the political arena with the hope of getting a larger role in decision-making processes after the national elections in 1978. Particular attention has been devoted in 1976 to attacking the Costa Rican family planning program, which has been labeled as an imperialist scheme to limit the strength of the people of the small Central American republic. It seems doubtful that its position on this issue will help the PVP achieve the third objective, because of overriding problems coupled with its aging party leadership and the stigmas which date back to the 1948 revolution.

The party's Twelfth Congress was dedicated to the memory of Carlos Luis Fallas, author of a locally famous novel, *Mamita Yunai*, whose title is taken from the name popularly applied in the banana-growing regions to the United Fruit Company. The congress was chiefly marked by the speech of a University of Costa Rica mathematician, Francisco Ramírez, who outlined in detail the PVP program at that institution, including literature distribution, seminars, and the politization of students. The speech attracted attention in the national press and led to the defeat of the mathematician when he ran in an election for the University Council.

The PVP continued to support Soviet policies. It has received indirect support in some circles through the purchase by the USSR of some $8 million's worth of Costa Rican coffee in 1976. The PVP newspaper, *Libertad*, devoted considerable space to proclaiming the importance of détente between the USA and the USSR and decrying the policies of the People's Republic of China.

Publications. The weekly *Libertad* is the official PVP newspaper. The CGTC publishes *El Orientador.*

National University of Costa Rica, Heredia, Costa Rica   Charles F. Denton

Cuba

The Communist Party of Cuba (Partido Comunista de Cuba; PCC), is Cuba's ruling party and the only one permitted to function in the country under the 1976 constitution. The PCC was formed in August 1925 by Cuban and non-Cuban Moscow-trained Communists who were members of the Comintern. For the next thirty years, Cuban Communist leaders followed faithfully the policies of Stalin. They collaborated closely with the regime of Fulgencio Batista, opportunistically adapting their line to the prevailing mercurial political situations in Cuba. In 1940 the PCC supported Batista's candidacy for president; in return, Batista during his 1940-44 presidential term rewarded the Communists with high positions in his government and allowed them to seize control of a number of key posts in the labor movement. In 1944, Carlos Rafael Rodríguez, one of the most prominent pro-Moscow Communist leaders (today a member of the PCC's Political Bureau and vice president of the Council of Ministers), became one of Batista's ministers without portfolio. In that year, the party took the name of the People's Socialist Party, which it retained through a period of legal existence, 1944-52, and of clandestine activities, 1952-59. In July 1961 it merged with Fidel Castro's victorious 26th of July Movement and the Revolutionary Directorate (a student anti-Batista militant group) to form the Integrated Revolutionary Organizations, which in 1961, after a purge of members, became the United Party of the Socialist Revolution. On 5 October 1965 that Party was dissolved and in its place the PCC was formed along orthodox Soviet-Communist lines. After ten years of slow organizational work and slow building up of its cadres and leadership, the PCC held its First Congress in December 1975.

According to Fidel Castro, in early 1976 the PCC had 204,115 members and alternate members. (*Granma*, 4 January.)

The population of Cuba is about 9,300,000.

Leadership and Organization. The leadership of the PCC remained unchanged in 1976. It emerged from the First Congress, whose delegates elected the Central Committee's 112 members and 12 alternates. The new Central Committee at its first meeting, late December 1975, elected the first and second secretaries of the party, along with the other members of the Political Bureau and the Secretariat.

The 13-member Political Bureau consists of Fidel Castro Ruz (first secretary), Raúl Castro Ruz (second secretary), Juan Almeida Bosque, Osvaldo Dorticós, Guillermo García Frías, Armando Hart Dávalos, Ramiro Valdés Menéndez, Sergio del Valle Jiménez, Blas Roca Calderío, José Ramón Machado Ventura, Carlos Rafael Rodríguez, Pedro Miret Prieto, and Arnaldo Milián Castro. The nine members of the Secretariat are Fidel Castro Ruz, Raúl Castro Ruz, Blas Roca Calderío, Carlos Rafael Rodríguez, Pedro Miret Prieto, Isidoro Malmierca Peoli, Jorge Risquet Valdés, Antonio Pérez Herrero, and Raúl García Peláez. (*Granma*, 4 January 1976.)

Lower on the pyramid-like structure of the PCC are 14 provincial and 169 municipal party "executive bureaus." The basic party cells are organized in virtually all centers of work and military offices. The PCC has 37 schools, attended by 6,144 students. The educational level of the party has continued to be very low, however, and the leaders plan, at best, to have "most members" complete at least the eighth grade of elementary school by 1980. In 1976, 9 percent of the members had completed high school and 4 percent had a university education. Despite efforts to increase the number of women in the party, less than 15 percent of the members are women.

Despite its admitted shortcomings, the PCC holds the leading role in the country under the new constitution.

According to Fidel Castro,

> The party is a synthesis of everything. Within it, the dreams of all the revolutionaries in our history are synthesized; within it, the ideas, principles and strength of the Revolution assume concrete form; within it, our individualism disappears and we learn to think in terms of the collective; it is our educator, our teacher, our leader and our vigilant conscience when we ourselves are unable to detect our errors, our defects and our limitations; within it, we are closely knit together, and among us we shape every one of us into a Spartan soldier of the fariest of causes, all of us together forming an invincible giant; within it are guaranteed our ideas, our experiences, the behests of our martyrs, the continuity of our work, the interests of the people, the future of our homeland and our indestructible ties with the proletarian builders of a new world all over the world. The party today is the soul of the Cuban Revolution. (Ibid.)

Cuba's new "socialist constitution," which replaced the constitution of 1940, was a creation of the December 1975 party congress. Cubans approved the constitution by a 97.7 percent vote, in a referendum which also confirmed the Constitutional Transition Law. The constitution was officially proclaimed on 24 February 1976. In April and May a new politico-Administrative division at the municipal level was put into effect, reducing the country's municipal units to 169 (from 407). There are 14 provinces. The Isle of Pines is a separate municipal entity under the direct supervision of the government in Havana. In elections on 10 and 17 October, 95 percent of some 5.6 million registered voters chose 10,725 delegates to the municipal assemblies. The February referendum and October elections—part of a process called the "institutionalization of the Revolution"—marked the first time since 1959, when Castro came to power, that Cubans were able to participate in nationwide balloting. On 31 October 1976, the municipal assemblies were set up, and on 7 November the provincial ones. On 2 December was held the first meeting of the National Assembly of People's Power, a body described as "the highest expression of state power, composed of representatives of the people elected throughout the country." A total of 481 deputies were elected to the National Assembly in special meetings of the 169 municipal assemblies. The breakdown of deputies—who serve for five years, meet once a year mainly to approve the state budget, and represent 20,000 persons each—is as follows: City of Havana, 101; Isle of Pines, 3; and for the provinces, Pinar del Río, 32; Havana, 28; Matanzas, 26; Villa Clara, 36; Cienfuegos, 17; Sancti Spiritus, 21; Ciego de Avila, 15; Camagüey, 31; Las Tunas, 21; Holguín, 42; Granma, 38; Santiago de Cuba, 44; Guantánamo, 26. On 3 December the National Assembly elected a 30-member Council of State which has legislative powers while the Assembly is not in session, executive powers because it names and removes ministers and heads of state agencies, and judicial powers because it gives instructions of "general character" to the courts and the attorney general. The Council of State also appoints Cuba's diplomatic representatives abroad. It watches over the performance of 43 central organizations, 34 of which are state committees or ministries, whose heads hold ministerial ranks and, along with the president of the Council of State and the vice presidents, comprise the Council of Ministers.

The Council of State has an Executive Committee comprised of Fidel Castro, president; Raúl Castro, first vice-president; and vice-presidents Juan Almeida Bosque, Ramiro Valdés Menéndez, Guillermo García Frías, Blas Roca Calderío, and Carlos Rafael Rodríguez. The secretary of the Council is Celia Sánchez Manduley.

The Council of Minsters has an Executive Committee consisting of Fidel Castro, president; Raúl Castro, first vice-president; and vice-presidents Osvaldo Dorticós Torrado, Carlos Rafael Rodríguez,

Ramiro Valdés Menéndez, Guillermo García Frías, Diocles Torralba González, and Belarmino Castilla Mas. The secretary is Osmany Cienfuegos Gorriarán. Other Council members include:

Central Planning Board — Humberto Pérez González
State Committee for Material and Technical Supply — Irma Sánchez Valdés
State Committee for Science and Technology — Zoilo Marinello Vidaurreta
State Committee for Economic Cooperation — Héctor Rodríguez Llompart
State Committee for Construction — Levi Farah Balmaseda
State Committee for Statistics — Fidel Basco González
State Committee for Finances — Francisco García Valls
State Committee for Normalization — Ramón Darías Rodríguez
State Committee for Prices — Santiago Riera Hernández
State Committee for Labor and Social Security — Oscar Fernández Padilla
Cuban National Bank — Raúl León Torras
Ministry of Agriculture — Rafael Francia Mestre
Ministry of Foreign Trade — Marcelo Fernández Font
Ministry of Domestic Trade — Serafín Fernández Rodríguez
Ministry of Communications — Pedro Guelmes González
Ministry of Construction — José López Moreno
Ministry of Culture — Armando Hart Dávalos
Ministry of Education — José Ramón Fernández Alvarez
Ministry of Higher Education — Fernando Vecino Alegret
Ministry of the Revolutionary Armed Forces — Raúl Castro Ruz
Ministry of Food Industry — José A. Naranjo Morales
Ministry of the Sugar Industry — Marcos Lage Coello
Ministry of the Construction Materials Industry — José Valle Roque
Ministry of the Fish Industry — Aníbal Velaz Suárez
Ministry of the Iron and Steel Industry — Lester Rodríguez Pérez
Ministry of the Chemical Industry — Antonio Esquivel Yedra
Ministry of Interior — Sergio del Valle Jiménez
Ministry of Justice — Armando Torres Santrayl
Ministry of Mines and Geology — Manuel Céspedes Fernández
Ministry of Foreign Relations — Isidoro Malmierca Peoli
Ministry of Public Health — José A. Gutiérrez Muñiz
Ministry of Transportation — Antonio E. Lusson Batlle
Ministry of Light Industry — Nora Frometa Silva
Ministry of Electrical Industry — José L. Bentrán Hernández

Substantial changes in the economic direction took place as the new Economic Management System was introduced. A new national accounting method was made mandatory; credit and debit relations between enterprises and units of the state sector were reestablished and, as of January 1977, the country was scheduled to have its first national budget in almost ten years. The management system is to be gradually applied in all economic sectors and activities, and the process, under the direction of the PCC, is to be completed by 1980. Heretofore a near anarchy existed in Cuba's economic management. According to Castro, in the middle and late 1960s charges and payments between units of the state sectors were abolished, the state budget was eliminated, the connection between salaries and output sales was severed, interest of loans and taxes collected from farmers were ended, and even, in 1967, courses of public accounting were abolished at the University of Havana. (Ibid.)

Mass Organizations. Cuba's mass organizations are the Confederation of Cuban Workers (Central de Trabajadores de Cuba; CTC), the National Association of Small Farmers (Asociación de Agricultores Pequeños; ANAP), the Committees for the Defense of the Revolution (Comités de Defensa de la Revolución; CDR), and the Federation of Cuban Women (Federación de Mujeres Cubanas; FMC). Four other groups, the Union of Young Communists (Unión de Jovenes Comunistas; UJC), the Union of Cuban Pioneers (Unión de Pioneros de Cuba; UPC), the University Student Federation (Federación Estudiantil Universitaria, and the Federation of High School Students (Federación de Estudiantes de Enseñanza Media), are not regarded as mass organizations. Rather, they are institutional steppingstones in the selection process of the ruling élite—the PCC and the governmental officialdom.

The mass organizations have two basic functions set by the party: they constitute a source of cadres and militants, and they enable the party leadership to keep in touch with and exercise control of every sector of the population whose specific interests these groups represent.

The CTC. The Confederation of Cuban Workers is headed by PCC Central Committee member Roberto Veiga Menéndez as secretary general of its National Committee. The CTC's principal task is to improve the country's production and productivity through "improving the revolutionary subconsciousness" of the working class and fostering a "new collective attitude toward work and social property." The CTC consists of 23 national trade unions and about 2.2 million workers. Another task of the CTC is to improve the educational level of its members, half of whom have not completed six grades of elementary school.

Various methods are applied to stimulate production. The "millionaire movement" is a drive to cut a million "arrobas" or more of sugar cane per harvest per "brigade" of 21 cane cutters. (One arroba equals 25 pounds.) The Vanguard Movement is concerned with volunteer labor, national "emulation," and the like. There is a "National Hero of Labor" medal for the best workers; it has been awarded to some 60 persons.

The ANAP. The National Association of Small Farmers, has been headed since its inception in May 1961 by Central Committee member José Ramírez Cruz. In 1976 the ANAP had about 230,000 members, on more than 6,000 private farms. About 160,000 were farm owners and the rest were their relatives.

The ANAP seeks to exercise control over Cuba's private agricultural sector, which makes up 20 percent of the land under cultivation. Private farmers have to sell all their produce—mostly vegetables, coffee, tobacco, and some sugar cane—to the state, which sets up prices. In contrast to most Communist countries in Eastern Europe, the state does not allow for free public sale of surplus agricultural products. The government, which admittedly plans to incorporate private farms into the state sector, acts gingerly pursuant to that policy, apprehensive that any drastic move would result in a drop of the already less than satisfactory agricultural output.

The CDR. There are 4.8 million members of the Committees for the Defense of the Revolution, comprising 80 percent of the country's population over the age of 14 years. Organized initially to combat all manifestations of "counter-revolutionary activities" and as an open vigilante branch of the Ministry of Interior, the CDRs have recently been performing primarily economic and social functions. There are CDR committees for every city block, factory, farm, and office in the country. At the government's orders, the CDRs can on short notice produce crowds for public rallies and the "spontaneous" receptions arranged for foreign leaders. The CDRs are headed by Jorge Lescano Pérez, their national Coordinator, who is a member of the PCC Central Committee.

The FMC. The Federation of Cuban Women, constituted in 1960, had in 1976 about 2.2 million members, approximately 80 percent of Cuba's female population over 14. Its principal aim is to incorporate women into productive work and to mobilize them for educational, social, and political tasks set by the government. The FMC is headed by Vilma Espín, member of the PCC Central Committee and wife of Raúl Castro. Of late, Mrs. Castro has been acting more like the first lady of Cuba, since her brother-in-law Fidel Castro (who became 50 in August 1976) is not married. The principal work load at the FMC is now carried on by Dora Carcaño Araujo, an alternate member of the Central Committee. Mrs. Castro is FMC president, and Mrs. Carcaño secretary-general. Despite the FMC's efforts and the growing number of women in all productive sectors of the economy, "machismo" remains strongly entrenched in Cuba. There are almost no women in the high echelons of the government and the party. Women continue to occupy positions in the administration traditionally regarded as being in the female domain: clerical, accounting, menial, and the like. Since shortages of every kind oblige women to perform also their traditional chores at home, Cuban women are probably more burdened today with work and social obligations, and less rewarded as individuals, than at any time in recent years.

The UJC. The Union of Young Communists, the Cuban counterpart of the Soviet Komsomol, is a steppingstone for every ambitious Cuban youth on the way to a position of relevance in the party, armed forces, or administration. It was created in 1962. Officially, the UJC is designated as the "organization of vanguard youth and a militant source and reserve" of the PCC. The first secretary of this elitist group is Luis Orlando Domínguez Muñiz, a member of the Central Committee. It has about 320,000 members, 30 percent of whom are girls. Cuban youths can join the UJC at the age of 17 and can be members until the age of 27. Those who pass the ideological test join the PCC. Since 1972, about 20,000 UJC members have joined the party. Every year, about 60 percent of the UJC members who reach the age of 27 are dropped from the organization because they are not regarded as suitable party material. The UJC is possibly the most radical political group in Cuba. It directly supervises the activities of the Union of Cuban Pioneers (headed by Juan Mock) and the Federation of High School Students, and indirectly those of the University Student Federation, whose president in 1976 was Carlos Lage.

The UPC. The Union of Cuban Pioneers, equivalent to the Soviet Pioneers, was created in 1961 to control activities of school children between the ages of 5 and 14. In 1976 some 1.9 million children, almost 100 percent of the school population of the 5 to 14 age group, were members of the UPC. According to the PCC platform, the UPC "contributes to the Communist education of the younger generation." It also organizes the children's leisure time, part of which is spent in the so-called school garden where, under supervision, the Pioneers cultivate vegetables and fruit.

The Revolutionary Armed Forces. The Revolutionary Armed Forces (Fuerzas Armadas Revolucionarias; FAR) had in 1976 about 120,000 men on active service and 180,000 reservists, according to Western intelligence estimates. In time past it has been a much larger force, but since 1970 about 150,000 men and 5,000 vehicles have been deactivated and transferred into the state economic sector. Thousands of former recruits have become members of the so-called Army of Working Youth, formed in 1973. Still, the FAR is considered the strongest military force in Latin America.

According to the Strategic Service Institute of London, Cuba can mobilize up to 300,000 men in 48 hours and over a million during a first week of conflict. The FAR is now in the process of being resupplied with more modern arms from the USSR, which already has given Cuba—free of charge, according to Castro (*Granma*, 4 January 1976)—modern weapons worth "several" billion dollars. One problem of the FAR is the low educational level of recruits, since students are exempt from the draft. In fact, the draft is admittedly used as a threat by parents and teachers against youths who get poor marks and as a punishment for those who fail scholastically. About 85 percent of Cuban officers are members of the PCC or UJC, and the FAR has a considerable number of Soviet advisers, who reportedly reach down to the battalion level. In November 1976, Cuba ended a 20-year-old tradition of having commander as the highest officer rank in the FAR, and introduced the ranks of general in the army and of admiral in the navy.

Beginning in late 1975 a large contingent of the FAR, estimated at 20,000 by some experts, became involved in the civil war in Angola, in what the USA saw as a sign of a new aggressive posture of Fidel Castro. Intelligence observers did not discount the possibility that the Cuban army could become the source of other Soviet bloc expeditionary forces in situations similar to that in Angola.

According to Castro, the decision to send troops to Angola was made by Cuba in November 1975 "at the urgent request" of Agostinho Neto, leader of a militant pro-Soviet group that dominated Luanda, the capital of the former Portuguese colony. Cuban soldiers, witnesses reported, arrived in Angola on Soviet transports and were armed only with light weapons, but were equipped there with tanks, artillery, and other war matériel which the Soviets had dispatched to Africa. This, military analysts wrote, suggested that Cuba's Angolan involvement was coordinated if not actually ordered by Moscow. Cuban troops clearly turned the tide in the civil war and as a result Dr. Neto became president of Angola.

Even though Castro in mid-1976, promised in a letter to former Swedish prime minister Olof Palme that Cuban troops would be rapidly withdrawn from Angola (*Manchester Guardian*, 13 June), by the end of the year there were indications that their stay would be long and possibly bloody. In July, Cuba signed an agreement with Angola under which Cuban soldiers would help organize the Angolan army. Later reports had it that Cuban troops, estimated between 14,000 and 18,000 men at the end of 1976, were being used to combat against anti-Neto guerrillas in various parts of Angola (*NYT*, 12 December), and that the "pacification" was causing casualties among members of the expeditionary FAR contingent.

Domestic Affairs. The year 1976 brought the "20th Anniversary of Granma" (Castro's landing in Cuba where he arrived from Mexico on board the boat *Granma*) and marked also a period of growing economic problems, after several years of apparent recovery prompted by high sugar prices. In a revealing, if not alarming speech delivered in October, Castro said that the sharp decline in sugar prices on the world market (from some 40 cents a pound in 1975 to about 8 cents in late 1976), the drastic drop in Cuba's projected 1976 sugar output due to a severe and prolonged drought, and the world-wide inflation will force the Cubans to make new sacrifices, the government to scale down the 1976-80 economic plans, and the economy to produce more for export in order to maintain credit and purchase goods indispensable for the country's functioning. Another casualty of the sugar price slump, Castro indicated, will be the trade with non-Communist countries. (*Granma*, 10 October.)

Thus Cuba is expected to rely more than ever on trade with the USSR and other Communist countries, and on the Soviet subsidy, which is believed to have increased now to $2 million a day. Among other products, the Soviet Union sends to Cuba annually 8.5 million tons of petroleum and other fuels. Cuba's 1976 sugar production was estimated at 5.7 million tons, virtually the same as during the two preceding years, but worth only a fifth as much as the 1974 and 1975 harvests. "The purchasing power of a pound of sugar on the world market today," said Castro, "is the same or less than it was in 1931 and 1932, at the time of the last great world crisis, which was a terrible time of starvation in our country—these factors are going to have an adverse effect, in the first place, on the directives for economic development during the present five-year period (1976-80) . . . and, without doubt, are going to have an adverse effect on annual output during that period. And we must recognize this honestly, frankly, openly and valiantly." (Ibid.) As part of a general belt-tightening, consumer goods became scarcer, with more bad economic news expected in early 1977.

International Positions. Cuba was very active during 1976 in international affairs, chiefly because of its military involvement in Angola. As a consequence of that involvement, and of Havana's support for anti-colonial struggle in Africa, a posture which closely followed the Moscow line, many countries, especially in Latin America, were apprehensive of aggressive Cuban designs for other parts of the world. Castro tried to assuage those concerns. In a speech in April he said: "No country in Latin America, regardless of its social system, will have anything to fear from the Armed Forces of Cuba. . . . The Government of Cuba has never thought of taking the revolution to any nation in this Hemisphere with the arms of its military units. Such an idea would be absurd and ridiculous. No country of Black Africa has anything to fear from Cuban military personnel." Indicating that the Angolan venture was an isolated case, Castro said that Cuba "would be even willing to maintain normal relations with the United States." (*Granma*, Havana, 20 April.) But in June, Cuba's UN representative, Ricardo Alarcón, sounded more aggressive than Castro, declaring that "armed struggle is the only way in Rhodesia" (*Juventud Rebelde*, 11 June).

In July, Cuba broadened its interest in Angolan affairs. The two countries signed a series of agreements for political, economic, scientific, and technical cooperation which established a firm, long-range basis for Cuban permanence in Angola.

The Cuban government clearly has the aim of becoming a leader of the Third World. Since 1970 Havana has established diplomatic relations with about 25 African nations. Besides Angola, Cuban troops are said to be stationed in Sierra Leone, the People's Republic of Congo, Guinea, Equatorial Guinea, Guinea-Bissau, Mozambique, Tanzania, and Somalia, according to U.S. sources. There are also medical teams in Algeria.

In furthering Soviet goals in Africa, Havana crossed swords, verbally, with Peking. In three strongly worded editorials, *Granma* (3 February, 13 March, 5 April) went to the extent of calling Chinese statements "Maoist, Goebbels-like lies," replete with "shameless cynicism," and expressions of an "outrageous counter-revolutionary, anti-Socialist and anti-nationalist policy."

The 15 October sabotaging of a Cuban jet airliner which crashed into the sea after taking off from Barbados, killing all 78 persons aboard, prompted Castro to renounce a three-year-old Cuban-U.S. agreement to prevent hijacking. At the same time, he said that the USA was indirectly responsible for the sabotage. He added that the U.S. Central Intelligence Agency had supported anti-Communist activities by Cuban refugees and other nationals held in custody in Caracas, among whom were persons accused of placing a bomb aboard the Cuban jet. In November, the U.S. State Department, responding to Castro, denied responsibility for the crash, reiterated U.S. opposition to all acts of terrorism, and called the Cuban renunciation of the anti-hijacking agreement "arbitrary and unjustified" (*NYT*, 13 November). Neither side appeared to be intransigent and some observers believed that the anti-hijacking agreement could be renegotiated after the new U.S. administration of President-elect Jimmy Carter has taken over.

International Contacts. The year was a busy one for visitors to Cuba and for Cubans traveling abroad. In January 1976, General Omar Torrijos, head of government of Panama, Prime Minister Pierre Trudeau of Canada, and Mme Simone Veil, French minister of health, visited Havana. In February and March Cuba had few important foreign guests because Casto was away, first attending the 25th Congress of the Communist Party of the Soviet Union in Moscow and later, on his way home, stopping in Bulgaria, Yugoslavia (where he met with Marshal Tito), Guinea, and Algeria. In May, Cuban defense minister Raúl Castro visited Moscow, and Politburo member Blas Roca represented Cuba at the 9th Congress of the Socialist Unity Party of Germany in East Berlin. In June, Raúl Castro traveled to Brazzaville, capital of the People's Republic of Congo, and in September to Poland, where he observed the maneuvers of Warsaw Treaty Organization troops. Also in June, Fidel Castro received in Havana Felipe González, head of the Spanish Socialist Party. Agostinho Neto, president of Angola, visited Cuba in July, as did Luis Carlos Prestes, secretary-general of the Brazilian Communist Party. In August, Politburo member Armando Hart met with Jamaica's prime minister in Kingston.

The September visitors to Cuba were Kaysone Phomvihane, secretary-general of the People's Party of Laos; the defense minister of Yugoslavia; the Hungarian foreign minister; and the prime minister of Saõ Tomé and Principe. In October the president of Guinea-Bissau was a visitor, and delegations from Chad and Mauritius traveled to Havana to formally initiate relations with the Castro government. In November, Soviet army general Victor G. Kulikov, chief of the general staff, led a military delegation to Cuba. A December visitor to Havana was the prime minister of Angola.

Publications. *Granma*, the official organ of the PCC Central Committee is published six times a week at Havana; the editor is Jorge Enrique Mendoza, a Central Committee member. *Granma* also appears in weekly editions in Spanish, English, and French, which circulate widely abroad. Its daily average domestic circulation is 600,000. The UJC publishes the daily *Juventud Rebelde*, the country's second national newspaper, with a circulation of 200,000. In June 1976, to save paper, *Granma* was reduced to 6 pages (from 8) and *Juventud Rebelde* to 4 pages (from 6). There are several small PCC provincial newspapers. National weeklies are *Verde Olivo*, the organ of the FAR, and *Bohemia*, a general news magazine whose circulation is 300,000.

University of Miami   George Volsky

Dominican Republic

Intense disagreement over leadership and policy issues, especially since the civil war of 1965, has led to fragmentation of the Communist movement of the Dominican Republic. The three principal organizations are the Dominican Communist Party (Partido Comunista Dominicano; PCD), more or less officially recognized by the USSR; the Dominican People's Movement (Movimiento Popular Dominicano; MPD), which has been pro-Chinese, and the Revolutionary Movement of 14 June (Movimiento Revolucionario 14 de Junio; MR-1J4), pro-Chinese, but also the group most sympathetic toward Cuba. Splits within these groups have created several new factions and parties, including the Popular Socialist Party (Partido Socialista Popular; PSP), the Communist Party of the Dominican Republic (Partido Comunista de la República Dominicana; PCRD, or PACOREDO), and the Red Flag (Bandera Roja), Red Line (Linea Roja), Red Fatherland (Patria Roja) and Proletarian Voice (Voz Proletaria) factions of MR-1J4. Only the PCD appears clearly to enjoy recognition within the international movement.

Communism is officially proscribed in the Dominican Republic, under laws covering propaganda and subversive activities. President Joaquin Balaguer has allowed the various groups to operate with relative freedom, although a bill he sent to Congress in 1974 to give legal recognition to the PCD has not been acted upon. For their part, most of the Marxist-Leninist groups have tended to seek respectability in recent years; the more important of them have denounced terrorism.

Estimates of membership vary widely (see *YICA, 1976*, p. 472). The PCD has perhaps 400 members and the MPD, the largest of the Communist groups, perhaps 2,000. The MR-1J4 may have 300 members, the PCRD 150, the PSP about 40. The population of the Dominican Republic is about 4,700,000.

Politically motivated murders became an established feature of the Dominican scene after the 1965 civil war. Most victims were members of Communist groups or of the major opposition party, the Dominican Revolutionary Party (Partido Revolucionario Dominicano; PRD). The killings were attributed both to feuds among Communist groups and to actions by paramilitary gangs reportedly organized by the military and the police, particularly the latter. There were few assassinations during 1976, although protests continued over the inability of the government to control the violence of the security services.

Communist Politics among Students. Sources of Communist support include the universities, secondary schools, and labor unions, and reflect the fragmentation of the movement. At the university level, "Fragua" is led by the Red Line of the MR-1J4, the Liga de la Juventud Democrática or Juventud Comunista by PCRD members, the Comité Universitario "Julio Antonio Mella" by PCD members, and the Comité Flavio Suero by MPD members. The powerful Federation of Dominican Students (Federación de Estudiantes Dominicanos; FED), which is said to enroll about 200,000 university and secondary school students, has since 1969 oscillated between control by non-Communist but left-wing students of the PRD, and by the MPD. The Communist movement in the secondary schools is represented by the Union of Revolutionary Students (Unión de Estudiantes Revolucionarios [UER]).

In January 1976, Red Line students sought to promote a student strike in protest against examinations. Their attitude was repudiated by a number of other student groups, and there was considerable violence on the campus on 5 February (Radio Clarin, Santo Domingo, 5 February).

In June the student group of PACOREDO seized the office of the Rector of the University of Santo Domingo, forcing him to leave. The aggressors claimed that he was "Balaguer's rector, the agent of imperialism," although in fact he was a partisan of former President Juan Bosch. The press reacted strongly against the PACOREDO action and supported expulsion of six members of the group from the university. The PCD also announced its support for the Rector. (*Renovación*, Santo Domingo, 30 June.)

Student elections in September showed a sharp drop in support for the MPD, which until then had controlled the FED, and for the PACOREDO, together with a strong increase in support for the followers of the Linea Roja and a rise of 100 percent in the votes for the PCD student group (ibid., 28 September).

Student groups were the principal ones to take note of the death of Mao Tse-tung. The UER mounted sound trucks to broadcast a translation of the official statement of Chinese authorities on Mao's death. Memorial meetings were organized by the UER and Comité Flavio Suero. (*Peking Review*, 15 October.)

Communist Influence in Organized Labor. Within the labor movement, which generally has been weak since the 1965 civil war, Communist support is more limited. The "Foupsa-Cesitrado" labor confederation, reportedly in MPD hands, is only one of several central labor bodies. There is also some Communist influence in the General Confederation of Workers (Confederación General de Trabajadores; CGT). The largest is the Confederación Autónoma Sindical Cristiana, more or less associated with the Revolutionary Social Christian Party (Partido Revolucionario Social Cristiano; PRSC). The powerful "Unachosin" chauffeurs' union includes Communist members, mostly of the MPD.

In March 1976 the CGT issued a denunciation of the labor policies of the government of President Balaguer, and also charged that the political section of the U.S. embassy had interfered in CGT internal affairs. It particularly accused the American Institute for Free Labor Development of trying to "buy leaders and divide the democratic and progressive trade unions." It also claimed that the national police were preventing the CGT "from freely exercising unionism in this country." (Radio Clarin, 26 March.)

In July the CGT sent a two-man delegation to Canada, to try to rally labor support there for its activities. The delegation particularly denounced the allegedly anti-union policies of the Falconbridge Nickel Mines in the Dominican Republic. (*Guardian*, New York, 14 July.)

Communists and the Military. In February 1976 the Communists in general seemed to receive support from a very unlikely source. General Manuel Antonio Cuervo Gómez, chief of the Army Support Command, speaking at a military graduation ceremony, after commenting that "We soldiers cannot become mercenaries, nor can we lazily and with cowardice hide behind obsolete concepts of military apoliticism," went on to say: "The struggle begun between an ideology as resolute, vigorous and revolutionary as communism, and a social organization as unjust, decadent and materialist as capitalism is a struggle to the death" (LATIN, 21 February). Two days later the Minister of the Armed Forces repudiated the speech, but there was no indication that Cuervo Gómez was in any way disciplined for it.

The PCD. The PCD was founded clandestinely in 1942. As the Popular Socialist Party (Partido Socialista Popular), it came into the open for a short while in 1946; in 1947 it was suppressed by the Trujillo dictatorship. During the military-civilian revolt in April 1965, the party took the PCD name, which it has used since. In 1967 the PCD adopted (verbally but not in practice) a Castroite line, advocating armed struggle for most Latin American countries, but soon abandoned that position. In recent years it has advocated the kind of popular front characteristic of the pro-Soviet parties in Latin America.

Narciso Isa Conde is the PCD secretary-general. The party claims to be organized on a national scale, with cells in most cities and in the countryside. It has a committee operating in New York City among persons of Dominican origin.

In March 1976, Isa Conde gave an interview to a TASS correspondent. Sketching the activities of the party, he said: "Now we are publishing legally the magazine *Impacto Socialista*, we have been given access to radio and television, we can publish articles in the press, make statements, and give interviews. However, all this is very unsteady, for the apparatus of terror and repression has not been liquidated." He added that the basic objectives of the party for the moment were aimed toward "uniting the urban workers' movement with the wave of peasant demonstrations." He said that this would raise the "mass struggle in the Dominican Republic" to a "qualitatively new level."

In January the PCD came out in favor of a sugar price rise as the only way to "prevent a short-term increase in the country's foreign debt" (EFE, 17 January). In April it attacked the Alcoa and Falconbridge mining firms for cutting back on their output (Radio Clarin, 1 April). Throughout the year the party continued to demand "definitive action" to find and punish the killers of two PCD journalists, Orlando and Edmundo Martínez Howley, murdered in 1975.

As the maneuvering for the 1978 presidential election began, the PCD strongly attacked Luis Julian Pérez, an independent oppositionist, who was seeking to rally all opposition behind his candidacy. In March the PCD accused him of being "an extreme rightist and ultra-reactionary politician" (ibid., 26 March). In April the Political Committee of the PCD accused Pérez of intending to persecute the Communists if elected (ibid., 2 April).

In September, Narciso Isa Conde, in a radio interview, emphasized the PCD's intention to continue to push for its own legalization. He added that the party would support "the desire of the Dominican majority for the democratization of the political life of the country" (*Granma*, Havana, 6 September).

The PCD continued its close alignment with the USSR. A PCD delegation attended the 25th Congress of the Communist Party of the Soviet Union, and the PCD sent a message to the congress (Radio Mil, Santo Domingo, 17 February; *Pravda*, 8 March).

Until 1976 the PCD published a clandestine weekly, *El Popular*. Now it is issuing a legal magazine, *Impacto Socialista*.

The PSP. When the PCD adopted Castroite views and tactics—mostly limited to verbal declarations—in 1967, a split occurred within the party. More moderate members, proclaiming support for the USSR and "peaceful coexistence," formed a new party, using the PCD's former name, Partido Socialista Popular. Despite its pro-Soviet stance, the PSP has not been recognized by the USSR, but it seems to maintain friendly relations with some pro-Soviet parties in Latin America.

The PSP was apparently relatively inactive during 1976.

The MPD. The MPD was formed by Dominican exiles in Havana in 1956. Originally its leaders included many persons who did not have Communist sympathies. After the death of Trujillo in 1961 and the return of the founders to Santo Domingo, it quickly took on a Marxist-Leninist orientation and those opposed to this left the party.

The MPD became a formal party only in August 1965. It was then pro-Chinese and was one of the most active and violent leftist groups, with considerable support among students and slum dwellers and some following in organized labor. More recently, like the PCD, it has sought a more respectable image, a development which has led to the desertion of its ranks by more violence-prone elements.

Among the leaders of the MPD is Julio de Peña Valdés, who has been secretary general of the Foupsa-Cesitrado trade union group. The party has some influence also in the CGT.

During 1976 the MPD experienced considerable internal dissension, which one observer characterized as a "crisis" (*Renovación*, 28 September). Little is known about the details.

In February the MPD denounced the Balaguer government as not favoring free elections. At the same time the MPD issued a statement calling on the PRD to "forget past experiments" and "return to reality" in preparation for the next electoral struggle. (LATIN, 21 February.)

In February also, on the 20th anniversary of the founding of the MPD, an interview with its top leadership appeared in the magazine *Ahora*. The leaders admitted that the party had committed "great and grave errors," but said it was "frankly on the road to their rectification" (*Renovación*, 24 February).

In October a document was circulated by a faction of the MPD calling itself "MPD Legalista." It attacked the party leadership for having centered its policies exclusively on opposition to President Balaguer, which it said had led the MPD into alliance with elements of the "pro-imperialist oligarchy in the opposition," and into mistaken involvement in guerrilla activities. It also accused the party of not having studied Marxism adequately and of paying insufficient attention to "class consciousness." (Ibid., 26 October.)

The MPD publishes an irregular clandestine paper, *Libertad*.

The 12th January Liberation Movement. As the MPD has sought a more respectable and recognized position in national politics, some more extremist elements have abandoned it. One such group formed the 12 January Liberation Movement in 1973 and subsequently participated in several terrorist actions. There were no evidences of its being active in 1976.

The PCRD. The Communist Party of the Dominican Republic was formed by MPD dissidents after the 1965 civil war, and is considered very extreme. The secretary-general is Luis Adolfo Montas Gonzalez. Membership is limited mostly to the city of Santo Domingo. The PCRD has defined itself as a Marxist-Leninist party "created in conformity with the thoughts of Mao Tse-tung," and proclaimed that its objective is to install socialism and then communism, through a "democratic revolution" (Radio Continental, Santo Domingo, 17 January 1971).

Aside from activities in the student field, already noted, the PCRD does not seem to have attracted much attention in 1976. Despite its supposed Maoist orientation, it was not reported by the Chinese as having sent condolences at the time of the deaths of Chinese Communist Party leaders, although several other Dominican groups were noted as having done so.

The MR-1J4. The Revolutionary Movement of 14 June derives its name from an unsuccessful attempt to overthrow the late dictator Trujillo on that day in 1959 by an invasion from Cuba. Although helped by Castro, many of the early leaders of the MR-1J4 felt that Cuban leaders had betrayed them, and the party was not pro-Communist until October 1963, when the government of President Juan Bosch was overthrown. Soon thereafter, the MR-1J4 attempted a guerrilla insurrection which resulted in the death of its original leaders. Those who took over evolved quickly in the Communist direction, particularly toward the then Castro version of Marxism-Leninism. The MR-1J4 has subsequently split into several factions, most of which were Maoist by the middle 1970s. These include the so-called Red Flag, headed by Juan B. Mejia; the Red Line, headed by Juan Rodríguez; the Red Fatherland; and the Proletarian Voice.

The Red Line group made considerable gains in student elections in 1976. It was also reported by *Peking Review* to have sent official condolences on the deaths of Chinese Communist Party leaders during the year, as were the Red Flag and Proletarian Voice groups.

Immediately after the death of Trujillo, the MR-1J4 was one of the three major political groups in the Dominican Republic, along with the PRD and the Unión Cívica Nacional. By 1976 all MR-1J4 factions were fringe groups in national politics with only marginal influence in the student and labor movements, and little or no general political impact.

According to *Peking Review* (30 September) the Red Line, Red Flag, and Proletarian Voice factions of the MR-1J4, together with an otherwise unidentified " Via ML," formed a "Committee for the Founding of the Workers Party of the Dominican Republic" and sent a message in the name of its constituent groups to Chinese party chairman Hua Kuo-feng on the occasion of the death of Mao Tse-tung.

Guerrilla Activity. Although most of the extreme left groups were for a number of years formally committed to the use of guerrilla war as the road to power, virtually all of them have abandoned that idea, at least as an immediate tactic. None of the traditional far-left factions made any guerrilla efforts in 1976.

In May, however, a hitherto unknown group calling itself the People's Revolutionary Army (Ejército Revolucionario del Pueblo; ERP) claimed credit for a shootout with a group of soldiers. In a note sent to the newspaper *El Sol* it claimed that it had killed two soldiers as "a forceful reply by the oppressed, with a dual purpose: defensive and offensive." It described itself as "an armed branch directed and oriented by the revolutionary vanguard." (EFE, 11 May.) There is no information as to whether or not the Dominican ERP has any connection with the Argentine Trotskyist guerrilla group which uses the same name.

Rutgers University   Robert J. Alexander

Ecuador

On 23 May 1926 the National Socialist Assembly proclaimed the creation of the Socialist Party of Ecuador (Partido Socialista Ecuatoriano; PSE), which immediately joined the Third Communist International. Two years later the "Friends of Lenin" group left the PSE and in October 1931 adopted the name of Communist Party of Ecuador (Partido Comunista del Ecuador; PCE) A Maoist splinter group, the Marxist-Leninist Communist Party of Ecuador (Partido Comunista Marxista-Leninista del Ecuador; PCMLE) dates from 1963. Factional divisions of the PSE have periodically produced other Marxist-Leninist groups, most notably the Revolutionary Socialist Party of Ecuador (Partido Socialista Revolucionario Ecuatoriano; PSRE), which broke away in 1962 as a frankly fidelista movement.

The PCE is estimated to have 600 members, although this figure may be conservative, and PSE membership is comparable. The PCMLE numbers no more than 200. The population of Ecuador is 7,014,000 (estimated 1976).

The military junta that assumed power in 1963 declared the PCE illegal, but the party remained intact through clandestine activities and its representation in various mass organizations. After 1966, when the government returned to civilian control, the party again began to function openly. In 1968 elections the PCE organized a coalition movement, the Popular Democratic Union (Unión Democrática Popular; UDP). Its candidates for president and vice-president both finished last in a five-man race, with about 2 percent of the votes. In 1970 the UDP was reorganized by the PCE and other small leftist groups in anticipation of elections scheduled for June 1972. Their efforts were halted by a military coup led by General Guillermo Rodríguez Lara on 15 February 1972 and elections were canceled.

The PCE promptly praised the regime as "revolutionary and nationalist." Legalized in 1973, it was the only party to back the Rodríguez government. It continued its support until Rodríguez was deposed by fellow military officers on 11 January 1976.

The new junta, called the Supreme Council of Government (Consejo Supremo de Gobierno), was headed by Vice-Admiral Alfredo Poveda Burbano, although the dominant figure was the former army commander, General Guilermo Durán Arcentales. The PCE Central Committee announced that, since it viewed the junta's policies as consistent with those of Rodríguez, it would "resolutely support all steps of the government to translate into reality the aspirations of the people," while opposing "any intentions of the oligarchic and imperialist forces to maintain their positions in the national economy" (*IB*, 31 January).

The government soon promised that power would be returned to civilian leadership no later than February 1978. In February and March 1976 the Minister of Government conducted an extensive series of meetings with representatives of political and economic groups as a precondition to the reestablishment of civilian rule. Following this "dialogue," the PCE objected to elections until it could be certain that progressive development would continue. In June the PCE reiterated its belief in the urgency of first realizing "fundamental revolutionary transformations that assure the country and the people a better life, social progress, sovereignty and independence" (*Granma*, Havana, 5 June).

The PCE Central Committee enumerated specific demands upon the junta. Among these were achievement of a democratic agrarian reform; total nationalization of the oil industry; defense of the

200-mile territorial sea; distribution of essential commodities by state agencies; price control on industrial items and popular consumer goods; rent reduction; attention to regional and provincial needs; and maintenance of an independent, sovereign, pro-peace foreign policy. The PCE called for "a great patriotic front that will fight for the revolutionary changes that have been pointed out and that will prevent the Plan for Reorganization from being utilized by the oligarchies and imperialism." (*El Universo,* Quito, 9 June.)

The PCE maintained a sympathetic posture toward the junta, occasionally voicing criticisms. In August it expressed reservations over a speech by Admiral Poveda, noting that his recent discussion of government programs had omitted any reference to agrarian reform and oil nationalization. Nonetheless, the party praised the "philosophy and plan of action of the revolutionary and nationalist government." (*Granma,* 11 August.) Two months later it was among those parties naming representatives to the three commissions created by the government to prepare a new constitution and draft laws for subsequent elections (*Latin America,* 22 October).

On 6 November the PCE suddenly announced in *El Pueblo* its break with the military government, charging that CIA agents had infiltrated what was "obviously heading toward a fascist regime of terror and bloodshed." This followed a wave of agitation and a strike by electrical workers in Quito, Guayaquil, and Riobamba, during which several party members were beaten. By the close of the year, with the government delaying the process outlined for a return to democracy, the PCE stood in unequivocal opposition.

Organization and Leadership. The Central Committee of 27 full and 15 alternate members chosen at the PCE's 9th Congress (November 1973) has remained stable. Pedro Antonio Saad continues as general secretary, a position he has held over three decades.

Saad was a founder of the Communist-dominated Confederation of Ecuadorean Workers (Confederación de Trabajadores Ecuatorianos; CTE) in 1944, and has served as its general secretary. The CTE, oldest of Ecuador's three national labor organizations, also claims to be the largest, with some 60,000 members. It is led by Juan Basquez Bastidas. The CTE is a member of the Communist-front World Federation of Trade Unions (WFTU).

In 1976 there was greater labor agitation than had occurred under the military in earlier years, and the CTE played a central role. This had been signaled on 13 November 1975 when the CTE joined with the other two labor organizations in a nationwide 12-hour strike calling for a wide array of concessions to labor. The collaboration proved effective, with trade union leaders explaining their action as directed "against the oligarchies, against imperialism and fascism" (*WFTU Flashes,* December). More often, however, the three union centers competed for support. The CTE also directed its fire at alleged Maoism.

This concern was suggested in a joint declaration of the CTE and the Central Council of Soviet Trade Unions which denounced Maoism for its anti-Sovietism and "its collaboration with the forces of reaction, imperialism and fascism in Latin America and other parts of the globe" (ibid., 17 March 1976). In April, at the congress of the Federación de Trabajadores de Pichincha (FTP), a statewide organization, police broke into the meeting hall to arrest some 50 workers, an act denounced by the FTP vice-president as the work of Maoist agitators. It was charged that members of a pro-Peking "Peoples Committee" had joined the police in the action. While CTE leaders ultimately retained control of the FTP, they attacked opponents as Maoists guilty of provocation and misguided ambition. The latter responded that the pro-Soviets had actually been responsible, aided by members of the "so-called Communist Party of Ecuador" who prevented many delegates from entering the hall.

The CTE remained publicly active through such events as the August meetings in Babahoyo and Cuenca to demand the nationalization of oil. Again working with the other two labor entities, the CTE through its weekly *El Pueblo* protested government petroleum policy and accused Gulf Oil of abuse and aggression against national interests (*Granma,* 5 August). In another venture the CTE called a general strike for 15 October in Quito and Guayaquil. Neither of the other two federations joined in, however, and the intended 24-hour work stoppage failed.

In addition to the CTE, PCE influence over labor is exercised through two of the nation's peasant organizations, the Coastal Farm Workers Federation (Federación de Trabajadores Agrícolas del Litoral) and the Ecuadorean Federation of Indians (Federación Ecuatoriana de Indios).

Of greater importance is the PCE youth wing, the Communist Youth of Ecuador (Juventud Comunista Ecuatoriana; JCE). The JCE is often embroiled in conflict with groups of pro-Chinese students.

A typical case arose in April on the eve of a Latin American student conference scheduled for Quito. The JCE Central Committee attacked the meeting as an effort to create a counterweight to the Communist Continental Latin American Student Organization (Organización Continental Latino-americana de Estudiantes; OCLAE). It charged that a small band of Maoists in the leadership of the national Federation of Ecuadorean University Students (Federación Estudiantil Universitaria Ecuatoriana; FEUE) was betraying the student movement through divisionist tactics, (Ibid., 7 April.) JCE influence in FEUE has generally been dominant, but such periodic clashes remain common.

Party Internal Affairs. In 1976 the most important PCE event was a special meeting in Guayaquil on 23 May commemorating the party's fiftieth anniversary. Congratulations were received from the USSR, and Pedro Saad pledged PCE efforts on behalf of peace and against imperialist aggression and cold war policies; unqualified support for the USSR was also promised (*Granma,* 26 May). In an interview with *Pravda,* Saad declared: "Broad perspectives are open to the communists of Ecuador, composed of the forces of the people, whose consciousness and level of organization are growing. We enjoy the certain support of the socialist camp and of the glorious Soviet Union." (Ibid., 24 May.)

Domestic Views. The "Political Resolution" of the 1973 PCE congress viewed some policies of the military government as at least partly constructive. This attitude continued in 1976 until the PCE break with the government in November. In addition, the party continued to attack domestic non-progressive elements. It demanded continued suppression of those involved in General González Alvear's September 1975 rightist coup attempt (*IB,* 31 January 1976). The local oligarchy was denounced for attempting to impose fascism on the masses (*Granma,* 28 February). Ecuadorean capitalists were attacked for complicity with transnational interests in attempting to strengthen the ties of dependency (ibid., 12 May).

A detailed statement following the 24-25 January plenum of the Central Committee warned of increasing activity by "imperialism and the domestic oligarchy" and urged "political unity with the broadest possible forces," in which a political alliance with the "Revolutionary-Socialist parties is of the utmost importance." Maoist tendencies were again cited as responsible for "division and discord in the popular movement." (*IB,* 30 April.)

International Views. Pedro Saad, in March 1976, attended the 25th Congress of the Communist Party of the Soviet Union (CPSU). A month earlier the PCE newspaper *El Pueblo* editorialized that the CPSU was fulfilling its internationalist duty in supporting movements for liberation and national independence. The PCE also sent a lengthy encomium to the congress, and Saad expressed the debt of Ecuador's Communists to the CPSU and to Marxist-Leninist principles. (*FBIS,* 10 March.)

Saad also attended the 1st Congress of the Cuban Communist Party. Cuba's dispatching of troops to Angola was hailed as an appropriate response to the "criminal" intervention by international imperialist and reactionary forces. Criticism was frequently directed toward the Chilean government, which was accused of torturing political prisoners (*Granma,* 17 July). The message to the CPSU congress also proclaimed PCE sympathy with "progressive forces" fighting for freedom and socialism in Brazil, Chile, Guatemala, Haiti, Paraguay, and Uruguay (*FBIS*, 10 March).

Publications. The PCE publishes the weekly *El Pueblo* in Guayaquil. Since the 1972 military coup it has appeared with occasional interruptions because of financial difficulties.

The PCMLE. In January 1976 a delegation from the Marxist-Leninist Communist Party of Ecuador visited six Chinese cities. Shortly thereafter the PCMLE expressed condolences over the death of Chou En-lai. (*Peking Review*, 9, 30 January.) In September the PCMLE sent a wreath to the mourning hall following the death of Mao Tse-tung.

The PCMLE organ is *En Marcha*.

The University of North Carolina   John D. Martz

El Salvador

The Communist Party of El Salvador (Partido Comunista de El Salvador; PCES) was officially founded in March 1930 and has been illegal since its attempted revolt in 1932. It currently operates through participation in the legal party known as the National Democratic Union (Unión Democrática Nacionalista; UDN) and is influential with the National Revolutionary Movement (Movimiento Nacional Revolucionario; MNR). Various guerrilla groups have been linked to the PCES.

The PCES is pro-Soviet. It is estimated to have 100 to 200 members. El Salvador, the smallest and most densely populated country on the mainland of the Western Hemisphere, has a population of more than four million.

Within the country there is a pronounced and growing gap between rich and poor, while the government, behind its democratic façade, is a one-party dictatorship with a revolving presidency. The current president is Colonel Arturo Armando Molina. Elections are scheduled for February 1977 and the ruling Party of National Conciliation (Partido Conciliación Nacional; PCN) has nominated General Carlos Humberto Romero, whose election is assured.

Leadership and Organization. The PCES secretary-general continues to be Jorge Shafick Handal; the deputy secretary-general is Roberto Castellanos Calvo. Luis Suarez, of the Political Commission of the Central Committee, and Lorenzo Vásquez are also prominent in party affairs. The party controls a newspaper, *Voz Popular*, and the major labor union of the country, the United Federation of Salvadorian Unions (Federación Unida de Sindicatos Salvadoreños; FUSS), with some 12,000 members.

There are a number of active guerrilla movements, the most important being the People's Revolutionary Army (Ejército Revolucionario del Pueblo; ERP), which was formerly linked to the

PCES but has split several times and currently appears to be dominated by Maoists. The most recent split of the ERP produced the Armed Forces of the National Resistance (Fuerzas Armadas de Resistencia Nacional; FARN), a group supposedly loyal to the late Roque Dalton Garciá, a leader of the PCES and the ERP who was murdered in an ERP dispute in May 1975. The FARN is pro-Soviet and pro-Cuban. Possibly the most violent and active of the revolutionary guerrilla movements is the Popular Liberation Force (Fuerzas Populares de Liberación; FPL), which is Maoist-Castroite in orientation. The Workers' Revolutionary Organization (Organización Revolucionario de Trabajadores; ORT) also remains active and is hostile to the PCES.

Domestic Activities. During 1976 the activiites of the PCES and its splinter groups were conditioned by four major events: the elections of 14 March, the arrest of the Armed Forces chief of staff in New York in May, the renewed hostilities with Honduras in July, and the government's land reform program, which began in August.

The period before the elections for the unicameral legislature and the mayorial posts of the *municipios* was marked by continuing revolutionary violence (*Latin American Report,* March). The ERP had warned the government in November 1975 not to try to prevent its activities, or else to expect a "fighting reply" (*FBIS,* 1 December). Soon the ERP was engaged in a distruptive campaign which included the killing of two customs police, while its rival, the "Farabundo Martí" group of the FPL kidnapped and later released the socially prominent Benjamín Sol Millet. Early March saw both groups planting bombs in the capital, including one set off by the ERP at the headquarters of the PCN.

Meanwhile, the legally constituted parties of the National Opposition Union (Union Nacional Oppositaria; UNO), which includes the UDN and MNR along with the Christian Democrats, attempted to contest the election, but soon found that new electoral laws made its participation a virtual impossibility. Although the MNR advocated continued efforts to elect candiates, the UNO decided to withdraw from all races. "If they tried that in a fascist regime," said President Molina, "they would be forced to participate in the elections." (*FBIS,* 2 March.) Shortly thereafter, the government refused the UNO permission to withdraw its candidates, and their names appeared on the ballots. The PCN won every seat in congress and every contest for mayor (*Latin America,* 2 April).

These high-handed actions of the government caused considerable protest from the PCES and all opposition groups, but no sooner had this indignation subsided than the country was stirred by reports that the chief of staff of the Armed Forces, Colonel Manuel Alfonso Rodríguez, had been arrested by the FBI in New York for allegedly trying to sell 10,000 submachine guns to the Mafia for $2.5 million. The UDN and MNR quickly demanded an investigation. (*Latin America,* 21 May.)

During July, border tension between El Salvador and Honduras rose to a higher pitch than at any time since 1970, and fighting broke out. The PCES, through its newspaper *Voz Popular,* denounced the fighting and demanded a peaceful solution to the border problem (*FBIS,* 29 August). Also in July, the left staged demonstrations to honor the memory of those killed in the "Miss Universe" riots of 30 July 1975.

The government of President Molina created a difficult situation for the PCES when it launched a land reform scheme in August. This scheme created the Institute of Agrarian Transformation, which set out to buy or expropriate parts of large landholdings in the eastern part of the country for the benefit of the landless peasants. At a discussion of this project at the Agronomy Department of the National University, PCES leader Roberto Castellanos Calvo supported the reform and accused the landholders of trying to block it.

This drew a disclaimer from President Molina, who said that PCES support did not mean that the government and the Communist party were in agreement (ibid., 23 August). More militant organizations, such as the FPL, attacked not only the government's program, but also the PCES and *Voz Popular* for approving it. As so often in the past, the more radical leftist groups were attempting to cast the PCES in the unwelcome role of a government stooge. As a result Jorge Shafick Handal clarified his party's position in a five-hour speech at the National University on 28 September, terming the government's land reform scheme "radical only in appearance" and calling upon all left-wing groups to provide a suitable alternative plan (ibid., 1 October).

Despite their experience in the last elections, the UNO parties decided in early October to contest the coming presidential election, naming the exiled Christian Democratic leader José Napoleón Duarte as their candidate.

International Activities and Contacts. In November 1975, TASS interviewed Lorenzo Vásquez, who obligingly denounced the Peking government as flirting with U.S. imperialism and promised solidarity with the USSR (*FBIS,* 24 November). The next month, Roberto Castellanos Calvo led a delegation of the PCES to Cuba, where they visited such installations as the Laboratorio Central de Telecomunicaciones in Havana (*Granma,* Havana, 20 December). PCES secretary-general Handal visited Romania in 1975, and in May 1976 a PCES delegation led by Luis Suarez went to that country to consolidate the links between the two Communist parties.

Eastern Connecticut State College   Thomas P. Anderson

Guadeloupe

Guadeloupe's Communist party, the Parti Communiste Guadeloupéen (PCG), was born in 1944. In 1958, under pressure from nationalist movements to change Guadeloupe from a French Overseas Department to an autonomous or independent state, it transformed itself from a federation within the French Communist Party (PCF) to an autonomous party with close links with its former parent. Since the May 1968 general strike in France the PCG, like the PCF, has been challenged as too conservative and bureaucratic by an assortment of small groups of pro-Chinese, nationalists, Trotskyites, and others collectively called "gauchistes."

Unlike some of these far-left movements, however, the PCG is legal and is represented in the French legislature as well as in the local General Council. For example, Hégésippe Ibéné, PCG mayor of Sainte-Anne, is one of Guadeloupe's representatives in the National Assembly; Marcel Gargar, allied with the party, represents Guadeloupe in the Senate. In the March 1976 elections for half of the 36 members of the General Council, three out of four Communist incumbents won, and one new PCG member took his seat. As a result, the body is dominated by seven Communist councillors allied with seven socialist, five progressive, and two unaffiliated councillors. Since its main purpose is to approve the local budget submitted by the appointed prefect, its influence is not great.

The PCG's reported 3,000 members account for less than one percent of Guadeloupe's population of 325,000. The party nonetheless succeeds in maintaining the above elected officials in office and also the mayors of major towns and cities such as Basse-Terre, the capital, and Point-à-Pitre, the major port and industrial center.

Leadership and Organization. Guy Daninth, first secretary of the PCG, celebrated his 50th birthday and the 31st anniversary of his party membership in 1976.

At the base of party structure are very small cells named after prominent personalities in party history. For example, the cell Amédée Fengarol is named after a former Communist mayor of Point-à-Pitre. Most party members are workers and professionals.

Linked with the PCG is Guadeloupe's largest trade union, the General Confederation of Labor of Guadeloupe (CGTG), which has ties with the French General Confederation of Labor (CGT). Other PCG groupings, such as those of youth and women, have little influence.

More important, the PCG has followed the lead of the French Communist Party in allying itself with socialists and progressives in the island. The three parties form the Permanent Committee of the Guadeloupan Left (Comité Permanent de la Gauche Guadeloupéen). The party also supports actions and meetings of the League for the Rights of Man.

On 18 January 1976 all PCG elected officials met to evaluate their activities over the preceding eight years and to plan for the future. Among other projects was the Sixth Congress of the party, held in October.

Guadeloupe's economic crisis dominated discussions at the Congress: unemployment of almost 30 percent of the work force; the increasing dominance of the tertiary sector—69 percent of GNP in 1970 (*L'Etincelle*, 24 July); the decline in exports to about 25 percent of imports; the weight of civil service salaries and equipment on the budget—about 56 percent annually; an inflation rate of about 14 percent. Any improvement was considered to be dependent on political change. Therefore the party continued its demand for recognition of Guadeloupe as an autonomous entity or nation within the French Republic. Concretely, this change would mean the establishment of an executive responsible to an elected assembly with significant powers plus an organism for ensuring close ties with France.

Domestic Attitudes and Activities. The goal of autonomy dominated other activities during 1976 as the party sought to wed nationalist and socialist ideas. The failures of departmentalization, which had been supported by the Communists in 1946, were underscored in speeches and publications and resolutions. Failure meant the refusal of the French government to provide the same services and protections to French citizens in the Overseas Departments that were provided to French citizens in Paris; it meant the failure of government-controlled local radio and television stations, F.R. 3 or France Région 3, to carry news of interest to the PCG; and it most significantly meant the helplessness of the island in regard to control of prices and cultural activities.

Frequent visits by French government ministers—including the Prime Minister and the President himself—were seen as empty gestures or as efforts to offset the growing importance of the united left in France. Thus, strikes continued in almost every sector of the economy, as they have for the past several years. The PCG complained in particular about the fact that the minimum hourly wage in Guadeloupe stood at 6.80 francs, compared with 8.58 francs in metropolitan France. Dockers were successful, however, in winning a 12 percent increase in their wages.

The party blamed the government's closing of some sugar mills for the decline in sugar production which has hurt the economy. From a production of 1,847,000 tons in 1965, sugar declined to 923,000 tons in 1975. For this and other reasons young people have been leaving the island with government help; the estimated exodus is now about 6,000 per year. The PCG saw agreements between the Common Market and the associated independent states of Africa, the Caribbean, and the Pacific for the purchase of agricultural products such as bananas as another threat to Guadeloupe.

Most dangerous, however, was the threatened eruption of La Soufrière, a previously dormant volcano near Basse-Terre. At the end of March the volcano seemed to be coming back to life, prompting the prefect, who lived near it, to depart for Point-à-Pitre. At the beginning of July ashes began to fall on Saint-Claude, the closest settled area, and on 15 August the prefect ordered the evacuation of about 70,000 persons from the surrounding area. The absence of adequate schools, lack of new jobs, and forced removal of farmers and small businessmen from their land and shops strained the economy further, raising social tensions to new heights. When, after all the panic and hardship, the volcano did not erupt, the PCG denounced the prefect for incompetence and claimed the government had evacuated the area in order to weaken further its economy.

International Views and Policies. The PCG tended to ignore direct reference to the Sino-Soviet dispute although its support for the USSR was clear from its activities and statements. The party focused much more explicitly on friendship with Cuba. Guadeloupan delegates attended the First Congress of the Cuban Communist Party in December 1975. A Guadeloupe-Cuba Friendship Organization supplied information about the reported successes of Fidel Castro. And, in honor of the Cuban revolutionary poet José Martí, the city of Point-à-Pitre opened a cultural center. Delegates from Cuba arrived to participate. Articles in *L'Etincelle*, the party newspaper, informed readers about Cuba. Relations with other pro-Soviet parties were also close: in addition to meetings with the French party, the PCG sent representatives to meetings and congresses of the parties of the Soviet Union, Bulgaria, Czechoslovakia, and East Germany.

On the other hand, the PCG denounced French government aid programs in neighboring Dominica, Saint Lucia, and Haiti. The party saw the increased interest as part of a Franco-American agreement to control the Caribbean area in order to extract resources from the ocean and to preserve markets.

The Soviet party sent "fraternal greetings" to the delegates at the PCG congress (*Pravda*, 18 December).

Publications. The PCG's positions are made known to the public through its weekly newspaper, *L'Etincelle*. The island has always had difficulty sustaining a local press over a long period of time so that party newspapers tend to be the only ones that survive, and Guadeloupans depend on them for news about events of local interest. The PCG founded *L'Etincelle* in 1944 and inaugurated a new and modern printing plant at the end of December 1975 (*L'Etincelle*, 20 December). Each issue of the newspaper is ordinarily printed in 12,000 copies, and on special occasions the issues may run to 16,000.

The most important single yearly event for the PCG is the "Fête de l'Etincelle," a popular two-day fair held to support the newspaper and give publicity to PCG activities. Bad weather threatened the receipts in 1976, but as usual the affair attracted many thousands of Guadeloupans who, while not members of the PCG, are questioning the island's status and who also wanted to enjoy this rather attractive festival.

Howard University   Brian Weinstein

Guatemala

The Communist party in Guatemala, which since 1952 has been called the Guatemalan Party of Labor (Partido Guatemalteco del Trabajo; PGT), originated in the predominantly Communist-controlled "Socialist Labor Unification," founded in 1921. This group became the Communist Party of Guatemala (Partido Comunista de Guatemala; PCG) in 1923 and joined the Communist International in 1924. Increasing Communist activities among workers during the mid-1920s were cut off by the end of the decade and were kept at a minimum throughout the dictatorship of Jorge Ubico (1931-44). In 1946-47 new Marxist groups appeared in the trade union and student movements, organized in the clandestine "Democratic Vanguard." At an underground congress in 1949 this group took the name PCG. A prominent Communist labor leader founded a second and parallel Communist party in 1950, called the "Revolutionary Workers' Party of Guatemala." The two groups merged into a single PCG in 1951. In 1952 the PCG adopted the name PGT, which it has continued to use.

The PGT operated legally between 1951 and 1954 and played an active role in the administration of Jacobo Arbenz. Outlawed in 1954 following the overthrow of Arbenz, it has operated underground since then. Although the party has some influence among students, intellectuals, and workers, it does not play any significant role in national affairs. In the most recent national election, March 1974, the Conservative coalition candidate General Kjell Laugerud García won a disputed victory over his non-Communist left opponent.

The PGT is estimated to have 750 members. The population of Guatemala is 6,016,000.

Violence. Various guerrilla groups have operated in Guatemala in recent years, including the Revolutionary Armed Forces, which is the military arm of the PGT, and the Rebel Armed Forces (Fuerzas Armadas Rebeldes; FAR), at least some of whose members claim affiliation with the PGT. (See the next section.) The 13 November Revolutionary Movement (MR-13) is apparently defunct. The Revolutionary Armed Forces and the FAR are believed to have fewer than 100 members each, plus several hundred sympathizers.

The most active of the guerrilla organizations in 1976, and possibly the largest, was the self-styled Guerrilla Army of the Poor (Ejército Guerrillero de los Pobres; EGP). The EGP began its operations in late November 1975 when it assumed responsibility for the murder of an anti-Communist leader and proclaimed in bulletins to the news media "a war to the death on U.S. imperialism and its local representatives." Its membership is believed to contain remnants of leftist guerrilla groups who succumbed to the effective counterinsurgency tactics of the Guatemalan military during the "law and order" administration of General Carlos Arana Osorio (1970-74). Although the EGP has not claimed any direct affiliation with the PGT, a connection can be inferred (for this reason, the EGP's operations are discussed below in connection with the PGT's domestic activities). The guerrilla situation remains complicated by the continued existence of non-ideological groups of common criminals who engage in kidnappings for ransom and other acts of violence.

The high level of political violence that has characterized national life in recent years was only temporarily abated by the calamitous earthquake which struck the country on 4 February 1976. An estimated 25,000 persons were killed, 80,000 injured, and more than a million left homeless. Rampant looting necessitated the immediate declaration of a national state of emergency. By May the escalation of politically motivated acts of violence by leftist organizations and clandestine movements of the right prompted President Laugerud to threaten the imposition of a state of siege (*El Imparcial,* Guatemala City, 4 May).

Although spokesmen for the National Police continue to deny its existence, the self-named "Death Squad" continued its vigilante actions against known and suspected criminal elements. The group made its first appearance in 1974 as the successor to similar-styled right-wing organizations. In the crime wave which followed the earthquake, the Death Squad claimed to have carried out more than 30 executions of alleged criminals for their underworld connections (*Los Angeles Times,* 4 April). After several months of relative inactivity, the squad resumed its "execution of enemies of the regime" with the murder in Esquintla Department of a man accused of being a "dangerous criminal" (*Prensa Libre,* 26 August). It is widely believed that the group is composed of off-duty policemen secretly organized by supporters of former president Arana Osorio to maintain arbitrary order.

The resurgence of violence in the months following the earthquake created concern among political leaders of all tendencies. On 27 March the former mayor of Guatemala City and leader of the United Revolutionary Front (Frente Unido de la Revolución; FUR), Manuel Colóm Argueta, survived an assassination attempt, presumably by right-wing elements (*El Imparcial,* 30 March). In a press release on 13 April Colóm's group cited the indiscriminate nature of the violence and its effect on individuals of diverse social sectors (ibid., 14 April). Death threats were reported by leaders within both opposition and pro-government parties, including Mario Sandoval Alarcón, vice-president of the republic and director general of the National Liberation Movement (MLN), the country's leading anti-Communist party (ibid., 7 May).

The victims of terrorist acts have by no means been confined to politicans and members of the military. Persons with little influence in the nation's political or economic life but with some standing in their local communities have been the victims of torture and murder by unidentified elements. According to Amnesty International, during a four-day visit by two of their representatives in May the local press reported more than 30 killings, with evidence that the great majority of them were politically motivated. According to the mission's preliminary report, an average of 11 bodies were found daily throughout the country (*Latin America,* 25 July).

During a news conference in San José, Costa Rica, President Laugerud accused international communism of "dragging the country into a bloodbath." When he was asked about his responsibility for the violence in Guatemala in recent years, he replied that it was brought into the country by "Communists who are being directed, financed, and incited by the Cuban government" (*El Imparcial,* 18 May). The following week, Defense Minister Vassaux Martínez declared at a press interview that the National Police had achieved "a considerable degree of success" in reducing the level of common criminal activity. However, he added that 6,000 more officers and equipment costing $20 million would be necessary to combat the most recent surge of violence. He attributed the violence to "long-standing social and economic problems that cannot be eradicated simply by means of coercive measures," and said that the principal cause was "the failure for many years to extend an effective system of social justice to all the people." (Ibid., 22 May.)

On 28 May the National Police director disclosed what he termed "a vast conspiracy" on the part of a group allegedly planning to overthrow the government. Arms were seized from farms in Esquintla and from several houses in Guatemala City. The group was also charged with having participated in kidnappings, extortion, and murder. The ringleader was identified as Jorge Antonio Zimeri, one of three brothers belonging to a family of industrialists and ranchers that is closely associated with former president Arana Osorio. (Ibid., 29, 30 May.) According to outside sources, the Zimeri family has been repeatedly accused of involvement with right-wing terrorism in recent years, going as far back as the Mano Blanca extermination squads of the late 1960s (*Latin America,* 11 June).

On 15 June a former leader of the National Teachers' Front (FNM) was the murder victim of an unidentified group. The discovery of Rosa Barrera's bullet-riddled body in El Progreso Province prompted various teachers' unions to request international investigations of "the wave of rampant violence in Guatemala" (*El Imparcial,* 18 June). In his second state-of-the-union address before Congress, on 25 June, President Laugerud expressed his government's concern with the increase in "civil and political delinquency" (ibid., 26 June). Meanwhile, representatives from more than 20 popular organizations began meeting to consolidate their efforts toward the creation of a national front to combat violence. Spokesmen for the National Committee of Labor Unity (CNUS), the Association of University Students (AEU), the National Teachers Front, peasant groups, and numerous other organizations joined forces in rejecting violence "irrespetive of its origins" and calling for an investigation of "the constant violation of human rights" (ibid., 5 July). On 30 July, the president of Guatemala's prestigious Newspapermen's Association (APG) declared that it was "the government's duty to bring a halt to the whirlwind of violence that is leading Guatemala down the path of sterile sacrifice" (ibid., 30 July).

Subsequent events suggest that neither the government nor the popular civilian organizations have been more than nominally successful in reducing the level of violence. On 31 August, while Guatemalan police were receiving orders to undertake one of the biggest anti-crime operations in recent years, a government official was fatally shot by unknown assassins. The victim, Sergio Dávila Ramírez, was a leader of the MLN and a legal consultant to the National Institute for Agrarian Transformation. (Ibid., 1 September.)

The PGT. Leadership and Organization. Little information is available on the present leadership of the PGT or the party's structure. According to Central Committee member Otto Sánchez, two general secretaries and 19 ranking members of the Central Committee have been assassinated by "repressive agencies" of Guatemala since 1972 (*WMR,* March 1976). Following Humberto Alvarado Arrellano's murder in December 1975, Isías de León became general secretary (*YICA, 1976,* p. 484). Other prominent members of the Central Committee besides Sánchez are Antonio Fuentes and Pedro Gonzáles Torres.

The PGT has a youth auxiliary, the Patriotic Youth of Labor (Juventud Patriótica del Trabajo). Student agitators are active at the secondary and university levels, although direct affiliation with the PGT is disclaimed. Student leaders supported by the PGT have been unsuccessful in recent years in their efforts to gain control of the influential AEU. One such group, defeated in the May elections for a new AEU secretary, campaigned on a program of "revigorization of popular action within the university, accelerated transformation of basic university reforms, and a denunciation of systematic injustices and daily repression manifest in the country" (*El Imparcial,* 8 May).

The PGT also controls the clandestine Guatemalan Autonomous Federation of Trade Unions (Federación Autónoma Guatemalteca), a small and relatively unimporant labor organization. The federation became an affiliated member of the Communist-front World Federation of Trade Unions (WFTU) in October 1974. The most militant of Guatemala's union federations is the National Central of Workers (Central Nacional de Trabajadores; CNT). On 30 June the CNT issued a communiqué demanding "an immediate end to the pressures being put on the popular sectors" and protesting against the police raid on CNT headquarters on 25 June. The Central's secretary and other union members were arrested. (*Prensa Libre,* 30 June.)

The traditional military arm of the PGT, the Revolutionary Armed Forces, was virtually inactive in 1976.

On 11 March police reported the capture of a guerrilla cell which had been distributing Communist propaganda in Guatemala City. According to official sources, the group belonged to the Rebel Armed Forces. The FAR's activities have become more closely associated with the PGT in recent years.

Domestic Attitudes and Activities. Prior to the earthquake, most of the PGT's— and the nation's— interest was focused on the question of Guatemala's claim to Belize (British Honduras). The Belize question reached a crisis point of minor proportions toward the end of 1975. Guatemala reportedly sent armored troop carriers to a village near the border and increased the number of its troops in the region. Great Britain responded by increasing its level of direct troop support. On 29 November it was announced that Guatemala's foreign minister and the British minister of colonies had concluded a meeting to "establish the framework for broad negotiations" to take place in 1976 (*El Emparcial,* 29 November). Under the same date, a statement by the Political Commission of the PGT declared: "We Guatemalan Communists condemn the aggressive plans of Guatemalan reaction aimed at seizing Belize by force." The official position of the PGT is that the problem of Belize can and should be solved only by peaceful means. It charged that the "ruling reactionary classes" are guilty of exploiting the nationalist and patriotic sentiments of the people: "We are against the reactionary and anti-national policy of the Guatemalan ruling classes who are striving to seize Belize by force. . . . The struggle of Belize for self-determination is part of the fight against all forms of oppression and dependence." (*IB,* 15 January 1976.)

By late 1976, the Belize question was once again getting front-page attention in the Guatemalan press. Press reports in London referred to Guatemala's "warlike attitude" toward Belize. Guatemala's Foreign Minister reportedly attached little importance to such reports, pointing out that "Guatemala favors a negotiated and peaceful resolution of its sovereignty claims over the territory" (ACAN, Panama City, 11 October).

It is difficult to determine whether the PGT's Central Committee met on a regular basis during 1976, or where. Likewise, there is little data to reveal the content of any political resolutions that may have been adopted. Various party leaders continued to publish abroad, on an irregular basis. Otto Sánchez, the PGT's representative on the *World Marxist Review,* wrote in March of the "hundreds of leading and rank-and-file members of the PGT who paid with their lives in fighting for the liberation and independence of Guatemala." He indicated that the PGT had restored its leadership and unity "after the telling blows struck by reaction." He added that demonstrations "led by communists and other progressives" were taking place in Guatemala in spite of intimidation, and that they constituted "an open challenge by the working people to a government of usurpers." (*WMR,* March.)

On 2 May a group identifying themselves as members of the PGT seized control of a radio station in Quetzaltenango, Guatemala's second-largest city. In a recorded message the group assailed the government and called upon workers to fight for social justice. The previous night a mimeographed communiqué attributed to the PGT was distributed at Quetzaltenango's municipal theater, where a program had been organized by the AEU (*El Imparcial,* 3 May).

Observers reported evidence of PGT support for the celebration of International Workers' Day in Guatemala City. The large workers' parade and rally were organized by the National Committee of Labor Unity (CNUS), which includes some 70 unions. Speakers at the rally voiced demands for a system of social justice in Guatemala with equal distribution of wealth, effective freedom of union organizations, and an end to national violence and the persecution of organized workers. Workers also carried slogans demanding better working conditions and condemning "exploitation by the native oligarchy and Yankee imperialism" (*WFTU Bulletin,* 5 May). On 29 August, spokesmen for CNUS threatened to call a general workers' strike to support a walkout by state hospital employees. President Laugerud responded the following day with a national address in which he termed the strike by hosptial employees "illegal and immoral." He vowed that he was prepared to make use of "all the legal powers at my disposal to keep the peace." (*El Imparcial,* 31 August.)

The PGT intensified its propaganda activites during the week preceding the 28th anniversary of its founding. Terrorist bombs were exploded and propaganda pamphlets were distributed on the streets in Guatemala City, Quetzaltenango, and several towns in southern Guatemala. The PGT criticized the government and called on the people to "unite in defense of their rights and against the usurpers of power" (ACAN, Panama City, 27 September).

Without doubt, the most enigmatic aspect of the PGT's activities in 1976 concerns the degree of its involvement with the self-styled Guerrilla Army of the Poor. Considerable uncertainty exists as to the actual origin of the group, the composition of its leadership, its theaters of operation, and the basis of its support. However, given the ideological orientation of the EGP and the targets of its rural and urban attacks, some degree of PGT influence, if not control, appears highly feasible. The first two victims claimed by the EGP in late 1975 were strongly identified with anti-Communist activities. One of them, Jorge Hernández Castellón, served as a security adviser to former president Arana Osorio and was thought to have been responsible for the "disappearance" of many leftists (*Latin America,* 9 January). The government's initial response was to deny any official knowledge of the existence of guerrillas in the country. Defense Minister Vassaux Martínez characterized the murder of Hernández as "an isolated case of political violence" (*El Imparcial,* 13 December 1975). However, following the earthquake, persistent reports of both rural and urban guerrilla activity undermined his credibility. Much of the government's initial optimism may have been derived from the confirmed death of the peasant guerrilla leader Valentín Ramos, who was killed on 2 December 1975 during a skirmish with the army in Chiquimula (ibid., 3 December). However, it is generally believed that the organization's leadership was assumed by Romualdo Bueso, a former military commissioner, who proceeded to carry out several guerrilla operations in the region in March.

On 7 April an urban cell of the EGP stole an estimated $25,000 worth of arms from a sporting goods store in central Guatemala City. This action was closely followed by the assassination on 21 Arpil of Colonel Elías Ramírez Cervantes. In a communiqué sent to news media, the EGP declared that Ramírez had been "executed as an act of popular justice against those agents of repression who serve the interests of the rich and Yankee imperialism." Ramírez was also condemned for his service as a chief of the regional police during Arana Osorio's government. He was singled out as being responsible for the disappearance and assassination of six members of the PGT's Central Committee in 1972, including the then general secretary. (Ibid., 22 April.) In May the EGP took credit for the burning of vast sugar-cane fields on the country's southern coast as part of its strategy to "disrupt the economy of the people's enemies." In a similar action, the group assumed responsibility for the burning of four trucks transporting coffee in Sacatepéquez Province. The trucks belonged to a family whom the EGP accused of having threatened peasants with eviction from their lands. (Ibid., 17 May.) In late July police reported the discovery of a clandestine arms factory located in a small town near the capital. The announcement coincided with a statement by the EGP that three of its members had been killed on the same day and in the same town in an armed clash with government security forces. Two of the three were reportedly students at San Carlos University. (Ibid., 29 July.)

In a communiqué sent to *El Imparcial* in August, the EGP claimed responsibility for the assassination of Miguel Sánchez Herrador, a former army officer who had supervised anti-guerrilla operations on the southern coast. The EGP also took credit for the burning of six tractors on a large estate in the region of El Quiché. The incident was intended to serve as a warning to other large landowners in the region to "cease repressive measures against peasants and rural workers." (Ibid., 9 August.) At a subsequent press conference, the commander for the military zone of El Quiché announced that "Communist guerrillas have invaded the jungle areas of El Quiché and Huehuetenango and also the mountainous regions of Sololá." Peasants were reportedly being recruited and trained at various guerrilla base camps, while regular army patrols and special "green beret" counter-insurgency units were engaged in search and destroy missions. Newsmen were informed that recent skirmishes in the area had followed guerrilla attacks on the villages of La Joya and San Diego. The zonal commander, speaking with the authorization of the defense minister, indicated that the guerrillas had been active in the area since the previous October. They reportedly adopted the name of the "Guerrilla Army of the Poor" after previous names had lost their appeal among peasant groups. (Ibid., 26 August.) It was reported in October that the EGP had begun to operate a clandestine radio station calling itself Radio Rebelde, "the voice of the Poor People's Guerrilla Army" (ACAN, Panama City, 23 October).

International Positions and Contacts. The PGT's positions on international issues follow closely those of the USSR. In its message of greeting to the 25th Congress of the Communist Party of the Soviet Union (CPSU) the Central Committee praised the "consistent and realistic foreign policy of the Soviet Union that has led to the establishment of conditions favorable for the cause of international détente, peace throughout the world, and the broadest international cooperation." The PGT expressed its "profound gratitude" to the Soviet working people for their solidarity with the Communists and working people of Guatemala. The statement also hailed the successes of the peoples of Indochina and Angola "in their struggle for the independence and freedom of their motherland against the U.S. aggressors." Within the Western Hemisphere, the PGT affirmed its oppostiion to the "reactionary dictatorial regimes" in Chile, Uruguay, Brazil, Paraguay, and Nicaragua, and expressed approbation of the "liberation struggle of the fraternal peoples of Peru and Panama and the successes achieved in Mexico, Venezuela, and Costa Rica." (*Pravda,* 1 March.)

Delegates from Guatemala attended the World Conference of National Peace Movements held in Leningrad in late 1975. A PGT delegation headed by Antonio Fuentes attended the First Congress of the Communist Party of Cuba in December 1975. Fuentes expressed sentiments of fraternal admiration and respect for the Cuban people and cited the PGT's efforts to follow the "exemplary struggle" set by Cuba (*Granma,* English edition, 20 December). In July a PGT delegation met with officials of the CPSU Central Committee in Moscow. An unidentified spokesman for the delegation stated that the "policy of mass murders and cruel terror pursued by the dictatorship for many years has not broken the will of the Guatemalan communists" (*Pravda,* 17 July.) At the conclusion of a visit to Bulgaria in August, a PGT delegation expressed total support for the CPSU against "imperialism, reaction, and fascism" (*Granma,* Spanish edition, 31 August). A delegation of the Central Committee of the PGT visited the German Democratic Republic at the invitation of the Central Committee of the Socialist Unity Party.

Publications. The PGT publishes a clandestine newspaper, *Verdad.*

Washington College, Maryland   Daniel L. Premo

Guyana

The People's Progressive Party (PPP) of Guyana was founded in 1950. At its First Congress, in 1951, it declared itself a nationalist party, committed to socialism, national independence, and Caribbean unity. During nearly two decades following, the leadership of the PPP was predominantly Marxist-Leninist, but the party followers in general were not knowledgeably so. In 1969 the leader of the party, Cheddi Jagan, moved for the first time to align the PPP unequivocally with the Soviet Union and, in turn, the PPP was recognized by Soviet leaders as a bona fide Communist party. Party leaders say that the process of transforming the PPP into a Leninist party began in 1969 (*Mirror*, 28 March).

The PPP is a legal organization and represents the major opposition to the ruling People's National Congress (PNC), a party led by one-time PPP member and present Guyanese prime minister Forbes Burnham. Particularly since Burnham's break with the PPP in the mid-1950s, Guyanese politics has been heavily influenced, at times determined, by ethnic differences in the country—roughly 50 percent of the population is of East Indian descent (traditionally supporting the PPP), some 40 percent of African descent (generally supporting the PNC), and the remainder assorted Amerindians, Portuguese, Chinese, and racial mixtures. In 1973 Burnham was reelected for his third term while the PPP, still claiming to be the majority party in the country, received only 26 percent of the vote (and 14 out of 53 seats in parliament). Jagan (with some justification) protested that fraud and illegal maneuvers had prevailed. The PPP boycotted parliament until May 1976.

The membership of the PPP is unknown, though the number of active and influential Marxist-Leninists is probably no more than several hundred. In the past few years a number of blacks have joined the PPP, while many East Indians have drifted into the PNC.

The population of Guyana is approximately 825,000.

Leadership and Organization. In 1976, at its 19th Congress (see below), the PPP returned Cheddi Jagan to his long-held position as secretary general and elected its 32-member Central Committee. Among the prominent party leaders, all of whom are among the 14 PPP members of parliament, are Janet Jagan (PPP secretary for international affairs), Ram Karran (secretary for labor), Clinton Collymore (columnist for the *Mirror*), Reepu Daman Persaud (chairman of auditing and control commission), Narbada (secretary for economic affairs), Harry Persaud (organizing secretary), and Feroze Mohamed (secretary for youth affairs).

The Progressive Youth Organization (PYO) has traditionally been a source of strong personal support for Cheddi Jagan. The PYO held its 9th Congress in April and Chairman Halim Majeed sounded a familiar note in his Central Committee report: "Let us at this Congress assure our party and its general secretary, Dr. Cheddi Jagan, our unshakable and unqualified support. We have faith in the matured, able and dynamic leadership of the PPP." Then he added, ominously: "We must vigorously oppose all attempts by any force to liquidate our glorious party." Within two months Majeed and six other senior members of the PYO, including the leadership of the University of Guyana (UG) group, had broken relations with the PPP and the PYO, evidently along the lines of general dissension within the party (see below). Besides being head of the PYO, Majeed had been a member of the PPP for 15 years and a member of its Central Committee, Education Committee, and Propaganda Committee. He was secretary/manager of the New Guyana Co. Ltd., publisher of the PPP paper, *Mirror*. (*Guyana Chronicle*, Georgetown, 7 June.)

The Guyana Agricultural and General Workers' Union (GAWU), based in the sugar industry, claims to be the largest trade union in the country with 15,000 members. Ram Karran is president, Maccie Hamid is secretary-general, and Lallbachan Lalbahadur, a PPP delegate to the national parliament, is economic adviser. In June, Karran and Lalbahadur were appointed members of the Sugar Industry Labour Welfare Fund Committee. The GAWU became a full member of the Guyana Trade Union Congress (TUC) in June, but by the end of the year had become very critical of the organization. Although the GAWU represented 25 percent of TUC members, it was permitted only 17 percent of the delegates to the 23d Annual TUC Delegates Conference at the end of September. In contrast, 5 government-sponsored or -affiliated unions, representing 23 percent of the TUC membership, were allotted 23 percent of the delegates. In the September elections, the GAWU won no top leadership position, and only two of 26 positions on the Executive Committee. The GAWU immediately protested the nonproportional representation and called for changes in the structure of the TUC.

The PPP also sponsors the Women's Progressive Organization (WPO).

Party Internal Affairs. The core leadership of the PPP has been shaken on several occasions since Jagan's 1969 decision to become formally affiliated with the pro-Soviet Communist bloc. The first crisis occurred in 1969-70 and the second in 1975-76. Most of the recent dissension within the PPP was caused by Jagan's decision to respond to recent policies of the PNC with "critical support." Balchand Persuad, former organizing secretary, was expelled from the party in mid-1975. Harry Lall, former PPP leader in parliament and head of the GAWU, dropped out of the party in January 1976; Ranji Chandisingh, the party's top theoretician, editor of *Thunder*, who resigned his position as PPP deputy secretary-general in August 1975, withdrew from the party in March 1976. Over the next few months a series of other prominent members of the PPP and/or PYO resigned, including the aforementioned Halim Majeed. Chandisingh explained his resignation in a long open letter to the PPP leadership published in the *Sunday Chronicle* (Georgetown, 28 March). He wrote that his divergence had "centered particularly on crucial and far-reaching issues embracing ideological questions, the political line and policies of the party, and matters pertaining to the very substance of the party's development as a Marxist-Leninist party." He charged that productive discussion was no longer possible within the PPP because "certain leading members in authority are less concerned with the real possibilities for socialism than with the prospect of achieving personal power and prestige." The party, he said, had become prone to "unendurable temporizing, vacillating, and tedious rationalization." The PPP nourished "an almost pathological fear of becoming a political anachronism" and in response to recent PNC policies was seeking to be different for its own sake through offering the government a muddled "critical support." Finally, "the ideology of the working class" was "not deeply embedded in the membership or even in the leadership as a whole." The PPP responded that Chandisingh's charges were "spurious," asserting that he and his former comrades differed on tactics, not strategy. "His tactical position in practice virtually approximates that of the PNC; namely, unconditional support and little or no criticism of the PNC. . . . Chandisingh's tactical line would lead to the isolation of the Party and thus play into the hands of the PNC which has been using administrative and other methods in its attempts to liquidate the PPP." (*Mirror*, 28 March.)

PPP Program from 19th Congress. The PPP issued a statement at the beginning of the congress (31 July-2 August 1976) saying that the party was meeting this time "more purified and more united than ever, and in a stronger ideological position" (*Mirror*, 1 August). The congress was attended by representatives of fraternal parties from the Soviet Union, Cuba, the German Democratic Republic, Romania, Martinique, Colombia, Trinidad and Tobago, and Surinam. The PPP proclaimed its task to be

> the mobilization of all the revolutionary, anti-imperialist and progressive social forces into a powerful united front and the creation at this transitional stage of development of the economic, political, ideological, cultural, and social pre-requisites for the building of socialism. . . . The PPP will ensure that there is a close alliance and constant coordination between the working class and peasantry. The firmer this worker-farmer alliance, the greater will be the attraction of the middle strata to the united front." (*Mirror*, 22 August.)

More specifically, the objectives of the PPP are to: establish a new power structure from the grass roots by extending democracy at all levels and by organizing the masses for the broadest possible participation in political life; establish majority popular rule in place of minority, bureaucratic rule, at central and local government levels, through independently monitored free and fair elections; place political power at all levels effectively in the hands of the workers, the farmers, and the progressive sections of the middle strata and set up a national, revolutionary-democratic government; provide for control of members of the National Assembly and local authorities through the right of recall; democratize local government and extend powers of the local and regional councils; recognize and uphold the supremacy of parliament and make the National Assembly function as a truly deliberative body; ensure the observance of the fundamental rights laid down in the Constitution; guarantee all citizens inviolability of the person, freedom of residence, secrecy of correspondence, freedom of movement, and the right to work and rest and study; establish machinery for the speedy hearing and conclusion of all cases involving violations of constitutional rights; separate the state from the ruling party and party-affiliated and/or controlled organizations; provide for and enforce equality between the various ethnic groups and the sexes; repeal the National Security Act; substitute peaceful democratic methods for coercive bureaucratic-administrative methods of political struggle; enact legislation giving workers the right to elect the union of their choice for the purpose of collective bargaining; give state recognition to mass organizations which are the true, genuine representatives of the people and involve them at the relevant levels of the state; provide for workers' and farmers' control through democratic organizations in all enterprises relating to production, distribution, marketing; set up People's Action Committees in every factory, farm, neighborhood, office, or school for the mobilization of the people toward the conquest and maintenance of power; end compulsory national service for women and as a condition for entrance to the University of Guyana and other educational institutions, and for any form of employment. (Ibid.)

Domestic Attitudes and Activities. The policy of "critical support" for the PNC, initiated in August 1975 (see *YICA, 1976*, p. 489), led to the end of the PPP's three-year boycott of the national parliament. The party announced in May that it would henceforth send its 14 delegates to the chambers to fight for: (1) completion of the anti-imperialist process by the nationalization of foreign banks, insurance companies, and other monopolies; (2) ending semi-feudalism by a revolutionary land reform; (3) centrally controlled, planned proportional development of the economy with emphasis on industry and agriculture; (4) embarking on a non-capitalist road to socialism through expansion of the public cooperative sectors; (5) a massive education campaign at all levels for imbuing the people with revolutionary, scientific socialist (Marxist-Leninist) ideological consciousness; (6) training of administrative, scientific, technical, and diplomatic personnel in the socialist states; (7) respect for and observance of the fundamental rights laid down in the constitution; (8) implementation of peaceful democratic political processes; (9) separation of party, state, and mass organizations; (10) cessation of harassment and victimization of PPP members and supporters;

(11) recognition of truly representative mass organizations; (12) equal opportunity for all Guyanese; (13) special treatment for Amerindians to permit accelerated development; (14) democratization of local government; (15) creation of a democratically-run and people-managed national People's Militia, with branches in every city block, village, and settlement; (16) enactment of integrity legislation and a commission with "watchdog committees" to probe corruption and theft of public property; (17) development of the closest relations in all aspects with the world socialist community headed by the Soviet Union. (*Mirror*, 30 May.)

The PNC had incorrect stands on many of these issues, according to the PPP, and these constituted obstacles to real national unity (see *Mirror*, 9 May), though some PNC policies had been improved by the end of the year. The PPP gave its backing to the nationalization of the massive holdings of the British Booker McConnell at mid-year, but it was furious with Prime Minister Burnham for describing as "political morons" those (like the GAWU) who advocated no compensation (ibid., 30 May). The PNC decision to establish "people's militias" was praised (ibid., 11 April) though as the year progressed alleged discrimination against PPP volunteers led the party to write of the "PNC militia" (ibid., 14 November).

International Views and Positions. During 1976 the PPP repeatedly charged that the United States, upset by the leftward direction of events in Guyana, was trying to "destabilize" the country. Some allegations from the USA and elsewhere—as to, for example, the supposed presence of thousands of Chinese and Cuban troops in Guyana—should be refuted by calling for independent investigators from the UN or some such organization. Jagan said that Cuban troops should be invited to defend Guyana if it was threatened by neighboring countries with territorial claims (*Washington Post*, 13 March). Guyana would be still more secure if relations with the socialist world would be further developed. A party statement in early April called upon the PNC government to stop attacking the Soviet Union—with references to "two superpowers," "two imperialisms," and the like—and at the same time refrain from praising the People's Republic of China. (*Mirror*, 4 April.) Jagan put the PPP position with respect to the Soviet Union very clearly in his "Straight Talk" column in *Mirror* (29 February):

> Firstly, the USSR has demonstrated that it is a consistent champion for the liberation of the exploited and oppressed peoples everywhere, in particular in the "third world." Secondly, countries in Asia, Africa, the Middle East, Latin America and the Caribbean—as Cuba, Vietnam, Bangladesh, Angola, etc.—have shown that in the struggle against imperialism for necessary deep-going economic and social transformations, the help of the socialist community headed by the Soviet Union is vital. To take any other position is not only stupid but dangerous.

Publications. The PPP's newspaper, *Mirror*, is edited by Janet Jagan. Its theoretical journal, *Thunder*, was edited by Ranji Chandisingh until his resignation from the party.

William E. Ratliff

Hoover Institution
Stanford University

Haiti

The United Party of Haitian Communists (Parti Unifié des Communistes Haitiens; PUCH) was formed in 1969 by the merging of the Party of the Union of Haitian Democrats and the People's Entente Party. (For background on these parties, see *YICA, 1973*, p. 356.) The membership of the PUCH is unknown, but presumed to be less than several hundred persons, most of whom are in jail or exile. The population of Haiti in 1976 was approximately 5,000,000.

All political parties in Haiti have been outlawed since 1949. In April 1969 a law was passed declaring all forms of communist activity crimes against the state, the penalty for which would be both confiscation of property and death. The government's anti-communist campaign which followed, under François Duvalier (until his death in April 1971) and his son Jean-Claude, has decimated the ranks of the PUCH. Most PUCH activities have been carried on outside of Haiti among exiles in Europe (especially the Soviet Union) and Cuba. The PUCH says it is disseminating revolutionary ideas, starting more cells in industry and agriculture, and forging links between the party and the workers, peasants, and other sectors of the population. The main party spokesman during the year was Jacques Dorcilien.

Domestic and International Views. During 1976 the PUCH charged that the main problems in Haiti were the Duvalier regime itself and its repression of all opposition, as well as political corruption, inflation, and the influence of foreign capital and intelligence agencies. The party claims that the Duvalier government is becoming increasingly unpopular and that underground opposition is responding ever more favorably to clandestine PUCH organizational activities. The party claimed a major victory for itself and its international allies in March when the Duvalier government released a number of political prisoners, most of whom had been detained since 1969. According to a PCHU statement (*L'Humanité*, Paris, 23 March) the Duvalier regime was not changing its political policies but merely forced to act by a groundswell of public opinion. The PUCH went on to demand the release of all remaining political prisoners; the right for all exiles of all persuasions to return to the country; the end of the state of siege which has been in force for nearly two decades; the repeal of the 1969 anti-communist legislation; freedom of activity for trade unions; and the restoration of democratic rights for all sectors of the population.

The PUCH's pro-Soviet international position was evident in the party's message to the 25th congress of the Communist Party of the Soviet Union (Pravda, 9 March) which praised the "tremendous successes of the Soviet international "peace policy" and national development.

Publications. The PUCH publishes the irregular, clandestine *Boukan* for circulation in Haiti. Several PUCH press organs are published in Canada and other countries.

Palo Alto, Calif.   Lynn Ratliff

Honduras

The Communist Party of Honduras (Partido Comunista de Honduras; PCH) was organized in 1927, disbanded in 1932, and reorganized 10 April 1954. In 1967 a dispute over strategy and tactics led to a division of the PCH into rival factions. Since 1971 there has been a self-proclaimed pro-Chinese Communist Party of Honduras/Marxist-Leninist (PCH-ML). A later division within the PCH led to the formation of the Honduran Workers' Party (Partido de los Trabajadores Hondureños; PTH).

The PCH has been illegal since 1957. In December 1972 the armed forces of Honduras took over the government in a non-violent coup and under the leadership of General Oswaldo López Arellano (previously president 1963-71), the situation in Honduras relaxed. The PCH, although still formally illegal, was able to operate more openly than before with occasional public meetings, radio broadcasts, and the opportunity to distribute party and other Marxist-Leninist literature in bookstores in the largest cities. On 22 April 1975, General López was replaced by Colonel Juan Alberto Melgar Castro after charges that the former accepted a $1.25 million bribe from United Brands to reduce export taxes imposed on bananas in 1974. For almost a year the PCH looked favorably upon the new regime because its important decisions were made by the Supreme Council of the Armed Forces and "not settled at the whim of one man," and because of its "declared intention to lead the country along the road of progress, independence and sovereignty, carry out the national development plan and enforce the agrarian reform law" of 14 January 1975 (*WMR*, June 1976). However, by April 1976 the PCH leadership had become critical of the "government's rightward shift" to the "ideological orientation of the most conservative wing of the bourgeoisie" and of the U.S. Embassy (*IB*, no. 14) and on 31 May withdrew its support.

In early June the director of the PCH weekly, *Vanguardia Revolucionaria*, charged that the Department of National Investigation was "preventing the printing and circulation of this publication of leftist orientation" (*FBIS*, 9 June). The weekly has been replaced by *Adelante* and *Patria*, both of which have appeared sporadically, and it is expected that *Vanguardia Revolucionaria* will resume publication in 1977.

The membership of the PCH is estimated at 650. The PCH-ML and PTH have estimated memberships of 100 and 150 respectively. The population of Honduras is 2,823,000 (estimated 1976).

Leadership and Organization. The secretary-general of the PCH is Dionisio Ramos Bejarano. Other important leaders are Rigoberto Padilla Rush, secretary of the Central Committee and member of the Political Commission, Milton René Paredes, a Central Committee member, and Mario Sosa Navarro, a member of the Political Commission. Padilla and Paredes have been the PCH's principal spokesmen in international affairs and Sosa has been the principal spokesman in domestic affairs.

Information on the PCH/ML is scant. It has no known publications and its specific leadership is unknown.

The PCH has been active in recruiting and organizational work among university and secondary students, urban workers, banana workers on the North Coast plantations operated by United Brands and Standard Fruit Company, and the peasant movement, but was "often forced to work underground" in certain local areas, according to Paredes (*WMR,* April 1975).

The PCH claims that students make up 20 percent of the membership. The PCH sponsors the Socialist Student Front (Frente Estudiantil Socialista; FES), probably the second-most important university student organization in the country. The FES has operated freely on the campuses of the National Autonomous University of Honduras in Tegucigalpa, the capital, and San Pedro Sula, the most important city on the North Coast. On 28 August 1976, Juan Ramon Ardon noted in the conservative Tegucigalpa newspaper *El Cronista,* that the United University Students Democratic Front (FUUD) defeated the University Reform Front (FRU) in elections in several faculties, the most important of which was the Law Faculty. The FRU is an independent splinter organization to the left of the FES. Ardon indicated that it "follows the Moscow line sponsored by Mikhail Suslov, one of those entrusted with guiding the policies of Communist parties in the Western world." He also charged that the University was "publishing texts impregnated with Marxist-Leninist theory."

The PCH also sponsors the Federation of Secondary Students (FESS), now in its sixth year, which claims to have 40,000 membership, a probable exaggeration. On 6 August the archbishop of Tegucigalpa charged that Communists were making efforts to "control" elementary schools in the same way that the University and the secondary schools were controlled (*FBIS,* 9 August).

On 26 July the commander of the 5th Infantry Battalion charged that recent "incidents between students and troops in Comayagua," an important city in the central part of the country, had been prompted by the PCH in an attempt to create chaos (ibid., 3 August).

The PCH has tried to influence both the Innovation and Unity Party (Partido Inovación Unidad; PINU) and the Christian Democratic Party (PDC), neither of which has been able to obtain legal recognition.

On 9 March the Melgar Castro government issued Decree 368 which created an "Advisory Council to the Chief of State," to start functioning 15 June. The Council was to be made up of 48 representatives, three principal and three alternate representatives to be elected or appointed by the army, political parties, labor and peasant associations. On 10 March, Padilla Rush charged the government with descrimination for not considering the PCH or the Democratic Left faction of the Liberal Party as deserving of positions on the Council (ibid., 12 March). On 19 April the PCH Central Committee said that the creation of the Council was a "concession to the ultra right" and termed the barring of the PCH an "anti-democratic measure" (*IB,* no. 14). On 6 May the Liberal Party and the National Party in a joint manifesto refused to participate in the Advisory Council until "free and honest elections" were held (*FBIS,* 7 May).

The PCH continues to recognize that the Supreme Council of the Armed Forces is a "heterogeneous body" in which some members "are more or less agreeable to structural changes intended to end poverty, backwardness and dependence," while others, "with conservative backgrounds, hold rightist views." (*WMR,* June). It did not comment publicly about the radicals or *peruanistas* who have looked to Peru for models of reform, especially in the area of agrarian reform, that might be implemented in Honduras.

PCH nuclei were active in the first four months of 1976 in supporting a movement by Christian Democratic-oriented and younger leaders to oust old trade union leaders affiliated with the Inter-American Regional Organization of Workers (ORIT) from the leadership of banana workers of the Tela Railroad Company and Standard Fruit unions. The younger leaders accused them of "being opportunistic and siding with whatever government was in office." The head of the Honduran Workers Confederation (CTH) and Standard Fruit Union leaders denounced these efforts to take over the country's unions as the work of Communists, charging that "the country's most recalcitrant leftwing sector both publicly and clandestinely advocates a revolution" and that this situation was condoned by the labor and social security minister (*FBIS,* 1, 16 April; *El Día,* Tegucigalpa, 8 April).

In the fall, the president of the National Association of Honduran Peasants (ANACH) managed to heal a split which the Communists had hoped to use to their advantage. In the spring, some reports (*FBIS*, 9 April) had indicated that ANACH would withdraw from the North Coast Workers' Federation (FESITRANH) because of the gains of the Christian Democratic—PCH coalition, but that never occurred. It is expected that ANACH will support leaders affiliated with the ORIT and CTH in FESITRANH elections in April 1977, in which the PCH will be active. The PCH's Paredes indicated that party members had been elected to ANACH's Executive Committee in 1975 "despite fierce opposition from the reactionaries," "but PCH influence is limited there, although strong in certain *seccionales* (local organizations).

Domestic Views. As noted above, the PCH originally supported the Melgar Castro regime, especially the five-year National Development Plan and the agrarian reform law of 14 January 1975. On 20 August 1974 the party's Political Commission claimed that Decree 253 of 1975 abrogating concessions to U.S. banana corporations was the "direct result of the prolonged bloody battles of the Honduran people against U.S. imperialism" in which "Communists played the principal role." The PCH also considered it "vitally important that the people demand the immediate setting up of a national banana corporation. . . . Moreover, the Communist Party holds that abrogation of the provisions on concessions should not be limited to the banana industry. It must be extended to all foreign enterprises, mainly those exploiting our mineral resources, and to the companies prospecting for oil and other minerals on our sea shelf." (*IB*, no. 23, 1975.)

By February 1976 the government had established the Honduran Banana Corporation (COHBANA) and the chief of state had reaffirmed its full support for the Union of Banana Exporting Countries (UPEB) (*FBIS*, 9 February).

One indicator of the shift by the PCH away from earlier support for the regime was a 7 January statement of the Political Commission charging that "reformist aspects" of the "bourgeois-reformist" programs begun by former president López Arrellano had been gradually "eliminated" and the programs "eventually turned into a plan of private business projects pursuing purely *desarrollist* aims. According to the PCH, the "popular masses" were "clearly disappointed" with a four-point plan presented 31 December 1975 by Melgar Castro for (1) continuation of agrarian reform, (2) implementation of the Tornasol tourist plan, (3) acceleration of the construction of a paper and pulp factory, and (4) adoption of measures to realize the El Cajon Hydroelectric project: "This *desarrollist* plan implies abandoning structural reforms—which could be financed through our own sources—and only leads to dependence on foreign capital. As a result of the announced four projects our foreign debt has risen by almost 1,500 million lempira [U.S. $750 million], which in addition to the 1,000 million we already owe will increase our neo-colonial dependency still more." (*IB*, no. 4.)

Further, the PCH said, "peasants cannot agree with the agrarian reform law, which contains many bureaucratic provisions and lays stress on conservative rather than progressive aspects." As a result, "although the agrarian reform law was promulgated a year ago, land distribution is very limited" and peasants felt compelled to occupy plots of land. (Ibid., see *YICA, 1976*, p. 493, for details of the agrarian reform law). The PCH was referring to various occupations of land which occurred in October-November 1975, one of which resulted in the killing of 15 peasants occupying an uncultivated estate in the Department of Lempira the weekend of 8 November by gunmen in the pay of a local landowner (*Intercontinental Press*, New York, 8 December). The National Front of Peasant Unity—made up of ANACH, the Christian Democratic National Peasant Union (UNC), and the Federation of Honduran Agrarian Reform Cooperatives (FECORAH)—had demanded on 9 October that the government distribute 370,650 acres of land to 30,000 peasant families, setting a deadline of 22 October for distribution to begin. When the deadline passed after Melgar asked the Front for more time in which to make a "positive reply," peasants began occupying land in various parts of the country. The shootings were the second major set of killings over land occupations since 25 June 1975 when 15 activists, taking part in a march on the capital to demand land reform, were killed in Olancho Department.

Subsequently, Front leaders held more meetings with National Agrarian Institute (INA) officials to study landholdings in various areas, to investigate confrontations between landowners and peasants, and to expedite the distribution of land (*FBIS,* 22 January 1976). Probably the most symbolic expropriation during 1976 occurred 9 July when the new INA director announced expropriation of various tracts of land including 1,600 hectares belonging to the Honduran Sugar Company, which were to be given to some 700 families (ibid., 13 July). Occupation of land by ANACH-and UNC-affiliated groups continued into August-September (ibid., 10 August, 10 September).

On 11 December 1975 the Honduran Council of Private Enterprise (COHEP), which has opposed agrarian reform, enlisted the support of the Honduran Bar Association and the Liberal and National parties for agreement calling for a "national dialogue" to study the mechanisms of a return to early elections and guidance of the nation without delay toward the achievement of a juridical system that guarantees political stability and economic growth" (ibid., 8 January).

The PCH Political Commission denounced the moves of the COHEP and its allies as "part of the machinations of the ultra rights [to] stop the process of democratic transformation initiated in 1969." Honduras, it said, "cannot resolve the grave problems of the nation" by early elections, and the "impoverished masses cannot resolve their present problems through the ballot box." Hence "national dialogues" should pursue "a different aim, namely to discuss the question of how to extricate the country from its impoverished condition." It added: "More than ever before we need unity of the forces really interested in implementing the structural reforms necessary to end the dependence and backwardness of the country. A democratic front could be formed by workers and peasant organizations, the reformist bourgeoisie, patriotic-minded military, progressive factions of the traditional parties, Christian Democrats, the Party of Innovation and Unity (PINU) and other organizations or groups favoring changes." (*IB,* no. 4, 1976).

International Activities and Contacts. In December 1975 a three-man PCH delegation led by Dionisio Ramos attended the First Congress of the Cuban Communist Party. In a visit to the Alta Habana Hospital, Ramos praised the support by Cuba "toward the Honduran people during the floods" caused by Hurricane Fifi in 1974 (*Granma,* English, 20 December).

Ramos attended the 25th Congress of the Communist Party of the Soviet Union (CPSU), 24 February-5 March 1976. In a speech Ramos rejoiced at the successes of the CPSU, and hailed "the CPSU's principled and invariable position" toward Communist China and the USSR's "desire to normalize relations on the basis of the principles of peaceful coexistence" (*FBIS,* 5 March).

The pro-Chinese PCH-ML was named by the New China News Agency among those sending condolences on the death of Mao Tse-tung (ibid., 29 September).

Although the Honduran government announced on 9 October 1975 that it would "shortly reestablish commercial relations with Cuba and other socialist countries" in order to increase the country's export bases, damaged by Hurricane Fifi and the depressed international economic situation (*FBIS,* 10 October), in June 1976 it was still studying the "possibilities of trade with Cuba" (ibid., 11 June).

Publications. The PCH publishes *El Trabajo,* a theoretical, political, and informational journal. Its weekly newspaper, *Vanguardia Revolucionaria,* has suspended publication. Party statements are often found in the *World Marxist Review* and that journal's *Information Bulletin.*

Texas Tech University   Neale J Pearson

Martinique

The Martinique Communist Party (Parti Communiste Martiniquais; PCM) is one of the oldest Communist parties, having been founded in July 1921. However, it has never fully recovered from the highly publicized defection in 1956 of its leader Aimé Césaire, famous poet, deputy in the National Assembly, and Mayor of Fort-de-France, the capital. Today membership is only about 1,000. The population of Martinique is 359,000.

In 1957 another change took place. Under continuing pressure from nationalist groups to change Martinique from a French Overseas Department to an autonomous or independent state the party transformed itself from a federation within the French Communist Party (PCF) to an autonomous party with close links with its parent. And since the May 1968 general strike in France the PCM, like the PCF, has been challenged as too conservative and bureaucratic by an assortment of small groups of pro-Chinese, nationalists, Trotskyites, and others collectively called "gauchistes." In addition, the Martinique Progressive Party (Parti Progressiste Martiniquais; PPM), which Césaire founded after leaving the PCM, competes effectively for votes in Fort-de-France, thus weakening Communist appeal.

The PCM is as legal in Martinique as the PCF is in metroplitan France. Although it is not represented in the French legislature, it had four councillors in the local 36-member General Council before the elections of 7 and 14 March 1976, when one of its incumbents, Georges Fitte-Duval, mayor of Saint-Esprit, failed to be reelected. With 20.7 percent of the votes cast, the PCM received more support than any other single party. The united left received 19,991 votes, and a coalition of pro-government parties continued to dominate the General Council, with 23,475. While regretting the loss of one seat in the Council, whose main function is to approve the local budget submitted by an appointed prefect, party members could console themselves with the knowledge that they control several municipal governments.

Leadership and Organization. Jean-Claude Darnal is first secretary of the PCM. Under the Politburo are sections and very small cells of one or two dozen members.

Closely linked with the PCM is Martinique's largest trade union, the General Confederation of Labor of Martinique (CGTM), which also has ties with the Communist-dominated General Confederation of Labor (CGT) in France. Victor Lamon, secretary-general of the CGTM, is a Communist member of the General Council. The party is also closely tied with the tiny Union of Communist Youth and the Union of Martiniquan Women headed by Solange Fitte-Duval, sister of the Communist mayor of Saint-Esprit who lost his Council seat in the March 1976 elections. Communist attempts to elect its representatives to the executive comittee of the National Union of Teachers (Syndicat National des Instituteurs) failed. The PCM-backed list received only 156 votes to 967 for the opposition.

More important, the PCM has followed the lead of the French Communist Party in allying itself with socialists and progressives in the island. The PCM, the Socialist Party (Parti Socialiste), and Cesaire's

PPM maintained in 1976 their "Permanent Committee of the Martiniquan Left." Trade unions such as the CGTM and discussion groups such as the Cercle Victor Schoelcher also joined it.

The PCM Central Committee met on 13 January to discuss the March elections, and again on 25 April to plan for the party's Sixth Congress at the end of October. The island's economic crisis and political status dominated discussions at the Congress, the first since 1972. The European Economic Community was denounced for discriminating against Martinique's products. The political-administrative status of Martinique as a department was deemed a failure because of unemployment (90,000 out of 190,000 active persons), an inflation rate of more than 13 percent per year, béké (local white) control of professional organizations, cultural oppression, and continuing exploitation of the island by international capital.

The party members alleged that the goal of the capitalists is to destroy the island's productive capacity once and for all under the guise of President Giscard d'Estaing's program of economic integration or "départementalisation économique." The objective, they said, would be to transform Martinique into a distribution center for European goods destined for North America. The only solution to this chain of events is political change, in the party's view. Autonomy within the French state is desirable because it would lead to local control over the economy without losing French aid which would be granted by a new government of Socialists and Communists in France. Recognition of autonomy would mean the establishment of an executive responsible to an elected assembly with significant powers, plus an organism to ensure close ties with France.

Domestic Attitudes and Activities. During 1976 the PCM threw its support behind numerous local strikes, a general strike on 4 May, denunciations of the alleged partisanship of government-controlled local radio and television stations (F.R. 3, or France Région 3), and the failure of Paris to provide Martiniquans with the same rights and privileges as have been provided in metropolitan France.

The party denounced reported government plans to deprive Martiniquan civil servants of their 40 percent cost-of-living allowance maintaining it for metropolitans working in the Overseas Departments. It warned the population about the steady decline of sugar production, from 92,500 tons in 1963 to 20,000 in 1972 (*Justice*, 29 January), and supported efforts of small sugar cane planters to get 156 francs per ton for their cane. Plans to close two pineapple firms were denounced as a betrayal of an agreement to reserve 40 percent of the French market for Martinique in the face of stiff competition from Ivory Coast producers favored by lower wages and Common Market agreements. Further, the PCM warned the government that the loss of 20,000 young people who emigrated between 1967 and 1974 compromised the future of the department.

Construction workers who went on strike in April and May were backed by the PCM in their demands that fired or laid-off colleagues be reinstated and that they receive the benefit of health insurance and family assistance like construction workers in France. Hospital workers, school employees, and others also went on strike. These events provided opportunities for the PCM to call attention to many issues and problems in the island—for example, the fact that the hourly minimum wage is 6.80 francs, compared with 8.58 francs in Paris.

Despite these criticisms of French policy, the PCM turned around to attack far-left elements such as the Socialist Revolution Group (GRS) for proposing independence as an alternative.

International Views and Policies. Strongly pro-Soviet, the PCM in 1976 sent messages to the Soviet party congress and delegates to the 22d congress of the PCF, the First Congress of the Cuban Communist Party, and the congresses of Czechoslovak and East German parties. Ties with Cuba became closer as the Martinique-Cuba Friendship Association sponsored a visit to Havana for 60

PCM members and friends. Cubans visited Martinique to report on their progress. The PCM newspaper reported favorably about Jamaica (*Justice*, 3 June). Léopold Senghor, the President of Senegal, was denounced for his alleged neo-colonial positions.

The PCM sent a message of support, through Cuba, to the Popular Movement for the Liberation of Angola. It denounced Haiti and Chile, one of whose warships visited Fort-de-France.

Publications. The PCM's weekly newspaper, *Justice*, has, through the 57 years of its existence, played an important role in transmitting information to the general public. Although only 8,000 copies are printed each week, they reach a wide audience.

The annual "Fête de Justice," an important island-wide event to raise money and publicize PCM activities, was celebrated on 4 and 11 July with Cuban participation.

Howard University   Brian Weinstein

Mexico

The Mexican Communist Party (Partido Comunista Mexicano; PCM) was founded in 1919. Originally it was called the Communist Party of the Mexican Proletariat to distinguish it from another Communist organization then in existence. When the other group collapsed in the spring of 1920, the party changed its name to the Mexican Communist Party, and it was recognized as such by the Comintern.

Since its inception, the PCM has been composed primarily of intellectuals, students, and elements of the middle class. Over the past few years, the estimated size of the party has been approximately 5,000 members. The PCM is tolerated, but it is not legally registered as a political party. According to the federal electoral law, a party must meet the legal membership requirement of 60,000 to enter registered candidates in national elections; it must also provide lists with data on all members to the government. The PCM has been unable or unwilling to provide this information.The party claimed that its presidential candidate in the 1976 election, Valentín Campa, received more than 500,000 votes. The government did not publish official figures because he ran as an unregistered candidate. The PCM does not have representation in Congress.

There are several other Marxist-Leninist political parties and groups. The largest was founded in 1947 as the Partido Popular by the late Vicente Lombardo Toledano, and the following year it became the Popular Socialist Party (Partido Popular Socialista; PPS). In 1963 the party merged with the Communist-oriented Partido Obrero y Campesino de Mexico. Like the PCM, the PPS appeals primarily to some intellectuals and certain elements of the middle class. Because it has been able to meet the minimum legal number to be registered as a political party (claiming 75,000 members), the PPS has presented candidates in federal and local elections. In the 1976 election, the party claimed it received more than 1,000,000 votes.

Two political parties were formed by former leaders of the 1968 student movement: the Mexican Workers Party (Partido Mexicano de los Trabajadores; PMT) in 1974 and the Socialist Workers Party (Partido Socialista de los Trabajadores; PST) in 1975, made up of former members of the PMT who separated because of political differences. The PMT claims 45,000 members; the PST claims it registered more than 100,000 voters for the 1976 election but the deadline had passed.

In addition to the PST, several groups refer to themselves as socialist. These include the Unified Socialist Action Movement (Movimiento de Acción Unificada Socialista; MAUS), made up of former Communists and dissidents from the PPS; the Socialist Organization Movement (Movimiento de Organización Socialista; MOS), which separated from the PST; and the Socialist Popular Youth (Juventud Popular Socialista; JPS). Other groups include the Students' Popular Revolutionary Front (Frente Revolucionario Estudiantil Popular; FREP), the Revolutionary Workers Party, and the Socialist Flag Party. The latter two groups merged at the beginning of 1976.

The Trotskyite groups in Mexico consider themselves to be "sympathizing organizations" of the Fourth International. The Internationalist Communist Group (Grupo Comunista Internacionalista; GCI) was founded in 1968. The Socialist League (Liga Socialista; LS) was formed a few years later as a result of a split in the GCI. At the beginning of 1976, a split occurred ín the LS, the immediate cause of which was a series of measures taken by the Militant Tendency (Tendencia Militante; TM) which won a formal majority against the Bolshevik Leninist Fraction (Fracción Bolchevique Leninist 2; FBL). The FBL includes most of the founding leaders of the LS. Other Trotskyite groups are the Revolutionary Labor Party, which calls itself "of the Posadist persuasion," and the Trotskyite-Leninist Faction of the Marxist Labor League.

The 23 September Communist League (Liga Comunista 23 Septiembre; the League) carried on sustained activities in 1976 as the major guerrilla organization in the country. Established in 1967 and taking its name from an abortive guerrilla attack on a Chihuahua army post that same year, the League operated in 1976 through various affiliates—the Red Brigade (Brigada Roja), the Revolutionary Command, the Arturo Gamiz Command, and the Fidel Castro Command. The League reportedly succeeded in incorporating various guerrilla bands. The press mentioned other guerrilla groups—the Party of the Poor (Partido de los Pobres) of the late Lucio Cabañas Barrientos; the Vikings Group of Guadalajara; the People's Revolutionary Armed Forces (Fuerzas Revolucionario Armado del Pueblo; FRAP); and the Spartacus Leninist League, formed in 1971.

Four political parties are represented in Congress—the Institutional Revolutionary Party (Partido Revolucionario Institucional; PRI), the National Action Party (Partido de Acción Nacional; PAN), the Authentic Party of the Mexican Revolution (Partido Auténtico de la Revolución Mexicana; PARM), and the PPS. The Pri is the outgrowth of the political apparatus which has dominated Mexican politics and government since 1929. To the right is the conservative PAN and somewhat to the left of the PRI is the PARM. Of the four, only the PPS is a Marxist-Leninist party. In the 4 July 1976 presidential election, the PPS and the PARM continued their practice of supporting the PRI, whose candidate, José López Portillo, was elected president with 18.5 million votes (7.4 million voters, 28 percent, abstained). The PRI won 194 of the 230 seats in the Chamber of Deputies and 63 of the 64 seats in the Senate. The PAN experienced a serious internal conflict and did not present a candidate. The opposition presented token write-in candidates who gained approximately a million votes between them—Valentín Campa (PCM), Pablo Emilio Madero (an unofficial candidate of the rump of PAN), and Marina González del Boy (of the newly-created Feminist Party of Mexico).

During 1976 there were numerous violent confrontations between students and peasants on the one hand and the police and army on the other. Economic problems led the government to devalue the peso for the first time in 22 years. The population continued to grow at a high rate, approximately 3.5 percent. Mexico is estimated to have a population of 62,159,000.

The PCM. Leadership and Organization. The leading organizational bodies of the PCM are the Politburo, the Central Committee, and the Executive Commission of the Central Committee. Arnoldo Martínez Verdugo, a leader in the party since the 1940s, has been secretary-general since 1964. The Executive Commission members include J. E. Pérez, Arturo Martinez Nateras, Gerardo Unzueta, Gilberto Rincón Gallardo, and José Encarnación Pérez.

Auxiliary organizations of the party include the Mexican Communist Youth (Juventud Comunista Mexicana; JCM) and several regional organizations, such as the Nadiezha Krupaskaya in Morelos.

Party Internal Affairs. The 17th Congress of the PCM, 9-14 December 1975, discussed such subjects as tactics for the 1976 election, policy toward the working class and peasants, international relations, joint actions and alliances with other parties and groups, and political and electoral rights. In April 1976 the Third Plenum of the Central Committee addressed itself to conflicts within the ruling class, further discussion of the working class, the alliance of local capitalism and foreign capital, and the need to reform the federal electoral law.

Domestic Attitudes and Activities. In the 1970 presidential campaign the PCM encouraged passivity and abstention, coining the slogan of "active abstention." In the 1976 campagin, however, the party decided upon an active participation. The 17th Congress chose a veteran Communist, 72-year-old Valentín Campa Salazar, to be the party's presidential candidate. His candidacy was also supported by the MOS and the LS (Tendencia Militante faction). The joint platform (analyzed in *Intercontinental Press,* New York, 1 March 1976) called for freeing all those imprisoned for political motives and abolition of the present Federal Election Law; possession of the land by those who work it and the elimination of landed estates; nationalization of basic industries; withdrawal of Mexico from the OAS and membership in the Organization of Petroleum Exporting Countries; and autonomy for the National University and for all other institutes and schools of this level, even if they are not called universities.

The electoral bloc which supported Campa's candidacy was the result of PCM efforts over the past few years. In an extensive interview (ibid., 31 May), Martínez Verdugo explained the PCM support for such a bloc. He believed that unity of the left offered a democratic solution to the political crisis of the country, bringing together both the left and the democratic forces (advanced sectors within the Church, the university, and the army, progressive businessmen, and even some groups within PRI). He was opposed to the PPS advocacy of a "patriotic front" unifying the democratic and left forces under government leadership—such a tactic did not take into account the fact that the interests of the big bourgeoisie were beginning to prevail in the government or that Mexican state capitalism was being transformed into monopoly capitalism. Hence, he maintained, the alliance of left and democratic forces must act independently and not as an auxiliary of the government. According to an article by José Encarnación Pérez (*WMR,* July), the PCM knew that the presidential election was a foregone conclusion and it was using the campaign to expose the violation of civil rights, including the rights of the working class. "Our purpose is to increase our mass influence, first of all among the working class, organize it more effectively, strengthen our own ranks and win over new organized forces . . ."

Both the 17th Congress of the PCM and the Third Plenum of the Central Committee dealt with labor problems. The party supported the 15 November 1975 labor demonstration under the leadership of the United Union of Electrical Workers of the Republic of Mexico (SUTERM) and criticized those union leaders who practice *charrismo* (a term taken up by the Mexican trade union movement in the mid-1940s and applied to the conduct of conciliators, leaders of the "yellow trade unions," and corrupt union leaders). The 17th Congress called for two different tactics: participation in the executive committees of leading trade union bodies and at other levels, and support for the clandestine organizations that have been formed in factories.

The party also concluded that the country was experiencing a deepening political, social, and economic crisis. This was evident in the conflicts within the PRI, the government, and the officially recognized parties, and in the deterioration of the economic situation. The needs of workers, peasants, students and other groups were not being met, and the despotic, paternalist presidential regime dealt with problems by increased governmental repression. As a partial answer to the crisis, the PCM and the MOS called for the establishment of an urban reform program that would freeze rents on working-class housing. Urban growth should be planned on the basis of expropriation of the property of land speculators, and the workers should actively participate in development plans. The PCM-MOS program declared that a national institute should be created, by absorbing the already existing institutions, to assume the responsibility for housing construction.

The PCM relationship with other political parties and groups was very flexible. In addition to an electoral bloc with the MOS and LS (Tendencia Militante), the party participated in two regional alliances: between the PCM, the PST, and the PPS for the office of mayor of Poza Rica; and between the PCM, PPS, and the Papantleco Liberal Party for the office of federal deputy, under the registration of the PPS. Guerrilla and terrorist activities, in the PCM's view, did not help the development of the people's struggle. Such groups as still believed in armed struggle were not only losing ground, but also playing into the hands of the most reactionary forces, who were fighting for a return to government methods that gave priority to repressive over political measures. When President-elect José López Portillo received a Communist delegation led by Martínez Verdugo and Valentín Campa, the PCM reiterated its position on several issues: the necessity for electoral reform, the freeing of political prisoners, and a cessation of "government repression against the democratic movement" (*Granma*, Havana, 17 August).

International Views and Policies. The 17th PCM Congress strongly supported the actions of the Soviet Union, particularly the policies of peaceful coexistence and détente, and was very critical of the Chinese government and party: "Great harm to the international Communist movement and progressive forces is done . . . by the present policy of the Maoists, who are making attacks against the Soviet Union, maintaining relations with the fascists in Chile, conducting subversive activity among the left-wing movement in Portugal, and aiding the pro-imperialist groupings in Angola. Our party believes that the Chinese Communist Party's actions must be rebuffed. For it is no secret to anyone that the CCP is attempting to pursue subversive policy within certain Communist and workers parties or that it is supporting splittist groupings" (*PRAVDA*, 17 December 1975). Thus, in contrast to recent years, the PCM appeared to be more pro-Soviet and less neutral in the Sino-Soviet dispute.

The PCM asked the Mexican government to establish diplomatic relations with the People's Republic of Angola. The request included a declaration condemning the Angolan policy of the U.S. government as intervention against the peoples struggling for Angolan independence. The PCM also declared its solidarity with the Cuban revolution and condemned those who attacked Cuban officials in Mexico and other countries.

Although the 17th Congress stated that the Echeverría government's domestic and foreign policies upheld the interests of the bourgeoisie, the PCM believed that the new world situation and the efforts of the left and democratic forces obliged the government to pursue an independent foreign policy. Thus the party supported the severing of diplomatic relations with the Chilean military junta, improved relations with Cuba, Mexican support for the establishment of the Latin American Economic System (SELA), diplomatic relations with almost all socialist countries, and the government's friendly statements about Vietnam.

When a Cuban jet airplane was sabotaged, with many deaths resulting, the PCM deplored the tragedy and denounced the organizations or Cuban counter-revolutionaries in various Latin American countries as being sponsored by "U.S. imperialism."

International Activities and Contacts. In December 1975, Antonio Franco, secretary of the PCM Central Committee, visited Hungary at the invitation of its ruling party. In the spring of 1976, Martínez Verdugo headed a delegation to the 25th Congress of the Communist Party of the Soviet Union in Moscow. He praised Brezhnev's report and said that the successful five-year plans of the USSR and progress within that country contrasted greatly with the situation in the capitalist world, which was experiencing a profound economic, political, and social crisis, and proved the superiority of the socialist system.

Publications. The history of the Communist press in Mexico goes back some 50 years. The newspaper *El Machete*, founded in 1924, was succeeded by *La Voz de México* (1938-1970), a weekly of the PCM Central Committee. The current weekly journal *Oposición* goes back to the same period. The Central Committee also publishes a theoretical journal, *Nueva Epoca*. Several Mexican newspapers and journals are Communist-oriented or pro-Communist, including the newspaper *El Dia* and the bimonthly publications *Política* and *¡Siempre!*

Other Marxist-Leninist Parties and Groups. The PPS is the largest Marxist-Leninist political party. Jorge Cruickshank García has been secretary-general since 1968.

In the 1976 election, the PRI and PPS cooperated on several levels. PRI spokesmen attacked the oligarchy, particularly the industrialists of Monterrey, and their reputed links with U.S. imperialism. The PRI charged that "a small, plutocratic, and pro-fascist minority" of businessmen and industrialists was trying to destabilize the government. Cruickshank complained of what he called "the offensive of the oligarchy, the right and imperialism against Mexico and the progressive attitude of the president of the republic" (*The Times of the Americas*, New York, 28 April).

As it has done since 1958, the PPS supported the PRI presidential candidate. Cruickshank explained that this tactic was consistent with the global strategy of the PPS: to attain the creation of a democratic and revolutionary front with all the progressive and nationalist forces. The PPS ran its own candidates for the Chamber of Deputies and also presented senatorial candidates from 22 states.

In addition to participating in electoral regional alliances with the PCM, the PPS joined the PRI in filing a request for the registration of common candidates for the Senate. The PPS-PRI document stated that the electoral coalition would strengthen the basic unity of the country's popular and democratic forces. Jorge Cruickshank, of the state of Oaxaca, became the first Mexican senator in modern times who was not nominally a member of the official party. However, a meeting in Guadalajara of PPS leaders of 13 states rejected the national leadership of Cruickshank because of his electoral alliance with the PRI. This caused a serious split within the party and led to the expulsion of four prominent members.

The principal informational organ of the PPS is *Viva Mexico*. The party also publishes the bimonthly *Avante*.

The PMT secretary-general is Heberto Castillo, reportedly a former close aide of the late President Lázaro Cárdenas. A PMT front organization, the "Mexican Movement for Peace, Anti-Imperialism, and Solidarity Among Peoples," petitioned the government to have Mexico recognize the People's Republic of Angola and the Popular Movement for the Liberation of Angola.

The PST secretary-general is Rafael Aguiler Talamantes. Jorge Sánchez is secretary of the party's Agricultural Workers Front. On 17-18 January 1976 the party held its first national leadership council, to train rank-and-file leaders within the labor movement. The council also discussed election tactics. According to an article in *Excelsior* (Mexico City, 29 April), the PST was involved in student unrest at the national autonomous universities in Mexico City and Puebla. The article also accused the party of leading peasant land invasions in Castillo de Teaya, Veracruz, which resulted in the massacre of peasants. The PST leadership stated that the peasants were defending their legitimate property when they were attacked by the police and "white guards," who worked for the large landholders.

The secretary-general of the MOS is Roberto Jaramillo Flores. The MOS-PCM electoral alliance agreed on the following: support the candidacy of Valentín Campa, agreement on an urban reform program, agreement on a joint electoral platform. Jaramillo emphasized the importance of supporting a policy of unified action with all forces willing to fight against imperialism and reactionaries and for democracy and socialism.

At the beginning of the year, the police announced the arrest of Guillermo Rousset Banda, a member of the Spartacus Leninist League and former member of the PCM. He was charged with homicide and the use of falsified documents. Two leaders of the Students' Popular Revolutionary Front are Eulalio Espinoso Marmolejo and Carlos Castrejon Bustamente. They stated that the FREP will take necessary steps to conduct a dialogue with the state government of Guerrero and put forth the university and popular positions on problems that need to be resolved.

The split in the Socialist League, one of the Trotskyite groups, led to the formation of the Militant Tendency (TM) and the Bolshevik Leninist Fraction (FLB). Each faction published its version of the dispute in different issues of the LS newspaper. The dispute began at the Sixth Plenum of the LS Central Committee, 14-15 September 1975, and came to a head at the party congress in December. At the congress, the TM characterized the FLB as "petty bourgeois" and requiring "reeducation" inside the factories. The Central Committee and leading organs of the party were restructured to insure a TM majority.

In addition to an internal power struggle, the TM-FLB dispute involved electoral tactics and ideological differences which those tactics produced. The FLB was very critical of the joint PCM-MOS-LS (TM) electoral platform. Although the FLB approved the presidential candidacy of Valentín Campa, it rejected cooperation with the PCM, which it considered to be a Stalinist party that collaborated with the bourgeois forces to defeat the workers. It accused the TM of abandoning the basic concepts of revolutionary Marxism by adhering to a reformist program of immediate minimum demands. The FLB also criticized the platform's foreign policy, which called for collaboration with the bourgeois governments of Panama, Peru, and Ecuador; it denounced the idea of a popular front between workers' states and certain bourgeois governments; it rejected the concept of peaceful coexistence. Instead, the FLB called for a government of the workers and peasants. Both the TM and the FLB continued to express their views in the fortnightly newspaper *El Socialista*.

The other principal Trotskyite group, the GCI, has been encouraging the TM and the FLB to heal their rift so that the GCI can proceed with its efforts to unify the Mexican Trotskyite groups. The GCI newspaper is *Bandera Roja*.

Although the 23 September Communist League was the major guerrilla group in 1976, other organizations did carry on limited operations. Papers seized by the police uncovered links between the rural guerrilla group, the Guerrero-based Party of the Poor (Partido de los Pobres), and the League. The Party of the Poor has not recovered from the death of Lucio Cabañas. In September 1975, newspapers reported that his successor as leader had been killed. In May 1976 the police in Guadalajara reported that five members (two men, three women) of the People's Revolutionary Armed Forces (FRAP) had been captured. All of them confessed to four kidnappings, several murders, and other crimes. They also complained about the "torture to which they had been subjected since their arrest" (*Excelsior,* 6 May). According to the police, an undetermined number of FRAP members were fugitives and the investigations were being continued. In June, a group calling itself the Armed Vanguard of the Proletariat released the 8-year-old daughter of an American businessman after reportedly receiving a ransom of $200,000 to $400,000.

Mexican and foreign newspapers have raised questions concerning the authenticity of the urban guerrilla 23 September Communist League—whether it exists, whether it is a tool used by the government against its opponents, whether it is a right-wing organization which assassinates leftists, support by the Soviet Embassy. The League apparently carried out sustained activities in 1976. The police published names and photographs of several League members. One highly publicized action of the League was the kidnaping of 16-year-old daughter of the Belgian ambassador. She was held five days and released for a ransom reportedly amounting to $408,000. A few months later, in August, the League failed in an attempt to kidnap or assassinate the sister of then President-elect López Portillo. During the shootout, the police killed David Sarmiento Jimenez Sarmiento, the 26-year-old leader of the League. Throughout the year the league engaged in kidnappings, bombings, killings, and bank robberies. League members robbed a Monterrey bank of almost $500,000 in the largest bank robbery on record in Mexico. On 30 November, the day before López Portillo assumed the presidency, several bombings took place at public buildings in Mexico City. The police believed the League was responsible. The Mexican judiciary announced that it was going to create a highly specialized police corps to exterminate subversion in the country. The specialized corps will receive intensive training in psychology, sociology, investigation, and fingerprinting.

Grand Valley State Colleges   Donald L. Herman

Nicaragua

The Socialist Party of Nicaragua (Partido Socialista de Nicaragua; PSN) was founded in 1937. It was declared illegal a year later and has been a clandestine organzation ever since. The Sandinist Liberation Front (Frente Sandinista de Liberación Nacional; FSLN) is a Castroite guerrilla organization founded in 1961.

The PSN is pro-Soviet. In 1967 an internal struggle resulted in the expulsion of some party leaders who then organized the Communist Party of Nicaragua (Partido Comunista de Nicaragua; PCN), which is anti-Soviet.

The PSN has only about 160 members; the PCN is probably smaller. The FSLN has perhaps a force of 50.

The population of Nicaragua is 2,224,000.

The PSN. The PSN has a negligible effect on the national political situation. This is due to its small, scattered membership and internal splintering, and the thorough suppression of such groups by the government of President Anastasio Somoza. A slight rise in Communist activities followed the disastrous earthquake of December 1972.

Luis Domingo Sánchez, believed to be the head of the party, was captured by secret police in May 1976 and has not been heard from since.

At its Tenth Congress, sometime between late 1972 and late 1973 (*YICA, 1974*, p. 346), the PSN stated that the independence of Nicaragua was "entirely nominal, being merely the façade of a semi-colonial and feudal regime fully devoted to imperialism." The party program said that the immediate goal was to free Nicaragua from U.S. domination. Tactically, the PSN calls for a united front of workers, students, peasants, the middle class, and other "progressives" against the Somoza government. While the PSN believes in armed struggle, it considers that the appropriate conditions in Nicaragua are still lacking. At this stage, it prefers building up its influence. The General Confederation of Labor operates under Communist leadership.

Internationally, the PSN has consistently affirmed its pro-Soviet stance. It condemned the military coup that toppled the Allende government in Chile and has criticized those in Central America who have sought to initiate violent action.

In early 1976 Luis Sánchez celebrated the 25th Congress of the Communist Party of the Soviet Union by delivering a major address to his comrades, reprinted in *Pravda* on 6 March. Sanchez condemned the "bloody fascist tyranny" in Chile and praised the victories achieved by Communists in both Vietnam and Angola. The main point of his speech, however, was to emphasize the pro-Soviet orientation of the PSN. He concluded with an appeal for a counterattack "against the Maoist mavericks, who have betrayed the socialist camp and broken with Marxim-Leninism."

The FSLN. Founded in 1961 by Carlos Fonseca Amador as a Castroite guerrilla organization, the Sandinist National Liberation Front has consistently maintained the necessity for direct action against the Somoza government, but it has been largely inactive throughout most of its history. After the exile of Fonseca to Cuba in 1970, the FSLN went completely underground, confining its operations to propaganda statements by its leader. In a 1971 interview published in Chile (*Punto Final*, Santiago, 27 April), Fonseca said that armed struggle "involves the most difficult course" but is the "only sure one," and that when the FSLN "takes up the guerrilla rifle, it inculcates a class consciousness."

In attempting to establish a guerrilla foothold in the peasant society of northern Nicaragua, the FSLN is emulating the man after whom it is named, Augusto C. Sandino, a revolutionary killed by government forces in 1934. Sandino is a true hero to the Nicaraguan left and, indeed, has become a legendary figure among the present generation of Latin American revolutionaries. For six years, 1927 to 1933, Sandino and his band of rebels occupied northern and eastern Nicaragua and waged a classic guerrilla war against both the National Guard and the U.S. Marines. Although the contemporary movement does not evidence the power of Sandino, it parallels the earlier one in the nature of its operations and is reportedly winning sympathy among peasants in the north, students in Managua and Leon, and middle-class professional people.

Domestic Activities. The FSLN first achieved notoriety in December 1974 when it kidnapped a number of prominent citizens in a daring raid at a Christmas party in Managua. Directly afterward, several members flew to Cuba and received training in propaganda and insurgency techniques. Meanwhile the Somoza government declared a national state of emergency—still in effect—suspending all constitutional guarantees. This includes a strict censorship of all newspapers and radio stations. FSLN members have been able to achieve some degree of organization and support in the north.

The year 1975 was fairly quiet, but 1976 has seen a dramatic upsurge in the guerrilla war. A number of clashes were reported and, for the first time, government authorities admitted the existence of an insurgency. The Somoza government has been helped by U.S. military assistance, the FSLN has received doctrinal and material aid from Cuba, and as of the moment, government troops appear to have the FSLN on the defensive, although guerrilla propaganda has not let up in its constant barrage against both President Somoza and the USA.

The government received an important intelligence and psychological boost with the capture of guerrilla leader Tomás Barge Martínez. His three-day trial before a military court in August was the first major intelligence breakthrough for the Army and special police forces. Barge apparently made revelations as to the extent of Cuban training and assistance and the insufficiency of the aid that the guerrillas in the mountains were receiving, the existence of a serious division within the FSLN, and the degree and nature of FSLN contact with subversive groups in other parts of Latin America. The overall picture was one of a badly divided, semi-isolated guerrilla army of about 50 men.

Avowedly Castroite since its beginning in 1961, the FSLN has always been supported by Cuba. In a message sent to the Soviet party congress in 1971, Fonseca declared that the FSLN was "the successor of the Bolshevist October revolution."

Although the Castro government does not officially authorize the participation of Cubans in the FSLN, a number of Cubans have been actively involved in FSLN operations. The FSLN has also exchanged information with the Rebel Armed Forces in Guatamala, the Montoneros in Argentina, and the Tupamaros in Uruguay. Its propaganda pictures the USA as the chief support of the opposition to its war effort, together with Brazil, both countries having been accused by the FSLN of active involvement in counter-insurgency.

Publications. PSN and FSLN publications appear to have been discontinued.

Hoover Institution   John J. Tierney, Jr.
Stanford University

Panama

The Communist Party of Panama (Partido Comunista de Panamá) was founded in 1930 but was dissolved in 1943 in favor of the People's Party of Panama (Partido del Pueblo de Panamá; PDP). Since all political activity in Panama focuses on the Canal issue and the PDP strongly supports the government of General Omar Torrijos Herrera, the Communist organization enjoys some freedom of action despite the fact that it has been illegal since 1953. In 1975, for the first time since Torrijos took office in 1968, there was some opposition to his regime from the far left.

The PDP's membership is difficult to ascertain but may reasonably be put at between 350 and 500. The population of Panama is 1,700,000 (estimated 1976).

Other leftist groups in Panama include the Revolutionary Unity Movement (Movimiento de Unidad Revolucionario; MUR), the National Action Vanguard (Vanguardia de Acción Nacional; VAN), the Panamanian Revolutionary Union (Unión Revolucionaria Panameña; URP), and the National Liberation Movement of 29 November (MLN-29-11). During the past few years these groups have been generally inactive owing to the exile or imprisonment of many of the leading personalities.

In 1976 the Revolutionary Socialist League (Liga Socialista Revolucionaria) emerged, replacing the Revolutionary Socialist Faction (FSR).

The PDP. Leadership and Organization. Since 1951 the secretary-general of the PDP has been Rubén Darío Sousa. Other leaders are Miguel Parcell and Luther Thomas. Another leader, Hugh Víctor Escala, has dropped out of sight and is presumed to be either in poor health or deceased.

The PDP's labor affiliate, the Trade Union Federation of Workers of the Republic of Panama (Federación Sindical de Trabajadores de la República de Panamá; FST) was disbanded by the Torrijos government in 1968 along with other labor unions. The PDP works with students through the University Reform Front (Frente Reformista Universitario; FRU), and the Federation of Students of Panama (Federación de Estudiantes de Panamá; FEP).

Party Internal Affairs. The year 1976 marked the end of the PDP-student alliance, which had locked the relatively small Communist party into active support of the traditionally revolutionary student groups. Students turned on the government during the year because of Panama's tough economic situation, while the PDP continued to support General Torrijos and his fight for the Canal. Darío Sousa continued to have close ties with certain government officials.

Domestic Views and Activities. The Canal issue is a natural for any "anti-imperialist" organization and the PDP is no exception, lending its full support to the Torrijos government, which in other respects is pro-foreign investment, pro-private enterprise, and anxious to develop the country with the strong participation of the private sector. The Panamanian economy has been severely affected by a drought, by rising fuel prices, and by the uncertainties exacerbated by the negotiations with the USA. This situation in the economy has led PDP leaders and student factions into a quandary and to further splits on a position vis-à-vis the government. Late in 1976, student demonstrations broke out in the Panama City area, in some cases only blocks from the U.S.-controlled Canal Zone. Despite efforts by the government and at least one PDP leader to channel the dissent toward the American entanglement, the demonstrators insisted on focusing on the nation's economic situation.

The PDP has failed to establish a united front among all leftist and socialist groups in support of the Torrijos effort to obtain a new treaty, and the proliferation of these groups resembles the situation on the pre-1968 national political scene, when all that was needed to establish a party was a president, a secretary, and a rubber stamp. The radical left has turned against the government because of unaccomplished goals and compromise with the USA. The government's effort to blame U.S. agents for the 1976 riots was totally ignored by the radicals.

International Views and Contacts. The PDP was delighted at the prospect of General Torrijos's visit to Cuba early in the year, but although Fidel Castro paid lip service to the symbolic need for an end to "colonialism" in Panama and for the total evacuation of the USA from the isthmus, all reports indicate that the visit was not totally cordial. Issues between the two leaders ranged from the presence of an International Hotel chef in Torrijos's party to the Panamanian leader's private investments abroad.

Upon returning from the trip, government friends of the PDP were no longer as friendly, since it had become apparent that no tangible assistance for the Panamanian cause could be expected from Cuba. The PDP continues to be basically pro-Soviet in its policies and in the age of détente the Canal issue proves to be a thorny one for the Panamanian Communists. Only time will tell if the party's strong endorsement of the Torrijos government was a wise "anti-imperialist" strategy or if the PDP may find itself in the uncomfortable position of having backed an enemy of the people.

Publications. The PDP publishes a monthly newspaper, *Unidad.*

National University of Costa Rica, Heredia   Charles F. Denton

Paraguay

The Paraguayan Communist Party (Partido Comunista Paraguayo; PCP) was founded in 1928. It has been illegal since that time except for a six-month period in later 1946-early 1947. The party has traditionally been aligned with the Soviet Union. One-time secretary general Oscar Creydt formed a rival PCP in 1965, after being ousted from the main body of the party, and has maintained an essentially pro-Chinese stance.

The membership of the PCP, including all factions and sympathizers, is estimated at approximately 3500 persons, many of whom are exiled in various Latin American and European countries. The party claims to have been growing rapidly in the past few years. The population of Paraguay is 2,600,000 (estimated 1976).

Organization and Internal Party Affairs. The pro-Soviet PCP is headed by Miguel Angel Soler. Other party leaders, according to Paraguayan security forces, include: Obdulio Barthe, César Avalos, Sebastian Quereis, José Chilavert, Adolfo Acosta, and Luis Centurion. Teynaldo Marin, identified as PCP first secretary, is the most frequent contributor to international communist publications.

Between November 1975 and October 1976, some 150 PCP members were reportedly arrested, including Secretary General Miguel Angel Soler and Derliz Villagra, president of the Federación Juvenil Comunista. Several party members, including Antonio Maidana, periodically reported to have died, Julio Rojas, and Alfredo Alcorta, have been in prison for more than a decade.

The PCP has devoted much of its time in recent years to trying to resolve the disputes which have separated Paraguayan communists. According to the PCP, a major step forward occurred in December 1974 when a general agreement was reached among party members regarding the essential dedication of communists to Marxism-Leninism and proletarian internationalism. The agreement emphasized that the program, rules, and policies approved at the party's Third and most recent congress in 1971 were binding on party members. (*WMR*, June 1975.) A Fourth Congress is reportedly in preparation.

PCP leaders claim the party is operating clandestinely in Paraguay and confrontations with security forces and arrests during the year indicate that this is true. Reynaldo Marin wrote at mid-year that party members distribute PCP papers illegally in the country, put out and distribute leaflets on current events and Marxist-Leninist literature, and write slogans on walls. (*WMR*, May 1976.)

The PCP professes to believe that only the masses headed by the working class can radically change national conditions, and that their party is the vanguard of the working people's movement. The party's chief tasks are to strengthen the unity of the working class, the trade unions and other mass organizations, and to establish solid links with the masses and unite them. According to the PCP, the Stroessner regime realizes that only the communists are capable of uniting the masses, this explaining the relentless anti-communist campaign of the government. During the past year the government has repeatedly charged communist infiltration in the nation's political parties, schools, and among various sectors of the population. Widespread government arrests have drawn criticism from national political leaders, the bishops of Paraguay (in a pastoral letter of 12 June) and such international organizations as Amnesty International and the International League for Human Rights.

Domestic Views and Activities. The PCP describes Paraguay as one of the most backward countries in Latin America, held back by imperialism and the latifundist system. Lopsided capitalist development and growing dependence on imperialism are said to aggravate the already drawn-out economic crisis. Party documents repeatedly argue that a deliberate gearing of production to exports, coupled with a huge and growing foreign debt, increase hardships for the masses. The government of Alfredo Stroessner shuts its eyes to the mounting crisis and insists that rising national inflation is an imported commodity. The grim national conditions have set into motion large segments of the population, according to PCP analysts, and increase national opposition to Stroessner and his allies. The upsurge in the people's struggle has been manifested among workers and their main allies, the peasants, as well as in the political parties. The change is particularly marked in the Liberal Radical Party (LRP), according to the PCP. (*WMR*, December 1975.)

Communist Party tactics at this time do not lean toward elections on the one hand nor individual terror and actions by small armed groups isolated from the masses. The PCP calls for an anti-dictatorial front which will be open to a broad spectrum of the population, including: members of the Colorado, Liberal Radical, Febrerista, and Christian Democratic parties; communists, civilians, military men, Christians, atheists, workers, peasants, students, small and medium employers, and even, under specific circumstances, members of the ruling element. United action must be based on the following demands: an end to repression, the release of all political prisoners, a lifting of the state of emergency, an increse in pay for workers, teachers, and other salary-earners, an end to evictions of peasants from the land, fixed equitable prices for farm products, respect for trade union freedoms, and protection of national industry.

Publications. The pro-Soviet branch of the PCP publishes *Adelante* and *Patria Nueva* irregularly for clandestine distribution in Paraguay.

*   *   *

The pro-Chinese PCP under Oscar Creydt, located mainly in Argentina until the military coup, is reportedly led by Juan Dario Quinonez, Efrain Ibañez, Lorenzo Arrua, Julio Vargas, Teodulo Riveros, Justo Ramirez, and Raul Ramirez, among others. The Paraguayan Interior Minister alleges that this group receives aid from China and other sympathetic countries. The pro-Chinese group reportedly publishes *Unidad Paraguay* and *MODEPA*.

*   *   *

A guerrilla group reportedly formed during the year was the Political Military Organization (Organización Politico-Militar; OPM). The OPM, reportedly trained and financed by the Argentina People's Revolutionary Army (ERP), was involved in several shoot-outs with government forces during the year.

Palo Alto, Calif.   Lynn Ratliff

Peru

The Peruvian Communist Party (Partido Comunista Peruano; PCP) had its origins in the Peruvian Socialist Party founded by José Carlos Mariátegui in 1928. As a result of orders from the Communist International it took its present name in 1930. Since 1964 the movement has been divided into a pro-Soviet party and several pro-Chinese splinter groups, some of them using the PCP name.

There also exist in Peru various Marxist-Leninist organizations to the left of the PCP. These include the Castro-oriented Movement of the Revolutionary Left (Movimiento de Izquierda Revolucionaria; MIR) and Army of National Liberation (Ejército de Liberacíon Nacional; ELN), the Trotskyite Revolutionary Left Front (Frente de Izquierda Revolucionaria; FIR), the Partido Obrero Revolucionario (Trotskista), and the Revolutionary Vanguard (Vanguardia Revolucionaria; VR).

Membership of the pro-Soviet PCP has been estimated at 2,000 and that of the pro-Chinese PCP groups at 1,200. Other Marxist-Leninist groups are small, with the VR and the FIR having the largest memberships. The population of Peru is about 15,804,000 (1976 estimate).

A constitutional provision prohibits Communist parties from participating in Peruvian elections, which have not been held in any case since the military assumed power in October 1968. The Communists have been allowed to engage in political activities subject to varying degrees of police surveillance and harassment. General Juan Velasco Alvarado, who was ousted from the presidency in August 1975, permitted the pro-Soviet PCP to function freely, but kept considerable control over other leftist groups. Several pro-Chinese and Trotskyite leaders were deported. The Velasco government also sought to co-opt leaders of various Marxist-Leninist groups, such as ex-ELN leader Héctor Bejar. During 1976, government policies toward the PCP and other Communist groups became increasingly cautious under the more conservative presidency of General Francisco Morales Bermúdez.

The Pro-Soviet PCP. Leadership and Organization. The highest organ of the pro-Soviet PCP is officially the National Congress, which is supposed to meet every three years. Its Sixth Congress, the most recent, met in November 1973. The PCP is organized from cells upward through local and regional committees, to its Central Committee. Regional committees exist in at least 22 cities. Lima has the largest number of local committees, concentrated in low-income neighborhoods and in the slum areas which the government now refers to as "new towns." Seventeen regional and local conferences were held during the first half of 1976 for the purpose of rejuvenating the party's leadership and stimulating recruitment activities (*Unidad,* 9 June). The general secretary of the party is Jorge del Prado. Raúl Acosta Salas serves as under-secretary. Other prominent members of the Central Committee are José Ramirez, Julio Rodriquez, Alfonso Oblitas, Gustavo Espinosa, José Martínez, and Vicente Ramírez. The official organ of the PCP, the weekly newspaper *Unidad,* claimed a circulation of more than 10,000 before it was closed down by the government in early July.

The PCP's youth group, the Peruvian Communist Youth (Juventud Comunista Peruana; JCP), is relatively small and operates mainly in the universities. Jorge Tapia is the group's general secretary. The JCP held its Second National Congress in Febraury with more than 150 delegates and some 50 representatives attending. In addition, delegations of Communist youth were present from various foreign countries, including the Soviet Union, the German Democratic Republic, Bulgaria, Czechoslovakia, Vietnam, Cuba, and Chile. In accordance with the PCP's policy line, the Congress reaffirmed its "most resolute support for the intensification and defense of the anti-imperialist, revolutionary process which we are undergoing" (*Unidad,* 18 February). The Congress's final report referred to "the state of crisis and anarchy existing within the university movement," a situation attributed to the control over it exercised by "the feeble Trotskyite and Maoist leadership in an obvious alliance with the reactionaries." Other topics of discussion included the status of labor and peasant working youth, the status of women, and the efforts of voluntary work brigades among young people in the slums (ibid.). In his address to the Congress, Jorge del Prado said that the JCP has accomplished much in the past in the unification of "anti-imperialist and progressive forces of Peruvian youth." However, he urged the Congress to ensure the multiplication of such efforts to give larger numbers of young people "our ideology and experience" (ibid., 11 February). On 25 March, more than 25 youth organizations, including the JCP, met for the purpose of planning for the Third Peruvian-Soviet Youth Festival, to be held in August (ibid., 9 June). The JCP inaugurated a membership drive on 12 June, and PCP undersecretary Raúl Acosta Salas called upon the members to solidify their internal organization by overcoming sectarian divisions (ibid., 16 June). At the end of the year, the JCP protested the ransacking of its national headquarters in Lima and the arrest of some of its members by government security forces and warned revolutionaries about the "magnitude of the offensive of the most reactionary sectors of the country" (*Granma,* Havana, 29 October, 4 November).

A major source of the PCP's influence lies in its control over the General Confederation of Workers of Peru (Confederación General de Trabajadores del Perú; CGTP). The CGTP was organized three months before the military coup of 1968 and was given legal recognition a few months afterward. By the beginning of 1975 it had become the largest of Peru's trade union federations, largely as a result of sympathetic treatment it received from the Velasco government. The CGTP's strongest opposition within the trade union movement comes from the government-sponsored Central Organization of Workers of the Peruvian Revolution (Central de Trabajadores de la Revolución Peruana; CTRP), and the Confederation of Workers of Peru (Confederación de Trabajadores del Perú; CNT), whose political involvement is with the Aprista party (American Popular Revolutionary Alliance; APRA). In a report presented at a CGTP conference held on 24-25 January, Acosta Salas singled out "the deconcentration of unionized workers" as the major weakness within the Peruvian trade union movement. He attributed this situation to the low level of class consciousness among workers, the confusion engendered by adversary movements, and the difficulty inherent in a country of little capitalist development, high economic dispersion, and extensive territory (*Unidad,* 4 February).

The CGTP held its Fourth National Congress in Lima from 17 to 21 March. The meeting brought together delegates from 44 national unions, 300 trade unions, and 1,700 branches of the CGTP. The guests included representatives of the World Federation of Trade Unions (WFTU) and trade union centers of 13 countries. The Congress ratified Isidoro Gamarra as the CGTP's new president, replacing Gustavo Espinosa. Eduardo Castillo Sánchez, general secretary of the CGTP-controlled Federation of Bank Workers, was elected secretary. Enrique Pastorino, president of the WFTU, hailed the "patriotic struggle which the people and armed forces of Peru are carrying on against imperialism." He condemned the activity of multinational companies, which he contended "have doomed the peoples to ignorance, exploitation, poverty, and underdevelopment" (WFTU *Flashes,* 31 March). Among the important resolutions of the Congress was the decision to reiterate the support of the working class for the process of structural change and to promote a unity of the people with the armed forces capable of guaranteeing the stability and extension of the Peruvian revolution toward socialism (*Granma,* English edition, 4 April).

According to the Ministry of Labor, 50 to 60 percent of labor conflicts in Peru are related to the CGTP. On 1 March, 80,000 members of the Departmental Federation of Arequipa Workers (FDTA), a

CGTP affiliate, declared a general strike to demand amendments to the decree law setting ceilings on salary raises (AFP, Paris, 2 March). On 25 June, some 15,000 members of the Federation of Bank Workers went on strike for the implementation of a wage increase previously negotiated. This Federation is considered to be one of the most important bases of the CGTP. On 2 July, the Federation's general secretary, Castillo Sánchez, criticized the government's economic austerity measures, which he said had precipitated a "logical popular outburst of indignation" (*Excelsior,* Mexico City, 20 July). By mid-year labor confrontations had become increasingly bitter. The growing number of strikes suggested that economic austerity would not be accepted passively by the major union federations. By August ministerial statements were becoming perceptibly more threatening toward any form of organized opposition to government policies. A typical example was the announcement by the Labor Minister that legislation covering job security and the right to strike would have to be modified. The minister's attitude underscored the government's determination to control the activities of left-wing extremists in the trade union movement, including any criticism of the military's increasingly conservative policies (*Latin America,* London, 27 August).

The PCP has continued to exert some influence in the peasant sector through its participation in the National Agrarian Confederation (Confederación Nacional de Agricultores; CNA). Founded in 1974, the CNA claims to represent 3.5 million peasants with 19 federations operating throughout the country. The organization held its Third National Conference on 12-15 December 1975. About 200 peasant leaders of CNA branches reportedly attended. The conference declared in favor of stronger unity of the people and the armed forces. It expressed support for President Morales's proposal to establish a National Front for the Defense of the Revolution (Frente Nacional para la Defensa de la Revolución; FNDR) and for the struggle against imperialism. It also pronounced itself in favor of controlling the mass media to "defend the nation and its sovereignty" (WFTU *Flashes,* 21 January). The Agricultural Minister stated in May that the first phase of the agrarian reform program would be completed at the end of 1976. By that time, he claimed, nearly 10 million hectares of land would have been turned over to approximately 325,000 families (*El Comercio,* 28 May). Most of the land is located in the provinces of Cuzco and Puno in the southeastern Andes area, and in Cajamarca in the north. In August the CNA issued a protest over the arrest of miners and mine workers' leaders. It also called for respect for the right to strike and work security (*Granma,* English, 5 September).

The PCP's principal opposition in the peasant sector comes from the pro-Chinese orientation of several parties belonging to the Confederation of Peruvian Peasants (Confederación de Campesinos Peruanos; CCP). According to Acosta Salas, one faction of the CCP is under the direction of "Bandera Roja" and the other follows the dictates of the Revolutionary Vanguard. The latter managed to achieve majority strength within the CCP at one point, but has since been weakened by internal divisions (*Unidad,* 4 February). The CCP has demanded that the titles to land distributed under the government's agrarian reform program be delivered without any form of payment. Overall, the CCP maintains a class struggle policy and, in general, views the government as one of the main enemies of the people (*Intercontinental Press,* New York, 1 March).

Domestic Attitudes and Activities. The PCP was forced to redefine its domestic position by the removal of General Velasco Alvarado on 29 August 1975. At the Central Committee's plenary session in Lima on 27-28 September, Jorge del Prado presented the Political Commission's report outlining a readjustment of the party's line to conform with the new circumstances. The report referred to President Morales's speech of 5 September in which he announced the beginning of a new, second stage of the revolution. According to the PCP, the characteristic weakness of the Peruvian revolution is that it is developing without the necessary full support of the people: the major deficiency of the Velasco regime during the "first stage" of the revolution was that it did not promote mass participation, which, rather, it greatly hindered through discriminatory and repressive methods in domestic policy.

The report did not absolve the party from any responsibility for insufficient mass involvement: "We should not forget our own lack of audacity and persistency in working for trade union unity, and this applies even more to our work in the peasant movement, the youth movement, and among teachers, students, and intellectuals." (*IB,* 15 November.)

In mid-November 1975, President Morales called for the creation of a new movement of popular support for the military regime—a National Front for the Defense of the Revolution (*Granma,* English, 16 November). The PCP leadership immediately endorsed the proposed Front and took an active role through the CNA and the CGTP in the initial stages of its organization. The FNDR was viewed by the party as an ideal instrument to channel and invigorate the political participation of the working class, peasants, and other groups in which Communist influence has been only moderately successful (*Unidad,* 4 February 1976). By mid-January, thirteen departmental branches of the National Organizing Committee of the FNDR had been created. The CNA played a direct role in organizing the committees and was responsible for setting up the National Organizing Committee at its general assembly in December. Avelino Mar Arias, head of the Cuzco Agrarian Federation, was elected president of the Committee (*El Comercio,* 21 January). The National Organizing Committee met in February with General Jorge Fernández Maldonado, minister of war and the commanding officer of the army. Fernández stated that he did not wish to see the people filling the streets of Peru without complete identification with the revolution. He affirmed that Peru's revolutionary process is characterized by the construction of Peruvian socialism based on its own creative ability and the Peruvian people's desire for liberation (*La Crónica,* 13 February). On 28 February, President Morales declared that "the rise of the FNDR expresses the growing development of an ever clearer political consciousness in our people." He stated that the FNDR is the direct, organized expression of the workers. (Ibid., 28 February.)

Official rhetoric in support of the Front has far outweighed the ability of the National Committee to carry out its organization beyond the planning phase. Avelino Mar announced in March that the Front would be created on a national level to coincide with Peru's national holiday on 28 July (*La Prensa,* 12 March). However, in the Department of Lima, the eight Revolutionary Defense Fronts were not expected to be consolidated until August. And only then could work begin on the organization of District Fronts. Meanwhile, during the first half of 1976 the PCP continued to provide vigorous verbal support for the formation of the FNDR and the military government's positions in general. In April, the Central Committee called for continued vigilance in defense of those revolutionary gains and structural transformations already achieved. The statement added that it was "wishful thinking to hope that Yankee imperialism could resolve economic problems in Peru when it is incapable of doing so in its own country" (*Granma,* 7 April). Writing in the May edition of the *World Marxist Review,* Jorge del Prado praised the social, economic, and ideological progress of the second stage of the revolution, while implicitly criticizing those who envisaged a "humanitarian-Christian Socialism." According to del Prado, the PCP's main task was to step up its campaign against the enemies of the revolution, among whom he included both the ultra-leftists and the right.

On 30 April, President Morales announced full amnesty for political prisoners and exiles and appealed for unity to overcome the antagonisms between the armed forces and the APRA. The announcement was received with mixed reaction in political circles. A spokesman for the PCP said that the party was "studying the situation," but that in principle it considered the amnesty for some labor leaders and political exiles "healthy." According to an unidentified party source, the PCP agrees with a policy of freedom for various political groups (*Unidad,* 5 May).

Morales's unprecedented action in seeking a reconciliation with some of the old-line political parties such as APRA underscored the economic and social setbacks that have begun to erode the image of revolutionary development in Peru. Inflation, shortages, and wage controls contributed to the most widespread labor strikes in more than 10 years (*NYT,* 2 May). On 30 June the government announced a series of drastic economic measures, including a 44 percent devaluation of Peru's currency, the lifting of price ceilings, and the prohibition of strikes. The austerity decree set off a wave of protests in Lima on 1 July that resulted in mass arrests and the declaration of a national state of emergency. Magazines and newspapers representing both extremes of the political spectrum were closed down on 5 July, including the PCP's weekly, *Unidad* (*Latin America*, 9 July). The following day the PCP issued a communiqué absolving the government of any responsibility for the economic crisis affecting the country. The document attempted to justify the "sacrifices of the masses" and charged the right wing with taking advantage of the situation to oppose the "revolutionary process." Advocating greater development of the state enterprises, the PCP asked the government to expedite the use of credits granted by the socialist countries to ease the nation's currency problems. The communiqué made no reference to the government's order banning publication of *Unidad*. (AFP, Paris, 7 July.)

On 9 July an attempted coup by troops of the Military Instruction Center, led by General Carlos Bobbio Centurión, was quickly suppressed with no reported casualties. Bobbio was known to favor more drastic measures to solve the country's economic crisis. One week later, four cabinet members, including Fernández Maldonado, were forced to resign. The replacement of Fernández on 16 July by the vehemently anti-Communist General Guillermo Arbulu Galliani was considered by some observers as "the death-knell of the Peruvian revolution as a progressive movement" (*Latin America*, 23 July). After assessing these events, the Political Commission of the PCP's Central Committee issued a critical statement in August that reflected the party's growing concern over the "important modifications" to basic policies introduced by the new military leadership. The declaration reiterated the PCP's support for all measures taken by the government to deal with the "counterrevolutionary offensive," but it warned that "the basic requirement for a successful anti-fascist policy is the organized forces of workers and popular sectors." In perhaps its strongest criticism yet, the PCP stated that the most recent measures adopted by the government had led to a big increase in the cost of living and had resulted in limitations on some of the most important workers' rights. It stated that temporary measures would not solve the economic crisis, and called for broader structural reforms. The PCP was particularly concerned about the implications of a remark by President Morales to the effect that "the state will not necessarily seek exclusive control over the enterprises in which it is involved." The PCP warned against any efforts to transform the original principles of social reform in the field of workers' rights into a new version of "people's capitalism" (*Granma*, 13 August). The message also stated in concise terms the nature of the PCP's support for the military government: "It is obvious—as we have said repeatedly—that the ideology of the revolutionary process led by the armed forces has not been, nor is, the ideology of the Communist Party; but the objectives of obtaining the independence of the country from imperialist domination and of overcoming the backwardness generated by dependence and oligarchic control is an ample base for coincidence of all the revolutionary forces of the country. Among these forces we Communists consider ourselves to be in the first line." (*El Comercio*, 12 August.) Editorials in *El Comercio* (13 August) and *El Expreso* (8 September) were highly critical of the PCP's positions. They characterized most of the party's proposals to the government as being "incurably idealistic."

By the end of August the military government was reportedly stepping up efforts to halt subversive activity, increase production, and stimulate the revolution it began eight years ago. Against charges that the government had let the 1968 revolution turn toward the right, President Morales responded that the military was in the process of "making corrections" so that the revolution could continue (*NYT*, 20 August). The president has repeatedly stated that the government rather than the extreme left will determine the policies of the revolution—which rejects both traditonal capitalism and Marxism—and that more flexible methods will be used to achieve them. He continued to stress the need for political and ideological pluralism and condemn groups advocating class conflict.

Some observers considered that the government, in this "second stage" of the Peruvian revolution, was thinking of breaking away from the conditional Communist "support," but that it was unprepared for a direct confrontation with the CGTP. This may well have been the military's justification for the need to establish the National Front for the Defense of the Revolution with activists who firmly believe in the ideological basis of the revolution, but who reject the concept of class struggle. In any event, the Front continued to exist basically on paper and, as yet, had no weight of its own to serve as a base of mass support for the government. At the end of December the PCP called upon the revolutionary and progressive forces in the country to adopt an emergency platform designed to defend and consolidate the conquests achieved since 1968, and rejected many of the domestic and international policies of the Morales government (*Granma*, 23 December).

International Views and Positions. The PCP continued to follow closely the Soviet line in its international positions. At the Second Congress of the JCP in February, Jorge del Prado warned against "attempts being made to divide the revolutionary forces from abroad." He charged the multinational companies, the U.S. State Department, and the Pentagon with trying to "tighten the economic noose around Peru and at the same time attempting to threaten our government and people with a direct or indirect armed aggression." He added that "in a continent which imperialism has always considered its 'backyard,' the mere existence of the Peruvian revolutionary process is unbearable to the capitalist empire." (*Unidad*, 11 February.) The PCP reaffirmed its solidarity with Cuba and Panama, its independent position within the OAS, and its support for the governments in Latin America which are struggling to recover their natural resources and defend their sovereignty.

In commenting on the East Berlin Conference of European Communist and Workers' Parties, in June, del Prado assessed the impact of Europe's future on Latin America. He stated that if the possibility of war in the old world is postponed, there will be more chance to defeat imperialism in Latin America, particularly in Peru (TASS, 14 July).

In the wake of July's disturbances, the FNDR issued a statement denouncing interference by imperialism in Peru's internal affairs. The communiqué warned workers, peasants, students, and other "progressive sectors" about imperialism's and the CIA's design for liquidating the Peruvian revolution. The FNDR charged that the country's economic crisis had been fomented by the imperialist monopolies in an attempt to turn the workers against the military government (*Granma*, English, 18 July).

Jorge del Prado headed the PCP delegation that attended the First Congress of the Communist Party of Cuba in December 1975. The PCP also attended the 25th Congress of the Soviet party in March. In a speech before the Congress, del Prado gratefully acknowledged the friendship and support of the Soviet Union in the party's struggle against U.S. imperialism and its Chinese confederates. He condemned "traitorous Maoism for its shameless support of Chile's fascist regime and the puppets of imperialism and racism in Angola." (TASS, 4 March.) PCP delegations visited Romania and Hungary in May.

The Pro-Chinese Communists. Leadership and Organization. From their inception in the 1960s, the pro-Chinese groups have experienced continuous internal dissension and splits. In the 8 January 1976 issue of the Peruvian weekly *Marka*, some 20 Marxist political organizations were analyzed, many of which, strictly speaking, do not "exist."

In recent years there have been at least three major factions of the pro-Chinese PCP. The one which enjoys more or less official recognition from the Chinese Communist Party is headed by Saturnino Paredes Macedo and, from its somewhat sporadic periodical, *Bandera Roja*, is generally known as the PCP-Bandera Roja. The Red Fatherland faction, so-called because of its periodical, *Patria Roja*, is believed to have the largest following of all pro-Chinese groups among students and labor. It reportedly exercises control over national labor organizations with memberships in excess of 100,000. The Bandera Roja faction, on the other hand, heads only local organizations with fewer than 100,000 affiliates. (*Marka,* 8 January.) The Patria Roja group also controls one of the labor "unification organizations" (Comité de Coordinación y Unifcación Sindical Clasista; CCUSC), which has engaged in fierce competition with a similar unifying organization controlled by the CGTP (*Latin America,* 11 June). The Patria Roja and other pro-Chinese groups have had relatively little successs in acquiring influence within the peasant movement.

A third pro-Chinese faction, the PCP-Marxist Leninist (PCP-ML), held its 7th Congress on 17-18 January. According to pro-Soviet sources, the Congress unanimously approved a declaration proclaiming its self-dissolution. A spokesman for the party stated that "a revolutionary organization of the working class cannot be built on the basis of Maoism." Members of the dissolved party were advised to join the ranks of the "genuine Marxist-Leninist Party — the PCP." (*Unidad,* 28 January.) In commenting on the self-disbandment of the PCP-ML, Jorge del Prado stated that the Peking leaders' attempts to turn Maoism into an international force and to weaken the ideological basis of the world Communist movement are "doomed to failure" (*Pravda,* 19 February).

In addition to the pro-Chinese groups, there are several Marxist-Leninist parties and movements of Castroite and Trotskyite orientation in Peru. Although these groups are now small compared to their size in the early 1960s, they retain some ideological influence, particularly among students. Like their Maoist counterparts, these Marxist groups operate underground and have remained steadfast in their opposition to the military government and the pro-Soviet PCP.

Washington College   Daniel L. Premo

Puerto Rico

The Puerto Rican Communist Party (Partido Comunista Puertorriqueño; PCP) is closely associated with the Communist Party of the United States of America (CPUSA) and continues to share its pro-Soviet views. The Puerto Rican Socialist League (Liga Socialista Puertorriqueña; LSA) has ties with the Progressive Labor Party (PLP) of the United States, and although it has been reported to be leaning somewhat toward the Chinese Communist camp (*Militant,* New York, 16 July 1976), like the PLP, it dropped its pro-Chinese platform in 1971. The Popular Socialist Movement (Movimiento Socialista Popular; MSP) has been reported to maintain a Maoist stance, and was recently described as having a guerrilla orientation (ibid.). The Armed Forces of Puerto Rican National Liberation (Fuerzas Armadas de Liberación Nacional Puertorriqueña; FALN) appears to have its origins in earlier terrorist groups, and continues to seek independence, allegedly through U.S. mainland bombings for the most part. The Puerto Rican Socialist Party (Partido Socialista Puertorriqueño; PSP), formerly the Pro-Independence Movement (Movimiento Pro-Independencia; MPI), maintains close ties with Cuba, and appears to continue independent in the Sino-Soviet dispute. The Puerto Rican Revolutionary Workers Organization (PRRWO) has operated since 1973 as an "underground revolutionary group committed to the twin goals of creating a revolutionary Communist Party in the United States and achieving Puerto Rican independence." It is Maoist in orientation. (U.S., Senate, Committee on the Judiciary, Subcommittee to Investigate the Administration of the Internal Security Act and Other Internal Security Laws, Staff Study, *The Puerto Rican Revolutionary Workers Organization*, 1976; hereinafter referred to as Staff Study). The Social Revolutionary Party (Partido Socialista Revolucionario; PSR) is a Marxist-Leninist group (*Intercontinental Press*, New York, 2 February 1976; *San Juan Star*, 7 November). The International Workers League (Liga Internacionalista de los Trabajadores; LIT), reported to be Trotskyist (*Militant*, 16 July 1976), is associated with the Fourth International (*Intercontinental Press*, 12 April, 28 June 1976).

Most of these organizations have relatively few members. In 1975, PCP membership was estimated at slightly over 100. That same year, FALN was reported to have around a dozen members (*NYT*, 28 October). A police official recently suggested that FALN members actually involved in bombings might be as few as five or six (ibid., 23 September 1976). Toward the end of 1975, PSP membership was estimated at several thousand (ibid., 9 November). According to preliminary figures, that party polled approximately 11,000 votes in the gubernatorial election held in Puerto Rico on 2 November 1976 (*San Juan Star*, 7 November). With the exception of the PSP, none of these groups has ever participated in a gubernatorial election, and at least since 1948 none but PSP has been represented in either legislative house.

The population of Puerto Rico is estimated at 3,200,000.

The PCP. *Organization.* The Puerto Rican Communist Party was founded in 1934, dissolved in 1944, and refounded in 1946. The PCP appears to have a party structure similar to that of other communist parties. Organs include the national party congress (the Second Congress was held in December 1975), Central Committee, Politburo, and General Secretariat. During 1976, PCP suffered the death of two leaders. On 22 April, Félix Ojeda, general secretary and editor in chief of the party's newspaper, passed away. A member since 1952, he was elected secretary of the Executive Committee twelve years ago, and was named general secretary at the start of this decade. He was close to the Soviet Union, and was reported to have withdrawn from the Socialist Party because of its anti-Soviet policies (*WMR*, June 1976). Moscow TASS noted that he was a leader in the Puerto Rican independence struggle, seeker of unity among Communist and workers' movements, and advocate of Puerto Rican friendship with the Soviet Union (*FBIS*, 27 April).

This party also lost José Enamorado Cuesta, at the age of 84. He was an ardent *independentista*, a member of the Partido Nacionalista, a founder of the Puerto Rican Peace Council, and a leading figure in the PCP (*Granma*, English, 17 October).

International Views and Policies. During September 1975, PCP members attended and supported the "International Conference of Solidarity with the Independence of Puerto Rico," held in Havana. Toward the end of the year, PCP organizing secretary Franklin Irizarri spoke at the Institute of Nuclear Investigations, San José, Cuba. He praised the work of the Cuban people which had culminated in the First Party Congress of Cuba. On behalf of the Puerto Rican Communists, he stated that Puerto Rico would be free and thanked the Cubans for their support (*Granma*, 20 December).

As acting general secretary, Irizarri attended the 25th Congress of the Communist Party of the Soviet Union (CPSU). He commented upon his return about the publication of a new book, *Facts about Puerto Rico*, by Soviet author Nelly Pallavskova, and reported on the resolutions seeking release of federally imprisoned *nacionalistas*. He added that CPSU first secretary Brezhnev had promised to maintain support for Puerto Rican independentistas (*San Juan Star*, 26 March 1976).

While in Moscow, Irizarri apparently delivered an address emphasizing that the PCP is seeking to further the goals of Soviet foreign policy. He strongly attacked the policies of the Maoists, whom he accused of tricking some Puerto Rican students and of being joined with the West in their anti-Soviet line and their stance on Angola. He championed détente, acknowledged lessons learned from CPSU, and pledged support of proletarian internationalism. (*FBIS*, 11 March.)

Domestic Views. In the speech apparently given in Moscow, Irizarri claimed that the PCP was only quasi-legal, and that members were repressed. He stated that Puerto Rico had been exploited economically and politically by the USA and utilized as a base for hemispheric military aggression. He described the negative impact of mainland economic control, including ecological damage, high unemployment, low wages, and widespread poverty. (Ibid.)

During 1976, police reported that the PCP was party to a thwarted attempt to occupy consular offices in San Juan of six of the nations scheduled to engage in an economic summit conference at Dorado, Puerto Rico in June (*NYT*, 25 June). Subsequently the PCP was reported to have joined several political groups in a "Revolutionary Anti-Electoral Front," formed to boycott the November elections (*Militant*, 16 July; see also *Claridad*, 18 June). The *Militant* claimed that the PCP was relatively small and had been left behind by other independentista bodies.

The PCP publishes *El Pueblo* and *El Proletario*.

The LSP. The Puerto Rican Socialist League is led by Secretary General Juan Antonio Corretjei, a former assistant to the late Pedro Albizú Campos, leader of the Partido Nacionalista. In the past the LSP was said to advocate a "people's war" in Puerto P'co. During 1976 it joined the plot to occupy the consular offices during the economic summit (*NYT*, 25 June), and joined the aforementioned Revolutionary Anti-Electoral Front (*Militant*, 16 July).

The MSP. The Popular Socialist Movement, a Marxist-Leninist organization, was created as a breakaway movement from the Puerto Rican Independence Party (Partido Independentista Puertorriqueña; PIP) in 1973. It held its First Congress in November 1974 and has claimed to be the only Marxist-Leninist party in Puerto Rico. It considers the island in "industrial colony," lacking peasantry, patriotic bourgeoisie, and petty bourgeoisie who seek freedom and who comprise a "classical" colony. The MSP goal has been socialism and independence, to be achieved through a war of national liberation. It has been active in the United Workers' Movement (Movimiento Obrero Unido; MOU), formed in 1971 as a militant federation of unions and locals, which appears to seek to create a national trade union (see *W.T.U. Movement*, November 1975).

During 1976, the MSP was also a party to the consular offices occupation plot and the Revolutionary Anti-Electoral Front (*NYT*, 25 June; *Militant*, 16 July). It has been reported that among its leaders is Luis Angel Torres, the 1972 PIP gubernatorial candidate who has since left that party (*Guardian*, New York, 17 December 1975).

The FALN. The Armed Forces of National Liberation acts as an underground revolutionary group seeking national independence for Puerto Rico. The origins, organization, and leadership of the FALN remain obscure. One study, utilizing information from unnamed detectives and FBI agents, reported that this terrorist organization may be the outgrowth of the Armed Revolutionary Independence Movement (MIRA), apparently organized in Cuba in 1966. The MIRA began incendiary raids on the U.S. mainland and in Puerto Rico in 1969 but was rendered inoperative by arrests in 1971. Investigators suggest that remaining MIRA members may have then formed the United Armed Revolutionary Force for Independence (FURIA), which subsequently became the Armed Commandos for Liberation (CAL). Former militants of FURIA and CAL formed the FALN (see *NYT*, 7 February 1975). FALN goals appear generally to include independence for Puerto Rico and freedom for Puerto Rican nationalists imprisoned for attempted assassinations of President Harry S. Truman and members of the U.S. House of Representatives. Puerto Rico's governor, Rafael Hernández Colón, claimed FALN had perhaps only ten members, with up to three-person cells in Chicago, New York, and Washington (*NYT*, 13 July).

During 1976, FALN members were suspected of or took credit for a number of mainland bombings. On the night of 7-8 June, four bombs exploded at business establishments and the police headquarters in Chicago. The blasts came close to the first anniversary of simultaneous bombings in Chicago and New York for which the FALN took credit. (*NYT*, 9 June; see also *Christian Science Monitor*, 9 June.) Later that month, the FALN seemed to claim responsibility for bombings of three business establishments and a police station in New York (*NYT*, 26 June).

The FALN took credit for planting a dozen bombs in Manhattan department stores during the National Democratic Convention, a number of which exploded. The bombs were believed to have been intended to protest the presence of the Puerto Rican delegation to the convention. (*NYT*, 13, 29 July.) In September, the FALN claimed to have planted a bomb which exploded at the New York Hilton Hotel, in protest of a political dinner appearance by Governor Hernández (*NYT*, 22, 23 September; *Granma*, English, 3 October). In November, FBI agents discovered an alleged FALN "bomb factory" in a Chicago apartment (*San Juan Star*, 7 November).

The PSR. In an announcement by Secretary General Narciso Rarbell Martínez, the PSR stated that it seeks a united front among all Puerto Rican independentista groups. The party claims that differences between such groups must be laid aside for present in the struggle against a common foe. The secretary general announced that PSR does not subscribe to the electoral system in its quest for power, and criticized PSP's participation in the recent elections. (Ibid.)

The PRRWO. The Puerto Rican Revolutionary Workers Organization has "developed a reputation as the foremost Maoist advocate among the organizations which comprise the Puerto Rican revolutionary movement in the United States." It evolved from a Chicago gang to the Young Lords Organization (1968-70) and the Young Lords Party (1970-72). Following its only national congress (1972) the PRRWO allegedly has gone underground, "working in a clandestine manner . . . in an attempt to infiltrate labor unions (Staff Report, citing *New York Post*, 23 March 1973). They have also participated in a number of rallies, demonstrations, and marches (Staff Report).

The PSP. The Puerto Rican Socialist Party was founded in November 1971 at the Eighth Annual Assembly of the Pro-Independence Movement. It is reported to have an organizational presence in every important population center of Puerto Rico, with the largest and most active organizations in the key industrial areas. The party's general secretary stated that 1976 was expected to be a year of expansion and further organizational refinement (*Guardian*, 17 December 1975).

Organization and Leadership. The PSP has held two party congresses, the first in 1971, and the second on 28 November-7 December 1975. Nearly 300 delegates attended the Second Congress, and 8,000 to 10,000 persons attended the closing session. The party elected a fifteen-member Central Committee at its latest congress, and also has a Political Commission. Among its leaders are Julio Vivres Vásques (chairman), Juan Marí Braz (general secretary and 1976 gubernatorial candidate), Pedro Grant (member of the Political Commission, national coordinator of MOU and 1976 candidate for senator at large), Carlos Gallisá (during 1976 a *representante* who won office in 1972 as a member of PIP and PSP candidate for representative at large), Ramón Arbona (member of the Political Commission and editor of *Claridad*, the party newspaper), Gervasio Morales (assistant director of *Claridad*), Manuel de Jesús González (member of the Political Commission), José Alvarez (first secretary of the mainland U.S. branch of the PSP), Florencio Merced Rosa (secretary of information and propaganda and 1976 mayoral candidate for San Juan), Alberto Pérez (secretary of exterior relations and member of the Central Committee), and Carlos Rivera (head of the PSP mission in Cuba and member of the Central Committee).

Domestic Attitudes and Activities. The PSP maintains that Puerto Rico is a colony which serves to further the interests of U.S. imperialists and local reactionaries. At its Second Congress the PSP developed its program. "Socialist Alternative," to move from a national liberation front to the "workers republic" and the foundations of socialism. Marí Bras declared that Puerto Rico would soon be entering the era of revolution, that the overwhelming majority of Puerto Ricans would be included in the effort, and that other organizations supportive of the independence movement would be invited to participate. (*Guardian,* 17, 24 December 1975).

During 1976 the general secretary called upon the PIP to join with the PSP in a united election front, claiming that present differences were insufficient to prevent such a basic and wise move (*Granma,* 2 April, 22 July). He also indicated a willingness to appoint non-PSP *independentistas* to government positions (*San Juan Star,* 31 October).

Despite the opposition of approximately a third the delegates to the Second Congress (*Intercontinental Press,* 27 December 1975), the PSP decided to field a slate of candidates for the 1976 insular elections. This represents the first effort by the party in electoral politics. The party leadership made it clear that they did not expect to gain independence through the ballot. Rather, the electoral process and positions won would be used for propaganda purposes and to demonstrate that, as an integral part of colonial oppression, the process seeks to dilute the strength of socialism and independence. (Ibid., 22 December 1975; *Guardian,* 17, 24 December; *Granma,* 7 February, 18 May 1976.) Further, electoral participation did not imply that PSP was renouncing its right of armed struggle, which it maintains must be preserved until the defeat of imperialist oppression (*Granma,* 9 December 1975). Nevertheless, Marí Bras rejected isolated instances of terrorist acts, especially those injurious to the cause and its supporters. He noted disagreement with bombings such as that, allegedly by the FALN, of Fraunces Tavern in New York City. (*Guardian,* 24 December 1975; *Time,* 16 February 1976.)

Thousands marched in North Philadelphia on the U.S. Bicentennial and called for the independence of Puerto Rico. Marí Bras addressed a three-hour rally which followed the parade (*Militant,* 16 July).

The PSP launched a series of calls for the termination of what it considered harassment and repression of party activists and other independentistas and socialists, including alleged political assassinations, arrests, imprisonments, and torture. These have been reportedly engaged in by federal authorities such as the FBI and CIA and by insular officials (see *Granma,* 2 April, 18 May). The PSP claimed that the death by shooting of Santiago Marí Pesquera, son of General Secretary Marí Bras, was a political assassination (*NYT,* 29 March; *Intercontinental Press,* 12 April). José Alvarez charged that in recent years there have been in excess of 200 acts of violence against independentistas, and that not a single conviction has resulted (*Intercontinental Press,* 12 April).

The PSP sponsored the TV broadcast in Puerto Rico of the Cuban motion picture *La nueva escuela,* the first post-revolutionary Cuban documentary shown on the island. The station's studios were bombed after the broadcast (*Granma,* English, 17 October).

The PSP newspaper, *Claridad,* and the party leadership have brought charges that the publicly owned Puerto Rican telephone company has, for political purposes, illegally wiretapped conversations of private citizens. Actual tapes were made public by Marí Bras in November 1976. The telephone company denied the charges, claiming that brief wiretappings were conducted for purposes of testing quality of service. The Puerto Rican government has claimed that the charges have been raised by the PSP purely for its own political benefit. Nevertheless, several investigations have ensued, including one by the insular Civil Rights Commission. By fall 1976, the questions were being considered by a somewhat controversial Puerto Rican special prosecutor and by federal authorities. The PSP general secretary called for the removal of the telephone company president and indicated an unwillingness to cooperate with the Puerto Rican prosecutor, demanding a different, impartial investigation. (*Granma,* 5, 6, 11 August; *NYT,* 27 November).

Preliminary and incomplete figures concerning the Puerto Rican gubernatorial election, indicated that PSP candidate Marí Bras received approximately 11,000 votes. This would appear to be around one percent of the total. No PSP legislative or mayoral candidates seem to have been successful. The general secretary indicated prior to the election that, regardless of the outcome, the party would reevaluate its stand with regard to participation in the present electoral system (*San Juan Star,* 31 October).

The PSP has been active in the United Workers Movement and assorted efforts to create a broadly based general confederation of workers, in the Puerto Rican Peace Council, and among students, faculty, and staff in educational institutions. Reportedly, the Independent Union of Telephone Employees of Puerto Rico supplied the controversial telephone company wiretap tapes to Marí Bras.

International Views and Attitudes. The PSP maintains an independent stance in international affairs with regard to splits in world Communist ranks. Marí Bras has denied that the party is either pro-Soviet or pro-Chinese. He maintains that it seeks further harmony within the socialist camp but is free to support or criticize policies of member groups (*Guardian,* 24 December 1975). The PSP has accepted, with reservations, the Soviet concept of détente, spoken against the invasion of Czechoslovakia by Soviet troops, and disagreed with China's policies on Angola and Chile and lack of participation in the 1975 UN committee vote concerning Puerto Rico. (Ibid., 17 December; *Intercontinental Press,* 27 December.)

At the party's Second Congress, it announced support of the new government of Angola and the People's Movement for the Liberation of Angola, the People's Republic of Congo, the reunification of Vietnam, the return of the canal to Panama, and resistance to the government of Chile (*Intercontinental Press,* 27 December). In September 1976, PSP general secretary Marí Bras sent a congratulatory message to Le Duan, secretary-general of the Vietnamese Communist party (VWP) upon the reunification of that nation (*FBIS,* 4 October). The congress continued firm support of Cuba (*Intercontinental Press,* 27 December 1975), though it should be noted that past PSP support of Cuba has not been totally uncritical. The general secretary led a PSP delegation to the First Congress of the Cuban Communist Party (*Granma,* 20 December).

In May 1976, Governor Hernández Colón accused Cuba of assisting Puerto Rican extremists in attempts to overthrow the government. He also linked the PSP with Cuba, claiming that party leaders were even obtaining training in that nation (*NYT,* 20 May), although a member of the Ford administration expressed a lack of knowledge of any direct physical assistance that Cuba might be supplying to Puerto Rican radicals (ibid., 20 May). While attending the economic summit meeting in Puerto Rico, President Ford, in a message which appeared to be directed toward Cuba, warned those endeavoring to interfere with the U.S.-Puerto Rican relationship that they were involving themselves in U.S. internal affairs (ibid., 26 June). U.S. secretary of state Henry Kissinger had previously indicated that renewal of U.S.-Cuban discussions would depend, in part, on Cuba's ceasing its active support of the independence of Puerto Rico (ibid., 23 April).

Puerto Rico continued as an issue before the UN Special Committee on the Situation with Regard to the Implementation of the Granting of Independence to Colonial Countries and People (Decolonization Committee). However, despite independentista efforts to pass a Cuban-sponsored resolution supporting the Puerto Rican right to independence, the committee, without a formal vote, delayed consideration of the issue until 1977. The PSP general secretary, who has continued efforts to make the independence of Puerto Rico a matter of international concern (Marí Bras in *Granma,* English, 14 September 1975), made a number of appearances before the committee, and the PSP continually supported the Cuban resolution.

Publication. The PSP publishes *Claridad,* which in late 1975 was reported to have a daily circulation of 20,000 and a weekend circulation of 30,000 (*Guardian,* 17 December). In May 1976, Governor Hernández Colón stated his belief that *Claridad* received Cuban funds (*NYT,* 20 May).

The LIT. The International Workers League supported participation in the electoral process of Puerto Rico in 1976. Due to scant membership it chose not to run candidates and supported the PSP slate, despite some reservations concerning its platform (*Militant,* 16 July). It offered to join in the protest over the alleged assassination of Santiago Marí Pesquera (*Intercontinental Press,* 12 April).

Described as revolutionary, the LIT has been reported to be the victim of slander and searches which violated members' rights. On 14 June it dispatched an open letter of protest to Governor Hernández Colón (ibid., 28 June).

St. John's University   Frank Paul Le Veness
Jamaica, New York

United States of America

The Communist Party, USA (CPUSA) is the largest and most influential Marxist-Leninist organization in the United States. It is descended from the Communist Labor Party and the Communist Party, both formed in 1919. At various times the CPUSA has also been called the Workers Party and, for a brief period during World War II, the Communist Political Association.

The Socialist Workers Party (SWP) is the leading Trotskyite party. Organized in 1938, it traces its origin to 1928, when several CPUSA members were expelled for supporting Leon Trotsky. The SWP has spawned numerous other Trotskyite groups, including the Workers' World Party, the Spartacist League, and the Revolutionary Marxist Organizing Committee.

The Progressive Labor Party (PLP) came into existence in 1965 following the expulsion of several CPUSA members for ultra-leftism. The PLP strongly supported Maoism until 1971. Its present ideological posture is rigidly Stalinist.

The two most important Maoist sects are the Revolutionary Communist Party (RCP), formerly the Revolutionary Union, and the October League (OL). A commitment to Marxism-Leninism is also proclaimed by such groups as the Weather Underground Organization (WUO), Prairie Fire-Organizing Committee (PFOC), the Marxist-Leninist Organizing Committee, the Communist Labor Party, the Revolutionary Student Brigade, the Revolutionary Workers' Congress, the August 29th Movement, the Revolutionary Socialist League, and the Proletarian Unity League. All of these emerged, at least in their Marxist-Leninist guise, in the early 1970s, usually under the direction of veterans of the now defunct Students for a Democratic Society (SDS).

The CPUSA is a legal party. Restrictive laws which hindered access to the ballot in some states have been removed or are under legal attack. In 1976 the party's presidential ticket of Gus Hall and Jarvis Tyner was on the ballot in 19 states and the District of Columbia. At present it has no representation either in Congress or in any state legislature.

The CPUSA claims to have about 18,000 members; outside estimates give it only about 5,000 (*Nation,* New York, 25 September 1976). Membership is mainly concentrated in a few industrial states, and recruitment efforts are particularly aimed at minorities (blacks, Puerto Ricans, Chicanos) and young industrial workers.

The SWP, like the CPUSA, runs candidates for state, local, and national office. While none have been elected, the SWP has drawn more votes than the CPUSA. The SWP claims 2,500 members (*NYT,* 11 October); other estimates are around 1,500 (*Nation,* 25 September). The SWP, although concentrated in the industrial states, has established strong local chapters in some areas of the South and Southwest where the CPUSA has made no headway.

The PLP does not run candidates for office. Neither does it provide information about membership. It is unlikely that there are more than 1,000 members. Neither the RU nor the OL provides such information, but neither has more than a thousand members. The other groups are smaller.

The CPUSA and SWP are active in broad-scale left movements, such as support of school busing and black causes, attacks on the Chilean junta and support for the MPLA in Angola. The smaller sects, whose origins go back to the campus turmoil of the 1960s, no longer appear to wield much influence in the colleges and universities. In general, the continuing economic problems in the United States have not stimulated any noticeable growth in Marxist-Leninist influence, but an increasing attraction toward Marxism-Leninism is apparent among the remnants of the New Left.

The population of the USA is about 215 million.

The CPUSA. Leadership and Organization. The leadership of the CPUSA remained largely intact in 1976. Gus Hall remains as general secretary and Henry Winston as national chairman. Arnold Bechetti is organizational secretary, Betty Smith is national administrative secretary, and Sid Taylor is national treasurer. Other important party leaders include: Helen Winter (international affairs secretary), James Jackson (national education director), Grace Mora (chairwoman, Puerto Rican Commission), Alva Buxenbaum (chairwoman, Commission for Women's Equality), George Meyers (chairman, National Labor Commission), Lorenzo Torres (chairman, National Chicano Commission), Arnold Johnson (public relations director), William Patterson and Roscoe Proctor (co-chairmen, Black Liberation Commission), Victor Perlo (chairman, Economics Commission), Alex Kolkin (chairman, Jewish Commission), Carl Bloice (editor, *People's World*). Danny Rubin (chairman, Commission on Unemployment and Inflation), and Si Gerson, Claude Lightfoot, Angela Davis, Charlene Mitchell, and Herbert Aptheker (Central Committee members). Hyman Lumer, member of the Political Commission and editor of *Political Affairs,* died in 1976.

Among the party leaders in important states are Jarvis Tyner (New York), Jim West (Ohio), Ishmael Flory and Jack Kling (Illinois), William Taylor and Al Lima (California), Tom Dennis (Michigan), Thomas Crenshaw (Missouri), Lee Dlugin (New Jersey), Ed Teixeira (New England), Rasheed Storey and Sondra Patrinos (Pennsylvania).

While the CPUSA does not officially have any affiliated organizations, the Young Workers Liberation League (YWLL) is, in fact, the party's youth arm. Henry Winston has proclaimed that "the ideology and the outlook in the CP and the YWLL membership are the same" (*Daily World,* 18 February 1976). An independent estimate puts YWLL membership at 3,000 but notes that the organization is plagued by "high turnover and dues delinquency." A commitment to socialism is not a prerequisite for membership. (*Nation,* 25 September.) The national chairman is Jim Steele. Other leaders include Roque Ristorucci (executive secretary), Jay Schaffner (organizational secretary), and

Jill Furillo (editor, *Young Worker*). The YWLL gave its efforts a Bicentennial flavor in 1976 in an effort to get beyond a sectarian approach. The goal for new members was put at 1976. The organization sponsored Youth Bicentennial Festivals which drew 3,000 participants in New York and 800 in Chicago in February with the aim of teaching American youth "the Bicentennial's correct lessons" (*Daily World,* 18 February).

A number of other organizations, while not as directly tied to the CPUSA, are dominated by the party and largely led by party functionaries. They represent the CPUSA's united front policies in different areas of American life. The most prominent and successful has been the National Alliance against Racist and Political Repression (NARPR). Charlene Mitchell, onetime CPUSA candidate for President, is executive director. Co-chairmen include Bert Corona and Angela Davis and Clyde Bellecourt of the American Indian Movement. The NARPR has focused its efforts on North Carolina, alleging that this state has instituted anti-labor and anti-black repression. In addition to protesting the conviction of a number of activists in the state, the NARPR called for a boycott of the J.P. Stevens firm, a large non-union textile manufacturer, and of all tourism. A Labor Day march in Raleigh to protest repression drew some 5,000 demonstrators.

The National Coalition to Fight Inflation and Unemployment (NCFIU), led by Sidney Von Luther, sponsored a march in Washington, D.C., on 3 April for jobs and lower prices which attracted 5,000 participants (*Daily World,* 6 April). The National Co-ordinating Committee for Trade Union Action and Democracy (TUAD) was founded in 1970 to help increase party influence in the trade union movement. Rayfield Mooty and Fred Gaboury are TUAD leaders.

The CPUSA's principal front in the women's field is Women for Racial and Economic Equality (WREE), led by Georgia Henning and Sondra Patrinos. At a national organizational conference in March, 65 delegates decided to hold a founding convention in 1977. WREE sees "corporate monopoly as the source of inequality for women." It opposes the Equal Rights Amendment to the U.S. constitution as at present written but supports a Women's Bill of Rights which focuses on economic issues, educational opportunities, and availability of day care for children (ibid., 17 March). Other party-dominated organizations include the Committee for a Just Peace in the Middle East, the National Council of American-Soviet Friendship, the Chile Solidarity Committee, the Metropolitan Council on Housing, and the National Anti-Imperialist Movement in Solidarity with African Liberation.

Party Internal Affairs. In 1976 the CPUSA began publication of *Black Liberation Journal* and a weekly Spanish-language supplement to its principal organ, *Daily World.* Party recruitment efforts continued to be directed towards minorities. Party officials were heartened by sizable crowds listening to Gus Hall and Jarvis Tyner during the election campaign and took this as a sign that U.S. communism was no longer beyond the pale (*NYT,* 29 October).

Stresses within the party over the Equal Rights Amendment and Zionism (see *YICA, 1976,* p. 524), apparently caused no changes in party positions. The promised reexamination of the ERA resulted only in a denunciation of the amendment for its vagueness and potential impact (*Political Affairs,* March). Gus Hall has admitted that the party's opposition to Zionism has probably cost it members (*Wall Street Journal,* 29 October).

Domestic Attitudes and Activities. The CPUSA gave much attention in 1976 to the Presidential election. The party campaigned extensively and attacked both major political parties. Although failing to gain its goal of ballot status in 35 states, the Hall-Tyner ticket did better than in 1972, when it was listed in 14 states but received about 60,000 votes in 19 states. Gus Hall saw the vote as an indication people are prepared for a new political movement. The Central Committee called the results "a major breakthrough, establishing the Party as a recognized current in U.S. political life" (*Daily World,* 24 November). There was frequent CPUSA criticism of laws which hinder minority parties from easy access to the ballot, and it was charged that conspiracy to keep the CPUSA off the ballot existed in some states (ibid., 10 June). Moreover, Gus Hall charged that refusal of the TV networks to expand the broadcasts of Presidential debates to minor-party candidates was another example of "limiting the election to the two-party system of big business" (ibid., 2 September).

None of the major-party candidates met with CPUSA approval. During the primary elections the CPUSA criticized President Ford for carrying out reactionary policies designed by Richard Nixon (ibid., 9 April). Ford's chief rival for nomination by the Republican Party, Ronald Reagan, was termed a man whose views had "more than a streak of the fascistic" (ibid., 7 January). The Democratic Party's Jimmy Carter was a bête noir of the CPUSA from the beginning of the campaign. Carter's ethnic purity remark was "a form of modified apartheid" and his apology "only proved how deep his racism really is" (ibid., 8, 10 April). Although the *Daily World* (25 March) was pleased by George Wallace's poor showing in the primary elections, it later remarked (8 April) that behind Carter's mask stood the Alabama governor. The CPUSA labeled Carter a reactionary millionaire, a conservative, anti-labor cold-warrior, and a racist (ibid., 14 October).

Seeing both parties as dominated by monopoly capitalism, the CPUSA declared: "independent political action is a major key to people's progress" (ibid., 21 January). In this view, the bankruptcy of the two major parties was making clearer the need for a new, anti-monopoly party of the working-class, blacks, and Puerto Ricans (ibid., 3 April). The CPUSA gave much attention to the Committee on Independent Political Action and suggested that the CIPA could be a harbinger of future independent campaigns for political office (ibid., 25 September). Gus Hall discerned signs of a new radicalization in the USA in the increase in "class struggle unionism" and a widening fight against racism and discrimination (ibid., 21 January).

The CPUSA campaigned on the grounds that neither major party was a lesser evil. The broadcast debates showed that their candidates agreed on support for the military budget and a jingoistic foreign policy (ibid., 8 October). Hall called for a $100 billion cut in defense spending, a reduction of the work week to 30 hours with no cut in pay, legislation to make racism a crime, and independence for Puerto Rico (ibid., 29 April). His running mate, Jarvis Tyner, suggested that the USA should have a House of Nationalities like the Soviet Union's to give fair representation to oppressed groups (ibid., 25 March). The party suggested that a large Communist vote would gain the attention of the government and force it to respond to various problems (ibid., 3 April).

On other domestic issues, the CPUSA continued its attacks on labor leaders George Meany and I.W. Abel as class collaborationists (ibid., 18 March). George Meyer claimed that "a qualitatively new situation is maturing in the trade union movement" as a result of rank and file revolts against union leadership. Labor's new militancy was not based, as in the 1930s, on organizing the unorganized, but on class-struggle unionism for job security and a shorter work week and against racism. Meyer added that the CPUSA was active in rank-and-file united fronts in such unions as the Steelworkers (ibid., 5 May; *Political Affairs,* January).

The CPUSA continued its criticism of U.S. intelligence agencies. The CIA murder plots revealed by congressional committees were part of an "anti-democratic conspiracy" and warranted the CIA's abolition as "an instrument for imperialism's undeclared war against democracy and people's causes' (*Daily World,* 22 January). The FBI was called a "police-state, anti-labor, racist instrument of the ruling class" (ibid., 23 March). The party charged that the chief targets of the FBI's disruption campaign were "labor, the Black liberation movement and the Communist Party" (ibid., 11 May), but ignored almost totally the revelations of the FBI campaign against the SWP. Moreover, the CPUSA did not make any comparable effort to force release and publication of documents on FBI programs directed against itself.

The party supports school busing to achieve racial balance and has demanded that Boston opponents of busing be punished (ibid., 16 June). The New York City fiscal crisis was "a phony" concocted to enable banks to save their money at the expense of the poor (ibid., 3 May).

International Views and Policies. Although Gus Hall reportedly has argued in private with Soviet leaders about internal Soviet policies, his and his party's public posture is one of complete and total approval of the USSR's domestic foreign policy (*Wall Street Journal,* 29 October 1976). Hall told the 25th CPSU Congress that "the Communist Party of the Soviet Union . . . serves as the working pattern for the revolutionary movements throughout the world" (ibid., 4 March). The ferment among European Communist parties barely touched the CPUSA. Hall insisted that differences between Communist parties such as Italy's and the CPSU were merely tactical. Differences that went further, however, were "based on opportunistic considerations" that lead to Maoism (ibid., 18 March). The CPUSA accused the West of ignoring the "new level of unity" among Communists, and insisted that proletarian internationalism "gives the working class strength" (ibid., 2 July), but argued that Communist parties have always been independent and autonomous (ibid., 16 July).

The CPUSA remained a staunch advocate of détente. It argued that détente is "deeply rooted" among average Americans despite growing attacks on it by political and labor leaders (ibid., 3 January). Countering criticism that it has been a one-sided process the *Daily World* (3 April) argued that détente had brought increased benefits to the USA in "trade, science, culture, technology." President Ford was criticized for the gap between accepting détente in principle and carrying it out (ibid., 6 January). The delay in signing an arms limitation agreement with the USSR was blamed on the USA (ibid., 16 January). Anti-détente forces included those protesting the "alleged plight of Soviet Jews" (ibid., 4 May).

China continued to be criticized. Former President Nixon's trip there was described as part of an intensified collaboration between Maoists and U.S. imperialists to destroy détente (ibid., 24 February). According to Gus Hall, "at the murky bottom of the swamp of opportunism there is counter-revolution," and "Maoism reached to that bottom" (ibid., 31 March).

The party's Middle East position remained unchanged. The CPUSA urged the reconvening of the Geneva conference with the Palestine Liberation Organization present (ibid., 8 May). Israel was attacked for murdering Palestinians, costing the USA money, being a threat to peace, bankrupting its own citizens, and refusing to deal with the PLO (ibid., 14 January). The Israeli raid at Entebbe was "state terrorism" (ibid., 7 July). The Lebanese crisis was a result of the Ford Administration's "playing power politics on behalf of big business" (ibid., 19 June).

In other policy positions also, the CPUSA faithfully echoed the Soviet line. It urged a "quarantine of genocidal South Africa" and the breaking of diplomatic relations (ibid., 14, 18 June). Cuban troops "do not restrict" Angola's freedom but "help safeguard it" (ibid., 25 June). South Korea was a repressive "terrorist dictatorship," while North Korea was "one of the most advanced and progressive of Asian states" (ibid., 25 June). The CPUSA called for reparations to Vietnam, an end to the blockade of Cuba, and an end of support for "fascist" Chile (ibid., 27 May).

International Activities and Contacts. Gus Hall, Henry Winston, and Helen Winter headed the U.S. delegation to the 25th Congress of the CPSU. The congresses of the ruling Communist parties in Czechoslovakia, Poland, and Bulgaria were attended by Winston and James Jackson, Betty Smith, and Claude Lightfoot, respectively. In March Roscoe Proctor attended a conference in Angola to support the MPLA. Carl Boice and Michael Meyerson were in South Yemen for discussions early in the year. During 1976 Winston was awarded the Soviet Order of the October Revolution.

Publications. The *Daily World,* published five times a week in New York, is the CPUSA's major publication (claimed circulation, 30,000). *Political Affairs* is a theoretical journal. Other party-linked papers are *People's World,* a San Francisco weekly: *Freedomways,* a black quarterly; *New World Review,* a bimonthly journal on international affairs; *Jewish Affairs,* a bimonthly newsletter; *Cultural*

Reporter; African Agenda; Labor Today; Korea Forum; and *Black Liberation Journal.* International Publishers has long been identified as the party's publishing outlet.

The SWP: Leadership and Organization. Jack Barnes is national secretary and Barry Shepard is organizational secretary of the Socialist Workers Party. Other party leaders include Malik Miah (black liberation director); Mary-Alice Waters (editor, *Militant*); Cindy Jaquith (women's liberation director) Olga Rodriguez (Chicano liberation director); Tony Thomas, Doug Jenness, Frank Lovell, Ed Shaw, George Breitman Fred Halstead, Gus Horowitz, Lew Jones, and Catarino Garza.

The most important party auxiliary is the Young Socialist Alliance, with about 1,350 members. Membership grew by about 15 percent during 1975. About 40 percent of the members are college students. Nan Bailey is national chairperson and Ilona Gersh national secretary. The 15th YSA Convention, held in December 1975, attracted 950 delegates from 30 states. The largest representation was from New York, California, and Wisconsin. (The YSA has 90 chapters around the country.) The convention adopted a reorganization plan which will base its local chapters on college campuses (*NYT,* 2 January 1976).

An important party organization which has attracted support from non-party figures is the Political Rights Defense Fund (PRDF), headed by Syd Stapleton. The PRDF was founded to raise money to fight the SWP's $37 million damage suit against the FBI for illegal surveillance of party activities over the years. During 1976 the government admitted to almost 100 burglaries against the SWP in 1960-66 (*Militant,* 9 April). The Attorney-General's order to end the FBI investigation was hailed by SWP presidential candidate Peter Camejo as "a victory for the democratic rights of all Americans." The party is now demanding to learn the names of some 66 FBI informers who are still members (ibid., 24 September). Gus Hall of the CPUSA charged that the SWP was "the main staging area for the FBI in the left movement in general," while the SWP taunted the CPUSA for its reluctance to obtain files of the FBI's campaign against itself (ibid., 10 September).

Other party-connected groups are the National Student Coalition Against Racism, led by Maceo Dixon, and the U.S. Committee for Justice to Latin American Political Prisoners.

Party Internal Affairs. The SWP convention in August 1976 attracted 1,650 delegates and guests. The party was optimistic about its growth and viability. Three-quarters of its members are reported to be 30 or under, 40 percent are women. Only 6 percent, however, are black, and only one in three is a union member (*Nation,* 25 September). Recruitment was a major effort throughout the year. The SWP instituted a provisional membership for a three-month period to acquaint potential members with the organization, and gained 200 new recruits in six-months. Most new members are recruited from the YSA, but the percentage joining without exposure to the youth group is rising (*Militant,* 20 February, 18 June). The SWP is shifting its orientation to smaller branches in working-class districts as opposed to large city-wide units. In June the party reported 59 branches and 13 locals (several branches in one city) (ibid., 18 June).

Tim Wohlforth, one-time YSA leader who subsequently joined the Workers League, returned to the SWP during the year. The SWP continued its conflict with the majority of the parties in the Trotskyite Fourth International, supporting the minority Leninist-Trotskyist tendency (ibid., 24 September).

Domestic Attitudes and Activities. The SWP placed major emphasis on the 1976 election. The Presidential ticket of Peter Camejo and Willie Mae Reid was on the ballot in 26 states, a few more than in 1972. Complete returns gave the SWP a total of 91,000 votes. Moreover, numerous party candidates ran for offices ranging from governor to congressman. The SWP campaign focused on economic and racial issues. Camejo supported busing, huge public works projects, free medical care, free education through college, and 30 hours' work for 40 hour's pay. He also called for a moratorium on interest payments on federal borrowing. (*NYT,* 11 October.) The SWP sees the beginning of the radicalization of the U.S. working class as a result of military adventures abroad, curtailment of democratic rights at home, and attacks on the standard of living of the working class. In this light, the SWP charged that the most oppressed U.S. sectors were stirring. Party members gave active support to the activities of the United Farm Workers, Coalition of Labor Union Women, New York Teachers, insurgents in the Steelworkers Union, and La Raza Unida (Chicano) political parties (*Militant,* 20 February).

One of the SWP's central objectives was organizing to win passage of the Equal Rights Amendment. There was a steady drumbeat of criticism of the CPUSA for its oppostion to ERA (ibid., 5 March). Another focus was an effort to build a movement to defend busing in Boston. There were attacks on the Ford Administration for allegedly supporting racist opponents of school desegregation (ibid., 28 May).

International Views and Policies. The SWP is critical of both the USSR and the USA, but directs the bulk of its attacks on the latter. During 1976 the SWP opposed any U.S. involvement in Angola and gave critical support to the MPLA even while criticizing it for being allied with imperialism (*Militant,* 23, 30 January). Détente was regarded as a ploy (a) grasped at by a weakened U.S. ruling class facing an upsurge of class struggle around the world and (b) pushed by an equally eager Soviet Union faced with domestic tensions caused by "socialism in one country." This effort to freeze the class struggle was, the SWP charged, doomed as a result of the economic disarray of world capitalism. The ferment among European Communists was "simply old vinegar in new bottles." The USSR was a degenerated workers' state which rejected workers' democracy, accepted class collaboration and détente, and persecuted dissidents. (Ibid., 2 July, 13 February.)

On the Middle East, the SWP insisted that "only the dismantling of the Zionist colonial-settler state and its replacement by a democratic, secular Palestine where Arab and Jew can live in equality" would bring peace (ibid., 26 March). Israel's raid at Entebbe was called "illegal" and "racist," and skyjacking criticized as playing "into the Zionists' hands" (ibid., 16 July). The SWP supported the PLO and its leftist allies in the Lebanese civil war (ibid., 16 April).

The SWP publishes *The Militant* every week. *Young Socialist* and *International Socialist Review* are monthlies.

The PLP. The Progressive Labor Party provides virtually no information about its membership or leading cadres. The party's founders, Milt Rosen and Mort Scheer, apparently still play leading roles. The PLP is seemingly rent by factionalism and disputes. A February report to its National Committee charged that many comrades had slipped on theoretical questions and doubted the militancy of the working class (*Challenge,* 26 February). Later the PLP admitted that members harbored strong tendencies of nationalism and racism which were responsible for their not understanding that economic cutbacks and layoffs were racist. Teachers who were PLP members were criticized for focusing on their own conflicts with school boards and ignoring those of students, and for failing to introduce communist ideas in the classroom. (Ibid., 4 March.)

In January, PLP-sponsored conferences in Detroit and San Francisco each drew some 1,500 people. The party's main effort was to "win workers to build a base around communist ideas." This was to be accomplished by organizing communist factions and caucuses in industrial shops. (Ibid., 12 February.) Also emphasis was placed on school organizing, in addition to rank-and-file organizing (ibid., 15 January). The PLP disdained united fronts and criticized the CPUSA as reformist (ibid., 12 February, 20 May).

The PLP's major front group is the Committee Against Racism (CAR). In July, 500 delegates attended CAR's convention in New York, which claimed the growth of a working-class leadership as one of its major accomplishments (ibid., 29 July). CAR and PLP support a six-hour work day with eight hours pay, a hike in the minimum wage, support of busing, no cutbacks in social services, national health insurance, and full rights for all aliens (ibid., 13 May). PLP urges the end of advocacy of "racist lies" in high school and college courses. CAR has disrupted talks by such speakers as Arthur Jensen and William Shockley (ibid., 20 May). While not focusing on international relations, PLP regards both the USSR and the USA as imperialist powers. The civil war in Angola indicated the USA's decline as imperialism's leader and replacement in Africa by the USSR (ibid., 8 January). As a consequence of "imperialist competition." the U.S. bosses were said "to be sinking rapidly into fascism" (ibid., 13 May).

The PLP publishes *Challenge-Desafio,* an English-Spanish weekly, and *Progressive Labor,* a theoretical journal.

Maoist Groups. The Maoist movement in the USA is splintered into a number of sects which have been groping toward unity but exchanging ever more vitriolic words with each other. The two largest organized groups are the Revolutionary Communist Party and the October League. The *Guardian* represents an independent Maoist line.

The OL chairman is Michael Klonsky, formerly an SDS activist. Other OL leaders include Sherman Miller, Jeff Berger, Arlene Schumacher, Larry Miller, Odis Hyde, Eileen Klehr, and Jill Gemmil. Many of OL's cadres were once active in the Southern Student Organizing Congress. OL sponsored a "National Fight Back Conference" in Chicago at the end of 1975 which was attended by 1,000. The conference's slogan was "unite against the two superpowers." Among the other organizations represented were the Congress of African People, the August 29th Movement (a largely Chicano group), and the Marxist-Leninist Organizing Committee (from the San Francisco Bay Area). OL hopes to form a new communist party by spring 1977 (*Guardian,* New York, 14 January 1976).

OL has revived the old CPUSA theme of self-determination in the black belt. Harry Haywood, longtime black CPUSA leader associated with that doctrine is now in the OL. On other civil rights issues, OL urged armed self-defense against Ku Klux Klan terror and opposed the death penalty. OL has also succeeded in capturing the Southern Conference Educational Fund (SCEF), a former CPUSA front group (ibid., 7 May). In foreign policy, OL insists with China that Soviet imperialism is the major world danger. It has criticized the independence movement in Puerto Rico and attacked the MPLA in Angola as an agent of Soviet social imperialism (ibid., 14 January). OL publishes *The Call.*

The Revolutionary Communist Party leadership is a combination of Old and New Left. Bob Avakian and Nick Unger were prominent in SDS, Barry Romo was a national coordinator of the Vietnam Veterans Against the War, Leibel Bergman is a former CPUSA activist, and William Hinton, a long-time supporter of China, is reportedly close to party leaders. Among groups heavily influenced by the RCP are the Vietnam Veterans Against the War, the Unemployed Workers Organizing Committee, and the party's youth group, the Revolutionary Student Brigade. The RCP, fervently suypporting China's policies, has attacked Cuba as a Soviet puppet and refused to support the MPLA in Angola (ibid., 19 May).

The RCP has been criticized by the Maoist *Guardian* for being isolated from black revolutionaries and for its allegedly backward position on the woman question. U.S. Maoists have been feuding bitterly over Chinese foreign policy, particular its opposition to the MPLA in Angola. The *Guardian* has supported the MPLA and attacked the OL and the RCP. The Chinese purge of leftists has created confusion among Maoist groups. After some hesitations, the *Guardian* (3 November) endorsed the purge. The OL has totally endorsed the Chinese line, while the RCP has not finished debating the guilt of the leftists. The RCP publishes *Revolution* and the *Worker.*

Prairie Fire Organizing Committee. The PFOC emerged in 1975 as a support group for the Weather Underground Organization (WUO). In early 1976 it sponsored a "National Hard Times

Conference" in Chicago which drew more than 2,000 people and, with various radical sects, co-sponsored a Bicentennial rally in Philadelphia which drew 15,000 (*Guardian,* 11 February). The PFOC underwent an internal upheaval as a result of the Hard Times conference. Clayton van Lydegraf, a former CPUSA figure, assumed a dominant role along with Arlene Eisen Bergman. Jennifer Dohrn, Russell Newfeld, Alan Berkman, and others were forced to engage in self-criticism. The victors attacked the previous emphasis on mass work and stressed the danger of right opportunism. The errors of the conference were said to be "pragmatism, tailing spontaneity, opportunism," and lack of support for blacks. The PFOC admitted that its internal struggle had consumed its attention and isolated it from other groups. (*Ossawatomie,* June.) The PFOC has set itself two tasks: "to build an anti-imperialist working class movement" and to build a communist party to lead that struggle (*Guardian,* April). It publishes *Ossawatomie* and *Groundswell.*

Emory University   Harvey Klehr

Uruguay

The Communist Party of Uruguay (Partido Comunista del Uruguay; PCU) dates from September 1920, when a congress of the Socialist Party voted to join the Comintern. The present name was adopted in April 1921. The PCU is firmly pro-Soviet. In December 1973 the PCU was declared illegal for the first time in its history. On 1 January 1975 a presidential decree made the 1973 outlawing of the PCU permanent.

Numerous leftist organizations operate in Uruguay and display Soviet, Chinese, Cuban, or nationalist leanings or combinations thereof. Among the more important are the Socialist Party of Uruguay (Partido Socialista del Uruguay; PSU), the Movement of the Revolutionary Left (Movimiento de Izquierda Revolucionaria; MIR), and the National Liberation Movement (Movimiento de Liberación National, MLN), the latter better known as the Tupamaros.

The Revolutionary Workers' Party (Partido Obrero Revolucionario; POR), originally formed in 1944 as the Revolutionary Workers' League, and the Socialist Workers' Party of Uruguay (Partido Socialista de los Trabajadores del Uruguay; PSTU), are Trotskyist in orientation.

Except for the PCU, these groups are apparently small (no precise membership figures are known). The PCU is estimated to have 30,000 members, with workers accounting for about 73 percent; with its youth group and sympathizers added, the total may be 35,000 to 40,000.

The population of Uruguay is 2,800,000 (1976).

The Broad Front. PCU electoral strength long resided in the Leftist Liberation Front (Frente Izquierda de Liberación; FIDEL), founded by the PCU in 1962 and composed of 10 small political groups. In an extremely complex electoral system which discouraged voting for minority party candidates, FIDEL never did well (less than 6 percent of the vote in 1966). In the 1971 national election FIDEL became part of a larger coalition, the Broad Front (Frente Amplio; FA), made up of 17 leftist and anti-government parties and groups, including the PSU, POR, the Christian Democratic Party (Partido Demócrata Cristiano; PDC), and extremist factions of the Colorado and National (Blanco) parties. The FA won 18 percent of the vote. It had 18 members in the Chamber of Deputies and 5 in the Senate until 27 June 1973 when President Juan Bordaberry with military backing dissolved the Congress, charging the FA congressmen with criminal conspiracy against the constitution.

The PCU. Organization and Leadership. PCU first secretary Rodney Arismendi in January 1975 was exiled to Moscow. The PCU Central Committee has 48 members and 27 alternates. The five-member Secretariat consists of Arismendi, Enrique Pastorino, Jaime Pérez, Enrique Rodríguez, and Alberto Suárez. Pastorino remains president of the pro-Soviet World Federation of Trade Unions (WFTU), and, through the International Labor Office of Geneva, has been given United Nations diplomatic immunity. During 1976 Pastorino has used the publication *WFTU Flashes,* the Cuban news service *Presnsa Latina,* and various Third World forums to attack the Uruguayan government's policies.

In December 1975, Arismendi went to Havana and indicated he would spend much of 1976 in Eastern European capitals and Moscow (*Granma,* Havana, 20 December). Pérez was imprisoned in Montevideo on 24 October 1974, and during 1975 and 1976 has been the object of a "Freedom for Jaime Pérez" propaganda campaign directed by Arismendi in news releases periodically appearing in *L'Unitá* of Rome, *Granma* of Havana, and information bulletins of the *World Marxist Review.*

Rodríguez in late 1975 surfaced in East Berlin, where Albert Norden, of the Politburo of the Socialist Unity Party of the German Democratic Republic, was his host (East Berlin Radio, 28 November).

Suárez was organization secretary until deposed by the PCU Central Committee for not preparing the party to cope with being outlawed. The PCU has publicly ignored Suárez since January 1975, but in early 1976 the ad hoc Marxist "Committee for the Defense of Political Prisoners of Uruguay," in Paris, demanded the restoration of the PCU as a legal party and did so in the name of the five-member Secretariat, inlcuding the name of Suárez (AFP, 4 January).

Among the 15 members of the PCU Executive Committee are José Luis Massera, Jorge Mazzarovich, and Wladímir Turiansky. Martha Valentini de Massera, wife of Luis Massera, was arrested late in 1975 for circulating petitions for the release of her husband; she was released in early 1976 (*Granma,* 13 February). Turiansky was arrested by Uruguayan police late in 1975 (*Christian Science Monitor,* 26 December) for directing a propaganda campaign for the outlawed PCU.

The secretary of the Apostolic Legation in Montevideo conferred with the Uruguayan Defense Minister in January 1976 about the grounds for jailing Mazzarovich and Massera. After reading the testimony of 100 PCU members arrested with Massera and Mazzarovich, who admitted possession of 927 weapons plus explosives, the Church spokesman ended his campaign for clemency. (*El País,* Montevideo, 23 January.)

Massera, an Italian born in Geneva, became an Uruguayan citizen, was elected a deputy from the PCU under the FIDEL banner, then a senator from the FA, and finally first secretary of the PCU after Arismendi went into exile.

From files that the police received from Turiansky, the attorney general on 11 February got an indictment against Juan José Crottogini, vice-president of the FA, charging him with coordinating PCU activities of medical students under the cloak of the FA in 1971. Dr. Crottigini was a professor of medicine at the University of Montevideo. (*Prensa Latina,* Havana, 12 February.)

The Crottogini arrest was also linked to the arrest for subversion on 7 January of Dr. Eduardo Grosso García, director of the PCU "health cadres," who were offering free medical treatment for prospective PCU members (*Latin,* Buenos Aires, 8 January).

The National Convention of Workers (Convención Nacional de Trabajadores; CNT), established in 1966 as the largest federation of labor unions, was led by PCU officials, including Pastorino and Turiansky. After calling a general strike, the CNT had all its activities suspended on 30 June 1973. In October 1975 a clandestine report on the CNT by Alvaro Marino was circulated among Marxist groups in Buenos Aires (*Nuestra Palabra,* Buenos Aires, 15 October). In mid-1976 the Uruguayan Ministry of Labor indicated to reporters that when unions and federations hold elections in either 1977 or 1978, CNT candidates will not be recognized because of ties to the outlawed PCU.

The PCU's youth organization, the Union of Communist Youth (Unión de la Juventud Comunista; UJC), was founded in 1955. It had a claimed membership of 22,000 when it was outlawed in 1973. The UJC and the PCU Central Committee held a clandestine plenary meeting in September 1975 to plan a long-range program to overthrow the anti-Communist government. The UJC program pledged to encourage "militancy of the working classes, deepen differences among the armed forces leaders, and work for a Marxist front of all forces" of the left (*IB,* no. 1, 15 January 1976).

General (ret.) Liber Seregni, head of the FA, was released from jail 2 November 1974 after serving a one-year term for sedition, and on 11 January 1976 was arrested again at his home in Punta del Este in conjunction with new PCU activities, in which he was accused of being a communications link (*Granma,* 10 February). Seregni's former executive secretary, Colonel (ret.) Carlos Zufriátegui, was arrested 9 February and charged with aiding the clandestine communications between Seregni and PCU (*Prensa Latina,* Montevideo, 9 February).

Ricardo Saxlund, one of the editors of the outlawed PCU daily newspaper *El Popular,* disappeared in 1974 and resurfaced in November 1975 with an article on the 75th anniversary of Lenin's founding of the Communist newspaper *The Spark* (*WMR,* November 1975). No clue as to Saxlund's residence was given. Then in mid-1976, a Brazilian underground Communist periodical quoted Saxlund on how clandestine literature should be circulated; neatly and tightly folded to fit into a sleeve and passed on hand to hand (*A Classe Operaria,* Rio de Janeiro, 1 August).

A leader of the PCU women's groups, Julia Arévalo, was arrested late in 1975, and in early 1976 she and her daughter were jailed for outlawed activities (*Granma Weekly Review,* Havana, 8 February). Mrs. Arévalo is a vice-president of the Women's International Democratic Federation, a Communist front, and in 1975 was named winner of the Ana Betancourt prize of the Federation of Cuban Women. Her arrest led police to the hideout of another PCU leader, Luis Tourón.

Domestic Attitudes and Activities. The major political events in Uruguay during 1976—the ousting of President Juan Bordaberry on 12 June by the armed forces, the selection of Aparicio Méndez as president of Uruguay by the Council of the Nation (Consejo de la Nación; COSENA), which succeeded the Council of State as the surrogate for the suspended Congress in July, and the decision of the Council and the military leaders to cancel the scheduled 1976 elections—evoked clandestine leaflets from the PCU protesting these happenings. The PCU has been demanding since its 1973 outlawing that it be allowed to campaign openly and that it be on the ballot for the elections which were to have been held in November 1976.

On 11 March, in Buenos Aires, the PCU announced that Jorge Mazzarovich and Gerardo Cuesta, both of the PCU Executive Committee, had been arrested again in Montevideo, after being in hiding following their release on probation early in the year.

In mid-March, in Salto and Paysandú, 58 labor union and municipal employees were arrested on charges of being active in the PCU. Some were released after questioning, but some were detained on charges of sediiton or being accessories to armed robberies (*Prensa Latina,* Buenos Aires, 15 March). In Moscow the labor newspaper *Trud* denounced these arrests.

Security forces announced 28 March that they had dismantled the PCU's logistical apparatus in Montevideo with the uncovering of an explosives factory and two storehouses with weapons. The factory had been disguised as a detergent plant. (*Latín,* Buenos Aires, 28 March.)

On 5 April the armed forces issued a 27-page report on Communist subversion in Uruguay, linking the PCU with the MLN, and with agents and funds from Cuba and the USSR. Among foreign agents charged with aiding the PCU was Marian Aishmat, a Dutch woman claiming to be a student of folklore until arrested as a paymaster for outlawed Marxist groups. (*El Espectador,* Montevideo, 5 April.)

A former police officer, Rubén Pérez González, who had worked for the National Information and Intelligence Directorate of the armed forces, was arrested in April after a Tupamaro admitted that Pérez was working with the MLN and the PCU (*El País,* 29 April).

The Committee for Defense of Political Prisoners, in Paris, on 4 May denounced what it charged was the disappearance from Libertad jail in Uruguay of Raúl Cariboni de Silva, history professor and PCU activist (AFP, 4 May).

Police on 7 May arrested eight UJC members for PCU activities (*Prensa Latina,* Buenos Aires, 8 May). They were arrested while sending a telegram to the UJC of Cuba via a courier en route to Buenos Aires. Police said that 70 percent of the UJC members came from the university and preparatory school areas.

On 1 September, after his inauguration, the new President of Uruguay, Aparicio Méndez, canceled the political rights of the leaders of political parties, including not only the FA and its affiliated PCU and PSU, but also former President Bordaberry of the Colorado Party, and Jorge Batlle, leader of a Colorado faction rivaling Bordaberry's faction. The order stressed that non-Marxist parties are not considered outlawed but "in recess" until new leadership can show responsibility to Uruguay for preserving its nationhood (*El País,* Montevideo, 2 September).

In mid-August, combined security forces arrested former senator and National (Blanco) Party presidential candidate Wilson Ferreira, who was charged with collaborating with the PCU. In mid-September the attorney general's office criticized the testimony Ferreira had volunteered in Washington before a U.S. congressional subcommittee, in which the Uruguayan urged no further U.S. aid to his country because of restrictions on political rights.

On 4 September the Ministry of the Interior announced that 1,300 Uruguayan political prisoners had been released during the past two years, including PCU and PSU members but not any Tupamaros (AP, Montevideo, 5 September). The ministry supplied names and descriptions of those released, but the Marxist press and the Third World press in general did not run the announcement. U.S. newspapers which have been critical of Uruguay's abridgement of civil rights likewise did not run the official announcement, a spot check of fourteen leading dailies revealed.

On 21 September, to commemorate the 56th anniversary of its founding, the PCU held a press conference, not in Montevideo where the PCU is outlawed, but in Havana, The main speaker for the celebration was Aníbal Hernández, political editor of the suspended PCU daily *El Popular.* (*Granma,* 23 September.)

On 28 October, police announced that some former Tupamaros and PCU Uruguayans living in Argentina had organized a "Party for the Victory of the People," but that its 14 leaders had been arrested in Montevideo with PCU literature and weapons, plus funds obtained from Europe in 1975 by Luis Presno, who had claimed that the money would "fight police torture of Marxist prisoners." The party's agents in Buenos Aires kidnapped Federico Hart, a leader of the Argentine Jewish community and extorted ransom from that community for his release. (*Latín,* Buenos Aires and Montevideo, 28 October.)

International Views and Positions. The biggest event of 1976 for the PCU, in terms of statements by Uruguayan Communists in exile and in clandestine leaflets, seemingly did not concern Uruguayans but a Venezualan. A Venezuelan woman Marxist who had joined the MLN left Uruguay secretly in 1975, then returned in 1976. When police pursued her in Montevideo, she got to the grounds of the Venezuelan Embassy, hoping for asylum, but was captured before she could get inside. The Venezuelan ambassador argued that she was entitled to remain at the Embassy grounds gate, whereupon the Uruguayan Foreign Ministry declared the ambassador persona non grata on 5 July. The next day, Uruguay and Venezuela mutually broke diplomatic relations, and the PCU got various leftist spokesmen in Latin America to denounce the Montevideo government, ranging from the Cuban, Venezuelan, and Mexican ambassadors to the UN to exiles of the former Allende regime of Chile. (*Prensa Latina,* Havana, 7 July.)

The Foreign Ministry issued a statement on 7 July that the entire imbroglio was a minor incident built up to proportions of international tensions by those seeking to injure the Uruguayan government (*El País,* 7 July). The Mexican Marxist periodical *Oposición* quoted Uruguayan, Cuban, and Central American Communist spokesmen as feeling that the incident justified the breaking of relations with Uruguay by all "anti-imperialist" nations (TASS, Mexico City, 23 July).

Another major event of 1976 in terms of PCU emphasis was Fidel Castro's successful intervention in Angola. The PCU issued a statement on 4 February asserting that the "Angolan people's struggle for liberation against aggression from imperialism was accomplished by the heroic struggle of Angolans under Agostinho Neto and the Popular Movement for the Liberation of Angola, with the solidarity and help of the Soviet Union, Cuba, and other socialist countries" (TASS, Buenos Aires, 5 February).

The factor of Communists versus anti-Communists was raised in the dispute between the U.S. and Uruguayan governments. The Democratic majority in the U.S. Congress formally pressured the State Department to invoke the so-called Koch Amendment (after its originator, Representative Edward I. Koch, of New York), and suspend all military aid to Uruguay for 1976-77 because Koch's Foreign Operations Subcommittee contended that human rights were not fully respected in Uruguay, according to the testimony of opponents of the Uruguayan government. The pro-government newspaper *El Pais* (25 September) described the dispute as "squabbles among friends," but two high-ranking Uruguayans, an air force and an army general, criticized Koch for forgetting about the PCU and MLN attacks against Uruguayan governments since 1969. The PCU welcomed the suspension of aid (AFP, 25 September), although the amount involved totaled only $3 million.

In connection with the 25th Congress of the Communist Party of the Soviet Union, in Moscow, PCU first secretary Rodney Arismendi on 25 February pledged the solidarity of Uruguayan Marxists with the USSR in its struggle against capitalism (*FBIS,* 25 February).

On 9 January the Central Committee of the Revolutionary Communist Party of Uruguay (Partido Revolucionairio Comunista del Uruguay; PRCU), a pro-Chinese group, sent a letter to the Chinese Communist Party expressing grief over the death of Chou En-lai (*Peking Review,* 30 January). On 23 September, the PRCU sent a message to Peking mourning the death of Mao Tse-tung (*FBIS,* 28 September).

The PRCU sent a delegation to Albania in January at the invitation of the Central Committee of the Albanian Workers' Party. The Uruguayans reported the PRCU secretary general Mario Ekilite had been imprisoned in Montevideo (ibid., 23 January).

On 25 June, 45 political detainees connected with the PCU flew from Montevideo under diplomatic protection of the Mexican ambassador to Uruguay. The group had been at the Mexican Embassy three months. Mexican president Echeverría called them "political refugees" when he met their airplane in Mexico City, but the Uruguayan foreign ministry answered that each Uruguayan had a passport stamped with a Mexican visa granting them permanent resident in Mexico, "hardly the documents found on refugees said to be fleeing" (AFP, Mexico City and Montevideo, 25 and 26 June).

The UN High Commission for Refugees on 21 November asked the Uruguayan government to report on Uruguayan exiles who had been living in Argentina but later turned up in Uruguayan jails. Some 20 Uruguayans are involved. (*NYT*, 22 November).The UN Commission did not ask about anti-Marxist Uruguayans whom the MLN kidnapped in 1970 and took to La Plata in Argentina and later ransomed.

PCU first secretary Arismendi, in Sofia, on 5 September was awarded the Dimitrov Peace Prize jointly from the government of Bulgaria and the Central Committee of the Bulgarian Communist Party (*FBIS*, 5 September).

Publications. To replace the outlawed daily newspaper *El Popular*, during 1974 and 1975 the PCU published the weekly *Carta*, printing 10,000 copies on offset plates at a hidden laboratory and duplicating the press run at a printing shop disguised as a store selling cardboard containers, both in Montevideo. At the end of 1975, police discovered the two printing plants, arrested PCU personnel at both sites, and impounded a rotoprint machine, cases of offset type, and a photocopier. The PCU members arrested were the former assistant manager of *El Popular*, a printer, and the circulation manager of *Carta*. (*El País*, 4 January.) Also in early 1976 police found the hiding place for back copies of the defunct PCU magazine *Discusión*.

The MLN (Tupamaros). From 1969 to 1971 the MLN made headlines by kidnapping officials for ransom, holding up banks, destroying buildings by fire, and killing police officers. By 1975 most of these urban guerrillas were in prison 30 miles west of Montevideo, in exile, or dead. In March 1976 the founder and leader of the MLN, Raul Sendic, was moved from the military jail in Montevideo to the Paso de los Toros prison in Tucuarembo (*Prensa Latina*, Buenos Aires, 10 March).

Arizona State University   Marvin Alisky

Venezuela

The Communist Party of Venezuela (Partido Comunista de Venezuela; PCV), the oldest of the extreme leftist groups in the country, was founded in 1931. In recent years two serious splits have greatly undermined the party's strength and influence. One took place in December 1970, when most of its youth organization and substantial elements of the adult party broke away to form the Movement Toward Socialism (Movimiento al Socialismo; MAS), the other in mid-1974 when a group of party leaders split away to form what was called first the Vanguardia Comunista (VC) and later the Vanguardia Unitaria Comunista (VUC).

Another Marxist-Leninist group, the Movement of the Revolutionary Left (Movimiento de Izquierda Revolucionaria; MIR), originated in 1960 from a split in the Democratic Action Party

(Acción Democrática; AD), which controlled the government from 1959 to 1969 and returned to power early in 1974. Other elements on the far left, Maoists and Trotskyists, have appeared in recent years.

There remain some active remnants of the urban and rural guerrilla movement, which had its high point in the early 1960s when both the PCV and MIR participated. The major elements of both parties withdrew from guerrilla activities in 1965-66.

The PCV may have about 3,000 members, the MAS perhaps more. Strength of the other groups is not known.

The population of Venezuela is about 11 million.

The PCV. Organization and Leadership. The top leadership of the PCV is its 13-member Politburo. This body includes Gustavo Machado, party chairman; Jesús Faría, secretary-general; and Radamés Larrazabal, who in recent years has been the principal public spokesman for the party.

Until the December 1970 split, the PCV's Venezuelan Communist Youth (Juventud Comunista Venezolana; JCV) was the largest political group in the student movement. The split deprived the JCV of most of its leaders and members, and threw it into such confusion that it was not until February 1972 that the JCV held its Third National Congress. The split reduced PCV influence in the student movement to minor proportions, the leading position being taken by the MAS youth group.

The principal center of PCV influence in the labor movement is the United Workers Confederation of Venezuela (Confederación Unitaria de Trabajadores de Venezuela; CUTV), established in the early 1960s when the PCV lost virtually all influence in the majority Confederation of Workers of Venezuela (Confederación de Trabajadores de Venezuela; CTV). The Communists apparently had no representation in the Seventh Congress of the CTV in May 1975, although Larrazabal had indicated a desire for rapprochement.

The CUTV held its own Seventh Congress on 25-26 March 1976. The agenda included discussion of wage increases, inflation, and unemployment, as well as the "stuggle for full national independence against imperialism" and the specific problems of women workers. A new executive committee was chosen, and Cruz Villegas was reelected president.

The CUTV congress was used as a major device for attempting to regain Communist prestige. It was attended by Enrique Pastorino, president of the Communist-front World Federation of Trade Unions (WFTU), and Roberto Prieto, secretary-general of the Latin American Workers Permanent Congress for Trade Union Unity (CPUSTAL), as well as by fraternal delegates from trade union groups in the USSR, Cuba, Czechoslovakia, Romania, Algeria, Vietnam, Iraq, Yugoslavia, Hungary, and Poland.

Domestic Attitudes and Activities. The most important event in Venezuela during 1976 was the nationalization of the oil industry in January. A considerable part of the political controversy of the year centered on the way the nationalized industry was being organized by the government of President Carlos Andrés Pérez, and the PCV participated in this discussion.

On the day of nationalization, the PCV secretary-general announced that the party was "ready to cooperate with the Venezuelan government if it has any trouble as a result of . . . nationalization" (*Ultimas Noticias,* Caracas, 2 January). Early in April, Larrazabal, who had been the PCV representative on the committee to study oil nationalization and make proposals for organization of the nationalized industry, commented that "it is premature to pass judgment on the financial results of the nationalized industry and, consequently, criticism should be constructive" (Caracas Diplomatic Information Service, 6 April).

Jerónimo Carrera of the PCV Central Committee wrote an extensive article in the July *World Marxist Review* about the oil issue. After noting PCV support for the nationalization law, and admitting that "it might well be that for some time nationalization will prove less profitable," he hailed the "progressive action by the government, for by eliminating the neo-colonial system of oil concessions the country has taken a significant step toward genuine independence." However, he complained against appointment of people formerly associated with the international companies to run the nationalized industry, and charged that the companies were "openly violating their agreements and cutting back oil purchases."

The first plenum of the PCV Central Committee, apparently held in January, expressed support for the Popular Movement for the Liberation of Angola and demanded that the Venezuelan government recognize it, urged a stepped-up campaign for the release of Chilean Communist leader Luis Corvalán, and expressed support for Panama's attempt to get control over the Canal (*IB,* 15 February). The sixth plenum, in June, reportedly decided to convert the party paper *Tribuna Popular* into a daily and to begin to lay plans for the 1978 election (*El Nacional,* Caracas, 29 June).

The PCV continued its campaign of several years to gain respectability. In June it thanked the Foreign Minister for his efforts to get the Chilean government to release Corvalán. In September, when police officials of the Policía Técnica Judicial (PTJ) implicated Vanguardia Comunista members in involvement in a robbery of the Zulia Regional Development Bank, the PCV rushed into print to "flatly reject the equivocal situation that could result from the information issued by the PTJ, which, if used maliciously, could involve the good name of the Communists in this matter" (ibid., 26 September).

International Views and Positions. The PCV was represented by Jesús Faría at the First Congress of the Communist Party of Cuba, in December 1975. Three months later he was in Moscow, where he addressed the 25th Congress of the Communist Party of the Soviet Union. After hailing the USSR's "growing economic and military might" as a "guarantee for the peoples struggling to gain and preserve their independence," Faría asserted that "In our publications, our messages to the people, and all mass events in which we participate, we speak about our friendship and admiration for the USSR, its leading party, and its people" (*FBIS,* 12 March 1976). A representative of the PCV Politburo was received by officials of the Polish ruling party in April and another was the guest of the Hungarian party in September.

Aside from the continuing campaign on behalf of Luis Corvalán, the PCV demanded the liberation of Miguel Angel Soler, secretary-general of the pro-Moscow faction of the Paraguayan Communist Party, when Soler was arrested early in 1976.

Publications. The PCV's principal organ is the newspaper *Tribuna Popular.* Its theoretical periodical, *Documentos Políticos,* has had some difficulty in coming out since the MAS split.

The VUC. The launching of the Vanguardia Comunista in June 1974 was significant because it represented a split in the "old guard" of the Venezuelan Communist movement. Particularly interesting was the presence in its leadership of Eduardo Machado. In all previous divisions of the Communist party, the Machado brothers, Gustavo and Eduardo, had always been aligned together. Another member of the PCV old guard who helped form Vanguardia Comunista was Guillermo Garcia Ponce.

The VC's First Congress, November 1974, proclaimed the new group to be a "Marxist-Leninist party . . . faithful to the traditions of international solidarity." It urged nationalization of all basic industries of Venezuela. Eduardo Machado was elected president, and Guillermo Garcia Ponce secretary-general (*El Nacional,* 4 November). Negotiations during most of 1975 for unification of the VC and the MIR came to nothing. In February 1976 the officially registered name of the party was changed to Vanguardia Unitaria Comunista. Although a small group, it further undermined the already reduced ranks of the PCV. Its following seems to be largely confined to Caracas.

In March 1976, when the Panamanian government canceled a conference of Latin American heads of state which it had called, the VUC issued a statement saying that this action—"the downfall of a weak and timid diplomacy incapable of surmounting the political struggles which have constantly disturbed Latin America"—would serve the interests of the USA.

In September, when police charged that VUC elements were involved in a bank robbery in Maracaibo, the party leadership issued a statement saying that the VUC "had nothing to do with the matter" and added:"The VC also firmly protests against attempts to implicate members of our political organization in actions that do not correspond to our political guidelines or our revolutionary practices" (ibid., 26 September).

In October, VUC Politburo member Carlos del Vecchio issued a statement attacking the party leadership for the same elitism and cult of personality the old PCV leaders had suffered from. He claimed also that some VUC leaders were seeking an alliance with the Copei Party (ibid., 4 October).

The MAS. The Movement Toward Socialism was formed late in 1970 as the result of a split in the PCV. Former PCV Politburo member Pompeyo Márquez is the MAS secretary-general. The MAS took with it a large part of the intermediary leadership cadres of the PCV, a majority of the former PCV rank-and-file, and virtually all of the JCV.

The MAS youth organization is the Juventud Comunista-MAS (JC-MAS), which initially dominated most of the student bodies of Venezuelan universities. Although its influence has somewhat declined, the JC-MAS remains the largest political group in the student movement.

In June 1976, MAS leaders in the student federation of the Central University of Caracas were involved in a confrontation with extreme leftist elements, whom they blamed for incidents on 27 May when three buses were set on fire. In response, the extremists demonstrated on the university campus and prevented the holding of a scheduled meeting of student delegates from various parts of the country (*El Nacional,* 5 June).

The MAS at its inception had some influence in the CUTV trade union movement. Those who went with MAS first formed the "CUT Clasista" as a rival organization. In July 1974 the MAS Central Committee decided to have its supporters enter the CTV, the majority union group. The MAS won at least one seat on the executive committee of the CTV at the confederation's congress in Arpil 1975. In July 1976 MAS members were involved in leadership of a strike of hospital workers in Caracas (EFE, 15 July).

Internal Dissension. For the first time, serious dissension appeared within the MAS in 1976. At the meeting of its National Directorate in March, there was a vigorous controversy over the possible party candidate for president in 1978. The two men most spoken about were José Vicente Rangel, the party's 1973 nominee, an independent who is closely associated with the MAS; and Teodoro Petkoff, one of the party's principal leaders. MAS secretary-general Márquez also indicated the possibility that he might be a candidate for the nomination. (*El Nacional,* 29 March.)

Several months later, Jesús Urbieta, MAS labor under-secretary and member of the Executive Committee of the CTV, was banned from any party leadership position for two years. At the same time, Gilberto Pinto, member of the Executive Committee of the Metal Workers Federation and of the MAS labor bureau, was suspended from holding office in the party for eight months. In addition, 18 regional MAS leaders were punished by party disciplinary committees. All of these measures followed from the MAS labor leaders having taken a position strongly in favor of the candidacy of Rangel. (Ibid., 3 August.)

Domestic Attitudes and Activities. In the beginning of the administration of President Carlos Andrés Pérez, early in 1974, the MAS adopted a position of "critical support" of the government. During 1976 the attitude of MAS was more pragmatic.

In December 1975 the MAS members of Congress had voted with the rest of the opposition against the government's bill to compensate foreign oil companies whose properties were to be expropriated on 1 January. However, three months later, on the occasion of Pérez's annual message to

Congress, the MAS leadership observed that the government had "made very positive achievements as regards international matters" (Radio Continente, Caracas, 13 March).

In June, when the Comptroller General resigned in a dispute with Pérez, Teodoro Petkoff, speaking for the MAS, expressed his party's support for the Comptroller General. He commented: "I have no doubt that more than one of those officials President Pérez recently described as swindlers sighed with relief at the resignation of the Comptroller General" (*El Nacional,* 22 June).

That same month, when the president announced a governmental reorganization and the establishment of two new ministries, the MAS was again in the opposition. Freddy Muñoz, although noting that governmental reorganization was required to foster economic development, observed that mere cabinet reorganization created doubt "as to whether it will contribute to a greater hypertrophy of the administration" (AFP, 14 June).

The Copei Party rejected AD suggestions for a united front against the MAS, arguing that this would only strengthen the MAS (*El Nacional,* 2 October).

International Views. The MAS continued during 1976 to maintain an independent attitude on foreign issues and in its relations with foreign parties.

Márquez was particularly preoccupied with relations with Brazil. In February he accused Brazil of trying to bring about failure of the Andean Pact, of which Venezuela is a member. He also warned against the "gendarme" role which he claimed the USA had assigned Brazil in the hemisphere (EFE, 23 February). In April, discussing the national defense bill, he expressed worry about Brazilian colonization efforts along the border. He also urged that Venezuela remain non-aligned, "that is, estranged from the United States, the USSR, and the People's Republic of China." (Ibid., 29 April.)

When U.S. secretary of state Henry Kissinger visited Venezuela in February, Freddy Muñoz expressed his party's skepticism about the visit and suggested that the government use the visit to "affirm the national principles and those of the Third World" (Radio Latin, Buenos Aires, 14 February). In April, an MAS deputy attacked the New Tribes Mission sect from the USA for allegedly concentrating its activities in areas rich with strategic mineral deposits (AFP, 17 April).

Publications. The principal MAS organ is the newspaper *Punto,* edited by Pompeyo Márquez.

The MIR. The MIR was established in 1960 by dissidents from the AD, including most of the party's youth movement. In 1962 the MIR joined in the launching of a guerrilla effort which lasted for several years. A large element of the party leadership and rank and file, headed by Domingo Alberto Rangel, withdrew from guerrilla activities in 1965-66 and later quit the party. However, the MIR officially foreswore participation in the guerrilla only in 1969.

During 1976 the activities of the MIR received only modest public attention. In December 1975 the MIR representation in Congress had opposed the government's bill to provide compensation for international oil companies whose properties were to be expropriated. In January 1976 the MIR denounced alleged efforts of the companies to buy Venezuelan oil at low prices.

In February the Supreme Electoral Council referred to its legislation committee a request of the MIR to be recognized as a national party. The MIR is recognized in several states. The question was whether it had sufficient support to justify recognition on a national basis.

In May the MIR issued a statement opposing Venezuelan participation in the general assembly at the Organization of American States, scheduled to take place in Chile in June. It denounced Venezuelan foreign policy in general and claimed that the countries which were to attend the OAS meeting would be working against the principles they claimed to defend (AFP, 28 May).

In August, when two party members were arrested while distributing literature, the MIR leadership termed this a violation of the national constitution and added: "We want to publicly charge that the police are harassing the MIR" (*Ultimas Noticias,* 2 August).

The Maoists. Until 1976 the Maoist elements in Venezuela were divided into two groups: the Patria Nueva movement and the Party of the Venezuelan Revolution (Partido de la Revolución Venezolana; PRV), the latter reportedly led by Douglas Bravo, one-time PCV Politburo member. During 1976 two new Maoist groups seem to have been established.

There was no evidence of activity on the part of the Patria movement during the year, but a PRV delegation visited China, headed by Ali Rodríguez, on invitation of the Central Committee of the Chinese Communist Party. The delegation visited various cities and was received by Yao Wen-yuan, member of the Politburo of the Chinese party (*Peking Review,* 8 September).

The two new Maoist groups were the Ruptura movement and the Popular Struggle Committees (CLP). The Ruptura held its first national congress in Caracas on 23-25 January (*Ultimas Noticias,* 2 February). The CLP had its first national meeting in June (ibid., 21 June). Neither had any influence in organized labor or general politics. The CLP apparently had some marginal following among students at the Central University.

Peking Review (15 October) reported that 2,000 persons attended a meeting on 24 September at the Central University to "honor the memory of the late Chairman Mao Tse-tung." The principal speaker was Armando Díaz, not identified as to party, who proclaimed that "Mao Tse-tung Thought is Marxism-Leninism of our epoch."

The Trotskyists. The first evidence of a Trotskyist movement in Venezuela was the appearance on 1 May 1972 of *Voz Marxista,* organ of the Grupo Trotskista Venezolano (Venezuelan Trotskyist Group). In 1973 this group took the name Socialist Workers Party (Partido Socialista de Trabajadores). It supported the candidacy of José Vicente Rangel in the 1973 election, but appears to have merged late in 1974 with a number of groups which had advocated abstention or a blank vote. These formed the Socialist League (Liga Socialista; LS). The LS is the Venezuelan section of the United Secretariat of the Fourth International. It publishes a fortnightly, *Voz Socialista.*

In February 1976 the LS was denied recognition as a political party by the Supreme Electoral Council, because it "did not comply with the stipulations of the law, such as the timely correction of the lists" (Radio Rumbos, Caracas, 5 February).

Rumors circulated in March that LS secretary-general Jorge Rodríguez had been arrested, but the LS denied this as being designed to "justify the wave of repression unleashed across the nation" (*Ultimas Noticias,* 5 March). However, Rodríguez was arrested in July and died at the hands of the police, with the result that several police officials were placed under arrest (Radio Rumbos, 26 July). Juan Medina Figueredo was chosen as his successor (*Ultimas Noticias,* 10 August).

In October the LS reportedly held a meeting to "mourn the passing of Mao Tse-tung," attended by 500 persons and addressed by Carmelo Laborit, the LS president (*Peking Review,* 15 October).

The Guerrillas. Isolated guerrilla groups continued sporadic activities during 1976, with no noticeable impact on the country's general political situation.

The most spectacular guerrilla action of the year was the kidnapping of William Niehous, vice-president and general manager of Owens-Illinois in Venezuela, a U.S.-owned glass processing company, on 27 February. The PCV, MIR, and MAS condemned the kidnapping.

By the end of the year, Niehous had still not been discovered by the authorities. His kidnapping had the result that Venezuela agreed to buy out the Owens-Illinois investment.

Several minor guerrilla incidents occurred during the year and some leaders were captured.

Rutgers University   Robert J. Alexander

MIDDLE EAST AND AFRICA

Egypt

The first Communist group in Egypt was formed in 1921. It subsequently developed into the Communist Party of Egypt (al-Hizb al-Shuyu'i al-Misri; CPE). Beset by factionalism and political fragmentation, the CPE was also proscribed from its inception. In 1965 it dissolved itself and urged members to join the Arab Socialist Union (ASU), the only legal political organization at the time. In 1975 party activities were reportedly resumed. Recent liberalization has provided Communists with new opportunities.

In March 1976 three *Manabir* (platforms or forums) were established within the ASU to represent the right, the center, and the left. Each platform has its own membership, structure, and activities; each nominates its own candidates to parliament.

The leftist platform, al-Tajammu'al-Watani al-Taqaddumi al-Wahdawi (National Progressive Unionist Organization), is headed by Khalid Muhyi al-Din, who was a "free officer" and member of the Revolutionary Command Council and is now a member of the ASU Central Committee (*Middle East Intelligence Survey*, 31 May). The exact membership of the platform is not known. It won two seats in the parliamentary elections in October (one seat going to Muhyi al-Din).

According to its program, the group does not aim at the immediate establishment of socialism. At this stage, it regards as its main task the defense of workers' rights and political freedoms. It demands the protection of the Egyptian economy from foreign domination and asserts the importance of planning and the role of the public sector.

When Muhyi al-Din once remarked that abrogation of the treaty with the USSR accorded with neither the immediate nor the long-term interest of Egypt, he was vehemently attacked as a Communist. The Egyptian press has unceasingly assailed the leftist platform as a Communist one. The platform, however, is more of a front which includes a diversity of Nasserite, social-democratic, and Marxist elements.

Communist underground activities continue. Small revolutionary organizations include a group that publishes the underground paper *Conflict*; the Beirut-based Egyptian Communist Party responsible for publishing the underground journal *Victory*; the Arab Communist Organization; and some Trotskyite factions. Apparently, no major organization has been active. CPE membership figures are unknown, but certainly the party is small.

In March 1976 a woman was charged with attempting to smuggle a number of pamphlets published by the Egyptian Communist Party of Beirut (*al-Ahram*, Cairo, 29 March). In April, members of a Communist organization were accused of inciting a disturbance and acts violating public order (*al-Akhbar*, Beirut, 4 April). In September the Prime Minister blamed the bus drivers' strike in Cairo on Communists. The official communiqué, however, named nobody and referred to "hostile elements" (*Al-Ahram*, 22 September).

Marxist writers continue to contribute to Egypt's intellectual life, through the monthly *al-Tali'ah* (Vanguard). In 1976 they were engaged in two major debates of similar nature. The first was conducted on the pages of the weekly *Rose al-Yusuf* in response to Dr. F. Zakaria, who criticized Nasser's era. The second was published in *al-Tali'ah* as a round-table discussion. Marxist contributors continued to defend the Nasserite experience against its rightist critics. The Communist movement, however, has in Egypt never constituted a real threat to the regime.

Cairo University and   Ali E. Hillal Dessouki
the American University
in Cairo

Iran

Precursors of organized Communist activity in Iran were organized in Tiflis and Baku early in the century, the Persian Social Democratic Party in 1904 and the Hezb-e'Adalat(Justice Party) in 1917. At the first major party congress, convened in Pahlavi(Enzeli) in 1920, the Justice Party changed its name to the Communist Party of Iran. In 1931 the government of Iran banned Communist activity in the country. This, combined with the Stalinist purges in the neighboring Soviet Union, caused the party to disband.

In 1941 a group of German-educated Marxist intellectuals formed the present Communist Party of Iran, known as the Tudeh Party ("Party of the Masses"). During the 1941-53 period of relative political freedom in Iran, the Tudeh burgeoned in size and influence until it became the largest party in the country.

A major split in the organized Communist movement developed in 1945-46. The Tudeh organization in the province of Azerbaijan broke away from the main party and formed the Democratic Party of Azerbaijan. This division stemmed both from the reluctance of the Tudeh Party to emphasize the ethnic problems peculiar to Azerbaijan and from the Soviet drive to support a friendly provincial government to counter the pro-Western central government in Tehran. In 1946, the Democratic Party of Azerbaijan was outlawed. In 1949 the Tudeh Party itself was banned when a member of the Central Council of United Trade Unions attempted to assassinate the Shah. Despite the ban, the Tudeh Party grew during the Mosaddeq period between 1951 and 1953. After the coup d'état and the return of the Shah to power in late 1953, the Tudeh Party was effectively suppressed. Some 500 army officers who belonged to the party were arrested; of these, 27 were executed. A number of the party leaders managed to escape to Europe and reorganized the Tudeh Party in East Germany.

Today Tudeh Party activity is confined almost entirely to organizations operating outside Iran. Within a country whose 1976 population approaches 34 million, Tudeh Party membership probably does not exceed a couple of thousand. There are, however, perhaps 15,000 to 20,000 Iranians associated with other Marxist-Leninist groupings and engaged in opposition activities of various kinds. Among them are the following four organizations, all of which have been formed since 1960 and all of which have a presence both within and outside the country:

(1) The Revolutionary Tudeh Party (Hezb-e Tudeh-e Iran) was formed in 1965 by a Maoist group that had been expelled from the Tudeh Party. This group publishes *Setareh-i Sorkh* (Red Star).

(2) The Organization of Marxist-Leninists (Sazman-e Marxist-Leninist) was formed in 1967 by two Maoist members of the Central Committee of the Tudeh Party. This group publishes the periodical *Tufan* (Storm).

(3) The Guerrilla Organization of the Devotees for the People (Cheraki Feda-ye Khalq) was formed in Iran in 1971. A number of its founders were former members of the Tudeh Party's youth organization. These individuals had left the party because of its opposition to guerrilla warfare. This group is well organized and has been responsible for a number of violent incidents directed against the government. Since 1971, approximately 200 members of this organization have been either killed in action or executed. This group tends to identify more with Latin American revolutionaries than with either the USSR or China.

(4) A section of the National Front (Jebheh-e Melli) which supported Dr. Mosaddeq has become Marxist since 1972. This group publishes *Bakhtar-e Emruz* (Today's West).

In 1976 the domestic Marxist guerrilla groups stepped up their activities considerably and carried out a number of dramatic acts of sabotage and assassination. Iranian security forces were busy throughout the year and although they were able to arrest, imprison, and execute a number of guerrilla leaders, they were unable to root out what appeared to be both a growing and dedicated opposition. Shootouts between police and guerrillas became a regular occurrence, especially in the Tehran area. Although Marxist-oriented opposition groups such as these have gained significantly in strength and appeal in Iran, the Tudeh Party remains the major Communist organization directly concerned with Iran in the international context.

Tudeh Party Leadership and Organization. Iradj Eskandari has been first secretary of the Tudeh Party since 1971. The party seldom publishes names of members, partly because of the government's repressive policy toward this particular group. Most pronouncements are issued in the name of the Central Committee of the Iranian Tudeh Party.

The leadership of the Tudeh Party places great stress on the need to turn the Iranian masses against the government. The party works to implement this goal primarily through its operation of the clandestine radio station, "Radio Iran Courier." This station, which is believed to be broadcasting from the German Democratic Republic, continues to harass the Iranian government through its programs of sharp social and political criticism. Major policy pronouncements concerning opposition tactics are also communicated through this channel. Increasingly, the party urges opposition members within Iran to join the government at all levels and from there they are encouraged to destroy the monarchical system through subversion from within.

The Tudeh Position on Domestic Issues. The Tudeh Party has consistently attacked the leadership of the Shah while stressing his regime's alleged oppression, injustice, backwardness, and corruption. The major goal of the party continues to be the overthrow of the Shah, and with him, the Pahlavi dynasty. Throughout 1976 the Tudeh leadership consistently stood by this position and criticized the government for coercive measures taken against opposition elements in the society as well as for the general absence of political and personal freedom in the country. Special criticism was directed against the harsh measures taken against indigenous "freedom fighters."

The Tudeh Position on International Issues. The Tudeh Party has been a strong supporter of the Soviet Union in the competition among the superpowers. The USA and the People's Republic of

China are considered implacable enemies of both the people and the Tudeh Party itself, and China has become a major target of Tudeh attack. In March 1976, First Secretary Eskandari attacked Peking for subverting the world communist movement and declared: "We will fight Maoist policy in our country, Iran, and in the Middle East." He later stated that "the Tudeh Party sharply condemns the policy of the Peking leadership as an anti-socialist, counterrevolutionary policy directed against the cause of peace and the interest of the peoples." Tudeh Party leaders lavishly praised Soviet Communist leadership at the 25th Congress of the Communist Party of the Soviet Union.

Tudeh spokesmen also made particularly forceful statements and especially long presentations in condemning Iranian political leaders for "colluding" and "compromising" with the international oil consortium. The Shah was criticized for directing "the lion's share" of oil revenues towards military expenditures. In August the party sharply attacked the United States for its economic and military policies toward Iran. According to the Tudeh analysis, the U.S. government is "worried lest the regional gendarme, Mohammed Reza Shah, while drowning and taking Iran under with him, will also entangle and endanger the United States."

Publications. The two major publications of the Tudeh Party are *Mardom* (People) and *Donya* (World). These papers are published in Eastern Europe. They contain a mixture of articles that deal with Marxist-Leninist theory, international politics and economics, and the Iranian social and political scene.

University of Texas, Austin   James A. Bill

Iraq

The Iraqi Communist Party (ICP) was officially founded in 1934. For many years, the party was severely persecuted. For almost a decade, from the revolution of 1958 to the revolution of 1968, the ICP and the Ba'th Party (now in power) were engaged in bitter competition; this weakened both groups and allowed other parties to govern for most of the time. Both Communists and Ba'thists concluded therefore that the right-wing groups had benefited from Communist-Ba'thist rivalry. The ICP offered to collaborate with the Ba'thist Party within the framework of a united national front. After the Ba'th Party achieved power in 1968, the ICP welcomed the new regime.

In 1970, the ICP held its Second National Convention, considered to be a landmark in the Iraqi Communist movement by its members. 'Aziz Muhammad, first secretary of the Central Committee, presented the party's program, which corresponded to accepted Marxist-Leninist principles. The ICP considers that the Communist Party of the Soviet Union (CPSU) forms the spearhead of the international Communist movement; any attempt to obstruct the CPSU should be considered as contrary to Marxist-Leninist teachings and against the interests of the international proletarian movement. The ICP also offered once more to cooperate with the Ba'th Party and called for the elimination of all repressive measures.

Meanwhile, the Ba'th Party consolidated its regime by liquidating its opponents and by appeasing the Kurds through a promise of self-rule. The ICP welcomed this policy and urged the Kurds to accept it.

In 1973, after an attempted coup was crushed, the Progressive Nationalist Front was formally established, composed of all "progressive" elements though initially only the Ba'th and the Communist parties joined it. For the first time in its history, the ICP was legalized, licensed and recognized as a political party. Two members of the party — 'Amir 'Abd Allah and Mukarram al-Talabani (the first an Arab, the other a Kurd) — were given cabinet posts. 'Aziz Sharif, head of the Partisans for Peace, a sympathizer with though not a member of the ICP, was also given a cabinet post (which he resigned in 1976).

From 1973 to 1975, agreement between the ICP and the Ba'th Party reached perhaps the peak in their relationship. Following the conclusion of a treaty of alliance with the Soviet Union (1972), the Ba'th leaders sought support of the ICP in foreign policy. Isolated from almost all neighbors, especially from Iran because of the dispute on the Shatt al-Arab, the Ba'th leaders cooperated with Communist and other radical groups. After agreement with Iran in 1975 and after the settlement of the Kurdish problem, the Ba'th Party ceased to be as dependent on Communist support as before. The ICP nevertheless maintained friendly relations with the Ba'th leaders. Although Iraq's need for Soviet economic assistance was reduced, the government still remained dependent on Soviet arms and equipment.

Domestic Attitudes and Activities: During 1976 the ICP continued to operate with a fair degree of freedom, despite growing restrictions. ICP literature continued to circulate.

In May the party held its Third Naitonal Convention in Baghdad. The convention accepted the party rules and the draft program prepared by the Central Committee.

A report submitted to the convention by 'Aziz Muhammad paid special attention to the further consolidation of the Progressive National Front, whose creation constituted "the greatest achievement" of the revolutionary movement. The ICP, in cooperation with the Ba'th Party and other progressive elements, would continue to strive for the ultimate victory of socialism.

In comparison with the Ba'th Party, the ICP has made relatively little progress. The Communist movement remains essentially confined to minority groups and to intellectuals, despite efforts to influence workers in urban and rural areas. As in other Arab countries, Islam and nationalism deter Muslims who consider joining the Communist party. There seems to be no serious struggle for power within the ICP at the present, but lack of leadership and differences on personal and procedural matters appear to have weakened the party to a greater degree than has been the case with Communist parties in other Arab counties. For a while, the Iraqi Communists followed the guidance of Khalid Bakdash, secretary-general of the Syrian Communist Party, whom they held in high respect. In recent years, however, Bakdash's leadership has often been challenged by Communists even in his own country.

Arab Policy. In his report to the ICP National Convention, 'Aziz Muhammad stated that since 1970 a fundamental change in political forces had brought greater influence for the world's socialist system through consolidation of its alliance with the national liberation movement and all "peace-loving and progressive" forces, expansion of the revolutionary-democratic and anti-imperialism movements, and intensification of the working class struggle against monopolies.

The ICP convention sent "congratulations to our Soviet Comrades for their success in all fields." Warning of the power that the international Communist movement holds, the ICP condemned the activities of the Peking leadership. Maoism, the report stated, is contrary to Marxist-Leninist teachings and against the interests of the working class all over the world, and therefore opposition to Maoism is a duty of all Communists and progressive forces.

In the Arab world, the report stated, a fierce struggle continues between the Arab liberation movement and its allies—the forces of progress and socialism—and imperialism, especially the imperialism of the USA and its client, Israel, and the reactionary regimes. This struggle was said to center on the consequences of "Israeli Aggression" and on the legitimate rights of the Arab people of Palestine. The differences and contradictions within the Arab world make it possible for Israel to continue the occupation of Arab lands. The Sinai agreement, signed behind the back of the Arabs, inflicted a blow on the Arab liberation movement which has led to the continuation of Israeli occupation of Egyptian lands and the consolidation of the U.S. military position, virtually terminating Egypt's role in the struggle for the liberation of captured Arab lands. The Soviet Union, according to the ICP, is a guarantee and source of strength for the Arab liberation movement in the struggle against Israel and imperialism. Therefore the party is opposed to the forces that work against Soviet support for the Arab liberation movement.

The Persian Gulf, the report argued, is being exploited by foreign oil companies and is subject to domination by the imperialists. Attempts are being made to suppress the national liberation movement in Uman (Oman) and the People's Democratic Republic of Yemen, and to turn the Indian Ocean into a strategic zone in support of imperialist and reactionary influences in that area. To achieve these objectives, the imperialists have reinforced their military bases in the Gulf by supplying reactionary regimes with huge quantities of arms and technological assistance. The USA was said to be operating hand in glove with reaction, with the aim of setting up a security system in the Gulf area for conducting its aggressive strategy. The ICP called for the elimination of foreign military bases and the U.S. and British military presence in the Gulf area, and the expulsion of Persian and British mercenaries from Uman.

Relations with Other Communist Parties. In December 1975, the ICP participated in a regional conference with the Saudi Arabian Communist Party and some Persian Gulf Communist parties. In a public statement, the delegates denounced imperialism and the oil companies and called upon their countries to operate their own national oil industries. In 1976, Saddam Husayn, vice-president of the Revolutionary Command Council, which governs Iraq, and Aysani, assistant secretary-general of the National Command, attended observances of the ICP's founding anniversary. Na'im Haddad, secretary-general of the Progressive Nationalist Front, made a speech at the ceremony praising Communist-Ba'thist cooperation.

The ICP has always kept close relations with the Syrian and Lebanese Communist parties, despite occasional differences on personal and procedural matters. Iraqi Communist leaders have often visited Damascus and exchanged views with Syrian leaders on the Arab liberation movement and the national fronts in Syria and Iraq. The ICP has supported the Lebanese Communist Party, and attacked the "reactionary" forces in Lebanon as contrary to Arab interest. In 1976 the Syrian Communists kept a low profile when the Syrian Ba'th regime intervened on behalf of right-wing elements in Lebanon. The ICP, on the other hand, backed the Iraqi Ba'th Party. It has also supported the Palestine Liberation Organization, with which the Syrian Ba'th Party has come into conflict.

On 12 December 1975 a five-member delegation of the ICP led by 'Aziz Muhammad visited Moscow and met Mikhail Suslov and Boris Ponomarev of the CPSU.

In February 1976, 'Aziz Muhammad led an Iraqi delegation to the 25th CPSU Congress. 'Aziz Muhammad, in an interview on 3 March, said that the ICP supported the Soviet policy of coexistence among nations with different social systems because it had proved successful in reducing international tension and promoting détente. This policy, he added, had helped to intensify the conflict with capitalism and the liberation struggle against capitalism, Zionism, and neo-colonialism.

On 30 May, Soviet premier Kosygin, during his visit to Baghdad, met 'Aziz Muhammad.

The ICP has also participated in the activities of other socialist countries.

In January, 'Aziz Muhammad visited Sofia at the invitation of the Bulgarian Communist Party. In July, another ICP delegation was in Sofia. In July, ICP leaders also visited in Bucharest, at the invitation of the Romanian Communist Party.

Publications. The ICP publishes *Tariq al-Sha'b* (People's Road), a daily newspaper, and a number of other periodicals.

The Johns Hopkins University   Majid Khadduri

Israel

The Communist movement in Palestine dates back to 1920, when the Socialist Workers' Party (Mifleget Po'alim Sozialistim) was established. This party disapeared in 1921, and a "proletarian Zionist" group, the Workers of Zion (Po'alei Zion), became the center of Communist activity. Failing to take control, Communists broke away in 1922 and established the Palestine Communist Party (Palestinische Kommunistische Partei; PKP), which became a member of the Comintern in 1924. Following the periodic appearance of factional divisions, the PKP split along ethnic lines in 1943. While the Jewish group retained the original name, the Arab faction called itself the League for National Liberation ('Usbah al-Tahrir al-Watani). In October 1948, with the newly established state of Israel in control of most of Palestine, the PKP and the League for National Liberation reunited to form the Israeli Communist Party (Miflaga Kommunistit Isrd'elit; MAKI).

The Communist movement split again in 1965, partly along Arab-Jewish lines. The "New Communist List" (Reshima Kommunistit Hadasha; RAKAH) — pro-Moscow, strongly anti-Zionist, and drawing a majority of its members from the Arab population — emerged as the main Communist party and increasingly gained international recognition as the Communist party of Israel. MAKI, which became an almost completely Jewish organization and moderate in its opposition to government policies, was eclipsed, and in 1975 it disappeared as a separate organization when it merged with MOKED ("Focus"), a Zionist (though dovish in the conflict with the Arabs) socialist organization. MOKED continued the publication of the former MAKI monthly, the Yiddish *Frei Isro'el* (Free Israel).

In keeping with Israel's competitive political party system, Communists have been free to organize and to participate in public life. The system of proportional representation according to which members of the Knesset (Parliament) and other representative bodies are elected has facilitated the election of candidates of small parties, including the Communists. Although Prime Minister Itzhak Rabin accused RAKAH of inciting violence in March 1976, he rejected proposals to outlaw the party.

From the beginning of the state, MAKI (and later RAKAH) found its main support among the Arab minority. This resulted from the absence of an Arab nationalist party in Israel—which left the

Communists as the only alternative to Zionist parties—and from the Communists' strong stand against official policies toward the Arab minority and toward the Arab world, and not from any espousal of Marxism-Leninism by large numbers of Arab voters. Increasingly, the Communists have gained the support of young educated Arabs. Although RAKAH's membership is about 70 percent Arab, many of its leaders (including a majority of its Central Committee) are Jews.

In recent years, RAKAH has gained unprecedented electoral strength among the Israeli Arabs, who now form about 15 percent of the population and are concentrated mainly in Galilee (in the north). In the general election of December 1973, RAKAH got 32 percent of the total Arab vote. In December 1975 the RAKAH-led "Democratic Front," which included non-Communist Arab intellectuals and merchants, won 67.3 percent of the vote and 11 out of 17 Council seats in the municipal elections in Nazareth (Israel's largest Arab city, population 40,000). One of RAKAH's leaders, Tawfiq Ziyad, was elected mayor by a large majority.

According to a 1976 Israeli government estimate, RAKAH has 1,100 members. Israel's population in September 1976 (not incuding the occupied territories) was 3,549,000.

RAKAH is isolated from the mainstream of Israeli politics. No Communist party has ever participated in the cabinet. RAKAH has had four seats (out of a total of 120) in the Knesset since the 1973 election. The less radical MOKED has had one seat. The Labor Alignment, with 51 seats, dominates the government. The right-wing Likud ("Unity") group, with 39 seats, is the main opposition party.

Leadership and Organizaton. The RAKAH Congress meets at four-year intervals. The 17th Congress (actually the fourth Congress of RAKAH, which sees itself as the direct successor to the 1920 organization, the PKP, and pre-1965 MAKI as the Communist party of Israel) met in 1972 in Tel Aviv and elected the Central Committee, the Supervisory Board, and the secretary-general.

The 18th RAKAH Congress, attended by 481 delegates, was begun in Haifa in December 1976. Seventeen parties, including delegations from Cyprus, Czechoslovakia, the German Democratic Republic, Great Britain, Hungary, Italy, Mongolia, Poland, the USSR, and the United States, were scheduled to attend. The Soviet delegation was headed by Aleksandr Aksenov, member of the Central Committee of the Communist Party of the Soviet Union (CPSU). The Congress aimed at the creation of a "peace front" to be directed "against the onslaught of the Israeli big bourgeoisie and their mentors, U.S. monopoly capital." It also aimed at a peace plan that would entail the establishment of a Palestinian state on the West Bank and in the Gaza Strip, as well as Israel's withdrawal from all territories occupied in the June war of 1967 (al-Ittihad, 4, 7, December). The party also condemned the buildup of Israeli military forces along the Lebanese frontier and looked to the prevention of a new war in the Middle East. The Congress was expected to make a special electioneering appeal to the Arab population of Israel; Israeli experts anticipated that the party might look forward to electing perhaps 13 Knesset members.

In 1976 Meir Vilner was secretary-general and members of the Politburo included David Khenin, Tawfiq Tubi (Secretary of the Central Committee), Benjamin Gonen, Uri Burnstein, Ruth Lubitz, Emile Habibi, Avraham Levenbraun, and Emile Tuma. The four RAKAH members in the Knesset were Vilner, Tubi, Levenbraun, and Tawfiq Ziyad. Organized on the principle of "democratic centralism," RAKAH's structure includes regional committees, local branches, and cells.

Auxiliary and Mass Organizations. RAKAH provides the dominant core of the Nazareth Democratic Front (see above) and other anti-establishment electoral lists in smaller towns. It also is in the forefront of the National Committee for the Defense of Arab Land (see below). RAKAH sponsors an active Young Communist League.

Party Internal Affairs. The 22d plenary session of the RAKAH Central Committee met in Haifa on 15-18 December 1975. Reports were presented by Vilner and Gonen, and discussion centered on Israel's policy in the Middle East conflict and on economic problems within Israel. Plans were made for the 18th Congress. The 23d plenary meeting, 7-8 February 1976, dealt with the Brussels Congress on Soviet Jewry, in addition to the Middle East conflict and Israeli-U.S. relations.

Domestic Attitudes and Activities. Speaking to the Central Committee in December 1975, Vilner stressed that militarization was responsible for severe inflation, sharp rises in taxes and the cost of public services, and the reduction of public expenditures on non-military items. He called for wage increases and a 40-hour work week.

RAKAH's main domestic focus during 1976 was on the position of the Israeli Arabs. Tubi accused the "Zionist ruling circles" of openly discriminating against the Arab population," whom he described as "second-class citizens . . . in any sphere" (TASS, in *FBIS*, 19 March). More specifically, emphasis was put on the government's plan to develop Galilee, involving the expropriation of Arab-owned land and interpreted as a "thinly disguised effort to 'Judaicize' the predominantly Arab area" (Ziyad, quoted in *Baltimore Sun*, 30 December 1975). Government authorization for such a plan on 29 February 1976 was followed by a RAKAH-led "emergency meeting" of Israeli Arab leaders in Nazareth and the announcement by the National Committee for the Defense of Arab Land of a one-day general strike and demonstrations (the "Day of the Land") for 30 March. RAKAH's Central Committee denounced the government decision as "infamous and racist" (TASS, in *FBIS*, 4 March).

The Day of the Land witnessed unprecedented clashes between Israeli Arabs and the security forces in Nazareth and several other Arab towns and vilages. Amid mutual accusations of responsibility for this violence, RAKAH members of the Knesset proposed a motion of no confidence against the government. The motion was defeated, with only the four RAKAH members voting for it and with two abstentions. During the Knesset debate, Vilner called 30 March "the day of the pogrom" and labeled Prime Minister Rabin a "mass murderer." This harsh language evoked proposals for the establishment of a Knesset committee to consider a temporary suspension of the right of RAKAH members to participate in the body. (*Arab Report and Record*, London, 16-30 March, p. 208.) An Israeli military court later found an army major guilty of manslaughter in the death of one local RAKAH official during the March disturbances. The police, upheld by the Supreme Court of Justice, refused to permit a May Day march in Nazareth. Nevertheless, a rally was held, which turned into a peaceful pro-Palestinian demonstration by 4,000 persons.

Local elections in seven small Israeli Arab towns in May resulted in gains for RAKAH. In all, 17 RAKAH-supported candidates were elected out of a total of 65 Council seats. RAKAH candidates were elected as heads of three towns. Of the seven towns, only two did not elect any RAKAH-supported Council members. Arab anger over the expropriation of land was a major factor working to RAKAH's advantage.

In May, responding to RAKAH's growing influence among the Israeli Arabs, the government announced the establishment of three bodies, including a ministerial committee, to be concerned with the Arabs' problems. RAKAH welcomed this development but demanded suspension of land expropriation, investigation of the 30 March incidents, and recognition for Arabs as a national minority entitled to participate in the government. At a Tel Aviv press conference in July, the Committee for the Defense of Arab Land reiterated its claim that the land expropriation was designed solely to transform Galilee into a Jewish area, not for develpment per se, and demanded cancellation of all expropriations, calling off the trials of people detained during the Day of the Land disturbances, compensation for those who were injured, and establishment of an investigatory committee.

In September a leaked confidential memorandum became public, written by Isra'el Koenig, the Minister of the Interior's representative in the Northern District. Koenig had proposed measures to prevent the emergence of an Arab majority in Galilee, including limitations on the admission of Arabs to Israeli universities and efforts to prevent Arab students from returning to Israel after completing their studies abroad, curbing the Arab birth rate by depriving Arabs of child welfare benefits, and limiting the proportion of Arabs in the labor force. Koenig also suggested that the government watch RAKAH closely. RAKAH joined other Israeli groups in condemning the memorandum as "racist" and demanding Koenig's resignation. The govenment denied that the proposals reflected official policy, but Koenig was not dismissed. Ziyad described the government's reaction as worse than the original proposal. Following a call made by a meeting of Arab municipal council heads, a two-hour commercial and transport strike was staged on 28 September in Arab towns to protest the proposals and the government's failure to take action against Koenig.

International Activities and Contacts. Vilner led a RAKAH delegation to the 25th CPSU Congress in Moscow, in February-March 1976. He addressed the Congress, and speeches by him and Tubi were broadcast by Moscow radio to the Middle East. On 9-20 August a RAKAH delegation visited Moscow, Leningrad, and the Uzbek Republic as guests of the CPSU Central Committee. Khenin visited Hungary in April and the German Democratic Republic in September. Another delegation, including Vilner, Lubitz, and Habibi, visited the GDR and held talks with party officials in June.

Moscow radio reported that delegations of RAKAH and the Jordanian Communist Party met in July (in an unspecified place) and issued a joint communiqué expressing agreement on Middle Eastern issues and reaffirming that RAKAH was the only Israeli party "struggling firmly against the Tel Aviv chauvinist and aggressive policy" (*FBIS*, 2 August). Groups of RAKAH leaders met with officials of the Palestine Liberation Organization in Moscow during the CPSU Congress, in Athens in March, and in New York (informally during a lecture tour) in October.

International Views and Policies. During 1976 RAKAH repeatedly attacked Israeli policies toward the Arab world, including "violence and repression" in the occupied territories (Tubi, from TASS, in *FBIS*, 4 March). In an article, "Israel's Violation of Human Rights" (*WMR*, June, pp. 118-22), Felicia Langer, an Israeli lawyer and prominent member of RAKAH, condemned imprisonment, confiscations, demolition of houses, deportation, colonization, torture, and other "terroristic measures" as violations of the Hague Convention of 1899 and the Geneva Convention of 1949. RAKAH's Politburo condemned Israel's boycott of the UN Security Council debate in January in which the Palestine Liberation Organization participated as contrary to "Israel's genuine national interests" (TASS, in *FBIS*, 5 January). RAKAH called for complete withdrawal from occupied territories, recognition of the PLO as the sole legitimate representative of the Palestinian people, the reconvening of the Geneva Conference (with PLO participation), and the establishment of a Palestinian state on the West Bank and the Gaza Strip. RAKAH's Central Committee issued a statement applauding the victory of candidates of the militant National Front in the April West Bank elections.

While condemning Zionism as "reactionary" (Vilner, quoted by TASS, in *FBIS*, 16 January), RAKAH leaders denied that theirs was an Arab nationalist party and affirmed Israel's right to sovereignty and territorial integrity. RAKAH rejected the PLO's concept of a "secular democratic state" that would replace Israel, and Ziyad emphasized his loyalty to Israel by participating in the state's annual Independence Day celebration.

RAKAH leaders warned against Israeli provocations toward Lebanon or any intervention in its civil war. They also denounced "reactionary forces in Lebanon and other Arab countries" (Moscow radio, in *FBIS*, 5 August) and called for an end to "outside interference" (TASS, in *FBIS*, 20 April).

RAKAH strongly expressed its support for Soviet positions. Tubi lauded Soviet "support . . . for a just peace in the Middle East" and contrasted it with U.S. actions that "perpetuate Israeli occupation and the serious crisis" (Moscow radio, in *FBIS*, 4 March). He accused Israeli leaders of using "slander" against the Soviet Union in order to undermine the relaxation of international tensions. He described the "so-called 'conference in defense of the rights of Soviet Jewry' . . . staged by the Zionists in Brussels in February" as the "latest example," and ridiculed charges of discrimination against Jews in the Soviet Union (TASS, in *FBIS*, 19 March). Vilner praised Soviet progress, condemned China's "Maoist leaders" and their "unprincipled policy," and defined "a person's attitude toward the Soviet Union as a principle of paramount importance" (*Pravda*, in *FBIS*, 10 March).

Publications. The RAKAH newspaper *al-Ittihad* (Union), an Arabic bi-weekly published in Haifa and edited by Tubi and Habibi, is widely read by Israeli Arabs. A Hebrew weekly, *Zo Ha-Derekh* (This Is the Way), is edited by Vilner in Tel Aviv. Other party publications are *al-Darb* (The Way), an Arabic theoretical magazine edited by Habibi and published irregularly in Haifa; *al-Jadid* (The New), a literary and cultural monthly magazine published in Haifa; *al-Ghad* (Tomorrow), a youth magazine; the Yiddish *Der Weg* (The Way), published weekly by Vilner in Tel Aviv; the Bulgarian *Tovaye Putnam* (This Is The Way), published every two weeks in Jaffa; *Arakim-Be'ayot ha-Shalom ve-ha-Soatziyalizm* (Values-Problems of Peace and Socialism), published irregularly in Tel Aviv; and a sporadic English *Information Bulletin*.

Other Marxist Organizations. Several other Marxist groups exist in Israel, but none of them is comparable to RAKAH as a political force. Excluding MOKED (despite the Marxist elements in it), each group consists of a handful of members, mostly young Jews, who propagate their views but do not, in most cases, offer their own lists of electoral candidates.

The most radical trend is represented by the Israeli Socialist Organization (Irgun Sotziyalisti Isra'eli; ISO), formed by a group of people who were expelled from MAKI in 1962. Widely known by the name of its monthly Hebrew publication, *Matzpen* (Compass), issued from Tel Aviv, the ISO condemns the creation of Israel at the expense of the Palestinian Arabs and its "open alliance with . . . imperialism, and collusion with the most reactionary forces in the Arab world." The ISO recognizes the continued existence of a Hebrew nation in Palestine, but calls for "de-Zionification" and "a socialist revolution," and "integration into a unified, socialist Middle East." It criticizes the USSR's policy of "peaceful coexistence," Soviet "bureaucracy," and RAKAH's acceptance of the Soviet line. It has also censured Peking's policies. (Arie Bobor, *The Other Israel: The Radical Case Against Zionism*, New York, 1972, *passim*, which is a collection of official ISO statements.) The *Matzpen* viewpoint has received most attention outside Israel. Several splits in the organization occurred during the early 1970s. Breakaway splinter groups include the Revolutionary Communist League (Brit Kommunistit Mahapkhanit), which is associated with the Fourth (Trotskyite) International; the Workers League (Brit ha-Po'alim), also Trotskyite; and the Maoist-oriented Revolutionary Communist Alliance-Struggle (Brit Kommunistit Mahapkhanit-Ma'avak).

The Israeli New Left (Smol Yisrael Chadash; SIAH) was created in 1968. It consists of a few youths (mainly students) previously associated with (and dissatisfied with) MAKI and MAPAM (the United Workers' Party, formerly a far-left party but now a part of the Labor Alignment). SIAH, which identifies with the radical student movement in Europe, professes devotion to a combination of Zionism and Marxism and calls for the creation of an independent Palestinian state to exist alongside Israel. Its publications include *Siah* (published irregularly in Hebrew) and *Israleft*, a bi-weekly English newsletter that disseminates statements by various leftist and peace groups.

Indiana State University
Terre Haute

Glenn E. Perry

Jordan

The Communist Party of Jordan (al-Hizb al-Shuyu'i al-Urdunni; CPJ) was officially established in June 1951. However, Communist activity on the West Bank of the Jordan River, annexed by the Hashemite kingdom of Jordan after the 1948 Arab-Israeli war, can be traced back to the founding in September 1943 of the Palestinian National Liberation League (PNLL) in Haifa. The partition of Palestine, supported by the Soviet Union, caused splits among local Communists. The PNLL initially opposed Jordan's takeover of the West Bank and denounced the "Hashemite army of occupation." Nonetheless, members of the PNLL joined ultimately with like-minded Jordanians to form the CPJ.

Under constant government pressure since the early 1950s, the party has operated under the guise of various popular front organizations. Its center of activity has been on the West Bank, where it has drawn support from students, teachers, professional workers, and the "lower middle classes." Although it had probably no more than 1,000 members at the time, mostly Palestinians, the CPJ was reportedly the strongest party in Jordan during the country's first decade of independence beginning in 1946.

The CPJ has been illegal since 1957, although the government's normally repressive measures occasionally have been relaxed. For example, two Communist deputies were elected to parliament as "independents" in 1961. More significantly, under a political amnesty granted at the outbreak of the 1967 Arab-Israeli war, all Communists were released from Jordanian jails and the party's secretary-general, Fu'ad Nassar, was allowed to return from exile. For a time the CPJ operated semi-legally. Repressive measures were resumed in 1972, and at present Communist party membership is punishable by jail sentences of from 3 to 15 years. Few radical organizations other than the Communists are active in Jordan. Various Palestinian groups, such as the Marxist-oriented Popular Front for the Liberation of Palestine, embittered by "repression" of the Palestinians during 1970-71, urge the overthrow of King Husain, but they appear to have little overt influence in Jordan itself.

The CPJ has perhaps no more than 500 members, mostly Palestinians. Jordan's population of about 2,789,000 includes more than 700,000 in Israeli-occupied East Jerusalem and the West Bank.

Leadership and Organization. The CPJ is said to be a "tightly organized, well disciplined network of small cells" (*NYT,* 23 August 1974). Secrecy is highly valued, and little information on party leadership is available. The current secretary-general, and only one thus far to hold that position, is Fu'ad Nassar, born in 1915, a Palestinian of Christian origin without formal education. Other prominent party members reportedly include 'Abd al-Muhsin Abu Maizar, also of the Palestine National Front (PNF), and Ishaq al-Khatib. 'Arabi 'Awad, a member of the CPJ's Central Committee and PNF leader, reportedly leads the West Bank branch of the CPJ and has spent more than 10 years in Jordanian and Israeli jails. Other members of the Central committee include 'Isa Madanat, Na'im Ashhab, and Ya'qub Diya' al-Din. Jiryas Qawwas, a former teacher, is an associate of 'Awad and also a prominent West Bank Communist and PNF official; he claims to have spent more than 13 years in Jordanian and Israeli jails.

Since its decline in the late 1950s, the CPJ has been known as a "passive political underground movement" confined to the West Bank (*NYT,* 23 August 1974). In recent years, however, activities have increased, and the CPJ claims to be the only party really functioning in Jordan. Fu'ad Nassar declared in an interview late in 1973 (Budapest radio, 29 December) that the party operates "under very difficult circumstances" on both sides of the river. He alluded to the frequent arrests of CPJ members by the authorities in Amman and the difficulties imposed by the Israelis, who have regularly rounded up Communists, among others, and deported them to the East Bank.

A CPJ statement in early 1976 (*FBIS*, 15 March) declared that "dozens and dozens" of party members, including the "best cadre workers and rank-and-file members," had been "imprisoned, exiled and subjected to brutal tortures." In January 1975, Bashir Barghuti, a West Bank resident, was tried by the Israelis on charges of spying for the "Communist-led" PNF. The Soviet news agency Tass denounced the "trumped-up charges," stating that Barghuti had simply written a letter to Amman referring to Israeli news accounts of the arrest and torture of PNF members. (*Arab Report and Record*, London, 16-31 January 1975.) Bashir Barghuti was released later in 1975, and was reported to be an editor of the Israeli-sanctioned Jerusalem Arabic newspaper *al-Fajr* (The Dawn) (*FBIS*, 29 January 1976).

Auxiliary and Mass Organizations. The Palestine National Front, composed of professional and labor union representatives and "patriotic personalities," was established on the West Bank in August 1973, evidently at CPJ instigation. The PNF generally follows the Palestine Liberation Organization (PLO) line: it advocates creating an independent Palestinian state on the West Bank together with the Gaza Strip and urges Palestinian participation in the Geneva peace talks. Its program includes mass political struggle and armed resistance in the occupied territories.

After the October 1973 Arab-Israeli war the PNF emerged as an "active pro-Palestinian organization." In an "Interview with the Palestine National Front" (*MERIP Reports*, Beirut, November 1974), Jiryas Qawwas and 'Arabi' Awad said that the PNF had organized the Arab boycotts of the Israeli trade union elections in Jerusalem in September 1973 and the Israeli parliamentary elections the following December. During the October war the PNF issued leaflets opposing the Israeli war effort and organized strikes of Arab workers in Israeli factories. Other activities have included campaigns against high Israeli taxes and prices, opposition to Jewish settlement in Nablus, and attacks on Israeli police posts, labor offices, and the banks in occupied West Jordan. The PNF reportedly organized the "popular uprising" of 13-23 November 1974 on the West Bank, on the occasion of Yasir 'Arafat's speech to the UN General Assembly.

Although the PNF's precise relationship to the CPJ is unknown, Israeli officials have stated that the CPJ is the core of the group's strength. The PNF is a member of the PLO, and its central committee includes representatives of most Palestinian factions and commando organizations. At least some of its leadership comes from the CPJ. It is clear, therefore, that West Bank Communists have become closely associated with Palestinian nationalist forces. According to Qawwas and 'Awad, the PNF mission "is to lead the struggle from inside the occupied territories" (ibid). Further evidence supports the belief that the CPJ's West Bank faction belongs to the PNF, and Ya'qub Diya'al-Din has stated that the CPJ plays a "large part" in that organization (*FBIS*, 29 January, 15 March 1976). The CPJ Central Committee has "appeal[ed] to the popular masses in the occupied territories to unite even more closely around the PLO and the National Palestinian Front" (*IB*, no. 2, 31 January).

Party Internal Affairs. In 1975, Na'im Ashhab described the CPJ as "the working-class party of two fraternal peoples—Jordanian and Palestinian" (*WMR*, June). Ya'qub Diya' al-din also views the CPJ as a party of Jordanian and Palestinian Communists (*FBIS*, 15 March 1976). Yet the CPJ, despite its support of Palestinian statehood, remains somewhat suspicious of the PLO, an attitude reciprocated by the PLO. In 1975, West Bank Communists began signing official statements with the name "Communist Party of the West Bank," as did affiliated student, labor, and women's associations, and the newspaper *al-Watan* appeared under the name "Palestine Communist Party." This name was evidently adopted by West bank cells without prior approval by the CPJ Central Committee. (*Le Matin-An-Nahar Arab Report*, Beirut, 3 February 1975.)

Domestic Attitudes and Activities. As a party oriented more toward Palestine than toward Jordan, the CPJ seemingly has devoted little attention to purely domestic issues. Like other anti-Husain Palestinians of whatever ideological persuasion, Fu'ad Nassar has denounced the "reactionary regime" in Amman and its links to "imperialism." He has advocated the establishment in Jordan of "a democratic, independent state" whose goal is social development. An April 1975 "Voice of Oman" statement (*FBIS*, 10 April) denounced the "agent regime" in Jordan which was said to deny general liberties, suppress the "masses' struggle," and render military aid to Sultan Qabus of Oman. In addition, the statement referred to the "national liberation movement" in Jordan and proposed the establishment of "a national progressive regime" in Amman, and of a "national front" which would be closely allied with the Palestinian and Arab national liberation movements.

The CPJ considers its "tireless" efforts to establish a national front in Jordan a "precondition for the establishment of a national liberation regime" (ibid., 15 March 1976). These activities are designed, among other things, to eliminate "imperialism" on the East Bank and to encourage a new Jordanian government to resist the Israeli occupation of the West Bank. Ya'qub Diya' al-Din has stated, with considerable exaggeration, that the CPJ has not only influenced various youth and intellectual organizations but has also had an "impact on all major political events in Jordan," including the struggles of the vocational and labor unions (ibid., 5 March).

The Palestine issue has vexed the party since its inception. As a generally pro-Soviet organization, the CPJ evidently has not been entirely free to take an independent stand on Palestine and consequently has lost support to more committed and radical Palestinian liberation movements, although its basic position on Palestine is similar to that of the main Palestinian groups. The party recognizes the PLO as the sole representative of the Palestinian people. In mid-1976, in a joint communiqué with Israel's Rakah or New Communist List party the CPJ demanded complete Israeli withdrawal from the occupied territories and "recognition of the legitimate rights of the Palestinian people, including the right to national self-determination and the establishment of an independent Palestinian state" (Moscow radio, 30 July, in *FBIS*, 2 August). The communiqué also urged resumption of the Geneva conference on the Middle East and the participation of the PLO on an equal footing with other delegations. A statement by Ya'qub Diya' al-Din (*FBIS*, 15 March) said that the anti-Israel struggle on the West Bank was aimed in part "against acts of desecration of religious objects and cultural values of our people."

International Activities and Attitudes. A former deputy adviser to Israel's prime minister has suggested that the CPJ may have coordinated activities with RAKAH to incite the Palestinians during the spring 1976 riots on the West Bank (*FBIS*, 2 April).

CPJ relations with the Lebanese Communists were said to have deteriorated in 1975 because of the latter's alleged encouragement of the West Bank Communists to break with the CPJ (*Le Matin-An-Nahar Arab Report*, 24 March). Later in 1975 the CPJ Central Committee took note of "the worsened situation in Lebanon [which was] generated by the dastardly conspiracies of the imperialist-reactionary alliance" (*IB*, no. 2, 31 January 1976). Reflecting the Soviet position, the aforementioned CPJ-RAKAH communiqué declared that the Lebanese civil war should be ended, as it did not serve the interests either of the Lebanese or the Palestinian peoples (*FBIS*, 2 August). The communiqué went on to denounce "reactionary forces" in Lebanon, U.S. imperialism, various Arab states, and Israel.

Fu'ad Nassar visited the German Democratic Republic at least twice in 1976 (*FBIS*, 11 February, 12 July), and Central Committee member Ya'qub Diya' al-Din visited the Soviet Union (*FBIS*, 5 March), where he stated in Minsk that the CPJ "continuously seeks to strengthen and develop [Soviet-

CPJ] relations on Marxist-Leninist and international proletariat foundations in the interests of peace, progress and democracy." An article by Na'im Ashhab discussed the imperialists' responsibility for the global arms race and its adverse economic impact on the developing countries (*WMR,* July).

Publications. The CPJ publishes a journal, *al-Jamahir* (The Masses), and an underground newspaper, *al-Watan* (The Homeland), both of which appear irregularly. The party also issues a political and theoretical journal, *al-Haqiqah* (The Truth), and special pamphlets. These publications are distributed clandestinely on both sides of the Jordan River, except for *al-Watan,* which seems to be restricted mainly to the West Bank. The PNF publishes its own newspaper, *Filastin* (Palestine). News of CPJ activities also appears in the organs of the Lebanese Communist Party, *al-Akhbar* and *al-Nida'.*

U.S. Department of Commerce   Norman F. Howard
Washington, D.C.

(Note: the views expressed in this article are the author's own and do not represent those of the Department of Commerce.)

Lebanon

The Lebanese Communist Party (al-Hizb al-Shuyu'i al-Lubnani; LCP) was established in 1924. During the period of the French mandates it accepted members from both Lebanon and Syria. What is generally considered its First Congress was held in January 1944, a little more than two years after Syria and Lebanon were first proclaimed independent states. This congress decided to establish separate Lebanese and Syrian Communist parties. The fighting in Lebanon in 1975-76 has led the LCP to emphasize its Lebanese origins. Thus, George Hawi asserted "We are from the Lebanese left. Bikfayya and al-Hadath are the two towns which saw the birth of our party at the hands of genuine Lebanese, such as Yusuf Yazbik and struggler Fu'ad al-Shamali and others from the pioneers of the modern ideological and nationalist renaissance." (*al-Sayyad,* Beirut, 8 January 1976.)

In 1965 the LCP decided to break away from its policy of working independently of other Lebanese political groups. Since then it has become a member of the Front of Progressive Parties and National Forces (FPPNF) under the leadership of the Progressive Socialists, a party headed by Kamal Jumblat. The LCP is also a member of the Arab Front for Participation in the Palestine Revolution (AFPPR). The LCP was banned by the government until 13 August 1970, when it gained recognition along with other controversial parties. It has been an active participant in the civil war of 1975-76.

Recent estimates of LCP strength count 2,000 to 3,000 Lebanese among its members and sympathizers. The Lebanese population in 1975 was about 2,500,000.

Leadership and Organization. The Congress, which is to be convened every four years, is the supreme organ of the LCP. The most recent, the Third Congress, was held in Beirut in January 1972 with delegates from more than 30 foreign Communist parties attending (*YICA, 1972,* pp. 252-59). This was the first formal congress ever held openly by an Arab Communist party. The Fourth Congress was supposed to be held in 1976. The fighting in Lebanon, however, made such an open meeting impossible. Between congresses, authority is vested in the 24-member Central Committee, which in turn selects and invests authority in the 11-member Politburo and the 5-member Secretariat. The secretary-general, Niqula al-Shawi, and his second in command, George Hawi, who is head of the Secretariat, are both Greek Orthodox. Other members of the Secretariat include Nadim 'Abd al-Samad, who is head of the party's foreign department, Karim Muruwwah, and Khalil al-Dibs.

Domestic Views and Activities. Stating the general domestic goals of the LCP, George Hawi said in January 1976, "The maximum we strive for is democratic reform of the political system to organize, by democratic methods, the question of the struggle over power" (*al-Sayyad,* 8 January). The Lebanese war, which began in the spring of 1975, is seen by the LCP as, internally, a crisis of the political and socio-economic system brought about by rightist extremist groups to prevent needed reforms and defeat the progressive forces. In the LCP's interpretation, this crisis has been provoked and perpetuated to distract the Arabs from the struggle for Palestinian rights and against Israeli occupation, to paralyze the Palestinian refugees, and to destroy the Palestine Liberation Organization (PLO). The Communist militia, a paramilitary arm of the LCP led by George Hawi, has been a significant fighting force in the Lebanese war, fighting alongside the Progressive Socialist Party of Kamal Jumblat and the Independent Nasserite Movement led by Ibrahim Kalilat. Hawi has justified this, saying that the party has fought "in solidarity with the Palestinian resistance," "in reply to aggression," and "in self-defense." He claims that if all the participants in the conflict agree to stop fighting and begin discussing in a framework of purely political struggle, the LCP will be the first to support this (ibid.). The LCP holds that the Lebanese themselves should resolve the crisis alone, on the basis of "safeguarding the independence, sovereignty and unity of Lebanon." The LCP has also called for the "freedom of movement and activity of Palestinians, not only in Lebanon, but also in all Arab territories around Israel." ('Abd al-Samad interview, Moscow radio, 19 August.) When a ceasefire in February seemed to be holding, Nadim 'Abd al-Samad presented a list of political tasks that needed to be tackled: "securing domestic peace, strengthening the democratic freedoms for the press, the trade unions and the parties, dismantling the anachronistic division by religion, changing the proportional representation in parliament, and creating a new election law . . . based on the actual balance of forces in the country" (interview, *Neues Deutschland,* East Berlin, 18 February).

The most significant foreign element involved in the Lebanese conflict has been Syria. In October 1976 the LCP lauded Syria for giving support to the broad masses of Lebanon who oppose internationalizing the conflict. However, Syria had lost favor with the party in mid-1976, after it sent forces into Lebanon, and especially after Syrian troops began to fight openly in concert with the Phalangists. A statement issued by the Central Committee of the LCP in August condemned the Syrian military intervention, charging that serious responsibility "devolves on all progressive patriots and communists in Syria and in the Syrian army, officers and ranks" (Iraqi News Agency, 13 August). In September the LCP accused Syria, Egypt, and Saudi Arabia of leading a reactionary Arab plot to wipe out the Palestinian resistance in Lebanon and head off the creation of an independent Palestinian state. Only Iraq was singled out among Arab countries for maintaining a coherent stand on behalf of the Palestinian cause. (ANSA, Rome, 16 September.)

The LCP has condemned the USA, France, and West Germany for giving aid to the Phalangists. However, it considers that "the ugliest aspect of the present situation is the increasing Israeli intervention in the civil war in Lebanon at the side of the right-wing forces," both as a supplier of weapons and as the agent imposing a maritime blockade against supply lines of the Lebanese leftist forces and the Palestinians (Moscow radio, 19 August). The LCP expressed its appreciation of the Communist parties of France, Italy, and other Western European countries who supported the domestic policy of the LCP. Most LCP communications in 1976 praised the support of the Communist Party of the Soviet Union (CPSU). But an LCP delegation in Rome disclosed that the LCP had a difficult time in August trying to persuade the Soviet Union to come out against Syria, with whom Moscow has had close ties (ANSA, 16 September). However, a joint communiqué was issued by the CPSU and the LCP declaring that "the Lebanese crisis could and should be resolved without the intervention of foreign forces but by the Lebanese themselves" (Moscow radio, 19 August).

International Views and Activities. The LCP continued in 1976 to follow the Soviet Union's general policy on the Middle East conflict, holding that a just and lasting peace in the region must be based on the withdrawal of Israeli troops from all occupied territories and the guarantee of the legitimate national rights of the Palestinian people. The LCP, however, emphasized the interrelationship of the Lebanese civil war and the Middle East conflict. Thus it joined with the Palestinian Rejection Front in September in calling for greater solidarity between the Lebanese nationalist movement and the Palestinian resistance (Iraqi News Agency, 23 September).

LCP contact with the Syrian Communist Party (SCP) has fluctuated according to Syrian military activity in Lebanon. Late in December 1975 the Egyptian press reported that 300 Communists had been arrested in Syria and that the SCP leader Khalid Bakdash had fled the country. The LCP denied the reports. It charged that Egypt was trying to undermine the Syrian National Progressive Front and damage friendly relations between Damascus and Moscow. The LCP claimed that "the political leadership of the sisterly land of Syria would not carry out measures of this sort, which would throw into disorder the unity between the nationalist and progressive forces, harm the progressive Syrian regime's accomplishments, and also damage the status of Syria on the Arab and international levels (*An-Nahar Arab Report,* 5 January). Syria's intervention in Lebanon in mid-June 1976 affected LCP interaction with the SCP. The LCP had supported the faction of the SCP which participated in the National Progressive Front. But with Syrian intervention the LCP found its views more in line with the faction that is opposed to the Syrian government, that supports the Palestinian cause, and that follows an independent line regarding the Soviet Union.

The LCP met with the Iraqi Communist Party in July. A joint communiqué condemned the Syrian forces and reaffirmed support of the Palestinian resistance and its right to exist on Lebanese territory (Iraqi News Agency, Baghdad, 2 July). In late October a delegation of the LCP, which included Nadim 'Abd al-Amad, again visited Iraq, but this time it met with leaders of the ruling Ba'th Party to discuss the latest developments in the light of the resolutions regarding Lebanon passed by the summit conferences of Arab leaders in Riyad and Cairo. Samad also attended meetings of the permanent secretariat of the Arab Popular Conference in Support of the Palestinian Revolution and the Lebanese National Movement. (Ibid., 30 October.)

A delegation led by Niqula al-Shawi participated in the 25th Congress of the CPSU in March. In his speech to the congress, Shawi praised the Soviet Union for its domestic achievements as well as its support of the Arabs against Israeli aggression. Shawi hailed the presence of the Cuban and Vietnamese delegations and praised the victories of the Portuguese and Greek people for putting "an end to dictatorship." (Radio Peace and Progress, Moscow, 4 March.) LCP leaders visited the Soviet Union again in August to discuss Syrian intervention in Lebanon. During the year LCP delegations also met with Communist party leaders in Cyprus, Italy, Hungary, Czechoslovakia and Bulgaria. In February, a delegation of the Communist Party, USA visited Lebanon at the invitation of the LCP.

The LCP reaffirmed opposition to the Sinai Agreement, on the grounds that it has caused chaos and delayed a real solution, and that its supporters have been isolated from the rest of the Arab world (TASS, Moscow, 22 July). The LCP was among those listed by the PLO in Aden, 15 January, as opposing Iran's military offensive in Oman. Also in January, the LCP joined with the Progressive Party of the Working People of Cyprus in welcoming the final acts of the Helsinki Conference and in demanding the implementation of its principles in the interest of peace and cooperation both in Europe and throughout the world (ibid., 5 June). In July the LCP denounced Peking for "opposing the relaxation of tensions and support[ing] the racists in South Africa and the fascist junta in Chile" (ibid, 22 July).

Publications. The LCP publishes a daily newspaper, *al-Nida* (The Call), a weekly magazine, *al-Akhbar* (The News), and a literary and ideological monthly, *al-Tariq* (The Road). These organs also serve as general information media for the illegal Communist parties of the Middle East.

Other Communist Organizations. The Organization of Communist Action in Lebanon (OCAL) is led by its secretary-general, Muhsin Ibrahim. Like the LCP, it is a member of both the FPPNF and the AFPPR. The OCAL has been actively involved in the war in Lebanon, fighting alongside the Progressive Socialists, the Independent Nasserite Movement, and the Iraqi Communist Party.

In June 1976 the U.S. ambassador to Lebanon was ambushed and killed. It was reported that his car disappeared near the area called al-Barbir where there were barricades manned by OCAL and other leftist groups. The OCAL, however, was not directly implicated in the incident.

In August, representatives of the Socialist Arab Ba'th Party, the LCP, and the OCAL met to discuss the current situation and the relations among the three organizations. It was reported that "an atmosphere of frankness and identity of views on the current situation prevailed at the meeting" (Iraqi News Agency, 19 August).

Three other Communist organizations were mentioned by rightist news media during the year. No details were provided, however, and their existence could not be substantiated. The names given were the Communist Labor Organization, the Revolutionary Communist Organization, and the Lebanese Communist Union.

Hoover Institution   Michel Nabti
Stanford University

The Maghreb

ALGERIA

The Algerian Communist Party (Parti Communiste Algérien; PCA) was founded in 1920 in the French colonial era. It has not been able to eliminate the stigma of having once been a virtual branch of the French Communist Party which entered the anti-colonial struggle late and reluctantly.

On 27 June 1976, Algerian president Houari Boumedienne submitted to a popular referendum a 60,000-word national charter to provide guidelines for a new constitution. This opened the way for presidential and legislative elections in December, in which Boumedienne's unopposed election was anticipated, although the newly elected National People's Assembly, the first parliament since the 1965 coup, was expected to give some scope for legal opposition activity.

The outlawed PCA was replaced in 1974 by the barely tolerated Socialist Vanguard Party (Parti de l'Avant-Garde Socialiste; PAGS). Its secretary-general is Sadiq Hadjeres. In 1976, PAGS activity was minimal, limited to reported contacts with extremist Palestinian groups, the Polisario independence movement in the western Sahara, and some Communist parties and factions abroad.

The number of Communists in Algeria is perhaps 500. The total population is about 17,300,000.

The official National Liberation Front (FLN) remains Algeria's ruling organization and the only party in 1976 with full political rights. This follows the one-party pattern of rule seen in other "socialist" Arab states such as Egypt, Iraq, and the People's Republic of Southern Yemen.

The Communist Party of the Soviet Union (CPSU) has party-to-party relations with the FLN. Since the late 1960s, the USSR has made every effort to consolidate its relations with Algeria, continuing a large program of economic and military aid down through 1976. The Boumedienne government has, however, consistently refused to grant any Soviet military, air, or naval base facilities, after totally ending the French military presence in the country before 1970.

Domestic Attitudes and Activities. The PAGS remained silent, possibly indicating tacit approval, during a wave of arrests of "bourgeois" elements that began in March 1976. Among those arrested were Ferhat Abbas, pre-1962 president of the Provisional Revolutionary Algerian Government-in-Exile (GPRA) and Ben Youssef ben Khedda, a prime minister of the GPRA, both living in retirement, and also Muhammad Kheriddine, an industrialist. The three had been among the signers of an anti-Boumedienne manifesto. In a speech at Tiaret on 19 March, Boumedienne made a strong appeal for leftist support for the FLN. He defended the FLN's achievements in industrial and agricultural development, and praised its "solid alliance" of "workers, peasants, soldiers and revolutionary intellectuals," which he termed the "shield of the revolution."

During the run-up to the campaign for the elections, the PAGS was reported to have encouraged its followers to back a government campaign against the "plague of bureaucracy" by entering citizens' suggestions on a questionnaire published by the ruling Council of the Revolution, the FLN's inner governing body.

International Activities and Attitudes. During 1976 Algeria played a leading role in the Paris "North-South" discussions between "rich" and "poor" nations, which it helped to initiate when Foreign Minister Abdel Azziz Bouteflika served as president of the UN General Assembly in 1975.

The country's foreign relations, however, were dominated by its dispute and occasional armed clashes with Morocco and Mauretania over the former Spanish Sahara. By agreement with Spain, Morocco and Mauretania partitioned this region between them over strong Algerian protests, in February 1976. Algeria also took a stand in favor of the Palestinian-Leftist alliance in the Lebanese civil war. The Algerian ambassador in Beirut, Muhammad Yazid, who was GPRA information minister before 1962, tried to mediate in that war.

In both the Saharan and Lebanese conflicts, the PAGS supported Algerian government policy, which coincided with Soviet policy (although Soviet opposition to Morocco was muted and expressed mainly through foreign Communist parties). With the FLN, the PAGS cooperated with the Polisario (Front for the Liberation and Independence of the Sahara) movement, which proclaimed an "independent Saharan republic" in April 1976 and waged guerrilla warfare against the Moroccan and Mauretanian armies in the western Sahara.

At the 25th Congress of the CPSU, in February and March, Algeria was represented only by the official FLN delegation, led by Muhammad ben Yahia, former Algerian ambassador to the USSR. Ben

Yahia praised Soviet policy and the growth of Algerian-Soviet relations and affirmed that Algeria is "indefatigably fighting to create a socialist society." He said that its land reform, which has suffered many delays, was aimed at restoring "the land to those who till it," and that an educational and cultural revolution would continue with Soviet assistance. He did not refer to Algeria's growing economic and trade relationships with the USA and Western Europe in the fields of oil, natural gas, and industrialization.

On 8 March, after the CPSU congress, ben Yahia and other Algerian delegates, including Salah Goudjil, FLN national commissar for regional organization, conferred in Moscow with Boris Ponomarev and other CPSU officials.

At the end of 1975 the USSR and Algeria signed a two-year working agreement to exchange radio and televison films and programs. Under a new scientific and technical accord reached in January 1976, the USSR agreed to support desalination plants, heavy electrical industries and electric power projects, mining operations at the Gara Jebilet iron works, and railroad construction, both of the latter in the strategic area adjoining the zone of conflict with Morocco in the western Sahara.

In July a joint Algerian-Soviet commission was set up to supervise Soviet-aided agriculture and hydropower projects, and a team of Soviet geo-botanical experts was assigned to survey Algeria.

In January, China agreed to help set up a rice-processing plant near Algeria's new industrial zone at Skikda.

Publication. The PAGS was reported in 1976 to be still issuing at infrequent intervals its clandestine journal *Saut al-Sha'b* (The Voice of the People).

MOROCCO

The Moroccan Communist Party (Parti Communist Marocain; PCM) was founded in 1943 as a branch of the French Communist Party. Like the Algerian and Tunisian Communist parties, it was originally organized and staffed by Europeans. Moroccans first joined it after 1944, when the nationalist Istiqlal (Independence) Party launched the drive for Moroccan independence from French and Spanish rule.

In 1945 'Ali Yata became the party's leader and secretary-general, and he has retained leadership until the present. The French Protectorate authorities banned both the PCM and Istiqlal in 1952, at the onset of active resistance against French rule which continued until Morocco won independence in 1956. King Muhammad V again banned the PCM in 1959. After many vicissitudes and some legal tests of the ban in the Moroccan courts, the PCM resurfaced in 1968 as the Party of Liberation and Socialism (Parti du Libération et du Socialisme), but it was soon outlawed again, by King Hasan II in 1969. As 'Ali Yata cooperated increasingly with the monarchy, the government rewarded the party in August 1974 by granting it legal status. Renamed the Party of Progress and Socialism (Parti du Progrès et du Socialisme; PPS), it participated in the Moroccan national elections of November 1976, but won no offices.

The number of Communists in Morocco in 1976 was estimated at under 1,000. The country's population is about 18,000,000.

Leadership and Domestic Activities. The PPS leadership derives largely from the old group with which 'Ali Yata worked through his years of resistance to the French Protectorate and early militancy in independent Morocco. A PPS party congress in 1975 confirmed Yata as secretary-general and created a secretariat consisting of himself, 'Abd Allah Layashi, and 'Abd al-Salam Bourquia, who with four others comprise the Politburo. Some 338 delegates attended the congress, which was also attended by Bu 'Abid, leader of the Socialist Union of Popular Forces (USFP) and by representatives of 16 foreign Communist parties, including the Communist Party of the Soviet Union (CPSU), and of other groups such as the Palestine Liberation Organization. (*WMR*, July 1975.)

The PPS participated in the November 1976 national elections on a platform emphasizing national unity behind King Hasan on the Sahara issue, and of facing the possible military threat from Algeria. The PPS domestic goals include nationalization of Moroccan banks, insurance companies, public utilities, and sugar, cement, and pharmaceutical industries. The PPS also advocates nationalization of mining industries in which foreign banks hold interests, the end of "feudal land tenure," support of Moroccan workers and students in Europe, and elimination of wage discrimination and other forms of discrimination against women.

Before 1975, the PPS consistently followed a pro-Soviet line. By the time of the November 1976 elections, however, 'Ali Yata had begun clearly to oppose Soviet policy with regard to Morocco, as the Soviet Union objected to Morocco's policy regarding the Spanish Sahara, a land rich in phosphates that was partitioned between Morocco and Mauretania early in 1976.

'Ali Yata received permission from King Hasan to form the PPS only after he had toured Eastern Europe (except for the USSR) in mid-1974 to explain and support Morocco's position in the Spanish Sahara issue. His emergence as a Moroccan patriot has contributed largely to the relative unity and harmony between the King and the opposition parties, including Istiqlal on the right and the USFP on the left. 'Ali Yata was one of the nine Moroccan party leaders consulted by the King in preparation for the elections for 830 local councils and for the parliamentary election.

The PPS appears to have disapproved of a wave of strikes, demonstrations, and unrest leading to the arrest of many secondary school and university students in January-March 1976, mainly in Rabat, Tangier, Fez, and Tetuan, with some worker involvement reported in Rabat. Small dissident leftist factions, such as that of Serfaty, referred scornfully to the PPS as part of the Moroccan "establishment" because of its orthodox patriotic views on the Sahara question.

Relations with Other Left-Wing Groups. The USFP consists of several factions. Its more or less pro-monarchist "Rabat" wing is led by former economy minister 'Abd al-Rhman Bou 'Abid. Its small and more independent "Casablanca" wing is headed by former premier Abdallah Ibrahim. Muhammad Basri probably heads its clandestine and largely exiled faction. At various times since 1970 Basri has broadcast anti-Hasan propaganda on the Libyan state radio in Tripoli, mainly during periods of violent antagonism between Hasan and Libya's Colonel Muammar al-Qaddafi, who was accused of encouraging one of the abortive army conspiracies against Hasan in 1972. None of the USFP factions actively cooperate with the PPS, but there has been little friction between the USFP and the PPS.

More of an irritation to the PPS are several other small Marxist-Leninist groups. One is led by veteran former PCM leader Abraham Serfaty, a Moroccan Jewish intellectual who was once one of Yata's close companions. Another, rather less Marxist, is the small Progressive Liberal Party; a third is the Action Party, consisting of a few intellectuals and professional men in Casablanca, Rabat, Fez, and Meknes.

As the elections drew near, Moroccan historian Abd 'Allah Laroui commented: "Curiously, the groups furthest to the left are those which are most moderate toward reform of our institutions. The USFP and the PPS are playing the game, while the other parties are afraid of change. Istiqlal is one of those which will find it difficult to adapt to the new situation created in Morocco by the elections." (*Jeune Afrique*, 15 October.)

International Attitudes and Activities. Unrest in the Moroccan student movement extended abroad to the 8,000 Moroccan students in France who in January 1976 held elections to their government council. 'Ali Yata expressed satisfaction with the victory of PPS and USFP-sponsored candidates and with the council's platform. This included "liberation of the Moroccan Sahara and the other territories" (meaning the Spanish-governed enclaves on the northern Moroccan coast) and "democratic elections and union of the national and progressive forces [in Morocco]." "It is known," wrote Yata, "that the student organization [before the student elections in France] had been literally torpedoed by the leftists who had, by their adventurist and provocative behavior, given an opening to repression, banning, and the loss of a large number of gains of the student movement." (*al-Bayan*, 16 January.)

The PPS supported King Hasan's "Green March" of 350,000 Moroccans into the Spanish Sahara in November 1975 and subsequent moves which hastened Spain's handover of the western Sahara to Morocco and Mauretania. This stand has placed the PPS in opposition to Moscow. Soviet statements backed the Algerian position, while refraining from open attacks on Morocco. These were left to West European Communists and Algerian commentators. The Algerian newspaper *La République* on 5 October 1975 described 'Ali Yata as a "pseudo-revolutionary . . . atop his throne as leader of a phantom party." Yata responded in an article, quoted by Morocco's official Maghreb Arabe Presse service on 11 November, saying that the Sahara was part of Morocco and that "a revolutionary who would like to lead the Moroccans of the western Sahara to break with their own country would be straying from Marxism-Leninism."

At the 25th Congress of the CPSU in Moscow in February-March 1976, 'Ali Yata stressed the "victory of the Angolan people over the imperialists and their reactionary henchmen" more than the Saharan question. But in April he repeated his 1974 tour of Czechoslovakia, Romania, Poland, Hungary, and East Germany, meeting Communist party leaders and reporting to them on "the evolution of the situation in the area following return of the Moroccan Sahara to the motherland" (PAP, Warsaw, 13 April; *al-Bayan*, 14 April).

The Sahara issue brought the PPS into bitter conflict with the French Communist Party (PCF), which like other West European Communist parties backed Polisario (Front for the Liberation and Independence of the Sahara) and the Algerian position. At the June conference of West European Communist and workers' parties in East Berlin, PCF secretary-general Georges Marchais expressed solidarity with "the struggle of the Saharan people for their national liberation." 'Ali Yata's rejoinder came in a report to the PPS Central Committee in Casablanca in August: "We remind Comrade Georges Marchais that the Saharan question is our affair." Marchais, Yata added, had not applied correct Marxist-Leninist principles of analysis to the study of the western Sahara and its population. Instead, Marchais had been "content to adopt Boumedienne's stance." (*Le Monde*, 3 August.)

Publications. 'Ali Yata edits *al-Bayan* (The Bulletin), a weekly appearing in Rabat, and *al-Mukafih* (The Fighter), appearing in Casablanca daily in Arabic and monthly in French.

TUNISIA

The Communist Party of Tunisia (Parti Communiste Tunisien; PCT) was founded by Europeans as a component of the French Communist Party. After its creation in 1919, its early militants were Frenchmen, Italians, and a few Tunisian Jews. It became independent in 1934 and at its peak period during World War II, when it took part in some pro-Allied resistance activities against the German and Italian forces, it probably had more than 2,000 members. The PCT was permanently outlawed in 1963, when all parties, except the Destourian Socialist, were banned. The PCT never succeeded in infiltrating the Tunisian Labor Federation, which received guidance and funds from the Western-oriented International Confederation of Free Trade Unions. Party congresses of the PCT in 1956, 1957, and 1962 adopted a program called "Tunisia's Path to Socialism." But the PCT produced no leaders worthy of mention and rallied little support, despite occasional outbursts of dissident student activity in Tunisia and France and some illegal workers' strikes.

There are at present perhaps no more than 200 Communists in Tunisia. The estimated population of the country in 1976 was 5,900,000.

Domestic Attitudes and Activities. Tunisian president Habib Bourguiba, national hero and father-figure, became president for life in 1974. In August 1976 the Tunisian National Assembly, after many years of hesitation and false starts, passed a law for reform of the 1959 constitution. It provided for a referendum procedure, revision of relations between the executive and legislative branches of the government, and regulation of the succession to the presidency.

In various clandestine publications the PCT has generally "supported progressive government measures aimed at consolidating national sovereignty and independence [and] establishing a state sector in the economy" (a course which has some partisans in the ruling Socialist Destourian party leadership). The PCT also has called for a policy of "restricting and easing out foreign monopoly capital." It supports the Destourian Socialist party's foreign policy, "especially as regards the struggle against imperialism and Zionism and development of friendly relations with the socialist countries" (*WMR*, October 1975).

In 1976 Tunisian Communists showed support for Ahmed ben Salah, the former leftist economic planner who, stripped of his ministerial posts and arrested for alleged corruption in 1969, escaped to Europe to become President Bourguiba's main critic in exile. On 13 January 1976 the French Communist newspaper *L'Humanité* published a PCT communiqué marking the 13th anniversary of the outlawing of the party. It denounced the "scandalous anti-democratic and anti-Communist practices of the authorities and the overtly pro-capitalist orientation of the Tunisian government." It demanded "an end to the systematic repression besetting the progressive, democratic, and trade union forces; respect for the basic freedoms of organizations and opinion laid down in the Tunisian constitution; and the lifting of the arbitrary ban imposed on the Tunisian Communist Party and the left-wing press."

On 30 March 1976, *L'Humanité* published a "joint document of Communists and friends of Ahmed ben Salah," outlining a plan to reorient Tunisian political and economic life along socialist lines. It urged a "policy of real development . . . consistent with the aims of economic independence and satisfying the most under-privileged social strata," the granting of "real exercise of all democratic freedoms, including the freedom of assembly inscribed in the constitution," and "an end to all forms of repression and an amnesty for all political prisoners."

Inside Tunisia the most notable public manifestation of opposition to Bourguiba's manner of governing came not from the left, but from a group headed by five former ministers. On 19 March they called for an end to one-party rule and for authorization to form a legal party opposing the Destourian Socialist Party.

In June seven civil servants were sentenced to six months' imprisonment after strikes in the postal services and government tobacco monopoly. Junior judges also went on strike for better working conditions and promotion prospects.

International Activities and Attitudes. Though no Tunisian delegates were apparently seated, the 25th Congress of the Communist Party of the Soviet Union, February-March 1976, heard a message from the PCT supporting the USSR, Angola, and the Palestinians, and denouncing the "pro-capitalist" orientation of Tunisia (*Pravda*, 1 March).

No apparent position was taken by the Communists in the crisis with Libya which arose in March when eleven Libyan diplomats were expelled from Tunisia after President Bourguiba announced on 22 March a conspiracy to kill him and Premier Hedi Nouira. Relations with Libya have gradually worsened since former Tunisian foreign minister Muhammad Masmoudi in 1972 tried and failed to bring about a union of Tunisia with Libya.

Though it remained neutral in the Lebanese civil war, Tunisia took a lead in Arab League efforts to end that conflict. It energetically supported the Palestine Liberation Organization in international forums, though it disassociated itself from terrorist activities widely reported to be supported by Libya and Algeria. Several times in 1976, President Bourguiba repeated his well-known proposal that the Arab-Israeli conflict should be settled by a return to the 1947 UN resolution partitioning the former territory of Palestine into an Arab and a Jewish state—in other words, confining Israel to its pre-1949 boundaries.

Several Soviet aid projects in irrigation and public works, begun in former years, were continued in 1976. In September, Czechoslovakia granted Tunisia a credit of $30 million in Swiss francs, with more credits stated to be available in the future if needed for joint ventures in agriculture and water projects.

At the end of March, a North Korean deputy foreign minister visited Tunis and conferred with the Tunisian foreign minister on undisclosed subjects.

Publications. The PCT has had no official organ since its banning and the proscription of its publications, *al-Tali'ah* (The Vanguard) and *Tribune du Progres*, in 1963. Leftists, mainly students, have sporadically produced *Tunisian Perspectives* and *The Tunisian Worker*. Ahmed ben Salah and his friends have occasionally published interviews in European publications.

Christian Science Monitor   John K. Cooley
Athens

Réunion

The Réunion Communist Party (Parti Communiste Réunnionais; PCR) was founded in 1959 by the transformation of the Réunion federation of the French Communist Party into an autonomous organization.

The PCR is legal. In 1967 the party claimed 3,500 members. More recently the U.S. State Department estimated the number at 800 (*World Strength of the Communist Party Organizations*, Washington, D.C., 1973).

Réunion has a population of about 500,000. As one of France's overseas departments, it is an integral part of the French Republic.

Politics in Réunion tends strongly toward the left, as indicated by the fact that in the 1974 French presidential election more than 50 percent of the votes on the island went to Socialist Party leader François Mitterrand. The PCR is an active participant in political life, on both local and departmental levels, and is the only party with a Réunion-based organization.

The PCR won 5 (of 36) seats in the General Council in the March 1976 elections, but party chief Paul Vergès lost his seat in what the PCR called a "fraudulent, fascist-type" election. On 18 March the five successful Communist candidates announced that in protest they would not attend the first session of the Council. (*Temoignages*, 18 March.)

Vergès, who is also mayor of one of the main towns, Le Port, was reelected PCR secretary-general at the party's Fourth Congress, in September 1976. No other leadership positions were announced.

The PCR controls the largest trade union, the General Confederation of Labor of Réunion (Confédération Général du Travail de la Réunion; ÇGTR), and is also influential in the Réunion Front of Autonomous Youth (Front de la Jeunesse Autonomiste de la Réunion; FJAR) and the Union of Réunion Women.

The PCR Fourth Congress had a reported attendance of 655 party delegates and more than 70 observers. Among the latter were representatives of the Communist parties of France and Martinique and observers from the CGTR, the FJAR, and other organizations in Réunion. (Ibid., 29 September.)

The PCR seeks autonomy for Réunion to achieve "freedom for our people and development for our country" (ibid., 2 September). The two-day visit to Réunion of French president Giscard d'Estaing in mid-October was taken by the Communists as an occasion for forceful presentation of their position. In a talk before some 10,000 people in the Communist- and Socialist-governed town of Saint-Louis, the president spoke out against autonomy. PCR members, who had arrived early and occupied all the seats in the front of the platform, waved banners and shouted slogans in support of autonomy in a highly charged atmosphere. According to Paris domestic Radio (21 October), the president won the crowd over to his view. Whereas the French government maintains that the people of Réunion profit from their status as an overseas department, the PCR insists that the past colonial exploitation of the island has been expanded by the relationship, and by French and other European monopolies. It argues that the traditional production sector—agriculture—has fallen off and that the industrial sector is also in regression. (*Témoignages*, 1, 3 October.)

The PCR says there is discontent among the workers, youth, consumers, functionaries, and people generally due to economic conditions, particularly the rise in the cost of living, and that resolution of the problems will have to come through unified struggle incorporating workers and planters, artisans and businessmen, intellectuals and democrats (ibid., 2, 28 September). In his report to the Fourth Congress, Vergès pointed to what he considered second-class treatment of Réunion by the government in France and called for many economic and political changes, ranging from unemployment benefits to lower fares on Air France (ibid., 1 October). Similar demands were made by the CGTR (ibid., 4 October).

The PCR holds periodic meetings (the most recent at the end of November) with leaders of the Communist parties of France, Guadeloupe, and Martinique in order to coordinate critiques of the French government and to formulate policies toward international issues. It devotes much attention to the "irreversible liberation from colonial oppression in Africa" (ibid., 19 September). At its congress, the party continued its promotion of "anti-imperialist solidarity among the peoples of the area for the Indian Ocean Zone of Peace" (ibid., 29 September; see also *Afrique-Asie*, Paris, 1-14 November).

The PCR publishes a daily paper, *Témoignages*.

Palo Alto, California   Lynn Ratliff

Senegal

The African Independence Party (Parti Africain de l'Indépendance; PAI) of Senegal was founded in 1957. In July 1960 it was dissolved by order of the government immediately after the municipal elections. Originally the PAI carried out activities in several French possessions in Africa, but since 1962 it has restricted its activities to Senegal on the grounds that France had by then been forced to grant autonomy or independence to the territories of its former colonial federations. On 9 August 1976 the party was declared legal.

Senegalese politics are dominated by President Léopold Sédar Senghor and his Senegalese Progressive Union (UPS). All opposition parties were outlawed and many political opponents incarcerated during the 1960s and early 1970s. In 1974 President Senghor authorized the formation of one opposition party, the Senegalese Democratic Party (PDS), under the leadership of Abdoulayé Wade, which held its first congress in early 1976. On 1 April 1976 the Senegalese National Assembly adopted a constitutional amendment which permitted three political parties to operate in Senegal. These parties were to profess different ideologies— liberal democratic, social-democratic, and Marxist-Leninist. Senghor, who regards himself as a socialist, declared that his UPS would constitute the social-democratic party; the PDS, also socialistically inclined, reluctantly accepted the liberal-democratic label. In August the minister of the interior officially approved the PAI's petition to be the Marxist-Leninist party. The April constitutional amendment stipulates that any party deviating from its "chosen" ideology may be dissolved. Critics of the government are, however, allowed considerable freedom of expression.

No membership figures have been released by the PAI. The population of Senegal is about 4,100,000.

Party Organization and Internal Affairs. The PAI is run by its Central Committee, Political Bureau, and Secretariat. Its most recent congress was held in 1972. A PAI National Conference held in Dakar on 7 August 1976 elected a five-member Provisional Secretariat comprised of: President Majmout (Majhemout) Diop (president), Bara Goudiaby (secretary-general), Malick Sow (financial affairs), Balla Ndiaye (mass movements), and Nguirane Ndiaye (press) (*Le Soleil,* Dakar, 19 August). Amath Dansoko is the PAI representative on the board of the *World Marxist Review* in Prague and was the party's chief spokesman over the past year in that publication and at European Communist party meetings.

The PAI is believed to draw its support primarily from intellectuals, particularly students, though party president Diop considers that the PAI is by no means simply a party of a few intellectuals. Members are not selected because of their adherence to any specific religious or philosophical doctrine, but on the basis of support for the PAI's political, economic, social, and cultural programs. (*Africa,* Dakar, 30 September.) Although forced by the government to operate in a clandestine fashion PAI leaders deny that the party has ever engaged in conspiratorial activities (*IB,* no. 24, 1975).

Domestic Policies and Activities. The PAI accuses President Senghor of being a relentless foe of revolutionary democrats and Communists, a leader given to "shoddy reactionary propaganda" (*WMR,*

December 1975). According to a Central Committee statement in November 1975, most Senegalese oppose the "unconstitutional and unlawful . . . political persecution" waged by the government. The Central Committee asserts that the present situation affords opportunities for restoring and extending social liberties in Senegal through domestic popular struggle in conjunction with the powerful upsurge of the international democratic movement. (*IB*, no. 24, 1975.) The party repeatedly calls for a broad alliance of all national, democratic, patriotic, and anti-imperialist forces for "democratic renovation." It rejected Senghor's first proposal in late 1975 that Senegal become a three-party state, calling instead for the simultaneous recognition of the PAI and the elimination of all restrictions on the formation of other political parties (*FBIS*, 19 November 1975). When the party was legalized some nine months later, Diop acknowledged that having three legal parties was better than having only one (*Africa*, 30 September 1976).

The PAI's stated objectives are to consolidate Senegalese independence and the construction of a Senegalese socialist society. More specifically, the party directs its interests and efforts toward four main problem areas: religion, democracy, unity, and internationalism. Although some 85 percent of the Senegalese people are Muslims, the PAI declares its independence from any specific religious belief. It professes to believe that power must be won and exercised by democratic means and that the issue of genuinely democratic and national government must be settled by the politically mature Senegalese people as a whole. The party affirms its support for unity among the Senegalese people and states as its primary immediate objective the pulling together of the Senegalese left. It calls for international unity of the progressive countries and peoples. (*IB*, no. 24, 1975; *Le Soleil*, 19 August 1976; *Africa*, 30 September.)

Publications. The PAI publishes the monthly *La Lutte* (Struggle) and the weekly *Momsarev* (Independence). Reports of party activities and positions appear periodically in the Senegalese press generally and in the publications of pro-Soviet parties and organizations abroad.

Palo Alto, California   Lynn Ratliff

South Africa

The South African Communist Party (SACP) was formed in 1953. It is the underground successor to the Communist Party of South Africa, Africa's first Marxist-Leninist party, a legal organization set up in 1921, outlawed and dissolved in 1950. The SACP continues to operate clandestinely in the country. Its leading officials, and almost certainly the bulk of its Central Committee, reside in exile, but party activists maintain some form of organization and conduct propaganda in major South African cities in the face of relentless government opposition. The SACP is a non-racial party with membership drawn from all South African racial groups, yet Africans constitute "the overwhelming majority of the leadership and membership" of the party (*African Communist,* no. 65, p. 28). Under present conditions it is impossible to estimate the numerical strength of the SACP.

The SACP remains closely allied with the African National Congress (ANC), headed by Alfred Nzo, its scretary-general. The ANC, the country's oldest African nationalist organization, has operated both underground internally in Africa and externally in Europe since its banning in 1960. The SACP recognizes the ANC as the head of a national liberation front which also includes the South African Coloured People's Congress, the South African Indian Congress (SAIC), and the South African Congress of Trade Unions (SACTU); sections of the latter two bodies operate on the margin of legality within South Africa under constant police surveillance. Members of the SACP participate in the component organizations of the national liberation front as well as in the activities of the party itself.

The population of South Africa is about 26 million.

Leadership and Organization. Prominent exiles remain the publicly visible spokesmen of the SACP. The post of chairman has been held since December 1972, by Dr. Yusef M. Dadoo, a 67-year-old Indian leader who has been active in the party since the 1940s, but in exile since 1960. Moses Kotane, a 71-year-old African under medical care in the Soviet Union since suffering a heart attack in Dar es Salaam in 1968, retains the post of party secretary, a position which he has held since 1939. Other leading party officials, most of whom undoubtedly also live outside the country, use pseudonyms when writing in the party press.

At a plenary session of the Central Committee in late 1975 it was reaffirmed that the party had an "indispensable political role to play both as an independent organization and as part of the liberation front headed by the African National Congress." It was reiterated that the "main content of the present phase of our struggle remains a national democratic revolution whose main contingent is the most oppressed and exploited section of the people—the Africans." Yet it was also asserted that "South Africa's proletariat occupies a special place in the coming struggle; a place that would be swamped, diluted and emasculated in the absence of its independent political instrument." (*African Communist,* no. 64, pp. 30-31.)

Domestic Activities and Attitudes. The SACP considers that in 1976 white supremacy in South Africa was further undermined both by international and by domestic events. Unusual significance was attached to the failure and retreat of the South African defense forces in Angola. In the view of a party editorialist, "a truly qualitative change has taken place in Africa as a result of the events in Angola." The victories of the Popular Movement for the Liberation of Angola (MPLA) and its allies have not only "taught a number of lessons about the nature of social and political struggle," but also "opened up gigantic new perspectives the possibilities of which are breathtaking." (*African Communist,* no. 65, p. 6.) When urban disturbances spread through the major South African townships in mid-1976 and police action resulted in an African death toll of more than 300 in bringing the disturbances to a halt, SCAP chairman Dadoo saw this as evidence that "the struggle is mounting and broadening with every passing day" (*FBIS,* 15 September).

The success of the MPLA with the aid of Soviet, Cuban, and other Communist powers was welcomed for exposing the vulnerability of the South African regime. The MPLA victory was also seen as confirmation of the strategy followed by the SACP and its allies in the national liberation movement who "have also been the joint recipients of fraternal aid and solidarity from the same world forces which helped consolidate the power of the People's Republic of Angola." Simultaneously, however, the SACP cautioned against misreading the lessons of Angola; the revolution would not come "at the tip of a Cuban or a Russian bayonet," and would only succeed by the efforts of the "vanguard parties and liberation organizations," which must have "a firm base among the people" (*African Communist,* no. 65, pp. 9-10).

To achieve this end the SACP advocates multifaceted activity on all fronts, utilizing strike actions, demonstrations, and other semi-legal opportunities, as well as disciplined underground organization, sabotage, and guerrilla struggle. The arrest and conviction of two small groups of white supporters of the party in Durban and Cape Town in late 1975 and mid-1976 for organizing clandestine cells and distributing party propaganda and material testified to ongoing efforts to build underground. The SACP and its ally, the ANC, also generally welcomed the stance of the South African Student Organization (SASO) and the Black People's Convention (BPC) and the growth of the Black Consciousness Movement, of which they are the organizational vanguard. At the same time, the ANC criticized the "go it alone" policy of younger militants and charged that the Black Consciousness Movement had "overlooked the laying down of a firm basis of principle on which it will cooperate with all other anti-racist groups, irrespective of colour" (*Sechaba*, Third Quarter, 1976, p. 17). Nevertheless, in Dr. Dadoo's estimation, "the organizations of our party within the country have considerably grown and strengthened of late. And, though anti-racist actions are in some localities spontaneous, nobody doubts today the role of the South African Communist Party and the African National Congress of South Africa in guiding the people's struggle against apartheid and racism" (*FBIS*, 15 September).

Yet the party was also sensitive to the potential appeal of government blandishments on behalf of participation in the institutions of separate development; it was likewise aware of the attraction of an exclusively African nationalism in an atmosphere of racial confrontation. To counter the former, the SACP continued its implacable opposition to Transkeian independence and the Bantustans, including Chief Gatsha Buthelezi of KwaZulu . . . The SACP also urged that the "liberation movements should continue to consolidate the broadest possible alliance—cutting across simple class lines" (*African Communist*, no. 64, p. 30). The SACP reserved equally scathing condemnation for those who invoke anti-communism and assert that the liberation movement is under non-African domination. This was done by eight prominent members of the ANC who were expelled from the organization after making public their charges in December 1975. In the view of the Central Committee of the SACP, "nationalism" of this type is analogous to that "paraded under slogans of true black nationalism, anti-Communism, anti-Sovietism, etc." by the African opponents of the leaderships of the MPLA and the Mozambique Liberation Front (FRELIMO) (ibid., no. 65, p. 21). Particular vigilance was necessary to "guard against the importation into the national movement of bourgeois ideology even when it is camouflaged to serve black interests in the guise of nationalism" (ibid., no. 64, pp. 29-30).

International Views and Activities. Always loyally pro-Soviet, the SACP saw its stance practically vindicated by the actions of the USSR in Angola. The links between the MPLA and its supporters were depicted as a model in which, "through thick and thin all parties to this relationship . . . openly discharged their fraternal responsibility to one another, not shirking any of its implications, nor overstepping its legitimate boundaries" (*African Communist*, no. 65, p. 7). The SACP also warmly praised Cuba and devoted considerable space to coverage of the First Congress of the Communist Party of Cuba. In contrast, its previously generally veiled criticism of the Chinese Communist leadership was made explicit on a number of occasions, extending well beyond its disagreements with Chinese policy on Angola. Dr. Dadoo represented the SACP at the 25th Congress of the Communist Party of the Soviet Union, where he completely identified himself with that party's policies.

In November 1975 an SACP delegation headed by Dr. Dadoo visited the People's Republic of Congo at the invitation of the Congolese Workers' Party.

Publications. Within South Africa the SACP irregularly mimeographs and distributes an underground journal, *Inkululeko-Freedom*. Its ANC ally also publishes clandestinely, including a newspaper, *Amandla-Matla* (Power), in which attacks on the government appear along with instructions for the organization of underground cells. Externally, the SACP issues the *African Communist*, a quarterly printed in the German Democratic Republic and distributed from London. *Sechaba,* the organ of the ANC, is published as a quarterly in London.

Duke University   Sheridan Johns

Sudan

The Sudanese Communist Party (al-Hizb al-Shuyu'i al-Sudani; SCP) traces its origins to 1944. In 1947, Communists formed a political party, the Sudanese Movement for National Liberation, with 'Abd al-Khaliq Mahjub as its secretary-general. The SCP, as it was later named, operated clandestinely at times, and at other times in relative freedom and with considerable power and influence. Some of its members were elected representatives to the national legislature. Even Ja'far Numairi, president of the Sudan since May 1969, at one time had two Communist members in his cabinet. The SCP gradually became a focal point of opposition, successfully infiltrating a number of professional, student, and labor groups. Implication in the abortive coup d'état of 19 July 1971 led to severe repression of the party(see *YICA, 1972,* pp. 290-92). Numerous SCP leaders were executed, including Mahjub. Thousands of party members were arrested and held without trial. The SCP has also been accused of participating in more recent abortive plots against the government, in September 1975 and July 1976.

No reliable figures exist concerning present SCP membership. Before the 1971 coup attempt the party was estimated to have from 5,000 to 10,000 active members. An unknown number are continuing party activities in exile or clandestinely within Sudan.

Leadership and Organization. Names of party leaders have generally been absent from international press reports on the SCP. One exception to this was the publication of a speech in Moscow's *Pravda* which was attributed to Ibrahim Zakariya, member of the Central Committee of the SCP. Since the suppression of the party in Sudan, statements issued by the party itself have withheld names. However, leading figures identified in 1974 were Ibrahim Nuqud, then in exile; Mahjub 'Uthman and al-Fajjani al-Tayyib, arrested in October 1974 after returning from exile; and Dr. 'Izz al-Din 'Ali 'Amir and Ibrahim Zakariya, whose whereabouts were unknown.

Domestic Views and Activities. A coup d'état was attempted against the government of Ja'far Numairi in September 1975. During the trial of Muhammad Bakhit Muhammad Adam, allegedly one of the planners and leaders, the defendant was reported to have named the SCP, along with the National Unionist Party, the Umma Party, the Moslem Brotherhood, and the People's Democratic Party as members of the Nationalist Front (al-Jabhah al-Qawmiyah), which staged the abortive coup. According to the confessions of various participants in the attempt, the Front was directed by 10 leaders within Sudan and four outside the country. One of the four named as working outside was the Communist leader 'Izz al-Din 'Ali 'Amir (MENA, Cairo, 30 November 1975, in *FBIS*, 2 December). Another, more serious coup attempt came on 2-3 July 1976. According to Numairi, the Sudanese Communists played a role in this, but substantial evidence of their involvement has not been provided. In an interview for the Egyptian periodical *al-Ahram*, Numairi disclosed his belief that "the communists are still working underground to change the present regime" (*Kuwait Times*, 7 August).

International Views and Activities. The SCP twice addressed the 25th Congress of the Communist Party of the Soviet Union (CPSU), February-March 1976. A message signed by the SCP Central Committee, Khartoum, February, followed the general CPSU line, praising the Soviet Union profusely both for its domestic achievements and its international policies. It specifically noted Soviet "support for the battle for freedom in Vietnam, Indochina, the Arab East and Angola." The Central Committee condemned the "vile position of China's Maoist leadership" as shown in its "subversive activities against the anti-imperialist front and the unity of the world Communist movement, in their cooperation with the racist regimes in Africa, and their support for any government that persecutes Communists and revolutionaries in Africa, Asia and Latin America." Except for the opening phrase "On behalf of the Sudanese Communists," the address could have been written by Soviet supporters anywhere in the world. There were no specific references to Sudan. Even more general issues relevant to the whole Arab world were given no more emphasis than Angola and far less than the Soviet Union's 10th Five-Year Plan. (*Pravda*, 2 March.) The other communication was a speech attributed to SCP leader Ibrahim Zakariya. According to this address, the SCP had an official delegation at the CPSU Congress. Zakariya's speech was generally the same in content as the Central Committee's message. It did, however, make specific reference to the SCP and to Sudan: "It is a great honor for us to represent our party at the 25th CPSU Congress. Our presence here confirms the friendship and solidarity between our parties and our peoples. We rate this friendship highly and are aware of the role it plays in the development of our country, helping Sudan to overcome its backwardness. We are sincerely grateful to you for your solidarity with us Sudanese Communists." (Ibid.) As already noted, many Sudanese Communists are living in exile in the Soviet Union and Eastern Europe because of President Numairi's anti-Communist policies.

On 18 August the Central Committee of the East German Communist party (SED) sent a congratulatory message extending "to all Sudanese Communists cordial fraternal militant greetings on the 30th anniversary of the founding of the Sudanese Communist Party." It praised the SCP's "outstanding contribution to the struggle for the national independence of Sudan and for the liberation of the country from colonial and neocolonial dependence." (*Neues Deutschland*, 18 August.) Numairi responded by asking the ambassador of East Germany to leave Sudan (MENA, 14 September).

In regard to one Middle East issue, the SCP was listed on 15 January by the Palestine Liberation Organization (PLO) in Aden as one of those in opposition to Iran's military involvement in Oman (*Afro-Asian Affairs*, London, 29 January).

Publications. As the SCP is under severe repression in the Sudan, the party does not have a regular party organ, but rather, publishes and distributes leaflets clandestinely. News of the party has generally been printed in publications of the Lebanese Communist Party, *al-Nida'* and *al-Akhbar*.

Stanford University   Patricia Mihaly

Syria

The Syrian Communist Party (al-Hizb al-Shuyu'i al-Suri; SCP) is an offshoot of the Lebanese Communist Party established in 1924 (see *Lebanon*). Under the French mandates all Communist activity was proscribed in 1939. This ban was continued after Syria and Lebanon were proclaimed independent states in 1943, and the separate SCP was formed in 1944. Despite illegality, the SCP has enjoyed several periods of considerable political freedom. In 1966 a Communist was named to a cabinet post for the first time. The Communist position improved even further after the bloodless coup of Lieutenant General Hafiz al-Asad in November 1970. As a result of changes brought about by al-Asad, two cabinet posts have been held by Communists since 1971. In March 1972 the SCP gained de facto legality through its participation in the National Progressive Front formed by al-Asad. Plagued with internal disputes since early 1971, the SCP finally split into two parties in December 1973 (see *YICA. 1974* and *1975*).

Combined membership in the SCP is believed to range between 3,000 and 4,000 with perhaps another 10,000 sympathizers, although one source has made an estimate of 30,000 card-carrying members. The population of Syria is about 7,500,000 (estimated 1975).

Leadership and Organization. The SCP is led by Khalid Bakdash, a Syrian Kurd who has been secretary-general of the SCP—except for a brief period in 1968—since its inception. At the party's Fourth Congress in 1974 Bakdash was reelected secretary-general and Yusuf Faisal was elected deputy secretary-general, a new post created by the Congress. The following were elected to the new Politburo: Bakdash, Ibrahim Bakri, Khalid Hammami, Daniel Ni'mah, Maurice Salibi, Dhahir'Abd al-Samad, Ramu Shaikhu, 'Umar Siba'i, and Murad Yusuf. Siba'i is minister of communications and 'Abd al-Samad minister of state in the Syrian cabinet. Bakdash and Ni'mah are the SCP representatives in the National Progressive Front.

In 1973, a faction that also identifies itself as the SCP split from the parent party. This faction still operates in a clandestine fashion under the leadership of Riyad al-Turk, its first secretary. It has no representatives either in the Syrian cabinet or in the National Progressive Front (a coalition of the Ba'th Party, the SCP, and other "progressive" and nationalist forces, formed in 1971).

Domestic Views and Activities. Khalid Bakdash outlined the basic domestic policies of the SCP in October 1975: (1) "Consolidation of the progressive national regime, promotion of its policy of liberation and progress, strengthening of the Progressive National Front and its role in national life," and (2) "Continued improvement of living standards, measures against profiteers and speculators and rising prices, solution of the housing and transport crises, etc." (*WMR,* October.) While the first point implies greater cooperation with the ruling Ba'th Party, tensions between the SCP and the Ba'th intensified toward the end of 1975. The SCP demanded separate representation at international conferences. Thus the SCP spoke in the name of Syria at the International Women's Congress in East Berlin in November, despite the presence of a Syrian Ba'th delegation. The Syrian government responded by preventing Khalid Bakdash from attending the First Congress of the Cuban Communist

Party later that month. In a spirit of defiance, a delegation of the SCP then in Eastern Europe went to Cuba at the instructions of Bakdash.

The Ba'th Party has apparently felt threatened by growing SCP influence, as in the trade union elections, where the Communists scored significant gains. The government therefore asked the SCP to dissolve its women's and popular organizations. The authorities also tried to prevent the SCP from forming alliances with leftist elements within the Ba'th Party and imposed travel restrictions on SCP leaders.

Late in 1975 some SCP officials were arrested prior to a visit from King Khalid of Saudi Arabia in order to prevent Communist-inspired demonstrations (*An-Nahar Arab Report*, Beirut, 5 January 1976). During the king's visit, on 26 December, newspapers in Cairo announced in front-page headlines that Syrian authorities had arrested 300 Communists and that SCP leader Khalid Bakdash had fled the country. The Egyptian newspapers reported that this marked the end of cooperation between the Ba'th and the SCP, and of their alliance in the National Progressive Front. The Syrian government, the SCP and the Lebanese Communist Party (LCP) swiftly denied these reports. The LCP accused Egypt of trying to sabotage Syria's National Progressive Front and the relations between Damascus and Moscow. Some speculated that the reports had been published to substantiate Egyptian claims that Syria was interfering in the Lebanese crisis to cover up serious domestic problems, or to promote acceptance of Egyptian policies by showing that Syria also was moving away from the Communists and Moscow and closer to Washington (*An-Nahar Arab Report*, 5 January).

Although the Cairo reports were apparently politically motivated, tension between the SCP and the ruling Ba'th Party continued in 1976. The SCP criticized the Syrian government for granting oil concessions to American companies. The SCP likewise opposed Syria's intervention in support of right-wing Christians in Lebanon. (*Middle East Intelligence Survey*, Tel Aviv, 16-31 May.) According to diplomatic sources, Bakdash was prevented from accepting official invitations to visit the Soviet Union and Bulgaria. For a while the government issued general instructions prohibiting Communists, even upper echelons of the party, from leaving the country Thus, in April, SCP leader and Syrian minister of communications 'Umar Siba'i was not allowed to leave for a conference of Arab ministers of communications in Cairo until President Asad himself intervened to permit his departure (*An-Nahar Arab Report*, 24 May). The SCP nevetheless continued to emphasize the importance of an alliance of progressive forces within the country. In a meeting in June with Soviet premier Kosygin, SCP leaders "stressed the invariability of the SCP's principal line of further strengthening and developing cooperation with the Arab Socialist Renaissance Party (Ba'th Party) and other Syrian parties and organizations within the framework of the Progressive National Front" (*TASS*, 3 June, in *FBIS*, 4 June).

The SCP and the Middle East. The basic policies of the SCP regarding the Middle East were outlined by Khalid Bakdash in October 1975: "cementing of anti-imperialist contingents, above all the Communist Party, the Ba'th Party and other progressive forces, for the liberation of the occupied territories and for ensuring the legitimate national rights of the Palestinian people" and "strengthening of fraternal bonds and cooperation with progressive Arab countries, settlement of possible differences and controversial issues on the basis of the principles of Arab brotherhood and the supreme national interests of our Arab people in the struggle against imperialism and aggression, the utilization of all Arab potentialities irrespective of the type of regime, opposition to attempts by reactionaries and imperialists to force our country, Syria, to retreat from its policy of national liberation." The SCP listed Syria, Iraq, Algeria, and the People's Democratic Republic of Yemen as the revolutionary Arab countries which have launched out on far-reaching social change. (*WMR*, October.)

In early 1976, at the 25th Congress of the Communist Party of the Soviet Union, Ramu Shaikhu condemned "American imperialism," "Zionism," and "Arab reactionaries" for seeking to "impose partial and separate solutions in the Middle East." He charged that the "Sinai agreement crowned this class alliance hostile to the interests of the Arab peoples and social progress in the Middle East." With the goal of achieving a comprehensive solution of the Middle East crisis he declared his party's support of the Soviet proposal on the resumption of the Geneva conference (TASS, 2 March, in *FBIS*, 8 March). In July the SCP expressed its approval of the Syrian-Palestinian agreement; the SPC specially emphasized the "right of the Palestine resistance movement to operate on any Arab territory, including Lebanese territory." Hoping that this agreement would end the Lebanese conflict, the SCP declared: "Their national patriotic duty demands that all national-patriotic forces and detachments of the Palestine resistance movement stop their extraneous struggle and resume their main struggle for the liberation of the occupied Arab lands, for securing the legitimate national rights of the Arab people of Palestine—including their right to a national independent state" (*Pravda,* 3 August).

The SCP blamed the Lebanese crisis on right-wing Lebanese forces. It charged them with trying to eliminate the Palestinian resistance movement and trying to make Lebanon a base from which Israel and American imperialism could sabotage the liberation movement in Arab countries. According to an editorial in *Nidal al-Sha'b* (16 September), the Lebanese rightists had been conspiring with Arab reactionaries and imperialists to set Arabs against each other and undermine inter-Arab cooperation in their fight against imperialism and Zionism.

The SCP was listed on 15 January by the Palestine Liberation Organization in Aden as one of the political parties and movements opposed to Iran's military involvement in Oman (*Afro-Asian Affairs,* London, 29 January).

Publications. The party organ of the SCP is the fortnightly newspaper *Nidal al-Sha'b* (People's Struggle), which is officially banned but has been circulated freely since the party joined the National Progressive Front. The SCP also disseminates its news through the two legal publications of the Lebanese Communist Party in Beirut, *al-Nida'* and *al-Akhbar.*

Stanford University   Patricia Mihaly

INTERNATIONAL COMMUNIST FRONT ORGANIZATIONS

Afro-Asian Peoples' Solidarity Organization. The Afro-Asian People's Solidarity Organization (AAPSO) was set up at Cairo in 1958 as an anti-colonialist offshoot from the World Peace Council (WPC). During the first few years of its existence it was jointly controlled by the USSR, China, and the United Arab Republic. The Sino-Soviet dispute led to disruption of AAPSO conferences at Moshi, Tanzania, in February 1963 and Winneba, Ghana, in May 1965 and finally to a split in the organization following the WPC meeting at Nicosia, Cyprus, in February 1967. The Chinese boycotted that meeting, which decided to hold the fifth AAPSO conference in Algiers the same year, rather than in Peking as originally planned. Since then, Soviet domination of AAPSO has continued, the aim of each component organization being to support USSR policies through mobilization of various segments of society. Indeed these efforts have been carried to the point where the internal and ideological disputes within the Communist camp find their reflection in front activities.

Structure and Leadership. From the AAPSO's beginning, its organizational structure has been rather loose. Although Congress and Council meetings have been held during this period, in a practical sense the secretariat has been the key organizational unit. The 11th Council meeting, held in March 1974, established the Presidium, which apparently bears responsibility, along with the Secretariat, for development and execution of policy.

Yusuf el-Sebai, AAPSO's secretary-general since its foundation, was reelected at the 11th Council and made chairman of the Presidium. Since he is secretary-general not only of AAPSO, but also of the AAWPB-Cairo (see next section), these two organizations actually have an overlapping directorate. Additional linkages are noticeable if the AAPSO and the AAWPB-Cairo are juxtaposed, both having headquarters in Cairo and focusing on problems of the same geographical area, possessing thus to an extent analogous functions. At present, AAPSO appears to be the more active and important of the two.

Views and Activities. During the AAPSO secretary-general's visit to Moscow in early December 1975, at the invitation of the Soviet Afro-Asian Solidarity Committee, the world situation was analyzed, emphasizing the struggle against colonialism, imperialism racism, and reaction. Also full support was given the Arab liberation movement, the accent being on liberation of Israeli-held lands (*TASS,* 4 December).

It was reported that Yusuf el-Sabai had talks on cooperation at the beginning of December 1975 with a member of the Socialist Alliance of the Working People of Yugoslavia and that he had invited a delegation from that group to visit AAPSO Secretariat in Cairo for further discussions. Concomitantly it was also reported that Sebai had conducted similar talks on strengthening relations with the East German and Soviet Asian Solidarity Committees. (Tanyug, 9 December; *Neues Deutschland,* East Berlin, 6-7 December; Moscow radio, 9 December.)

During a visit to Angola by an AAPSO delegation in mid-December 1975, support for the Angolan people was discussed, including matters in connection with the Afro-Asian People's Solidarity Organization's planned "International Conference of Solidarity with Angola" to be held in Luanda in early February 1976 (*Neues Deutschland,* 18 December).

At the beginning of January 1976, AAPSO called on African nations which have not yet recognized Angola to do so, demanding the immediate withdrawal from Angola of foreign troops on the occasion of the emergency Summit of the Organization of Africa Unity (OAU), being held in Aden to discuss this problem (TASS, 4 January).

An AAPSO Presidium meeting in Aden on 19-20 January was attended by delegations from Afro-Asian countries, Eastern Europe, Finland, and Chile, representatives of national liberation movements and mass organizations, and ambassadors of states accredited to South Yemen. Joseph Nhanhla, "rapporteur of the African section," presumably the AAPSO, reported on preparations for the International Conference of Solidarity with Angola, the Angolan question generally, and the results of the OAU meeting. A general statement expressed support for the struggle of the Popular Front for the Liberation of Oman, for the Palestine Liberation Organization, the Popular Movement for the Liberation of Angola (MPLA), and the UN resolution condemning Zionism; condemned the racialist regimes in South Africa, South West Africa, and Rhodesia; and called both for complete disarmament and for the limitation of strategic arms. (Aden radio, 18-20 January; *Ta Nea,* Nicosia, 18 January; INA 19 January, *Neues Deutschland,* 21 January.)

More than 80 national and international organizations including several Soviet-controlled front organizations, were represented at the International Conference of Solidarity with Angola, 2-4 February, in Luanda. The AAPSO delegation led by Facima Bangura of Guinea, described as secretary, arrived on 26 January to prepare for the conference. At a press conference the delegations condemned the armed aggression of the forces of imperialism and the FNLA and UNITA against the people of Angola, as well as China's stand on the Angolan question—it was, allegedly, now an open secret that the Peking leaders were linking up with the enemies of the national liberation movements (Luanda radio, 27 January; TASS, 29 January). Leonid Brezhnev (USSR), Erich Honecker (German Democratic Republic), and Fidel Castro (Cuba) sent goodwill messages. The Angolan president, Dr. Agostinho Neto, stated that the MPLA's "victory over Portugal's colonialism" would have been "very difficult if the Socialist camp, which has always been the main provider of material for our people, had not existed" (Luanda radio, 2 February).

The conference adopted an appeal to world public opinion, calling on member states of the UN and the OAU to recognize Angola under the leadership of President Neto. It sought a vigorous campaign by "progressive and peace-loving forces, particularly in Western Europe," for an end to the recruitment of mercenaries to fight in Angola, an end to military aid to the anti-MPLA groups and to the supply of arms to South Africa, and for fraternal help for Angola's reconstruction (*Morning Star,* London, 5 February; *Neues Deutschland,* 5 February).

Describing the anti-MPLA groups as "agencies of imperialism," a general statement said that there was no basis for a reconciliation or coalition between them and the MPLA. It also condemned Peking for allying itself with South Africa, the USA, and their "puppets," and spoke of "the support which the socialist countries, in particular the USSR and Cuba, give the Angolan people in their defense of the young republic." The liquidation of the Portuguese colonial system by the liberation movement was said to have altered the balance of power in Africa in favor of the force of freedom and progress. Solidarity was also expressed with the "patriots in Chile, Spain, Namibia, and the Middle East." (Maputo radio, 5 February; *Neues Deutschland,* 5 February).

The AAPSO condemned the holding in Brussels on 17 February of a conference on the protection of the rights of Soviet Jews, claiming that it was "being mounted by Zionists who wanted to conceal the crimes committed by the Israeli invaders in occupied Arab territories" (*Morning Star,* 14 February). In March, AAPSO sent warm congratulations to the 25th congress of the Communist Party of the Soviet Union, praising Soviet assistance to young African states and the Arab people of Palestine (*Pravda,* 12 March), and was represented at a symposium of non-aligned nations on news and information held in Tunis (*Patriot,* New Delhi, 31 March).

Delegates from AAPSO and 15 countries attended a seminar organized by the Ghana Council for Peace and Solidarity, at Accra, 23-25 April; among the participants were Joseph Nhanhla (South Africa), AAPSO Secretary, and Anatoli Kuznetsov (USSR). The seminar appealed for unity in the anti-imperialist struggle and for the liquidation of colonialism, neo-colonialism, and apartheid. (Ghana News Agency, 23 April; *Ghanaian Times,* 24 April; *Neues Deutschland,* 27 April; Moscow radio, 28 April.)

In June the Soviet Afro-Asian Solidarity Committee called on the world public to mount a world movement of solidarity with the struggle of the people of South Africa for freedom, and to demand that their governments sever all diplomatic, eonomic, military and cultural relations with the Republic of South Africa and give all possible assistance and support to the national liberation movement of South Africa—the African National Congress—as the true representative of the country's people (TASS, 19 June).

The 4th session of the AAPSO Presidium met in Brazzaville in late July, the main topic of which was the strengthening of anti-imperialist unity. Yusuf el-Sebai stressed the need for expansion of anti-imperialist struggle, and a representative of the Congolese Labor Party said it was imperative to call on world public opinion for intensified support of the peoples of Rhodesia, South West Africa, and the Republic of South Africa, who were fighting against the oppression of racism and colonialism. Members of the more than 25 delegations attending proclaimed their high appreciation for the role the USSR and other socialist countries in behalf of the peoples, struggling for peace and freedom of the peoples, particularly the representatives of the People's Democratic Republic of Yemen and the African National Congress. (TASS, 24 July, in *FBIS.)* The Presidium adopted a closing resolution proposing a convocation of an international conference to examine issues pertaining to eradication of racialism and apartheid in South Africa and liberation of peoples in that part of the continent (ibid., 31 July, in *FBIS*).

A month later, AAPSO called on all peace champions to contribute in every way possible toward the admission of the People's Republic of Angola to the UN (ibid., 29 August, in *FBIS*).

An AAPSO statement on 16 October, the "international day of solidarity with political prisoners in South Africa," said that the oppressed peoples demand revolutionary transformations, refusing to live as they used to as privileged slaves in their own country (TASS, 13 October).

At the end of October an "extraordinary" international conference of solidarity with the people of South Africa was held in Addis Ababa on AAPSO initiative and was attended by delegations from 60 countries. The head of the Soviet delegation declared that the meeting would contribute to the liberation of the people of South Africa, outlining concrete ways of giving moral and political support and practical aid to the patriotic forces. James Jackson, of the Communist party in the USA and leader of the American delegation, said that he represented 30 million Afro-Americans in his country as well as the working class, intellectuals, and all progressive forces who were against imperialism in general and US imperialism in particular, which he condemned in strong terms. On behalf of "revolutionary Ethiopia," the chairman of the Provisional Military Administrative Council of the country voiced confidence that the meeting would help the struggle of the peoples of Asia, Africa, and Latin America for freedom and independence. The AAPSO secretary-general called for, among other things, more vigorous action against the establishment of imperialist military bases in the Indian Ocean. (TASS, 29, 30 October, 1 November; Addis Ababa domestic service, 29 October; AFP, 1 November.)

Afro-Asian Writers' Permanent Bureau. The Afro-Asian Writers' Permanent Bureau (AAWPB) was originally set up by the Soviets at an "Afro-Asian Writers' Conference" in Tashkent in October 1958. Following a second conference, at Cairo in February 1962, a "Permanent Bureau" was established with headquarters in Colombo, Ceylon, now Sri Lanka. The Chinese Communists gained control of the organization at a meeting ot its executive committee in Bali, Indonesia, July 1963 and established a new executive secretariat in Peking, 15 August 1966. Officially still based in Colombo, the AAWPB operates exclusively from Peking. A pro-Soviet faction—the AAWPB-Cairo—broke away after the Chinese began to dominate the organization. The AAWPB-Peking, which has not yet held a third conference, appears to have no activities outside its irregular publication, *The Call,* and occasional statements carried by the New China News Agency.

The AAWPB-Cairo. The pro-Soviet AAWPB was founded on 19-21 June 1966 at an "extraordinary meeting" attended by delegations from Cameroon, Sri Lanka, India, Sudan, the USSR, and the United Arab Republic. Its relatively successful "Third Afro-Asian Writers' Conference," held at Beirut in 1967 and attended by some 150 delegates from 42 countries, was the first serious blow to the pro-Chinese AAWPB. since then the pro-Soviet organization appears to have consolidated and augmented its base of support.

The secretary-general of the AAWPB-Cairo is Yusuf el-Sebai (Egypt), who is also secretary-general of AAPSO and a member of the Presidential Committee of the WPC. The assistant secretary-general is Edward el-Kharat (Egypt). The ten-member Permanent Bureau has members from India, Japan, Lebanon, Mongolia, the former Portuguese colonies, Senegal, South Africa, the USSR, Sudan, and Egypt. There is also a 30-member Executive Committee. The organ of the group is a "literature, arts and sociopolitical quarterly," *Lotus,* in English, French, and Arabic editions. Books by various Afro-Asian "men of letters" have been published in the USSR by the AAWPB-Cairo.

The AAWPB-Peking. The pro-Chinese AAWPB, the continuation of the original body, is led by Frederik L. Risakotta (Indonesia), of the Peking-based Delegation of the Communist Party of Indonesia's Central Committee, as "acting head ad interim" of the AAWPB Secretariat. The group was relatively inactive in 1976. It issues *The Call* at irregular intervals.

International Association of Democratic Lawyers. The International Association of Democratic Lawyers (IADL) was founded at an "International Congress of Jurists" held in Paris in October 1946 under the auspices of a para-Communist organization, the "Mouvement National Juiciaire," and attended by lawyers from 25 countries. Although the IADL originally included elements of various political orientations, the leading role was played by leftist French lawyers and by 1949 most non-Communists had resigned. The IADL was orginally based in Paris, but was expelled by the French government in 1950. It then moved to Brussels, where it remains, although some organizational work has also been carried out from Warsaw.

Membership is open to lawyers' organizations or groups and to individual lawyers and may be on a "corresponding," "donation," or "permanent" basis. Lawyers holding membership through organizations or individually are estimated to number about 25,000. The IADL claims to be supported by membership fees and donations, but no details of its finances are published.

The IADL holds consultative status Category C with the UN Economic and Social Council.

Structure and Leadership. The highest organ of the IADL is the Congress, in which each member organization is represented. There have been ten congresses to date, the latest in Algiers in April 1975. The Congress elects the IADL Council, which is supposed to meet yearly and consists of the Bureau, the Secretariat, and a represnetative of each member organization. Robert Dachet (Belgium) is secretary-general; Pierre Cot (France), president; Joë Nordmann (France), deputy president; and Heinrich Toeplitz (German Democratic Republic), treasurer.

Views and Activities. An "International Conference of Human Rights in Namibia," was held in Dakar, Senegal, on 5-8 January 1976, jointly organized by the IADL, the International Commission of Jurists, and the Institute of Human Rights in Strasbourg. About 300 lawyers and others from various countries and national liberation movements attended, including Dustan Kamana (Zamiba), president of the UN Council for Namibia, Zambia's foreign minister Rupiah Banda, and Sam Nujoma of the South West Africa People's Organization (SWAPO). The meeting condemned South Africa's armed intervention in Angola and use of Namibia as a base for this, and called for support for SWAPO. (Lusaka radio, 5-6 January; *Neues Deutschland.* 6, 13 January.)

An IADL delegation to Chile during the first fortnight of June reported an increase in the number of arrests and disappearances in that country. The IADL sent a list of those arrested or missing to inernational organizations and appealed to journalists to initiate moves to save their lives. (*L'Humanité,* Paris, 13 July.) The IADL described the raid carried out by Israel in Uganda at Entebbe as a "crime against international law" (*Neues Deutschland,* 4 July).

Publications. The principal IADL publications, *Review of Contemporary Laws* and *Information Bulletin,* appear irregularly in English and French.

International Federation of Resistance Fighters. The International Federation of Resistance Fighters (Fédération Internationale des Résistants; FIR) was founded in 1951 in Vienna as the successor to the International Federation of Former Political Prisoners (Fédération Internationale des Anciens Prisonniers Politiques). With the name change, membership eligibility was widened to include former partisans and resistance fighters, and all victims of Nazism and fascism and their descendants.

In 1959 the FIR had a membership of four million; no recent figures have been announced, but in 1971 the FIR claimed affiliated groups and representation in every country of Europe (*Résistance Unie,* no. 14). The headquarters is in Vienna, and a small secretariat is maintained in Paris. In 1972 the FIR was granted B status with the UN Economic and Social Council.

Structure and Leadership. The organs of the FIR are the Congress, General Council, Bureau, and Secretariat. The Congress, which is supposed to meet every four years, elects the president, vice-president, and members of the Bureau, and determines and ratifies members of the General Council after they have been nominated by national associations. The General Council is supposed to meet at least once a year. The Bureau supervises the implementation of the decisions reached by the Congress and the General Council, and is responsible for the budget; from among its members it elects the Secretariat. Arialdo Banfi (Italy) is president and Alex Lhote (France) is secretary-general.

Views and Activities. On 27 November 1975 a European symposium on the problems of disarmament was held in Paris in the UNESCO building, under the initiative of the FIR, the World Veterans Federation, the International Confederation of Former Prisoners of War, and the European Veterans Confederation. The speakers called for cessation of the arms race, general and complete disarmament, and elimination of military blocs. It was also emphasized that the Helsinki Accords inspired all champions of peace, security, and cooperation. Among those attending the symposium were representatives of the Soviet Veterans Committee, the WPC, and the International Organization of Journalists. (TASS, 27 November.)

The FIR was represented at a rally in Strasbourg on 13 March 1976 against "closed professions" in West Germany (*Informationsdienst,* no. 3). Also an FIR delegation had talks in Vienna with the UN Secretary-General's representative concerning the repatriation of Greek political prisoners. At the same time the FIR protested to the Chilean Embassy in Vienna about the planned trial of Luis Corvalán and other leaders of the Popular Unity Party (ibid).

Representatives of the FIR, the World Veterans' Federation (WVF), the International Confederation of Former Prisoners of War, and the European Confederation of Former Combatants (CEAC) attended the meeting of the Coordinating Committee of the European Disarmament Symposium in Paris on 10-11 March. The meeting completed the symposium's final document and decided to reconvene early in October at the same time as a meeting of the Union of French War Veterans (UFAC), or of the WVF (ibid., no. 4).

Alex Lhote (France) attended a meeting in Paris on 8-9 March, called by the WVF, which adopted a joint FIR/WVF memorandum on the status of resistance fighters and national freedom fighters, addressed to the president of the Diplomatic Conference on Human Rights, meeting in Geneva from 21 April to 12 June (ibid.).

The FIR Bureau met in Warsaw on 4-5 September to observe the 25th anniversary of its founding and issued a warning of increased neo-Nazi activities, a resolution on job discrimination in West Germany, an appeal for "true democracy" in Spain, and a message of greeting to U.S. former servicemen on the U.S. Bicentennial. A resolution on disarmament called for a world meeting of former servicemen and resistance fighters on the problems of peace and disarmament, and for close cooperation between the FIR and UN organizations. (Tanjug, 3 September; PAP, 4-6 September; special issue of *Résistance unie.*)

Publications. The FIR announced in 1976 that its quarterly magazine *Résistance unie/Wiederstandskämpfer* and its *Service d'information de la FIR/Informationsdienst der FIR* would be merged as a monthly.

International Organization of Journalists. The International Organization of Journalists (IOJ) was founded in June 1946 in Cophenhagen. Merging with it at the time were the International Federation of Journalists (IFJ) and the International Federation of Journalists of Allied and Free Countries. By 1952 the participating non-Communist unions had withdrawn in order to refound the IFJ. Since 1955 the IOJ has made unsuccessful overtures to the IFJ for forming a new world organization of journalists. It was for the purpose of bridging differences with the IFJ that the IOJ founded in 1955 the International Committee for Cooperation of Journalists (ICCJ). No IFJ member is known to have become affiliated with the ICCJ, perhaps because most ICCJ officers are also leading members of the parent IOJ. The IOJ headquarters, originally in London, was moved to Prague in 1947.

A rival organization established in 1963 by pro-Chinese journalists, the Afro-Asian Journalists' Association, appears to have drawn little other support (see *YICA, 1976,* p. 580).

The IOJ was awarded consultative and information Category B status with UNESCO in 1969. It also holds consultative status, Category II, with the UN Economic and Social Council.

Structure and Leadership. National unions and groups are eligible for membership in the IOJ, as are also individual journalists. A total of 150,000 members in 67 organizations and 58 countries is claimed.

The highest IOJ body, the Congress, is supposed to meet every four years. It elects the Executive Committee, made up of the Presidium (president, vice-president, and secretary-general), other officers (secretaries and treasurer), and ordinary members. Jean-Maurice Hermann (France) is president and Jiří Kubka (Czechoslovakia) is secretary-general. New elections were held in September 1976 (see below).

Views and Activities. The second "International Conference on the Training of Journalists," in Budapest on 2-5 December 1975, was organized by the IOJ in cooperation with UNESCO and attended by 58 journalists from 24 countries, including 10 from developing countries (MTI, 2 December 1975). The first conference was held in Budapest in June 1973. The director of the Department of Free Flow of Information and Development of Communication, UNESCO, stressed in a letter to the IOJ the success of the second conference and welcomed new opportunities for cooperation on other projects (*Journalists' Affairs,* no. 2, 1976).

A two-member IOJ delegation visited Cyprus in December 1975 and discussed the broadening of international solidarity with Cyprus and stronger contacts with the Cyprus Journalists' Union (*Cyprus Press Digest.* 7 December).

Young journalists from eleven Afro-Asian and Arab countries participated, on behalf of the IOJ, in a six-month course for journalists from developing countries, begun on 13 January 1976, at the School of Solidarity's International Institute for Journalism, East Berlin. The Union of East German Journalists has held courses in Syria, Somalia, Guinea, Iraq, and Egypt. So far, 300 students from developing countries have attended courses. (*Neues Deutschland,* East Berlin, 14 January.)

At the end of the course, Ernst Otto Schwabe, chief editor of the East German foreign affairs magazine *Horizont,* said that the German Democratic Republic (GDR) was proud to contribute to the strengthening of the anti-imperialist movement. The courses are financed by GDR journalists. (ADN, East Berlin, 23 July.)

A statement by the IOJ Secretariat on 16 January claimed that a press campaign in some Western countries was distorting facts about the situation in Angola to divert attention of the world public from the efforts of the leaders of the Popular Movement for the Liberation of Angola.

An article in the IOJ monthly *Democratic Journalist* (no. 2, February) by Wolfgang Kleinwachter (GDR) stated: "The essence of peaceful coexistence is . . . that it is conducted through different forms in the sphere of economics, politics, science, technology, culture, education, etc. . . . The extensive practical application of peaceful coexistence relations leads to broader cooperation . . . although there is no 'middle way' between bourgeois and socialist ideologies. . . . The present development of peaceful coexistence and ideological struggle therefore is not contradictory, but represents a logical dialectical unity that increasingly determines international relations at the present time. . . . On the basis of peaceful coexistence, opportunities increase for socialism to spread its ideology and views throughout the whole world." On the other hand Klienwachter concluded: "Through the 'free flow of information,' which is nothing but the free flow of information for imperialist ideas, imperialism is trying to obtain a state of 'ideological coexistence' with the socialist countries . . ."

According to the same journal (no. 3), on the basis of proposals by the IOJ, the Czechoslovak Union of Journalists was offering places in hospitals and sanatoria to Palestinian and Lebanese journalists, members of the IOJ affiliates, who were wounded during the fighting in Lebanon. Journalists' unions of the other Communist countries, it said, would also provide medical aid to wounded journalists particularly to members of the Union of Palestinian Journalists.

A statement by the secretary-general on 5 February demanded the closing of Radio Free Europe and Radio Liberty, as being under the control of the U.S. Central Intelligence Agency and hindering the relaxation of international tensions and the promotion of mutual understanding between the peoples. Journalists working at these radio stations were said to be violating all norms of professional honor. The statement said there was need for journalists of all countries to launch an international campaign for the purity of their profession. (*Pravda,* 15 February.)

Jean-Maurice Hermann and other IOJ figures were present at a meeting of Czechoslovak and foreign journalists, organized by the IOJ, in Prague on 31 March. The meeting called for the release of Luis Corvalán and other political prisoners (CTK, March 31). Earlier the IOJ issued a statement on the lack of press freedom in Latin America and called on member unions to voice solidarity with persecuted journalists (ibid., 15 March).

The Union of Journalists in Finland assigned its president to the post of observer at the IOJ to "ensure permanent contact between both organizations in the spirit of and in order to carry out those tasks set out in the final document of the Helsinki Conference" (*Journalists' Affairs,* no. 3).

President Echeverría of Mexico inaugurated the First Congress of Latin American Journalists, held in Mexico City on 4-7 June, a meeting previously scheduled for Lima in October 1975. Delegates from 23 countries attended, the IOJ being represented by a guest observer. The "Latin American

Federation of Journalists" (FELAPE) was set up on this occasion, under the presidency of Eleazer Diaz Rangel (Venezuela) Genaro Carnero Checa (Peru), an IOJ Executive Committee member, was named secretary-general. The FELAPE will be based in Mexico. (*El Universal, Grafico,* Mexico City, 4 June; Havana radio, 4, 8 June).

The IOJ's 8th Congress opened in Helsinki on 21 September, attended by 300 delegates from 80 countries. A message from Leonid Brezhnev stated that it is the lofty duty of the democratic press to continue activity for a stronger world peace and international security. Viktor Afanasyev, chairman of the board of the USSR Union of Journalists and chief editor of *Pravda,* spoke on behalf of 60,000 Soviet journalists, stressing that international democratic journalism is an effective instrument of peace, cooperation, and socialist progress. The Congress elected Kaarle Nordenstreng from Finland as new president of the IOJ and Viktor Afanasyev as vice-president; Jiří Kubka was reelected as secretary-general (TASS, 23 September).

A correspondent of the *Guardian* (London, 29 September) commented that it was "against considerable opposition from Finland's non-communist parties" that the IOJ was allowed to hold its Congress in Helsinki. The IOJ is trying hard to achieve respectability in the non-Communist world, and there was much talk of the wickedness of the Western media, managed and controlled by monopolies and infiltrated by imperialist agents, all combining to pervert the Third World and perpetuate neo-colonialism. There was, the correspondent noted, a "marked absence of any suggestions that the press of the communist world was anything less than absolutely free."

Publications. The IOJ fortnightly, *Journalists' Affairs,* and monthly, *Democratic Journalist,* appear in English, French, Spanish, and Russian editions.

International Union of Students. The International Union of Students (IUS) was founded in August of 1946 at a congress in Prague attended by students of varying political persuasions. In 1951 most of the non-Communist student unions withdrew because of domination of the IUS by pro-Soviet groups. The 1960s were marked by bitter debates between pro-Soviet and pro-Chinese students. In the middle 1960s the Chinese withdrew from active participation.

The IUS has consultative Category C status with UNESCO. Applications for Category B status have been repeatedly deferred. It is based in Prague.

Structure and Leadership. The highest governing body of the IUS is its Congress, which is supposed to meet every three years. Each affiliated and associated organization is permitted to send delegates. The Congress elects the national unions to be represented on the Executive Committee; the national unions then determine which individual(s) will represent them. The Executive Committee meets once a year. The Eleventh Congress (Budapest, May 1974) increased the number of national unions represented on the Executive Committee to 51 (from 47) and in the Secretariat, which is part of the committee, to 34 (from 23). Dusan Ulcak (Czechoslovakia) is the IUS president, and Fathi Muhammad al-Fadl (Sudan) is secretary-general.

Views and Activities. In December 1975 delegates to the biannual conference of the British National Union of Students (NUS) reportedly voted to censure Sue Slipman, NUS secretary and its most prominent Communist, and to remove all responsibility for overseas affairs from her because she had used her position to "swing the Union behind Soviet-oriented policies toward other students' unions abroad." One delegate declared: "The executive will take up international issues only after getting the OK from Moscow through the IUS in Prague." (*Daily Telegraph,* London, 8 December.)

The IUS, the All-Africa Students' Union, and the National Union of Ghana Students jointly organized a "Seminar on the Neo-Colonialist Penetration of African Universities," held at Accra on 5-8 January 1976. It was attended by 100 delegates from 30 national student unions in Africa, Asia, Latin

America, and Europe and from international organizations. The seminar, opened by the head of state of Ghana, envisaged plenary and working sessions, the adoption of a communiqué, and an evening devoted to solidarity with the youth and students of Angola and the Popular Movement for the Liberation of Angola. (*Ghanaian Times,* 5, 7-9, 12 January; British NUS *Bulletin,* 23 January.)

According to the *Irish Times* (Dublin, 13 January), a "further allegation that the Union of Students in Ireland (USI) is Moscow-dominated" appeared in a pamphlet by the League for a Workers' Republic—a Trotskyist organization. The pamphlet claimed that the Communist Party of Ireland and the Sinn Fein were vitally interested in maintaining their link with the USI, because of its link with the IUS in Prague, described as being composed of all East European students' unions, some of the unions dominated by the Communist parties in under-developed countries, and a handful of West European unions "of which USI is the most important and holds a seat on the Secretariat." It added that the "IUS is less a union than a diplomatic tool of the Kremlin bureaucracy, as it devotes more attention to endorsing [Soviet] foreign policies than discussing the problems of students."

An IUS delegation visiting South Yemen warned in a joint statement with the General National Union of Yemen Students that the Gulf area had become the "target of expansionist imperialist conspiracies" (Aden radio, 24 January).

An article in the IUS *World Student News* (no. 3, March) by the IUS president, entitled "Students for Disarmament," recalled:

> Mass movements—and this also includes the international democratic student movement—have made a palpable contribution to the improvement in the international climate. This could be seen in the many moves in favor of peace and disarmament that were made after the Second World War and at the time of the imperialist-inspired cold war. This has also been evident in more recent years in such events as the important World Congress of Peace Forces in Moscow. . . . The Youth and Student Movement has acted through such events as the World Festival of Youth and Students, the Youth Security Conference, the European Student Meetings, the youth and student meetings in the framework of the Moscow World Congress and . . . many similar events.

A delegation from the British NUS attended a "Consultative Meeting of Educational Officers" in Bulgaria, jointly organized by the National Students' Council of Bulgaria and the IUS, on 2 March (NUS *Bulletin,* 5 March).

According to a broadcast by the China-based "Voice of the Malayan Revolution" on 20 April, "Soviet-controlled International Union of Students recently sent its vice-president, Labeed Abbawi (Iraq) to carry out activities in some Asian countries and regions . . . in an attempt to infiltrate and control the student movements." The broadcast said that in recent years the IUS, "working in coordination with Soviet revisionism's ambition of establishing world hegemony," had "undermined the struggle of people and students of the Third World countries against imperialism, colonialism and hegemony." The IUS, according to the broadcast, regarded the Asian Students' Federation as the main target for infiltration, but the three student organizations in Singapore had refused to join the IUS and to establish any ties with it, and Labeed Abbawi while visiting Hong Kong in February had been exposed and denounced by the Asian Students' Federation and the student organizations there.

Marking its 30th anniversary on 17 August, the IUS issued a statement to the effect that despite reactionary attempts to disrupt the unity of the international democratic student movement, the IUS had emerged from three decades of struggles as the only democratic mass representative international students' organization. It added: "We congratulate the students of the socialist countries . . . who build a society of equality and socialism on the ruins of misery, poverty and exploitation, thus proving that socialism is the only valid alternative. . . . We lend our support to the progressive students in capitalist countries, fighting against the domination of monopoly capital and to the students in Africa, Asia and Latin America . . ." (Prague radio, 26 August.)

A meeting of Latin American students for "strengthening anti-imperialist unity" was held in San José, Costa Rica, on 21-24 September under the patronage of the IUS, the Latin American Continental Organization of Students (OCLAE), and the Central American Federation of University Students (FEUCA). It was attended by representatives of Latin American and Caribbean student organizations and guests from Vietnam, Romania, and the USSR. The meeting supported the Federation of Students of Panama in its struggle for defense of the revolutionary process and against an alleged U.S. policy of destabilization. (*Granma,* Havana, 4, 24 September.)

Publications. The IUS issues a monthly magazine, *World Student News,* in English, French, German, and Spanish and a fortnightly bulletin, *IUS News Service,* in English, French and Spanish.

Women's International Democratic Federation. The Women's International Democratic Federation (WIDF) was founded in Paris in December 1945 at a "Congress of Women" organized by the Communist-dominated Union des Femmes Françaises. The WIDF had headquarters in Paris until 1951, when it was expelled by the French government. It then moved to East Berlin. It holds Category A status with the UN Economic and Social Council, and Category B with UNESCO. It is also on the Special List of the International Labor Organization and chairs the Non-Governmental Organization (NGO) sub-committee on the Status of Women in the framework of the NGO's Human Rights Commission. The WIDF has 120 national affiliated organizations in 130 countries. (*International Associations,* Brussels, no. 8/9, 1975.)

Structure and Leadership. The WIDF's highest governing body is the Congress, which meets every four years. Next in authority is the Council, which meets annually and is in control between congresses; it elects the Bureau and the Secretariat. The Bureau meets at least twice a year and implements decisions taken by the Congress and the Council, and is assisted by the Secretariat. Fanny Edelman (Argentina) continued in 1976 as secretary-general. Freda Brown (Australia) was elected president at the Seventh Congress, East Berlin, October 1975.

Membership in the WIDF is open to all women's organizations and groups, and in exceptional cases to individuals. In 1971, total membership was said to exceed 200 million. The organization seeks to maintain contact with non-affiliated women's groups through its International Liaison Bureau, which has its general headquarters in Copenhagen and a secretariat in Brussels.

Views and Activities. A "Radio Peace and Progress" broadcast (Moscow, 1 December 1975), on the occasion of the WIDF's 30th anniversary, regretted the lack of Chinese representation in the Federation for several years and blamed this on Mao Tse-tung's foreign policy. Interviewed on the same occasion by the East German news agency, Rita Sath, secretary, said that the Federation's 121 national organizations in 106 countries had increased in strength, influence and scope. It now had a say in the community of international organizations in the UN Economic and Social Council and UNESCO, as well as in various UN specialized agencies. (*Neues Deutschland,* East Berlin, 2 December.)

The WIDF-sponsored World Congress for International Women's Year took place in East Berlin on 20-24 October 1975 (see *YICA, 1976* pp. 584-85). It adopted an action program for 1976-80 which includes a great number of international conferences, regional conferences, and seminars, on many subjects, to be held in Europe, the USA, Africa, Asia, Australia, Latin America, and the Middle East. The main topics to be brought into discussion deal with the status of women "in the democratic process," welfare of children in order to rear them "in a spirit of international solidarity, peace, friendship and understanding among peoples," and the usual themes of opposition to imperialism, colonialism, and neo-colonialism, renewed struggle for national independence and help to newly liberated peoples, total disarmament in view of universal peace, and prohibition of all nuclear weapons of mass destruction. (*Women of the Whole World,* no. 1, 1976.)

Concomitantly it was announced that since its Sixth Congress, in June 1969, the WIDF had accepted 21 new organizations, among them the Bangladesh Women's Congress, Cambodia Association of Democratic Khmer Women, General Federation of Iraqi Women, Jordan Women's Organization for Struggle against Illiteracy, Federation of Puerto Rican Women, and, in the USA, Women for Racial and Economic Equality (ibid.).

The WIDF, beginning in February 1976, made a call to women all over the world to launch a broad campaign for peace and disarmament in order to remove the existing causes of tensions and conflicts and start collecting signatures under the Stockholm Appeal of 1975 (TASS, 9 February).

In a statement for the "International Day for the Abolition of Racial Discrimination"—21 March, the anniversary of the Sharpeville massacre—the WIDF called for intensified campaigns of solidarity with political prisoners in South Africa. It added that protests and petitions should be directed to the governments in Pretoria and Salisbury (ADN, 8 March).

In statements issued on 18 March the WIDF declared its solidarity with "democratic forces" in Brazil and with the "just struggle" of the Palestinian people for their legitimate national rights under the leadership of the Palestine Liberation Organization. It also condemned the "dangerous military moves" by the USA in South Korea and demanded the immediate evacuation of all foreign military personnel and arms from that country. ("Voice of the GDR," East Berlin, 18 March.)

Freda Brown attended celebrations organized on 2 March by the Organization of Angolan Women (OMA). She announced a series of measures for political and material support of Angola. (*Neues Deutschland,* East Berlin, 24 March.)

The WIDF welcomed an "international week of solidarity with the Panamanian people," 9-14 January (TASS, 10 January); protested to Chile about the violation of human rights there and in a message to the UN expressed the hope that it would adopt appropriate resolutions against the "terror" ("Voice of the GDR," 4 February); denounced in a message to the UN Israel's "expansionist policy" and expressed solidarity with the struggle for the "legitimate rights" of the Palestinian people (ADN, 2 April); protested to Paraguay about the "escalation of repression" there and appealed to the UN to use its influence to save the lives of four prisoners on hunger strike (ibid., 7 April); protested the Spanish government's "repressive measures," appealing for solidarity with the struggle for democracy and freedom in Spain (ibid., 12 April); and protested against South Africa's "bloodbath" at Soweto, accusing the regime of genocide and stating that Dr. Vorster's visit to West Germany gave "encouragement to the apartheid regime to maintain its fascist policy" ("Voice of the GDR," 23 June).

In July a WIDF statement declared that the Helsinki Conference held a year ago has been a major stage on the path of peaceful coexistence and relaxation of tension, and called for women all over the world to take every measure to bring the realization of the final act of the agreement (TASS, 31 July).

Publications. The WIDF publishes a quarterly, *Women of the Whole World,* in English, French, Spanish, German, and Russian, and issues various pamphlets and bulletins.

World Federation of Democratic Youth. The World Federation of Democratic Youth (WFDY) was founded in November 1945 at a "World Youth Conference" convened in London by the World Youth Council. Although the WFDY appeared to represent varying shades of political opinion, key offices were fast taken by Communists, and by 1950 most non-Communists had withdrawn and established their own organization, the World Assembly of Youth. Originally based in Paris, the WFDY was expelled by the French government in 1951. Its headquarters has since been in Budapest.

All youth organizations that contribute to the safeguarding of the activities of young persons are eligible for membership in the WFDY, which claims to enroll 150 million persons from 210 organizations in 104 countries.

Structure and Leadership. The highest governing body of the WFDY is the Assembly, which convenes every three years and to which all affiliated organizations send representatives. The Assembly elects the Executive Committee, which meets at least twice a year. Day-to-day work is conducted by the Bureau and the Secretariat. Piero Lapiccirella (Italy) is president and Jean-Charles Nègre (France) is secretary-general.

Views and Activities. Representatives from 60 affiliates in 50 countries attended a meeting of the WFDY Executive Committee in Kladno, near Prague, 13-15 December 1975. Négre reported on the importance of the Helsinki Conference and of WFDY activities in support of the people of Chile, the youth of Palestine and the Middle East, the Vietnamese people, and the youth movement in capitalist countries. The meeting discussed the struggle of young people for peace, détente, and social progress. Two WFDY subsidiary bodies, the International Committee of Children's and Adolescents' Movements and the International Voluntary Service for Youth Solidarity and Friendship (SIVSAJ), also held sessions in Kladno. The meeting adopted a general resolution praising the "consistent peace policy" of the Soviet bloc and 20 resolutions on individual areas including Angola, Chile, Indochina, Portugal, and the Middle East, on disarmament and economic relations, and on a program of action for 1976. (CTK, December; *Neues Deutschland,* 16 December.) The resolution on Chile demanded the restoration of human rights and release of all political prisoners in Chile, and called for a "Youth of the World for Chile" campaign (CTK, 15 December). New affiliates included the Communist Youth of Portugal, the Revolutionary People's Youth of Laos, and organizations in Sweden, Mexico, and Ghana.

More than 120 representatives of national and international youth organizations attended the first preparatory meeting, in Oslo, 11-13 January 1976, for the European Youth Assembly, to be held in Warsaw on 20-26 June.

The International Preparatory Committee (IPC) asked the Cuban Federation of University Students (FEU) and other Cuban youth organizations to prepare for the World Youth Festival, to be held in Havana in 1978. Work reportedly has already begun on the buildings and international voluntary work brigades were being set up, with travel expenses to be paid by the International Union of Students and internal expenses by the FEU (NUS *Bulletin,* 23 January).

A statement issued by the WFDY for International Women's Day on 8 March said that the movement for equal rights of women could not be separated from the fight against imperialism, colonialism, and racial discrimination, and for peaceful coexistence, disarmament, national independence, and social and economic progress (MTI, 4 March).

In Havana, 4-15 March, Lapiccirella and Négre were among 200 delegates representing 16 international organizations at the second preparatory meeting for the World Youth Festival. The meeting adopted the slogan "For Anti-Imperialist Solidarity, Peace and Friendship" and decided to set up a permanent commission of the IPC in Havana in 1977.

Dominique Vidal, head of the international section of the French Communist Youth Movement and coordinating secretary for the World Youth Festival, accused the West German Social-Democratic Party (SPD) of using the European Youth and Student Meeting in Warsaw as a testing ground for its "imperialist strategy . . . which is to freeze and even to block the process of détente." He claimed that the SPD was "planning by means of its youth organization (JUSO) and the international Union of Socialist Youth (IUSY), which it dominates, to exclude national youth and students' organizations from the preparation and running of this meeting . . ." According to Vidal, the SPD's aim was to impose "bloc versus bloc" cooperation upon European youth and to "force the WFDY into the role of a Communist Youth International, dominated by the youth of the socialist countries," and to attempt at the same time to "achieve recognition for social-democratic organizations and the associations influenced by them, such as the Council of European National Youth Committees (CENYC), as the only representatives and spokesmen of West European youth." In the face of SPD "maneuvers" the position of the French Communist Youth Movement, according to Vidal, was clear: European youth cooperation required "a big mass meeting initiated by all its national organizations, prepared by broad-based national committees adapted to the conditions prevailing in each country and bringing together vast national delegations representing fighting youth . . ." (*L'Humanité,* Paris, 8 March.)

Lapiccirella was among some 100 representatives of 18 international, regional, and national youth organizations of different political leanings taking part in a preparatory session in Sofia, 10-12 April, which decided to hold a meeting on 19-24 June, with about 1,500 participants, under the slogan "European Youth and Students in the Struggle for Lasting Peace, Security, Cooperation and Social Progress." An appeal to the youth and students of Europe was adopted (BTA, 10 April; *Neues Deutschland,* 12, 13 April).

About 1,500 delegates, representing 200 youth and student organizations in 31 European countries, attended the European Youth and Students' Meeting, held in Warsaw on 19-24 June, jointly organized by the WFDY and the Council for European National Youth Committees (CENYC). Three organizations— the Democratic Youth Community of Europe(DEMYC), European Democrat Students (EDS), and the European Union of Young Christian Democrats— refused to send delegates, because although the meeting's main task was to define the objectives of youth cooperation in the light of the Conference on Security and Cooperation in Europe (CSCE), the scope and phraseology of many points in the program revealed the partisan nature of the meeting, which led to their suspicions of Communist attempts to manipulate the meetings for propaganda purposes (*Guardian,* London, 5, 11, 18 June). The French Communist movement said it would not attend because right-wing movements were invited (*L'Humanité,* 10 June).

Leonid Brezhnev (USSR), President Kekkonen of Finland, Edward Gierek (Poland), Erich Honecker (German Democratic Republic), János Kádár (Hungary), Gustav Husák (Czechoslovakia), and Todor Zhivkov (Bulgaria), sent messages to the meeting. Its main task was to define the objectives of youth cooperation in the light of the results of the Helsinki Conference and to outline future joint youth activities by different political forces at national and international levels. (PAP, 13, 19 June; Moscow radio, 19 June; *Neues Deutschland,* 21 June). Young liberal delegates read a statement from an underground group, "Polish Youth Committee for the Implementation of the Helsinki Agreement," attacking the Polish authorities for not implementing Clause Three of the Agreement. This resulted in a purge among Polish secret policemen, whose job it had been to prevent such contacts. A list of student arrests in Warsaw, Lublin, and Szczecin was also given. (*Guardian,* 29 June; *Le Point,* Paris, 5 July.)

At talks held in Mogadiscio, delegations of the WFDY and the Somali Youth League emphasized the need for unity among young people of developing countries in the common anti-imperialist struggle of the people. the participants protested the "unceasing provocations of the racist regimes of the Republic of South Africa and Rhodesia" against independent African countries and expressed solidarity with the peoples of Zimbabwe, Namibia, and South Africa for their freedom and independence. (TASS, 20 August.)

In mid-October an international conference of youth and students for turning the Indian Ocean into a zone of peace was held in Madras, India, on the initiative of the WFDY and Indian organizations, with about 40 national and international youth associations participating.

Publications. The WFDY publishes a bimonthly magazine, *World Youth,* in English, French, German, and Arabic. The monthly *WFDY News* appears in English, French, and Spanish.

World Federation of Scientific Workers. The World Federation of Scientific Workers (WFSW) was founded in London in 1946 at the initiative of the British Association of Scientific Workers, with 18 organizations of scientists from 14 countries taking part. Although it purported to be a scientific rather than a political organization, Communists obtained most official posts at the start and have kept control since. The headquarters is in London, but the secretary-general's office is in Paris.

WFSW membership is open to organizations of scientific workers everywhere and to individual scientists in countries where no affiliated groups are active. The WFSW claims to represent 300,000 scientists in 30 countries, most of the membership deriving from 14 groups in Communist-ruled countries. The only large non-Communist affiliate, the British Association of Scientific Workers, has 21,000 members. Scientists of distinction who do not belong to an affiliated organization may be nominated for "corresponding membership." The WFSW has a constitution and a "Charter for Scientific Workers" to which affiliates must subscribe.

Structure and Leadership. The governing body of the WFSW is the General Assembly, in which all affiliated organizations are represented. Ten Assembly meetings have been held, the most recent in September 1973 at Varna, Bulgaria. Between these, the Executive Council and its Bureau are responsible for operations. There are three standing committees: the Science Policy Committee, the Socio-Economic Committee, and the Committee on Peace and Disarmament. Eric Burhop (United Kingdom) is president and chairman of the Executive Council; Pierre Biquard (France) is secretary-general.

The WFSW has consultative status Category A with UNESCO.

Views and Activities. The WFSW and the World Federation of Trade Unions (WFTU) made a joint statement in December 1975 continuing the theme of the WFSW-sponsored Disarmament Symposium in Moscow in July 1975 (see *YICA, 1976,* pp. 588-89) and appealing to the scientists of the world to halt the devlopment, accumulation, and deployment of nuclear weapons in these times of détente (WFTU brochure). A further joint statement in December declared that ecological problems can be solved only within the framework of a political and economic democracy. Eric Burhop was among signatories to a letter to the British Prime Minister asking him to cooperate with the USSR in seeking a universal ban on nuclear weapons (*Morning Star,* London, 19 December).

Burhop (UK), president, Pierre Biquard (France), secretary-general, and Horst Sander (GDR) attended meetings of the Bureau, the Peace and Disarmament Committee, and the Science Policy Committee, in East Berlin on 23-26 January 1976, which were called to evaluate the results of the WFSW's Disarmament Symposium held in Moscow in July 1975 and to discuss the implications for the WFSW of the Conference for Security and Cooperation in Europe (*Voice of the GDR,* 23 January; *Neues Deutschland,* 24-25 January).

The WFSW Socio-Economic Commission met in Paris at the UNESCO building in January and discussed with a WFTU representative the scope of possible joint work with international bodies. Also discussed were a UNESCO recommendation on the status of scientific researchers, two forthcoming UNESCO conferences, and a study on the influence of multinational enterprises on science and technology (*Scientific World,* no. 2).

The Bureau meeting at East Berlin in January discussed preparations for the 11th Assembly, to be held in London in September, on the theme of the "inter-relation of current economic and social developments with science and technology." Also discussed were a projected symposium in India in 1977, the significance of the Final Act of Helsinki for the WFSW, job discrimination in West Germany, and joint activity with international trade union centers, particularly in relation to work in the International Labor Organization, UNESCO and the UN. (Ibid.)

Publications. The official publication of the WFSW is the quarterly *Scientific World,* issued in English, French, German, Spanish, Russian, and Czech. The WFSW *Bulletin* is issued irregularly and only to members, in English, French, German, and Russian.

World Federation of Trade Unions. The World Federation of Trade Unions (WFTU), set up at the initiative of the British Trade Union Congress, held its founding congress in October 1945 in Paris, where its first headquarters was established. Expelled from Paris and next from Vienna for subversive activities, the headquarters has been in Prague since 1956. Louis Saillant (France), the first WFTU secretary-general, is generally considered responsible for bringing the WFTU Secretariat and other ruling bodies under Communist control. Some non-Communist affiliates gave up their membership in 1949 to found an alternative organization, the International Conference of Free Trade Unions (ICTFU). In 1975 the WFTU claimed to have 160 to 170 million members in 68 countries (TASS, 4 October).

Structure and Leadership. The highest WFTU authority, the Congress, meets every four years and is composed of delegates from affiliates in proportion to the number of their members. The Congress, which has no policy-making function and is too large to transact much specific business, elects the General Council, Executive Bureau, and Secretariat. The General Council has about 66 regular and 68 deputy members representing the national affiliates and 11 Trade Union Internationals (TUIs). The latest Congress, held in Varna, Bulgaria in the fall of 1973, reelected Enrique Pastorino (Uruguay) as president and Pierre Gensous (France) as secretary-general. Two seats on the General Council have been left vacant for China and Indonesia. The Executive Bureau is the most powerful body of the WFTU, having assumed much of the authority which before 1969 was enjoyed by the Secretariat, which was revamped by the 1969 Congress and reduced to six members, including the secretary-general.

The TUIs represent workers of particular trades and crafts, one of their main purposes being to recruit local unions which do not, through their national centers, belong to the WFTU. Though the TUIs are in theory independent (each TUI has its own offices and officials, holds its own meetings, and publishes its own bulletin), their policies and finances are actually controlled by the WFTU department having supervision over their particular areas. The WFTU General Council in December 1966 decided that each TUI should have its own constitution; this move, taken to bolster the appearance of independence, had the purpose of allowing the TUIs to join international bodies as individual organizations.

The WFTU's "Special Commission on UN Agencies," created in 1967 to facilitate WFTU activities in the UN agencies, has permanent representatives at the UN, the International Labor Organization (ILO), the Food and Agriculture Organization (FAO), and UNESCO.

Views and Activities. The WFTU has published a booklet, *Thirty Years in the Workers' Services,* containing an account of the 26th General Council session in Paris, 7-9 October 1975 (See *YICA, 1976,* pp. 592-94).

An Executive Bureau meeting in Budapest on 10-11 November 1975 dealt with preparations for the TUIs' 5th Conference, to be held in Sofia in October 1976. It also approved applications for membership from the Union of Commercial Representatives and Collectors of Panama and the left-wing section of the Austrian Union of Commercial, Clerical, and Technical Employees. (*TUI News,* no. 230.)

The French Communist-controled General Confederation of Labor (CGT) invited the WFTU's affiliated centers in Europe to meet in Champigny on 7-9 October 1975, preceding the above-mentioned General Council meeting, to discuss WFTU problems, particularly concerning the advancement of the class struggle in "capitalist Europe" and the giving of "class content" to international workers' solidarity (*Le Peuple,* organ of the CGT, 1-15 December).

Gensous led a delegation to Africa, 30 November-15 December 1975, visiting Mali, Ghana, Zambia, and Tanzania. In Zambia it met representatives of the South African Congress of Trade Unions (SACTU) and the South-West Africa People's Organization (SWAPO), and in Tanzania with a delegation from the National Union of Tanganyika Workers (*Flashes,* 5 December). Gensous said later that he had been seeking a better knowledge of the African trade unions' current objectives and to foster cooperation in ending underdevelopment, establishing a new economic order, and struggling against multinational companies and the effects of the economic crisis (ibid., no. 1-2, 1976).

In its monthly organ, *Free Labor World* (December 1975), the International Confederation of Free Trade Unions asked:

> ... whether and to what extent unity of action can reach beyond our free trade union movement: whether in fact the ICFTU could and should actively cooperate with Communist-inspired organizations and, in particular, with the WFTU and its affiliates.... It may be true that we and the WFTU have common enemies, but we think that we have not much of a common platform.... We may agree on what we want to destroy, but not on what we want to build in its place. We free trade unionists detest the inhuman practices of the capitalistic system, but we would not see any advantage in replacing this system by an equally inhuman bureaucratic and monopolistic State power—the type of society found in East European countries. For us human and trade union rights are indivisible—we fight against violation of these rights wherever they occur and irrespective of who commits them: The WFTU and the forces it represents are very selective in their approach. We are working for the liberation of oppressed people from fascist or military tyranny. ... We are not going to assist in the setting of another form of dictatorship. ... We look at these matters as trade unionists, whereas the WFTU considers them from the political point of view.

Late in 1975, the WFTU condemned Indonesia's action in East Timor and called for an immediate withdrawal of its troops (CTK, 10 December) and sent a solidarity telegram to the Japanese General Council of Trade Unions (Sohyo) on the occasion of a public workers' strike and also a message to the Japanese government urging it to respect ILO conventions and to guarantee trade union rights to public service workers (*Flashes,* no. 45-46).

A four-man WFTU delegation attended a UNESCO-sponsored symposium of the three international trade union centers—the WFTU, ICFTU, and World Confederation of Labor—in Paris on 8-12 December. The WFTU recommended the convening of a world union conference on adult education (ibid., no. 1-2, 1976).

Early in January 1976, the WFTU said that steps were being taken to set up an "International Trade Union Committee of Solidarity with Chile" and appealed for 12 February to be declared a day of action in support of Chile (ibid., no. 3).

The East German party organ *Neues Deutschland* (27 January) said that Gensous, visiting Damascus at the invitation of the Union of Palestinian Workers, had declared that preparations were going ahead for an "International Conference of Solidarity with the Struggle of the Palestinian People."

In response to an invitation from the UN Industrial Development Organization (UNIDO), Vaclav Holub (Czechoslovakia), member of WFTU's UN and Specialized Agencies' Affairs Department, represented the WFTU at a meeting of the Inter-Governmental Committee in charge of drafting the constituent act of UNIDO in January in Vienna (this body is to be transformed into a specialized agency) (ibid., no. 6).

The WFTU Bureau, meeting in Moscow on 27-30 January, analysed its activities since its 6th Conference (Budapest, May 1974) and examined the consequences of the "capitalist crisis" for workers. It decided to prepare for an "International Conference on Collective Bargaining" early in 1977 (ibid., no. 7-8).

In February the WFTU called on the working people and trade unions of all countries to demand the immediate ending of nuclear tests, particularly in the People's Republic of China, and to pursue an international campaign for complete disarmament, peace, and social progress (TASS, 12 February).

An article in the Bulgarian trade union newspaper *Trud* (February) described the training of trade union cadres from a number of Asian, African, and Latin American countries as an "extremely important manifestation of international and class solidarity" by the Bulgarian trade unions. It mentioned that more than 1,800 trade union functionaries from almost 60 countries had so far received training (BTA, 13 February).

It was announced on 17 February that the "International Trade Union Committee for Solidarity with Chile" had been set up jointly by the WFTU, the International Confederation of Arab Trade Unions, the Organization of American Trade Union Unity, and the Permanent Congress of Latin American Trade Union Unity (CPUSTAL) in agreement with the External Committee of the Single Center of Chilean Workers (CUTCH), and will be based in Prague. The committee will try to obtain increased support for the release of all political prisoners in Chile, the dropping of proceedings against Luis Corvalán, and the restoration of democratic rights and freedoms. (*Neues Deutschland,* 18 February.)

WFTU chairman Enrique Pastorino, addressing the 25th Congress of the Communist Party of the Soviet Union, hailed the USSR as the "principal bastion of peace . . . and of the struggle for consolidation of the international unity of working people" (*Pravda,* 7 March).

The French National Trade Union of Teachers in Higher Education (SNES-FEN), in collaboration with the World Federation of Teachers' Unions (FISE), held an international symposium of the higher education trade unions and organizations of European and Arab countries of the Mediterranean. The meeting, in Paris, 6-8 February, brought together representatives from organizations in Algeria, France, Italy, Libya, Morocco, Portugal, Spain, Tunisia, Yugoslavia, the FISE, and the WFSW. The symposium adopted several recommendations on the equivalents and recogniton of diplomas, to be presented to UNESCO, and a resolution calling for cooperation between the teachers' unions of the Mediterranean countries "on fundamental international issues." (MTI, 8 March.)

A delegation from the UN Committee on Apartheid had talks with representatives of the WFTU, the IUS, the IOJ, and the Czechoslovakian Afro-Asian Solidarity Committee in Prague on 6-9 March (CTK, 10 March).

Gensous met with the executive director of the UN Industrial Development Organization in Vienna on 16 February to discuss ways of raising cooperation between the WFTU and UNIDO "to a level comparable to that attained in recent years . . . between the WFTU and the International Trade Union movement as a whole." The WFTU has consultative status with UNIDO. (*Flashes,* 10 March.)

The WFTU Secretariat on 4 March resolved to form a permanent working commission for matters bearing on multinational companies and to set up a special WFTU body for trade union work in connection with these companies. The Secretariat also discussed a meeting to be held with spokesmen of the Spanish Workers' Commissions on an unspecified date. It decided to contribute $5,000 to the victims of "reaction" in Lebanon and $3,000 to Sahara refugees. (Ibid., 17 March.)

Representatives of trade union centers, both members of the WFTU and others, from France, Guinea, Chile, India, Iraq, Italy, Cuba, the USSR, and Czechoslovakia attended a working group meeting in Prague, 7-8 April, on problems of women workers. The meeting was called to evaluate the activity of the WFTU in International Women's Year and its tasks in behalf of working women in the period leading up to the 9th WFTU Congress, due in October 1977 (CTK, 7 April).

A delegation of Spanish Workers' Commissions and a delegation of the WFTU Secretariat met in Prague on 13 April to discuss the situation in Spain after Franco's death. The Secretariat assured the Workers' Commissions that it is determined to help their economic struggle and that of all democratic opposition forces in Spain (TASS, 13 April).

The 14th Bureau Session of the WFTU, at Tatranska Lomnica in Czechoslovakia on 21-22 April, was attended by delegates from 23 countries. Pastorino contrasted the achievements of the socialist countries with the deepening crisis in the capitalist world. Gensous stressed the important role played by the WFTU in the struggle of the working people in capitalist and developing countries. The training of cadres, especially in the developing countries, was discussed. The Bureau also "looked at the . . . tragic situation in Lebanon and decided to make greater efforts to help the Lebanese people in their struggle for their just demands." Palestine received close attention, particularly the preparations for the International Solidarity Conference to be held in October. The Bureau approved the request for affiliation from the National Workers' Federation of Guinea Bissau. (CTK, 21-22 April; Prague radio, 21-22 April; TASS 23 April.)

The WFTU called for the immediate withdrawal of US arms and troops from South Korea and for solidarity with the struggle of the Korean people for their country's reunification (CTK, 9 March).

The WFTU vigorously protested the decision of the French government to sell an atomic power station to South Africa, stating that such a sale was a "flagrant violation of the United Nations decisions which have condemned the South African regime as being racist and inhuman." It called on trade unions and workers in all countries to demonstrate with force their condemnation of the French government's decision, and to demand annulment of the contract and an end to collaboration of any kind with South Africa. (CTK, 2 June.)

Gensous led the WFTU delegation to the 61st session of the International Labor Conference, which opened in Geneva on 2 June. Statements and protests were made by the WFTU against arrest of unionists and politicians in Bangladesh, attacks on a workers' demonstration in Athens, murders of political prisoners by the Chilean military junta, and the "puppet regime" in South Korea (*Flashes,* no. 22-23-24).

Pierre Gensous in a letter to the UNESCO director-general on 29 June made suggestions concerning the UNESCO draft program and budget for 1977-78, saying that the WFTU was convinced that UNESCO should play an increased role with regard to such problems as peace, détente, peaceful coexistence, disarmament, protection of human rights, and the establishment of a new international economic order. He added that the WFTU shared the general idea announced by the director-general, namely that UNESCO should become an international organization, really serving the peoples. Cooperation between UNESCO and the big international trade union organizations was important, he said, because without real and effective participation by the big mass organizations, no national or international action could bear fruit. (Ibid., no. 27).

Through the year, the WFTU issued statements on the topics already noted, expressing solidarity with and calling for support of the Palestine resistance movement, the trade unions, and "other progressive forces" in Lebanon (e.g., TASS, 9 July; Prague radio, 11 August; *Flashes,* no. 30); the People's Republic of Angola (TASS, 24, 31 August); and withdrawal of U.S. forces from South Korea (Prague radio, 23 August; TASS, 25 August). The WFTU hailed the "31st anniversary of the Socialist Republic of Vietnam (Hanoi radio, 6 September) and called for 11 September to be observed as a "great day of solidarity" with the workers and people of Chile (CTK, 27 August).

The second "International Trade Union Conference for Solidarity with the Workers and People of Palestine" was opened on 25 October in Karl Marx Stadt, East Germany, by Pierre Gensous of the WFTU and was attended by representatives of some 70 trade unions in Europe, Africa, Asia, and Latin America (ADN, 25 October).

A WFTU statement in November denounced the U.S. veto of admission of the Socialist Republic of Vietnam to the United Nations (CTK, 23 November).

The 15th session of the WFTU Bureau, in Delhi, in early December, drew representatives of TUIs in 24 countries. The meeting passed a special resolution in support of the coming "World Forum of Peace Forces" in Moscow. (TASS, 4 December; *Trud,* Moscow, 4 December.)

Publications. The most important publication of the WFTU is an illustrated magazine, *World Trade Union Movement,* circulated in some 70 countries, in English, French, Spanish, German, Russian, and other languages. *Flashes,* published several times a month in four languages, is an information bulletin of 4-5 pages.

World Peace Council. The "world peace movement" headed by the World Peace Council (WPC) dates from August 1948 when a "World Congress of Intellectuals for Peace" in Wroclaw, Poland, set up an organization called the International Liaison Committee of Intellectuals. This committee in April 1949 convened a "First World Peace Congress" in Paris. The Congress launched a "World Committee of Partisans of Peace" which in November 1950 was renamed the World Peace Council. Originally based in Paris, the WPC was expelled in 1951 by the French government. It moved first to Prague and then in 1954 to Vienna, where it adopted the name "World Council of Peace." Although outlawed in Austria in 1957, it continued its operations in Vienna under the cover of a new organization, the International Institute of Peace (IIP), subsequently referred to by WPC members as the "scientific-theoretical workshop of the WPC" (CTK, 16 December 1971). In September 1968 the World Council of Peace transferred its headquarters to Helsinki, while the IIP remained in Vienna. Although no formal announcement was made, the World Council of Peace has reverted to its earlier name, the World Peace Council.

Structure and Leadership. The WPC is organized on a national basis with Peace Committees and other affiliated groups in more than 80 countries. No precise figure is available on the total individual membership. The highest authority is the 600-member Council, which elects the 101-member Presidential Committee, which in turn elects the 24-member Bureau and 18-member Secretariat, with memberships divided among representatives from various countries. Communist-front organizations such as the IUS, WFDY, WFSW, WFTU, and WIDF are represented on the Presidential Committee.

Amendments adopted at the February 1974 meeting of the Council require it to meet every three years instead of every two and urge the national peace movements—Peace Committees—to meet annually, while the Presidential Committee will meet only once a year instead of twice. The Bureau will normally meet three or four times a year to review international events and the Council's work and to execute decisions of the Presidential Committee. It appears that the Bureau has authority to act independently on a wide range of matters. The executive bodies of the IIP—ostensibly independent of those of the WPC, but in fact elected by the Council—are the 7-member Presidium and 30-member Executive Committee. Romesh Chandra (India) is the WPC secretary-general.

The WPC has "Consultation and Association—Category A" status with UNESCO.

Views and Activities. In the latter part of November 1975 the "WPC Congress Committee Conference" met for four days in Vienna under the chairmanship of Romesh Chandra; Sean McBride, chairman of the UN Commission for Namibia; and Knut Nielsen, president of the International Association of World Federalists. The discussions centered on what must be done to anchor the decisions and results of the Conference on Security and Cooperation in Europe (CSCE) in the minds of a broad strata of people, and what possibilities exist after the Helsinki conference for international economic cooperation (*Volksstimme,* Vienna, 27 November).

At the "Second Annual Conference of National Peace Movements," held in Leningrad on 21-24 November, Chandra called for strong solidarity with the peoples of Bangladesh and said that the WPC would appoint an international commission of inquiry into "crimes perpetrated by the Bangladesh junta and the CIA behind them" (*Patriot,* New Delhi, 22 November). Chandra described the conference as an "event of historic significance for the development of the entire world peace movement." The year 1976, he said, would be devoted to the search for collective security in Asia and the next meeting of the Presidential Committee would take place in New Delhi. A special "Asia week" was called for in the first half of April and an appeal issued for an end to the "crimes" being committed in Bangladesh (*Moscow News,* 6 December). Chandra added that the WPC's cooperation with the UN had reached new heights, a WPC delegation having recently visited UN headquarters in New York where it presented medals to the Special Committees on Apartheid and Decolonization. This was the first time the UN had "accepted an award from a non-governmental organization." (Ibid.)

The WPC held an "International Conference against Fascism" in Patna, India, on 4-7 December, attended by some 6,000 delegates, of whom 114 came from outside India. The conference was held under the initiative of the WPC and organized by an Indian preparatory committee which included leaders of the Congress and Communist parties and other "patriotic political forces," federal and state ministers, and leaders of trade unions, women's, youth and student organizations. Among the participants were representatives of the IUS, the Afro-Asian Peoples' Solidarity Organization (AAPSO), the African National Congress (ANC) of South Africa, and the Palestine Liberation Organization (PLO). Messages were received from President Dórticos of Cuba, party chief Erich Honecker of the German Democratic Republic (GDR), the president of the People's Republic of Angola, Archbishop Makarios of Cyprus, Prime Minister Indira Gandhi of India, and the GDR Committee of Anti-Fascist Resistance Fighters. The following problems were discussed within the four commissions of the conference: (1) imperialism and fascism, (2) the socio-economic base of fascist and neo-fascist forces, (3) fascist and neo-fascist forces in developing countries, and (4) unity and peace forces as the key to victory over fascism. A number of resolutions were adopted, including a declaration of solidarity with the Indian people. This declaration claimed that "U.S. imperialism" was compensating for its failures elsewhere by counterattacking in the Indian sub-continent: "Imperialism and reaction, acting through agencies like the CIA, are aiming at deestablishing developing countries." Developments in Bangladesh were said to "make it amply clear that India's national freedom and sovereignty are being threatened in a planned manner from the outside." Chandra described the conference as a landmark in the united effort to promote positive tendencies in international life and said that it had "mapped out a program of concrete actions for the forces of peace and progress." (*Neues Deutschland,* 4-8 December 1975; *Guardian,* London, 5 December; *Patriot,* New Delhi, 6 December; TASS, 6, 8, December; *Times of India,* New Delhi, 8 December; *New Age,* New Delhi, 14 December.)

Harald Edelstam, Swedish ambassador in Algiers, has, according to the Stockholm *Svenska Dagbladet* (24 December), become one of the "most prominent Swedes in the front ranks of the Moscow-controlled WPC." The paper criticized his attendance at the Conference against Fascism in Patna, and the Stockholm *Aftonbladet* reported (6 January 1976) that the Embassy staff had complained about him and that an inspector had been sent to investigate.

Visiting Hungary at the invitation of the national Peace Committee, Chandra attended a meeting of the national Peace Council on 8 January 1976 and called at the WFDY's headquarters in Budapest where he discussed the "consolidation of peace and security and the promotion of disarmament," with WFDY president Lapiccirella (MTI, 7-8 January).

The WPC on 9 January expressed full support for the struggle of the Panamanian people to restore their sovereignty over the Panama Canal Zone and appealed to all governments and peoples to pledge solidarity with the people of the Panama fighting for its legitimate rights (TASS, 9 January).

On 16-18 January an emergency Bureau meeting of WPC in Helsinki discussed international solidarity with the Angolan people against "imperialist aggression," the new Stockholm movement to end the arms race and for disarmament, and the WPC program for the year 1976. Delegates from 38 countries attended, including a five-member delegation led by Jose Eduardo dos Santos, Angolan foreign minister.

Dos Santos called for the immediate world-wide recognition of the Popular Movement for the Liberation of Angola (MPLA). He proposed an eight-point plan of solidarity, including an international conference (presumably the AAPSO one in Luanda, 2-4 February), and fund raising for the MPLA. "What is taking place in our country," he declared, "is not a civil war, but a clear-cut aggression and imperialist intervention by Zaire, South Africa, and world imperialism, headed by the USA." He commended particularly the USSR and Cuba for their "selfless aid" and thanked the WPC for its award of the Joliot-Curie gold medal to Angolan president Neto. A resolution stated that Neto's was the legitimate government and condemned the USA, South Africa, and Zaire for their "aggression" and China for its support for the "reactionary forces" in Angola. (PAP, 8, 18, 19, 21 January; MTI, 14 January; Havana radio, 15 January; *Neues Deutschland,* 17-18 January; TASS, 17, 19 January.)

The WPC Bureau appealed to world public opinion on 20 January to contribute actively toward normalization of the situation in Lebanon (TASS, 20 January). The WPC strongly protested the Chilean junta's staging of a trial of Luis Corvalán and other Chilean Communist leaders, and asked world public opinion to take urgent measures to save their lives and secure their release (ibid., 29 January).

Romesh Chandra was among representatives of peace movements from 13 countries at a preparatory meeting in Frankfurt, West Germany, on 30-31 January to discuss the role of social organizations in solving the disarmament problem. An "international conference" of WPC members took place in Frankfurt at about the same time. (*Neues Deutschland,* 31 January; 1, 4 February; "Voice of the GDR," 31 January.)

A second meeting of "Latin American Universities for Solidarity with Chile" was held in Caracas, Venezuela, on 18-22 February under the auspices of the WPC, WFTU, WFDY, IUS, and WFSW (the first was held in Colombia in March 1975). Some 500 delegates from Latin American countries and representatives of international organizations examined ways of intensifying solidarity with persecuted academics, students, and officials in Chile's unviersities. (*Tribuna Popular,* Caracas, 27 February-4 March; *Resistance,* Chilean exiles' bulletin, Algiers, 1-7 March.)

Chandra said in an interview (*New Times,* Moscow, March) that the program of "further struggle for peace and international cooperation for freedom and independence of peoples," advanced at the 25th Congress of the Communist Party of the Soviet Union, had set "concrete targets that are clear and understandable to all those who realize how disastrous would be the consequences of a destructive world war." He added that "the call issued by Leonid Brezhnev for new initiatives and new actions on this most urgent question of disarmament facing mankind today will certainly become a source of new inspiration for public organizations of different countries." (TASS, 4 March.)

Neues Deutschland announced on 17 March that Volodia Teitelboim, member of the Central Committee of the Chilean Communist Party and WPC Presidential Committee member, had been awarded the Soviet Order of Friendship "for his services to the international Communist movement."

Representatives from 10 international organizations and 19 countries participated in a meeting of the WPC Executive Committee in Athens on 9-10 March to discuss the Middle East and adopt a program of action. They elected a presidium composed of prominent figures from various countries and charged Romesh Chandra with coordinating its work (WFTU *Flashes,* no. 12; *Peace Courier,* no. 3).

The WPC lodged a sharp protest on 16 March with the Israeli prime minister for reprisals against the population on the west bank of the Jordan River and other occupied Arab territories. It also called for the release of all "Palestinian patriots" and an end of "Israeli atrocities." (TASS, 17 March.) Experts and witnesses from more than 20 countries participated in Helsinki in the fourth meeting of the "International Commission for the Investigation of the Crime of the Chilean Military Junta" (set up at a meeting in the same city in September 1973) under the auspices of the WPC and a number of Finnish organizations. The session took the form of a hearing on "arbitrary arrests and imprisonments in Chile." Its final declaration condemned the projected trial of Luis Corvalán and other Popular Unity leaders and urged that efforts be made to stop it. It was decided that the member countries of the Organization of American States should be asked to reconsider their intention to hold their next meeting in Chile, "in view of the continued violence of human rights" there. (*Neues Detuschland,* 29-30 March.)

The British government's refusal of visas for four leading figures in the peace movement from the USSR, Poland, and the GDR led the "International Continuing Liaison Committee of the World Congress of Peace Forces" to withdraw from the "International Forum on Disarmament," to be held in London in late March. The Forum's secretary said that it would still be a "very international Forum," its two main aims being to increase public awareness of the dangers of the arms race and of the social and economic consequences of growing military expenditure, as well as to appeal to the United Nations to convene a world disarmament conference. (*Morning Star*, London, 6 March; *Pravda*, 28 March.)

About 300 delegates from more than 20 countries and from international organizations attended the Forum (1,000 delegates were originally expected). A message from Soviet dissident Andrei Sakharov, Nobel prize winner, was made available to delegates afterward, but was not read out as he had requested; the organizers alleged that it was too late, too long, and of a "different nature" from the other messages. According to one report, the official Soviet delegates threatened to walk out if it were read. (*Morning Star*, 23, 26 March; *Guardian*, 31 March.) The Forum adopted a "York Declaration" which stressed that a general improvement of the international situation opened up prospects for a better future for mankind. It also pointed to the urgent need to seek universal and complete disarmament, demanded the early signing of an international convention to ban nuclear and all other types of mass destruction weapons, supported an appeal for a world disarmament conference under UN auspices, and stressed the importance of deepening the process of détente. (TASS, 1 April.)

In April, the Patriarch of Moscow and All the Russias was presented with a medal of the WPC, instituted to mark the 25th anniversary of the peace movement (ibid., 27 April). The same WPC medal was presented to President Neto of Angola (ibid., 29 April).

Romesh Chandra was busy throughout March and April visiting Iraq, the GDR, Romania, and Angola. Many appeals, messages, and statements continued to be sent out. While the General Assembly of the OAS was preparing to meet in Santiago, the WPC accused once more the Chilean junta of increasing its aggression against the people of Chile (PAP, 21 April). Also the WPC drew the attention of the UN to alleged violations of its resolutions by Turkish forces in Cyprus (PAP, 28 April). In connection with the "Week for Security and Disarmament in Europe" (9-16 May), the WPC appealed to all peace organizations to strive for the realization of the Helsinki Agreements (*Neues Deutschland*, 28 April). A four-day session of the WPC Presidium opened in Athens on 18 May, attended by representatives of 60 national and international organizations, to discuss problems of the "people's struggle for peace and international cooperation, freedom, and independence." Implementation of the Helsinki Conference's decisions was prominent on the agenda. (TASS, 18, 21 May.)

Chandra in a statement reported by TASS on 27 May announced that the Joliot-Curie gold medal, the highest decoration of the peace movement, was being conferred on Leonid Brezhnev for, among other things, the great part played by him in the defense of peace and security.

Ever so active, Chandra attended an international seminar in Havana devoted to the struggle against apartheid and race oppression. He declared that the non-aligned movement was expected to play a prominent role in solving these problems. Chandra emphasized that the peaceful policy of the USSR and other members of the socialist community fully accords with the interests of the non-aligned movement and hailed the contribution of Brezhnev in the drafting and implementation of the peace program. (TASS, 27 May.)

A "Colloquium for a Just Peace in the Middle East" was held in Coimbra, Portugal on 26-29 May, organized by the Portuguese Council for Peace and Cooperation in conjunction with the WPC and Coimbra University. Fifteen foreign participants represented peace movements in the Middle East and Europe (*Peace Courier*, no. 5-6).

Delegates from about 30 countries and representatives of international organizations attended a seminar on the theme "Development Problems and the Struggle for a New International Economic Order" in Baghdad on 1-4 June. The seminar was organized by the Iraqi National Council for Peace and Solidarity in cooperation with the WPC and the AAPSO. Three commissions discussed the problems of the developing countries, multinational companies in the Third World, and the struggle for a new international economic order. (Ibid.; Iraqi News Agency, 1 June.)

Chandra headed a WPC delegation to the "First Conference of Latin American National Peace Movements" in Bogota, Colombia. This conference acclaimed 16 June as a "day of international solidarity with Guyana" to be sponsored, organized and supported by the WPC, national Peace Committees, and "world progressive forces" (Havana radio, 5, 8 June).

In a statement given out in Helsinki at the end of June, the WPC denounced the USA for using the veto in the UN Security Council to prevent admission of the People's Republic of Angola (TASS, 28 June).

A WPC delegation, led by its secretary-general, met in Geneva at the beginning of July with members of the Disarmament Conference, telling them about the efforts made by peace supporters and stressing that the problems discussed in the conference are closely linked with the tasks of the peace movement (ibid., 3 July). Also in July, representatives from the WPC, WFDY, IUS, WIDF, the Peace Committees, the UN, and other national and international organizations attended an international symposium in Geneva to discuss political prisoners in South Africa. This symposium was held on the initiative of the Federation of Non-Governmental Organizations, including the World Council of Churches and the Red Cross ("Radio Peace and Progress," Moscow, 2, 13 July).

In a letter dated 20 July, the WPC condemned "security screening" in West Germany, which "violated the regulations of the Final Act of the Helsinki Conference," and called for solidarity with the "champions of democratic freedom" in West Germany and for support for their struggle against "political discrimination" (TASS, 20 July).

According to Soviet sources, top Soviet leaders Brezhnev, Kosygin and Podgorny are among more than 150 million persons who have signed the New Stockholm Appeal, other signatories including the Finnish prime minister, 200 Indian MPs and 800 members of legislative bodies in the Indian states, and members of provincial legislatures and trade union councils in Canada (ibid., 15, 16, 20, 22, 24 July). A WPC statement on the Appeal said that the campaign has already spread to more than 80 countries and that the national peace organizations of these countries had collected millions of signatures (ibid., 22 July). A statement circulated a few days later stressed the enormous importance of the Appeal and added that it established a new economic structure (ibid., 27 July).

An article in *Pravda* (6 August) marked the start of the WPC "week of actions against weapons of mass destruction," to include rallies and meetings in the USSR and throughout the West. The article said that the USSR has put forward many important initiatives aimed at reducing armament, and that these initiatives have met with broad support in the West, although the governments of the Western powers were still not displaying a proper desire to adopt and implement them, while the USSR was in the forefront of the fighters for a world without weapons and wars.

The Presidium of the WPC Bureau in an "emergency session" in Paris in early September discussed the situation in Lebanon with representatives of 27 countries. The Presidium called for the immediate withdrawal of Syrian troops and appealed to all peace champions to strengthen solidarity with the Lebanese (TASS, 7 September). An international conference was held in Helsinki at the end of September to expose the "imperialist conspiracy" against the people of Lebanon and Palestine. Sponsored by the WPC, it was attended by 150 delegates, including parliamentarians, trade unionists, and representatives of "progressive" movements and parties from 60 countries. The delegates endorsed the text of the conference statement condemning U.S. and Israeli policy, which was said to be trying to split Arab anti-imperialist unity, eliminate the Palestinian resistance movement, and isolate the Arab people from the USSR and other socialist countries. An "action program" was adopted, urging the world public to launch a wide struggle exposing U.S. imperialism, Zionism, and internal Arab reaction in the Middle East. (TASS, 28 September.)

Christian Peace Conference. The Christian Peace Conference (CPC), which has been under Soviet domination since 1968, is noted here because it operates in tandem with the WPC.

An international Secretariat meeting of the CPC, held in Prague on 14-16 January 1976, decided that during the coming year it would support all constructive efforts toward international détente and the implementation of the resolutions of the Helsinki Conference (CTK, 16 January). Later that month, the CPC called for support for the Popular Movement for the Liberation of Angola (*CPC Information,* no. 190).

An "Anti-Racism Study Commission" meeting in Arnoldsheim, West Germany, on 2-6 February was attended by Karoly Toth (Hungary), CPC secretary-general; and Dr. Herbert Mochalski (West Germany), CPC vice-president. The meeting drafted a statement on the situation in South-West Africa and a circular letter to churches on Angola (ibid., no. 191, 12 February).

An international preparatory committee for a "World Conference of Religious Leaders," to be held in 1977, was set up in Moscow after a meeting attended by 116 religious leaders from 29 African and European countries. The idea for the conference rose from a meeting of representatives of the CPC and religious communities in the USSR in Zagorsk in 1975. (TASS, 31 March.)

Seventy participants from 24 countries, including the CPC secretary-general, attended a seminar in Sofia on 17-19 June which discussed the Conference on Security and Cooperation in Europe and its significance for the Third World. A communiqué stressed the significance of the CSCE Final Act, but warned that the conference had not done away with the forces opposed to détente, so that it was important for peace forces to remain vigilant. The Helsinki Accords, it added, did not signify any diminution of the efforts of socialism to combat capitalism in order to secure a better future for mankind. (BTA, 19 June; *CPC Information,* no. 198.)

Thirty commission members and guests from 13 countries heard CPC leader Toth at the "Sub-Commission on Disarmament" meeting in Japan on 23-26 June when he told of CPC efforts toward disarmament. The delegates expressed support for a UN Disarmament Conference and an "Ecumenical Conference of Churches and Christians for Disarmament and against Hunger." (Ibid., no. 199.)

Publications. The WPC issues a semimonthly bulletin, *Peace Courier,* in English, French, Spanish, and German; a quarterly journal, *New Perspectives,* in English and French; an occasional *Letter to National Committees;* and a *Letter* to members.

Hoover Institution
Stanford University   George Duca

CONFERENCE OF COMMUNIST AND WORKERS' PARTIES OF EUROPE

The Conference of Communist and Workers' Parties of Europe, held in East Berlin on 29-30 June 1976, was the second conference of that type, the first having taken place at Karlovy Vary, Czechoslovakia, on 24-26 April 1967 (see *YICA, 1968*, pp. 753-57). The subject of the East Berlin Conference was: "For Peace, Security, Cooperation and Social Progress in Europe." In conclusion of its deliberations, the Conference adopted a final document under the same name. Delegations from 29 Communist and workers' parties were present in East Berlin, while 24 participating parties attended the Karlovy Vary meeting.

Background. The Karlovy Vary European Conference was followed by the International Meeting of Communist and Workers' Parties, gathering in Moscow on 5-17 June 1969. (See *YICA, 1970*, pp. 789-95.) This was the third world conference since the dissolution of the Communist International, the first and the second having been held in 1957 and 1960. It was the result of a consultative meeting of Communist and workers' parties on 26 February-5 March 1968 in Budapest. (See *YICA, 1969*, pp. 997-1007.)

In early December 1973, János Kádár, the first secretary of the Hungarian Socialist Workers' Party, and Todor Zhivkov, the head of the Bulgarian Communist Party, advanced the idea of a new Communist world conference. They were supported by a *Pravda* article (5 June 1974) written on the occasion of the fifth anniversary of the Moscow 1969 world conference. Since apparently several Asian and European parties opposed the holding of a new world conference, wanting to avoid a possible condemnation of the Chinese Communist Party by a Soviet-dominated majority, the idea of a world conference was abandoned. Instead, on an Italian-Polish initiative, a preliminary consultative conference with the task of discussing the organization of a gathering of European Communist parties convened on 16-18 October 1974 in Warsaw. Representatives of 28 European parties attended and unanimously decided to hold the conference not later than June of 1975.

That date was not kept because a special editorial commission (composed of representatives of all of the participating parties) as well as a smaller editorial subcommittee (whose members were delegates of the Soviet, East German, Romanian, Yugoslav, Italian, French, Spanish, and Danish parties), needed some 16 sessions over a period of 20 months to reach agreement on a text which the East Berlin conference would endorse. (For a review of the work of some of the editorial commission and subcommittee meetings see *Keesing's Contemporary Archives*, 30 April, 24 September 1976.) The representatives of the Communist Party of the Soviet Union (CPSU) were reportedly eager to see the conference take place before the 25th Congress of their party (February-March 1976), and since interparty disagreements made this impossible, there were hints in the press that the Soviets were considering writing off the "unity" conference (*Christian Science Monitor*, 6 April). In fact, Soviet party leader Leonid Brezhnev in his report to the 25th CPSU Congress sounded vague about the conference's chances, and had nothing more to say than that it was in the process of preparation. At the subsequent congress, in May, of the East German party (which was in charge of the European conference), differences of opinion were publicly vented, and doubts about the general conference persisted. As late as 12 June, after the final preparatory meeting in East Berlin, discords appeared to dim the prospects for the long-awaited conference (*NYT*, 13 June).

The disagreements mentioned above revolved essentially around the problem of relations between the CPSU and some other Communist parties, East and West, such as the Yugoslav, Romanian, Italian, Spanish, and French. Various Western commentators used the terms "centralizers" and "autonomists" to describe those who differed on the future internal relationships within the international Communist movement. The concept of "proletarian internationalism" figured most prominently in the debates, becoming the touchstone for those who favored or rejected the role and the right of the CPSU to be "the center" of the movement, i.e., continuing to have the prerogative of establishing the general line and imposing collective discipline on all other parties.

This was certainly not the only controversial issue. The concept of "Eurocommunism," that is, of some specific distinguishing qualities of the Communist parties of Western Europe, putting them apart from those of Eastern Europe, and used most often by the Italians, was another one. It was not only unacceptable to the CPSU (and therefore unmentionable in any official Conference documents) but was criticized by some Western European Communist leaders otherwise in league with the Italians. Santiago Carrillo, the head of the Spanish party, argued that the very name would eliminate the Japan Communist Party, in many respects very close to the West Europeans. Georges Marchais, the secretary-general of the French party, objected to the "emergence of a new center within the international Communist movement" (in his interview given to the Rome newspaper *Paese Sera*, 13 June). The French Communists, moreover, while sharing the "autonomist" views of some others, insisted on a more militant document, with a strong emphasis on "the aggravation of the crisis of Capitalism" and the necessity to "combine détente with resolute struggle against imperialism" (*L'Humanité*, Paris, 14 May). Soviet diplomatic praises for the foreign policy of President Giscard d'Estaing were pointedly referred to by a French Communist spokesman as "lacking proletarian internationalism" (*Le Monde*, Paris, 28-29 March). Finally, Tito and the LCY representative at all the East Berlin conference preparations, Aleksandar Grličkov, adamantly insisted on their usual "autonomist" themes, the best known of which is probably the formula that "every party is responsible for its policy exclusively to its own working class and its own people."

Under these circumstances the mere holding of a general conference depended on compromises and quid pro quos. It is believed that the Italians were the "master compromisers," stressing Communist consensus as the pre-condition to everybody's participation. This was clearly stated by a member of the Italian party's Central Committee who asserted that "a document acceptable to all could only be one that identified points of convergence, without claiming to delineate general lines and strategies, to take on a binding character, or to tackle themes—including ideological questions—on which there exist diverse and divergent positions" (*L'Unità*, Rome, 14 February). Likewise, visits to Romania at the end of May, and to Yugoslavia on 7 June, by Konstantin Katushev, the CPSU secretary for relations with ruling parties, are credited with clearing up the path to (nearly) everyone's trip to East Berlin.

Participants. All the controversies notwithstanding, and as already noted, the East Berlin Conference was better attended than the preceding one at Karlovy Vary. On that occasion the absentee parties included those of Albania, Romania, Yugoslavia, Iceland, Netherlands, Norway, and Turkey. This time the only parties which did not send representatives to East Berlin were the Albanian Party of Labor, and the United Socialist Party of Iceland. The Communist Party of Netherlands did not take part in the preparatory work of the conference but sent its delegate to the East Berlin meeting.

Here is then the list of who represented which party in East Berlin:

Communist Party of Belgium, headed by Jean Terfve, vice-chairman of the party
Bulgarian Communist Party, headed by Todor Zhivkov, first secretary of the Central Committee

Communist Party of Denmark, headed by Knud Jespersen, chairman of the party

German Communist Party, headed by Herbert Mies, chairman of the party

Socialist Unity Party of Germany, headed by Erich Honecker, general secretary of the Central Committee

Communist Party of Finland, headed by Aarne Saarinen, chairman of the party

French Communist Party, headed by Georges Marchais, general secretary of the party

Communist Party of Greece, headed by Harilaos Florakis, first secretary of the Central Committee

Communist Party of Great Britain, headed by Gordon McLennan, general secretary of the party

Communist Party of Ireland, headed by Michael O'Riordan, general secretary of the party

Italian Communist Party, headed by Enrico Berlinguer, general secretary of the party

League of Communists of Yugoslavia, headed by Josip Broz Tito, chairman of the party

Communist Party of Luxembourg, headed by Dominique Urbany, chairman of the party

Communist Party of the Netherlands, headed by Henk Hoekstra, chairman of the party

Communist Party of Norway, headed by Martin Gunnar Knutsen, chairman of the party

Communist Party of Austria, headed by Franz Muhri, chairman of the party

Polish United Workers' Party, headed by Edward Gierek, first secretary of the Central Committee

Portuguese Communist Party, headed by Alvaro Cunhal, general secretary of the party

Romanian Communist Party, headed by Nicolae Ceauşescu, general secretary of the party

San Marino Communist Party, headed by Ermenegildo Gasperoni, chairman of the party

Left Party—Communists of Sweden, headed by Lars Werner, chairman of the party

Swiss Party of Labor, headed by Jakob Lechleiter, member of the Politburo and secretary of the Central Committee

Communist Party of the Soviet Union, headed by Leonid I. Brezhnev, general secretary of the Central Committee

Communist Party of Spain, headed by Santiago Carrillo, general secretary of the party

Communist Party of Czechoslovakia, headed by Gustav Husák, general secretary of the Central Committee

Communist Party of Turkey, headed by Ismail Bilen, general secretary of the Central Committee

Hungarian Socialist Workers' Party, headed by János Kádár, first secretary of the Central Committee

Socialist Unity Party of West Berlin, headed by Erich Ziegler, deputy chairman of the party

Progressive Party of Working People of Cyprus (AKEL), headed by Christos Petas, member of the Politburo of the Central Committee

Speeches. The Conference was opened on 29 June, in the big conference room of the 39-story Stadt Berlin Hotel, and in the presence of 114 delegates. The host, Erich Honecker, general secretary of the East German Socialist Unity Party, stated in his opening remarks that the 29 delegations represented more than 29,000,000 Communists. Since no special agenda was established, and no time for debate foreseen, the two days of the Conference were filled with speeches prepared in advance: the head of each delegation had 30 minutes to develop his views, the sole exception being Leonid Brezhnev, who spoke for more than an hour.

Brezhnev's address, accommodating and non-polemical vis-à-vis other Communist parties, but tough toward domestic and international "class enemies," covered essentially three themes. First, he reiterated the main tenets of Soviet foreign policy, and spoke proudly of the "stable, dynamic and united" society created in the Soviet Union. He stressed that the USSR and other socialist states were complying much more faithfully with the conclusions of the 1975 Helsinki Conference than the countries of the West. He attacked bourgeois propaganda for inventing a myth of a Socialist "closed society," but warned that "we shall not give freedom for subversive actions against our system, our society." Second, he depicted in highly optimistic terms the development of events in the world, seeing them as "increasingly determined by the anti-imperialist forces." There were several categories of such forces which Brezhnev warmly praised or favorably commented upon. He was most assertive while speaking of the "fraternal solidarity of the socialist countries," and the "profound, organic and ever-growing friendly ties between party and state organs." This was, according to him, "an absolutely new phenomenon—a truly fraternal union of peoples that have commonly held views and goals. The comradeship in arms of the Marxist-Leninist parties constitutes the strong foundation of this union, its cementing force." (It should be noted that Communist China and Albania were never mentioned in his speech.) Then came the "ardent greetings" to all the participants in the national liberation movement, to whom Brezhnev pledged "our invariable support to their just struggle for the freedom, independence and progressive development of their countries." Besides expressing his satisfaction that "Socialism is already deeply rooted in many countries" of Asia, Africa, and Latin America, he had kind words for "a considerable role in international life played by the non-alignment movement." Next, Brezhnev declared that "We, for our part, always solidarize with the struggle waged by our class brothers in the camp of capitalism and strive to give them moral and political support." He congratulated especially the Italian Communist Party for its "outstanding success" in the recent parliamentary elections. Finally, in a sort of a "united front" anti-capitalist appeal, Brezhnev said that it was "of special importance [to unite] in the struggles against reactionary imperialist circles with broad democratic streams, including Social Democrats and Christians."

The third and most important theme of Brezhnev's speech—the relations among European Communist parties—had two main characteristics. One was his readiness not only to compromise with the "autonomist" current, but even to accept as his own their chief arguments, including terminology. At one point he sounded like a "Titoist," saying that "Every Communist party is . . . responsible for its actions first of all before the working people of its own country, whose interests it expresses and defends." He went on then to assuage all those who feared that he might harbor a desire to recreate some organizational center:

> Strange apprehension. So far as is known, no one and nowhere has put forth the idea of creating such a center. As to proletarian internationalism, that is, the solidarity of the working class, of the Communists of all countries in the struggle for common goals, their solidarity with the struggle of the peoples for national liberation and social progress, the voluntary cooperation of fraternal parties, while strictly observing the equality and independence of each of them—we believe such comradely solidarity of which the Communists have been the standard-bearers for more than a hundred years, preserves all its great significance also in our time. It was and remains the powerful and tested tool of the communist parties and the working-class movement in general.

The second characteristic of this part of Brezhnev's speech was his reminder to his listeners that "proletarian internationalism"—to which he expressly referred several times in his text—was a concept he continued to hold essential for a proper understanding of Marxism-Leninism: "Our party," he said, "being loyal to the great ideas of proletarian internationalism, has never separated the destinies of the Soviet Union from those of other countries of Europe and the rest of the world." Mixing, no doubt intentionally, the terms "proletarian internationalism" and "voluntary cooperation" of all the Communist parties, he ended his address with another optimistic note: "We are convinced that the results of our conference, which raised high the banner of unity of European communists, will help to pool our efforts, to activise our joint struggle for the vital interests of working people, for democracy and socialism, and lasting peace in Europe." (All preceding quotations from Brezhnev's speech are taken from the English text broadcast by TASS on 29 June, as reproduced in *FBIS*, 30 June; the *NYT* of the same day also printed excerpts from the speech.)

Brezhnev's approach was strongly supported by the majority of the Conference's speakers, belonging to both the ruling and the non-ruling Communist parties. They unreservedly hailed the Soviet Union and the CPSU, endorsed "proletarian internationalism," and assailed "anti-Sovietism" as a weapon used by the enemies of the entire Communist movement. For Gustav Husák the fight against anti-Sovietism was "a matter of honor." Erich Honecker asserted that while there might be different opinions on certain questions, "what is decisive is what unites us." He also extolled the "close fraternal alliance with the USSR in particular." János Kádár and Edward Gierek followed suit in somewhat more subdued and conventional terms. The leaders of many non-ruling parties sounded even more determinedly pro-Soviet, especially those of the Portuguese, Norwegian, Austrian, West German, Greek, Turkish, and Cypriot parties. The general secretary of the Turkish party, for example, regretted that the term "proletarian internationalism" was excised and replaced by that of "international solidarity" in the basic document of the Conference, and that no mention of the Soviet Union had been made while referring to the international revolutionary process. (*Keesing's Contemporary Archives*, 24 September, contains large excerpts of many speeches made at the Conference, as does the *NYT* of 1 July.)

The speeches of the "autonomist" party leaders drew large public attention around the world, and some of their formulations were not printed in the Soviet press. They also were of different intensity and originality. Tito's speech reaffirmed "the principles of independence, equality and non-interference, as the foundations for cooperation among communist and workers' parties." At the same time the head of the LCY offered statements which could only please the Soviet leaders. He spoke, for example, of the "deep crisis of the capitalist system which aggravates old and new contradictions," stressed the "extended assistance [Yugoslavia had offered in recent years] to the liberation struggle of the peoples of Vietnam, Cambodia, Laos, Angola, and in general to all national liberation movements and imperiled peoples," and endorsed the Marxist postulate that "class struggle is waged on a worldwide scale." He ended his speech with the averment that "socialism as a world process is breaking new ground and winning new victories." (The full text of Tito's speech in English may be found in Belgrade's *Review of International Affairs*, 30 June.)

The Romanian party chief, Nicolae Ceauşescu, delivered a speech of a pure "national communism" vintage. He stated bluntly that "it is definitely no longer either possible or necessary to have an international [Communist] center." In his view "the nation has had and will continue to have for a long period of time a fundamental importance in the life of human society." He then tempered that statement by adding that "between national duties and those pertaining to the international solidarity of the Communist parties there is a complete dialectical unity, as the two of them condition each other." (AGERPRES, in English, 29 June; *FBIS*, 30 June.)

The most unorthodox speeches came, as expected, from the leaders of the three most important Western European parties: Italian, French, and Spanish. The founding father of "Eurocommunism," Enrico Berlinguer, general secretary of the Italian Communist Party, reviewed his favorite topics about the necessity for Communist—domestic and international, doctrinal and tactical—innovations. In his eyes the East Berlin Conference was "a free gathering of independent and equal parties, a meeting which does not impose directives or obligations on any party. . . . Each party independently works out its own domestic and international political line and decides on it in complete independence." Calling for "the abandonment of obsolete methods," he argued that the entire movement for social and political liberation, in each country and internationally, extends beyond the Communist parties, and that aspirations toward socialism do not stem only from the working class. After paying tribute to the October Revolution of 1917, which "opened up a completely new road not only for the peoples of the Soviet Union but also for the whole of mankind," he asserted that today "the task again arises . . . of seeking new roads to socialism in the countries of the European West." The roads followed by the Social Democratic parties had proved incapable of overcoming capitalism, while Eastern European socialist models do not correspond to the particular conditions of Western European societies. Development in the elaboration of Marxism had not kept pace with the transformations taking place in the world. Mentioning his party's criticism of Soviet behavior in Czechoslovakia in August of 1968, Berlinguer concluded that only free and open discussions on the basic issues could help the progress of the workers' movement, making socialism more attractive particularly for the younger generation. (East Berlin Radio, 30 June; *FBIS*, 1 July.)

Berlinguer's French counterpart, Georges Marchais, discoursed along similar lines albeit with different, Gallic, emphases. He linked together socialism, democracy, and liberty, and explained that this was the reason why the 22d Congress of the French Communist Party, held in February 1976, eliminated from its program the concept of the dictatorship of the proletariat. "Socialism in France," he exclaimed, "will be a socialism in the colors of France." With greater bluntness than Berlinguer, Marchais stated that "as far as we are concerned conferences such as this no longer meet the requirements of our time," adding that "the elaboration of a strategy common to all our parties is completely out of the question." He went on, then, to outline the efforts of his party to consolidate "the unity of the left," and to remain "the vanguard of social and human progress." Again with greater vigor than the Italian leader, Marchais insisted on the friendship with the ruling Communist parties and on the French party's internationalist solidarity, while criticizing—without mentioning its name—the Soviet Union for cooperating in the name of peaceful coexistence with the capitalist regimes, hindering in this way "the struggle we are waging against the might of big business, for democracy and socialism." (East Berlin Radio, 30 June; *FBIS*, 1 July.)

But it remained for the Spanish Communist leader, Santiago Carrillo, to make the most original and resounding speech, one of whose paragraphs will probably be quoted in the years to come:

> We Communists were born and grew up in conditions of struggle and persecution comparable only to the conditions experienced by the primitive Christians. . . . The sufferings which our parties have borne and still do . . . have created among our rank and file an alloy made of scientific socialism and a kind of mysticism based on sacrifice and predestination. We have built a sort of new church with our martyrs and prophets. Moscow, where our dreams first began to come true, was for a long time a kind of Rome for us. We spoke of the Great October Socialist Revolution as if it were our Christmas. This was the period of our infancy. Today we have grown up. . . . We are beginning to lose the characteristics of a church. The scientific content of our theories is taking on aspects of faith and the mysticism of predestination.

While agreeing with Berlinguer and Marchais that "Today we Communists have no leadership center, and are not tied to any international discipline," Carrillo saw the intra-Communist differences as "a sign of maturity and strength." The nuances of his formulations were both more subtle and candid than those of his Italian and French colleagues. He admitted, for example, that singling out national peculiarities was also a helpful device against "the reactionary forces which are bent on combating us by alluding to non-existent international discipline." Likewise, ruling out the achievement of socialism with dictatorial measures, rejecting the one-party system, and accepting the verdict of universal suffrage, Carrillo warned that "We do not rule out that democratic liberties must be defended with the use of force if they are exposed to the danger of a coup d'état on the part of reactionary minorities which have been defeated in elections." And more insistently than anyone else, the Spanish Communist leader argued in favor of "reaching an agreement with socialists, social democrats, Christians, radicals and all others of a democratic nature, in order to create a bloc of those forces having roots in the people." (Radio independent Spain [clandestine], 30 June; *FBIS*, 1 July.)

The Final Document. The special character of the East Berlin Conference could also be seen in the fact that its final document, 47 pages long, was not signed, or endorsed by vote, but merely issued without any usual titles such as "declaration" or "communiqué" or even "joint statement" (*NYT*, 1 July). The document consists of a long preamble ending with an appeal to the broadest masses of the

European population to work actively for the following four objectives (each developed into a series of concrete proposals): (1) For strengthening the process of détente by taking effective measures toward disarmament and toward strengthening security in Europe; (2) For extirpating fascism, defending democracy and national independence; (3) For the development of mutually beneficial cooperation, for better understanding among peoples; and (4) For peace, security, cooperation, national independence and social progress in the whole of the world.

The very length of the document, as well as its repetitiousness, precludes its full reproduction here. Since the preamble contains the most significant formulations of agreement on basic issues among all the participants at the East Berlin Conference, five points will be quoted here, with added subtitles (not existing in the original text):

The Present Crisis of Capitalism

The difficulties imperialism is going through are the result of the further aggravation of the general crisis of the capitalist system which affects all spheres of capitalist society — economic, social, moral and political — and manifests itself in various forms and dimensions in different countries. Such characteristic features of the current serious crisis as chronic inflation, the crisis of the monetary system, the fact that productive capacities are increasingly underused, and the unemployment of millions of working people are making themselves felt with particular intensity. Everywhere the crisis entails serious consequences for the working and living conditions of the working class, peasants and farmers, and the middle strata, hitting young people, women and foreign workers especially severely. It is accompanied by manifestations of moral decay and by upheavals which testify to its political nature.

The crisis leads to profound contradictions in international political and economic relations. It is also manifest in serious trade conflicts, in merciless competition between the monopoly groups of various countries, including those of the EEC countries, and in the contradictions between the capitalist monopolies and the developing countries.

All this proves that the economic and social structure of capitalist society is becoming more and more inconsistent with the needs of the working and popular masses and with the requirements of social progress and of democratic political development.

The working class and all working people in the capitalist-dominated part of Europe are struggling for a democratic way out of the crisis which would correspond to the interests of the broad mass of the people and open up the way for a socialist transformation of society.

The Independence of Communist Parties

The Communist and Workers' Parties of the European countries . . . will develop their internationalist, comradely and voluntary cooperation and solidarity on the basis of the great ideas of Marx, Engels and Lenin, strictly adhering to the principles of equality and sovereign independence of each Party, non-interference in internal affairs, and respect for their free choice of different roads in the struggle for social change of a progressive nature and for socialism. . . .

. . . The participants in the Conference emphasize that their Parties, on the basis of a political line worked out and adopted by every Party in complete independence in accordance with the socio-economic and political conditions and the specific national features prevailing in the country concerned, are firmly resolved to continue waging a consistent struggle in order to achieve the objectives of peace, democracy and social progress, which is in line with the general interests of the working class, the democratic forces and the mass of the people in all countries.

Peaceful Coexistence and Détente

The participants state with all clarity that the policy of peaceful coexistence, active cooperation between states irrespective of their social systems, and international détente correspond both to the interests of each people as well as to the cause of progress for the whole of mankind and in no way mean the maintenance of the political and social status quo in the various countries, but on the contrary create optimum conditions for the development of the struggle of the working class and all democratic forces as well as for the implementation of the inalienable right of each and every people freely to choose and follow its own course of development for the struggle against the rule of monopolies, and for socialism.

The participants in the Conference note that essential positive changes have taken place in the international situation which are the result of the shift in the balance of forces in favor of the cause of peace, democracy, national liberation, independence and socialism, and the result of the intensified struggle by the mass of the people and broad political and social forces. This has led to the process of transition from a policy of tension and confrontation to the implementation of the course toward détente and the normalization and all-round development of new relations and cooperation between states and peoples.

Anti-communism and Anti-sovietism

The Communist and Workers' Parties consider it their duty to direct the attention of all popular forces to the damage done by aggressive anti-communism to the development of the movement for peace and progress. The Communist Parties do not consider all those who are not in agreement with their policies or who hold a critical attitude toward their activity as being anti-communist. Anti-communism is and remains an instrument which imperialist and reactionary forces use not only against Communists but also against other democrats and against the Communist Parties, the socialist countries, beginning with the Soviet Union, against the forces of socialism and progress, campaigns which aim to discredit the policy and the ideals of Communists among the mass of the people and to prevent unity within the working-class movement and cooperation among the democratic and popular forces. It is in the interests of the aspiration of the popular forces for progress and for democratic development to isolate and overcome anti-communism.

Relations with Other Political Forces

The participants consider dialogue and cooperation between Communists and all other democratic and peace-loving forces as necessary. In this, they base themselves on what they all have in common and stand for the removal of mistrust and prejudices which may hamper their cooperation. . . .

. . . The participants in the Conference welcome the successes achieved in a number of countries and at international levels in developing cooperation between Communist and socialist or social-democratic parties. They consider that the basic interests of the working class and of all working people require the overcoming of the obstacles which stand in the way of cooperation and which complicate the struggle of the mass of working people against monopoly capital and against the reactionary and conservative forces. . . .

. . . The influence of the working class is growing through the unification of efforts by its trade union organizations both at national and international levels. Communists will continue in every respect to support the drive for unity which is growing in the trade union organizations and their independent activities.

Ever broader Catholic forces, members of other Christian communities and adherents to other faiths play an important role in the struggle for the rights of the working people and for democracy and peace. The Communist and Workers' Parties recognize the necessity of dialogue and joint action with these forces, which is an inseparable part of the struggle for the development of Europe in a spirit of democracy and in the direction of social progress.

In the following four specific parts of the final document, the European Communist parties enumerated at length the measures that should be taken "to guarantee the durability of détente," in both military and political fields. They pleaded for an end to the arms race in all forms, particularly nuclear armament; the dismantling of foreign military bases; and a systematic reduction of the military budgets of all states. They called for "an immediate end to repression in Spain," welcomed "the progressive development taking place in the new Portugal," and expressed their solidarity with the people of Cyprus. The same feelings of solidarity were extended to the struggle of democratic forces in Greece and Northern Ireland. They "emphatically demanded the legalization of the Communist Party of Turkey," and expressed opposition to "any discrimination against and persecution of Communists and other progressive forces, and to anti-democratic legislation barring Communists and other democrats from certain types of employment in the Federal Republic of Germany." In many places of the final document the holding and the results of the 1975 Helsinki Conference on Security and Cooperation in Europe were hailed in most emphatic terms.

The participants in the Conference also pleaded for "a just overall settlement of the Middle East conflict guaranteeing the withdrawal of Israeli troops from all Arab territory occupied since 1967." They expressed support for the peoples of Vietnam, Laos, and Cambodia "in their endeavors to repair the damage suffered by them in the war of aggression." Support was also promised to the government and people of the People's Republic of Angola, the Democratic People's Republic of Korea, and the anti-imperialist struggle of the Arab peoples, the peoples of South Africa, Namibia, and Zimbabwe. They asked for the release of "all Chilean patriots and democrats imprisoned by the fascist junta," as well as "an immediate end to the acts of terror and reprisal being perpetuated against Communists and other democrats in Uruguay, Paraguay, Guatemala and a number of other Latin American countries." They also advocated "strict compliance with the trade embargoes imposed on racist regimes under UN resolutions, severance of relations with the government of the Republic of South Africa by all states, and, most important, a complete stop to all arms supplies to that government." They upheld the elimination of colonialism and neo-colonialism and the establishment of a new international economic order. (Identical texts of the Conference's final document were printed in *World Marxist Review*, vol. 19, no. 8, August 1976, and in *FBIS*, 1 July.)

Reactions to the Conference and Its Significance. The East Berlin Communist summit has caused countless comments, East and West, many of which have been recorded in the profiles of individual Communist parties prepared for this Yearbook. To complete, however, the survey of the Conference itself, it may be appropriate to mention some of the most typical reactions to a reunion which took so long to be arranged and then unfolded in ways unprecedented in the history of the international Communist movement.

Soviet official comments on the Conference were uniformly positive. Boris Ponomarev, secretary of the CPSU Central Committee in charge of relations with the non-ruling Communist parties, wrote an article for the journal *Kommunist*, organ of the CPSU Central Committee, about the East Berlin gathering. According to him the Conference has added to the prestige of the Communist and Workers' parties — "the most influential political force of the times." Among many of the Conference's merits which the author enumerated, three appeared outstanding: it was "the broadest communist forum in the history of the revolutionary working-class movement in Europe"; it achieved "unanimity on major problems of the times"; and it projected "organic integration of the struggle for peace and the struggle for social progress." (TASS, 30 July; *FBIS*, 2 August.) Identical views, only discussed on a broader basis, were expressed on Moscow's TV program "Studio Nine" on 20 July. Among the discussants of the East Berlin Conference was Vadim Zagladin, first deputy chief of the International Section of the CPSU Central Committee. He and two of his colleagues highly placed in the CPSU hierarchy reviewed practically all the aspects of the Conference. Discussing at one point the issue of Communist China, they noted that "the mass media of that country were as silent as a tomb during the Conference," but insisted that "our policy is not one of excommunicating China, it is a policy for the return of the Chinese Communist Party to the bosom of the Communist family." Their only intra-Communist polemical remark concerned the term "Eurocommunism" which one of them described as "an attempt to isolate the communist parties [i.e., Western European, but without singling out any one specifically] into a separate and isolated group." (It is interesting to note that in the same context a reference was made to Professor Zbigniew Brzezinski as a promoter of Communist divisions.) The discussants emphasized Leonid Brezhnev's "internationalist" speech at the Conference, and informed the viewers that he had 13 meetings with individual Communist leaders while in East Berlin. Zagladin also stated that "in recent years our party has held more than 200 meetings annually with communist parties from other countries." (*FBIS*, 3 August.)

Four members of the editorial board of the *World Marxist Review*, who are also high officials of the Danish, Irish, Bulgarian, and Greek Communist parties, offered their appraisal of the Conference in the September issue of the magazine. They carefully balanced the successful and the problematic aspects of the Conference, maximizing the former and reducing the impact of the latter. Their favorable comments referred especially to three items: "A maximum number of participants, including parties which for a long time and for various reasons had stayed away from such meetings"; their certainty that "in spite of divergences over this or that issue, the Communists of Europe *are at one on the principal and fundamental problems of today*" (italics in the text); and, another certainty, that "Now as in the past, the Communists are firm primarily in their principled, uncompromising class stand on capitalism and the imperialist system." On the other hand, the authors dealt in general terms with "divergent views" among participants, and assailed "the imperialist agents-provocateurs, who wanted to foment centrifugal trends in the communist movement at all costs." Claiming that these disruptive attempts failed and that the capitalist press will be proven wrong in suggesting that the East Berlin meeting was "the 'swan song' of internationalism and that it had 'neither a past, nor a future,' " the authors glorified Leonid Brezhnev's "forceful and profound speech" at the Conference: "The speech, which deeply impressed the participants in the Conference, was inspired by genuine proletarian internationalism. It contained an in-depth Marxist-Leninist analysis of the problems of the struggle for peace, security and social progress facing the communist movement of Europe and the world."

The Yugoslav press, unanimously, praised the "autonomist" aspects of the Conference, and the same was largely true for the other parties with the same inclinations. The Western, especially American, commentators put in general their emphases—with idiosyncratic variations—on two elements: Communist diversity and militancy, emerging in an unusual light both before and at the East Berlin conclave. Many observers had expected a new, European Communist schism like the one that developed between Moscow and Peking in 1960. They concluded, however, that Moscow's concessions to the near-heretics in the West averted—at least for the time being—the new split. Without entering into details one may describe two manners of viewing the significance of the East Berlin meeting according to Western observers.

For one school of thought, the unity of the movement was threatened by the dissident Western European Communists, personified in Santiago Carrillo—"a sort of collective Martin Luther demanding radical change" (from an editorial entitled "Red Reformation?" in the *NYT* of 14 August). The same idea was put differently by C. L. Sulzberger who wrote that "A new generation of Titoism—Western and non-Slavic—is dividing the Communist world" (ibid., 30 June). Brezhnev's acceptance of the open rejection of the Kremlin's control by the most prominent Western Communist leaders, codified in the Conference's final document, had "permanently weakened the Soviet Union as a center of world communism" for a commentator of the *Baltimore Sun* (1 July). Quoting "senior U.S. government analysts," an influential conservative weekly ran a survey entitled "In Next Decade—Breakup of Communist World?" (*U.S. News and World Report*, 9 August). Three main reasons were given for such an appraisal: an unending Sino-Soviet conflict; the dissension of Western European Communists parties, and an uneasy Soviet domination of Eastern Europe. To reinforce the importance of that last element, one should add the often advanced argument that insistence on personal freedoms and political pluralism on the part of Western Communist leaders could have a profound impact on the political situation in Eastern Europe.

Proponents of the other school of thought would advance different arguments. Without denying Brezhnev's problems with the obstreperous Western European parties, they would insist on his success in maintaining Communist solidarity against the West (see James Burnham's article "The International Party" in the *National Review* of 24 December). Brezhnev's recognition of Communist diversity while calling for Communist unity has allowed him to end Yugoslavia's 19-year boycott of international Communist conferences, and to rivet Fidel Castro, once a critic, more firmly than ever to the Communist bloc (see Peter Osnos's dispatch from Moscow in the *Washington Post*, 12 July). Likewise, the endorsement by the participants of the East Berlin Conference of the basic tenets of Soviet foreign policy would prove that "the conflicts between the Italian Communist Party and the Soviet Union have virtually nothing to do with foreign policy" (*Commentary*, New York, vol. 62, no. 5, November, p. 51). This brings forward the factor of "electoralism," namely the awareness of the experienced and intelligent Western European Communist leaders that the most effective way to break their decades-long and sterile situation of political isolation is to dispel popular apprehension of their traditional loyalties to Moscow. As for their new democratic terminology, "The Communist parties [in the West] maintain their authoritarian internal discipline, and 'popular front' tactical alliances with other 'progressive' forces are an old game" (*Wall Street Journal*, 6 July).

It is impossible, of course, to know which of these predictions and observations will prove to be correct in a longer perspective. Conflicts among the Communists are as old, and sometimes as intensive, as their enmity toward the "class" enemies. Consequently, the future only will tell whether the East Berlin Conference was the catalyst of that historically momentous Communist break-up, or on the contrary a new departure for a better-adjusted militant movement.

The Hoover Institution   Milorad M. Drachkovitch
Stanford University

SELECT BIBLIOGRAPHY 1974-75

GENERAL ON COMMUNISM

Baechler, Jean. *Revolution*. New York, Harper & Row, 1975. 206 pp.

Bertsch, Gary K., and Thomas W. Ganschow. *Comparative Communism: The Soviet, Chinese, and Yugoslav Models*. San Francisco, Freeman, 1976. 463 pp.

Brus, Wlodzimierz. *Socialist Ownership and Political Systems*. London, Routledge & Paul, 1975. 222 pp.

Cassinelli, C. W. *Total Revolution: A Comparative Study of Germany under Hitler, the Soviet Union under Stalin, and China under Mao*. Santa Barbara, Ca., Clio Press, 1976. 244 pp.

Chambre, Henri. *De Karl Marx à Lénine et Mao Tse-toung*. Paris, Aubier Montaigne, 1976. 413 pp.

Claudin, Fernando. *The Communist Movement: From Comintern to Cominform*. New York, Monthly Review Press, 1976. 2 v.

Cohan, A. S. *Theories of Revolution*: An Introduction. New York, Halsted Press, 1976. 250 pp.

Craipeau, Ivan, et al. *Detente and Socialist Democracy: A Discussion with Roy Medvedev*. New York, Monad Press, 1976. 163 pp.

Crozier, Brian (ed.). *Annual of Power and Conflict 1975-76*. London, Institute for Study of Conflict, 1976. 232 pp.

Desfosses, Helen, and Jacques Levesque. *Socialism in the Third World*, New York, Praeger, 1975. 338 pp.

Duve, Freimut. *Kommunismus ohne Wachstum?* Reinbek bei Hamburg, Rowohlt, 1975. 206 pp.

Fedoseyev, P. N., et al. *Leninist Theory of Socialist Revolution and the Contemporary World*. Moscow, Progress, 1975. 447 pp.

Feiwel, George R. *Growth and Reform in Centrally Planned Economies*. New York, Praeger, 1976. 375 pp.

Feuer, Lewis S. *Ideology and the Ideologists*. New York, Harper & Row, 1975. 220 pp.

Field, Mark G. (ed.). *Social Consequences of Modernization in Communist Societies*. Baltimore, Md., Johns Hopkins University Press, 1976. 277 pp.

Griffith, William E. (ed.). *The World and the Great-Power Triangles*. Cambridge, Mass., MIT Press, 1975. 480 pp.

Hajek, Milos. *Storia dell'Internazionale Comunista (1921-1935)*. Rome, Riuniti, 1975. 334 pp.

Holzman, Franklyn D. *International Trade under Communism*. New York, Basic Books, 1976. 239 pp.

Leonhard, Wolfgang. *Was ist Kommunismus?: Wandlungen einer Ideologie*. Munich, Bertelsmann, 1976. 269 pp.

Longley, Alcander. *What is Communism?* New York, AMS Press, 1976. 413 pp.

Losovsky, Drizdo. *L'Internationale Syndicale Rouge*. Paris, Maspero, 1976. 213 pp.

Low, Alfred D. *The Sino-Soviet Dispute: an Analysis of the Polemics*. Rutherford, N.J., Fairleigh Dickinson University Press, 1976. 364 pp.

Mazlish, Bruce. *The Revolutionary Ascetic: Evolution of a Political Type*. New York, Basic Books, 1976. 261 pp.

Rummel, R. J. *Peace Endangered: The Reality of Détente*. Beverly Hills, Ca., Sage, 1976. 189 pp.

Salert, Barbara. *Revolutions and Revolutionaries*. New York, Elsevier, 1976. 161 pp.

Sarkesian, Sam C. (ed.) *Revolutionary Guerrilla Warfare*. Chicago, Precedent, 1975. 623 pp.

Simon, Jeffrey. *Ruling Communist Parties and Detente: A Documentary History*. Washington, D.C., American Enterprise Institute, 1975. 314 pp.

Staar, Richard F. (ed.) *1976 Yearbook on International Communist Affairs*. Stanford, Ca., Hoover Institution Press, 1976. 636 pp.

Szawlowski, Richard. *The System of the International Organizations of the Communist Countries*. Leyden, Sijthoff, 1976. 322 pp.

Thornton, Judith. *Analysis of the Soviet-Type System*. New York, Cambridge University Press, 1976. 372 pp.

Todd, Emmanuel. *La Chute finale: essai sur la décomposition de la sphère soviétique*. Paris, Laffont, 1976. 323 pp.

Ulam, Adam. *Ideologies and Illusions: Revolutionary Thought from Herzen to Solzhenitsyn*. Cambridge, Mass., Harvard University Press, 1976. 335 pp.

Vincent, Jean-Marie, et al. *L'Etat Contemporain et le Marxisme*. Paris, Maspéro, 1975. 232 pp.

Wesson, Robert G. *Why Marxism? The Continuing Success of a Failed Theory*. New York, Basic Books, 1976. 218 pp.

SOVIET UNION

Abosch, Heinz. *Trotzki und der Bolschwismus*. Basel, Edition Etcetera, 1975. 199 pp.

Afanasev, Viktor G. *The Scientific and Technological Revolution: Its Impact on Management and Education*. Moscow, Progress, 1975. 320 pp.

Andrle, Vladimir. *Managerial Power in the Soviet Union*. Lexington, Mass., Saxon House Books, 1976. 176 pp.

Ascher, Abraham (ed.). *The Mensheviks in the Russian Revolution*. London, Thames & Hudson, 1976. 147 pp.

Avtorkhanov, Abdurakhman. *Zagadka smerti Stalina*. Frankfurt, Possev, 1975. 316 pp.

Barghoorn, Frederick C. *Detente and the Democratic Movement in the USSR*. New York, Free Press, 1976. 229 pp.

Berliner, Joseph S., *The Innovation Decision in Soviet Industry*. Cambridge, Mass., MIT Press, 1976. 561 pp.

Besançon, Alain. *Court traité de soviétologie*. Paris, Hachette, 1976. 125 pp.

Bocca, Geoffrey. *The Moscow Scene*. New York, Stein & Day, 1976. 192 pp.

Brezhnev, Leonid I. *Report of the CPSU Central Committee and the Immediate Tasks of the Party in Home and Foreign Policy*. Moscow, Novosti, 1976. 112 pp.

Brown, Archie, and Michael Kaser (eds.). *The Soviet Union Since the Fall of Khrushchev*. New York, Free Press, 1976. 294 pp.

Carmichael, Joel. *Stalin's Masterpiece: the Show Trials and Purges of the Thirties*. New York, St. Martin's Press, 1976. 238 pp.

Churchward, L. G. *The Soviet Intelligentsia: An Essay on the Social Structure and Roles of Soviet Intellectuals During the 1960's*. London, Routledge & Paul, 1973. 204 pp.

Claudin-Urondo, Carmen. *Lénine et la Révolution Culturelle*. The Hague, Mouton, 1975. 119 pp.

Coates, Ken (ed.). *Détente and Socialist Democracy: A Discussion with Roy Medvedev*. New York, Pathfinder Press, 1976. 163 pp.

Cocks, Paul, Robert V. Daniels, and Nancy Whittier Heer (eds.). *The Dynamics of Soviet Politics.* Cambridge, Mass., Harvard University Press, 1976. 427 pp.

Communist Party of the Soviet Union. *Documents and Resolutions of the XXVth Congress of the CPSU.* Moscow, Novosti, 1976. 270 pp.

———. *Zur Rolle der KPdSU und der Sowjetunion im Revolutionaeren Weltprozess.* Berlin, Dietz, 1975. 339 pp.

Daix, Pierre. *Le socialisme du silence: de l'histoire de l'URSS comme secret d'Etat, 1921-19. .* Paris, Seuil, 1976. 285 pp.

Ellenstein, Jean. *Histoire du phénomène stalinien.* Paris, Grasset, 1975. 224 pp.

Feshbach, Murray. *Soviet Manpower, Supply and Demand, 1950-1980.* New York, Praeger, 1976. 200 pp.

Gerasimov, I. P. et al. (eds.). *Man, Society and the Environment.* Moscow, Progress, 1975. 343 pp.

Gilison, Jerome M. *The Soviet Image of Utopia.* Baltimore, Md., Johns Hopkins University Press, 1975. 192 pp.

Ginsburgs, George. *Sino-Soviet Territorial Dispute.* New York, Praeger, 1976. 150 pp.

Glassman, Jon D. *Arms for the Arabs: The Soviet Union and War in the Middle East.* Baltimore, Md., Johns Hopkins University Press, 1976. 243 pp.

Gouré, Leon. *War Survival in Soviet Strategy: USSR Civil Defense.* Coral Gables, Fla., Center for Advanced International Studies, University of Miami, 1976. 218 pp.

Griffith, William E. (ed.). *The Soviet Empire: Expansion & Detente.* Lexington, Mass., Lexington Books, 1976. 417 pp.

Grigorenko, Major General P. G. *The Grigorenko Papers.* Boulder, Colo., Westview Press, 1976. 320 pp.

Gromyko, A. A., and B. N. Ponomarev (eds.). *Istoria vneshnei politiki SSSR.* Moscow, Nauka, 1976. 2 vols.

Gupta, Bhabani Sen. *Soviet-Asian Relations in the 1970's and Beyond: An Interperceptional Study.* New York: Praeger, 1976. 384 pp.

Hazan, Baruch A. *Soviet Propaganda: A Case Study of the Middle East Conflict.* New Brunswick, N.J., Transaction Books, 1976. 293 pp.

Hutchings, Raymond. *Soviet Science, Technology and Design.* New York, Oxford University Press, 1976. 320 pp.

Israel, Gerard. *The Jews in Russia.* New York, St. Martin's Press, 1975. 329 pp.

Kaiser, Robert G. *Russia: The People and the Power.* New York, Atheneum, 1976. 499 pp.

Khodorovich, Tatiana (ed.). *The Case of Leonid Plyushch.* Boulder, Colo., Westview Press, 1976. 152 pp.

Kirby, E. Stuart. *Russian Studies of China: Progress and Problems of Soviet Sinology.* London, MacMillan, 1975. 209 pp.

Konstantinov. F. V. (ed.). *Borba idei v sovremennom mire.* Moscow, Politizdat, 1975 and 1976. 2 vols.

Korionov, Vitaly. *Policy of Peaceful Coexistence in Action.* Moscow, Progress, 1975. 116 pp.

Lazitch, Branko. *Le Rapport Khrouchtchev et son histoire.* Paris, Editions du Seuil, 1976. 192 pp.

Lecourt, Dominique. *Lysenko; Histoire réelle d'une "Science Prolétarienne."* Paris, Maspero, 1976. 255 pp.

Leonhard, Wolfgang. *Am Vorabend einer euen Revolution? Die Zunkunft des Sowjetkommunismus.* Munich, Bertelsmann, 1975. 431 pp.

Levesque, Jacques. *L'URSS et la Révolution Cubaine.* Montreal, Les Presses de L'Université de Montréal, 1976. 220 pp.

Lewis, Robert A. *Nationality and Population Change in Russia and the USSR. New York, Praeger, 1976. 456 pp.*

Linhart, Robert. *Lénine, les paysans, Taylor.* Paris, Seuil, 1976. 172 pp.

Mamoulian, Armand. *Les fils de Gulag.* Paris, Presses de la Cité, 1976. 220 pp.

MccGwire, Michael (ed.). *Soviet Naval Influence: Domestic and Foreign Dimensions.* New York, Praeger, 1976. 500 pp.

Medvedev, Roy A., and Zhores A. Medvedev. *Krushchev: The Years in Power.* New York, Columbia University Press, 1976. 198 pp.

Meissner, Boris, and Georg Brunner (eds.). *Gruppeninteressen und Entscheidungsprozess in der Sowjetunion.* Cologne, Wissenschaft & Politik, 1975. 264 pp.

Narochnitskiy, A. L., et al. (eds.). *Sovetskiy Soyuz i Organizatsiya Obedinennykh Natsii, 1966-1970.* Moscow, Nauka, 1975. 536 pp.

Nord, Pierre. . . . *et Staline decapita l'Armée Rouge.* Paris, Librairie des Champs-Elysees, 1975. 251 pp.

Panine, Dimitri. *Soljenitsyne et la réalité.* Paris, Table Ronde, 1976. 188 pp.

——. *The Notebooks of Sologdin.* New York, Harcourt Brace Jovanovich, 1976. 320 pp.

Pipes, Richard (ed.). *Soviet Strategy in Europe.* New York, Crane Russak, 1976. 316 pp.

Rabinowitch, Alexander. *The Bolsheviks Come to Power: The Revolution of 1917 in Petrograd.* New York, Norton, 1976. 393 pp.

Reck, Vera T. *Boris Pilniak: A Soviet Writer in Conflict with the State.* Montreal, McGill-Queen's University Press, 1975. 243 pp.

Revel, Jean François. *La tentation totalitaire.* Paris, Laffont, 1976. 369 pp.

Rychener, Hans. . . . *und Estland, Lettland, Litauen? Eindrucke aus dem freien und Dokumente aus dem sowjetischen Baltikum.* Frankfurt/M., Herbert Lang, 1975. 106 pp.

Sacks, Michael Paul. *Women's Work in Soviet Russia: Continuity in the Midst of Change.* New York, Praeger, 1976. 240 pp.

Sakharov, Andrei D. *My Country and the World.* New York, Knopf, 1975. 109 pp.

Samizdat Vingtième Siècle. *Une Opposition Socialiste en Union Soviétique Aujourd'hui.* Paris, Maspero, 1976. 211 pp.

Shishkin, V. F. *Velikii Oktiabr i proletarskaia moral.* Moscow, Mysl, 1976. 260 pp.

Shtrik-Shtrikfeldt, Wilfrid. *Protiv Stalina i Gitlera.* Frankfurt, Possev, 1975. 439 pp.

Singleton, Fred (ed.). *Environmental Misuse in the Soviet Union.* New York, Praeger, 1976. 250 pp.

Smith, Hedrick. *The Russians.* New York, Quadrangle, 1976. 527 pp.

Sokoloff, Georges. *L'Economie Obéissante: Décisions politiques et vie économique en URSS.* Paris, Calmann-Lévy, 1976. 352 pp.

Solzhenitsyn, Aleksandr I. *Amerikanskie rechi.* Frankfurt, Posev, 1975. 107 pp.

——. *Arkhipelag Gulag.* Paris, YMCA Press, 1976. Vol. 3. 581 pp.

——. *Détente: Prospects for Democracy and Dictatorship.* New Brunswick, Transaction Books, 1976. 112 pp.

——. *Lenin in Zurich.* New York, Farrar, Straus & Giroux, 1976. 309 pp.

——. *Rasskazy.* Frankfurt/Main, Possev, 1976. 373 pp.

——. *Warning to the West.* New York, Farrar, Straus & Giroux, 1976. 146 pp.

Solzhenitsyn, Aleksandr I., et al. *From Under the Rubble.* Boston, Mass., Little Brown, 1975. 308 pp.

Stepanyan, Ts. A. (ed.). *Rabochy klass SSSR i ego vedushchaya rol v stroitelstve kommunizma.* Moscow, Nauka, 1975. 568 pp.

Suliny, François. *Le piéton de Stalingrad.* Paris, Fayard, 1975. 406 pp.

Svirski, Grigor. *Hostages: the Personal Testimony of a Soviet Jew.* New York, Random House, 1976. 305 pp.

Sylvestre, M. and Pierre S. *La "Liberté" des Communistes: Police, prisons et camps soviétiques.* Paris, Les Sept Couleurs, 1975. 276 pp.

Taylor, Telford. *Courts of Terror: Soviet Criminal Justice and Jewish Emigration.* New York, Knopf, 1976. 187 pp.

Thorwald, Jurgen. *The Illusion: Soviet Soldiers in Hitler's Armies.* New York, Harcourt, Brace, Jovanovich, 1975. 342 pp.

Trotsky, Leon. *L'Appareil Policier du Stalinisme.* Paris, Union Générale d'Editions, 1976. 315 pp.

___ . *The Challenge of the Left Opposition (1922-1925).* New York, Pathfinder Press, 1975. 428 pp.

Uvachan, V. N. *The Peoples of the North and Their Road to Socialism.* Moscow, Progress, 1975. 227 pp.

Vasileva, E. K. *The Young People of Leningrad: School and Work Options and Attitudes.* White Plains, N.Y., International Arts & Science Press, 1976. 220 pp.

Vereeken, G. *La Guépéou dans le Mouvement Trotskiste.* Paris, La Pensée Universelle, 1975. 377 pp.

Vigor, P. H. *The Soviet View of War, Peace and Neutrality.* London, Routledge & Paul, 1975. 256 pp.

Wortman, Richard S. *The Development of a Russian Legal Consciousness.* Chicago, University of Chicago Press, 1976. 345 pp.

EASTERN EUROPE

Bakarić, Vladimir. *Theoretical Foundations of Social Reproduction in Socialism.* Belgrade, Socialist Thought and Practice, 1976. 141 pp.

Bertsch, Gary K. *Values and Community in Multinational Yugoslavia.* New York, Columbia University Press, 1976. 160 pp.

Bryson, Phillip J. *Scarcity and Control in Socialism: Essays on East European Planning.* Lexington, Mass., Lexington Books, 1976. 202 pp.

Denitch, Bogdan Denis. *The Legitimation of a Revolution: The Yugoslav Case.* New Haven, Conn., Yale University Press, 1976. 254 pp.

Dolanc, Stane. *The League of Communists in the System of Socialist Self-management.* Belgrade, Socialist Thought and Practice, 1976. 268 pp.

Duzević, Stipe (ed.). *Tenth Congress of the League of Communists of Yugoslavia.* Belgrade, Komunist, 1975. 210 pp.

Dziewanowski, M. K. *The Communist Party of Poland.* Cambridge, Mass., Harvard University Press, 1976. 2nd ed. 423 pp.

Faber, Bernard L. *The Social Structure of Eastern Europe: Transition and Process in Czechoslovakia, Hungary, Poland, Romania, Yugoslavia.* New York, Praeger, 1976. 423 pp.

Fallenbuchl, Zbigniew M. *Economic Development in the Soviet Union and Eastern Europe.* New York, Praeger, 1975. 2 vols.

Flavien, Jean, and André Lajoinie. *L'Agriculture dans les pays socialistes d'Europe.* Paris, Editions sociales, 1976. 288 pp.

Frolik, Josef. *The Frolik Defection.* London, Leo Cooper, 1975. 184 pp.

Furtak, Robert K. *Jugoslawien: Politik, Gesellschaft, Wirtschaft.* Hamburg, Hoffman & Campe, 1975. 242 pp.

Gati, Charles. *International Politics of Eastern Europe.* New York, Praeger, 1976. 400 pp.

George, Richard T. de, and James P. Scanlan (eds.). *Marxism and Religion in Eastern Europe.* Dordrecht, Reidel, 1976. 181 pp.

Granick, David. *Enterprise Guidance in Eastern Europe: A Comparison of Four Socialist Economies.* Princeton, N.J., Princeton University Press, 1975. 505 pp.

Gransow, Volker. *Kulturpolitik in der DDR.* East Berlin, Volker Spiess, 1975. 170 pp.

Gronowicz, Antoni. *Polish Profiles: the Land, the People and Their History.* Westport, Conn., Lawrence Hill, 1976. 220 pp.

Grothusen, Klaus-Detlev (ed.). *Suedosteuropa-Handbuch; Jugoslawien*. Goettingen, Vandenhoeek & Ruprecht, 1975. 566 pp.

Harasymiw, Bohdan (ed.). *Education and the Mass Media in the Soviet Union and Eastern Europe*. New York, Praeger, 1976. 134 pp.

Hoehmann, Hans-Hermann, Michael C. Kaser, and Karl C. Thalheim (eds.). *The New Economic Systems of Eastern Europe*. Berkeley, Ca., University of California Press, 1976. 423 pp.

Herder Institut. *Polen: Laenderberichte II*. Munich, Hanser Verlag, 1976. 282 pp.

Hermann, A. H. *A History of the Czechs*. Totowa, N.J., Rowman & Littlefield, 1975. 324 pp.

Honecker, Erich. *Reden und Aufsaetze*. East Berlin, Dietz, 1975. vol. 2. 552 pp.

Horsky, Vladimir. *Prag: Systemveraenderung und Systemverteidigung*. Munich, Koesel, 1975. 534 pp.

Horvat, Branko. *The Yugoslav Economic System: The First Labor-Managed Economic System: The First Labor-Managed Economy in the Making*. White Plains, N.Y., International Arts & Sciences Press, 1976. 400 pp.

Hoxha, Enver. *Selected Works*. Tirana, 8 Nentori, 1976. Vol. 2. 879 pp.

_____. *Speeches, 1971-1973*. Tirana, 8 Nentori, 1974. 343 pp.

Institut d'Histoire de l'Academie des Sciences de la R. P. d'Albanie. *La Lutte antifasciste de libération nationale du peuple Albanais; Documents principaux (1941-1944)*. Tirana, 8 Nentori, 1975. 558 pp.

Isusov, Mito, et al. (eds.). *Problems of the Transition from Capitalism to Socialism in Bulgaria*. Sofia, Academy of Sciences, 1975. 365 pp.

Jambrek, Peter. *Development and Social Changes in Yugoslavia: Crises and Perspectives of Building a Nation*. Lexington, Mass., Lexington Books, 1975. 280 pp.

Jurgela, Constantine R. *Lithuania: Outpost of Freedom*. St. Petersburg, Fla., Valkyrie Press, 1976. 387 pp.

Kardelj, Edvard. *The Nation and International Relations*. Belgrade, Socialist Thought & Practice, 1975. 211 pp.

Kaslas, Bronis J. *The Baltic Nations: The Quest for Regional Integration and Political Liberty*. Pittston, Pa., Euramerica Press, 1976. 319 pp.

Kiera, Hans-Georg. *Partei und Staat im Planungssystem der DDR*. Duesseldorf, Droste, 1975. 230 pp.

Kiraly, Bela K. (ed.). *Tolerance and Movements of Religious Dissent in Eastern Europe*. New York, Columbia University Press, 1975. 227 pp.

Koch, Hans-Gerhard. *Staat und Kirche in der DDR: Stellung, Quellen, Ulbersichten*. Stuttgart, Quell-Verlag, 1975. 262 pp.

Kosinski, Leszek (ed.). *Demographic Developments in the Soviet Union and Eastern Europe*. New York, Praeger, 1976. 300 pp.

Kulski, W. W. *Germany and Poland: From War to Peaceful Relations*. Syracuse, N.Y., Syracuse University Press, 1976. 336 pp.

Lamm, Hans Siegfried, and Siegfried Kupper. *DDR und Dritte Welt*. Munich, Oldenbourg, 1976. 328 pp.

Loebl, Eugen. *My Mind on Trial*. New York: Harcourt, Brace & Jovanovich, 1976. 235 pp.

Ludz, Peter C. (ed.). *DDR Handbuch*. Cologne, Wissenschaft & Politik, 1975. 991 pp.

_____. *Ideologiebegriff und marxistische Theorie*. Cologne, Westdeutscher Verlag, 1976. 370 pp.

Mihajlov, Mihajlo. *Underground Notes*. Kansas City, Sheed, Andrews and McMeel, 1976. 204 pp.

Milazzo, Matteo J. *The Chetnik Movement and the Yugoslav Resistance*. Baltimore, Md., Johns Hopkins University Press, 1975. 208 pp.

Myrdal, Jan, and Gun Kessle. *Albania Defiant*. New York, Monthly Review Press, 1976. 185 pp.

Nikiforov, L. A., et al. (eds.). *Sotsialisticheskaya Federativnaya Respublika Yugoslaviya*. Moscow, Nauka, 1975. 180 pp.

Obrebski, Joseph. *The Changing Peasantry of Eastern Europe.* Cambridge, Mass. Schenkman, 1976. 102 pp.

Parrot, Cecil. *The Tightrope.* London, Faber & Faber, 1975. 223 pp.

Pelikan, Jiri. *S'ils me tuent.* Paris, Grasset, 1975. 293 pp.

Radde, Juergen. *Die aussenpolitische Fuehrungselite der DDR.* Cologne, Wissenschaft & Politik, 1976. 239 pp.

Rakowski, Mieczyslaw F. *The Foreign Policy of Polish People's Republic.* Warsaw, Interpress, 1975. 211 pp.

Reuter-Hendrichs, Irena. *Jugoslawische Aussenpolitik, 1948-1968.* Cologne, Heymanns, 1976. 363 pp.

Shapiro, Jane P., and Peter J. Potichnyj (eds.). *Change and Adaptation in Soviet and East European Politics.* New York, Praeger, 1976. 252 pp.

Sik, Ota. *Das kommunistische Machtsystem.* Hamburg, Hoffman & Campe, 1976. 357 pp.

Simo Zotos, Aglaia. *Nuages gris sur la Bulgarie, pays des roses.* Paris, Librarie du Merveilleux, 1976. 208 pp.

Singleton, Fred. *Twentieth-century Yugoslavia.* New York, Columbia University Press, 1976. 346 pp.

Skilling, H. Gordon. *Czechoslovakia's Interrupted Revolution.* Princeton, N.J., Princeton University Press, 1976. 924 pp.

Stantchev, Michail. *Sous le joug du libérateur.* Moudon, Editions du Bourg, 1975. 213 pp.

Stehle, Hansjakob. *Die Ostpolitik des Vatikans, 1917-1975.* Munich, Piper, 1975. 487 pp.

Szporluk, Roman (ed.). *The Influence of East Europe and the Soviet West on the USSR.* New York, Praeger, 1976. 272 pp.

Timar, Matyas. *Reflexions on the Economic Development in Hungary, 1967-1973.* Budapest, Akademia Kiado, 1975. 219 pp.

Tomasevich, Jozo. *The Chetniks.* Stanford, Ca., Stanford University Press, 1975. 508 pp.

Unger, Peter. *Die Ursachen der politischen Unruhen in Polen im Winter 1970/71.* Berne, Herbert Lang, 1975. 287 pp.

Wallace, William V. *Czechoslovakia.* Boulder, Colo., Westview Press, 1976. 400 pp.

Wettig, Gerhard. *Community and Conflict in the Socialist Camp: The Soviet Union, East Germany and the German Problem 1965-1972.* New York, St. Martin's Press, 1975. 161 pp.

Wyniger, Willy. *Demokratie und Plan in der DDR.* Cologne, Pahl-Rugenstein, 1975. 140 pp.

Zhivkov, Todor. *Selected Articles and Speeches, 1965-1975.* Moscow, Politizdat, 1975. 580 pp.

WESTERN EUROPE

Akarli, Engin D., (ed.). *Political Participation in Turkey: Historical Background and Present Problems.* Istanbul, Bogazici University, 1975. 192 pp.

Amendola, Giorgio. *Una scelta di vita.* Milan, Rizzoli, 1976. 264 pp.

Badaloni, Nicola. *Pour le communisme: question de théorie.* The Hague, Mouton, 1976. 264 pp.

Badie, Bertrand. *Stratégie de la grève.* Paris, Fondation nationale des sciences politiques, 1976. 262 pp.

Baget Bozzo, Gianni. *Il partito cristiano, il comunismo e la societa radicale.* Florence, Vallecchi, 1976. 155 pp.

Balibar, Etienne. *Sur la dictature du proletariat.* Paris, Maspero, 1976. 280 pp.

Bartoli, Domenico (ed.). *Gli italiani nella terra di nessuno.* Milan, Mondadori, 1976. 273 pp.

Bauermann, Rolf. *Das Elend der "Marxologie."* Frankfurt/Main, Marxistische Blaetter, 1975. 279 pp.

Berlinger, Enrico, and Carillo Santiago, *Una Spagna libera in un'Europa democratica*. Rome, Riuniti, 1975. 68 pp.

Bilstein, Helmut, et al. *Organisierter Kommunismus in der Bundesrepublik Deutschland*. Opladen, Leske Verlag, 1975. 3rd rev. ed. 141 pp.

Boggs, Carl. *Gramsci's Marxism*. London, Pluto, 1976. 145 pp.

Bosi, Mariangela, and Hugues Portelli. *Les P. C. espagnol, français, italien face au pouvoir*. Paris, Bourgois, 1976. 256 pp.

Boyle, Kevin, Tom Hadden, and Paddy Hillyard. *Law and State: The Case of Northern Ireland*. London, Martin Robertson, 1975. 194 pp.

Brancoli, Rodolfo. *Gli USA e il PCI*. Milan, Garzanti, 1976. 193 pp.

British and Irish Communist Organization. *The Two Irish Nations*. Belfast, The Organization, 1975.

Calhoun, Daniel F. *The United Front! The TUC and the Russians, 1923-1928*. New York, Cambridge University Press, 1976. 450 pp.

Cambria, Adele. *Amore come revoluzione*. Milan, Sugar, 1976. 275 pp.

Carollo, Vincenzo. *Borghesia rivoluzionaria per il comunismo*. Milan, Mursia, 1976. 210 pp.

Chao, Ramon. *Après Franco: L'Espagne*. Paris, Stock, 1975. 378 pp.

Chatelet, François, et al. *Les marxistes et la politique*. Paris, Presses universitaires, 1975. 730 pp.

Communist Party of Ireland. *Communist Party of Ireland: Outline History*. Dublin, New Books, 1975. 64 pp.

Cunhal, Alvaro. *Pela revolução democrática e nacional*. Lisbon, Editorial Estampa, 1975. 227 pp.

Daix, Pierre. *J'ai cru au matin*. Paris, Robert Laffont, 1976. 480 pp.

Dewar, Hugo. *Communist Politics in Britain, 1919-1939*. London, Pluto, 1976. 169 pp.

Documents from the First Joint Meeting of Nordic Marxist-Leninists, January, 1975. Oslo, Duplotrykk, 1975. 53 pp.

Domes, Alfred (ed.). *Ost-West Kontakte: Gefahren und Moeglichkeiten*. Bonn, Atlantic Forum, 1975. 235 pp.

Duclos, Jacques. *Ce que je crois*. Paris, Grasset, 1975. 251 pp.

Dufour, Jean Marc. *Prague sur Tage: Chronique de la révolution portugaise depuis avril 1974*. Paris, Nouvelle Aurore, 1975. 283 pp.

Dugos, Carlos. *Descolonização portuguesa: O Malogro de dois planos*. Lisbon, Edições Acropole, 1975. 124 pp.

Ehlermann, Claus-Dieter, et al. *Handelspartner DDR: Innerdeutsche Wirtschaftsbeziehungen*. Baden-Baden, Nomos, 1975. 336 pp.

Fajon, Etienne (ed.). *L'Union est en combat*. Paris, Editions sociales, 1975. 127 pp.

Fajon, Etienne. *Ma vie s'appelle liberté*. Paris, Laffont, 1976. 304 pp.

Ferreira, Serafim (ed.). *Citaçoes de Vasco Gonçalves*. Amadora, Fronteira, 1975. 125 pp.

Fields, Rona M. *The Portuguese Revolution and the Armed Forces Movement*. New York, Praeger, 1976. 291 pp.

Fondation Nationale des Sciences Politiques. *Sociologie du communisme en Italie*. Paris, Armand Colin, 1974. 248 pp.

Foubert, Charles. *Portugal 1974-1975: Les années de l'espoir*. Paris, Centre international d'information et de documentation sur l'Eglise conciliaire, 1975. 123 pp.

Freymond, Joel. *Le P.C.F., un parti pas comme les autres*. Paris, Veritas, 1976. 160 pp.

Galli, Giorgio. *Storia del Partito comunista italiano*. Milan, Il Formichiere, 1976. 391 pp.

Gonçalves, Vasco. *Discursos; Conferências de imprensa; Entrevistas*. Lisbon, Augusto Paulo da Gama, 1976. 507 pp.

Green, Gil. *Portugal's Revolution*. New York, International Publishers, 1975. 100 pp.

Ginsburg, Shaul. *Raymond Lefebvre et les origines du communisme français*. Paris, Tête de feuilles, 1975. 261 pp.

Groupe pour la fondation de l'Union des communistes français (marxiste-leniniste). *Le livre des paysans pauvres*. Paris, Maspero, 1976. 302 pp.

Hamrin, Harald. *Between Bolshevism and Revisionism: The Italian Communist Party, 1944-1947*. Stockholm, Esselte Studium, 1975. 341 pp.

Hinton, James, and Richard Hyman. *Trade Unions and Revolution: Industrial Politics of the Early British Communist Party*. London, Pluto, 1975. 78 pp.

Historische Kommission beim ZK der KPOe. *Beitraege zur Geschichte der Kommunistischen Partei Oesterreichs*. Vienna, Globus, 1976. 112 pp.

Internationale Kommunisten Deutschlands & Kommunistische Jugendorganisation Spartacus. *Die Grundlagen der bolschewistischen Parteitheorie*. Berlin, Unser Wort, 1976. 156 pp.

Jaeggi, Max, et al. *Das rote Bologna*. Zurich, Verlagsgenossenschaft, 1976. 304 pp.

Jara, Jose Manuel. *Maoismo em Portugal*. Lisbon, Ediçoês sociais, 1975. 79 pp.

Jocteau, Gian Carlo. *Leggere Gramsci: una guida alle interpretazioni*. Milan, Feltrinelli, 1975. 167 pp.

Kleinheyer, Gerd, and Bernard Stasiewski (eds.). *Rechts-und Sozialstrukturen im europaeischen Osten*. Cologne, Boehlau, 1975. 100 pp.

Kommunistische Partei Oesterreichs. *Protokoll der Konferenz der KPOe, 30. Nov. 1974, Wien*. Vienna, KPOe, 1975. 87 pp.

Korbel, Josef. *Détente in Europe, Real or Imaginary?* Princeton, N.J., Princeton University Press, 1976. 312 pp.

Kuhlman, James A., and Louis J. Mensonides (eds.). *American and European Security*. Leiden, Sijthoff, 1976. 190 pp.

Kunz, Rainer, et al. (eds.). *Programme der politischen Parteien in der Bundesrepublik*. Munich, C. H. Beck, 1975. 312 pp.

Lagoa, Vera. *Crónicas do Tempo(5/6/75-2/10/75)*. Porto, Livraria Internacional, 1975. 162 pp.

Lagroye, J. (ed.). *Les Militants politiques dans trois partis français: Parti communiste, Parti socialiste, Union des démocrates pour la République*. Paris, Pedone, 1976. 186 pp.

Lajolo, Davide. *Finestre aperte a Botteghe oscure*. Milan, Rizzoli, 1975. 245 pp.

Landis, Arthur H. *Spain! The Unfinished Revolution*. New York, International Publishers, 1975. 452 pp.

Longchamp, Jean Paul de. *La Garde de Fer*. Paris, SEFA, 1975. 133 pp.

Lourenco, Eduardo. *Os militares e o poder*. Lisbon, Arcadia, 1975. 168 pp.

Mahon, John. *Harry Pollitt*. London, Lawrence & Wishart, 1976. 567 pp.

Mammach, Klaus (ed.). *Die Bruesseler Konferenz der KPD*. Berlin, Dietz, 1975. 621 pp.

Mammarella, Giuseppe. *Il Partito comunista italiano, 1945-1975*. Florence, Vallecchi, 1976. 286 pp.

Marchais, Georges (introd.). *La Crise, Journées d'étude organisées par le Parti communiste français les 23, 24 et 25 mai 1975 à Nanterre*. Paris, Editions sociales, 1975. 271 pp.

Martinet, Marcel. *Culture prolétarienne*. Paris, Maspero, 1976. 163 pp.

Martinez Val, Jose Maria. *Españoles ante el comunismo*. Barcelona, Dopresa, 1976. 258 pp.

Meissner, Boris (ed.). *Moskau-Bonn: Dokumentation*. Cologne, Wissenschaft & Politik, 1975. 2 vols.

Mendel, Gerard. *Pour une autre société*. Paris, Payot, 1975. 220 pp.

Moreira Alves, Marcio. *Les soldats socialistes du Portugal*. Paris, Gallimard, 1975. 248 pp.

Morselli, Guido. *Il comunista*. Milan, Adelphia, 1976. 359 pp.

Naville, Pierre. *L'entre-deux guerres: la lutte des classes en France, 1927-1929*. Paris, Etudes et documentation internationales, 1975. 624 pp.

Noirot, Paul. *La memoire ouverte*. Paris, Stock, 1976. 370 pp.

Parti communiste français. *Les entreprises publiques en France*. Paris, Editions sociales, 1975. 253 pp.

——. *Les principes de la politique du Parti communiste français*. Paris, Editions sociales, 1975. 123 pp.

——. *Le socialisme pour la France: 22ème Congrès du Parti communiste français du 4 au 8 fevrier 1976*. Paris, Editions sociales, 1976. 217 pp.

Partido comunista portuguès. *Conferencia nacional do P.C.P.* Lisbon, Ediçôes Avante, 1976. 216 pp.

——. *Documentos do Comite Central*. Lisbon, Avante, 1975 and 1976. Vols. 2 and 3.

——. *O PCP e a luta sindical, 1935-1973*. Lisbon, Ediçôes Avante, 1975. 311 pp.

——. *Programa e estatutos do PCP aprovados no VII Congresso (extraordinario) em 20/10/74*. Lisbon, Avante, 1975. 111 pp.

Partido Revolucionario do Proletariado. *Brigadas Revolucionarias 1971-1974; Documentos*. Lisbon, Ediçôes Revoluçâo, 1975. 233 pp.

Partito comunista italiano. *14. Congress-Rome, March 18-23, 1975*. Rome, Riuniti, 1975. 911 pp.

Partito comunista marxisto-leninista italiano. *La Posizione del Partito comunista marxista-leninista italiano*. Milan, Lavoro liberato, 1976. 191 pp.

Pelling, Henry. *The British Communist Party: a Historical Profile*. London, Black, 1975. 204 pp.

Polverini, Giorgio. *Benedetto Croce e il comunismo*. Como, Nani, 1975. 207 pp.

Ragionieri, Ernesto. *Palmiro Togliatti*. Rome, Riuniti, 1976. 786 pp.

Ravines, Eudocio. *Capitalismo o comunismo*. Madrid, Libreria Editorial San Martin, 1976. 374 pp.

Robrieux, Philippe. *Maurice Thorez: vie secrète et vie publique*. Paris, Fayard, 1975. 660 pp.

Rodano, Franco. *Sulla politica dei comunisti*. Turin, Boringhieri, 1975. 132 pp.

Rodrigues, Urbano Miguel. *Da resistencia a revoluçâo (1903-1975)*. Lisbon, Ediçôes Avante, 1975. 225 pp.

Salvetti,Patrizia. *La stampa comunista da Gramsci a Togliatti*. Turin, Guanda, 1975. 414 pp.

Shipley, Peter. *Revolutionaries in Modern Britain*. London, Bodley Head, 1976. 256 pp.

Slaughter, Cliff. *Marxism and the Class Struggle*. London: New Park, 1975. 166 pp.

Tiso, Aida. *I comunisti e la questione femminile*. Rome, Riuniti, 1976. 151 pp.

Vene, Gian Franco. *La borghesia comunista*. Milan, Sugar, 1976. 199 pp.

Verdier, Robert. *Parti socialiste, parti communiste: une lutte pour l'entente*. Paris, Seghers, 1976. 320 pp.

Vloyantes, John P. *Silk Glove Hegemony: Finnish-Soviet Relations, 1944-1974*. Kent, Ohio, Kent State University Press, 1975. 208 pp.

Widgery, David. *The Left in Britain, 1956-1968*. Harmondsworth, England, Penguin, 1976. 549 pp.

Williams, Gwyn A. *Proletarian Order: Antonio Gramsci, Factory Councils and the Origins of Italian Communism, 1911-1921*. London, Pluto, 1975. 368 pp.

Woodhouse, Michael, and Brian Pearce. *Essays on the History of Communism in Britain*. London, New Park, 1975. 248 pp.

ASIA AND THE PACIFIC

Barnds, William J. (ed.). *The Two Koreas in East Asian Affairs*. New York, New York University Press, 1976. 267 pp.

Bartke, Wolfgang. *China's Economic Aid*. New York, Holmes & Meier, 1975. 215 pp.

Bhushan, Sh. (ed.). *Twenty Years of Bandung and Problems of Peace and Security in Asia*. New Delhi, Allied Publishers, 1975. 151 pp.

Black, Cyril E., et al. *The Modernization of Japan and Russia: A Comparative Study*. New York, Free Press, 1975. 386 pp.

Carrier, Fred J. *North Korean Journey: The Revolution against Colonialism*. New York, International Publishers,1975. 120 pp.

Chang, Parris H. *Power and Policy in China*. University Park, Pennsylvania State University Press, 1975. 276 pp.

Chang, Y. C. *Factional and Coalition Politics in China*. New York, Praeger, 1976. 235 pp.

Chari, A. S. R. *Memoirs of an Unrepentant Communist*. Bombay, Orient Longman, 1975. 172 pp.

Chesneaux, Jean, and Francoise le Barbier. *La Marche de la révolution 1921-1949: de la fondation du parti communiste à la libération*. Paris, Hatier Universite, 1975.

Chin, Tsai. *Peiping's International Propaganda Activities: A United Front Plot*. Taipei, Asian Peoples' Anti-Communist League, 1975. 100 pp.

Communist Party of India. *Report on Party Organisation and Amendments to Party Constitution, Adopted by the Tenth Congress of the Communist Party of India, Bhowanisennagar, Vijayawada, 27 January to 2 February 1975*. New Delhi, CPI, 1975. 53 pp.

Copper, John Franklin. *China's Foreign Aid: An Instrument of Peking's Foreign Policy*. Lexington, Mass., Heath, 1976. 197 pp.

Crozier, Brian. *The Man Who Lost China: The First Full Biography of Chiang Kai-shek*. New York, Scribner's, 1976. 430 pp.

Davin, Delia. *Woman-Work: Women and the Party in Revolutionary China*. New York, Oxford University Press, 1976. 244 pp.

Duiker, William J. *The Rise of Nationalism in Vietnam, 1900-1941*. Ithaca, N.Y., Cornell University Press, 1976. 313 pp.

Eckstein, Alexander. *China's Economic Development: The Interplay of Scarcity and Ideology*. Ann Arbor, The University of Michigan Press, 1975. 399 pp.

Evans, Les, and Block Russell (eds.). *Leon Trotsky on China*. New York, Monad Press, 1976. 687 pp.

Fitzgerald, C. P. *Mao Tse-tung and China*. New York, Holmes & Meier, 1976. 160 pp.

George K. C. *Immortal Punnapra-Vayalar*. New Delhi, Communist Party of India, 1975. 171 pp.

Gheddo, Piero. *Vietnam, Cristiani e Comunisti*. Turin, Societa Editrice Internazionale, 1976. 359 pp.

Gollan, Robin. *Revolutionaries and Reformists: Communism and the Australian Labour Movement, 1920-1955*. Richmond, England, Richmond Publishing Co., 1975. 330 pp.

Griffin, Patricia E. *The Chinese Communist Treatment of Counter-revolutionaries, 1924-1949*. Princeton, N.J., Princeton University Press, 1976. 257 pp.

Guillermaz, Jacques. *The Chinese Communist Party in Power, 1949-1974*. Boulder, Colo., Westview Press, 1976. 700 pp.

Immortal Heroes: Lives of Communist Leaders. New Delhi: Communist Party of India, 1975. 165 pp.

Israel, John, and Donald W. Klein. *Rebels and Bureaucrats: China's December 9ers*. Berkeley, University of California Press, 1976. 305 pp.

Jain, Jagdish Prasad. *After Mao What? Army-Party Group Rivalries in China*. Boulder, Colo., Westview Press, 1976. 276 pp.

Karan, Pradyumna P. *The Changing Face of Tibet: The Impact of Chinese Communist Ideology on the Landscape*. Lexington, University Press of Kentucky, 1976. 114 pp.

Kau, Michael Y. M. (ed.). *The Lin Piao Affair: Power Politics and Military Coup*. White Plains, N.Y., International Arts & Sciences Press, 1975. 591 pp.

Kiyosaki, Wayne S. *North Korea's Foreign Relations*. New York, Praeger, 1976. 135 pp.

Kommunistischer Bund Wien. *Dokumente zum Befrieungskampf der Indochinesischen Voelker*. Vienna, Wieser, 1975. 126 pp.

Konovalov, E. A., et al. (eds.). *Koreiskaya Demokraticheskaya Respublika*. Moscow, Nauka, 1975. 156 pp.

Kuo, Leslie T. C. *Agriculture in the People's Republic of China*. New York, Praeger, 1976. 320 pp.

Kuo, Thomas C. *Chen Tu-hsiu (1879-1942) and the Chinese Communist Movement*. South Orange, N.J., Seton Hall University Press, 1975. 428 pp.

LaPorte, Robert, Jr. *Power and Privilege: Influence and Decision-Making in Pakistan*. Berkeley, University of California Press, 1976. 225 pp.

Laushey, David M. *Bengal Terrorism and the Marxist Left: Aspects of Regional Nationalism in India, 1905-1942*. Columbia, Mo., South Asia Books, 1975. 187 pp.

Lieberthal, Kenneth. *A Research Guide to Central Party and Government Meetings in China, 1949-1975*. White Plains, N.Y., International Arts & Sciences Press, 1976. 322 pp.

Liu, Alan P. L. *Political Culture and Group Conflict in Communist China*. Santa Barbara, Ca., Clio Books, 1976. 205 pp.

Maitan, Livio. *Party, Army and Masses in China: A Marxist Interpretation of the Cultural Revolution and Its Aftermath*. Atlantic Highlands, N.J., Humanities Press, 1976. 373 pp.

Mesquita, Bruce Bueno de. *Strategy, Risk and Personality in Coalition Politics: The Case of India*. New York, Cambridge University Press, 1976. 198 pp.

Milton, David, and Nancy Dall Milton. *The Wind Will Not Subside: Years in Revolutionary China —1964-1969*. New York, Pantheon, 1976. 397 pp.

Mozingo, David. *Chinese Policy Toward Indonesia, 1949-1967*. Ithaca, N.Y., Cornell University Press, 1976. 303 pp.

Murugesan, K., and C. S. Subramanyam. *Singaravelu, Furst Communist in South India*. New Delhi, People's Publishing House, 1975. 246 pp.

Nee, Victor, and James Peck (eds.). *China's Uninterrupted Revolution: From 1840 to the Present*. New York, Pantheon, 1976. 480 pp.

Niloufer, Wajid Ali. *Communist China and South and Southeast Asia (October 1949-June 1972)*. Lahore, Ferozsons Ltd., 1975. 296 pp.

Ognetov, I. A., et al. (eds.). *Demokraticheskaya Respublika Vietnam*. Moscow, Nauka, 1975. 144 pp.

Perkins, Dwight (ed.). *China's Modern Economy in Historical Perspective*. Stanford, Ca., Stanford University Press, 1975. 344 pp.

Perrolle, Pierre M. (ed.). *Fundamentals of the Chinese Communist Party*. White Plains, N.Y., International Arts & Sciences Press, 1976. 205 pp.

Price, Jane L. *Cadres, Commanders, and Commissars: The Training of the Chinese Communist Leadership*. New York, Columbia University Press, 1976. 250 pp.

Pye, Lucian W. *Mao Tse-tung: The Man in the Leader*. New York, Basic Books, 1976. 346 pp.

Rousset, Pierre. *Le Parti Communiste Vietnamien*. Paris, Maspero, 1975. 2nd ed. 355 pp.

Roy, Asish Kumar. *The Spring Thunder and After: A Survey of the Maoist and Ultra-Leftist Movements in India, 1962-1975*. Columbia, Mo., South Asia Books, 1976. 303 pp.

Scalapino, Robert A. *Asia and theRoad Ahead: Issues for the Major Powers*. Berkeley, University of California Press, 1975. 452 pp.

Seymour, James D. *China: The Politics of Revolutionary Reintegration*. New York, Crowell, 1976. 329 pp.

Shaha, Rishikesh. *Nepali Politics: Retrospect and Prospect*. New York, Oxford University Press, 1975. 208 pp.

Solomon, Richard H. *A Revolution is Not a Dinner Party: A Feast of Images of the Maoist Transformation of China*. New York, Anchor, 1976. 200 pp.

Suh, Dae-Sook, and Chae-Jin Lee. *Political Leadership in Korea*. Seattle, University of Washington Press, 1976. 272 pp.

Taylor, Jay. *China and Southeast Asia: Peking's Relations with Revolutionary Movements*. New York, Praeger, 1976. 403 pp.

Terzani, Tiziano. *Giai Phong! The Fall and Liberation of Saigon*. New York, St. Martin's Press, 1976. 317 pp.

Tung, Shih-chin. *Communist China and the Chinese Problem*. Taipei, China Publishing Co., 1975. 196 pp.

Uhalley, Stephen Jr. *Mao Tse-tung: A Critical Biography*. New York, New Viewpoints, 1975. 233 pp.

U.S. Congress, Joint Economic Committee. *China: A Reassessment of the Economy—A Compendium of Papers*. Washington, D.C., U.S. Government Printing Office, 1975. 737 pp.

Vladimirov, Peter. *The Vladimirov Diaries; Yenan, China: 1942-1945*. Garden City, N.Y., Doubleday, 1975. 538 pp.

Whiting, Allen S. *The Chinese Calculus of Deterrence: India and Indochina*. Ann Arbor, University of Michigan Press, 1975. 299 pp.

Wilson, A. Jeyaratnam. *Electoral Politics in an Emergent State: The Ceylon General Election of May 1970*. New York, Cambridge University Press, 1975. 240 pp.

Wilson, Richard W., Sidney L. Greenblatt, and Amy Auerbacher Wilson. *Deviance and Social Control in Chinese Society*. New York, Praeger, 1976. 470 pp.

Woodside, Alexander. *Communism and Revolution in Modern Vietnam*. Boston, Mass., Houghton Mifflin, 1976. 352 pp.

THE AMERICAS

Aizcorbe, Roberto. *Argentina, the Peronist Myth: an Essay on the Cultural Decay in Argentina after the Second World War*. Hicksville, N.Y., Exposition Press, 1975. 313 pp.

Arnaudo, Florencio José. *Las principales tesis marxistas*. Buenos Aires, Editorial Pleamar, 1975. 171 pp.

Bonachea, Ramon L., and Marta San Martin. *The Cuban Insurrection, 1952-1959*. New Brunswick, N.J., Transaction Books, 1974. 451 pp.

Brown, Phil. *Toward a Marxist Psychology*. New York, Harper & Row, 1974. 186 pp.

Castro, Fidel. *Educacíon y revolucíon*. Mexico, Nuestro Tiempo, 1975. 165 pp.

——. *Imperialismo, tercer mundo y revolucíon*. Barcelona, Editorial Anasrama, 1975. 136 pp.

——. *La primera revolucíon socialista en América*. Mexico, Siglo Veintiuno Editores, 1976. 327 pp.

Chadwick, Lee. *Cuba Today*. Westport, Conn., Lawrence Hill, 1976. 212 pp.

Communist Party U.S.A. *Toward Peace, Freedom, and Socialism: Main Political Resolution, 21st National Convention*. New York, New Outlook, 1976. 131 pp.

Diggins, John P. *Up From Communism: Conservative Odysseys in American Intellectual History*. New York, Harper & Row, 1975. 522 pp.

Dill, H. O. *El ideario literario y estético de José Martí*. Havana, Casa de las Américas, 1975. 206 pp.

Eagleson, John. *Christians and Socialism: Documentation of the Christians for Socialism Movement in Latin America*. Maryknoll, N.Y., Orbis, 1975. 246 pp.

Farber, Samuel. *Revolution and Reaction in Cuba, 1933-1960: A Political Sociology from Machado to Castro*. Middletown, Conn., Wesleyan University Press, 1976. 283 pp.

Garay, Blas. *El comunismo de las misiones; La revolucíon de la independencia del Paraguay*. Asuncíon, Instituto Colorado de Cultura, 1975. 252 pp.

Genta, Jordan B. *Acerca de la libertad de ensenar y de la ensenanza de la libertad*. Buenos Aires, Ediciones Dictio, 1976. 580 pp.

Gerson, Simon. *Pete: The Story of Peter Cacchione, New York's First Communist Councilman*. New York, International Publishers, 1976. 215 pp.

Hall, Gus. *The Crisis of U.S. Capitalism and the Fight-Back: Report to the 21st convention of the Communist Party, U.S.A.* New York, International Publishers, 1975. 93 pp.

Halperin, Ernst. *Terrorism in Latin America.* Beverly Hills, Ca., Sage, 1976. 90 pp.

Halperin, Maurice. *The Rise and Decline of Fidel Castro.* Berkeley, University of California Press, 1975. 392 pp.

Levesque, Jacques. *L'URSS et la Révolution Cubaine.* Paris, Presses de la Fondation nationale des sciences politiques, 1976. 220 pp.

McCarthy, Joseph Raymond. *Major Speeches and Debates of Senator Joe McCarthy Delivered in the United States Senate, 1950-1951.* New York, Gordon Press, 1975. 354 pp.

O'Brien, Philip (ed.). *Allende's Chile.* New York, Praeger, 1976. 225 pp.

Partido Comunista de Colombia. *¿De donde venimos, hacia donde vamos, hacia donde debemos ir?* Medellín, Editorial 8 de junio, 1975. 586 pp.

Partido Comunista de Colombia (Marxista-Leninista). *Documentos.* Medellín, Editorial 8 de junio, 1975.

Peery, Nelson. *The Negro National Colonial Question.* Chicago, Workers Press, 1975. 2nd ed. 190 pp.

Petras, James F. *The United States and Chile: Imperialism and the Overthrow of the Allende Government.* New York, Monthly Review Press, 1975. 217 pp.

Polanco, Jorge Rodríguez. *A un senador norteamericano: la verdad sobre el processo chileno.* Santiago, Polanco, 1975. 325 pp.

Radosh, Ronald (ed.). *The New Cuba: Paradoxes and Potentials.* New York, Morrow, 1976. 248 pp.

Ratliff, William E. *Castroism and Communism in Latin America, 1959-1976: The Varieties of Marxist-Leninist Experience.* Washington, D.C., AEI-Hoover Policy Studies, 1976. 240 pp.

Rojas, Robinson. *The Murder of Allende and the End of the Chilean Way to Socialism,* New York, Harper and Row, 1976. 274 pp.

Rudich, Norman (ed.). *Weapons of Criticism: Marxism in America and the Literary Tradition.* Palo Alto, Ca., Ramparts Press, 1976. 389 pp.

Starobin, Joseph Robert. *American Communism in Crisis.* Berkeley, University of California Press, 1975. 331 pp.

Stave, Bruce M. *Socialism and the Cities.* Port Washington, N.Y., Kennikat Press, 1975. 212 pp.

Stepan, Alfred. *The Military in Politics: Changing Patterns in Brazil.* Princeton, N.J., Princeton University Press, 1976. 328 pp.

Suchlicki, Jaime. *Cuba from Columbus to Castro.* New York, Scribner's, 1975. 242 pp.

Valenzuela, Arturo, and J. Samuel (eds.). *Chile: Politics and Society.* New Brunswick, N.J. Transaction Books, 1976. 399 pp.

Vieira, Gilberto. *Escritos Políticos.* Bogotá, Ediciones Sur-américa, 1975. 198 pp.

Weinstein, James, *Ambiguous Legacy: The Left in American Politics.* New York, New Viewpoints, 1975. 179 pp.

MIDDLE EAST AND AFRICA

Adamolekun, Ladipo. *Sekou Touré's Guinea.* New York, Barnes & Noble, 1976. 250 pp.

Andrade, Mario de, and Marc Ollivier. *The War in Angola: a Socio-Economic Study.* Dar es Salaam, Tanzania Publishing House, 1975. 128 pp.

Bailey, Martin. *Freedom Railway.* London, Rex Collings, 1976. 168 pp.

Damachi, Ukandi, et al. (eds.). *Development Paths in Africa and China.* Boulder, Colo., Westview Press, 1976. 251 pp.

De Souza Clington, Mario. *Angola Libre?* Paris, Gallimard, 1975. 318 pp.

Elazari-Volcani, Isaac Avigdor. *The Communistic Settlements in the Jewish Colonisation in Palestine.* Westport, Conn., Hyperion Press, 1976. 139 pp.

Encausse, Helène Carrère de. *La Politique soviétique au Moyen-Orient, 1955-1975.* Paris, Fondation nationale des sciences politiques, 1975. 327 pp.

First, Ruth. *Libya: The Elusive Revolution.* New York: Africana Publishing Company, 1975. 294 pp.

Hall, Richard, and Hugh Peyman (eds.). *The Great Uhuru Railway, China's Showpiece in Africa.* London, Gollancz, 1976. 208 pp.

Heikal, Mohamed Hasanayn. *The Road to Ramadan.* New York, Quadrangle, 1975. 285 pp.

Hutchison, Alan. *China's African Revolution.* Boulder, Colo., Westview Press, 1976. 313 pp.

Isaac, Rael Jean. *Israel Divided: Ideological Politics in the Jewish State.* Baltimore, Md., Johns Hopkins University Press, 1976. 227 pp.

Jacqz, J. W. *Iran: Past, Present and Future.* New York, Aspen Institute for Humanistic Studies, 1976. 481 pp.

Jureidini, Paul A., and William E. Hazen. *The Palestinian Movement in Politics.* Lexington, Mass., Lexington Books, 1976. 141 pp.

Kiernan, Thomas. *Arafat: The Man and the Myth.* New York, Norton, 1976. 281 pp.

McLaurin, Ronald D. *The Middle East in Soviet Policy.* Lexington, Mass.: Lexington Books, 1975. 206 pp.

Nahas, Dunia Habib. *The Israeli Communist Party.* London, Croom Helm, 1976. 113 pp.

Offenberg, Mario. *Kommunismus in Palaestina.* Meisenheim am Glan, Hain, 1975. 369 pp.

Rubinstein, Alvin Z. *Red Star on the Nile: The Soviet-Egyptian Influence Relationship Since the June War.* Princeton, N.J., Princeton University Press, 1976. 388 pp.

Shivji, Issa G. *Class Struggles in Tanzania.* New York, Monthly Review Press, 1976. 182 pp.

Sivan, Emmanuel. *Communisme et nationalisme en Algérie 1920-1962.* Paris, Fondation nationale des sciences politiques, 1976. 262 pp.

Starushenko, Gleb. *Africa Makes Choice: The Development of Socialist-Oriented States.* Moscow, Novosti, 1975. 119 pp.

Stevens, Christopher. *The Soviet Union and Black Africa.* New York, Holmes & Meier, 1976. 236 pp.

Tibi, Bassam. *Militaer und Sozialismus in der Dritten Welt.* Frankfurt/M., Suhrkamp, 1973. 352 pp.

Weinstein, Warren (ed.). *Chinese and Soviet Aid to Africa.* New York, Praeger, 1975. 290 pp.

Yu, George T. *China's African policy, a Study of Tanzania.* New York, Praeger, 1975. 200 pp.

INDEX OF NAMES